Sixth Edition

CHILD DEVELOPMENT AND EDUCATION

TERESA M. MCDEVITT
University of Northern Colorado

JEANNE ELLIS ORMROD
University of Northern Colorado, Emerita

PEARSON

Boston   Columbus   Indianapolis   New York   San Francisco   Hoboken
Amsterdam   Cape Town   Dubai   London   Madrid   Milan   Munich   Paris   Montreal   Toronto
Delhi   Mexico City   Sao Paulo   Sydney   Hong Kong   Seoul   Singapore   Taipei   Tokyo

Vice President and Editorial Director: Jeffery W. Johnston
Vice President and Publisher: Kevin M. Davis
Development Editor: Gail Gottfried
Editorial Assistant: Marisia Styles
Executive Field Marketing Manager: Krista Clark
Senior Product Marketing Manager: Christopher Barry
Project Manager: Lauren Carlson
Procurement Specialist: Carol Melville
Senior Art Director: Diane Lorenzo
Cover Designer: Candace Rowley
Cover Art: Shutterstock
Media Project Manager: Tammy Walters
Full-Service Project Management: Kelli Jauron, S4Carlisle Publishing Services
Composition: S4Carlisle Publishing Services
Printer/Binder: RR Donnelley
Cover Printer: RR Donnelley
Text Font: ITC Garamond Std

Credits and acknowledgments for material borrowed from other sources and reproduced, with permission, in this textbook appear on the appropriate page within the text.

Every effort has been made to provide accurate and current Internet information in this book. However, the Internet and information posted on it are constantly changing, so it is inevitable that some of the Internet addresses listed in this textbook will change.

Library of Congress Cataloging-in-Publication Data
McDevitt, Teresa M.
  Child development and education / Teresa M. McDevitt & Jeanne Ellis Ormrod. — Sixth Edition.
    pages cm
  Includes index.
  ISBN 978-0-13-354969-0 — ISBN 0-13-354969-0 1. Child development. 2. Adolescent psychology.
  3. Educational psychology. I. Ormrod, Jeanne Ellis. II. Title.
  LB1115.M263 2015
  305.231—dc23
                                                                    2014032007

4   16

PEARSON

ISBN 10:   0-13-354969-0
ISBN 13: 978-0-13-354969-0

To the many teachers, principals, counselors, psychologists, nurses, and other educational professionals who cherish every child in their care.

TERESA M. MCDEVITT (left) is a psychologist with specializations in child development and educational psychology. She received a Ph.D. and M.A. in child development from Stanford University's Psychological Studies in Education program, Ed.S. in educational evaluation from Stanford University, and B.A. in psychology from the University of California, Santa Cruz. Since 1985 she has served the University of Northern Colorado in a variety of capacities—in teaching course in child psychology, human development, educational psychology, program evaluation, and research methods; advisement of graduate students; administration and university governance; and research and grant writing. Her research focuses on child development, families, and teacher education. She has published articles in *Child Development, Learning and Individual Differences, Child Study Journal, Merrill-Palmer Quarterly, Youth and Society,* and *Science Education,* among others. She has gained practical experiences with children, including by raising two children with her husband and working as an early childhood teacher of toddlers and preschool children, early childhood special education teacher, and volunteer in school and community settings. Teresa enjoys spending time with her children and husband and, when she has the chance, traveling internationally with her family.

JEANNE ELLIS ORMROD (right) is an educational psychologist with specializations in learning, cognition, and child development. She received a Ph.D. and M.S. in educational psychology at The Pennsylvania State University and an A.B. in psychology from Brown University; she also earned licensure in school psychology through postdoctoral work at Temple University and the University of Colorado, Boulder. She has worked as a middle school geography teacher and school psychologist and has conducted research in cognitive development, memory, problem solving, spelling, and giftedness. She is currently Professor Emerita of Psychological Sciences at the University of Northern Colorado; the "Emerita" means that she has officially retired from the university. However, she can't imagine ever *really* retiring from a field she enjoys so much, and so she continues to read and write about current research findings in educational psychology and child development. She is the author or coauthor of several other Pearson books, including *Educational Psychology: Developing Learners; Essentials of Educational Psychology; Human Learning; Practical Research: Planning and Design,* and *Our Minds, Our Memories: Enhancing Thinking and Learning at All Ages.* Jeanne has three grown children and three young grandchildren.

Preface

As psychologists and teacher educators, we have been teaching child and adolescent development for many years. A primary intention for us has been to help students translate developmental concepts into practical implications in their own teaching. In past years, the child development textbooks available to our students were typically quite thorough in their descriptions of theory and research but limited in concrete suggestions for working with infants, children, and adolescents.

With this book, now in its sixth edition, we bridge the gap between theory and practice. We draw from innumerable theoretical concepts; research studies conducted around the world; and our own experiences as parents, teachers, psychologists, and researchers to identify strategies for promoting young people's physical, cognitive, and social-emotional growth. As in the previous editions, this book focuses on childhood and the adolescent years and derives applications that are primarily educational in focus.

A primary goal for the sixth edition was to convert the information into an electronic format. Achievement of this goal reduced production costs and allowed us to use a dynamic format with powerful pedagogical features. With integrated electronic features, readers are guided through numerous interactive exchanges and provided with feedback along the way.

The shift to digital format inspired an overhaul to the structure of each chapter, elevating clear learning objectives, which are now in one-to-one correspondence with major sections of each chapter. For each objective, readers can engage with several exercises that solidify conceptual understandings and practical knowledge. As readers encounter concepts in the narrative, they can deepen understandings by examining illustrations of various kinds. Readers can review children's artwork and essays, observe children's actions in video clips, and check their comprehension at the end of each section, with explanations immediately accessible to confirm expectations and correct misconceptions.

As we wrote the sixth edition, we took to heart suggestions from reviewers, instructors, and readers about the need to elaborate on the experiences of children from a multitude of backgrounds and with characteristics that are commonly misunderstood in society. We added information about children from families with gay and lesbian parents, adolescent parents, military parents, and incarcerated parents. We also embellished on information about English language learners and children with disabilities.

With growing awareness about the crucial role of self-control in a child's life, we expanded treatment of self-regulation and methods for cultivating it throughout the book. Self-regulation is discussed in the context of parenting, brain development, learning, motivation, and morality.

Several features of the book make it different from other textbooks about child and adolescent development. In particular, the book

- Continually relates abstract theories to educational practices in schools
- Not only describes but also *demonstrates* developmental phenomena
- Guides observations of children
- Facilitates analysis of what children say, do, and create
- Offers concrete strategies for effective teaching of, and working with, children
- Fosters a thorough understanding of children's growth from infancy to late adolescence within the domains of physical, social-emotional, and cognitive development.

In the next few pages, we explain and illustrate how the book helps readers learn how to:

- Apply developmental insights in their work with children
- Refine their observations, assessments, and decisions
- Appreciate and accommodate children's upbringing
- Take a strategic approach to learning concepts in child development

APPLICATION

Readers are shown how to apply concepts. *Child Development and Education* spells out the educational and practical implications of developmental perspectives for those who teach and work with children.

Development and Practice

In addition to formulating recommendations for teachers and other professionals throughout the text, we provide *Development and Practice* features that offer concrete techniques for facilitating children's development. To help readers move from research to practice, each strategy is followed by examples of a professional implementing it in a classroom or other setting. You will find examples of the *Development and Practice* feature on pages 147, 160, 251, and 345 of this text.

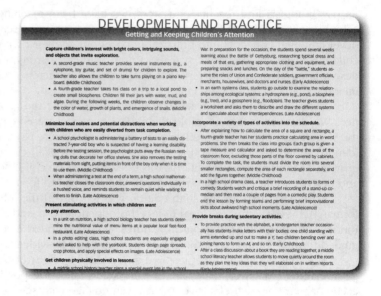

Developmental Trends Tables

Six-year-olds often think and act differently than 11-year-olds do, and 11-year-olds are, in turn, quite different from 16-year-olds. Most chapters have one or more *Developmental Trends* tables that highlight developmental differences between infancy (birth–2 years), early childhood (2–6 years), middle childhood (6–10 years), early adolescence (10–14 years), and late adolescence (14–18 years). In the Developmental Trends tables, diversity of potential characteristics is also highlighted, and implications for practice are offered. See pages 263–264, 349–350, and 365–366 for examples.

Preparing for Your Licensure Examination

Many prospective teachers are required to demonstrate their knowledge of child development on teaching tests. To prepare for these assessments, readers can focus on key theorists and concepts in the field of child development. As they read through the book, readers will be alerted with margin notes to specific concepts that they might encounter on the *Praxis II™* and other licensure tests. In addition, end-of-chapter exercises pose realistic scenarios and ask readers to prepare brief essays and answer multiple-choice questions, in formats similar to many teacher examinations. Find examples of *Preparing for Your Licensure Examination* on pages 240, 250, and 317, and of *Practicing for Your Licensure Examination features* on pages 273, 311, and 403–404, and 485.

> **Preparing for Your Licensure Examination**
> Your teaching test may ask you how to address children's basic cognitive processes during instruction.

PRACTICING FOR YOUR LICENSURE EXAMINATION

Many teaching tests require students to use what they have learned about child development in responses to brief vignettes and multiple-choice questions. You can practice for your licensure examination by reading the following case study and answering a series of questions.

The Library Project

In the final year of her teacher education program, Jessica Jensen is a teacher intern in four eighth-grade social studies classes. She has recently assigned a month-long group project that involves considerable library research. Midway through the project, Jessica writes the following entry in her journal:

Within each group, one student is studying culture of the region, one has religion, one has economy, and one government. The point is for the students to become "experts" on their topic in their region. There are a lot of requirements to this assignment. I'm collecting things as we go along because I think a project this long will be difficult for them to organize . . .?

So we spent all week in the library. I collected a minimum of two pages of notes yesterday, which will be a small part of their grade. The one thing that surprised me in our work in the library was their lack of skills. They had such difficulty researching, finding the information they needed, deciding what was important, and organizing and taking notes. As they worked, I walked around helping and was shocked. The librarian had already gotten out all of the appropriate resources. Even after they had the books in front of them, most did not know what to do. For instance, if they were assigned "economy," most looked in the index for that particular word. If they didn't find it, they gave up on the book. After realizing this, I had to start the next day with a brief lesson on researching and cross-referencing. I explained how they could look up commerce, imports, exports, and how these would all help them. I was also shocked at how poor their note-taking skills were. I saw a few kids copying paragraphs word for word. Almost none of them understood that notes don't need to be in full sentences. So, it was a long week at the library.

Next week is devoted to group work and time to help them work on their rough drafts. With the difficulty they had researching, I can imagine the problems that will arise out of turning their notes into papers. (Journal entry courtesy of Jessica Jensen)

Constructed-Response Question

1. Initially, Jessica realizes that her students will need some structure to complete the project successfully. In what ways do she and the librarian structure the assignment for the students?

Multiple-Choice Questions

2. How does the students' prior knowledge influence the effectiveness of their strategies?
   a. Students' lack of knowledge about such terms as *economics* makes it difficult for them to use the index and to cross-reference terms.
   b. Students' limited knowledge about their topic makes it difficult for them to make sense of the material they read.
   c. Students' lack of exposure to the topics they are researching makes it difficult for them to paraphrase and summarize what they've read.
   d. All of the above.

3. Given the information on metacognition in this chapter, how might Jessica teach students about strategy usage?
   a. Jessica needs to realize that due to their age, the eighth-grade students are not yet capable of acquiring learning strategies.
   b. Jessica can model and give students practice in using such strategies as identifying the main point of a passage, paraphrasing the material they read, referring to an index in a book, and keeping notes organized.
   c. None, because with additional reflection, Jessica will come to the conclusion that students already know how to use learning strategies and simply need to be told to try harder.
   d. Jessica should teach students to memorize the assertions of experts and repeat these comments verbatim in their reports.

ENHANCEDetext *licensure exam*

Basic Developmental Issues Tables

To understand particular developmental concepts, theories, and instructional practices, readers can identify positions on significant issues—the degree to which development is presumed to draw from nature and nurture, reflect qualitative and quantitative changes, and represent trends that are universal or varied. Examples of particuar developments and theories analyzed in terms of these key issues can be found on p. 70, 232, and 435.

For Further Exploration

Educators periodically become perplexed with how to motivate a child, resolve a problem with group dynamics, or address another dilemma. When initial strategies are ineffective and colleagues don't have a satisfactory answer, teachers and practitioners may search for expert advice. *For Further Exploration* exercises give readers a chance to refer to specialized topics and consider their relevance for important issues in education. For examples, see pages 48, 243, and 340.

BASIC DEVELOPMENTAL ISSUES
Contrasting Piaget and Vygotsky

ISSUE	PIAGET	VYGOTSKY
Nature and Nurture	Piaget believed that biological maturation probably constrains the rate at which children acquire new thinking capabilities. However, his focus was on how interactions with both the physical environment (e.g., handling concrete objects) and the social environment (e.g., discussing issues with peers) promote cognitive development.	Vygotsky acknowledged that children's inherited traits and talents affect the ways in which they interpret the environment. But his theory primarily addresses the environmental conditions (e.g., engagement in challenging activities, guidance from more competent individuals, exposure to cultural interpretations) that influence cognitive growth.
Universality and Diversity	In Piaget's view, children make similar advancements in their logical reasoning capabilities despite the particular environment in which they grow up. Children vary in the ages at which they acquire new abilities, however.	From Vygotsky's perspective, the specific cognitive abilities that children acquire depend on the cultural contexts in which the children are raised and the specific activities in which they are encouraged to engage.
Qualitative and Quantitative Change	Piaget proposed that children's logical reasoning skills progress through four qualitatively distinct stages. Any particular reasoning capability continues to improve in a gradual (quantitative) fashion throughout the stage in which it first appears.	Vygotsky acknowledged that children undergo qualitative changes in their thinking. Much of his theory points to gradual and presumably quantitative improvements in skills. A child may initially find a task impossible, later be able to execute it with adult assistance, and eventually perform it independently.

> **FOR FURTHER EXPLORATION . . .**
> Read about the properties of three interventions in character education.
> ENHANCEDetext
> *content extension*

OBSERVATION

Readers are encouraged to refine their interpretations of children. Foundational to effective teaching is the ability to identify children's thoughts, feelings, and abilities from their drawings, work samples, statements, and behavior. *Child Development and Education* provides numerous exercises for readers to watch and listen to children and examine their work. As they make independent judgments from what they see, readers can sharpen their interpretations with viewpoints from the authors.

Observation Guidelines

To work productively with children, educators must first be able to draw appropriate inferences from their behavior. *Observation Guidelines* tables help readers recognize developmental nuances in infants, children, and adolescents with whom they work. By learning how to recognize particular qualities in each area of growth, readers gain a deeper capacity for recognizing milestones and states to accommodate. As you can see on pages 213, 361, and 416, these tables offer specific characteristics to look for, present illustrative examples, and provide specific recommendations for practitioners.

OBSERVATION GUIDELINES
Assessing Piagetian Reasoning Processes in Children and Adolescents

CHARACTERISTIC	LOOK FOR	EXAMPLE	IMPLICATION
Concrete Thought	• Heavy reliance on concrete objects to understand concepts • Difficulty understanding abstract ideas	Tobey solves arithmetic word problems more easily when he can draw pictures of them.	Use concrete objects, drawings, and other realistic illustrations of abstract situations, concepts, and problems.
Abstract Thought	• Ability to understand strictly verbal explanations of abstract concepts and principles • Ability to reason about hypothetical or contrary-to-fact situations	Elsa can imagine how two parallel lines might go on forever without ever coming together.	When working with adolescents, occasionally use verbal explanations (e.g., short lectures) to present information, but assess students' understanding frequently to make sure they understand.
Idealism	• Idealistic notions about how the world should be • Difficulty taking other people's needs and perspectives into account when offering ideas for change • Inability to adjust ideals in light of what can realistically be accomplished	Martin advocates a system of government in which all citizens voluntarily contribute their earnings to a common "pool" and then withdraw money only as they need it.	Engage adolescents in discussions about challenging political and social issues.
Scientific Reasoning Skills	• Formulating multiple hypotheses for a particular phenomenon • Separation and control of variables	Serena proposes three possible explanations for a result she has obtained in her physics lab.	Have middle school and high school students design and conduct simple experiments in which they are shown how to control variables. Include interventions related to their interests.
Mathematical Reasoning Skills	• Understanding abstract mathematical symbols (e.g., π, the variable x in algebraic equations) • Understanding proportions in mathematical problem solving	Giorgio uses a 1:240 scale when drawing a floor plan of his school building.	Initially, introduce abstract mathematical tasks using simple examples (e.g., when introducing proportions, begin with fractions such as ½ and ¼). Progress to more complex examples only when youngsters are ready.

Observing Children 2-8

Observe a first-grade teacher guide children's nonfiction writing with a rubric.

ENHANCEDetext *video example*

Observing Children

New for this edition, the *Observing Children* feature illustrates particular characteristics and conditions described in the book with videos. As readers learn about a developmental concept, such as toddlers becoming scared with the presence of a stranger, a child being aware of memory limitations, or a classroom of children learning how to write with a rubric, they can see one or more children in a relevant situation. You can find examples on p. 52, 125, 168, 220, and 332.

Assessing Children

In another new tool for this edition, readers are provided with videos and students' creations and asked questions that guide their interpretations. By carefully inspecting children's activities, readers gain experience in analyzing children's facial expressions, body language, and behavior for clues as to their needs and abilities. Readers also have the opportunity to compare their judgments with interpretations from the authors. You can find examples on pages 184, 228, 287, and 346.

Assessing Children 8-1

Practice identifying intellectual abilities that are tapped in academic lessons.

ENHANCEDetext *application exercise*

Artifacts

Interspersed throughout the book, artifacts provide windows into children's development. Each artifact is described in terms of applicable chapter concepts. You will find examples of children's artifacts on pages 72, 211, 285, 329, and 471.

ARTIFACT 8-1 Examine 10-year-old Amaryth's sketches for use of several distinct abilities.

SENSITIVITY

Readers are shown how to demonstrate acceptance for children's upbringing. *Child Development and Education* situates children in the contexts of their lives and articulates how adults can address this personal knowledge. Through numerous illustrations of distinct family, cultural, and socioeconomic backgrounds, readers gain a practical understanding of adjustments that meet the needs of individual children.

Bioecology of Child Development

Skilled teachers and practitioners appreciate that a child is embedded within the interrelated contexts in which he or she grows. Within every chapter, one or more illustrations of a breadth of bioecological factors are identified as influences on a particular aspect of children's growth. You can see examples of the bioecological notation on pages 68, 262, 346, and 364.

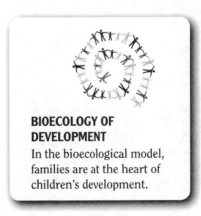

BIOECOLOGY OF DEVELOPMENT
In the bioecological model, families are at the heart of children's development.

DEVELOPMENT IN CULTURE
Immigrant Children

Individual children in immigrant families have a few similar experiences. They go to school, make friends, learn about two or more cultures, and master increasingly difficult concepts and skills. Often they learn a second language and adjust to discrepant expectations at home and in the dominant community. But children from immigrant families are by no means fully alike. They have quite different experiences depending on their personal characteristics and the circumstances of their family's immigration, their parents' jobs and income, and their culture's standing in the adopted society (Akiba & García Coll, 2003; Glick & Bates, 2010; Hernandez, Denton, & Macartney, 2010; Urdan, 2012).

Such similarities and differences are evident among children from immigrant families in Providence, Rhode Island (García Coll & Marks, 2009). Many of the immigrant families there had moved from Cambodia, the Dominican Republic, or Portugal. Children from these three cultural groups had somewhat comparable experiences in that they grew up in low-income families, had parents with high expectations for their education, and achieved at relatively high levels at school. Yet the three groups also varied in their beliefs and customs. Cambodian, Dominican, and Portuguese American children ate the foods of their ancestors, celebrated holidays compatible with their separate heritages, and worshipped in their own churches or temples. Within each group, individual children developed unique habits and self-perceptions.

Families from Cambodia had moved to the United States to escape war, starvation, and persecution. Two parents with approximately 4 years of formal education were typical heads of Cambodian American families. Parents spoke Khmer to their children and were somewhat segregated from others in the new society. Teachers perceived Cambodian American parents to be uninvolved because the parents rarely came to school. However, from the parents' perspective, parents should defer to teachers' authority and not interfere with instruction. Teachers saw these children as attentive, conscientious, and socially skilled.

Families from the Dominican Republic had usually moved to the United States for economic opportunities and a safe environment for their children. Single-parent and two-parent families were both common in Dominican immigrants. Families remained closely connected with extended family members back on the island, traveling back and forth between Providence and the Dominican Republic for birthdays, weddings, funerals, and family crises; likewise Dominican relatives often came to visit families in Providence. A strong network of Dominicans in the United States eased the adaptation of new immigrants and enriched children with role models, festivals, and other cultural resources. With their typically dark skin, Dominican American youngsters were perceived to be black by others, yet the Dominican American children generally identified with their Dominican heritage and not as African Americans. The children tended to do well in school but frequently received lower grades as they grew older, and they had relatively high rates of absenteeism from school.

Families from Portugal tended to enter long-standing communities of Portuguese Americans. Recently emigrating Portuguese families had moved to the United States for economic opportunities. Most families had two parents in the home. Members of the Portuguese American community celebrated their cultural heritage but also moved in and out of the mainstream society with ease, in part because their white, European American facial features resembled the appearance of local residents. Established Portuguese sports clubs and religious societies welcomed new immigrants, and numerous Portuguese Americans had penetrated positions of authority, including as police, political officials, and teachers. Two parents with little formal education were the typical heads of family.

Development in Culture

Every child acquires the values and traditions of one or more cultures, and these cultural frameworks give meaning to everything the child experiences. It is crucial for teachers and practitioners to gain a cultural perspective, in which they develop insights into their own backgrounds and learn how to identify, respect, and adjust to the practices of children and their families. In the *Development in Culture* feature, a particular aspect of development is illustrated in one or more cultural settings. You can find examples of this feature on pages 48, 342, and 378.

Case Studies

Case studies reveal how a particular facet of a development, for example language or morality, unfolds in a particular child. Each chapter begins with a case study and related questions that illustrate and frame chapter content. You will find examples of the introductory case studies on pages 115, 313, and 350.

CASE STUDY: Mario

As a young boy growing up in rural Vermont, Mario had the good fortune to learn two languages. At home, his parents spoke Spanish almost exclusively, communicating to one another in their shared native tongue and passing along their cultural heritage to their son. Most of Mario's early exposure to English was in the child care centers and preschools he attended off and on from the time he was 2 years old.

When Mario was 5, his dominant language was Spanish, but he was proficient in English as well. After his first 2 months in kindergarten, his teacher wrote the following in a report to Mario's parents:

[Mario is] extremely sociable. He gets along fine with all the children, and enjoys school. He is quite vocal. He does not seem at all conscious of his speech. His slight accent has had no effect on his relations with the others. Whenever I ask the class a question, he is always one of the ones with his hand up.

His greatest problem seems to be in the give and take of conversation. Since he always has something to say, he often finds it difficult to wait his turn when others are talking. When he talks, there are moments when you can see his little mind thinking through language—for he sometimes has to stop to recall a certain word in English which he might not have at his finger tips. (Fantini, 1985, p. 28)

The "slight accent" in Mario's English led a speech therapist to recommend speech therapy, which Mario's parents declined. In fact, all traces of an accent disappeared from Mario's speech by age 8, and his third-grade teacher was quite surprised to learn that he spoke a language other than English at home.

Standardized tests administered over the years attested to Mario's growing proficiency in English. Before he began kindergarten, his score on a standardized English vocabulary test was at the 29th percentile, reflecting performance that, although a little on the low side, was well within the average range. Later, when he took the California Achievement Test in the fourth, sixth, and eighth grades, he obtained scores at the 80th percentile or higher (and mostly above the 90th percentile) on the reading, writing, and spelling subtests. When Mario spent a semester of fifth grade at a Spanish-speaking school in Bolivia, he earned high marks in Spanish as well, with grades of 5 on a 7-point scale in reading, writing, and language usage.

As Mario grew older, his vocabulary and written language skills developed more rapidly in English than in Spanish, in large part because most of his instruction at school was in English. His father described the situation this way:

[B]y about fifth grade (age ten), he had entered into realms of experience for which he had no counterpart in Spanish. A clear example was an attempt to prepare for a fifth grade test on the topic of "The Industrial Revolution in England and France." It soon became clear that it was an impossibility to try to constrain the child to review materials read and discussed at school—in English—through Spanish. With this incident,

INVIGORATE LEARNING WITH THE ENHANCED PEARSON ETEXT

The Enhanced Pearson eText provides a rich, interactive learning environment designed to improve student mastery of content with the following multimedia features:

- **Overall design** that fosters readers' self-regulated learning with objectives, clear explanations, concrete illustrations, applications, and feedback.
- **Embedded videos** in the *Observing Children* feature show one-on-one interviews with children and adolescents and also students in the classroom and playground. These videos help readers actually see development, not simply read about it. (See pages 119, 124, 198, and 204 for examples.)
- **Scaffolded video analysis exercises** in the *Assessing Children* features challenge readers to apply chapter content to reflect upon teaching and learning in real classrooms. (See pages 128, 139, 228, and 229 for examples.)
- *Practicing for Your Licensure Exam* assessments, modeled after questions found on teacher licensure tests, help readers prepare for their certification exams. (See page 150 for example.)
- **Embedded assessments with feedback** throughout the eText help readers assess how well they have mastered the content. (See pages 215, 228, and 234 for examples.)

CURRENCY

More than a thousand new citations are included with this edition, reflecting the many important discoveries that have been made in recent years. Every chapter includes updates that together offer a cutting-edge perspective on children's growth. With this up-to-date knowledge, readers will be better prepared to meet the needs of children from many walks of life. Selected examples are as follows.

- New information on classroom assessment, including an example of a rubric and recommendations for advising children how to prepare for standardized tests, examining performance over time, and supplementing testing with other measures (Chapter 2, now retitled Research and Assessment).
- New sections on families with gay and lesbian parents, families with adolescent parents, families with military parents, and families with incarcerated parents (Chapter 3).
- New emphasis on special education and children with disabilities (e.g., Chapter 4, Chapter 7, Chapter 15)
- Reorganization and reframing of content on cognitive sciences and information processing (Chapter 7), with new emphasis on executive processing and exceptionalities (Chapter 8).
- Recent research on second language learners, in particular English Language Learners in the classroom (Chapter 9).
- Description of the Common Core standards and academic standards frameworks, along with recommendations for applying standards in a developmentally appropriate manner (Chapter 10).
- Reorganization of content focused on development of the self (Chapter 12) and self-regulation and motivation (Chapter 13), with increased attention to diversity.
- Emphasis on contemporary topics such as cyber-bullying (Chapter 14), self-control (Chapter 13), emergent literacy and expository writing (Chapter 10), and health and nutrition (Chapter 5).
- New and expanded material on instruction with advanced technology and integration of electronic media into peer relationships (Chapter 15)

SUPPLEMENTARY MATERIALS

The following supplements are available to help instructors organize, manage, and enliven their courses and to enhance students' learning and development as teachers.

Online Instructor's Manual

Available to instructors for download at www.pearsonhighered.com/educator is an *Instructor's Manual* with suggestions for learning activities, supplementary lectures, group activities, and class discussions. These have been carefully selected to provide opportunities to support, enrich, and expand on what students read in the textbook.

Online PowerPoint® Slides

PowerPoint slides are available to instructors for download on www.pearsonhighered.com/educator. These slides include key concept summarizations and other graphic aids to help students understand, organize, and remember core concepts and ideas.

Online Test Bank

The *Test Bank* that accompanies this text contains both multiple-choice and essay questions. Some items (lower-level questions) simply ask students to identify or explain concepts and principles they have learned. But many others (higher-level questions) ask students to apply those same concepts and principles to specific classroom situations—that is, to actual student behaviors and teaching strategies. The lower-level questions assess basic knowledge of development and its implications in educational settings. But ultimately it is the higher-level questions that can best assess students' ability to use principles of child and adolescent development in their own teaching practice.

TestGen

TestGen is a powerful test generator available exclusively from Pearson Education publishers. You install TestGen on your personal computer (Windows or Macintosh) and create your own tests for classroom testing and for other specialized delivery options, such as over a local area network or on the web. A test bank, which is also called a Test Item File (TIF), typically contains a large set of test items, organized by chapter and ready for your use in creating a test, based on the associated textbook material. Assessments—including equations, graphs, and scientific notation—may be created for both print and testing online. The tests can be downloaded in the following formats:

TestGen Testbank file — PC
TestGen Testbank file—MAC
TestGen Testbank—Blackboard 9 TIF
TestGen Testbank—Blackboard CE/Vista (WebCT) TIF
Angel Test Bank (zip)
D2L Test Bank (zip)
Moodle Test Bank
Sakai Test Bank (zip)

ACKNOWLEDGMENTS

Although we are listed as the sole authors of this textbook, in fact many individuals have contributed in significant ways to its content and form. Our editor, Kevin Davis, recognized the need for an applied child development book and nudged us to write one. Kevin has been the captain of our ship throughout all six editions, charting our journey and alerting us when we drifted off course. We thank Kevin for his continuing encouragement, support, insight, vision, and high standards.

We have been equally fortunate to work with a series of expert development editors: Julie Peters (on the first and second editions), Autumn Benson (on the third edition), Christie Robb (fourth edition), Linda Bishop (early planning and fifth edition), and Gail Gottfried (sixth edition). It was a special treat to work with Gail on the current edition given her expertise in research perspectives in child development. Julie, Autumn, Christie, Linda, and Gail have seen us through the day-to-day challenges of writing the book—for instance, offering creative ideas for improving the manuscript, locating artifacts to illustrate key concepts, pushing us to condense when we were unnecessarily wordy, insisting that certain concepts be clarified, overseeing the quality of the book's increasingly sophisticated online resources, being a willing ear whenever we needed to vent our frustrations, and, in general, coordinating our writing efforts until books went into production. We thank Julie, Autumn, Christie, Linda, and Gail for their advice, support, and good humor, and also for their willingness to drop whatever else they were doing to come to our assistance at critical times—even on subsequent editions of the book!

Others at both Pearson Education and S4Carlisle Publishing Services have been key players in bringing the book to fruition. Lorretta Palagi worked diligently to keep the manuscript focused, concise, and clear. Lauren Carlson, Norine Strang, and Kelli Jauron guided the manuscript through the production process; without a complaint, they let us continue to tweak the book in innumerable small ways even as production deadlines loomed dangerously close. Carrie Mollette, with the help of Lauren Carlson, secured permissions for the excerpts and figures we borrowed from other sources and was flexible when we added to our list at the eleventh hour. Caitlin Griscom, Jorgensen Fernandez, and Sandeep Ramesh sifted through possible photos to identify those that could best capture key developmental principles in a visual form. Marisia Styles resolved a range of operational issues, for which we are grateful. Marketing whizzes Joanna Sabella and Maggie Waples helped us get out the word about the book. Pearson Education sales representatives across the country offered us encouragement and relayed invaluable recommendations they had heard from instructors using the book.

We are also deeply indebted to the children, teachers, and other adults who appear in the videos that are included in the book. Recordings of children's images and actions allow us to better understand and address the needs of children generally. We greatly appreciate the assistance of Gail Gottfried, who helped us sort through possible videos, and the many professionals who applied arranged environments and conducted interviews in which children could be themselves and relay their thoughts and feelings. Thanks to Jayne Downey, Stuart Garry, Jason Cole, Greg Pierson, Keli Cotner, Dana Snyder, Kelle Nolke, Stacey Blank, Tara Kaysen, Addie Lopez, Laura Sether, Lisa Blank, and many others for their creative and technical assistance.

Children, Adolescents, Teachers, and Other Professionals Equally important contributors to the book were the many young people and practitioners who provided the work samples, written reflections, photographs, other artifacts, and verbal responses that appear throughout the 15 chapters and other resources for the book. The work of the following young people and adults contributed immeasurably to the depth and richness of our discussions:

Davis Alcorn	Geoff Alkire	Madison Blank	Eric Campos
Jacob Alcorn	Brenda Bagazuma	Brent Bonner	Leif Carlson
Curtis Alexander	Andrew Belcher	Diamond Bonner	Zoe Clifton
Kyle Alexander	Katie Belcher	Ricco Branch	Wendy Cochran
David Alkire	Kayla Blank	Marsalis Bush	Jenna Dargy

Noah Davis	Tyler Hensley	Dustin O'Mara	Connor Sheehan
Shea Davis	Elisabet Deyanira	Alex Ormrod	Aftyn Siemer
Mayra de la Garza	Hernandez	Jeff Ormrod	Karma Marie Smith
Brandon Doherty	Lauryn Hickman	Shir-Lisa Owens	Alex Snow
Daniel Erdman	Sam Hickman	Isiah Payan	Sam Snow
Rachel Foster	William Hill	Isabelle Peters	Connor Stephens
Tina Ormrod Fox	Brandon Jackson	Michelle Pollman	Megan Lee Stephens
Eddie Garcia	Rachel Johnson	Laura Prieto-Velasco	Joe Sweeney
Palet Garcia	Jordan Kemme	Cooper Remignanti	Emma Thompson
Veronica Garcia	Marianne Kies	Ian Rhoades	Grace Tober
James Garrett III	Sarah Luffel	Talia Rockland	Sarah Toon
Amaryth Gass	Jessica Lumbrano	Oscar Rodriguez	David Torres
Andrew Gass	Dave Magnacca	Elizabeth Romero	Joseph Torres
Tony Gass	Joan Magnacca	Corey Ross	Samuel Torres
Dana Gogolin	Maria Magnacca	Katie Ross	Madison Tupper
Ivy Gogolin	Krista Marrufo	Trisha Ross	Danielle Welch
Kenton Groissaint	Steven Merrick	Amber Rossetti	Brady Williamson
Acadia Gurney	Margaret Mohr	Bianca Sanchez	John Wilson
Amanda Hackett	Tchuen-Yi Murry	Daniela Sanchez	Joey Wolf
Jared Hale	Mike Newcomb	Corwin Sether	Lindsey Woollard
Cody Havens	Malanie Nunez	Alex Sheehan	Anna Young

To ensure that we included children's work from a wide variety of geographic locations and backgrounds, we contacted organizations north and south, east and west to obtain work samples that would reflect ethnic, cultural, and economic diversity. We want to thank several individuals for their assistance and coordination efforts: Don Burger at Pacific Resources for Education and Learning (PREL), Michelle Gabor of the Salesian Boys' and Girls' Club, Rita Hocog Inos of the Commonwealth of the Northern Mariana Islands Public School System, Bettie Lake of the Phoenix Elementary School District, Heidi Schork and members of the Boston Youth Clean-Up Corps (BYCC), Ann Shump of the Oyster River School District, and Chelsie Hess and Laura Pool from Eyestone Elementary School in Fort Collins, Colorado. Furthermore we thank the many professionals—a child welfare case worker, a neurologist, a public health educator, and many others—who were so helpful to our efforts to identify artifacts, anecdotes, dialogues, and strategies to illustrate developmental concepts; key among them were Janet Alcorn, Rosenna Bakari, Trish Belcher, Paula Case, Michael Gee, Jennifer Glynn, Evie Greene, Diana Haddad, Betsy Higginbotham, Betsy Hopkins, Dinah Jackson, Jesse Jensen, Mike McDevitt, Erin Miguel, Michele Minichiello, Andrew Moore, Dan Moulis, Tina Ormrod Fox, Annemarie Palincsar, Kellee Patterson, Elizabeth Peña, Jrene Rahm, Nancy Rapport, Lori Reinsvold, Gwen Ross, Karen Scates, Cindy Schutter, Karen Setterlin, Jean Slater, Julie Spencer, Nan Stein, Pat Tonneman, Peggy Torres, Sally Tossey, Pat Vreeland, and Cathy Zocchi.

Colleagues and Reviewers In addition, we received considerable encouragement, assistance, and support from our professional colleagues. Developmental scholars, educational psychologists, and teacher educators at numerous institutions around the country have offered insightful reviews of one or more chapters. We are especially indebted to the following reviewers for this edition:

Gary Bingham, Georgia State University
John Corey Steele, Loyola University Chicago
Tami Dean, Illinois State University
Ithel Jones, Florida State University
Nanci Monaco, Buffalo State College

Elizabeth Pemberton, University of Delaware
Lisa Pescara-Kovach, University of Toledo
Valerie Roderick, Arizona State University
Julia Torquati, University of Nebraska- Lincoln

We continue to appreciate the guidance of reviewers for earlier editions of the book. These individuals helped guide our early efforts:

Karen Abrams, Keene State College

Daisuke Akiba, Queens College

Jan Allen, University of Tennessee

Lynley Anderman, University of Kentucky

Patricia Ashton, University of Florida

David E. Balk, Kansas State University

Thomas M. Batsis, Loyola Marymount University

Brigid Beaubien, Eastern Michigan University

Jennifer Betters-Bubon, University of Wisconsin–Madison

Doris Bergen, Miami University

Irene Bersola-Nguyen, California State University–Sacramento

Donna M. Burns, The College of St. Rose

Jean Clark, University of South Alabama

Heather Davis, University of Florida

Teresa K. DeBacker, University of Oklahoma

Michael Cunningham, Tulane University

Heather Davis, North Carolina State University

Deborah K. Deemer, University of Northern Iowa

Karen Drill, University of Illinois at Chicago

Eric Durbrow, The Pennsylvania State University

William Fabricius, Arizona State University

Daniel Fasko, Morehead State University

Suzanne Fegley, University of Pennsylvania

Kathleen Fite, Texas State University

Hema Ganapathy-Coleman, Indiana State University

Connie Gassner, Ivy Tech Community College

Sherryl Browne Graves, Hunter College

William Gray, University of Toledo

Michael Green, University of North Carolina–Charlotte

Glenda Griffin, Texas A&M University

Deborah Grubb, Morehead State University

Linda L. Haynes, University of South Alabama

Melissa Heston, University of Northern Iowa

James E. Johnson, The Pennsylvania State University

Joyce Juntune, Texas A&M University

Michael Keefer, University of Missouri–St. Louis

Judith Kieff, University of New Orleans

Nancy Knapp, University of Georgia

Jennie Lee-Kim, University of Maryland

Carol A. Marchel, Winthrop University

Mary McLellan, Northern Arizona University

Sharon McNeely, Northeastern Illinois University

Kenneth Merrell, University of Iowa

Marilyn K. Moore, Illinois State University

Tamera Murdock, University of Missouri–Kansas City

Bridget Murray, Indiana State University

Kathy Nakagawa, Arizona State University

Virginia Navarro, University of Missouri–St. Louis

Terry Nourie, Illinois State University

Larry Nucci, University of Illinois–Chicago

Debra S. Pierce, Ivy Tech Community

Jennifer Parkhurst, Duke University

Sherrill Richarz, Washington State University

Kent Rittschof, Georgia Southern University

Linda Rogers, Kent State University

Richard Ryan, University of Rochester

Candy Skelton, Texas A&M University–Corpus Christi

Sue Spitzer, California State University, San Bernardino

Benjamin Stephens, Clemson University

Bruce Tuckman, The Ohio State University

Rob Weisskirch, California State University–Monterey Bay

Kathryn Wentzel, University of Maryland–College Park

Andrew R. Whitehead, East Stroudsburg University of Pennsylvania

Allan Wigfield, University of Maryland–College Park

Thomas D. Yawkey, The Pennsylvania State University

Increasingly, we have heard from colleagues at other institutions who have taken the time to let us know what they think about the book and how it might be improved. We are grateful for such very helpful feedback. In addition, staff and administrators at the University of Northern Colorado—especially staff at the Michener Library and Mark Alcorn, Carolyn Edwards, Helen Reed, Eugene Sheehan, and Robbyn Wacker—unselfishly provided advice, resources, and time.

Our Families   Finally, our families have been supportive and patient over the extended period we have been preoccupied with reading, researching, writing, and editing. Our children gave of themselves in anecdotes, artwork, and diversions from our work. Our husbands picked up the slack around the house and gave us frequent emotional boosts and comic relief. Much love and many thanks to Eugene, Connor, and Alex (from Teresa) and to Richard, Tina, Alex, and Jeff (from Jeanne).

T.M.M.
J.E.O.

Brief Contents

Contents

Part 4 • Social and Emotional Development

Chapter 11 Emotional Development 406

Chapter 12 Development of Self and Social Understandings 448

Chapter 13 Self-Regulation and Motivation 486

Special Features

Basic Developmental Issues

Development in Culture

CHILD DEVELOPMENT AND EDUCATION

CHAPTER ONE

Making a Difference in the Lives of Children and Adolescents

CASE STUDY: Tonya

At any given moment, in almost every classroom, at least one child is having difficulty in adjusting to the demands of school. The struggling child may be delayed in academic skills, careless in following classroom rules, or rejected by peers. Mary Renck Jalongo remembers one first-grade child, Tonya, who had faced each of these problems (Jalongo, Isenberg, & Gerbracht, 1995).

Fortunately for Tonya, Mary was knowledgeable about child development. Mary realized that Tonya, like every child, had positive qualities and, with the right support, would be able to overcome her challenges. To determine how best to help Tonya, Mary considered the little girl's circumstances. Academically, Tonya was delayed. She had been retained in kindergarten and was not catching up as quickly as Mary would have liked. Physically, Tonya received inadequate nutrition and was chronically hungry at school. Socially, Tonya had few friends, having previously badgered classmates into giving her their snacks and prized possessions and, when they refused, having pilfered the items from their desks.

Mary reports that Tonya's mother was sick, at a debilitating point, with lupus, and not able to work outside the home or attend school functions. To compound her problems, Tonya lacked the support of her principal, who thought that a harsh punishment—no recess for a month—was an appropriate response to Tonya's thefts.

In spite of these challenging conditions, Tonya was eager to develop productive skills and solve some of her own problems. When Mary asked Tonya why she took other children's snacks, she answered simply that she was hungry. When asked if she ate breakfast, Tonya replied that she had not because she needed to take care of her younger brother. After Mary invited her to think about possible solutions, Tonya volunteered that she and her brother might be able to get breakfast at their aunt's house. Tonya followed through with this solution, walking daily with her brother to her aunt's house for an early morning meal.

Mary also realized that Tonya had the capacity to repair her relationships with peers. After obtaining Tonya's promise that she would stop taking other children's things, Mary stood proudly by Tonya's side and announced to the class that Tonya had agreed not to take anyone's belongings. Afterward, Tonya earned the acceptance of the other children and began to concentrate on her schoolwork. Ultimately Tonya blossomed into a healthy, well-adjusted young woman (M. R. Jalongo, personal communication, June 12, 2007).

- What kind of impact did Mary Jalongo have on Tonya's life?
- How did Mary apply her understanding of child development in her work with Tonya?

In drawing on her knowledge of child development, Mary realized that Tonya could grow and change if given sensitive, loving care. By encouraging Tonya and her brother to eat breakfast with their aunt, Mary helped meet Tonya's physical needs and paved the way for closer ties to extended family. By repairing Tonya's damaged reputation with the other children, Mary helped Tonya earn their acceptance. Feeling comfortable physically and secure emotionally, Tonya was better prepared to tackle academic tasks and develop a healthy sense of who she was and how she fit in the world around her. Thanks, in part, to Mary Jalongo's thoughtful intercession, Tonya would ultimately thrive.

THE STUDY OF CHILD DEVELOPMENT

The study of human development helps us understand how human beings change from the time of conception, through the childhood and adolescent years, and on into adulthood, old age, and death. This book covers the early part of the human journey—beginning with the union of sperm and ovum and including prenatal growth, birth, infancy, childhood, and

OBJECTIVES

1.1: Describe the study of child development and three basic issues that characterize developmental change.

1.2: Differentiate among the seven theoretical perspectives on child development in terms of essential principles and educational implications.

1.3: Identify the characteristics and educational implications of the five developmental periods.

1.4: Formulate developmentally appropriate practices that teachers and other professionals can use.

adolescence. The field of **child development** seeks to identify and explain changes in the physical, cognitive, and social-emotional development of children and adolescents.

The developmental changes of childhood have three essential qualities. First, the abilities that emerge during developmental changes tend to be *persistent*: Once a new developmental ability is introduced, it typically remains in the child's repertoire of skills, as with abilities to walk and talk. Second, developmental changes are *cumulative*: A new ability builds on the previous one, as when a toddler shifts from eating with his fingers to using utensils, first occasionally and then consistently. Finally, developmental changes are *progressive:* Children gradually become more capable and responsible, even though they sometimes revert to less mature forms, as when a 4-year-old girl, who has learned the need to express her disagreements verbally, every now and then regresses to hitting a classmate during a heated argument.

As you will learn in this chapter, a child's developmental journey is guided by four factors:

* *Nature*—the genetic inheritance guiding the child's growth
* *Nurture*—the influences of the social and physical environment in which the child lives
* *Existing conditions for the child*—the physiological and psychological foundations upon which new advancements can be built
* *The child's own activity*—the child's choices, mental processes, emotional responses, and behaviors

As you will also discover in your reading, development includes changes that are common to most children as well as those that are specific to particular individuals, groups, or those who share a particular characteristic. At times, we talk about developments that nearly everyone undergoes, such as acquiring complex language skills and becoming increasingly considerate of other people's feelings. At other times, we discuss developments that differ considerably among youngsters. For example, some children respond to difficulties at school by seeking support from peers, teachers, and family members, whereas others withdraw from teachers and classmates and participate in risky behaviors (M. B. Spencer, 2006).

To describe the many specific influences on children's growth, scholars of child development draw from several academic disciplines. In this book, our descriptions pull from research primarily in psychology but also in biology, sociology, anthropology, and the applied fields of early intervention, education, child and family studies, juvenile justice, counseling, social work, and medicine. We emphasize research that is relevant to children's experiences in schools.

Our primary goal is to help you support healthy, optimal development in all children in your care. We pursue this goal by focusing on two objectives. First, we want you to learn how children think, feel, and act at various ages. This information can help you understand children with whom you work. Second, we want you to be able to apply what you learn in your classroom, school, and community. We will show you how you can integrate practical ideas from the field of child development into your instruction, classroom routines, and relationships with children.

Three Developmental Domains

The study of child development is organized into three domains, or broad areas of study: physical development, cognitive development, and social-emotional development. **Physical development** is concerned with the biological changes of the body. It includes genetics, a fetus's growth in the mother's womb, the birth process, brain development, and the acquisition of such motor skills as throwing a ball and cutting paper with scissors. It also encompasses behaviors and environmental factors that promote and impede growth and health. **Cognitive development** refers to the age-related transformations that occur in children's reasoning, concepts, memory, language, and intellectual skills—changes that are cultivated by children's involvement in families, schools, and communities. **Social-emotional development** includes the many modifications that occur in emotions, self-concept, motivation, social relationships, and moral reasoning and behavior—advancements that depend in large part on children's interactions with other people.

Although the three domains may appear to be independent areas, they are in fact closely intertwined. An increase in the ability to look at situations from multiple perspectives, a cognitive ability, enhances social skills. A second-grade girl becomes more skilled at pursuing personal goals (e.g., wanting to tell Natalie about her upcoming birthday party) while respecting others' needs (e.g., realizing that she should comfort Natalie about her dog having died last night before mentioning the birthday get-together). The three domains are also inseparable such that every activity by the child has ripple effects. An exercise break allows for better concentration, second-language instruction permits new friendships, and, as occurred with Tonya, emotional support from a teacher enables academic progress.

Effects of Context on Development

All areas of development depend on the **context** of children's lives—their experiences in families, schools, neighborhoods, community organizations, cultural and ethnic groups, and society at large. Child development research has shown that some sort of "family" or other cluster of close, caring relationships is a critical condition for optimal development. Schools, too, play a significant role, not only by fostering cognitive skills but also by supplying a teacher and peers whose relationships are influential. As a member of one or more ethnic groups and **cultures**—long-standing groups with defined values, traditions, and symbol systems—children form interpersonal relationships and enter into daily activities with a sense of purpose. And in their local communities and broader societies, children gain access to peers, adult role models, recreation, the media, and such institutions as social services, banks, and medical clinics.

In preparing to teach or in some other way care for children, you are about to become a vital part of their context. Your productive role in that setting will be strengthened by a thorough foundation in child development. One of the ways you can gain this foundation is by becoming familiar with three key issues that child development theorists have grappled with, but not yet resolved. First, experts wonder how genetic factors and the environment combine to influence development. Second, they speculate about which developmental paths are true for everyone and which others are unique to specific groups and individuals. Third, they debate about the developmental changes that can be characterized as major transformations or, alternatively, as a series of gradual trends. Let's now look more closely at these three issues, which are referred to as questions of (a) nature and nurture, (b) universality and diversity, and (c) qualitative and quantitative change.

Nature and Nurture

In the study of development, **nature** refers to the inherited characteristics that influence growth. **Nurture** consists of the environmental conditions that additionally affect the progression of changes. Nature and nurture are partners in a child's growth.

Nature contributes to both common human traits and individual differences in children. Some genes (the basic units of heredity) appear in virtually everyone. Almost all children have the capacity to learn to walk, understand language, imitate others, use simple tools, and draw inferences about how other people view the world. Other characteristics, including stature, eye color, and facial appearance, vary among children and are also strongly determined by heredity. Similarly, children's **temperaments**—their characteristic ways of responding to emotional events, novel stimuli, and impulses—are affected by their individual genetic makeup (Rothbart & Bates, 2006; Wang & Deater-Deckard, 2013). Likewise, being slow or quick to learn from everyday experiences has a partial genetic basis (Calvin et al., 2012; Kan, Wicherts, Dolan, & van der Maas, 2013; Petrill et al., 2004).

Heredity is powerful, but it has limits. For one thing, the child's present developmental level affects which genes come into play. Whereas some hereditary instructions, such as the chromosomes that determine sex, exert an influence from the beginning, other instructions emerge only gradually through the process of **maturation**, the genetically guided changes that occur over the course of development. For example, puberty begins when the pituitary gland in the brain senses it is time to release certain hormones, the excretion of which initiates sexual maturation.

Preparing for Your Licensure Examination
Your teaching test might ask you to distinguish the kinds of growth that children exhibit in the three developmental domains.

Children's experiences affect all aspects of their being, from the health of their bodies to the curiosity of their minds. *Nurture* affects children's development through multiple channels: physiologically through nutrition, activity, affection, and exposure to light, viruses, and stress; intellectually through informal experiences and formal instruction; and socially through exposure to adult role models and participation in peer relationships. However, nurture faces definite limits. Even the best environments cannot overpower every possible defective gene. And, unfortunately, optimal conditions in the environment do not always exist. Abuse, neglect, poor nutrition, pollution, and racism are just a few threats that children may encounter.

Historically, many theorists saw nature and nurture as separate and rival factors. Several early theorists believed that biological factors are ultimately responsible for growth. Other theorists assumed that children become whatever the environment shapes them to be. In recent decades, developmental theorists have learned that nature and nurture intermesh dynamically in the lives of busy, active children. Consider the following principles of how nature and nurture exert their effects in development.

Nature and nurture are constrained by the developmental process. Genes and environment alone are not sufficient to explain the complex sequences of events that occur in the changing brain and body. The *developmental process* itself is a factor in growth. In other words, current structures in the child's brain and body constrain the handiwork of nature and nurture (Champagne, 2009; Stiles, 2008). For example, during a child's prenatal growth in the womb, new cells specialize in particular ways and move to appropriate locations depending on signals from nearby cells. In the globular hands that first emerge during prenatal development, cells respond to certain chemicals by duplicating, taking on certain properties, and in boundaries between fingers, perishing to separate the digits. This cascade of reactions allows fingers to sprout, project from the palm, elongate, and differentiate into the elegant digits that will permit buttoning a shirt and drawing with crayons.

The relative effects of heredity and environment vary for different areas of development. Some abilities are strongly influenced by genetically controlled systems in the brain. For example, the abilities to distinguish among various speech sounds and use appropriate grammatical structures develop without formal training under a wide range of environmental conditions (Archer & Curtin, 2011; Gallistel, Brown, Carey, Gelman, & Keil, 1991). In contrast, abilities in traditional school subject areas (e.g., reading, geography, and music) rely heavily on instruction (Bruer, 1999; R. K. Olson, 2008).

Inherited tendencies make individual children more or less responsive to particular environmental influences. Because of their genetic makeup, some children are easily affected by certain conditions in the environment, whereas others are less affected (Bugental, 2009; La Greca, Lai, Joormann, Auslander, & Short, 2013; Rutter, 1997). Children who are, by nature, inhibited may be quite shy around other people if they have few social contacts. However, if their parents and teachers arrange for them to make friends, these otherwise shy children may become more socially outgoing (Arcus, 1991; Kagan & Fox, 2006). Children who have more extroverted temperaments may be sociable regardless of their specific environment because they will seek out peers with whom they can talk, laugh, and play.

Some genes exert their effects only in certain environments. Children are sometimes born with particular genes that put them at risk for developing psychological problems. For example, a certain chemical, serotonin, is produced in the brain and influences a person's mood. Some people have a short form of a gene (known as 5-HTT) that makes it difficult for their brains to recycle serotonin, such that insufficient amounts of it are available for maintaining positive emotions. As a result, these individuals are at risk for becoming chronically sad and irritable. Yet the short form of this gene does not cause emotional depression unless these individuals are also maltreated as children or grow up in a stressful environment (Caspi et al., 2003). Conversely, being raised in a potentially traumatizing environment is associated with later depression mainly in individuals who have this short gene.

Individual differences in heredity may exert stronger effects when environments are favorable than when environments are impoverished. When youngsters have decent experiences in their culture, community, and age-group, heredity often plays a strong role in their individual characteristics. Thus, when children grow up with adequate nutrition, a warm and stable home environment, and appropriate educational experiences, heredity affects how quickly and thoroughly they acquire new skills. But when they have experiences that are quite unusual—for instance, when they experience extreme deprivation—the environment outweighs heredity (D. C. Rowe, Almeida, & Jacobson, 1999; Sameroff, 2009). When children grow up deprived of adequate nutrition and stimulation, they may fail to develop advanced intellectual skills, even though they had been born with such potential (N. A. Fox, Almas, Degnan, Nelson, & Zeanah, 2011; Plomin & Petrill, 1997).

Timing of environmental exposure matters. When children are changing rapidly in any area, they are especially prone to influence by the environment. Early in a mother's pregnancy, her use of certain drugs may damage her future offspring's quickly growing organs and limbs. Just prior to birth, exposure to the same drugs may adversely affect the baby's brain, which at that point is forming the neurological connections needed for survival and learning in the outside world. In a few cases a particular stimulation *must* occur during a brief period if a prospective ability is to become functional (C. Blakemore, 1976; Hubel & Wiesel, 1965). In such cases there is a *critical period* for stimulation.

At birth, certain areas of the brain are tentatively reserved for processing visual patterns—lines, shapes, contours, depth, and so forth. In virtually all cases, infants encounter adequate stimulation to preserve these brain circuits. However, when cataracts are present at birth and not removed for a few years, a child's vision is obstructed, and areas of the brain that otherwise would be devoted to these visual functions are redirected for other purposes.

In many and probably most other developmental areas, however, children may be most receptive to a certain type of stimulation at one point in their lives but remain able to benefit from it to some degree later as well. Many theorists use the term **sensitive period** when referring to such a long time frame of heightened receptivity to particular environmental experiences. Sensitive periods appear to be more common than critical periods, reflecting nature's fortunate practice of giving children second chances to learn important skills. During early childhood, children are naturally predisposed to tune in to the sounds, structure, and meaning of language, suggesting a sensitive period for learning language. Educators can realistically expect to make meaningful progress with children who are delayed in language as long as missing experiences are provided.

Children's actions affect their environment. In addition to being affected by nature and nurture, children's growth is influenced by their own behaviors. Youngsters make many choices, seek out information, and, over time, refine their knowledge and beliefs. Children often request information ("What does *cooperate* mean, Mommy?") and experiences ("Uncle Ignacio, can I play on your computer?"). Children even create environments that intensify their genetic tendencies. Those with irritable dispositions might pick fights, thereby creating a more aggressive climate in which to interact.

As children get older, they become increasingly able to seek stimulation that suits their tendencies. Imagine that Marissa has an inherited talent for verbal processing. As a young child, Marissa depends on her parents to read to her. As she grows older, Marissa chooses her own books and begins to read to herself. Marissa's experience would suggest that genetic tendencies become more powerful as children grow older—an expectation that is consistent with genetic research (Haworth & Plomin, 2012; Scarr & McCartney, 1983; Trzaskowski, Yang, Visscher, & Plomin, 2014; Tucker-Drob & Harden, 2012).

Universality and Diversity

Developmental changes that occur in just about everyone are said to reflect a certain degree of **universality**. Unless significant disabilities are present, all young children learn to sit, walk, and run, almost invariably in that order. Other developmental changes are highly individual or are different between groups—for example, in boys and girls or among members of different cultures. These variations reflect **diversity** and remind us of the many healthy manifestations of children's growth—and, unfortunately, of a few maladaptive pathways.

Theorists differ in their beliefs regarding the extent to which developmental accomplishments are universal among human beings or unique to individuals and groups. Some scholars propose that shared genes and maturational processes contribute to universality in development (e.g., Gesell, 1928). They point out that despite widely varying environments, virtually all human beings acquire basic motor skills, proficiency in language, and the ability to inhibit immediate impulses. Certain consistencies in children's environments provide an additional route to universality. In all corners of the world, children observe objects falling down rather than up and people getting angry when someone intentionally hurts them. In the same manner, children commonly participate in everyday cultural activities, for example, household chores, which prepare them for adult roles.

Yet other theorists have been impressed by diversity in child development. They point out that nature permits variations in genes affecting facial features, physical characteristics, and intellectual abilities. Still other scholars view the environment (nurture) as weighing heavily in diversity. They propose that factors as global as the historical period of one's upbringing and as personal as one's family relationships generate individuality (Baltes, Lindenberger, & Staudinger, 2006; Bornstein & Lansford, 2010; Giallo, Cooklin, Wade, D'Esposito, & Nicholson, 2014). Many theorists also see culture as a significant source of diversity: Children differ in the competencies they acquire based on the particular tools, communication systems, and values they encounter in society (Göncü & Gauvain, 2012; Griedler & Shields, 2008; Rogoff, 2003).

Earlier we mentioned that the relative influences of nature and nurture vary from one area of development to another. The same pattern is true for universality and diversity. Development tends to be similar in some aspects of physical development, such as the sequences in which puberty unfolds. In other areas, including many aspects of cognitive and social-emotional development, diversity is prevalent. Nevertheless, there is always *some* diversity, even in physical development. Obviously, children vary in height, weight, and skin color, and some are born with physical disabilities or become seriously injured.

Throughout this book you will find instances of developmental universality, but just as often, you will see divergence in developmental pathways. Gaining an appreciation for both common trends and the many exceptions will help you meet the needs of children.

Qualitative and Quantitative Change

Sometimes development reflects dramatic changes in the essence or underlying structure of a characteristic. Such major reorganizations are called **qualitative changes**. When children learn to run, they propel their bodies forward in a way that is distinctly different from walking—they are not simply moving faster. When they begin to talk in two-word sentences rather than with single words, they are, for the first time, using rudimentary forms of grammar. And when they shift from obeying a teacher because they do not want to be punished to following classroom rules because it is the right thing to do, they are transforming the way they look at morality.

But not all development involves dramatic change. In fact, development frequently occurs as a gradual progression, or *trend,* with many small additions and modifications to behaviors and thought processes. These progressions are called **quantitative changes**. For example, children gradually grow taller and learn more and more things about such diverse realms as the animal kingdom and society's rules for showing courtesy.

Stage Theories

Theorists who emphasize qualitative changes often use the term **stage** to refer to a period of development characterized by a particular way of behaving or thinking. According to a **stage theory** of development, individuals progress through a series of stages that are qualitatively different from one another.[1]

Some stage theories include *hierarchical* levels. In hierarchical models, each stage is seen as providing the essential foundation for modifications that follow. After observing children in a wide variety of thought-provoking situations, the eminent psychologist **Jean Piaget** (1896–1980) proposed a stage theory to describe transformations in children's logical

---

[1] Note that developmental scholars have a more precise meaning for the term *stage* than is communicated by the same word in everyday speech. Parents often make comments like "He's at the *terrible twos stage.*" Such comments reflect the idea that children are behaving typically for their age group. When developmental scientists say a child is in a certain stage, they additionally assume that the child is undergoing a series of age-related qualitative transformations.

reasoning. His observations led him to conclude that as infants, children interact with the world primarily through trial-and-error behavior, for example, in discovering the properties of a rubber ball as they mouth it and roll it on the floor. As children mature, they begin to symbolically represent concepts and make mental predictions about objects and actions in the world around them. They know that the ball will bounce when they drop it on a wooden floor. Later they begin to derive logical deductions about concrete, real-world situations, perhaps inferring that the ball must be made out of a pliable substance. And once they reach adolescence, they become capable of thinking systematically about abstract ideas—for instance, by thinking about the unseen physical factors (e.g., *momentum, gravity*) influencing the ball's bounce.

Another famous stage theorist, **Erik Erikson** (1902–1994), focused on a set of primary challenges that individuals face at different points in their lives. During their infancy and early childhood years, youngsters learn first to trust others and then to act self-sufficiently. As adolescents, youngsters reflect on their *identities* as boys or girls, members of particular ethnic groups, and individuals with defined interests and goals for the future. In Erikson's theory, stages are "soft": People do not fully replace earlier developments with new modes of thinking (Kohlberg, Levine, & Hewer, 1983). Instead, earlier struggles persist—and sometimes intrude—in the form of new challenges. Hence a young adult who has failed to develop a clear identity may be confused about the kind of role to play in a romantic relationship (J. Kroger, 2003).

Historically, stage theories emphasized *universal* progressions: All children were thought to go through the same sequence of changes, with slight variations in timing due to dissimilarities in environmental support. Piaget was a strong believer in universal progressions in children's thinking. However, research has *not* entirely confirmed the idea that young people proceed through general stages one at a time or that they always move in the same direction (e.g., Ceci & Roazzi, 1994; K. W. Fischer & Bidell, 2006; Voutsina, 2012). A 9-year-old girl may easily plan ahead while playing chess (her hobby) but have difficulty organizing a complex essay (an unfamiliar activity). Nor do stage progressions always appear to be universal across cultures and educational contexts (e.g., H. Keller, 2011; Sachdeva, Singh, & Medin, 2011; S.-C. Li, 2007). Youngsters raised in vastly different cultures often learn to think in significantly different ways. Given these and other research findings, few contemporary developmental theorists endorse strict versions of stage theories (Parke, Ornstein, Rieser, & Zahn-Waxler, 1994).

Many theorists now believe that qualitative changes do exist—not as inevitable, universal, and hierarchical patterns, but rather as dynamic and somewhat individual states of thinking and acting that evolve as children mature and try new things. It is obvious that the actions of adolescents differ from those of 2-year-old children. Fifteen-year-olds are not simply taller and more knowledgeable about the world; they go about their day-to-day living in qualitatively different ways. Maturation-based developments, such as the brain's increases in memory capacity, plus ever-expanding knowledge and experience, permit both gradual and occasionally dramatic changes in thinking and behaving (Barrouillet, Gavens, Vergauwe, Gaillard, & Camos, 2009; Morra, Gobbo, Marini, & Sheese, 2008). Thus, contemporary developmental theorists tend to see both qualitative and quantitative changes in children's development.

Applying Lessons from Basic Issues in Child Development

As you read this book, you will find that the three basic developmental issues of nature and nurture, universality and diversity, and qualitative and quantitative change surface periodically within individual chapters. They also are presented in Basic Developmental Issues tables in each chapter. The first of these tables, "Illustrations in the Three Domains," provides examples of how these dimensions are reflected in the domains of physical, cognitive, and social-emotional development. These big ideas also have several broad implications for your work with children:

• **Accept the powerful influences of both nature and nurture.** A child's fate is never sealed—it always depends on care from adults and the child's own efforts. Again and again, nurture matters. But so does nature. How children respond to guidance depends, in part,

BASIC DEVELOPMENTAL ISSUES
Illustrations in the Three Domains

ISSUE	PHYSICAL DEVELOPMENT	COGNITIVE DEVELOPMENT	SOCIAL-EMOTIONAL DEVELOPMENT
Nature and Nurture	Nature guides the order and timing in which specific parts of the brain and body are formed. Genetic factors undergird individual dispositions, such as a tendency toward thinness or a susceptibility to diabetes. All growth depends on nurture. Nutrition, exercise, athletic training, and protection from excessive stress influence health and motor skills (Chapters 4 and 5).	Some capacities for intelligence, learning, and language seem to be guided by genes. However, many contemporary theorists emphasize environmental influences, including informal learning experiences, adult modeling and mentoring, family relationships, and formal schooling (Chapters 3, 6, 7, 8, 9, and 10).	The basic capacity to form attachments with other people is made possible by genes and altered by social experience. Environmental influences are strong in self-esteem and motivation. Becoming especially aggressive, empathic, shy, or outgoing occurs due to the combined influences of nature and nurture (Chapters 11, 12, 13, and 14).
Universality and Diversity	The emergence of key physical features (e.g., gender-specific characteristics during puberty) is highly similar. Diversity is evident in the ages at which children accomplish motor milestones (e.g., becoming able to sit, stand, and walk), as well as in their general state of physical health (Chapter 5).	The basic components of language (e.g., an ability to combine words according to grammatical rules) and thinking (e.g., mechanisms that allow new information to be compared with existing knowledge) are nearly universal. Diversity is evident in the effectiveness with which children acquire academic information (Chapters 6, 7, 8, and 9).	The need for peer affiliation represents a universal aspect of development in children. There are considerable individual differences in the kinds of social groups that young people form and the degree to which peers accept one another as desirable companions (Chapter 15).
Qualitative and Quantitative Change	Some aspects of physical development (e.g., transformations during prenatal development and puberty) reflect dramatic qualitative change. Most of the time, however, physical development occurs gradually as a result of many small changes (e.g., young children slowly grow taller) (Chapters 4 and 5).	Children's logical reasoning skills show qualitative change; for instance, children develop new, more sophisticated ways of solving problems that integrate but also restructure previous methods. Quantitative change occurs as children gradually gain knowledge in various academic subjects (Chapters 6, 7, and 10).	Some evidence suggests that with appropriate social experiences, children's understanding of morality undergoes qualitative change. In a quantitative manner, children gradually come to understand how other people's minds work and discover that others' perspectives may be different from their own (Chapters 12 and 14).

on their genetic inheritance. An important implication is that when children show unusual talents, you can offer extra challenges. And when children's natural inclinations become stumbling blocks to positive growth, you can provide additional support.

• **Become familiar with general developmental trends and common variations.** Common tendencies at a particular age level guide the daily work of educators. An elementary teacher familiar with Piaget's theory knows that young children have difficulty with abstract ideas and so arranges many concrete, hands-on experiences. Yet unique patterns in developmental pathways—the timing, appearance, and form of changes—must also be accommodated. By growing familiar with the developmental diversity among children, you can learn to give individual youngsters the specific instruction they need.

• **Look for both quantitative and qualitative changes in children's characteristics.** As you teach children academic concepts, the benefits of physical activity, ways to get along with peers, and so on, you might find that children learn information in a quantitative fashion. That is, they soak up facts and skills incrementally, sometimes rapidly. You can support such learning by providing children with rich and varied resources. On other occasions children need to revamp their basic ways of thinking before they are able to progress. Much of the momentum for qualitative change comes from the child, but teachers and other professionals can support new ways of thinking by exposing children to increasingly sophisticated reasoning. For example, a class discussion about school rules can prompt children to learn that disregarding directions at home or school not only leads to punishment (an understanding that comes early in life) but undermines order in the group and can upset other people (which are later acquisitions). With these new insights, many children become more considerate of others.

Summary

The field of child development examines how human beings change beginning at conception and extending throughout prenatal development, infancy, childhood, and adolescence. Each child's journey is guided by four factors: nature, nurture, existing conditions in the child's brain and body, and personal activity. Developmental theorists typically focus on the progression of children in three domains—physical, cognitive, and social-emotional—and look at how a variety of contexts affect growth in these areas and in their overall adjustment.

Developmental theorists wrestle with three basic issues related to children's development. First, they wonder how much development is influenced by nature (heredity) and nurture (environment). Second, they speculate about the extent to which developmental paths are universal (true for everyone) or diverse (unique to individuals and groups). And third, they debate whether the form of developmental changes can be characterized as qualitative (involving major transformations) or quantitative (reflecting gradual trends). Clearly, development is influenced by nature and nurture; certain aspects of development are universal and others reflect diversity; and the course of development is characterized by both qualitative and quantitative change.

Now that you have read about basic features of child development, you are ready to check your knowledge of these essential concepts. In the summary of each major section, you will see a Testing Your Understanding feature in the margin. Click on the icon in the margin to find out how well you understand the concepts in this first section. In addition, the following Assessing Children features, which are found in every chapter, allow you to identify significant developmental concepts in videos and artifacts from children. The first two of these, which you can access by clicking on the icons immediately below, focus on universality and diversity and on qualitative and quantitative change.

ENHANCEDetext *self-check*

Assessing Children 1-1

Practice assessing universality and diversity in children's development.

ENHANCEDetext *application exercise*

Assessing Children 1-2

Practice assessing qualitative and quantitative changes in children's development.

ENHANCEDetext *application exercise*

THEORIES OF CHILD DEVELOPMENT

To guide their research questions, methods, and interpretations of data, developmental scholars construct **theories**, integrated collections of principles and explanations regarding particular phenomena. Seven theoretical approaches have dominated academic discussions of child development. We examine the theories and their practical implications here, one by one, and then refer to them selectively in later chapters as they become relevant to specific topics.

Biological Theories

Biological theories focus on the adaptive capacity of children's brains and bodies in supporting their survival, growth, and learning. We can reasonably expect that it helped our ancestors, and their predecessors before them, to have brains that disposed them to notice patterns in the world, to form lasting and productive relationships with family members, to use and invent tools, and to acquire language and learn from one another. Human genes helped to sculpt brains that enabled these important abilities. When heredity increases chances for survival, young people live into their adult years, have children of their own, and pass on adaptive genes to the next generation.

Historically, biological theories emphasized the *maturation* of children's bodies, perceptual abilities, and motor skills (Gesell, 1928). Early theorists compiled detailed charts of the average ages at which children learn to sit, crawl, reach for objects, and so forth. According to this view, children walk when they are physiologically ready, and puberty begins when a biological clock triggers the appropriate hormones. In some instances maturation also establishes sensitive periods for learning. Italian physician and educator **Maria Montessori** (1870–1952) noticed that infants are perceptive of order in the physical world and that preschool-aged children eagerly soak up details about language (Montessori, 1936, 1949). In the many Montessori schools now in existence in North America and Western Europe, teachers are urged to become careful observers of children's natural tendencies and to provide stimulating materials that entice children to engage in activities suited to their up-and-coming abilities.

Montessori's analysis aside, a limitation of early biological perspectives was that they largely overlooked the effects of children's experiences. In comparison, contemporary biological theorists emphasize that genes are flexible instructions that blend with environmental experiences in their effects on the child. Hence biological perspectives are now balanced in their regard for nature and nurture (Bjorklund, 2003; Carnell, Kim, & Pryor, 2012; Gottlieb, Wahlsten, & Lickliter, 2006; Konner, 2010; Szyf & Bick, 2013).

Three key principles that a practitioner can take away from biological theories are that (a) children's maturational levels impose limits on their abilities and interests; (b) children's age-related motivations serve valuable functions for them, such as prompting exploration; and (c) individual children are born with unique dispositions that interact with environmental experiences to influence learning, emotional expression, and interactions with other people. Your awareness of abilities that are heavily limited by maturation, for example, reaching for objects during infancy handling small objects during early childhood, will convince you that these skills can be encouraged but not rushed. Similarly, if you realize that children are predisposed to be physically active, you will understand that they need regularly scheduled time for play in safely equipped yards. And if you accept that each child has a one-of-a-kind profile of genes, you will strive to design flexible educational environments that allow everyone to be successful.

Behaviorism and Social Learning Theories

Whereas biological theorists see heredity (nature) as a principal driving force behind development, advocates of behaviorism and social learning theories propose that developmental change is largely due to environmental influences (nurture). Conducting research with humans and other species (e.g., dogs, rats, pigeons), these theorists have shown that many behaviors can be modified through environmental stimuli. As a proponent of a perspective known as **behaviorism**, American psychologist **B. F. Skinner** (1904–1990) suggested that children actively "work" for rewards, such as food, praise, or physical contact, and tend to avoid behaviors that lead to punishment (Skinner, 1953, 1957). Other behavioral theorists have revealed how children learn emotional responses to certain stimuli (e.g., a fear of dogs) based on experience (e.g., having been bitten by a dog).

A serious limitation of behaviorism is that it focuses exclusively on children's visible behaviors, with little consideration for how internal thought processes influence those actions. Another problem with some behavioral applications is that children can become overly focused on rewards and lose sight of their own interests in learning or behaving.

Contemporary **social learning theories** portray children's beliefs and goals as having crucial influences on their actions. Researchers in the social learning tradition have shown that behavior is not simply a response to a reward or punishment in the immediate environment. Instead, children regularly anticipate the consequences of their actions and choose their behaviors accordingly, whether or not they have ever been rewarded or punished for these actions. Moreover, children learn a great deal by observing what other people do and what consequences follow those behaviors, and they develop expectations for the kinds of tasks they themselves are likely to achieve. In recent years social learning theory has increasingly incorporated thought processes into explanations of learning; accordingly, the succeeding framework is sometimes called *social cognitive theory* (Bandura, 2012; Schunk, 2012).

Numerous practical applications have been derived from behaviorism, social learning theory, and social cognitive theory, and you will encounter many of them as you study child development. For now, let's look at three overarching principles. First, environmental stimuli, such as rewards and punishments, clearly influence children's actions and feelings. Mary Jalongo, in the opening case study, chose not to follow the advice of her principal to punish Tonya harshly because Mary realized this response would do Tonya more harm than good. Second, children's actions are affected by what they see others doing. Children often imitate others' behaviors, whether those behaviors are desirable (e.g., the hoop shots of a famous basketball player) or disagreeable (e.g., a teacher's condescending actions toward the school custodian). Finally, children's confidence in their ability to achieve certain standards is based largely on their past experiences on similar tasks. Adults can help children be successful, notice the results of their hard work, and set goals for future improvements.

Psychodynamic Theories

Psychodynamic theories focus on the interaction between a person's internal conflicts and the demands of the environment. These frameworks assert that early experiences play a critical role in later characteristics and behavior. They typically focus on social and personality development and, often, on abnormal development.

The earliest psychodynamic theorist, **Sigmund Freud** (1856–1939), was an Austrian physician who argued that young children continually find themselves torn by sexual and aggressive impulses, on the one hand, and desires to gain approval from parents and society, on the other (Freud, 1905, 1910, 1923). Freud proposed that as an outgrowth of children's personal motives and family relationships, they progress through a series of qualitatively distinct stages, ideally learning to channel their impulses in socially appropriate ways. Another psychodynamic theorist, Erik Erikson, who was born in Germany and eventually moved to the United States, suggested that people grow as a result of resolving their own internal struggles. Compared to Freud, Erikson focused less on sexual and aggressive impulses and more on other parts of the developing personality, especially desires to feel competent and sure of one's values, commitments, and direction in life (Erikson, 1963).

Psychodynamic perspectives have made a lasting contribution by highlighting the significance of children's social-emotional needs. Several psychodynamic ideas remain influential today: Early social experiences affect later well-being; first relationships strongly influence children's sense of security; children defend themselves from criticism, neglect, and traumatic events in complex ways that they cannot always verbalize; concerted efforts are needed to dislodge children from unhealthy paths; and children wrestle with specific issues during certain phases of life (Josephson, 2013; Ludwig-Körner, 2012; Malberg, Stafler, & Geater, 2012).

A significant weakness of psychodynamic theories has been the difficulty of supporting claims with research data. For one thing, it is difficult to verify what internal conflicts a particular person might have, in part because many of these conflicts are hidden from self-awareness. If we ourselves are not consciously aware of a conflict, we are unable to talk about that feeling with another person. In addition, generalizations cannot necessarily be made from the studies that theorists conducted. Freud developed his ideas from in-depth interviews with troubled adults—individuals whose childhoods do not necessarily reflect typical experiences. Critics additionally point out that desires to restrain sexual urges (Freud's theory) and define one's personal identity (Erikson's theory) may be central motives for some people but not others. Finally, research has refuted several ideas central to psychoanalytical perspectives. Although Freud recommended that children perform mildly aggressive acts as a way to release inborn aggressive tendencies, research indicates that encouraging such acts can actually *increase* aggressive behavior (Mallick & McCandless, 1966; C. E. Smith, Fischer, & Watson, 2009).

Despite these serious problems, psychodynamic theories remind educators of two things. First, children often have mixed and confusing emotions. Adults can help children by teaching them to express their feelings in ways that both honestly reflect their experience and are acceptable to other people. Second, children who have gotten off to a rough start in family relationships need extra support in child care and at school. Teachers and other professionals can support families, model sensitive caregiving, form their own affectionate relationships with children, teach missing social skills, and, when children exhibit serious mental health problems, seek therapy for them.

Cognitive-Developmental Theories

Cognitive-developmental theories emphasize thinking processes and how they change, qualitatively, over time. According to these views, children play an active role in their own development: They seek out new and interesting experiences, try to understand what they see and hear, and endeavor to reconcile any discrepancies between new information and what they previously believed to be true. Through these reflections, children's thinking becomes increasingly logical and abstract with age.

The earliest and best-known cognitive-developmental theorist was Swiss scientist Jean Piaget. With a career that spanned decades and spawned thousands of research studies around the world, Piaget focused primarily on children's cognitive development (Piaget, 1928, 1929, 1952a, 1952b). Using detailed observations, in-depth interviews, and ingenious experimental tasks, Piaget investigated the nature of children's logical thinking about such topics as numbers, physical causality, and psychological processes. Another prominent cognitive-developmental theorist, American psychologist **Lawrence Kohlberg** (1927–1987), is known for his extensive research on children's moral reasoning (Kohlberg, 1963, 1984).

Piaget, Kohlberg, and their colleagues have suggested that taking a developmental perspective means looking sympathetically at children and understanding the logic of their thinking. Although adult-like reasoning may be the eventual, desired outcome for young people, cognitive-developmental theorists believe that it is a mistake to hurry children beyond their current capacities—that one cannot *make* a child think in ways beyond his or her current stage. They also believe that adults who try to push children beyond their present abilities create stress and fail to augment children's existing reasoning skills.

Many cognitive-developmental ideas are well regarded by contemporary developmental scholars. Present-day experts recognize that children's thinking reflects a reasonable attempt to make sense of puzzling information. Nevertheless, the various tenets of cognitive-developmental theories are not accepted across the board. A central criticism is that researchers rarely find that children's performance reflects clear-cut stages. Instead, children often move back and forth between more and less advanced ways of thinking. Critics point out that simply because children do not think abstractly about a particular topic does not mean that they are *incapable* of abstract reasoning. As we mentioned in our earlier discussion of stage theories, children are sometimes able to reason at a very high level with certain topics, while simultaneously being incapable of advanced reasoning in other areas.

Perhaps the most important principle that emerges from cognitive-developmental theories is that teachers need to understand children *as children*. To facilitate children's learning, educators must listen closely to children's conversations, permit them to actively explore their environment, observe their actions, and gently probe their ideas. Only when adults appreciate children's thinking can they hope to enhance it.

Cognitive Process Theories

Cognitive process theories focus on basic thinking processes. Central concerns are how people interpret and remember what they see and hear and how these processes change during childhood.

Cognitive process researchers conduct detailed analyses of what children think and do. For instance, investigators have studied the eye movements of children in the process of scanning pictures, the length of time it takes them to read text, and their strategies in completing puzzles. Detailed models of how children attend to information, find meaning in it, and use it in a range of settings guide these analyses.[2]

---

[2] Information processing theories, a family of theoretical perspectives that are examined in Chapter 7, offer influential frameworks for conducting precise analyses of children's thinking.

Research by American psychologist **Robert Siegler** illustrates the cognitive process approach. Siegler has found that children often spontaneously use several different strategies when first learning to complete tasks in arithmetic. For instance, in solving the problem "2 + 4 = ?" children may count on their fingers, starting with the first number and then counting on from there ("two . . . then three, four, five, six—six altogether"), or simply recall the number fact ("2 + 4 = 6") from memory. The same versatility is present as children begin to tackle such tasks as telling time, spelling, and reading. Children's general tactic of trying out a few solutions is often quite useful in determining which methods work effectively on particular kinds of problems (Siegler, 2006; Siegler & Alibali, 2005; van der Ven, Boom, Kroesbergen, & Leseman, 2012).

Cognitive process theories now dominate research in cognitive development. A key contribution of this perspective has been to describe children's thinking in painstaking detail, but critics suggest that there is a price to pay for taking a delimited view on learning. Cognitive process researchers can easily overlook the larger issue of *why* children think as they do. For instance, cognitive process approaches often neglect social-emotional factors and contexts of children's lives, factors that many other theorists consider significant.

Another contribution of cognitive process theories has been the wealth of concrete, research-tested instructional strategies they have generated. Cognitive process theories offer techniques for keeping children's attention; helping them use deliberate mental processes, for example, organizing and elaborating on new information; making the most of their limited memory capabilities; and challenging their misconceptions related to a lesson (Mayer, 2012; Muijs, Kyriakides, van der Werf, Creemers, Timperley, & Earl, 2014).

Sociocultural Theories

Cognitive developmentalists and cognitive process theorists have focused squarely on how intellectual skills develop in an individual. By and large, both have paid little attention to the roles played by the broader social and cultural settings in which individuals live. **Sociocultural theories**, on the other hand, concentrate on the impact of *social systems* (e.g., families, teacher–child relationships, and community agencies) and *cultural* traditions (e.g., customs with print, types of household chores, and uses of memory aids). These theories portray development as the process of children becoming full participants in the society into which they were born.

Russian psychologist and educator **Lev Vygotsky** (1896–1934) is the pioneering figure credited with advancing our knowledge of how children's minds are shaped by everyday social experiences. Having studied the learning of both children and adults, Vygotsky concluded that people grow intellectually by taking part in routine activities and gradually assuming higher levels of responsibility for their completion (Vygotsky, 1962, 1978). Vygotsky believed that guidance with tools, especially advice on using such tangible materials as a protractor in mathematics or lined paper in writing, and such mental prompts visualizing procedures for dissecting an angle, foster cognitive growth. Because different cultures impart distinct ways of performing daily tasks, children's thoughts and behaviors develop in culturally specific ways.

The last two decades have seen a virtual explosion of research conducted within sociocultural perspectives (Göncü & Gauvain, 2012; Griedler & Shields, 2008; Lillemyr, Søbstad, Marder, & Flowerday, 2011; Salomo & Liszkowski, 2013). This evidence is often well received by teachers because it focuses on real children in real settings and has clear implications for how teachers can support learning. Another strength of sociocultural theories is that they show concretely how specific cultural groups encourage children to use different modes of thinking.

As with any theoretical approach, however, sociocultural theories have limitations. Vygptsky and his heirs have described children's thinking with less precision than have investigators working within cognitive process perspectives. In some cases sociocultural theorists have taken for granted that children learn important skills simply by taking part in an activity; in reality, some children merely go through the motions without being accountable for making discernible contributions to the task.

As we have suggested, sociocultural theories offer useful applications for educators. A key principle is that children learn valuable skills by being engaged in authentic tasks (Gauvain, 2001). Depending on their society, children may learn to weave, hunt, raise crops, care for livestock, look after younger children, worship in a religious community, barter and trade, read and write, program computers, or acquire some combination of these or other skills. In the classroom, teachers can give children chances to tackle real-world tasks that were previously beyond their capabilities.

Sociocultural perspectives also offer implications as to how children's practices at home influence their learning and behavior at school. Teachers can reach out to families to share home traditions, such as board games and hobbies, and encourage children to make choices in the classroom tasks, for example selecting autobiographies of interest to them. Teachers can further incorporate children's cultural pastimes in the classroom, perhaps their greetings, a few songs, and customs for celebrating birthdays; they can also make their own expectations transparent by communicating school rules and procedures.

Developmental Systems Theories

Developmental systems theories help clarify how multiple factors combine to promote children's development. A child's body is an active, living *system*, an organized assembly of parts that work together and draw from the environment to keep the child alive. The child is an integral member of multiple, interconnected social groups (Baltes et al., 2006; K. W. Fischer & Bidell, 2006). From this perspective, the child's own initiative contributes to changes in and among these various systems.

Urie Bronfenbrenner (1917–2005), a native of Russia and immigrant to the United States at age 6, is undoubtedly the most widely known developmental systems theorist. In his *bioecological model* of human development, Bronfenbrenner described the influences that people, institutions, and prevailing cultural practices have on children. Of utmost importance are the immediate and extended family members that children interact with every day (Bronfenbrenner & Morris, 2006). Parents and other primary caregivers form close bonds with children, meet their emotional needs, and arrange for them to take on increasingly mature roles in society. Yet children also clearly have influential relationships with people outside the family. In our introductory case Mary Jalongo played an important role in Tonya's life because she expressed faith in Tonya and took a few practical steps to guide the young girl. Teachers, peers, and neighbors regularly support children and in some cases compensate for disadvantages at home or in the community (Criss, Pettit, Bates, Dodge, & Lapp, 1992; Crosnoe & Elder, 2004; Rhodes & Lowe, 2009).

Also important in the bioecological model are other elements of society. Institutions that parents participate in, such as the workplace and political systems, trickle down to influence children (Bronfenbrenner, 1979, 2005; Bronfenbrenner & Morris, 2006). Parents who have decent wages and close relationships with coworkers, friends, and family generally have adequate resources to care for children. Those who don't may find it difficult to provide food and housing and in some cases are under such stress themselves that they struggle in meeting children's needs for attention.

As in the sociocultural framework, the bioecological model emphasizes the importance of culture. Culture essentially tells children whether they should be obedient and devoted or independent and self-assertive in their family, school, and society. Moreover, their culture tells them whether they are members of a valued group or, alternatively, part of a persecuted collection of people that continually fight discrimination (M. B. Spencer, 2006; M. B. Spencer et al., 2012). As a result of personal, familial, and cultural influences, every child has access to protective factors—perhaps strong family relationships or close relationships with neighbors—as well as risk factors—possibly economic poverty or racism in the community—that jointly influence his or her outlook on life.

Finally, the bioecological model suggests that children partly determine their own environment (see Figure 1-1). A boy who is quiet and reflective elicits a different style of instruction than does another who is disruptive and inattentive. Thus dynamic relationships exist between the child and the environment and among all systems in which the child develops. For example, if parents and teachers develop mutually respectful relationships, they are likely to magnify each other's support for the child. When parent–teacher relationships are poor, the adults may blame one another for a child's limitations, with the result that no one teaches the child needed skills. Because the child, parents, teachers, and other people

Preparing for Your Licensure Examination
Your teaching test might ask you about the basic ideas of B. F. Skinner, Jean Piaget, Erik Erikson, Lev Vygotsky, Urie Bronfenbrenner, and other key developmental theorists.

FIGURE 1-1   The bioecological model examines development in an interactive, multi-layered, and changing environment. The framework was developed by Urie Bronfenbrenner (Bronfenbrenner, 2005; Bronfenbrenner & Morris, 2006) and has since been elaborated on by other theorists (e.g., M. B. Spencer, 2006; M. B. Spencer et al., 2012).

in the environment are themselves maturing and changing, the child's relationships evolve over time.

The power of developmental systems theories is that they capture it all—nature, nurture, and the child's developmental level, activity, and personal characteristics. Ironically, the integrative character of this type of framework generates its own weaknesses. It is difficult to make predictions about any single factor in development because the effects of each factor are inextricably intertwined with other elements.

Like the other theoretical perspectives, developmental systems theories offer valuable ideas for teachers. Contemporary ecological theorists suggest that educators can exert beneficial effects on children by considering children's perceptions of their interrelated environments (M. B. Spencer, 2006). It is always important to listen to a child's ideas, as Mary did with Tonya in the introductory case, and to look at each child as facing definite strengths and limitations. Because youngsters can change dramatically after a transition (e.g., moving to a new school, encountering a bully at recess), educators must monitor youngsters' evolving experiences and adjust services accordingly. Moreover, educators can form their own close relationships with children and consider how they can help children address any serious challenges.

Taking a Strategic Approach to Theory

Table 1-1 summarizes the seven theoretical perspectives. With so many theories, the question arises, "Which one is right?" The answer is that, to some extent, they all are. Each perspective provides unique insights that no other approach offers. At the same time, no single framework can adequately explain all aspects of child development, and increasingly, experts must draw from more than one camp to account for all they know about children. In a sense, any theory is like a lens that brings certain phenomena into sharp focus but leaves other phenomena blurry or out of the picture.

Research on **self-regulation**, the processes by which children direct their own actions, learning, and emotions to meet their personal goals and standards, illustrates the value of a comprehensive theoretical approach. A child exercises self-regulation skills when resisting the urge to shove an annoying classmate, listening to the teacher despite distractions,

TABLE 1-1 Theories of Child Development

THEORETICAL PERSPECTIVES	POSITIONS	BASIC DEVELOPMENTAL ISSUES	REPRESENTATIVE THEORISTS[a]
Biological theories	Investigators focus on genetic factors, physiological structures, and inborn dispositions that help the child adapt to the environment. As an illustration, compared to young adolescents who slept well for relatively long periods at night, youngsters of the same age who slept less and reported interrupted sleep exhibited less activity in the part of the brain that is associated with positive emotions and sensations of feeling rewarded (S. M. Holm et al., 2009).	*Nature and nurture:* Genes support characteristics that enhance an individual's chances for survival and reproduction. Adequate nutrients, supportive social relationships, and exploration in the environment are essential for normal growth. *Universality and diversity:* Children typically form bonds with caregivers and have brains that make it relatively easy for them to learn about language, numbers, basic properties of physics, and other people's intentions and feelings. Diversity in physical characteristics and abilities occurs through variations in genes and experience. *Qualitative and quantitative change:* Qualitative changes are seen in transformations at puberty and sensitive periods in perceptual development and language learning. In many other respects the child grows gradually, reflecting quantitative transformations.	Charles Darwin Arnold Gesell Maria Montessori Konrad Lorenz John Bowlby Mary Ainsworth Sandra Scarr Robert Plomin David Bjorklund Susan Gelman Elizabeth Spelke Renée Baillargeon Melvin Konner
Behaviorism and social learning theories	Investigators focus on the effects of environmental stimuli on behavior. In one investigation a group of girls with cystic fibrosis were more likely to engage in health-promoting exercise for 20-minute segments when they were given small, immediate rewards (e.g., special snacks) and allowed to earn points that could be exchanged for other prizes (e.g., playing their favorite game with parents; Bernard, Cohen, & Moffet, 2009).	*Nature and nurture:* Emphasis is on nurture. When children act, the environment responds with rewards or punishments or ignores the behavior. Children modify their actions based on their experiences, goals, and beliefs about whether an action will lead to desirable or undesirable consequences. *Universality and diversity:* Children work for generally similar rewards (e.g., food, praise, physical contact). Yet preferences for incentives are somewhat individual, and because environments vary in how they respond to children's actions, diversity in behavior is expected. *Qualitative and quantitative change:* Development is quantitative: Children undergo countless incremental changes in behaviors.	B. F. Skinner John B. Watson Ivan Pavlov Sidney Bijou Donald Baer Albert Bandura Dale Schunk Barry Zimmerman
Psychodynamic theories	Investigators focus on how early experiences and internal conflicts affect social and personality development. In an investigation in which divorced parents and their children were studied over a 10-year period, researchers detected sibling rivalries that were based, in part, on unconsciously held allegiances to one parent (Wallerstein & Lewis, 2007).	*Nature and nurture:* Sexual and aggressive urges are inborn. Family and society affect how children express instinctual urges, trust others, and perceive themselves as individuals. *Universality and diversity:* Universally, children struggle with strong feelings (aggression and sexuality, according to S. Freud) and personal challenges (the belief that they can or cannot make things happen, according to Erikson). Relationships with other people are highly varied and result in diversity in children's coping skills. *Qualitative and quantitative change:* Through a series of distinct stages, children learn to resolve mixed feelings and gain a sense of identity.	Sigmund Freud Anna Freud Erik Erikson Donald Winnicott Joan Berzoff Tom Billington

TABLE 1-1 Theories of Child Development (*continued*)

THEORETICAL PERSPECTIVES	POSITIONS	BASIC DEVELOPMENTAL ISSUES	REPRESENTATIVE THEORISTS[a]
Cognitive-developmental theories	Investigators focus on major transformations in thinking. One researcher found that young children focused on their own concrete views of an event, whereas older children and adolescents were able to consider how several individuals could see a single event from distinct points of view (Selman, 1980).	*Nature and nurture:* Children are biological organisms strongly motivated to make sense of their worlds (nature). Access to a reasonably complex environment is vital to development (nurture). Young people actively contribute to their own learning. *Universality and diversity:* Universality is emphasized. Variations among youngsters are most common at the highest stages of development, which require advanced education. *Qualitative and quantitative change:* Children's reasoning undergoes transformations in its underlying essence; new methods of classifying information build on previous mental processes but also involve reorganizations. Quantitative additions to the knowledge base occur within stages.	Jean Piaget Bärbel Inhelder Lawrence Kohlberg John Flavell David Elkind Robbie Case Juan Pascual-Leone Kurt Fischer Sergio Morra Camilia Gobbo
Cognitive process theories	Investigators focus on the precise nature of cognitive operations. In one study 7-year-old Dutch children who were learning one-digit multiplication problems used a variety of strategies: counting on their fingers, drawing items and then counting them, using repeated addition (e.g., $5 \times 7 = 7 + 7 + 7 + 7 + 7$), using short-cuts such as doubling (for 6×4, start with $4 + 4 + 4 = 12$; then add $12 + 12$ to get 24), and retrieving answers from long-term memory (van der Ven et al., 2012).	*Nature and nurture:* Both nature and nurture are important. Children are born with capacities to perceive, interpret, and remember information; these abilities are refined with brain maturation, experience, and reflection. *Universality and diversity:* The desire to make sense of the world is universal. Diversity is present in educational experiences and, to some degree, in children's natural talents. *Qualitative and quantitative change:* The methods by which children perceive, interpret, and remember information change qualitatively (e.g., inventing new rules for solving arithmetic problems) and quantitatively (e.g., becoming more proficient with a strategy).	David Klahr Deanna Kuhn Robert Siegler Ann L. Brown Henry Wellman Susan Gelman John Flavell Robbie Case Alison Gopnik Erik Thiessen
Sociocultural theories	Investigators focus on acquisition of tools, communication systems, intellectual abilities, and social-emotional skills as children take part in familiar tasks with other people. In one study children's ability to plan informal activities (such as deciding what to eat for breakfast and do after school) improved over the elementary years and depended on cultural experiences (Gauvain & Perez, 2005).	*Nature and nurture:* Emphasis is on nurture. Children become familiar with tools used by their families as they take part in daily activities. The underlying capacity that allows children to acquire the traditions and ideas of one or more cultures is inherited. *Universality and diversity:* All children learn language, beliefs espoused in their communities, and practical life skills. Variation is present in the particular tools, customs, and ideas that children acquire in society. *Qualitative and quantitative change:* Children shift qualitatively in how they carry out tasks. Initially, a child may look to a teacher for help when completing a difficult task and later independently follow the teacher's strategies. Quantitatively, children gradually take on responsibility in social groups.	Lev Vygotsky A. R. Luria James Wertsch Barbara Rogoff Patricia Greenfield Mary Gauvain Jerome Bruner Michael Cole Alex Kozulin Jose Medina Virginia Martinez

(continued)

TABLE 1-1   Theories of Child Development (*continued*)

THEORETICAL PERSPECTIVES	POSITIONS	BASIC DEVELOPMENTAL ISSUES	REPRESENTATIVE THEORISTS[a]
Developmental systems theories	Investigators focus on the multiple influences in children's development. In one study a wide range of factors were associated with hours children slept at night, including children's own activities (excessive television viewing was associated with little sleep), family functioning (eating meals together on weekdays was associated with lengthy sleep), and demographic factors (older African American children slept fewer hours than did children from other groups; Adam, Snell, & Pendry, 2007).	*Nature and nurture:* Multiple factors in the child (nature) and outside the child (nurture) combine in development. The child's own activity is also an essential factor. *Universality and diversity:* Developmental changes occur in all individuals from conception to death. Some changes are common across children of particular age, yet historical events, types of interactions with adults, and other personal circumstances contribute to individual patterns. *Qualitative and quantitative change:* Most change is quantitative, but shifts occur that result in entirely new ways of behaving. A baby may use her arm to swat awkwardly at a toy and later learn to pick it up in a precise finger grip.	Urie Bronfenbrenner Arnold Sameroff Margaret Beale Spencer Suzanne Fegley Richard Lerner Kurt Fischer Esther Thelen Gilbert Gottlieb Paul Baltes Theodore Wachs

[a]Several theorists have contributed to two or more theoretical perspectives.

and evaluating options for solving a difficult mathematical problem rather than following the first tactic that comes to mind. Self-regulation is best understood by casting a wide net. Neurological researchers, taking a *biological perspective*, find that specific abilities, including inhibiting impulses, sustaining attention, and planning for the future, are supported by maturing structures in the brain (Hosenbocus & Chahal, 2012; Zhou, Chen, & Main, 2012). Investigators working within *behaviorist and social learning* frameworks examine the rules that children learn to follow (e.g., looking at the teacher when she is giving instructions), methods by which they keep tabs on personal actions (e.g., using a checklist), and rewards they receive or give themselves when achieving a high standard (perhaps being praised by the teacher or taking pride themselves in a good performance; Mace, Belfiore, & Hutchinson, 2001; Schunk, 2012). *Cognitive process* theorists emphasize children's understanding of the demands of learning (e.g., what they should do when confused while reading) and the strategies they actually employ (e.g., going back to reread a difficult passage; Dimmitt & McCormick, 2012). *Sociocultural* theorists show that children organize their activities by talking themselves through challenging tasks and using materials as they have been shown (Vygotsky, 1962). Together, these separate perspectives converge on a picture of children learning to regulate behavior as their brains mature and they gain practice in working toward certain goals.

As you proceed through the text, you will see that we refer to ideas included in the seven main theories but also summarize more focused theoretical perspectives on particular aspects of children's development—for example, theories explicitly focused on moral development or language acquisition. Inevitably, however, any single theory omits crucial information. We attempt to redress this limitation by periodically reminding you to take a bigger perspective, one that reveals the dynamic ways in which children's own characteristics and multilayered environments influence their learning. Whenever you notice the bioecological symbol in the margin (as you can see next to this paragraph), consider how children are growing and changing based on a complex blend of factors, including biological trends, relationships with others, and cultural practices and beliefs.

BIOECOLOGY OF DEVELOPMENT

The bioecological model asserts that the child's personal activity, temperament, and abilities are affected by relationships with family members, peers, teachers, and neighbors. The child in turn influences these others, and he or she grows in the process.

Summary

Developmental theorists have proposed a variety of explanations as to how and why children change over time. These explanations can be categorized into seven theoretical frameworks: biological, behaviorism and social learning, psychodynamic, cognitive-developmental, cognitive process, sociocultural, and developmental systems perspectives. The seven frameworks focus on different domains of development and place greater or lesser importance on nature versus nurture, universality versus diversity, and qualitative versus quantitative change. Teachers and other practitioners may find that several frameworks are relevant to their work.

ENHANCEDetext *self-check*

Assessing Children 1-3

Practice assessing children's activities from a theoretical perspective.

ENHANCEDetext *application exercise*

DEVELOPMENTAL PERIODS

We can make our task of exploring child development more manageable by dividing the developmental journey into specific time periods. Age cutoffs are somewhat arbitrary, yet we know that children act in very different ways as they grow. In our discussions of changes in various abilities, we usually consider five periods: infancy (birth–2 years), early childhood (2–6 years), middle childhood (6–10 years), early adolescence (10–14 years), and late adolescence (14–18 years). Here we give an overview for each period, identify typical abilities of youngsters at that age level, and derive implications for teachers and other practitioners. As we proceed, we also refer to video clips that illustrate environments designed for each age group.

Infancy (Birth–2 Years)

Infancy is a truly remarkable period. It is a time when basic human traits, such as emotional bonds with other people, nonverbal communication, language expression, and motor exploration, burst onto the scene.

A newborn baby is completely dependent on others. But the baby is equipped with an arsenal of skills—a distinctive cry, physical reflexes, an interest in human faces, and a brain alert to novelty and sameness—that elicit comfort and stimulation from caregivers. In a matter of weeks, the baby smiles broadly during good-humored exchanges with familiar caregivers. As caregivers respond warmly and consistently, attachments grow.

A sense of security nourishes infants' desire to learn. Babies want to know everything: what car keys taste like, what older family members do in the kitchen, and what happens when they drop a bowl of peas. Infants' growing facility with language builds on interests in concrete experiences, such as a parent's laughter and the sensation of warm water in the bathtub.

Intellectual curiosity fuels babies' drive to use physical skills. Babies reach, crawl, and climb to get objects they desire. The urge to explore coincides with a budding sense of mastery ("I *can* do it!") and independence ("*I* can do it!"). Emotional reactions, such as a legitimate fear of heights and uneasiness in the presence of strangers, limit exploration and occasionally prompt withdrawal.

Caregivers who work effectively with infants realize that each baby is unique, develops at his or her own rate, and is hungry for loving interaction. Dedicated caregivers emphasize quality of care, giving individualized, responsive, and affectionate attention to babies and their families (Chazan-Cohen, Jerald, & Stark, 2001; Recchia & Shin, 2012). They find time to respond warmly to each infant's bids for attention, patiently provide for their physical needs, and share attention to objects and events, for example, while paging through a picture book together.

Observing Children 1-1

Observe a child care setting that is safe and interesting for infants.

ENHANCEDetext *video example*

In addition, knowledgeable caregivers design the environment so that infants can explore objects and surroundings freely. A video example shows a setting where crawling infants can speed up and down cushioned ramps, and walking infants (*toddlers*) can swagger around open spaces. When infants stumble, furniture poses little threat because it has been crafted with soft, rounded edges. Notice a mirror that attracts attention; colorful toys with complex textures that beg to be touched; mobiles over cribs that encourage inspection; a tunnel that invites entering, exiting, and playing peekaboo games; and simple books to be examined while cuddling with an adult in a rocking chair.

High-quality care prepares an infant for the expanded learning opportunities of early childhood. The infant is ready to venture from the caregiver's lap.

Early Childhood (2–6 Years)

Early childhood is a period of incredible creativity and fantasy. Preschool-aged children see life as a forum for invention, imagination, and drama. They continually try on new roles and work hard to play their parts in harmony.

Language and communication skills develop rapidly. New vocabulary, sensitivity to communication rules, and facility with syntax (grammar) are noticeable advancements. Language builds on observations about the world and, especially, the habits and patterns of daily life. High levels of energy radiate from preschool-aged children's activities. The cautious movements of infancy give way to fluid rolling, tumbling, running, and skipping. Socially and emotionally, preschoolers are endearing, trusting, and affectionate in their relationships with familiar adults. Young children become progressively more interested in peers, infuse fantasy into play, and contend with aggressive and self-centered impulses.

Effective teachers channel children's natural energy with gentle guidance. They are respectful of young children's curiosity, spontaneity, and desire to try on new roles. They realize that children learn a great deal as they play (Hirsh-Pasek, Golinkoff, Berk, & Singer, 2009; Lillard et al., 2012). Efforts to instruct children in basic academic skills such as recognizing and forming letters of the alphabet are balanced with opportunities for children to take initiative in their own learning (Hauser-Cram & Mitchell, 2012).

Environments for young children are designed to encourage active and purposeful learning (National Association for the Education of Young Children [NAEYC], 1997, 2009). In a video example, you can see a classroom where children are able to draw and paint creatively. Play structures encourage children to climb, hide, and search for one another. Tables and chairs make it possible for children to sit and converse during mealtimes and group activities. A dramatic play area, furnished with kitchen appliances and dress-up clothes, encourages imagination. Elsewhere in the room children can sit and look at books and take turns on a computer. Mats let children recharge their batteries with rest; a separate bathroom area is available for toilet needs and hand washing. Outdoors, children can scoot on vehicles, ride bicycles, and play in the sand.

Observing Children 1-2

Observe a preschool that encourages creative movement, pretend play, and hands-on learning in young children.

ENHANCEDetext *video example*

Given occasions to explore the environment and interact with friendly peers and adults, young children gain valuable knowledge about themselves and their world. They become ready to take on the responsible roles of middle childhood.

Middle Childhood (6–10 Years)

Children continue to play during the elementary years, but they now also learn through formal instruction (Bergen & Fromberg, 2009; S. G. Paris, Yeung, Wong, & Luo, 2012).[3] Children at this age level invest considerable effort in mastering the customs, tools, and accumulated knowledge of their community. Typically they learn to read and write, apply rules in games and sports, care for younger brothers and sisters, and use computer technology.

---

[3] Many children retain qualities typical of early childhood, including an interest in pretend play, until age 8 or older, which has led the NAEYC to classify children from birth until age 8 as "young children" (NAEYC, 1997). We have used age 6 as the cutoff between early and middle childhood. Although age 6 is somewhat arbitrary, it marks the typical age for first grade, during which time schools introduce an academic curriculum. We also wanted to distinguish middle childhood from the early adolescent years, as some youngsters (girls in particular) begin the first phases of puberty as early as age 8 or 9.

Serious commitments to peers, especially to playmates of the same age and gender, emerge during middle childhood. Friendships are important, and children learn much from spending time together and getting into—and out of—scuffles. Children also begin to compare their performance to that of others: Am I the slowest reader in my class? Am I good enough to be picked for the baseball team? When they routinely end up on the losing side in such comparisons, children become hesitant to take on new challenges.

In the elementary school years, children internalize many admonishments they've previously heard (e.g., "Don't play near the river," "Keep an eye on your little brother"). They gain a sense of what is expected of them, and most are inclined to live up to these standards. Motor skills are polished, and many children become proficient in athletic skills.

In middle childhood, children do their best thinking when familiar with a topic and given access to concrete objects. Teachers can nurture children's skills by observing them, identifying their talents and areas in which they are less knowledgeable, and implementing instructional methods that allow them to handle objects and make connections to prior understandings (Association for Childhood Education International, 2009; National Board for Professional Teaching Standards, 2001).

You can see a classroom that provides noticeable support for children's academic learning in a video example. Maps are visible in several places, suggesting the importance of geography. Frequently used words are posted on cabinets for children to refer to while writing. Small objects can be manipulated, counted, and classified according to shape. Books, a computer, chalkboards, and other resources are available to extend learning. Tables and chairs permit group work, and sofas encourage relaxation while reading.

Having begun to think systematically, children are ready for some particularly challenging tasks: growing an adult body and speculating on what it means to hold a job, date, become intimate, and raise a family. This transition between childhood and adulthood takes time, and there are growing pains along the way.

Observing Children 1-3
View an elementary school setting that supports children's academic learning with concrete objects, displays of language rules, tables and chairs for group work, couches for relaxed reading, and other resources.
ENHANCEDetext *video example*

Early Adolescence (10–14 Years)

In early adolescence, a youngster enters the transition of growing a reproductively mature body. Physical changes are accompanied by equally dramatic reorganizations in learning and relating to parents, teachers, and peers.

The physical changes of puberty are orderly and predictable, but many boys and girls alike experience them as disconcerting events. Young adolescents sometimes look and feel awkward. Hormonal changes can lead to mood swings. Adolescents reflect on their changing selves and worry about how their peers perceive them. Adults have accelerating expectations for young people, which are not easy to meet. Peers become a sounding board through which adolescents seek assurance that their appearance and behavior are acceptable.

Adolescents begin to think in a far-reaching, logical, and abstract manner (Anderman, 2012). The interests of young adolescents broaden well beyond family and peer group. Feeling powerful and idealistic, adolescents challenge the existing order, wondering why schools, governments, and the earth's ecosystem cannot be improved overnight.

Diversity is present in every developmental phase, but individual differences are especially pronounced in early adolescence. The age at which puberty begins varies considerably from one individual to the next. Thus not all young adolescents start puberty during the 10-to 14-year-old age range. Some, girls especially, may begin puberty before age 10. Others, boys in particular, may not begin puberty until the end of this age span.

Middle school educators recommend that every student is supported by one adult (an *adviser*) who keeps an eye on his or her academic and personal development (Association for Middle Level Education, 2011). The adviser–student relationship, when warm and stable, can help young adolescents weather rapid developmental changes. In addition to being personal advocates, teachers can educate learners with flexible instructional methods and ample time for learning during the regular school day and in after-school programs. Breadth in the curriculum accommodates adolescents' need for autonomy by allowing students to choose a couple of elective classes (Anderman, 2012).

Observing Children 1-4

Observe a setting that encourages young adolescents to focus on academic learning, work together in groups, talk privately with advisers, and follow a code of conduct emphasizing kindness and respect.

ENHANCEDetext *video example*

Several environments designed to meet the developmental needs of young adolescents are shown in a video example. Classrooms are equipped with a rich array of instructional resources, including clocks, an easel, chalkboards, maps, binders, and a computer. Adolescents' artwork, papers, and a diorama are displayed for all to admire. A code of conduct reminds adolescents to treat themselves, others, and the environment with respect. A small room with two desks is set aside for private conversations with adults. Hallways are clean and uncluttered, school colors are prominent, and rows of lockers give adolescents places to store personal supplies and congregate between classes.

First steps toward maturity are often hesitant ones. With affection from parents and teachers, young adolescents gradually gain confidence that the adult world is within reach.

Late Adolescence (14–18 Years)

As teenagers continue to mature, they lose some of the gawky, uneven features of early adolescence and blossom into attractive young adults. Increasingly, they feel entitled to make their own decisions. Common refrains often include the word *my*: "It's *my* hair, *my* body, *my* clothes, *my* room, *my* education, *my life!*"

Late adolescence can be a confusing time due to the abundance of mixed messages that society communicates. Teenagers may be encouraged to abstain from sexual activity by parents while encountering provocative sexual images in the media. Similarly, adults urge healthy eating habits, yet junk food is everywhere—in vending machines at the convenience store, at the refreshment stand at the movie theater, and often in kitchen cabinets at home.

Fortunately, many high school students make wise decisions. They try hard in school, gain job experience, and refrain from seriously risky behaviors. Some students are less judicious in their choices: They experiment with alcohol, drugs, sex, and violence and in general think more about here-and-now pleasures than long-term consequences.

Peer relationships remain a high priority in late adolescence. Affiliations with age-mates can have either a good or bad influence, depending on the typical pastimes of the group. Most adolescents continue to savor their ties with trusted adults and preserve fundamental values championed by parents and teachers, such as the importance of a good education and the need to be honest and fair.

Individual differences in academic achievement are substantial in high school. Indeed, wide variations in students' abilities are among the biggest challenges faced by high school teachers today. Some low-achieving students drop out of high school altogether, looking for other environments where they can be successful. Many low achievers who stay in school hang out with students who share their pessimistic views of education.

Observing Children 1-5

Watch a setting that encourages adolescents to become proficient in core academic subjects, achieve proficiencies in areas of personal interest, and follow a code of conduct emphasizing good citizenship.

ENHANCEDetext *video example*

Older adolescents need intelligent, behind-the-scenes support from adults. Schools that offer personalized services to adolescents—for example, those that ensure that the aspirations, strengths, and limitations of each student are known by a teacher or another school staff member—are especially successful in meeting high school students' needs (Mero & Hartzman, 2012; National Association of Secondary School Principals, 2004).

Schools can help meet adolescents' needs for personalized attention by doing several things. As you can see in a video example, classrooms can be arranged so students face one another, making it hard for anyone to remain anonymous. In the science classrooms in this clip, numerous types of equipment, resources, and materials are present; these can be used flexibly to meet individual learning needs. Statements of responsibility and citizenship are posted on a wall. A mural contains images appealing to a range of interests, including music, drama, and athletics. The message seems to be that *everyone* belongs here.

The five periods of development just identified appear in the following Developmental Trends table, "Accomplishments and Diversity at Different Age Levels," which gives an overview of the domains of physical, cognitive, and social-emotional development. In addition, it derives implications for teachers and other practitioners working with young people.

Summary

Infancy (birth to 2 years) is a remarkable time characterized by rapid growth and the emergence of essential human traits, including emotional bonds with other people, language, and mobility. Early childhood (2–6 years) is a time of imaginative play, rapid language development, advancing motor skills, and expanding social skills. During middle childhood (6–10 years), children tackle in earnest the abilities that they need to participate effectively in adult society; they also develop friendships and internalize many of society's rules and prohibitions. In early adolescence (10–14 years), youngsters are preoccupied with the physical changes of puberty and sensitive about how they appear to others; at the same time, they are thinking in increasingly abstract and logical ways. Late adolescence (14–18 years) is a period of intensive interaction with peers and greater independence from adults. Although many older adolescents make wise choices, others engage in risky and potentially dangerous behaviors.

ENHANCEDetext *self-check*

Assessing Children 1-4

Practice identifying a distinct developmental period from children's characteristics.

ENHANCEDetext *application exercise*

FROM THEORY TO PRACTICE

The practical applications in this book build on a single concept: Children are nurtured most effectively when adults understand how they *generally* progress but also show sensitivity to *individual* needs. In other words, teachers engage in **developmentally appropriate practice**, instruction and caregiving adapted to the age, characteristics, and developmental progress of individual youngsters.

Developmentally appropriate practice enables children to be active learners. Sensitive practitioners recognize that adult-level functioning is not usually worthwhile for children to imitate, and encourages children to work together in an ethical and democratic fashion (Kohlberg & Mayer, 1972). In our view, teachers and other staff who are most likely to make a positive difference for children are optimistic about their individual abilities, learn about their unique backgrounds, nurture personal strengths, and try to address or compensate for weaknesses, risks, and challenges. Moreover, they are strongly committed to supporting all children with a high-quality education.

By knowing the typical characteristics and thinking abilities of children at a particular age, adults set the groundwork for effective instruction. By further considering the uniqueness of individual children and the ways in which family, culture, and community contribute to diversity, educators can refine their support for children in age-graded groups. The Development and Practice feature on pages 26 to 28, "Engaging in Developmentally Appropriate Practice with Infants, Children, and Adolescents," provides illustrations of educators guiding young people of various ages while responding to their individual needs.

Applying Knowledge of Child Development in the Classroom and Community

Seven general strategies will help you get started in nurturing children's potential for positive growth:

• **Develop warm relationships with children.** Affectionate relationships with teachers and other caregivers promote children's emotional well-being, academic achievement, and acceptance by peers (Gagnon, Huelsman, Kidder-Ashley, & Ballard, 2009; Ly, Zhou, Chu, & Chen, 2012). As you can see in her drawing in Artifact 1-1 on page 28, 11-year-old Melanie represents her teacher, Mrs. Lorenzo, as exuding warmth at school: Mrs. Lorenzo puts her arm around a student and posts a happy face on the bulletin board. Adults can reach out to children by expressing affection, responding sensitively to children's needs, and advocating for children's welfare.

DEVELOPMENTAL TRENDS
Accomplishments and Diversity at Different Age Levels

AGE	WHAT YOU MIGHT OBSERVE	DIVERSITY	IMPLICATIONS
Infancy (Birth–2 Years) 	**Physical Development** • Motor skills that include rolling over, sitting, crawling, standing, and walking • Growing ability to reach, grab, manipulate, and release objects • Rudimentary self-feeding by end of infancy **Cognitive Development** • Ability to distinguish among different faces (beginning in the first months) • Rapid growth in communication with gestures, facial expressions, synchronization of attention with others, babbling, and mostly one-word and a few multiple-word sentences • Ability to imitate simple gestures from the conversational partner, progressing to imitation of complex patterns from memory • Increasing ability to remember people and things out of sight **Social-Emotional Development** • Formation of close bonds with affectionate caregivers • Use of words to label needs and desires • Playing side by side with peers and interacting at times • Increasing awareness of ownership and boundaries of self ("Me!" "Mine!") • Developing sense of personal will ("No!")	• Variation occurs in age when, and manner in which, babies develop motor skills. • Self-help skills emerge later in families that encourage children to rely on adults for meeting basic needs. • Children's temperaments and physical abilities affect their exploration of environment. • Infants receiving restricted nutrition may be less alert and energetic than those with adequate nutrition. • Presence of dangers in the environment may lead families to limit children's exploration. • Some young children begin to learn two or three languages. • Ability to pretend is displayed early by some children and later by others. • Depending on customs, a child may be either encouraged or discouraged from making eye contact with an elder. • Children who have little contact with peers may appear tentative, curious, or aggressive. • Some children are encouraged by families to share possessions, and others are asked to respect individual property rights.	• Provide a safe and sensory-rich environment so infants can explore surroundings and handle objects. • Hold infants gently, and care for their physical needs in an attentive manner. • Respond sensitively to each infant's distinctive style in approaching or resisting new people, objects, and events. • Encourage but do not rush infants to acquire new motor skills. • Learn what each family wants for its children, and try to provide culturally sensitive care. • Recognize that children's early images of themselves are influenced by unconscious messages from adults (e.g., "I enjoy holding you" or "I'm sad and cannot attend to your needs"). • Speak to infants regularly to enrich their language development. • Communicate regularly with families about infants' daily activities, including how much and what they ate and drank, how well they slept, and what their moods were during the day.
Early Childhood (2–6 Years)	**Physical Development** • Increasing abilities in such motor skills as running and skipping, throwing a ball, building block towers, and using scissors • Growing competence in basic self-care and personal hygiene **Cognitive Development** • Dramatic play and fantasy with peers • Ability to draw simple figures • Some knowledge of colors, letters, and numbers • Recounting of familiar stories and events **Social-Emotional Development** • Developing understanding of gender and ethnicity • Emerging abilities to defer immediate gratification, share toys, and take turns • Rudimentary appreciation that other people have their own desires, beliefs, and knowledge • Some demonstration of sympathy for people in distress	• Children coordinate separate movements (e.g., in skipping) at different ages. • Individual differences in fine motor proficiency and gross motor agility are substantial. • Some children enter kindergarten having had few social experiences with age-mates; others have been in child care with peers since infancy. • Family and cultural backgrounds influence the kinds of skills that children master by the time they begin school. • Some children have had a lot of experience listening to storybooks, whereas others have been read to rarely. • Many children at this age have difficulty following rules, standing quietly in line, and waiting for their turns.	• Provide sensory-rich materials that encourage exploration (e.g., with a water table, sandbox, textured toys). • Arrange a variety of activities (e.g., assembling puzzles, coloring, building with blocks, dancing) that permit children to exercise fine motor and gross motor skills. • Encourage children to engage in fantasy play by providing props and open play areas. • Read to children regularly to promote vocabulary and literacy skills. • Encourage children to participate in games that allow them to distinguish speech sounds, identify letters, and count objects. • Communicate expectations for behavior so that children learn to follow rules. • Communicate regularly with families about children's academic and social progress.

DEVELOPMENTAL TRENDS (continued)

AGE	WHAT YOU MIGHT OBSERVE	DIVERSITY	IMPLICATIONS
Middle Childhood (6–10 Years)	**Physical Development** • Successful imitation of complex physical movements • Ability to ride a bicycle • Participation in organized sports **Cognitive Development** • Mastery of basic skills in reading, writing, mathematics, and other academic subject areas • Ability to reason logically about concrete objects and events **Social-Emotional Development** • Growing awareness of how one's own abilities compare with those of peers • Desire for time with age-mates, especially friends of same gender • Increasing responsibility for household chores • Adherence to rules of games • Understanding of basic moral principles (e.g., fairness and equity)	• Children begin to compare their academic and physical performance to that of others, and those who perceive they are doing poorly may have less motivation to achieve. • Some children have few chances to exercise with their families or friends. • Many children are unable to sit quietly for long periods. • Individual differences are evident in children's performance in academic areas. • Children differ in temperament and sociability; some are outgoing, whereas others are more reserved and shy. • A few children may show unacceptable levels of aggression. • Some children are given a lot of responsibility in their family whereas others are expected to be dependent on parents.	• Tailor instruction (e.g., with co-operative groups, individualized assignments, and choices in activities) to accommodate diversity in talents, background knowledge, and interests. • Address delays in basic skills (e.g., in reading, writing, and mathematics) before they evolve into serious delays. • Provide moderately challenging tasks that inspire children to learn new skills, study hard, and attempt increasingly difficult activities. • Provide the guidance necessary to help children interact successfully with peers (e.g., suggest ways to resolve conflicts, and find a "buddy" for a newcomer to school). • Prohibit bullying and enforce codes of conduct.
Early Adolescence (10–14 Years)	**Physical Development** • Onset of puberty • Significant growth spurt • Increased appetite • New sleep habits (with some youngsters wanting to stay up later at night and others feeling tired during periods of rapid growth) **Cognitive Development** • Emerging capacity to think and reason about abstract ideas • Preliminary exposure to advanced academic content in specific subject areas **Social-Emotional Development** • Increasing interest in peer relationships • Self-consciousness about appearance • Emerging sexual interest in the opposite gender or same gender, depending on orientation • Challenges to parents, teachers, and other authorities regarding rules and boundaries • Occasional moodiness and rashness	• Young adolescents exhibit considerable variability in the age at which they begin puberty. • Academic problems often become more pronounced during adolescence; students who encounter frequent failure typically become less engaged at school. • Adolescents seek out peers whose values are compatible with their own and who give them recognition and status. • Some young adolescents begin to engage in deviant and risky activities (e.g., unprotected sex, cigarette smoking, use of drugs and alcohol).	• Suggest and demonstrate effective study strategies as adolescents begin to tackle difficult subject matter. • Give struggling adolescents the extra academic support they need to be successful. • Provide a regular time and place where young adolescents can ask about academic or social matters (e.g., offer your classroom or office as a place where students can occasionally eat lunch). • Provide opportunities for adolescents to contribute to decision making in clubs and recreation centers. • Impose appropriate consequences when adolescents break rules.

DEVELOPMENTAL TRENDS (continued)

AGE	WHAT YOU MIGHT OBSERVE	DIVERSITY	IMPLICATIONS
Late Adolescence (14–18 Years)	**Physical Development** • Progress toward sexual maturity and adult height • For some teens, development of a regular exercise program • Development of specific eating habits (e.g., becoming a vegetarian, consuming junk food) **Cognitive Development** • In-depth study of certain academic areas • Consideration of career tracks and job prospects **Social-Emotional Development** • Dating • Increasing independence (e.g., driving a car, making choices for free time) • Frequent questioning of existing rules and societal norms • Increasing commitment to personal values, career prospects, ethnic affiliations, and other elements of an identity	• Older adolescents aspire to widely differing educational and career tracks (e.g., some aspire to college, others anticipate employment immediately after high school, and still others make no plans for life after high school). • Some teens participate in extracurricular activities; those who do are more likely to stay in school until graduation. • Some adolescents make poor choices regarding the peers with whom they associate and initiate risky behaviors. • Some teens become sexually active, and a few become parents. • Teenagers' neighborhoods and communities offer differing opportunities and temptations. • Some adolescents are keenly aware of prejudice and discrimination to themselves and others who share their culture, ethnicity, gender, or sexual orientation.	• Communicate affection and respect for all adolescents. • Allow choices in academic subjects and assignments, but hold adolescents to high standards for performance. • Provide the assistance that low-achieving students need to be more successful. • Help adolescents explore a variety of career paths and options for higher education. • Encourage involvement in extracurricular activities. • Arrange opportunities for adolescents to make a difference in their communities through volunteer projects.

ARTIFACT 1-1   A child's view of the classroom. This child's drawing shows a warm and friendly classroom.

Around the world, sympathetic adults conscientiously meet children's physical, cognitive, social, and emotional needs according to their society's customs. Thus, *developmentally appropriate practices* are to some degree culturally defined. As you can see in the Development in Culture feature "Developmentally Appropriate Practice in Japan," adults express their compassion according to customs in their society.

• **Consider children's age-related abilities.** Children exhibit predictable sequences of growth, such as noticing that one pile of cookies has more than another during infancy, counting a small number of objects during early childhood, performing basic numerical calculations in elementary school, and understanding abstract mathematical principles in adolescence (Berthold & Renkl, 2009; Bussi & Boni, 2009; M. Carr, 2012). By matching children's evolving levels of thinking with comparable demands in the curriculum, adults maximize the likelihood that children will find lessons informative and motivating.

• **Capitalize on each child's strengths.** Individual children have different strengths, depending on their genes, interpersonal relationships, and past experiences. A child who is particularly curious about the physical world may, as an infant, carefully observe patterns of light, and at later ages become a determined explorer in the sand, an industrious builder of blocks, and, eventually, a bioengineer who designs lifesaving medical equipment. Adults can support this child's curiosity by encouraging exploration and providing relevant educational experiences.

• **Recognize that children's immaturity serves a purpose.** When we compare children's abilities to our own, children inevitably come up short. Yet from a developmental perspective, the "immaturities" youngsters display often serve a purpose (Bjorklund, Periss, & Causey, 2009; Bruner, 1972; Nielsen, 2012). For instance, children's play often appears to adults to be a waste of time but in reality allows children to explore the properties of objects, coordinate their activities with peers, exercise physically, solve problems, and work through emotions.

• **Nudge children toward advanced thinking and behaving.** To some extent, adults must meet children *where they are,* at children's current levels of functioning. But to promote

DEVELOPMENT AND PRACTICE

Engaging in Developmentally Appropriate Practice with Infants, Children, and Adolescents

Infancy

Set up a safe and stimulating environment for exploration.

- A caregiver in an infant center designs her environment so babies and toddlers can safely crawl, walk, and climb both inside and on the playground. A quiet corner is reserved for small infants not yet able to move around. Various materials are carefully arranged to be in reach. Duplicates of popular toys are available.

Arrange clean and quiet areas for meeting physical needs.

- A teacher in an early intervention program sets up his environment so that he can help toddlers meet their physical needs in a hygienic and quiet area. He talks to children while feeding, diapering, and toileting, explaining what's happening and praising children when they take small steps toward self-care.

Provide culturally sensitive care, and support families' home languages.

- A family child care provider who is bilingual uses both Spanish and English with toddlers in her care. She has cloth and cardboard books in both languages (some of the books are homemade), as well as recordings of songs and stories.

Early Childhood

Provide reassurance to children who have difficulty separating from their families.

- A child care provider establishes a routine for the morning. After children say good-bye to their parents, they stand at the window with their teacher, watch their parents walk to their cars, and then find an activity to join.

Create a classroom environment that permits children to explore their surroundings.

- A preschool teacher makes several "stations" available to children during free-choice time. The stations include a water table and areas for playing with blocks, completing puzzles, doing arts and crafts, engaging in dramatic play, and listening to audio recordings of books.

Introduce children to the joys of literature.

- A preschool teacher reads to children at least once each day. She chooses books with entertaining stories and vivid illustrations that capture everyone's attention, interest, and imagination.

Middle Childhood

Encourage family members to become active participants in their children's activities.

- A religious educator invites parents and other family members to contribute in some small way to one of the classes. Different parents assist with musical performances, bake cookies, and give hands-on help during lessons.

Ensure that all students acquire basic academic skills.

- A second-grade teacher individualizes reading instruction for her students based on their knowledge and skills. With the help of a classroom aide, she works on mastery of letter identification and letter-sound correspondence with some, comprehension of simple stories with others, and selection of appropriate books with students who are already reading independently.

Give children the guidance they need to establish and maintain positive relationships with peers.

- When two children are quarreling, their teacher asks them to generate a few possible ways to settle the dispute.

Early Adolescence

Design a curriculum that is challenging and incorporates knowledge and skills from several content areas.

- A middle school teacher designs a unit on "war and conflict," integrating writing skills and knowledge of social studies. He encourages students to bring in newspaper clippings about current events and to write about political controversies.

Assign every young adolescent an adviser who looks after the adolescent's welfare.

- During homeroom with her advisees, a seventh-grade teacher makes sure that each student is keeping up with assignments. She also encourages her advisees to talk with her informally about their concerns about coursework, school, and interactions with other classmates.

Show sensitivity to youngsters who are undergoing the physical changes of puberty.

- A sports coach makes sure that adolescents have privacy when they dress and shower after team practice.

Late Adolescence

Expect students to meet high standards for achievement, but give them the support they need to meet those standards.

- An English composition teacher describes and then posts the various steps involved in writing—planning, drafting, writing, editing, and revising—and asks his students to use these steps in their essays. He then monitors his students' work, giving feedback as necessary and making sure that students execute each step in a way that enhances the quality of their writing.

Encourage adolescents to give back to their communities.

- A high school requires all students to participate in 50 hours of volunteer work or service learning in their town.

Educate adolescents about the academic requirements of jobs and colleges.

- A high school guidance counselor posts vacant positions in the area, listing the work experience and educational requirements for each.

DEVELOPMENT IN CULTURE
Developmentally Appropriate Practice in Japan

In Japan, teachers express their sensitivity by carefully observing and anticipating the needs of children. They interpret subtle facial cues that children exhibit and situational factors that hint at children's motivations (Rothbaum, Nagaoka, & Ponte, 2006). A Japanese preschool teacher who observes a worried young child staring intently at a juice box would not wait for the child to ask for help but would rather infer the child's difficulty and discretely demonstrate how to insert the straw into the box and sip the juice. Japanese teachers generally value empathy and emotional closeness and believe that they should help children *before* children verbalize their concerns (Rothbaum et al., 2006).

Japanese teachers also demonstrate compassion while encouraging children to get along with peers. They ask children to respond sympathetically when classmates appear isolated (Hayashi, Karasawa, & Tobin, 2009). Teachers may unobtrusively ease a shy child into a group of children playing together—for example, by asking the child to join a pretend tea party in the housekeeping area of the classroom. Because preschool class sizes are large in Japan, children have many occasions to solve conflicts on their own, teach one another rules of etiquette, and assist peers in distress (Hayashi et al., 2009). When arguing children require intervention from adults, teachers do not confront children directly about their misdeeds but rather tactfully demonstrate or explain proper behavior (Peak, 2001; Tobin, Wu, & Davidson, 1989).

Japanese teachers of older children express their concern for children by communicating high expectations and providing engaging learning

I CAN HELP. Many Japanese teachers anticipate the needs of children in their care.

activities. In Japan, all children are considered capable but not necessarily equally motivated (Ansalone, 2006). As a result, teachers often remind children to work diligently. When individual differences in achievement levels become obvious, exceptionally skilled students are invited to tutor their less proficient peers. Thus, mistakes are opportunities for learning and not signs of weakness. By emphasizing effort, teachers communicate their optimism about children's prospects for high academic achievement while also preparing them to fit into a society that sees hard work as the primary means to achievement.

development, adults must also introduce tasks of increasing complexity. Adults can help children set goals that can be achieved with hard work and modest levels of support. A school counselor, for instance, may work with an isolated child to promote her effective interaction with peers. One such tactic might be to stand close to a group of children and make a point of saying something complimentary or relevant to the conversation. Initially, children may need reminders but eventually they will initiate the behaviors on their own. Other strategies for extending children's current abilities depend largely on the specific duties that professionals have, as you read about in a For Further Exploration feature.

• **Integrate children's cultural values and customs into lessons.** By learning about the cultures of children in your care, you gain an important route to make activities meaningful. One way to learn about their upbringings is to invite children to share their backgrounds, for example, information about hobbies, traditions, and family origins. After learning about their backgrounds, you can incorporate these themes into the curriculum, for example, the aspirations of local refugees, and allow children the freedom to select projects that reflect their cultural values.

• **Consider how you might accommodate bioecological factors in children's lives.** Many children follow similar developmental pathways, but exceptions are everywhere. Children have personal experiences—perhaps growing up in poverty, having a chronic illness, or losing a family member to death or incarceration—that present unique challenges. Likewise, all children have their own advantages—maybe an exceptional talent in music or advocacy from a concerned relative—that can leverage positive growth. Educators can consider children's risks and protective factors and tailor support accordingly.

FOR FURTHER EXPLORATION . . .

Learn about the kinds of concerns that various categories of professionals have about children.

ENHANCEDetext
content extension

Strengthening the Commitment

A commitment to developmentally appropriate practice isn't something that can be applied automatically or that necessarily lasts forever. Teachers and other practitioners must continually discern the group characteristics *and* individual needs of young people. Furthermore, researchers continue to advance the frontiers of knowledge about child development. Therefore, educators can—and must—continue to learn more about the advantages and disadvantages that children of various ages face. Following are three useful things you can do:

• **Continue to take courses in child development.** Additional course work is one sure way of keeping up to date on (a) the latest research results on child development and (b) their practical implications for work with young people. Such course work has been shown to enhance professional effectiveness with children (Algozzine et al., 2011; Darling-Hammond & Bransford, 2005).

• **Find colleagues who share your concerns about children.** New teachers sometimes feel overwhelmed with pressures to accomplish their many responsibilities and may temporarily lose sight of developmental perspectives. Working together, teachers can remind one another to focus on children's needs by selecting age-appropriate curricula and designing settings suitable for the children with whom they work (Early et al., 2007).

• **Obtain perspectives from colleagues.** Many professional organizations hold regular meetings at which you can hear researchers and practitioners exchange ideas. Such meetings enable everyone to learn about the latest research findings and discover new methods for supporting children. Professional organizations also publish journals and magazines about research and standards for the instruction, care, and guidance of young people.

Summary

Effective care of youngsters is based on an understanding of typical developmental pathways and respect for individual differences. As a future educator, counselor, or other type of professional, you can identify and capitalize on individual children's strengths and nudge them toward increasing responsibility. Through ongoing education, conversations with colleagues, and participation in professional organizations, you can keep up to date on advancements in child development and maintain an optimistic outlook on your ability to help children.

ENHANCEDetext *self-check*

PRACTICING FOR YOUR LICENSURE EXAMINATION

Many teaching tests require students to apply what they have learned about child development to brief vignettes and multiple-choice questions. You can practice for your licensure examination by reading the following case study and answering a series of questions.

Latisha

Latisha, who is 13 years old, lives in a housing project in an inner-city neighborhood in Chicago. An adult asks her to describe her life and family, her hopes and fears, and her plans for the future. She responds as follows:

> My mother works at the hospital, serving food. She's worked there for 11 years, but she's been moved to different departments. I don't know what my dad does because he don't live with me. My mother's boyfriend lives with us. He's like my stepfather.

> In my spare time I just like be at home, look at TV, or clean up, or do my homework, or play basketball, or talk on the phone. My three wishes would be to have a younger brother and sister, a car of my own, and not get killed before I'm 20 years old.

> I be afraid of guns and rats. My mother she has a gun, her boyfriend has one for protection. I have shot one before and it's like a scary feeling. My uncle taught me. He took us in the country and he had targets we had to like shoot at. He showed us how to load and cock it and pull the trigger. When I pulled the trigger at first I feel happy because I learned how to shoot a gun, but afterward I didn't like it too much because I don't want to accidentally shoot nobody. I wouldn't want to shoot nobody. But it's good that I know how to shoot one just in case something happened and I have to use it.

> Where I live it's a quiet neighborhood. If the gangs don't bother me or threaten me, or do anything to my family, I'm OK. If somebody

say hi to me, I'll say hi to them as long as they don't threaten me. . . . I got two cousins who are in gangs. One is in jail because he killed somebody. My other cousin, he stayed cool. He ain't around. He don't be over there with the gang bangers. He mostly over on the west side with his grandfather, so I don't hardly see him. . . . I got friends in gangs. Some of them seven, eight years old that's too young to be in a gang. . . . They be gang banging because they have no one to turn to. . . . If a girl join a gang it's worser than if a boy join a gang because to be a girl you should have more sense. A boy they want to be hanging on to their friends. Their friends say gangs are cool, so they join.

The school I go to now is more funner than the school I just came from. We switch classes and we have 40 minutes for lunch. The Board of Education say that we can't wear gym shoes no more. They say it distracts other people from learning, it's because of the shoe strings and gang colors.

My teachers are good except two. My music and art teacher she's old and it seems like she shouldn't be there teaching. It seem like she should be retired and be at home, or traveling or something like that. And my history teacher, yuk! He's a stubborn old goat. He's stubborn with everybody.

When I finish school I want to be a doctor. At first I wanted to be a lawyer, but after I went to the hospital I said now I want to help people, and cure people, so I decided to be a doctor. (J. Williams & Williamson, 1992, pp. 11–12)[a]

Constructed-Response Question

1. How does the context in which Latisha is growing up affect her development? Describe at least three elements of Latisha's environment that seem to influence her.

[a] "Case Study: Latisha" by J. Williams and K. Williamson, from "I Wouldn't Want to Shoot Nobody: The Out-of-School Curriculum as Described by Urban Students" from ACTION IN TEACHER EDUCATION, Volume 14, No. 2, pp.11–12, 1992. Copyright © 1992 by J. Williams and K. Williamson. Reprinted with permission of Action in Teacher Education, published by the Association of Teacher Educators, Manassas Park, VA.

Multiple-Choice Questions

2. Which of the following theoretical accounts of Latisha's characteristics would most likely focus on the active role that Latisha plays in her own development and the stage-like changes that may periodically take place in her thinking?

   a. A biological theory
   b. A behaviorist or social learning theory
   c. A psychodynamic theory
   d. A cognitive-developmental theory

3. Which of the following theoretical accounts of Latisha's characteristics would most likely explain her characteristics as being the outcome of her personal activity and the numerous factors interacting inside her and in her multilayered social environment?

   a. A cognitive-process theory
   b. A sociocultural theory
   c. A developmental systems theory
   d. A biological theory

ENHANCEDetext *licensure exam*

Key Concepts

child development (p. 4)
physical development (p. 4)
cognitive development (p. 4)
social-emotional development (p. 4)
context (p. 5)
culture (p. 5)
nature (p. 5)
nurture (p. 5)

temperament (p. 5)
maturation (p. 5)
sensitive period (p. 7)
universality (p. 7)
diversity (p. 7)
qualitative change (p. 8)
quantitative change (p. 8)
stage (p. 8)

stage theory (p. 8)
theory (p. 11)
biological theory (p. 11)
behaviorism (p. 12)
social learning theory (p. 12)
psychodynamic theory (p. 13)
cognitive-developmental theory (p. 14)

cognitive process theory (p. 14)
sociocultural theory (p. 15)
developmental systems theory (p. 16)
self-regulation (p. 17)
developmentally appropriate practice (p. 25)

CHAPTER TWO

Research and Assessment

CASE STUDY: Jack's Research

Jack Reston, an elementary school principal, had recently joined a district committee charged with reducing student absenteeism. He realized that research could inform the work of his committee and guide new policies at his school. He carefully considered a productive direction for an investigation. Looking back, he wrote:

I began by asking three questions:

1. What student characteristics are associated with student absenteeism?
2. What are some longitudinal effects of student absenteeism?
3. What are some effective strategies to prevent student absenteeism?

I reviewed current studies, literature, local and national profiles, written surveys, and interviews. I found that absenteeism was highly associated with dropping out of school, academic failure, and delinquency. I learned what students and parents in our school believed about the relationship between school and absenteeism. I concluded that I really did not understand the belief systems of families at risk for poor attendance in school. I conducted a massive survey of students and parents within a four-day period of time. Surveys gathered data concerning such things as respectfulness of students, safety in school, conflict management, discipline, school rules, self-esteem, and academics. In addition, the survey gathered data on mobility rates, volunteerism, and levels of education in parents. The identity of the families surveyed was kept unknown. . . .

Student teachers from a nearby university and local educators with experience in action research interviewed selected students and parents. The interviews were conducted over the telephone or face-to-face. (Reston, 2007, pp. 141–142)[a]

After collecting and analyzing his data, Jack realized that, by and large, his students were not motivated by such extrinsic rewards as for prizes or certificates. He also concluded that students did not perceive rules to be fair or effectively enforced by the school. In reflecting on these observations and the relatively low achievement of numerous students, Jack realized that he needed to change his policies and style of interacting with students:

This information led to major changes in our approach to improving attendance in our school. First, we stopped spending large sums of money for rewards and drawings. Although these are nice things for students, they are ineffective in dealing with the problem of poor attendance. Second, we recognized punitive measures were having little effect on attendance. This led us to the belief that students succeeding in school were more likely to attend school regularly.

We began a concentrated effort to improve the success of students at school both academically and emotionally. This included the use of student/parent/teacher/principal contracts, daily planners for students, individual conferences between the student and the principal every 14 days to review grades and behaviors, better assessments to locate students having academic problems, improved instructional techniques and alignment of curriculum, and more concentrated efforts to improve the self-esteem of students. . . .

Based on these findings, I worked with teachers and parents to develop quick responses that unite the student, parent, educator, and community in a preventive effort to minimize absenteeism. (Reston, 2007, p. 142)[a]

- How did Jack ensure that his research was of high quality?
- What ethical practices did Jack use as he conducted his research?

[a]Excerpts from "Reflecting on Admission Criteria" by J. Reston. In *Action Research: A Guide for the Teacher Researcher* (3rd ed., pp. 141–142), by G. E. Mills, 2007, Upper Saddle River, NJ: Merrill/Prentice Hall. Reprinted with permission of the author.

Jack Reston safeguarded the quality of his data by first examining relevant investigations and then gathering comprehensive responses from children and parents. He also followed ethical practices by protecting the confidentiality of participants' individual responses and engaging all members of the community in a search for solutions. In the end Jack's research was the basis for strengthening relationships with students, monitoring their progress, and offering structure to their organizational skills.

PRINCIPLES OF RESEARCH

To contribute to knowledge of child development, researchers must follow three basic principles. First and foremost, they must obey a strict ethical code. Second, they must follow the steps of the scientific method. Finally, they must select children and adolescents who can provide needed information. We examine each of these principles in turn.

Ethical Protection of Children

A paramount concern for scholars of child development is that they conduct research in an ethical manner, in particular, that they are honest and respectful of the rights of children (American Psychological Association, 2002; Dalli & One, 2012; C. B. Fisher & Vacanti-Shova, 2012; Palaiologou, 2014; Society for Research in Child Development, 2007). To protect children's rights, researchers aspire to these ethical standards:

- *Do no harm.* Researchers prioritize the welfare of children over their own desires for information. They avoid procedures that cause children stress, embarrassment, or pain.
- *Get approval from authorities.* Before collecting data from children, researchers prepare a proposal of the kinds of data children will provide, any risks and benefits children might encounter, plans for reducing danger and threat to minimal levels, and measures for advising children and families about the research. They then obtain approval for their proposed study from authorities at their university, school district, or other organization.
- *Obtain consent from participants and their families.* Also before collecting data, researchers explain to parents and children what the study entails in time and involvement and ask for written permission that children be able to take part in the research. Children are also asked to give their assent either orally or in writing, depending on their age. If permission is unnecessary because researchers will not intrude on children's customary activities, for example, if researchers plan to observe children's spontaneous play at the park, appropriate institutional authorities would review the study but not require written consent.
- *Preserve children's privacy.* Investigators usually describe group trends in their results. When they single out a particular child, they use a fictitious name and withhold identifying information.
- *Be honest.* Children expect adults to be honest. Researchers do not exploit or undermine this assumption. Thus deception with children is almost always avoided. Exceptions are evaluated by authorities and generally require an explanation to children afterwards and efforts to regain their trust.
- *Communicate openly.* After children provide the data that will be used in the investigation, researchers respond to any questions or concerns children or parents might have. When investigators write up their results, they often send families a brief description of their findings. Investigators also share the results with other scholars and, if appropriate, with the public.

The Scientific Method

The **scientific method** is a powerful strategy for acquiring and refining insights about children because it requires researchers to think critically about the data they collect and the conclusions they draw. For developmental scholars, the scientific method includes these general steps:

1. *Pose a question.* Researchers clearly state the question they want to answer. When they are able to make predictions about the outcomes of their study, they also state hypotheses.

2. *Design an investigation*. Once the question is clear, researchers must figure out what kinds of information will help answer their question and, if applicable, test the hypotheses. With specific methods in mind, they obtain guidance on ethical dimensions, as we explained previously.

3. *Collect data*. Researchers recruit children and gather information using carefully defined procedures.

4. *Analyze the data*. Researchers organize the data, categorize children's responses, look for themes, and, when appropriate, perform statistical tests. After making sense of the data, they draw conclusions relevant to their research question.

5. *Share the results*. Researchers write up the study's purpose, methods, results, and conclusions and present the paper at a conference, submit it to a journal, or both. Scientific peers evaluate the manuscript on its merits, identify any flawed arguments, and build on new ideas in the research that they find especially convincing. This give-and-take among scientists leads to scientific progress.

Research Participants

In most types of developmental research, investigators wish to make fairly broad claims about children of a certain age or background. To make their work manageable, they limit their attention to a reasonable number of children. Thus researchers first define a population and then select a subgroup, or **sample**, of that population, from which they collect data. The sample provides a reasonable basis for making conclusions about the larger population, which it presumably resembles but is more cost-effective to examine. For example, imagine that a team of psychologists wants to know what adolescents in public high schools in San Francisco, California, think about desirable careers. With the help of administrators in San Francisco schools, the researchers obtain a list of homeroom teachers and randomly select 10 percent of these teachers. Next, the researchers ask the selected teachers to distribute letters, consent forms, and surveys. If the return rate of materials from students and parents is high, investigators can be reasonably confident that their *sample* of adolescents is representative of the larger *population* of adolescents in public schools in San Francisco. If instead a good number of potential participants decide not to join the study, or they drop out before data collection is completed, the resulting sample may be so small that the results cannot be said to represent trends in the population.

In other kinds of studies, generalizing to a large population is not the goal. For instance, a team of scholars may study one child or a small group of children intensively. These researchers hope to analyze children's experiences in enough depth that they can draw accurate conclusions about the experiences of *these children*—not about children overall. In this kind of investigation, researchers recruit children who have characteristics of interest (for example, being from a certain cultural group) and then follow them closely. In their reports, the investigators would conscientiously describe the experiences of these children while protecting their confidentiality and not presuming that their experiences inevitably apply to others with similar circumstances.

Regardless of whether investigators want to obtain a large representative sample or a small number of children for in-depth analysis, they must consider the role that children's backgrounds play in the phenomenon of interest, be it self-esteem, achievement, or something else. Historically, children from middle-income, white European American backgrounds were overrepresented in research, whereas children of and those who are learning English as a second language and growing up in low-income communities were underrepresented (M. H. Bornstein, Jager, & Putnick, 2013; García Coll et al., 1996; McCubbin & McCubbin, 2013; McLoyd, Aikens, & Burton, 2006). Fortunately, many developmental researchers now recruit participants more inclusively, such as those from diverse ethnic and economic backgrounds and from such traditionally neglected populations as children whose parents are migrant, homeless, or incarcerated. These outreach efforts are currently enriching our knowledge of diversity in the daily challenges children face and the assets they have. In writing this book, we have made special efforts to include research with diverse samples of children, and we encourage you to watch for information about the characteristics of research participants when you read investigations yourself. When the backgrounds of participants differ significantly from those of children in your care, you will want to be especially cautious in accepting the researchers' conclusions.

Summary

Research with children needs to be guided by strong ethical standards, the scientific method, and access to willing children. The manner in which researchers integrate these principles into their investigations depends largely on the kinds of methods they use.

ENHANCEDetext *self-check*

METHODS OF RESEARCH

Investigators convert general principles of research into specific features of a study that fit their research questions. Usually they make good choices, implementing sound methods that adequately answer their questions. Occasionally, though, researchers make short-sighted decisions, collect data haphazardly, or draw unwarranted interpretations from their data. To interpret developmental research critically, you need to become familiar with common data-collection techniques and research designs.

Data-Collection Techniques

Researchers gather data using four kinds of techniques: self-reports, tests and other assessment tasks, physiological measures, and observations of behavior. Each of these methods offers a unique window into the minds and habits of children.

Self-Reports

Observing Children 2-1

Observe an interviewer use several types of requests for information from Claudia about her classification of seashells.

ENHANCEDetext *video example*

Researchers often ask children to explain their beliefs, attitudes, hopes, and frustrations. In fact, some of the most informative research data comes in the form of youngsters' own statements about themselves—that is, in the form of **self-reports**. Self-reports take two primary forms, interviews and questionnaires.

During **interviews**, researchers ask questions to explore the reasoning of children. Interviewers who succeed in making children feel safe and comfortable can learn a lot about how these young people think about things. Interviewers may sit beside children on the floor, ask children about their interests, and, when beginning the interview, reassure children that whatever they tell them is fine. Interviewers often start with general questions before asking for specific information, as you can see in an Observing Children video, in which an interviewer gently but persistently asks 12-year-old Claudia questions about why she grouped seashells precisely as she did. Initially, Claudia describes her reasoning in a fairly general way. After several questions, Claudia elaborates on her strategy.

Investigators typically conduct interviews through face-to-face conversations, which allow them to communicate directly with children. Researchers occasionally interview young people over the telephone, reducing costs of travel and involving participants who might avoid a face-to-face interview on the topic. For example, one group of researchers interviewed 14- to 16-year-old adolescents by telephone and found that many youth willingly reported being able to purchase alcohol by showing fake driver's licenses or getting help from others, behaviors they might not have revealed in face-to-face interactions (M.-J. Chen, Gruenewald, & Remer, 2009).

Developmental researchers use **questionnaires** when they need to gather responses from a large number of participants. When young people complete questionnaires, they typically read questions or statements and choose from defined options that best express their feelings, attitudes, or actions. In studies of motivation, researchers have occasionally asked adolescents to indicate how much they agree that they want to learn as much as possible in school or, alternatively, just want to avoid failing there. From such responses, researchers have learned that adolescents' motivational beliefs are related to the courses they select in high school and the levels of achievement they attain (Crosnoe & Huston, 2007; Witkow & Fuligni, 2007).

As we have said, youngsters usually complete questionnaires through a paper-and-pencil format, but in some situations they answer questions on the computer or listen to questions through earphones (Langhaug, Cheung, Pascoe, Hayes, & Cowan, 2009). Researchers have tried other technologies as well, including beepers that emit signals at regular intervals throughout the day to remind adolescents to record their experiences in notebooks or respond to a text message on their mobile phone (Hedin, 2014; Larson & Richards, 1994).

Self-reports have advantages and disadvantages. Valuable insights emerge from interviews when researchers ask children about their views, probe their understandings in a thorough yet sensitive fashion, and confirm what they say with other types of data. However, interviews are time-consuming and highly dependent on the interviewer's skill. Questionnaires are an efficient means to collect data yet exceed many children's reading abilities, do not allow researchers to probe, and provide no mechanism for children to express confusion or mixed feelings. In addition, when researchers are unaware of children's thinking about a topic, they may unintentionally create response options that are out of sync with children's views or experiences. Computers and other technologies can lend efficiency to the research enterprise but are costly and depend on youngsters' familiarity with the equipment. Both interviews and questionnaires are vulnerable to **social desirability**, the tendency of children to give answers that will be perceived favorably by others. For instance, adolescents may underestimate their use of illicit drugs or number of sexual partners if they perceive that the researchers view these behaviors negatively. Researchers can reduce the effects of social desirability by establishing rapport with their research participants, advising them that they are not being judged, letting them know that their responses will be kept confidential, and encouraging their honesty. Such tactics improve the likelihood that self-reports provide accurate glimpses into the thoughts and actions of youngsters.

Tests and Other Assessments

A **test** is an instrument designed to assess children's knowledge, abilities, or skills in the same manner from one individual to the next. Some tests use paper and pencil, whereas others do not, but all typically yield a result in the form of a number (e.g., a score on an intelligence test) or category (e.g., "alert" or "proficient").

Tests are frequently used to gauge the effectiveness of educational programs. In an intervention for children from low-income families, participants regularly completed tests of cognitive ability from ages 3 months to 12 years and again at age 21 and 30 (F. A. Campbell et al., 2002; F. A. Campbell et al., 2012). Scores indicated that individuals who participated in a full-time high-quality child care program as infants not only exhibited larger cognitive gains in the first few years of life but also had higher reading and math scores at age 21 compared to individuals who did not participate in the program. A second intervention, beginning at age 5 and lasting for 3 years, was less effective. These tests are valuable in revealing that interventions are most effective when initiated at a young age.

Developmental scholars sometimes measure children's abilities with **assessments**, samples of things they say or create that reveal their knowledge, abilities, and other characteristics. Researchers conducting separate investigations might collect children's artwork, examine their essays, record children's efficiency in navigating through a maze, or analyze their understanding of commonly used verbal expressions. Some assessments involve spoken language—not the in-depth interviews described earlier but brief question-and-answer exchanges that reveal the child's knowledge. In an Observing Children video, you can listen to an assessment of 14-year-old Alicia's understanding of proverbs:

Observing Children 2-2
Listen to an assessment of Alicia's understanding of proverbs.
ENHANCEDetext *video example*

Interviewer: What does it mean when someone says, "Better to light a candle than to curse the darkness"?

Alicia: Well, it means, probably, that you're actually getting somewhere than just complaining about it and not doing anything about it.

Interviewer: What does it mean when someone says, "An ant may well destroy a dam"?

Alicia: I think it probably means that even though they're really small, they can still change things.

An advantage of tests and assessments is that they provide clues to children's thinking. From her responses, we know that Alicia can look beyond common expressions to determine their underlying meanings. Assessments tell us only so much, however—we cannot tell *how* Alicia was able to decipher the proverbs. Had she previously encountered them, or did she apply strong reasoning skills on the spot? Nor can single assessments tell us how children might change their skills if given particular kinds of instruction. Accordingly, researchers sometimes administer several assessments, perhaps before, during, and after instruction.

Physiological Measures

To learn about children's physical development, researchers often turn to **physiological measures**, systematic appraisals of such bodily conditions as heart rate, hormone levels, bone growth, brain activity, eye movements, body weight, and lung capacity.

Physiological measures yield important information about children's well-being. They allow us to monitor indicators of health—cardiovascular fitness, obesity, stress levels, and malnutrition. Physiological measures also enable us to uncover valuable information about infants' cognitive development. Infants cannot use words to tell us what they know but they can show us from their behavior and physiological reactions. Researchers have learned a great deal about infants' attention, perception, and memory by exploiting infants' tendency to respond differently to familiar and unfamiliar stimuli. When infants are shown the same object or pattern repeatedly, they grow accustomed to it and lose interest. You can see an infant grow tired of a rattle in an Observing Children video. This tendency, called **habituation**, can be assessed through changes in heart rate, sucking, and eye movements. Studies in habituation have shown that infants perceive depth from visual cues and can discriminate among particular consonants and vowels, number and size of objects, and types of movements (Cantrell & Smith, 2013; Fais, Kajikawa, Shigeaki, & Werker, 2009; Granrud, 2006; Hespos, Dora, Rips, & Christie, 2012; Kavšek, 2013).

Observing Children 2-3
Observe an infant undergo habituation to a rattle.
ENHANCEDetext *video example*

Other technologies have improved our understanding of children's brain development. We have learned of fascinating developmental patterns through animal research, analyses of brains of individuals who died during childhood, and new technologies that can be safely implemented with living children. An example of the last of these methods is magnetic resonance imaging (MRI), which measures the varying magnetic densities of different parts of the brain (Paus, 2005; see Figure 2-1 for an example of MRI scans of a child's brain). One investigation examined MRIs of the brains of healthy individuals from age 7 to age 30 and found that compared to the children's brains, adults' brains showed fewer but stronger connections in areas of the brain that support judgment, restraint, and the ability to plan for the future (Sowell, Delis, Stiles, & Jernigan, 2001).

An advantage of physiological measures is that they give precise indications of how children's bodies and brains are functioning. A disadvantage is that the meaning of the data they yield is not always clear. The fact that infants perceive differences among various perceptual stimuli (e.g., "two and three items") does not necessarily indicate that they are consciously aware of patterns or that they can act on them in any meaningful way. Another limitation is that many physiological tests cannot be administered often because they cause discomfort (e.g., some brain-scan procedures can be quite noisy) or may be harmful if done too frequently (as is the case with X-rays).

Observations

Researchers conduct **observations** when they carefully watch the behavior of youngsters. Observations offer rich portraits of children's lives, particularly when they take place over an extended time and are supplemented with interviews, tests, and other data.

Researchers who conduct observations generally keep a detailed record of meaningful events that take place in a particular setting, perhaps the family home, a classroom, or a

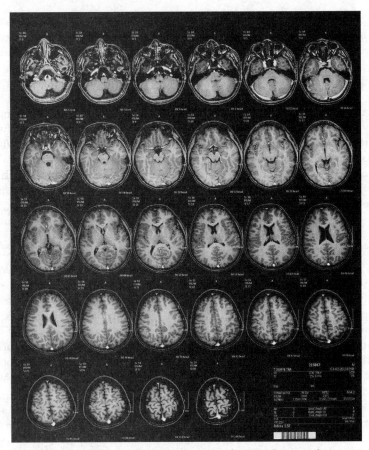

FIGURE 2-1   MRI of a child's brain taken from various angles.

neighborhood playground. The following observation reveals interactions between a father and his 5-year-old daughter, Anna:

11:05 a.m.   Anna looks at her father, who is sitting on the couch reading the newspaper: "Wanna play Legos, Dad?" Dad says, "Sure," and puts down the paper and gets on the floor. Anna pushes a pile of Legos toward Dad and says, "Here. You can build the factory with the volcanoes."

11:06 a.m.   Dad looks puzzled and says, "What factory?" Anna laughs and says, "The one where they make molten steel, silly!" Dad says, "Oh, I forgot," and picks up a gray Lego and fits a red one to it. (Pellegrini, 1996, p. 22)

Although observers hope to describe events as faithfully as possible, they must make decisions about what to record and what to ignore. The observer who writes about Anna and her father may focus on the pair's negotiations over what to play and what to pretend. Other events, such as Anna dropping toys or her father scratching his head, would receive less attention.

Researchers frequently use observations to document characteristics and behaviors (e.g., hairstyles, dress codes, bullying behaviors) that young people display in public settings. Observations are also helpful in identifying actions that individuals may be unaware of or unable to articulate (e.g., the types of questions directed toward boys vs. girls, or the interests of small children) and behaviors that violate social rules (e.g., temper tantrums, petty thefts). In an Observing Children video, you can watch 7-month-old Madison inspect the visual properties of toys and books, exhibiting her strong interest in these objects, which she certainly would not have been able to articulate with words.

The contribution of observations is their ability to tell us what children actually *do*—not what children *say* they do or what parents report about children's actions. Observations have their weaknesses, however. For one thing, the presence of an observer might change the

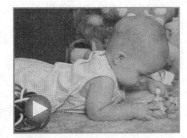

Observing Children 2-4
Observe an infant inspecting the visual properties of objects.
ENHANCEDetext *video example*

behaviors under investigation. Children may misbehave or, alternatively, stay on task more than usual. Some young people become self-conscious or even anxious in the company of a stranger. To minimize these reactions, researchers often spend considerable time in a setting before they collect data. That way, children grow accustomed to the researchers and eventually carry on as they normally would.

Another weakness of observations is that researchers' expectations can influence their conclusions. An observer who perceives children as hostile may categorize an interaction between two boys as "hitting," whereas an observer who perceives children as friendly may see the same scuffle as "energetic play." Researchers handle this problem by spending as much time as possible in the setting, carefully defining the events and behaviors they observe, and discussing their observations with other observers. Finally, some actions, such as extreme temper tantrums in third-grade classrooms, would require a lengthy and expensive period of time for trained observers to obtain a record that might generalize to other settings.

Integrity in Data Collection

Regardless of exactly how scholars collect their information, they continually ask themselves *how* they know their data-collection methods are of high quality. The specific terms for quality vary somewhat with type of investigation. In studies with relatively large samples and statistical analyses, researchers typically are concerned with **validity**, the extent to which data-collection methods actually assess what the researchers intend to assess. To address validity, investigators must show that they are examining the essential parts of a well-defined domain. For instance, researchers who see mathematical ability as being comprised of both computational proficiencies (adding, subtracting, multiplying, dividing) and problem-solving skills (making sense of situations by determining underlying mathematical patterns) must make a point to include *both* types of competencies in their assessments.

Researchers must also rule out the influence of irrelevant traits. For instance, do scores on a test of mathematical ability reflect children's knowledge of a particular culture—for instance, are there too many questions about American sports? Are children expected by test developers to answer questions hurriedly even though they have been socialized to be cautious and introspective? Does a test of scientific reasoning assess children's desire to please the experimenter as much as it assesses finesse in thinking skills? Only when researchers can say no to such questions do they have an assurance that their methods are valid.

The validity of data can be enhanced by the researcher considering how children understand the the purpose of the activities from which data were collected. Skilled investigators recognize that children must be rested and attentive during experimental tasks. Investigators also recognize that young people bring their own expectations and agendas to interactions with adults. Some participants (adolescents especially) may give responses to shock a researcher or in some other way undermine the research effort. Others may tell a researcher what they think he or she wants to hear (recall the concept of *social desirability*). Furthermore, youngsters may understand words and phrases differently than researchers do. Probing sensitively, searching for confirmation through a variety of sources, and reassuring children that they are not personally being judged, are strategies investigators use to improve the validity of data.

As we suggested earlier, developmental researchers who conduct observations try to put children at ease by allowing the children to grow accustomed to their presence before collecting data. Observers also realize that they cannot record all aspects of children's behavior and must instead focus on a limited number of carefully defined actions. In addition, investigators know that they could be biased in their interpretations of children's behavior and therefore ask colleagues to independently record children's actions and interpret what they see.

Researchers must also ask whether their data-collection techniques are yielding consistent, dependable results—in other words, whether their methods have **reliability**. Data are reliable when the same result is obtained in a variety of circumstances. In general, reliability is lower when unwanted influences (usually temporary in nature) affect the results. Children and adolescents inevitably may be more or less rested, attentive, cooperative, honest, or articulate depending on their circumstances. Their performance can also be influenced by characteristics of the researcher (e.g., gender, educational background, ethnic origin, appearance) and conditions in the research setting (e.g., how quiet the room is, how instructions are worded, and what kinds of incentives are given for participation).

Preparing for Your Licensure Examination
Your teaching test might ask you to identify the characteristics of valid and reliable tests and assessments.

TABLE 2-1 Types of Developmental Designs

TYPE OF DESIGN	FOCUS	EXAMPLE
Experimental studies	Identifying causal effects in interventions	What are the effects of a counseling treatment on children's level of aggression?
Correlational studies	Documenting associations	What is the correlation between number of hours per week children view aggressive television and number of acts of physical and verbal aggression at school?
Developmental studies	Revealing developmental change and stability	What is the association between children's exposure to a punitive style of parenting and children's later aggressiveness?
Naturalistic studies	Describing children's daily experiences and perspectives	How do children justify having committed violent acts?

Sometimes the instrument itself influences the reliability of scores, as can occur when two different forms of an assessment yield dissimilar conclusions about children. This could happen if one form is more difficult or if two researchers interpret the same responses differently. When researchers are making subjective judgments (e.g., about the sophistication of children's artistic skills), they must establish clear standards or run the risk of making idiosyncratic decisions.

In studies with small sample sizes in which investigators aim to portray the experiences of children with sensitivity and insight, different terms for the integrity of data collection, analysis, and interpretation are used. Scholars might suggest that they have tried to produce *trustworthy* or *credible* results by spending a long time observing children, reflecting on their own biases, asking participating children for their interpretations of events, getting input from colleagues, and corroborating the results with several kinds of information—perhaps children's interview responses, their behavior, comments from teachers and parents, and the assignments they complete at school.

Having carefully collected information from children and caregivers, researchers must also consider the meaning of the data within the broader context of the study. To a large extent, the research design directs the collection and interpretation of data.

Research Designs

The *research design* translates the research question into the concrete details of an investigation. The design specifies the procedures and schedule of data collection and strategies for analyzing the data. In child development research the design typically focuses on one of four themes: (a) the effects of new interventions on children, (b) the elements of children's development that occur in close association, (c) the particular aspects of children's behavior that change with time and those others that stay the same, or (d) the nature of children's experiences in carrying out routines in familiar groups. In Table 2-1, you can see the kinds of questions researchers attempt to answer with these four designs.

Identification of Causal Effects

In an **experimental study**, the investigator manipulates one aspect of the environment and measures its impact on children. Experiments typically involve an intervention, or *treatment*. Participants are divided into two or more groups, with the separate groups receiving different treatments or perhaps with one group (a **control group**) receiving either no treatment or a presumably less effective one. Following the treatment(s), the investigator looks for differences between the groups' performances.

In a true experimental design, participants are assigned to groups on a *random* basis; they have essentially no choice in the treatment (or absence of treatment) that they receive.[1] Random assignment increases the likelihood that any differences in individuals (perhaps in

[1]Ethical considerations may lead researchers to give members of the control group an alternative treatment—something of value that will not compromise the experimental comparison. For example, in an investigation into the effects of a new tutoring program for delayed readers, children who do not participate in the program might receive a collection of children's books, extra help in mathematics, or some other resources known to be valuable to them. In other circumstances researchers make the experimental treatment available to children in the control group *after* the study has been completed.

the motivations or personalities of group members) are evenly distributed between groups. With the exception of administering a particular treatment, the experimenter makes all conditions of the experience identical or very similar for all groups. The researcher thus tries to ensure that the only major difference among the groups is the experimental treatment itself. For example, during a month-long experiment with third graders, the treatment group receives a new science unit whereas the control group receives the regular science unit long used in the district. The treatment and control lessons are each taught by equivalently enthusiastic and experienced teachers; both groups of children participate in science instruction for the same period of time. Therefore, any differences in children's subsequent scientific understandings are almost certainly the result of differences in the curricula.

In many situations experiments are impossible, impractical, or unethical. When random assignment is not a viable strategy, researchers may conduct a **quasi-experimental study**, in which they administer one or more experimental treatments to existing groups (e.g., classrooms or schools; D. T. Campbell & Stanley, 1963). Because researchers cannot make sure that the groups are similar in every respect, the possibility exists that some other variable (e.g., presence of gangs at one school but not the other) may account for differences in the characteristics of the participants at the end of the treatment.

An illustration of a quasi-experimental design can be found in an investigation examining the effectiveness of different treatments for aggression with 904 elementary and junior high students in Israel (Shechtman & Ifargan, 2009). Three classrooms at a single grade level in 13 schools were randomly assigned to one of three 4-month-long treatments. A counseling group included activities addressing circumstances that commonly provoke aggression in children and coached children in controlling these urges. Students who participated in an in-class intervention read literature and took part in activities fostering empathy for classmates and emphasizing the inappropriateness of aggression. Students who participated in a control group took part in their regular classes and completed the research instruments. This study is considered a quasi-experiment because the children as individuals were not randomly assigned to treatments—rather, they were members of a particular classroom and shared the same treatment (or no treatment) with their classmates. Before and after the 4-month period, students rated their own behavior on a seven-point scale in terms of how typical various aggressive behaviors were of them (with 1 being "is not characteristic of me at all" and 7 being "is very characteristic of me"). Among the key findings were that children who had been previously identified by teachers as being especially aggressive rated themselves as significantly less aggressive after participating in either the counseling or in-class intervention group, whereas children in the control group did not, as you can see in the following data:

Average Scores on Levels of Aggression Before and After Treatment[2]

Type of Aggression	Counseling Group		In-Class Intervention		Control Group	
	Before	**After**	**Before**	**After**	**Before**	**After**
Verbal aggression	4.49	4.06	4.45	3.90	4.23	4.37
Physical aggression	4.09	3.28	4.28	3.28	4.04	3.89

Another variant on experiments is the single-subject design, in which a child's behavior is studied intensively as interventions are introduced and removed. For example, investigators might look at the effects of a certain strategy, such as temporarily removing children from interaction with peers, after they have acted aggressively. The investigators would keep a careful chart of the frequency of the target behavior before the intervention, note its frequency immediately after the intervention, and continue to record the behavior after the intervention is removed and then reinstated (C. Wilson, Robertson, Herlong, & Haynes, 1979). With this kind of methodical analysis, the investigators can be reasonably confident that the intervention is having an effect on aggressive behavior.

---

[2]The averages in this table are *means*, which if you are familiar with statistics, you will understand are calculated by adding up all scores in a group and dividing by the number of individuals in that group. Separately, a judgment would be as to whether the groups are statistically different by comparing the means to the variation (or spread among scores) in the groups.

True experiments are unique among research designs in the degree to which outside influences are regulated and therefore eliminated as possible explanations for results. For this reason, experiments are the method of choice when a researcher wants to identify cause-and-effect relationships. Another strength of experiments is that their rigorous procedures allow other researchers to replicate the conditions of the study. A common limitation, however, is that to ensure adequate control of procedures, researchers regularly conduct their interventions in artificial laboratory settings that are considerably different from conditions in the real world. Ethical and practical considerations make it impossible in many situations to conduct true experiments, and when quasi-experiments and single-design studies are carried out instead, causal effects cannot be fully certain.

Documentations of Associations

Some studies uncover patterns already present in children's lives. In an investigation examining associations, a researcher collects information on one variable, such as the amount of time per week parents read to children, and sees if it is related to another variable, such as the size of children's vocabulary. Associations often are examined with a **correlation**, a statistic that measures the extent to which two variables are related to each other. If a correlation exists, one variable changes when the other variable does, in a somewhat predictable fashion.

In correlational studies, associations are often measured with a particular statistic known as the *correlation coefficient*, a number that is typically between −1 and +1. The sign of the coefficient (+ or −) tells us about the direction of the relationship. Among a group of children at a particular age level, height and weight tend to be positively correlated—taller children tend to weigh more than shorter children. In comparison, children's age and the number of hours they sleep at night tend to be negatively correlated; as children grow older, they tend to sleep somewhat less. The size of the coefficient tells us how strong the relationship is. A coefficient that is close to either +1 or −1 (e.g., +.89 or −.76) indicates a strong link between the variables, whereas coefficients that are close to zero (e.g., +.15 or −.22) indicate a weak connection between the variables. Coefficients in the middle range (e.g., those in the .40s and .50s, whether positive or negative) indicate moderate associations.

In a **correlational study**, investigators look for naturally occurring associations among existing characteristics, behaviors, or other variables. In a study with ninety 10- to 11-year-old girls in a rural community in the northwestern part of the United States, the amount of time girls watched physically aggressive programs on television was associated with teachers' reports of the girls being aggressive. Viewing a lot of aggressive content on television was associated with frequency of verbal aggression (e.g., calling children names, in a coefficient of +.38), with physical aggression (e.g., hitting or kicking peers, in a coefficient of +.25), and relational aggression (e.g., spreading rumors or gossiping about classmates, in a coefficient of +.21) (Linder & Gentile, 2009). Because these data are correlational and not experimental, they do not give definitive clues as to what factors might have led girls who had been exposed to high levels of violence to become aggressive. Although televised aggression might have provoked aggression in the girls, other conditions, such as parents' difficulty in maintaining warm relationships with their daughters, may have prompted the girls to watch television *and* become aggressive at school. Note also that the associations are weak, suggesting that additional factors account for the degree to which girls became antagonistic with classmates.

Correlational studies have the advantages of being relatively inexpensive to conduct and permitting the analysis of several relationships. One disadvantage, however, is that cause-and-effect relationships cannot be determined from correlational data alone. This is a serious limitation: Although correlational studies may demonstrate an association between two or more variables, they can never tell us the specific factors that explain *why* it exists. In other words, correlation *does not* confirm causation. For example, although being exposed to stressful circumstances is negatively associated with children's achievement in school, it's not fully clear why this connection occurs. Is it that traumatic events undermine children's ability to concentrate at school, or is it that stressful events are more common in certain families, perhaps those with substance abuse or mental health problems, such that it is not stress itself but these other factors that reduce children's opportunities in learning (Goodman, Miller, & West-Olatunji, 2012)? Or is a combination of factors at work? Correlational studies provide fascinating clues but not definitive answers to these questions.

Documentation of Developmental Change and Stability

Some investigations, known as *developmental studies*, examine how children grow, change, or stay the same as they grow. One approach is a **cross-sectional study**, in which a researcher compares individuals at two or more age levels at the same point in time. In a study with first- and third-grade boys, Coie, Dodge, Terry, and Wright (1991) found that first graders were more likely to be targets of aggression than were third graders.

Another option for studying developmental stability and change is the **longitudinal study**, in which a researcher examines one group of children over a lengthy period of time, often for several years and sometimes for decades. Longitudinal studies allow us to see changes in a characteristic when the same measurement is taken on repeated occasions. Longitudinal designs also allow us to examine the factors in children's early lives that forecast their later performance. An example of a longitudinal study is Eron's (1987) investigation into factors related to aggressive behavior. Eron collected data at three points in time, first when the participants were in third grade, a second time 10 years later, and a third time 12 years after that. Factors evident when the participants were children, including parents punitive style of discipline, the children's own preferences for watching violent television shows, and the children's lack of a guilty conscience in hurting others, were associated with their aggressiveness and criminal behavior 10 and 22 years later.

To strengthen inferences that can be made about change and stability in child development, some researchers have creatively modified developmental designs. A few have tried *microgenetic methods*, which you might think of as brief but thorough longitudinal designs. Researchers implementing these methods may study children's responses after training or while learning a new task over a few hours, days, or weeks (Siegler, 2006; Vygotsky, 1978). Other variations include a combination of cross-sectional and longitudinal designs. A *cohort-sequential design* replicates a longitudinal study with new *cohorts*—that is, with one or more additional groups of people born in certain subsequent years. Suhr (1999) conducted a cohort-sequential study to examine children's scores in mathematics, reading recognition, and reading comprehension. Scores had been collected every 2 years for children who were born in 1980, 1981, 1982, and 1983. Suhr found that growth in skills was rapid between ages 5 and 10 but slowed down after age 10. Because the design included children from four different birth years, Suhr could be reasonably confident that the spurt of learning that occurred between 5 and 10 years was a reasonably accurate result and not an anomaly of one particular group.

The particular strengths and limitations of developmental studies are design-specific. Cross-sectional studies offer an efficient snapshot of how characteristics or behaviors differ with age, but these age differences can be attributed to a variety of factors, including maturation, exposure to schooling, and general changes in society. Longitudinal studies allow prediction of later characteristics based on earlier qualities but are expensive, time-consuming, and of questionable relevance to unstudied populations. The hybrid projects that combine the features of cross-sectional and longitudinal designs, for example, the microgenetic and cohort-sequential designs mentioned earlier, have definite advantages, but they are also expensive to carry out and create demands for continued involvement in waves of data collection that many potential participants would rather avoid.

Descriptions of Children's Everyday Experiences

In a *naturalistic study*, researchers examine children's experiences in families, peer groups, schools, clubs, and elsewhere. In this type of investigation, researchers try not to prejudge children's ideas and instead listen carefully to views expressed by the children. In a recent study with adolescents from low-income families who were attending middle schools in an urban community, interviewers asked students to talk about how they might respond to particular conflicts (Farrell et al., 2008). Adolescents regularly described their emotional responses (e.g., "If they just keep on coming and coming . . . I lose my temper," p. 402) and personal goals (e.g., "I want to be able to stay on a good record like I got. I don't want to stay in fights and stuff. Because that's the way that you won't get in college and you won't get a good job," p. 403). The themes that are found in a naturalistic investigation are not necessarily those that are expected by the researchers, which contributes to a sense of discovery in the research.

In some naturalistic studies, known as **ethnographies**, scholars look at the everyday rules of behavior, beliefs, social structures, and other cultural patterns of an entire group of people—perhaps a community, classroom, or family. Researchers who conduct ethnographies typically spend many months and occasionally even a year or more collecting detailed notes in an ordinary setting, getting to know the people who congregate there and the meaning of their ways (Mears, 2013; Warming, 2011; Wolcott, 1999).

In another type of naturalistic investigation, a researcher conducts a **case study**, wherein a single person's or a small group's experiences are documented in depth. (Research case studies are not to be confused with the case studies that begin the chapters in this book, which are more limited in scope.) Other naturalistic designs take the form of **grounded theory studies**, in which researchers typically collect in-depth data on a particular topic—often one related to young people's experiences with a particular phenomenon—and use those data to develop a theory about that situation (Corbin & Strauss, 2008). For example, a researcher might ask young children to describe and draw pictures of enjoyable playgrounds in an attempt to capture children's perspectives of play (Hyvönen & Kangas, 2007).

The results of naturalistic studies usually appear as verbal assertions, often with quotations from research participants, and are less reliant on statistical tests than are the three other designs we've examined.[3] As an example, two researchers conducted interviews with 17 adolescent boys living in either a residential treatment center or a halfway home and summarized the kinds of justifications the boys gave for their aggression (V. A. Lopez & Emmer, 2002). Using a grounded theory approach, the researchers asked the boys about their violent crimes and identified two motives. In "vigilante crimes," the boys used physical aggression to avenge another person's actual or perceived wrongful act. Sixteen-year-old Tax used a vigilante motivation in trying to protect his cousin:

> We had went over there to go use the phone and I went to go use the restroom. And when I came out, they had beat him [cousin] down, and hit him with a brick in his head, and cracked his skull open. So I got into a fight with one of them. I hit him with a lock and broke his jaw. He had to get three stitches in his head. (V. A. Lopez & Emmer, 2002, p. 35)

In "honor crimes," the boys used violence to protect themselves or their gang. Seventeen-year-old Muppet gave this explanation for his participation in a drive-by shooting:

> Around my birthday me and a bunch of my cousins [fellow gang members] found out about B [name of rival gang] named A who was talking shit and had jumped one of my cousins so we found out where he [rival gang member] lived and we went by and shot up his trailer house. We don't like Bs [members of rival gang] to begin with. (V. A. Lopez & Emmer, 2002, p. 37)

A key strength of naturalistic studies is their sensitivity to children's own views of everyday events and relationships. In the study we just examined, the young people interpreted their aggressive acts as reasonable ways to preserve their identities and solve conflicts. Such studies also make it possible to capture the complexities and subtle nuances of children's involvement in complex environments, making naturalistic studies informative windows into the bioecology of children's development. Naturalistic studies have several limitations, however. They are difficult and time-consuming to carry out, usually require extensive data collection, and produce results that fail to disentangle causes and effects in children's lives.

In the description of investigations in this section, we included several studies focusing on one topic, children's aggression. We learned that conscientiously planned interventions can diminish aggression in children, that watching violence on television is associated with children's own fighting, that punitive child rearing by parents is connected with aggressiveness later in life, and that violent youth see their aggressive acts as justified. Each of the designs we've examined affords valuable insights, and together they give us a more complete picture into the dimensions of children's lives.

Becoming a Thoughtful Consumer of Research

As you examine research studies, you will want to get in the habit of critically reading methods, results, and conclusions. If you ask a few simple questions of the investigations, you can begin to distinguish studies that are worthy of your consideration from those that are not.

BIOECOLOGY OF DEVELOPMENT
Investigators who ask children about their experiences in families, peer groups, schools, and communities contribute to an understanding of the bioecology of child development.

---

[3] Naturalistic studies are sometimes called *qualitative studies* because their analyses draw heavily on verbal interpretations. Of course, many qualitative studies do report numerical results, including the number of children who articulate a particular theme.

FOR FURTHER EXPLORATION . . .

Read about the properties of three interventions in character education.

ENHANCEDetext
content extension

BIOECOLOGY OF DEVELOPMENT

Some educational programs work effectively in particular settings but not others because of children's needs are intertwined with their cultural values, quality of relationships, resources, and risk factors.

As an illustration, imagine that a group of elementary teachers wants to improve children's ability to get along with peers and teachers at school. In their initial conversations, the teachers decide that what they most want to do is increase the frequency of kind, respectful, and cooperative behaviors toward one another and school staff. A committee is appointed to study the matter in greater depth, and in particular to look at the impact of existing programs. The committee addresses the following questions:

What Is the Purpose of the Research?

The committee wants to find research into effective educational programs that foster respectful and cooperative behaviors. With the help of a librarian, the committee identifies promising electronic databases and keywords (e.g., *character education, moral education, prosocial behavior*) to include in its search. It soon finds articles examining three widely used programs: the Ethics Curriculum for Children (Leming, 2000), Positive Action program (Flay & Allred, 2003), and Caring School Community (Solomon, Watson, Delucchi, Schaps, & Battistich, 1988), as well as an Internet site that compares the effectiveness of these and other similar programs (Institute of Education Sciences, 2006). The committee focuses on three articles, which you can read more about in a *For Further Exploration* reading.

Who Participated in the Investigations?

The committee notes that all three investigations had fairly large samples. The projects drew from different parts of the country and recruited children from families with varying income levels and ethnic backgrounds. However, none of the samples is as diverse as the population at the committee's own school, which includes many children from immigrant families, several ethnic backgrounds, and varying income levels.

What Are the Designs of the Studies?

Each of the studies used a quasi-experimental design. Because participants were not randomly assigned to treatment and control groups, the committee cannot know for sure whether any group differences in outcomes were due to program content, preexisting differences between groups, or some other factor.

What Information Is Presented About the Integrity of the Data?

The strength of the data varied across the three studies. The evaluation of the Ethics Curriculum for Children depended on participating teachers' ratings of students' behaviors; in making their ratings, the teachers may have been affected by *observer bias*—that is, they may have seen what they *expected* to see in students. The evaluation of Positive Action involved school records related to disciplinary referrals, suspensions, and absentee rates. Absenteeism can be recorded accurately, but administrators' disciplinary actions could have been influenced by personal biases toward or against particular students. The investigators examining the Caring School Community program appeared to have been especially thoughtful about the quality of their data in that observers did not know which children were members of the program.

Are the Studies Published in Reputable Journals?

Most journals use the process of sending manuscripts out to specialists in the field to comment on strengths, limitations, and suitability for publication. The committee determines that each of the three articles was published in a reputable journal that accepts only articles that have been favorably reviewed by experts in the field.

Do the Analyses Suggest Significant Results in Areas of Concern?

Results were not consistently favorable in the Ethics Curriculum for Children study. Results were generally promising for the Positive Action and Caring School Community programs. Furthermore, the committee finds additional support for the Positive Action and Caring School Community programs in other resources it examines (Battistich, 2003; Institute of Education Sciences, 2006). After considerable discussion, the committee decides that the outcomes for the Positive Action program are only tangentially related to the goals of fostering cooperative and helping behaviors. The committee concludes that the Caring School Community yielded results that most closely align with its own goals for children.

After completing its analysis, the committee recommends the Caring School Community to the school faculty because of its favorable outcomes in fostering children's cooperative behaviors, the high validity and reliability of the data, and the extensive data available on effects. Committee members realize that they should cautiously examine how the program works for children at their school given that sample in the research is different from their own population of children.

As you read research articles and reports, you can ask yourself questions similar to the ones the committee addressed. You will find that it takes practice to identify the strengths and limitations of data-collection techniques and the designs of investigations. With experience, you will be able to gain expertise in distinguishing dependable information about child development from untrustworthy sources.

Summary

Developmental researchers use various methods for collecting data, including interviews and questionnaires, tests and other assessment tasks, physiological measures, and observations. Regardless of the particular method, credible data must be shown to be accurate measures of the characteristics or behaviors being studied (a matter of *validity*) and minimally influenced by temporary, irrelevant factors (an element of *reliability*). Investigators also need research designs that match their questions. Designs are available that allow conclusions about cause-and-effect relationships, find associations among two or more variables, trace age trends over time, and observe children in natural environments. To make the most of developmental investigations, you must judge whether their conclusions are warranted and applicable to your own work with young people.

ENHANCEDetext *self-check*

CLASSROOM ASSESSMENTS

As you have seen, academic researchers work diligently to collect information about children in ways that are ethical, sensitive, valid, and reliable. Teachers and other school professionals do the same, although their objectives and strategies are somewhat different.

Purposes of Classroom Assessments

Assessments are a familiar feature in every modern classroom. Teachers and other practitioners have many purposes in mind as they collect information from children.

Learning About Children's Abilities

Teachers regularly conduct their own assessments to determine what children know and can do. One productive avenue is in implementing **formal assessments**, tasks that adults have created ahead of time to evaluate students' learning—for instance, through an essay about causes of the U.S. civil war or a fill-in-the-blanks test of the defining features of a peninsula, isthmus, island, and continent. Teachers also learn a lot about children from **informal assessments**, spontaneous observations of what children do, say, and create. For example, a teacher might observe children's social-emotional abilities during recess, watching for which children do and do not find a play partner (C. Gibson, Jones, & Patrick, 2010; Squires, 2012).

Guiding Instruction

Teachers design their lessons with the expectations that children are able to follow instructions, have the necessary prerequisites to carry out assignments, and are sufficiently motivated and attentive that they are able to absorb new information and apply it appropriately. Yet these assumptions do not always hold true. In fact, some children benefit from lessons and others do not, and over time, individuals vary in their academic accomplishments in particular subjects. **Formative assessments** are implemented before or during instruction in order to determine what children know and can do. Teachers might ask children to write

Observing Children 2-5

Observe a fifth-grade teacher implement a worksheet at the end of a lesson.

ENHANCEDetext *video example*

Observing Children 2-6

Observe a therapist administer a test of verbal ability to determine the accommodations that will help a girl reach her potential at school.

ENHANCEDetext *video example*

a few sentences about a topic they will be studying or summarize what they have learned partway through a lesson or unit. If students have obvious misconceptions, teachers can challenge them as well as validate and extend children's productive understandings and skills. **Summative assessments** are implemented after a lesson or unit of instruction and determine what children have learned. A variety of summative assessments are commonly used, including tests, essays, oral reports, music recitals, and athletic performances. As you can see in an Observing Children video, teachers can use this information to reflect on how children have responded to instruction and what their needs might be in future lessons.

Encouraging Children's Learning

Classroom assessments can motivate children to try harder and employ their learning strategies. Students generally study harder if they know they will be tested on assigned material than if simply asked to read it (Dempster, 1991; Roediger, Putnam, & Smith, 2011). Students also typically achieve at higher levels than they would otherwise when they have been advised of the objectives of a lesson and receive specific feedback that addresses their progress (I. Clark, 2012; Roediger et al., 2011; Wiggins, 2012). Telling 16-year-old Henley that he has done a "good job" in writing a story is far less effective than explicitly describing his progress in meeting a standard: "The words you use in the first half of your story give me a picture of the setting, characters, and plot. The second half of your story is less clear. Can you revise that part so your readers better understand what is going on and how the story ends up?"

Identifying Strengths and Limitations in Children's Abilities

Periodically, teachers encounter children who are significantly delayed in **developmental milestones**, those basic abilities that are age-related and usually appear in a predictable sequence. Most children walk by 18 months, after first crawling and then teetering around the edges of furniture. Academic milestones in counting, recognizing letters, and reading, and social-emotional landmarks in imitating another's motions, making eye contact, and taking turns in a game, are also important advancements. Wide variation in age is normal for most milestones, yet when a child is exceedingly slow, it is possible that he or she will benefit from special services. Medical personnel regularly screen infants for potential problems in vision and hearing, assessments that are warranted because of the critical role that sensory learning plays in early learning. In the toddler and preschool years, other specialists identify children with delays in physical, cognitive, and social-emotional abilities (Bagnato, McLean, Macy, & Neisworth, 2011; Cangialose & Allen, 2014). In the elementary and secondary years, students undergo formal testing by professionals when they are not learning effectively without individualized instruction. In an Observing Children video, you can watch a girl taking a verbal ability test that will help her teachers determine instructional strategies for maximizing her classroom learning.

Evaluating Learning and Instruction

In addition to guiding instruction, assessments are frequently used in evaluating how well children have learned. One type of summative evaluation, the **standardized achievement test**, a formal assessment of knowledge and skills in academic areas, is periodically implemented in schools, usually at the end of the year. Results are used to determine how well children have achieved academic **standards**, the knowledge and skills in particular subjects that are established as targets by public officials for children of a particular grade level.

Some schools use the results of students' scores on standardized achievement tests as an indicator of whether students should be promoted to a higher grade or receive a high school diploma. Ensuring that students are making good progress is an important function of annual achievement tests. Every student deserves a high-quality education with effective instruction in academic skills, and standardized test scores are one indication of which students need either additional challenges or interventions to accelerate learning.

Yet these tests have definite disadvantages in evaluating learning. The particular tests administered do not always align with the curriculum implemented at school. Thus students who have been challenged in the expressive arts will not be able to show these proficiencies on a test devoted solely to reading, mathematics, science, and social studies. Another problem is that some students have not received the help they have needed to rebound from a history of poor performance. One high school student in Texas described his concerns with the Texas Assessment of Knowledge and Skills (TAKS):

> In general, like, school is easy, but the TAKS test . . . make you feel like if you don't pass it you're like, "Why am I going to school?" . . . I have friends who doesn't pass the TAKS and they don't even want to come because they're not going to graduate, 'cause the tests. So they feel like, "oh, I spent my whole, my three, my four years here for nothing. . . ." They want to drop out. (Heilig, 2011, p. 2658)

Obviously, students who believe that they have no real option besides dropping out of school need guidance as to how they can succeed academically.

Many teachers appreciate the value of standardized tests in revealing how well children have mastered important educational standards. Yet they worry about such unintended consequences as students disengaging from school after recurrent low performances. Also, a number of teachers, who invariably want their students to be successful and feel that they themselves are being judged by students' performance, overemphasize material that is tested and lose sight of other important parts of the curriculum. In fact, a few teachers have felt such extreme pressure to raise children's test scores that they have administered achievement tests dishonestly—for example, giving students hints or more time than should be allowed, tampering with test results, or inappropriately excluding low-performing students from the testing session (American Teacher, 2012; Hardy, 2013). Other teachers implement tests scrupulously yet find it unfair that students' performance weighs so heavily in their own evaluations, especially when they work in seriously distressed communities, where children have not previously achieved foundational skills. Several teachers, weary of the pandemonium surrounding standardized tests, have left education altogether.

As we have discussed, assessments can be implemented and interpreted properly or improperly. We now look more carefully at formal and informal assessments and offer recommendations for both.

Formal Classroom Assessments

Teachers have many options to choose from when evaluating students' learning. Let's look at common formal assessments that teachers use.

Paper-and-Pencil Assessments

Teachers frequently use **paper-and-pencil assessments**, in which students answer questions or solve problems on worksheets and other documents. Examples of formats for paper-and-pencil assessments include true/false items, multiple-choice items, matching items, short-answer items, interpretations of material (e.g., a table or graph), and essay tasks.

Performance Assessments

Performance assessments are arranged when teachers want to ask students to demonstrate skills, as in giving an oral presentation, programming a computer, performing a piece of music, and conducting a science experiment.

Authentic Assessments

In an **authentic assessment**, students apply their knowledge and skills in a real-life context, perhaps writing a persuasive letter to the principal about the appropriateness of requiring school uniforms, baking a cake, or changing the oil in a car.

Criterion-Referenced Tests

Criterion-referenced tests reveal what students know and can do related to a specific standard or criterion. A third-grade student accurately spells 18 out of 20 words, only forgetting the apostrophe in "can't" and the second "i" in "fishing." Criterion-referenced tests

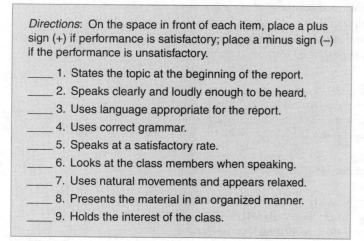

Directions: On the space in front of each item, place a plus sign (+) if performance is satisfactory; place a minus sign (−) if the performance is unsatisfactory.

_____ 1. States the topic at the beginning of the report.

_____ 2. Speaks clearly and loudly enough to be heard.

_____ 3. Uses language appropriate for the report.

_____ 4. Uses correct grammar.

_____ 5. Speaks at a satisfactory rate.

_____ 6. Looks at the class members when speaking.

_____ 7. Uses natural movements and appears relaxed.

_____ 8. Presents the material in an organized manner.

_____ 9. Holds the interest of the class.

FIGURE 2-2 Checklist for evaluating an oral presentation. *From Gronlund's Writing Instructional Objectives for Teaching and Assessment (8th ed., pp. 86–87), by Norman E. Gronlund and Susan M. Brookhart, 2009, Upper Saddle River, NJ: Pearson Education. Copyright 2009 by Pearson Education. Reprinted with permission.*

Preparing for Your Licensure Examination
Your teaching test might ask you about how rubrics help students learn how to complete important tasks.

Observing Children 2-7
Observe a first-grade teacher guide children's nonfiction writing with a rubric.

ENHANCEDetext *video example*

give teachers and students an indication of how well students have mastered a particular standard—correct spelling of a word list, accurate awareness of the sounds of particular consonants, and the ability to graph simple equations. Criterion-referenced tests are developed regularly by teachers to determine how well children have mastered specific academic standards. Theoretically, all children can perform well on a criterion-referenced test if they understand and apply the relevant skills.

Norm-Referenced Tests

Norm-referenced tests show how well an individual student performs in one or more subjects in comparison to a norm group—a large and carefully defined collection of age-mates. If you have ever taken a standardized test and received the feedback that you did better on the test than a certain percentage of other students in the country, you took a norm-referenced test. Norm-referenced tests are typically designed by commercial test developers and include a large assortment of individual items that vary in difficulty level, such that students spread themselves out in their total scores. Thus, unlike criterion-referenced scores, norm-referenced tests almost always show dispersion in achievement.

Recommendations for Formal Classroom Assessments

To gain accurate information about children's abilities from formal classroom assessments, try these strategies:

• **Consider what you know about children's ages when designing assessments.** Ideal formats for assessments are to some degree age-dependent. Young children can sometimes draw pictures of their understandings of complex matters, say, the life cycle of a frog, that are exceedingly difficult for them to articulate orally or in writing (N. Chang, 2012). Older children, in comparison, may be able to express their understandings through a variety of formats. Similarly, older children are capable of concentrating for longer periods of time and complete lengthier and more complex assessments than can younger children.

• **When evaluating children's responses to assessments, use explicit scoring criteria.** You are most likely to be accurate in the judgments you make about children's performance when you use carefully designed evaluation criteria. Teachers sometimes use *checklists* when they wish to evaluate the degree to which children's behaviors or work products reflect specific criteria. Figure 2-2 shows a checklist that a debate teacher might use to evaluate a student's oral presentation.

Designing a **rubric**, a list of the ideal features of a completed task, is another tactic that increases the fairness of grading. If you have shared the criteria with children ahead of time (and we encourage you to do so), children will be able to guide their learning toward clear standards and will better understand your feedback after you have evaluated their performance (E. J. Lee & Lee, 2009; Stiggins, 2007). In Figure 2-3, you can see a rubric for a third-grade writing assignment. And in an Observing Children video, you can see a first-grade teacher introduce a rubric for writing a nonfiction report with her students.

• **Use assessment strategies that guide students' learning.** Children are more likely to learn from assessment results when they receive feedback that articulates their specific successes and limitations (e.g., "You gave an excellent summary of the chapter in your biology book. You hit all the major points and did a nice job of saying them in your own words. Remember that the assignment also required you to think of some practical implications of what you learned about energy. If you're having trouble with thinking of examples, I can help you.").

Student _____ Name of Story _____

Element	Needs to Work on Element (0 points)	Meets Expectations (1 points)	Exceeds Expectations (2 points)
Organization	The paper does not make sense.	Most of the sentences stick to a single topic and are placed in a reasonable order.	All of the sentences are about the same topic and unfold in a logical order.
Content	The paper includes few details that help the reader visualize the story.	A few of the paragraphs include details about the story.	Every paragraph includes details that communicate rich information about the story.
Language Usage	It is difficult to read the paper because of numerous errors in punctuation. Numerous words are misspelled.	Most but not all beginning capitals and ending punctuation is correct. Only a few words are misspelled.	Beginning capitals and ending punctuation are all correct. No words are misspelled.
Story Elements	Setting, characters, story problem, and resolution are not clearly described.	Some story elements are clearly described and others are not.	Setting, characters, story problem, and resolution are all clearly described.
Legibility	It is difficult to decipher the words in the story due to sloppy handwriting.	Most but not all of the story is neatly written.	The entire story is legible and carefully written.
Style	The story does not include varied language or any interesting phrases.	The story includes a few instances of a unique and interesting style.	The story uses good attention-grabbing mechanisms, creative dialogue, and varied language.

FIGURE 2-3 Third-grade rubric for story assignment.

• **Keep in mind both the advantages and limitations of paper-and-pencil tests.** Paper-and-pencil tests are often an efficient way of determining what children have and have not learned. However, appraisals of children that rely exclusively on test scores can paint a lopsided picture of their abilities. In particular, children who have limited reading and writing skills (perhaps because they have a learning disability or have only recently begun to learn English) are likely to perform poorly on a test in spite of their relevant knowledge. Furthermore, paper-and-pencil tests, by their very nature, can tell us little if anything about children's self-confidence, motor skills, ability to work well with others, or expertise at using equipment.

• **Use multiple sources of information.** Because no single source of data ever has absolute validity, teachers and other school personnel often patch together several different sources of information when drawing conclusions about children's needs. A high school teacher who obtains low scores in one of her science sections may realize there are other explanations besides students not studying. Did the students not have the prerequisite understandings, were they inattentive the day of testing, or did they struggle for other reasons? To gather additional information, the teacher could talk informally with the students, perhaps individually, or ask them to write about their confusions about the subject.

• **Watch for bias in assessments.** Children often interpret test questions differently than do adult examiners. As an example, one team of researchers analyzed the science scores of a culturally and linguistically diverse group of elementary children (Luykx et al., 2007). Many of the children misinterpreted questions because of their cultural and language backgrounds. Several of the Spanish-speaking children confused the abbreviations of *F* and *C* (intended to stand for Fahrenheit and Celsius) with the Spanish words *frío* and *caliente*, and a few Haitian children misconstrued an item that asked how long they would be able to play between 4 P.M. and a 6 P.M. dinner, probably because they typically would have had their

Preparing for Your Licensure Examination
Your teaching test might ask you if it is advisable to make a decision about a child based on a single test score.

B. Declaration of independence
1. written in 1776 By thomas Jefferson and presented to the Second continental congress for Approval
2. Declaration gives reasons why the U.S. wished to rebel against the British
3. the declaration presents some Basic Ideals the US Adopted
A. Popular Sovereignity - Belief that people choose their own government.
B. Natural rights - All People have a certain right that no one could take Away (life, Liberty Happiness)
C. Social Contract - In order to Be Safe people needed to form govts But the People Should Be able to choose the government
4. the declaration officially Created the United States.

ARTIFACT 2-1   Connor's history notes. A teacher examining 14-year-old Connor's history notes might conclude that Connor has been exposed to key doctrines in U.S. history. To determine what Connor truly understands about these concepts, the teacher would need to ask Connor to explain these ideas in his own words.

Observing Children 2-8

Observe a sixth-grade teacher prepare her students for their statewide achievement test in mathematics.

ENHANCEDetext *video example*

own main meal (which they called "dinner") earlier in the day. This assessment seems to have been unfairly biased against children who did not speak English or had different everyday experiences than did the test developers.

In general, an assessment is tainted with **cultural bias** when it offends or unfairly penalizes some individuals because of their ethnicity, gender, socioeconomic status, or cultural background. When examining children's responses yourself, you can consider how children's apparent errors may arise because of a language difference or distinct cultural perspective. If you suspect a cultural bias, you will need to obtain additional information from children before drawing any firm conclusions about their abilities.

• **Remember that validity and reliability apply to all assessments.** Never over-interpret any single product a child has created. For example, imagine that a 6-year-old draws a self-portrait with a frowning face, as one of Teresa's sons once did. The boy's teacher concluded that he was unhappy and had low self-esteem, but nothing could have been further from the truth: The child was (and continues to be) a happy, self-confident individual. Perhaps on that single occasion he was simply having a bad day or was annoyed with the teacher who asked him to draw the picture.

• **Ask children to help you interpret their work.** Children regularly take notes, write essays, and create projects that reflect their underlying understandings. Yet it is not always clear what children mean from what they write. A teacher can ask children about their intentions with significant projects. A case in point can be seen in Artifact 2-1, in which 14-year-old Connor has taken notes about U.S. history. Rather than assuming Connor understands the abstract concepts, his teacher might ask him to explain his understanding of "popular sovereignty" and "social contract."

• **Assess environments to determine the extent to which they support children's well-being.** In our opening case study, Jack Reston learned that his school was not initially meeting the needs of all students as well as he hoped. With the data he collected, he was better able to motivate students. Other educators may focus on whether their school is actively engaging children, perhaps looking for indicators that school policies "reinforce citizenship and civic behaviors by students, family members, and staff and include meaningful participation in decision making" (Association for Supervision and Curriculum Development, 2013). Specific features of the school environment, such as the safety of playgrounds, can also be assessed (Botsoglou, Hrisikou, & Kakana, 2011).

• **Teach children how to take standardized tests.** Part of what tests measure, beyond the obvious academic concepts, is what children know about taking tests. Yet not every child has this knowledge. To prepare students for a standardized test, you can provide practice in taking tests with a similar layout, which might include multiple-choice items and other structured-response formats. You can also coach them in using their time efficiently, bubbling in answer sheets properly, and avoiding stray pencil marks on answer sheets. Many students are unaccustomed to reasoning through questions for which they have only partial information and can be taught how to eliminate alternatives. In an Observing Children video, you can watch a sixth-grade teacher prepare her students to answer extended-response items in mathematics, in which they must solve a mathematical problem, apply a specific concept, and show and explain steps in their work.

• **Interpret the results of standardized tests cautiously.** An important implication of single assessments not having perfect validity and reliability is that major decisions about children, such as whether they are promoted to the next grade or allowed to graduate from high school, should *never* be made on the basis of a single test score (American Educational Research Association, 2000; Elliott, Kurz, & Neergaard, 2012). Standardized tests have other limitations that we've discussed, including being incomplete reflections of the skills students have learned in the curriculum.

• **When evaluating instruction, focus on students' performance over time and supplement with other measures**. School officials increasingly use students' test scores as a reflection of teaching effectiveness. Yet a one-time shot of standardized test scores is an imperfect indication of how well teachers have taught. As we have already said, any given test has advantages and disadvantages in revealing students' abilities. In addition, students' learning during a unit depends in large part on their prior achievement levels. Based on end-of-the-year test scores, a teacher who began the year with high-achieving students might appear to be more effective than a teacher working with low-achieving students, even though both teachers could have held high standards, instructed expertly, been enthusiastic, and fostered considerable progress. Many officials are moving to growth models that show trends in students' scores over a several-year period. Growth models are not fully satisfactory, either, for a number of reasons (especially with reliability), and in any case, good teaching includes but is not limited to effective instruction of academic skills (Di Carlo, 2012). For these reasons, many schools address teacher evaluation in a multifaceted way, including observations of classroom lessons made by the principal, observations by other teachers, self-assessments by teachers, and data on the teacher's improvement over time (Johnson & Fiarman, 2012; Mielke & Frontier, 2012).

• **Stay focused on children's needs.** In all the commotion over testing, teachers may find it easier to remain level headed if they concentrate on *children's needs* rather than succumbing to the pressures around them. One research team identified three priorities of teachers that helped them contend with testing pressures: (1) teaching with students' "hearts and heads" in mind, such that teachers continually communicate faith in students' abilities, individualize instruction as necessary, and acknowledge any concerns about how well students are performing; (2) teaching in a culturally sensitive fashion, such that teachers and students regularly share how and what they have learned at home and in their community, and how academic skills are useful in those contexts; and (3) establishing a productive learning environment, with students learning concepts and practicing skills in realistic tasks rather than acquiring them for the primary purpose of passing tests (Elish-Piper, Matthews, & Risko, 2013, p. 12).

Recommendations for Informal Classroom Assessments

From a developmental perspective, all aspects of a child's development are important. Although fostering children's academic skills has been presumed to be the primary responsibility of teachers, teachers who are developmentally sensitive strive to monitor additional aspect of development, including children's language abilities, reasoning skills, physical well-being, and social-emotional welfare. Informal assessments provide worthwhile clues as to children's overall adjustment and their progress in specific domains. In this section, we suggest actions teachers can take to obtain valuable information from informal assessments of what children say and do.

Listening to What Children Say

From a young age, children are motivated to tell adults what makes them feel relaxed, interested, or happy on the one hand, and angry, bored, or sad, on the other. It is up to adults to set aside the time, put youngsters at ease, and let them speak their minds. Here's how you can gain access to children's perspectives:

• **Let children know you care.** The surest way into a child's heart is to express affection sincerely and dependably. When you have earned a child's trust, the child is more likely to articulate what's on his or her mind.

• **Develop your interviewing skills.** Too often, conversations between adults and children are short, ask-a-question-and-get-an-answer exchanges. Yet lengthier dialogues, perhaps with an individual child or a small group of children, can be far more informative. Getting children to talk takes experience, but there are a few specific things you can do (D. Fisher & Frey, 2007; Graue & Walsh, 1998; C. Green, 2012; Koekoek, Knoppers, & Stegeman, 2009). First of all, you can try a combination of open-ended questions ("How was your day?") and close-ended questions ("Did you watch TV when you went home from school?"). Also, include some general requests for information that are not in question form ("Tell me more about that.") Try not to ask a long series of questions, or your probing may seem like an inquisition. Make sure you pause after asking a question to give children plenty of time to formulate their thoughts, and communicate that you really care about what they have to say. Sometimes it is appropriate to ask children how *other children* view a situation; this tactic can be an effective way to help them feel safe in speaking their minds. For example, rather than asking children how they feel about achievement tests, ask them how *other children* feel ("How did kids at your school feel last week when they took the state achievement test?"). For some children, being allowed to carry on with an activity, for example, building blocks, playing with puppets, or eating a snack, puts them at ease while talking with adults (C. Green, 2012).

• **Listen intently to children's perspectives.** Unless adults truly listen to young people, they cannot fully understand young people's experiences. Sometimes children see the world in the same way as adults, but perhaps more often children have different viewpoints that we don't learn about until we ask the right questions and listen with an open mind. In a study with sixth graders in the Philadelphia public schools (B. L. Wilson & Corbett, 2001), young adolescents appeared to share many priorities and goals with sympathetic adults. The students stated that they wanted teachers to push them to complete assignments (even when they resisted), to maintain order (even when they misbehaved), and to teach them difficult material (even when they struggled). Despite their apparent desire to succeed, these youngsters were unaware of what it took to do well when subjects became challenging, and they were naive about skills needed for success in college. From these results, we realize that teachers need to be persistent in explaining concepts, teaching study skills, and preparing adolescents for the reality of college.

• **Develop classroom routines that foster self-expression.** Teachers can establish classroom procedures that encourage children to share their interpretations (D. Fisher & Frey, 2007). Bringing in provocative materials, such as works of art from other cultures, inspires children's storytelling, conversation, and analysis (Mulcahey, 2009). Some teachers use the Think–Pair–Share discussion strategy, in which they stop midway through a lesson, ask children to think about a particular question or issue, pair up children to discuss their responses, and finally ask them to share their ideas with the rest of the class (Alanís, 2013; Lyman, 1981). Other teachers use the Whip Around technique, a structured activity at the end of a lesson. They pose a question, ask children to write their responses on a piece of paper, and then "whip around" the group asking everyone for brief responses (D. Fisher & Frey, 2007). From such replies teachers gain a sense of what children have learned and are in the process of learning. These techniques foster self-expression in children, provided that teachers communicate that everyone is encouraged to participate and no one will be ridiculed for what he or she says.

Preparing for Your Licensure Examination
Your teaching test might include items about promoting children's participation in discussions.

Observing Children

If you carefully watch children interacting in classrooms, after-school programs, and other settings, you can learn a lot about their interests, values, and abilities. Here are some suggestions to enhance your observation skills:

• **Observe how children respond in different settings.** On a daily basis, teachers and other practitioners see children moving in and out of the classroom, cafeteria, and playground. When you are able to make observations across separate settings, you gain deeper insights into the needs of children. For example, a child who appears happy and carefree on the playground but fearful and tense in the classroom may need tutoring or other assistance in order to become academically successful.

- **Observe children's nonverbal behaviors.** Careful observation of children's postures, actions, and emotional expressions can yield valuable clues about their preferences and abilities. An infant caregiver may learn that one 18-month-old toddler slows down, pulls at his ear, and seeks comfort when he's sleepy, whereas another child speeds up, squirms, and becomes irritable when ready for a nap. During an interview with a teenage boy, a school counselor might notice that he seems withdrawn and discouraged. In response, the counselor inquires sympathetically about how things are going for him at home and school.

- **Consider children's developmental states.** When you sense an unmet need in a child, you can analyze the child's circumstances with your knowledge of child development. The Observation Guidelines table, "Learning from Informal Assessments of What Children Say and Do" on page 58 suggests some general things to look for as you interact with young people.

- **Form multiple hypotheses.** When observing children, never be content with a single interpretation, no matter how obvious that explanation might seem. Always consider multiple reasons for the behaviors you observe, and resist the temptation to settle on one of them as "correct" until you've had a chance to eliminate other possibilities. With their daily contact with children, teachers actually have an advantage over professional researchers in their awareness of long-term patterns in children's behavior.

- **Distinguish observations from inferences.** To observe accurately, you need to differentiate what you see from what you think it means. It is not possible to be entirely objective, but you can make some headway in reflecting on your reactions to events. One strategy that may help is to keep separate records of what you see and how you make sense of the experience. Here are some notes from a student teacher, Ana, who recorded her observations in a "Notetaking" column and her interpretations in a "Notemaking" one:

Notetaking	Notemaking
A child is working at the computer. There are fourteen students working at their desks. Six students are working with another teacher (aide) in the back of the room. It is an English reading/writing group she is working with—speaking only in English. I see a mother working with one child only and she is helping the student with something in English. There is a baby in a carriage nearby the mother. I hear classical music playing very lightly. I can only hear the music every once in a while when the classroom is really quiet. I stand up and move around the room to see what the children at their desks are working on. They are writing scary stories. The baby makes a funny noise with her lips and everyone in the class laughs and stares for a few seconds, even the teacher. . . .	The class seems to be really self-directed. . . . I am not used to seeing students split up into different groups for Spanish and English readers because in my class they are Spanish readers, but it is really good for me to see this because it happens in a lot of upper grade settings, and I will be working in an upper grade bilingual setting next placement. I really like the idea of putting on music during work times. I know that when I hear classical music it really helps me to relax and calm down, as well as focus. I think that it has the same effect on the students in this class. I'm noticing more and more that I really cherish the laughter in a classroom when it comes from a sincere topic or source. It is also nice to see the students *and* the *teacher* laughing. . . . (C. Frank, 1999, pp. 11–12)[4]

Trying to notice order in children's activities without jumping to conclusions can help you become a perceptive observer. By distinguishing what you see from what it might mean, you can also learn about your own priorities as a teacher, as Ana might have done when rereading her "Notemaking" comments.

- **Try out different kinds of observations.** The types of observations you conduct will depend on what you hope to gain from watching children. *Running records* are narrative summaries of a child's activities during a single period of time (Nicolson & Shipstead, 2002).[5] Running records provide teachers and other professionals with opportunities to focus on a particular child.

Preparing for Your Licensure Examination
Your teaching test might ask you what you can infer from children's hand gestures, eye gaze, facial expressions, and tone of speech.

---

[4]From *Ethnographic Eyes: A Teacher's Guide to Classroom Observation* (pp. 11–12), by Carolyn Frank, 1999, Portsmouth, NH: Heinemann. Copyright 1999 by Carolyn Frank. Reprinted with permission.

[5]The term "running records" is also used by literacy specialists to refer to a structured technique for detecting accuracy and errors in a child's oral reading of a written passage.

OBSERVATION GUIDELINES
Learning from Informal Assessments of What Children Say and Do

CHARACTERISTIC	LOOK FOR	EXAMPLE	IMPLICATION
What Children Say	• *Verbal expressions* of likes and dislikes • *Thoughtful questions* about topic (probably indicates high engagement and motivation) • *Previously answered questions* (might stem from inattentiveness or lack of understanding) • *Complaints* about difficulty with an assignment (might indicate low motivation, lack of confidence, or overloaded schedule)	In a whining tone, Danielle asks, "Do we really have to include *three* arguments in our persuasive essays? I can only come up with one!"	Read between the lines in the questions children ask and the comments they make. Consider what their statements might reveal about their knowledge, skills, motivation, and self-confidence.
What Children Do	• *Exploration of the environment* through manipulation of objects, focused attention, and attempts to make sense of events by talking about them (may indicate inquisitiveness about certain kinds of situations) • *Preferred activities during free time* (may show children's foremost desires and interests) • *Interest in people*, including initiating interactions and responding to others' social gestures (may indicate comfort in social situations) • *Quiet self-absorption* (may demonstrate either thoughtful self-reflection or sadness) • *Facial expressions* (reflecting enjoyment, excitement, boredom, sadness, confusion, anger, or frustration) • *Tenseness of limbs* (might signify either intense concentration or excessive anxiety) • *Slouching in seat* (might indicate fatigue or resistance to an activity)	Whenever his teacher engages the class in a discussion of controversial issues, James eagerly participates. When she goes over the previous night's homework, however, he crosses his arms, droops low in his seat, pulls his hat low over his eyes, and says nothing.	Provide a safe environment with interesting and attractive objects for active exploration. Periodically make changes to the environment that offer intriguing new options for study. Get to know individual children's preferences for activities during free time. Use children's body language as a rough gauge of interest, and modify activities that do not appear to be eliciting children's attention. Speak confidentially with children who frequently appear sad or angry.

In Figure 2-4 you can see an excerpt from a running record of a child with a hearing impairment prepared by a language specialist. After carefully scrutinizing the running record, the language specialist concluded that Taki understood some aspects of spoken language as she followed directions. However, Taki needed help when completing the Listening Lotto game. These kinds of interpretations can suggest next steps. Possibly, the language specialist realized from the observation that she needed to look further into Taki's hearing ability.

Anecdotal records are descriptions of brief incidents observed by teachers and other professionals (McClain, Schmertzing, & Schmertzing, 2012; Nicolson & Shipstead, 2002; Paley, 2007). An anecdotal record is typically made when an adult notices a child take an action or make a statement that is developmentally significant. Anecdotal records are made of specific accomplishments, physical milestones, patterns in social interaction, ways of thinking, and concerns. Anecdotal records tend to be much briefer than running records and may be written up later in the day. Teachers often gather up these notes about children and share them with family members during conferences. Seven-year-old Matthew's teacher made this anecdotal record of his insights:

> While discussing *In a Dark, Dark Room and Other Scary Stories* by Alvin Schwartz, Matthew thoughtfully shared, "Do you know what kind of scary things I like best? Things that are halfway between real and imaginary." I started to ask, "I wonder what. . ." Matthew quickly replied, "Examples would be aliens, shadows, and dreams coming true."[6] (Nicolson & Shipstead, 2002, p. 139)

One means of recording observations is not necessarily better than another. Instead, each observational system has a distinct purpose. As you gain experience in observing youngsters,

---

[6] *From* Through the Looking Glass: Observations in the Early Childhood Classroom *(3rd ed., p. 139), by S. Nicolson and S. G. Shipstead, 2002, Upper Saddle River, New Jersey: Merrill/Prentice Hall. Copyright 2002 by Pearson Education. Reprinted with permission.*

Center/Age Level:Center for Speech and Language/3- to 6-Year-Olds

Date:	7/17	Time:	10:20–10:26 AM
Observer:	Naoki	Child/Age:	Taki/5;1
		Teacher:	Camille

	Comments
	10:20
Taki is seated on the floor with Kyle (4;8) and Camille, the teacher, in a corner of the classroom; both children have their backs to the center of the room. Taki sits with her right leg tucked under her bottom and her left leg bent with her foot flat on the floor. The Listening Lotto card is in front of her on the floor, and she holds a bunch of red plastic markers in her right hand. Camille begins the tape.	No intro of game. Hearing aid working.
The first sound is of a baby crying. Taki looks up at Camille, who says, "What's that?" Taki looks at Kyle, who has already placed his marker on the crying baby. Camille says, "That's a baby crying," and points to the picture on Taki's card. Taki places the marker with her left hand as the next sound, beating drums, begins.	
Taki looks at Kyle as the drumming continues. Camille points to the picture of the drums on Taki's card, and Taki places her marker.	Understands process.
The next sound is of a toilet flushing. Taki looks at Kyle and points to the drums. Kyle says, "Good, Taki. We heard drums banging." Taki smiles. Camille says, "Do you hear the toilet flushing?" as she points to the correct picture. Taki places her marker and repositions herself to sit cross-legged. She continues to hold the markers in her right hand and place them with her left. . . .	10:22 Kyle supportive of Taki.

Conclusions: Taki's receptive language was on display when she followed the teacher's directions in Listening Lotto (put markers on the appropriate spots), but she did not demonstrate success on her own. Her fine motor control was in evidence as she adeptly handled small markers.

FIGURE 2-4 **Running record for Taki during Listening Lotto.** Specialists in child development often list a child's age in years and additional months, separating the two numbers by a semicolon. Taki's age of 5 years and 1 month is indicated as "5;1." *From* Through the Looking Glass: Observations in the Early Childhood Classroom *(3rd ed., pp. 118–119), by S. Nicolson and S. G. Shipstead, 2002, Upper Saddle River, New Jersey: Merrill/Prentice Hall. Copyright 2002 by Pearson Education. Reprinted with permission.*

you are likely to see how your own understanding of individual children grows when you use several observational methods and supplement them by listening to what children say.

Conducting Action Research

Teachers sometimes conduct systematic studies of children's experiences in school and then revise their instruction based on what they learn. In our introductory case study, Jack Reston conducted research in order to evaluate and improve absenteeism policies at his school. Such practically focused investigations, known as **action research** studies, take numerous forms. Examples include assessing the effectiveness of a new teaching technique, gathering information about adolescents' opinions on a schoolwide issue, conducting an in-depth case study of a particular child, and gaining insight into one's own teaching (Cochran-Smith & Lytle, 1993; Harnett, 2012; Hopkins, Stringfield, Harris, Stoll, & Mackay, 2014; G. E. Mills, 2007; Ponder, Vander Veldt, & Lewis-Ferrell, 2011).

Action research employs the following steps:

1. *Identify an area of focus.* The teacher-researcher begins with a practical problem at school and gathers preliminary information that might shed light on the situation. Usually this involves perusing the research literature for investigations into similar problems and perhaps surfing the Internet and talking with colleagues. He or she develops a research plan that addresses a research question and specifies data-collection techniques, the research design, and so forth. At this point, the teacher seeks guidance from supervisors and experts in research ethics.

2. *Collect data.* The teacher-researcher collects data relevant to the research question, perhaps in the form of questionnaires, interviews, observations, achievement tests, journals, portfolios, or existing records (e.g., school attendance patterns, rates of referral for discipline problems, hours spent on school projects). Many times the teacher-researcher uses two or more sources to address the question from various angles.

3. *Analyze and interpret the data.* The teacher-researcher looks for patterns in the data. Sometimes the analysis involves computing simple statistics (e.g., percentages, averages, correlation coefficients). At other times it involves a non-numerical inspection of the data. In either case, the teacher-researcher relates observed patterns to the original question.

4. *Develop an action plan.* The final step distinguishes teachers' research from more traditional research: The teacher-researcher uses the information collected to formulate a new practical strategy—for instance, a change in instructional techniques, advising practices, home visiting schedules, or school policies. In many cases, the teacher will then study the outcome of the revision.

A good example of action research is a case study conducted by Michele Sims (1993). Initially concerned with why intelligent middle school students struggle to comprehend classroom material, Sims began to focus on one of her students, a quiet boy named Ricardo. She talked with Ricardo, had conversations with other teachers and university faculty, wrote her ideas in her journal, and made notes of Ricardo's work. The more she learned, the better she understood who Ricardo was as an individual and how she could foster his development. She also became increasingly aware of how often she and her fellow teachers overlooked the needs of quiet students:

> We made assumptions that the quiet students weren't in as much need. My colleague phrased it well when she said, "In our minds we'd say to ourselves—'that child will be all right until we get back to him.'" But we both wanted desperately for these children to do more than just survive. (Sims, 1993, p. 288)

Action research serves many positive functions. It can solve problems, broaden perspectives on adults' relationships with children, clarify children's understandings of and attitudes toward learning particular academic topics, foster a community spirit among adults, and make schools more humane (Buck, Cook, Quigley, Prince, & Lucas, 2014; Chant, 2009; Harnett, 2012; Noffke, 1997). The Development and Practice feature "Getting a Flavor for Conducting Research as a Teacher" suggests some initial steps you can take. Action research can be especially informative about the characteristics of children from unfamiliar cultures, which you can learn about in the Development in Culture feature "Using Action Research to Learn About the Culture of Children and Families."

Ethical Guidelines for Teacher-Researchers

Regardless of your specific techniques in collecting data from children, you must protect their welfare. Consider the following guidelines:

• **Keep your supervisor informed of your research initiatives.** Principals and other supervisors can advise teachers and counselors on how to protect the rights of children and families. Supervisors can inform you of regulations in your district or community and procedures for getting your research plan approved. School leaders can also give you a fresh set of eyes in interpreting results and generating implications for any needed changes in practice.

• **Be tentative in your conclusions.** Careless observations of children can do more harm than good. For instance, a teacher might wrongly infer that children have poor comprehension skills because they scored at low levels on a reading test, even though they had in fact been distracted by a fire alarm during the test's administration. Acting on a false perception, the teacher might attempt to remediate children's alleged weaknesses. Therefore, you should try not to put too much weight on any single piece of information. Instead, you can look for consistent trends across a range of data sources—possibly written essays, test scores, projects, and informal observations of behavior. Finally, when sharing your perceptions of children's abilities with parents, acknowledge that these are your *interpretations*, based on the data you have available, rather than irrefutable facts.

• **Administer and interpret tests or research instruments only if you have adequate training.** Many instruments, especially psychological assessments, physiological measures, and standardized achievement tests, must be administered and interpreted only by individuals trained in their use. In untrained hands tests can yield erroneous conclusions that might

DEVELOPMENT IN CULTURE
Using Action Research to Learn About the Culture of Children and Families

Misunderstandings occasionally arise in people from different cultures, including teachers and children from dissimilar backgrounds. For example, some teachers wonder why children from immigrant families do not learn English quickly, actively participate in lessons, or achieve at advanced levels, whereas children may be puzzled as to why their teachers are insensitive and strange (Rothstein-Fisch, Trumbull, & Garcia, 2009).

Such a clash of cultures is not inevitable. Teachers can gain an appreciation for children's traditions by observing children at school and encouraging them to talk and write about their cultural origins. However, everyday observation and social exchange are not always enough. When teachers' initial efforts prove insufficient, teachers can turn to action research as a way to delve into children's customs and frames of mind.

Action research with three elements can be especially effective in fostering teachers' cultural sensitivity. First, teachers can acquire new understandings about children by remaining open to using entirely new ways of interpretation. Tiffany, an experienced elementary teacher, conducted research in her second-grade classroom of ethnically diverse children from low-income families, the majority of whom were Mexican American (Riemer & Blasi, 2008). Tiffany had previously mandated which classroom centers individual children could visit during the day but wondered how the children would respond if they were able to make some of their own decisions. The children surprised her with their maturity:

> I began to notice that they were taking control of their learning. They researched and learned what they wanted to learn about, they worked with other students that they or I would normally not group them with,

GAINING INSIGHT. Teachers and other practitioners can learn a great deal about children's cultural beliefs and traditions by reflecting on their own values, remaining open to new interpretations of children's abilities, and spending time with children in their community.

and they even created their own organizational tool to keep track of the centers they visited. They gave themselves choices between working on research projects, preparing presentations of the research collected, and/or visiting centers. . . . I gave them more independence and therefore, they did not need me as much. They also relied more on one another. . . . I have had increased awareness as to what my students are truly capable of, owning their education. (Riemer & Blasi, 2008, p. 58)

Second, teachers may increase their understanding of children when given time to reflect on their own values and biases. One kindergarten teacher joined a research team of university faculty and other teachers who were hoping to learn more about the needs of students and their immigrant Latino families (Rothstein-Fisch et al., 2009). As a result of her introspection and discussions with colleagues, she realized that these parents had a valid perspective that was different from her own:

> It was a revelation that the parents weren't wrong, just different, because it never felt right to me to think they were wrong. But deep down I thought they were wrong and I knew that was racist and that was eluding me (Rothstein-Fisch et al., 2009, p. 477).

After conducting her research, the teacher and her colleagues began to open up to families in new ways, talking informally with parents as they dropped off and picked up their children, taking photographs of families at open houses, experimenting with formats for conferences, and building on families' desires for a relaxed atmosphere during school meetings.

Finally, teachers can learn a lot by spending time with children and their families (Lahman, 2008). Bernie, a sophomore preparing to teach, conducted an in-depth observational study of Amish children in Ohio (Glasgow, 1994). Early in her research Bernie was judgmental, confessing that she thought of the Amish as "a simple, unsophisticated people with very naive ideas about the ways of our world" (Glasgow, 1994, p. 43). She noticed a sense of peacefulness in their lives but also believed that "the Amish culture stifles personal growth, intellectual advancement, and creativity" (p. 43). As she spent more time in the Amish community, Bernie became increasingly attuned to cultural traditions and values, gaining permission from an Amish elder to visit a one-room schoolhouse and take careful field notes about what she saw. With increasing contact with people in the Amish culture, Bernie came to appreciate the integrity of their customs. At the end of her observations, she planned to explore new ways to reach Amish children in her future classroom.

By being open to new interpretations, reflecting on their own biases and values, and collecting data over an extended period of time, teachers and other practitioners can acquire a thoughtful understanding of children and families from different cultures. This heightened sensitivity can pay enormous dividends in relationships between teachers and children.

DEVELOPMENT AND PRACTICE
Getting a Flavor for Conducting Research as a Teacher

Keep a journal of your observations and reflections.

- A kindergarten teacher regularly makes notes of the centers that children visit when they have a free choice, using the information to make adjustments in unpopular areas. (Early Childhood)
- A high school English teacher keeps a daily log of students' comments about the novels they are reading. The teacher reassigns novels that provoke the most interest the following year and replaces books that do not engage students. (Late Adolescence)

Talk with your colleagues about what you are noticing.

- A middle school teacher observes that a new student who has been homeless comes to class late without a notebook or pen and appears distracted. The teacher wonders about the family's financial resources and speaks privately with the principal to see if the school can secure school supplies for the young man. (Early Adolescence)
- A school counselor notices that a group of low-achieving girls are excited about their work in a community service club. She asks colleagues for their ideas about how they might capitalize on the girls' involvement in blood drives, senior visits, and animal shelter work as a catalyst to success at school. (Late Adolescence)

Invite children and families to contribute to your inquiry.

- A teacher in an infant room hears parents complain that their employers do not grant them time off to care for sick children. She asks three parents who have been most vocal to help her look into family leave regulations. (Infancy)
- A high school principal notices that a high number of students have been referred to her this year for physical aggression. She asks a school improvement team of teachers, school counselors, parents, and students to examine possible reasons for the increase in violence and discuss possible solutions. (Late Adolescence)

Inquire into the circumstances of children who appear sad, inattentive, or disengaged at school.

- A preschool teacher is concerned about a 3-year-old girl who has recently appeared unhappy at school. During free play, the young girl quietly and repeatedly puts a doll in a box and places the box under a toy crib. The teacher talks with the girl's mother at the end of the day and learns that the mother, who had been a full 5 months along in her pregnancy, recently had a miscarriage. Her 3-year-old daughter knew about the pregnancy and was upset about the family's loss. The teacher expresses her sympathy to the mother and suggests that the little girl seems to be coping through play. (Early Childhood)
- A middle school teacher observes that a few students sit in the back of the room and appear to be mentally "tuned out." She talks privately with the students, learns about their backgrounds and interests, and tries out new strategies that might capture their attention. (Early Adolescence)

Enlist the assistance of children or families.

- An elementary teacher wonders what her children are thinking about during independent learning time. She asks the children to interview one another and take notes on each other's answers. In analyzing the children's responses, the teacher realizes that only some of the children are using the time effectively. (Middle Childhood)
- A career counselor would like to help high school students explore career interests and gain employment experience. She enlists the help of adolescents to survey local businesses about possible opportunities for after-school jobs and internships. (Late Adolescence)

harm or inconvenience children. For example, a teacher who interprets an achievement test wrongly might offer instruction that duplicates children's previous knowledge or alternatively surpasses their current abilities.

• **Be sensitive to children's perspectives.** Children are apt to notice any unusual attention you give them. When Michele Sims was collecting data about Ricardo, she made the following observation:

> I'm making a conscious effort to collect as much of Ricardo's work as possible. It's difficult. I think this shift in the kind of attention I'm paying to him has him somewhat rattled. I sense he has mixed feelings about this. He seems to enjoy the conversations we have, but when it comes to collecting his work, he may feel that he's being put under a microscope. Maybe he's become quite accustomed to a type of invisibility. (Sims, 1993, p. 285)

When data collection makes children feel so self-conscious that their performance is impaired, a teacher-researcher must seriously consider whether the value of the information collected outweighs possible detrimental effects. Otherwise, teachers' good intentions can actually put children at a disadvantage.

• **Maintain confidentiality.** When teachers have obtained the necessary permissions and clearances, they are permitted to share the general results of their research with colleagues. Some teachers also make their findings known to an audience beyond the walls of their institution; for instance, they may make presentations at conferences or write journal articles describing what they have learned. However, they must not broadcast research findings in ways that violate the confidentiality of children's responses. Children would naturally feel betrayed if teachers were to disclose the responses that they as individuals have made. Teachers must likewise protect their data sources from examination by onlookers: It would be unwise to leave a notebook containing records of individual children on a table where other children would have access to them.

Summary

Teachers and caregivers often gather data about children. Educators can learn a great deal from their conversations with youngsters, analyses of the assignments they complete, and everyday observations of their behavior. Systematic action research can also provide useful information, in which teachers address a specific question and strive to improve their ability to meet children's needs. As with other kinds of investigations, research carried out by teachers and other practitioners must be conducted with concern for ethics and the integrity of the data.

ENHANCEDetext *self-check*

Assessing Children 2-1

Practice assessing children's learning during a lesson.

ENHANCEDetext *application exercise*

I went
to davis's
house
Alex

Assessing Children 2-2

Practice making several different interpretations of a single assessment.

ENHANCEDetext *application exercise*

PRACTICING FOR YOUR LICENSURE EXAMINATION

Many teaching tests require students to apply what they have learned about child development to brief vignettes and multiple-choice questions. You can practice for your licensure examination by reading the following case study and answering a series of questions.

The Study Skills Class

Read the case and then answer the questions that follow it.

As a last-minute teaching assignment, Deborah South took on a study skills class of 20 low-achieving and seemingly unmotivated eighth graders. Later she described a problem she encountered and her attempt to understand it through action research (South, 2007):

My task was to somehow take these students and miraculously make them motivated, achieving students. I was trained in a study skills program before the term started and thought that I was prepared....

Within a week, I sensed we were in trouble. My 20 students often showed up with no supplies. Their behavior was atrocious. They called each other names, threw various items around the room, and walked around the classroom when they felt like it....

Given this situation, I decided to do some reading about how other teachers motivate unmotivated students and to formulate some ideas about the variables that contribute to a student's success in school. Variables I investigated included adult approval, peer influence, and success in such subjects as math, science, language arts, and social studies, as well as self-esteem and students' views of their academic abilities.

I collected the majority of the data through surveys, interviews, and report card/attendance records in an effort to answer the following questions:

- How does attendance affect student performance?
- How are students influenced by their friends in completing schoolwork?
- How do adults (parents, teachers) affect the success of students?
- What levels of self-esteem do these students have?

As a result of this investigation, I learned many things. For example, for this group of students attendance does not appear to be a factor—with the exception of one student, their school attendance was regular. Not surprisingly, peer groups did affect student performance. Seventy-three percent of my students reported that their friends never encouraged doing homework or putting any effort into homework.

Another surprising result was the lack of impact of a teacher's approval on student achievement. Ninety-four percent of my students indicated that they never or seldom do their homework to receive teacher approval. Alternatively, 57 percent indicated that they often or always do their homework so that their families will be proud of them.

One of the most interesting findings of this study was the realization that most of my students misbehave out of frustration at their own lack of abilities. They are not being obnoxious to gain attention, but to divert attention from the fact that they do not know how to complete the assigned work.

When I looked at report cards and compared grades over three quarters, I noticed a trend. Between the first and second quarter, student performance had increased. That is, most students were doing better than they had during the first quarter. Between the second and third quarters, however, grades dropped dramatically. I tried to determine why that drop would occur, and the only common experience shared by these 20 students was the fact that they had been moved into my class at the beginning of the third quarter.

When I presented my project to the action research class during our end-of-term "celebration," I was convinced that the "cause" of the students' unmotivated behavior was my teaching.... This conclusion, however, was not readily accepted by my critical friends and colleagues ...who urged me to consider other interpretations of the data. (pp. 1–2)[a]

Constructed-Response Question

1. Describe one potential strength and limitation for each method Deborah used.

Multiple-Choice Questions

2. What kind of research did Deborah conduct?

   a. Action research
   b. An experimental study
   c. A correlational study
   d. A cross-sectional study

3. Deborah tentatively concluded that her own teaching led to the dramatic drop in grades from the second quarter to the third. Is her conclusion justified?

   a. Yes, Deborah's conclusion is justified because she collected several different kinds of data.
   b. Yes, Deborah's conclusion is justified because she is in the best position to understand her students best.
   c. No, Deborah's conclusion is not fully justified because without an experimental design, a variety of reasons for the change in students' behavior are possible.
   d. No, Deborah's conclusion is not fully justified because teachers are never able to collect data of any merit.

ENHANCEDetext *licensure exam*

[a]From "What Motivates Unmotivated Students?" by D. South. In *Action -Research: A Guide for the Teacher Researcher* (3rd ed., pp. 1–2), by G. E. Mills, 2007, Upper Saddle River, NJ: Merrill/Prentice Hall. Reprinted with permission of the author.

Key Concepts

scientific method (p. 36)
sample (p. 37)
self-report (p. 38)
interview (p. 38)
questionnaire (p. 38)
social desirability (p. 39)
test (p. 39)
assessment (p. 39)
physiological measure (p. 40)
habituation (p. 40)

observation (p. 40)
validity (p. 42)
reliability (p. 42)
experimental study (p. 43)
control group (p. 43)
quasi-experimental study (p. 44)
correlation (p. 45)
correlational study (p. 45)
cross-sectional study (p. 46)
longitudinal study (p. 46)

ethnography (p. 46)
case study (p. 47)
grounded theory study (p. 47)
informal assessment (p. 49)
formal assessment (p. 49)
formative assessment (p. 49)
summative assessment (p. 50)
developmental milestone (p. 50)
standardized achievement
    test (p. 50)

standards (p. 50)
paper-and-pencil assessment (p. 51)
performance assessment (p. 51)
authentic assessment (p. 51)
criterion-referenced test (p. 51)
norm-referenced test (p. 52)
rubric (p. 52)
cultural bias (p. 54)
action research (p. 59)

CHAPTER THREE

Family, Culture, and Community

CASE STUDY: Cedric and Barbara Jennings

Cedric Lavar Jennings and his mother Barbara are a close-knit family of two. One night during Cedric's senior year, he and his mother go to his high school to pick up his first-semester grade report. Knowing that he is one of the top students—perhaps *the* top student—in his physics class, Cedric is shocked to discover a B for his semester's work. He's furious, because, as he tells his mother, other students cheated on class examinations, all the while he took tests honestly. At first Barbara isn't overly concerned, but as Ron Suskind reports in *A Hope in the Unseen* (1998), when Cedric asks what *they* will do, she soon realizes that he needs her to act as the vigilant protector she has always been.

The two of them go in search of Cedric's physics teacher, Mr. Momen. After finding him, Cedric complains that Mr. Momen allows rampant cheating when leaving the room unattended. Although Mr. Momen doubts Cedric and defends himself, Barbara stands firm, insisting that her son would not lie about something so important. Mr. Momen eventually agrees to give Cedric a retest over the semester's material.

Afterward, Barbara advises her son that he *must* get an A. Cedric studies hard for the test, earns a perfect score, and ultimately receives an A for the semester. He brings home the test for her to examine, and as she looks at it, it dawns on her that their relationship is changing, that she will no longer be able to stand at his side after he heads off to college. Cedric is relieved to realize that he is now ready to advocate for himself. He points to the test score and suggests that the paper certifies Barbara's accomplishments—as mother.

- Why was Cedric able to assume his mother would help him at school?
- What qualities might Cedric have learned from his mother?

As a child, Cedric had found his mother to be a loving caregiver. Having grown accustomed to her faithful care, Cedric could now safely assume that she would back him up when he needed her. Like Cedric, most children depend on their families for love and reassurance, food and shelter, oversight and guidance. In this chapter, you will learn that the family's care has profound effects on children. From Barbara, Cedric had learned to work hard, act with integrity, and confront injustice. Having benefited from his mother's support, and having learned to make good choices on his own, Cedric was ready to enter society as a productive young man.

CRADLES OF CHILD DEVELOPMENT

A happy and healthy childhood depends on a loving relationship with family, regular exposure to the traditions of a culture, and participation in a responsive community. The *bioecological model* and other related frameworks reveal how children draw from relationships and resources in the three inter-related settings.

Family

A **family** consists of two or more people who live together and are related by such enduring factors as birth, marriage, adoption, or long-term mutual commitment. Families with children usually have one or two adults (most often the parents) who serve as heads of family. Heads of family exercise authority over children, take responsibility for their welfare, and interact affectionately with them over a period of years if not decades.

According to the bioecological model, every child needs at least one adult devoted to his or her health, education, and welfare (Bronfenbrenner, 2001). Typically, heads of family have the necessary dedication to meet the child's many needs. Caring for offspring ideally

OBJECTIVES

3.1: Identify the primary contributions of family, culture, and community for a child's development.

3.2: Describe variations that exist in family membership and their implications for teachers' work with children and families.

3.3: Define key elements of family interaction, influential conditions in the family, and qualities of effective educational partnerships with families.

3.4: Portray unique assets and challenges of children from a range of backgrounds.

BIOECOLOGY OF DEVELOPMENT

In the bioecological model, families are at the heart of children's development.

begins before birth, when prospective parents take protective measures to increase their chances of having a healthy conception and pregnancy. After birth, sensitive care makes it possible for infants to form close bonds with parents, explore the world, and develop harmonious relationships with people outside the family (Ainsworth, 1963, 1973; Bloch, 2014; Booth-LaForce & Kerns, 2009; Bowlby, 1969/1982; Kok et al., 2013).

Families continue to feed, clothe, and attend to children's basic needs. But just as important, family members are key figures in the **socialization** of children. That is, by encouraging certain behaviors and beliefs (and *dis*couraging others), parents and other heads of family help children learn to act and think in ways society deems appropriate. Heads of family teach and model proper ways of behaving in various situations; reward certain behaviors and punish others; arrange for children to participate in worthwhile pastimes and avoid unproductive ones; and advise them how to communicate and cope with emotional feelings (Gauvain & Parke, 2010; Kehoe, Havighurst, & Harley, 2014; Trommsdorff & Heikamp, 2013).

Culture

A culture is the defined values, traditions, and symbol systems of a long-standing social group. In the bioecological model, culture gives meaning to the activities, accomplishments, and policies of the society in which the child lives. In this manner, culture helps children experience events as predictable and worthwhile. Culture also adds an intellectual dimension by exposing children to mental tools (e.g., alphabets, musical notation, calculators), instruction in school, advanced discoveries, and creative works of their society.

Children become familiar with important routines as they participate with families in work and play, maintance of the household, and conversation. Children are also inducted into traditional rituals, such as those for worshipping and celebrating holidays. The effects of culture are especially evident when comparing practices of people from distinct groups and separate regions. Cultural groups exhibit variations in mealtime habits (what and with whom they eat), division of responsibility (who goes out to work and who looks after the children), and social practices (how children play and how marital partners relate to one another). Separate groups also encourage children's education in distinct ways. For instance, one parent volunteers at school by reading to children, helping out at a school carnival, and doing odd jobs for teachers, whereas another parent helps children with school assignments at home and shows respect to teachers by *not* interfering with their work (García Coll & Marks, 2009).

Cultural beliefs, although not as obvious as behaviors, are an equally important part of a group's heritage. Core beliefs vary among societies. For example, **individualistic cultures** encourage independence, self-assertion, competition, and expression of personal needs (Greenfield & Quiroz, 2013; Markus & Hamedani, 2007). Many families from the United States and Western Europe raise their children in an individualistic manner. Core ideas in **collectivistic cultures** are that people should be obedient to and dependent on authority figures, honorable and cooperative, and invested in accomplishments of the group rather than in personal achievements. Many families in Asia, Africa, and South America raise their children in a collectivistic manner.

The two bookends of culture—behaviors and beliefs—are closely related. Common practices are grounded in beliefs about what is true, healthy, appropriate, and rational (Kitayama, Duffy, & Uchida, 2007). Adults within a culture, therefore, justify their typical ways of raising children by asserting familiar values. As an example, consider how families defend their sleeping practices. Many European American parents have children sleep alone in their own rooms and explain that this practice ensures nighttime privacy for adults and fosters independence in children. Other parents, particularly those in certain Asian and Caribbean cultures, sleep beside children and say that co-sleeping arrangements foster intimacy and solidarity in family members (S. Li et al., 2009; Luijk et al., 2013; Shweder et al., 1998).

Of course, *differences* between cultures in beliefs and behaviors are only half of the story. Many cultural groups share such fundamental principles as commitments to achieving academically and treating others respectfully. Hence, within a single classroom, children from separate cultures may be more similar than different in values and behaviors. Thus children from different backgrounds may accept the value of working independently during a designated reading time as well as working collaboratively on a poster in another lesson (Greenfield & Quiroz, 2013).

In addition, dissimilarities *between* groups are often eclipsed by prominent individual differences *within* groups. Within a classroom each child may adhere to individualistic principles in distinct ways, with one student excelling academically, another achieving advanced levels in computer games, and a third raising an unprecedented amount of money for a local charity (Gauvain, 2009; Goodnow, 2010). Finally, a group's strong commitment to a particular worldview does not prevent its members from endorsing other beliefs. Plenty of Western parents encourage children to assert their personal rights (an individualistic orientation) but also live by a code of honor (a collectivistic orientation). Likewise, numerous non-Western parents augment a primarily collectivistic orientation with individualistic ideals, socializing children to be mindful of the family's needs while asserting their private wishes.

Although we have implied that children grow up in a single albeit complex culture, increasingly children become familiar with several cultures due to such factors as the family's immigration, multiple heritages being represented within the family, and frequent exchanges occurring between the family and members of a different society. When children become acquainted with more than one culture, they often acquire some beliefs and practices from each. In such a circumstance, a family may socialize children to develop an allegiance to one or more aspects of their ancestries, for instance, by encouraging an immigrant child born in Riyadh, Saudi Arabia, and currently residing in Toronto, Canada, to identify as a Saudi Arabian, a Saudi immigrant, a Canadian, a Muslim, or a Canadian Muslim—or some combination, depending on circumstances. As they grow, children develop their own preferences for customs and determine how they fit within their various groups (Acevedo-Polakovich et al., 2014; García Coll & Marks, 2009; Gonzales-Backen, 2013; Suárez-Orozco, Suárez-Orozco, & Todorova, 2008).

Community

A child's **community** includes the local neighborhood and surrounding areas, which together create a bridge from the family to the outside world. Particularly when children are young, they make friends in their neighborhood, at the local school, on a hometown sports team, or as part of a nearby club or center. As they grow older, youngsters continue to spend spare time in activities that are reasonably close by as they: venture farther from home. You can see how important recreational opportunities are by listening to 14-year-old Brendan in an Observing Children video. Here's how Brendan describes his neighborhood:

Observing Children 3-1
Listen to Brendan talk about recreational opportunities.
ENHANCEDetext *video example*

> There's a lot of people. Nice people. And there's fun stuff to do around here. . . . We play football or sports in the backyards, and we have playgrounds and a basketball court.

Local neighborhoods vary in their characteristics, of course. Some neighborhoods are able to provide nicely furnished schools and safe spaces for children's play. Yet in a number of economically disadvantaged neighborhoods, youngsters attend run-down schools and interact with peers who participate in criminal acts (Duncan, 2013; Leventhal, Dupéré, & Brooks-Gunn, 2009). When neighbors partake in illegal activities, prey on youth, and turn the other way when youngsters get into trouble, young people are at increased risk for exhibiting such negative behaviors as bullying peers, destroying others' property, cheating and telling lies, and being disobedient at school (Eamon & Mulder, 2005). Fortunately, support from teachers, parents, and other family members, when available, reduces harm from a dangerous neighborhood (Gauvain & Parke, 2010).

The bioecological model presumes that the community, through its provisions of resources to parents, also influences children. Parents obtain salaries, employment benefits, and services from community agencies, which collectively enhance their ability to meet children's needs. Unfortunately, inadequate resources can lead to problems for children, as when parents are forced to work excessively long hours and not given sufficient sick leave (Repetti & Wang, 2010). The social environment also affects parents' ability to care for children. Parents generally have their own friends who step in to supervise children's activities, offer advice on parenting strategies, and provide emotional support (Algood, Harris, & Hong, 2013; Bronfenbrenner, 2005).

BIOECOLOGY OF DEVELOPMENT

In the bioecological model, communities influence children by supplying friends and neighbors with whom they interact and resources for parents that affect the family's standard of living.

Addressing Contexts in Children's Lives

Children enter school having already taken part in formative experiences in their family, culture, and community. In the best of circumstances, these contexts are fountains of nurture: The family has cared for children, the culture has given meaning to children's lives, and the community has supplied valuable social contacts and decent living conditions. With optimal support, children enjoy good health, exercise their natural talents, and evolve into responsible citizens, as Cedric was in the process of doing in our chapter-opening case study. The Basic Developmental Issues table "Considering Family, Culture, and Community" describes the many favorable ways in which nature and nurture, universality and diversity, and qualitative and quantitative change are manifested in family, culture, and community.

Amidst these benefits are assorted challenges. A few minor problems instigate growth, but many serious trials overwhelm children. Skilled teachers consider both the strengths and difficulties that children encounter. Following are five basic ways to address children's involvement in families, cultures, and communities:

• **Use a variety of strategies to learn about children's backgrounds.** At the beginning of the school year, teachers can telephone parents to get acquainted. During initial contacts, they can ask about the family (e.g., who is in the family, what languages are spoken at home) and child (e.g., what his or her interests are, what he or she likes to do in spare time). Later in the year, children might be asked to send in a photograph of themselves with their families, write about the family's heritage, or invite their parents and extended family to share their traditions at school. As the year progresses, educators can validate children's backgrounds, for example, by marking each country on a world map with pins for family origins.

• **Consider children's individual risks and protective factors.** In a theoretical extension to the bioecological model, American psychologist **Margaret Beale Spencer** and her

BASIC DEVELOPMENTAL ISSUES
Considering Family, Culture, and Community

ISSUE	FAMILY	CULTURE	COMMUNITY
Nature and Nurture	At a child's conception, parents pass on genes for basic human traits (e.g., for language) and individual characteristics (such as dispositions to be healthy or frail) (nature). Families care for children, serve as role models, form affectionate relationships, and encourage participation in shared routines (nurture).	The general capacity for culture has evolved over millions of years and is inscribed in the human genetic code. In the daily lives of children and families, cultural traditions nurture children by giving meaning, purpose, and predictability to interpersonal relationships, activities, and tool use.	Human beings are a social species with a natural inclination to congregate in groups. When a community contains friendly neighbors, decent housing, accessible playmates, safe playgrounds, and reasonably stable and well-paying jobs, it exerts beneficial influences on development.
Universality and Diversity	Children universally need one or more adults to advocate for their welfare, and heads of family usually serve in this manner. Families differ considerably in membership and styles of expressing affection and authority.	Children need (and almost always have) opportunities to participate in cultural activities. Diversity occurs in beliefs (such as to whether young children are capable of reasoning) and practices (such as how men and women contribute to the household).	Communities universally create a link to the outside world for children. Communities vary in population density, industries, parks, libraries, access to fresh food, medical centers, and other types of support for children and families.
Qualitative and Quantitative Change	Some changes in family roles occur in a trend-like fashion, as when children slowly master the steps in preparing a meal (e.g., washing the vegetables, buttering the bread, and grilling the meat). Other changes facilitate entirely new ways of thinking and behaving, as when an 8-year-old boy is asked to look after his 4-year-old sister for the first time.	Some cultures institute abrupt qualitative changes; for instance, certain rituals signify passage from childhood to adulthood and are accompanied by major changes in young people's roles. Other cultures view development as a series of small, gradual steps; for instance, children are gradually given more independence in fulfilling chores without adult supervision.	Children's experiences in communities show a few qualitative changes. Getting a driver's license or part-time job allows for entirely new choices in transportations, pastimes, and purchases. Many changes are incremental, as when children gradually learn about a city's neighborhoods through walks and bus rides.

colleagues have examined *risks* in children's environments, conditions that increase vulnerability to problematic outcomes (e.g., dropping out of school, being incarcerated, becoming an adolescent parent) and *protective factors*, conditions that help children deal with hardship, mitigate their harm, and catalyze positive growth (Cicchetti, Spencer, & Swanson, 2013; D. Patton, 2013; M. B. Spencer, 2006; M. B. Spencer & Spencer, 2014; M. B. Spencer et al., 2012; Swanson, Cunningham, Youngblood, & Spencer, 2009). Risk factors include economic poverty, unstable family conditions, restrictive gender stereotypes, racial discrimination, and underfunded schools. Protective factors include being intelligent and physically attractive, having involved immediate and extended families, and living in a close community.

Teachers should look at *every* child as having a unique profile of assets that impel growth and risks that deter progress. For example, a teacher may approach a girl who is generally self-reflective but occasionally rude to peers with suggestions for expressing anger productively. Having gotten to know the girl personally, the teacher realizes that the girl is well able to address her own social limitations if given a modicum of guidance.

• **Help children adjust to transitions between settings.** Usually children can move easily from one setting to the next, but occasionally children become distressed when separated from loved ones or when dealing with animosities between key people in their lives. Thus an adolescent girl whose parents dislike her friends may feel torn by conflicting loyalties (A. C. Fletcher, Hunter, & Eanes, 2006). Teachers can empathize with children who articulate such concerns and also watch for nonverbal signs of distress, such as being withdrawn or acting out, which may indicate difficulty in adapting to incompatible pressures. Teachers can also help children who have just joined their classroom ease into the new setting by explaining expectations and introducing them to classmates (Ackesjö, 2013; García Coll & Marks, 2009).

• **Appeal to children's initiative.** Staying optimistic about improving the world is a valuable resource that can be cultivated at school. An elementary teacher might ask children who complain about a dirty playground to take part in a clean-up effort (Howard, 2007). A high school teacher might respond to an adolescent's concerns about inequities in society by advising her about local coalitions dedicated to protecting human rights.

• **Provide extra support when children face serious risks.** Sadly, some children are exposed to grave threats, for example, a non-nutritious diet, lack of medical care, *and* neglect at home. Children are hardy, yet when serious threats are present, the collection of stresses can easily exceed children's ability to cope, with the result of emerging problems in health, social relationships, concentration, and self-control (G. W. Evans, Li, & Sepanski Whipple, 2013; J. Patterson & Vakili, 2014). In these situations, support from teachers needs to be supplemented with resources from other professionals, for example, food supplements from community services and counseling by mental health experts.

Summary

Family, culture, and community together create foundations for child development. These contexts teach children who they are as human beings, how they should relate to others, and what they can aspire to become as adults. Educators can help children by learning about their backgrounds, building on their strengths, and reducing the harmful effects of risks.

ENHANCEDetext *self-check*

FAMILY MEMBERSHIP

A child's **family structure** refers to the makeup of the family—those individuals who live in the family home, including the one or more adults who care for the child and any siblings. Consider these statistics compiled on family structures of American children:

- 65 percent live with two married parents.
- 4 percent live with two unmarried parents.
- 24 percent live with their mother only.

ARTIFACT 3-1 My family. Children from countless types of families enjoy affection from their loved ones. In this drawing, 5-year-old Alex, who was adopted, includes (clockwise, from top) his older brother, father, himself, and mother holding hands in a circle. Also represented are the family goldfish, house, and driveway.

- 3 percent live with their father only.
- 4 percent live without a parent in their household and instead reside in some other living arrangement, such as with grandparents, other relatives, or foster parents (Federal Interagency Forum on Child and Family Statistics, 2013a).

Keep in mind that many family conditions defy such cut-and-dried categories. At any given time, a child may be in the process of adjusting to one or more family changes, perhaps the addition of a new stepparent, the marriage of previously unmarried parents, or the coming or going of a parent's unmarried (*cohabiting*) partner. A child may live with one parent yet stay in contact with the second parent, in accordance with custody agreements or informal arrangements.

Regardless of their family type, children eagerly soak up affection from responsive adults and siblings. Five-year-old Alex, who was adopted, portrays a sense of unity in his drawing of the family home in Artifact 3-1. Yet as they gain strength from their families, children also encounter difficulties. Although you would never want to pigeon-hole a child based on his or her family type, you can learn to be sensitive to the advantages and challenges that children are apt to have in particular family structures.

Mothers and Fathers

When a mother and father are present in the home, children tend to form close bonds with both parents (Kochanska & Kim, 2013; M. E. Lamb, Chuang, & Cabrera, 2005). Having two adults in the home magnifies the affection children receive and allows one parent to compensate when the other one is unable (Meteyer & Perry-Jenkins, 2009). In large part due to the emotional and financial resources generally present in two-parent families, children living with a mother and father tend to achieve at higher levels in school and show fewer behavior problems than is the case with children in other kinds of families (Magnuson & Berger, 2009).

Being in a two-parent family also exposes children to two approaches to parenting. Mothers generally tend to children's physical needs (e.g., feeding, bathing, scheduling doctors' appointments), watch over the children, and display affection (Belsky, Gilstrap, & Rovine, 1984; L. Craig & Powell, 2013; Phares, Fields, & Kamboukos, 2009). As children grow, relationships with mothers tend to be more intimate than those with fathers, and mothers are more likely to encourage children to open up about personal matters (Harach & Kuczynski, 2005; Smetana, Metzger, Gettman, & Campione-Barr, 2006).

Fathers, in contrast, are more physically playful and instrumental in guiding children to get along with people outside the family (M. E. Lamb et al., 2005; Parke & Buriel, 2006; Phares et al., 2009). Nevertheless, fathers are not simply playmates; most spend substantial amounts of time caring for their children and are quite competent in feeding, bathing, and in other ways nurturing children (M. E. Lamb, Frodi, Hwang, Frodi, & Steinberg, 1982; Mackey, 2001; McFadden & Tamis-LeMonda, 2013). In many societies fathers become more involved as children grow older, especially in disciplining, encouraging self-reliance, and modeling subtle masculine qualities, such as being a dependable source of financial support for the family (Munroe & Munroe, 1992; Pruett & Pruett, 2009).

In addition to providing two caregivers, two-parent families show children how to carry out adult relationships. A man and woman have much to work out on a daily basis as an intimate couple and as **coparents**, partners in raising their children (Feinberg, Kan, & Goslin, 2009; Palkovitz, Fagan, & Hull, 2013). Many parents air their differences constructively and search for solutions that are mutually beneficial, giving children valuable lessons in cooperation and conflict resolution (Cummings & Merrilees, 2010; J. P. McHale & Rasmussen, 1998). Children benefit in another way from their parents healthy relationships. Emotionally close couples are inclined to shower affection on their children (Holland & McElwain, 2013; Ward & Spitze, 1998).

The lessons other children receive are different. Some children frequently overhear heated arguments. Loud and bitter exchanges can frighten children and be poor standards for conflict resolution. When parents' disputes are intense and protracted, young children tend to become upset and blame themselves, and older children feel insecure (Goeke-Morey, Papp, & Cummings, 2013). Arguments also put parents in a foul mood, which can quickly spill over into harsh interactions with children (S. G. O'Leary & Vidair, 2005; Yoo, Popp, & Robinson, 2013). As a result, intense marital conflict is associated with assorted problems in youngsters, including physical aggression, depression, anxiety, and difficulties in personal relationships (Bornovalov et al., 2014; Feinberg, Kan, & Hetherington, 2007; Finger, Hans, Bernstein, & Cox, 2009; Koss et al., 2013).

An increasing number of unmarried heterosexual couples have children together. Compared to married parents, *cohabiting parents* are (on average) younger, less educated, and less financially stable; less warm and attentive to their children; less satisfied with their relationships with their partners; and more apt to break up and enter new intimate relationships (Aronson & Huston, 2004; Klausi & Owen, 2009; Kotila & Kamp Dush, 2012). Children of cohabiting couples tend to achieve lower grades in school and exhibit more behavior problems, but these disadvantages disappear when cohabiting couples have good social support from extended family and access to adequate financial resources (Parent, Jones, Forehand, Cuellar, & Shoulberg, 2013; C. J. Patterson & Hastings, 2007).

Divorcing Parents

Once an infrequent occurrence, divorce is now commonplace. In the United States more than 4 to 5 in 10 marriages end in divorce, and approximately half of American children are affected by this change in family relationships (Lansford, 2009; M. M. Stevenson, Braver, Ellman, & Votruba, 2013).

For children, the divorce of parents is not a single event but a series of occurrences, each requiring adjustment. News of a divorce can be a blow for children, even though they may have previously witnessed parents' strained communication or animated disagreements. Immediately after being told about the separation, children may receive less attention than before due to parents' own distress (Kaslow, 2000). Custodial parents—one or both parents who look after the children in their homes—often struggle to complete all the tasks involved in maintaining an organized household, including shopping, cooking, cleaning, paying bills, and monitoring children's activities (Wallerstein & Kelly, 1980). Financial setbacks can complicate everyone's adjustment. Parents who previously owned a house may have to sell it, and so, on top of everything else, children must move to new (and inevitably smaller) quarters, with an accompanying loss of proximity to friends and familiar neighbors (Austin, 2012; J. B. Kelly, 2007; Schramm et al., 2013).

As the coparents establish separate households, children learn how their parents will get along (or not) and what role each parent will now play for them. One parent may withdraw from the children and eventually invest, both emotionally and financially, in a new life and perhaps a new family. Thus one unfortunate consequence of some divorces is that children lose contact from one of their parents, most often the father (J. B. Kelly, 2007; M. M. Stevenson et al., 2013). Fortunately, this trend is by no means universal. Many fathers actively seek joint custody arrangements after a divorce (R. A. Thompson, 1994b; M. M. Stevenson et al., 2013).

Many children struggle with all of these changes. Divorce is especially troubling for young children, who may erroneously believe that their own naughty behavior caused the family's breakup (Fausel, 1986; Lansford, 2009). Older children usually respond reasonably well, even though they may initially find their parents' divorce quite painful and subsequently perceive it as unnecessary (Hetherington, Bridges, & Insabella, 1998; Lansford, 2009). Given time and support, most youngsters ultimately learn to accept their parents' divorce and avoid significant psychological problems (Fergusson, McLeod, & Horwood, 2014; Lansford, 2009; M. M. Stevenson et al., 2013).

Children's adjustment to divorce is facilitated by several factors. Coparents and other adults assist children by maintaining affectionate relationships with them; enforcing rules consistently; listening to their concerns sympathetically; and encouraging their continued contact with friends, nonresident parents, and extended family members (Hetherington & Clingempeel, 1992; Kushner, 2009). Children who have good coping skills, for example, those who are inclined to talk with a friend when upset rather than let their anxiety escalate, are more likely to adjust favorably to the breakup (Lansford, 2009; Pedro-Carroll, 2005).

Children are also likely to adapt effectively when coparents establish reasonably productive relationships, agree on expectations and disciplinary measures, keep a lid on their own disputes, and seek counseling for their children (Hetherington, Cox, & Cox, 1978; Regev & Ehrenberg, 2012; M. M. Stevenson et al., 2013). When children are removed from dangerous situations, such as ongoing abuse, divorce can result in their entry into a healthier environment (Lansford, 2009; Sarrazin & Cyr, 2007).

Single Parents

Families headed by one parent are especially diverse in their characteristics. Most single parents are divorced or have never been married, but a few are widowed, separated, or have a spouse who is temporarily absent (U.S. Census Bureau, 2013a). The vast majority are women. Some single mothers, particularly older unmarried mothers who are highly educated, are well able to provide adequate food, shelter, and opportunities for their children, whereas other single mothers, especially those who are young and uneducated, are apt to have limited financial resources and undesirable housing arrangements (C. J. Patterson & Hastings, 2007; M. Wen, 2008).

Single parents carry out the tasks of parenting with the realization that much responsibility falls on their shoulders (Beckert, Strom, Strom, Darre, & Weed, 2008). This realization often leads them to make their children's needs top priority. Perhaps because of this clear focus, many single-parent families function extremely well, particularly if they have a reasonable standard of living and the support of a stable network of family and friends (Fennimore, 2013; C. J. Patterson & Hastings, 2007). In fact, the simple structure of single-parent families has advantages: Children may be shielded from intense conflict between parents, observe strong coping skills in their custodial parent, and enjoy the intimacy of a small family.

Single-parent families do experience unique challenges, though. Single parents, mothers and fathers alike, often express reservations about their ability to "do it all"—juggle children, home, and work responsibilities (Beckert et al., 2008; R. A. Thompson, 1994b). Unless they have the support of extended family members, neighbors, and friends, single parents may have difficulty in remaining affectionate and patient, especially when tired or sick, and offering children the rich range of roles, activities, and relationships known to maximize positive developmental outcomes (Garbarino & Abramowitz, 1992; Magnuson & Berger, 2009; Miljkovitch, Danet, & Bernier, 2012). Fortunately, single parents tend to be well aware of their personal limitations and inclined to reach out to others for assistance.

Parents and Stepparents

Many divorced parents eventually remarry. When they do, they and their children become members of a **stepfamily**, a single-parent family that is expanded to include a new adult and any children in his or her custody.[1] Approximately 6 percent of children in two-parent families live with a biological or adoptive parent and a stepparent (Federal Interagency Forum on Child and Family Statistics, 2013b).

As is true for all family structures, children in stepfamilies are exposed to benefits and challenges. A new adult may bring additional income to the family and help with household duties. Children forge relationships with a new parent figure and, sometimes, with new brothers and sisters as well. Yet children may feel that they must now share their parent's time and affection with the new spouse. They may believe, too, that the new stepparent is interfering with a possible reunion of the divorced parents and that by showing affection to the stepparent, they are betraying the nonresident parent (R. Berger, 2000; Bigner, 2006).

For a stepfamily to blend successfully, it must establish its own identity and traditions. Whereas a couple without children can initially focus on one another, the newly married parent and stepparent must attend to the needs of the children as well as to their own relationship. Having entered the marriage with habits of their own, the man and woman must decide how to spend money, divide household chores, prepare and serve meals, and celebrate holidays. Initially the stepparent is apt to defer to the biological parent when the child needs to be disciplined, but the couple must eventually agree on rules and discipline (Pettigrew, 2013).

---

[1]Stepfamilies are also known as *reconstituted, re-partnered, remarried,* and *blended families.*

Most children in stepfamilies ultimately adjust well to their new family situation (E. R. Anderson & Greene, 2013; R. Berger, 2000). In many (probably most) instances, stepparents soon become important parts of children's lives. As you can see in the poem by 9-and-a-half-year-old Shea shown in Artifact 3-2, Shea became deeply attached to her stepmother, Ann, who had been a family member for 3 years.

Extended Family

Many children have strong ties with relatives, particularly grandparents. In the United States, about 6 percent of all children live with at least one grandparent (U.S. Census Bureau, 2013b). Grandparents often become primary guardians when a child's parents are young and economically poor, neglectful, imprisoned, deployed in the military, and incapacitated by illness or substance abuse, and when a parent dies (Bertera & Crewe, 2013; Dolan, Casanueva, Smith, & Bradley, 2009; O. W. Edwards & Taub, 2009). Custodial grandparents sometimes worry that they do not have adequate energy and funds to raise a second generation of children, yet their mature outlook and parenting experience often lead them to be competent caregivers, especially when offered social support from teachers and other family members (C. B. Cox, 2000; Y. R. Green & Gray, 2013; Letiecq, Bailey, & Dahlen, 2008). For some children, other extended family members assume central roles. Aunts, uncles, and cousins regularly step forward to raise children when they are the only viable parent figure (Milardo, 2010; Sear & Mace, 2008).

Adoptive Parents

Two out of every 100 children in the United States are adopted (Federal Interagency Forum on Child and Family Statistics, 2013c). Adoption is almost always a positive arrangement for children, especially when the new parents have thoughtfully chosen to expand their family and embrace the adopted children's individual qualities. Adoption is also almost invariably a blessing for adoptive parents and siblings, as these individuals find themselves with a new child to love. As you can see in the journal entry from newly adoptive brother Connor shown in Artifact 3-3, siblings can quickly appreciate the qualities of new siblings.

The past few decades have seen several changes in adoption policies. One growing practice is *open adoption,* in which the birth mother (perhaps in consultation with the birth father) chooses the adoptive family with help from an agency. Adoptive families often gain access to medical records through open adoption, and adopted children may have a chance someday to meet their birth parents. In *international adoption,* families in one country adopt children orphaned or relinquished in another country. Since 1990, China and Russia have permitted the most adoptions by U.S. families (U.S. Department of State, 2013). In a third trend, many adoption agencies are increasingly flexible in evaluating potential adoptive parents; the result is a growing number who are single, older, gay, lesbian, from lower-income groups, and from a different racial background than the adopted child (Bigner, 2006; Logan, 2013).

Although adopted children are at slightly greater risk for emotional, behavioral, and academic problems compared to children reared by biological parents, most adopted children grow up to be well-adjusted individuals (Christoffersen, 2012; Freeark, 2006; Palacios & Sánchez-Sandoval, 2005). Adopted children seem to cope best when family members talk openly about the adoption yet provide the same love and nurturance that they would offer biological offspring (Bigner, 2006; Brodzinsky, 2006).

Occasionally children adopted at an older age have physical or mental disabilities or require special services due to preexisting conditions or poor care earlier in life (Julian, 2013; Follan & McNamara, 2014; Rutter, 2005; Rycus, Freundlich, Hughes, Keefer, & Oakes, 2006). In extreme cases children were abused or neglected or had several different placements before being adopted and later have trouble in forming secure relationships with new family

MOM is WOW

She is great at hide-and-seek
She takes me to look at an antique
I get to see her three times a week

MOM is WOW

She helped teach me multiplication
She encourages my imagination
She is involved when it comes to participation

MOM is WOW

She's a great stepmom, I guarantee
She lets us watch Disney TV
She is an important part of the family tree

MOM is WOW

No matter what, she is never late
If I have a question, she will demonstrate
When it comes to stepmoms, she's great

MOM is WOW

ARTIFACT 3-2 Mom is Wow. In her fourth-grade class, Shea wrote a Mother's Day poem for her stepmother, Ann, using the "Mom is Wow" structure the teacher provided. Notice that Shea perceives Ann as a kind and reliable caregiver who enriches her life, helps her learn productive skills, and shares enjoyable leisure time with her.

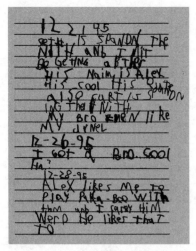

ARTIFACT 3-3 **I got a brother, cool, huh?** In his journal, 7-year-old Connor communicates his excitement about becoming a big brother. Eight-month-old Alex is placed in Connor's family on December 20, originally in a foster arrangement, and by December 28, Connor is aware of some of Alex's likes, such as playing peekaboo and being carried by him.

members. Elementary school students who have spent their infancy and early childhood neglected in stark orphanages sometimes exhibit problems paying attention in class, relating to peers, and forming secure attachments to adults. Teachers can use resources at their bestowal to assess and address these needs, including collaborating with school counselors and psychologists (F. S. Baker, 2013).

Adolescent Parents

Adolescent mothers are at risk for being under intense stress and lacking awareness of children's emotional, cognitive, and social needs (Borkowski et al., 2002; Lee Smith, Gilmer, Salge, Dickerson, & Wilson, 2013). Teenage mothers who are anxious and unrealistic about child development are apt to be inattentive, inconsistent, and critical with their children. The unhappy result is that their children face risks for delayed language development and lower-than-average academic achievement (Borkowski et al., 2002; Lefever, Nicholson, & Noria, 2007). Nevertheless, numerous adolescent mothers are competent caregivers, and educators can better the odds for young mothers and their offspring by motivating mothers to complete high school, teaching them about child development, and advising them of local programs that support new mothers (Jahromi, Guimond, Umaña-Taylor, Updegraff, & Toomey, 2014; Lee Smith et al., 2013; Robbers, 2008).

Much less is known about adolescent fathers, but they also face challenges as new parents. Before the birth of their baby, adolescent fathers may encounter disapproval from others, struggle to maintain a good relationship with their pregnant girlfriend, and worry about their ability to fulfill the responsibilities of raising a child (T. T. Williams, Mance, Caldwell, & Antonucci, 2012). After the baby is born, teenage fathers may find that these fears were well founded, as the relationship with the baby's mother is likely to become strained and well-paying jobs difficult to find (T. T. Williams et al., 2012). Young fathers can benefit from support, especially from their own families but also from professionals who understand their pressures, offer practical advice in staying involved with their children, and validate their age-typical need to develop a sense of identity.

Gay and Lesbian Parents

Growing numbers of children live with gay or lesbian parents. In the United States, approximately one in five male couples and one in three female couples are raising children from adoption, donor insemination, a previous marriage, or other arrangements (H. Bos, 2013; R. H. Farr & Patterson, 2013; Tasker, 2013). Children who have gay or lesbian parents have many assets, including being as intelligent and well adjusted as other children (Crowl, Ahn, & Baker, 2008; Golombok et al., 2014; C. J. Patterson, 2009). They are also inclined to become tolerant and open-minded adults who are respectful of diversity in its many forms (Goldberg, 2007; Telingator, 2013).

Prejudice, discrimination, and stigma are challenges that gay and lesbian parents and their children confront. Children of homosexual parents may encounter peers teasing their parents but are usually able to develop healthy friendships and cope with this prejudice without too much problem (C. J. Patterson, 2009). Unfortunately, some children are persistently bullied because of their parents' sexual orientation, and they sometimes shield their parents from the derogatory remarks so as not to trouble them (Telingator, 2013). Because of concerns about stigmatization, gay and lesbian parents may be reluctant to share their sexual orientation with teachers and other personnel at school. The children themselves are apt to be cautious in whom they confide about their parents. When they do "come out" about having gay parents, they often feel relieved to be able to share this part of themselves (M. G. Welsh, 2011, p. 63).

Although being condemned can obviously trouble both parents and children, both parties generally cope effectively, especially when there is a close and loving relationship within the family (C. J. Patterson, 2009; Telingator, 2013; M. G. Welsh, 2011). Experts suggest that an inclusive school climate and a curriculum that is openly accepting of gay, lesbian, bisexual, and transgender (GLBT) individuals helps not only students with this orientation but also the children of GLBT parents (Byard, Kosciw, & Bartkiewicz, 2013; J. E. Hart, Mourot, & Aros, 2012).

Foster Parents

In *foster care,* children are placed with families in a legal but temporary arrangement, commonly necessitated by their birth parents' neglect, maltreatment, or substance abuse (P. A. Fisher, Kim, & Pears, 2009; J. Smith, Boone, Gourdine, & Brown, 2013). Children in foster care must deal with several difficult circumstances—often, inadequate care from birth parents, the ordeal of being separated from their first families, the need to form relationships with entirely new caregivers, and the uncomfortable feeling of conflicting loyalties to separate families (Mehta, Baker, & Chong, 2013). Court officials generally try to keep siblings together, although this unified arrangement is not always possible, as when the family size is large or sibling relationships are destructive (Summers, Gatowski, & Dobbin, 2012).

Foster parents also face challenges. They must build a trusting relationship with a child who puts up barriers, has been a victim of abuse, and currently exhibits emotional and behavioral problems (M. E. Cox, Orme, & Rhoades, 2003; Orme & Buehler, 2001). In addition, foster parents receive minimal financial support yet must deal with numerous social service agencies. Fortunately, many foster parents take in children for the right reasons—because they themselves grew up in foster care or are committed in caring for children who have faced difficult conditions (Barber & Delfabbro, 2004).

Many children in foster care grow attached to their new families but nevertheless long to return to their birth families (Mehta et al., 2013; Samuels, 2009a). In fact, the majority of children in foster care are reunited with birth families within the first year (U.S. Department of Health and Human Services, 2007). Nevertheless, some birth parents are unable or unwilling to resume duties as parents, or they may have died, and their children are kept in foster care or eventually adopted, on average at about 6 or 7 years of age, often by their foster parents and sometimes by other adults who decide to adopt older children (U.S. Department of Health and Human Services, 2007). Unfortunately, because of heavy caseloads in agencies, crowded court dockets, and the typical preference of adoptive parents for newborn infants, foster children are sometimes shuffled among temporary arrangements before being placed into permanent homes (McKenzie, 1993). Such a transitory existence is particularly detrimental when children have already faced challenges—perhaps neglect, abuse, or exposure to drugs and violence.

Despite the odds, many children in foster care form healthy relationships with foster parents, do well in school, develop friendships with peers, and grow up as productive adults with good jobs and stable relationships (L. Jones, 2012; Kufeldt, Simard, & Vachon, 2003; G. Schofield & Beek, 2009). Foster parents who have specialized training from social workers are especially likely to help children achieve good developmental outcomes (P. A. Fisher et al., 2009; Van Andel, Grietens, Strijker, Van der Gaag, & Knorth, 2014).

Teachers can encourage children in foster care to overcome their challenges and give extra attention during periods of transition. Teachers can also reach out to foster parents, who are typically proficient in expressing affection and disciplining children yet appreciate status reports of their children's adjustment and academic progress at school (Crum, 2010). Realistically, teachers should also look for manifestations of the significant stress children experience in those rare but tragic situations when foster parents themselves have difficulty adjusting, as when they succumb to their own vulnerabilities in maltreating children or abuse alcohol or other substances (Courtney, Piliavin, Grogan-Kaylor, & Nesmith, 2001).

Accommodating the Full Range of Family Structures

Most school professionals place a high value on being inclusive and respectful of children and their families. Following are some specific tactics educators can use to be supportive of a wide range of family circumstances:

• **When organizing activities, make them inclusive to children from varied backgrounds.** School assignments and extracurricular activities sometimes involve one or more family members. With a little creativity, teachers can broaden activities so that they accommodate diverse family structures. Recall the Mother's Day poem Shea wrote to her stepmother (p. 75). Shea's teacher gave her enough time to write two poems, one for her mother and one for her stepmother.

• **Foster a climate of acceptance for diverse family structures.** As you have learned, children occasionally tease classmates from nontraditional families. At the preschool and elementary levels, teachers can counteract such intolerant attitudes by reading stories about children in different family structures and expressing the view that loving families are formed in many ways. Obviously, tormenting peers about family membership should not be tolerated. In the secondary grades adolescents tend to be more accepting about diverse family structures; nevertheless, at this age level as well, teachers should keep an ear open for, and emphatically discourage, any derogatory comments about a student's family.

• **Include mothers, fathers, custodial grandparents, and other heads of family at school.** By equalizing communications to children's coparents, teachers validate the incredibly influential roles that various parent figures play. It is also important to acknowledge the presence of other heads of family, such as grandparents serving as guardians. And whenever possible, extended family members should be welcome at school open houses, plays, and concerts.

• **Be supportive when children undergo a major family transition.** Many events, including divorce, remarriage, departure of a parent's nonmarital partner, death of a family member, or movement from one foster family to another, can change a child's life dramatically. In each case one or more caregivers may become unavailable, and other new relationships may begin (Adam, 2004; Dush, 2013; Fergusson et al., 2014). Adjustment to family transitions takes time, and practitioners should be prepared to offer long-term support. Adults can help children express their feelings, realize that they are not being abandoned and did not cause the family change, distinguish events that they can and cannot control, consider benefits to being in the new family structure, and find relationships outside the immediate family that are sustaining during these transitions (Pedro-Carroll, 2005; Recker, Clark, & Foote, 2008).

• **Remain patient while children are figuring out how to adjust to new family structures.** Many youngsters must adapt to moving back and forth between two houses (Smart, Neale, & Wade, 2001). In such circumstances teachers can express sympathy for any distress or frustration but also encourage the child to come up with a plan for adjusting to the transitions and keeping track of belongings (including homework) during moves between residences.

• **Let children say what they want; don't pry.** Children often prefer to keep family matters to themselves. They may feel that teachers and counselors are snooping into their personal lives by asking questions about their family life. It is desirable, therefore, for adults to lend a sympathetic ear without being too inquisitive. When children bring up family problems, you can help them generate options for dealing with their problems, such as compiling a portfolio of schoolwork when anticipating a move to a new school.

• **Anticipate children's needs based on what you know about their families.** A student with a grandparent living with the family may be able to come to school meetings when her single mother is away on business trips. A child whose family has recently moved to the school needs information about the school day and procedures for gathering supplies for a lesson, getting in line for lunch, getting settled after recess, etc. Another child with a chronically sick parent may need help in getting to school on time; perhaps a classmate's parent would be willing to drive the child to and from school.

• **Extend an extra hand to students living in foster care.** A number of children in foster care are emotionally burdened yet have trouble asking for assistance. Some may have profound social needs and as a result engage in behaviors that upset even experienced professionals. Others desperately miss their birth parents and any brothers and sisters staying with other families. Because of such overwhelming challenges, children in foster care may need guidance in coping skills to help them relax and gradually adjust to separations and new caregivers.[2] Predictable routines at school can be therapeutic to children dealing with a family trauma, especially when teachers take time to express their concern, communicate expectations, and advise them of services. Teachers can also offer practical help with homework and assignments when children miss school because of attending court hearings or moving between residences.

---

[2]Coping skills are examined in Chapter 11.

Summary

Families come in many forms, including those with two parents, single parents, stepparents, adoptive parents, parent figures from extended families, adolescent parents, gay or lesbian parents, and foster parents. Many youngsters experience one or more changes in family structure (e.g., as a result of divorce, remarriage, or death of a parent) at some point during their childhood. Particular family structures present unique benefits and challenges for children, but ultimately the quality of family relationships exceeds family membership in significance. Teachers can be inclusive of children and their families by welcoming everyone, reassuring children during family transitions, discouraging discriminatory remarks by children, and respecting children's privacy.

ENHANCEDetext *self-check*

FAMILY INTERACTION

How parents raise their children has profound effects on children's adjustment. By virtue of their personalities and activities, children influence parents and other family members in return. In this section we examine the mutually influential interchanges that family members have. We also examine temporary disruptions in families, family maltreatment, and strategies for establishing productive relationships with families.

BIOECOLOGY OF DEVELOPMENT
Children thrive when they have loving relationships with parents and are given the chance to take on increasing responsibilities at home.

Families' Influences on Children

As agents of socialization, parents and other heads of family blend affection with discipline as they interact with children. They also encourage children to participate in everyday routines and become involved in their education.

Parenting Styles

The foundation of parenting is love. Parents communicate affection by responding sensitively to children's initiatives, comforting them when distressed, and celebrating their accomplishments. A second vital element of parenting is discipline. Children have strong wills of their own but lack foresight and self-restraint. In response, parents teach children to rein in their impulses, anticipate the outcomes of their actions, follow rules, and make amends for wrongdoings. Parents use a variety of techniques for disciplining children, including reasoning, scolding, withdrawing affection, removing privileges, imposing restrictions, and, occasionally, spanking children. A reasonable balance between affection and discipline fosters children's self-regulation, their ability to direct and control personal actions and emotions (Maccoby, 2007; K. E. Williams, Ciarrochi, & Heaven, 2012).

Most parents around the world manage to find acceptable, balanced ways to love and wield authority over their children (R. H. Bradley, Corwyn, McAdoo, & Coll, 2001; Rohner & Rohner, 1981; Scarr, 1992). Yet parents vary in the ways in which they express affection and implement discipline; that is, they develop individual **parenting styles**. Research on parenting styles was pioneered in the 1960s by American psychologist **Diana Baumrind** and has been subsequently refined by Baumrind and her colleagues (Baumrind, 1967, 1971, 1980, 1989, 1991, 2013).

Considerable evidence indicates that a style of parenting that blends steady affection with firm discipline is associated with children's mature, competent, confident, cheerful, independent, and considerate behavior and their commitment to achieving in school (Baumrind, 2013; Dornbusch, Ritter, Leiderman, Roberts, & Fraleigh, 1987; A. L. Gonzalez & Wolters, 2006; Lamborn, Mounts, Steinberg, & Dornbusch, 1991; Simons-Morton & Chen, 2009; Steinberg, Elmen, & Mounts, 1989). Parents who use this approach, called an **authoritative parenting style**, are affectionate and responsive, promote age-appropriate behavior, communicate high expectations, assert their authority when children misbehave, give reasons children understand for why they should act in a certain way, and consider children's perspectives when establishing rules. Authoritative parenting seems to foster healthy development because it provides valuable guidance, is tailored to the child's age and abilities, is accompanied by warm regard, and nurtures the child's sense of autonomy

(Baumrind, 2013; Gauvain, Perez, & Beebe, 2013; Grolnick & Pomerantz, 2009; Uji, Sakamoto, Adachi, & Kitamura, 2014).

In a second, very different approach, known as the **authoritarian parenting style**, parents demand immediate compliance but withhold affection, give very few reasons for requests ("Clean your room because I told you to—and I mean *now!*") and allow little chance for negotiation. Like authoritative parenting, authoritarian parenting reflects efforts to direct children's behavior, but authori*tative* parents guide children with warmth and flexibility, whereas authori*tarian* parents are harsh and rigid. Children of consistently authoritarian parents tend to be withdrawn, mistrusting, and unhappy; they are apt to have low self-esteem, little self-reliance, and poor social skills; and they have a greater-than-average tendency of acting aggressively (Baumrind, 2013; Coopersmith, 1967; Gauvain et al., 2013; Lamborn et al., 1991; Simons, Whitbeck, Conger, & Conger, 1991). Authoritarian parents offer structure for the child but fail to support his or her sense of autonomy (Grolnick & Pomerantz, 2009).

In a third pattern, parents exert *little control* over children, and children generally suffer from this lack of direction. Parents who use a **permissive parenting style** appear to care about their children but relinquish important decisions to children (even fairly young ones)— allowing them to decide when to go to bed, what chores (if any) to do around the house, and what curfews to abide by (e.g., "Okay. Stay up later, but try to get *some* sleep tonight."). Children in such families are typically immature, impulsive, demanding, dependent on parents, and, not surprisingly, disobedient when parents ask them to do something they do not want to do. These children also tend to have difficulty in school, are aggressive with peers, and engage in delinquent acts as adolescents (C. Christopher, Saunders, Jacobvitz, Burton, & Hazen, 2013; Lamborn et al., 1991; Pulkkinen, 1982; Tucker, Ellickson, & Klein, 2008). Apparently, these generally warm family environments do not adequately compensate for their lack of guidance.

A few parents are not only permissive but also indifferent to children. When using a fourth pattern, the **uninvolved parenting style,**[3] parents make few demands and respond to children in an uncaring and even rejecting manner. Children of uninvolved parents frequently exhibit serious difficulties, including problems with school achievement, emotional control, tolerance for frustration, and delinquency (Lamborn et al., 1991; Rothrauff, Cooney, & An, 2009; Simons, Robertson, & Downs, 1989). These children receive neither adequate affection nor the supervision they need to develop essential skills.

Altogether, the evidence overwhelmingly suggests that children fare best when parents use an authoritative style. But there are qualifications to this conclusion. For one thing, parents are not fully consistent from one situation to the next. Instead, they adjust their tactics depending on their moods, children's misbehaviors, and the demands of the situation (Grusec & Davidov, 2007; Solem, 2013). For instance, in the morning, a father may reason with his 4-year-old son about bringing a jacket, advising him of the weather but allowing him to make the final decision. Yet in the afternoon, when the boy ventures into a busy street, his father forcefully removes him from harm's way. Thus, rather than being the adult's only method of caregiving, parenting style is more accurately thought of as a parent's predominant techniques for expressing affection and controlling behavior.

Conclusions about the powerful effects of parenting style must be tempered additionally because children are active partners in disciplinary exchanges. Through their temperaments and actions, children elicit certain reactions from parents. For instance, parents generally reason with characteristically compliant children and use harsh discipline with easily angered children (K. E. Anderson, Lytton, & Romney, 1986; Kochanska & Kim, 2013; A. S. Morris, Cui, & Steinberg, 2013). As you might expect, the discipline that parents use also affects individual children differently depending on their personal characteristics. Children whose temperaments predispose them to be irritable, when raised by harsh parents, are likely to develop high levels of aggression and oppositional behavior (Kochanska & Kim, 2013). In comparison, children who are generally agreeable cope more easily with severe and punitive parents.

Children are active in another important way that mediates the influence of discipline. How children make sense of parents' actions and gestures affects their overall adjustment. Specifically, children view parents' discipline as being legitimate (if not always welcome)

---

[3]Some scholars use the term *disengaged* or *rejecting-neglecting* for uninvolved parenting (Baumrind, 2013).

to the degree that parents have previously been involved, affectionate, and respectful with them (Grusec & Davidov, 2007; Maccoby, 2007; C. R. Martinez & Forgatch, 2001). Through a variety of tactics, parents demonstrate their concern and persuade children that they are imposing restrictions for children's own good. As a result, children usually accept parents' authority, even though they sporadically—and sometimes recurrently—haggle over limitations (Hoffman, 1994). In comparison, when parents come across as demeaning, cruel, or hostile, children may comply with parents' demands only when parents are present to enforce them.

The effects of parenting styles are also mediated by culture and community (Baumrind, 2013; Chao, 1994; Deater-Deckard, Dodge, Bates, & Pettit, 1996; Pomerantz & Wang, 2009; Steinberg, Lamborn, Darling, Mounts, & Dornbusch, 1994). Authoritative parenting is broadly associated with good developmental outcomes, but some aspects of authoritarian parenting are productive in certain settings. In collectivistic cultures, including some East Asian and Middle Eastern societies, demands for immediate compliance are associated with parental warmth and acceptance—not rejection—and generate healthy outcomes in children (Chao, 1994, 2000; Dwairy et al., 2006; Rudy & Grusec, 2006). This positive result is probably due to children's perceptions that their strict parents are helping them by insisting that they abide by the obligations of society.

Other aspects of families' lives make the authori*tative* style ineffective or difficult to use. When families live in dangerous neighborhoods, parents protect children in some situations by issuing stern commands (Baumrind, 2013; Hale-Benson, 1986; McWayne, Owsianik, Green, & Fantuzzo, 2008). In other circumstances parents are strict not because they are preparing children to survive in hazardous environments, but rather because economic stresses provoke them to be short tempered (Bronfenbrenner, Alvarez, & Henderson, 1984; L. F. Katz & Gottman, 1991; Ricketts & Anderson, 2008). Unless they receive substantial support, these latter parents may find it difficult to reason calmly or enforce rules dependably.

Such qualifications aside, a parent's inclinations to be loving, responsive, and thoughtful with discipline facilitate the child's development. How, then, are child-rearing strategies acquired? Several factors are important, including parents' own childhood experiences, the behaviors they have become familiar with in their culture, any advice or training they have received about parenting, and the amount of stress they have in their lives (D. Gross et al., 2009; Kitamura et al., 2009). Parents' own relationships are also important. When families are reasonably harmonious, parents find it relatively easy to be authoritative with their children (A. S. Morris et al., 2013).

Daily Activities

When children are ready to make strides in caring for themselves or interacting with others, parents teach specific skills, for example, how to tie their shoes, brush their teeth, and greet their grandmother. **Guided participation**, in which a child engages in everyday adult tasks and routines, typically with considerable supervision, is another method by which parents support children's learning. Parents include children in such activities as cooking, completing errands, worshipping, gardening, and volunteering in the community. As they learn, children are allowed to take on progressively higher levels of responsibility for planning and carrying out tasks (Gauvain et al., 2013; Perez & Gauvain, 2009; Rogoff, 2003).

The activities parents arrange, both inside and outside the home, affect children's academic learning, expectations about school, and knowledge of work-related skills. Many parents comment on the purposes and patterns of language and expose children to books, art, music, computer technology, and scientific and mathematical thinking (Eccles, 2007; Farver, Xu, Lonigan, & Eppe, 2013; Hess & Holloway, 1984; LeFevre et al., 2009). Children observe parents exhibiting occupational skills as well, perhaps balancing expenses on a spreadsheet, building a cabinet, or answering the telephone politely (Denmark & Harden, 2012; González, Moll, & Amanti, 2005).

Families offer a further contribution to children's academic learning through their involvement in schooling. When children enter school, their families advise them on how to behave, what goals to strive for, how hard to try, and so on. As children progress through the grade levels, heads of family may discuss school activities with children, assist with homework, and give feedback about in-class projects. At school, heads of family may volunteer in the classroom, participate in parent advisory groups, join fund-raising projects, and confer with teachers about children's progress. Students whose parents are involved at school generally achieve at higher levels than those whose parents are not, perhaps because involved parents convey high value for education, communicate effectively with teachers, and gain insights into the kinds of help children need most at home (Crosnoe, 2009; Eccles, 2007; T. T. Williams & Sánchez, 2013).

Although family involvement in schooling is usually constructive, there are exceptions. In some cases, parents intrusively direct the child's schoolwork, give assistance that is misaligned with the child's abilities, and put excessive pressure on the child to achieve (Silinskas, Niemi, Lerkkanen, & Nurmi, 2013; E. T. Tan & Goldberg, 2009). Furthermore, not every family finds it easy to become involved at school or sees their presence there as welcome. Parents in some cultures believe that they should offer tangible assistance at home and *not* interfere at school (García Coll & Marks, 2009). These families offer considerable support by setting aside a quiet place at home for school work, providing help with assignments, and monitoring children's academic progress.

Employment and Child Care

The majority of children in the United States have working parents, a pattern that holds true in many other nations as well (U.S. Department of Labor, 2013). Among U.S. families with children, 87.8 percent have at least one employed parent. In single-mother families, 67.1 percent of women are employed; in single-father families, 81.6 percent of men are employed. In two-parent families, 59 percent have both parents working.

Employment by parents and guardians influences children in several ways. Jobs give the family income, occupy parents' schedules, and, in some cases, provide sick leave and health insurance. Parents also talk with children about their experiences at work and in this manner socialize children as to what they have to look forward to—or might wish to avoid—in the world of work. Long work hours can mean that parents have little remaining time for relaxing with children, checking homework, and cooking nutritious meals (K. W. Bauer, Hearst, Escoto, Berge, & Neumark-Sztainer, 2012).

Employment is also significant in that others typically care for children when parents are working. From middle childhood and on, schools fulfill this role for some of the day. Yet many children are cared for by extended family, neighbors, or employed caregivers for 10 to 40 hours per week or more, depending on their age. Caregivers provide oversight and structure activities that can be either developmentally attuned or incongruent with children's emerging needs, interests, and motivations.[4] This wide variation in quality of care means that children must be able to adjust to numerous situations, some of which are growth-promoting and others of which increase children's stress.

Children's Influences on Families

You have learned that parents are powerful forces in children's development through expressions of love, enforcement of discipline, and inclusion in enriching activities. Yet as children comply with parents' guidance, they also express their own desires, often quite emphatically, as Cedric did when spurring his mother into action in our chapter-opening case study.

Children's Effects on Parents

As you found when reading about parenting styles, socialization involves *reciprocal influences,* whereby children and parents simultaneously affect one another from the beginning of life (R. Q. Bell, 1988). Babies demand comfort by crying, but they also coo, chatter, and lure their parents into contact in a most disarming manner. A father intent on sweeping the kitchen floor will find it hard to resist the antics of his 6-month-old daughter who wriggles, chatters, and smiles at him.

Reciprocal influences continue as children grow. Preschoolers frequently play games that elicit imitation and turn taking with parents (Kohlberg, 1969). In everyday interactions, children respond to parents in much the same way as they have been treated, as you

---

[4]We examine types and effects of child care in Chapter 15.

can see in the note from 10-year-old Samuel to his mother, shown in Artifact 3-4. Children also develop desires, skills, and viewpoints outside the family and bring them home. For example, children plead for certain kinds of fast foods and noisy toys that parents might otherwise avoid (Chaudhary & Gupta, 2012). At school, on the Internet, and in their peer groups, adolescents encounter varying perspectives on people's rights and responsibilities. To make sense of discrepant viewpoints on how society should be governed, adolescents ask parents for their opinions and some-times express outlandish views so as to solicit parents' explanations (M. McDevitt & Ostrowski, 2009). Over time, both parents and adolescents refine their political views, having listened to one another's reasoning.

Reciprocal influences on one another's emotions are similarly evident in daily exchanges. When parents treat their children warmly, the children usually respond with affectionate gestures, as you can see in Artifact 3-5, a note from Alex to his bereaved father. In contrast, when parents establish a negative climate, children may learn to challenge, accuse, and ridicule their parents. In some families, parents and children intensify demands as they interact, as shown in this interchange:

ARTIFACT 3-4   Thank you, Mom. Children's and parents' behaviors are mutually influential, as you can see in Samuel's loving card to his affectionate mother.

Mother:	I told you to clean your room. This is a *disaster*.
Daughter:	Get outta *my* room!
Mother:	*(raises her voice)* You clean up that mess or you're grounded! *(stamps her foot)*
Daughter:	Hah! You can't make me!
Mother:	For a month! *(shouting now)*
Daughter:	You stink! *(stomps out of her room and marches to the front door)*
Mother:	For two months! *(shouting louder)*
Daughter:	As if you'd notice I was gone! *(slams door)*

During this exchange, things go from bad to worse: The daughter is blatantly disobedient, the mother escalates in her demands, and both mother and daughter explode with anger. Such exchanges are common in troubled families (G. H. Brody et al., 2013; G. R. Patterson & Reid, 1970). When patterns of negative interaction become habitual, it is difficult for family members to ease up on their ultimatums. However, both parents and children *can* grow and change, often in response to intensive counseling (Bugental, 2009; Shayne & Miltenberger, 2013).

Parents largely set the tone of these family dynamics, but children contribute im-mensely to interactions through their emotional expressions and expressions of interests. For instance, children who are easily frustrated tend to provoke severe and intrusive be-havior in adults (Bornstein, 2009; Kochanska & Kim, 2013). Children who have exceptional verbal abilities regularly ask for verbal explanations, storybook readings, and other intel-lectual enrichment from parents (Lugo-Gil & Tamis-LeMonda, 2008; Scarr, 1992).

ARTIFACT 3-5   Taking care of Dad. Children take initiative when they see beloved family members in distress. Six-year-old Alex wrote this sympathy card to his father the day Alex's grandfather (his father's father) died.

Siblings' Responses to One Another

Children have an impact not only on their parents but also on any siblings in the family. Approximately 80 percent of children in the United States and in Europe live in a household with at least one sibling (J. Dunn, 2007; U.S. Census Bureau, 2013a).

Siblings serve many purposes for children. Close sibling relationships supplement parent–child bonds, especially during such difficult transitions as divorce (Ehrenberg, Regev, Lazinski, Behrman, & Zimmerman, 2014; K. Jacobs & Sillars, 2012; Seibert & Kerns, 2009). Other influences by siblings depend on the relative ages of children. In Western society, older siblings often look after young children when parents do brief errands. In many other societies, older children are the primary caregivers for younger brothers and sisters for a sig-nificant part of the day, serving as role models, tutors, and playmates (Hafford, 2010; Weisner & Gallimore, 1977; Zhang et al., 2009).

Sibling relationships allow children many chances to practice social skills. During early and middle childhood, children spend more time with siblings than with parents or peers (J. Dunn, 2007). The relationships that evolve among siblings are often quite close but can introduce conflict and stress into the family (J. Dunn, 2007; Tucker & Kazura, 2013). Children compete for limited resources, including parents' attention, and occasionally become downright combative over seemingly trivial issues (such as who gets to select first from a full plate of freshly baked cookies: "*Lemme* go first!" "No, it's *my* turn!"). Competition probably has some benefits, including helpful lessons from parents about attending to the sibling's perspective, and social insights gained in outsmarting or cooperating with brothers and sisters (Recchia & Howe, 2009; Tucker & Kazura, 2013). However, resentment may brew if one child feels slighted by a parent (G. H. Brody, Stoneman, & McCoy, 1994; J. Dunn, 2007).

Within a family, individual children can encounter quite different child-rearing strategies by their parents. The intellectual and social experiences of children depend partly on *birth order*—that is, on whether children were born first, second, or later down the line. Older siblings tend to have a slight advantage academically, perhaps because of the exclusive time they had with their parents before siblings came along, benefits from teaching younger siblings, or other factors (Chiu, 2007; Härkönen, 2014; Kanazawa, 2012; Zajonc & Mullally, 1997). Yet younger siblings enjoy their own rewards: They show greater skill in interacting with peers than do older siblings, probably as a result of learning to assert themselves with older siblings (J. Dunn, 1984; N. Miller & Maruyama, 1976; B. C. Wright & Mahfoud, 2012).

Despite their influences, siblings are by no means essential for healthy development. *Only children*—children without brothers or sisters—are often stereotyped as lonely, spoiled, and egotistical, but research findings consistently suggest healthy adjustment. On average, only children perform well in school, enjoy strong relationships with their parents, and have good mental health, possibly because the close attention they receive from parents fosters effective coping skills (Falbo & Polit, 1986; Riordan, Morris, Hattie, & Stark, 2012).

Other Significant Conditions in Families

We have seen that several factors within the family affect the child's development—family membership, transitions in families, styles of caregiving, and sibling relationships. Outside circumstances also impinge on the family. Here we look at two very different conditions, military deployment and imprisonment, which can both result in a parent's absence from the family home and the child's need to adjust to these changes.

Children with Military Parents

In the United States, approximately 1.2 million children have one or more parents in military service, and 2 million children have lived through a parent's deployment, the assignment of the parent to a remote location, often overseas, in order to accomplish a military mission (De Pedro et al., 2011; Ohye, Rauch, & Bostic, 2012).

Having an enlisted parent is a source of pride for many children, a feeling that is often validated at school through such initiatives as honoring wounded warriors and sending care packages to troops separated from their loved ones. Yet interruptions punctuate military life. For children, being raised by a military parent often requires one or more moves to a new base, each of which requires adjustments to new schools, peer groups, and communities. Teachers and counselors can help the child by suggesting ways to stay in touch and making sure families have appropriate records, including report cards, test scores, the school's grading scales and curriculum, and verification of the child's extracurricular activities, community service hours, academic recognitions, and individual accommodations (Military Child Education Coalition, 2013). After the move, new teachers can learn as much as possible about the child's education history, introduce the child to the class, and identify a buddy to accompany him or her around the building for a couple of days.

In a situation of a parent's deployment, in which the child remains at home, additional services may be necessary. Children with a deployed parent face numerous challenges—separation from the parent, concern about his or her welfare, reactions to anxiety in the at-home parent, and distress if the military parent returns with a significant injury or trauma (De Pedro et al., 2011). Children who encounter these problems are vulnerable to mental health problems, behavioral disorders, and academic delays (De Pedro et al., 2011). Young children, given their undeveloped coping skills, regularly become overwhelmed by such separations. Older children can more easily understand the purposes of their parent's work and the time frame for the deployment. In fact, adolescents may take on extra household chores and support the at-home parent and younger siblings (Huebner & Mancini, 2005). Educators can communicate their ongoing concern to children and watch for serious manifestations of stress that might be addressed with counseling.

Children with Incarcerated Parents

With increased drug use and mandatory sentencing laws, growing numbers of parents are separated from their children by imprisonment (B. J. Myers, Smarsh, Amlund-Hagen, & Kennon, 1999). In the United States, 10 million children have experienced a parent being incarcerated (D. Johnston, 2012). Fathers are more frequently incarcerated than are mothers, but children are more deeply affected by mothers' detention because mothers are typically primary caregivers (B. J. Myers et al., 1999; Newell, 2012). In the case of an incarcerated father, the child would usually live with the mother, whereas under the circumstance of an incarcerated mother, the child is apt to reside with a grandparent, aunt, or other relative (Kjellstrand, Cearley, Eddy, Foney, & Martinez, 2012; Mackintosh, Myers, & Kennon, 2006).

Children who have a parent in prison face substantial risks. Those who witness their parent's arrest are apt to find the confrontation disturbing (Dallaire & Wilson, 2010; B. J. Myers et al., 1999). Even if the child is not present during the arrest, he or she is likely to be devastated by the sudden departure. After the arrest, the child may feel anxious about the separation and challenges in adjusting to a new caregiver and household (B. J. Myers et al., 1999). When the arrest, verdict, sentencing, and incarceration become public knowledge, the child may feel ashamed; if the family's circumstances are kept a secret, he or she is apt to feel alone and isolated (Gust, 2012; Newell, 2012; E. B. Nichols & Loper, 2012). These difficulties add to existing hardships, including economic poverty, exposure to community violence, family stress, and impaired caregiving emanating from a parent's mental illness, alcoholism, or drug abuse (D. Johnston, 2012; B. J. Myers et al., 1999; Newell, 2012). Thus, it appears that the separation, stigma, and other risks associated with the parent's incarceration undermine the child's already troubled family life. Under these profoundly difficult conditions, it is not surprising that children of incarcerated parents sometimes develop emotional problems, academic delays, and adjustment difficulties at school (Kjellstrand et al., 2012).

As you might expect, the developmental level of the child affects his or her adjustment to the incarceration. Young children find a parent's incarceration especially upsetting if they are nearby when the parent is arrested, have previously observed the parent committing a crime, are concerned about the parent's wrongdoing, and have previously developed only rudimentary coping skills (D. Johnston, 1995; B. J. Myers et al., 1999). Older children face cumulative stresses if the parent has been imprisoned several times. Resulting emotional difficulties are manifested in nightmares, restlessness, aggression, and other problems. During adolescence, the young person may be lured into joining gangs, stealing, disengaging from school, failing classes, and consuming drugs or alcohol; some adolescents with incarcerated parents believe that going to prison is an inevitable part of growing up (Gust, 2012; D. Johnston, 2012; B. J. Myers et al., 1999).

Fortunately, many children with incarcerated parents have protective factors that help to offset these risks. Examples include the child's own intelligence and interests, a high-quality relationship and continued contact with the incarcerated parent, ongoing support from the new caregiver, a strong alliance between the incarcerated parent and the new caregiver, support from faith-based groups, and services in the community (Loper, Phillips, Nichols, & Dallaire, 2013; Mackintosh et al., 2006; Newell, 2012).

Community organizations and prisons have tried to make children's visits to parents easier by arranging transportation and child-friendly rooms in the prison for family get-togethers and attending to age-related needs with other services (D. Johnston, 2012; B. J. Myers et al., 1999). Educational instruction for pregnant prisoners and preschool programs for young children have aided both parents and children. After-school programs for older children have included peer support, academic lessons, and recreational activities and proven effective in increasing children's academic skills and decreasing their behavior problems. Training in job skills, career planning, and cultivation of entrepreneurial abilities have fostered adolescents' knowledge of business, self-confidence, and employment experience.

Maltreatment in Families

Unfortunately, not all families provide good environments for children. **Child maltreatment** is the most serious outcome of an unhealthy family environment and takes four major forms (Benbenishty & Schmid, 2013; Centers for Disease Control and Prevention, 2009b; English, 1998). *Neglect* occurs when caregivers fail to provide food, clothing, shelter, health care, or affection and do not adequately supervise children's activities (the *uninvolved* parents we described earlier would be considered neglectful if they were truly disengaged from their children). Caregivers engage in *physical abuse* when they intentionally cause physical harm to children, perhaps by kicking, biting, shaking, or punching them. If spanking causes serious bruises or other injuries, it, too, is considered physical abuse. Caregivers engage in *sexual abuse* when they seek sexual gratification from children through such acts as genital contact or pornographic photography. Caregivers engage in *emotional abuse* when they consistently ignore, isolate, reject, denigrate, or terrorize children or when they corrupt them by encouraging substance use or criminal activity. Sadly, some parents submit children to more than one form of abuse.

Approximately one in seven U.S. children has been maltreated by a family member or other caregiver (Centers for Disease Control and Prevention, 2013; Finkelhor, Ormrod, Turner, & Hamby, 2005; Wulczyn, 2009). The occurrence of maltreatment seems to be related to characteristics of both the adult and the child. Adults who maltreat children suffer from such serious psychological problems as depression, anxiety, and substance abuse (Ayoub, 2006; Barth, 2009; Egeland, 2009). Many have little contact with extended family or friends, are economically disadvantaged, move around a lot, were maltreated themselves as children, have large families to care for, and believe that physical punishment is justified by religious or cultural beliefs. Some abusive parents are quite naive about children's development and become angry when children fail to meet their unrealistic expectations.

Children most likely to be maltreated are those who are very young (premature infants are especially at risk); others with disabilities; and individuals who are irritable, not easily soothed, aggressive, or exceedingly noncompliant (Ayoub, 2006; Barth, 2009; U.S. Department of Health and Human Services Administration for Children and Families, Administration on Children, Youth and Families, Children's Bureau, 2012). Within a single family, one child may be maltreated and others not, although some parents, such as those with a substance abuse problem, are uniformly neglectful or harsh with all of their children.

Tragically, children can suffer long-term consequences from being neglected or assaulted by family members (Centers for Disease Control and Prevention, 2013; Raposa, Hammen, O'Callaghan, Brennan, & Najman, 2014; Wulczyn, 2009). Children who have been maltreated are at risk for becoming aggressive, withdrawn, and depressed, for viewing themselves negatively, and for developing maladaptive ways of coping and interacting with other people. These children are also at risk for physical problems and even death.

Occasionally, children describe the anguish of abuse with a teacher. Generally, children will do this only when they feel safe and expect that they will be believed. Such a conversation is best responded to with empathic concern. The teacher's proper role is to listen and support, and later to follow up with authorities, not to try to verify or delve into the details of the abuse (Collin-Vézina, 2013). In fact, asking leading questions (e.g., about whether a parent touched the child's private parts when the child did not mention being touched) can jeopardize a later prosecution because of the possibility that these questions planted false memories (Otgaar, Verschuere, Meijer, & van Oorsouw, 2012). Even prior to any disclosures, teachers can advise children of resources in the school—especially counselors, psychologists, nurses, and social workers. Whoever is told about abuse will want to express concern, emphasize that it is not the child's fault, and advise the child that a plan will be developed to get help (Collin-Vézina, 2013).

Educators and others working with children and adolescents must, by law, contact proper authorities (e.g., the school principal or Child Protective Services) when they suspect child abuse or neglect, regardless of whether the child has described the abuse to them. Two helpful resources are the National Child Hotline (1-800-4-A-CHILD®, or 1-800-422-4453)[5] and the Internet website for Childhelp USA®, childhelpusa.org. When a concern is expressed to Child Protective Services, the authorities may be able to verify the maltreatment and provide the family with counseling, parent education, housing assistance, substance treatment, home visits, and referrals for other services. Unfortunately, reports to Child Protective Services do not always lead to immediate services for maltreated children or their families. Sometimes authorities cannot find sufficient evidence to substantiate suspicions, and at other times high caseloads prevent authorities from intervening promptly (Larner, Stevenson, & Behrman, 1998; Wolock, Sherman, Feldman, & Metzger, 2001).

---

[5]The National Child Abuse Hotline receives calls from the United States, U.S. Territories, and Canada. Many other countries have similar organizations.

As they wait for intervention, maltreated children desperately need stable, caring relationships with adults outside the family. Teachers can help by expressing their confidence in children's abilities, building on such protective factors as individual talents, and providing a sense of normalcy during upheaval in the family (Bernard & Popard Newell, 2013; Phasha, 2008). Sadly, many maltreated children have acquired negative social behaviors that elicit rejection from other adults, and possibly for this reason are at risk for developing low-quality relationships with teachers (Pianta, Hamre, & Stuhlman, 2003). Teachers are advised to make special efforts that address children's reactions to maltreatment (e.g., inattentiveness, disruptive behavior, or withdrawal from activities). When an investigation is under way, continued sensitivity is essential because children must adjust to disruptions in family structure (e.g., a child might be placed with a foster family) or family climate (e.g., a mother might become depressed when she learns she could lose custody of her children). After Child Protective Services intervenes, the child must adjust to new family conditions and may need individualized support for trouble in learning, paying attention, expressing emotions appropriately, and controlling aggressive behaviors.

Forming Partnerships with Families

Parents and teachers have much in common. They both take on tough responsibilities that demand long hours, unwavering devotion, and flexible methods. When teachers and families communicate effectively (as Barbara and Mr. Momen eventually did in our opening case study, with help from Cedric), they are likely to magnify their positive effects on students. Ideally, teachers and heads of family become partners who collaborate in support of children's learning.

Joyce Epstein, an American sociologist, has examined family–school partnerships and identified methods for establishing, and benefits accrued from, successful relationships among educators, parents, and other members of the community (J. L. Epstein et al., 2009; J. L. Epstein, Galindo, & Sheldon, 2011; Hutchins, Greenfield, Epstein, Sanders, & Galindo, 2012). Based on the work of Epstein, her colleagues, and many other experts in the field, we offer the following recommendations on forming constructive partnerships with families:

• **Make schools family friendly.** One of the best things you can do to establish effective relationships with families is to set up an environment that is conducive to interactions among parents, teachers, students, and siblings in the school building. Teachers, psychologists, and other personnel sometimes devote a room for families to drop in and have a cup of coffee or tea; occasionally they provide babysitters for special events at the school and arrange for transportation for families that are not otherwise able to visit. With a family-friendly environment, parents and other family members are more inclined to attend school events.

• **Get to know who is in children's families.** As you have learned, families come in many forms. Thus an important first step is to determine who the guardians are and whether other family members care for children on a daily basis. The Observation Guidelines table "Identifying Family Conditions" lists family membership and other characteristics that teachers can take into consideration.

• **Communicate with each primary caregiver.** When two parents are actively involved in a child's life—whether they live in the same household or not—teachers should try to get to know both and show respect for the role that each plays in the child's life. A good first step when meeting parents and guardians is to ask them how they like to be addressed and keep a record of these preferences ("Señora Torres, thank you for coming to Davey's conference," "Good afternoon, Jillian.").

• **Accommodate family transitions.** Families undergoing significant transitions invariably appreciate being kept informed. For example, a teacher might encourage a third-grade boy to send photographs of an exemplary diorama to his father, who is deployed in a military assignment. Children also need support under special family circumstances. For instance, a teacher might help a fourth-girl make up homework after spending a couple of days out of town to visit her incarcerated mother.

• **Recognize siblings.** Teachers can validate children's close-knit relationships with siblings, especially when children face a loss or challenge. In times of family crisis (e.g., with the death of a grandparent or a parent's imprisonment), children may appreciate contact with siblings,

OBSERVATION GUIDELINES
Identifying Family Conditions

CHARACTERISTIC	LOOK FOR	EXAMPLE	IMPLICATION
Family Structure	• *Single versus multiple caregivers* • *Presence or absence of siblings* • *Extended family members* living in the home • *Nonrelatives* living in the home • *Children's relationships* with other family members	Alexis's chronic kidney disease causes periodic bouts of pain and fatigue. During flare-ups, she finds comfort in being with her older sister. Teachers arrange for the girls to be together at lunch when Alexis is feeling poorly.	Accept all heads of family as valued, legitimate caregivers of children. Invite extended family members to school functions. Give youngsters time to be with siblings in times of personal crisis.
Cultural Background	• *Language(s)* spoken at home • *Routines* in eating, bathing, sleeping, and carrying out chores • *Loyalty* to and sense of responsibility for other family members • *Attitudes* toward cooperation and competition • *Communication styles* (whether they make eye contact and ask questions)	Carlos is reserved in class. He follows instructions and clearly wants to do well in school. However, he rarely seeks his teacher's help. Instead, he often asks his cousin (a classmate) for assistance.	Remember that most children and parents value academic achievement, despite what their behaviors may make you think. Try to determine children's preferred ways of interacting and communicating. Consider how families' cultural knowledge and skills can enrich the classroom. Invite families to share their traditions at school.
Family Livelihood	• *Family business* (e.g., running a farm or cottage industry) that requires children's involvement • *Parental unemployment* or job turnover • *Older children and adolescents with part-time jobs* (e.g., grocery store work, paper routes)	April completes several chores on the family farm before going to school each morning. She keeps records of the weight and health of three calves born last year. She constructs charts to show their progress as a project for her science class.	Take outside work commitments into account when assigning homework. For example, give students at least 2 days to complete short assignments and a week for longer ones.
Parenting Styles	• *Parents' warmth or coldness* toward children • *Parents' expectations* for children's behavior • *Parents' willingness to discuss issues* and negotiate solutions with children • *Parents' disciplinary techniques* • *Effects of children's temperaments* on parents' discipline • *Children's interpretations* of parents' motives with discipline • *Cultural values*, such as honoring elders, that affect discipline • *Dangers and opportunities* in the community that influence parenting methods	At a parent–teacher conference, Julia's parents express their exasperation about trying to get Julia to do her homework: "We've tried everything—reasoning with her, giving ultimatums, offering extra privileges for good grades, punishing her for bad grades—but nothing works. She'd rather hang out with her friends every night."	Realize that most parents have children's best interests at heart when they discipline children. Recognize that parents adapt their parenting styles to children's temperaments. With all children, communicate high expectations, show sensitivity to children's needs, and give reasons for your requests. Explain your rationale for the particular disciplinary methods you use because children may be accustomed to entirely different techniques at home.
Disruptive Influences	• *Change in family membership* (e.g., as a result of death, divorce, or remarriage) • *Residential mobility* due to parents looking for work, being deployed in the military, or being incarcerated • *Physical or mental illness*, alcoholism, or substance abuse • *Economic poverty* and its associated deprivations and challenges for the family • *Stress* in the family affecting parents' sensitivity and responsiveness	Justin has had trouble concentrating since his parents' divorce, and he now shows little enthusiasm for class activities. He has moved to a new neighborhood and has yet to make new friends there.	Show compassion for children undergoing a family transition. Listen patiently if children want to talk. Realize that some families may quickly return to healthy functioning after a change, but others may be in turmoil for lengthy periods. Seek the assistance of a counselor when children have a serious or prolonged difficulty.

OBSERVATION GUIDELINES (continued)
Identifying Family Conditions

CHARACTERISTIC	LOOK FOR	EXAMPLE	IMPLICATION
Maltreatment	• *Frequent injuries* attributed to "accidents" • *Age-inappropriate sexual knowledge* or behavior • *Extreme negative emotions*, perhaps withdrawal, anxiety, or depression • *Excessive aggression and hostility* (e.g., with name calling and hitting) • *Untreated medical or dental needs* • *Chronic hunger* • *Poor hygiene* • *Lack of warm clothing in cold weather*	Johnny often has bruises on his arms and legs, which his mother says are the result of a "blood problem." He recently broke his collarbone, and soon after that he had a black eye. "I fell down the stairs," he explained, and refused to say more.	Immediately report signs of possible maltreatment to a school counselor or principal. Contact Child Protective Services for advice about additional courses of action that are warranted.

perhaps on the playground, in the lunchroom, or in the nurse's office. Educators can welcome brothers and sisters during school events by reserving a room and making durable toys and child-friendly snacks available. During parent–teacher conferences, teachers can refrain from making comparisons between students and their siblings.

• **Put heads of family at ease during conversations.** Most parents want to be heard rather than just "talked at," yet some are anxious, distrustful, or reluctant to voice their perspectives (Hoover-Dempsey & Sandler, 1997; Janssen, Bakker, Bosman, Rosenberg, & Leseman, 2012). Educators can look for signs of discomfort, use friendly body language, comment optimistically about children's abilities, display a sense of humor, treat parents as authorities about children's needs, and assure parents that they should feel free to call whenever they have questions or concerns.

• **Ask heads of family about their goals, concerns, and strategies for supporting children.** During conversations with families, teachers can invite parents to talk about their philosophies of parenting and priorities for children. Some teachers invite parents to come to the classroom to talk about their ancestors and cultures, which can be an excellent way to honor students and their family heritage (Kersey & Masterson, 2009).

• **Advise parents about children's age-related assets and challenges.** Being familiar with children of a particular age level, teachers have special insights into typical developmental needs. For example, teachers realize that infants regularly protest separation from parents at the child care center, young children exhibit oppositional behavior when frustrated, elementary school children worry when they don't read as well as peers, and so on. Teachers can help parents understand age-related characteristics and constructive ways to address them. In Artifact 3-6 a teacher helps parents recognize their middle school children's developmental qualities. You can find a list of typical concerns of parents and ways teachers might address them in the Developmental Trends table "The Family's Concerns for Children of Different Ages."

• **Remember that most parents view their children's behavior as a reflection of their own competence.** Parents typically feel proud when their children are successful in school and get along well with friends. Conversely, they may respond to children's academic difficulties or behavior problems with embarrassment, shame, anger,

To understand your adolescent, you need to consider . . .
. . . the child's basic individuality.
. . . what is expected of anyone of his or her particular age level.
. . . what environment your child finds himself or herself in.

Eleven-year-olds can be . . .
egocentric,
energetic,
always "loving" or "hating";

as well as . . .
not as cooperative or accepting as in the past
more angry than in the past
inattentive
hungry all the time
more interested in the clothes they wear (but not in cleaning them!)
uncertain
more apt to cry
fearful
rebellious
very interested and involved in family activities

ARTIFACT 3-6 Understanding your adolescent. Teachers can be valuable sources of information about child and adolescent development. In this flier for parents, middle school teacher Erin Miguel describes several common characteristics of young adolescents.

DEVELOPMENTAL TRENDS
The Family's Concerns for Children of Different Ages

AGE	TOPICS	DIVERSITY	IMPLICATIONS
Infancy (Birth–2 Years)	**Physical Development** • Ensuring infants' safety by instituting precautions such as placing gates on stairs • Meeting infants' physical needs (e.g., feeding on baby's schedule, diapering when soiled, and easing baby into a sleep schedule that conforms to adults' patterns) • Giving proper nutrition to match physiological needs and pace of growth **Cognitive Development** • Talking with infants and responding enthusiastically to smiling and babbling • Encouraging infants to take turns in conversations and make simple games • Providing appropriate sensory stimulation **Social-Emotional Development** • Abiding by infants' preferences (e.g., after noticing that an infant likes vehicles, sharing picture books with trucks) • Arranging for responsive caregivers during parents' work • Affirming infants' feelings • Responding sympathetically with reasonable promptness to infants' cries	• Some parents promote independence by encouraging infants to try self-help actions, such as picking up bits of food and feeding themselves; others prefer to do these things for infants. • Nap time depends on parents' beliefs about desirable sleeping practices. • Parents may differ in how much they talk with infants. Some verbalize frequently; others focus on nonverbal gestures. • Families differ in beliefs about out-of-home care. Some parents leave infants only for brief periods with familiar relatives. Other parents are comfortable with employed caregivers. • Concerns of parents depend partly on the temperament and health status of infants. When infants are difficult to soothe or sick, parents may be quite concerned.	• Complete daily records of physical care so parents are aware of how their infants' needs are met and the kind of day they have had. • Talk with parents about the developmental milestones you notice in infants. For example, tell parents when you see a new tooth breaking through the gums. • Post a chart of typical developmental milestones (e.g., rolling over, sitting up, uttering a first word) so that parents can watch for emerging skills. Select a chart that emphasizes wide variation in ages at which milestones are attained. • Ask parents to share concerns about their infants, and offer reassurance and, if appropriate, names of local specialists.
Early Childhood (2–6 Years)	**Physical Development** • Ensuring basic safety (e.g., protecting children from street traffic and household chemicals) • Helping children with self-care routines (e.g., dressing, brushing teeth) • Finding appropriate outlets for physical energy **Cognitive Development** • Answering children's incessant questions • Channeling curiosity into constructive activities • Reading stories and promoting foundations for literacy • Preparing for transition to formal schooling **Social-Emotional Development** • Curbing temper tantrums • Promoting sharing with siblings and peers • Addressing conflicts and aggressive behavior • Forming relationships with teachers	• Some parents, worrying about their children's safety, are reluctant to leave them in the care of others. • Low-income families have little or no discretionary income with which to purchase books. • Some kindergartners and first graders have had little or no prior experiences with other children; for instance, they may be only children or may not have previously attended child care or preschool. • Some parents (especially those from higher-income, professional backgrounds) give children many intellectually challenging activities but too few chances to play.	• Suggest possible approaches to teaching young children about self-care habits, social skills, and impulse control. • Keep parents regularly informed about their children's progress in academic and social skills. • Make books available that parents can check out and use at home. • When highly educated parents seem overly concerned about accelerating children's cognitive development, suggest research-based literature that indicates a need for balance between stimulation and relaxation.

AGE	TOPICS	DIVERSITY	IMPLICATIONS
Middle Childhood (6–10 Years) 	**Physical Development** • Fostering healthy eating habits • Using safety equipment (e.g., seat belts in the car, helmets for cycling) • Establishing exercise routines and limiting television and electronic games **Cognitive Development** • Helping children acquire good school habits (e.g., setting goals and checking on progress in assignments) • Promoting mastery of basic academic skills • Enhancing children's education through family involvement **Social-Emotional Development** • Promoting increasing responsibility (e.g., for waking up on time, doing homework) • Monitoring interactions with siblings and playmates • Instilling moral values (e.g., honesty)	• Some parents are under stress from pressures at work. • Some neighborhoods have few playgrounds or other safe places where children can play. • Children's special talents and interests influence their choices of leisure activities. • Some children look after themselves after school, and they may or may not use this time wisely. • Some parents may worry that children are not receiving a sufficiently high-quality education. • Some parents whose children have disabilities are concerned that children's needs are not being met at school.	• Distribute literature about safety measures from local pediatricians, police departments, and fire stations. • Provide resource materials (perhaps through the school library) focused on children's development. • Encourage parents' involvement in school activities and parent–teacher groups. • Suggest programs in the community (e.g., soccer leagues, scout organizations) with opportunities for after-school recreation and skill development.
Early Adolescence (10–14 Years) 	**Physical Development** • Dealing with early stages of puberty • Encouraging physical fitness • Affording new clothing during periods of rapid growth **Cognitive Development** • Supporting expectations for advanced academic performance • Fostering young adolescents' talents and interests **Social-Emotional Development** • Showing sensitivity to self-consciousness about appearance • Accommodating requests for more leisure time with peers • Dealing with increased conflict as adolescents seek greater autonomy • Protecting young people from exploitation on the Internet	• Adolescents differ widely in the age at which they begin puberty. • Some youngsters have little access to recreation. • Some parents have difficulty allowing their adolescents greater independence. • Overt parent–teenager conflicts are rare in some cultures, especially in those that cultivate respect for elders. • Various peer groups encourage unproductive behaviors. • Some students need an extended time to adjust to middle school. • Some parents worry that adolescents indulge in video games rather than finish homework.	• Inform parents about athletic and social programs in the community. • To avoid overload for students, create a coordinated homework program (e.g., math assignments on Monday and Wednesday; writing on Tuesday; others on Thursday). Post due dates on the school's website so that parents can help monitor adolescents' assignments. • Share with parents your expectations for independence and responsibility in young adolescents.
Late Adolescence (14–18 Years) 	**Physical Development** • Keeping track of teenagers' whereabouts • Encouraging students to maintain realistic schedules that allow adequate sleep • Worrying about inexperienced and risky driving • Concern about possible alcohol and drug use **Cognitive Development** • Encouraging youth to persist with challenging assignments • Understanding adolescents' expanding capacity for logical thinking • Educating adolescents about employment and college requirements **Social-Emotional Development** • Worrying about loss of control over teenagers' social activities • Finding a reasonable balance between supervision and independence	• Alcohol and drugs are readily available in most communities, but their use is more frequent and socially acceptable in some families and peer groups than others. • Some parents refuse to believe that their children could be involved in risky behaviors, even when faced with convincing evidence. • Families differ in their knowledge of, and experiences with, higher education, vocational training, and job prospects. • Parents differ in the extent to which they encourage teenagers' employment.	• Advise parents of extracurricular activities and recreation centers for youth. • Share information about part-time job vacancies, internships, and community service openings. • Provide information about possible careers and educational opportunities after high school; address numerous options, including part-time and full-time vocational programs, community colleges, and 4-year colleges and universities.

Sources: Borgen & Hiebert, 2014; W. A. Collins, 1990; V. Davis, 2012; Gallo, Hadley, Angst, Knafl, & Smith, 2008; Guttman, 2013; A. Kirby, Edwards, & Hughes, 2008; Kong et al., 2013; Kutner, Olson, Warner, & Hertzog, 2008; Maccoby, 1984; Montemayor, 1982; Mortimer, Shanahan, & Ryu, 1994; Nesteruk, Marks, & Garrison, 2009; Paikoff & Brooks-Gunn, 1991; Pipher, 1994; Warton & Goodnow, 1991; Youniss, 1983.

or denial. Teachers are more likely to have productive discussions with parents if they avoid placing blame for students' struggles and instead propose that students, parents, and teachers work as a team to identify solutions. Whenever possible, teachers and other practitioners can share at least one favorable comment about a child each time they contact his or her parent (Kersey & Masterson, 2009).

• **Foster leadership in parents.** Parents and other heads of family have important perspectives on how well schools are serving children and how they could be improved. Parents can participate on a school management team, participate in hiring of teachers, and help plan school-wide events (J. Bryan & Henry, 2008; Halgunseth, 2009; C. Rush, 2012).

• **Ask for help.** Parents know their children intimately and are likely to have insights they can share with teachers. They have a right to know about the significant challenges their child encounters and may be able to offer suggestions that will help him or her at school. Parents of children with disabilities are generally informed about their children's condition and might be able to recommend customized educational strategies (Ray, Prewitt-Kinder, & George, 2009; V. Tucker & Schwartz, 2013).

• **Respect cultural differences.** When conferring with parents about children's achievement and classroom behaviors, educators should keep in mind that people from different cultures inevitably have distinct ideas about how children should be educated and disciplined. For example, some immigrant Chinese parents abroad have great respect for teachers yet tutor their children in mathematics to help them achieve high standards that are consistent with accomplishments in their homeland (Wong-Lo & Bai, 2013). As educators talk with family members, they can tell them about their own instructional strategies and find out about how parents help at home. With an open mind, educators can learn about the worthwhile customs that have jump started children's learning.

• **Build positive relationships with families of all ethnic backgrounds.** Children and parents from ethnic minority groups are less likely to enjoy supportive relationships with teachers than are children and parents from European American backgrounds (J. Hughes & Kwok, 2007). Weak or conflicted relationships are particularly likely to occur when teachers are unaware of families' cultural perspectives and communication styles. Knowing that good parent–teacher and teacher–child relationships are beneficial for *all* children, teachers can make extra efforts to reach out to individuals with backgrounds different from their own. Written notes to families about the school schedule, curriculum, and activities can be a good way to set a tone of respect for parents' role in children's education. Afterward, invitations to visit the school, attend parent–teacher–student conferences, and advise the teacher of any concerns are desirable.

• **Accommodate language and literacy differences.** Many immigrant parents are not yet fluent in the dominant languages of their new society. When parents speak a language other than English, educators can invite a bilingual interpreter to meetings. Educators should also have newsletters and other written messages translated whenever it is reasonable to do so.

• **Invite families to join in school activities.** Many family members have special abilities (such as woodworking, calligraphy, and storytelling) that they would happily demonstrate at school. Likewise, some parents are bilingual, and they might step forward to translate school materials (Finders & Lewis, 1994). To benefit from these talents, you may wish to ask families at the beginning of the year about their interests in sharing their expertise at school. Teresa recalls that when her son Connor was in middle school, she and her husband received a booklet containing tear-sheets with occasions for contributing to school activities (such as driving on field trips, volunteering in the classroom, and bringing in treats for special events); it was easy to go through the booklet, choose a few activities, and send the sheets back.

• **Accommodate schedules when asking for help.** Encouraging parents to attend meetings or help at school is most likely to be effective when teachers recognize obstacles in parents' way. Some parents have exhausting work schedules, inadequate child care, and difficulty communicating in English. Still others may be actively involved when their children are in elementary school but inclined to withdraw as adolescents move to middle and secondary levels (J. L. Epstein, 1996; Finders & Lewis, 1994; Roderick & Camburn, 1999). Thus, invitations must be sincere and include a variety of things that could be done during the day, in the evening, or over the weekend.

• **Visit families in their homes and in the community.** Home visits are a relatively common way of supporting parents' efforts at home, especially in families with young children (Gomby, Culross, & Behrman, 1999; S. Smith, 2013). Home visiting programs typically focus on getting to know parents and seeing children's routines. To make home visits maximally effective, educators can present themselves as friendly and nonjudgmental, share a small gift of school supplies, begin the conversation with compliments about the child, ask about the child's chores and hobbies, and offer practical suggestions for this age. Some experts recommend bringing a colleague if possible. When home visits are not possible or appropriate, teachers can learn more about families by getting involved in their community. Educators can attend festivals, community events, and meetings of local groups—in fact, such community involvement is a good idea regardless of whether home visits can be conducted.

• **Advise parents of educationally worthwhile activities that children can do at home.** In general, families that are actively involved in their children's education have children who are academically and socially competent (Toldson & Lemmons, 2013). To help parents choose activities that are especially productive, teachers can offer developmentally supportive guidance. With young children, teachers can encourage engaging children in regular conversation; reading children's books to them; teaching them basic concepts such as shapes, colors, numbers, and the alphabet; and taking them on visits to zoos, farms, museums, concerts, and theatrical performances (Clair, Jackson, & Zweiback, 2012). Parents can support older children's studies by setting aside quiet areas for reading and doing schoolwork, limiting television and electronic games, and expressing interest in children's academic accomplishments. Parents' school involvement tends to decline during adolescence, but parents continue to serve important roles by showing an interest in their sons' and daughters' schoolwork and extracurricular activities. In newsletters and at conferences, school professionals can advise parents of the kind of age-appropriate guidance that is advantageous for children. Educators can also contrast assistance that is generally helpful (e.g., reading daily with younger children, periodically reminding older children over the summer to complete summer packets) with gestures that are less productive (e.g., writing an essay *for* the child, insisting that a mathematical problem be solved with a procedure familiar to the parent but not to the child).

• **Validate the beneficial effects that parents have on children's learning.** For various reasons, including a feeling of discomfort in visiting school and a cultural tradition of showing respect to teachers by not intruding there, some parents avoid school events. Yet many of these parents work tirelessly at home to back up their children's education. Some of these parents will have left their native country to ensure decent opportunities for their children, and others do everything they can at home to teach children relevant skills. In newsletters and during informal conversations with parents picking up and dropping off children, teachers can let parents know about the skills children have learned at home that are paying dividends at school (S. W. Nelson & Guerra, 2009). To keep parents informed, teachers might also post a link to videotapes of children's work at school or send home photographs of their children in a play or other event (Kersey & Masterson, 2009).

• **Inform parents of services available to them.** Parents in distress are sometimes unaware of free and low-cost community services for which they are eligible. Teachers and other professionals can advise them of potentially helpful services, such as outlets for family recreation. A variety of parent education programs, such as those teaching parents how to maintain their composure when provoked by children, have proven effective in improving parents' behaviors (Knerr, Gardner, & Cluver, 2013).

• **Use a variety of communication formats.** Families appreciate hearing about children's accomplishments, and they deserve to know about children's behaviors that consistently interfere with their learning. Likewise, teachers can learn a lot about a child's needs from talking with family members. Here are a few helpful forms of communication:

- *Meetings.* In most schools parent–teacher–student conferences are scheduled one or more times a year. These meetings are an excellent forum for celebrating children's successes and identifying areas that need additional attention. At a conference it may be mutually agreed that the teacher will find new assignments that better match the child's needs, the child will begin keeping track of due dates for homework, and the family will reserve a quiet place at home for the child to do homework uninterrupted.
- *Written communications.* Educators can fill out structured forms to let parents know what their children are doing. Prepared forms that specify activities and leave space for individual comments can be helpful. A growing number of mobile applications also allow teachers to send home notes to parents (Whitehead, 2013). More commonly, paper newsletters communicate about school events, resources, and policies.
- *Telephone conversations.* Telephone calls are useful for introductions and for addressing issues that require immediate attention. Teachers might call parents to express concern when a student's behavior deteriorates unexpectedly, and they might also call to express their excitement about an important step forward. Parents, too, should feel free to call teachers. Keep in mind that many parents are at work throughout the school day; hence it is often helpful for teachers to take calls at home during the early evening hours.
- *E-mail and websites.* Increasingly, educators find that they can maintain regular contact with parents electronically—for instance, by sending e-mail messages and creating web pages that list events, policies, and assignments (D. Johnson, 2013; S. Mitchell, Foulger, & Wetzel, 2009). In Artifact 3-7 you can see a newsletter sent by two elementary school counselors to parents electronically at the end of the school year. Notice the many good suggestions the counselors had for helping children have a fun and enriching summer. Consider, also, that electronic communication can be a two-way form of communication. Parents can be encouraged to send e-mails to teachers and complete brief forms online. Such electronic communication, of course, can be used only when families have easy access to computer technology and the Internet.
- *Parent discussion groups.* In some instances teachers, counselors, and principals may want to assemble a group of parents to discuss mutual concerns. School leaders might want to use a discussion group as a sounding board for evaluating possible school improvement plans. Or, a school counselor might convene a school involvement committee to plan such events as a career night or Black History Month concert (J. Bryan & Henry, 2008).

None of the strategies just described will, in and of itself, guarantee a successful working relationship with heads of families. Meetings with parents occur somewhat infrequently. Written communication is unrealistic for parents who have limited literacy skills. Some families do not want to be visited at home. And, of course, not everyone has a telephone, let alone e-mail. Despite difficulties with staying in touch, effective teachers and other practitioners do their best to form productive partnerships with families (e.g., see the Development and Practice feature "Making Schools Family Friendly" on page 96).

Summary

Parents influence children's development by building relationships, engaging children in activities, showing affection, and disciplining children. Children influence their families, in turn, by virtue of their temperaments, interests, and abilities. Children also influence one another as siblings, but having a sibling is not vital to healthy development. Most

Parent Newsletter

Summer 2015 Vol. 12, No. 5

TIPS FOR STUDENT LEARNING

Early June means the end of the school year, and with it, a lot of kids without much to do. Summer should be relaxing and a fun time for kids, but at the same time they still need to keep their minds and bodies active. The following Tips for Parents will help you plan fun summer activities for your kids.

Keep Their Minds Active

Summer shouldn't mean taking a break from learning, especially when it comes to reading. Studies show that most students experience a loss of reading skills over the summer months, but children who continue to read actually gain skills. During the summer, parents can help children sustain (and even bolster) reading skills, strengthen their vocabulary, and reinforce the benefits of reading for enjoyment.

- Read aloud together with your child every day. Make it fun by reading outdoors. For younger children, be sure to practice letter–sound correspondence, do lots of rhyming and clapping out of syllables, and explore the relationships between oral language and print.
- Set a good example! Keep lots of reading material around the house. Turn off the TV and have family reading time.

- Let kids choose what they want to read. Every so often, read the same book your child is reading and discuss it together.
- Buy books on tape or check them out at the library.
- Visit the library regularly with your children.
- Set a reading goal with your child, such as reading five books, with a reward at completion.

Keep Their Bodies Active

The American Academy of Pediatrics (AAP) warns that more than 2 hours a day in front of the TV leads to increased obesity and lowered academic achievement. The AAP recommends no more than 1 to 2 hours a day of screen time (TV, video games, computer).

- Set limits for how much time they're allowed to watch TV and movies, or play video or computer games.
- Visit the local library for books, videos, music, games, activities, story times, and summer reading programs. For tips and ideas, visit the American Library Association, www.ala.org.
- Sports: Have the kids join a team. If that's not possible, encourage them to play basketball, soccer, baseball, badminton, volleyball, or croquet in the yard or with friends who live nearby.
- Outdoor fun: Tree climbing, jumping rope, camping in the backyard, bike riding, sidewalk chalk, building forts out of cardboard boxes, playing with pets, swimming, jumping on a trampoline, or running through the sprinkler are all great outdoor activities. Check out Family Education's Outdoor Activities, http://fun.familyeducation.com/play/outdoor-activities/33394.html, for tons of great ideas for kids 6 to 10 years old.
- Projects: Encourage children to undertake a project, such as planting a vegetable or flower garden, writing a book or journal, painting a series of paintings on a theme, planning and performing a play, making a movie with a camcorder, etc.
- Learn a new sport or musical instrument, study geology or geography with field trips, or study astronomy and stargazing.
- Arts and crafts activities: Visit Creative Kids at Home's Summer Activities, www.creativekidsathome.com/summerkidsactivities2.html, for fun ideas.
- Start a collection: Kids can collect bugs, rocks, dried plants or flowers, books, or found objects.
- Help children plan, advertise, and run a small summer business, such as babysitting; lawn mowing; pet sitting; or selling baked goodies, crafts, or jewelry they've made;

or have them start plants from seeds and sell them. Read the Money Instructor's Child Business Tips, http://content.moneyinstructor.com/664/kids-starting-business.html.
- Volunteer: Kids learn a lot from helping others. They can help an elderly neighbor, coach a younger team, be a teen volunteer at the local hospital, or organize a charity event such as car wash, barbecue, or mothers' luncheon. Teens can visit Do Something, www.dosomething.org/volunteer, for volunteer opportunities near them.
- Summer camp: Have children go to an accredited camp for a week or two for a change of scenery and good fun. Visit the American Camp Association, www.acacamps.org/, for accredited camps in your area.
- Planned outings: Visit the zoo, museum, planetarium, beach, park, or swimming pool, or go camping or hiking, stargazing, or fishing.
- Cooking: Have children plan, shop, and prepare for a family dinner each week. They can visit the award-winning kids cooking website Spatulatta, www.spatulatta.com/, for measuring instructions, safety tips, recipes, and more.
- Community events: Check your local paper or visit your library to find out about fairs, festivals, and other community events to do as a family.
- Board games: Encourage children to make games exciting by having neighborhood chess tournaments, for example. Or have a family game night.
- Chores: OK, doing chores is rarely fun, but it's important for kids to take part in the family's chores. They learn responsibility, and feel proud that they can contribute. Require that kids clean up after themselves, and have them help out with laundry or watering the garden. Reward them for a job well done.

ARTIFACT 3-7 **Tips for parents.** In this handout, two elementary school counselors advise parents of many constructive options for children over the summer.
Courtesy of Laura Pool and Chelsie Hess, Fort Collins, Colorado.

DEVELOPMENT AND PRACTICE
Making Schools Family Friendly

Learn about families.

- An elementary teacher hosts a Family Welcome Night at the beginning of the school year and asks parents to complete a questionnaire (available in English and a few other common languages) about children's interests, abilities, and hobbies (Kersey & Masterson, 2009). (Middle Childhood)
- A high school adviser calls parents at the beginning of the school year. The adviser asks the parents about any special needs, informs parents of his cell phone number and e-mail address, and encourages their contact with questions or concerns. (Late Adolescence)

Help children and their families feel that they are appreciated members of the school.

- A caregiver of toddlers provides storage boxes ("cubbies") for each child. Each box is adorned with photographs of the child and his or her family. Children point to their parents and other family members throughout the day. (Early Childhood)
- A middle school principal sets up a school improvement team of a few teachers, the school counselor, a group of parents, and a couple of students. The principal treats the team with utmost respect and sends everyone letters of appreciation for their time and efforts. (Early Adolescence)

Recognize the significance of families in children's lives.

- A music teacher asks students to bring in the lyrics from a favorite family song. She posts the words of the songs on a bulletin board labeled "My Family and Me." (Middle Childhood)
- A middle school social studies teacher invites parents and other family members to come to class and describe their jobs and the history of their ancestors. (Young Adolescence)

Acknowledge the strengths of family backgrounds.

- An elementary teacher asks a community leader to come to class and talk about the cultural traditions of immigrant families. (Middle Childhood)
- When planning a lesson on the history of farming in Colorado, a middle school social studies teacher encourages families to send in photographs of the farm tools they use while planting and harvesting crops. (Early Adolescence)

Use a variety of formats to communicate with parents.

- A fourth-grade teacher works with the children in his class to produce a monthly newsletter for parents. Two versions of the newsletter are created, one in English and one in Spanish. (Middle Childhood)

- A high school drama teacher takes photographs of individual students during play practice and sends home the images with e-mail messages. (Late Adolescence)

Acknowledge children's strengths, even when communicating about shortcomings.

- An elementary teacher is concerned about a child's disruptive behavior in class. In a phone call to the girl's parents, the teacher asks for the parents' insights, "Although I appreciate your daughter's energy and sociability, I'd like to work with you to find a way to increase her time on task" (Christenson, Palan, & Scullin, 2009, p. 11). (Middle Childhood)
- A high school counselor talks on the phone with parents of a student. She describes several areas in which the student has made considerable progress but also asks for advice about strategies that might help him be more agreeable with peers. (Late Adolescence)

Be sensitive to parents' concerns.

- A 3-year-old girl's parents are concerned with her speech. They mention to her teacher that she says "sool" for "school" and "hairpane" for "airplane." The teacher reassures the parents that such mispronunciations are common in young children, but also advises the parents that a speech therapist is available at the district office if they want an expert opinion. (Early Childhood)
- A school counselor talks with worried parents of a 16-year-old girl who has begun smoking and possibly experimenting with drugs. Thinking about the girl's interest in photography, the counselor informs the parents about an after-school photography club, with hopes that companionship with more academically oriented peers will get the student back on track. (Late Adolescence)

Encourage parents and guardians to get involved with school activities.

- An infant caregiver asks for volunteers to give their input into decisions about programs for children, such as how to staff a new room when enrollment grows or the kind of outdoor play space that makes the most sense given toddlers' needs and the limited budget of the center (J. Daniel, 2009). (Infancy)
- A high school principal sends home a book of "coupons" printed with assorted activities that parents might assist with at school (e.g., tutoring in the classroom, baking goodies for an open house, serving on the parent advisory group). She supplements the book with a letter expressing her hope that all parents who have time will return at least one coupon. (Late Adolescence)

families provide safe and nurturing environments. However, some families maltreat children, either by neglecting them or by subjecting them to physical, sexual, or emotional abuse. Such maltreatment can have negative long-term effects, which can be ameliorated with intervention.

Effective partnerships between educators and families are grounded in mutual respect and ongoing communication. Toward these ends, teachers can validate the contributions of families. They can also accommodate major transitions in the family (e.g., a parent's military deployment or incarceration), diversify their methods of communication (e.g., parent–teacher–student conferences, newsletters, the telephone), and encourage parents to become—and stay—actively involved in their children's education.

Assessing Children 3-1

Practice assessing membership and support in families and methods for establishing effective partnerships with heads of family.

ENHANCEDetext *application exercise*

ENHANCEDetext *self-check*

CHILDREN IN A DIVERSE SOCIETY

Increasingly diverse populations attend school, creating an opportunity—and a responsibility—for teachers to adapt their methods for the betterment of all children. In this section we focus on the range of experiences children have as members of defined races, social groups, and residents of particular communities.

Children's Experiences in Diverse Groups

Across the world, children attending school include individuals who are growing up with different skin colors, religions, traditions, and primary languages. In the United States, about 23 percent of children live with at least one foreign-born parent, 22 percent speak a language other than English at home, and 5 percent have limited mastery of English (Federal Interagency Forum on Child and Family Statistics, 2013d). As you can see in Table 3-1, the population is becoming more varied in its ethnic and racial backgrounds.

TABLE 3-1 Percentages of U.S. Children in Racial and Ethnic Groups

RACE AND ETHNICITY	ESTIMATES FOR YEAR		PROJECTIONS FOR YEAR			
	2000	2010	2020	2030	2040	2050
American Indian and Alaska Native	1.0	0.9	0.9	0.9	0.8	0.8
Asian	3.5	4.4	4.7	5.0	5.6	6.0
Black	14.8	14.1	13.0	12.5	11.8	11.2
Native Hawaiian and Other Pacific Islander	0.2	0.2	0.2	0.2	0.2	0.2
White	61.2	53.6	50.9	46.4	41.7	38.0
Two or More Races	2.2	3.7	3.4	4.0	4.5	4.9
Hispanic	17.2	23.2	26.9	31.1	35.5	38.8

Note: Figures are for U.S. children 17 years and under. Accumulated percentages may not equal 100 due to rounding error. Hispanic children may be of any race but have parents who have identified them as being Hispanic. The percentages shown for children who are American Indian and Alaska Native, Asian, Black, Native Hawaiian and Other Pacific Islander, White, and Two or More Races are those whose parents did not identify them as being of Hispanic heritage. Children whose parents identified them as Hispanic are counted in this table as being Hispanic regardless of any race they might also have selected.

Source: Federal Interagency Forum on Child and Family Statistics, 2013e.

Ethnicity and Race

A child's **ethnicity** refers to the group of people with whom he or she identifies as having a common heritage, tribe, geographical origin, language, religious faith, or combination of characteristics. A child's **race** refers to the group of people with whom he or she has shared physical features such as skin color, eye hair texture, and facial bone structure. Both factors are influential, ethnicity primarily because it affects children's exposure to traditions and beliefs, and race because of the tendency for people in society to hold expectations and biases about others based on appearance.

Ethnicity has a complex connection to culture. Typically, an ethnic group includes people from several different cultural roots. For example, people who are *Hispanic* tend to speak Spanish or Portuguese (or are descended from individuals who spoke these languages) and originate (or whose ancestors originated) from one of several very different regions (Spain, Portugal, Mexico, Central and South American countries, and Spanish-speaking Caribbean nations); as a result, individual Hispanics share a few common values but follow many distinct cultural practices (C. B. Fisher, Jackson, & Villarruel, 1998; García & Jensen, 2007). In addition, people who are Hispanic can come from any racial group. The implication of this heterogeneity is that knowing a child comes from a Hispanic American background gives only a rough idea as to what his or her cultural practices and beliefs might be.

Children from a single race (e.g., Asians) have, by definition, certain physical features in common but may or may not have a common ethnic heritage. For example, people in the United States who are white (also known as Caucasians or European Americans) generally have ancestors from such dissimilar cultural groups as the Irish, French, or Slovaks, and may, a generation or two after being in the country, draw on selected customs of their ancestors while typically thinking of themselves as Americans. For centuries white people have been the dominant group in American society. Today, to the extent their financial circumstances allow, individuals who are white have a range of options from which to choose professions, residences, and lifestyles. Many individuals in the United States who are black (often called African Americans) have ancestors who were brought to North America as slaves from western Africa. Despite being discouraged from exercising their African customs, black Americans have successfully infused traditions related to spirituality, storytelling, and extended family networks into their daily lives. Today, many of their descendants take pride in this resilience (Elmore & Gaylord-Harden, 2013; Vereen, Hill, & Butler, 2013). Struggles by black families for full access to American resources persist, however, due to a long history of economic hardship and present-day discrimination.

Children's perceptions of their ethnicity and race can change across contexts and with development. A boy with two Korean parents who is raised in Australia and whose family moves to England during his adolescence may initially identify as Australian, gradually perceive himself as Australian *and* English, and be seen by others as Asian. Today numerous children are *multiethnic* or *multiracial,* claiming ancestry from more than a single ethnic or racial group. A girl whose mother has both African American and Native American heritages and whose father emigrated from Spain will be exposed to several family traditions. Multiethnic and multiracial children may affiliate with two or more distinct groups and selectively carry out particular traditions depending on the context (e.g., speaking English at school and Spanish at home; Henriksen & Paladino, 2009; Kennedy & Romo, 2013). Multiethnic and multiracial children tend to become flexible and skillful in navigating through different cultural environments but occasionally confront pejorative comments about their blended heritage (Henriksen & Paladino, 2009).

Immigration

Ethnicity is especially salient when people move from one environment to another—for instance, when they immigrate to a new country. When different cultural groups exist in the same region, people interact and learn about one another. As immigrants participate in new customs and take on the values of their adopted culture, **acculturation** occurs. Acculturation takes four different forms:

- **Assimilation**. Some individuals totally embrace the values and customs of the new culture, giving up their original identity in the process. Assimilation is typically a gradual

BIOECOLOGY OF DEVELOPMENT

A child's ethnicity, race, and culture afford distinct opportunities and occasionally noticeable hardships.

process that occurs over several generations when immigrants feel accepted by the host society.[6]

- **Separation**. Sometimes people move to a new culture without taking on any of their new community's cultural practices. Complete rejection of a new culture may occur when individuals have little need to interact with people in that culture or when the new society segregates immigrants to isolated regions.
- **Selective adoption**. Sometimes immigrants acquire some customs from the new culture while retaining other customs from their homeland. For example, families begin to celebrate a few holidays of their new culture while continuing to observe other traditions from their country of origin. Children are likely to adopt the host society's customs when parents encourage them to embrace their new community's traditions and when they feel accepted as valued participants.
- **Bicultural orientation**. Some people retain their original culture yet also acquire beliefs and master practices of their new culture, and they readily adjust behaviors to fit the particular contexts in which they find themselves. A bicultural orientation is promoted when the new society is tolerant of diversity. (Delgado-Gaitan, 1994; Mana, Orr, & Mana, 2009; Yoon et al., 2013)

In previous decades total assimilation was considered by many people in the United States to be the optimal situation for immigrants. The route to success was presumed to be a "melting pot" in which people of different backgrounds become increasingly similar. More recently, researchers have discovered that when young immigrants give up their family's cultural values and traditions, they are at greater risk for developing serious conflicts with their parents, achieving at lower levels in school, and engaging in such risky behaviors as consuming alcohol and drugs, having unprotected sex, and engaging in criminal activities (Hwang, 2006; Roche, Ghazarian, & Fernandez-Esquer, 2012; Roosa et al., 2009; Ying & Han, 2007).

Therefore, the idea that societies with large immigrant populations are melting pots is giving way to the idea that civilizations can be more productively thought of as a "mosaics" of cultural and ethnic pieces that all legitimately contribute to the greater good of society (C. B. Fisher et al., 1998). Consistent with this view, many immigrant children and their families adjust most successfully when they learn certain aspects of their new culture while also retaining other aspects of their original culture—that is, when they show a pattern of either *selective adoption* or *bicultural orientation* (Rutland et al., 2013; Upegui-Hernández, 2012). You can read more about children from different countries in the Development in Culture feature "Immigrant Children."

Environmental Challenges and Coping Strategies

Children from immigrant families and those from ethnic and racial minority backgrounds face distinct risks and assets. One unnecessary hardship is that children's abilities and motivations are easily misunderstood by others. Unless they come from a similar background, or make an effort to learn about children's everyday experiences, educators may be unaware of the skills and traditions that children bring to school (C. Brown & Chu, 2012; Olmedo, 2009; Riojas-Cortez, Huerta, Flores, Perez, & Clark, 2008).

All children possess what Puerto Rican American psychologist **Luis Moll** and his colleagues have called *funds of knowledge*, the information and traditions that are essential for completing activities in a child's household and local community (Moll, Amanti, Neff, & González, 2005). Examples include knowledge needed to plan and prepare the family's meals, celebrate traditions at home, take part in hobbies, get along with others in the community, and so on. Such personal knowledge defines how children see the world and determines their expectations about values that are important and ways in which relationships are to be carried out. When children's funds of knowledge go unrecognized at school, children may feel confused or disengaged (Hogg, 2011).

---

[6]Developmental scholars use the term *assimilation* in two separate ways. In Piaget's theory *cognitive assimilation* refers to a process of learning. In studies of immigration, *cultural assimilation* is a gradual progression by which settlers take on customs and beliefs of their adopted society, giving up their original cultural patterns in the process.

DEVELOPMENT IN CULTURE
Immigrant Children

Individual children in immigrant families have a few similar experiences. They go to school, make friends, learn about two or more cultures, and master increasingly difficult concepts and skills. Often they learn a second language and adjust to discrepant expectations at home and in the dominant community. But children from immigrant families are by no means fully alike. They have quite different experiences depending on their personal characteristics and the circumstances of their family's immigration, their parents' jobs and income, and their culture's standing in the adopted society (Akiba & García Coll, 2003; Glick & Bates, 2010; Hernandez, Denton, & Macartney, 2010; Urdan, 2012).

Such similarities and differences are evident among children from immigrant families in Providence, Rhode Island (García Coll & Marks, 2009). Many of the immigrant families there had moved from Cambodia, the Dominican Republic, or Portugal. Children from these three cultural groups had somewhat comparable experiences in that they grew up in low-income families, had parents with high expectations for their education, and achieved at relatively high levels at school. Yet the three groups also varied in their beliefs and customs. Cambodian, Dominican, and Portuguese American children ate the foods of their ancestors, celebrated holidays compatible with their separate heritages, and worshipped in their own churches or temples. Within each group, individual children developed unique habits and self-perceptions.

ALIKE, DIFFERENT, AND UNIQUE. Immigrant children face some similar developmental tasks but also different experiences and family circumstances.

Families from Cambodia had moved to the United States to escape war, starvation, and persecution. Two parents with approximately 4 years of formal education were typical heads of Cambodian American families. Parents spoke Khmer to their children and were somewhat segregated from others in the new society. Teachers perceived Cambodian American parents to be uninvolved because the parents rarely came to school. However, from the parents' perspective, parents should defer to teachers' authority and not interfere with instruction. Teachers saw these children as attentive, conscientious, and socially skilled.

Families from the Dominican Republic had usually moved to the United States for economic opportunities and a safe environment for their children. Single-parent and two-parent families were both common in Dominican immigrants. Families remained closely connected with extended family members back on the island, traveling back and forth between Providence and the Dominican Republic for birthdays, weddings, funerals, and family crises; likewise Dominican relatives often came to visit families in Providence. A strong network of Dominicans in the United States eased the adaptation of new immigrants and enriched children with role models, festivals, and other cultural resources. With their typically dark skin, Dominican American youngsters were perceived to be black by others, yet the Dominican American children generally identified with their Dominican heritage and not as African Americans. The children tended to do well in school but frequently received lower grades as they grew older, and they had relatively high rates of absenteeism from school.

Families from Portugal tended to enter long-standing communities of Portuguese Americans. Recently emigrating Portuguese families had moved to the United States for economic opportunities. Most families had two parents in the home. Members of the Portuguese American community celebrated their cultural heritage but also moved in and out of the mainstream society with ease, in part because their white, European American facial features resembled the appearance of local residents. Established Portuguese sports clubs and religious societies welcomed new immigrants, and numerous Portuguese Americans had penetrated positions of authority, including as police, political officials, and teachers. Two parents with little formal education were the typical heads of family.

Children in each of these three immigrant cultures generally coped well, drew on rich traditions from the cultures of their families, and took advantage of opportunities in the new land. In other respects the children were unique. They developed personally distinct ways of expressing themselves and combining the various cultural practices in which they were immersed.

Another challenge many racial minority children face is *discrimination,* inequitable treatment as a result of group membership. Unfortunately, numerous children from racial minority groups encounter insults and exclusion by peers, rude treatment from storeowners, and low academic expectations from teachers (G. H. Brody et al., 2006; T. R. Coker et al., 2009; Killen, Mulvey, & Hitti, 2013). Some parents of color have few options with housing and employment due to truncated schooling, limited income, and biases of bank lenders and hiring authorities (Roscigno, Karafin, & Tester, 2009; J. C. Ziegert & Hanges, 2005). Due in part to these circumstances, ethnic minority families are more likely than European American families to live in undesirable neighborhoods and lack sufficient income to purchase fresh food, adequate health care, and such educational materials as books, magazines, calculators, and computers.

Many children from ethnic and racial minority backgrounds learn to cope with being misunderstood and discriminated against (García Coll et al., 1996; Gaylord-Harden, Burrow, & Cunningham, 2012; McAdoo & Martin, 2005). One effective coping strategy is to develop a clear sense of accomplishments by their ancestors; another is to deflect any assaults on their race or ethnicity with pride in family heritage. For example, many children develop strong **ethnic** and **racial identities** in that they embrace their membership in an ethnic or racial group, gain a sense of being like others who share this classification, and adopt values and behaviors that are characteristic of the group. Having a strong understanding of, and commitment to, one's origins, including a well-defined sense of self with multiethnic and multiracial heritages, is positively related to adjustment in youth, as for example, is the case with qualities of leadership and responsibility being present in those Latino and Latina adolescents with strong bicultural identities (Acevedo-Polakovich et al., 2014).

As you might expect, it takes time to develop such identities. Young children tend to see their ethnicity and race in fairly simple terms, for example, as being Latino because of speaking Spanish or African American because of having dark skin. As they develop cognitively, children increasingly understand messages they hear from parents and others about people with whom they share an ethnicity or race. They may hear tales of ancestors' struggles and victories in discriminatory contexts and see media portrayals of predecessors they identify with in particular roles—perhaps as leaders and trailblazers for humane causes or, alternatively, as violent and deviant troublemakers (C. B. Fisher et al., 1998; M. B. Spencer, 2006). Eventually, many youngsters form a coherent set of beliefs about their ethnic and racial groups, take pride in their cultural traditions, and reject demeaning messages from others (Luster, 1992; Ogbu, 1994; Phinney, 1990; L. O. Rogers et al., 2012; M. B. Spencer, Noll, Stoltzfus, & Harpalani, 2001).

A second important coping strategy is to take advantage of confidence-building strategies that are present in some form in every culture. For example, many African American families cultivate positive personal qualities, such as deep religious convictions and commitments to extended family members, which sustain them in difficult environmental conditions, including high unemployment and poverty (R. L. Coles, 2006; McBride, 2013; McCreary, Slavin, & Berry, 1996). Similarly, many children in Latino families benefit from the tradition of *familism*, a priority for collective decision making, such that the needs of the family as a whole are more important than the desires of any individual family member (Brittian et al., 2013).

Creating Supportive Environments for All Children

With growing diversity in our population, teachers can expect that, regardless of the actual community within which they work, they will have an opportunity to support youngsters from diverse ethnic and racial groups. You can see some illustrations of adults nurturing students in the Development and Practice feature "Supporting Children from Culturally and Linguistically Diverse Backgrounds." Here are some related strategies for helping children from varied backgrounds achieve academic and social success:

• **Reflect on how your own cultural experiences affect your responses to people from different ethnicities and races.** Like all human beings, teachers generally see their own customs as sensible, and others' traditions as quaint and occasionally bizarre (P. J. Miller & Goodnow, 1995). Reflecting on your upbringing, privileges, and experiences with other groups can sensitize you to any personal biases you might harbor about children from an unfamiliar culture (Tilley & Taylor, 2013; H. Wang & Olson, 2009). To gain self-insight, you can talk with your family and read about your own cultural origins as well as those of other groups in your community. With a clearer recognition of the values and traditions that you have come to take for granted, you are ready to learn about others with an open mind, By immersing yourself in community events, reading historical biographies of prominent figures,

Establish connections with local communities.

- An elementary school in a Mexican American community in Chicago reaches out to families by inviting children, parents, and teachers to take part in Mexican folkloric dance classes (Olmedo, 2009). The school includes both Mexican and American flags on an outdoor mural and celebrates the holidays of both nations at school. (Middle Childhood).

- A high school teacher encourages adolescents to take part in community service projects. The students may choose from a wide range of possibilities, including neighborhood cleanups, story time with preschoolers at the library, and volunteer work at a food bank. (Late Adolescence)

Learn about the *funds of knowledge* children develop at home.

- A preschool invites families to describe how they use plants as ingredients in health remedies and meals (Riojas-Cortez et al., 2008). The family's strategies for using plants are integrated into science lessons, and the families are invited to take part in the lessons. (Early Childhood)

- A team of educators visits the family of fourth grader Jacobo (Genzuk, 1999). The team learns that Jacobo's father is a skilled hydraulics mechanic and that Jacobo himself is interested in mechanics. His teacher asks Jacobo to create an automotive journal that can be used as a resource in the classroom. Jacobo enthusiastically writes in his journal and shares it with others in the class. (Middle Childhood)

Endorse children's background experiences in the classroom.

- An infant caregiver purchases tunes of lullabies in Spanish and Mandarin Chinese, the two languages that are most often spoken by the immigrant families she serves. She encourages the babies to clap their hands and sway with the music. (Infancy)

- A teacher asks her second-grade children to bring in lyrics from rap songs and then screens out those that are offensive. The children perform the selected songs and analyze them in terms of their literal and figurative meanings, rhyme scheme, and principles of alliteration (Ladson-Billings, 1995). (Middle Childhood)

Adapt to the cultural beliefs and practices of children.

- A Japanese family has recently placed their 8-month-old son in part-time child care. The baby is accustomed to his mother hand feeding him. His new caregiver holds him during mealtime and offers him small pieces of food. (Infancy)

- A third-grade teacher notices that only a few of the children are willing to answer her questions about common pets, even though it is clear from individual conversations that most have pets. She discovers that bringing attention to oneself is not appropriate in the children's culture and so modifies her style to allow for group responses. (Middle Childhood)

Use materials that represent all ethnic groups in a competent light.

- An elementary school librarian examines history books in the school's collection for the manner in which various cultural groups are represented. The librarian orders a few additional books to balance the treatment of groups that are excluded or misrepresented in the compendium. (Middle Childhood)

- A middle school history teacher peruses a textbook to make sure that it portrays all ethnic groups in a nonstereotypical manner. He supplements the book with readings that highlight important roles played by members of various ethnic groups throughout history. (Early Adolescence)

Arrange for children of different backgrounds to get to know one another.

- A teacher invites heads of family to celebrate their children's birthdays at school on one Friday afternoon each month, with summer birthdays celebrated in August and May. The teacher also arranges for volunteers to bring in healthful treats on each Birthday Friday so that no one is inadvertently left out due to diet restrictions. The birthday celebrants are encouraged to bring in photographs of their families and tell the class who everyone is. (Middle Childhood)

- To promote awareness of and involvement in community issues, a high school teacher engages his class in a large-scale public service project. He forms small groups with students from different backgrounds that work on the various phases of the project, for instance, collecting data about public opinions, identifying relevant community agencies, and contacting local officials who might be willing to speak to the class. (Late Adolescence)

Expose youngsters to successful models from various ethnic backgrounds.

- A kindergarten teacher in an ethnically diverse school collaborates with a third-grade teacher in the building to establish a reading program. The older children come to kindergarten once a week to read to their younger buddies. Older children gain experience in reading aloud, and younger children enjoy the stories and attention. (Early Childhood)

- A middle school teacher invites several successful professionals from minority groups to tell her class about their jobs. When some youngsters seem interested in particular career paths, she arranges for them to spend time with these professionals at their workplaces. (Early Adolescence)

Be neutral, inclusive, and respectful regarding children's religious practices.

- A preschool teacher encourages children in her class to bring in decorations and other materials showing how they celebrate holidays during the winter months. Children bring in decorations related to Christmas, Ramadan, Kwanzaa, Hanukkah, and the winter solstice. The teacher passes around the materials and explains that children in her class celebrate many different holidays. (Early Childhood)

- A social studies middle school teacher asks students to select a figure in history who struggled against religious persecution. After the students have conducted individual investigations, they take part in a class discussion and learn about the wide range of religious groups that have experienced persecution. (Early Adolescence)

Orient recent immigrants to the expectations and institutions of their new society.

- A middle school principal tries to meet with every new immigrant family. At a New Arrivals meeting, the principal hands out a simple welcome basket with a couple of pieces of fruit donated by a local company. The principal also hands out a list of community resources in the area. (Early Adolescence)

- A high school offers a Newcomer Program for recent immigrants. The program introduces incoming students to practices in American society and advises students about the school's calendar, extracurricular activities, and sponsored social events (National Clearinghouse for English Language Acquisition, 2006). (Late Adolescence) and studying anthropologists' reports, you can enhance your sensitivity to the customs and heritages of the children and families you serve.

• **Accept that what you do (and fail to do) can perpetuate inequities.** Although very few professionals intentionally discriminate against young people based on their ethnicity or skin color, their actions sometimes perpetuate group differences (Howard, 2007; McGrady & Reynolds, 2013). For instance, some teachers rarely modify instruction for students with diverse needs; instead, they present instruction in a take-it-or-leave-it manner. Clearly, teaching children from diverse backgrounds requires more than giving lip service to cultural diversity; it requires a genuine commitment to modifying interactions with children so they can achieve their full academic potential (Bakari, 2000).

• **Recognize the variation that exists *within* social groups.** It is human nature to see cultural groups as simple, uniform entities. The reality is that any given group (e.g., children who are Native Americans or those whose parents are Hawaiian natives) is usually quite heterogeneous. For example, immigrant parents hold beliefs about education that vary depending on their country of origin and their personal experiences—some might be seasonal migrant workers and others diplomats, foreign-born university students, or political asylum seekers (Kağitçibaşi, 2007). And, of course, children have varied interests, skills, and views that transcend their group's typical patterns. Teachers can get to know children as individuals by asking them about their hopes for the future, preferences for spending free time, interests at school, responsibilities at home, and prior experiences with academic subjects (Hogg, 2011; Villegas & Lucas, 2007).

• **Expect children to follow practices from two or more cultures.** Earlier we introduced the idea that immigrant children often adjust well when they hold onto their family's cultural beliefs and practices while incorporating values and practices favored by the new society. The same principle holds for multiethnic children: Children raised by parents from different ethnic cultures are likely to value traditions from both sides of the family. Teachers and other practitioners can recognize that children who are exposed to more than one culture need tolerant settings in which they can safely explore the separate parts of their multifaceted cultural heritage.

• **Integrate children's *funds of knowledge* into the curriculum.** Practitioners increase their effectiveness with youngsters by tailoring their services to children's cultural backgrounds and personal experiences (Howard, 2007; McMillan, 2013; G. M. Rodriguez, 2013). Being careful not to stereotype children, teachers can regularly allow children to make choices that include a range of cultural materials, work styles, and traditions. One elementary teacher learned that children sold candy to contribute to family income and developed an interdisciplinary lesson on confectionery (Moll, Amanti, & Neff, 1992). In an elementary school in Canada, children who were Punjabi Sikh interviewed their grandparents and then prepared picture books about family upbringings (Marshall & Toohey, 2010). A secondary school teacher arranged for students in grades 8 and 9 to use clay animation to tell about their lives in a compelling visual arts demonstration (Henderson & Zipin, 2010). The Observation Guidelines table "Identifying Cultural Practices and Beliefs" on page 104 lists some values and learning methods that teachers and other school personnel can accommodate.

• **Include a spectrum of cultural perspectives in instructional materials and strategies.** As societies become the multicultural mosaic we spoke of earlier, it is essential that schools support this diversity. In **culturally responsive teaching**, teachers learn about children's cultural backgrounds and individual characteristics and use this information as they select curricula and instructional strategies (A. Gunn, Bennett, Evans, Peterson, & Welsh, 2013; N. L. Norton, 2014; Santamaria, 2009; Villegas & Lucas, 2007). Hence, a teacher might examine immigration during a social studies unit and invite parents to relay their experiences in moving from one society to another. Children can learn a lot from materials that include the practices, experiences, and contributions of people from more than one culture, as 9-year-old

FOR FURTHER EXPLORATION . . .

Read about how parents and teachers can develop distinctly different beliefs about children.

ENHANCEDetext
content extension

Preparing for Your Licensure Examination

Your teaching test might ask you to identify classroom accommodations for cultural differences in language, communication, and interpersonal relationships.

OBSERVATION GUIDELINES
Identifying Cultural Practices and Beliefs

CHARACTERISTIC	LOOK FOR	EXAMPLE	IMPLICATION
Individualism	• *Independence,* assertiveness, and self-reliance • *Eagerness to pursue individual assignments* and tasks • *Willingness to compete* against others • *Pride in personal accomplishments*	When given the choice of doing a project either by herself or with a partner, Melissa decides to work alone. She is thrilled when she earns a third-place ribbon in a statewide competition.	Provide time for independent work, and accommodate children's individual achievement levels. Give feedback about individual accomplishments in private rather than in front of peers.
Collectivism	• *Willingness to depend on others* • *Emphasis on group accomplishments* over individual achievements • *Preference for cooperative rather than competitive tasks* • *Concern about bringing honor* to one's family • *Strong sense of loyalty* to other family members	Tsusha is a talented and hard-working seventh grader. She is conscientious about bringing home her graded assignments to show her parents but appears uncomfortable when praised in front of classmates.	Emphasize group progress and achievement more than individual successes. Make frequent use of structured cooperative learning activities in heterogeneous groups with specific roles and expectations for everyone.
Behavior Toward Authority Figures	• *Looking down* in the presence of an authority figure versus looking an authority figure in the eye • *Observing an adult quietly* versus asking questions when one doesn't understand	A Native American child named Jimmy never says a word to his teacher. He appears frightened when his teacher looks him in the eye and greets him each morning. One day, the teacher looks in another direction and says, "Hello, Jimmy" as he enters the classroom. "Why hello Miss Jacobs," he responds enthusiastically (Gilliland, 1988, p. 26).	Recognize that different cultures show respect for authority figures in dissimilar ways; don't misinterpret lack of eye contact or nonresponse as an indication of disinterest or disrespect.
Valued Activities	• *Hopes for high achievement* in traditional academic areas • *Personal values* for school achievement but lack of confidence in performing academically • *Expectations for excellence* in culture-specific activities, such as art or dance • *Enjoyment in retelling or making up stories* or preference for factual accounts	Clarence is obviously a very bright young man, but he reveals considerable ambivalence about showing his knowledge in front of peers. He often earns high marks in papers he writes, but he rarely participates in class discussions and does not show his knowledge on tests.	Show how academic subjects relate to children's lives. Acknowledge youngsters' achievement in nonacademic as well as academic pursuits. Continually communicate confidence in the potential of youngsters and encourage hard work and good study habits. Encourage children to share music and artwork from their society.
Conceptions of Time	• *Concern for punctuality* and acknowledgment of deadlines for assignments • *Relaxed feelings about specific times* and schedules	Lucy and her parents are diligent about going to parent–teacher conferences but often arrive well after their scheduled time.	Encourage punctuality in order to enhance children's long-term success in Western society. At the same time, recognize that not all children are concerned about clock time. Advise parents that they can help you by being punctual if they repeatedly arrive late.

Sources: Banks & Banks, 1995; Basso, 1984; García, 1994; Garrison, 1989; Gilliland, 1988; C. A. Grant & Gomez, 2001; Heath, 1983; Irujo, 1988; Losey, 1995; Maschinot, 2008; N. L. Norton, 2014; McAlpine & Taylor, 1993; L. S. Miller, 1995; Ogbu, 1994; Oyserman & Lee, 2007; Raval, 2013; N. Reid, 1989; Shweder et al., 1998; M. B. Spencer, 2006; Stoicovy, Fee, & Fee, 2012; Tharp, 1994; Torres-Guzmán, 1998; Trawick-Smith, 2010.

Dana reveals in her school notes in Artifact 3-8. Following are additional illustrations of what teachers might do:

- In history, look at wars and other major events from more than one perspective (e.g., the Spanish perspective of the Spanish-American War and Native American groups' views of pioneers' westward migration in North America).
- In social studies, examine discrimination and oppression.
- In mathematics, use numerical problems that refer to traditional legends and calendars.
- In literature, present the work of minority authors and poets.
- In art, consider creations and techniques by artists from around the world.
- In music, teach songs from many cultures and nations.
- In physical education, teach games or folk dances from other countries and cultures. (Asai, 1993; Averill et al., 2009; Boutte & McCormick, 1992; McMillan, 2013; N. L. Norton, 2014; NCSS Task Force on Ethnic Studies Curriculum Guidelines, 1992; Sleeter & Grant, 1999)

ARTIFACT 3-8 **Light.** In the elementary years, children are able to understand basic differences in the way people of different cultures live. Nine-year-old Dana learned about how people in two societies use natural and artificial light. Art by Dana.

As you might expect, children of different ages have varying abilities to understand the symbolic meaning of another culture's customs. Thus teachers should adjust their culturally responsive strategies to the age range of their students. During middle childhood, children can learn about the tangible, concrete customs and livelihoods of different cultures. As children grow older, they become increasingly able to learn the details, motivations, and underlying symbolism of people's traditions.

- **Address gaps in children's understandings—in the contexts of their strengths.** Some children who have missed a lot of school or previously studied in culturally *un*responsive schools lack basic skills. Teachers can help these children by addressing their academic delays while also recognizing personal talents and interests—maybe a fascination with monkeys, captivation with technology, or an ability to speak multiple languages. You could encourage children to write a short book on a topic in which they hold unusual expertise conduct a presentation for class, or apply their talents in a group project. In this manner, children get to shine while improving their basic skills.

- **Foster respect for diverse cultures and ethnic groups.** When talking about cultural practices, teachers can emphasize the merits of traditions practiced by families. Similarly, teachers can select materials that represent groups in a positive light—for instance, by choosing books and movies that portray people of varying ethnic backgrounds as legitimate participants in society rather than as exotic "curiosities" who live in a separate world. Educators should avoid (or at least comment critically on) materials that portray members of minority groups in an overly simplistic, romanticized, exaggerated, or otherwise stereotypical fashion (Banks, 1994; Boutte & McCormick, 1992; Pang, 2007).

- **Arrange for children from different backgrounds to interact.** When youngsters have positive interactions with people from backgrounds other than their own, they often gain respect for these cultures. In schools in which children come from several distinct backgrounds, teachers and school counselors might promote friendships among students by implementing cooperative learning activities, teaching simple phrases in represented languages, and encouraging schoolwide participation in extracurricular activities. In culturally homogeneous schools, professionals might take youngsters beyond school boundaries—perhaps engaging them in community service projects or arranging a visit to an inclusive center for the arts.

Preparing for Your Licensure Examination
Your teaching test might ask you to identify ways to integrate children's cultural backgrounds into curricula.

• **When conflicts occur, find constructive ways to address them.** Occasionally, children follow cultural practices that are contradictory—at least on the surface—to those adhered to in the classroom. When this happens, it is a good idea to learn more about these customs. Investing in such an effort can help practitioners understand why children act as they do and what accommodations are necessary ("OK, avoiding certain foods shows religious devotion; I can certainly offer other snack choices").

Showing respect for diverse perspectives does not necessarily mean that "anything goes" or that there are no moral judgments to be made. No one, for example, needs to embrace a tradition in which some people's basic human rights are blatantly violated. Showing respect does mean, however, that adults and children must try to understand another group's behaviors from within the entirety of their beliefs and traditions (M. N. Cohen, 1998).

• **Confront inequities.** As you have learned, children of color and those from immigrant groups face misunderstanding and discrimination. Educators can take the stand that inequities will *not* be tolerated at school. To profess its commitment to fairness and justice, one school district displays a statement of its "Equity Vision":

> Roseville Area Schools is committed to ensuring an equitable and respectful educational experience for every student, family, and staff member, regardless of race, gender, sexual orientation, socioeconomic status, ability, home or first language, religion, national origin, or age. (Howard, 2007, p. 20)

Of course, children and families want to see such words backed up with fair, respectful, and compassionate deeds. Teachers and principals must confront any practices that inadvertently favor one group or another (e.g., assigning inexperienced teachers to work with students who need the most help, having low expectations for students from ethnic minority backgrounds, and preferentially treating subgroups of students when selecting recipients for awards) (Villegas & Lucas, 2007).

Community Resources

Communities affect children in a number of ways. Here we examine the impact of the community and family income on children's development and offer recommendations for working with children from low-income families.

Type of Community

Communities vary in their population density and geographical features, including their climate, natural resources, and predominant cultures. Children in large cities live side by side with thousands and sometimes millions of others in a relatively confined region. Here children frequently have access to ongoing events and resources related to music, art, drama, science, sports, and culture. You can see 6-year-old Lee's enthusiasm for a museum he visited in his drawing in Artifact 3-9. Not every child in a big city can take advantage of its splendors, however. Forced to live in unsafe neighborhoods, economically disadvantaged families encounter such problems as drugs, violence, crime, racial segregation, and low-performing schools (S. Griffin & Green, 2012; Juon, Evans-Polce, & Ensminger, 2013; S. Massey & Denton, 1993; Schaefer-McDaniel, 2007). Nevertheless, urban centers, churches, recreation centers, and other institutions advocate for low-income youth and exert positive influences on children's lives (Farmer-Hinton, Lewis, Patton, & Rivers, 2013).

In comparison, families living in rural settings typically share their community with 2,500 or fewer citizens (B. K. Lawrence, 2009). Rural families, particularly those residing in farming communities, structure chores so that all family members contribute to the family's economic livelihood and help neighbors with such seasonal projects as harvests. As a result, rural families are apt to foster a cooperative spirit and strong work ethic in children (García, 1994; B. K. Lawrence, 2009). A downside of rural environments is that students must travel many miles to attend school each day and may not be able to participate in extracurricular activities (North Central Regional Educational Laboratory, 2008).

ARTIFACT 3-9   Day at the museum. Children learn a lot from visiting institutions in their community. After visiting an art museum, 6-year-old Lee drew this picture, representing themes of religion and warfare that he perceived in the museum's paintings.

A number of rural schools spend a high proportion of available funds on transportation services and have insufficient resources remaining to invest in computers, Internet access, and professional development for teachers (Provasnik et al., 2007; Ullman, 2010b).

Rural parents regularly work long hours and do not always have time for events at school, making it worthwhile for teachers to keep families informed through newsletters, telephone calls, e-mail messages, and other methods of outreach. Rural populations are becoming increasingly diverse in their ethnicity, especially when certain industries are present and actively recruit immigrants, as sometimes occurs in meat processing plants (A. Walker, 2012). Educators can sponsor after-school activities that give adolescents options for leisure, as adolescents in rural settings need constructive outlets for their time; these individuals are at least as prone as their urban and suburban counterparts to engage in such risky activities as drinking alcohol to excess, taking drugs, and having unprotected sex (Rishel, Cottrell, & Kingery, 2012).

Families living in suburban communities reside in residential areas that are generally within commuting distance from a large city. On average, families in suburban communities have higher incomes than those who live in inner cities or rural areas, schools are often of higher quality, children are able to visit the cultural sights of the big city, nearly everyone has a bit of backyard, and children can play safely outdoors. As a result of these and other advantages, more high school students from suburban cities attend college than do students from big cities or rural areas (National Center for Education Statistics, 2007). However, not all young people have an optimistic outlook about their chances for future success, and students in suburban schools are as likely as their counterparts in larger cities to engage in risky behaviors (Greene & Forster, 2004; Luthar & Goldstein, 2008; V. Robbins, Dollard, Armstrong, Kutash, & Vergon, 2008). Although much of suburban population is relatively well off, a growing number of suburban families lives in poverty without access to the safety net of community resources that are seen in densely populated areas (D. M. Wilson, 2012).

Family Income

A child's experience in a community is strongly affected by the family's personal and financial resources. This idea is captured in the notion of the family's **socioeconomic status (SES)**, that is, its standing in the community based on income level, the prestige of parents' jobs, and parents' levels of education. A family's socioeconomic status—whether high-SES, middle-SES, or low-SES—gives us a sense of how much flexibility family members have with regard to where they live and what they buy, how much influence they have in political decision making, and what educational opportunities they can offer children.

Children from high- and middle-SES families enjoy material comforts and usually go to well-equipped schools with teachers who are experienced and highly prepared in the subjects they teach. Children are typically encouraged by parents to learn productive skills in after-school activities, for example, in soccer leagues, music lessons, and ballet classes. Families also socialize children to cooperate in structured teams and negotiate with authority figures (Lareau, 2003). Advantaged parents converse regularly with young children, expose them to sophisticated vocabulary, and foster their reasoning skills. Yet children in these families face disadvantages, including frequently being overcommitted and having little time to play. Despite attending good schools and living in safe neighborhoods, children are at risk for emotional problems and substance abuse when parents put excessive pressure on them and stay on the periphery of their day-to-day activities (Luthar & Latendresse, 2005; Weissbourd, 2011).

Children from low-income families have fewer material resources but nevertheless encounter definite advantages. In many low-income families, children receive substantial emotional support, are allowed discretion in how they spend their free time, and consequently learn to manage their freedom creatively and effectively (Lareau, 2003). Even so, children from low-income families are not always prepared for the academic demands of school. Some low-income parents do not regularly engage their children in extended verbal give-and-take or encourage them to ask questions of, or assert themselves with, authority figures (Willingham, 2012).

Preparing for Your Licensure Examination
Your teaching test might ask you about the kinds of risks experienced by children in low-income families.

Children Living in Economic Poverty

Some families do not merely scrape by with limited means. They go without. Families in economic poverty have so little in financial resources that their ability to nurture children can be compromised (Dawson-McClure et al., 2014; G. W. Evans & Kim, 2007; Willingham, 2012). Approximately 22 percent of U.S. children live in poverty (Federal Interagency Forum on Child and Family Statistics, 2013d).

Children and adolescents living in poverty face serious challenges. Typical problems include these:

- *Corrosive physical environment.* Compared to their well-to-do peers, children in economically disadvantaged families are more likely to be exposed to factory pollution, toxic waste dumps, allergens that trigger asthma, and excessive noise.
- *Inadequate housing and material goods.* Many children live in tight quarters, perhaps sharing one or two rooms with several other family members. Some children have no place to live at all, except, perhaps, the family car or a homeless shelter. Children from homeless families are sometimes reluctant to go to school because they lack bathing facilities and presentable clothing. Even the most basic school supplies are beyond the family's reach.
- *Poor nutrition and health care.* Some children are poorly fed and have little access to adequate health care; as a result, they may suffer from malnutrition and other chronic health problems.
- *Increased probability of disabling conditions.* Children who live in poverty are more likely to have physical, mental, or social-emotional disabilities. Low-income families do not always have an adequate support network to address these disabilities.
- *Gaps in background knowledge.* Teachers assume that children have had certain kinds of experiences before they begin school—for instance, that they have been read to, have seen many kinds of animals at farms or zoos, and have had many occasions to explore the physical environment. Some children who live in extreme poverty miss out on these foundational experiences. At home, poor children are, on average, less often spoken to and receive less overall cognitive stimulation than do children from economically advantaged families.
- *Emotional stress.* Many poor families live in chronically stressful conditions, constantly worrying about where their next meal is coming from, how to find transportation from one place to another, how to afford electricity to heat or cool the house, where to find clothes for growing children, and how long the landlord will wait before evicting them for not paying the rent. Low-income parents who are under continual stress sometimes struggle with remaining calm and attentive with their children, and children easily absorb parents' anxieties. Exposure to serious hardships over an extended period of time when unaccompanied by adequate reassurance from familiar adults can culminate in the child's **toxic stress**. Toxic stress is a prolonged physiological reaction that leaves the child in a state of constant worry and triggers stress-related conditions later in life, including heart disease, depression, and substance abuse. Toxic stress also undermines the health of certain structures of the brain, especially those that support memory, attention, and coping skills.
- *Lower-quality schools.* Schools in low-income neighborhoods are often poorly funded and equipped, and they have high teacher turnover rates. Unfortunately, some teachers in these schools have low expectations for students, offer an undemanding curriculum, assign little homework, and set low standards for performance.
- *Public misconceptions.* People from economically advantaged backgrounds often have mixed feelings about low-SES families: They may feel pity yet simultaneously believe that poor people are responsible for their misfortunes because of laziness, promiscuity, or overdependence on social welfare programs. (L. M. Berger, Paxson, & Waldfogel, 2009; Berliner, 2009; G. W. Evans & Kim, 2007; G. W. Evans & Schamberg, 2009; A. S. Garner et al., 2012; Gershoff, Aber, & Raver, 2005; Graff, 2014; Linver, Brooks-Gunn, & Kohen, 2002; McLoyd, 1998a; McLoyd et al., 2009; Murnane, 2007; Payne, DeVol, & Smith, 2006; Willingham, 2012)

Some children and adolescents find the challenges of poverty so overwhelming that they engage in behaviors—dropping out of school, abusing drugs and alcohol, participating in criminal activities—that create further problems. However, many other children and adolescents from poor families do well despite the adversities they face: They are relatively hardy in confronting their many hardships (Abelev, 2009; Felner & FeVries, 2013; Kim-Cohen, Moffitt, Caspi, & Taylor, 2004). These youngsters show **resilience**, an ability to thrive despite adverse environmental conditions. Let's examine strategies educators use to nurture resilience in low-income youngsters.

Working with Children from Low-Income Families

Adults who want to make a difference in children's lives are especially likely to do so in schools serving low-SES populations. But to be effective, teachers and other school personnel must fully commit to their jobs, think creatively about how they can make the most of limited resources, show a contagious enthusiasm for learning, and work with families and other members of the community (L. W. Anderson & Pellicer, 1998; S. Griffin & Green, 2012; E. H. Ogden & Germinario, 1988). Experts offer these recommendations for working with children from low-income families:

• **Invest in children's strengths.** Youngsters may become discouraged when teachers have concentrated on their weaknesses. In contrast, focusing on what's *right* with children can generate optimism, excitement, and a definite commitment to learning in children. It doesn't take long to figure out children's strengths when you are intentionally looking for them. Many children of poor immigrant families have two parents at home who support them, are physically healthy, and have extended families concerned with their welfare (Shields & Behrman, 2004). Young children from low-income families are apt to be curious, eager to acquire language and literacy skills, and receptive to forming close relationships with teachers (Maier, Vitiello, & Greenfield, 2012). Adolescents who work part time to help their families make ends meet have a sense of purpose and a good understanding of the working world (Schilling, 2008). Children of single, working parents may know far more than peers about cooking, cleaning, and taking care of younger siblings (Whiting & Edwards, 1988).

• **Foster a sense of community.** Children from low-income backgrounds benefit from teachers' efforts to build a **sense of community**—a collection of shared beliefs that individuals in the group (e.g., a class or school) have common goals, respect one another's efforts, and believe that everyone makes an important contribution (L. W. Anderson & Pellicer, 1998; Sayer, Beaven, Stringer, & Hermena, 2013; Watson & Battistich, 2006). Teachers can assign chores on a rotating basis, use cooperative learning activities, involve children and adolescents in cross-grade tutoring, and encourage everyone's participation in extracurricular activities (Downey, 2000). Because youngsters often feel more connected to their community when, in some small way, they give something back, educators can also sponsor community service projects. Children might conduct a neighborhood cleanup, volunteer in a nursing home, serve as readers at the local library, or raise funds to benefit community causes (Ladson-Billings, 1994).

• **Convey clear expectations for children's behavior.** For all children, and especially for those who have had more than their share of life's challenges, knowing what's expected is important. Hence adults need to describe their expectations in clear, concrete terms (Downey, 2000; Reinke, Herman, & Stormont, 2013). For instance, when finishing lunch in the cafeteria, children might be asked to "empty the napkins and leftovers into the trash bin, put the trays and dishes on the counter, and go quietly outside." When working in cooperative groups, young people might be reminded, "Everyone needs to participate in discussions and contribute to the project."

• **Establish a warm, predictable, and safe environment.** Children who face harsh and adverse circumstances, especially over a long period of time, above all else need to feel safe and loved. Teachers can establish pleasant routines, such as greeting them with affection first thing in the morning and saying goodbye to them personally, by name, in the afternoon. Adults can also show their affection for children by encouraging them to pursue their interests and providing constructive individualized feedback on their learning progress (C. Howes, Fuligni, Hong, Huang, & Lara-Cinisomo, 2013). When children manifest exceptionally high levels of stress, for example, by biting their fingernails, sucking their fingers, clinging to adults, having daytime toileting accidents, complaining of headaches and stomach pains, developing rashes, and being withdrawn or acting out, they need extra support from adults.

• **Show relevance of academic skills to children's lives and needs.** Finding personal relevance in classroom activities and subject matter is important for any child, but it may be especially critical for children from low-SES backgrounds (L. W. Anderson & Pellicer, 1998). Helping children see how they can use skills in their everyday lives makes learning meaningful, as well as motivating.

• **Acquaint children with local institutions.** Students who have not had the opportunity to see institutions in their society can learn a lot from brief visits. Teachers can take their classes on field trips to a zoo, museum, post office, fire station, and so forth, and thereby create new knowledge for children to build on in academic lessons. When field trips are too expensive or logistically impractical, an alternative is to bring the community to children—perhaps by having a representative of the local zoo bring some of the zoo's smaller residents or by asking a police officer to come describe the many public services that the police department provides.

• **Encourage children to get involved in extracurricular activities.** Participation in sports and after-school activities appears instrumental in exposing children to worthwhile skills and discouraging such problematic behaviors as drug use, thefts, and violence (McLoyd et al., 2009). Teachers can inspire young people to get involved in fun and rewarding activities while advising them of community resources that could offset any expenses required for participation. The timing of events is also an issue for some students in immigrant families, who may be reluctant to spend too much time away from their parents; organized activities right after school might be considered (Simpkins, Delgado, Price, Quach, & Starbuck, 2013).

• **Communicate high expectations for children's success.** Some children from low-SES backgrounds do not expect much of their own academic skills. Yet teachers can communicate a can-do attitude, urge students to challenge themselves, and provide support for reaching personal goals. Offering tutoring sessions for challenging classroom material, finding low-cost academic enrichment programs available during the summer, helping adolescents fill out applications for college scholarships, and arranging for them to take college admission tests are just a few examples of useful assistance (Kunjufu, 2006).

• **Give homeless children school supplies and help them adjust to school.** Children who are homeless reside in a range of settings, for example, motels, campgrounds, temporary shelters, cars, parks, abandoned buildings, and bus stations. Educators who work with children of homeless families can first of all help them adjust to school. Teachers, principals, and school counselors might provide a notebook, clipboard, or other portable "desk" on which children can do their homework at the temporary residence; ask civic organizations to donate school supplies; meet with parents at the shelter or other setting rather than at school, if desired by the family; and pair homeless children with classmates who can explain school procedures and introduce them to peers (Bowman & Popp, 2013; Pawlas, 1994). Educators can make another valuable contribution for children when they move again by planning for this eventuality, keeping a portfolio of children's assignments, and sending it to the new school.

In the United States, homeless children have rights under the McKinney-Vento Act for a free and appropriate public education. Teachers and other school personnel must determine children's individual needs, clues of which may surface during conversations with children about their previous educational experiences (e.g., whether they had a teacher who worked with them individually or in small groups outside the regular classroom, which might indicate a customized intervention; Bowman & Popp, 2013). Tutoring may be helpful and can be provided with help from school psychologists, special education teachers, and other personnel. A school counselor may address any serious difficulties in adjustment, and a nurse might be able to arrange for showering facilities, clothing, and medical care. Discretion is essential with these services because homeless children are apt to feel uncomfortable in discussing their personal and family situations.

• **Be a mentor.** Young people from low-income families often benefit from assistance in navigating through difficulties at school. A trusted teacher, counselor, or coach can show children how to express their needs and interests in educational environments. Particularly when youngsters encounter serious obstacles in their schooling, for example, failing subjects, missing school, or becoming a teenage parent, mentors can suggest practical ways to overcome difficulties (Abelev, 2009; Schilling, 2008).

• **Advocate for improvement of schools.** Teachers and other practitioners can join community groups that are striving to improve schools. Various initiatives have been productive, including efforts to work within existing school systems and others that develop charter or alternative schools with high expectations and clear objectives for family involvement (Fruchter, 2007; Kunjufu, 2006).

Summary

Children and families are profoundly affected by their experiences in ethnic, racial, cultural, and immigrant groups. To a large extent, children's ethnicity affects their values, actions, and styles of communicating; race affects other people's perceptions, biases, and responses. Children also are influenced by their community's character and by the incomes of their families. Educators can build on children's experiences in the community and help economically disadvantaged children by providing support, resources, and validation of children's personal strengths.

ENHANCEDetext *self-check*

Assessing Children 3-2

Practice assessing children's experiences in their neighborhood and community.

ENHANCEDetext *application exercise*

PRACTICING FOR YOUR LICENSURE EXAMINATION

Many teaching tests require students to use what they have learned about child development in responses to brief vignettes and multiple-choice questions. You can practice for your licensure examination by reading the following case study and answering a series of questions.

Four-Year-Old Sons

A common behavior displayed by preschoolers is asking a lot of *why* questions. *Why are carrots orange? Why does Daddy have a beard? Why do I have to go to bed now?*

In a study about the lives of women, Belenky and her colleagues interviewed several mothers (Belenky, Bond, & Weinstock, 1997). The authors found distinct perspectives on how mothers viewed questions by their children. Elizabeth describes her son Charles as being disrespectful in questioning her authority. For example, when Elizabeth tells Charles not to touch a dead bug, he questions her about why the insect is dead and why he shouldn't touch it. She believes his frequent questions reflect his intention to anger her by not listening respectfully or accepting her statements.

In contrast, Joyce describes her son Peter as having an insatiable curiosity. She believes that his frequent questions are a natural outgrowth of his need to analyze the world around him. She sees his responses to her requests as a natural outgrowth of his mental reflection. She admires and appreciates her son's questions because she believes that he sees dimensions to things that she misses, and his questions help her to think through what they are doing together.

Constructed-Response Question

1. How do the two mothers interpret their sons' questions? How might they have developed their different orientations to children's queries?

Multiple-Choice Questions

2. How might a teacher form a partnership with each of these mothers?

   a. A teacher could let the mothers know how happy she is to have the boys in her class and see if either mother has any concerns to discuss.

   b. A teacher could advise the mothers about how she addresses typical characteristics of children this age, including their natural curiosity and frequent question asking.

   c. A teacher could use a variety of formats to inform the mothers of the preschool curriculum, policies, and events by sending home newsletters about classroom activities and getting these reports translated if possible for families who speak another language.

   d. A teacher could try all of the strategies listed above.

3. Should a teacher be concerned that Elizabeth is maltreating her son?

   a. No, because emotional abuse, which Elizabeth is exhibiting, does not reach the threshold for maltreatment.

   b. No, because although Elizabeth expresses frustration with her son's frequent questioning, she does not say anything that indicates she is harming her son physically or emotionally.

   c. Yes, Elizabeth's dislike of her son's questioning is proof that she is physically maltreating him.

   d. Yes, because impatience with a child's questioning is an indication of emotional maltreatment.

ENHANCEDetext *licensure exam*

Key Concepts

family (p. 67)	self-regulation (p. 79)	ethnicity (p. 98)	racial identity (p. 101)
socialization (p. 68)	parenting style (p. 79)	race (p. 98)	culturally responsive teaching (p. 103)
individualistic culture (p. 68)	authoritative parenting style (p. 79)	acculturation (p. 98)	
collectivistic culture (p. 68)	authoritarian parenting style (p. 80)	assimilation (p. 98)	socioeconomic status (SES) (p. 107)
community (p. 69)	permissive parenting style (p. 80)	separation (p. 99)	toxic stress (p. 108)
family structure (p. 71)	uninvolved parenting style (p. 80)	selective adoption (p. 99)	resilience (p. 109)
coparents (p. 72)	guided participation (p. 81)	bicultural orientation (p. 99)	sense of community (p. 109)
stepfamily (p. 74)	child maltreatment (p. 85)	ethnic identity (p. 101)	

CHAPTER FOUR

Biological Beginnings

CASE STUDY: Maria

Joan and Dave longed for a baby. Time and again they were disappointed when a conception did not occur. Months turned to years, and the couple gradually accepted that their future would be childless. Joan and Dave invested in their marriage, faith, jobs, community service, and precious time with family and friends. Their lives were full and meaningful.

One day they were astonished to find that they were expecting a baby. Disbelief gave way to excitement as medical tests, morning sickness, and a little bump protruding from Joan's abdomen convinced the couple of the reality of their growing child. Midway through her pregnancy, Joan's doctor advised the prospective parents that because of Joan's age (39) and the presence of an irregular feature in the ultrasound scan, they had an elevated risk for having a baby with a birth defect. Although apprehensive about their baby's condition, Joan and Dave decided to avoid any intrusive medical tests. Instead, they resolved to love their baby.

And love her they did. Joan and Dave adored baby Maria. At birth, Maria was beautiful, healthy, and snuggly. She relaxed in their arms, was happily comforted when distressed, and eased into a sleep schedule that quickly resembled their own. Being informed about her medical status did throw a wrinkle into the family's adjustment, however. The new parents were advised that Maria had Down syndrome.

In the years ahead, Dave and Joan were to learn a great deal about Down syndrome. Just as important, they were to learn about Maria's individuality and appreciate her radiant, buoyant, and demonstrative personality. The new parents cared for Maria at home during her infancy. They tended to her needs, showered her with affection, enjoyed her antics, read to her, and encouraged her mastery of the developmental milestones of sitting, crawling, walking, and eating independently. At 18 months, Maria entered an early childhood intervention center and received numerous services that effectively nurtured her understanding of language and her speech, cognition, and desire to explore the world. She thrived.

The move to kindergarten was unexpectedly difficult. Her teacher was an experienced educator in a private school who agreed to include Maria in her classroom. It turned out that she was unfamiliar with the needs of children with special needs and accommodations that help them reach their potential. Maria had a special knack for sensing how people judged her, and with this teacher she felt unaccepted, perhaps even rejected, a perception that was difficult for her to articulate to her parents. Fortunately, Joan and Dave were perceptive themselves and became increasingly concerned about the tension they perceived in Maria related to school.

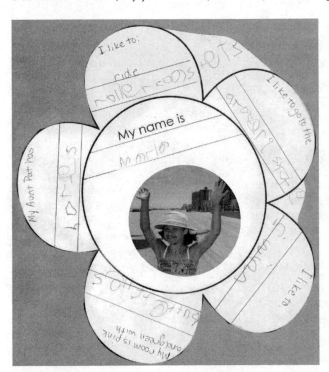

ARTIFACT 4-1 Maria at age 10 writes that she likes to ride roller coasters, go to the grocery store, and swim, and she has a pink and green bedroom with butterflies and an Aunt Pat who has horses.

Joan, Maria (age 11), and Dave.

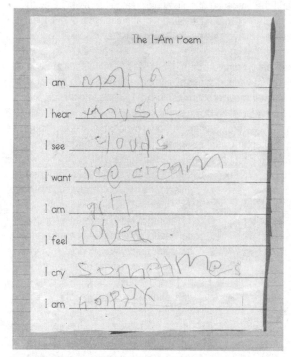

ARTIFACT 4-2 Maria at age 11 filled in the blanks in an I-Am Poem, writing that she hears music, sees clouds, wants ice cream, is a girl, feels loved, cries sometimes, and is happy.

One day, as they approached school, Maria protested, "No. No. *No!!!*" It was a turning point for Joan and Dave, who moved Maria to a new school, where she was sincerely welcomed, accepted, and loved. Again she would flourish. Maria bonded with her teachers and several classmates, including both typical students and others classified as having special needs. Maria divided her school day between lessons with a special education teacher, specialists, and her regular classroom teacher. Shifts between the settings were seamless, especially when the different educators were able to communicate regularly. There were a few occasions when Joan had to remind the school that Maria could be—and therefore *should be*—included in more activities in the regular classroom—in classroom photographs, for example, and particular lessons that could be easily adapted to Maria's abilities. Fortunately, the principal and teachers were receptive to such revisions.

Maria progressed well during the elementary school years. She worked hard. She learned to read and write, studied spelling lists, and absorbed many important concepts. She made and kept friends. She swam, rode horses, and enjoyed roller coasters. Although Maria struggled with certain things—forming letters, following multistep instructions, and grasping abstract ideas, customized goals and strategies allowed her to succeed.

Now she is ready for the next major transition, entry into middle school. There will be significant challenges ahead, not the least of which are adjusting to a new building, facing a different schedule of classes, coping with intensified academic demands, and adjusting to adolescence. Yet continued advocacy from Joan and Dave, a principal who has reached out to the family, long-standing friends who will accompany her to the new school, and, of course, Maria's own cheerful self and good health—are assets that will ease the transition.

- How did her parents contribute to Maria's well-being?
- How did biological structures and processes influence her development?

Maria had a happy childhood in large part because her parents, Joan and Dave, loved her, accepted her individuality, and advocated for her rights. Maria contributed to her own positive growth with a loving and joyful personality, willingness to work hard, and capacity for friendship. Teachers, principals, and other specialists provided invaluable support, effectively nurturing her abilities and confidence. Of course, natural biological processes were also an essential part of Maria's growth. Nine months of healthy prenatal development, modestly deterred by the chromosomal condition of Down syndrome, culminated in the birth of a beloved child who would benefit from inclusion in a regular school environment supplemented with customized educational support.

In this chapter we show that genetic foundations, prenatal growth, and childbirth reflect extraordinary symphonies of developmental processes, each orchestrated by a harmonious blend of nature and nurture. We find that there are many things prospective parents and caring professionals can do to give children healthy beginnings.

GENETIC FOUNDATIONS

Like Maria, every child has a unique profile of hereditary instructions that support his or her life, growth, human traits, and individuality. These guidelines are contained in a child's **genes**, the basic units of heredity.

Structure of Genes

Each gene tells the body to create one or more proteins or to regulate the operations of other genes. Proteins produced by genes create life-sustaining reactions that, with adequate nutrition and a favorable environment, culminate in a healthy child. Some proteins guide the production of new cells (e.g., elastic skin cells or message-sending brain cells). Other proteins tell the body to increase in size, fight infection, repair damage, carry chemical signals throughout the body, and activate or inhibit other genes.

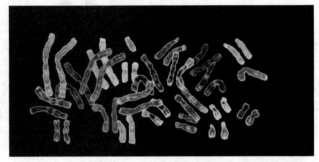

FIGURE 4-1 One person's chromosomes. Photograph of human chromosomes, which have been extracted from a human cell, colored, and magnified.

The 21,000 to 25,000 or so genes that exist in the human body are laid out in an orderly way on rod-like structures called **chromosomes** (Pennisi, 2012; U.S. Department of Energy Office of Science, 2008). Chromosomes are organized into 23 distinct pairs that are easily seen with a high-powered microscope (Figure 4-1). These 46 chromosomes reside in the center of virtually every cell in the body. One chromosome in each pair is inherited from the mother, the other from the father.

Genes are made up of deoxyribonucleic acid, or **DNA**. A DNA molecule is structured like a ladder that has been twisted many times into a spiral staircase (see Figure 4-2). Pairs of chemical substances comprise each step on the staircase, with a gene being comprised of a series of these steps. Location on the staircase helps scientists determine the identity of particular genes. Above and below genes on the ladder are other instructions that tell genes when they should turn on and off and do other things that have yet to be discovered. The hierarchical relationships among cells, chromosomes, genes, and DNA molecules are represented in Figure 4-2.

Operation of Genes

Most genes are identical—or at least very similar—across children. Among these universal genes are those that make it possible for children to develop basic human abilities, such as communicating with language, walking and running, and forming social relationships. The remaining genes vary among children. These variable genes predispose individual children to be relatively tall or short, heavy or thin, active or sedentary, eager to learn new things or content to rely on existing knowledge, emotionally agreeable or combative, and healthy or vulnerable to disease. Remarkably, universal and individual genes blend together in their effects, such that a given child develops a distinctive appearance, temperament, and style of interacting with others.

Both universal and variable genes initiate chains of events during development. Genes directly affect the operations of individual cells present in the child's organs, brain, and other physiological systems. These structures and processes in turn affect the child's

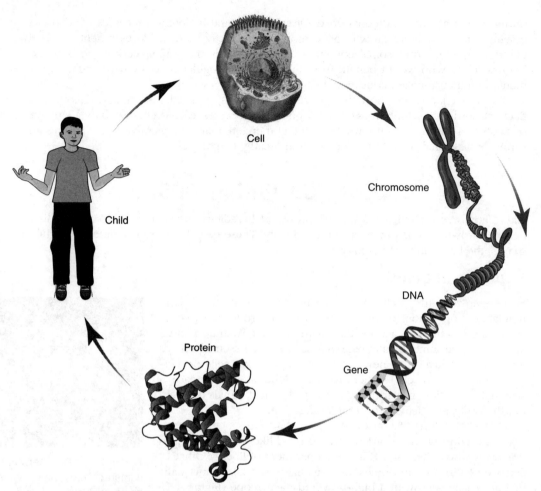

FIGURE 4-2 Relationships in genetic structures. The body contains billions of cells, most of which contain 46 chromosomes. Each chromosome contains thousands of genes. Genes are long sequences of DNA that assemble proteins. Proteins are released and affect activities in the cell and, physiological processes throughout the body, health, and growth.

behavior, relationships, and learning. Thus genes are powerful, but they are *not* simple recipes or blueprints for traits. Rather, the proteins that originate from genetic instructions are released into the child's cells, and their effects depend partly (largely, in some cases) on the child's health and activity. To illustrate, an 8-year-old boy genetically predisposed to asthma may rarely have respiratory flare-ups because his family gives him proper medical care and shields him from the hair and dander of dogs, his personal trigger for wheezing and coughing.

The causal chain also operates in reverse, with the environment affecting genetic expression. That is, the environment provides opportunities for learning and exposure to nutrition and toxins; these factors affect the body; and the health and operations of physical systems activate (or suppress) particular genes. For example, a 1-year-old boy who has been exposed to high levels of lead may not be able to fully express genes that would otherwise have permitted good motor skills and insatiable learning.

Developmental stage and still other factors also affect genetic expression. In fact, only a subset of genes is active in a cell at any given moment. Responding to the body's health, maturational state, and chemicals circulating within the body, cells activate a limited collection of genes. Other genes remain dormant until it is their turn to be called into action. This fact helps explain the order of changes in physical appearance and motor skills. As an example, maturational state affects genetic expression through the age-related release of hormones. As you can see in an Observing Children video, hormones are chemical messengers that flow through the bloodstream and generate reactions in cells with matching receptors. For example, a child is born with genes for sexual maturation but the body waits to release relevant hormones until adolescence. The delay in the action of genes also explains why some diseases and mental health conditions appear seemingly out of nowhere: Genes that make people vulnerable to certain conditions remain silent until maturational states and environmental circumstances elicit their effects.

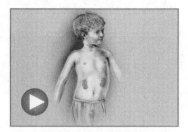

Observing Children 4-1
Watch an animated video depicting the effects of hormones in the endocrine system on children's growing bodies.
ENHANCEDetext *video example*

Formation of Reproductive Cells

Normal human cells contain 46 chromosomes. There is an important exception: Male and female reproductive cells, called **gametes**, have only 23 chromosomes each—one from each chromosome pair. Gametes, which take the form of *sperm* in men and *ova* in women, are created in a process of cell division called **meiosis** (see Figure 4-3).

Meiosis

Nature forms new reproductive cells that conserve most of the genetic characteristics of the parent cell but also generate a few novel features. Meiosis begins when the 46 chromosomes within a male or female *germ cell* (a precursor to a gamete) pair up into 23 matched sets. The germ cell duplicates each chromosome, and pairs of chromosomes line up side by side. Next, segments of genetic material are exchanged between each pair. This *crossing-over* of genetic material shuffles genes between paired chromosomes generating new hereditary combinations that do not exist in either parent's chromosomes.

After crossing-over takes place, the pairs of duplicated chromosomes separate, and the cell divides into two new germ cells with half from each pair. Chance determines which of the duplicated chromosomes from each of the 23 pairs moves to one or the other of the two new cells. This phase thus provides a second route to genetic individuality. During the first cell division, one of the two new female germ cells gets the bulk of the cell matter and is strong and healthy whereas the second, smaller cell disintegrates. Both new male germ cells are viable.

A second cell division takes place, and the duplicated chromosomes separate. Each new cell receives one of the duplicate chromosomes from each pair. The resulting male germ cells are ready to mature and become male gametes (sperm). The female germ cells undergo this second division only after being fertilized by sperm. When the female cell divides, once again, only one of the two new cells, a female gamete (an ovum), is viable. The process of meiosis thus produces one ovum and four sperm.[1]

The multiple steps of meiosis ensure that most traits are preserved across generations as well as that a few entirely new constellations of traits are created. Children share some features with both of their parents because they inherit half of their chromosomes from each parent. Children are unlike their parents (and siblings) in other respects because parts of chromosomes change slightly during meiosis; the chromosomal structures that children inherit are *not* exact duplicates of parents' chromosomes.[2] Furthermore, a single gene transmitted from parent to child (and shared by both) may operate differently in the two family members because other genes (not shared by both) intensify or weaken its effects.

Gender

When one sperm and one ovum unite at conception, the 23 chromosomes from each parent come together and form a new being (the **zygote**) with 46 chromosomes. The 23rd chromosome pair determines the gender of the individual: Two *X chromosomes* (one each from

---

[1] Sperm are produced continuously throughout a male's reproductive years. In girls, up to 2 million germ cells are present at birth. Many subsequently decay, and only about 40,000 remain at the beginning of adolescence. About 400 ova will be released over the woman's lifetime.

[2] For any given parent, each event of meiosis begins with the exact same chromosomes. The process of meiosis tweaks the structure of chromosomes slightly; no two meiotic events alter chromosomes in precisely the same way.

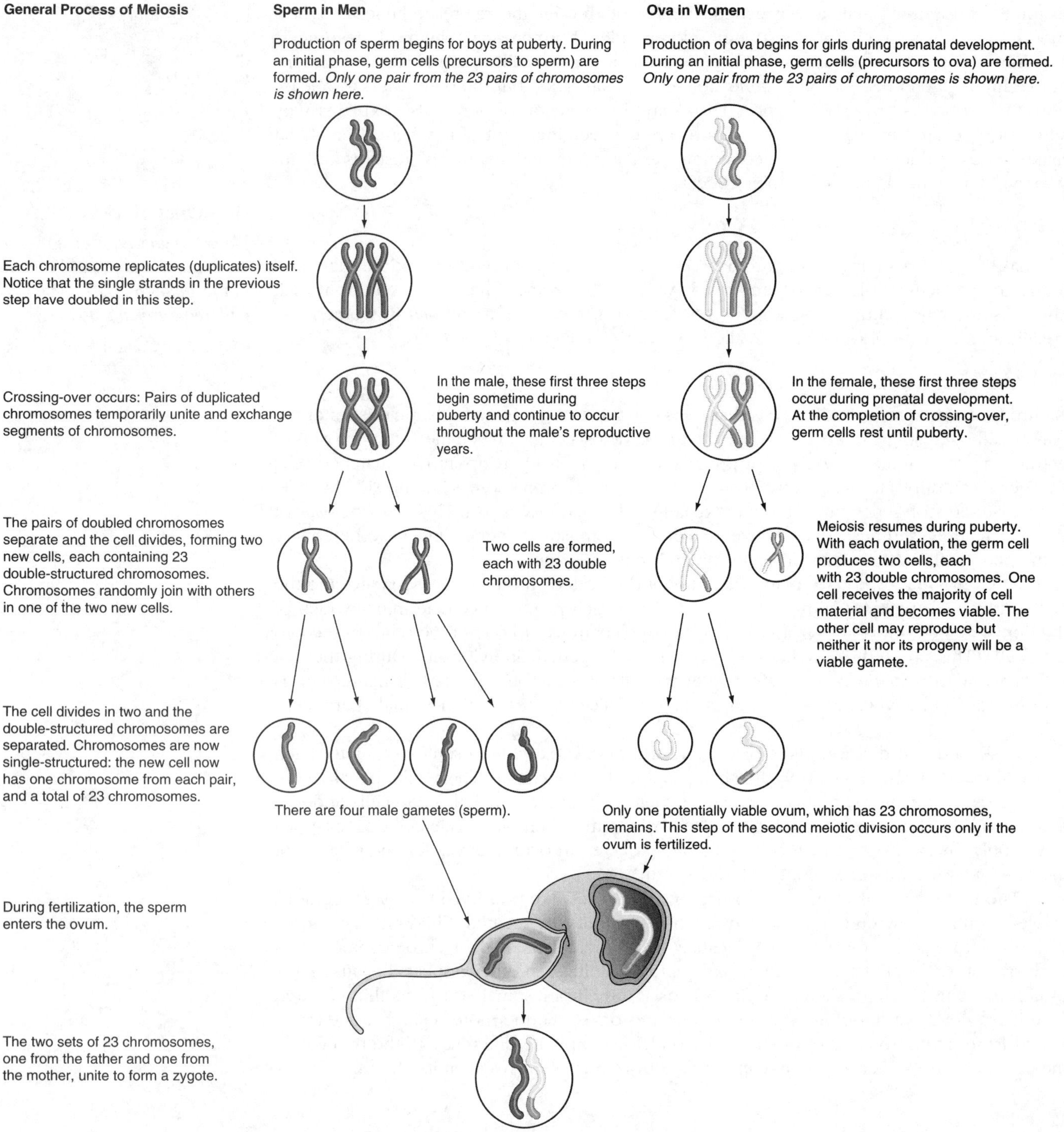

General Process of Meiosis

Sperm in Men

Production of sperm begins for boys at puberty. During an initial phase, germ cells (precursors to sperm) are formed. *Only one pair from the 23 pairs of chromosomes is shown here.*

Ova in Women

Production of ova begins for girls during prenatal development. During an initial phase, germ cells (precursors to ova) are formed. *Only one pair from the 23 pairs of chromosomes is shown here.*

Each chromosome replicates (duplicates) itself. Notice that the single strands in the previous step have doubled in this step.

Crossing-over occurs: Pairs of duplicated chromosomes temporarily unite and exchange segments of chromosomes.

In the male, these first three steps begin sometime during puberty and continue to occur throughout the male's reproductive years.

In the female, these first three steps occur during prenatal development. At the completion of crossing-over, germ cells rest until puberty.

The pairs of doubled chromosomes separate and the cell divides, forming two new cells, each containing 23 double-structured chromosomes. Chromosomes randomly join with others in one of the two new cells.

Two cells are formed, each with 23 double chromosomes.

Meiosis resumes during puberty. With each ovulation, the germ cell produces two cells, each with 23 double chromosomes. One cell receives the majority of cell material and becomes viable. The other cell may reproduce but neither it nor its progeny will be a viable gamete.

The cell divides in two and the double-structured chromosomes are separated. Chromosomes are now single-structured: the new cell now has one chromosome from each pair, and a total of 23 chromosomes.

There are four male gametes (sperm).

Only one potentially viable ovum, which has 23 chromosomes, remains. This step of the second meiotic division occurs only if the ovum is fertilized.

During fertilization, the sperm enters the ovum.

The two sets of 23 chromosomes, one from the father and one from the mother, unite to form a zygote.

FIGURE 4-3 **Reproductive cells.** *Meiosis* is the multistep process of forming gametes, cells that join in reproduction to form a new organism. *Based on information in K. L. Moore, Persaud, & Torchia (2013) and Sadler (2010).*

the mother and father) produce a female, and a combination of an *X chromosome* and a *Y chromosome* (from the mother and father, respectively) produces a male.

How Twins Are Created

Occasionally, a zygote splits into two separate cell clusters, resulting in two offspring instead of one. *Identical,* or **monozygotic twins**, come from the same fertilized egg and so have the same genes. At other times, two ova simultaneously unite with two sperm cells, again resulting in two offspring. These **dizygotic twins**, also known as *fraternal* twins, are as similar to one another as ordinary siblings. They share some genetic traits but not others.

Because monozygotic and dizygotic twins differ in the degree to which they have overlapping genes, researchers have studied them extensively. Twin studies permit rough estimates of the relative effects of heredity and environment on human characteristics. Considerable data indicate that monozygotic twins are more similar to one another than are dizygotic twins in their ability to learn new concepts and their tendency to be cooperative or aggressive (Ganiban, Ulbricht, Saudino, Reiss, & Neiderhiser, 2011; Knafo & Plomin, 2006; Mikolajewski, Allan, Hart, Lonigan, & Taylor, 2013; Tuvblad, Bezdjian, Raine, & Baker, 2014). Monozygotic twins are more alike in intelligence and personality than are dizygotic twins because these characteristics are partly genetically determined. Even so, "identical" twins are *not* indistinguishable in all psychological characteristics or even in their physical features—an indication that environment, experience, children's own choices, and even random factors affect development.

Genetic Basis of Individual Traits

So far, you have learned that children have both uniform genes (that bestow common human abilities) and variable genes (that contribute to individuality). Unvarying human genes, carried by all parents, are transmitted to every child. Genes that fluctuate among children are transmitted through systematic patterns of inheritance as well as by less common mechanisms and biological errors. Let's look more closely at how children receive traits that contribute to their individuality.

Common Mechanisms of Genetic Transmission

When the two sets of 23 chromosomes combine into matched pairs during conception, the corresponding genes inherited from each parent also pair up. Each gene pair includes two forms of the protein-coding instructions—two **alleles**—related to a particular physical characteristic. Sometimes the two genes in an allele pair give the same instructions ("Have dark hair!" "Have dark hair!"). At other times they give very different instructions ("Have dark hair!" "Have blond hair!"). When two genes give different instructions, one gene is more influential than its counterpart. A **dominant gene** manifests its characteristic, in a sense overriding the instructions of a **recessive gene** with which it is paired. A recessive gene influences growth and development primarily when its partner is also recessive. For example, genes for dark hair are dominant and those for blond hair are recessive. Thus a child with a dark hair gene and a blond hair gene will have dark hair, as will a child with two dark hair genes. Only when two blond hair genes are paired together will a child have blond hair.

However, when two genes of an allele pair disagree, one gene doesn't always dominate completely. Sometimes one gene simply has a stronger influence than others, a phenomenon known as **codominance**. *Sickle cell disease*, a blood disorder, is an example. The disease develops in its full-blown form only when a person has two (recessive) alleles for it. Nevertheless, when an individual has one recessive allele for sickle cell disease and one healthy allele, he or she may experience temporary, mild symptoms when short of oxygen; only occasionally develop more serious health problems; and have greater-than-average resistance to malaria (Aneni, Hamer, & Gill, 2013; Jorde, Carey, & Bamshad, 2010).

For many characteristics, the influence of genes is even more complex. Many physical traits and most psychological ones are dependent on multiple genes rather than on a single pair of alleles. With a **multifactorial trait**, many separate genes work together with environmental factors in the expression of the characteristic. Height and vulnerability to certain illnesses, including some kinds of diabetes, epilepsy, obesity, gastrointestinal disorder, and cancer, are determined by several genes acting together and interacting with such environmental factors as nutrition, activity, and toxins (J. W. Ball, Bindler, & Cowen, 2010; Dibbens, Heron, & Mulley, 2007; Keir & Wilkinson, 2013; Marques, Oliveira, Pereira, & Outeiro, 2011).

Problems in Genetic Instructions

Sometimes problems occur in genetic instructions, with resulting exceptionalities in one or more areas of growth (see Table 4-1). There are two primary types of genetic disorders, chromosomal abnormalities and single-gene defects. A child with a *chromosomal abnormality* has an extra chromosome, a missing chromosome, or a wrongly formed chromosome. Because each chromosome holds thousands of genes, a child with a chromosomal abnormality has many affected genes, and as a result major physical and cognitive problems. Chromosomal abnormalities occur when chromosomes divide unevenly during meiosis. Errors can also occur *after* meiosis, if the zygote's cells divide unevenly, such that the zygote has some cells with normal chromosomes and others with abnormal chromosomes. Chromosomal abnormalities are caused by a variety of factors, including a parent's exposure to viruses, radiation, toxins, or drugs.

TABLE 4-1 Common Chromosomal and Genetic Disorders in Children

DISORDER	INCIDENCE	CHARACTERISTICS[a]	IMPLICATIONS FOR CARE
Chromosomal Abnormalities Children have an irregular number of chromosomes (more than or fewer than 46) or one or more chromosomes with irregular structures.			
Down syndrome	1 per 700 births	Children with an extra 21st chromosome or an extra part of one develop distinctively shaped eyes, a protruding tongue, thick lips, a flat nose, short neck, wide gaps between toes, short fingers, a risk for heart problems and hearing loss, an intellectual disability that can range from mild to severe, good visual discrimination skills, and better understanding than production of verbal language.	Build on strengths in social, visual, and self-help skills. Provide explicit instruction in any delayed skills (e.g., in language). Supplement concepts with visual representations when possible. Address health issues such as heart problems and potential feeding difficulties.
Klinefelter syndrome	1 per 500–1,000 boys	Boys have one Y chromosome and two or more X chromosomes. They tend to have long legs, modest breast tissue, and lower-than-average verbal ability. Diagnosis may not occur until adolescence, when testes fail to enlarge.	Offer an enriched verbal environment. Medical treatment may be given to support development of male sexual characteristics.
Turner syndrome	1 per 2,500–5,000 girls	Girls have one X chromosome unaccompanied by a second sex chromosome. Affected girls have broad chests, webbed necks, short stature, health problems, typically normal verbal ability but lower-than-average visual and spatial abilities, and difficulty in making friends.	Provide instruction and support related to visual and spatial processing. Hormone therapy helps with bone growth and development of female characteristics. Provide social skills training.
Prader-Willi syndrome	1 per 10,000–25,000 births	Children are missing a segment of chromosome 15 from the father. They tend to become obese, show an intellectual disability, have small hands and feet, become short in stature, and develop maladaptive behaviors such as throwing temper tantrums, picking at their skin, eating excessively, and consuming unappealing substances (e.g., dirt).	Create appropriate plans to help children follow a well-balanced diet, decrease inappropriate behaviors, and increase acceptable emotional expression. Seek medical care as necessary.

TABLE 4-1 Common Chromosomal and Genetic Disorders in Children (*continued*)

DISORDER	INCIDENCE	CHARACTERISTICS[a]	IMPLICATIONS FOR CARE
Angelman syndrome	1 per 10,000–30,000 births	A deletion of a segment on chromosome 15 is inherited from the mother. Children show an intellectual disability and have a small head, seizures, jerky movements, and unusual, recurrent bouts of laughter not associated with happiness.	Provide appropriate educational support suited to children's skills and developmental levels. Seek medical care as necessary.

Single-Gene Defects

Children have an error on a dominant gene on one of the 22 paired chromosomes, a recessive defect on both chromosomes in one of the 22 matched pairs, an anomaly on a recessive gene on the X chromosome (boys), or a problem on a gene on both X chromosomes (girls).[b]

Neurofibromatosis	Mild form occurs in 1 per 2,500–4,000 births; severe form occurs in 1 per 40,000–50,000 births	Children develop tumors in the central nervous system and in some cases exhibit learning disabilities or a significant intellectual disability. Most individuals experience only minor symptoms, such as having colored, elevated spots on their skin.	Address learning disabilities; offer adaptive services to children with an intellectual disability. Tumors may be removed or treated. Surgery or braces may be provided if the spine becomes twisted.
Huntington disease (HD)	3–7 per 100,000 births	Children develop a disorder of the central nervous system typically by age 35 to 45, although age of first symptoms varies between 2 and 85 years. A protein destroys brain cells, causing irritability, clumsiness, depression, and forgetfulness and eventually may result in loss of motor control, slurred speech, and mental disturbances.	Remove sharp edges from the physical environment. When memory deteriorates, provide visual instructions about daily tasks. Medication may be given to alleviate movement problems and depression.
Phenylketonuria (PKU)	1 per 15,000 births, with rates highest in people of Celtic origin (e.g., from Ireland and Scotland)	Children are at risk for developing an intellectual disability, eczema, seizures, motor problems, aggression, self-mutilation, and impulsivity. Children's livers cannot produce an enzyme necessary for breaking down phenylalanine (an amino acid), which accumulates and becomes toxic to the brain.	Teach planning and memory skills. When phenylalanine is restricted from the diet, an intellectual disability can be avoided but subtle problems with fine motor control and learning may occur in children.
Sickle cell disease	1 per 500–600 children of African lineage; rates are also elevated in Mediterranean descendants	Children develop blood cells that are rigid and can't pass through small blood vessels. Children may experience pain, stroke, infection, tissue damage, and fatigue. Symptoms become obvious during the first or second year of life.	Be alert to medical crises, such as strokes. Offer comfort to children who are tired or in pain. Treatments include blood transfusions and medication for pain and infections.
Cystic fibrosis (CF)	1 per 3,300 children from European backgrounds and 1 per 9,500 children from Hispanic backgrounds	Children develop glands that produce thick, sticky mucus that creates serious problems with breathing and digestion. Usually beginning in infancy, children exhibit persistent coughing, wheezing, pneumonia, and a big appetite with little weight gain. Many individuals with CF now live well into their 40s.	Be aware of symptoms that require medical care. The condition is often treated with physical therapy, medication, and bronchial drainage.

(continued)

TABLE 4-1 Common Chromosomal and Genetic Disorders in Children (*continued*)

DISORDER	INCIDENCE	CHARACTERISTICS[a]	IMPLICATIONS FOR CARE
Tay-Sachs disease	1 per 2,500–3,600 children among Ashkenazi Jews (of Eastern European ancestry)	Children develop a fatal, degenerative condition of the central nervous system because they lack an enzyme required to break down a fatty substance in brain cells. At about 6 months of age, children slow down in growth, lose vision, and develop an abnormal startle response and convulsions. Other functions are gradually lost, and children develop an intellectual disability, can no longer move, and die by age 3 or 4.	Offer love and attention as you would to other children. Be alert to new accommodations that are needed, such as securing the surroundings when children lose sight. There is no known cure or treatment.
Thalassemia (Cooley's anemia)	1 in 800–2,500 individuals of Greek or Italian descent in the United States; rates are lower in other groups	Children develop blood cells that do not transmit oxygen effectively and as a result become pale, fatigued, and irritable within their first 2 years of life and may also develop feeding problems, diarrhea, enlargement of the spleen and heart, infection, and unusual facial features and bone structures. Young people sometimes die by early adulthood.	Help children cope with health problems. Treatment may include blood transfusions, antibiotics, and bone marrow transplants.
Duchenne muscular dystrophy	1 per 3,000–4,000 boys	Boys develop a progressive muscular weakness because of the absence of an essential protein needed by muscle cells. Between ages 2 and 5, they stumble and walk on their toes. They may lose the ability to walk between ages 8 and 14 and eventually die from respiratory and cardiac problems.	Watch for respiratory infections and heart problems. Treatments include physical therapy, orthopedic devices, surgery, and medications to reduce muscle stiffness.

[a]This table describes typical symptoms. Children's actual functioning depends on medical treatments; experiences with families, teachers, and other children; and their other genes.
[b]X-linked defects based on a single dominant gene also occur but are rare. For example, children who receive the gene for hypophosphatemia on their X chromosome produce low levels of phosphate and develop soft, easily deformed bones.

Sources: Austeng et al., 2013; J. W. Ball et al., 2010; Blachford, 2002; Burns, Brady, Dunn, & Starr, 2000; Cody & Kamphaus, 1999; Dykens & Cassidy, 1999; Hazlett, Gaspar De Alba, & Hooper, 2011; Jorde et al., 2010; Lepage, Dunkin, Hong, & Reiss, 2013; Massimini, 2000; J. L. Miller, Lynn, Shuster, & Driscoll, 2013; S. Mills, & Black, 2014; K. L. Moore et al., 2013; Nilsson & Bradford, 1999; M. P. Powell & Schulte, 1999; Prows, Hopkin, Barnoy, & Van Riper, 2013; J. T. Smith, 1999; Waisbren & Antshel, 2013; Wynbrandt & Ludman, 2000.

Chromosomal abnormalities occur in about 1 in 150 births (March of Dimes, 2013). One such abnormality, an extra 21st chromosome or extra piece of one, causes *Down syndrome.* Children with Down syndrome show delays in mental growth and are susceptible to heart defects and other health problems. Apparently, the extra 21st chromosome causes biochemical changes that redirect brain development. The severity of disabilities caused by Down syndrome and many other chromosomal abnormalities varies considerably from one affected child to the next. Yet educational strategies and medical treatments have improved considerably in recent years, such that life expectancy has increased to nearly 60 years, and a growing number of young people with Down syndrome are earning their high school diplomas, attending college, holding down jobs, and living independently (Prows et al., 2013). You can watch an Observing Children video about the special medical needs of children with Down syndrome.

The second type of genetic disorder occurs when a child inherits a *single-gene defect* from one or both parents. Resulting physical problems tend to be more specific and subtle than those caused by chromosomal abnormalities. Nonetheless, some single-gene defects are quite serious. The usual pattern of inheritance is that children who inherit a dominant-gene defect show the problem. Those who inherit a recessive-gene defect show the problem only if both genes in the allele pair are defective (transmission is slightly different in X-chromosome-linked defects).

Observing Children 4-2

Watch a video about the characteristics of children with Down syndrome.

ENHANCEDetext *video example*

Some genetic problems do not fit neatly into the categories of chromosomal abnormality or single-gene defect. For instance, a few conditions are mild or severe depending on the particular sequence of chemical compounds on a gene. An example is *fragile X syndrome,* which results from a genetic defect on the X chromosome. When this defect is small and limited, people who carry the problem gene are able to produce some of the necessary protein, and as a result they may show no symptoms or only mild learning disabilities. But the defect can intensify as it is passed from one generation to the next and lead to full-blown fragile X syndrome (Narayanan & Warren, 2006). Children with this condition develop severe learning disabilities, emotional problems, and intellectual disabilities (J. W. Ball et al., 2010; Hagerman & Lampe, 1999; McDuffie, Kover, Hagerman, & Abbeduto, 2013). Children tend to have prominent ears, long faces, double-jointed thumbs, and flat feet, and they are prone to sinus and ear infections. They also tend to be socially anxious, sensitive to touch and noise, and inclined to avoid eye contact and repeat certain activities over and over (e.g., spinning objects, waving their arms, and saying a particular phrase). The problems of girls with fragile X are generally less serious than those of boys because girls have a second X chromosome that is usually healthy enough to produce the missing protein.

Other physical problems are the result of multifactorial influences. *Spina bifida* (in which the spinal cord is malformed) and cleft palate (in which a split develops in the roof of the mouth) are examples of such conditions, which tend to run in some families but do not typically follow simple patterns of genetic transmission. Instead, affected children have genes that made them susceptible to particular risks, such as their mother's vitamin deficiency (especially, the shortage of folic acid, a B vitamin), illness, or medications such as anticonvulsant drugs taken by their mother as their bodies were being formed (J. W. Ball et al., 2010; K. L. Moore et al., 2013; Wallingford, Niswander, Shaw, & Finnell, 2013). You can watch an Observing Children video about a couple's experiences in raising a child with spina bifida.

All children require individualized care, but those with chromosomal abnormalities, single-gene defects, and other genetic conditions and birth defects strongly benefit from customized interventions. In fact, children who have significant biologically based disabilities can, with systematic instruction tailored to their individual needs, make dramatic gains in intellectual and social development.

Increasingly, parents and teachers have realized that these accommodations can usually be made in the regular classroom. In a practice called **inclusion**, children with exceptional needs are educated with their nondisabled peers in the general education classroom for all or part of the school day. Many teachers and specialists have found that when they keep an open mind about what their students can accomplish, intervene first when children are young, set specific goals, and think creatively about how they can adapt the curriculum, instruction, and activities for individual students, almost everyone can participate effectively in the regular classroom (Grosche & Volpe, 2013; Rao, Ok, & Bryant, 2014; Zigmond, Kloo, & Volonino, 2009).

In the United States and in many other nations around the world, children with identified special needs are entitled to accommodations. The student, his or her parents, the classroom teacher, and other specialists collaborate in a meeting to establish an **individualized education program (IEP)**. In the United States, the Individuals with Disabilities Education Act mandates that an IEP be prepared for children with designated disabilities, including a cognitive disability; emotional disorder; autism; an impairment in hearing, vision, language; or another characteristic that interferes with learning. After the IEP has been prepared, designated professionals contribute to the student's educational program, whenever possible in the regular classroom. You can listen to a special education teacher, speech therapist, and interpreter describing the services they provide for Star, a girl with an intellectual disability, in an Observing Children video.

The Awakening of Genes

Earlier we explained that only some genes are active within cells at any given time. As a result, some genes have an almost immediate influence on the development of physical characteristics, but many others don't manifest themselves until later. For example, the infant's body length at birth is determined largely by exposure to prenatal conditions in the mother's

Observing Children 4-3
Watch a video about a couple's experiences in raising a child with spina bifida.
ENHANCEDetext *video example*

Preparing for Your Licensure Examination
Your teaching test might ask you about the educational rights of students with exceptional learning needs.

Observing Children 4-4
Listen to several educational professionals talk about their goals and services for Star.
ENHANCEDetext *video example*

uterus and is only minimally influenced by heredity. By 18 months of age, however, we see a definite correlation between children's heights and the heights of their parents, presumably because genetic factors have begun to exert an influence (Tanner, 1990).

Maturational influences in genetic expression are also seen in *sensitive periods* age ranges dictated by heredity during which time highly specific environmental experiences are necessary for normal development. For the duration of a sensitive period, the child is biologically primed to develop a specific ability as long as these conditions are present. For example, children are especially sensitive to language input during infancy and early childhood. By regularly participating in conversation, young children easily learn one or more languages. Children deprived of language during early childhood require considerable intervention if they are to acquire a first language later in life.

In other areas, such as reading and engaging in productive social relationships, there is no single restricted time frame for learning. Children who have had inadequate experiences in these areas can frequently make up for lost time. However, educators should not wait for delayed children to catch up in fundamental academic and social skills. Such competencies build cumulatively over time, and without appropriate intervention, children may easily fall further behind and develop self-perceptions of being incapable.

Numerous emerging characteristics are tightly controlled by genetic instructions, a phenomenon known as **canalization** (Waddington, 1957). Growth and basic motor skills are highly canalized: Getting taller and crawling, sitting, and walking appear under a wide range of circumstances and almost invariably without training or encouragement. Only extremely unusual environmental conditions can stifle them, such as when a young child exposed to heavy doses of a toxic substance (e.g., lead paint and pesticides) is seriously behind age-mates in mastering basic motor and psychological skills (C. Cole & Winsler, 2010; de Wit, Sas, Wit, & Cutfield, 2013; Gottlieb, 1991). Spared from such poisons and allowed to move freely for even small amounts of time, children almost always grow taller and develop such motor skills as handling objects and walking proficiently.

Many skills are *not* tightly canalized, however. Most of the abilities that children acquire at school—reading, writing, mathematical problem solving, and so on—are modified by experiences both inside and outside the classroom. Social skills also rely on environmental support. Deciphering other people's intentions, learning to anticipate others' actions, and taking turns during conversation are competencies that are refined with social involvement. Thus, genes that support these particular abilities are flexible in the learning outcomes they permit.

The Blending of Heredity and Environment

In addition to responding to maturational states *inside* the child, genes react to conditions that originate in the *outside* environment. Children who participate in progressively challenging activities and obtain nutritious meals, affection from caregivers, and encouragement to act with self-control are apt to achieve their full genetic potential (Brant et al., 2009; W. Johnson, Deary, & Iacono, 2009; Rutter, 2013). Other environmental involvement, including opportunities for physical activity, exposure to light, protection from certain viruses, and medication also influence children's genetic expression.

The tendency for a child's genes to be dynamically influenced by so many factors means that few developmental outcomes can be anticipated with certainty. In other words, genes make particular characteristics likely but do not guarantee their manifestation. Furthermore, the interactions across domains of development means that genes guiding a distinct area of growth can affect progress in other areas. A 6-year-old girl with a healthy diet and regular physical activity will refine her motor skills, perhaps learning to ride a bicycle and play basketball. These new skills open the door for other developments, perhaps making new friends and exploring surrounding neighborhoods. Another 6-year-old girl who has a weak diet and leads a sedentary life will not find it as easy to acquire athletic skills or leverage sports for social purposes.

Evidence from multifactorial traits indicates that environmental factors nudge certain genes into action. People appear to have genetic predispositions to various temperaments—becoming particularly cheerful, outgoing, moody, anxious, or aggressive (P. T. Davies,

Cicchetti, Hentges, & Sturge-Apple, 2013; Glahn & Burdick, 2011; Rothbart, Posner, & Kieras, 2006; A. C. Wood, Saudino, Rogers, Asherson, & Kuntsi, 2007; M. U. Zuckerman, 2007). Yet these traits are clearly influenced by the environment, especially when children are young and gaining foundational skills for coping with emotions and relating to other people (Lemery-Chalfant, Kao, Swann, & Goldsmith, 2013; Plomin, Owen, & McGuffin, 1994). We're not born wild or shy; instead, we're born with certain tendencies that our environments may or may not promote.

As children grow, their environment continues to influence genetic expression but children themselves become progressively capable of altering their surroundings to serve their natural abilities, a phenomenon known as **niche construction** (E. G. Flynn, Laland, Kendal, & Kendal, 2013; Laland, Odling-Smee, & Feldman, 2000; Saltz & Nuzhdin, 2014; T. Ward & Durrant, 2011). Think about an athletic boy who joins a baseball team, organizes neighborhood games, requests sports equipment from parents, and in other ways creates occasions for practicing athletic skills. Consider another young man who is especially quick-witted, joins the drama club at school, entertains peers with his antics, and organizes a comedy night at school. By altering their environments, both young men essentially arrange for the refinement of their own genetically based talents. As you might expect, there is a developmental trend in niche construction—with age, children become increasingly persistent in choosing their pastimes and therefore more and more capable of expressing their unique characteristics.

It should now be clear to you that genes do not dictate appearance, behavior, or even cell functioning in any simple way. Genes operate in concert with one another; are affected by nutrition, stress, and other environmental agents; and are activated by hormones and physiological circumstances. Individual genes are influential at particular points in development; occasionally characteristics emerge that *seem* to come "from nowhere," having been dormant for many years and then brought into play.

Acknowledging Nature and Nurture in Children's Lives

Genetics may appear far removed from the responsibilities of teachers. Yet the reality of working in a busy classroom is that children learn and react differently in large part because of variations in heredity. At the same time, evidence of strong environmental influences inspires optimism in our ability to make a difference for children. We offer the following recommendations:

• **Make allowances for individual differences.** Teachers who value a multitude of physical characteristics, personality types, and talents are apt to put youngsters at ease. Children who are tall and short, chubby and thin, coordinated and clumsy, shy and outgoing, and calm and irritable all have a rightful place in the hearts of adults who educate them.

• **Remember that environmental factors influence virtually every aspect of development.** Children's development is *not* simply an outgrowth of biology. Even when children have inherited a tendency toward certain talents, temperaments, and deficits, their paths can be steered one way or another with physical activity, social interaction, school instruction, and the like. Children who are genetically predisposed to be irritable or distractible can, with guidance, learn more productive ways of responding (Beauchaine et al., 2013; Reiss, 2005; A. E. West & Weinstein, 2012). Guidance can take a variety of forms, including informal coaching from others and structured programs that teach children how to interact appropriately with peers, express their emotions constructively and gain control over their attention during task completion.

• **Intervene when children struggle.** There is an extended window of time for most types of learning, but we cannot leave it to chance that delayed children catch up on their own. Basic intellectual, social, and emotional skills affect many aspects of life, making it important to offer extra guidance when progress is unusually slow. Furthermore, without appropriate intervention, children who straggle behind peers may come to doubt their capability for learning, leading to even more serious problems, such as dropping out of school. Fortunately, classroom teachers, special education teachers, counselors, and school

BIOECOLOGY OF DEVELOPMENT

Evidence that children who share a genetic anomaly (e.g., Down syndrome or Phenylketonuria) exhibit variations in relevant characteristics attests to the complexity and malleability of genetic expression.

psychologists can work with students and families to design instruction that facilitates good progress.

• **Be mindful of your own reactions to demanding temperaments in children.** Evidence suggests that parents adapt their caregiving styles to individual children's temperaments (Deater-Deckard, 2009; Pener-Tessler et al., 2013). Those with mild temperaments and good self-control elicit calm reactions from parents, whereas others who are irritable push parents' buttons. This same tendency may occur to some extent with teachers, who also adjust to children based on their characteristic behaviors. Consequently, teachers and other professionals must try to remain calm while interacting with oppositional children (Keogh, 2003; Rudasill, Pössel, Winkeljohn Black, & Niehaus, 2014).

• **Encourage children to make growth-promoting choices.** Especially as they grow older, youngsters actively seek out experiences compatible with their natural tendencies. Adults can present options for cultivating youngsters' talents and remediating any pronounced weaknesses. For instance, a socially outgoing boy with an excessive amount of energy and little self-control often interrupts lessons. His teachers may remind him to hold his tongue and give others a chance to speak.

• **Consult with parents and specialists for a child with an exceptional need.** Children with identified needs will typically be assigned a team of experts a classroom teacher can consult on goals and strategies. Contributing your own insights is important, and you can practice determining these needs in an Assessing Children exercise.

Summary

All children have a set of genetic instructions that influence their characteristics at birth and their emerging physical and psychological features. Most of the genes that children inherit are ones they share with other children, giving them a common human heritage. Other genes contribute to children's individuality by prompting them to look and act in unique ways. Genes exert their effects on children through complex and interactive processes in cells and systems in the body. Children's health, physiological processes, and experiences mediate the effects of genes. Teachers and other professionals can keep in mind that all children have genetically based characteristics that make certain kinds of relationships, behaviors, and accomplishments relatively easy or difficult for them. Adults can express their confidence that, whatever children's natural abilities, they have the potential to achieve high personal standards.

ENHANCEDetext *self-check*

Assessing Children 4-1

Practice assessing the needs of a child with a genetic disorder.

ENHANCEDetext *application exercise*

PRENATAL DEVELOPMENT

During **prenatal development**, the period of growth between conception and birth, a simple, single cell is transformed, step by step, into a complex human being. During this remarkable journey, the organism undergoes a series of changes in an environment especially suited to its fragile capabilities.

Phases of Prenatal Growth

The developing baby-to-be must accomplish several important tasks, including growing new cells, moving through the mother's body, settling into the interior wall of the mother's uterus, taking in nutrition and expelling wastes, forming and refining basic body structures, and activating rudimentary learning abilities. Following *conception*, there are three phases of prenatal growth: the periods of the *zygote*, *embryo*, and *fetus* (see Figure 4-4).

Development of the Zygote

During the middle of a woman's menstrual cycle, an *ovum* (female gamete) emerges from one of her two *ovaries*. The ovum enters the adjacent *fallopian tube*, a narrow and curved pipe that connects the ovary to the uterus. The ovum is guided toward the uterus by pliant fringes in the fallopian tube. When a man ejaculates during sexual intercourse, he releases 200 to 600 million sperm into the woman's vagina, with about 200 finding their way into the uterus and through the fallopian tube (K. L. Moore et al., 2013). When fertilization takes place, a single sperm attaches to the ovum and enters it (Figure 4-5). The ovum cooperates by rearranging its exterior layers so that no other sperm can enter. The ovum and the sperm then combine their chromosomes, and the zygote, a new being, is formed.

The zygote creates additional cells as it travels downward through the fallopian tube and toward the uterus. In a process called **mitosis**, the zygote adds new cells through a duplication process that preserves the original 46 chromosomes. During mitosis, the spiral staircase of DNA straightens itself up and splits down the middle, and each half re-creates the original structure. After two exact copies of the chromosome have been formed, one copy from each pair moves to opposite sides of the cell, with the two sides gradually splitting apart into new cells. This process of mitosis continues throughout the life span and permits both growth and replacement of worn-out cells.

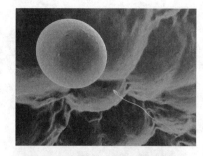
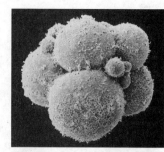
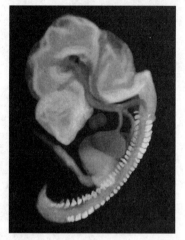
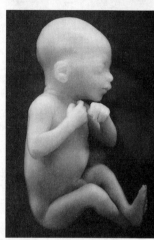

FIGURE 4-4 Miracles of prenatal growth. Human prenatal development begins at fertilization (top left) and then progresses through the periods of the zygote (top right), embryo (bottom left), and fetus (bottom right).

In the zygote, the first cell separates into two cells; these two cells divide to make four cells; four split into eight; and by the time the zygote has 16 cells, it is entering the uterus. These cells align themselves as the exterior lining of a sphere. Now about a week old, the zygote attaches itself to the wall of the uterus. The zygote separates into two parts, one a tiny being that will develop further into an embryo, and the other the *placenta*, the spongy structure in the uterus that provides nourishment. Cells begin to specialize and merge with other similar cells to form distinct structures, such as the nervous system and brain. The implanted zygote releases hormones, telling the ovaries that a conception has occurred and that menstruation should be prevented. In two short weeks, the new being has initiated its own growth, taken a journey, and found a hospitable home.

Development of the Embryo

The period of the **embryo** extends from 2 through 8 weeks after fertilization. Tasks of the embryonic period are to instigate life-support systems and form basic body structures. The placenta becomes larger, stronger, and more elaborate as it goes about its job of supplying food, liquid, and oxygen; removing wastes; and secreting hormones that sustain the pregnancy. An *umbilical cord* forms and connects the embryo to the placenta.

The embryo itself undergoes rapid structural changes and increases in size. During prenatal development, growth tends to occur from top to bottom (head first, feet last) and from

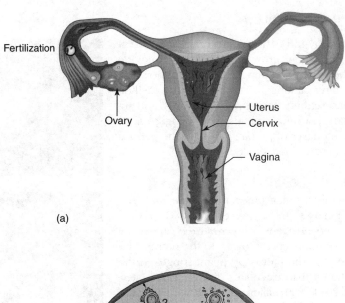

(a)

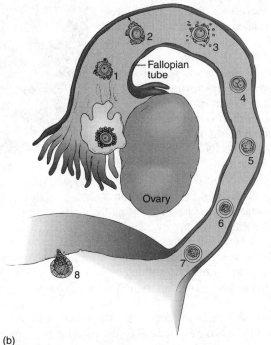

(b)

FIGURE 4-5 **Fertilization and the zygote.** (a) *Fertilization* occurs after sperm are deposited in the vagina and make their way into the uterus and Fallopian tubes. One sperm enters the ovum and releases its chromosomes; fertilization occurs. (b) The fertilized egg (1), now called the *zygote*, begins its journey in the fallopian tube (2), fusing its two sets of chromosomes into one nucleus. About 30 hours after fertilization, the organism starts to grow through cell division (3), first slowly and then more rapidly until the zygote resembles a ball of tiny cells (4, 5, and 6). Cells adhere to one another, leaving room for a fluid-filled cavity that provides space for growth, extension outward for emerging appendages, and formation of the placenta. The zygote enters the uterus (7) and implants in the uterine wall (8) where, conditions permitting, it will grow for 9 months and be born.

inside to outside (torso before limbs, arms and legs before hands and feet). Consistent with these trends, the head and heart are among the first structures to develop (see Figure 4-6). The growth of the neural tube that will give rise to the brain and spinal cord is well under way. Neurons—the cells that form connections in, and to and from, the brain—emerge and move to their proper places. Buds of limbs begin to develop, and by the eighth week, fingers and toes are recognizably distinct as separate digits. Internal organs appear and begin to develop.

Week 4	Week 5	Week 6	Week 7	Week 8
(28–32 days)	(35–38 days)	(42–44 days)	(48–51 days)	(54–58 days)

FIGURE 4-6 **Development of the embryo.**

Development of the Fetus

The period of the **fetus** lasts from week 9 until birth. During this period, the developing being grows rapidly, refining structures and receiving finishing touches that permit life outside the womb (see Figure 4-7). The many organs and structures that were initiated earlier are now expanded, and they become coordinated with other systems in the body. The fetus's body is elaborated through a series of specific changes:

- *Third month*—the head is large in comparison to the rest of the body and now allows other parts of the body to catch up. The eyes move to their proper places, and the fetus becomes increasingly human looking. The external genitalia grow. The fetus begins to show reflexes and muscular movement. The mother does not yet feel these movements.
- *Fourth month*—the fetus grows rapidly in length (height). Weight increases slowly. Hair grows on the head and eyebrows. Eye movements occur.
- *Fifth month*—the fetus continues to increase in length. Fine hair covers the body, and a greasy substance protects the fetus's delicate skin. The mother can usually feel the fetus's movement by now.
- *Sixth month*—the fetus has red, wrinkled skin and a body that is lean but gaining weight. Fingernails are present. The respiratory system and central nervous system develop and synchronize their operations.
- *Seventh month*—eyes open and eyelashes are present. Toenails grow. The body begins to fill out. The brain has developed sufficiently to support breathing.
- *Eighth month*—skin is pink and smooth. Fat grows under the skin. The testes (in males) descend. (K. L. Moore et al., 2013; Sadler, 2010)

During the final months of prenatal development, the fetus hones its basic body structures and also gains weight, slowly at first and more steadily as birth approaches. On average, the fetus at 6 months of prenatal growth weighs approximately 1 pound, 13 ounces; at 7 months, 2 pounds, 14 ounces; at 8 months, 4 pounds, 10 ounces; and at 9 months, 2 weeks (full term), 7 pounds, 8 ounces (K. L. Moore et al., 2013). These last few weeks of weight gain increase the chances of an infant's survival after birth. In fact, infants rarely survive when they are born before 5½ half months of prenatal development or at weights of less than 1 pound, 6 ounces.

9–12 weeks	13–18 weeks	19–24 weeks	25–36 weeks

FIGURE 4-7 **Development of the fetus.**

The brain makes steady progress toward maturation during the final weeks and months of prenatal growth. Structurally, the outer layers of the brain (those closest to the skull) bunch up into folds and creases, creating a staggering number of potential circuits for transmitting information. Functionally, the fetus's brain prepares to carry out such vital reflexes as sucking, swallowing, and looking away from bright lights. In the weeks before birth, the fetus's brain also activates pathways for sensing stimulation, including sounds and visual patterns, and learning about the world.

In fact, studies now show definite learning taking place during these final prenatal weeks. In one study, mothers from Ontario, Canada, who were in the final weeks of pregnancy were randomly assigned to one of two treatments (Kisilevsky et al., 2009). Both groups of mothers lay on their backs with audio speakers placed about 10 centimeters above their abdomens. One group of mothers rested while listening to guitar music and while a prerecording of a passage they had previously recited from *Bambi* was played through headphones above their abdomen. The second group also rested and listened to guitar music as a different prospective mother's prerecording of the same *Bambi* passage was emitted over their abdomen. As the mothers rested, their fetus's heart rate was examined. Results indicated that the heart rates of fetuses exposed to their own mother's voice were higher than those of fetuses exposed to an unfamiliar woman's voice. Presumably, fetuses recognized their own mother's voice, having been previously exposed to her conversation. Studies such as this one suggest that rudimentary abilities to learn simple patterns are present before birth.

As you have seen, the formation of a human life is the outcome of many changes. Growth is carefully managed by nature, constantly drawing from nurture. In spectacular feats of coordination, new cells extend body parts such that structures become increasingly defined—for example, simple paddles turn into elongated arms, arms add hands, and hands add fingers. Genetic expression and prenatal development show wonderful balances between nature and nurture, universality and diversity, and qualitative and quantitative change, as you can read more about this in the Basic Developmental Issues table "Biological Beginnings."

Medical Care

Prospective parents invariably hope for healthy children. To enhance their chances of giving birth to strong, well-formed infants, prospective mothers and fathers can look after themselves and obtain medical advice.

Preparing for Pregnancy

A woman can increase her chances of having a healthy infant by caring for herself *before* becoming pregnant. Physicians and nurses may suggest that a woman hoping to conceive watch her diet, take approved vitamin supplements, exercise moderately, and avoid alcohol and drugs. Medical experts will review her prescriptions and over-the-counter medicines because some are harmful to embryos and fetuses. For example, the acne medication Isotretinoin appears to cause serious malformations in some offspring (M. R. Davidson, London, & Ladewig, 2008; Organization of Teratology Information Specialists [OTIS], 2013a). Medical personnel may also address particular health problems that can become complicated during a pregnancy, such as hypertension or diabetes. Finally, physicians and nurses may discuss any concerns related to the woman's age. Pregnant women under age 17 sometimes have poor nutrition and give birth to infants with low birth weight. Advanced age in mothers and fathers (35 or older for mothers, 40 or older for fathers) is associated with slightly elevated risks for genetic problems, and older mothers are at minor risk for complications during the pregnancy and for giving birth to a baby with a physical malformation (Centers for Disease Control and Prevention, 2013; M. R. Davidson et al., 2008; Vaughan, Cleary, & Murphy, 2014).

Yet the responsibility for avoiding toxic substances must not rest entirely on mothers-to-be. Prospective fathers, too, should take precautions in the days, weeks, and months before conceiving a child. Evidence is growing that men's exposure to mercury, lead, alcohol, cigarettes, and other substances is associated with miscarriage (spontaneous loss of the

BASIC DEVELOPMENTAL ISSUES
Biological Beginnings

ISSUE	GENETIC FOUNDATIONS	PRENATAL DEVELOPMENT
Nature and Nurture	Nature forms sperm and ova and fuses them to form an organism with a unique genetic makeup. Nurture is evident in environmental effects on parents' chromosomes, as occurs when radiation creates errors in reproductive cells. During prenatal development, nature and nurture work in concert: Particular genes are activated according to nutrition and the organism's maturation.	Nature and nurture are closely intertwined during prenatal development. The effects of nature are evident in predictable, ordered changes to body structures and in the formation and operation of supporting physical structures, such as the placenta. The effects of nurture are seen in nutrition, protection from harmful substances, and the mother's stress management.
Universality and Diversity	The vast majority of children are born with 46 chromosomes. Most genes are uniform instructions across children for building bodies and brains. Some genes vary systematically across children and permit individual differences in height, weight, physical appearance, motor skills, health, intellectual abilities, and temperament. Errors in chromosomes and genes are another source of diversity.	In healthy organisms, there is considerable universality in the sequence of changes. The organism proceeds through phases of the zygote, embryo, and fetus, and ultimately is born after approximately 9 months. Diversity occurs because of variations in mothers' health and exposure to or protection from harmful substances, the genetic vulnerability of the fetus, and the efficiency with which physical structures in the womb sustain life.
Qualitative and Quantitative Change	Qualitative changes are made possible by the careful sequence with which particular genes are triggered. At appropriate times, selected genes spring into action and create qualitative changes in the child's body, including the makeover of puberty. As genes direct the body to mature, they also permit quantitative changes, including steady increases in height and weight.	The future baby undergoes a series of qualitative transformations. As a zygote it moves through the fallopian tubes, grows new cells, and burrows into the inside wall of the uterus; as an embryo it forms the basic organs and structures of the body; and as a fetus it builds and refines these preliminary structures and activates physiological processes for survival. Quantitative changes are present in the rapid production of new cells, particularly in the brain and body prior to birth.

offspring), low birth weight, and birth defects in their offspring (Engeland et al., 2013; Sadler, 2010). The expectant father's prior exposure to certain chemicals and substances is also associated with birth defects in offspring (Desrosiers et al., 2012).

A man and woman concerned about conceiving a child with significant problems may consult a genetic counselor. The genetic counselor examines the couple's medical records and those of siblings, parents, and other biological relatives. Diagnostic tests may be conducted, including an analysis of the potential parents' chromosomes. Genetic counselors inform the couple of medical facts, inheritance patterns, estimated risks for having a child with a birth defect, and ways to deal with risks. Counselors may recommend that prenatal diagnostic tests be conducted during a pregnancy and refer to parents for counseling should they want it.

Avoiding Harmful Substances

During prenatal development, some babies-to-be are unfortunately exposed to potentially harmful substances, or **teratogens**. Examples of teratogens include many prescription and nonprescription drugs; alcohol; infectious agents such as rubella, syphilis, and human immunodeficiency virus (HIV); and dangerous environmental chemicals, including lead and polychlorinated biphenyls.

Prenatal development includes a series of *sensitive periods* for forming physical structures. Body parts are especially vulnerable when they are first emerging, growing speedily, and laying the foundation on which more refined extensions can be built. Thus the timing of exposure to teratogens partly determines their impact. A newly formed *zygote* has not yet begun to form separate body parts and tends not to sustain structural defects when exposed to teratogens. Occasionally, exposure to teratogens can cause death of the zygote, or alternatively a few cells will die or become damaged, with these cells being replaced with healthy cells (K. L. Moore et al., 2013). For the *embryo,* damage can be serious. The principal parts of the body, including the limbs and the internal organs, are formed during this phase, and exposure to drugs, alcohol, and other teratogens can cause major problems. Limbs are particularly sensitive to harm 24 to 36 days after conception. Keep in mind that during this early phase of the pregnancy, women may not yet know they are pregnant. As a general rule, the *fetus* is less susceptible to serious structural damage, although there are many exceptions: Notably, the brain continues to grow until (and after) birth and, as a result, it is susceptible to damage late in pregnancy and during infancy.

The genetic makeup of both mother and baby moderates the effects of teratogens. For example, phenytoin is an anticonvulsant medication prescribed for some people who have epilepsy. Between 5 and 10 percent of children exposed to phenytoin as embryos develop a small brain, an intellectual disability, wide spaces between eyes, a short nose, and other distinctive facial features (K. L. Moore & Persaud, 2008). About a third of exposed embryos show minor congenital problems, and approximately half are unaffected. Presumably, genetic factors are partly responsible for these different outcomes.

The amount of teratogen exposure is important: The greater the exposure, the more severe and widespread the effects. Clearly, women who are pregnant must exercise caution in the food and substances they ingest and the toxins they are exposed to in the environment. In fact, this need for caution extends to all women who are sexually active and capable of being pregnant, because women are not always aware that they are carrying rapidly growing offspring. Here are some examples of particular teratogens and their potential effects on offspring:

- *Alcohol*—women who drink alcohol excessively during pregnancy are prone to have infants with *fetal alcohol syndrome.* Cells in the brain are disrupted, physical development is delayed, facial abnormalities occur, intellectual disabilities are common, and children become impulsive and exhibit other behavioral problems. In less severe cases, children may develop learning disabilities and minor physical problems.
- *Nicotine*—women who smoke cigarettes are in danger of giving birth to small, lightweight babies and (less often) to losing their offspring through miscarriage.
- *Marijuana*—women who smoke marijuana regularly during pregnancy are at risk for giving birth to infants with low birth weight and having children with attention problems.
- *Cocaine*—women using cocaine during pregnancy are likely to have a miscarriage; give birth prematurely; and have babies with low birth weight, small head size, lethargy, and irritability.
- *Methamphetamines*—babies exposed to methamphetamines may be born early, small, and light and have risks for problems in respiration, hearing and seeing, and learning.
- *Organic mercury*—pregnant women who ingest high levels of mercury from diets rich in fish are at risk for giving birth to children with abnormal brains, intellectual disabilities, attention problems, and motor disabilties.
- *Rubella*—pregnant women who become infected with the virus rubella (also known as German or three-day measles) early in their pregnancy may give birth to children with cataracts, heart problems, and deafness.
- *Toxoplasmosis*—toxoplasmosis is an infection contracted by exposure to a parasite found in cat feces and undercooked infected meat. Infants who have been exposed prenatally to this condition may develop such serious problems as abnormal growth of the brain, heart, kidneys, or other internal organs, and they may have trouble seeing and hearing.
- *Herpes simplex*—pregnant women with the herpes simplex virus are vulnerable to having a miscarriage or giving birth prematurely to infants with physical problems.
- *HIV infection and AIDS*—unless treated medically, pregnant women with the HIV virus are in jeopardy of passing on the condition to their children, and children who

become infected may initially show delays in motor skills, language, and cognitive development, and they may ultimately develop more serious health impairments. (Boucher et al., 2014; Buka, Cannon, Torrey, Yolken, and the Collaborative Study Group on the Perinatal Origins of Severe Psychiatric Disorders, 2008; M. R. Davidson et al., 2008; K. S. Montgomery et al., 2008; OTIS, 2013b, 2013c, 2013d; Slotkin, 2008; C. B. Smith, Battin, Francis, & Jacobson, 2007; Tzilos, Hess, Kao, & Zlotnick, 2013)

Maternal anxiety can also create problems for the fetus. Pregnant women who experience high levels of stress may develop complications and are apt to give birth to infants with low birth weight and short-tempered dispositions and, later in life, difficulties in focusing attention and dealing with negative emotions (Bekkhus, Rutter, Barker, & Borge, 2011; Guardino & Dunkel Schetter, 2014; Huizink, Mulder, & Buitelaar, 2004; Wakeel, Wisk, Gee, Chao, & Witt, 2013). Of course, most women experience some stress during their pregnancy, and mild emotional strain is probably harmless and may even help stimulate growth of the fetus's brain (DiPietro, 2004).

Implementing Medical Procedures

Several medical procedures are available for checking on the status of prenatal offspring. With requests from parents for diagnostic information, medical personnel schedule the tests for the particular periods of pregnancy that yield the most accurate results.

Some parents, like Joan and Dave in our introductory case study, permit only noninvasive tests, which do not involve probes or needles being inserted into the uterus. Examples of noninvasive include examining maternal blood samples, the relative size and structure of particular parts of the fetus's body from the ultrasound scan, and the mother's age to identity risks for certain chromosomal abnormalities such as Down syndrome, spina bifida, and defects in the abdominal wall.

The *ultrasound examination* (also known as ultrasonography) has become a routine part of obstetric care for pregnant women in many countries. Ultrasound devices emit high-frequency sound waves that bounce off tissues of varying densities in the fetus, typically after 6 to 7 weeks of prenatal development. The apparatus is passed over the woman's abdomen or inserted in her vagina. Echoes from the waves are converted into two-dimensional images and displayed on a television monitor, providing an image such as that in Figure 4-8. Ultrasound examinations provide good estimates of the age of the fetus, detect multiple fetuses, and reveal major abnormalities. Ultrasounds are also used as anatomical guides during the implementation of other prenatal tests. No long-term risks to the fetus from an ultrasound test have been found, although the procedure is recommended only if necessary (American Pregnancy Association, 2013a). Images confirm the reality of the pregnancy for expectant parents, as one father reported:

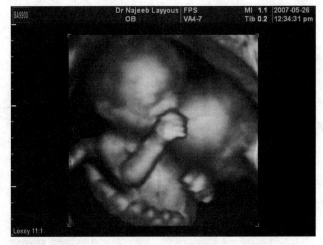

FIGURE 4-8   Image of fetus in an ultrasound scan.

> Yes, when (she) got pregnant I didn't really understand it. But after we had the ultrasound I did. . . . It was the most exciting thing I have done as far as the baby is concerned. It was more exciting than when I heard that we were going to have a baby. (Ekelin, Crang-Svalenius, & Dykes, 2004, p. 337)

Several other prenatal diagnostic techniques are available but generally avoided except by women with high-risk pregnancies. *Chorionic villus sampling* (CVS) is an invasive diagnostic procedure performed between 10 and 12 weeks after conception (London et al., 2007). A needle is inserted into the woman's abdomen, or a tube is guided through her cervix, and tiny amounts of chorionic villi (blood vessels that grow on the membrane surrounding the developing fetus) are collected. Abnormalities detected by CVS include chromosomal abnormalities, X-chromosome-linked disorders such as Tay-Sachs disease, and some diseases of the blood, for example sickle cell disease. Results are typically available within a few days. The procedure entails a small risk for damage to an arm or leg of the embryo or fetus, and miscarriage is possible but unlikely (Sadler, 2010).

Amniocentesis is an invasive diagnostic procedure usually performed sometime between 14 and 20 weeks after conception. A needle is inserted into the woman's abdomen to draw a small amount of fluid from the uterus. The fluid is analyzed for high concentrations of a fetal protein, which are present when fetuses have *neural tube defects* and certain abdominal problems. Fetal cells floating in the amniotic fluid are analyzed for possible chromosomal abnormalities. Other problems detected by amniocentesis are biochemical defects, prenatal infections, gene defects, chromosomal errors, and blood diseases. Results from cell cultures usually take 2 to 4 weeks to analyze. Risks associated with amniocentesis are trauma to the fetus, infection, and miscarriage (fetal loss rates are less than 1 percent; Sadler, 2010).

Medical researchers are now working on diagnostic tests that are not invasive and can instead be conducted with a simple blood test from the mother, since fetal cells are cast off and circulate in the mother outside the uterus. Non-invasive blood tests can identify chromosomal and genetic defects in the fetus (Daley, Hill, Lewis, & Chitty, 2014; Chiu & Lo, 2013). Other tests are performed only as certain conditions are suspected. In consultation with the mother, a physician may use a *fetoscope,* an instrument with a tiny camera and light, to examine the fetus for defective limbs or other deformities. Corrective surgery is performed in rare circumstances.

When couples learn that their offspring has a chromosomal abnormality or other serious defect, they may be shocked initially and subsequently ask for support from counselors, medical personnel, and family and friends (C. L. Anderson & Brown, 2009; Balkan et al., 2010; Farrelly et al., 2012; Lalor, Begley, & Galavan, 2009). Depending on their values and circumstances, some couples choose to terminate the pregnancy, concerned that they will not be able to care adequately for a child with special needs. Other couples want practical tips and emotional support in preparing for the birth of a child with a disability, believing in the fetus's right to life and their ability to be caring parents for the child.

Supporting Parents, Protecting Babies

If you work with prospective parents, you may be able to educate them about prenatal development and their future child's need for protection. Here are some specific tactics to take, should the opportunity arise:

• **Encourage women to evaluate their health *before* becoming pregnant.** Women who are planning a pregnancy or capable of becoming pregnant can consult with a physician. Women who take over-the-counter or prescription medications can ask about risks for a pregnancy and alternative ways of managing chronic conditions. Women can also begin to watch their diet carefully and, if medically warranted, take particular vitamin supplements.

• **Remind sexually active women and men to take care of themselves.** Women may be several weeks along (or longer) in a pregnancy before they become aware of it. Consequently, women who might be pregnant should watch their diet and restrict their exposure to teratogens, including alcohol, and avoid x-rays. Men may need to be advised that they, too, can put their future children at risk by exposing themselves to harmful substances.

• **Urge pregnant women to seek medical care.** Some pregnant women are reluctant to see a nurse practitioner, physician's assistant, or doctor. Yet prenatal care is necessary to detect and treat problematic conditions in mothers and offspring. For example, pregnant women with HIV can be treated with antiretroviral therapy, helping control the infection and in many cases preventing transmission of the virus to their offspring. Under the guidance of a doctor, pregnant women often begin or alter an existing exercise program. Getting regular exercise can help pregnant women keep up their stamina, prepare for birth, and ease stress. Getting adequate rest is another important goal for pregnant women, even though doing so is sometimes difficult, especially when they have other children, jobs, and ongoing household responsibilities.

- **Use well-researched strategies when reaching out to young women who need prenatal care.** Outreach is critical but it must be done effectively. Public health officials who have consulted with pregnant women have found that effective strategies include toll-free hotline numbers, radio spots, posters in visible locations, and materials written in the language spoken by expectant mothers (P. A. Doyle et al., 2006; Torres, Smithwick, Luchok, & Rodman-Rice, 2012). When women make their first prenatal visit, health care professionals can make the experience pleasant and informative. In one program targeting women who faced various risks such as being adolescent or uninsured, participants met four times with a registered nurse and wrote out their goals; attended childbirth classes; and received books, a car seat, maternity clothes, and a few other materials (Kapka, 2013). These young women had healthier babies than did women with similar risks who did not participate in the program.

- **Advise pregnant women about nutritional resources.** All expectant mothers need healthful diets. Yet some women may not remember to eat well, and others cannot afford to do so. With encouragement, expectant mothers can set goals for eating nutritiously, and, if they need it, for registering with community agencies. For example, the U.S. Special Supplemental Nutrition Program for Women, Infants, and Children (WIC) offers supplemental foods with nutrients that are generally lacking in the diets of low-income populations but vital for healthy prenatal development (e.g., protein, iron, folic acid, calcium, and vitamins A and C).

- **Urge pregnant women to stay clear of teratogens.** Smokers can be encouraged to reduce the number of cigarettes they smoke or, better, quit smoking altogether. Twenty-year-old Veronica, first-time mother and smoker since the age of 13, was concerned that her smoking would harm her baby and decided to phase out cigarette smoking one cigarette at a time, until the fourth month of her pregnancy, when she quit altogether and commented, "I have done what I can, now the rest is up to God" (Nichter et al., 2007, p. 754).

Expectant women who drink alcohol or take drugs can be confronted with the permanent damage these substances can cause in children. Obviously, pregnant women who are physiologically dependent on alcohol or drugs need immediate professional help. For their own sake and that of their children, women who continue to abuse substances after their babies are born also need professional treatment. Many of these mothers additionally need guidance with parenting skills (J. A. Bailey et al., 2013; J. V. Brown, Bakeman, Coles, Platzman, & Lynch, 2004; Slesnick, Feng, Brakenhoff, & Brigham, 2014). Community counselors and family educators can advise parents about helpful programs in their area.

- **Ask pregnant women to speak their minds.** Many expectant mothers have experiences they want to share. They may have concerns about possible birth defects, labor and delivery, and the costs of raising a child. Or they may simply want to communicate excitement about the sensation of the fetus stirring within. These women appreciate sympathetic listeners who let them talk about their changing and occasionally conflicting feelings.

- **Ask fathers to talk about their experiences.** Many fathers are mystified with the physical changes their partners undergo during pregnancy. Some feel excluded during pregnancy. Although they had an obvious hand in creating the new being, they may believe they are not needed in further development (Genesoni & Tallandini, 2009). In reality, fathers play an enormously important role in supporting expectant mothers. Prospective fathers gain just as much as mothers from having a sensitive listener with whom to share their worries and hopes related to the baby.

- **Help pregnant adolescent girls address the many challenges in their lives.** Pregnant teenage girls have typical age-related needs, including forming a sense of their own identity, navigating the complex social world of school, mastering a complex academic curriculum, and asserting their autonomy at home. Pregnant teens must also cope with the physical and hormonal transformations of pregnancy, the imminent changes awaiting them at the baby's arrival, and the need to negotiate with the baby's father over responsibility for the child. At school, teachers and other professionals can encourage prospective mothers to make academic progress, learn about child development, and protect their health as well as that of their baby by eating well, trying to relax, getting good sleep, exercising, obtaining regular medical care, and avoiding harmful substances.

FOR FURTHER EXPLORATION . . .

Learn how you can work effectively with children who have learning challenges as a result of prenatal alcohol exposure.

ENHANCEDetext
content extension

• **Advise new parents about appropriate care when children have been exposed to teratogens.** Sadly, the brains and bodies of some children are impaired due to prenatal exposure to drugs, alcohol, infection, and other teratogens. A few effects are lasting, but even so, affected children benefit from responsive, predictable, and developmentally appropriate care. For example, many children who have been exposed to cocaine and other serious teratogens develop proficient language, communication, and interpersonal skills when they receive sensitive and high-quality care from parents, foster families, and other caregivers (J. V. Brown et al., 2004; Tsantefski, Parkes, Tidyman, & Campion, 2013). Special educational services can likewise enhance the academic and social skills of teratogen-exposed children.

Unlike many developmental accomplishments, for instance, learning to talk, walk, and ride a bicycle, most aspects of prenatal development cannot be observed directly. Nevertheless, scientific evidence and the mother's firsthand experience provide benchmarks as to what is happening to the baby-to-be during the various phases of growth. The Developmental Trends table "Prenatal Development" provides a useful synopsis of key prenatal developments and discernible signs of growth.

DEVELOPMENTAL TRENDS
Prenatal Development

PHASE OF PRENATAL GROWTH	WHAT YOU MIGHT OBSERVE	DIVERSITY	IMPLICATIONS
Zygote (Fertilization until 2 Weeks After)	• The zygote begins to develop at conception with the fusing of the sperm and ovum. The offspring's first cell divides into two cells, two divide into four, four divide into eight, and so forth. The zygote is a ball of cells as it travels down the fallopian tube and into the uterus. • No signs of pregnancy are typically noticeable to the prospective mother.	• Couples vary in their chances of conceiving a child. • Some children are conceived with the assistance of reproductive technologies. • Large numbers of zygotes perish because errors in chromosomes cause them to be seriously malformed and unable to grow. • Hormonal factors in the woman can cause loss of zygotes.	• Encourage prospective parents to plan for pregnancy by first taking stock of their health, talking with a physician, and, if they have concerns about potential genetic problems, seeing a genetic counselor. • Persuade prospective parents to follow the physician's recommendations regarding prescription medications, over-the-counter drugs, and vitamins. • Advise sexually active women to avoid alcohol and drugs.
Embryo (2 Through 8 Weeks After Fertilization)	• Body parts and organs are being formed as the embryo rapidly develops. At the end of the period, the little being shows a head structure and limbs that are recognizably human. • The prospective mother may notice that her menstrual period is late. She may experience early signs of pregnancy, including nausea, fatigue, abdominal swelling, and tender breasts.	• The embryo is especially susceptible to damage from harmful substances. The extent of harm done by teratogens depends on the timing and duration of exposure, the amount of the dose, and the biological vulnerability of the embryo. • Miscarriage is fairly common during this period.	• Encourage a prospective mother to see a nurse or physician if she believes she might be pregnant. • Encourage pregnant women to shield themselves from potentially harmful substances. Educate prospective mothers and fathers about the impact of teratogens on developing offspring.
Fetus (9 Weeks After Fertilization Until Birth)	• Organs and body parts continue to grow and mature. • The mother can feel the fetus moving, lightly at first and vigorously over time. • The mother's abdomen swells, and the mother gains weight.	• Many pregnant women feel strong and healthy during the final months of pregnancy, but some experience nausea and fatigue. • Fetuses vary in their movements, growth rates and birth weights, and readiness for survival at birth.	• Advise pregnant women to follow the advice of their nurse, physician, and midwife regarding diet, exercise, and weight gain. • Listen to prospective mothers and fathers talk about their hopes, fears, and expectations related to the baby. • Advocate for abstinence from alcohol and drugs; discourage cigarette smoking. • Encourage pregnant women to manage their stress levels. • Inform pregnant women about prepared childbirth classes in their area.

Source: Browne, O'Brien, Taylor, Bowman, & Davis, 2014; Harden et al., 2014; K. L. Moore et al., 2013.

Summary

At conception, the new offspring inherits a unique genetic makeup that guides the lifelong process of growing, changing, and interacting with the environment. Development begins at fertilization, when the *zygote,* a one-celled being, divides multiple times and becomes a ball of cells that burrows into the uterus. From weeks 2 through 8, the *embryo* grows rapidly, forming structures needed to sustain future growth and developing rudimentary organs and body parts. Between week 9 and birth, the *fetus* continues to grow quickly, now receiving the finishing touches on body and brain and becoming sufficiently heavy and strong to live in the outside world. Professionals can support healthy prenatal growth by informing prospective parents (and all sexually active individuals) about the damaging effects of teratogens; the need to evaluate health and medical regimens before a pregnancy; and the value of stress management, a healthful diet, appropriate exercise, and ongoing medical care throughout the pregnancy.

ENHANCEDetext *self-check*

Assessing Children 4-2

Practice assessing the psychological needs of adolescent girls who are pregnant.

ENHANCEDetext *application exercise*

BIRTH OF THE BABY

Childbirth is a complex series of events. The steps that culminate in birth are affected by the health of mother and baby; the relationships the mother has with family members, friends, midwives, medical personnel, and her partner, should she have one; her preferences for managing the physical strain of labor and delivery; and her cultural traditions and beliefs.

In many societies, childbirth is a natural event, unaccompanied by drugs or medical procedures. Numerous women in Western societies strive for a natural childbirth yet frequently use medical practices that ease their discomfort or protect their baby from complications. Women who choose to take medication and permit one or more procedures typically have good outcomes. In some cases, medical interventions save the life of mother or baby. However, in a sizable number of births women are pressured into medical procedures that are probably unnecessary and in some cases potentially harmful to them or their babies (Janssen et al., 2009).

In Western and non-Western societies alike, a clash often arises between traditional customs and the procedures of modern medicine. As you can see in the Development in Culture feature "Having Babies in Nepal," numerous contemporary health providers invite women to select from the best features of traditional methods and medical techniques.

Preparation for Birth

The birth of a child provokes a range of feelings in parents—excitement, fear, pain, fatigue, and joy. The events of birth are managed best when families prepare ahead of time, obtain adequate care, and hold reasonable expectations about the baby's abilities.

Some anxiety is common, but other than that parents are highly individual in their feelings about pregnancy and birth. One first-time mother may be eager to have her baby but worried about changes to her life, new financial pressures, and her lack of experience with children. Another prospective woman has plenty of support from her family and takes the momentous changes in stride. Such feelings, along with any concerns about controlling pain, can influence the actual birth experience (Guszkowska, 2014; Hall et al., 2009; Soet, Brack, &

BIOECOLOGY OF DEVELOPMENT
Childbirth is affected by biological processes and by the mother's choices, experiences, and cultural traditions.

DEVELOPMENT IN CULTURE
Having Babies in Nepal

Nepal is a small developing country nestled between China and India. Three rivers and a rough mountainous terrain make it difficult for the Nepalese to grow crops and travel between villages. These harsh conditions have given rise to a hardy people, most of whom are Hindus or Buddhists who advocate for loyalty in the family, respect for elders, nonviolence, and a commitment to meditation (Rolls & Chamberlain, 2004).

Sex roles are clearly demarcated in Nepalese culture, especially in the sparsely populated regions. In rural areas, women collect water, prepare meals, wash clothes, and aspire to live by ethics of modesty, obedience, and self-sacrifice. Men make the major decisions for the family, carry out strenuous agricultural tasks, and trade with other men in the village. Marriages typically take place between young women in their teens and young men in their early 20s. Most newly married couples eagerly await their first child and proceed to have three or more additional offspring.

Nepalese women are expected to remain self-sufficient during pregnancy and childbirth. Prenatal development is presumed to be a natural process that progresses with divine help (Matsuyama & Moji, 2008). Medical care was not historically available in the rural areas, nor could women easily travel to hospitals or for that matter did they want to be examined by unfamiliar doctors, nurses, or midwives. In recent years, more and more clinics have been built but are not always used. When pregnant women decide that they need help, they generally ask mothers-in-law for practical advice and traditional healers for assistance in banishing evil spirits (Justice, 1984; Regmi & Madison, 2009). However, when men and women are both educated about the need for prenatal care, expectant mothers are more likely to obtain prenatal care (Joshi, Torvaldsen, Hodgson, & Hayen, 2014).

Most Nepalese women are strong and robust. They work throughout their pregnancies, have smooth deliveries, and resume household toils soon after their babies are born. More than 9 out of 10 deliveries occur at home or in a cowshed (Regmi & Madison, 2009). Nepalese women typically give birth without medication, using such postures as kneeling, squatting, or standing (Carla, 2003). They regularly take herbal remedies to ease recovery after the birth.

But not every Nepalese woman has an easy time with pregnancy or birth. Occasional serious problems, including poor nutrition and health complications, go untreated and as a result, the mortality rate of Nepalese pregnant mothers is distressingly high—539 deaths per 100,000 live births (Kulkarni, Christian, LeClerq, & Khatry, 2009; Matsuyama & Moji, 2008). Moreover, almost 1 in 20 infants dies during childbirth due to serious difficulties during the delivery or before their first birthday because of such problems as inadequate nutrition, impure water, prolonged exposure to the cold, and contraction of infectious diseases (Central Intelligence Agency, 2010; Justice, 1984).

In recent decades, international agencies and local authorities have tried to prevent and treat medical problems of Nepalese women. Medical personnel have had mixed success, in part because their interventions have failed to address barriers in local conditions and have been seen as incompatible with cultural practices. In one program young women trained as midwives came primarily from the urban areas and were shunned in the villages because of the widespread belief that young women should not travel on their own or work side by side men (Justice, 1984). Some women have avoided going to hospitals because of the reputation of medical staff in discouraging local childbirth traditions, including beneficial delivery postures that allow mobility (Carla, 2003; Regmi & Madison, 2009).

Health initiatives have begun to accommodate the traditions and beliefs of Nepalese culture while offering mothers the benefits of modern medicine. A few programs are educating mothers-in-laws about maternal health, prenatal care, and danger signs during pregnancy and labor (Regmi & Madison, 2009). Many health care workers are now showing respect for cultural traditions, encouraging women to make their own choices, and selectively implementing intrusive medical procedures only for mothers with defined risks (Barker, Bird, Pradhan, & Shakya, 2007; Safe Motherhood Network Federation, 2010).

A BLESSING. Many Nepalese women have their first child during their teenage years, welcome a baby as a divine blessing, and bear the discomforts of pregnancy and childbirth without complaint.

Dilorio, 2003). Excessive levels of stress make for an unpleasant experience for parents and prolong the early stages of labor, raise the mother's blood pressure, and decrease oxygen to the baby. Parents can reduce their anxiety by getting organized for the baby, reaching out to loved ones, practicing relaxation exercises, and preparing other children in the family for the new arrival.

Health care providers and family educators can give useful information and needed reassurance to prospective parents. They might teach relaxation techniques; offer tips for posture, movement, and exercise; and persuade women to eliminate potentially risky behaviors. In Western societies, *prepared childbirth classes* are common. These programs typically include the following elements:

- Information about changes in, and nutritional needs of, the prospective baby
- Preparation for the baby's arrival, including arrangements for the baby at home and decisions about breastfeeding or bottle feeding
- Relaxation and breathing techniques that encourage the mother to stay focused, manage pain, reduce fear, and use muscles effectively during the various phases of labor
- Support from a spouse, partner, friend, or family member who coaches the mother throughout labor and delivery, reminds her to use the breathing techniques she has learned, massages her, and encourages her
- Education about the physiology and mechanics of delivery, types of positions during delivery, and pain medications and common medical interventions. (American Pregnancy Association, 2013b; Dick-Read, 1944; Jaddoe, 2009; Lamaze, 1958)

The pregnant woman and her partner, if she has one, may decide ahead of time where the birth will take place and who will attend to it. Hospitals offer the latest technology, well-trained medical staff, arrangements for insurance coverage, and pain medication, but they have definite disadvantages. Some parents perceive hospitals as instituting unnecessary treatments and as creating an impersonal climate that separates rather than unites family members during a momentous occasion. Hospitals have responded to concerns about their lack of family orientation by creating birthing rooms that are attractive, comfortable, and large enough to accommodate several family members. Community birth centers are home-like, inexpensive, and welcoming of extended contact with the newborn; however, they are less appropriate for women with high-risk deliveries, those who need emergency care or do not have adequate insurance to cover costs. Home settings offer families a familiar and comforting environment, allow family members to participate, are inexpensive, and give extended contact with the newborn. They have disadvantages similar to those of community birth centers and in many cases offer no pain medication, few emergency procedures, and minimal access to trained birth attendants (Brintworth & Sandall, 2013; Cheyney, Burcher, & Vedam, 2014; Symon, Winter, Inkster, & Donnan, 2009).

In North America, physicians most often deliver babies, but other common attendants include certified *midwives* who may or may not be trained as nurses. Midwives typically assume responsibility for advising the mother on prenatal care, delivery, and recovery after the birth. Increasingly mothers also turn to *doulas*, attendants at the birth who do not provide medical care but do offer emotional and physical support. Doulas help the mother develop a birth plan ahead of time and then stay by a mother's side throughout the childbirth, guiding her in effective breathing techniques, massaging her back, and coaching her through the process (Deitrick & Draves, 2008; Devereaux & Sullivan, 2013; Hye-Kyung, 2014).

In addition to seeking conventional medical treatment, many women avail themselves of *complementary therapies* during pregnancy and childbirth (J. Byrne, Hauck, Fisher, Bayes, & Schutze, 2014; M. R. Davidson et al., 2008; Fontaine, 2011; K. L. Madden, Turnbull, Cyna, Adelson, & Wilkinson, 2013; M. Mitchell, 2013). Complementary therapies supplement standard medicine and offer some benefits in health and relaxation. In other cases, women use *alternative therapies*, healing practices that are tried *instead* of conventional treatments. As complementary therapies or in lieu of conventional medical procedures, numerous women obtain *acupuncture*, a traditional Chinese treatment in which thin stainless steel needles stimulate precise locations on the body so as to relieve pain and promote wellness; *biofeedback*, a method for controlling muscle tension; or *self-hypnosis*, a self-induced state of relaxation and receptivity to suggestions about reducing distress. Many women derive a sense of well-being from *prayer*, during which they address (silently or vocally) the divine being of their faith, or from *meditation,* a quiet transcendent state during which the mind is still, peaceful, and uncluttered. Other common complementary and alternative therapies include *massage therapy*, relaxing manipulation of the body's soft tissues to reduce tension and promote comfort; *hatha yoga,* an Eastern practice of gentle exercises and breathing techniques; and use of herbs and essential oils.

Complementary and alternative therapies offer the advantages of being relatively low in cost, emphasizing wellness, and being noninvasive. Unfortunately, childbirth risks cannot always be anticipated and do not always respond to natural therapies. In rare situations medical procedures are needed to save the life of the mother or infant.

The Birth Process

Amazingly, medical researchers are still not able to pinpoint the cascade of changes necessary to trigger the uterine contractions that begin a woman's labor. Currently, medical researchers believe that a combination of factors precipitates labor, including hormonal changes in the mother's uterus and placenta and substances released by the baby's brain and lungs (L. Dixon, Skinner, & Foureur, 2013a). Some evidence indicates that up until the time of labor, a couple of genes suppress contractions with the help of the hormone progesterone. These genes lose that ability to prevent contractions when progesterone wanes late in pregnancy; as a result, the hormone oxytocin can unleash contractions (Zakar & Mesiano, 2013).

Typically, the mother's uterus begins preparations for birth 38 to 40 weeks into the pregnancy. Here is the incredible sequence of events that constitutes the birth process:

- As the pregnancy advances, the mother experiences *Braxton Hicks contractions*. These irregular contractions exercise the mother's uterine muscles without causing the cervix to open.
- In most cases, the baby settles in a head-downward position, which facilitates its passage through the birth canal. When babies are in breech position (situated to come out buttocks or legs first) or in a sideways position (a shoulder would likely come out first), the mother is monitored closely and often undergoes a *cesarean delivery*, a surgical procedure in which the baby is removed after an incision is made in the mother's abdomen and uterine wall.
- A few events may occur in the days immediately before labor begins. The mother may experience a descent of the baby into the pelvis, feel a rush of energy, lose 1 to 4 pounds as her hormonal balance changes, and notice vaginal secretions. Sleep is difficult at this time. Accordingly, health providers may coach mothers in using relaxation techniques and reassure them that sleep disturbances prior to labor rarely interfere with its progression.
- Uterine contractions, which widen the cervix opening, mark the beginning of childbirth, which progresses through four stages (Figure 4-9A–D). These stages are significant to midwives and medical personnel but are not necessarily experienced as distinctly different periods by mothers, with the exception of the baby's arrival, of course.
- In the *first stage of labor*, the mother experiences regular contractions. These contractions last until the cervix is dilated to about 10 centimeters (approximately 4 inches). Mothers feel pain during contractions, especially in their pelvis and back. This first stage typically takes about 12 to 16 hours for mothers who are having their first baby and 6 to 8 hours for mothers who have previously delivered one or more babies. Medical personnel keep track of the cervix opening and monitor the fetal heartbeat. They may offer pain medication and encourage the mother to walk around. At the beginning of the first stage of labor, contractions are spaced widely apart (e.g., every 15 to 30 minutes) and are mild to moderate in intensity. When the cervix dilates to 3 centimeters, an "active" phase begins and lasts until full dilation. Contractions become stronger and longer (they last 30 to 60 seconds) and occur every 2 to 3 minutes.

- In the *second stage of labor*, the cervix is fully dilated, the baby proceeds down the birth canal, and the child is born. This stage may take about half an hour, but in first pregnancies it often lasts up to two hours. Contractions come often and hard. They appear every other minute and last for a minute at a time. Mothers must push hard to help move the baby down and out. Medical personnel continue to watch the fetal heartbeat. The doctor may use forceps or call for a cesarean delivery if uterine contractions slow down or the baby does not move quickly enough. Too fast is not good either because the pressure might tear the mother's tissues or the baby's head. Thus, the doctor or midwife may place a hand on the part of the baby coming out and ease it out methodically. Medical personnel may also help rotate the baby's head so that it can get past the mother's pelvic bones. As the head comes out, the doctor or midwife checks to make sure the umbilical cord is not wrapped around the head, and if it is, the cord is removed. The nose and mouth are cleansed of fluids. The mother continues to push to eject the baby's shoulders and the rest of the body. The baby is gently wiped dry, and after the blood has drained from the umbilical cord into the baby's body, the cord is clamped and cut. The baby is born! The baby is placed on the mother, and the father or other coach may take a turn holding him or her. Oftentimes the baby is alert and looks around the room—a stunning and memorable event for the mother, father or other partner, and accompanying friends and family. You can watch the final moments of a normal birth and the extensive testing of the newborn that takes place in many hospitals immediately afterwards in an Observing Children video.

- In the *third stage of labor*, the placenta and fetal membranes (collectively known as the *afterbirth*) are expelled from the uterus (see Figure 4-9D). Usually, this process happens without assistance, although medical personnel must watch to make sure it happens. The mother is checked to see if lacerations have occurred and if medical treatment is needed.

- In the *fourth stage of labor*, one to four hours after birth, the mother's body begins to readjust after its exertion. Having lost some blood, the mother may experience a slight decrease in blood pressure, shake and feel chilled, and want to drink water and get something to eat. (M. R. Davidson et al., 2008; Demarest & Charon, 1996; L. Dixon, Skinner, & Foureur, 2013b; Sherwen, Scoloveno, & Weingarten, 1999)

Observing Children 4-5
Observe the final moments of a birth and the testing of a newborn infant.

ENHANCEDetext *video example*

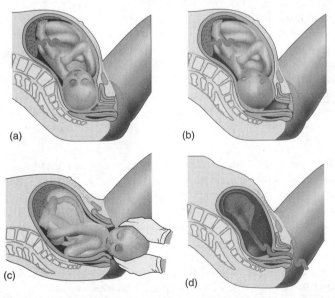

(a)   (b)

(c)   (d)

FIGURE 4-9 **Stages of a typical birth.** In the first stage of labor, the mother's cervix dilates (a). After numerous contractions the cervix opens completely, the baby's head moves down the vagina, and the second stage of labor begins (b). The second stage continues with the mother pushing with each contraction, the baby moving down the vagina, the baby's head appearing, and, gradually, the rest of the body emerging (c). The third stage of labor is the delivery of the placenta (d).

Medical Interventions

Medical personnel, midwives, and the mother's partner can do many things to comfort the mother as she goes through labor and delivery. Following are examples of procedures that are typical in many Western societies:

- Physicians may *induce labor*—that is, start it artificially—with medications (e.g., Pitocin). Candidates for an induced labor include women past their due dates and those with diabetes or pregnancy-induced hypertension.

FIGURE 4-10 Water Birth. This new mother delivered her baby in relaxing warm water at the hospital with help from a midwife.

- Midwives, doulas, partners, and medical staff may address the mother's pain with methods that do not require medication. Some mothers are assisted by a warm whirlpool bath, visual images of the cervix opening, music, hypnosis, biofeedback, and massage. You can see a setting for a water birth in Figure 4-10.
- Physicians sometimes offer *analgesics,* medicines that reduce pain without loss of consciousness. Medications injected into the mother's spine (such as *epidural analgesia*) are an especially common method of relief. Generally, these medications are not offered early in labor, because they may slow progress, but also not too late, because physicians want the medicine to be metabolized by mother and baby prior to birth. Some analgesic medications can increase the need for other medical interventions, such as use of forceps and cesarean deliveries, and they may reduce breathing in the newborn.
- Physicians may offer *anesthetics* to women in active labor if extreme pressure must be applied (such as occurs in the use of forceps) or when a cesarean delivery must be performed. Anesthetics cause loss of sensation and in some cases lead to loss of consciousness.

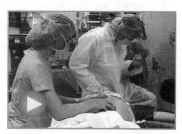

Observing Children 4-6

Watch a cesarean delivery.

ENHANCEDetext *video example*

- Women sometimes take *opioids* (also known as narcotics), medicines that reduce the sensation of pain by changing the way it is perceived by the brain. Opioids have several disadvantages, including limited effectiveness in reducing pain, occasional side effects such as nausea and drowsiness, and tendency to adversely affect the baby's breathing and breastfeeding.
- Slightly over 30 percent of babies born in the United States are delivered through cesarean surgery, a rate that many people suggest is higher than it should be (B. E. Hamilton, Martin, & Ventura, 2011). Cesarean deliveries are performed when the physician believes the safety of the mother, child, or both is at stake. Examples of conditions that might lead to a cesarean delivery are fetal distress, health problems of the mother, failure to progress in labor, infections in the birth canal, and the presence of multiple babies. You can watch a cesarean delivery in an Observing Children video.

Regardless of the specific medical treatments expectant mothers receive, they and their families invariably appreciate consideration for their needs and preferences. Nurses, midwives, doulas, and other attendants offer sympathetic reassurance to women in dealing with the pain and loss of control that accompanies the birthing process. Depending on their cultural traditions, women may also appreciate support from their husbands, other partners, friends, or close family members during labor and delivery.

Many medical personnel and attendants consciously strive to accommodate women's cultural practices. For example, some Latinas prefer to stay at home during the early stages of labor, and when they do arrive at the hospital, may want to pray with partners and family members (Callister, Corbett, Reed, Tomao, & Thornton, 2010; Champion, 2013; Spector, 2004). The hospital staff will try to respect prayer, meditation, and devotion by not interrupting them. Muslim women might become distressed when unfamiliar male doctors and nurses see them uncovered; thus medical personnel take measures to ensure that mothers are covered and accompanied by other women during examinations (Abushaikha & Massah, 2013; Rassin, Klug, Nathanzon, Kan, & Silner, 2009). Chinese mothers may wish to follow cultural traditions of eating traditional foods, drinking tea, and asking for extra blankets to stay warm (Callister, Eads, & See Yeung, 2011). When they can, nurses adapt to these wishes. Women from a few cultural groups (e.g., some Native Americans and the Hmong from Laos) may ask to take the placenta home for burial in the ground in alignment with their religious beliefs, and medical personnel who understand the cultural significance will help them make these arrangements (M. R. Davidson et al., 2008; Fadiman, 1997).

Babies at Risk

Some babies are born before they are able to cope with the demands of life outside the womb. Two categories of babies require special care:

- *Babies born early*—a baby is considered full term at 38 weeks. The **premature infant** is born before the end of 37 weeks after conception (Sherwen et al., 1999). Premature labor may be precipitated by several factors, including infection, presence of two or more babies, abnormalities in the fetus, death of the fetus, abnormalities in the mother's uterus or cervix, and serious disease or infection in the mother. Extremely early babies (born after only 32 or fewer weeks of prenatal growth) face serious risk factors, including higher-than-usual rates of death during infancy. After birth, premature infants are at risk for health problems, including breathing problems, anemia, brain hemorrhages, feeding problems, and temperature instability.
- *Babies born small for date*—some infants are small and light given the amount of time they have had to develop in the mother's uterus. These babies are at risk for many problems, including neurological deficiencies, structural problems in body parts, breathing difficulties, vision problems, and other serious health problems (Charkaluk et al., 2012; Sadler, 2010). Small babies may have chromosomal or genetic abnormalities or may have been exposed to infections or harmful substances or received inadequate nutrition during their prenatal development.

Developmental Care for Babies at Risk

Babies born especially early or small may not have the physical maturity to breathe independently, regulate their temperature, or suck adequately to meet nutritional needs. Despite these challenges, babies can often survive with access to life-sustaining devices and medicines. Physicians and nurses strive to create a therapeutic atmosphere that is nurturing and developmentally appropriate. The following guidelines are recommended for those who care for a fragile infant:

- Reduce the infant's exposure to light and noise.
- Regulate the amount of handling of the infant by medical staff.
- Position the baby to increase circulation.
- Encourage parents to participate in the care of the infant.
- Inform parents about the infant's needs.
- Arrange diapering, bathing, and changing of clothes so that interruptions to sleep and rest are minimized.
- Encourage mothers and fathers to cuddle with the infant and carry him or her often and for long periods.
- Swaddle the baby in a blanket or with arms bent and hands placed near the mouth to permit sucking on fingers or hands.
- Massage the baby.
- Educate parents about the infant's condition and methods for caring for him or her. (L. F. Brown, Pridham, & Brown, 2014; L.-L. Chen, Su, Su, Lin, & Kuo, 2008; T. Field, 2001; E. C. Hall, Kronborg, Aagaard, & Brinchmann, 2013; Helth & Jarden, 2013; Sherwen et al., 1999)

When fragile babies become strong enough to leave the hospital and go home with their families, they may need specialized treatments. Their families may also benefit from support because these babies are not easily soothed. If parents of premature and health-impaired infants learn to fulfill infants' needs confidently and tenderly, however, these infants generally calm down and develop healthy habits in responding to distress (J. M. Young, Howell, & Hauser-Cram, 2005).

Thus, the developmental journeys of premature and sick newborn infants are typically *not* destined to be rocky ones. In fact, many early and small infants go on to catch up with peers in their motor, intellectual, and communication skills, particularly when families, educators, and other professionals meet their special needs (de Wit et al., 2013; Sheffield, Stromswold, & Molnar, 2005). Some premature children do have intellectual delays or persisting medical problems, such as visual problems or asthma, and they benefit from appropriate medical care, advocacy from families, and educational services that help them progress academically and socially. As they grow older, the children may require continued services, such as speech therapy and other individualized interventions. Without sensitive care and, if needed, effective intervention, some premature and low-birth-weight infants continue to face later problems in coping with negative emotions and in learning at school (Hack et al., 2012; Nomura, Fifer, & Brooks-Gunn, 2005; Shenkin, Starr, & Deary, 2004).

Enhancing Parents' Sensitivity to Newborn Infants

To give infants a healthy start on life, parents and other caregivers must recognize infants' abilities, interests, and styles of self-expression. Family educators and other professionals can support infants indirectly—yet powerfully—when they teach family members how to observe their infants closely and respond sympathetically to infants' individual needs. To get a sense of how you might enhance caregivers' awareness of these needs, see the examples in the Development and Practice feature "Showing Sensitivity to the Needs of Newborn Infants." Also consider these recommendations:

• **Reassure new mothers that they will be able to find the necessary energy and insight to care for their babies.** Many new mothers return home from the hospital feeling tired, sore, and overwhelmed by the demands of an infant, as reflected in these comments:

- "I guess I expected that our lives would change dramatically the moment we walked in the door with him . . . which they did!"
- "It's hard, and sometimes I don't want the responsibility."
- "I felt very much like I didn't know what to do!"
- "Some people are giving too much advice." (George, 2005, pp. 253–254)

These accounts reveal the need for a series of adjustments by new parents. Although mothers and fathers may want information about infants and their care, they are best able to act on this information when they have caught up on their rest and feel supported by friends, family, and health care professionals. When they need it, parents can reach out to others for support.

• **Share what you know about infants' sensory and perceptual abilities.** Infants learn a lot about the world from their sensory and perceptual abilities. **Sensation** refers to the infant's detection of a stimulus; for example, a newborn baby may sense a father's stroking movements on her hand. Infants sense many things that they don't necessarily focus on or think about. When infants do attend to and interpret a sensation, **perception** takes place, such as when a 6-month-old baby watches a moving image and perceives it to be his father.

At birth, many newborn infants look intently at the faces of parents and others, giving people the impression that infants are learning from the beginning of life. In fact, they are. What newborn infants actually *perceive* cannot be determined with certainty, but researchers have established that newborn infants are able to *sense* basic patterns and associations. The majority of infants can see well-defined contrasts and shapes, such as large black-and-white designs on checkerboards, but it takes time for the various parts of the eye to work efficiently and connect with brain structures that interpret visual stimuli.

During the first year of life, vision improves dramatically (D. L. Mayer & Dobson, 1982; Perone & Spencer, 2014; Ricci et al., 2007; van Hof-van Duin & Mohn, 1986). Infants can see

DEVELOPMENT AND PRACTICE
Showing Sensitivity to the Needs of Newborn Infants

Carefully observe the sensory abilities of newborn infants.

- A pediatric nurse watches a newborn infant scanning her parents' faces. The nurse explains that infants can see some shapes and patterns, are especially attracted to human faces, and rapidly gain visual acuity in their first few months. (Infancy)
- A doctor notices a 3-day-old infant turn his head after his mother begins speaking. The doctor comments softly to the baby in front of the mother, "Oh, you hear your mother talking, don't you, young man?" (Infancy)

Point out the physiological states of newborn infants.

- A family educator talks with parents about their newborn infants, commenting that infants commonly sleep for long periods but usually have brief periods each day when they are receptive to quiet interaction. (Infancy)
- A child care director watches the gaze of a newborn infant as her parents tour the child care center. "Hello little one," says the director. "You are taking it all in now, aren't you?" (Infancy)

Notice the kinds of stimuli that attract infants' attention.

- A mother watches her newborn infant while he is awake and alert. She notices that her son intently inspects her face and certain other stimuli, such as the edges of the bassinet. (Infancy)
- A 2-week-old infant stares at his father's face while sucking on the bottle. His father smiles back at him. (Infancy)

Encourage parents to watch for infants' preferences in being soothed.

- A pediatrician asks a new mother how she is getting along with her baby. When the mother reports that the baby cries a lot, the doctor asks her how the baby likes to be comforted. The doctor explains that most infants find it soothing to be held tenderly, but some relax while riding in a car or stroller. The doctor suggests that the mother keep informal records of the infant's fussy times and the kinds of care that eventually prove calming. (Infancy)
- A visiting nurse asks a new mother and her partner about the infant's frequent crying. The parents express their frustration and listen appreciatively when the nurse demonstrates several ways for calming the baby. (Infancy)

Model sensitive care for new parents.

- A family educator shows a new father how to hold the baby, change her diaper, and interact quietly and sensitively with her. (Infancy)
- A grandmother demonstrates to her daughter how to bathe her newborn son. The grandmother carefully tests the temperature of the water in the kitchen sink and assembles all of the bathing supplies before immersing him in a few inches of warm, sudsy water and gently patting down his skin with a clean cloth. (Infancy)

Offer appropriate care to fragile infants.

- A hospital offers lifesaving care to fragile infants and attends to their sensory abilities and psychological needs by reducing light, noise, and unnecessary medical procedures, and by massaging the infants a few times each day. (Infancy)
- In the neonatal intensive care unit of the hospital, mothers and fathers are allowed to hold their premature infants for a couple of hours every day in a procedure known as Kangaroo Care. One parent lies down on a bed and holds the infant on his or her bare chest. The baby's head is placed to one side to allow detection of the parent's heartbeat. A blanket is then placed over the baby, and the parent is encouraged to relax and allow the baby to do the same. (Infancy)

---

best from a distance of about 6 to 12 inches, quickly develop a preference for looking at faces, and explore the visual properties of objects. The sense of hearing is more advanced at birth than is vision. Recall that late in prenatal development, fetuses begin to hear and recognize their mothers' voices. Typically developing infants are born with the ability to experience touch, taste, and smell. Sensory and perceptual abilities continue to develop, and these abilities will, of course, make critical contributions to rapidly expanding knowledge about the world.

• **Point out the physiological states of newborn infants.** Unless they have previously had a child or been around newborn infants, parents may be surprised at how their infants act, how long they sleep, and how they respond to stimuli. Family educators and medical personnel can educate parents by explaining the nature of infants' **states of arousal**, the physiological conditions of sleepiness and wakefulness that they experience throughout the day. Infant practitioners can also point out their **reflexes**, those automatic motor responses to stimuli. One example of a reflex is an infant blinking his eyes when his father moves him close to a bright light. You can learn more about infants' reflexes in an Observing Children video. Also take a look at the Observation Guidelines table "Indicators of Health in Newborn Infants" on page 149 for descriptions of physical states you can share with parents.

Observing Children 4-7
Watch newborn infants exhibiting reflexes.
ENHANCEDetext *video example*

• **Encourage families to watch infants' responses to particular stimuli.** Infants give off clues about what they like and dislike, find interesting, and experience as pleasant or painful. However, it may take a while for caregivers to decipher infants' signals and the circumstances that elicit them. When infants are drowsy, asleep, or agitated, they do not show curiosity. When they are rested, comfortable, and awake, they may scan the visual environment, intently study the properties of a mobile over the crib, and smile at familiar vocalizations from a parent. By observing the textures, tastes, sounds, and visual properties that attract infants' sustained attention, parents and other caregivers can guess about things that interest infants—perhaps that the blanket feels soft, the juice tastes sweet, the melody is pleasing, and the rubber duck is visually attractive.

• **Discuss the kinds of stimulation infants might find soothing.** Babies have distinct preferences for being comforted. Different babies relax to varying sensations—listening to the rumble of the clothes dryer, nursing at Mother's breast, sleeping on Father's chest, or going for a ride in the car. Mothers and fathers who have not yet found the antidote to their infants' fussy periods may be grateful for suggestions about a range of soothing techniques.

• **Model sensitive interactions with infants.** Not all caregivers know how to interact in a gentle, reassuring manner with infants. Practitioners can show parents and other caregivers how to slow their pace, hold the baby gently but firmly, speak quietly, and watch for signs that the baby is ready to interact (e.g., the baby looks into caregivers' faces) or is distressed by the interaction (e.g., the baby looks away).

• **Show parents how to care for the baby.** First-time parents may appreciate some hands-on tips for administering to the needs of a new baby. Unless they have seen a baby being bathed, nursed, fed a bottle, diapered, or carried, new parents may not know how to perform these caretaking functions. You can watch a nurse show a new mother how to breastfeed her baby in an Observing Children video.

• **Offer early and continued support to parents of fragile infants.** Infants who are at risk for one reason or another—for example, those who are premature or have serious disabilities—can require unusually high levels of attention. Infants might cry often, be difficult to console, or need an intensive medical treatment. Some infants with health problems may be sluggish and solicit little interaction. In such cases family members may have practical questions about optimal care for their children, and they may also benefit from counseling and parent education.

Observing Children 4-8

Watch a nurse show a new mother how to hold her baby while breastfeeding.

ENHANCEDetext *video example*

Summary

The birth of the baby is an exciting and sometimes nerve-racking event for parents, who can reduce their stress by preparing for childbirth. Birth is a multistage process that is grounded in culture and often assisted by family members and doctors, nurses, midwives, and doulas. The health and medical needs of newborn infants depend on their birth weight, size, prior exposure to teratogens, and genetic vulnerabilities. Family educators and other professionals can help parents develop realistic expectations about their newborn infants and respond sensitively to their physical and psychological needs.

ENHANCEDetext *self-check*

OBSERVATION GUIDELINES
Indicators of Health in Newborn Infants

CHARACTERISTIC	LOOK FOR	EXAMPLE	IMPLICATION
Adjustment After Birth	• First breaths are taken within a half minute after birth (the doctor may suction fluid from the mouth and throat). • Attempts to nurse at the breast occur within a few hours after birth (the baby may lose a few ounces of weight during the first few days). • First urination and bowel movements occur within first 2 days. • In some babies, elongated head after birth that gradually regains round appearance; skin may be scratched and contain discolored spots that disappear within a few days.	Immediately after birth, Trinisha begins crying. Her head is misshapen and she has some blotchy spots on her skin. Her mother places Trinisha on her chest, and the baby quiets down, opens her eyes, and scans the room.	Before birth, encourage parents to arrange for appropriate medical care for their newborn babies. After birth, reassure parents about the appearance of their infant.
States of Arousal	• *Quiet sleep:* The infant lies still with closed eyelids and relaxed facial muscles. • *Active sleep:* Although the infant is sleeping, eyes may open and shut and move from side to side, facial expressions change and include grimaces, and breathing is irregular. • *Drowsiness:* The infant's eyelids may open and close without focus, and breathing is regular and rapid. • *Quiet alert:* The infant is awake, calm, happy, and engaged with the world. • *Active waking:* The infant wriggles in bursts of vigorous movements, breathes in an irregular tempo, has flushed skin, and may moan or grunt. • *Crying:* The infant cries and thrashes and has a flushed and distressed face.	In the first few days after birth, Kyle spends most of his time sleeping. Some of his sleep appears peaceful, and at times he appears to be dreaming. When Kyle is awake, he sometimes looks intently at people and objects close to him. At other times he appears agitated, and these episodes often escalate into loud and persistent crying.	Help parents notice infants' distinct states of arousal. Encourage them to develop a sensitive style of responding to infants' distress. Advise parents that when infants are in the quiet, alert state, this is a good time to interact calmly.
Reflexes	• *Rooting:* When touched near the corner of the mouth, the infant turns toward the stimulus, as if in search of a nipple. • *Sucking:* When a nipple or finger touches the infant's mouth, he or she begins to suck it. • *Swallowing:* Liquids are transferred from mouth to stomach with muscles in the throat. • *Grasping:* The infant grasps onto a finger or other small object placed in his or her hand. • *Moro reflex:* When startled, the infant stretches arms outward and then brings them together in a hugging motion. • *Babinski reflex:* When the inner side of the infant's foot is rubbed from heel to toe, the infant's big toe moves upward and the other toes fan inward toward the bottom of the foot. • *Stepping:* When the baby is held upright under the arms with feet touching a hard surface, the legs take rhythmic steps. • *Tonic neck reflex:* If the infant is lying on his or her back and the head is moved toward one side, the arm on that side extends out and away from the body, and the other side is flexed close to the head with clenched fist (resembling a fencing position).	Little Josefina lies on her back on a blanket as her mother washes the dishes. When her mother accidentally drops and breaks a dish, Josefina appears alarmed, extends her arms, and seems to be grasping for something in midair.	Gently demonstrate infants' reflexes to family members. Family members, including the baby's siblings, may begin to use the finger grasping reflex as a way to interact with the baby. Explain that reflexes indicate that the infant's brain and body is operating as it should.

Sources: Adamović, Sovilj, Ribarić-Jankes, Ljubić, & Antonović, 2013; Adolph & Berger, 2011; Jadcherla, Gupta, Stoner, Fernandez, & Shaker, 2007; Shevell, 2009; C. W. Snow & McGaha, 2003; Wolff, 1966.

PRACTICING FOR YOUR LICENSURE EXAMINATON

Many teaching tests require students to use what they have learned about child development in responses to brief vignettes and multiple-choice questions. You can practice for your licensure examination by reading the following case study and answering a series of questions.

Nadia's Horses

Autism spectrum disorders are a group of related disabilities in communicating and acquiring basic social and cognitive skills (Centers for Disease Control and Prevention, 2007; National Institute of Mental Health, 2008a). The most severe of the autism spectrum conditions is commonly known as *autism*. Children with autism typically have difficulty learning to speak and comprehending language. They generally withdraw from eye contact and other social interaction; do not understand social gestures or participate in pretend games; repeat particular actions incessantly (e.g., repeatedly turning the pages of a book); resist changes in routine; and exhibit unusual reactions to sensory experiences (e.g., they may shudder at the sensation of being draped with silk yet not react with pain after running into a wall). Autism appears to be caused by both genetics and exposure to teratogens (Aigner, Heckel, Zhang, Andreae, & Jagasia, 2014; Arndt, Stodgell, & Rodier, 2005; Freitag, 2007).

Nadia, an English child of Ukrainian immigrants, was identified as being autistic at age 6 (Selfe, 1977). By age 3, Nadia had spoken only 10 words, which she uttered rarely. Her language did not progress much further in the following years, and she found it especially difficult to learn abstract and superordinate concepts (e.g., "furniture") (Selfe, 1995). Nadia was clumsy, showed no concern for physical danger, and displayed regular temper tantrums. Yet like a small minority of other children with autism (Treffert & Wallace, 2002; Winner, 2000), Nadia was an exceptionally talented artist. After noticing her unusual artistic ability, Nadia's parents and a psychologist gave her paper and pens. Nadia drew several times a week, reproducing pictures she had studied days before in children's books, newspapers, or other printed material. Nadia's drawings were realistic but also creative representations of images she had seen—she occasionally reversed the orientation, changed the size, or constructed a composite of several images. As you examine two of her drawings, answer the questions on the next page.

Artwork by Nadia. Horse; age 3 ½ years (left). Horse and rider; age 5 ½ years (below).

Originally published in Selfe, Lorna (1977). *Nadia: A Case of Extraordinary Drawing Ability in an Autistic Child*. London: Academic Press. Used with permission of Lorna Selfe.

Constructed-Response Question

1. How might you as a teacher support Nadia's interest in drawing horses?

Multiple-Choice Questions

2. Which of the following statements most effectively represents how *nature* played a complex role in Nadia's abilities?

   a. Nadia's amazing ability to represent the contours of moving animals; realistic details in their faces, legs, and hooves; and depth and perspective may have had some genetic basis.

   b. Nadia's genes may have contributed to her autism.

   c. Nada's genes may have contributed to her delayed language ability.

   d. Genetic factors may have played a role in Nadia's artistic ability, autism, and language delays.

3. If Nadia had an individualized education program (IEP), who would contribute to the plan and what would it contain?

   a. Nadia's psychologist would prepare the IEP given that he or she would have the necessary expertise to determine Nadia's needs; the IEP would contain educational goals and strategies.

   b. Nadia's parents would advise her teacher and specialists about what they want Nadia to achieve. The teacher and specialists would convert the parents' wishes into educational jargon that would be acceptable to district officials. The IEP would contain educational goals and strategies.

   c. Nadia's teacher would prepare the draft of the IEP, with Nadia's parents and specialists subsequently having the right to veto separate sections. The IEP includes motivational aspirations for career goals for the student to achieve after completing school.

   d. Nadia's parents, teacher, other specialists, and perhaps Nadia herself would participate in the IEP meeting. The IEP would include educational goals and strategies for achieving these goals based on Nadia's abilities and experiences.

ENHANCEDetext *licensure exam*

Key Concepts

gene (p. 117)
chromosome (p. 117)
DNA (p. 117)
gamete (p. 119)
meiosis (p. 119)
zygote (p. 119)
monozygotic twins (p. 120)

dizygotic twins (p. 121)
alleles (p. 121)
dominant gene (p. 121)
recessive gene (p. 121)
codominance (p. 121)
multifactorial trait (p. 121)
inclusion (p. 125)

individualized education program
  (IEP) (p. 125)
canalization (p. 126)
niche construction (p. 127)
prenatal development (p. 128)
mitosis (p. 129)
embryo (p. 129)

fetus (p. 131)
teratogen (p. 133)
premature infant (p. 145)
sensation (p. 146)
perception (p. 146)
state of arousal (p. 147)
reflex (p. 147)

CHAPTER FIVE

Physical Development

CASE STUDY: Project Coach

Sam Intrator and Donald Siegel, professors in exercise and sports science, have devoted their careers to getting children actively involved in high-quality athletic programs. For Sam and Donald, helping children develop proficiency in sports is not an end in and of itself but rather a means to foster children's health, confidence, academic achievement, and communication skills (Intrator & Siegel, 2008).

As one of their initiatives, Sam and Donald reviewed children's involvement in sports in Springfield, Massachusetts, an economically distressed city with numerous adolescents not exercising, achieving in school, or protecting themselves from such risks as a pregnancy. Young people had few prospects to immerse themselves in sports, primarily because they were not accustomed to exercising and adults were not available to supervise their leagues. Few parents were able to serve as coaches, and no one else stepped forward to volunteer.

The situation seemed bleak to Sam and Donald until one day, in a conversation with Jimmy, the parks and recreation director, they came up with a creative solution: Ask teenagers in the community to work as coaches. The teenagers could benefit from the leadership training, and the children would finally have a viable sports league. Jimmy was enthusiastic about the idea, and *Project Coach* was launched.

As a training program, adolescents were recruited into an after-school program that taught them rules of sports, methods of coaching, and benefits of being a leader. The adolescent coaches acquired other advantages as well. They found themselves on a more productive path for their lives and restored their reputations as responsible citizens, rather than, as formerly, "problems to be managed" (Intrator & Siegel, 2008, p. 22). They learned how to solve problems, communicate clearly, and give effective feedback to children.

The elementary children who became involved loved the program. With teen leaders now trained, elementary children had a chance to play soccer and other sports. They had somewhere to go after school. And they had adolescent mentors from their own neighborhoods expressing interest in their welfare.

Having proven successful for both the adolescent coaches and their younger athletes, Project Coach drew interest from the local community, where it took roots and expanded. As of 2013, Project Coach had educated over a hundred coaches and a thousand young athletes (Project Coach, 2013).

- What kinds of physical needs did the children in Springfield have?
- How did the sports league affect children and their mentors?

As children develop, they undergo physical changes. They learn to crawl, walk, run, and play sports. They grow taller and stronger. They become increasingly proficient at handling small objects.

These and other physical developments depend on good nutrition, ample physical activity, and protection from harm. Thus children, and the adults who care for them, must prioritize nutritious food and address challenges to health. For some children, hazards come in the form of junk food. Other children cope with chronic illnesses or injuries. Many lack opportunities to exercise. Adolescents confront temptations with drugs and alcohol. In the case of young people in Springfield, they were inactive, bored, and careless.

Fortunately, Sam and Donald believed in the power of youth. They realized that the children could become physically fit and that local adolescents were part of the solution. New sports leagues allowed elementary school children to rehearse athletic skills, forge friendships, and have fun. Participating adolescents gained important lessons in leadership as well as productive outlets for their time.

As the Springfield youth demonstrate, health depends on conditions at school and in the community. In this chapter we examine age-related changes in physical development, brain growth, and the many strategies adults can implement to foster young people's physical well-being.

OBJECTIVES

5.1: Outline principles of physical development and the primary characteristics of children during each of the five developmental periods.

5.2: Summarize basic issues related to children's physical health, and explain how professionals can assist children in acquiring health-promoting habits and avoiding health-compromising behaviors.

5.3: Identify the brain's basic structures and developmental processes, and derive implications for educating children.

PHYSICAL DEVELOPMENT

Principles of growth underlie children's physical development. One modification after another transforms the newborn infant bundled in a parent's arms into an independent young adult.

Principles of Growth

The changes that occur during physical development are methodical. Patterns of growth follow these key principles:

Each part of the body has its own rate of growth. Genes tell particular parts of the body to grow quickly during distinct time periods. As a result, the relative proportions of different body parts change over childhood (see Figure 5-1). Early in development heads are closer to adult size than are torsos, which are more advanced than arms and legs. In the upper limbs, the hand approaches adult size sooner than the forearm does; the forearm approaches adult size before the upper arm does. Likewise in the lower limbs, the foot is more advanced than the calf, which is more mature than the thigh. You can see systematic changes in one boy's development in a series of Observing Children photographs.

Internally, separate systems also grow at different rates (London, Ladewig, Ball, Bindler, & Cowen, 2011; J. M. Tanner, 1990). The lymphoid system (e.g., tonsils, adenoids, lymph nodes, and the lining of the small intestines) grows rapidly throughout childhood and then slows in adolescence. Lymphoid organs help children resist infection, which is particularly important during the early and middle childhood years when children are exposed to many contagious

6 mos.   2 yrs.   5 yrs.   8 yrs.

11 yrs.   14 yrs.   16 yrs.

FIGURE 5-1 Physical development during childhood. Children grow taller and heavier as they develop, and the relative proportions of their body parts change as well.

Observing Children 5-1

This boy is wearing the same t-shirt in photographs taken at ages 1, 5, 9, 13, and 17. Notice that the boy's head is well developed during his first couple of years, after which time the torso and limbs accelerate in size. With time the boy grows taller, his arms and legs get longer, his face shifts from bring round to angular, and his hair color darkens.

illnesses for the first time. Following their own trajectory, reproductive organs expand slowly until adolescence, at which time they undergo a substantial burst of growth.

The outcome of separate systems growing at distinct rates is the body as a whole increasing in size, albeit with its parts progressing unevenly. Typical growth curves for height and weight reveal rapid increases during the first 2 years, slow but steady growth during early and middle childhood, an explosive spurt during adolescence, and a leveling off to mature levels by early adulthood (Hamill et al., 1979). Patterns of growth are similar for boys and girls, although girls on average have their adolescent growth spurts a year and a half earlier, and boys end up taller and heavier.

Functioning becomes increasingly differentiated. Every cell in a person's body (with the exception of sperm and ova) contains the same genetic instructions. As cells grow, they take on specific functions, some aiding with digestion, others transporting oxygen, still others transmitting signals, and so on. Thus individual cells "listen" to only a subset of the many instructions they have available. This progressive shift from having the *potential* to become many things to actually carrying out a specialized function is known as **differentiation**.

Differentiation characterizes many aspects of development. During prenatal development, the arms first protrude as tiny, round shoots, which gradually become longer buds and sprout globular hands, and eventually differentiate into fingers. After birth, fingers continue to elongate, with each one becoming distinct. In Artifact 5-1, you can see further differentiation in the hand over the childhood years. Motor skills, too, become increasingly specialized: They first appear as rough, unsteady actions but gradually evolve into precise, controlled motions.

Functioning becomes increasingly integrated. As cells and body parts differentiate, they begin to work together. Their increasingly coordinated efforts are known as **integration** (J. M. Tanner, 1990). The various parts of the eye coordinate their mechanical movements to permit vision; separate areas of the brain form connections for exchanging information; and fingers become more adept at synchronizing movements while handling small objects, as you can see in a series of Observing Children videos.

Each child follows an overall growth curve. Children's bodies pursue predetermined heights—not as specific as 4′9″ or 6′2″, but with definite ballpark targets for stature. Increases in height and weight show rapid growth during infancy, a slower rate of growth in middle childhood, and a spurt during adolescence. For individual children, growth curves, with the trajectory of height or weight plotted against age, are especially revealing when things go awry. Circumstances such as a serious illness or poor nutrition may briefly halt height increases. But when health and adequate nutrition are restored, children grow rapidly again. Before you know it, they're back on track—back to where we might have expected them to be, given their age and original rate of growth.

Sadly, exceptions to this self-correcting tendency occur when severe malnutrition is present early in life or extends over a lengthy time. Thus, children who were seriously undernourished during their prenatal phase may become shorter than they would have been

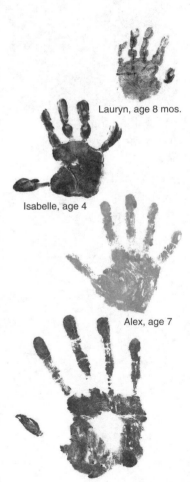

Lauryn, age 8 mos.

Isabelle, age 4

Alex, age 7

Connor, age 15

ARTIFACT 5-1 Growing apart. The separate fingers on a child's hand start out similar looking but become increasingly distinct (differentiated).

Observing Children 5-2

Observe developmental progression in hand grips by comparing three children, Corwin (16 months), Zoe (4 years old), and Elena (9 years old).

ENHANCEDetext *video example*

Observing Children 5-3

Observe Madison reaching for objects.

ENHANCEDetext *video example*

otherwise and might develop brain damage, mental and behavioral deficiencies, and motor difficulties (Belluscio, Berardino, Ferroni, Ceruti, & Cánepa, 2014; Rees, Harding, & Inder, 2006; Roseboom, de Rooij, & Painter, 2006; Shonkoff & Richter, 2013; M.-Q. Xu et al., 2009).

Physical development is characterized by both quantitative and qualitative changes. Quantitative changes are perhaps most obvious. Children continually eat, of course, and in most cases gain weight steadily. Motor skills, which may seem to the casual observer to emerge overnight, typically result from numerous gradual advancements, as when a young girl slowly improves in manual dexterity and eventually ties her shoes independently. Yet qualitative changes in motor skills occur as well (see Figure 5-2). As they grow from infants to toddlers to preschoolers, children walk not only more quickly but also in a series of transformations to posture, center of gravity, and rhythm (Gallahue & Ozmun, 1998; C. Hyde & Wilson, 2011; Wiebler, 2013).

Children's bodies function as dynamic systems. As you have learned, the specific parts in the body change over time, as do the connections among the parts, and children's own activity is an important element in maturation. To illustrate, infants apply considerable effort in coordinating the various muscles needed for reaching objects with arms and hands. Having moved their limbs spontaneously during the prenatal period and immediately after birth, infants gradually gain experience with voluntary movement and by 3½ to 4 months of age, they begin to reach for objects, first shakily and eventually smoothly (Rocha, de Campos, dos Santos Silva, & Tudella, 2013; Thelen & Smith, 2006). After some small improvements, infants often exhibit temporary *declines* in speed, directness, and smoothness in reaching, as if they must figure out how to address changes in muscle tone or deal with another new factor. With considerable practice and typically before 12 months of age, most infants can reach easily and quickly. You can see 7-month-old Madison adeptly reach for objects and transfer them from one hand to the other in an Observing Children video.

Children gradually discover how to offset personal limitations while coordinating their body parts. Infants who make vigorous, spontaneous movements in their first few months of life must learn to control their arms before they can successfully make contact with objects. In contrast, infants who generate few and slow movements have a different set of problems to solve: They must learn how to exert muscle tone in holding arms stiffly while extending them forward. The act of reaching, like so many motor skills, shows dramatic individual differences in pathways to proficiency.

Children's health is affected by their involvement in the environment. The bioecological model identifies the numerous people and settings that influence children's health-related decisions and habits (Gardiner & Kosmitzki, 2008; Naar-King et al., 2013; Pfefferbaum, Pfefferbaum, & Norris, 2010; Senefeld & Perrin, 2014). In their families, children learn to like certain foods and dislike others, follow an energetic or inactive lifestyle, and take or avoid physical risks. Parents' jobs indirectly affect children's health by generating resources for food, housing, and medical insurance (Y. R. Harris & Graham, 2007; Repetti & Wang, 2010; Ziol, Guest, & Kalil, 2012). Peers incite outdoor play and, as they grow older, gather at fast-food restaurants, in the park, at the gym, or on a street corner. School personnel may restrict or encourage children's movement and allow access to wholesome or non-nutritious

FIGURE 5-2 Qualitative changes in walking. In walking, children progress from (a) having difficulty maintaining balance and using short steps in flat-footed contact, to (b) a smoother pattern, where arms are lower and heel-toe contact occurs, to (c) a relaxed gait with reflexive arm swing (Gallahue & Ozmun, 1998).

meals on the lunch line. Neighbors are overweight, of normal weight, or underweight and demonstrate pastimes, perhaps playing Frisbee in the park, walking from one errand to the next, or sitting all day watching television and playing video games.

Growth During the Developmental Periods

Accompanying the orderly changes that take place in children's bodies are chances to practice motor skills, develop healthy habits, engage in physical activity, and relate to peers in new ways. We now describe the developmental periods in terms of their physical characteristics and health-related issues.

Infancy (Birth–Age 2)

Infancy is a period of rapid growth that builds on the foundations of prenatal development. Before the umbilical cord is cut, the first reflex, *breathing*, begins, providing oxygen and removing carbon dioxide. Breathing and a few other reflexes begin in infancy and operate throughout life. Additional reflexes, such as automatically grasping small objects placed in hands and responding to loud noises by flaring out arms and legs, last only a few months.

As infants grow older, they add motor skills to their physical repertoire. In the first 12 to 18 months, infants hold up their heads, roll over, reach for objects, sit, crawl, and take first steps. In the second year, they walk with increasing coordination and manipulate small objects with their hands. In an Observing Children video, you can see 16-month-old Corwin walking confidently. Corwin holds his arms high to maintain balance and is agile enough to stay upright while reaching down into a bag. He is also able to handle a toy adroitly.

Motor skills emerge in a particular order, following *cephalocaudal* and *proximodistal* trends (W. J. Robbins, Brody, Hogan, Jackson, & Green, 1928). The **cephalocaudal trend** refers to the vertical order of emerging skills, proceeding from the head downward. Infants first learn to control their heads, then shoulders and trunk, and later their legs. The **proximodistal trend** refers to the inside-to-outside pattern in which growth progresses outward from the spine. Infants first learn to control their arms, then their hands, and finally, their fingers.

Because infants cannot use words to communicate needs, practitioners must observe infants carefully and ask families about sleeping, eating, drinking, diapering, and comforting preferences. We offer ideas of what to look for in the Observation Guidelines table "Assessing Physical Development in Infancy."

Early Childhood (Ages 2–6)

Dramatic changes occur in gross motor and fine motor skills during early childhood. **Gross motor skills** (e.g., walking, running, hopping, tumbling, jumping, climbing, and swinging) permit movement throughout the environment. **Fine motor skills** (e.g., drawing, writing, cutting with scissors, and manipulating small objects) involve more limited, controlled, and precise movements, primarily with the hands.

During the preschool years, children master several gross motor skills, for instance riding a tricycle and throwing and catching a ball. Motor skills become smoother and better coordinated over time as a result of several factors—practice, development of longer arms and legs, and genetically guided increases in muscular control. Optimism, determination, and pleasure in using new skills also contribute to the learning process. When Teresa's son Alex was 4, he repeatedly asked his parents to throw him a baseball as he stood poised with a bat. Not at all deterred by an abysmal batting average (about 0.05), Alex would frequently exclaim, "I almost got it!" His efforts paid off, as he gradually did learn to track the ball and coordinate his swing with its path.

A lot of chatter, fantasy, and sheer joy accompany gross motor movements in early childhood. Often young children infuse pretend roles into physical play. They become superheroes and villains, cowboys and cowgirls, and astronauts and aliens. You can see creative and cooperative interactions between two 4-year-old children, Acadia and Cody, as they play on climbing equipment in an Observing Children video. The two children practice a variety of gross motor skills—running, climbing, throwing a ball—all in the name of play.

Young children also make major strides in fine motor skills. They dress and undress themselves and eat with utensils. They build blocks, put small pieces of puzzles together, and

BIOECOLOGY OF DEVELOPMENT
The bioecological model examines children's immersion in settings that influence their health-related decisions and habits.

Preparing for Your Licensure Examination
Your teaching test might ask you about major milestones in physical development during childhood.

Observing Children 5-4
Watch Corwin walking with good balance as he deftly handles a toy.
ENHANCEDetext *video example*

Observing Children 5-5
Watch Acadia and Cody playing actively and spontaneously at the park.
ENHANCEDetext *video example*

OBSERVATION GUIDELINES
Assessing Physical Development in Infancy

CHARACTERISTIC	LOOK FOR	EXAMPLE	IMPLICATION
Eating Habits	• *Ability to communicate hunger* to adults by crying, pointing, reaching, and using a few words • *Developing ability to suck, chew, and swallow* • *Ability to enjoy and digest food* without abdominal upset • *Cultural and individual differences* in how families feed infants	Wendy Sue is a listless eater who doesn't seem as interested in food as are the other infants. The caregiver tells her supervisor she is worried, and the two decide to talk with Wendy Sue's parents.	Talk with parents to learn about any individual health needs of the infant. Ask parents for their thoughts on infants' preferences for drinking, eating, and sleeping.
Mobility	• *Coordination of looking and touching* • *Emerging ability to move* toward objects • *Temperamental factors* that affect speed and amount of movement • *Physical challenges,* including hearing and visual impairments, that affect exploration • *Temporary disruptions* to exploration, as when separating from parents in the morning	Due to neurological damage during birth, Daniel's left arm and leg are less strong than the limbs on his right side. His teacher notices that he seldom moves around in the center. During a home visit, the teacher finds that Daniel's movements are lopsided, but he crawls energetically. The teacher realizes that Daniel needs to feel secure before he is confident enough to explore in the center.	Set up the environment so infants find it safe, predictable, attractive, and interesting. Help individual children find challenges in the environment that match their interests.
Resting Patterns	• *Typical moods and responses* prior to napping • *Families' expectations* for sleeping arrangements • *Difficulty falling asleep* • *Evidence that families understand risk factors* for sudden infant death syndrome (SIDS)	Angie cries a lot when falling asleep, in part because she is used to napping on her stomach at home. Her teacher explains to her parents that he places babies on their backs in order to reduce the risk of SIDS. He rubs Angie's forehead as she adjusts to her new sleeping position.	Talk to parents about risk factors for SIDS (see upcoming section on "Rest and Sleep"). Explain why babies should be placed on their backs rather than abdomens when falling asleep.
Health Issues	• *Possible symptoms of infections,* such as unusual behavior, irritability, fever, and respiratory difficulty • *Suspicious injuries and unusual behaviors* that may result from abuse • *Possible symptoms of prenatal drug exposure,* including extreme sensitivity and irritability • *Physical disabilities* requiring accommodation	A teacher enjoys having 18-month-old Michael in her care. Michael has cerebral palsy, making it difficult for him to scoot around. His teacher encourages him to move toward objects, but she also occasionally brings faraway toys to him to examine. When he has a fever, she calls his mother or father, as she would with any child.	Remain alert to signs of illness and infection in children. Contact family members when infants have a fever or show other unusual physical symptoms.

 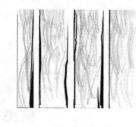

ARTIFACT 5-2   Cutting and writing. Isabelle, age 3½, traced shapes and wrote her name in the artwork on the left. Just learning to spell her name, Isabelle included two *E*s and two *L*s. In the artwork on the right, she practiced her cutting, attempting to follow the black lines and, showing her desire to cut in a straight line, correcting her work in the third rectangle from the left.

string beads. Some children spend considerable time drawing and cutting, forming creative shapes (e.g., by combining circles and lines to represent human beings), and mimicking adults' cursive writing with wavy lines or connected loops (Braswell & Callanan, 2003; Kellogg, 1967). In Artifact 5-2, you can see 3½-year-old Isabelle's creations in writing, drawing, and cutting.

Educators of young children notice pronounced individual differences in their fine motor skills. Children born with certain disorders (e.g., Turner syndrome or autism) and those exposed to alcohol during prenatal development show delays in fine motor skills (Connor, Sampson, Streissguth, Bookstein, & Barr, 2006; M. Lloyd, MacDonald, & Lord, 2013; Provost, Lopez, & Heimerl, 2007; Starke, Wikland, & Möller, 2003). Girls sometimes find certain fine motor activities (e.g., cursive handwriting) easier than do boys, although many girls have trouble with fine motor skills, and plenty of boys find it easy and even pleasurable to write, draw, and cut. Fortunately, explicit instruction can help delayed children improve in fine motor skills, even if minor limitations in dexterity persist (Case-Smith, 1996; S. Chang & Yu, 2014; Maraj & Bonertz, 2007).

Middle Childhood (Ages 6–10)

Over the course of middle childhood, youngsters typically show slow but steady gains in height and weight. Their bodies grow larger without undergoing major alterations to basic structures. As a result, proportions of separate body parts change less than in infancy or early childhood. With these slow, continuous gains come a few losses: Children lose their 20 primary ("baby") teeth one by one, replacing them with permanent teeth that at first appear oversized in the small mouths of 6-, 7-, and 8-year-olds. Girls mature somewhat more quickly than do boys, erupting permanent teeth sooner and progressing earlier toward skeletal maturity.

In middle childhood, children improve in their physical capabilities. Many gross motor skills, once uncertain and awkward, are now executed smoothly. Elementary schoolchildren put running to use in games and sports and intensify their speed and coordination in running, kicking, catching, and dribbling. Movement remains highly enjoyable for many children, as you can see in the five activities 6-year-old Alex selected in Artifact 5-3. You can also notice the pleasure that 9-year-old Kyle and 10-year-old Curtis experience as they practice basketball skills in an Observing Children video.

Children in this age range become capable of refined fine motor skills. Their drawings, supported by physiological maturation and cognitive expansions, are more detailed, and their handwriting becomes smaller, smoother, and more consistent. They also begin to tackle such fine motor activities as sewing, model building, and arts and crafts projects.

As children proceed through middle childhood, they become more sensitive about their physical appearance. In a variety of cultures, a person's physical attractiveness is connected with his or her self-esteem, and other people tend to treat an attractive individual better than they do a less attractive person (Bale & Archer, 2013; Dohnt & Tiggemann, 2006; R. A. Gordon, Crosnoe, & Wang, 2013; Harter, 1999). Thus, although many children exaggerate their own physical flaws, the reality is that appearance *is* influential in social relationships and influences how children feel about themselves.

Teachers and other practitioners can support the healthy physical development of children. In the Development and Practice feature "Accommodating the Physical Needs of Children," we give examples of strategies for addressing children's physical needs.

Early Adolescence (Ages 10–14)

The most obvious physical change in early adolescence is the beginning of **puberty**. Ushered in by a cascade of hormones, puberty entails a series of biological developments that lead to reproductive maturity. Puberty is accompanied by a **growth spurt**, a rapid increase in height and weight. The release of hormones has other physiological repercussions as well, such as increases in bone density, facial oil production (often manifested as acne), and sweat secretions (Styne, 2003; Wilk, Pender, Volterman, Bar-Or, & Timmons, 2013).

Girls typically progress through puberty before boys do. Puberty begins in girls sometime between ages 8 and 13 (on average, at age 10). It starts with a growth spurt, "budding" of the breasts, and emergence of pubic hair. These changes are typically gradual; however, first menstruation, **menarche**, is an unprecedented event that can be either exciting or frightening depending on a girl's preparation. The first menstrual period occurs late in puberty, usually between 9 and 15 years of age. Nature apparently delays menstruation, and with it the possibility of conception, until girls are close to their adult height and strong enough to bear a child.

For boys, puberty starts between 9 and 14 years (on average, at 11½ years), when the testes enlarge and the scrotum is modified in texture and color. A year or so later, the penis grows larger, and pubic hair appears; the growth spurt begins soon after. At about 13 to 14 years, boys have their first ejaculation, the **spermarche**, often while sleeping. Boys seem to receive less information about this milestone than girls do about menstruation, and little is known about boys' feelings about it. Later developments for boys include growth of facial hair, deepening of the voice, and eventually attainment of adult height.

ARTIFACT 5-3   I like to move. When asked to choose five things he likes to do, 6-year-old Alex drew pictures of himself kicking, running, swimming, skating, and boating.

Observing Children 5-6
Watch Kyle and Curtis practicing basketball skills.

ENHANCEDetext *video example*

DEVELOPMENT AND PRACTICE
Accommodating the Physical Needs of Children

Meet the requirements of each infant rather than expecting individuals to conform to a universal schedule.

- A caregiver keeps a schedule of times each infant usually wants to be fed. That way, she can plan her feeding rotations, giving every baby as much attention as possible during bottle feedings. (Infancy)
- A child care director recruits volunteers from a local senior group to drop in during the early afternoon when the majority of infants want to be held before falling asleep. The director encourages the seniors to partner with the same couple of infants each visit. (Infancy)

Integrate physical needs into the curriculum.

- An infant caregiver understands the importance of meeting children's physical requirements in ways that deepen relationships. She uses one-to-one activities, such as diaper changing, as occasions to interact. (Infancy)
- A preschool teacher involves children in the preparation of healthful midmorning snacks by asking them children to place crackers and apples slices on plates, serve peers, and sponge down the table. (Early Childhood)

Make sure the environment is safe for exploration.

- After a new carpet is installed in his classroom, a preschool teacher notices that a few children complain of headaches. He wonders if the recently applied adhesive is to blame and asks the director to evaluate the situation. Meanwhile, he conducts activities outdoors and in other rooms. (Early Childhood)
- The principal in a new elementary school reviews designs for a playground structure to ensure specifications for secure anchoring in the ground, accessibility for children in wheelchairs, and a cushioning surface for reducing injuries. During the selection process, the principal establishes a schedule for inspection and guidelines for playground supervisors. (Middle Childhood)

Provide frequent opportunities for children to engage in physical activity.

- A preschool teacher schedules "Music and Marching" for midmorning, "Outdoor Time" before lunch, and a nature walk after nap time. (Early Childhood)
- Elementary school teachers organize a walking club in which students stroll around the school grounds three times a week with pedometers (small instruments that measure number of steps taken; Satcher, 2010). (Middle Childhood)

Plan activities that help children develop their fine motor skills.

- A teacher introduces spoons and bowls when toddlers begin to show an interest in feeding themselves with utensils. (Infancy)

- An after-school caregiver invites children to make mosaics of vehicles. The children glue a variety of small objects (e.g., beads, sequins, beans, colored rice) onto line drawings of cars, trains, boats, airplanes, and bicycles. (Middle Childhood)

Design physical activities so that students with widely differing skill levels can participate.

- During an outdoor play session, a teacher provides balls of varying sizes so that individual children with different levels of proficiency can throw and catch balls. (Early Childhood)
- During a unit on tennis, a physical education teacher has children practice the forehand stroke with tennis rackets. First, she asks them to practice bouncing and then hitting the ball against the wall of the gymnasium. When students master the basic skills, she asks them to see how many times in succession they can hit the ball against the wall. When they reach five successive hits, she suggests they shift the height of the ball from waist high to shoulder high (Logsdon, Alleman, Straits, Belka, & Clark, 1997). (Middle Childhood)

Add physical activity into selected academic lessons.

- When teaching about molecules and temperature, a second-grade teacher asks children to stand in a cluster in an open area of the classroom. To show children how molecules behave when something is cold, she asks them to move slowly while staying close together. To show them how molecules behave when something is hot, she asks them to spread farther apart and move more quickly. (Middle Childhood)
- A preschool teacher reads *Alphabet Under Construction* by D. Fleming (2002) and then takes the children for a walk to examine the architecture of local buildings (Bredekamp, 2011). (Early Childhood)

Give children time to rest.

- After a full-day kindergarten class has been playing outside, their teacher offers a snack of apple slices, crackers, and milk. Afterward, the children gather around him on the floor while he reads a story. (Early Childhood)
- A third-grade teacher arranges for children to read books quietly after returning from lunch. (Middle Childhood)

Respect children's self-care.

- A teacher shows toddlers how to wash their hands after toileting and before eating. The teacher stands with the children, uses warm and soapy water, and helps them rub their hands together before rinsing. (Infancy)
- In an after-school program, a teacher allows the children to go to the restroom whenever they need to. He asks children to hang a clothespin with their name on an "out rope" when they leave the room and then return the pin to the "in rope" when they get back. (Middle Childhood)

In addition to differences in reproductive organs, boys and girls become increasingly distinct in height and muscle mass. On average, boys end up taller than girls. Boys also have a longer period of steady prepubescent growth, and they add a bit more height during their growth spurt. With the onset of puberty, boys also gain more muscle mass than girls, courtesy of the male hormone *testosterone*. The course of puberty for boys and girls is depicted in Figure 5-3.

IN GIRLS	IN BOYS
Initial elevation of breasts and beginning of growth spurt (typically between 8 and 13 years; on average, at 10 years)	Enlargement of the testes and changes in texture and color of scrotum (typically between 9 and 14 years; on average, at 11$\frac{1}{2}$ years)
Appearance of pubic hair (sometimes occurs before elevation of breasts)	Increase in penis size and appearance of pubic hair
Increase in size of uterus, vagina, labia, and clitoris	Beginning of growth spurt (on average, at 12$\frac{1}{2}$ years)
Further development of breasts	*Spermarche*, or first ejaculation
Peak of growth spurt	Peak of growth spurt, accompanied by more rapid penis growth
Menarche, or onset of menstrual cycle (typically between 9 and 15 years)	Appearance of facial hair
	Deepening voice, as size of larynx and length of vocal cords increase
Completion of height gain (about two years after menarche), breast development, and pubic hair growth	Completion of penis growth, height gain, and pubic hair growth

FIGURE 5-3 Maturational sequences of puberty.

Heredity, primarily, and nutrition, exercise, and stress, secondarily, influence the age at which puberty begins (R. Carter, Jaccard, Silverman, & Pina, 2009; Mustanski, Viken, Kaprio, Pulkkinen, & Rose, 2004). Some adolescents are pleased to see the first signs of puberty, whereas others are not at all happy with their changing bodies. They may believe they are too thin, fat, flabby, or unattractive, or developing too quickly or slowly. Youngsters who begin puberty early, girls especially, are often dissatisfied with their bodies and vulnerable to anxiety, eating disorders, and precocious sexual activity (Benoit, Lacourse, & Claes, 2013; Zehr, Culbert, Sisk, & Klump, 2007). Children entering puberty later than peers are apt to be self-conscious about their appearance and worried that something is wrong with them (Lindfors et al., 2007). Yet adjustment for early and late developers depends on the full spectrum of strengths, resources, and risks in their lives. Those who have weak coping skills, have been exposed to more than their share of stressful experiences, affiliate with trouble-making peers, and have been rejected by parents are especially likely to find untimely puberty stressful (Benoit et al., 2013; J. Hamilton et al., 2014). Those who enter puberty well adjusted typically weather an early or late maturation without too much distress.

Whenever it begins, puberty has far-reaching effects on the young person. Dramatic new cognitive capacities, social relationships, and self-perceptions emerge (Brooks-Gunn & Paikoff, 1992; Peper & Dahl, 2013; E. Reese, Yan, Fiona, & Hayne, 2010). Modifications to thinking, acting, and feeling are partly due to brain maturation. Hormones that are released during puberty intensify the level of activity in areas of the brain that process rewards, emotions, and reasoning about why people act as they do (Peper & Dahl, 2013). Puberty loosens restraints on problematic behaviors, in part because brain changes accentuate the pleasure adolescents feel when taking risks, especially in the presence of peers. In many cultures the onset of puberty is associated with experimentation with alcohol, drugs, and cigarettes and the misbehaviors of lying, shoplifting, and stealing (R. Carter et al., 2009; Martino, Ellickson, Klein, McCaffrey, & Edelen, 2008; Peper & Dahl, 2013).

School personnel can help youngsters adjust during adolescence by giving advance warning about physiological changes, reassuring youngsters that wide variations in timing are normal, encouraging them to work hard in school, and restricting their access to unhealthy experiences. In the Development and Practice feature "Accommodating the Physical Needs of Adolescents," we give additional examples of strategies for accommodating the changes of puberty and the diversity that exists among young adolescents.

DEVELOPMENT AND PRACTICE
Accommodating the Physical Needs of Adolescents

Anticipate concerns adolescents have about developing normally.

- A middle school basketball coach gives students plenty of time to shower in stalls that have curtains for protecting privacy. (Early Adolescence)
- A high school teacher advising the Yearbook Club asks student photographers to take pictures of boys and girls from different ethnicities and of varying heights, weights, and appearances so as to represent the full diversity in the student population. (Late Adolescence)

Be sensitive to adolescents' feelings about early or late maturation.

- A middle school's health curriculum describes the sequences of puberty for boys and girls. It also stresses that the timing of these changes varies widely from one person to the next. (Early Adolescence)
- During an advising session, a high school teacher asks a late-developing freshman boy about his goals for the year. The adviser admits that his primary goal at the same age was to grow a few inches, which makes the boy smile. (Early Adolescence)

Keep in mind that menstruation, which is sometimes accompanied by discomfort, can begin at unexpected times.

- An eighth-grade girl comes into class obviously upset, and her best friend approaches their teacher to explain that the two of them need to go to the nurse's office. The teacher realizes what has probably happened and gives them permission to go. (Early Adolescence)
- A high school nurse allows girls to rest on a sofa in her office when they have menstrual cramps. (Late Adolescence)

Make sure adolescents understand what sexual harassment is, and do not tolerate it.

- A middle school includes a sexual harassment policy in its student handbook. Homeroom teachers explain the policy at the beginning of the school year. (Early Adolescence)
- When a high school junior teases a classmate about her "big rack," his teacher takes him aside and explains that his comment not only constitutes sexual harassment (and so violates school policy) but also makes the girl feel embarrassed. The boy admits that he spoke without thinking and, after class, tells the girl he's sorry. (Late Adolescence)

Late Adolescence (Ages 14–18)

On average at about age 15 for girls and 17 for boys, the growth spurt ends and sexual maturity is attained. By this age level many young people have shed the gawky appearance of younger adolescence, now presenting as attractive young adults, comfortable in their own skin and balanced in the relative sizes of their facial features, torso, limbs, and hands and feet. Those who eat well and exercise are apt to enjoy their peak in fitness, strength, and flexibility. With sexual maturation comes increasing interest in close relationships and sexual activity, including hugging, kissing, and, for many teens, intimate sexual contact (DeLamater & MacCorquodale, 1979; Szielasko, Symons, & Lisa Price, 2013).

For some teens, the motivation to engage in dangerous behaviors, which emerged during early adolescence, intensifies during the high school years. In fact, numerous young people engage in one or more behaviors that could undermine their long-term physical health—for instance, by abusing alcohol and drugs or not wearing a seat belt while riding in an automobile (Briggs, Lambert, Goldzweig, Levine, & Warren, 2008; Hale, Fitzgerald-Yau, & Mark Viner, 2014; Wallander, Eggert, & Gilbert, 2004). Table 5-1 presents the prevalence of risky behaviors in American high school students. Given their significance, we examine several of these behaviors in more detail in an upcoming section.

The Developmental Trends table "Physical Development at Different Age Levels" on pages 164–165 summarizes the key characteristics of each age group and provides implications for teachers and other professionals. In the next section we examine practices that contribute to good health and, conversely, undermine it.

Summary

The body is a complex, dynamic system that matures while acting and interacting in a multilayered environment. Over time, physiological functioning becomes increasingly *differentiated* (e.g., cells take on discrete roles depending on maturational state and their location in the body) and *integrated* (e.g., separate body parts work closely together). Children's bodies esssentially aim for general targets in size and height, goals that can be temporarily disrupted by mild illnesses or moderate nutritional inadequacies and disregarded with more serious health problems.

TABLE 5-1   Percentages of U.S. Students in Grades 9–12 Who Reported Engaging in Risky Behaviors

RISKY BEHAVIOR	GIRLS	BOYS
Substance use		
Alcohol (in last 30 days)	37.9	39.5
Cigarettes (in last 30 days)	16.1	19.9
Marijuana (in last 30 days)	20.1	25.9
Cocaine (in last 30 days)	1.8	4.1
Inhalants (in lifetime)	12.3	10.5
Heroin (in lifetime)	1.8	3.9
Methamphetamine (in lifetime)	3.0	4.5
Ecstasy (MDMA; in lifetime)	6.5	9.8
Hallucinogenic drugs (e.g., LSD, mescaline, or angel dust; in lifetime)	5.9	11.3
Illegal steroids (in lifetime)	2.9	4.2
Sexual behaviors		
Had sexual intercourse (in lifetime)	45.6	49.2
Sexually active (had intercourse in past 3 months)	34.2	33.3
No method of birth control during last intercourse (among sexually active adolescents)	15.1	10.6
Alcohol or drug use at last sexual intercourse (among sexually active adolescents)	18.1	26.0
Had four or more sexual partners (in lifetime)	12.6	17.8
Behaviors that contribute to unintentional injuries		
Rarely or never wore seat belts in car	6.3	8.9
Rarely or never wore helmet on bicycle (in those who rode bike in last year)	85.9	88.8
Rode with a driver who drank alcohol (in last 30 days)	24.9	23.3
Drove car after drinking alcohol (in last 30 days)	6.7	9.5
Texted or sent email while driving a car or other vehicle (in last 30 days)	34.9	32.8
Weapon use		
Carried a weapon (e.g., knife, club, gun; in last 30 days)	6.8	25.9
Carried a gun (in last 30 days)	1.4	8.6

Source: Centers for Disease Control and Prevention (CDC), 2012.

Predictable changes in physical functioning occur during childhood. In infancy, survival mechanisms, such as reflexes, are introduced, and motor skills compel exploration. Early childhood is marked by vigorous physical activity and the acquisition of purposeful motor skills. Middle childhood is a time of consolidation, when children's growth continues but decelerates, and children put motor skills to purposeful use. Puberty marks the onset of adolescence and extends over several years' time. Adult height, sexual maturation, and a typically more mature outlook on personal health are attained in late adolescence.

ENHANCEDetext *self-check*

DEVELOPMENTAL TRENDS
Physical Development at Different Age Levels

AGE	WHAT YOU MIGHT OBSERVE	DIVERSITY	IMPLICATIONS
Infancy (Birth–2 Years)	• Emergence of reflexes • Rapid growth and weight gain • Increasing ability to move around, first by squirming; then rolling, crawling, creeping, or scooting; finally by walking • Increasing ability to coordinate hand movements with vision • Increasing self-help skills in feeding, dressing, washing, toileting, and grooming	• Children vary in timing and methods for rolling over, crawling, and sitting up depending on genetic and cultural factors. • Fine motor skills and eye–hand coordination appear earlier or later depending on genetic makeup and opportunities for practice. • Self-help skills appear earlier when encouraged.	• Celebrate each child's unique patterns of growth, but watch for exceptional delays that may require a specialist's assessment and intervention. • Encourage movements of squirming, rolling, scooting, crawling, and walking. • Don't *push* infants to reach milestones. Instead, allow them to experience each phase of physical development thoroughly and try new skills when ready.
Early Childhood (2–6 Years)	• Loss of rounded, babyish appearance, with arms and legs lengthening • Boundless energy for practicing such new gross motor skills as running, hopping, tumbling, climbing, and swinging • Occasional collisions while children learn to coordinate movements • Rudimentary pencil grip (child might use fist to hold pencil at age two and pincer grip with three fingers at age 5) • Transition away from afternoon nap, initially marked by fussiness in the afternoon	• Individual children differ considerably in the ages at which they master motor skills. • On average, boys are more active than girls, but girls are healthier. • Some home environments (e.g., small apartments) limit vigorous physical activity; others present hazardous conditions (e.g., lead paint, toxic fumes). • Children with intellectual disabilities may have delayed motor skills.	• Provide frequent opportunities to play outside or (in inclement weather) in a large indoor space. • Intersperse vigorous physical exercise with rest and quiet time. • Encourage use of fine motor skills through puzzles, blocks, and arts and crafts. • Choose activities that accommodate diversity in gross and fine motor skills.
Middle Childhood (6–10 Years)	• Steady gains in height and weight • Loss and replacement of primary teeth with occasional chewing on objects to relieve tenderness in gums • Refinement and consolidation of gross motor skills in structured play activities • Participation in organized sports • Increasing fluency in fine motor skills, such as in handwriting and drawing	• Variations in weight and height are apparent. • Some children show exceptional athletic talents and interests. • Gender differences appear in preferences for sports. • Some neighborhoods lack safe play areas. • Some children have delays in fine motor skills. • Children with some conditions (e.g., autism) are uncertain of, or resistant to, active social games. • Some children prioritize video games over outdoor pursuits.	• Integrate physical movement into selected academic activities. • Provide daily opportunities for play. • Teach children the basics of sports, and encourage them to participate in organized athletic programs. • Encourage practice with fine motor skills, but don't penalize children whose fine motor precision is delayed.
Early Adolescence (10–14 Years)	• Periods of rapid growth • Beginnings of puberty • Self-consciousness about physical changes • Some risk-taking behavior	• Onset of puberty varies over several years among individual adolescents; puberty typically occurs earlier for girls than boys. • Leisure activities may or may not include regular exercise. • Adolescents differ in strength, endurance, and talent for sports. • Boys are generally faster, stronger, and more confident than girls in physical skills. • Peer groups may engage in risky behavior.	• Be a role model for physical fitness and nutritious eating. • Arrange for privacy while changing clothes and showering. • Explain what sexual harassment is, and do not tolerate it in jokes, teasing, or contact. • Encourage after-school clubs that help teenagers spend time constructively. • Supervise adolescents and restrict their access to risky activities.

DEVELOPMENTAL TRENDS (continued)

AGE	WHAT YOU MIGHT OBSERVE	DIVERSITY	IMPLICATIONS
Late Adolescence (14–18 Years)	• In girls, attainment of mature height • In boys, ongoing increases in stature • Ravenous appetites • Sexual arousal and in some cases intimate sexual activity • Some risky behaviors (e.g., drinking alcohol, taking drugs, engaging in unprotected sexual contact, driving while impaired, revealing personal information on the Internet) • Adolescents are less likely than younger children to get regular medical care.	• Gender differences in physical abilities increase; boys are more active in organized sports programs. • Some teens begin to limit their risky behaviors and now make better decisions. • Eating disorders may appear, especially in girls. • Adolescents differ in consumption of drugs and alcohol depending on personality, peer norms, and parent behaviors. • An emphasis on self-improvement or competition influences physical activity. • Some adolescents prioritize the Internet over physical activity	• Make sure that adolescents know "the facts of life" about sexual intercourse and conception. • Encourage abstinence when adolescents are not sexually active. • When adolescents are sexually active, encourage them to use protective measures and restrict number of partners. • Encourage young people to form worthwhile goals (e.g., going to college, developing athletic skills). • Reduce adolescents' exposure to potentially risky situations. • Develop and enforce policies related to sexual harassment.

Sources: Bredekamp, 2011; Bredekamp & Copple, 1997; Gallahue & Ozmun, 1998; Iivonen & Sääkslahti, 2014; G. King et al., 2013; Moreno, Jelenchick, & Christakis, 2013; Potvin, Snider, Prelock, Kehayia, & Wood-Dauphinee, 2013; V. F. Reyna & Farley, 2006; Steinberg, 2007; J. M. Tanner, 1990; C. Wood, 2007.

HEALTH AND WELL-BEING

With age, children become more aware of what it takes to remain healthy, but they don't always use measures that safeguard their personal welfare. In the following sections, we consider eating habits, physical activity, rest and sleep, and health-compromising behaviors. We also identify strategies that adults can use to encourage healthful lifestyles.

Eating Habits

Food affects all aspects of well-being. In many but unfortunately not all circumstances, the nutrition children consume is sufficient to enable growth, energy, and an ability to learn and remember.

At birth, breastfeeding is the preferred source of nutrition because breast milk is rich in vitamins, provides antibodies against illness, nourishes the growing brain, and is easier to digest than infant formulas (London et al., 2011; Lutter & Lutter, 2012). Of course, some mothers cannot easily breastfeed, others do not want to, and a few (e.g., mothers who carry the human immunodeficiency virus [HIV] or are undergoing certain medical treatments) cannot breastfeed safely because infections and medications are passed to the baby. As an alternative, many families select one of the iron-fortified formulas that have been commercially prepared from cow's milk or soybeans to match infants' digestive abilities and requirements for protein, calories, vitamins, and minerals. Other formulas are available for infants with food allergies and intolerances. Infant caregivers generally try to support families' preferences but also suggest medically advisable strategies, for example, introducing nutritious soft cereals and fruits at around 4 to 6 months and avoiding hard foods that infants cannot chew or swallow.

As children grow, they remain strongly influenced by food served by families. For some children, mealtime is a chance to refuel, follow cultural customs, and talk about the day. For others, meals are unhealthy, especially when parents have few financial resources or are homeless, mentally ill, or too tired to cook. When children are underfed or given primarily non-nutritious foods, consequences can be serious. Anemia (iron deficiency) is the most common nutritional problem and a contributor to delays and behavioral disturbances in children (Domellöf & Szymlek-Gay, 2012; Killip, Bennett, & Chambers, 2007; S. P. Walker et al., 2007). Other outcomes are less grave but still serious, as when children raised on fast food develop an unwavering preference for meals that are high in fat, sugar, and salt (Azzam, 2009/2010).

What, exactly, *should* children be eating? The U.S. Department of Agriculture recommends that half a person's plate be covered with fruits and vegetables, and that water and nonfat or 1 percent milk be offered as beverages instead of sugary drinks and whole milk (U.S. Department of Agriculture Center for Nutrition Policy and Promotion, 2013). A 10-year-old boy who is

51 inches tall (4 feet 3 inches), 71 pounds in weight, and inclined to consume about 1,800 calories per day is advised to eat 6 ounces of grains (at least half of which are whole grains), 2½ cups of vegetables, 1½ cups of fruits, 3 cups of milk, and 5 ounces of meats, beans, or other low-fat proteins. A few small snacks (e.g., cookies and potato chips) are considered acceptable as long as children are physically active and obtain needed nutrition. There are many opportunities for schools to encourage this kind of healthy diet, as you can see in Figure 5-4.

10 tips
Nutrition Education Series

the School Day just got Healthier
United States Department of Agriculture

Nearly 32 million children receive meals throughout the school day. These meals are based on nutrition standards from the U.S. Department of Agriculture. New nutrition standards for schools increase access to healthy food and encourage kids to make smart choices. Schools are working to make meals more nutritious, keep all students hunger-free, and help children maintain or reach a healthy weight.

1 healthier school meals for your children
Your children benefit from healthier meals that include more whole grains, fruits and vegetables, low-fat dairy products, lower sodium foods, and less saturated fat. Talk to your child about the changes in the meals served at school.

2 more fruits and vegetables every day
Kids have fruits and vegetables at school every day. A variety of vegetables are served througout the week including red, orange, and dark-green vegetables.

3 more whole-grain foods
Half of all grains offered are whole-grain-rich foods such as whole-grain pasta, brown rice, and oatmeal. Some foods are made by replacing half the refined-grain (white) flour with whole-grain flour.

4 both low-fat milk (1%) and fat-free milk varieties are offered
Children get the same calcium and other nutrients, but with fewer calories and less saturated fat by drinking low-fat (1%) or fat-free milk. For children who can't drink milk due to allergies or lactose intolerance, schools can offer milk substitutes, such as calcium-fortified soy beverages.

5 less saturated fat and salt
A variety of foods are offered to reduce the salt and saturated fat in school meals. Main dishes may include beans, peas, nuts, tofu, or seafood as well as lean meats or poultry. Ingredients and foods contain less salt (sodium).

6 more water
Schools can provide water pitchers and cups on lunch tables, a water fountain, or a faucet that allows students to fill their own bottles or cups with drinking water. Water is available where meals are served.

7 new portion sizes
School meals meet children's calorie needs, based on their age. While some portions may be smaller, kids still get the nutrition they need to keep them growing and active.

8 stronger local wellness programs
New policies offer opportunities for parents and communities to create wellness programs that address local needs. Talk with your principal, teachers, school board, parent-teacher association, and others to create a strong wellness program in your community.

9 MyPlate can help kids make better food choices
Show children how to make healthy food choices at school by using MyPlate. Visit ChooseMyPlate.gov for tips and resources.

10 resources for parents
School meal programs can provide much of what children need for health and growth. But for many parents, buying healthy foods at home is a challenge. Learn more about healthy school meals and other nutrition assistance programs at www.fns.usda.gov.

United States Department of Agriculture Center for Nutrition Policy and Promotion

Go to www.ChooseMyPlate.gov for more information.

DG TipSheet No. 21
August 2012
USDA is an equal opportunity provider and employer.

FIGURE 5-4 Healthy Meals at School. The U.S. Department of Agriculture presents guidelines for meals and beverages at school that offer children essential nutrition and hydration without excessive calories. *Reprinted from the U.S. Department of Agriculture (USDA). (2012). The school day just got healthier. USDA Center for Nutrition Policy and Promotion 10 Tips Education Series. Retrieved from http://www.choosemyplate.gov/food-groups/downloads/TenTips/DGTipsheet21SchoolDayJustGotHealthier.pdf*

Most children between ages 2 and 17 do *not* meet the full complement of dietary requirements established by the U.S. Department of Agriculture (Federal Interagency Forum on Child and Family Statistics, 2013). The diets of young American children (between 2 and 5 years of age) generally include adequate amounts of fruit, milk, and meat but insufficient servings of dark green vegetables, beans, and whole grains. Children also eat far too much "bad" stuff—the fatty, sugary, and salty foods. With growth many children become less inclined to eat breakfast, resulting in difficulty concentrating at school (CDC, 2005a).

Teachers can foster inclinations to eat healthfully as part of their health education curriculum. The National Health Education Standards are a good place to start for identifying relevant behaviors that can be fostered at school (CDC, 2013a). For example, one of the standards is that "Students will demonstrate the ability to use goal-setting skills to enhance health." First-grade children might meet this standard by aspiring to increase their consumption of fresh fruits and vegetables one evening during the week. High-school students could conduct a comprehensive analysis of their own diets, maintain a weeklong chart of the foods they ate, and evaluate the alignment of their diet with the recommended regimen.

Overweight Youth

In part because of children's increasing reliance on processed foods, a staggering number of children have become overweight during the past few decades. Children are considered *overweight* when their body mass index (BMI), a measure of weight in relation to height, is at or above the 85th percentile for children of the same age and sex (CDC, 2013b). Obviously, there is significant variation among overweight students. Children are considered **obese** if their BMI is at or above the 95th percentile for someone of the same age and gender. Approximately 17 percent of children between ages 2 and 17 are obese (CDC, 2013c). Comparable rates are high in many other countries as well. In fact, obesity is now considered a global health crisis (Y. Wang & Lim, 2012; World Health Organization, 2000).

Obesity is a concern because it is associated with serious health risks in childhood, including asthma, and even deadlier problems in adulthood, for example, continued weight problems and diabetes, elevated blood pressure, and high cholesterol (CDC, 2013d; Jelalian, Wember, Bungeroth, & Birmaher, 2007). Obesity also has detrimental social consequences. Sadly, some peers torment overweight youngsters, calling them names and excluding them from social activities.

For some obese children, weight problems may have a genetic basis, but environmental experiences, especially the family's customs in eating high-fat meals and rarely exercising, are major factors in most cases (H. Thomas, 2006). Acquiring an appetite for unhealthy foods, eating too much and too often, sitting for long periods in front of televisions and computers, and spending little time in physical activity all contribute to obesity in children. Fortunately, interventions in clinics, dietary counseling, goal setting for optimal calorie levels, increases in physical activity, and use of behavioral techniques (e.g., recognizing and rewarding progress toward specific goals) reduce weight in obese children (Lochrie et al., 2013).

Increasingly, educators are realizing that schools are an important setting for tackling children's weight problems. Many educators are making sure that water is available for drinking (rather than carbonated sodas), adjusting cafeteria menus, and replacing the sweet, salty, and fatty snacks in vending machines with more nutritious items (Cluss, Fee, Culyba, Bhat, & Owen, 2014; Fetro, Givens, & Carroll, 2009/2010; Lumeng, 2006). Schools regularly provide breakfast to children whose families cannot easily afford it, and not only does breakfast provide essential nutrients and energy, allowing children to concentrate on schoolwork rather than on debilitating hunger, it increases the chances that children eat more healthily at other meals during the day (Affenito et al., 2013). Some schools have asked students to set dietary goals and keep track of their fat intake, soft drink consumption, and physical activity (Haerens et al., 2006). Such record keeping, when coupled with motivational techniques, can have highly beneficial effects on youngsters' weight and health.

A more controversial program has been for schools to issue BMI (Body Mass Index) report cards to children. Intended to help children and families keep track of children's weight and to be alerted when diet changes are necessary, BMI report cards can embarrass children and are not always accompanied by opportunities at school for physical activity or a school climate that warmly accepts all body shapes and sizes (Nihiser et al., 2009).

Eating Disorders

Whereas some young people eat too much, others eat too little and develop eating disorders that seriously threaten their health. People with **anorexia nervosa** eat hardly anything. In contrast, people with **bulimia** eat voraciously, especially fattening foods, and then purge their bodies by taking laxatives or forcing themselves to vomit. Unfortunately, extreme weight control methods, such as drastically reducing calories, taking diet pills or laxatives, and vomiting, are fairly widespread among adolescents. Approximately 10 percent of high school girls and 4 percent of boys in the United States are anorexic (Austin et al., 2008; Stice, Marte, & Rohde, 2013).

Individuals with eating disorders often have a distorted body image (believing they are "fat" when they appear dangerously thin to others) and exercise compulsively to lose additional weight. In addition to jeopardizing health, eating disorders tend to slow down the bodily changes of puberty (London et al., 2011). Moreover, the malnutrition that accompanies anorexia can, in extreme cases, cause heart failure. Tragically, anorexia is also associated with thoughts related to, and attempts at, suicide.

Many experts believe that society's obsession with thinness is partly to blame for anorexia nervosa and bulimia (Ahern & Hetherington, 2006). Images of attractiveness in the media are unrealistic for most young people, and those individuals who are extremely dissatisfied with their bodies are at risk for developing an eating disorder (A. S. Hartmann, Greenberg, & Wilhelm, 2013). Psychological factors, some of which may be partly inherited, also come into play. Individuals with eating disorders are apt to be lonely, depressed, and anxious, and some have experienced child abuse or personal problems with substance abuse (Brietzke, Moreira, Toniolo, & Lafer, 2011; Dominé, Berchtold, Akré, Michaud, & Suris, 2009; Manuel & Wade, 2013; U.S. Department of Health and Human Services, 2000). You can listen to a young woman describing her experience with anorexia nervosa in an Observing Children video.

Educators should be alert to common symptoms such as increasing thinness, complaints of being "too fat," unusual eating habits, and lack of energy. When they suspect an eating disorder, teachers can consult with a counselor, school psychologist, or principal. Fortunately, many young people with eating disorders respond favorably to intensive and long-term intervention from specialists.

Observing Children 5-7

Watch a video of a young woman describing her experience with anorexia nervosa.

ENHANCEDetext *video example*

Promoting Wholesome Diets

We end this section with thoughts about what teachers and other practitioners can do to encourage good nutrition:

• **Promote children's health as a priority for your school.** Health advisory councils can be established at school to promote children's physical welfare. Representative teachers, parents, community members, and students can make recommendations for cafeteria menus, guidelines for birthday celebrations, and opportunities for physical activity (e.g., minutes of exercise per week in physical education, the relative emphasis on self-improvement versus competition, time for recess, and inclusion of movement in academic lessons; CDC, 2011).

• **Provide between-meal snacks for young children.** Crackers, healthy cookies, and fruit slices can invigorate active preschool and elementary children. Nutritious snacks are particularly important for children who are growing rapidly yet receive inadequate meals at home. In providing refreshments, educators can accommodate food allergies and possible limitations in chewing and swallowing.

• **Offer nourishing food at school.** Teachers and other school personnel can advocate for healthful foods and drinks on the cafeteria line, in vending machines at school, at concession stands at school events, and at meetings with families (Azzam, 2009/2010; Budd & Volpe, 2006; CDC, 2011). When children are permitted to bring snacks, teachers can send home guidelines for appropriate items (e.g., carrot sticks, pretzels, and granola bars). As a fourth grader, Teresa's son Alex was advised that chocolate (a passion for him) was *not* a good idea for a midmorning snack. He began to bring other snacks instead, such as granola bars and, as you might suspect, he was happy to find granola bars sprinkled with chocolate chips.

• **Encourage children to try new foods.** Children who have grown accustomed to processed food may initially resist fresh food. Young children may not want to try a new food until they have seen it multiple times, sometimes only after 10 to 15 presentations (Blissett & Fogel, 2013; Zero to Three, 2010). Strategies that successfully encourage culinary exploration include offering new foods next to preferred foods; using such healthy dips as yogurt, hummus, ketchup, and low-fat salad dressings side by side new vegetables and fruits; and enlisting the involvement of children in preparation of the meal (Zero to Three, 2010). Educators in the Baltimore City public schools have included a piece of fresh fruit in every lunch and implemented a program called "No thank you bites," in which children can try small portions of a new fruit, vegetable, or entrée item; children can ask for more if they like it or say "No thank you" and move down the cafeteria line if they don't (Geraci, 2009/2010). Another strategy of Baltimore schools has been to open an organic farm that produces fresh food and allows students to work there, instilling an interest in the crops they have grown together.

Finally, it can be effective to reward children for tasting new foods, for example, by pasting a sticker next to the child's name every time he or she tries a new dish. What is *not* effective is to restrict the child's preferred food, for example, chocolate chip cookies, until he or she eats a portion of an alternative substance, for example, broccoli. Children who are controlled in this manner may very well eat broccoli in order to gain access to cookies but typically will never like or select broccoli unless accompanied by an incentive (Blissett & Fogel, 2013).

• **Educate children about good and bad diets.** Children can learn about nutrients that are essential for health, the ideal amounts of certain foods, and the consequences of eating excessive calories and too many sweet, salty, and fatty foods. Many activities, including electronic games, activity sheets, videos, and songs, are available through the USDA's ChooseMyPlate.Gov programs (choosemyplate.gov/kids/ParentsEducators.html). Lessons in nutrition are available for grades 1 through 6, including the one in Figure 5-5, which gives students practice in reading and comparing the nutritional contents indicated by food labels.

• **Ask children to set goals for improving eating habits.** A reasonable first step is to ask children to evaluate their own diets based on recommended servings in basic food groups. In Artifact 5-4, 8-year-old Charlotte realizes she has been consuming too many sugary snacks. After analyzing their diets, young people can set specific goals (e.g., substituting salty snacks with an apple or yogurt) and chart their progress toward these goals (Lochrie et al., 2013; Schinke, Moncher, & Singer, 1994; D. K. Wilson, Nicholson, & Krishnarmoorthy, 1998).

• **Make referrals when you suspect students have eating disorders.** Youngsters with eating disorders urgently need medical intervention. If you suspect a student has an eating disorder, you will want to contact your principal or supervisor. Even after beginning medical care, children may require services from counselors at school to help them cope with the trials and tribulations of being in an academically challenging, complex social environment.

• **Follow up when you suspect serious nutritional problems.** Malnutrition can occur as a result of many factors. When low family income is the cause, practitioners can help families obtain free or reduced-cost lunches at school. When parental neglect or mental illness is possibly involved, teachers can report their suspicions to principals, counselors, or school nurses to find the best approach for supporting families and protecting children.

• **Convey respect for the feelings of children and adolescents.** Youngsters who struggle with obesity or eating disorders are certainly as distressed as their peers—and often even more so—when others make unflattering comments on their appearance. Unfortunately, rude remarks are occasionally made, as recalled by these overweight adolescents: "'Kids make fun of me, they say, 'You fat ugly cow, you make a whale look small,' 'In the gym, they laugh and talk behind my back,' and 'It hurts me when they say, Hey there, fat kid. I try to ignore them, but it does not stop" (M. J. Smith & Perkins, 2008, p. 392). Adults must insist that classrooms and after-school programs are "no-tease zones" about weight.

I think I have ate to many sweets on Sunday. I had 1 to many things from the dairy groop. I had the right amount of meat, but not anof vegetables, I had only one vegetble. You wone't belve this, I had no fruits at all! I realy need to eat more fruits and vegetbles. If I ate two more things from bread groop I would have had anof.

ARTIFACT 5-4 Too many sweets. Charlotte (age 8) reflects on her eating habits over the weekend.

NUTRITION LABEL
Comparison

THIRD COURSE • REPRODUCIBLE 1

Name:_____Date:_____

The **Nutrition Facts label** on food packages can give you helpful information about what's inside. Below is a group of labels for snack foods. Work with a partner to read and compare the labels. Which is the healthier snack alternative?

YOGURT, FAT-FREE, PLAIN

Nutrition Facts
Serving Size 1 cup (245g)
Servings Per Container 4

Amount Per Serving	
Calories 140	
	%Daily Value*
Total Fat 0g	0 %
Saturated Fat 0g	0 %
Trans Fat 0g	
Cholesterol 5mg	0 %
Sodium 175mg	7 %
Total Carbohydrate 19g	6 %
Dietary Fiber 0g	0 %
Sugars 13g	
Protein 14g	

Vitamin A 0%	•	Vitamin C 4%
Calcium 50%	•	Iron 0%

* Percent Daily Values are based on a 2,000 calorie diet.

YOGURT, WHOLE MILK, VANILLA

Nutrition Facts
Serving Size 1 cup (245g)
Servings Per Container 4

Amount Per Serving	
Calories 230 Calories from Fat 70	
	%Daily Value*
Total Fat 8g	12 %
Saturated Fat 5g	25 %
Trans Fat 0g	
Cholesterol 30mg	10 %
Sodium 125mg	5 %
Total Carbohydrate 30g	10 %
Dietary Fiber 0g	0 %
Sugars 29g	
Protein 8g	16 %

Vitamin A 6%	•	Vitamin C 0%
Calcium 30%	•	Iron 0%

* Percent Daily Values are based on a 2,000 calorie diet.

APPLE SLICES

Nutrition Facts
Serving Size 1 bag (68g)
Servings Per Container 1

Amount Per Serving	
Calories 35 Calories from Fat 0	
	%Daily Value*
Total Fat 0g	0 %
Saturated Fat	0 %
Trans Fat 0g	0 %
Cholesterol 0mg	0 %
Sodium 0mg	6 %
Total Carbohydrate 9g	3 %
Dietary Fiber 2g	8 %
Sugars 7g	
Protein 0g	

Vitamin A 0%	•	Vitamin C 30%
Calcium 2%	•	Iron 2%

* Percent Daily Values are based on a 2,000 calorie diet.

FRENCH FRIES, SMALL

Nutrition Facts
Serving Size 1 serving (68g)
Servings Per Container 1

Amount Per Serving	
Calories 210 Calories from Fat 90	
	%Daily Value*
Total Fat 10g	15 %
Saturated Fat 1.5g	8 %
Trans Fat 0g	
Cholesterol 0mg	0 %
Sodium 135mg	6 %
Total Carbohydrate 26g	9 %
Dietary Fiber 2g	8 %
Sugars 0g	
Protein 3g	

Vitamin A 0%	•	Vitamin C 15%
Calcium 0%	•	Iron 2%

* Percent Daily Values are based on a 2,000 calorie diet.

Study the labels. Use your notebook to record the data for all four snack foods, and then answer the questions.

	PLAIN YOGURT	VANILLA YOGURT	APPLE SLICES	FRENCH FRIES
Serving size				
Calories in entire container				
% DV for saturated fat per serving				
% DV for calcium per serving				
% DV for sodium per serving				

Which snack food has the most calcium with the lowest amount of calories? _____

Which snack foods are the lowest in saturated fat? _____

Which snack food is the lowest in sodium (salt)? _____

Which snack foods are healthier alternatives? _____

Explain how you came to your conclusion. Were any of your results surprising? _____

USDA **Serving Up MyPlate** — Grades 5 & 6
U.S. Department of Agriculture • Food and Nutrition Service • September 2012 • FNS-446

http://teamnutrition.usda.gov

FIGURE 5-5   Food labels. In this lesson, children learn to analyze the nutritional labels for three snacks. *From U.S. Department of Agriculture. (2012, September).* Serving up Myplate: A yummy curriculum (grades 5 and 6). *Standards-based nutrition education. FNS 446. Available at http://www.choosemyplate.gov/ kids/downloads/ServingUpMyPlate-level3-TeachersGuide.pdf*

Physical Activity

Infants and toddlers are highly motivated to learn new physical skills. As they wiggle, squirm, reach, and grasp, they improve their motor abilities. For preschool children, physical activity is so enjoyable—and increasingly controllable—that children become even more active. After the preschool years, there is a decline in physical activity, even though children need to move their bodies regularly.

Unfortunately, children are not always given sufficient chances to move. One of the problems is that adults tend to want children to remain still and quiet, particularly while in groups, whereas children are apt to prefer rambunctious activities. A common type of physical activity in early and middle childhood is **rough-and-tumble play**, or good-natured mock "fighting" (Harvey, 2011; A. P. Humphreys & Smith, 1987; Lindsey & Colwell, 2013; Pellegrini, 2006). Children often derive considerable pleasure from rough housing, find it a healthy release from intellectually demanding tasks, and defend it as just "playing" or "messing around." Ideally, playground supervisors set reasonable rules that reduce the chances of injury while still allowing children to run and shout.

As children grow older, they may develop sedentary habits. Some youngsters watch a lot of television or spend their free time on the Internet. Too many young people prioritize electronic games over playing outside with friends, occasionally deferring homework, activities with friends, and even meals and sleep until they've finished with the game—and the next game, and others after that (Moreno et al., 2013).

Another deterrent to physical activity is the perception of policy makers that physical education and outdoor play take time away from academic lessons. In fact, a series of studies showed that reductions in physical education do *not* culminate in higher levels of academic achievement (Ahamed et al., 2007; Trost & van der Mars, 2009/2010). In fact, evidence indicates that physical activity and participation in physical education can actually *increase* achievement (S. A. Carlson et al., 2008; Kristjánsson, Sigfúsdóttir, & Allegrante, 2010; Tremarche, Robinson, & Graham, 2007). Research findings also demonstrate that recess and other breaks help children regain energy and refocus attention (Cook-Cottone, Tribole, & Tylka, 2013; Pellegrini & Bjorklund, 1997; Pellegrini & Bohn, 2005). With older children, organized walks or other energetic breaks can allow children to relax and concentrate on school learning (Jeffrey, 2009/2010). In many schools, children are given a chance to move around within the classroom between and sometimes during lessons.

Numerous educators are now re-introducing recess, if they previously eliminated it, and looking closely at the implementation of their physical education curriculum. In a national study with U.S. high school students, just over half of students in grades 9 through 12 reported enjoying their physical education classes (Brener et al., 2013). Movement and sports can become more fun and effective when guidelines for high-quality physical education are followed. Experts recommend daily physical education in kindergarten through 12th grade; a curriculum that is based in national standards and features carefully sequenced skills (from easy and low intensity to difficult and strenuous); encouragement for children to set personal goals and evaluate progress; the inclusion of exercises, for example, dancing, jumping rope, and aerobic games, that children can do outside school as well as inside it; movement in selected lessons (e.g., students might be allowed to walk around the room as the teacher reads a book aloud); and adaptive devices such as oversized bats and balls that facilitate involvement of children with disabilities (CDC, 2011).

Organized Sports and Individual Athletic Activities

In this chapter's opening case study, a group of adolescents were trained as coaches, creating an outlet for their exercise and that of local elementary children. Organized sports offer the means for enhancing physical strength, endurance, and agility. Sports can promote social development by fostering communication, cooperation, and leadership skills. Particularly when parents and coaches encourage children to try hard and work together as a team, children enjoy sports and see themselves as competent athletes (Ullrich-French & Smith, 2006).

Organized sports have a downside when adults promote unhealthy competition, put excessive pressure on children to perform well, and encourage athletically talented children at the expense of their less gifted teammates. Well-meaning coaches can bolster children's athletic skills but rob children of their intrinsic enjoyment of sports and, when they fail to implement safety procedures, put children at risk for injury (Holt, Tink, Mandigo, & Fox, 2008; R. E. Smith & Smoll, 1997; N. Waters, 2013).

Many children do *not* like team sports but nevertheless want to exercise. A few are drawn to such individual athletic activities as running, skateboarding, snowboarding, and mountain biking. Although not necessarily part of teams, youngsters who engage in individual sports often spend time with peers while exercising. Personal athletic pursuits have the advantages of requiring initiative and at least moderate levels of physical activity and, when unsupervised, the occasional disadvantage of incurring risk for injury. You can watch an Observing Children video about youngsters' participation in risky sports and the kinds of guidance adults can offer about protective measures.

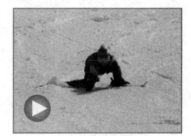

Observing Children 5-8

Watch a video about youngsters' participation in risky sports (e.g., ski racing, rock climbing, and snowboarding) and the kinds of guidance nurses offer about protective measures.

ENHANCEDetext *video example*

ARTIFACT 5-5 Recess. Eleven-year-old Grace draws a picture of children during recess.

Encouraging Physical Activity

Physical activity is an essential part of every child's day. Here are some specific strategies educators can follow to promote movement and sports:

• **Be "pro-ACTIVE."** Teachers can incorporate physical movement into several activities, particularly at the preschool and elementary school levels. Regular breaks that include physical activity can actually increase children's attention to more sedentary, cognitively demanding tasks (Pellegrini & Bjorklund, 1997; Pellegrini & Bohn, 2005; Springer, Tanguturi, Ranjit, Skala, & Kelder, 2013). For 11-year-old Grace, recess is a favorite time at school, as you can see in Artifact 5-5. Teachers can also resist the temptation to punish children by eliminating recess, as movement is essential to all children, especially those who are naturally boisterous.

• **Provide appropriate equipment and guidance so children can safely engage in physical activity.** Open space, playground equipment, balls, and other athletic props encourage physical exercise. Equipment should be chosen carefully to allow children to experiment safely, ideally minimizing times when adults have to say no to particular choices of movement (Bronson, 2000). Equipment and exercise facilities should also be properly designed to fit children's body sizes and abilities (Frost, Shin, & Jacobs, 1998; Nolte, Krüger, Els, & Nolte, 2013).

• **Make exercise an enjoyable pastime.** By the time they reach high school, many young people have had unpleasant experiences with physical workouts and, as a result, associate exercise with regimentation, discomfort, failure, embarrassment, competitiveness, boredom, and injury (Rowland, 1990). Furthermore, many adolescents see exercise as missing from the daily lives of family members. Educators have their work cut out for them in instilling a new commitment to exercise, but one effective way to begin is to capitalize on children's interest in activities (e.g., in karate), pleasure in physical self-expression (e.g., through dance), and camaraderie during group activities (e.g., exercising together in an aerobics class; W. C. Taylor, Beech, & Cummings, 1998).

• **Plan physical activities with diversity in mind.** Not everyone can be a quarterback or baseball pitcher. But nearly all children can find enjoyment in exercise of some form. Offering a range of activities, from dance to volleyball, and modifying them for children with special needs can maximize the number of students who participate. A child who is unusually short might look to such activities as soccer, cycling, or gymnastics because they do not require exceptional height (Rudlin, 1993). Another child in a wheelchair might go up to bat in a softball game and then have a classmate run the bases for her.

Ensuring that boys and girls are encouraged to participate in athletic activities is imperative. According to *Title IX* of the Educational Amendments of 1972, educators in the United States must give boys and girls the same opportunities to participate in athletic programs and, in fact, in all aspects of academic life. Thus, boys and girls must receive comparable quality in coaching, practice, locker facilities, and publicity for their athletic events and accomplishments.

The distinct needs of boys and girls during recess are also important to consider. In general, boys tend to be more active physically (A. M. Woods, Graber, & Daum, 2012). Boys typically play ball games, often in large groups, whereas girls spend time jumping rope and sitting together talking in small groups (Blatchford, Baines, & Pellegrini, 2003). Allowing children to make their own choices is an important feature of recess, although adult supervisors may wish to encourage both boys and girls to join games and activities that require moderate levels of physical activity (C. A. Howe, Freedson, Alhassan, Feldman, & Osganian, 2012).

• **Focus on self-improvement rather than on comparison with peers.** Focusing on their personal improvement is, for most children, far more motivating than attending to relative standing with peers. Dwelling too much on competition leads children to believe that physical ability is largely a matter of "natural talent," when in fact most physical skills require considerable practice (Ames, 1984; R. W. Proctor & Dutta, 1995). Thus adults can direct children to focus on progress they are making as individuals (e.g., "Wow, Libby, you have become one fine kicker this week"). Adults can also encourage children to record their own accomplishments on worksheets and in electronic programs.

Another way to promote self-improvement is to teach skills in progression, from simple to complex (CDC, 2011; Gallahue & Ozmun, 1998). A preschool teacher could ask children to hop on one foot as they pretend to be the "hippity hop bunny." Once they have mastered that skill, the teacher might demonstrate more complex skills, such as galloping and skipping. Carefully sequenced lessons give children feelings of success and make physical activities enjoyable.

• **Make sure that children don't overdo it.** Becoming fanatically involved in exercise can create medical problems for children. The soft and spongy parts of bones in growing children are susceptible to injury from repeated use (R. H. Gross, 2004; S. Jenny & Armstrong, 2013; Micheli, 1995). Weight-training machines are almost always designed for adult-sized bodies, increasing children's chances for injury. Overuse injuries are frequently seen in distance running, competitive swimming, and gymnastics. Medical experts recommend that children be discouraged from concentrating solely on one sport before adolescence, never be asked to "work through" stress fractures, and receive regular care from a physician who can monitor the possible health effects of intensive training (e.g., delays in sexual maturation; American Academy of Pediatrics [AAP] Committee on Sports Medicine and Fitness, 2000).

Rest and Sleep

Rest and sleep are essential to growth and health. Sleep helps young people grow, because growth hormones are released at higher rates as children snooze than when they're awake. In addition to promoting growth, sleep may help the brain maintain healthy functioning (N. R. Carlson, 2014).

Infancy

Newborn babies spend a long time sleeping—16 to 18 hours a day (Wolff, 1966). Gradually, infants develop wake–sleep cycles that correspond to adults' day–night cycles (St. James-Roberts & Plewis, 1996). Individual infants begin to sleep through the night when they are ready, depending in part on their own biological rhythms. Teresa recalls that her sons were oblivious to a pediatrician's guideline that they should be able to sleep through the night by 10 weeks of age and 10 pounds in weight. Sleeping habits are also affected by cultural practices, suggesting that there is no single "best" way to put babies to sleep (Shweder et al., 1998).

Although there may be no best way, there is definitely one *wrong* way to put babies to sleep. Medical experts advise caregivers *not* to place babies on their stomachs for sleeping because this position puts babies at risk for **sudden infant death syndrome (SIDS)**, a loss of life that occurs (usually during sleep) in infants without an apparent medical cause. SIDS is a leading cause of death among infants from 1 month through 1 year in age (American Academy of Pediatrics Task Force on Infant Sleep Position and Sudden Infant Death Syndrome, 2000). During the period that SIDS is most common (between 2 and 4 months), infants' brains are developing circuits for controlling arousal, breathing, heart rate, and other basic physiological functions. Minor abnormalities in these areas may prove fatal if infants are under physical stress, for example, if they have a respiratory infection, are especially warm due to excessive clothing or blankets, or have an obstructed airway as their faces are nestled into the mattress (Kinney, 2009; E. A. Mitchell, 2009; Rohde et al., 2013; F. M. Sullivan & Barlow, 2001).

Infant caregivers need to be aware of current advice not only for reducing the risk of SIDS but also for preventing suffocation generally. Recommendations include placing babies on their backs (face up) to sleep, refraining from smoking nearby, keeping babies at a comfortable temperature, using a firm mattress, and avoiding soft surfaces and loose bedding (Task Force on Sudden Infant Death Syndrome, 2011). Room-sharing but not bed-sharing is considered ideal by medical experts because of the increased chance for SIDS when infants sleep in the same bed with parents. Some parents use a cot that attaches safely to the parents' bed. You can watch an Observing Children video on measures to reduce the risk for SIDS.

Observing Children 5-9

Learn more about practices to reduce the risk of sudden infant death syndrome (SIDS).

ENHANCEDetext *video example*

Early Childhood Through Adolescence

Time spent sleeping decreases steadily over the course of childhood. Two-year-olds typically need 12 hours of sleep; 3- to 5-year-olds, 11 hours; 10- to 13-year-olds, 10 hours; and 14- to 18-year-olds, 8½ hours (Roffwarg, Muzio, & Dement, 1966). These figures are averages, of course. The number of hours of sleep children of a particular age need to feel rested varies among individuals.

Occasional sleep problems occur. Nightmares are widespread between ages 3 and 6, and children may ask adults to help them battle the demons of the night. Pronounced sleep disturbances (e.g., waking repeatedly during the night) may be due to serious health problems, excessive stress, use of street drugs, or side effects from prescribed medications. Repeated nightmares are common among children who have experienced abuse or traumatic incidents or witnessed domestic violence (Durand, 1998; C. Humphreys, Lowe, & Williams, 2008; Insana, Foley, Montgomery-Downs, Kolko, & McNeil, 2013). Also, children with certain disabilities (e.g., cerebral palsy, severe visual impairment, autism, attention-deficit hyperactivity disorder) regularly have difficulty sleeping (Cotton & Richdale, 2010; Durand, 1998; Mannion, Leader, & Healy, 2013).

Especially as they grow older, children may get insufficient sleep because of poor sleep habits. Adolescents in particular are at risk for *sleep deprivation*, a state of being tired after not sleeping sufficiently and as a result having difficulty in reasoning, learning, and remembering. Although they require less sleep than they did in their earlier years, adolescents are still growing rapidly, and their brains and bodies need sleep and rest (Bei et al., 2013; Mitru, Millrood, & Mateika, 2002). Yet out-of-school obligations—extracurricular activities, part-time jobs, social engagements, homework assignments, and the ubiquitous World Wide Web—may keep teenagers up until the wee hours of the morning.

When young people lose sleep, they are likely to become short tempered and impatient. Depending on their age, sleep-deprived youngsters may become aggressive and depressed, have trouble concentrating, perform at low levels academically, and engage in high-risk behaviors (Bergin & Bergin, 2009/2010; Dahl & Lewin, 2002; Hildenbrand, Daly, Nicholls, Brooks-Holliday, & Kloss, 2013; Perkinson-Gloor, Lemola, & Grob, 2013; Sadeh, Gruber, & Raviv, 2002).

Accommodating Children's Needs for Rest and Sleep

Educators often have youngsters in their classrooms who do not sleep well, including some who are truly sleep deprived. With this situation in mind, we offer the following suggestions:

• **When appropriate, provide time for sleep during the day.** Infants and toddlers *must* sleep during the day. It is a common custom, and most certainly good practice, to include an optional naptime in the schedule of preschoolers who attend child care or school in the afternoon. A few older children and adolescents—for instance, youngsters with brain injuries or other chronic health conditions—may need an hour or two of sleep as well, perhaps on a couch in the school nurse's office (Lewandowski & Rieger, 2009; Ormrod & McGuire, 2007).

• **Include time for rest in the daily schedule.** Young children typically give up their afternoon nap sometime between ages 2 and 5, but for quite some time after that, they need to recharge their batteries with quiet and restful activities (e.g., listening to stories or music) in the afternoon. Older children also learn most effectively when they take an occasional, restful break from intense academic learning.

• **Communicate with families about the importance of sleep.** Teachers and other practitioners can speak tactfully with family members when they think chronic fatigue is causing a child's difficulty in concentrating, maintaining good spirits, and resisting aggressive impulses. The topic of sleep can also be addressed in tips to parents in school newsletters with such recommendations as turning off the television and computer an hour or two before bedtime and setting and enforcing reasonable bedtimes.

• **Encourage youngsters to start early and make steady progress on lengthy assignments.** At the high school level, adolescents may have several hours of homework each night. Add to this workload extracurricular events, social activities, family commitments, and part-time jobs, and you get adolescents who are seriously overstretched. When assigning major projects, teachers can encourage regular progress by giving interim deadlines for various *parts* of the assignment.

- **Schedule school events with reasonable ending times.** Athletic practices, plays and musical performances, club meetings, and other school events can be planned with definite starting and ending times that allow students to wrap up commitments early enough to go home at sensible hours (Bergin & Bergin, 2009/2010). Occasionally, events as school dances extend far into the night (and into the morning), but late-night activities should be the exception rather than the rule.

- **Deliberate over the starting time for high school.** Some high schools delay the start of morning classes to allow students to sleep in an extra hour or so (Bergin & Bergin, 2009/2010; M. Short et al., 2013; Wahlstrom, Davison, Choi, & Ross, 2001). These schedule revisions have been well received, especially by adolescents, who generally sleep more rather than staying up later at night (M. Short et al., 2013; Wolfson & Carskadon, 2005). However, the implications of schedule changes for families and school personnel must also be considered during discussions.

- **Recognize that sleep problems can be a sign of illness or emotional stress.** Words of acknowledgment and kindness ("You look tired today, Darragh. Did you sleep all right last night?") may give tired children permission to share their troubles and, as a result, take the first step toward resolving them. With seriously disturbed children, guidance from a counselor or psychologist may be necessary.

As you have seen, advances that occur in physical development take many forms and depend on several distinct factors, including maturational processes, adequate nutrition, physical activity, and sleep. In the Basic Developmental Issues table "Physical Development," we summarize how growth shows nature and nurture, universality and diversity, and qualitative and quantitative change. Because good health comes not only from acquiring health-promoting habits but also from avoiding negative substances, we now focus on the important topic of health-compromising behaviors.

Health-Compromising Behaviors

Especially as they grow older and gain independence from direct supervision, students face many choices for leisure time. With freedom comes an element of danger: Young people sometimes make decisions that undermine their health. Here we look at three health-compromising behaviors: cigarette smoking, alcohol and drug use, and unsafe sexual activity.

Cigarette Smoking

Every year, a number of young people begin to smoke cigarettes (see Table 5-1). Unfortunately, teens often continue to use tobacco when they become adults. Because the health risks are so well publicized, it is difficult to understand why adolescents choose to smoke. Undoubtedly, "image" is a factor. Teens may smoke cigarettes to look older, rebel, and affiliate with certain peer groups. Advertising plays a role as well. The majority of teen smokers choose from only a few cigarette brands, perhaps because of the youthful, sophisticated, and fun-loving images that tobacco companies project in the media. Regardless of the reasons adolescents begin smoking, those who make it a habit are at risk for developing health problems they might otherwise avoid.

Alcohol and Drug Use

Alcohol and drugs are among the most serious threats to physical health faced by adolescents. Occasionally a single episode of sufficient dosage with a particular drug leads to permanent brain damage or even death. While impaired under the influence of these substances, adolescents become vulnerable in other ways, such as engaging in unprotected sexual activity. Those who are intravenous drug users sometimes share needles, putting themselves at risk of contracting hepatitis C and the human immunodeficiency virus (HIV; described later in the chapter), and other infections (J. L. Evans, Hahn, Lum, Stein, & Page, 2009; Newland & Treloar, 2013). Figure 5-6 describes substances used by a number of adolescents.

Given the hazards of alcohol and drugs, why do adolescents use them? For some, it's a matter of curiosity: After hearing about alcohol and drugs, not only from their peers but also from adults and the media, teens may want to experience the effects firsthand. For others, trying alcohol and drugs is an impulsive event with little forethought.

BASIC DEVELOPMENTAL ISSUES
Physical Development

ISSUE	PHYSICAL GROWTH	MOTOR SKILLS	HEALTH AND ACTIVITY
Nature and Nurture	Genetic instructions specify the particular changes that occur as bodies grow larger and provide individual targets for mature appearance, height, and weight. Normal progressions depend on adequate nutrition, movement, stimulation, affection, sleep, and protection from toxic substances.	Nature sets firm boundaries as to the motor skills a child can execute at any age range. A 6-month-old cannot run and a 10-year-old cannot clear 15 feet in the standing high jump. Nurture allows children to maximize their athletic achievements.	Nature influences children's individual activity level and susceptibility to illness. Nurture affects children's daily activities. Children learn habits related to eating and exercising from parents, peers, teachers, coaches, and others in their community.
Universality and Diversity	Children tend to show similar sequences in physical development (e.g., in the emergence of male and female characteristics during puberty) across a wide range of situations. The rate of development differs from one child to the next as a result of genetic factors, personal choices, family stresses, and cultural variations.	Motor skills often develop in a similar sequence. Children can, on average, pick up crumbs at age 1, scribble with a crayon at age 2, and build a tower 10 blocks high at age 4 (Sheridan, 1975). Diversity is present in the exact ages at which children master motor skills, due to genetic differences and variations in environmental support.	All children need good nutrition, plenty of rest, and a moderate amount of physical activity. Diversity exists in the kinds of meals that children obtain at home and in the encouragement they receive to exercise. Children also vary in their susceptibility to illness, physical disabilities, and accommodations at school.
Qualitative and Quantitative Change	Many physical advancements result from quantitative changes (e.g., gradual increases in strength and dexterity). Qualitative changes are implicated in the physical characteristics of puberty.	As a general rule, children must practice motor skills for a long time before they can execute them smoothly. Some motor skills, such as throwing a ball, are transformed qualitatively, such that new styles emerge and replace previous ones.	During middle childhood, children gradually gain control over what they eat and how they spend their leisure time (a quantitative change). Reorganizations in thinking about danger and acting on impulses occur during adolescence.

Adult behaviors, too, influence substance abuse. Many adolescents who use drugs or alcohol have parents who fail to supervise their whereabouts and do little to promote their self-confidence, willingness to abide by society's rules, or ability to stay focused on long-term goals (Branstetter & Furman, 2013; Jessor & Jessor, 1977; P. Wu, Liu, & Fan, 2010). Drug and alcohol use is more typical when people in the local community are tolerant of such behavior (Poresky, Daniels, Mukerjee, & Gunnell, 1999). Peer group norms and behaviors are yet another factor affecting adolescents' substance abuse (Lai et al., 2013; P. Wu et al., 2010). To a great extent, use of alcohol and drugs is a social activity, and teenagers may partake to a certain extent as a means of "fitting in."

Regardless of their initial reasons for trying alcohol and drugs, youngsters' continued use often creates serious problems. If these substances give adolescents pleasure, satisfy a desire for thrills, alleviate anxieties, or deaden feelings of pain and depression, they may begin to use the substances regularly (Conner, Hellemann, Ritchie, & Noble, 2010; Ozechowski & Waldron, 2010; R. C. Palmer et al., 2013). Unfortunately, some users eventually develop an **addiction** to, or dependence on, drugs or alcohol. Thus they grow physiologically accustomed to using the substance and need increasing quantities to produce a desired effect. If they try to stop, addicts experience intense cravings and unpleasant reactions (Hussong, Chassin, & Hicks, 1999; National Institute on Drug Abuse, 2009).

Unsafe Sexual Activity

Learning about sexuality is an important part of coming of age, and many adolescents become sexually active during the secondary school years.[1] On average, 4 or 5 in every 10 high school students in the United States report having had sexual intercourse (CDC, 2012;

[1]Sexual intimacy is examined in Chapter 15.

- *Alcohol* depresses the central nervous system, incites a feeling of elation, and impairs coordination, perception, speech, and judgment; inebriated drinkers may talk incoherently and walk with a staggered gait. Teens who drink heavily are more likely to have car accidents and commit rape than those who do not.

- *Methylene dioxymethamphetamine* (MDMA, or "ecstasy") gives users a sense of euphoria and exuberance, sensory enhancements and distortions, and feelings of being at peace with the world and emotionally close to others (it is sometimes called the "hug drug"). However, the sense of euphoria often leads users to ignore bodily distress signals, such as muscle cramping and dehydration; more serious effects include convulsions, impaired heart function, and death. It is often available at dance clubs ("raves"), where its effects are intensified with music and flashing lights.

- *Inhalants* are attractive to many adolescents because they cause an immediate "high" and are readily available in the form of such household substances as glue, paint thinner, aerosol paint cans, and nail polish remover. These very dangerous substances can cause loss of sensation, brain damage, and death.

- *Marijuana* delays reaction time, modifies perception, and instills a mild feeling of bliss, but it can also heighten fears and anxieties and impair thinking. Teens who smoke marijuana may have red eyes, dry mouths, mood changes, and loss of interest in former friends and hobbies, and they may exhibit impaired driving.

- *Methamphetamine* ("speed") is a stimulant that gives users a sense of energy, alertness, confidence, and well-being. Overdoses are possible, addiction frequently results, and changes to the brain and heart can occur. People who use speed regularly combat psychiatric problems, such as becoming violent and confused and believing that "everyone is out to get me."

- *Cocaine* (including *crack*, a particularly potent form) overstimulates neurons in the brain and gives users a brief sense of energy and intense euphoria; it can also cause tremors, convulsions, vomiting, respiratory problems, overheating, strokes, and heart failure. Cocaine users may be energetic, talkative, argumentative, and boastful; long-time users may appear anxious and depressed. Crack users are prone to violence and crime.

- *Bath salts (designer cathinones)* are synthetic stimulants contained in a white powder that is typically snorted. The salts can cause rapid heart racing (and sometimes heart attacks), dizziness, paranoia, seizures, delusions, and suicidal thoughts.

- *Rohypnol* is a central nervous depressant that causes muscle relaxation, a sense of euphoria, impaired judgment, amnesia, and slow breathing (which in extreme cases can culminate in death). It has been called the "rape drug" because it has been placed in alcoholic drinks of unsuspecting women to render them defenseless during a sexual assault.

- *Prescription medications* are used improperly by a growing number of adolescents because of their effects on the body. Prescription painkillers, such as OxyContin and Vicodin, are potentially addictive narcotics that reduce sensations of discomfort and increase feelings of relaxation and pleasure. Stimulants such as Adderall and Ritalin that treat attention and hyperactivity disorders are sometimes sold by adolescents to peers who want to get "high." Anabolic steroids, another type of medication for which there is an illicit market among teenagers, increase muscle development, but regular users experience unwanted side effects (e.g., in boys, shrinking testicles and breast development; in girls, growth of facial hair and menstrual changes; in both, liver damage and high blood pressure).

FIGURE 5-6 **Examples of substances abused by some adolescents.** *DanceSafe, 2000a, 2000b; Gunderson, Kirkpatrick, Willing, & Holstege, 2013; L. D. Johnston, O'Malley, Bachman, & Schulenberg, 2007; Kulberg, 1986; National Institute on Drug Abuse, 2010a, 2010b, 2010c, 2010d, 2010e, 2010f, 2010g, 2010h; Neinstein, 2004; Patnode et al., 2014; P. Stevens & Smith, 2013; J. M. Taylor, 1994; U.S. Department of Justice Drug Enforcement Administration, 2011.*

see Table 5-1). More than 1 in 10 students have had four or more sexual partners, and more than 1 in 10 who are sexually active did not use any precautions during last intercourse. From the perspective of physical health, early sexual activity is problematic because it can lead to infections, pregnancy, or both.

Sexually Transmitted Infections. Sexually transmitted infections (STIs) vary in long-term effects. Syphilis, gonorrhea, and chlamydia can be treated with antibiotics, but affected teens do not always seek prompt medical help. Without treatment, serious problems can occur, including infertility and sterility, heart problems, and birth defects in future offspring. Genital herpes has no known cure, but medication can alleviate the severity of symptoms.

Undoubtedly the most life-threatening STI is acquired immune deficiency syndrome (AIDS), a medical condition in which the immune system is weakened, permitting severe infections, pneumonias, and cancers to invade the body. AIDS is caused by HIV, which can be transmitted through the exchange of body fluids (e.g., blood and semen) during a single contact. Sexual transmission is the most common means of HIV transmission in both men and women (CDC, 2013e; Harper & Riplinger, 2013). (Of course, adolescents also contract HIV from contaminated needles during intravenous drug use and, rarely, from transfusions and organ transplants).

Pregnancy. Pregnancy rates in U.S. adolescents have decreased slightly during the past few decades in large part due to increased use of condoms and other contraceptive methods (Santelli, Orr, Lindberg, & Diaz, 2009). Nevertheless, numerous pregnancies occur in teens, some of which end in miscarriage or abortion, and others of which go to full term. The current rate is 15 births per 1,000 American girls ages 15 to 17 (Federal Interagency Forum on Child and Family Statistics, 2013). Girls who become teenage mothers are apt to come from low-income families, have weak academic performance, believe they have few career options, be prone to depression, achieve status within their community with the birth of the baby, and yearn for an emotional connection (Coley & Chase-Lansdale, 1998; C. Y. Huang, Costeines, Kaufman, & Ayala, 2013; Madkour, Harville, & Xie, 2014; Sieger & Renk, 2007).

Addressing Health-Compromising Behaviors

Schools and community organizations can do a great deal to reduce physical risk. We offer a few thoughts on support:

BIOECOLOGY OF DEVELOPMENT

Health-compromising behaviors and their prevention are affected by numerous bioecological factors.

• **Provide healthy options for free time.** Children are less likely to engage in health-compromising behaviors when they have better things to do with their time. In our chapter-opening case study, a new program afforded productive activities for both children and their adolescent coaches. Community leaders can choose from numerous kinds of after-school programs and community athletic leagues depending on resources and the preferences of local youth.

• **Prevent problems.** It is much easier to teach adolescents to resist cigarettes, alcohol, and drugs than it is to treat dependence on these substances. Schools are important sites for prevention because they serve so many young people (Hale, Fitzgerald-Yau, & Viner, 2014; Pokhrel et al., 2013). Effective programs take advantage of the protective factors that young people have, for example, strong family ties are assets that educators can leverage by sending home newsletters about drug prevention (Bukstein & Deas, 2010; National Institute on Drug Abuse, 2003).

Effective programs also address age-typical abilities and risk factors. At the elementary level, programs reduce the possibility that problems with aggression and academic failure put children on a trajectory of troubled behavior. Activities foster children's self-control, emotional awareness, communication skills, social problem solving, and academic achievement. In middle, junior high, and high school, successful programs address similar abilities as well as drug-resistance skills, antidrug attitudes, and commitments for avoiding drugs and alcohol. Repeated exposure to the same antidrug messages across multiple settings, for example, at school and home, in faith-based organizations, and in the media, can also be valuable. What *doesn't* work are simple scare tactics or information about drugs that fails to address the developmental needs of young people, their beliefs and attitudes, options for leisure time, and goals for future careers and family life. Because not all drug prevention programs are successful, it behooves school leaders to investigate the effectiveness of interventions they are considering.

• **Discourage drug and alcohol use in all settings.** The kinds of programs educators implement are determined largely by their duties and the needs of youngsters with whom they work. Coaches and other staff members in the Forest Hills School District in Cincinnati, Ohio, designed a productive drug prevention program (see Figure 5-7). Participation was encouraged by school coaches, principals, other school staff, team captains, parents, and the adolescents themselves (U.S. Drug Enforcement Administration, 2002). Coaches spoke openly about substance use. Peer pressure was enlisted in discouraging alcohol and drug use. When athletes did break the rules, they were given defined consequences, in a way that communicated hope that they would try harder next time.

• **Encourage adolescents to protect themselves.** Approaches to preventing adolescent pregnancy and transmission of STIs can be contentious. Parents may object to the school's distribution of condoms and advocacy of "safe sex." (And, of course, at the present time condom use is no guarantee of protection against either infection or pregnancy.) Evidence suggests, however, that having condoms available in schools

Student's Pledge

As a participant in the _____ High School Athletic Program, I agree to abide by all training rules regarding the use of alcohol, tobacco, and other drugs. Chemical dependency is a progressive but treatable disease, characterized by continued drinking or other drug use in spite of recurring problems resulting from that use. Therefore, I accept and pledge to abide by the training rules listed in the athletic handbook and others established by my coach.

To demonstrate my support, I pledge to:

1. Support my fellow students by setting an example and abstaining from the use of alcohol, tobacco, and other drugs.

2. Not enable my fellow students who use these substances. I will not cover up for them or lie for them if any rules are broken. I will hold my teammates responsible and accountable for their actions.

3. Seek information and assistance in dealing with my own or my fellow students' problems.

4. Be honest and open with my parents about my feelings, needs, and problems.

5. Be honest and open with my coach and other school personnel when the best interests of my fellow students are being jeopardized.

Student _____ Date _____

**PARENTS: We ask that you co-sign this pledge to show your support.

Sample Letter from Coach to Parent about a Drug or Alcohol Violation

Dear Parent:

Your daughter _____ has violated the _____ High School extra-curricular activities code of conduct. She voluntarily came forward on Thursday afternoon and admitted her violation of the code, specifically, drinking alcohol. The code is attached.

We respect her honesty and integrity and hope you do as well. Admitting a mistake such as this is very difficult for her. Not only does she have to deal with authorities such as us, she must face you, her parents, as well as her peers—which is probably the most difficult. We understand that no one is perfect and that people do make mistakes. Our code, and the resulting consequences of violating the code, is a nationally recognized model and is designed to encourage this type of self-reporting where the student can seek help and shelter from guilt without harsh initial penalties. She has admitted to making a mistake and is willing to work to alleviate the negative effects of the mistake.

As you can see in the enclosed code, we require that your daughter complete 10 hours of drug and alcohol in-service education and counseling. In addition, she must sit out 10 practice days of competition. She is still part of the team and must attend practices and competition; she is just not allowed to compete or participate in games for 10 days.

We hope you understand and support our effort to provide a healthy athletic program for the students. If you have any questions, please call either one of us at the high school.

Sincerely,

FIGURE 5-7 **Team Up drug prevention materials from high school athletic coaches.** *From* Team Up: A Drug Prevention Manual for High School Athletic Coaches, *by the U.S. Drug Enforcement Administration, 2002, Washington, DC: U.S. Department of Justice Drug Enforcement Administration.*

moderately increases condom use for those students who are already sexually active (and so offers some protection against infections and pregnancy) and does not necessarily increase rates of sexual activity (Alan Guttmacher Institute, 2001; Fonner, Armstrong, Kennedy, O'Reilly, & Sweat, 2014; D. Kirby & Laris, 2009). Programs that encourage sexual abstinence are a less controversial alternative that discourage sexual intercourse in the short run but are relatively ineffective over the long run (Dreweke & Wind, 2007; D. Kirby & Laris, 2009; B. McCarthy, & Grodsky, 2011; Raghupathy, Klein, & Card, 2013).

Some programs encourage both abstinence and use of contraception, and it appears that young people easily grasp the merits of these two strategies for different situations (D. Kirby & Laris, 2009; Lindberg & Maddow-Zimet, 2012). All things considered, young people seem to benefit from sex education that is comprehensive, includes information about risks and methods of protection, and portrays sexuality as a healthy part of human development.

• **Get help for young people who have become addicted to drugs or alcohol.** Teachers and other practitioners can share suspicions with parents and counselors that youngsters have become dependent on drugs or alcohol. Various kinds of treatment, including medication, counseling, and residential programs, can help young people manage painful withdrawal symptoms and learn to resist these substances in the future (National Institute on Drug Abuse, 2009; Pokhrel et al., 2013). Some adolescents go through treatment voluntarily, whereas others are required by families and court orders to participate. Relapses in drug and alcohol use are relatively common and signify the need for additional intervention.

The four areas we've discussed in this section—eating habits, physical activity, rest and sleep, and health-compromising behaviors—all have major effects on youngsters' physical development. In the Observation Guidelines table "Assessing Health Behaviors and Characteristics of Children," we identify attributes of good and poor health. Obviously, practitioners should not provide treatment for which they are untrained, but they can help young people acquire habits of self-care that are health-promoting and life-sustaining.

Special Physical Needs

Some children have long-term physical conditions that affect school performance, friendships, and leisure activities. Here we look at chronic medical conditions, serious injuries, and physical disabilities in children and adolescents. We then identify strategies for accommodating these conditions.

Chronic Medical Conditions

All children get sick now and then, but some have ongoing, long-term conditions because of genetic legacies (e.g., cystic fibrosis), environmentally contracted illnesses (e.g., AIDS), or an interaction between the two (e.g., some forms of asthma and cancer). As many as 1 or 2 in 10 children have a chronic condition that causes them to experience noticeable limitations in strength, vitality, relaxation, or alertness (Nabors, Little, Akin-Little, & Iobst, 2008).

Teachers come face to face with children's health flare-ups and lapses in self-care. For instance, a fourth-grade girl with diabetes needs to monitor her blood sugar levels and take appropriate follow-up action. Her teacher will find out from the girl and her parents what her schedule for testing is and will accommodate her daily trip to the nurse's office. Yet children with chronic conditions are not always reliable in assessing their own symptoms and sometimes forget to take prescribed medication (D. J. Bearison, 1998; S. Kirk et al., 2013; Koinis-Mitchell et al., 2009). Accordingly, educators may need to seek family help or medical assistance when conditions deteriorate.

In addition to facilitating self-care in chronically sick children, teachers can support children's peer relationships. Some children who are ill feel so "different" that they are hesitant to approach peers (Alison, Negley, & Sibthorp, 2013; M. Jackson, 2013; A. Turnbull, Turnbull, & Wehmeyer, 2010). They may blame their physical condition (perhaps accurately, perhaps not) for any problems they have with friendships (Kapp-Simon & Simon, 1991).

Unfortunately, some healthy children actively reject peers with serious illnesses. To some extent, such reactions reflect ignorance. Many children, young ones especially, have naive notions about illness. For instance, preschoolers sometimes believe that people contract cancer by being in the same room as someone else with that condition (Bibace & Walsh, 1981; M. Jackson, 2013). As children get older, their conceptions of illness gradually become more accurate. They grow more attuned to internal body cues, better understand the effects of germs, and differentiate types of illness (T. K.-F. Au et al., 2008; D. J. Bearison, 1998; Sigelman, 2012). Children also absorb many of their community's ideas as to how health conditions are contracted and best addressed. You can learn more about cultural differences in an Observing Children video.

Teachers and other professionals can address the special needs of sick children. Practitioners can help a child with unfinished work, explain the concepts in homework if necessary, find a sympathetic peer the child can talk with when returning to the classroom, and contact a school counselor when he or she is sad or withdrawn. When necessary, teachers can remind the youngster about visiting the nurse to take scheduled medicine.

Serious Injuries and Health Hazards

Injuries represent a major threat to children. Young children are at risk for ingesting poisons, drowning in pools, falling from heights, and getting burned from the stove. As children get older, their increasing independence makes them susceptible to other kinds of injuries. In the United States, injuries from firearms, motor vehicle crashes, unintentional drowning or poisoning, and suicide are the primary causes of death during the adolescent years (CDC, 2013f).

Preparing for Your Licensure Examination

Your teaching test might ask you about exceptionalities in physical development.

FOR FURTHER EXPLORATION . . .

Read how children of various ages cope with chronic illnesses.

ENHANCEDetext

content extension

Observing Children 5-10

Learn about cultural practices and beliefs regarding care of sick children.

ENHANCEDetext *video example*

OBSERVATION GUIDELINES
Assessing Health Behaviors and Characteristics of Children

CHARACTERISTIC	LOOK FOR	EXAMPLE	IMPLICATION
Eating Habits	• *Frequent consumption* of junk food (candy, chips, carbonated beverages, fast food, etc.) • *Unusual heaviness or thinness*, especially if these characteristics become more pronounced over time • *Lack of energy* • *Reluctance or inability to eat* at lunchtime	Melissa is a good student, an avid runner, and a member of the student council. She is quite thin, though, eats only a couple of pieces of celery at lunch, and wears baggy clothes that hide her figure. Her school counselor suspects an eating disorder and contacts Melissa's parents to share her suspicion.	Observe what children eat and drink during the school day. Seek free or reduced-cost breakfasts and lunches for children from low-income families. Consult with parents and specialists when eating habits seem to be seriously detrimental to children's health.
Physical Activity	• *Improvements in speed, complexity, and agility* of gross motor skills (e.g., running, skipping, jumping) • *Restlessness, lethargy, or inattention* during lengthy seatwork (possibly reflecting a need to take a break) • *Overexertion* (increasing the risk of injury)	Before beginning a soccer game during field day, a teacher asks children to run up and down the field, accelerating and decelerating while taking turns kicking a ball. She then has them practice evading another player. Only after such practice does she begin the game (Logsdon et al., 1997).	Incorporate regular physical activity into the daily schedule. Choose tasks and activities that are enjoyable and allow for a range of skill levels. Make sure youngsters have mastered prerequisite skills before introducing more complex abilities.
Rest and Sleep	• *Listlessness* and lack of energy • *Inability to concentrate* • *Irritability* and overreaction to frustration • *Lashing out to peers* when frustrated, and other signs of poor self-control • *Sleeping in class*	A teacher in an all-day kindergarten notices that some of his students become cranky during the last half-hour of school, and so typically reserves this time for storybook reading and other quiet activities.	Provide regular opportunities for rest. When a youngster seems unusually tired day after day, talk with him or her (and perhaps with parents) about how lack of sleep can affect attention and behavior. Together seek possible solutions.
Health-Compromising Behaviors	• *Smell of cigarettes* on clothing • *Physiological symptoms of drug use*, possibly red eyes, dilated pupils, tremors, convulsions, respiratory problems, slurred pronunciation, fast talking, incoherence, poor coordination, impaired decision making, mood changes, or unusual energy • *Change in personality and friends* • *Rapid weight gain* and a tendency to wear increasingly baggy clothes (in girls who might be pregnant) • Conversation and writing about sexual activities	A school counselor notices a dramatic change in James's personality. Whereas he used to be eager to engage in conversation, he now begins to "zone out" during counseling sessions. He slumps in his chair, looks out the window, and speaks unintelligibly. The counselor asks James if he is using drugs, which he denies. The counselor advises his parents about her fears and mentions a range of treatment options in the community.	Prevent health-compromising behaviors by providing opportunities to be successful academically and socially. Educate young people about the dangers of substance abuse and unprotected sexual activity; teach behaviors for resisting temptations, tailoring instruction to age and cultural background. Enforce alcohol and drug policies on school grounds and in extracurricular activities. Arrange productive leisure activities. Consult with a mental health professional when you worry that a youngster is pregnant or abusing drugs.

Although some injuries heal quickly, others have long-term effects that must be accommodated at school. **Traumatic brain injuries (TBIs)** are hits or jolts to the head that alter brain functioning; TBIs range from mild concussions to severe wounds. Children sustain TBIs from playground falls, bicycle mishaps, skiing and motor vehicle accidents, sports injuries, assaults, and other harrowing events (CDC, 2013g; McKinlay et al., 2008). Depending on location in the brain and the severity of the wound, TBIs can have temporary or lasting effects. Children with mild concussions experience a brief loss of consciousness or sense of being disoriented and may have memory lapses for events immediately before or after the accident. Youngsters frequently have headaches, nausea, and trouble concentrating for several months after the injury. Depending on the student's symptoms, a teacher might minimize distractions in the classroom, allow extra time to complete assignments, or adjust expectations for performance, at least for the first few weeks (A. Turnbull et al., 2010). Children who have had a more serious brain injury experience a lengthy period of unconsciousness and amnesia and afterwards exhibit difficulties in learning, controlling emotions, speaking, walking, and seeing or hearing. These children generally require therapy and modifications to the curriculum.

Many childhood injuries are avoidable, of course, and schools can play a key role in educating children about preventive measures. Teachers can advise children to use seat belts while riding in motor vehicles and wear helmets while cycling, snowboarding, and skating (CDC, 2013h; Klassen, MacKay, Moher, Walker, & Jones, 2000). Coaches can instruct athletes on how to reduce risks for head injuries, recognize signs of concussions, and get help after a possible TBI (CDC, 2010). After an injury, an athlete should be given ample time to recover before returning to the field and reminded to take precautions in avoiding collisions in the future.

Physical Disabilities

Preparing for Your Licensure Examination
Your teaching test might ask you about accommodations that allow children with physical disabilities to participate in sports.

Children with physical disabilities, such as cerebral palsy, muscular dystrophy, and blindness, have the same essential physical needs as other children, namely, a good diet, regular exercise, and adequate rest and sleep. Because exercise is central to health, adults must find ways to adapt physical activities for children with special sensory and physical conditions. Adaptation essentially involves giving the type of support that enables successful movement. For example, a teacher can assist students who have visual impairments by guiding their bodies into correct positions and inserting bells or other noisemakers inside playground balls (Poel, 2007). For a student who likes baseball but lacks strength and endurance, a teacher might allow another student to run around the bases after a hit (Pangrazi & Beighle, 2010). For students with hearing impairments, teachers need to ask parents whether any assistive devices, such as hearing aids and cochlear implants, should be removed during vigorous physical activity. While conducting the physical activity, they can use illustrations, enlist the help of an interpreter, demonstrate movements, and confirm that students understand the objectives (Schultz, Lieberman, Ellis, & Hilbenbrinck, 2013).

Promoting Physical Well-Being in All Children

As you are learning, children with chronic illnesses, serious injuries, and physical disabilities often require individualized accommodations to achieve optimal health. Several guidelines apply to *all* children but especially to those with special physical needs:

• **Seek guidance from parents and specialized organizations about accommodations that help children be actively involved in sports.** Parents and guardians often have helpful suggestions about adjustments that enable their children to participate in exercise. Professional organizations—most are easily found on the Internet—also offer a wealth of ideas about adapting instruction and equipment for children with chronic conditions and disabilities. Two broadly focused organizations are the American Alliance for Health, Physical Education, Recreation and Dance, and the National Consortium for Physical Education and Recreation for Individuals with Disabilities. Specific disabilities are the focus of other organizations, such as the American Athletic Association for the Deaf and the U.S. Association for Blind Athletes.

• **Encourage children to monitor their health.** Children gradually learn to cope with the everyday demands of chronic health conditions, but they may need reminders to carry out required procedures (e.g., to test blood glucose levels if they have diabetes), go to the nurse's office at appropriate times (e.g., to take medicines), and look after their recurring physical needs (e.g., to eat nutritious snacks and use the toilet regularly).

• **Encourage children and their families to take protective measures.** Caregivers and teachers can teach young children safety precautions, such as how to handle certain emergencies, for example, how and under what circumstances to make an emergency phone call, what to do when lost or approached by a stranger, and how to respond if they find a gun (S. O'Neill, Fleer, Agbenyega, Ozanne-Smith, & Urlichs, 2013; Pan-Skadden et al., 2009; M. C. Roberts, Brown, Boles, & Mashunkashey, 2004). In elementary school, teachers can explain (and enforce) safety rules for climbing and using slides and distribute safety brochures on seat belts, bicycle helmets, and fire and smoke safety.

- **Design environments to minimize injuries.** Careful attention to equipment can reduce children's injuries (M. C. Roberts et al., 2004). An infant caregiver can purchase cribs with slats close together to prevent babies' heads from getting stuck between them. He or she can also examine toys for choking hazards, set the temperature of water heaters below what would cause scalding, and confirm that the refrigerator door will not lock from the inside (M. C. Roberts et al., 2004). A principal can ensure that a playground has no sharp edges; that the ground's surface has soft, cushioning materials; and that smoke detectors are installed properly and regularly checked for capacity.

- **Know what to do in a health emergency.** Some children have conditions that could result in life-threatening situations. A child with diabetes could go into insulin shock, a child with asthma might have trouble breathing, and a child with epilepsy could have a serious seizure at school. When teachers learn that a child has a chronic health condition, they can consult with parents to find out ahead of time how to respond in emergencies.

- **Educate children about physical disabilities.** Children are more likely to show kindness to a peer with a physical impairment if they understand the nature of the disability. Children should know, for example, that cancer cannot be spread through breathing the same air and that epileptic seizures, although frightening, are only temporary. Keep in mind, however, that a teacher should talk about a child's physical condition *only* if he or she and the parents have given permission to do so (Shapiro & Manz, 2004).

- **Keep lines of communication open with children who are hospitalized or homebound.** Sometimes children's health conditions keep them out of school for lengthy periods of time. In such circumstances, children can participate in classroom lessons, activities, and social events by telephone or a video and voice conferencing system such as *Skype* or *FaceTime*. When children cannot stay in touch regularly, they may be especially appreciative of correspondence and photographs from classmates and other important people in their lives.

- **Teach social skills to children who find themselves excluded from friendship groups.** School absences and the stresses of a chronic condition (and occasional overprotection from parents) can put a strain on children's peer relationships. Teachers can keep an eye out for the inclusion of children with chronic illnesses who are reentering school after repeated or lengthy absences. Teachers can also coach sick children to try particular social skills, such as listening sympathetically, resolving conflicts, and gaining entry into an existing group of children (Kapp-Simon & Simon, 1991).

- **Address any problems in learning that accompany children's illnesses.** Depending on their conditions and the medicines they take, children with chronic illnesses may develop attention and organizational problems (Shapiro & Manz, 2004). Teachers can encourage children to stay focused and teach them how to organize their work and set interim goals for complex assignments. Teachers can also arrange for hospitalized children to make up missed work when they regain their strength.

- **Use appropriate precautions when caring for children.** Educators can teach children basic safety precautions, such as sneezing into their own elbow, staying away from a friend's bloody knee, and washing hands after using the toilet. Adults also need to take precautions themselves. The use of appropriate barrier precautions for blood (e.g., latex gloves) is advisable when helping children who have suffered open wounds. Experts also direct caregivers to wash their hands after changing diapers and wiping noses (American Academy of Pediatrics Committee on Pediatric AIDS and Committee on Infectious Diseases, 1999). Teachers may need to refer children to the school nurse when they appear feverish and hence need to be home, where they can recover without spreading the illness to other children.

Summary

Health depends on eating habits, physical activity, and rest and sleep. Children can benefit from overtures by adults that affirm health-promoting behaviors and discourage hazardous actions. Some children exhibit behavior that jeopardizes their physical well-being (e.g., with eating disorders, overreliance on sedentary activities, and over-commitments that result in insufficient sleep). In adolescence, additional health-compromising behaviors may emerge as youth partake in cigarette smoking, alcohol and drug use, and unprotected sexual activity. Prevention can be emphasized at school, supplemented by individualized treatment, counseling, and other services for young people who are actively engaged in risky behaviors.

Youngsters with chronic illness, serious injuries, and physical disabilities often benefit from modifications in instruction, equipment, and the physical environment. Ultimately, educators should strive to include these children in physical activity and social interactions with peers.

ENHANCEDetext *self-check*

Assessing Children 5-1

Practice assessing a student's records of exercise.

ENHANCEDetext *application exercise*

Assessing Children 5-2

Practice assessing children's behavior during recess.

ENHANCEDetext *application exercise*

BRAIN DEVELOPMENT

Now that you have a foundation in basic features of physical development, you are ready to learn about the human brain, an extraordinary organ that senses information in the environment, guides movement, and regulates other systems in the body. The brain also permits advanced human abilities: It forms associations among environmental stimuli and previously learned ideas, fills everyday experience with emotional meaning, translates thoughts and feelings into words and behaviors, and determines actions needed to achieve desired outcomes.

How is this amazing organ structured? Altogether, the brain is made up of trillions of cells, the two primary kinds of which are *neurons* and *glia*. Historically scientists have emphasized the 100 billion **neurons**, the cells that transmit information to other cells (Naegele & Lombroso, 2001; R. W. Williams & Herrup, 1988). Each neuron has a long, arm-like **axon** that sends information on to other neurons and numerous branchlike extensions called **dendrites** that absorb chemicals released by nearby neurons (Figure 5-8).

Dendrites and axons come close to one another at junctions called **synapses**. When any neuron is stimulated by a sufficient amount by a chemical, it either "fires," generating an electrical impulse that triggers the release of its own substance (culminating in the stimulation and subsequent firing of adjacent neurons), or it is inhibited from firing. Neurons fire or are inhibited from firing depending on the amount and types of chemicals that neighbors send their way.

Most of the brain's neurons have thousands of synapses, so obviously a great deal of cross-communication occurs. Groups of neurons grow together as "communities" that specialize in certain functions. Following the principle that there is strength in numbers, these communities, called *circuits* or *networks,* are laid out in side-by-side wires that reach out to other groups of neurons. The result is that important processes of the brain (such as feeling emotions, paying attention, and learning new ideas) are supported by robust structures.

Intermingling with neurons are a trillion or more **glial cells**. Glial cells perform numerous functions (Figure 5-9). *Oligodendrocytes* coat the axons of neurons with insulating myelin, allowing electrical signals to propagate rapidly. *Microglia* rid the brain of damaged neurons, bacteria, and viruses. **Astrocytes** are glial cells that regulate blood flow to the brain, bring nutrients to neurons, metabolize chemicals released by neurons, and communicate with one another and with neurons. When stimulated, individual astrocytes release calcium, triggering other nearby astrocytes to activate. Scientists have begun to speculate that astrocytes may partly control the actions of neurons and help integrate information in the brain (Fields, 2009; Koob, 2009; Tong, Shigetomi, Looger, & Khakh, 2013; Volterra, Liaudet, & Savtchouk, 2014). Clues to the special role played by glial cells are found in research with different types of animals. Compared to other species, human beings have a higher ratio of astrocytes to neurons as well as larger and more complex astrocytes. Moreover, astrocytes are especially plentiful in areas of the brain responsible for higher-thinking processes. Ultimately scientists may find that it is the close interplay between neurons and glial cells, rather than the separate functions of either cell type, that is at the root of thinking.

Structures and Functions

Taking a broader scale, we can see that individual neurons and glial cell are organized into three main sections: the hindbrain, midbrain, and forebrain (Figure 5-10). Each of these sections has identifiable functions:

- The **hindbrain** controls basic processes that sustain survival, including breathing, blood pressure, sleep, arousal, balance, and movement (thank your hindbrain for your slow, methodical breathing as you sleep blissfully at night).
- The **midbrain** connects the hindbrain to the forebrain and acts as a kind of relay station between the two; for instance, it sends messages to the forebrain about priorities for attention ("Hello! Alarm clock ringing! Time to rise!").
- The **forebrain** produces complex thinking, emotional responses, and the forces of motivation ("Ugh! I can sleep another 10 minutes if I skip breakfast. No . . . I better get up.").

The *forebrain* is of special relevance to educators and other practitioners because it allows children to learn concepts of all kinds and develop distinct personalities. The forebrain contains the **cortex**, a wrinkled cap that rests on the midbrain and hindbrain. Physiologically, the cortex is extremely convoluted. Bundles of neurons repeatedly fold in on

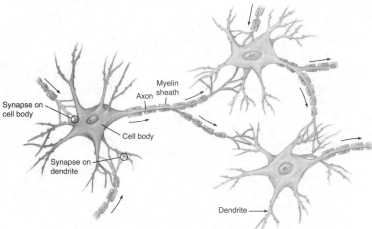

FIGURE 5-8   **Neurons.** The neuron at left is receiving information from other cells and will subsequently fire and incite neurons at right to fire. Arrows show the direction of messages being sent. *Adapted with permission from Carlson, N. R. (2014). Foundations of behavioral neuroscience (9th ed.). Boston, MA: Pearson. Reprinted with permission.*

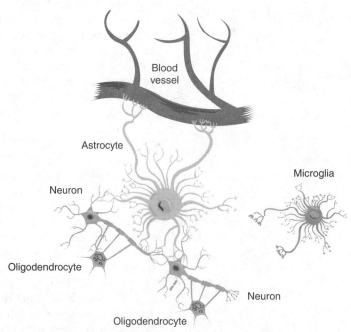

FIGURE 5-9   **Glial cells take numerous forms, three of which are represented here.** *Oligodendrocytes* insulate neurons and increase efficiency in firing. *Microglia* rid the brain of infectious and damaged material. *Astrocytes* play numerous roles, including communicating with one another and nourishing and regulating neurons.

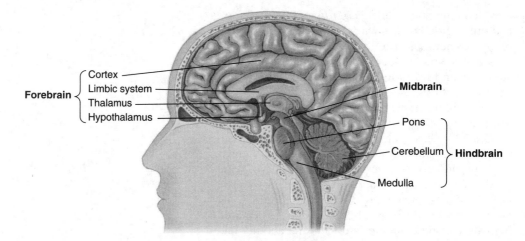

FIGURE 5-10 Structure of the human brain. The human brain is an intricate organ with three main parts: the hindbrain, midbrain, and forebrain. *Adapted with permission from* Carlson, N. R. (2014). Foundations of behavioral neuroscience (9th ed.). Boston, MA: Pearson.

themselves. This arrangement permits a huge capacity for storing and transmitting information throughout the brain.

The cortex enables interpreting, reasoning, communicating, and deliberate thinking processes: planning and decision making, collectively known as **executive functions**. The cortex is also the seat of many personality traits, such as being enthusiastic and sociable or quiet and introverted, and of habitual ways of responding to events and novel information. The cortex of one 10-year-old girl would control the way she snuggles up to her father on the sofa in the evening, her exuberant style in social groups, her understanding of how to read, and, of course, much more.

Areas of Specialization Within the Cortex

Consistent with the principle of differentiation, various parts of the cortex take on responsibility for psychological processes. The cortex consists of regions (called *lobes*) that specialize in particular functions, notably decision making and planning (front), understanding and production of language (sides), and visual processing (rear). In addition, the cortex is divided into two halves, or *hemispheres*. In right-handed individuals, the **left hemisphere** controls the right side of the body, and the **right hemisphere** manages the left side. In most people the left hemisphere dominates in *analysis,* breaking up information into constituent parts and extracting order in a sequence of events, as occurs in talking, understanding speech, reading, writing, mathematical problem solving, and computer programming (N. R. Carlson, 2014; Pinel & Dehaene, 2009). It is usually the right hemisphere that excels in *synthesis,* pulling together information (especially nonlinguistic information) into a coherent whole, as when we recognize faces; detect geometrical patterns; read body language; and appreciate musical melodies, humor, and emotions (N. R. Carlson, 2014; Gainotti, 2007). Left-handed individuals often have reversed patterns, with the right hemisphere dominant in analysis and the left hemisphere involved in synthesis (Toga & Thompson, 2003). A few individuals (particularly those who use both hands equally well) blend psychological functions within hemispheres in unique configurations (Sheehan & Smith, 1986).

Apparently, some of the many genes that guide brain development during the prenatal phase direct separate circuits to be formed in each side of the brain (Pinel & Dehaene, 2009). After birth and continuing throughout childhood, the two hemispheres become progressively distinct (Zhou, Lebel, Evans, & Beaulieu, 2013). Despite their separate specialties, the two hemispheres are in constant communication, trading information through a thick bundle of connecting neurons. For example, the right hemisphere processes a complex emotion, the mixed feelings people experience at a high school graduation, while the left hemisphere searches for the right words to communicate these feelings.

Supplementing the numerous circuits *within* the cortex are connections *between* the cortex and other parts of the brain. As an illustration, basic "energizing" activities that reside partly in areas of the brain outside the cortex (e.g., certain aspects of attention, emotion, and motivation) regularly interact with reflective "intellectual" processes that take place in the cortex. Hence, children who feel alert and happy readily grasp a classroom lesson, whereas children who are sleepy or distracted do not. An important method the brain uses is to relegate distinct functions—visualization, auditory analysis, verbal reasoning, musical recognition, and so on—to discrete areas dedicated to their unique processing needs, and then share the results with other areas, which help interpret the meaning of the experience (Bassett & Gazzaniga, 2011). Thus, once a little boy determines that the nighttime rustling he hears is only the family dog turning over, he realizes he can return to sleep.

Developmental Changes in the Brain

The magnificent intricacy of the human brain is made possible by a lengthy course of forming, refining, and connecting its parts. Together, nature and nurture guide this sculpting process throughout prenatal development, infancy, childhood, adolescence, and the adult years.

Prenatal Development

During prenatal development, the brain's most basic parts are formed. The brain begins as a tiny tube approximately 25 days after conception, as illustrated in Figure 5-11. This seemingly simple tube grows longer in places and folds inward to form pockets (Tierney & Nelson, 2009). Three bulges appear early on and become the forebrain, midbrain, and hindbrain. Soon the brain takes on more complex features, with the forebrain cleaving down the middle and specializing into the left and right hemispheres (Stephan, Fink, & Marshall, 2007).

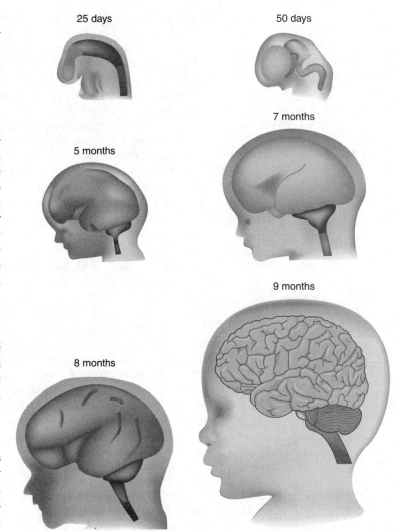

FIGURE 5-11 Prenatal brain growth. During the first few months, the basic structures appear (for 25 and 50 days, the relative sizes of which have been increased to show detail in forms). During the middle months of prenatal development, basic structures are refined. During the final weeks prior to birth, the cortex folds in and out of itself, preparing for learning as a baby.

Before the brain can develop any further, it must become a factory for neurons. Beginning in the fifth week, neurons reproduce in the inner portion of the tube. Production peaks between the third and fourth prenatal months, when several hundred thousand new neurons are generated *each minute* (C. A. Nelson et al., 2006). The vast majority of neurons that will ever be used by a person are formed during the first 7 months of prenatal development (Rakic, 1995).[2]

Once formed, neurons move, or *migrate,* to specific brain locations where they will do their work. Some young neurons push old cells outward, creating brain structures underneath the cortex. Others actively seek out their destination, climbing up pole-like glial cells and forming the cortex. When in place, neurons send out axons, which grow together as teams, reaching toward other groups of neurons (their targets) that attract them by secreting certain chemicals. As axons get close to neighboring neurons, they generate branches that become the dendrites, which in turn form synapses with other cells. The target cells do their part, forming small receptors with dendrites at the point of synapse. Only about half of

---

[2]Some new neurons are formed later in development, including during the adult years, in a structure of the brain that forms memories (C. A. Nelson et al., 2006). Astrocytes continue to duplicate throughout life.

neurons ultimately make contact with other cells. Those that do, survive; the others atrophy and die. Nature's tendency to overproduce neurons and eliminate those that fail to connect ensures that the brain invests in connections that actually work (M. Diamond & Hopson, 1998; P. R. Huttenlocher, 1990).

In the last few months of prenatal growth, the brains of developing babies form circuits for breathing, sucking, swallowing, crying, forming simple associations, and learning about people and the physical world. These final touches prepare newborn infants to survive and learn.

The rapid changes that occur in the prenatal offspring's brain make this phase of life highly susceptible to environmental influence and a *sensitive period*. Disruptions in cells can occur due to infection, genetic irregularities, poor nutrition, and exposure to toxins. Such problems can permanently affect the number of neurons, the circuits they build, and the chemical reactivity of neurons later in life. Therefore, practitioners who have the opportunity to advise pregnant women can emphasize the crucial need for adequate nutrition; protection from toxins, drugs, alcohol, and excessive stress; and prenatal medical care.

Infancy and Early Childhood

At birth and for a couple of days afterward, astrocytes and other glial cells proliferate and find their places near neurons. Neurons reach out for one another in countless new connections (synapses), a phenomenon known as **synaptogenesis**. In the first few years of life, so many new synapses appear that their number far exceeds adult levels (C. A. Nelson et al., 2006).

Following this fantastic proliferation of synapses, frequently used connections become stronger, and rarely used connections wither away in a process known as **synaptic pruning**. Particular regions of the brain take their turns growing and shedding synapses (P. R. Huttenlocher, 1990; Muftuler et al., 2012). Psychologists speculate that by generating more synapses than will ever be needed, human beings can adapt to a wide variety of conditions and circumstances. Synaptic pruning, then, is Mother Nature's way of customizing a brain to work efficiently in its particular circumstances.

Early brain development is also marked by **myelination**, a process in which glial cells grow around the axons of neurons to form a fatty coating (*myelin*) that insulates axons and enables rapid firing by neurons. Just as synaptic proliferation and pruning proceed in order through areas of the brain, myelination also occurs in this same general sequence (Yakovlev & Lecours, 1967). It actually begins during the prenatal period, with the coating of neurons involved in basic survival skills. Myelination then takes place around neurons that activate sensory abilities during infancy, followed by those involved in motor skills later in childhood, and eventually (well into adolescence) with those responsible for complex thinking processes, judgment, planning, and restraint (M. Diamond & Hopson, 1998; C. A. Nelson et al., 2006; Sanchez et al., 2012).

The *sensitive period* for brain growth that begins during the prenatal period persists into infancy, with the brain now devoted to identifying and learning patterns in the physical and social world. Infants spot uniformities as they are in the midst of taking initiative, inspecting the environment, developing a mutually responsive relationship with one or more caregivers, discerning the meaning of words, and otherwise discovering patterns around them. American psychologist Alison Gopnik has studied these amazing abilities of infants in forming generalizations from regularities in experience (A. Gopnik, 2009a, 2009b, 2009c; R. Wu, Gopnik, Richardson, & Kirkham, 2011). Infants notice such things as their parents being special people who lovingly care for them; toys being colorful, shiny, and made of hard, durable substances; and their native language being composed of ordered sounds (e.g., "p" and "t" often occur together within English words, as in "Peter," but not in direct succession, as in "Pteer"). Infants can form such generalizations because their brains are primed to detect patterns, sequences, and configurations.

If you have ever watched an 18-month-old child play with a new toy, you have seen the child pick it up, rotate the toy carefully while looking at its various sides, watch the results of it being shaken, and listen for any sounds. Gopnik argues that a child's brain specializes in *exploration*, whereas an adult's mind concentrates on *exploitation* of resources toward particular goals (A. Gopnik, 2009c; C. M. Walker & Gopnik, 2013). In other words, a young child's brain plays in order to learn, whereas an adult's brain works to achieve specific purposes.

As infants interact in their world, regularities in perceptions are transformed into brain networks. As the idle neurons atrophy and networks that fire together strengthen, the resulting operating circuits essentially obligate the child to notice features of stimuli that are consistent with the patterns he or she has previously perceived. The brain's tendency to convert preliminary distinctions into networks that support and constrain future learning has been described as making *neural commitments* (Kuhl, 2007; Kuhl, Conboy, Padden, Nelson, & Pruitt, 2005). When infants regularly hear certain sounds in their native language (e.g., the sound *ba* in English), they form neural commitments for these sounds, aiding the infants in recognizing them in full-blown words (e.g., *ba*ll). Such neural commitments help young children learn their native language but later *limit* their ability to learn a second language with different sounds.

If young children miss out on fundamental experiences with language, trusting relationships with caregivers, or occasions for listening, watching, and inspecting tangible objects, relevant areas in the brain do not develop normally. Depending on the severity of the deprivation, a child might later acquire language, learn to trust, and develop sensory abilities, but not as easily as would have been the case during infancy, and in some circumstances not as fully, because those networks in the brain that would have recorded these competencies have since been reallocated for other purposes.

As you may be realizing, research on early brain development has definite practical implications. Obviously, adults should do whatever they can to give children a good start in life. Yet during infancy and early childhood, much of the motivation for learning emanates from the children themselves. Instead of learning best with flash cards, teacher-directed lessons, or television programs, young children acquire knowledge most effectively when immersed in a reasonably complex environment and allowed to play, explore, and communicate with others. In fact, because neurological changes in certain areas do not take place until middle childhood or later, young children are typically not able to benefit from educational experiences that require sustained attention and inhibition of spontaneous responses.

Middle Childhood

By the time a child enters kindergarten, his or her brain is typically well formed, with some of its areas having already achieved full maturation and many others continuing to grow (Fusaro & Nelson, 2009; Taki et al., 2013). Sensory and perceptual functions reach adult levels of maturity during this period. Sections that permit other psychological processes, including memory and emotion, are also essentially complete although they continue to reach out and connect up with other parts of the brain during childhood and afterward. This progression of linking previously separate neurological centers makes it increasingly possible for children to reflect on their thoughts and persist in their attention.

Synaptic pruning of weak connections becomes a major force of change during childhood. Yet even as unused synapses are being pruned back, new ones continue to be formed with learning, especially in the cortex (National Research Council, 1999; Taki et al., 2013). The process of myelination also continues, protecting neurons and speeding up transmission of messages (Yakovlev & Lecours, 1967). This practice of solidifying useful neurological circuits allows children to become knowledgeable about whatever strikes their fancy—comic books, dance movements, cake decorating, or hunting strategies. In this manner, children also learn about the habits and motives of people in their lives, helping them fit comfortably into family and peer groups. Also during this period, children become increasingly proficient in their native tongue, now flexibly using sophisticated words and grammatical structures.

One other outcome of neurological changes is that children become capable of handling a growing number of ideas in mind and carrying out multiple mental tasks simultaneously. You can see this capacity being tapped by 6-year-old Brent as he recalls 6 out of 12 words in an Observing Children video. A year or so earlier he probably would have recalled fewer words, and in a few more years, he likely will recall more. Yet in part because their brain circuits are still under construction, children in the elementary grades have limited attention spans and restricted abilities to plan for the future. As a result, they cannot recall lengthy instructions and frequently forget belongings.

Elementary school teachers and other practitioners can accommodate the abilities and limitations of children's growing brains. Adults can ask children to identify the patterns in the changing seasons, tidal movements, holidays, artistic designs, musical rhythms, and historical events. Adults can also help children exercise fragile executive skills by posting a calendar, offering reminders, setting interim goals for complex tasks, and encouraging them to keep track of progress on projects. Moreover, adults can nurture children's initial efforts

Observing Children 5-11
Observe Brent as he tries to keep a few words in mind.
ENHANCEDetext *video example*

Preparing for Your Licensure Examination

Your teaching test might ask you about strategies for supporting children's organizational skills (e.g., encouraging them to set goals, manage time, and assemble learning materials for a lesson).

in regulating their emotions by talking with them about their feelings and teaching them productive ways to convey anger, disappointment, and sadness. Finally, children of this age continue to learn new vocabulary and grammatical structures and can benefit from exposure to literature, poetry, and second languages.

Adolescence

The cortex continues to change in important ways during adolescence (Casey, Giedd, & Thomas, 2000; Koolschijn & Crone, 2013; Sowell, Delis, Stiles, & Jernigan, 2001). Synaptic pruning and myelination continue in parts of the brain used in complex thought processes. As a result of these numerous long-term changes, adults' brains are more efficient than children's brains, both in terms of their connections (through synapses) and insulation (through myelination).

Given the significant transformations that brains are going through at this age, young people can now look beyond the surface of things. The capacity to consider multiple ideas simultaneously builds on the many insights children have acquired and now culminates in abstract thinking. Yet as adolescents are developing high-brow intellectual abilities, they also are gaining a taste for adventure (Banich, 2010; Carlisi, Pavletic, & Ernst, 2013; Steinberg, 2007). Many previously compliant youngsters suddenly violate basic rules, perhaps stealing, taking drugs, coloring their hair purple, or driving recklessly.

How is it that adolescents can act intelligently one minute and rashly the next? The answer seems to lie in a temporary imbalance that occurs in the adolescent brain. During this period, circuits in the brain devoted to enjoying immediate rewards (e.g., laughing uproariously with friends at the appearance of a classmate) mature before other circuits for avoiding adverse consequences (e.g., realizing that the classmate might overhear the remarks, anticipating his reaction, and telling friends to stop). Gradually, neurological systems curbing impulsive behavior catch up, making it easier for young people to control their impulses in the heat of the moment.

Of course, precisely how youth respond to impetuous feelings depends a great deal on the expectations of adults and the conduct of peers. Some societies tolerate testing of limits whereas others discourage, limit, or redirect this behavior. The Amish, a peaceful, traditional Christian sect in rural areas of Pennsylvania and Indiana, allow a period of "Rumspringa," a time when adolescents engage in such misbehavior as wearing nontraditional clothing, driving automobiles instead of horse-drawn vehicles, drinking alcohol, and engaging in premarital sex (Cates & Weber, 2012; Stevick, 2007). At the end of this period, Amish youth are encouraged to resume traditional ways, become baptized, and marry. Many other societies ask young people to profess their commitment to adult roles, albeit after education rather than a period for exploration as provided by the Amish, as you can learn about in the Development in Culture feature "Initiation Ceremonies."

The complex neurological changes of adolescence have implications for teachers and other professionals. Adults can foster abstract thinking by providing opportunities to test hypotheses in science, analyze characters' motivations in literature, and identify conflicting perspectives in history. They can similarly encourage adolescents to polish skills in individual areas of interest, perhaps computer programming, religious studies, or film production. Given the penchant for impetuous behavior at this age, adults must try to shield young people from harm by restricting their access to hazardous activities. Adolescents are generally able to appraise the risks of dangerous behaviors (e.g., drinking and driving, having unprotected sex), but they can easily lose good judgment when overwhelmed by immediate social pressures (Carlisi et al., 2013; Cauffman et al., 2010; V. F. Reyna & Farley, 2006; Somerville et al., 2010; Steinberg, 2007). As a result, efforts to educate adolescents about the consequences of risk-taking behaviors tend to be only modestly effective unless paired with mechanisms that limit exposure to temptations. Thus, adults can educate adolescents about problems with underage drinking but also make it not only illegal but also expensive and inconvenient for them to obtain alcoholic beverages.

Irregularities in Brain Development

In some cases, children's brains have unusual networks or distorted structures, malformations that can interfere with learning and behavior. Too many or too few cells form, connections among cells are laid out in unusual ways, or neurons become unusually slow or quick to fire (C. A. Nelson, Thomas, & de Haan, 2006). These neurological conditions affect children's ability to pay attention, learn efficiently, control impulses, and deal with negative emotions.

DEVELOPMENT IN CULTURE
Initiation Ceremonies

To help young people remain committed to a productive life despite temptations around them, some societies arrange for *initiation ceremonies*, rites of passage in which boys and girls are shepherded through an educational process and afterward accepted as men and women. In Latin American cultures, a 15-year-old girl may take part in a *Quinceañera* celebration after publically affirming her religious faith. A 13-year-old Jewish boy may become a *Bar Mitzvah* and a 12-year-old girl a *Bat Mitzvah* after reading from the Torah during a religious ceremony. Many Christian youth take part in *Confirmation* ceremonies, during which time they profess their faith and become full members of their religious community.

In nonindustrialized societies, initiation ceremonies prepare girls for womanhood and boys for manhood (H. Montgomery, 2009). In the Tswapong culture of Botswana, a girl who has had her first menstrual period is designated a "mothei" and secluded to a hut for 7 days. The mothei is ushered through several intense rituals, including observing village women dancing, being smeared with python dung and swatted on the back, eating special food, and listening to women recite codes of conduct (Werbner, 2009). The mothei is seen as undergoing the transformation from child to adult.

Many boys in nonindustrialized societies also take part in initiation ceremonies, often in groups (Lancy, 2008; Schlegel & Barry, 1980). For instance, the Tapirapé, an indigenous tribe in the Amazon rain forest of Brazil, bring young adolescent boys into the "takana," a men's club that socializes the boys for manhood (Wagley, 1977). Boys stay in the takana for several months—some for up to a year—and learn about such masculine traditions as making bows and arrows. When the boys are considered mature and

COMING OF AGE. Initiation ceremonies prepare adolescent boys and girls for adult roles. These Aboriginal boys in Arnhem Land, Australia, are heading into the bush with elders to celebrate their manhood.

ready to find a spouse, they undergo another ceremony, in which they dance for a full day and night and are then considered men.

Children mentally prepare for their personal transformation, having observed older siblings and cousins go through the process. The road to adulthood is not always an easy one, but guidance from adults in the form of initiation ceremonies can ease the transition by offering education and signaling the new mature status to others.

A neurological disorder that begins in childhood takes a distinct developmental course depending on the underlying genetic condition or other developmental cause. Children who are *autistic* are apt to be born with brains that are smaller than usual (N. R. Carlson, 2014). After birth until about age 2, their brains grow more rapidly than is normal and then slow down such that by adolescence their brains are only minimally larger than average. Specific regions involved in interpretation of verbal and social stimuli grow especially rapidly to begin with, and then more slowly than usual. The result is impaired language and social abilities.

Children with *Down syndrome* are born with brains that are lighter than usual and have a cortex that is less convoluted than normal; therefore, they have a slightly diminished capacity for interconnections among neurons. Particular areas are also affected: children with Down syndrome have small frontal lobes, regions that support executive functions, and a less advanced superior gyrus, which is crucial for language comprehension (N. R. Carlson, 2014). Children with this condition are affected in this manner because they have three rather than the customary two copies of the 21st chromosome and produce a larger than average amount of a specific protein that directs movement of young neurons to their final locations in the brain. With too much of the protein from this chromosome, cells developing into neurons are impelled to migrate before a sufficient number have grown (Dierssen, 2012). Consequently, they face intellectual delays.

Schizophrenia, a serious psychiatric disorder that affects 1 in 100 people, often surfaces during late adolescence or early adulthood (Anjum, Gait, Cullen, & White, 2010; N. R. Carlson, 2014). Individuals with schizophrenia display such symptoms as thought disorders (e.g., irrational ideas and disorganized thinking), hallucinations (e.g., "hearing" nonexistent voices), delusions (e.g., worrying that "everyone is out to get me"), and social withdrawal (e.g., avoiding eye contact or conversation with others). Genes, viral infections and malnutrition during prenatal development, childbirth complications, and stressful environments during childhood share responsibility for symptoms. Possibly, certain people are born with genes that contribute to this condition and then are exposed to teratogens during prenatal development or traumatic events in childhood that turn on or off genes that affect the dramatic transformations of adolescence. During young adulthood, individuals who develop symptoms of schizophrenia are apt to lose volume in the cortex, more so than occurs in the normal synaptic pruning processes at this age. Fortunately, medication can quell troublesome symptoms.

Applications of Research on Brain Development

We previously considered the needs of children during specific periods of brain development. Let's now look at broader applications.

• **Be optimistic that children can learn essential skills throughout childhood.** People need stimulation throughout life. Certainly early stimulation *is* necessary for normal development, especially in visual processing and depth perception. Some cats, monkeys, and people who have had reduced or abnormal visual stimulation in their first few months (perhaps due to a congenital cataract) have developed lifelong difficulties in visual perception, apparently as a result of irreversible neurological effects. On the other hand, varied experiences around the world provide sufficient stimulation for normal development in visual areas of the brain (Bruer, 1999; Greenough, Black, & Wallace, 1987; C. Harris, 2011). Equally important during this period (for other areas of the brain) is access to loving caregivers, chances to explore the environment, and exposure to language.

The preponderance of the evidence indicates that people remain able to learn throughout later years. Therefore, you can certainly have an important impact during the course of childhood if you offer such "brain-friendly" experiences as properly designed instruction, exposure to rich cultural contexts (visits to museums, libraries, and the like), and warm relationships with students.

• **Give children opportunities to exercise their emerging executive functions.** As you have learned, infants and toddlers are *not* best served through teacher-directed academic lessons. Instead, infants detect all kinds of regularities in the world by spontaneously exploring objects, listening to language, playing, and interacting with people (Denison, Reed, & Xu, 2013; S. Edwards & Cutter-Mackenzie, 2013; Golinkoff, Ma, Song, & Hirsh-Pasek, 2013; Thompson-Schill, Ramscar, & Chrysikou, 2009). Around age 3 or 4 and after, children become increasingly able to direct their behavior toward the goals that they and teachers establish. Executive skills remain fragile for some time, however, making it useful for adults to keep explanations brief, teach children steps for self-control (e.g., counting to 10 before responding when angry), and break up challenging assignments into manageable pieces (Calkins & Marcovitch, 2010).

• **Consider the connections that exist among cognitive processes, emotional experiences, and bodily sensations.** Although we adults (particularly we teachers) occasionally prioritize children's cognitive abilities over their social-emotional and physical needs, the reality is that children's thoughts trigger emotions, which in turn play out as sensations in the body (Immordino-Yang & Damasio, 2007). A group of third graders may become distressed as they listen to a teacher's description about a recent famine, with their faces tensing, fists clenching, and bodies fidgeting. Noticing their reaction, the teacher might talk about her own feelings, reassure them about the productive actions officials are taking in response to the tragedy, and solicit the children's ideas about how they, too, might address the problem. An exclusively intellectual focus violates the brain's desire for integration—children have physical and social-emotional selves that require outlets for expression.

• **Accommodate the needs of children with neurological delays and disabilities.** Individualizing instruction is especially important for children who have neurological conditions that hinder learning. Children with difficulty in distinguishing among various sounds of speech often benefit from intensive training in speech processing, presumably because of its effects in strengthening relevant brain pathways (T. A. Keller & Just, 2009; Simos et al., 2007). Similarly, children who have trouble performing basic numerical, verbal, or visual skills may have brain networks that do not easily process information in that area but that can be strengthened through intervention (Abitbol Avtzon, 2013; Posner & Rothbart, 2007).

Some children with genetic problems and those who were exposed to alcohol, cocaine, and other drugs during their prenatal development have brains that struggle in processing certain kinds of information. Children may need assistance in understanding abstract ideas (e.g., a teacher's request to be "responsible"), inhibiting inappropriate responses (e.g., hitting bothersome peers), and generalizing rules to multiple settings (e.g., "keep your hands to yourself" applies to the playground as well as to the classroom). Ultimately, adults must remember that, with proper guidance and instruction, most children with unusual brain networks can lead fulfilling lives.

• **Coach young children in sustaining their attention and regulating their impulses.** As they grow, children typically learn many skills related to *self-regulation,* the ability to direct and control personal actions that is supported by the prefrontal cortex. Yet not all children receive adequate support for self-control at home, and others develop genetically guided neurological networks that predispose them to be tense or combative and at a loss in expressing themselves in ways that others find acceptable (Eisenberg, 2006). By the time children enter school, major individual differences are obvious in children's self-regulatory abilities. Some children are able to deal productively with disappointment, distraction, and frustration, whereas others cannot easily restrain themselves (Blair, 2002). Children who lack self-regulatory skills need the same loving, sensitive care as do other children, but they also need extra guidance in waiting patiently in line, keeping their hands to themselves, and expressing their emotions in culturally appropriate ways.

• **Help children who have been neglected or abused to form warm, trusting, and stable relationships.** Children develop expectations, written into their neurological circuits, regarding relationships (e.g., whether caregivers are affectionate or rejecting), emotions (e.g., whether anger dissipates or explodes into a turbulent outburst), and themselves (e.g., whether they are intrinsically worthy people or not; W. A. Cunningham & Zelazo, 2010; S. Hart, 2011; Siegel, 2001). When children have had many negative lessons early in life it is up to caring adults to help them realize that other kinds of relationships, emotional expressions, and self-perceptions are possible. Early and repeated interventions are necessary when children have been subjected to repeatedly harsh and neglectful treatment.

• **Be skeptical about fads in brain-compatible education.** Enthusiasm about brain discoveries has outpaced critical analysis of what the results mean and do *not* mean. For example, well-meaning educators have espoused a model of instruction that tries to reach either students' "left brains" or "right brains." This model is based on evidence of distinct specializations in the two hemispheres but does not account for continual communications between the separate sides (Alferink & Farmer-Dougan, 2010). Other educators have assumed that children individually have distinct neurological styles of learning that must be accommodated, even though children's preferences for processing information do *not* indicate that worthwhile skills in other domains cannot be acquired. A reasonable tactic for educators is to look for evidence about the brain that originated in a stringent research program, that has since been replicated in other laboratories, and whose educational implications have been tested and validated as facilitating children's learning.

Summary

The human brain is an intricate organ that regulates physiological functions (e.g., heart rate), sensations of pleasure and pain, motor skills and coordination, emotional responses, and intellectual processes. The brain consists of millions of interconnected circuits of neurons and glial cells, which collectively make up the distinct parts of the brain.

During prenatal development, neurons form and migrate to places where they will do their work. During infancy, brain cells connect up, others whither away, and the brain as a whole concentrates on perceptual learning, exploration of the environment, first relationships, and language and communication. During early and middle childhood, the brain protects those connections that are used most often and lets the others fade away; particular refinements solidify language skills and complex learning processes. During adolescence, the brain makes new interests and passions possible, sparks impetuous behavior, and grows in areas that will play key roles in forethought and judgment.

ENHANCEDetext *self-check*

PRACTICING FOR YOUR LICENSURE EXAMINATION

Many teaching tests require students to use what they have learned about child development in responses to brief vignettes and multiple-choice questions. You can practice for your licensure examination by reading the following case study and answering a series of questions.

My Health by Nick

When Nick was 18 and getting ready to head to college, he agreed to describe his health during childhood, addressing his eating and sleeping habits, sports and exercise, major illnesses and injuries, and experiences with drugs, alcohol, and sex. Here is his essay:

My Health

by Nick

I've been fortunate to be healthy most of my life. I was born an average-sized baby, about seven pounds. At about a year and a half, I had pneumonia. I don't remember it but my Mom told me I had to take antibiotics and breathe through a nebulizer. After treatments, I used to run around the house bumping into walls until the jitteriness wore off.

I wasn't sick very much after that, in fact I got perfect attendance awards at school for a couple of years. During my senior year in high school I had the flu for 10 days. It was bad. I couldn't walk, I had a fever, and every bone in my body hurt. I felt weak for a couple of weeks but made a full recovery.

I love sports. I played soccer in preschool and then focused on football and basketball. It was so much fun to run around the field and court with my friends. Coaches told me I was talented and agile. I continued to play football and basketball through the beginning of middle school and then stopped. I was slow to get my growth spurt and got tired of being knocked down by bigger players. In high school I went to the gym and worked out instead and took up snowboarding.

I never broke an arm or a leg but did have a minor head injury at my 12th birthday party. We rented a local gymnastic center and my friends and I had fun running and jumping on the trampolines. At one point the manager turned off the lights. I ran full speed into a lateral pole and blacked out. I saw stars and bled from my forehead. I was disoriented and kept trying to wash off the blood even when it dried up, or so I have been told. I don't remember much except that my Dad tried to make a joke of it and took my photograph and my Mom freaked out. For a couple of weeks afterwards I was very tired and had a headache every day. My Mom made me go to the doctor, and he gave me some kind of brain test and

I passed it. I haven't had a concussion again, and don't want another one, either.

I finally started catching up in height with my friends during my junior year. Before then, I felt like something was wrong with me because I was so short and delayed. I used to worry about it. My doctor told me I was normal. I didn't believe him until I started going through puberty. Puberty was okay but I was hungry and tired all the time. There never seemed to be enough food in the house. My parents cooked weird stuff like fish and vegetarian lasagna. I prefer plain hamburgers and spaghetti and meatballs. At lunch I went out with my friends and usually we would order two-dollar cheese quesadillas, sometimes a burger and fries. I ate a lot of snacks as well—trail mix, chips, apples, Pop-Tarts, and cookies mainly. I'm now tall, thin, and muscular. I'd like to gain some weight.

In high school I started staying up late, playing video games, and hanging out with friends on the Internet. It was always hard to get enough sleep. On school days I woke feeling like I was drugged. It was a struggle to climb out of bed.

Speaking of feeling drugged, I tried marijuana during my junior year and liked it. I also drank alcohol a few times with friends. I am going to college next week and am looking forward to the freedom and the parties. But I've decided I won't smoke marijuana anymore. I don't think it's wrong but I don't want to be excluded from certain jobs in the future. I never tried the other drugs, like ecstasy, that I heard some kids talking about. Really, why would anyone purposefully kill brain cells?

I have a girlfriend but we haven't had sex yet. I'm in no hurry really. I want to wait until it's the right time. I know that sex can mess up your emotions and I don't need that right now. I know I should use a condom when the time comes.

I hope I can stay healthy in college. I will play Ultimate Frisbee, work out at the gym, and snowboard when I can. I have a meal plan, which should be good and keep me well fed. I know I have to be careful at college parties. My brother says you always have to have a DD (designated driver). My Dad showed me how you can walk around at a party with an empty beer can so no one pressures you to have another drink. My Mom says I should count the number of drinks I have so I keep track.

I will have a roommate, and we'll have to agree on a lights-out time. I'm not ready to give up video games at night but know I can get carried away when playing them. I guess I'll figure that out.

Constructed-Response Question

1. What did Nick do during his childhood to stay healthy? What kind of risks has he taken with his health? What challenges lie ahead for him as he enters college?

Multiple-Choice Questions

2. Nick engaged in some risky behaviors, and he has also shown restraint. Why do adolescents partake in potentially hazardous activities?

   a. Adolescents engage in risky behaviors because they like to experiment with new things.

   b. Adolescents engage in risky behaviors because their brains now have a heightened sensitivity to rewards and pleasure in interacting with peers, whereas the areas of the brains that inhibit impulses have not advanced sufficiently to exert strong control.

   c. Adolescents engage in risky behaviors because they do not understand the dangerous consequences that can result from such actions.

   d. Both *a* and *b* are reasons that adolescents engage in risky behaviors.

3. Nick was behind his peers in the age at which he began puberty. How does the timing of puberty affect the psychological development of boys and girls?

   a. The timing of puberty is entirely the result of existing distress in children's lives, with high levels of anxiety precipitating or delaying the onset of puberty, such that distress is the cause, rather than the effect, of an early or late puberty.

   b. Young people who are exceptionally early or late in their sexual maturation are inevitably maladjusted due to the stress involved.

   c. It is the changes of puberty, not the timing, that influence adolescents.

   d. Boys and girls who have an early or late puberty are apt to be self-conscious but their level of distress depends on their coping skills and the resources and risks in their lives.

ENHANCEDetext *licensure exam*

Key Concepts

differentiation (p. 155)

integration (p. 155)

cephalocaudal trend (p. 157)

proximodistal trend (p. 157)

gross motor skills (p. 157)

fine motor skills (p. 157)

puberty (p. 159)

growth spurt (p. 159)

menarche (p. 159)

spermarche (p. 159)

obese (p. 167)

anorexia nervosa (p. 168)

bulimia (p. 168)

rough-and-tumble play (p. 170)

sudden infant death syndrome (SIDS) (p. 173)

addiction (p. 176)

traumatic brain injury (TBI) (p. 181)

neuron (p. 184)

axon (p. 184)

dendrite (p. 184)

synapse (p. 184)

glial cell (p. 185)

astrocyte (p. 185)

hindbrain (p. 185)

midbrain (p. 185)

forebrain (p. 185)

cortex (p. 185)

executive functions (p. 186)

left hemisphere (p. 186)

right hemisphere (p. 186)

synaptogenesis (p. 188)

synaptic pruning (p. 188)

myelination (p. 188)

schizophrenia (p. 191)

CHAPTER SIX

Cognitive Development: Piaget and Vygotsky

CASE STUDY: Museum Visit

Four-year-old Billy is fascinated by dinosaurs. He and his mother have read many children's books about dinosaurs, so he already has some knowledge about these creatures and the geological time periods in which they lived. As Billy and his mother visit a dinosaur exhibit at a natural history museum, they have the following conversation:

Mother: This is a real dinosaur rib bone. Where are your ribs? Where are your ribs? No that's your wrist. Very close.

Billy: Oh, yeah, right here.

Mother: Yeah, that's right. Here. Protecting your heart . . . and your lungs. And this was one from a dinosaur from the Jurassic period, also found from our country. In a place called Utah.

Mother: And this one . . . [Mother picks up a piece of fossilized dinosaur feces, known as *coprolite*] Oh! You're not . . . guess what that is. Look at it and guess what that is.

Billy: Um, what?

Mother: Guess. What's it look like?

Billy: His gum? What? Mom!

Mother: It's dinosaur poop.

Billy: Ooooo! (laughs)

Mother: That's real dinosaur poop.

Billy: I touched it! (laughs)

Mother: It's so old that it doesn't smell anymore. It turned to rock. It's not mushy like poop. It's like a rock. And that's from the Cretaceous period but we don't know what dinosaur made it. And this was also found in our country in Colorado. I think that's pretty funny.

Billy: What's this?

Mother: So this one. . . . Oh, that's called . . . that's a stone that dinosaurs . . . remember in your animal book it says something about how sometimes chickens eat stones to help them digest—it helps them mush up their food in their tummy?

Billy: Yeah.

Mother: Well, dinosaurs ate stones to mush up their food in their tummy and this was one of the stones that they ate. They're so big, that to them this was a little stone. Right? And that also comes from Colorado. (Dialogue is from Crowley & Jacobs, 2002, p. 346; "Billy" is a pseudonym.)[a]

- What knowledge does Billy have that can help him understand what he sees in the dinosaur exhibit?
- What does Mother do to help Billy make sense of the exhibit?

[a]Excerpt from LEARNING CONVERSATIONS IN MUSEUMS by Kevin Crowley. Copyright © 2002 by Kevin Crowley. Reprinted with permission.

Thanks to the many books that 4-year-old Billy and his mother have read together, Billy knows a lot about dinosaurs. He understands that the words *Jurassic* and *Cretaceous* refer to earlier times and knows that some animals have stones in their stomachs to aid digestion. Mother helps him connect what he is seeing to his prior knowledge—not only about geological periods and stomach stones but also about commonplace concepts such as ribs and "poop." Yet Billy, like all children, is not simply a "sponge" who passively soaks up the information that his environment provides. Instead, his cognitive development is in large part the result of his *own active efforts* to make sense of his world.

OBJECTIVES

6.1: Describe Piaget's theory of cognitive development in terms of its seven principles, four stages, legacy into the present day, and implications for fostering children's learning.

6.2: Explain Vygotsky's theory, including its nine key principles, modern spin-offs, and ideas for promoting children's learning.

6.3: Outline similarities and differences between Piaget's and Vygotsky's views on cognitive development and appropriate educational practice.

As we begin to examine cognitive development in this chapter, we consider the classic developmental theories of Jean Piaget and Lev Vygotsky, both of whom studied the active manner in which children learn. The perspective of children energetically creating knowledge, rather than passively absorbing information, is known as **constructivism**. Formulated in the first few decades of the 20th century, these two constructivist theories have provided much of the foundation for our current understanding of how children think. Between them, the two frameworks tell us a great deal about how children make sense of everyday events both on their own and in collaboration with adults and peers. As you will find out, the two theories have much to say about how parents, teachers, and other adults can help children learn effectively.

PIAGET'S THEORY

Jean Piaget (1896–1980) was formally trained as a biologist. He had interests in philosophy and psychology as well and was especially curious about the nature of knowledge and its changes with development. In the 1920s he began observing the everyday actions of children and drew inferences about the reasoning that underlies their behavior. In his laboratory in Geneva, Switzerland, Piaget pioneered the **clinical method**, a procedure by which an adult presents a task or problem and asks a child a series of questions, tailoring subsequent questions to the child's previous responses. Drawing from these observations and interviews, Piaget developed a theory of cognitive development that transformed our understanding of how children and adolescents think and learn (e.g., Piaget, 1928, 1952b, 1959, 1985).

Key Ideas in Piaget's Theory

Central to Piaget's theory are seven principles:

Children are energetic and motivated learners. In the chapter-opening case study, Billy is eager to make sense of the fossils he sees in the natural history museum. Piaget proposed that children are naturally curious about their world and actively seek out information that can help them understand it (e.g., Piaget, 1952b). They often experiment with objects, manipulating them and observing the effects. We authors think back to the days when our children were in high chairs, experimenting with their food (pushing, squishing, dropping, and throwing it) as readily as they would eat it. As they grew older, they spent hours in the sandbox, shaping hills and valleys and pushing toy trucks through hidden passageways. According to Piaget, such initiatives—which of course change with age—are the engine of intellectual growth.

Observing Children 6-1

Watch 2-year-old Maddie act on her intrinsic motivation as she explores the properties of an intriguing new toy.

ENHANCEDetext *video example*

Contemporary theorists share Piaget's view that much of a child's motivation for learning comes from within. Children are naturally inclined to make sense of people, objects, and events around them (R. Brooks & Meltzoff, 2014; Hunnius & Bekkering, 2010; K. Nelson, 1996a). They comprehend the world by listening, watching, playing with materials, and interacting with people. You can see an example of 2-year-old Maddie's efforts to learn about the properties of a toy in an Observing Children video.

Children organize what they learn from their experiences. Children don't amass the things they learn into a collection of isolated facts. Instead, they pull their experiences together into an integrated view of how the world operates. By observing that food, toys, and other objects always fall down (never up), children construct a basic understanding of the effects of gravity. As they interact with family pets, visit zoos, look at picture books, and observe creatures around them, they develop an understanding of animal life.

In Piaget's terminology, the things that children learn and can do are organized as **schemes**, sets of similar actions or thoughts that are used repeatedly in response to the environment. Initially, children's schemes are largely behavioral in nature, but over time they become increasingly mental and, eventually, abstract (Inhelder & Piaget, 1958; Piaget, 1952b, 1954). An infant has a behavioral scheme for putting things in her mouth, an action that she uses in dealing with a variety of objects, including her thumb, toys, and blanket. A 7-year-old has a mental but relatively concrete scheme for identifying snakes, one that includes their long, thin bodies, a slithery nature and absence of legs. As a 13-year-old, Jeanne's daughter

Tina had her own opinion about what constitutes fashion, an abstract scheme that allowed her to classify articles of clothing at the mall as being either "totally awesome" or "really stupid."

Piaget proposed that children use newly acquired schemes over and over in familiar and novel situations. In an Observing Children video, you can observe 16-month-old Corwin repeatedly taking a toy out of a paper bag and returning it. In the process of repeating their schemes, children refine them and use them in combination. Eventually, they integrate schemes into broader systems of mental processes called **operations**. This integration allows children to think in progressively sophisticated ways. For example, a child may integrate schemes for ordering blocks by size, placing the largest block on the bottom, and adding successively smaller pieces into the new ability of building a stable tower.

Observing Children 6-2

Observe Corwin repeatedly using his "putting-in" and "taking-out" schemes.

ENHANCEDetext *video example*

Children adapt to their environment through the processes of assimilation and accommodation. According to Piaget, children's developing schemes allow them to adapt to their environment in ever more successful ways. Such adjustment occurs as a result of two complementary processes: assimilation and accommodation (Piaget, 1954). **Assimilation** entails responding (either physically or mentally) to an object or event in a way that is consistent with an existing scheme.[1] The process involves perceiving new information or objects in terms of existing schemes and operations. An infant assimilates a ball into her putting-things-in-the-mouth scheme, and a 7-year-old assimilates a new slithery creature in the backyard as a snake.

Yet children must typically adjust existing schemes and operations at least a little bit in order to respond to a new object or event. Thus **accommodation** is likely to occur. Children will either modify an existing scheme to account for the new object or event or else form an entirely new scheme to deal with it. An infant may have to open her mouth wider than usual to accommodate a teddy bear's paw. A 7-year-old may find a long animal with a snakelike body that cannot possibly be a snake because it has four legs. After making inquiries, he will develop a new scheme—*salamander*—for this creature.

Assimilation and accommodation work hand in hand. Children interpret each new event within the context of their existing knowledge (assimilation) but at the same time modify their knowledge as a result of the new event (accommodation). In the chapter-opening case study, Billy initially thinks that the piece of coprolite is a large wad of dinosaur gum—that is, he mistakenly assimilates the object into his "chewing gum" scheme. But with his mother's help, he creates a new scheme, "fossilized dinosaur poop," that more accurately accounts for what he is seeing. Later Mother helps Billy assimilate a large stone into a "stones-that-help-digestion" concept he has previously acquired. In the process, however, he must also modify this scheme so that it applies not only to chickens but also to dinosaurs.

Young children's play reflects this blend of the two processes. Children impose their existing ideas on the world (in other words, they *assimilate*) when they pretend that a banana is a cell phone or a block is their pet dog. Children *accommodate* to events in the world when they imitate patterns they have previously witnessed, for example, the business-like demeanor of an airline pilot or the doting style of a grandmother. During play, which Piaget (1962) viewed as an important means for children to make sense of the world, children try out adult roles, reflect on the various parts as they act them out, test what it feels like to be certain characters, infer intentions and feelings, and watch how other people react to their characterizations.

Interaction with the physical environment is critical for cognitive development. By exploring and manipulating the world around them—by conducting many little "experiments" with objects and substances—children learn the nature of their physical world and continue to revise their existing schemes. Thus a child's intuition for engineering is enriched by building towers and bridges with blocks.

Interaction with other people is equally crucial. Piaget suggested that children learn a great deal from interacting with their fellow human beings. As you will discover shortly,

[1]Note that Piaget's concept of *assimilation* is quite different from the process of *cultural assimilation* described in Chapter 3.

BIOECOLOGY OF DEVELOPMENT

Piaget testified to the informative lessons a child receives during dynamic interactions in the environment.

preschoolers occasionally have difficulty seeing the world from anyone's perspective. By conversing, exchanging ideas, and arguing with others, they gradually come to realize that individuals often see things differently and that their own view of the world is not necessarily completely accurate. Likewise, older children may begin to recognize logical inconsistencies in what they say and do when someone else points out discrepancies.

The process of equilibration promotes increasingly complex forms of thought. Piaget proposed that children are sometimes in a state of **equilibrium**: They comfortably address new situations using their existing schemes and operations. But equilibrium doesn't continue indefinitely. In their daily lives children regularly encounter circumstances for which their present knowledge and skills are inadequate. These circumstances create **disequilibrium**, a sort of mental "discomfort" that spurs children to try to deal with the situation at hand. By replacing or reorganizing certain schemes, children are better able to address the situation, and so they can return to equilibrium. This process of moving from equilibrium to disequilibrium and back to equilibrium again is known as **equilibration** (e.g., Inhelder & Piaget, 1958). In many instances the end result is a more integrated, inclusive, and stable set of schemes and operations than children had previously. Thus, the equilibration process gradually leads to increasingly complex levels of thought and knowledge.

Piaget was a bit vague about how the processes of assimilation, accommodation, and equilibration actually work (e.g., Karmiloff-Smith, 2012; Keating, 2012; Klahr, 1982). Nevertheless, contemporary developmental scientists accept that children's new ideas are based on their earlier ones and that inconsistencies can sometimes spur children to develop more sophisticated understandings and abilities. Developmentally speaking, then, more advanced knowledge, skills, and cognitive processes don't just appear out of thin air—they emerge out of children's quest for understanding, discontent with personal knowledge, and creative thinking processes.

Children think in qualitatively distinct ways at different age levels. Piaget proposed that as a result of brain maturation, environmental experiences, and children's natural desire to make sense of their world, cognitive abilities undergo qualitative change. He characterized youngsters' cognitive abilities as falling into four general stages (Piaget, 1971). Thinking begins during infancy with reflections on sensations, reflexes, and movements. Thereafter, all abilities are constructed out of the accomplishments of preceding thought. Thus, the four stages are *hierarchical*—each one depends on its predecessors—and so children progress through them in a predictable order. To a considerable degree, they are also assumed to be *universal,* characterizing the cognitive development of children throughout the world.

As you will discover later in the chapter, many psychologists question the notion that cognitive development is as universally stage-like as Piaget suggested. Nevertheless, Piaget's stages provide helpful insights into different age levels, and so we look closely at them.

Piaget's Stages of Cognitive Development

Piaget's four stages are summarized in Table 6-1. The ages of onset for all but the sensorimotor stage are *averages:* Some children show characteristics associated with a particular stage a bit earlier; others, a little later. According to the theory, at any given time some children are in *transition* from one stage to the next, displaying characteristics of two adjacent stages at the same time. Furthermore, children don't always take advantage of their advanced cognitive abilities, and so they may show considerable variability in sophistication of thinking in day-to-day activities (Piaget, 1960b). Figure 6-1 depicts the transitional and flexible nature of progress through stages.

Sensorimotor Stage (beginning at birth)

Piaget believed that in the first month of life, infants' behaviors are little more than biologically built-in responses to stimuli—that is, they are *reflexes* (e.g., sucking on a nipple)—that keep them alive. In the second month infants begin to exhibit voluntary behaviors that they repeat over and over, reflecting the development of perception- and behavior-based

TABLE 6-1   Acquisitions Associated with Each of Piaget's Four Stages

STAGE	AVERAGE AGE OF ONSET	DESCRIPTION	EXAMPLES OF ACQUISITIONS
Sensorimotor	Begins at birth	Schemes are based largely on behaviors and perceptions. Especially in the early part of the stage, children cannot think about things that are not immediately in front of them, and so they focus on what they are doing and seeing at the moment.	• *Trial-and-error experimentation:* Exploration and manipulation of objects to determine their properties • *Goal-directed behavior:* Intentional actions to bring about a desired result • *Object permanence:* Realization that objects continue to exist even when removed from view • *Symbolic thought:* Representation of physical objects and events as mental entities *(symbols)*
Preoperational	Appears at about age 2	Thanks in part to their rapidly developing symbolic thinking abilities, children can now think and talk about things beyond their immediate experience. However, they do not yet reason in logical, adult-like ways.	• *Language:* Rapid expansion of vocabulary and grammatical structures • *Extensive pretend play:* Enactment of true-to-life or fanciful scenarios with plots and assigned roles (e.g., mommy and daddy, hunter and prey, or hero and villain) • *Intuitive thought:* Some logical thinking based on "hunches" and "intuition" rather than on conscious awareness of logical principles
Concrete Operations	Appears at about age 6 or 7	Adult-like logic appears but is limited to reasoning about concrete, real-life situations.	• *Distinction between one's own and others' perspectives:* Recognition that personal thoughts and feelings may be different from those of others and do not necessarily reflect reality • *Class inclusion:* Ability to classify objects as belonging to two or more categories simultaneously • *Conservation:* Realization that amount stays the same if nothing is added or taken away, regardless of alterations in shape or arrangement
Formal Operations	Appears at about age 11 or 12	Logical reasoning processes are applied to abstract ideas as well as concrete objects and situations. Many capabilities essential for advanced reasoning in science and mathematics appear.	• *Reasoning about abstract, hypothetical, and contrary-to-fact ideas:* Ability to draw conclusions about situations with no basis in physical reality • *Separation and control of variables:* Ability to test hypotheses by manipulating one variable while holding others constant • *Proportional reasoning:* Conceptual understanding of fractions, percentages, decimals, and ratios • *Idealism:* Ability to envision alternatives to current social and political practices (sometimes with little regard for what is realistically possible in a given time frame)

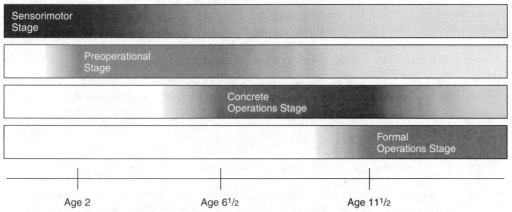

FIGURE 6-1   Emerging and continuing abilities. Children gradually develop new ways of thinking, and they don't entirely leave behind characteristics associated with previous stages.

Observing Children 6-3

Observe an infant's exploratory behavior.

ENHANCEDetext *video example*

Observing Children 6-4

Observe Corwin's searching behavior, revealing his awareness of object permanence.

ENHANCEDetext *video example*

Preparing for Your Licensure Examination

Your teaching test might ask you about the major cognitive advancements that children achieve during Piaget's four stages.

sensorimotor schemes. Initially, such behaviors focus almost exclusively on infants' own bodies (e.g., putting a fist in one's mouth), but eventually they involve nearby objects as well. For much of the first year, Piaget suggested, infants' behaviors are largely spontaneous and unplanned. Seven-month-old Madison, for example, is clearly intrigued by a variety of toys that happen to be nearby her in an Observing Children video.

Late in the first year, after having repeatedly observed that certain actions regularly lead to certain consequences, infants acquire knowledge of cause-and-effect relationships. At this point, they begin to engage in **goal-directed behavior**: They behave in ways that they know will bring about desired results. An infant who pulls a blanket to retrieve a small object lying on it shows goal-directed behavior. At about the same time, infants acquire **object permanence**, an understanding that physical objects continue to exist even when they are out of sight. In an Observing Children video, 16-month-old Corwin shows object permanence as he looks for a toy elephant that his mother repeatedly hides.

Piaget believed that for much of the sensorimotor period, children's thinking is restricted to objects in the immediate environment—that is, to the here and now. But in the latter half of the second year, young children develop **symbolic thought**, the ability to represent and think about objects and events as internal, mental entities, or *symbols* (Piaget, 1962). They may "experiment" with objects in their minds, first predicting what will happen if they do something to an object—say, if they give a toy car a hard push toward the edge of a tabletop—and then put their plans into action. They may also recall and imitate behaviors they have seen other people exhibit—for instance, "talking" on a toy mobile phone or "driving" with a toy steering wheel.

The acquisitions of the sensorimotor stage are basic building blocks that later cognitive development extends. The Observation Guidelines table "Assessing Cognitive Advancements in Infants and Toddlers" presents some of the behaviors you might look for with small learners.

Preoperational Stage (beginning at about age 2)

The ability to represent objects and events mentally (i.e., with symbolic thought) gives children in the preoperational stage a more extensive worldview than they had during the sensorimotor stage. They can now recall past events and envision future ones that might be similar to previous experiences. In addition, they can begin to tie their memories together into an increasingly intricate understanding of the world.

Language skills virtually explode during the early part of the preoperational stage. The words in children's rapidly increasing vocabularies provide labels for newly developed mental schemes and serve as symbols for thinking about objects and events even when not directly in sight. Children can express their thoughts and receive information from other people in a way that was not possible during the sensorimotor stage.

The emergence of symbolic thought is reflected not only in rapidly expanding language skills but also in the changing nature of children's play. Preschoolers often engage in fantasy and make-believe, using realistic objects or reasonable substitutes as props to supplement their imagination. Piaget proposed that such pretend play enables children to practice newly acquired symbolic schemes and familiarize themselves with the various roles they see others assume in society. This idea is illustrated in the following scenario, in which 5-year-olds Jeff and Scott construct and operate a "restaurant":

> In a corner of Jeff's basement, the boys make a dining area from several child-sized tables and chairs. They construct a restaurant "kitchen" with a toy sink and stove and stock it with plastic dishes and "food" items. They create menus for their restaurant, sometimes asking Jeff's mother how to spell certain words and sometimes using their knowledge of letter-sound relationships to guess how a particular word might be spelled.
>
> Jeff and Scott invite their parents to come to the new restaurant for lunch. The boys pretend to write their customers' meal orders on paper tablets and then scurry to the kitchen to assemble the requested lunch items. Eventually, they return to serve the meals (hamburgers, French fries, and cookies—all of them plastic—plus glasses of imaginary milk), which the adults "eat" and "drink" with gusto. After the young waiters return with the final bills, the parents pay for their "meals" with nickels and leave a few pennies on the tables as tips.

OBSERVATION GUIDELINES
Assessing Cognitive Advancements in Infants and Toddlers

CHARACTERISTIC	LOOK FOR	EXAMPLE	IMPLICATION
Repetition of Gratifying Actions	• *Repetition of actions involving the child's own body* • *Replication of actions on objects*, for example, persistently banging toy on floor • *Evidence that the child repeats an action* because he or she notices and enjoys it	Myra waves her arms, stops, and waves her arms again. She makes a sound and repeats it, as if she enjoys listening to her own voice.	Provide a variety of visual, auditory, and tactile stimuli. Play "This little piggy" with an infant's toes, hang a mobile safely over the crib, and provide age-appropriate objects (e.g., rattles, plastic cups). Be patient and responsive when infants repeat seemingly "pointless" actions (e.g., dropping favorite objects).
Exploration of Objects	• *Apparent curiosity about the effects* that different behaviors have on objects • *Use of multiple behaviors* (feeling, poking, dropping, shaking, etc.) to explore an object's properties • *Use of several sensory modalities* (i.e., seeing, listening, feeling, tasting, and smelling) in play	Paco reaches for his caregiver's large, shiny earring. The caregiver removes the earring and holds its sharp fasteners between her fingers while Paco touches the silver loop and multicolored glass beads that hang from it.	Provide objects that infants can explore using multiple senses, making sure they are free of dirt and toxic substances; lack sharp edges, loose cords, and bags that could cause strangulation or suffocation; and are large enough to prevent choking and swallowing.
Experimentation	• *Creativity and flexibility* in behaviors for discovering how things work • *Specific problems that the child tackles* and the approaches he or she uses to solve them	Jillian drags a step stool to her dresser so that she can reach toys on top of it. One by one, she drops the toys, watching how each one lands and listening to its impact.	Childproof the environment so that experiments and problem-solving activities are safe. Provide objects that require a sequence of actions (e.g., stacking cups, building blocks, and pulling toys). Closely supervise children's activities.
Imitation and Pretending	• *Imitation of actions modeled by another person* • *Imitation of actions when the model is no longer present* • *Use of one object to stand for another*	Darius holds a doll and sings to it in the same way his mother sings to him. He combs the doll's hair with a spoon and uses an empty plastic vitamin bottle to feed the doll.	Engage children in reciprocal, imitative games (e.g., peekaboo, hide-and-seek). Provide props that encourage pretend play (miniature shopping carts, plastic carpentry tools, dolls, etc.).

With the emergence of symbolic thought, young children are no longer restricted to the here and now and can think and act far more flexibly. At the same time, preoperational thinking has some definite limitations, especially when compared to the concrete operational thinking that emerges later. Piaget described young children as exhibiting **egocentrism**, an inability to view situations from another person's perspective.[2] Preschoolers may play games together without ever checking to be sure that they are all following the same rules. And they may say things without considering the perspective of the listener—for instance, leaving out critical details as they tell a story and giving a fragmented version that a listener could not possibly understand. Here we see one reason why, in Piaget's view, social interaction is so important for development. Only by getting repeated feedback from other people can children learn that their thoughts are unique to them and must be expressed in a certain way for others to understand them.

Preoperational thinking, especially during the preschool years, is illogical (at least from an adult's point of view). Following is an example of reasoning that characterizes preoperational thought:

We show 4-year-old Lucy the three glasses at the top of Figure 6-2. Glasses A and B are identical in size and shape and contain an equal amount of water. We ask Lucy if the two glasses of water contain the same amount, and she replies confidently that they do. We then pour

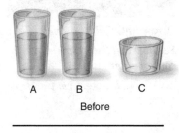

A   B   C
Before

After

FIGURE 6-2 Conservation of liquid. Do Glasses A and C contain the same amount of water after water in Glass B is poured into Glass C?

[2]Consistent with common practice in representing Piaget's work, we use the term *egocentrism* to refer to the egocentric thinking that characterizes preoperational thought. Piaget actually talked about different forms of egocentrism at *each* of the four stages of development. For instance, he described egocentrism in the formal operations stage as involving an inability to distinguish one's own logical conclusions from the constraints of the real world. Adolescents' idealism about social issues is one manifestation of formal operational egocentrism.

the water in Glass B into Glass C. We ask her if the two glasses of water (A and C) still have the same amount. "No," Lucy replies. She points to Glass A and says, "That glass has more because it's taller."

Piaget used this task to assess a logical thought process known as **conservation**, the recognition that an amount must stay the same if nothing is added or taken away, despite any changes in shape or arrangement. Lucy's response reveals that she is not yet capable of *conservation of liquid:* The differently shaped glasses lead her to believe that the actual amount of water has changed. Similarly, in a *conservation of number* task, a child engaging in preoperational thought might say that a row of five pennies spread far apart has more than a row of five pennies spaced close together, even though she has previously counted the pennies in both rows and found them to have the same number. Young children often confuse changes in appearance with changes in amount. Piaget suggested that such confusion is seen because the preoperational stage depends more on perception than on logic.

Another ability that young children find challenging is **class inclusion**, the recognition that an object can belong both to a particular category and to one of its subcategories simultaneously. Preschool-age children demonstrate lack of class inclusion in response to questions such as "Are there more brown beads or more wooden beads?" in a situation where there are 10 brown beads and 2 white beads and all beads are made of wood (Piaget, 1952a). They may insist that there are more brown beads whereas in reality there are more wooden beads.

Sometime around age 4 or 5 children show early signs of thinking more logically than they have previously. For example, they occasionally draw correct conclusions about conservation problems (e.g., the water glasses task) and class inclusion problems (e.g., the wooden beads task). But they base their reasoning on hunches and intuition rather than on any conscious awareness of underlying logical principles, and so they cannot yet explain *why* their conclusions are correct.

Concrete Operations Stage (beginning at about age 6 or 7)

In the early primary grades, children become capable of thinking about various perspectives on a situation. For example, children now know that other people have perceptions and feelings different from their own. Accordingly, they realize that their own views may reflect personal opinion rather than reality, and so they may seek out external validation for their ideas ("What do you think?" "Did I get that problem right?").

Observing Children 6-5

See how children respond to conservation tasks.

ENHANCEDetext *video example*

Children in the concrete operations stage show many forms of logical thought, and they can readily explain their reasoning. They can also easily classify objects into two categories simultaneously, making it easier for them to solve class inclusion problems. And they are capable of conservation: They readily understand that if nothing is added or taken away, an amount stays the same despite changes in appearance. For example, the second girl depicted in an Observing Children video is quite confident that juice poured from a short, wide glass into a tall, thin glass hasn't changed in amount: "Just because this is skinny doesn't mean it's . . . this one is just wider, this one is skinnier, but they have the same amount of juice."

Children continue to develop their newly acquired logical thinking capabilities throughout the elementary school years. Over time they become capable of dealing with increasingly complex conservation tasks. Some forms of conservation, such as conservation of liquid and conservation of number, appear at age 6 or 7. Other forms don't appear until later. Consider the task involving *conservation of weight* depicted in Figure 6-3. Using a balance scale, an adult shows a child that two balls of clay have the same weight. One ball is removed from the scale and smashed into a pancake shape. The child is then asked if the pancake weighs the same as the un-smashed ball or if the two pieces of clay weigh different amounts. Children typically do not achieve conservation of weight—that is, they don't realize that the flattened pancake weighs the same as the round ball—until age 9 or 10 (Piaget, 1950).

Although children displaying concrete operational thought show many signs of logical thinking, cognitive development is not yet complete. In particular, they have trouble reasoning about abstract or hypothetical ideas (hence the term *concrete* operations stage). In language, this weakness may be reflected in an inability to interpret the underlying, nonliteral meanings of proverbs. In mathematics, it may be reflected in confusion about such concepts

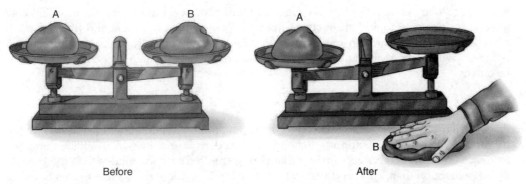

FIGURE 6-3 **Conservation of weight.** Balls A and B initially weigh the same. When Ball B is flattened into a pancake shape, how does its weight now compare with that of Ball A?

as *pi* (π), *infinity*, and *negative number*. And in social studies, it may limit children's comprehension of such abstract notions as *democracy, communism,* and *human rights.*

Formal Operations Stage (beginning at about age 11 or 12)

Piaget concluded that sometime around puberty children become capable of thinking and reasoning about things that have little or no basis in physical reality. They can think logically about abstract concepts, hypothetical ideas, and statements that contradict what they know to be true in the real world. Also emerging are scientific reasoning abilities that enable children to identify cause-and-effect relationships in physical phenomena. As an example, consider the following task:

> An object suspended by a rope or string—a pendulum—swings indefinitely at a constant rate. Some pendulums swing back and forth very quickly, whereas others swing more slowly. Design an experiment that can help you determine what factor or factors affect a pendulum's oscillation rate.

To solve this problem successfully, you must first *formulate hypotheses* about possible variables affecting a pendulum's swing. You might consider (a) the weight of the suspended object, (b) the length of the string that holds the object, (c) the force with which the object is pushed, and (d) the height from which the object is initially released. You must then *separate and control variables*, testing one factor at a time while holding all others constant. To test the hypothesis that weight makes a difference, you should try different weights while keeping constant the length of the string, the force with which you push each weight, and the height from which you release it. Similarly, if you hypothesize that the length of the string is critical, you should vary the length of the string while continuing to use the same weight and starting the pendulum in motion with constant force. If you carefully separate and control variables, your observations should lead you to conclude that only *length* affects a pendulum's oscillation rate.

Once formal operational thinking appears, more advanced verbal and mathematical problem solving is possible. Adolescents become able to see beyond literal interpretations of such proverbs as "A rolling stone gathers no moss" and "An ant may well destroy a dam" to identify their underlying meanings. Adolescents also become better able to understand such concepts as *negative number* and *infinity* because they can now comprehend how numbers can be below zero and how two parallel lines will never touch even if they go on forever. Furthermore, they can understand the nature of proportions (e.g., fractions, ratios, decimals) and correctly use them when working on mathematical problems. And they gain an appreciation for contrary-to-fact ideas.

The emerging capacity to think about hypothetical and contrary-to-fact ideas allows adolescents to envision how the world might be different from, and possibly better than, the way it is now. Thus they may be idealistic about and devoted to social, political, spiritual, and ethical issues—climate change, world hunger, animal rights, religious conversion, and so on. Sometimes they offer recommendations for change that seem logical but aren't practical in today's world. For example, they may argue that racism would disappear overnight if people would just "love one another." Piaget suggested that adolescent idealism reflects an inability to separate personal logical abstractions from the perspectives of others and from practical considerations. Only through experience do adolescents eventually begin to temper their optimism with some realism about what is possible in a given time frame and with limited resources.

Current Perspectives Related to Piaget's Theory

Piaget's theory has sparked a great deal of research about children's cognitive development. In general, this research supports Piaget's proposed *sequence* in which abilities emerge. Evidence confirms Piaget's conclusions that young children's reasoning depends more heavily on perception than logic, and that logical thinking is applied to concrete events before it is used with abstract ideas (Borst, Poirel, Pineau, Cassotti, & Houdé, 2013; Flavell, Miller, & Miller, 2002; Morra, Gobbo, Marini, & Sheese, 2008). However, many specific abilities, at least in a fragile and rudimentary form, appear considerably earlier than Piaget suggested.

Capabilities of Different Age-Groups

Using different research methods than those that were available to Piaget, present-day researchers have found that infants and preschoolers are more competent than portrayed in Piaget's descriptions of the sensorimotor and preoperational stages. When Piaget studied the development of object permanence, he focused largely on whether infants reached for an object that was no longer in view. Contemporary researchers look at more subtle measures, such as how long infants look at an object and how their heart rates change as they watch it. Modern-day scholars find that infants spend a lengthy time looking toward an object that disappears in one spot and immediately reappears elsewhere—a staged event that apparently violates their basic understandings of how physical objects should behave. Such innovative techniques reveal that infants show preliminary signs of object permanence as early as 2 to 6 months old and gradually solidify this understanding and use it to guide reaching behaviors (Baillargeon, 2004; Cacchione, 2013; Charles & Rivera, 2009).

FOR FURTHER EXPLORATION . . .

Read how four theoretical perspectives depict the weaknesses of young children's speech in adapting to listeners' needs.

ENHANCEDetext
content extension

Contemporary methods with preschoolers have taken a slightly different tact, with investigators making experiments less artificial and easing demands on children's memories. When tasks are modified in these ways, preschoolers are often quite capable of conservation and class inclusion (M. Donaldson, 1978; R. Gelman & Baillargeon, 1983; Rule, 2007). Young children also find it easier to reason about categories when they can inhibit an automatic response, such as feeling compelled to compare the number in two subordinate categories (e.g., daisies and roses) when the question is about the relative number in one subordinate category (e.g., roses) with the number in the superordinate category (e.g., flowers; Borst et al., 2013). Thus, children's performance is affected not only by their logical abilities (e.g., for class inclusion) but also by their capacity to resist such routine responses as attending to perceptually salient information. Furthermore, observations in everyday life suggest that children are far less egocentric than Piaget thought. Young children may have trouble relaying intricate stories to others, but they do alter the way they speak to babies and exhibit definite efforts at inferring the perspective of their listener (Shatz & Gelman, 1973).

Piaget may also have underestimated the capabilities of elementary schoolchildren. Many elementary students—and occasionally even 4-year-olds—show some ability to think abstractly and hypothetically about unobserved events (S. Carey, 1985; Schulz, Goodman, Tenenbaum, & Jenkins, 2008; Winkler-Rhoades, Carey, & Spelke, 2013). Even kindergarteners and first and second graders can understand simple ratios and proportions (e.g., fractions such as ½, ⅓, and ¼) if they can relate these concepts to everyday objects (Empson, 1999; Tobias & Andreasen, 2013). Many elementary students can understand ratios when presented with such familiar circumstances as people in a restaurant. Knowing that for every 12 customers, 4 are children, students can extrapolate that if there are 20 children, there must be 60 people. Similarly, elementary schoolchildren often control variables in science when the task is broken up and they are given hints about the importance of controlling all variables except the one they are testing (Danner & Day, 1977; Lazonder & Kamp, 2012; Strand-Cary & Klahr, 2008).

Yet Piaget probably *overestimated* what adolescents can do. Formal operational thinking processes emerge much more gradually than Piaget suggested, and adolescents don't use these skills as regularly as Piaget would have had us believe (Kuhn, Pease, & Wirkala, 2009; Pascarella & Terenzini, 1991). A related issue is whether formal operational reasoning is really the final stage of cognitive development. Some theorists have proposed that many adults progress to a fifth, post-formal stage in which they envision multiple approaches to a problem, each of which may be valid from a particular perspective, and the integration of which is often the most constructive response (Galupo, Paz, Cartwright, & Savage, 2010; Sinnott, 2009).

Effects of Experience

Piaget acknowledged that as children gain new logical thinking abilities, they may apply the skills in one content area but not necessarily in another (Piaget, 1940). It is becoming increasingly apparent that for people of all ages, their reasoning in a particular situation depends on relevant understandings (Croker & Buchanan, 2011; Seiver, Gopnik, & Goodman, 2013). Thus it appears that what young people learn, with support, is how to think systematically about particular concepts rather than how to use all-purpose logical principles across settings.

As an illustration of how prior knowledge affects formal operational thinking, consider the fishing pond shown in Figure 6-4. In a study by Pulos and Linn (1981), 13-year-olds were shown a similar picture and told, "These four children go fishing every week, and one child, Herb, always catches the most fish. The other children wonder why." If you look at the picture, it is obvious that Herb is different from the three other children in several ways, including the bait he uses, the length of his fishing rod, and his location at the pond. Children who had fished frequently identified variables for this situation more effectively than they did for the pendulum problem described earlier, whereas the reverse was true for children without fishing experience. In Observing Children videos, you can listen to two children consider potentially influential factors as they look at the picture in Figure 6-4. Notice how Kent, who appears to have some experience with fishing, considers several possible variables and remains open minded about the causal one. In contrast, Alicia, who is older but admittedly unfamiliar with fishing strategies, considers only two variables and jumps to a conclusion about causation:

Kent: He has live . . . live worms, I think. Fish like live worms more, I guess 'cause they're live and they'd rather have that than the lures, plastic worms. . . . Because he might be more patient or that might be a good side of the place. Maybe since Bill has a boombox thing [referring to the radio], I don't think

FIGURE 6-4   Gone fishing. What are some possible reasons why Herb is catching more fish than are the others? *Based on descriptions in Pulos & Linn, 1981.*

Observing Children 6-6

Listen to 10-year-old Kent and 14-year-old Alicia's attempts to identify influential factors in fishing, an activity in which they have had different levels of experience.

ENHANCEDetext *video example*

they would really like that because . . . and he doesn't really have anything that's extra . . . . But he's the standing one. I don't get that. But Bill, that could scare the fish away to Herb because he's closer . . . .

Alicia: Because of the spot he's standing in, probably. . . . I don't know anything about fishing. Oh, OK! He actually has live worms for bait. The other girl's using saltine crackers [she misreads *crickets*]. . . . She's using plastic worms, he's using lures, and she's using crackers and he's actually using live worms. So obviously the fish like the live worms the best.

One general factor that promotes advanced reasoning is formal education. Going to school and receiving instruction are associated with mastery of concrete operational and formal operational tasks (Artman & Cahan, 1993; Gauvain & Munroe, 2009; Sophian, 2013). For instance, you may be happy to learn that taking college courses in a particular area (in child development, perhaps?) leads to improvements in reasoning skills related to that area (Lehman & Nisbett, 1990; T. M. McDevitt, Jobes, Sheehan, & Cochran, 2010).

Effects of Culture

Piaget acknowledged that children grow intellectually as they reflect on their exchanges with other people and in handling objects in environment. He further recognized that cultural variations in intellectual opportunities could lead to modest differences in children's skills (Piaget, 1972). Yet many contemporary theorists now conclude that Piaget did not fully understand how powerfully culture shapes children's minds or how strongly his own theory reflected the Western position that scientific reasoning is the pinnacle of human development (H. Keller, 2011; Maynard, 2008).

Considerable research indicates that Piaget was more on target about younger children developing similar abilities than with older children. Infants in all known cultures learn a lot from exploring their physical environment, and young children in the preschool years represent their ideas with language and intuitive logic. In comparison, concrete and formal operational abilities are more susceptible to particular cultural experiences. For example, Mexican children whose families make pottery for a living seem to acquire conservation skills earlier than Piaget found to be true for Swiss children (Price-Williams, Gordon, & Ramirez, 1969). Apparently, creating pottery requires children to make frequent judgments about needed quantities of clay and water—judgments that must be fairly accurate regardless of the specific form of the clay or water container. In other cultures, conservation may appear several years later than Piaget proposed, and some aspects of formal operational reasoning—at least as measured by Piaget and colleagues—do not appear when abstract reasoning has little relevance to people's daily lives (Fahrmeier, 1978; H. Keller, 2011; Maynard, 2008).

Does Cognitive Development Occur in Stages?

In light of all the evidence, does it still make sense to talk about discrete stages of cognitive development? Even Piaget acknowledged that the characteristics of any particular stage don't necessarily hang together as a tight, inseparable collection of abilities (Piaget, 1940). Most contemporary developmental theorists believe that children do *not* universally go through stages in all-encompassing logical structures. Today's theorists suggest that Piaget's evidence about children's abilities may better describe how children *can* think, rather than how they typically *do* think (Borst et al., 2013; K. W. Fischer, Stein, & Heikkinen, 2009; Halford & Andrews, 2006).

Key Ideas in Neo-Piagetian Theories

Neo-Piagetian theorists share Piaget's belief that children's skills and understandings change qualitatively over time. Unlike Piaget, however, they suggest that children's abilities are strongly tied to personal experiences in particular contexts. Following are several principles that are central to neo-Piagetian approaches:

Cognitive development is constrained by the maturation of information-processing mechanisms. Neo-Piagetian theorists have echoed Piaget's belief that cognitive development depends on brain maturation. A fundamental capacity that develops in the brain is known as **working memory** (Blain-Brière, Bouchard, Bigras, & Cadoret, 2014; Case, 1985; Davidse, de Jong, Bus, Huijbregts, & Swaab, 2011; Pascual-Leone, 2013). Working memory is that part of the human memory system in which people hold and actively think about new information. Addition of two numbers might take three units of working memory—one for each of the two numbers, and a third unit for the process of addition. In comparison, comparisons of proportions are much more taxing of working memory, because two units are used for each of two numbers, for example, ⅖ and ⅜, and a fifth unit for judgments about the relative sizes of the fractions. Neo-Piagetian theorists propose that gradual expansion in working memory capacity allows for increasingly complex thinking, mathematics, and language skills (Dauvier, Bailleux, & Perret, 2014).

Children acquire new knowledge through both unintentional and intentional learning processes. Many contemporary psychologists agree that children learn some things with little or no conscious awareness or effort. Consider this question about household pets: "On average, which are larger, cats or dogs?" Even if you've never intentionally thought about this issue, you can easily answer "dogs" because of the many characteristics (including size) you've learned to associate with both species. Children unconsciously learn the consistent patterns and associations that characterize many aspects of their world. Yet, especially as children's brains mature in the first year or two of life, they increasingly think about their experiences and devote considerable mental attention to deliberately solving the little problems that come their way each day (Case & Okamoto, 1996; Pascual-Leone, 1970). This combination of implicit learning and intentional strategies for making sense of information is a central characteristic of children's development, the relations of which change with age, with children becoming increasingly intentional yet continuing to absorb information about patterns and relations (Case, 1985; Weinert, 2009; Yim & Rudoy, 2013).

Children acquire cognitive structures within particular domains of thought. Neo-Piagetian theorists reject Piaget's proposal that children develop general-purpose mental processes (operations) that they can apply to a broad range of tasks and content domains. Instead, they suggest, children acquire specific concepts and thinking skills that influence reasoning in particular areas. Hence, children think differently when trying to comprehend a story than when trying to figure out a mathematical problem.

Canadian psychologist **Robbie Case** (1944–2000) and his colleagues have proposed that integrated networks of thoughts and skills within certain areas, called **central conceptual structures**, form the basis of children's reasoning (Case, 1991; Case & Okamoto, 1996; S. Griffin, 2009). A central conceptual structure related to *number* underlies children's ability to reason about and manipulate mathematical quantities. This structure reflects a unified understanding of how numbers, counting, addition, and subtraction are interrelated.[3] A central conceptual structure related to *spatial relationships* underlies children's performance in such areas as drawing, construction and use of maps, replication of geometric patterns, and psychomotor activities (e.g., writing in cursive, hitting a ball with a racket). This structure enables children to align objects in space according to one or more reference points (e.g., the *x*- and *y*-axes used in graphing). A central conceptual structure related to *social thought* underlies children's analysis of interpersonal relationships, knowledge of common patterns in human interaction, and comprehension of motivations in short stories. This structure includes children's general beliefs about human beings' thoughts, desires, and behaviors. Case has found evidence indicating that the three conceptual structures develop in a wide variety of cultural and educational contexts (Case & Okamoto, 1996).

Cognitive growth depends on initial predilections in the brain that are refined with learning. Swiss scientist **Annette Karmiloff-Smith** (2012, 2013) agrees with her esteemed mentor, Jean Piaget, that children develop cognitive abilities as they interact with the world. Unlike Piaget, however, Karmiloff-Smith views changes in children's understandings as due to other factors besides the general processes of assimilation and accommodation. Karmiloff-Smith argues that tiny neurological features at birth evolve with experience into sophisticated networks in the brain that govern learning in particular areas. When a baby is born, slight

---

[3] See Chapter 10 for more details about a possible central conceptual structure in number.

variations exist in different regions of the brain, with certain localities being more facile than others in processing particular kinds of information—language, spatial ability, facial expressions, mathematics, etc. These circumscribed regions are transformed from being only marginally advantaged in dealing with particular stimuli into supercenters of specialized processing, especially as the child gains experience with relevant information. Thus, although Piaget's processes of assimilation and accommodation most certainly operate within language learning and other domains, dedicated neurological mechanisms, which are increasingly constrained by experience, also guide development. These mechanisms vary somewhat from one field of learning to another.

Advances in cognitive performance are enabled by progressions in executive functions. Research on brain development has shown that maturation of *executive functions*, neurologically based abilities for purposeful and conscious thinking processes, enable advancements in memory, planning, decision making, and reasoning. Recent evidence indicates that young people become increasingly able to focus their attention, resist counterproductive urges, and guide their intellectual efforts with strategies (Keating, 2012). Neo-Piagetians have integrated these results into frameworks of cognitive development, for example, showing that children exhibit conservation and class inclusion only after learning to inhibit such automatic responses as reacting to misleading perceptual information (Borst et al., 2013).

Development in specific content domains can sometimes be characterized with miniature stages. Although neo-Piagetian theorists reject Piaget's notion that a single series of global stages characterizes cognitive development, they speculate that cognitive development in specific content domains often has a stage-like character (e.g., K. W. Fischer & Immordino-Yang, 2002; G. Young, 2012). Children's entry into a particular stage is marked by the acquisition of new abilities, which children practice and gradually master over time. Eventually, they integrate these abilities into more complex structures that result in a transition into a higher stage.

Even in a particular subject area, however, cognitive development is not necessarily a simple sequence of stages through which children progress as if they were climbing rungs on a ladder. In some cases development might be better characterized as progression along "multiple strands" of skills that occasionally interconnect, consolidate, or separate in a weblike fashion (K. W. Fischer, 2008; K. W. Fischer & Immordino-Yang, 2002; Mascolo & Fischer, 2010). From this perspective, children acquire more advanced levels of competence in a particular area through any one of several pathways. For instance, as they become increasingly proficient in reading, children gradually develop word decoding skills, comprehension abilities, and so on and draw on these assorted skills when reading a book. Individual children vary in their competence with various skills and the speed with which they learn to coordinate them.

Applying the Ideas of Piaget and His Followers

Educators and practitioners who have taken Piaget's theory to heart respect the natural curiosity of children, give children opportunities to make choices, and appeal to children's interests. Adults who are inspired by Piaget have tried these specific strategies:

• **Encourage children to be curious.** A major tenet of Piaget's theory is that children are naturally curious learners. When allowed to explore on their own, children tinker around with objects in a manner that allows them to test hypotheses about how things work (C. Cook, Goodman, & Schulz, 2011; Yardley, 2014). Children push buttons, pull levers, and watch effects, and in the process notice patterns, alter their ideas, and formulate new questions. Children spontaneously exercise classification by placing objects with similar attributes together. They learn to conserve by noticing that as a lump of clay is flattened, its loss in height is compensated for by an increase in width. Teachers can remark on what the children seem to be noticing and pursuing ("Very nice . . . Are you watching how quickly the balls slide down the ramp?" "How will the color change if you add more red?" "What happens to the amount of clay you as you change its shape?").

Especially in the preschool years, children ask countless questions of adults about how the world works. Yet by the time children have entered elementary school, they have generally become sensitive to adults' expectations about when it is acceptable and inappropriate to ask questions (Engel, 2011). Children may come to believe that they

Preparing for Your Licensure Examination
Your teaching test might ask you about Piaget's contributions to educational practice.

should be mastering facts and skills rather than inquiring into dilemmas, incongruities, and issues of personal fascination. Thus, teachers need to encourage children's curiosity and validate questions (e.g., "What a wonderful question, Marcie! Let's see if we can explore that issue in science") rather than dismissing them because they are posed at inopportune times.

- **Let children play.** In infancy and early childhood, and to some degree in middle childhood as well, play is an active forum for learning. To facilitate play, teachers can provide interesting materials and allow a period or two of free choice during the day. At the preschool level, children might have access to a puzzle area, science corner, reading center, and the pretend area with such alternating themes as fire station, science laboratory, and doctor's office. With older children, teachers can arrange for daily recess. Children can also enjoy brief periods of exploration before instruction, as with making imaginative designs with pattern blocks before a structured geometry lesson. Similarly, children can be invited to fool around with concepts, words, and ideas, much like scientists, artists, and other experts do when inventing and creating. The performing arts in particular—drama, music, and dance—can engender a sense of playful discovery when children express themselves freely while acquiring new techniques.

- **Provide opportunities for children to experiment with physical objects.** Learners of all ages acquire a lot of information by exploring the physical world (H. P. Ginsburg, Cannon, Eisenband, & Pappas, 2006; B. Y. White & Frederiksen, 1998; Winkler-Rhoades, Carey, & Spelke, 2013). In infancy this might involve having regular access to objects with visual and auditory appeal, such as mobiles, rattles, stacking cups, and pull toys. At the preschool level, it might involve playing with water, sand, wooden blocks, and age-appropriate manipulative toys. During the elementary school years, hands-on exploration might entail working with clay, clustering objects with similar properties, handling worms, and building stick structures. Despite their increased capability for abstract thought, adolescents also benefit from opportunities to manipulate concrete materials—perhaps equipment in a science laboratory, food and cooking utensils, or woodworking tools. Such activities allow teens to discover laws of the natural world firsthand and tie their emerging abstract ideas to the physical world. Fifteen-year-old Habtom applies advanced reasoning in designing a circuit board (in Artifact 6-1) that he was later able to construct and test.

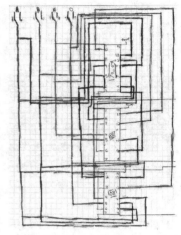

ARTIFACT 6-1 Habtom's circuit board. Fifteen-year-old Habtom designed a circuit board with the help of his engineering teacher, who advised him about the characteristics of electronic chips (see vertical boxes with internal numbers toward the middle-right of the artifact) and connections among the binary switches. Using advanced reasoning skills, Habtom designed the circuit board, built it, and confirmed that it worked.

A potential downside of hands-on activities is that children sometimes misinterpret what they observe, either learning the wrong thing or confirming their existing misconceptions about the world (Fitzsimmons, Leddy, Johnson, Biggam, & Locke, 2013; Legare, Gelman, & Wellman, 2010; Schauble, 1990). Consider the case of Barry, an 11th grader whose physics class was studying the idea that an object's mass and weight do *not,* in and of themselves, affect the speed at which the object falls. Students were asked to build an egg container for studying the effects of weight on falling speed. Convinced that heavier objects fall faster, Barry added several nails to his egg's container. Yet when he dropped it, classmates recorded its fall at 1.49 seconds, a time very similar to that for other students' lighter containers. Rather than concluding that weight did not matter, Barry decided that his classmates were not accurately timing the drops (Hynd, 1998).

At the elementary and secondary levels, the misconceptions that arise from spontaneous explorations can be addressed by adding structure to activities. Carefully planned lessons that allow both exploration and guided interpretation can help children construct appropriate understandings (R. G. Fuller, Campbell, Dykstra, & Stevens, 2009; Hardy, Jonen, Möller, & Stern, 2006; D. T. Hickey, 1997; Lillard et al., 2013). Encouraging children's interest is also helpful because children are more likely to learn from experiences when they are intrigued with forces in the domain—what makes eggs float, objects fall, and planets revolve around the sun (Hadjiachilleos, Valanides, & Angeli, 2013). The Development and Practice feature "Facilitating Discovery Learning" illustrates several recommendations for enhancing the effectiveness of exploration.

- **Probe children's reasoning.** By presenting a variety of tasks and probing students' reasoning with a series of follow-up questions—that is, by using Piaget's clinical method—adults can gain valuable insights into how young people think about their world. The

DEVELOPMENT AND PRACTICE
Facilitating Discovery Learning

Make sure students have the necessary knowledge for appreciating new explanations.

- A first-grade teacher asks students what they already know about air (e.g., people breathe it, wind is air that moves). After ascertaining that the students have some awareness that air has substance, she and her class conduct an experiment in which a glass containing a crumpled paper towel is turned upside-down and completely immersed in a bowl of water. The teacher eventually removes the glass from the water and asks students to explain why the paper towel didn't get wet. (You can see part of this lesson in an Observing Children video.) (Middle Childhood)

Observing Children 6-7

Listen to a teacher help children prepare for a hands-on lesson.

ENHANCEDetext *video example*

- Before asking students to build a simulated volcano, a high school science teacher introduces types of magma and defines important terms such as *cinder cone, lava dome, caldera,* and *flood basalt*. (Late Adolescence)

Show puzzling results to create disequilibrium.

- A middle school science teacher shows her class two glasses of water. In one glass an egg floats at the water's surface. In the other glass an egg rests on the bottom. The students give a simple explanation for the difference: One egg has more air inside and so must be lighter. But then the teacher switches the eggs into opposite glasses. The egg that the students believe to be "heavier" now floats, and the "lighter" egg sinks to the bottom. The students are quite surprised and demand to know what is going on. (Ordinarily, water is less dense than an egg, so an egg placed in it will quickly sink. But in this demonstration, one glass contains salt water—a mixture denser than an egg and so capable of keeping it afloat.) (Early Adolescence)
- A high school social studies teacher asks students to decide whether adolescents in the past 60 years can be better characterized as conforming and obedient or rebellious and innovative. The teacher distributes two sets of readings that support each of the conclusions and asks students to examine the evidence, determine why there might be a discrepancy in viewpoints, and ultimately justify a position. (Late Adolescence)

Structure a discovery session so that students proceed logically toward discoveries you want them to make.

- Most of the students in an third-grade science class believe that some very small things (e.g., a tiny piece of Styrofoam, a single lentil bean) are so light that they have no weight. Their teacher asks them to weigh a pile of 25 lentil beans on a balance scale, and the students discover that the beans together weigh approximately 1 gram. In the ensuing class discussion, the students agree that if 25 beans have weight, a single bean must also have weight. The teacher then asks them to use math to estimate how much a single bean weighs. (Middle Childhood)
- Students in a high school chemistry class bring in samples of household water and then analyze the amount of various chemicals in the fluids. After it is determined that the fluids contain unhealthful levels of acid, the teacher asks the students to brainstorm ways that their community can reduce acid rain. (Late Adolescence)

Help students relate their findings to concepts in an academic discipline.

- A teacher distributes slices of five kinds of apples—Granny Smith, Golden Yellow, Red Delicious, Fuji, and McIntosh—for purposes of taste testing. The teacher asks the children to indicate their first preference for apples, and together they aggregate the results into a graph, identifying the most and least favorite apples. Afterward, the teacher shows the class other examples of graphs and explains how diagrams have many uses. (Middle Childhood)
- After students in a social studies class have collected data on average incomes in counties within their state, their teacher asks, "How can we interpret these data in economic terms?" (Late Adolescence)

Sources: Blevins, 2010 (apple chart example); Bruner, 1966; Center for History and New Media, 2006 (teenage conformists and rebels example); de Jong & van Joolingen, 1998; Frederiksen, 1984; Hardy et al., 2006; D. T. Hickey, 1997; Lillard et al., 2013; R. E. Mayer, 2004; Minstrell & Stimpson, 1996; Palmer, 1965 (egg example); C. L. Smith, 2007 (Styrofoam example); Smithsonian National Museum of Natural History, 2010 (volcano example); Water Educational Training Science Project, 2002 (acid rain example); B. Y. White & Frederiksen, 1998, 2005.

Observation Guidelines table "Assessing Piagetian Reasoning Processes in Children and Adolescents" lists some of the characteristics you might look for.

In probing youngsters' reasoning, teachers and other practitioners need not stick to traditional Piagetian tasks. On the contrary, Piaget's clinical method is applicable to a wide variety of content domains—children's understandings about friendship, the animal kingdom, forms of government, phases of the moon, symbolism of maps, and so forth (e.g., diSessa, 2007; Ginsburg, 2009). Typically, an adult would begin a clinical interview by asking a child to explain a natural process, such as how mountains are formed, or to make a prediction about the effects of an intervention, for example, what might happen if a stout beaker of water is poured into a taller, thinner glass (S. J. Mayer, 2005). After the child responds, the adult asks for more information using the child's vocabulary (e.g., if the child says that mountains are formed by God shoveling dirt into piles, the adult might ask where God gets the

OBSERVATION GUIDELINES
Assessing Piagetian Reasoning Processes in Children and Adolescents

CHARACTERISTIC	LOOK FOR	EXAMPLE	IMPLICATION
Concrete Thought	• *Heavy reliance on concrete objects* to understand concepts • *Difficulty understanding abstract ideas*	Tobey solves arithmetic word problems more easily when he can draw pictures of them.	Use concrete objects, drawings, and other realistic illustrations of abstract situations, concepts, and problems.
Abstract Thought	• *Ability to understand strictly verbal explanations* of abstract concepts and principles • *Ability to reason about hypothetical or contrary-to-fact situations*	Elsa can imagine how two parallel lines might go on forever without ever coming together.	When working with adolescents, occasionally use verbal explanations (e.g., short lectures) to present information, but assess students' understanding frequently to make sure they understand.
Idealism	• *Idealistic notions* about how the world should be • *Difficulty taking other people's needs and perspectives into account* when offering ideas for change • *Inability to adjust ideals* in light of what can realistically be accomplished	Martin advocates a system of government in which all citizens voluntarily contribute their earnings to a common "pool" and then withdraw money only as they need it.	Engage adolescents in discussions about challenging political and social issues.
Scientific Reasoning Skills	• *Formulating multiple hypotheses* for a particular phenomenon • *Separation and control of variables*	Serena proposes three possible explanations for a result she has obtained in her physics lab.	Have middle school and high school students design and conduct simple experiments in which they are shown how to control variables. Include interventions related to their interests.
Mathematical Reasoning Skills	• *Understanding abstract mathematical symbols* (e.g., π, the variable x in algebraic equations) • *Understanding proportions* in mathematical problem solving	Giorgio uses a 1:240 scale when drawing a floor plan of his school building.	Initially, introduce abstract mathematical tasks using simple examples (e.g., when introducing proportions, begin with fractions such as ⅓ and ¼). Progress to more complex examples only when youngsters are ready.

dirt or how many shovels full of dirt he [or she] uses). This method is revealing of the child's thinking because it follows the lead of the child. In an Observing Children video, you can hear an interviewer asking 12-year-old Claudia a series of questions to probe her reasoning during a categorization task (e.g., "How did you decide which shells to put where?" "What makes [those shells] different from the other ones?").

• **Keep Piaget's stages in mind when planning activities, but don't take the stages too literally.** Although Piaget's four stages are not fully accurate descriptions of children's capabilities, they do provide a rough idea of the reasoning processes you are apt to see at various age levels (Crain, 2011; Feldman, 2004; Kuhn, 1997; Lefmann & Combs-Orme, 2013). Thus, infant caregivers should remember that repetitive behaviors, even those that make a mess or cause inconvenience (dropping food, throwing toys), are an important means through which infants master basic motor skills and learn about cause-and-effect relationships. Preschool teachers should not be surprised to hear young children arguing that the three pieces of a broken candy bar constitute more candy than a similar, unbroken bar (a belief that reflects lack of conservation). Elementary school teachers should recognize that their students have trouble with proportions (e.g., fractions, decimals) and with such abstract concepts as *time* in astronomy and *negative number* and *pi* in mathematics (B. Adams, 2008; Kaufmann, 2008; Tourniaire & Pulos, 1985). With high school students, educators can expect to hear passionate arguments from adolescents that reflect idealistic notions about how schools, cities, and society should operate.

Piaget's stages also provide implications for strategies that are apt to be effective in teaching children of different age levels. For instance, given the abstract nature of historical time, elementary teachers planning history lessons should probably limit talk about specific

Observing Children 6-8
Observe the use of probing questions with 12-year-old Claudia.

ENHANCEDetext *video example*

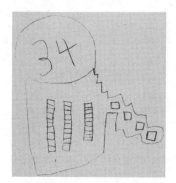

ARTIFACT 6-2 Thirty-four. Eight-year-old Noah uses rows of 10 squares and single squares to depict the number 34.

dates in favor of active investigations into people's motivations, conflicts, and accomplishments (Barton & Levstik, 1996; K. Greene, 2014; Levstik, 2008). Especially in the elementary grades (and to a lesser degree in middle and high school), instructors should find ways to make abstract ideas more concrete. As one example, a third-grade teacher, realizing that the abstract concept of *place value* might be a difficult, showed her students how to depict two-digit numbers with blocks, using 10-block rows for the number in the tens column and single blocks for the number in the ones column. You can see Noah's rendition of place value in Artifact 6-2.

• **Present situations children cannot easily explain using their existing understandings.** Events that conflict with youngsters' current understandings create disequilibrium that may motivate them to reevaluate and perhaps modify what they "know" to be true (e.g., Hadjiachilleos et al., 2013; Pugh, 2011; Vosniadou, 2009). If they believe that "light objects float and heavy objects sink" or that "wood floats and metal sinks," a teacher might present a common counterexample: a metal battleship (floating, of course) that weighs many tons. As we mentioned earlier, after being shown compelling information that conflicts with their present ideas, children sometimes discount it. To instill an open mind, teachers can encourage children's interest in the topic, ask the children to talk and write about their observations, and be very clear about how we know that an explanation new to children is more accurate, scientific, and comprehensive than what they might previously have thought.

• **Use familiar content when asking children to reason in sophisticated ways.** Earlier we presented evidence to indicate that children and adolescents display more advanced reasoning skills when they work with topics they know well. With such evidence in mind, teachers and other practitioners might ask young people to do the following:

- Conserve liquid within the context of a juice-sharing task.
- Separate and control variables within the context of a familiar activity (perhaps fishing, designing a paper airplane, or using various combinations of ingredients in baking cookies).
- Consider abstract ideas about subject matter that has already been studied in depth in a concrete fashion (e.g., introducing the concepts of *inertia* and *momentum* to explain such everyday experiences as throwing a ball and driving quickly around a sharp curve).

• **Informally assess the strategies that children use in solving problems.** Observing the learning procedures and struggles of individual children is an important feature of constructivist teaching. The neo-Piagetians have made an especially good case for determining and adjusting to the particular challenges that children face as they work on problems. Teachers might find that children have a pre-established idea about a task (e.g., mistakenly assuming that the arithmetic problem 4 + __ = 7 requires them to add the two numbers, thus writing "11" as the answer). Or children may have an inadequate memory capacity to complete the task (e.g., remembering only a few steps in a teacher's lengthy verbal instructions); misinterpret the requirements of a problem (e.g., not realizing that "=" in mathematics means "make the same"); or lack constituent skills (e.g., submitting the wrong answer on a long-division problem because of simple errors in subtraction; Case, 1980; Morra et al., 2008). Once teachers determine children's abilities and difficulties, they can tailor their assistance accordingly, perhaps instructing children in missing skills or alleviating the memory load.

• **Plan group activities in which young people share their perspectives with one another.** As noted earlier, Piaget proposed that interaction with peers teaches children that others view the world very differently than they themselves do and that their own ideas are not always reasonable or accurate. Interactions with age-mates that involve differences of opinion—situations that create **sociocognitive conflict**—can cause disequilibrium and spur children to reevaluate their current perspectives.

Many contemporary psychologists share Piaget's belief in the value of sociocognitive conflict. They have offered several reasons why interactions with peers may help promote cognitive growth:

- Peers speak at a level that children can understand.
- Whereas children may accept an adult's ideas without argument, they are more willing to disagree with the ideas of their peers.

- When children hear competing views held by peers—individuals who presumably have knowledge and abilities similar to their own—they may be motivated to reconcile the contradictions, especially when available information does not converge decisively on a single conclusion. (Damon, 1984; De Lisi & Golbeck, 1999; C. Howe, 2009; Murphy & Alexander, 2008; Rubin, Bowker, & Kennedy, 2009; A. G. Young, Alibali, & Kalish, 2012)

When sharing their views with one another, however, children can also acquire misinformation (Good, McCaslin, & Reys, 1992). It is essential, then, for teachers to monitor group discussions and correct any misinterpretations that youngsters may pass on to their peers.

Although children learn a great deal from their interactions with others, cognitive development is, in Piaget's theory, ultimately an individual enterprise: By assimilating information to present ideas and accommodating to new experiences, children develop increasingly advanced and integrated schemes over time. Thus Piaget's perspective depicts children as doing most of the mental "work" themselves. In contrast, Lev Vygotsky's theory, which we soon introduce, places much of the responsibility for children's development on adults.

Summary

Piaget portrayed children as active and motivated learners who, through numerous interactions with their physical and social environments, construct an increasingly complex understanding of the world around them. He proposed that children's thinking progresses through four stages: (a) the sensorimotor stage, when cognitive functioning is based primarily on behaviors and perceptions; (b) the preoperational stage, when symbolic thought and language become prevalent, but reasoning is "illogical" by adult standards; (c) the concrete operations stage, when logical reasoning capabilities emerge but are limited to tangible objects and events; and (d) the formal operations stage, when thinking about abstract, hypothetical, and contrary-to-fact ideas becomes possible.

Developmental researchers have found that Piaget probably underestimated the capabilities of infants, preschoolers, and elementary schoolchildren and overestimated the capabilities of adolescents. Furthermore, children's reasoning on particular tasks depends heavily on their prior knowledge, experience, and formal schooling relative to those tasks. Contemporary developmental scholars doubt that cognitive development can be consistently characterized as general stages. Several neo-Piagetians propose that children acquire specific concepts and thinking skills within particular domains, abilities that sometimes change in a stagelike manner. However, other neo-Piagetians suggest that children exhibit gradual trends in a variety of abilities. Virtually all present-day theorists acknowledge the value of Piaget's research methods, his portrayal of cognitive development as a constructive process, and his delineation of qualitative changes in cognitive development.

ENHANCEDetext *self-check*

VYGOTSKY'S THEORY

Whereas Piaget had a background in biology and philosophy, Russian psychologist **Lev Vygotsky** (1896–1934) had training in law, history, philosophy, literature, and education. Vygotsky was deeply influenced by Karl Marx's proposal that historical changes in society have a significant impact on how people think and behave. And like Marx's colleague Friedrich Engels, Vygotsky saw much value in the use of *tools* in moving a society forward (Gredler & Shields, 2008; Vygotsky, 1997e). According to Vygotsky, numerous tools influence thinking, many of which are tangible, including paper, writing utensils, stories, and books. In today's industrialized societies, we also recognize the transforming role of computers, calculators, mobile phones, and other electronic handheld devices. In Vygotsky's mind, *cognitive* entities—concepts, theories, problem-solving strategies, memory techniques, and methods for investigating hypotheses and reasoning about observations—were also influential tools.

Vygotsky believed that the adults in any society intentionally foster children's learning. Parents, teachers, and other grown-ups engage children in meaningful and challenging activities, show them how to use tools known to facilitate performance, and help them make sense of experience. Because Vygotsky emphasized the importance of adult guidance in promoting cognitive advancements—and more generally because he emphasized the influence of social and cultural factors in children's cognitive development—his perspective is known as a *sociocultural theory*.

With the assistance of his students, Vygotsky conducted numerous studies of children's thinking from the 1920s until his early death from tuberculosis in 1934. In his major writings, he typically described his findings in general terms, saving the details for technical reports that he shared with a small number of research psychologists working in Russia at the time (Kozulin, 1986). Although his own research was limited, Vygotsky's followers have been persuaded by the integrity of science that Vygotsky espoused as necessary for progress in the study of cognitive development. According to Vygotsky, research with children should have a coherent theoretical foundation instead of being based in a hodgepodge of ideas. He argued that investigations must focus on essential mental processes rather than on isolated responses, and they ought to track developmental changes in mental processes instead of taking single snapshots of thinking (Gredler & Shields, 2008; Vygotsky, 1987a, 1997a, 1997d).

In their investigations, Vygotsky and his collaborators gave primary attention to how children improve in their use of, and thinking about, cultural materials, especially when assisted by others. In Figure 6-5 you can see the types of materials Vygotsky included in his research. Interested in how children use external stimuli to augment their basic memory processes, Vygotsky told children he would show them a long list of words that would be impossible to remember without help. He encouraged children to form associations between words and pictures on cards, the latter of which could be used as clues later. For young children, the pictures did not help and in some cases were distracting, but older children were generally able to use the pictures effectively. An older child might associate the word "crab" with the picture of a theater by connecting the two together in an image: "The crab is looking at the stones on the bottom, it is beautiful, for him it is a theater" (Vygotsky, 1997c, p. 181). Later, this child would easily remember the word "crab" when shown a picture of the theater.

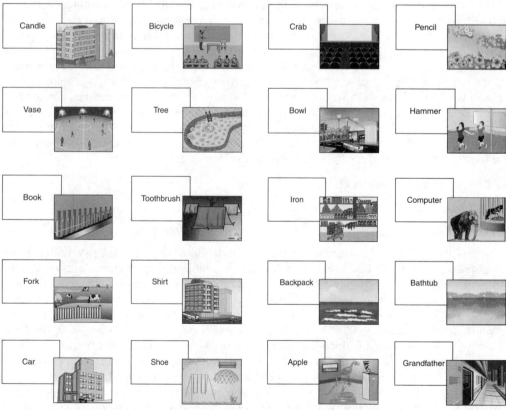

FIGURE 6-5 Learning how to use memory aids. Vygotsky showed two sets of cards to children, inviting them to think of a possible connection between each word and the picture with which it was paired (e.g., they might form an association between candle and trees by imagining trees next to a tall building lit up with candles). Afterward, cards with words were removed and the children were asked to recall as many words as possible. *Based on information in Vygotsky, 1997c.*

In his book *Thought and Language*, Vygotsky explained that his approach to studying children's cognitive development was radically different from frameworks by Piaget and other psychologists of his era. Rather than determine the kinds of tasks children could successfully perform *on their own* (as Piaget did), Vygotsky often examined activities that children could complete *only with adult assistance*. For example, he described two hypothetical children who could, without help, do things that a typical 8-year-old might be able to do. He would give each child progressively more difficult tasks and offer a little help, perhaps asking a leading question or suggesting a first step. With such assistance, both children could almost invariably tackle more difficult tasks than they could handle on their own. However, the *range* of tasks that the two children could complete with assistance might be quite different, with one child "stretching" his or her abilities to succeed at typical 12-year-old-level tasks and the other succeeding only with average 9-year-old-level tasks (Vygotsky, 1934/1986, p. 187).

Western psychologists were largely unfamiliar with Vygotsky's work until the last few decades of the 20th century, when his major writings were translated from Russian into English (e.g., Vygotsky, 1934/1986, 1978, 1997b). Although Vygotsky's premature death meant he did not have the chance to develop his theory fully, his views remain evident today in discussions about learning and development.

Key Ideas in Vygotsky's Theory

Vygotsky acknowledged that biological factors play a role in development. For example, he understood that brain development allows children to use complicated tools. He also realized that children bring certain genetically based characteristics to learning situations (Vygotsky, 1997b). Some children find it easier than others to acquire cultural skills based partly in heredity. However, Vygotsky's primary focus was on the role of nurture, and especially on the ways in which a child's social and cultural environments foster cognitive growth. Following are central ideas in Vygotsky's theory:

Some cognitive processes are seen in a variety of species; others are unique to human beings. Vygotsky distinguished between two kinds of mental processes, which he called *functions*. Many species exhibit *lower mental functions:* certain basic ways of learning and responding to the environment, such as discovering what foods to eat and how best to get from one location to another. Human beings are unique in their additional use of *higher mental functions:* deliberate intellectual processes that enhance learning, memory, and reasoning. In Vygotsky's view, the potential for acquiring lower mental functions is biologically built in, but society and culture are critical for the development of higher mental functions.

Children undergo developmental transitions in their thinking. Vygotsky's short life did not give him sufficient time to flesh out the developmental transformations he detected, but his writings do offer provocative images of development. According to Vygotsky, infants and young children react automatically to stimuli in their environment, without regard for symbols, words, and mental images (Vygotsky, 1997f). Presented with a complex array of objects, say, colored blocks of various shapes and sizes, young children play without clustering objects into categories. In a modest advancement, at about age 3 or 4, children classify objects according to simple properties but change their criteria spontaneously, perhaps first grouping blocks by color and then shifting to shape, or even changing the basis of classification midstream (Vygotsky, 1987b).

During middle childhood, a major transformation occurs, during which time children think and remember with the help of rules, concepts, and symbols. Given a piece of paper but no writing implement, and asked to remember a number, they might tear the sheets into the same number of pieces or create shapes that resemble the number. Shown a shape and told it is a "square," they can identify other squares printed on a piece of paper. In adolescence, young people are able to group and remember ideas with entirely mental connections. One of Vygotsky's colleagues found that an adolescent could remember the words *beach, hail,* and *dress* by creating associations among the elements with the sentence, "A lady walked on the beach; it began to hail and ruined her dress" (Leont'ev, 1959, p. 94). As young people learn to make such mental associations, they become capable of purposefully thinking, remembering, and regulating their mental activities. As a result, they are able to take full advantage of their society's rich heritage in science, mathematics, art, history, and other intellectual fields of study.

BIOECOLOGY OF DEVELOPMENT

Vygotsky proposed that guidance from adults is essential for children in learning to use cultural symbols, strategies, and tools.

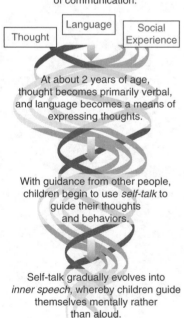

In infancy, thought is nonverbal in nature, and language is used primarily as a means of communication.

Language — Social Experience — Thought

At about 2 years of age, thought becomes primarily verbal, and language becomes a means of expressing thoughts.

With guidance from other people, children begin to use *self-talk* to guide their thoughts and behaviors.

Self-talk gradually evolves into *inner speech*, whereby children guide themselves mentally rather than aloud.

FIGURE 6-6 **Weaving of thought, social experience, and language.** Vygotsky proposed that these separate functions eventually become intertwined and regulate intellectual activity, behavior, and emotions.

Through both informal interactions and formal schooling, adults convey to children ideal methods for interpreting the world. In their interactions with children, adults share the *meanings* they attach to objects, events, and, more generally, human experience. As they do so, they actually *transform* the situations children encounter. This process of helping children make sense of experiences in culturally appropriate ways is known as **mediation**. Meanings are conveyed through a variety of mechanisms—language, mathematical symbols, art, music, and so on. In the "Museum Visit" case at the beginning of the chapter, Mother helps 4-year-old Billy make sense of several dinosaur artifacts. She points out how dinosaur ribs and human ribs serve the same function ("Protecting your heart . . . and your lungs"). She relates some of the artifacts to scientific concepts that Billy already knows (*Jurassic, Cretaceous* eras). And she substitutes everyday language ("dinosaur poop") for an unfamiliar scientific term (*coprolite*).

Informal conversations are one common method by which adults pass along culturally appropriate ways of interpreting situations. But no less important in Vygotsky's eyes is formal education, where teachers systematically impart the ideas, concepts, and terminology used in academic disciplines. Although Vygotsky, like Piaget, saw value in allowing children to make discoveries on their own, he emphasized the worth of adults passing along the technologies and discoveries of previous generations (Vygotsky, 1934/1986).

Every culture passes along physical and cognitive tools that make daily living more efficient. Not only do adults teach children ways of interpreting experience, they also instruct them about specific tools that can help them tackle challenges they are apt to face. Some tools, such as shovels, sewing machines, and computers, are physical objects. Others, such as writing systems, maps, and spreadsheets, are partly physical and partly symbolic. Still others, such as using rounding rules and mental arithmetic to estimate the cost of purchases at a store, have little physical basis at all. In Vygotsky's view, mastering tools that are partly or entirely symbolic—**cognitive tools**—greatly enhances learning.

Different cultures pass along different cognitive tools. Thus Vygotsky's theory leads us to expect greater diversity in children than Piaget's theory does. For instance, recall a point made earlier in the chapter: Children acquire conservation skills at a younger age if conservation of clay is important for their family's pottery business. Similarly, children are more likely to acquire map-reading skills if maps (perhaps of roads, subway systems, and shopping centers) are a prominent part of their community, family life, and personal experience (I. Hemmer et al., 2013; Liben & Myers, 2007). And children are more apt to have a keen sense of time if clocks and calendars regulate cultural activities (Burny, Valcke, Desoete, & Van Luit, 2013; Graesch, 2009; K. Nelson, 1996a). In the opening case study, Billy has some understanding of distant time periods—cognitive tools from the field of geology—because books, museums, and discussions have exposed him to these tools.

Thought and language become increasingly interdependent in the first few years of life. One very important cognitive tool is language. For us as adults, thought and language are closely interconnected. We often think by using the specific words that our language provides. When we think about household pets, our thoughts contain such words as *dog* and *cat*. We usually express our thoughts when we converse with others. In other words, we "speak our minds."

Vygotsky proposed that thought and language are separate abilities for infants and young toddlers. In the early years, thinking occurs independently of language, and when language appears, it is first used primarily as a means of communication and not as a mechanism for facilitating thinking. Sometime around age 2, thought and language start to become intertwined: Children express their thoughts when they speak and begin to think in words.

When thought and language first merge, children often talk to themselves, a phenomenon known as **self-talk** (you may also see the term *private speech*). Vygotsky suggested that self-talk serves an important function in cognitive development. By talking to themselves, children learn to guide their own behaviors through complex maneuvers in much the same way that adults previously guided them. Self-talk eventually evolves into **inner speech**, in which children "talk" to themselves mentally rather than aloud (Figure 6-6). They continue to direct themselves verbally through tasks and activities, but others can no longer see and hear them do it (Vygotsky, 1934/1986).

Recent research has supported Vygotsky's views regarding the progression and role of self-talk and inner speech. The frequency of children's audible self-talk decreases during the preschool and early elementary years, but this decrease is at first accompanied by an increase in whispered mumbling and silent lip movements, presumably reflecting a transition to inner speech (Bivens & Berk, 1990; Ostad, 2013; Winsler & Naglieri, 2003). Self-talk increases when children are performing more difficult tasks and helps them regulate their behavior by staying focused on certain steps ("First select puzzle pieces with straight edges . . . second place these in matching slots.") and standards ("Too messy. No smudges.") (Alarcón-Rubio, Sánchez-Medina, & Prieto-García, 2014; Berk, 1994; Vygotsky, 1934/1986). As you probably know from your own experience, adults also regularly talk to themselves when they face new challenges.

Complex mental processes begin as social activities and gradually evolve into internal mental processes that children can try on their own. Vygotsky proposed that complex strategies, including the use of cognitive tools, have their roots in social interaction. As children discuss objects and events with adults and other knowledgeable individuals, they gradually incorporate words, concepts, symbols, and strategies into their ways of thinking.

The process through which social activities evolve into internal mental activities is called **internalization**. The progression from self-talk to inner speech just described illustrates this process: Over time, children gradually internalize adults' directions so that they are eventually giving *themselves* directions.

Not all mental processes emerge as children interact with adults, however. Some develop as children interact with peers. For example, children frequently argue with one another about a variety of matters—how best to carry out an activity, what games to play, who did what to whom, and so on. According to Vygotsky, childhood arguments help children discover that there are often several ways to view the same situation. Eventually, he suggested, children internalize the "arguing" process, developing the ability to look at a situation from several different angles on their own.

Each child acquires a culture's tools in an individual manner. Recall that Vygotsky was a constructivist. He believed that children do not necessarily internalize *exactly* what they see and hear in a social context. Rather, they often transform ideas, strategies, and other cognitive resources to make these tools uniquely their own. You may sometimes see the term **appropriation** used to refer to this process of internalizing but also selectively implementing some skills rather than others and adapting the ideas and strategies of one's culture for personal use. Children do not necessarily learn all cultural pastimes easily or enthusiastically. Instead, individual children approach educational activities using their own motivations, prior understandings, and creative learning processes.

Children can perform more challenging tasks when assisted by advanced helpers. Vygotsky distinguished between two kinds of abilities that children are apt to have at any particular point in their development. A child's *actual developmental level* is the upper limit of tasks that he or she can perform independently, without help from anyone else. A child's *level of potential development* is the upper limit of tasks that he or she can perform with the assistance of a more competent individual. To get a true sense of children's cognitive development, Vygotsky suggested, teachers should assess children's capabilities both when performing alone *and* when performing with assistance.

As we noted earlier, Vygotsky found that children typically accomplish more difficult things in collaboration with adults than they can do on their own. With the assistance of a parent or teacher, young people may be able to read more complex prose than they comprehend independently. They can play more difficult piano pieces when an adult helps them locate some of the notes on the keyboard or provides suggestions about which fingers to use. And they can be coached to develop such basic arithmetic skills as addition, subtraction, multiplication, and addition (A. L. Petitto, 1985).

Challenging tasks promote maximum cognitive growth. The range of tasks that children cannot yet perform independently but *can* perform with guidance of adults or, in some

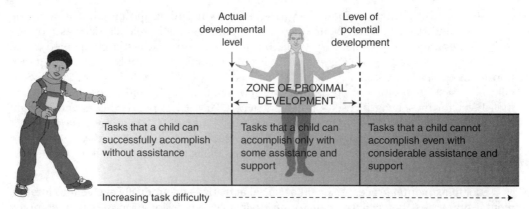

FIGURE 6-7 **In the zone.** Tasks within a child's zone of proximal development are optimal for promoting cognitive advancements.

Observing Children 6-9

Watch preschool children anticipate the next steps in a pattern with just a bit of help from their teacher.

ENHANCEDetext *video example*

cases, with help from peers or older children who are especially skilled in performing an activity, is, in Vygotsky's terminology, the **zone of proximal development,** or **ZPD** (see Figure 6-7). A child's zone of proximal development includes learning and problem-solving abilities that are just beginning to emerge. You can observe children working within their ZPD in an Observing Children video.

Vygotsky proposed that children learn very little from performing tasks they can already do independently. Instead, they develop primarily by attempting tasks they can accomplish only with modest guidance from a more competent individual—that is, when they attempt tasks within their zone of proximal development. In a nutshell, it is the shared challenges in life, not the easy or independent successes, that promote cognitive development.

Whereas moderately difficult tasks are educational for children, tasks that they cannot do even with considerable assistance are of no benefit whatsoever. For example, it is pointless to ask a typical kindergartner to solve for *x* in an algebraic equation. A child's ZPD therefore sets a limit on what he or she is capable of learning.

Naturally, any child's ZPD will change over time. As some tasks are mastered, other, more complex ones appear on the horizon. Furthermore, children's ZPDs vary considerably in "width." Whereas some children may, with assistance, be able to "reach" several years above their actual (independent) developmental level, others may be able to handle tasks that are only slightly more difficult than what they can currently do on their own.

Play allows children to stretch themselves cognitively. Recall the scenario of Jeff and Scott playing "restaurant" presented earlier in the chapter. The two boys take on several adult roles (restaurant manager, server, cook) and practice a variety of adult-like behaviors: assembling the necessary materials for a restaurant, creating menus, keeping track of customers' orders, and tallying final bills. In real life such a scenario would, of course, be impossible. Very few 5-year-old children have the cooking, reading, writing, mathematical, or organizational skills necessary to run a restaurant. Yet the element of make-believe brings these tasks within the boys' reach (e.g., Lillard, 1993). In Vygotsky's words:

> In play a child always behaves beyond his average age, above his daily behavior; in play it is as though he were a head taller than himself. (Vygotsky, 1978, p. 102)

Many contemporary psychologists share Vygotsky's and Piaget's belief that play provides an arena in which youngsters practice skills needed later in life. Not only does play promote social skills (e.g., cooperation, perspective taking, and conflict resolution strategies), it also helps children experiment with objects; identify cause-and-effect relationships; and practice use of tools (Gredler & Shields, 2008; Hedegaard & Fleer, 2013; Rubin, Fein, & Vandenberg, 1983; Sutherland & Friedman, 2013; Vygotsky, 1966).

To some degree, play serves distinct purposes for different age groups. For infants, one primary outcome of play activities is to discover what objects are like and can do, as well as what people can do *to* and *with* the objects. Through such discoveries, infants learn many properties of the physical world—which ones bounce, feel mushy, taste good, make a loud noise, and fit together (Gopnik, 2009b; Morris, 1977; Wu, Gopnik, Richardson, & Kirkham, 2011). Through social games, including peekaboo, pat-a-cake, and playful exchanges of sounds, infants practice imitation, learn the rhythms of interpersonal exchange, and acquire rudimentary skills with cooperation and turn-taking (Bigelow & Best, 2013; Bruner & Sherwood, 1976; Flavell et al., 2002; Powers & Trevarthen, 2009).

When play takes on an element of make-believe around age 2, children begin to substitute one object for another in imaginary actions—for instance, "eating" pretend food with an invented fork (Markova & Legerstee, 2012; Pederson, Rook-Green, & Elder, 1981). As Vygotsky suggested, pretense probably helps children distinguish between objects and their symbolic representations. In play, children respond to an internal representation (e.g., to the concept of *fork*) even more than to the immediate appearance of the actual object (Bodrova & Leong, 1996; S. M. Carlson, White, & Davis-Unger, 2014; W. L. Haight, 1999; Osório, Meins, Martins, Martins, & Soares, 2012). When, in the preschool years, children expand their pretend play into elaborate scenarios—sometimes called **sociodramatic play**— they practice such roles as "parent," "teacher," or "waiter," behave in ways that conform to cultural standards, and learn to anticipate other people's perspectives.

As children reach school age, role-playing activities gradually diminish, and other forms of play take their place. Elementary school children often spend time with friends constructing things from cardboard boxes or Legos, playing cards and board games, and engaging in team sports. Many of these activities continue into adolescence. While adhering to rules of games, youngsters learn to plan ahead, think before they act, cooperate and compromise, solve problems, and engage in self-restraint—skills critical for successful participation in the adult world (Christie & Johnsen, 1983; Hromek & Roffey, 2009; Sutton-Smith, 1979).

Play, then, is hardly a waste of time. Instead, it is a valuable training ground for the adult world. Perhaps for this reason it is seen in children worldwide. In the Development in Culture feature "Playing Around," you can learn how playing alone and with others helps children gain proficiency in cultural practices.

Current Perspectives Related to Vygotsky's Theory

As you have learned, Vygotsky's descriptions of developmental processes were imprecise. Despite this weakness, many contemporary theorists and practitioners have found Vygotsky's theory to be insightful. Advocates have taken Vygotsky's notions in many different directions, with much of their work addressing a few general ideas: the social construction of meaning, scaffolding, participation in adult activities, and acquisition of teaching skills.

Social Construction of Meaning

Contemporary psychologists have elaborated on Vygotsky's proposal that adults help children attach meaning to the objects and events around them. They point out that an adult (e.g., a parent or teacher) often helps a child make better sense of the world through joint discussion of their mutual experiences (Crowley & Jacobs, 2002; Feuerstein, 1990; Kozulin et al., 2010; Mahn & John-Steiner, 2013). Such an interaction, sometimes called a **mediated learning experience**, encourages the child to think about the event in culturally relevant ways: to attach labels to it, recognize its underlying principles, draw certain conclusions from it, and so on. In such a conversation, the adult must consider the prior knowledge of the child and tailor the discussion accordingly, as Billy's mother does in the chapter-opening case study (Newson & Newson, 1975).

In addition to co-constructing meanings with adults, children often talk among themselves to derive meaning from their experiences. School is one obvious place where children and adolescents can toss around ideas about a particular issue and conceivably reach consensus about how best to interpret and understand the topic in question. Children also acquire misconceptions from well-meaning peers who convincingly tout a false explanation, making it worthwhile for teachers to monitor children's discussions and interject other considerations.

Scaffolding

Theorists have given considerable thought to the kinds of assistance that help children accomplish challenging tasks and activities. The term **scaffolding** is often used to describe the

DEVELOPMENT IN CULTURE
Playing Around

From the perspective of cultural learning, play is a productive medium through which children voluntarily socialize themselves into their community's traditions (F. P. Hughes, 2010).

To some degree, lessons in cultural practices change as children grow. Early on, adults guide the direction of play. Mothers, fathers, and other adults invite infants to join games of peekaboo, pat-a-cake, and other good-humored exchanges that vary from one cultural group to the next. One psychologist, Heidi Keller, found distinct patterns in infant play in mothers and infants from urban German middle-class families and rural Camroonian Nso families (H. Keller, 2003). German mothers tended to spend a considerable amount of time interacting verbally with their infants—talking with them and encouraging their eye contact and play with toys. In comparison, Nso mothers attended to the physical needs of their infants by breastfeeding, soothing, and providing close body contact. The Nso mothers also gently jiggled and tugged at infants' limbs. As infants from both groups were enjoying their social interactions, they were simultaneously obtaining guidance in conducting themselves—developing verbal skills and playing with objects in German families and staying physically close to mothers and exercising new motor skills in Nso families.

Children continue to integrate familiar cultural routines into play as they grow. In societies that encourage serious chores in children, children pretend to be adult laborers (F. P. Hughes, 2010). In Botswana, men herd oxen, and boys regularly play the "cow game." Taking on complementary roles, boys pretend to be oxen yoked with twine and others act as drivers who control the oxen (Bock & Johnson, 2004). Girls pretend to pummel grain with reeds, sticks, dirt, and imaginary mortars (Bock & Johnson, 2004). In industrialized cultures that separate children from the daily work of adults, children are apt to include fantasy figures that they have seen on television and in video games (F. P. Hughes, 2010; Lehrer & Petrakos, 2011). Not every culture values or encourages pretend play, and in some groups children play creatively with objects and with one another without taking on defined roles (Farver & Shin, 1997; F. P. Hughes, 2010; Smilansky, 1968).

In middle childhood and after, youngsters often participate in structured games. Children in many societies play competitive games, wherein participants follow prescribed rules and vie to be winner (Bonta, 1997; F. P. Hughes, 2010). In hunting societies, children play games of physical dexterity, including foot races and contests of tracking and spear-throwing, pursuits that allow for practice of valuable motor skills. In nomadic groups, children frequently play games whose outcomes are determined by chance, perhaps preparing them for adjusting to largely uncontrollable environmental conditions, as their parents must do to survive. In cultures that are technologically advanced, children play games that require some degree of strategy (e.g., chess, checkers, and computer games with defined objectives and tactics), advancing their facility with complex systems (S. Elliott & Elliott, 2014). In societies that do not encourage competition, children may play cooperative games, tell one another stories, and copy adult roles (Bonta, 1997; F. P. Hughes, 2010).

PLAYTIME. These boys enjoy a morning swim at a lake in Sri Lanka. Even as the boys enjoy lighthearted moments, they are actively acquiring cultural knowledge about social interaction.

guidance provided by more competent individuals to help children perform tasks in their ZPD. To understand this concept, think of the scaffolding used in the construction of a new building. The *scaffold* is an external structure that provides support for workers (e.g., a place where they can stand) until the building itself is strong enough to support them. As the building gains strength and stability, the scaffold becomes less necessary and is gradually removed.

In much the same way, an adult guiding a child through a new task provides a scaffold to the child's early efforts. Scaffolding can take a variety of forms. Here are just a few of the many possibilities:

- Demonstrate the proper performance of the task in a way that children can easily imitate.
- Divide a complex task into several smaller, simpler tasks.
- Provide a structure or set of guidelines for how the task should be accomplished.
- Provide a calculator, computer software (word processing program, spreadsheet, etc.), or other technology that makes some aspects of the task easier.

- Ask questions that get children thinking in appropriate ways about the task.
- Keep children's attention focused on relevant dimensions.
- Give frequent feedback about how children are progressing. (Bodrova & Leong, 2009; A. Collins, 2006; Gallimore & Tharp, 1992; Pentimonti & Justice, 2010; Rogoff, 1990; Smit, van Eerde, & Bakker, 2013; Torres-Guzmán, 2011; D. Wood, Bruner, & Ross, 1976)

Children need customized scaffolding to support their success (Lodewyk & Winne, 2005; Puntambekar & Hübscher, 2005; Rittle-Johnson & Koedinger, 2005). As they become more adept at performing an activity, assistance is gradually phased out so that they eventually accomplish it entirely on their own. As you might expect, learning to offer just the right level of support takes skill and sensitivity. You can watch a preschool teacher scaffolding young children's efforts at assembling puzzles in an Observing Children video.

Observing Children 6-10

Watch a teacher scaffold a child's puzzle completion by encouraging him to study the cardboard layout, look for pieces that match the color of the external frame, and focus first on pieces with straight edges before trying to place inner pieces.

ENHANCEDetext *video example*

Participation in Adult Activities

Virtually all cultures allow—and in fact usually require—children to be involved in adult activities. Yet children's early experiences are often at the fringe of the pursuit. As children acquire greater competence, they gradually take a more central role in the activity until, eventually, they are full-fledged participants (S. Gaskins, 1999; Gregory, Choudhury, Ilankuberan, Kwapong, & Woodham, 2013; Lave & Wenger, 1991; Rogoff et al., 2007).

In most cases children's early involvement in adult activities is scaffolded through what is sometimes known as **guided participation** (Bhatia & Ebooks, 2014; Rogoff, 2003). When our own children were preschoolers, we authors often had them help us bake cookies by asking them to measure, pour, and mix ingredients, but we stood close by and offered suggestions about how to get the measurements right, minimize spilling, and so on. Similarly, when taking our children to the office with us, we had them press the appropriate buttons in the elevator, check our mailboxes, open envelopes, and deliver documents to the department secretary, but we kept a close eye on what they were doing and instructed them when necessary. In later years we gave them increasing responsibility and independence. By the time they were in high school, they were baking their own pastries, and they sometimes ran errands for us.

Parents are not the only ones who engage children in adult activities. Schools sometimes invite students to be members of faculty decision-making committees, and parent-teacher organizations ask students to help with school fund-raising efforts. Girl Scout troops introduce girls to salesmanship, accounting, and other adult business practices during annual cookie drives (Rogoff, 1995, 2003). Many local newspapers take on high school students as cub reporters, movie reviewers, and editorial writers, especially during the summer months.

In some instances adults work with children in formal or informal **apprenticeships**, one-on-one relationships in which adults teach young people new skills, guide their initial efforts, and present increasingly difficult tasks as proficiency improves and the ZPD progresses. Many cultures use apprenticeships as a way of gradually introducing children to particular skills and trades in the adult community—perhaps weaving, tailoring, or playing a musical instrument (D. A. Davis & Davis, 2012; D. J. Elliott, 1995; Lave & Wenger, 1991; Tsethlikai & Rogoff, 2013).

In apprenticeships, children learn not only useful actions but also the language of the skill or trade (Lave & Wenger, 1991). When master weavers teach apprentices their art, they might use such terms as *warp, weft, shuttle,* and *harness* to focus attention on a particular aspect of the process. Similarly, when teachers guide students through scientific experiments, they use words like *hypothesis, evidence,* and *theory* to help students evaluate their procedures and results (Perkins, 1992). Furthermore, an apprenticeship can show children how adults typically think about a task—a situation known as a **cognitive apprenticeship**. For instance, an adult and child might work together to accomplish a complicated task (perhaps sewing a patchwork quilt, solving a mathematical brainteaser, or collecting data samples in biology fieldwork). In the process of talking about various aspects of the task, the adult and child analyze the situation and develop the best approach to take, and the adult models effective ways of thinking about and mentally processing the situation (Bodrow & Magalashvili, 2009; Bouta & Retalis, 2013; A. Collins, 2006; Shreyar, Zolkower, & Pérez, 2010).

Acquisition of Teaching Skills

When learning new techniques from more experienced members of the community, children observe the teaching process and subsequently have occasions to teach other children basic skills (Gauvain, 2001; N. Howe, Recchia, Della Porta, & Funamoto, 2012). For instance, children in Gambia help peers or siblings learn new clapping games by giving verbal directions and moving younger children's hands into the appropriate position (Koops, 2010). Many older children have an intuitive sense of instructional formats that appeal to younger children and may use local materials, for example, seeds, sticks and stones, and familiar songs and stories, when imparting such fundamental skills as counting objects (Mweru & Murungi, 2013).

With age and experience, children become increasingly adept at teaching others what they themselves have learned. In a study in rural Mexico (Maynard, 2002), Mayan children were observed as they worked with younger siblings in preparing food and washing clothes. The children's earliest form of "instruction" (perhaps around age 4 or 5) was simply to let a younger brother or sister join in and help. At age 6 or 7, children tended to be directive and controlling, giving commands and taking over if something wasn't done correctly. By the time they were 8, however, they were proficient teachers, using a combination of demonstrations, explanations, physical guidance, and feedback to scaffold their siblings' efforts. When children help others, the "teachers" often benefit as much, or nearly as much, as the "students" (Bowman-Perrott et al., 2013; Karcher, 2009; Webb & Palincsar, 1996).

Applying the Ideas of Vygotsky and His Followers

Vygotsky's work and the advances it has spawned have numerous implications for teaching. Educators taking a Vygotskian perspective guide children in taking on increasing levels of responsibility for completing culturally important, challenging endeavors.

• **Help children acquire the basic cognitive tools they need to succeed in academic disciplines.** Obviously, children in an industrialized society need to learn to read, write, and do arithmetic. Children can also become better musicians when they can read music and understand what *keys*, *chords*, and *thirds* are. In the disciplines of science, mathematics, and social studies, our culture passes along other key concepts (e.g., *molecule, negative number, democracy*), symbols (e.g., H_2O, π, x^3), and visual representations (e.g., graphs, maps) that help children interpret advanced material.

• **Use group learning activities to help children internalize cognitive strategies.** Contemporary researchers have found that, as Vygotsky suggested, children often internalize—and so eventually use independently—the complex thinking processes they first use in social interaction (e.g., Andriessen, 2006; Murphy, 2007). We find an example in **reciprocal teaching**, a model of reading instruction that has had great success in enhancing children's reading comprehension skills (Alfassi, Weiss, & Lifshitz, 2009; A. L. Brown & Palincsar, 1987; Law, 2014; Mandel, Osana, & Venkatesh, 2013; Palincsar & Brown, 1984). This approach is designed to foster four effective reading strategies:

- *Summarizing.* Identifying the main ideas of a reading passage
- *Questioning.* Asking oneself questions to check comprehension of ideas
- *Clarifying.* Taking steps to better understand a confusing point
- *Predicting.* Anticipating what points an author is apt to make in later sentences or paragraphs

In this approach, a teacher and several students meet in a group to read a piece of text, occasionally stopping to discuss and process it aloud. Initially, the teacher leads the discussion, asking questions about the text to promote summarizing, questioning, clarifying, and predicting. He or she gradually turns this "teaching" role over to a few students, who for a short time take charge of the discussion and ask one another the same kinds of questions that their teacher has modeled. Eventually, the students can read and discuss a text almost independently of the teacher, working together to make sense of it and checking one another for comprehension.

Reciprocal teaching has been used successfully with a wide variety of students, ranging from first graders to college students, to teach effective reading and listening comprehension skills. In many cases students become far more effective readers and transfer their new reading strategies to other subject areas (A. L. Brown & Palincsar, 1987; Mandel et al., 2013; Palincsar & Brown, 1984, 1989; Stricklin, 2011).

Preparing for Your Licensure Examination

Your teaching test might ask you about the major contributions of Vygotsky to educational practice.

• **Provide tangible reminders about what children should be doing during the lesson.** Teachers can ask preschool children to draw a picture or write simple notes about their plans during a free-choice activity. A 4-year-old boy moving to the play center draws a picture of himself building blocks with a friend. He brings his picture to the block area and guides his play according to his plan (Bodrova, Leong, & Akhutina, 2011). Similarly, three first-grade children enter the science center, with each child taking a picture of an ear, lips, and pencil to remind them to be a listener, speaker, or recorder when completing the assignment. Their teacher reminds them to follow their plan when they drift away from it.

• **Provide effective scaffolding on challenging tasks.** For optimal learning, teachers and other adults need to present assignments that a child can perform successfully only with assistance—that is, tasks within the child's ZPD. Although it is not always practical to assess and accommodate every child's ZPD, teachers can offer assignments that are moderately challenging for most students and then make a range of scaffolds available, the selection of which will depend on individuals' skill levels. In Artifact 6-3, you can examine numerals written by a young child with the help of outlines of numbers prepared with dots. The Development and Practice feature "Scaffolding Children's Efforts at Challenging Tasks" presents several additional examples.

ARTIFACT 6-3   I can count! In this simple worksheet a preschool teacher scaffolds 4-year-old Hannah's attempt at writing numerals.

One powerful strategy, teaching children how to talk themselves through a complex new procedure, makes use of Vygotsky's concept of *self-talk* to enable children to create their *own* scaffolding. Children can learn how to follow five steps (Meichenbaum, 1977, 1985):

1. *Cognitive modeling.* An adult model performs the desired task while verbalizing instructions that guide performance.
2. *Overt, external guidance.* The child performs the task while listening to the adult verbalize the instructions.
3. *Overt self-guidance.* The child repeats the instructions aloud (*self-talk*) while performing the task.
4. *Faded, overt self-guidance.* The child whispers the instructions while performing the task.
5. *Covert self-instruction.* The child silently thinks about the instructions (*inner speech*) while performing the task.

In this sequence of steps, depicted in Figure 6-8, the adult initially serves as a model both for the behavior itself and for the process of self-guidance. Responsibility for performing the task is soon turned over to the child. Eventually, responsibility for guiding the performance is assumed by the child as well.

	TASK PERFORMANCE	TASK INSTRUCTIONS
Step 1	The adult performs the task, modeling it for the child.	The adult verbalizes instructions.
Step 2	The child performs the task.	The adult verbalizes instructions.
Step 3	The child performs the task.	The child repeats the instructions aloud.
Step 4	The child performs the task.	The child whispers the instructions.
Step 5	The child performs the task.	The child thinks silently about the instructions.

FIGURE 6-8   Self-talk. In a five-step process, a child shifts from adult help to independent self-regulation.

• **Assess children's abilities under a variety of work conditions.** To foster children's cognitive development, educators need to determine under what conditions the children are most likely to accomplish assignments successfully. For instance, can children accomplish a task entirely on their own? If not, can they do it in collaboration with one or two peers? Can they do it if they have some adult guidance and support? By addressing such questions, teachers can get a better sense of the tasks that are in each child's ZPD (Bodrova & Leong, 2009; Haywood & Lidz, 2007; Mahn & John-Steiner, 2013).

• **Provide opportunities to engage in authentic activities.** As we've already seen, children's participation in adult activities plays a critical role in their cognitive development. However, children spend much of their day at school, which is removed from the working world of adults. A reasonable alternative is **authentic activities**—classroom tasks and projects that closely resemble typical adult activities. Following are examples:

- Writing an editorial
- Participating in a debate
- Designing an electrical circuit
- Conducting an experiment
- Creating and distributing a class newsletter
- Organizing a volunteer campaign to address a community need
- Performing in a concert
- Planning a personal budget
- Conversing in a foreign language
- Creating a museum display
- Developing a home page on the Internet
- Filming and editing a video production

DEVELOPMENT AND PRACTICE
Scaffolding Children's Performance on Challenging Tasks

Ask questions that get children thinking about a task.

- A middle school teacher asks her students a series of questions as they prepare to deliver a persuasive speech: *What are the main points you want to make? Who will make them? What kind of objections and counterarguments can you anticipate? How will you respond to them?* (Early Adolescence)
- As students in a high school science class begin to plan their experiments for an upcoming science fair, their teacher encourages them to separate and control variables with the following questions: *What do I think causes the phenomenon I am studying? What other possible variables might influence it? How can I be sure which variables are influencing the results I obtain?* (Late Adolescence)

When learners are unfamiliar with a task, provide explicit guidance and give frequent feedback.

- A preschool teacher watches children attempt to write their names. With a girl who writes the sequence backward, the teacher puts a green dot under the first letter and tells her to start with it. With a boy who forgets a few letters, the teacher writes highlights missing letters with a color pen. With another boy, the teacher writes the letters he cannot remember and asks has him to add the letters he knows. (Early Childhood)
- When an outdoor educator takes 12-year-olds on their first camping trip, he has the children work in pairs to pitch their tents. Although he has previously shown the children how to put up a tent, this is the first time they've actually done it themselves, and so he provides written instructions that they can follow. In addition, he circulates from campsite to campsite and provides assistance as necessary. (Early Adolescence)

Provide a calculator, computer software, worksheet, or other material that reduces a little of the challenge of the task while still allowing children to gain experience in tackling it.

- Children in a third-grade class have mastered basic addition, subtraction, and multiplication facts. They are now applying their knowledge of arithmetic to determine how much money they would need to purchase a list of recreational items from a mail-order catalog. Because the list is fairly lengthy and includes varying quantities of each item, their teacher gives them calculators to do the necessary multiplication and addition. (Middle Childhood)
- A high school history teacher distributes a worksheet with a partially completed table of cultural inventions from ancient African and Middle Eastern societies. A few cells contain summaries that serve as models for notes students can take as they read their textbook. (Late Adolescence)

Teach children how to talk themselves through a complex procedure.

- A school psychologist teaches children with cognitive disabilities to classify shapes by asking themselves questions (e.g., Does the object have three or more sides? Is it round?). The children begin to ask themselves these questions and learn to classify shapes more accurately. (Middle Childhood)
- A physical education teacher shows beginning tennis players how to use self-instructions to remember correct form when swinging the racket:
  1. Say *ball* to remind yourself to look at the ball.
  2. Say *bounce* to remind yourself to follow the ball with your eyes as it approaches you.
  3. Say *hit* to remind yourself to focus on contacting the ball with the racket.
  4. Say *ready* to get yourself into position for the next ball to come your way. (Early Adolescence)

Divide a complex assignment into several smaller, simpler tasks, and ask children to tackle it in small groups.

- A fourth-grade teacher has his students create a school newspaper with news articles, a schedule of upcoming events, a couple of political cartoons, and classified advertisements. Several students work together to create each feature, with different students assuming distinct roles (e.g., fact finder, writer, editor) and occasionally switching parts. (Middle Childhood)
- A film analysis teacher helps high school students dissect movies by breaking up their assignments into manageable parts. After the class watches *Citizen Kane*, the teacher gives poster paper to groups of students. One group pieces together flashbacks of the life of Charles Foster Kane, another reads the screenplay, a third group examines the movie's filmmaking innovations, and a fourth group looks into the reception the movie originally received. (Late Adolescence)

Gradually withdraw guidance as children become proficient.

- A preschool teacher has 2- and 3-year-olds take turns distributing crackers, fruit, and napkins at snack time, and she asks all of them to bring their dishes and trash to the kitchen after they have finished eating. Initially, she must show them how to carry the food so that it doesn't spill. She must also remind servers to make sure that every child gets a snack. As the year progresses, reminders are less necessary, although she must occasionally say, "I think two of you have forgotten to bring your cups to the kitchen. I'm missing the ones with Big Bird and Cookie Monster." (Early Childhood)
- In an after-school service club, a teacher facilitates discussion and eventually encourages students to consider worthwhile program for their community. As the adolescents narrow the field of programs they might implement, the teacher is silent, allowing students to formulate an action plan on their own. (Late Adolescence)

Sources: Benko, 2012; Bodrova & Leong, 2009 (kindergarten writing example); Gallimore & Tharp, 1992; Helibronner, 2013; Kirshner, 2008 (persuasive speech example); Lajoie & Derry, 1993; Lou et al., 1996; Meichenbaum, 1985; Rosenshine & Meister, 1992; D. Wood et al., 1976; Ziegler, 1987 (tennis example).

By placing classroom activities in real-world contexts, teachers can enhance a variety of skills in students, including their mastery of classroom subject matter and ability to work effectively in groups (A. Collins, Brown, & Newman, 1989; Silva, Lopes, & Silva, 2013). For instance, students may show greater improvement in writing skills when they practice composing stories, essays, and letters to real people, rather than completing short, artificial writing exercises (Curwood, Magnified, & Lammers, 2013; Nail, 2007). Likewise, they may gain a more complete understanding of how to interpret maps when they construct their own rather than simply interpreting maps in workbook exercises (Gregg & Leinhardt, 1994a).

• **Scaffold children's play.** Many developmental theorists advocate for the inclusion of play in the curriculum, especially during the preschool and early elementary years. Following are several suggestions for promoting young children's play:

- Partition the classroom into small areas—perhaps a corner for blocks, a play center, an art table, a reading corner, and a science area. The play center is often set up as a small home because one of the chief themes for pretend play is being a mother or father and caring for a baby. Yet themes can be rotated through the center in alignment with topics being addressed in the curriculum (perhaps a hospital, hair salon, fire station, and veterinarian hospital).
- Furnish a play area with realistic toys (e.g., dolls, dress-up clothes, plastic dishes) that suggest certain activities and functions, as well as more versatile objects (e.g., Legos, wooden blocks, cardboard boxes) that encourage open-ended fantasy.
- Read a story to children (e.g., *Diary of a Worm* by Doreen Cronin, 2003) and then supply props (e.g., plastic worms, toy birds, paper, and crayons) for children to act it out.
- Expose children to in-depth information about a topic, for instance, by reading to them, inviting speakers (e.g., a paleontologist when learning about dinosaurs), showing videos, and supplying relevant props for the play area (e.g., plastic bones, shovels, brushes).
- Take a secondary role in children's pretend play. Help children integrate information they have been learning about (e.g., the job of an emergency responder or 911 operator), by spending a little time in the play center and temporarily taking on a part (e.g., a distressed victim seeking reassurance from a 911 operator).
- Encourage children to set a goal for their play, such as running a shop together. When conflicts escalate, remind the children of their goal and suggest how to compromise ("It sounds as if you both want to be the cashier. Your shop needs a cashier *and* a stocker. I wonder if you might trade off in these jobs.").
- Provide enough toys and equipment to minimize potential conflicts, but keep them limited enough in number that children must share and cooperate.
- Exercise sensitivity in responding to children's individual needs. A young child who is hesitant may appreciate reassurance about joining high-spirited peers, whereas another child who is fascinated with the intricacies of objects can be provided with new toys to inspect. (Bodrova & Leong, 2009; Bredekamp, 2011; Frost, Shin, & Jacobs, 1998; J. Jung & Recchia, 2013; Leong & Bodrova, 2012; Massey, 2013).

By observing children during play, teachers can gain insights into the abilities and skills that individual children are acquiring. Examples of things to look for are presented in the Observation Guidelines table "Observing the Cognitive Aspects of Young Children's Play."

• **Differentiate instruction for children with special needs.** Vygotsky believed that children with special needs need not be delayed in their development but do require adjustments with their tools (Vygotsky, 1993). A certain number of cultural tools, for example, Braille, lip reading, and sign language, are designed to facilitate communication for children with sensory impairments (Mahn & John-Steiner, 2013). Yet other accommodations can also be beneficial for learning, including adjustments to the presentation of concepts (e.g., using more visual materials than is customary), types of instruction (e.g., increasing the level of scaffolding in steps of a task), and alterations to pace and repetition (e.g., offering more practice than is usually necessary; Bøttcher & Dammeyer, 2012). In today's world, hand held devices and laptops, coupled with software resources on the World Wide Web, offer innumerable ways to customize material and instruction. Although teachers are not always familiar with devices that facilitate children's learning, they can consult experts and in some cases parents to determine how to integrate devices and materials for children with exceptional learning needs (M. Davis, 2013).

OBSERVATION GUIDELINES
Observing the Cognitive Aspects of Young Children's Play

CHARACTERISTIC	LOOK FOR	EXAMPLE	IMPLICATION
Exploratory Play with Objects	• *Interest in exploring objects* in the environment • *Ability to handle objects adeptly* • *Use of multiple senses* in exploratory play	When Tyler sees a new toy guitar in the playroom, he picks it up, inspects all sides, and turns the crank (although not enough to elicit any musical notes). After Tyler leaves it to play with something else, Sarah picks up the guitar, sniffs it, puts the crank in her mouth, and begins to suck and chew it.	Provide a wide variety of objects for infants and toddlers to explore, making sure that they are safe, clean, and non-toxic. Recognize that children may use these things in unexpected ways (and not necessarily how their manufacturers intended) and will typically move quickly from one object to another.
Group Play	• *Extent to which children play* with one another • *Extent to which children cooperate* in during play	LaMarr and Matthew are playing with trucks in the sandbox, but each boy seems to be in his own little world.	Give children opportunities to play together, and provide toys that encourage cooperation.
Use of Symbolic Thought and Imagination	• *Degree to which children use an object* to stand for another • *Imaginary objects* incorporated into play	Julia tells her friend she is going to the grocery store, opens an imaginary car door, sits on a chair inside her "car," steers her pretend steering wheel, and says, "Beep, beep" as she blows her "horn."	When equipping a play area, include objects (e.g., wooden blocks, cardboard boxes) that children can use for a variety of purposes.
Role Taking	• *Extent to which children use language* (e.g., tone of voice and specific phrases) *and behaviors* (e.g., mannerisms, characteristic actions) that reflect a particular role or job • *Extent to which children coordinate multiple roles* within the context of a complex play scenario	Mark and Alisa are playing doctor. Alisa brings her teddy bear to Mark's "office" and politely says, "Good morning, Doctor. My baby has a sore throat." Mark holds a Popsicle stick against the bear's mouth and instructs the "baby" to say "Aaahhh."	Provide toys and equipment associated with particular roles (e.g., toy medical kit, cooking utensils, play money).

Summary

Vygotsky suggested that human beings are different from other species in their acquisition of complex mental processes. In his view, adults promote children's cognitive development by sharing meanings that their culture assigns to objects and events, introducing children to the many tangible and cognitive tools that previous generations have generated, and assisting children with challenging tasks. Social activities are often precursors to, and form the basis of, complex mental processes: Children initially use new skills in the course of interacting with adults or peers and slowly internalize these skills for their own use.

Contemporary theorists have extended Vygotsky's theory in several directions. Some suggest that adults can help children benefit from their experiences through joint construction of meanings, guided participation, and cognitive apprenticeships. Others recommend that adults engage children in authentic, adult-like tasks, initially providing enough scaffolding such that youngsters can accomplish those tasks successfully, and gradually withdrawing support as proficiency increases.

ENHANCEDetext *self-check*

Assessing Children 6-1

Practice assessing children's play.

ENHANCEDetext *application exercise*

Assessing Children 6-2

Practice assessing a teacher's scaffolding of children's observations in science class.

ENHANCEDetext *application exercise*

COMPARING PIAGETIAN AND VYGOTSKIAN PERSPECTIVES

Together, Piaget's and Vygotsky's theories and the research they've inspired give us a more complete picture of cognitive development than either theory provides alone. Let's examine similarities and differences in these two prominent perspectives.

Common Themes

If we look beyond the very different vocabulary Piaget and Vygotsky used to describe the phenomena they observed, we notice four themes that their theories share: constructive processes, readiness, challenge, and social interaction.

Constructive Processes in Learning

Neither Piaget's nor Vygotsky's theory depicts cognitive development as a process of simply "absorbing" one's experiences. Rather, both frameworks portray the acquisition of new knowledge and skills as an energetic and constructive process. In Piaget's view, children increasingly organize their thoughts as schemes and, later, as operations that apply to a wide variety of circumstances. In Vygotsky's view, children gradually internalize—in their own creative and idiosyncratic ways—the interpretations and cognitive tools they first encounter and use in social contexts. In Artifact 6-4, you can see 6-year-old Laura's drawing of how fish breathe, inhaling and exhaling under water as people do above water, individually constructed in a Piagetian manner, and prepared with writing utensils, cultural tools from a Vygotskian perspective.

These two perspectives on constructivism are complementary. Piaget's theory focuses largely on how children construct knowledge *on their own;* his perspective is sometimes labeled **individual constructivism**. In contrast, the ideas of Vygotsky and his followers focus more on how children construct meanings in collaboration with adults and peers, processes sometimes called **social constructivism**. Without doubt, children acquire increasingly sophisticated thinking processes through *both* their own individual efforts and joint meaning-making efforts with others.

Readiness

Both Piaget and Vygotsky suggested that at any point in time a child is cognitively ready for some experiences but not others. Both theorists acknowledged that brain maturation places limits on what children can do at various points in development. Piaget proposed that children recognize new objects and events only when they can assimilate the information into existing schemes, and they can think logically about new problems only if they have constructed the relevant logical operations. Vygotsky, meanwhile, portrayed children's readiness for tasks as comprising an ever-changing zone of proximal development. As children master skills and abilities, other, slightly more advanced ones emerge in immature forms that are ready for adult nurturance and support.

For Piaget and Vygotsky, children are always prepared to learn *something*. For Piaget specifically, they are continually ready to learn based on their ample curiosity about the world. For Vygotsky, children are ready to learn concepts and skills used by people in their home and community especially in tasks that children can accomplish with a smidgen of help.

ARTIFACT 6-4   Under the sea. This drawing reflects 6-year-old Laura's personal conception of underwater ocean life. The air bubbles rising up from the fish and sea horse reveal her belief that sea creatures exhale in a manner similar to people. In representing her vision, Laura uses her acquired skill in drawing with materials made available to her.

Challenge

We see the importance of challenge most clearly in Vygotsky's concept of the zone of proximal development: Children benefit most from tasks that they can perform only with the assistance of more competent individuals. Yet challenge, albeit of a somewhat different sort, also lies at the heart of Piaget's theory: Children develop more sophisticated knowledge and thought processes only when they encounter phenomena they cannot adequately understand using existing knowledge—in other words, phenomena that create disequilibrium.

Importance of Social Interaction

In Piaget's eyes, the people in a child's life can present information and arguments that create disequilibrium and, as a result, foster greater perspective taking and logical thinking processes. For instance, when young children disagree with one another, they begin to realize that different people have discrepant yet equally valid viewpoints, and they gradually shed the egocentrism that characterizes preoperational thought. In Vygotsky's view, social interactions provide the very foundation for thought processes. Children internalize processes they use when conversing with others until ultimately, they use these processes independently. Tasks within the ZPD can, by definition, be accomplished only when others assist in children's efforts.

The four qualities that these two theories agree on culminate in a single coherent picture of children's reasoning. The Developmental Trends table "Thinking and Reasoning Skills at Different Age Levels" draws on elements of both perspectives to describe characteristics of youngsters in different age ranges.

Differences Between the Two Theories

Despite having similar basic ideas, Piaget and Vygotsky held opposing views on significant matters. In the Basic Developmental Issues table "Contrasting Piaget and Vygotsky," we compare the two perspectives in terms of our three general themes: nature and nurture, universality and diversity, and qualitative and quantitative change. Here we hone in on differences in convictions about the role of language and environment in cognitive growth.

Theoretical Differences

Following are four questions that capture distinctions between Piaget's and Vygotsky's theories:

To what extent is language essential for cognitive development? According to Piaget, language provides verbal labels for many of the concepts that children have already developed. It is also the primary means through which children interact with others and begin to incorporate multiple perspectives into their thinking. Yet in Piaget's view, much of cognitive development occurs independently of language.

For Vygotsky, language is critical for cognitive development. Children's thought processes are internalized versions of social interactions that are largely verbal in nature. Through two language-based phenomena—self-talk and inner speech—children begin to guide their actions in ways that others have previously guided them. In their conversations with adults, children learn the meanings that their culture imposes on events.

The truth of the matter probably lies somewhere between Piaget's and Vygotsky's perspectives. Piaget clearly underestimated the importance of language: Children acquire more complex understandings of phenomena not only through their own interactions with the world but also (as Vygotsky suggested) by learning how others interpret these occurrences. On the other hand, Vygotsky overstated the case for language. Some concepts clearly emerge *before* children have verbal labels to attach to them (R. Brooks & Meltzoff, 2014; Gopnik, 2009b; Halford & Andrews, 2006; Yermolayeva & Rakison, 2013). Furthermore, verbal exchanges may be less important for cognitive development in some cultures than in others. For instance, adults in some rural communities in Guatemala and India place heavy emphasis on gestures and demonstrations, rather than on verbal instructions, to teach and guide children (Rogoff, Mistry, Göncü, & Mosier, 1993).

What kinds of experiences promote development? Piaget maintained that children's independent, self-motivated explorations of the physical world form the basis for many developing schemes, and children often create these schemes with little guidance from others. In contrast, Vygotsky argued for activities that are facilitated and interpreted by

DEVELOPMENTAL TRENDS
Thinking and Reasoning Skills at Different Age Levels

AGE	WHAT YOU MIGHT OBSERVE	DIVERSITY	IMPLICATIONS
Infancy (Birth–2 Years)	• Exploratory actions in the environment becoming increasingly complex, flexible, and intentional over time • Growing awareness of simple cause-and-effect relationships • Emergence of ability to represent the world mentally (e.g., as revealed in daily conversations and make-believe play)	• Temperamental differences (e.g., the extent to which infants are adventuresome vs. timid) influence exploratory behavior. • Infants and toddlers who are securely attached to caregivers are more willing to venture out and explore the environment. • In some cultures adults encourage infants to focus more on people than on the environment, in which case children are less inclined to explore physical surroundings.	• Set up a safe, age-appropriate environment for exploration. • Provide objects that stimulate different senses—for instance, things that babies can look at, listen to, feel, and smell. • Suggest age-appropriate toys and activities that parents can provide at home. • Give physical comfort to infants not yet ready to explore their environments.
Early Childhood (2–6 Years)	• Rapidly developing language skills • Reasoning that is, by adult standards, often illogical • Limited perspective-taking ability • Frequent self-talk • Sociodramatic play	• Shyness may limit children's willingness to talk with others and engage in sociodramatic play. • Adult-like logic is more common when children have accurate information (e.g., about cause-and-effect relationships). • Children learn to interpret events in culture-specific ways.	• Provide numerous opportunities for children to interact with one another during play and other cooperative activities. • Introduce children to a variety of real-world situations through picture books and field trips. • Talk with children about their interpretations of events. • Expose children to basic tools, for example, paper and writing utensils, the alphabet, and numerals. • Encourage children to set goals for free-time activities, and provide concrete reminders (e.g., a picture of an ear when listening).
Middle Childhood (6–10 Years)	• Conservation, class inclusion, and other forms of adult-like logic • Limited ability to reason about abstract or hypothetical ideas • Emergence of group games and team sports that involve coordination of multiple perspectives • Ability to participate to some degree in many adult activities	• Development of logical thinking skills is affected by the importance of those skills in a child's culture. • Formal operational reasoning may occasionally appear for simple tasks and in familiar contexts, especially in 9- and 10-year-olds. • Roles for involvement in adult activities vary by culture.	• Use concrete objects and experiences to illustrate concepts and ideas. • Supplement verbal explanations with concrete examples, pictures, and hands-on activities. • Allow time for organized play activities. • Introduce children to various professions, and provide opportunities to practice authentic adult tasks.
Early Adolescence (10–14 Years)	• Increasing ability to reason about abstract ideas • Emerging scientific reasoning (e.g., formulating and testing hypotheses, separating and controlling variables) if taught • Increasing ability to reason about mathematical proportions • Some idealism about political and social issues, but often without taking realistic constraints into consideration • Increasing ability to engage in adult tasks	• Adolescents can think more abstractly on topics for which they have considerable knowledge. • Adolescents are more likely to separate and control variables for situations with which they are familiar. • Development of formal operational reasoning skills is affected by their integration in the culture. • Adolescents' idealistic notions may reflect religious, cultural, or socioeconomic backgrounds.	• Present abstract concepts central to academic disciplines, but tie them to concrete examples. • Have students engage in scientific investigations, focusing on familiar objects and phenomena. • Assign math problems that require use of simple fractions, ratios, or decimals. • While demonstrating how to do a new task, also talk about how to *think* about the task. • Scaffold challenging assignments with interim steps.

(continued)

DEVELOPMENTAL TRENDS (continued)

AGE	WHAT YOU MIGHT OBSERVE	DIVERSITY	IMPLICATIONS
Late Adolescence (14–18 Years)	• Abstract thought and scientific reasoning skills becoming prevalent, especially for topics about which adolescents have considerable knowledge • Idealistic notions tempered by realistic considerations • Ability to perform many tasks in mature manner	• Abstract thinking is more common in some content areas (e.g., mathematics, science) than in others (e.g., history, geography). • Formal operational reasoning skills are less likely to appear in cultures that don't enlist these skills. • Teenagers' proficiency in adult tasks varies considerably from individual to individual and from task to task.	• Study academic disciplines in depth; introduce complex explanations. • Encourage discussions about social, political, and ethical issues; elicit multiple perspectives regarding issues. • Involve adolescents in activities that are similar to tasks they will eventually do as adults. • Explain how experts in a field think about key operations. • Provide the minimal guidance adolescents need to complete difficult assignments.

BASIC DEVELOPMENTAL ISSUES
Contrasting Piaget and Vygotsky

ISSUE	PIAGET	VYGOTSKY
Nature and Nurture	Piaget believed that biological maturation probably constrains the rate at which children acquire new thinking capabilities. However, his focus was on how interactions with both the physical environment (e.g., handling concrete objects) and the social environment (e.g., discussing issues with peers) promote cognitive development.	Vygotsky acknowledged that children's inherited traits and talents affect the ways in which they interpret the environment. But his theory primarily addresses the environmental conditions (e.g., engagement in challenging activities, guidance from more competent individuals, exposure to cultural interpretations) that influence cognitive growth.
Universality and Diversity	In Piaget's view, children make similar advancements in their logical reasoning capabilities despite the particular environment in which they grow up. Children vary in the ages at which they acquire new abilities, however.	From Vygotsky's perspective, the specific cognitive abilities that children acquire depend on the cultural contexts in which the children are raised and the specific activities in which they are encouraged to engage.
Qualitative and Quantitative Change	Piaget proposed that children's logical reasoning skills progress through four qualitatively distinct stages. Any particular reasoning capability continues to improve in a gradual (quantitative) fashion throughout the stage in which it first appears.	Vygotsky acknowledged that children undergo qualitative changes in their thinking. Much of his theory points to gradual and presumably quantitative improvements in skills. A child may initially find a task impossible, later be able to execute it with adult assistance, and eventually perform it independently.

more competent individuals. The distinction, then, is one of primarily self-exploration versus guided study. Children almost certainly need both kinds of experiences: opportunities to manipulate and experiment with physical phenomena and chances to draw on the wisdom of prior generations (Brainerd, 2003; Karpov & Haywood, 1998; Silcock, 2013).

What kinds of social interactions are most valuable? Both theorists saw value in interacting with people of all ages. However, Piaget emphasized the benefits of interactions with peers (who could create conflict and disequilibrium), whereas Vygotsky placed greater importance on interactions with adults and other more advanced individuals (who could support children in challenging tasks and help them make appropriate interpretations).

Some contemporary theorists have proposed that interactions with peers and adults play different roles in children's cognitive development (Damon, 1984; S. A. Gelman, Ware, Manczak, & Graham, 2013; Hartup, 2009; Rogoff, 1991). When children's development requires that they abandon old perspectives in favor of new, more complex ones (e.g., regarding their understanding of the purposes of friendship in a person's life), the conflict that often occurs among age-mates may be optimal for bringing about change. But when children's development instead requires that they learn general knowledge and new skills (e.g., on how to operate a microscope), the thoughtful, patient guidance of an informed adult may be more beneficial.

How influential is culture? Although Piaget acknowledged that different cultural groups foster different ways of thinking, he gave only modest attention to culture as a factor in development (Chapman, 1988). In Vygotsky's view, culture is of paramount importance in determining the thinking skills that children acquire. Vygotsky was more on target here. Earlier in the chapter we presented evidence to indicate that children's reasoning skills do not necessarily appear at the same ages across countries. In fact, some reasoning skills (especially those involving formal operational thought) rarely appear unless a child's culture cultivates them.

Teachers and other practitioners must keep in mind, however, that there isn't necessarily a single "best" or "right" way for a culture to promote cognitive development (Rogoff, 2003). Despite their diverse instructional practices, virtually all of the world's cultures have developed effective strategies for helping growing children acquire the knowledge and skills they need to be successful participants in society.

Educational Differences

Divergences between Piaget's and Vygotsky's core ideas are manifested in their educational implications. As you have learned, Piaget believed that educators should honor the direction of children's curiosity and allow flexibility in exploring the physical world. Vygotsky professed that educators ought to guide children in using cultural tools. In Table 6-2, you can see how teachers firmly committed to either a Piagetian or Vygotskian perspective might respond differently to similar situations.

TABLE 6-2 Teachers Taking Piagetian and Vygotskian Perspectives

OPPORTUNITY FOR LEARNING	PIAGETIAN PERSPECTIVE	VYGOTSKIAN PERSPECTIVE
A second-grade class takes a field trip to see hands-on exhibits at an aquarium. As the children walk around exhibits, the teacher recalls her plans for interacting with the children.	At the aquarium, Miss Sánchez takes children to the hands-on tide pool, advises them of rules for touching marine life, encourages them to learn about the animals, and listens intently to their conversations. She asks the parent chaperones to enforce rules that ensure the safety of children and animals but otherwise allow children to explore freely. Miss Sánchez endorses Piaget's notion that children learn a great deal based on their own curiosity.	At the aquarium, Mr. Avraham reminds the children of the words they learned back at school: *camouflage*, *hide*, *enemy*, and *disguise*. He distributes pencils and sheets of paper and asks parent chaperones to encourage children to draw pictures of animals that seem to be hiding or are well camouflaged near sand, rocks, coral, and seaweed. Mr. Avraham accepts Vygotsky's ideas that children learn a lot from using cultural tools and receiving educational support from adults who are knowledgeable about a topic.
Five-year-old Berlinda sits at a table completing a puzzle that has imprints of the shapes of pieces. She frowns as she stares at the shapes of pieces and outlines in the tray. After a few unsuccessful attempts at inserting pieces, she grows frustrated and tosses the puzzle pieces onto the floor. She returns later in the day and inspects the puzzle.	Mr. Moses concludes that Berlinda is motivated to complete puzzles. Over the next few days, he continues to make puzzles available in the classroom and observes Berlinda. He notices that she continues to select puzzles during free time and systematically improves in puzzle completion. Mr. Moses applies Piaget's ideas that adults need to be sympathetic observers of children's initiatives and make available the kinds of experiences children find interesting.	Ms. de la Cruz sits next to Berlinda and demonstrates the strategy of first locating and inserting pieces that have straight edges on the periphery and then filling in other pieces. She then stands back and encourages Berlinda to try a few pieces by herself. When Berlinda struggles, Ms. de la Cruz gently directs the girl's attention to a particular shape in the inlaid outline, and together they search for its match. Ms. de la Cruz applies Vygotsky's ideas that adults should provide carefully attuned levels of help on worthwhile tasks.
A group of 3- and 4-year-old children sit side-by-side in the sandbox, moving their vehicles this way and that and building tunnels and towers. Elliott says, "I'm going to the rocky quarry." Roz says, "My castle is getting bigger."	Mrs. Dean smiles at the children, interpreting their language as being benignly self-centered, a charming quality of early childhood that will fade as they move into concrete operations. Mrs. Dean agrees with Piaget's conclusion that children's speech is often egocentric during the preschool years.	Mr. Sidorov interprets the speech of children as externalized thought that helps guide their activities. He shares Vygotsky's view that children generally emit less audible speech with development while continuing to talk themselves through difficult tasks.

Summary

Constructive processes, readiness, challenge, and social interaction are central to the theories of both Piaget and Vygotsky. However, the two perspectives differ on the role of language in cognitive development, the relative value of free exploration versus guided activities, the comparative importance of interactions with peers versus adults, and the influence of culture. The two theories also offer different educational applications, especially with regard to scaffolding of challenging tasks.

ENHANCEDetext *self-check*

PRACTICING FOR YOUR LICENSURE EXAMINATION

Many teaching tests require students to use what they have learned about child development in responses to brief vignettes and multiple-choice questions. You can practice for your licensure examination by reading the following case study and answering a series of questions.

Adolescent Scientists

Scott Sowell has just introduced the concept of *pendulum* in his seventh-grade science class. When he asks his students to identify variables that might influence the frequency with which a pendulum swings, they suggest three possibilities: the amount of weight at the bottom, the length of the pendulum, and the "angle" from which the weight is initially dropped. You can watch this lesson in the accompanying video.

Mr. Sowell divides his students into small groups and gives each group a pendulum composed of a long string with a paper clip attached to the bottom (Figure A). He also provides extra paper clips that the students can use to increase the weight at the bottom. He gives his students the following assignment: *Design your own experiment. Think of a way to test how each one of these variables affects the frequency of swing. Then carry out your experiment.*

Jon, Marina, Paige, and Wensley are coming to grips with their task as Mr. Sowell approaches their table.

Figure A

Marina: We'll time the frequency as the seconds and the . . . um . . . what? [She looks questioningly at Mr. Sowell.]

Mr. S.: The frequency is the number of swings within a certain time limit.

The group agrees to count the number of swings during a 15-second period. After Jon determines the current length of the string, Wensley positions the pendulum 25 degrees from vertical. When Jon says "Go" and starts a stopwatch, Wensley releases the pendulum. Marina counts the number of swings until, 15 seconds

later, Jon says "Stop." Jon records the data from the first experiment: length = 49 cm, weight = 1 paper clip, angle = 25°, frequency = 22.

The group shortens the string and adds a second paper clip onto the bottom of the first clip. The students repeat their experiment and record their data: length = 36 cm, weight = 2 paper clips, angle = 45°, frequency = 25.

Wensley: What does the weight do to it?
Marina: We found out that the shorter it is and the heavier it is, the faster it goes.

Mr. Sowell joins the group and reviews its results from the first two tests.

Mr. S.: What did you change between Test 1 and Test 2?
Marina: Number of paper clips.
Mr. S.: OK, so you changed the weight. What else did you change?
Wensley: The length.
Marina: And the angle.
Mr. S.: OK, so you changed all three between the two tests. So what caused the higher frequency?
Wensley: The length.
Marina: No, I think it was the weight.
Jon: I think the weight.
Paige: The length.
Mr. S.: Why can't you look at your data and decide? [The students look at him blankly.] Take a look at the two tests. The first one had one paper clip, and the second had two. The first test had one length, and the second test had a shorter length. Why can't you come to a conclusion by looking at the two frequencies?
Marina: All of the variables changed.

Mr. Sowell nods in agreement and then moves on to another group. The four students decide to change only the weight for the next test, so they add a third paper clip to the bottom of the second. Their pendulum now looks like Figure B. They continue to perform experiments but are careful to change only one variable at a time, or so they think. In reality, each time the group adds another paper clip, the pendulum grows longer. Mr. Sowell visits the students once again.

Figure B

Mr. S.:   One thing you're testing is length, right? And another thing is weight. Look at your system. Look at how you might be making a slight mistake with weight and length. [He takes two paper clips off and then puts one back on, hanging it, as the students have done, at the bottom of the first paper clip.]

Marina: It's heavier *and* longer.

Mr. S.:   Can you think of a way to redesign your experiments so that you're changing only weight? How can you do things differently so that your pendulum doesn't get longer when you add paper clips?

Jon: Hang the second paper clip from the bottom of the string instead of from the first paper clip.

When Mr. Sowell leaves, the students add another paper clip to the pendulum, making sure that the overall length of the pendulum stays the same. They perform another test and find that the pendulum's frequency is identical to what they obtained in the preceding test. Ignoring what she has just seen, Marina concludes, "So if it's heavier, the frequency is higher."

Constructed-Response Question

1. In what ways does Mr. Sowell scaffold students' efforts during the lab activity?

Multiple-Choice Questions

2. Which one of Piaget's stages is students' reasoning most representative of?

    a. The sensorimotor stage, because students are focusing on the sensory properties of objects and using proficient motor skills in manipulating them

    b. The preoperational stage, because students use language proficiently yet do not engage in a systematic analysis of the effects of separate factors

    c. The concrete operations stage, because students are systematic in inspecting the objects but are not able to separate and control variables in their experimentation

    d. The formal operations stage, because students are displaying the pinnacle of advanced human reasoning

3. Given current perspectives on Piaget's theory, how might a teacher help students to separate and control variables?

    a. Teachers might simply wait a few years until the students mature.

    b. Teachers ought to lecture students on the merits of scientific reasoning.

    c. Teachers could give students practice in pouring liquids to and from containers of various sizes and asking students if the volume remains the same.

    d. Teachers can give students practice in separating and controlling variables, for example, by growing sunflowers under varying conditions or charting their progress in a particular athletic skill with different training regimens.

ENHANCEDetext *licensure exam*

Key Concepts

constructivism (p. 198)
clinical method (p. 198)
scheme (p. 198)
operation (p. 199)
assimilation (p. 199)
accommodation (p. 199)
equilibrium (p. 200)
disequilibrium (p. 200)
equilibration (p. 200)
goal-directed behavior (p. 202)

object permanence (p. 202)
symbolic thought (p. 202)
egocentrism (p. 203)
conservation (p. 204)
class inclusion (p. 204)
neo-Piagetian theory (p. 208)
working memory (p. 209)
central conceptual structure (p. 209)
sociocognitive conflict (p. 214)
mediation (p. 218)

cognitive tool (p. 218)
self-talk (p. 218)
inner speech (p. 218)
internalization (p. 219)
appropriation (p. 219)
zone of proximal development (ZPD) (p. 220)
sociodramatic play (p. 221)
mediated learning experience (p. 221)

scaffolding (p. 221)
guided participation (p. 223)
apprenticeship (p. 223)
cognitive apprenticeship (p. 223)
reciprocal teaching (p. 224)
authentic activity (p. 225)
individual constructivism (p. 229)
social constructivism (p. 229)

CHAPTER SEVEN

Cognitive Development: Cognitive Processes

CASE STUDY: How the United States Became a Country

Our colleague Dinah Jackson worked for many years in the Colorado public schools. At one point she asked students in grades 2 through 8 to write essays addressing the following question: *The land we live on has been here for a very long time, but the United States has been a country for only a little more than 200 years. How did the United States become a country?* Here are some of their responses:

Second grader:

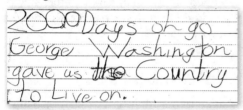

2000 Days oh go George Washington gave us the Country To Live on.

Third grader:

The pilgrims came over in 17 hundred, when they came over they bilt houses. The Idians tihout they were mean. Then they came friends and tot them stuff. Then winter came and alot died. Then some had babies. So thats how we got here.

Sixth grader:

The U.S.A. became a country by some of the British wanting to be under a different rule than of the kings. So, they sailed to the "new world" and became a new country. The only problem was that the kings from Britin still ruled the "new world". Then they had the revolutionary war They beat Britin, and became an independent country.

Eighth grader:

We became a country through different processes. Technology around the world finally caught up with the British. There were boats to travel with, navigating tools, and the hearts of men had a desire to expand. Many men had gone on expeditions across the sea. A very famous journey was that of Christopher Columbus. He discovered this land that we live. More and more people poured in, expecting instant wealth, freedom, and a right to share their opinions. Some immigrants were satisfied, others were displeased. Problems in other countries forced people to move on to this New World, such as potato famins and no freedom of religions. Stories that drifted through people grew about this country. Stories of golden roads and free land coaxed other families who were living in the slums. Unfortunately, there were slums in America. The people helped this country grow in industry, cultures, religions, and government. Inventions and books were now better than the Europeans. Dime-novels were invented, and the young people could read about heroes of this time. May the curiosity and eagerness of the children continue.

- What do the four compositions suggest about developmental changes in children's knowledge of written language?
- What do the responses indicate about growth in knowledge of American history?

Certainly the older children know *more* about the mechanics of writing and American history. But if you look closely at what the children have written, differences in the *quality* of children's writing and knowledge of history are evident as well. Whereas the third grader describes the nation's history as a list of seemingly unrelated facts, the sixth and eighth graders have pulled what they have learned into an integrated whole that hangs together. In addition, the younger children's descriptions reflect concrete understandings (e.g., the country was a gift from George Washington, the Pilgrims came over and built houses). In contrast, the eighth grader uses abstract concepts (e.g., technological progress, freedom of religion, and optimistic expectations for wealth) to explain immigration to the new land.

In this chapter our focus is on contemporary research on children's thinking. As you will discover, today's developmental scientists build on the foundational work of Piaget and Vygotsky.[1] Like these historically prominent figures, present-day theorists assume that children actively make sense of their worlds. In contrast to the methods of Piaget and Vygotsky, however, modern theorists use more precise research procedures, search for continuous changes in children's knowledge and skills within defined areas, document the efficiency of mental processes, and view children's thinking as being derived from specific experiences rather than as reflecting broadly applicable stages or social factors.

BASIC COGNITIVE PROCESSES

Do children become better able to control their attention as they grow older? Do they remember things more effectively? Does knowledge develop with age? How do changes in the brain enable improvements in learning? Such questions reflect a concern for the development of children's basic cognitive processes.

Developmental scholars in cognitive science are intrigued with these questions. **Cognitive science** is an interdisciplinary field that examines representations and operations of information in the human mind. It draws from research in psychology, neuroscience, linguistics, anthropology, artificial intelligence, and philosophy. Several frameworks within cognitive science have contributed to an understanding of children's thinking. Especially popular has been **information processing theory**, a family of perspectives that address how human beings mentally acquire, interpret, and remember information.

Information processing theories emerged in the late 1950s and early 1960s and continued to evolve in the decades that followed. Early information processing theorists drew parallels between how people think and how computers operate. As a result, computer terms are sometimes used to describe human thought processes, as with people *storing* (i.e., putting) symbolic information in memory and *retrieving* (i.e., finding) it when they need it at a later time.

Increasingly, cognitive scientists have found that people think in distinctly non-computer-like ways. Unlike most computer programs, human beings actively pursue self-chosen goals and create understandings in individual ways. Numerous information processing perspectives and other cognitive science frameworks have a *constructivist* flavor similar to that of Piaget's and Vygotsky's theories, in which children are credited with creating their own original ideas. As an example, consider the second grader's explanation in the opening case study:

> 2000 Days oh go George Washington gave us the Country to Live on.

Almost certainly, no one has told her that the United States was a gift from George Washington. Instead, she uses something she has learned—that Washington was a key figure in the country's early history—to construct what is, to her, a logical explanation of her country's origin. Furthermore, not knowing how to spell *ago*, she uses two words she does know (*oh* and *go*) to construct a reasonable (albeit incorrect) spelling. Following in the footsteps of Piaget and Vygotsky, cognitive scientists would notice the second grader's creative amalgamation of her existing ideas.

Unlike the encompassing theories of Jean Piaget and Lev Vygotsky, cognitive science has no single framework that speaks for the entire spectrum of changes we know about in

[1]Piaget's and Vygotsky's theories are examined in Chapter 6.

children's cognitive development. Yet taken together, the various perspectives offer complementary explanations of intellectual processes. Neuroscientists tell us about the networks of cells that are activated during mental and emotional processes. Scholars with expertise in artificial intelligence inform us as to the ideas and skills that appear necessary for certain transformations in thinking to occur. Information processing theorists tell us a great deal about *what* processes change over time, and sociocultural cognitive scientists explain *how* those changes occur (Gauvain, 2001; Mareschal et al., 2007; Q. Wang, 2013). In this chapter, we pull from many specific areas within cognitive science as we examine three types of abilities: basic cognitive processes, insights about thinking and strategic learning procedures, and personal theories.

Key Ideas in Cognitive Process Theories

The information processing framework portrays thinking as a sequence of mental events—an exchange of information with the environment, an internal dynamic of flowing sensations and ideas between and among separate storage systems, and the conscious oversight of mental processes by a watchful self. Figure 7-1 presents an influential representation of the human information processing system. Although information processing theorists don't always agree on the specific mechanisms involved in learning and remembering information, many of them subscribe to several points:

Input from the environment provides the raw material for learning and memory. Human beings encounter material from the environment through the senses (e.g., by seeing, hearing, or touching) and translate that raw input into more meaningful information. The first part of

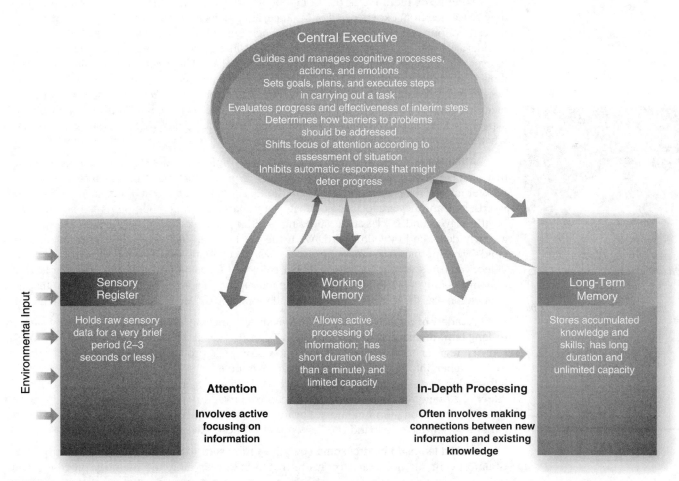

FIGURE 7-1 Model of the human information processing system. *Model based on R. C. Atkinson and Shiffrin (1968), Baddeley (1981), and Neisser (1976), with adjustments that incorporate recent emphases on executive functions (Cuevas & Bell, 2014; Garon, Bryson, & Smith, 2008; Korkman, Lahti-Nuuttila, Laasonen, Kemp, & Holdnack, 2013; Ursache, Blair, & Raver, 2012).*

Preparing for Your Licensure Examination
Your teaching test might ask you to identify key features of children's basic cognitive processes.

this process, detecting stimuli in the environment, is *sensation*. The second part, interpreting those stimuli, is *perception*.

Even the simplest interpretation (perception) of an environmental event takes time. Many theorists believe that human memory includes a mechanism that allows people to remember raw sensory data for a very short time (perhaps 2 to 3 seconds for auditory information and less than a second for visual information). This mechanism goes by a variety of names, but we'll refer to it as the **sensory register**.

In addition to a sensory register, human memory includes two other storage mechanisms: working memory and long-term memory. **Working memory** is that part of the human memory system in which people actively hold and think about new information.[2] Working memory is the mental system that allows children to solve a problem or make sense of what they are reading. It can keep information for only a very short time (probably less than a minute), so it is sometimes called *short-term memory*.[3] Working memory also appears to have a limited capacity—only a small amount of "space" in which people can hold and think about events or ideas. As an illustration, try computing the following division problem in your head:

$$59\overline{)49{,}383}$$

Did you find yourself having trouble remembering some parts of the problem while you were dealing with other parts? Did you ever arrive at the correct answer of 837? Most people cannot solve a multistep division problem like this unless they write it on paper or use a calculator. There simply isn't "room" in working memory to hold all the numbers in mind while simultaneously solving the problem.

Long-term memory is the component that allows human beings to save the things they've learned from experience. For instance, it might include such knowledge as where cookies can be found in the kitchen and how much 2 and 2 equal, as well as such skills as how to ride a bicycle and use a microscope. Things in long-term memory don't necessarily last forever, but they do last for a lengthy period, especially if revisited occasionally. In addition, long-term memory appears to have an unlimited capacity, "holding" as much information as a person could possibly need to save. To think about information previously stored in long-term memory, people must retrieve and reflect on it in working memory. Thus, although people's capacity to keep information in long-term memory may be boundless, their ability to *think about* what they've stored is limited to whatever they can hold in working memory at any one time.

Observing Children 7-1
Observe 10-year-old David's realization that attention affects memory.

ENHANCEDetext *video example*

Attention is essential to the learning process. Information processing theorists suggest that attention is the primary process through which information moves from the sensory register into working memory. When children pay attention to something, such as a teacher's words, it means they are focusing on that stimulus and ignoring other things—children outside on the playground; a classmate sneezing, sniffling, and coughing; and colorful pictures on a newly decorated bulletin board. What the teacher has said generally cannot move into a child's working memory unless he or she has paid attention to it. In an Observing Children video, you can see what happens when a child isn't focusing on the task. Ten-year-old David remembers only 3 of the 12 words that the interviewer reads to him. He realizes that his lapse in attention was the reason he did not recall more words: "My brain was turned off right now."

A variety of cognitive processes are involved in moving information from working memory to long-term memory. Whereas attention is instrumental in moving information from the sensory register to working memory, more complex processes are needed if people are to remember information for longer than a minute or so. Occasionally simply repeating information over and over (*rehearsing* it) is sufficient for its long-term storage. More often, effective storage requires making connections between new information and the ideas that already exist in long-term memory. For instance, people might use their existing knowledge either to *organize* or expand (i.e., *elaborate*) on newly acquired information.

A child learns to control some cognitive processes. Some sort of cognitive "supervisor" is almost certainly necessary to ensure that a child's learning and memory processes work

---

[2]Working memory is introduced in Chapter 6.

[3]In everyday language, people often use the term "short-term memory" to refer to memory that lasts for a few days or weeks. Notice how, in contrast, information processing theorists characterize working memory as lasting *less than a minute*.

effectively. This component, sometimes called the **central executive**, oversees the flow of information throughout the memory system and is critical for planning, decision making, and inhibition of unproductive thoughts and behaviors.[4] Executive functions have major implications for education, thus we'll give them ample consideration later in the chapter.

Cognitives development involves gradual changes in the components of the information processing system. Many information processing theorists reject Piaget's global stages. Instead, they propose that children's cognitive abilities develop primarily through ongoing *trends*. Children gradually develop efficient mental processes and strategies. Qualitative transformations that do emerge in information processing tend to be short-lived states that vary from child to child and domain to domain. In the following sections, we look at developmental trends in the human information processing system.

Sensation and Perception

Foundational development in sensory and perceptual abilities occurs during infancy and early childhood. Researchers have reached the following conclusions about this development during the early years:

Some sensory and perceptual capabilities are present at birth, and others emerge within the first few weeks or months of life. Even newborns can sense and discriminate among different sights, sounds, tastes, and smells (Turati, Gava, Valenza, & Ghirardi, 2013; Winberg, 2005). Their ability to perceive—that is, to *interpret*—this sensory information appears quite early as well. Newborns have some ability to determine the direction from which a sound originates (Morrongiello, Fenwick, Hillier, & Chance, 1994). From birth or soon afterward, infants are also sensitive to the convergence of sensory cues across different modalities (Colombo, Brez, & Curtindale, 2013). Infants prefer to watch videos of a ball bouncing and a face speaking that are synchronized with the sounds, respectively, of the bounce and actual voice, rather than to delayed or distorted recordings (Colombo et al., 2013; Streri, Coulon, & Guellaï, 2013).

Sensory and perceptual capabilities continue to improve after the newborn period. At birth visual acuity is less than 20/600, although infants can do a great deal with their limited eyesight (Courage & Adams, 1990). When they are only a few days old, they can recognize the contours of their mother's face (Colombo et al., 2013; de Heering et al., 2008; T. Field, Woodson, Greenberg, & Cohen, 1982; Werker, Maurer, & Yoshida, 2010). Vision develops rapidly, and by 6 months of age, acuity is close to 20/20 (Sokol, 1978). Visual perception is probably not fully developed until the preschool years or after, when the child's visual cortex—the part of the brain that handles complex visual information—becomes similar to that of an adult (T. L. Hickey & Peduzzi, 1987; Vedamurthy, Suttle, Alexander, & Asper, 2008).

Infants show consistent preferences for attending to certain types of stimuli, especially social ones. As early as the first week of life, infants are drawn to new and interesting stimuli, particularly social ones (Haith, 1990). Within 3 days of birth, they recognize their mother's voice and will suck vigorously on a synthetic nipple if doing so turns on a recording of her speaking (DeCasper & Fifer, 1980). In the first month, infants prefer to look at spatial configurations that look like faces, with large visible elements resembling eyes at the top (Werker et al., 2010). This early inclination to focus on social stimuli is, of course, advantageous for infants, who must focus on people in order to acquire essential social skills, language, and cultural traditions (Colombo et al., 2013).

Perceptual development is the result of biological maturation and experience. We find a clear illustration of the integration of nature and nurture in *depth perception*, the ability to perceive distances between objects in three-dimensional space. To determine when infants acquire depth perception, researchers sometimes use a *visual cliff*, a large glass table with a patterned cloth close beneath the glass on one side, and on the other side, the same pattern on the floor, farther from the glass (see Figure 7-2).

FIGURE 7-2 Visual cliff. By refusing to crawl onto the "deep" side of this glass-covered table, infants demonstrate a fear of heights.

[4]The central executive oversees the executive functions you learned about in Chapter 5.

In a classic study (E. J. Gibson & Walk, 1960), infants age 6 to 14 months were placed on a narrow platform between the "shallow" and "deep" sides of a visual cliff. Their mothers stood at one end of the table and actively coaxed them to crawl toward them, across the glass. Although most infants willingly crawled off the platform to the "shallow" side, very few ventured onto the "deep" side, suggesting that infants can perceive depth.

Certainly brain maturation is involved in depth perception. Visual acuity must be suitably developed to enable infants to perceive edges, inclines, and the relative distances between objects. Some animals that walk almost immediately after birth (e.g., chicks, lambs, baby goats) show avoidance of the deep side of a visual cliff within the first days of life (E. J. Gibson & Walk, 1960), suggesting that a neurological basis for fear of heights exists in the animal kingdom. But learning also appears to be involved. Infants who have had experience with self-locomotion, either through crawling or using a walker (a framed seat with wheels attached to the base),[5] show greater fear of drop-offs than infants without this motor experience (Bertenthal, Campos, & Kermoian, 1994; A. Dahl et al., 2013).

From an evolutionary perspective, it makes sense that both nature and nurture would leave their imprint on a child's perceptual development. Genes guide the formation of a child's brain to be receptive to certain kinds of perceptual information, such as faces, voices, and a warm, gentle touch. Actual experiences fine-tune the brain such that perceptual abilities can help the child interact in his or her world. In this manner, infants look intently at all faces from birth, quickly recognize the appearance of beloved caregivers, and later gradually distinguish among faces of individuals outside the family (Colombo et al., 2013; Werker et al., 2010).

Attention

As with changes in sensation and perception, developments in attention are due, in part, to brain maturation. The brain has three primary attention networks that emerge and interconnect over the course of development (Breckenridge, Braddick, & Atkinson, 2013; Posner, 2004; Posner & Rothbart, 2013). An *orienting system* develops in the first year of life and allows children to direct mental energies to interesting objects and events. The orienting system is at work when children look at one toy instead of another, visually track a moving ball as it rolls across the floor, and look away after inspecting a picture on the wall. An *arousal system* permits children to maintain a state of focused alertness when thinking about something. The arousal system becomes obvious when children exhibit increasingly long periods of sustained attention while exploring toys, conversing with others, and participating in lessons at school. Finally, the *executive control system*, which takes many years to mature, lets children plan ahead, keep their goals in mind, and disregard potentially distracting or irrelevant stimuli. The maturation of these three attention systems contributes to the following developmental trends:

Children's attention is affected by stimulus characteristics and, later, by familiarity. Watch as 16-month-old Corwin is captivated by an unusual, multicolored toy he finds in a paper bag in an Observing Children video. Like all human beings, infants quickly turn their attention to new, unusual, and intense stimuli—for instance, orienting to a flash of light, loud noise, or sudden movement. Once they have gained some knowledge about their everyday world, familiarity comes into play. Infants examine objects and events that are moderately different, but not too dissimilar, from those they have previously experienced, such as Daddy's face after shaving his moustache (J. Atkinson & Braddick, 2013; McCall, Kennedy, & Applebaum, 1977).[6]

With age, distractibility decreases and sustained attention increases. Children as young as 6 months exhibit focused attention for brief periods when captivated by an object or event (J. Atkinson & Braddick, 2013; Richards & Turner, 2001). Yet by and large, young children's

Observing Children 7-2
Observe how Corwin's attention is drawn to a novel object.
ENHANCEDetext *video example*

---

[5]Traditional walkers are now considered unsafe by many medical experts (Conners, Veenema, Kavanagh, Ricci, & Callahan, 2002).
[6]This tendency to prefer novelty in moderation is consistent with Piaget's belief that children can accommodate to (and learn from) new stimuli only to the extent that they can assimilate those stimuli into existing schemes.

attention moves quickly from one thing to another (Ruff & Lawson, 1990). You can see a young child's age-typical shifts in attention in an Observing Children video. As children move through the elementary school years, they become better able to sustain their attention on a particular task despite the presence of distractions (Merrill & Conners, 2013; Ruff & Lawson, 1990).

Attention becomes increasingly purposeful. By the time children are 3 or 4 months old, they show an ability to anticipate where a moving object will soon appear and focus their attention accordingly (Haith, Hazan, & Goodman, 1988; Reznick, 2009). In the preschool years they intentionally use attention to help them learn and remember something, and their ability to concentrate improves during the elementary and middle school years (Hagen & Stanovich, 1977; Kar & Srinivasan, 2013). Indeed, much of children's learning becomes a function of what they *want* to remember.

Attention develops in the context of social relationships. For two people to interact and communicate, they rely on shared understandings. Each member of the pair has an awareness of what the other person sees, knows, thinks, and feels. Such mutual understanding is first seen in shared attention and is known as **intersubjectivity**. The beginnings of this abiltiy are seen between 2 and 6 months of age, when infants and their caregivers focus on one another through eye contact, exchanges of smiles, and give-and-take in vocalizations (Adamson & McArthur, 1995; Legerstee, 2013; E. Nagy, 2008). Contributing to mutual focus are conditions in the brain and body—neurological networks devoted to social processing; the hormone oxytocin, which facilitates social recognition and bonding with other people; and *mirror neurons*, cells that activate both when a person performs a particular action and when watching another individual perform it, essentially allowing for a personal simulation of another's experience, as you might have when watching another person yawn or scratch his head (Arbib, 2005; R. Brooks & Meltzoff, 2014).

Sometime around 9 or 10 months of age, intersubjectivity takes the form of **joint attention**. At this point, an infant and caregiver can simultaneously focus on a single object, possibly a book, ball, or puppy, with both individuals monitoring each other's attention to the object and coordinating their behaviors toward the target (Deák, Triesch, Krasno, de Barbaro, & Robledo, 2013; Trevarthen & Hubley, 1978). You can see joint attention in action as 16-month-old Corwin and his mother read a book in an Observing Children video. Young children gather information about the identity, names, and characteristics of objects during joint attention. When an adult uses a word that a toddler has never heard before, the toddler is apt to look at the speaker's face and follow his or her line of vision to the object being inspected. In this way, children learn many new object labels (Kwisthout, Vogt, Haselager, & Dijkstra, 2008; Salley, Panneton, & Colombo, 2013).

At age 1, infants engage in **social referencing**, the act of looking at someone else for clues about how to respond to and feel about an object or event (Feinman, 1992; Schmitow & Stenberg, 2013). Children are most likely to engage in social referencing when they encounter a new and uncertain situation. In one study (Klinnert, 1984), 1- and 1½-year-old infants were shown three new toys to which their mothers had been instructed to respond with a happy, fearful, or neutral expression. Upon seeing each new toy, most infants looked at their mother and chose actions consistent with her response. They typically moved toward the toy if Mom showed pleasure, but moved away from it if she showed fear.

Working Memory and the Central Executive

Working memory and the central executive are closely connected and jointly responsible for what children pay attention to, how they think about information, and how well they remember things. Three developmental trends in working memory and the central executive enable children to handle increasingly complex cognitive tasks with age:

Processing speed increases. As youngsters move through childhood, they execute many cognitive processes more quickly and efficiently than they did in earlier years (Fry & Hale, 1996; Kail, McBride-Chang, Ferrer, Cho, & Shu, 2013). Some of this increased speed is undoubtedly due to the genetically driven *myelination* of brain neurons, whereby

Observing Children 7-3
Observe Maddie's age-typical shifts in attention.
ENHANCEDetext *video example*

Observing Children 7-4
Watch joint attention in a mother–infant pair.
ENHANCEDetext video example

FOR FURTHER EXPLORATION . . .

Read about the role of attention and other cognitive processes in social learning.

ENHANCEDetext
content extension

insulation grows around their axons, the long fibers that carry impulses to neighboring cells.[7] Experience and practice are involved as well. By practicing certain mental and physical tasks, children and adolescents develop **automatization** over relevant processes. In this manner, children learn to perform familiar tasks rapidly and with little or no conscious effort. Once thoughts and actions become automatized, they take up very little "space" in working memory, enabling children to think about other, more challenging elements of a task.

As an example of the benefits of automatization, consider how children's reading ability improves over time. When children first begin to read, they devote considerable mental effort to identifying the words on the page—for instance, figuring out what the letters *f-r-i-e-n-d* spell—and may recall little about the *meaning* of what they've read. But with increasing exposure to a variety of reading materials, word identification gradually becomes an automatized process, such that children immediately recognize most of the words they see. At this point, they can focus their efforts on understanding what they're reading.

The capacity of working memory increases with age. One common way of measuring the capacity of working memory is to ask people to remember a sequence of unrelated items, perhaps a series of digits or unrelated objects or words. Toddlers remember more items than infants can, older children remember more items than younger children can, and adolescents remember even more. Much of this increase in working memory capacity may be due to the fact that cognitive processes become faster and more efficient with age and so take up less "room" (Cowan, 2014). Basic maturational processes in the brain, including myelination, synaptic pruning, and increased connections among neurons, also contribute to the speed of processing and hence to working memory capacity (Luna, 2009; Myatchin & Lagae, 2013).[8]

The central executive increasingly takes charge of cognitive processes. Thanks in large part to continuing maturation of the brain, youngsters gain increasing control of their cognitive processes (Korkman et al., 2013; Zelazo, Müller, Frye, & Marcovitch, 2003). With such control comes a variety of new and improved abilities. Youngsters become better able to plan and direct their actions toward goals and standards. They also better inhibit inappropriate thoughts and behaviors. And they begin to reflect on their thinking, as we'll see in our discussion of *metacognition* later in the chapter. Keep in mind, however, that the central executive is still a "work in progress" at the end of the high school years and does not fully mature until well into adulthood.

Long-Term Memory

Some knowledge in long-term memory is virtually universal across children. Children around the globe learn that people typically have two legs but cats and dogs have four. Other understandings depend on children's unique experiences and the cultural contexts in which they grow. In the four children's compositions in the opening case study, we see a perspective on early European colonization rather than one on invasion and conquest, the latter of which might occur in children living in certain Native American communities. Regardless of their particular background, all children place a mounting number of ideas in memory. The following trends in long-term memory enhance children's ability to adapt in the world:

The capacity to remember information in long-term memory appears very early and improves with age. Before birth, children have simple abilities to learn and remember experiences. For instance, infants develop some initial taste preferences based on flavors they were exposed to prenatally in the amniotic fluid (as a result of their mother's diet; Mennella, Jagnow, & Beauchamp, 2001). Similarly, encounters with their mother's speech, muffled in the womb, help infants recognize their mother's voice after birth (Kisilevsky et al., 2009; Partanen et al., 2013).

In infancy, the capacity for long-term memory manifests itself in additional ways. When a ribbon connected to a mobile is tied to a 2-month-old baby's foot, the baby easily learns that kicking makes the mobile move and remembers the connection over a period of several days—even longer if given an occasional reminder (Rovee-Collier, 1999). At 6 months, infants can also recall and imitate actions they saw 24 hours earlier, and their ability to remember the movements increases in the months that follow. By the time children reach their second birthday, they are able

---

[7]Chapter 5 describes myelination, the maturational process in which a fatty sheath grows around neurons and allows messages to be transmitted rapidly.

[8]Chapter 5 introduces synaptic pruning as the universal process in brain development whereby unused synapses wither away.

to retain a complex sequence of actions for a year or more (Bauer, De-Boer, & Lukowski, 2007). Such advancements in long-term memory ability are probably due, in large part, to brain maturation (Fujioka, Mourad, & Trainor, 2011; Lavenex & Banta Lavenex, 2013).

Children gain conscious awareness of events. Early memories are by and large acquired through an *implicit memory* process—infants are not knowingly aware that they are learning information, and they cannot articulate their memories in words (Lloyd & Newcombe, 2009). Implicit memories are evident in infants' responses to parents over unfamiliar adults, preferences for some foods above others, and selection of a favorite blanket when tired. Yet as they grow, children cannot necessarily recall these memories in any detail. In fact, children typically have little if any *conscious* recall of things that happened during their first 2 years—a phenomenon known as **infantile amnesia.** For much of the preschool period as well, recall of past events continues to be sketchy. A variety of explanations for infantile amnesia have been offered, including the immaturity of brain structures and the absence of relevant cues later in life necessary for triggering recollections from infancy (Lavenex & Banta Lavenex, 2013; H. L. Williams & Conway, 2009). The condition of infantile amnesia is slowly overcome as the child develops symbolic thinking, an emerging sense of self, and related abilities for cataloging personal memories.

Of course, the fact that children cannot recall their earliest experiences does not mean that these memories do not serve a vital function in life. On the contrary, first experiences form the foundation of long-term knowledge (Hayne & Simcock, 2009). Rudimentary bonds with parents teach children about other people's trustworthiness. Regularities in the physical world let children anticipate the texture and properties of water, sand, wood, and plastic. Exposure to language and storybooks entice children to participate in conversation and consume literature. Thus the early years of life yield images, information, and habits that guide children's behavior and expectations for many years to come.

Particularly when people engage children in discussions about shared experiences, children's awareness of past events improves dramatically (M. L. Howe, Courage, & Rooksby, 2009; K. Nelson, 1996b). It appears that talking about events enables children to store the events in a verbal (language-based) form, making circumstances easier to recall. Initially, parents do most of the work, reminiscing, asking questions, and prompting recall, but by the time children are 3 years old, children are active participants in conversations about the past (Fivush, 2009). By the end of the preschool years, young children can typically give detailed narratives of important events, for example, what they did on their last birthday. These memories converge into an **autobiographical self,** a mental "history" of important events in one's life. The autobiographical self continues to change with development, adding details during middle childhood and coherence to life events during adolescence (Y. Chen, McAnally, & Reese, 2013). The manner in which adults interpret events for a child depends on cultural traditions, as you can read about in the Development in Culture feature "Memory."

The amount of knowledge stored in long-term memory increases many times over. This trend is an expected one, and the four essays in the opening case study illustrate it clearly. Yet the obviousness of this increase does not diminish its importance. Long-term memory provides the **knowledge base** from which children draw as they respond to new situations. As their knowledge base grows, children interpret new events with greater accuracy, sophistication, and maturity. A deeper knowledge base also allows for greater intricacy in how children represent aspects of their life. Artifact 7-1 allows you to compare the maps that three children drew of their hometown.

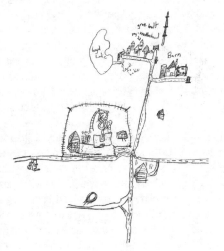

ARTIFACT 7-1 Developmental change in children's knowledge base. Three children drew maps of their hometown, Loveland, Colorado. The first grader's map (top) includes only a few features of her town that she knows well (her house and school, nearby mountains) and does not try to represent relative distances between locations. The third grader's map (middle) shows many features of his immediate neighborhood and their proximity to one another. The seventh grader's map (bottom) encompasses numerous town landmarks and their relative locations on major streets. It also makes greater use of symbols—single lines for roads, squares for buildings, and distinctive letter *M*s to indicate McDonald's restaurants. *Maps courtesy of Dinah Jackson.*

DEVELOPMENT IN CULTURE
Memory

Across a wide range of circumstances, children develop common memory characteristics, including an increasingly efficient working memory capacity and an expanding knowledge base. Coexisting with these common trends are cultural variations in memory.

Cultural settings give children distinct routines that affect the *content* of their memories. At the kitchen table, on city streets, and in the classroom, children form images and recollections of how institutions operate. Distinct *methods* of remembering are acquired during cultural exchanges. Repeated exposure to information is sufficient to form memories when meaningful patterns are present in the material. Children easily learn and remember songs, stories, dances, woodcarvings, games, and configurations of objects in familiar environments (Gaunt, 2006; Kearins, 1981; Rogoff, 2003). In industrialized societies, children are generally taught to use memory strategies for learning and retrieving abstract information (Bjorklund, Dukes, & Brown, 2009). They may be encouraged to listen for the main point, to take notes during lectures, and to use memory tricks.

Cultural experiences also influence children's autobiographical memory. As children reminisce with their parents and other adults, they learn customs related to sharing life stories (Q. Wang, 2013). Children regularly asked to talk about personal experiences retain especially early images of their lives. The Māori, an indigenous people of New Zealand, speak in great detail with children about such significant experiences as the occasion of their birth (E. Reese, Hayne, & MacDonald, 2008). Of course, children cannot recall their own births but these discussions prompt Maori children to conjure up past events. The earliest memories of Māori adults date back to 2½ years on average whereas other cultures exhibit later ages for first memories—typically at about 3½ to 4 years (E. Reese et al., 2008).

The focus of adults' questions affects the content of children's memories. Many mothers from European American families prompt children with numerous questions about how events unfolded and why people acted as they did. In the following interaction, a European American mother asks her 3-year-old son to expand on his description of their shared experience at a craft fair:

Mother:	Tell me about the craft fair. Mommy and Daddy went to the craft fair. What did we go there for, do you remember?
Child:	Yeah. Christmas time.
Mother:	It was Christmas time, we were getting some Christmas presents. Did you want to be there?
Child:	No.
Mother:	And what did you start to do?
Child:	Hit.
Mother:	And you started to hit and what else?
Child:	Scratch.
Mother:	Do you remember why you were so mad?
Child:	Yell.
Mother:	You were yelling very loud, I sure agree with that.
Child:	And crying.
Mother:	And crying too. Why were you so mad?
Child:	Because I just want to do whatever I want to do.
Mother:	You want to do whatever you want to do. I see.[a] (dialogue is from Q. Wang, 2006, p. 186)

DO YOU REMEMBER WHEN? As this girl talks with her mother about an event they experienced together, she develops memorable images of her childhood.

With each question and comment, the mother scaffolds an interpretation of the events—the boy hit, scratched, and yelled because he did not want to be at the fair. Parents from European American families ask a lot of questions that evoke details from children, particularly about children's personal feelings and motivations (Fivush, 2009; M. L. Howe et al., 2009; Q. Wang, 2006).

Parents from several other cultures do not request details and instead concentrate on other features of events. In the following conversation, a Chinese mother asks her 3-year-old son to focus on the moral dimensions of an event:

Mother:	What did Teacher Lin tell you at school?
Child:	"Qiu Shao-yun." He didn't move even when his body was on fire.
Mother:	The teacher taught you to follow the rules, right?
Child:	Um.
Mother:	Then why did you cry last night?
Child:	You and Grandma didn't let me watch TV.
Mother:	Do you know why we didn't let you watch TV?
Child:	You were worried that my eyes would get hurt. I wanted to watch "Chao-Tian-Men." I was mad. I insisted on watching it.
Mother:	So you got spanked, right?
Child:	Um.[a] (dialogue is from Q. Wang, 2006, p. 186)

This mother asks her son to articulate a moral lesson learned at school and infer its relevance to home life. She invites him to speculate on why she enforced a restriction on television viewing and encourages him to notice the connection between his misbehavior and the punishment he received. Many parents from Chinese families regularly ask their children to think about moral lessons and shared experiences with family members (Fivush, 2009; M. L. Howe et al., 2009; Q. Wang, 2006).

In large part through discussions with parents about past experiences, young children form distinct memories. These conversations convey all sorts of cultural principles, such as the significance of personal motivations or moral codes. Generally those parents who repeatedly ask young children to elaborate on past experiences foster their children's ability to narrate life experiences (Fivush, 2009).

An inspection of the maps reveals definite age-related increases in children's knowledge about their community (also see Forbes, Ormrod, Bernardi, Taylor, & Jackson, 1999; Liben, 2009; Liben & Downs, 2003).

On average, older children and adults learn new information and skills more easily than do younger children. A key reason is that they have more knowledge that they can use to make sense of new information and experiences (Kail, 1990). When the tables are turned—when young children know more about a particular topic than older children or adults do—the younger children are often the more effective learners (Chi, 1978; H. Waters, & Waters, 2010). In one classic study, elementary and middle school children who were expert chess players could better remember where chess pieces were located on a chess board than could college-educated adults who were relative novices at chess (Chi, 1978).

Children's knowledge about the world becomes increasingly integrated. Children begin categorizing their experiences as early as 3 or 4 months of age (more about this point a bit later). Even so, much of what young children know about the world consists of separate, isolated facts. In contrast, older children's knowledge includes many associations and interrelationships among ideas (Bjorklund, 1987; Darling, Parker, Goodall, Havelka, & Allen, 2014; M. Schneider & Hardy, 2013; M. C. Wimmer & Howe, 2009). This developmental change is undoubtedly one reason why older children can think more logically and draw inferences more readily: They have a more cohesive understanding of the world around them.

As an example, let's return to the essays in the opening case study. Notice how the third grader presents a chronological list of events without any attempt at tying them together:

> The Idiuns thout they were mean. Then they came friends, and tot them stuff. Then winter came, and alot died. Then some had babies.

In contrast, the eighth grader identifies and implies cause-and-effect relationships among events:

> More and more people poured in, expecting instant wealth, freedom, and a right to share their opinions. Some immigrants were satisfied, others were displeased. Problems in other countries forced people to move on to this New World, such as potato famins and no freedom of religions. Stories that drifted through people grew about this country. Stories of golden roads and free land coaxed other families who were living in the slums.

Children and adults alike organize some aspects of their knowledge into schemas and scripts. **Schemas** are tightly integrated ideas about specific objects or situations.[9] You might have a schema for what a typical horse looks like (e.g., it's a certain height, and it has a mane and an elongated head) and a separate schema for what a typical office contains (it probably has a desk, computer, bookshelves, and file cabinets). **Scripts** encompass knowledge about the predictable sequence of events related to particular activities. You may have a script related to how weddings typically proceed, and even many 3-year-olds can tell you what typically happens when you go to McDonald's for a meal (K. Nelson, 1997). Schemas and scripts help children make sense of their experiences, understand stories, and predict what is likely to happen on future occasions (Zampini, Suttora, D'Odorico, & Zanchi, 2013).

Schemas and scripts increase in number and complexity with development (Flavell, Miller, & Miller, 2002; Hudson & Mayhew, 2009). Toddlers can act out typical scenarios (scripts) with toys long before they have the verbal skills to describe what they are doing (Bauer & Dow, 1994). As children get older, their mental structures are less tied to physical actions and perceptual qualities and more detailed, organized, and flexible as representations (Schwartz & Shaul, 2013). Whereas a toddler boy has a simple script for ordering and eating at a fast-food restaurant, when he becomes a preschooler, he expands his script to include a drive-through option, slightly different routines for different restaurants, and a few other steps, including paying the bill and getting napkins ahead of time and using the restroom afterward.

Preparing for Your Licensure Examination
Your teaching test may ask you to recognize how children use organized networks of ideas to represent their knowledge.

---

[9]From an information processing perspective, schemas are similar, but not identical, to Piaget's *schemes*. From an information processing perspective, *schemas* are organized mental representations of a phenomenon. In Piaget's theory, a *scheme* is an organized group of similar actions or thoughts that are used repeatedly in response to something in the environment.

Reasoning

From an information processing perspective, many developmental changes occur in **reasoning**, the ability to think logically and weigh evidence soundly when drawing conclusions. Here we look at three trends in reasoning:

Logical thinking abilities improve with age. The initial manifestations of logical thinking appear in infancy and are related to perceptions of physical events. Long before their first birthdays children can perceive a cause-and-effect relationship in a sequence of events. When 6-month-olds see one object hit another and watch the second object move immediately after impact, they seem to understand that the first object has essentially "launched" the second one (L. B. Cohen & Cashon, 2006; Schlottmann, Ray, & Surian, 2012).

By preschool age, children can draw logical inferences from verbal information. For instance, they draw conclusions about events depicted in children's stories (M. Donaldson, 1978; R. Gelman & Baillargeon, 1983; McKie, Butty, & Green, 2012). However, preschoolers and elementary schoolchildren do not always draw *correct* inferences, and they have difficulty distinguishing between what *must* be true versus what *might* be true given the evidence before them (Galotti, Komatsu, & Voelz, 1997; Pillow, 2002). Even later in childhood and adolescence, reasoning ability varies widely from one young person to another, and it is often influenced by the circumstances of the situation as well as by personal motives, beliefs, and biases (Goswami, 2011; Kail, 2013; Kuhn & Franklin, 2006; Steegen & De Neys, 2012).

Reasoning increasingly incorporates symbols. In Piaget's influential theory of cognitive development, the content of infants' and toddlers' schemes is predominantly sensorimotor—that is, based on perceptions and behaviors.[10] Near the end of the sensorimotor stage (at about 18 months, Piaget suggested), children begin to think in terms of **symbols**, mental entities (e.g., words) that do not strictly reflect the perceptual and behavioral qualities of the objects or events they represent (e.g., a "ball" is called by different names in different languages). Such symbolic thought enables children to infer characteristics they haven't directly observed. When a 3-year-old who is familiar with common household pets hears her father use the word "cat," she might easily visualize a small animal that has pointy ears and whiskers, walks on four legs, and purrs.

Piaget was probably correct in believing that sensorimotor images of objects and events precede symbolic representations. However, the shift from one to the other is much more gradual than Piaget thought. For one thing, a great deal of learning occurs before children are able to use symbols. Infants sense all sorts of regularities in the world before they can put these observations into words. Infants detect regularities in the probabilities of certain events (e.g., if shown a box full of mainly red ping-pong balls and just a couple of white balls, 6- to 12-month-old infants appear surprised, and look longer, when an adult extracts mainly white balls (F. Xu & Kushnir, 2013).

Little by little, children become conscious of their observations in the world and the habits and presumed motivations of other people. Long before children reach school age, they begin to use such symbols as words, numbers, pictures, and miniature models to represent real-life objects and events (DeLoache, 2011; K. Nelson, 1996a; Tsubota & Chen, 2012). Yet when children begin elementary school, they struggle with some of the symbols they encounter. For example, elementary school teachers often use blocks and other concrete objects to represent numbers or mathematical operations, but not all kindergartners and first graders make the connection between these objects and the intended concepts (DeLoache, Miller, & Rosengren, 1997). As children grow older, they use symbols to think, remember, and solve problems more frequently and with greater expertise. Eventually, their symbolic abilities allow them to transcend everyday realities, think about what could or should happen in the future, and develop abstract understandings about their physical and social worlds (Bandura, 2006; Kuhn, 2009; Vallotton & Ayoub, 2010).

Gestures sometimes foreshadow more sophisticated reasoning. As children make the transition to more advanced forms of reasoning—perhaps about traditional Piagetian tasks or mathematical problems—they often show reasoning in their gestures before they show it in their speech (Goldin-Meadow, 2006; Pine, Lufkin, Kirk, & Messer, 2007). Gestures provide

---

[10] Piaget's description of sensorimotor thinking is introduced in Chapter 6.

a way for children to "experiment" (cognitively) with new ideas. Gestures may also alleviate the strain on working memory as children wrestle with more complex ways of thinking (Goldin-Meadow, 2006; G. O'Neill & Miller, 2013).

Facilitating Basic Cognitive Processes

Our discussion of information processing theories leads to several implications for working with children and adolescents:

Observing Children 7-5

See examples of safe environments for infants and young children.

ENHANCEDetext *video example*

• **Provide a variety of sensory experiences for infants and young children.** In the first years of life, children learn many things about the physical world through direct contact—by looking, listening, feeling, tasting, and smelling. Experiences required for perceptual development are *not* those that involve intense, nonstop stimulation, however. Instead, needed arrangements are ones that children encounter in any reasonably nurturing setting—everyday contact with the expressive faces and voices of caregivers, a loving touch, a warm bath, cheerful music, and a variety of objects—maybe toys, boxes, and pots and pans from the kitchen. Thus, adults can offer an interesting environment but not overdo it. You can see examples of safe environments for young children in an Observing Children video. In addition, the Development and Practice feature "Providing Appropriate Stimulation for Infants and Young Children" offers several suggestions for structuring materials and settings for small children.

• **Regularly engage infants in social exchanges.** In the early months, social interaction with infants may simply involve making eye contact, smiling and vocalizing, extending a finger to be grabbed, and holding infants in a different way in response to a shift in their

DEVELOPMENT AND PRACTICE
Providing Appropriate Stimulation for Infants and Young Children

Give children choice in sensory experiences.

- A home caregiver offers a variety of simple toys for infants to explore. She places several items within reach and respects infants' occasional rejection of one thing or another. (Infancy)
- A preschool teacher makes available a variety of sensory materials that children can observe, touch, smell, and handle. The teacher includes jars that contain various scents (e.g., herbs, vanilla, and orange slices), sound boxes with small objects (e.g., rice, beans, and coarse salt), and a water table with funnels, containers, and pouring toys. (Early Childhood)

Allow children periods of quiet and calm.

- A teacher in an infant center realizes that his room is usually busy and noisy. Knowing that too much stimulation can be unsettling, he monitors the sights, sounds, textures, and smells that are present at any one time. He tones down the environment a bit when introducing a new child to the center and in afternoon naptime. (Infancy)
- A preschool teacher includes a brief rest period after snack time to allow children to recharge their batteries. Children who need to sleep lie down on mats, while non-nappers complete puzzles or participate in other quiet activities. (Early Childhood)

Avoid the "better baby" trap.

- A child care provider attends a workshop on brain development, where several presenters make a pitch for products that are supposedly essential for superior intellectual growth. Fortunately, she knows enough about cognitive development to realize that children benefit from a wide variety of toys, and that an intensive "sensory stimulation" approach is *not* in children's best interest. (Infancy)

- A toddler teacher designs his curriculum carefully, exposing children to a wide range of developmentally appropriate objects, including blocks, dolls, trucks, durable books, and coloring materials. When parents ask about his plans to "multiply the intelligence" of children, he explains that he does not use flash cards or structured academic lessons with toddlers. Instead, he cultivates their intelligence through a carefully selected curriculum that fosters children's natural curiosity and nurtures their budding sense of self, language development, and knowledge of the world. (Infancy)

Recognize that a child's temperament and cultural experiences help determine the stimulation that is optimal for him or her.

- A teacher in a child care center has noticed that some of the toddlers in her group seem to respond to sensory overload by getting excited and animated, whereas others fuss, go to sleep, or in some other way indicate that they have had enough. Although she prefers a quiet, peaceful room, one of her coworkers enjoys lively salsa music and often plays it while the children are awake. The two teachers often compare notes about how individual children respond to quiet versus busy environments. (Infancy)
- A kindergarten teacher observes that children vary in how they respond to discussions during story time. Some children are animated and make spontaneous comments, whereas others remain still and quiet. The teacher realizes that the children have acquired customs at home for responding to authority figures that foster their quiet respect. The teacher makes a point to ask silent children about their perceptions of stories at the end of the lesson, as the large group disperses. (Early Childhood)

position. Later it is includes jointly looking at, manipulating, experimenting with, and talking about objects. Such activities, simple though they may be, foster the intersubjectivity essential for later information sharing (Hobson, 2004; K. Nelson, 2005; Øberg, Blanchard, & Obstfelder, 2014; R. A. Thompson & Virmani, 2010).

• **Watch for and address significant problems in perception.** By the time they enter preschool, most but not all children will have been previously screened by a pediatrician or nurse for limitations in seeing and hearing or unusual sensitivities to tastes, smells, sights, or tactile sensations (Rine & Wiener-Vacher, 2013; Turnbull, Turnbull, & Wehmeyer, 2010). Yet not every child with a perceptual impairment will have been identified, and teachers who suspect a limitation will want to advise appropriate specialists at the school about a conceivable need for assessment. Educators themselves can do a lot for children who have sensory and perceptual limitations. A teacher might relocate a girl who complains about the muted noises of a fan to a different part of the classroom. A school psychologist might refer a boy with limited language to an audiologist. Another girl with tactile sensitivities might dislike getting her hands dirty but be willing to tolerate a temporary mess when engaged in a cooking lesson.

• **Talk with children about their experiences.** Children begin to talk about their experiences almost as soon as they speak, and by age 2 they do it fairly often (van den Broek, Bauer, & Bourg, 1997). Adults should join in: Talking with children about shared experiences not only enhances children's memories of what they are seeing and doing but also helps children interpret their experiences in culturally rich ways (Fivush, 2009; Ota & Austin, 2013).

• **Encourage children to pay to attention to things that are important for them to know.** As we've seen, attention is a critical factor in learning. Yet many children, young ones especially, are easily distracted from planned activities by extraneous sights and sounds. Even highly motivated high school students can't keep their minds on a single task indefinitely. Several strategies for helping children focus their attention are presented in the Development and Practice feature "Getting and Keeping Children's Attention."

Preparing for Your Licensure Examination
Your teaching test may ask you how to address children's basic cognitive processes during instruction.

• **Relate new information to children's existing knowledge.** People of all ages learn new information more effectively when they relate it to what they already know. Yet children don't always make meaningful connections on their own. For instance, they may not realize that subtraction is simply the reverse of addition or that Shakespeare's *Romeo and Juliet* is in some ways similar to modern-day ethnic clashes around the world. By pointing out such connections, adults can foster a more integrated knowledge base (Ormrod, 2008; K. L. Roberts, 2013; Vosniadou, 2009).

• **Remember that children think about only a small amount of information at any one time.** Although working memory capacity increases during childhood, young people can think about only a limited amount of material at once. Thus teachers should pace any presentation of new information slowly enough that the children have time to "process" it all. Educators might also write complex directions or problems on a chalkboard or ask children to write them on paper or on mobile devices if available. Because individual differences in students' working memory capacity can be sizable, it behooves teachers to monitor everyone's comprehension of interim steps on complex tasks (Cowan, 2014). When teachers determine that students cannot complete a complicated learning objective because they have not mastered constituent skills (and therefore must use up scarce working memory on rudimentary parts of the task), teachers might scaffold the lower-level skills (e.g., with calculators or audio recordings of a written passage), provide practice on the skills ahead of time (e.g., with worksheets or computer programs), or assign another task in which the higher-order learning objective is maintained with less demand on prerequisite skills.

• **Give children ongoing practice in basic skills.** Some skills are so fundamental that children must be able to retrieve them effortlessly. To write well, children should be able to form letters and words without having to stop and think about how to make an uppercase *G* or spell the word *friend*. And to solve mathematical word problems, they should have such number facts as "2 + 4 = 6" and "5 × 9 = 45" on the tips of

DEVELOPMENT AND PRACTICE
Getting and Keeping Children's Attention

Capture children's interest with bright colors, intriguing sounds, and objects that invite exploration.

- A second-grade music teacher provides several instruments (e.g., a xylophone, toy guitar, and set of drums) for children to explore. The teacher also allows the children to take turns playing on a piano keyboard. (Middle Childhood)
- A fourth-grade teacher takes his class on a trip to a local pond to create small biospheres. Children fill their jars with water, mud, and algae. During the following weeks, the children observe changes in the color of water, growth of plants, and emergence of snails. (Middle Childhood)

Minimize loud noises and potential distractions when working with children who are easily diverted from task completion.

- A school psychologist is administering a battery of tests to an easily distracted 7-year-old boy who is suspected of having a learning disability. Before the testing session, the psychologist puts away the Russian nesting dolls that decorate her office shelves. She also removes the testing materials from sight, putting items in front of the boy only when it is time to use them. (Middle Childhood)
- When administering a test at the end of a term, a high school mathematics teacher closes the classroom door, answers questions individually in a hushed voice, and reminds students to remain quiet while waiting for others to finish. (Late Adolescence)

Present stimulating activities in which children *want* to pay attention.

- In a unit on nutrition, a high school biology teacher has students determine the nutritional value of menu items at a popular local fast-food restaurant. (Late Adolescence)
- In a photo editing class, high school students are especially engaged when asked to help with the yearbook. Students design page spreads, crop photos, and apply special effects on images. (Late Adolescence)

Get children physically involved in lessons.

- A middle school history teacher plans a special event late in the school year when all of his students will "go back in time" to the American Civil War. In preparation for the occasion, the students spend several weeks learning about the Battle of Gettysburg, researching typical dress and meals of that era, gathering appropriate clothing and equipment, and preparing snacks and lunches. On the day of the "battle," students assume the roles of Union and Confederate soldiers, government officials, merchants, housewives, and doctors and nurses. (Early Adolescence)
- In an earth systems class, students go outside to examine the relationships among ecological systems: a hydrosphere (e.g., pond), a biosphere (e.g., tree), and a geosphere (e.g., floodplain). The teacher gives students a worksheet and asks them to describe and draw the different systems and speculate about their interdependences. (Late Adolescence)

Incorporate a variety of types of activities into the schedule.

- After explaining how to calculate the area of a square and rectangle, a fourth-grade teacher has her students practice calculating area in word problems. She then breaks the class into groups. Each group is given a tape measure and calculator and asked to determine the area of the classroom floor, excluding those parts of the floor covered by cabinets. To complete the task, the students must divide the room into several smaller rectangles, compute the area of each rectangle separately, and add the figures together. (Middle Childhood)
- In a high school drama class, a teacher introduces students to forms of comedy. Students watch and critique a brief recording of a stand-up comedian and then read a couple of pages from a comedic play. Students end the lesson by forming teams and performing brief improvisational skits about awkward high school moments. (Late Adolescence)

Provide breaks during sedentary activities.

- To provide practice with the alphabet, a kindergarten teacher occasionally has students make letters with their bodies: one child standing with arms extended up and out to make a *Y*, two children bending over and joining hands to form an *M*, and so on. (Early Childhood)
- After a class discussion about a book they are reading together, a middle school literacy teacher allows students to move quietly around the room as they plan the key ideas that they will elaborate on in written reports. (Early Adolescence)

their tongues. Typically, children automatize basic skills by using and practicing them (J. C. Anderson, 1983; Ruitenberg, Abrahamse, & Verwey, 2013; W. Schneider & Shiffrin, 1977). This is definitely *not* to say that teachers should fill each day with endless drill-and-practice exercises involving isolated facts and procedures. Automatization can occur just as readily when the basics are embedded in a variety of stimulating, challenging (and perhaps authentic) activities—counting crops grown in the school garden, calculating profits in the school snack bar, or writing birthday wishes to the parent of a classmate who is stationed abroad on military assignment.

• **When it's important to obtain accurate recollections from children, ask questions that don't presume an answer.** Because young children are impressionable, what adults say to them can influence their memories. Imagine that a man identified as "Sam Stone" briefly visits a preschool classroom. He comments on the story the teacher is reading to the children, strolls around the perimeter of the room, waves good-bye, and leaves. Later another adult asks, "When Sam Stone got that bear dirty, did he do it on purpose or was it an accident?" and "Was Sam Stone happy or sad that he got the bear dirty?" When asked such questions, children may recall that Sam soiled a teddy bear, even though he never touched a stuffed animal during his visit (Leichtman & Ceci, 1995, p. 571). Such susceptibility to leading questions is more common in 3- and 4-year-olds than in 5- and 6-year-olds.

As you might expect, careful questioning is a serious concern for police officers and attorneys when young children are thought to be victims or witnesses of a crime. Rather than phrasing pointed questions about who did what, criminal justice professionals are advised to follow strict protocols, for example, by first establishing rapport and then asking children to tell them what happened in their own words and asking follow-up questions based on the children's lead (J. Anderson et al., 2010). Teachers can show the same restraint when talking with young children about injuries on the playground—not jumping to conclusions, talking with children individually, beginning with general requests for information, and so forth.

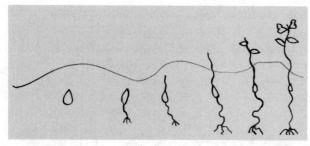

ARTIFACT 7-2 Noah's sprout. Eight-year-old Noah draws a seed becoming a plant. His picture reveals understandings that roots typically go down before a stalk grows up and that leaves gradually increase in size and number.

• **When assessing what children are ready to learn, consider not only what they say but also how they act and what they create.** Imagine a 6-year-old who said that a tall, thin glass had more water than a short, wide dish because of the height difference between the two containers. At the same time, she gestured that the tall container had a smaller diameter than the short one. Such discrepancies in what children say and do suggest a possible readiness for developing new ideas—for instance, a readiness for acquiring conservation of liquid (Goldin-Meadow, 1997; Goldin-Meadow et al., 2012). In some instances adults might assess children's current knowledge by asking them to draw rather than describe what they have learned. As you can see in Artifact 7-2, 8-year-old Noah understands sequences in plant germination and growth.

• **Solidify children's knowledge with brief classroom tests.** Considerable research indicates that taking tests can help children remember material (Roediger, McDermott, & McDaniel, 2011). Apparently, testing fosters mental processing as students search their memory banks for relevant clues. Although it can be time-intensive for teachers to develop and grade tests, many computer programs include assessments at the end of each lesson, the completion of which enhances students' learning (J. Jia et al., 2013). Even self-testing can improve memory of studied material, thus, students can be shown how to ask themselves pertinent questions as they read (M. Smith, Roediger, & Karpicke, 2013).

Exceptionalities in Information Processing

Every child learns in his or her own way. But the information processing capabilities of a few children are sufficiently different from those of peers that they require specially adapted instructional practices and materials.[11] Here we consider two kinds of exceptionalities in information processing: learning disabilities and attention-deficit hyperactivity disorder.

Learning Disabilities

A **learning disability** is a significant "ongoing difficulty with one or more cognitive processes that cannot be attributed to a sensory impairment, a general intellectual disability, an emotional or behavioral disorder, or lack of instruction. This difficulty interferes with academic achievement to such a degree that special educational services are warranted (E. K. Anderson, 2013; Sotelo-Dynega, Flanagan, & Alfonso, C. 2011).

Many learning disabilities have a biological basis. Some children have minor abnormalities in certain brain structures, and others seem especially vulnerable to interference from brain signals irrelevant to the task at hand (Ashkenazi, Black, Abrams, Hoeft, & Menon,

Preparing for Your Licensure Examination

Your teaching test may ask you about the needs of children with learning disabilities and attention disorders.

---

[11]In Chapters 8 and 9, respectively, we examine individual differences in intelligence and language. Children with these exceptionalities also respond well to customized interventions.

2013; Kovas, Haworth, Dale, & Plomin, 2007). In Artifact 7-3, you can see the difficulties that Nathan has in representing sounds with letters, a problem that is common in young elementary children with reading disabilities.

Children with learning disabilities are a diverse group, with a wide variety of talents, abilities, and personalities. Some children easily gain proficiency in mathematics but have significant difficulty with reading, whereas others show the reverse pattern.[12] Other children have trouble expressing their thoughts in language, interpreting visual information, spelling words, typing and forming letters, or performing in still other domains. Despite this variation, many children with learning disabilities have certain characteristics in common. They are apt to have trouble with executive functions—focusing attention, concentrating on learning goals, inhibiting inappropriate thoughts and behaviors, and so on (de Weerdt, Desoete, & Roeyers, 2013; Semrud-Clikeman, Fine, & Bledsoe, 2013). With few effective strategies at their disposal, children may take a rather "passive" approach to schoolwork—for instance, mindlessly staring at a textbook instead of actively thinking about what the words mean (Brownell, Mellard, & Deshler, 1993; Meltzer & Krishnan, 2007). Some children with learning disabilities have less working memory capacity than their age-mates, making it difficult for them to engage in several cognitive processes simultaneously (H. L. Swanson & Jerman, 2006; Wesley & Bickel, 2013). They may also suffer from low self-esteem and emotional problems, due at least partly to frustration over repeated academic failures (Al-Yagon, 2012; Horowitz, Darling-Hammond, & Bransford, 2005).

As students reach the secondary grades, the school curriculum becomes increasingly challenging, textbooks are written in more sophisticated language, and teachers expect greater independence. Unless they have considerable scaffolding to help them study and learn, students with learning disabilities become discouraged. Perhaps for this reason, adolescents with learning disabilities are often among those students most at risk for dropping out of school (Barga, 1996; L. Gonzalez, 2011).

Attention-Deficit Hyperactivity Disorder

Children with **attention-deficit hyperactivity disorder (ADHD)** have either or both of the following characteristics:

- *Inattention*—Children are easily distracted by either external stimuli or their own thoughts. They may daydream, have trouble listening to and following directions, or give up easily when working on difficult tasks.
- *Hyperactivity and impulsivity*—Children have an excess amount of energy. They may be fidgety, move around at inappropriate times, talk excessively, or have difficulty working or playing quietly. They may show impulsive behaviors, for example, blurting out answers, interrupting others, making careless mistakes, and acting without thinking about potential ramifications (American Psychiatric Association DSM-5 Task Force, 2013).

For a person to be classified as having ADHD, he or she needs to have exhibited several symptoms in a few settings before the age of 12. A weakness with executive functions, especially in the inhibition of inappropriate thoughts and actions, may be at the heart of ADHD (Denckla, 2007; Langberg, Dvorsky, & Evans, 2013). Limitations in reward mechanisms in the brain, especially favoring immediate over delayed rewards, seem to share responsibility (Carmona et al., 2009; Silvetti, Wiersema, Sonuga-Barke, & Verguts, 2013).

In large part because of their inattentiveness, hyperactivity, and impulsivity, children identified as having ADHD are apt to have difficulties with academic learning, interpersonal skills, and classroom behavior (Barkley, 1998; B. A. White, Jarrett, & Ollendick, 2013). Problems can escalate if not addressed effectively during early childhood. Adolescents with ADHD have greater difficulty than peers in meeting the strains of the teenage years—the physical changes of puberty, complex classroom assignments, and demands for responsible behavior. Compared to peers, young people with ADHD are more prone to use tobacco and alcohol, get in traffic accidents, and drop out of school (Barkley, 1998; Ramos Olazagasti et al., 2013).

[12]See discussions about *dyslexia* and *dyscalculia* in Chapter 10.

ARTIFACT 7-3 Halloween. A few days before Halloween, Nathan, age 7, created and illustrated the writing sample shown here. Writing in small print, his first-grade teacher recorded what he intended to say: "I drew this pumpkin" and "A bat." With the exception of the *L* in the first line, Nathan correctly captured some of the sounds he was trying to spell: the *d* in *drew*, the *s* in *this*, and the *b* and *t* in *bat*. He omitted several other consonants and all vowel sounds except the initial *l*. It is possible that Nathan has difficulty hearing all of the distinct sounds in spoken words and matching them with letters in written words.

Given the pervasive challenges children with ADHD experience—and create—at home and in the classroom, several types of interventions may be implemented. In consultation with parents, physicians often prescribe psychostimulants (e.g., Adderall, Ritalin), which help dopamine, a neurotransmitter operating in attention centers of the brain, work more effectively (M. D. Rapport, Orban, Kofler, & Friedman, 2013). This medication generally reduces inattention and disorderly behavior but can have side effects, and its long-term consequences are unknown. Mental health experts also offer training to parents in effective discipline and guidance to children in self-control. Despite these interventions, children may continue to have trouble in concentrating and resisting impulses, generating the need for teachers to promote attention in the classroom.

In this regard, typical developmental sequences of information processing abilities provide worthwhile educational targets. By becoming aware of common sequences in attention, memory, and learning, teachers can scaffold children's delayed skills. Recognizing strengths, too, is essential because a child's assets can leverage growth. For example, a young girl with an attention problem but a love of literature might gradually lengthen her focus while listening to stories. You can gain a sense of typical progressions and exceptionalities in the Developmental Trends table "Basic Cognitive Processes at Different Ages." When everyday tactics are insufficient to secure concentration from individual children, teachers can seek professional guidance from school psychologists and special educators, who can design personalized procedures.

Working with Children Who Have Information Processing Difficulties

Some children with learning disabilities and ADHD might stare out the window instead of working on assignments. Others may interrupt a lecture, pester a classmate, or get up out of their seats at all the wrong times. Yet it is generally a neurological deficit, rather than laziness or rudeness, that causes these problems. In fact, children with information processing

DEVELOPMENTAL TRENDS
Basic Cognitive Processes at Different Ages

AGE	WHAT YOU MIGHT OBSERVE	DIVERSITY	IMPLICATIONS
Infancy (Birth–2 Years)	• Some ability to learn and remember from before birth • Adult-like hearing acuity within hours after birth • Improvement in visual acuity during the first year • Preference for moderately complex stimuli • Attention easily drawn to intense or novel stimuli • By 3 or 4 months, an ability to integrate information into categories	• Variations in attention spans are partly due to differences in temperament, but persistent inability to focus on any one object may signal a cognitive disability. • Exploration tendencies vary considerably: Some infants consistently seek new experiences, whereas others are more comfortable with familiar objects. • Health, good nutrition, and loving care foster infants' physical stamina and interest in exploration.	• Change a sub-set of toys and materials regularly to re-capture infants' interests in exploration. • Provide objects that can be easily categorized (e.g., colored blocks, plastic farm animals). • Allow for differences in interest, attention span, and exploratory behavior; offer choices of toys and activities.
Early Childhood (2–6 Years)	• Short attention span • Distractibility • Conscious recall of past events • Some understanding and use of symbols • Limited knowledge base with which to interpret new experiences • Growing ability to sustain attention to favorite activities	• Children's prior knowledge differs markedly by cultural and socioeconomic background. • Young children who experience significant stress may find it difficult to concentrate at school. • First signs of ADHD might include difficulty in rhyming; learning basic literacy tools, such as the alphabet; following simple directions, such as placing the blue ball in a yellow cup; unusual delays in buttoning and snapping clothes; apparent inability to sit still; and excessive aggression.	• Change activities fairly often to meet the short attention spans of children. • Reduce unnecessary distractions. • Arrange experiences (field trips to the library, fire department, etc.) that enrich children's knowledge base. • Consult experts when delays in basic skills suggest a possible learning disability. • Enlist the help of parents or community volunteers to facilitate relaxing learning activities, such as by reading individually to children in a corner of the classroom with a throw carpet and pillows.

DEVELOPMENTAL TRENDS (continued)

AGE	WHAT YOU MIGHT OBSERVE	DIVERSITY	IMPLICATIONS
Middle Childhood (6–10 Years)	• Increasing ability to focus on important stimuli and ignore irrelevant information • Increasingly symbolic thought and knowledge • Gradual automatizing of basic skills • Increasing exposure to environments beyond the home and family, leading to an expanding knowledge base • Knowledge of academic subject matter consisting of a range of un-integrated facts, especially in science and social studies	• Many children with learning disabilities or attention disorders have short attention spans and are easily distracted. • Trouble learning to read, spell, and acquire basic arithmetic skills is sometimes due to learning disabilities. • Some children with learning disabilities have a smaller working memory capacity than that of their peers. • Mild cognitive disabilities may not be evident until the upper elementary grades. • Variations in home traditions affect learning and memory skills.	• Intersperse sedentary assignments with physically active activities. • Ask children to rehearse basic knowledge and skills (e.g., number facts, word recognition), often as part of authentic, motivating, and challenging tasks. • Establish routines to attract children's attention during transitions, for example, hand signals, music, or a particular phrase. • Recognize and reward concentration. Ask children to set goals for attention and evaluate their mental focus during lessons.
Early Adolescence (10–14 Years)	• Ability to attend to a single task for an hour or more • A core of automatized skills in reading, writing, and mathematics (e.g., word identification, common word spellings, basic math facts) • Growing (although not necessarily well integrated) knowledge base related to various topics and academic disciplines	• Individual differences in adolescents' proficiency with basic reading and numerical skills • Many adolescents with information processing difficulties have trouble paying attention for a typical class period. • Some adolescents with sensory disabilities (e.g., those with visual impairments) have less-than-average knowledge of the physical world. • Adolescents with learning disabilities may dislike school due to their history of academic struggle.	• Incorporate variety in learning activities as a way of keeping young adolescents' attention. • Frequently point out how concepts and ideas are related to one another, both within and across content domains. • Provide extra guidance and support for those with diagnosed or suspected information processing difficulties. • Teach and reward use of organization skills with time, materials, and learning tasks.
Late Adolescence (14–18 Years)	• Ability to attend to a single task of personal interest for lengthy periods • Extensive and moderately integrated knowledge in some content domains • Ability to engage in fairly sophisticated symbolic reasoning	• High school students have choices in course selection, leading to variations in their knowledge of science, mathematics, and other academic subjects. • Students' attention can vary considerably from one class to another, depending on their intrinsic interest in the subject matter at hand. • Students with disabilities may forget to turn in homework, fail to bring supplies to class, and exhibit other signs of disorganization.	• Occasionally give assignments that require focusing on a particular task for an extended period. • Consistently encourage adolescents to think about the "hows" and "whys" of what they are learning. • Assess learning in ways that require depiction of relationships among ideas. • Scaffold students' use of calendars, adding deadlines for major projects (e.g., a 5-page history essay), and dates for sub-tasks (e.g., an outline, first draft, and revision).

difficulties invariably *want* to learn and behave like their classmates. Fortunately, several broad-spectrum tactics, adapted to the unique needs of each child, can improve learning, attention, and behavior:

• **Examine children's work for clues as to how learning disabilities restrict academic progress.** Writing samples, math homework, and other academic work can be a rich source of information about cognitive deficits. A child who solves a subtraction problem this way:

$$\begin{array}{r} 85 \\ -29 \\ \hline 64 \end{array}$$

may be applying an inappropriate rule to subtraction ("Always subtract the smaller number from the larger one"). A child who reads the sentence *I drove the car* as *I drove the cat* may be having trouble in using context clues when deciphering words. Instruction that hones in on these particular "bugs" in thinking can be enormously beneficial to children.

• **Provide extra scaffolding in areas of weakness.** Children with significant delays in foundational subjects, especially reading and mathematics, need personalized lessons. One child needs one-on-one tutoring in basic arithmetic calculations whereas another requires extra practice with recognizing common words. Learning skills may also need to be taught. Such support might take the form of structured note-taking, handouts that list major ideas, memory techniques for recalling information, after-school homework programs, tips in breaking up ambitious projects into manageable steps, and the like (T. Bryan, Burstein, & Bryan, 2001; Meltzer, 2007).

• **Teach children organizational skills.** Children with learning disabilities and attention problem are apt to need assistance in keeping track of assignments, school supplies, and their schedule (Abikoff et al., 2013). A teacher might help a fourth-grade boy prepare colored folders labeled with each of his classes. With difficult projects, the teacher might prepare a checklist that allows the student to mark off parts as they are being completed. A monthly calendar can list projects, assignments, and tests. Children can be rewarded for consistently using the organizations tool and eventually, for developing and implementing their own.

• **Help children stay focused on the task at hand.** Many children with information processing difficulties are easily distracted. Adults should minimize the presence of distractions, and for those with attention disabilities, consider seating them away from the window, finding a quiet and uncluttered room for tasks requiring substantial concentration, and pulling down window shades when alluring events unfold outside. Many children benefit from training in attention-focusing strategies, such as keeping eyes on the speaker and moving to a new location if the current one presents disruptive sights and sounds (Buchoff, 1990).

• **Provide children with opportunities to practice learning strategies.** Many children with learning disabilities and attention problems need to learn how to acquire, store, and recall information (M. Montague, Enders, & Dietz, 2011; Turnbull et al., 2010). Teachers can ask students to use such learning strategies as formulating a goal when undertaking a task, dividing complex activities (e.g., reading a long passage) into easily handled units, and identifying key concepts to look for when starting a lesson.

• **Incorporate both movement and restful transitions in the daily schedule.** All children, but especially those with information processing difficulties, need regular opportunities to release pent-up energy through recess, sports, and hands-on activities (Cortese, 2013; Panksepp, 1998). After a period of high activity, adults might give children a "settling-in" time that allows them to calm down gradually (Pellegrini & Horvat, 1995). When children return from lunch, an elementary teacher could read a passage from a relaxing storybook before introducing new concepts. Some children remain fidgety regardless of these measures and may appreciate permission to stand at the back of the classroom or squeeze a stress ball or other pliable toy.

• **Teach strategies for controlling hyperactivity and impulsivity.** Children with ADHD are apt to behave productively when they receive clear expectations and earn rewards for such desirable behavior as turning in an assignment on time, waiting to speak instead of calling out an answer, helping peers during a group assignment, following lunchroom rules, and bringing supplies to class) (Center for Children and Families, 2013). A daily report card can be kept of targeted behaviors and shared with the child and his or her parents. At school, the child might select from an array of rewards, for instance, being a messenger for the office, caring for class animals, preparing popcorn, having extra time on the computer, choosing stickers, or eating at a special table. Parents can examine the report card and offer such rewards as having an extra bedtime story, eating dessert after dinner, choosing music in the car, or enjoying another privilege suggested by the child.

Summary

Information processing theories focus on how children acquire, interpret, and remember information and on how these cognitive processes change over the course of development. Infants have many sensory and perceptual capabilities at birth or soon thereafter. In general, children are less efficient learners than adults are. They have shorter attention spans, a smaller working memory capacity, and a less integrated knowledge base to which they can relate new information and events. Children's limitations in information processing can be addressed by breaking up tasks, arranging activities that are varied and attention-grabbing, and delivering interesting lessons that incorporate practice in fundamental skills.

The information processing capabilities of some children (e.g., those with learning disabilities and those with attention-deficit hyperactivity disorder) require specially adapted instruction and materials. Although children with such disabilities have diverse abilities and needs, virtually all benefit from explicit instruction in effective cognitive strategies and scaffolding of learning tasks.

ENHANCEDetext *self-check*

METACOGNITION AND COGNITIVE STRATEGIES

In the process of learning and remembering information, children gain insights into how the mind works. The capacity for understanding and controlling personal mental processes is known as **metacognition**. The related processes that children intentionally use to regulate their own thinking are known as **cognitive strategies**. In this section we look at development in four important elements of metacognition: learning strategies, problem-solving strategies, metacognitive awareness, and self-regulated learning.

> **Preparing for Your Licensure Examination**
> Your teaching test may ask you to distinguish metacognition from basic cognitive processes.

Learning Strategies

As you have learned, children are able to remember some but not all of the information they encounter on a daily basis. As they progress through school, it becomes necessary for children to learn information deliberately, with an intention to remember it later.

Toddlers begin to try to remember things when prompted (DeLoache, Cassidy, & Brown, 1985). When asked to remember where a doll has been hidden in their home, they may stare or point at the location where they saw it being placed until they are able to go get it. Preschool children are inclined to verbalize the object or location (L.A. Henry & Norman, 1996). Yet overall, young children rarely make a point of learning and remembering something. In fact, 4- and 5-year-olds can remember a set of objects more successfully by playing with the objects than by intentionally trying to remember them (L. S. Newman, 1990).

As they progress through the elementary and secondary grades, children and adolescents develop an increasing number of *learning strategies*—techniques that they deliberately use to learn or remember information. Three that appear during the school years are rehearsal, organization, and elaboration.

Rehearsal

What do you do if you need to remember a telephone number for a few minutes? Do you repeat it over and over as a way of keeping it in your working memory until you can dial it? Repetition of information in order to remember it is known as **rehearsal**.

Rehearsal is rare in preschoolers but increases in frequency and effectiveness throughout the elementary school years. By age 5 to 7, children rehearse information in order to remember it (Jarrold & Citroën, 2013). By age 9 or 10, they become more strategic, combining items into a list as they rehearse. If they hear the list "cat, dog, horse," they might say "cat" after the first item, "cat, dog" after the second, and "cat, dog, horse" after the third. Repeating items in this cumulative manner helps children remember items more successfully, at least for a minute or so (Bjorklund et al., 2009; Kunzinger, 1985). Although rehearsal becomes more polished with age and experience, it is actually a relatively *in*effective strategy for remembering information over the long run unless, in the process, children also make sense of the information by relating it to something they already know (Cermak & Craik, 1979; M. Lehmann & Hasselhorn, 2012).

Organization

Take a minute to study and remember the following 12 words, and then cover them and try to recall as many as you can:

shirt	table	hat
carrot	bed	squash
pants	potato	stool
chair	shoe	bean

In what order did you remember the words? Did you recall them in their original order, or did you rearrange them somehow? If you are like most adults, you grouped the words into three categories—clothing, furniture, and vegetables—and recalled them category by category. In other words, you used **organization** to help you learn and remember the information.

As early as 3 or 4 months old, children begin to organize their experiences into mental categories (Kovack-Lesh, Horst, & Oakes, 2008; Quinn, 2002). After seeing pictures of dogs, they may gradually lose interest, but their interest is apt to pick up again when, for a change, they see a picture of a cat.[13] Infants' initial categories are based on perceptual similarity (e.g., *balls* are round, *blocks* are cubes), but they also show emerging knowledge of more general, abstract categories (e.g., *vehicles, furniture*; Horst, Oakes, & Madole, 2005; Mash, Bornstein, & Banerjee, 2014). By age 2, children may physically pick up objects and sort them by theme or function, perhaps using classifications such as "things for the feet" or "kitchen things" (Cacchione, Schaub, & Rakoczy, 2013; DeLoache & Todd, 1988; Mandler, Fivush, & Reznick, 1987).

As children move through the elementary, middle school, and secondary grades, they become increasingly effective in using organization as a learning strategy (Lucariello, Kyratzis, & Nelson, 1992; Megalakaki & Yazbek, 2013; Pressley & Hilden, 2006). They may sort items into categories when they want to remember them, for example. Their organizational strategies become more sophisticated and prevalent, with children incorporating a variety of dimensions and increasingly using abstract categories. Children also become more flexible in their organizational schemes. For example, consider the several alternatives that 17-year-old Paul identifies for organizing shells in an Observing Children video:

> Yeah, I could do them by color, smoothness. Some are rough, some got little jagged edges on them. Some are just smooth. And these big ones, they could do like patterns and stuff.

Observing Children 7-6
Notice Paul's ability to consider multiple organizational structures for sorting shells.

ENHANCEDetext *video example*

Elaboration

If we authors tell you that we've both spent many years living in Colorado, you will probably conclude that we either live or have lived in or near the Rocky Mountains. In this situation you're not only learning the information we told you, you're also learning some information that you yourself supplied. This process of embellishing on new information with existing knowledge is known as **elaboration**. Expanding on new information by adding pertinent details usually facilitates learning and memory, sometimes dramatically.

Children elaborate on everyday experiences in preschool and while reading in the elementary years (Fivush, Haden, & Adam, 1995; van der Schoot, Reijntjes, & Lieshout, 2012). As a strategy that they *purposefully* use to help them learn, however, elaboration appears relatively late in development (usually around puberty) and gradually increases throughout the teenage years (Bjorklund et al., 2009; W. Schneider & Pressley, 1989). Yet this strategy is not a guaranteed outcome by any means. Even in high school, it is primarily students with high academic achievement who use existing knowledge to help them expand on and remember new information. Students who are low achievers or have intellectual disabilities are much less likely to use elaboration when they study, and students of all ability levels resort to rehearsal for difficult, hard-to-understand material (J. E. Barnett, 2001; Pressley, 1982;

---

[13] Children who grow bored with repeated exposure to the same stimulus are showing *habituation*, a process that is introduced in Chapter 2.

Rosende-Vázquez & Vieiro-Iglesias, 2013). The following interview with 15-year-old "Beth," who earns mostly As in her classes but must work hard to get them, illustrates how infrequently some high school students elaborate on classroom subject matter:

> Adult: Once you have some information that you think you need to know, what types of things do you do so that you will remember it?
>
> Beth: I take notes . . . [pause].
>
> Adult: Is that all you do?
>
> Beth: Usually. Sometimes I make flash cards.
>
> Adult: What types of things do you usually put on flash cards?
>
> Beth: I put words I need to know. Like spelling words. I put dates and what happened then.
>
> Adult: How would you normally study flash cards or your notes?
>
> Beth: My notes, I read them over a few times. Flash cards I look at once and try to remember what's on the other side and what follows it. (interview courtesy of Evie Greene)

Notice how Beth emphasizes taking notes and studying flash cards, approaches that typically require little or no elaboration. In fact, the use of flash cards is really just a form of rehearsal.

Why do some students learn to use advanced learning strategies whereas others do not? Instruction is key. When teachers talk about memory (e.g., "What are some good ways to remember that formula? Can you form a picture in your mind?") and encourage children to use memory strategies, children tend to deploy these techniques and achieve at high levels (Moely, Santulli, & Obach, 1995; Okoza, Aluede, & Owens-Sogolo, 2013; P. A. Ornstein, Grammer, & Coffman, 2010). Teachers can also instruct children in use of elaboration strategies by regularly asking children to develop analogies ("What is _____ like?"), paraphrase the material ("Say it in your own words; what does _____ mean?"), draw inferences ("What else might be true?"), and compare and contrast ("How is _____ similar to and different from _____?") (Weinstein, Ridley, & Dahl, 1988).

Problem-Solving Strategies

By the time children are a year old, they have some ability to think about and solve problems. Imagine that an infant sees an attractive toy beyond her reach. One end of a string is attached to the toy, and its other end is attached to a cloth closer at hand. But between the cloth and the infant is a foam rubber barrier. The infant puts two and two together, realizing that to accomplish her goal (getting the toy), she has to do several things in sequence. She removes the barrier, pulls the cloth toward her, grabs the string, and reels in the toy (Willatts, 1990).

Problem solving requires several steps to address a blocked goal: understanding the situation, developing a plan, identifying and carrying out the steps, and checking out the results (Bayazit, 2013). Initially, young children engage in a lot of trial-and-error experimentation, not fully understanding the problem until they have tinkered with relevant materials (Boncoddo, Dixon, & Kelley, 2010). The ability to break a problem into two or more steps and work toward each one develops during the preschool and elementary school years (e.g., Klahr & Robinson, 1981; Welsh, 1991). Children also learn to inhibit impulses for responding with a tactic that comes immediately to mind, instead generating a range of possible solutions and shifting attention flexibly during the steps of a complex plan (Agostino, Johnson, & Pascual-Leone, 2010; Mehnert et al., 2013; H. L. Swanson, 2011).

With familiar tasks, children's don't simply replace existing strategies with a newer tactic. Initially, they are likely to use a new strategy infrequently and ineffectively. With time and practice, they become more adept at applying the new tactic efficiently, flexibly, and successfully (P. A. Alexander, Graham, & Harris, 1998; L. P. Flannery & Bers, 2013; Siegler & Alibali, 2005). By the time children reach elementary school, they can envision several different strategies for dealing with a particular problem, and the specific tactic they use may vary from one occasion to another. Some strategies are apt to be more advanced than others, yet because children initially have trouble using the more advanced ones effectively, they may resort to less efficient but more dependable "backup" strategies. For example, even after children have learned their basic math facts ($2 + 4 = 6$, $9 - 7 = 2$, etc.), they sometimes resort

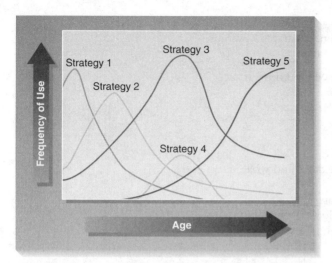

FIGURE 7-3 **Strategy development as a progression of overlapping waves.** Children gradually replace simple tactics with more advanced and effective strategies. Here we see how five different methods for dealing with the same task might change in frequency over time. *From Children's Thinking (4th ed., p. 98), by R. Siegler and M. W. Alibali, 2005, Upper Saddle River, NJ: Prentice Hall. Copyright 2005 by Prentice Hall. Adapted with permission of Prentice-Hall, Inc., Upper Saddle River, NJ.*

to counting on their fingers to solve simple addition and subtraction problems. Eventually, children acquire sufficient proficiency with more advanced strategies that they can comfortably leave the less efficient ones behind (P. A. Alexander et al., 1998; Kuhn & Pease, 2010; Siegler & Alibali, 2005).

American psychologist **Robert Siegler** and colleagues have observed that the rise and fall of various strategies is similar to the *overlapping waves* depicted in Figure 7-3 (Siegler & Alibali, 2005). Children use several strategies, gradually favoring ones that produce successful performances, in areas as diverse as crawling, spelling, and counting (Chetland & Fluck, 2007; Heineman, Middelburg, & Hadders-Algra, 2010; Kwong & Varnhagen, 2005; Young-Suk, Apel, Al Otaiba, Nippold, & Joffe, 2013).

Metacognitive Awareness

In addition to acquiring new learning and problem-solving strategies, children acquire increasingly sophisticated knowledge about the nature of thinking. This **metacognitive awareness** includes a conscious appreciation of thought processes, an understanding of the limits of human memory, and knowledge of the relative effectiveness of various learning strategies.

Awareness of Thought

By the time children are 3 years old, they are aware of thinking as an entity in its own right (Flavell, Green, & Flavell, 1995). Their initial understanding of thought is quite simplistic, however. They are likely to say that a person is "thinking" only when he or she appears to be physically engaged in a challenging task and has a thoughtful or puzzled facial expression. They also view thinking and learning as effortless activities (e.g., the mind acquires and holds information but doesn't do much with it), rather than as the active, constructive processes they actually are (Flavell et al., 1995; Wellman, 1990).

Conversations with adults help children learn about thinking (Salmon & Lucas, 2011). However, children don't automatically share adults' meanings for mental terms. Although many preschoolers learn the words *know, remember,* and *forget,* they don't fully grasp the nature of these mental phenomena. Three-year-olds use the term *forget* simply to mean "not knowing" something, regardless of whether they knew the information at an earlier time (Lyon & Flavell, 1994). And when 4- and 5-year-old children are taught a new piece of information, they may say that they've known it for quite some time (M. Taylor, Esbensen, & Bennett, 1994). The following interview, which a kindergarten teacher aide conducted with a bright 5-year-old whom we'll call "Ethan," illustrates the modest awareness that young children have of thought processes:

> Aide: When you learn a new song, like "The Horne Street School Song," how do you remember the words?
>
> Ethan: I just remember. I didn't know how to sing it for a while until I listened to the words enough to remember them.
>
> Aide: When I ask you during group time to "put on your thinking caps," what do I mean?
>
> Ethan: It means think. You think hard until you know what you are trying to think about. . . . I don't really know how you think, you just do. . . .
>
> Aide: How do you remember to give Mommy and Papa papers that we send home?
>
> Ethan: My good memory.
>
> Aide: Why do you have a good memory?
>
> Ethan: It's just good. It started when I turned three. I still had it when I was four, and now when I am five. (interview courtesy of Betsy Hopkins)

During the elementary and secondary school years, young people become better able to reflect on their own thought processes and are increasingly aware of the nature of thinking

(Jaswal & Dodson, 2009; K. E. Lyons & Ghetti, 2013; Wellman & Hickling, 1994). Metacognitive insights into academic learning are not automatic and instead depend on instruction and practice (Okoza et al., 2013).

Understanding of Memory Limitations

Young children tend to be overly optimistic about how much they can remember. As they grow older and encounter a wide variety of learning tasks, they discover that some things are especially difficult to learn or know, and they may not be as capable as they thought (Flavell et al., 2002; Grammer, Purtell, Coffman, & Ornstein, 2011; K. E. Lyons & Ghetti, 2013; Miele, Son, & Metcalfe, 2013). They also begin to realize that their memories are not perfect and they cannot possibly remember everything they see or hear. In one study (Flavell, Friedrichs, & Hoyt, 1970), preschoolers and elementary schoolchildren were shown pictures of 1 to 10 objects and asked to predict how many objects they could remember for a short time period. The average predictions of each of four age-groups and the average number of objects the children actually remembered were as follows:

Age-Group	Predicted Number	Actual Number
Preschool	7.2	3.5
Kindergarten	8.0	3.6
Grade 2	6.0	4.4
Grade 4	6.1	5.5

Notice that children in all four age-groups predicted that they would remember more objects than they actually did. But the older children were more realistic about the limitations of their memories.

Being naive is a mixed blessing for young children. Anticipating that they will be successful in remembering information, young children fail to apply extra procedures that might assist with memory. Yet their overly optimistic assessment of their mental abilities has a distinct benefit. It seems to give children the necessary confidence to try new and difficult tasks—challenges that are likely to promote cognitive growth (Bjorklund et al., 2009).

Knowledge About Effective Learning and Memory Strategies

Imagine that it's winter and you live in a cold climate. Just before you go to bed, some friends ask you to go ice skating with them after class tomorrow. What might you do to be sure you will remember to take your ice skates to class with you? Older children typically generate more strategies than younger children for remembering to take the skates to school. Yet even 5- and 6-year-olds can identify one or more effective strategies—perhaps writing a note to themselves, recording a reminder on a tape recorder, or leaving their skates next to their school bag (Kreutzer, Leonard, & Flavell, 1975).

Not only do children acquire more effective learning strategies (e.g., organization, elaboration) as they grow older, but they also become increasingly aware of what strategies are effective in different situations (Lovett & Flavell, 1990; J. Metcalfe & Finn, 2013; W. Schneider & Lockl, 2002). Consider the simple idea that when you don't learn something the first time, you need to study it again. This is a strategy that 8-year-olds use, but 6-year-olds do not (Masur, McIntyre, & Flavell, 1973). Similarly, 10th graders are more aware than 8th graders of the advantages of using elaboration to learn new information (H. S. Waters, 1982). Even so, many youngsters seem relatively uninformed about which learning strategies work most effectively for them in different situations (Joseph, 2010; Kuhn, Garcia-Mila, Zohar, & Andersen, 1995). The following interview with "Amy," a 16-year-old with a history of low school achievement, illustrates how metacognitively naive some adolescents are:

Adult: What is learning?
Amy: Something you do to get knowledge.
Adult: What is knowledge?
Amy: Any information that I don't know.
Adult: What about the things you already know?
Amy: That doesn't count.

Adult: Doesn't count?

Amy: As knowledge, because I already know it.

Adult: How do you know when you have learned something?

Amy: When I can repeat it, and it is the same as what the teacher said or what I read, and I can remember it forever or a really long time. (interview courtesy of Jennifer Glynn)

Notice how Amy thinks she has learned something when she can repeat what a teacher or textbook has told her. She says nothing about *understanding* classroom subject matter. And curiously, she thinks of knowledge as things she *doesn't* know.

Self-Regulated Learning

As children gain awareness of their learning and memory processes, they become more capable of **self-regulated learning**—that is, they become more proficient in directing and controlling their own learning. Self-regulated learning involves strategies such as these:

- Setting goals for a learning activity
- Planning effective use of study time
- Keeping attention on the subject matter to be learned
- Persisting while studying
- Identifying and using appropriate learning strategies
- Monitoring progress toward learning goals
- Adjusting goals or learning strategies depending on progress
- Evaluating knowledge gained from a learning activity (Boekaerts, 2006; Malmberg, Järvenoja, & Järvelä, 2013; Meltzer & Krishnan, 2007; Muis, 2007; S. M. Reis, 2011; B. J. Zimmerman & Schunk, 2004)

Rudimentary capacities for self-regulated learning are evident beginning in early childhood, when many children show flashes of self-control, perhaps by ignoring an annoying classmate instead of hitting him, looking at an array of items for a long time when trying to remember them later, or staying focused on building a tower after several pieces tumble (Demetriou, 2000; Kopp, 1982; U. Wagener, 2013). Some preschool teachers encourage children to make plans for their free time, as, for example, by asking children to verbalize their intentions for a specific activity (perhaps playing with a friend in the housekeeping area or riding a tricycle outside) beforehand and later asking them how they did (Bodrova & Leong, 2009; S. Jones, Bub, & Raver, 2013).

Self-regulatory skills are a long time in the making. In many circumstances, elementary school children and adolescents have difficulty regulating their learning on academic tasks (Bronson, 2000; B. J. Zimmerman & Risemberg, 1997). Fortunately, teachers can foster self-regulatory learning by allowing children numerous opportunities to set goals and ask questions (at least some of which should be of personal interest), monitoring their performance, and making adjustments to instruction as necessary (Cano, García, Berbén, & Justicia, 2014; Merritt, Wanless, Rimm-Kaufman, Cameron, & Peugh, 2012; Perels, Merget-Kullmann, Wende, Schmitz, & Buchbinder, 2009; Tracy, Reid, & Graham, 2009; Yoon, 2009).

Cultural Roots of Metacognition

Perhaps not surprisingly, an active mental engagement seems to be universally valuable for academic achievement (J. Lee, 2014). Yet specific metacognitive understandings and strategies are, in large part, the result of the particular social and cultural environments in which they live. From the perspective of mainstream Western culture, the acquisition of knowledge is largely for one's personal benefit: People learn in order to understand the world and acquire new skills and abilities. But for many people in China, learning has moral and social dimensions: It enables an individual to become honorable by making contributions to society.

From a traditional East Asian perspective, true learning is not a quick-and-easy process. Rather, it comes only with a great deal of diligence, concentration, and perseverance (Dahlin & Watkins, 2000; H. Grant & Dweck, 2001; J. Li & Fischer, 2004; Q. Wang & Pomerantz, 2009). As part of their emphasis on hard work, many East Asian parents and teachers encourage

BIOECOLOGY OF DEVELOPMENT

Children make strides in self-regulated learning with the help of neurological maturation; practice in setting and pursuing goals; and guidance from parents, teachers, and other adults.

rehearsal and rote memorization as learning strategies (Dahlin & Watkins, 2000; D. Y. F. Ho, 1994; Purdie & Hattie, 1996). Rehearsal and memorization are common in other cultures that commit oral histories or verbatim passages to memory (Alhaqbani & Riazi, 2012; MacDonald, Uesiliana, & Hayne, 2000; Rogoff et al., 2007; Q. Wang & Ross, 2007). In contrast, many schools in mainstream Western societies ask students to focus on making sense of classroom material rather than memorizing it word for word. Even so, Western schools typically insist that students commit certain things to memory (e.g., word spellings, multiplication tables; Q. Wang & Ross, 2007).

Of course, every culture offers valid ways to process information, and without discounting a society's traditions in learning, teachers can scaffold techniques that are worthwhile for the material they are presenting. For example, teachers might encourage children not yet accustomed to active self-regulatory strategies to try a few techniques that are age-typical. Children might be asked to draw pictures and write reflections about a story they have listened to, predict what will happen next, and discuss their ideas with classmates. On other occasions, teachers can validate the procedures that children bring from home, for instance finding occasions to rehearse certain information (e.g., poems) at school (Vassallo, 2013).

The Developmental Trends table "Cognitive Strategies and Metacognitive Understandings at Different Age Levels" summarizes developmental changes in children's cognitive strategies and metacognitive understandings, as well as some of the metacognitive diversity you are likely to see in any age group.

BIOECOLOGY OF DEVELOPMENT

Children acquire views about learning from their personal experiences in cultural communities.

DEVELOPMENTAL TRENDS
Cognitive Strategies and Metacognitive Understandings at Different Age Levels

AGE	WHAT YOU MIGHT OBSERVE	DIVERSITY	IMPLICATIONS
Infancy (Birth–2 Years)	• Use of one object to obtain another (in the second year) • Ability to plan a simple sequence of actions to accomplish a goal (appearing around age 1) • Absence of intentional learning strategies but preliminary ability to look or point at a location to remember where an object is hidden • Little awareness of thought processes but appreciation that other people have intentions[14]	• Emergence of early problem-solving strategies is dependent on opportunities to experiment with objects. • Willingness to engage in trial-and-error exploratory behavior is partly a function of temperament and motor abilities. • Health and nutrition influence how vigorously infants explore the environment, attend to language, and initiate interactions with caregivers.	• Model tool use and basic problem-solving strategies. • Pose simple problems for infants and toddlers to solve (e.g., place desired objects slightly out of reach), but monitor children's reactions to make sure they are not unnecessarily frustrated. • Be mindful of the tremendous strategies that infants use in mastering language and gaining information about their world, methods that are not necessarily intentional but are adaptive nevertheless.
Early Childhood (2–6 Years)	• Some rehearsal beginning in preschool, but with little effect on learning and memory • Occasional organization of concrete objects • An ability to learn simple strategies modeled by others • Growing awareness of thought in oneself and others • Overestimation of how much information one can remember	• Children's awareness of mental processes depends on the extent to which adults talk about thinking. • Many young children with autism have little conscious awareness of the existence of thought, especially in other people.[15] • Cultural preferences affect opportunities for memorization (e.g., with poetry, scripture, or the alphabet) and active interpretation (e.g., being asked about the moral lesson of a fable or the way a toy operates).	• Talk about thinking processes (e.g., "I *wonder* if . . .," "Do you *remember* when . . .?"). • Model strategies for simple memory tasks (e.g., pinning permission slips on jackets to remind children to get parents' signatures). • Ask children open-ended questions that engage their thinking (e.g., while reading: "What do you think is going to happen to Sam's homework?"). • Encourage children to ask questions as they play (e.g., ask, "What will happen if I mix blue and red on my paper?").

(continued)

[14] Children's understanding of other people's thoughts is explored in Chapter 12.
[15] The characteristics of children with autism are examined in Chapter 12.

DEVELOPMENTAL TRENDS (continued)

AGE	WHAT YOU MIGHT OBSERVE	DIVERSITY	IMPLICATIONS
Middle Childhood (6–10 Years)	• Use of rehearsal as the predominant learning strategy • Gradual increase in organization as an intentional learning strategy • Emerging ability to reflect on the nature of one's own thought processes • Frequent overestimation of personal memory capabilities • Little self-regulated learning in terms of goal setting and monitoring progress toward goals	• Some Chinese and Japanese children rely more heavily on rehearsal than do peers in Western schools; this difference continues into adolescence. • Children with cognitive disabilities struggle to organize material as they learn it. • A few high-achieving children are capable of sustained self-regulated learning.	• Encourage children to repeat and practice the things they need to learn. • To encourage organization as a learning strategy, ask children to categorize familiar themes and objects. • Ask children to engage in simple self-regulated learning strategies initially, perhaps setting a goal or talking about what strategies helped them understand a history document.
Early Adolescence (10–14 Years)	• Emergence of elaboration as an intentional learning strategy • Few and relatively ineffective study strategies (e.g., weak note-taking skills) • Increasing flexibility with learning strategies • Belief that knowledge consists of a collection of discrete facts	• Adolescents differ considerably in their use of effective learning strategies. • Some adolescents, including many with cognitive disabilities, have few strategies for engaging effectively in self-regulated learning. • Students may employ learning strategies when scaffolded by teachers in their use in particular academic subjects	• Ask questions that encourage adolescents to elaborate on new information. • Teach and model effective strategies within the context of subject areas. • Assign homework and other tasks that require independent learning, but provide sufficient structure to guide students' efforts. • Give adolescents frequent opportunities to set goals and assess their own learning.
Late Adolescence (14–18 Years)	• Increase in use of elaboration while learning • Growing awareness of which cognitive strategies are most effective in particular situations • Increasing self-regulatory learning strategies (e.g., setting of goals and keeping track of progress) • Increasing realization that knowledge involves understanding of connections among ideas • Emerging willingness to critically evaluate conflicting perspectives on an issue (in some students)	• High-achieving teenagers are likely to use sophisticated learning strategies (e.g., elaboration). • Low-achieving students typically resort to simple and ineffective strategies (e.g., rehearsal). • Many teenagers with cognitive disabilities have insufficient reading and study skills to learn successfully from typical high school textbooks. • Willingness to critically evaluate others' ideas is, in part, a function of cultural and religious upbringings.	• Continue to teach and model effective learning strategies both in and out of school. • Assign complex independent learning tasks, giving the necessary structure and guidance for those who are not yet self-regulating learners. • Teach specific criteria (e.g., presence of research evidence, logical consistency) by which to evaluate diverse perspectives.

Promoting Metacognitive and Strategic Development

Metacognition is worthwhile to foster because of the strong connection between this capacity and children's academic achievement (Afflerbach, Cho, Kim, Crassas, & Doyle, 2013; Roebers, Krebs, & Roderer, 2014). Following are several suggestions for fostering the development of metacognition and cognitive strategies.

• **Engage children in discussions about the mind.** As you've seen, even preschoolers have some awareness of the mind and its activities. Adults can enhance this awareness by regularly referring to mental activities—for example, by asking children to put on their "thinking caps," describing someone's mind as "wandering," and encouraging children to explain how they might learn to ride a bicycle (Grammer, Coffman, & Ornstein, 2013; Wellman & Hickling, 1994).

As children become more introspective in the elementary and secondary school years, they become better able to reflect on and describe the kinds of things they do mentally while learning. At earlier points in the chapter, we've presented interviews in which children described their views about thinking, learning, and studying to adults. Such interviews can shed light on young people's study strategies that adults in turn can accommodate in instruction. These conversations may also have educational value for children. Children's explanations in mathematics, for example, can help them identify inconsistencies and gaps in their understandings of concepts (M. Carr, 2010).

• **Demonstrate effective cognitive strategies.** Adults can foster more effective problem-solving strategies by modeling them for children. Infants as young as 6 to 10 months can overcome obstacles to obtaining an attractive toy if someone shows them how to do it (Z. Chen, Sanchez, & Campbell, 1997; Gerson, & Woodward, 2013). Learning strategies, too, can be modeled and taught. Three- to five-year-olds can be taught to organize objects into categories as a way of helping them remember them (Augustine, Smith, & Jones, 2011; Carr & Schneider, 1991; Lange & Pierce, 1992).

As children encounter increasingly challenging learning tasks at school and elsewhere, simple categorization alone is, of course, not enough. By the time they reach high school, students need to learn—and often must be explicitly taught—strategies such as elaboration, goal setting, note taking, and time management. Ideally, such instruction should be integrated into lessons about specific academic topics, rather than in a separate course or unit (Carr, 2010; R. E. Mayer, 2010; Pressley, El-Dinary, Marks, Brown, & Stein, 1992). Once adolescents become proficient in advanced strategies, they are apt to find these procedures more rewarding than simple rehearsal. In an Observing Children video, 16-year-old Hilary describes her feelings about rehearsal this way:

> Just felt like I was trying to memorize for a test or something. . . . Sometimes it's kind of boring or repetitious, [just] going over it.

Observing Children 7-7
Hear Hilary express her view of rehearsal.
ENHANCEDetext *video example*

Small-group learning and problem-solving activities, especially when structured to encourage effective cognitive processes, can also promote more sophisticated strategies (A. King, 1999; Kuhn & Pease, 2010; Palincsar & Herrenkohl, 1999; S. Vaughn et al., 2011). One approach is to teach children how to ask one another thought-provoking questions about the material they are studying. The following exchange shows two fifth graders using such questions as they study material about tide pools and tidal zones:

Janelle: What do you think would happen if there weren't certain zones for certain animals in the tide pools?
Katie: They would all be, like, mixed up—and all the predators would kill all the animals that shouldn't be there and then they just wouldn't survive. 'Cause the food chain wouldn't work—'cause the top of the chain would eat all the others and there would be no place for the bottom ones to hide and be protected. And nothing left for them to eat.
Janelle: O.K. But what about the ones that had camouflage to hide them? (A. King, 1999, p. 95)

Notice how Janelle's questions don't ask Katie to repeat what she has already learned. Instead, Katie must use what she's learned to speculate and draw inferences; in other words, she must engage in elaboration. Questioning like Janelle's promotes both better recall of facts and increased integration of ideas, undoubtedly because it encourages more sophisticated learning strategies.

Collaborative learning and problem-solving activities are beneficial for several reasons. For one thing, group members scaffold one another's efforts, providing assistance on difficult tasks. Second, group members describe and explain their strategies, allowing others to observe and possibly model them. Third, when students engage in mutual question asking, they may eventually ask *themselves*, and then answer, equally challenging questions as they read and study.

• **Encourage self-regulated and strategic learning.** On average, self-regulating learners achieve at higher levels in the classroom than do non-self-regulators (Blair & Razza, 2007; Duckworth & Seligman, 2005; Kaya & Kablan, 2013). But like so many developmental capacities, self-regulated learning is a complex endeavor that involves many components (goal setting, attention control, flexible use of cognitive strategies, etc.). Therefore, in order to help students take advantage of this wonderful resource, adults need to nurture its various elements over the course of childhood.

Preparing for Your Licensure Examination
Your teaching test may ask you how to foster children's metacognitive knowledge and strategies.

The roots of self-regulated learning are established in infancy, wherein tiny learners are impelled to notice basic patterns during personal interactions, play, and exploration. Even for a few years afterward, a great deal of learning occurs during spontaneous discovery. By early childhood and the early elementary years, children are ready for explicit guidance in self-regulation, which teachers may oblige by describing personal mental events (e.g., of trying to remember a certain name) and by asking children to set goals in their learning and play and evaluate their accomplishments toward these goals. Later in the elementary and secondary school years, teachers and other adults can scaffold self-regulation by instructing children in more sophisticated learning strategies. For instance, they might provide examples of questions that encourage elaboration (e.g., "Explain why _____," "What is a new example of _____?"). They might provide guidance about how to develop a good summary (e.g., "Identify the main idea," "Find three points that support the main idea"). As children develop increasing proficiency with each self-regulating strategy, the scaffolds can gradually be removed (Meltzer & Krishnan, 2007; Pressley et al., 1992).

• **Create opportunities for children to evaluate their own learning.** Depending on the lessons offered, students have numerous options to regulate their learning. You can observe 8-year-old Keenan's self-evaluation in an Observing Children video. By engaging in ongoing self-evaluation, Keenan is developing appropriate standards and applying those standards regularly to her accomplishments—true hallmarks of a self-regulating learner. Self-evaluation can be facilitated in several ways:

Observing Children 7-8
Observe 8-year-old Keenan's self-evaluation of her work.
ENHANCEDetext *video example*

- Teach children to ask themselves, and then answer, questions about the topic.
- Have children set specific objectives for each session and then describe how they've met each one.
- Provide specific criteria that children can use to judge their performance.
- Encourage children to evaluate their performance realistically, and then reinforce them (e.g., with praise or extra-credit points) when their accomplishments match an established standard.
- Have children compile portfolios that include samples of their work, along with a written reflection on the quality and significance of each sample. (Carr, 2010; McCaslin & Good, 1996; Nicolaidou, 2013; Paris & Ayres, 1994; Perry, 1998; Rosenshine, Meister, & Chapman, 1996; Schraw, Potenza, & Nebelsick-Gullet, 1993; Tracy et al., 2009; Winne, 1995b).

• **Regularly comment on the advantages of effective strategies.** If they are to achieve at high levels in high school and college, young people must believe that they can learn and achieve through effort and technique rather than assume that their level of performance is predetermined by existing abilities.

American psychologist **Carol Dweck** (2012) has demonstrated the power of children's belief that they can grow intellectually if they try hard and work effectively. Teachers can educate children that the brain changes with experience and can grow in capacity like a muscle. Rather than praising children for their intelligence, teachers can draw children's attention to strategies that seem to be working—persistence on a task, rereading of different materials, and methodical approaches to a difficult task (Dweck, 2008). Eventually, children will recognize strategies that increase their likelihood of academic success.

Teachers can also foster additional views that academic knowledge is not merely a cut-and-dried set of facts and that effective learning is not simply a process of mindlessly repeating facts. One way to foster more advanced understandings is to talk openly about the nature of learning and provide experiences that lead children to discover for themselves that knowledge is dynamic rather than static. Students might be given complex problems that have no clear-cut right or wrong answers; asked to read conflicting accounts of historical events, and shown how to compare several different explanations of a scientific phenomenon (Dutt-Doner, Cook-Cottone, & Allen, 2007; M. C. Linn, Songer, & Eylon 1996; Schommer, 1994b; Tabak & Weinstock, 2008; E. M. Walsh, 2013).

• **Teach children how to study.** Homework is a perfect time to exercise self-regulatory skills—but teachers had best provide the necessary scaffolding. A high school advisor might help students prepare a homework plan for the week, setting goals for a couple of nights during the week and checking off assignments when completed. A homework-helper tool might include tips for studying, such as setting reasonable goals for each study session; finding a quiet place to concentrate; breaking up a task into manageable chunks; taking brief breaks; and distributing study sessions over time rather than try to cram the night before a test (S. Carpenter, Cepeda, Rohrer, Kang, & Pashler, 2012; L. Rosen, Mark Carrier, & Cheever, 2013).

Summary

The term *metacognition* encompasses both the knowledge that people have about their own cognitive processes and their intentional use of strategies for learning and remembering. Children's metacognitive knowledge and cognitive strategies improve throughout the school years. When supported by educators, children become more proficient in rehearsal, organization, and elaboration, and they acquire increasingly powerful and effective ways of solving problems. With age, they become more aware of the nature of thinking, learning, and knowledge, and they develop strategies for regulating their own academic performance.

ENHANCEDetext *self-check*

Assessing Children 7-1

Practice assessing children's metacognitive insights.

ENHANCEDetext *application exercise*

Assessing Children 7-2

Practice identifying children's insights into their mental processes.

ENHANCEDetext *application exercise*

PERSONAL THEORY CONSTRUCTION

Piaget, Vygotsky, their heirs, and contemporary cognitive scientists have all suggested that children *construct* their own understandings of the world. Some developmental psychologists with specializations in cognitive science suggest that children gradually combine self-constructed understandings about particular matters into a succession of integrated and increasingly accurate belief systems, or *theories*. This approach to cognitive development is known as **theory theory**—a theoretical framework about how children form and revise their ideas when they confront new evidence (Gopnik & Meltzoff, 1997; Morton, 1980).

Children's theories about the world emerge early in life. As an illustration, by 5 to 8 months of age, children understand that human beings and other animals are different from inanimate objects—for instance, that living and nonliving entities move in distinctly different ways (L. B. Cohen & Cashon, 2006; Mandler, 2007b; Setoh, Wu, Baillargeon, & Gelman, 2013). As children grow older, they increasingly understand that the *insides* of living creatures are as important as, and perhaps more important than, outside appearance (S. A. Gelman, 2003). Even though they have not yet learned about genetics, DNA, and the like, they realize that biological entities are defined primarily by their origins and internal properties (Keil, 1989). In contrast, children understand that nonliving, human-made objects are largely defined by their functions, not their internal makeup (Greif, Kemler Nelson, Keil, & Gutierrez, 2006; Keil, 1989). Told that bowling balls are reshaped into objects that hold liquid for drinking, children conclude that these objects are really cups and not bowling balls.

Children busily form personal explanations on a range of topics, and by ages 3 to 5, they have theories for various aspects of the physical, biological, social, and mental domains (Geary, 2005; Wellman, Cross, & Watson, 2001; Wellman & Gelman, 1998). By age 5, children realize that living things grow and reproduce whereas nonliving things do not (Erickson, Keil, & Lockhart, 2010). As they grow older, they expand on and refine their theories, while integrating many of the facts, concepts, and beliefs they acquire (J. A. Dixon & Kelley, 2007; Gopnik & Wellman, 2012; Keil, 1994; Wellman & Gelman, 1998). We now explore children's ideas about the physical world as an example of growth in a personal theory.

Children's Theories of the Physical World

Young infants are amazingly knowledgeable about the physical world. By age 3 or 4 months, they show signs of surprise when one solid object passes directly through another one, when an object seems to be suspended in midair, or when an object appears to move immediately from one place to another without traveling across the intervening space (Baillargeon, 1994; Newcombe, Sluzenski, & Huttenlocher, 2005; Spelke & Kinzler, 2007). Such findings suggest that young infants know that objects (a) are substantive entities with definite boundaries, (b) fall unless something holds them up, and (c) move in a continuous manner across space.

ARTIFACT 7-4   Making a lake. Children's early theories often include naive beliefs about the world. When 4-year-old Isabelle is asked "How were lakes made?" she offers an explanation: "You get a bucket and you fill it up with water. You get lots and lots of buckets." She illustrates her theory with the picture shown here.

Several cognitive scientists presume that children are endowed at birth with basic knowledge of the physical world (Fodor, 2000; Spelke & Kinzler, 2007). The idea that some knowledge might be biologically preprogrammed is known as **nativism**. Built-in knowledge about the world would have an evolutionary advantage, of course—it would give infants a head start in learning about their environment—and evidence for it has been observed in other species as well (S. A. Gelman & Kalish, 2006; Spelke, 2000).

Nevertheless, many other theory theory theorists present a compelling case that infants are able to construct basic intuitions about objects, physics, living things, and the nature of thinking through a combination of neurological preferences and experiences in reflecting on statistical regularities in the world. Thus, the human brain is not necessarily hardwired with certain knowledge but may be "softly assembled" with primitive neurological capabilities that, when coupled with the child's ongoing perceptions and activity, give rise to definite ideas and abilities (Gopnik & Wellman, 2012; Thelen & Smith, 2006).

Whatever their origins may be, children's initial conceptions of objects provide a foundation for constructing an elaborate theory of the physical world. In the preschool and early elementary years, children's naive ideas about how the world works develop with little or no direct instruction from adults. A belief that people play a significant role in influencing physical phenomena (e.g., forming mountains, making clouds move, causing hurricanes) is common in the preschool and early elementary years (O. Lee, 1999; Piaget, 1929, 1960a). In Artifact 7-4, 4-year-old Isabelle has shown her idea that lakes are formed by a person pouring water into a large hole. Young children may also believe that natural objects and phenomena have a particular purpose. For instance, they may believe that pointy rocks exist so that animals can scratch themselves when they have an itch (Kelemen, 1999, 2004; Piaget, 1929).

Some misconceptions persist well into adolescence. For example, many high school and college students believe that an object persists in movement only if a force continues to act on it, and that an object dropped from a moving train or airplane will fall straight down (diSessa, 1996; diSessa, Gillespie, & Esterly, 2004; M. McCloskey, 1983). In reality, an object continues to move at the same speed in a particular direction unless a force acts to *change* its speed or direction (reflecting the law of inertia), and an object dropped from a moving train or plane not only falls but also continues to move forward (reflecting the laws of gravity and inertia).

Several factors probably contribute to inaccuracies in children's theories about the world (D. B. Clark, 2006; Glynn, Yeany, & Britton, 1991b; Keil, 2012; Vosniadou, 2009). For one, misconceptions result from how things appear to be. From our perspective here on Earth, the sun looks as if it moves around the earth, rather than vice versa. Several misconceptions are encouraged by common expressions in language (e.g., the sun "rises" and "sets"). Various cultural mechanisms—fairy tales, television shows, local folklore, occasionally even textbooks—also play a role. For example, after cartoon "bad guys" run off the edge of a cliff, they usually remain suspended in air until they realize that there's nothing solid holding them up, and at that point they fall straight down.

Students hold strongly onto their misconceptions, presenting a challenge for educators. Consider the fact that many children in the early elementary grades believe that the earth is flat rather than round. When adults tell them the earth is actually round, they may interpret that information within the context of what they already "know" and hence think of the earth as being *both* flat and round—in other words, shaped like a pancake (Vosniadou, 2009).

Facilitating Children's Theory Construction

Theory theory yields several practical implications for parents, teachers, and other adults who work with young people.

• **Encourage and answer children's questions.** Young children ask many *why* and *how* questions: "Why is the sky blue?" "How does a cell phone call know how to connect with another phone?" Such questions often pop up within the context of shared activities with adults (Callanan & Oakes, 1992; Frazier, Gelman, & Wellman, 2009; Siry & Max, 2013). These queries reflect children's genuine desire to make sense of their world and to refine their theories about why things are the way they are. Of course, children often need to see for themselves. Astute educators find ways to address children's questions by arranging for them to make focused observations relevant to their questions and by asking them pointed questions that scaffold their conclusions (Siry & Max, 2013).

• **When teaching a new topic, determine what children already know and believe.** Adults can more successfully address children's misconceptions when they know what those false impressions are (P. K. Murphy & Alexander, 2008). When beginning a new curriculum unit, teachers might assess students' existing beliefs about the topic, perhaps simply by asking a few informal questions that probe what students know and misunderstand. For instance, when asked if plants need food to survive, children may respond with a variety of ideas, for instance that plants need to make food for animals, don't have mouths and cannot eat, and use fertilizer as food (Keeley, 2012). Such ideas can help focus lessons on the correct mechanism, the biochemical processes of photosynthesis, by which food is produced for the plant.

• **When children have misconceptions about a topic, work actively to help them acquire accurate understandings.** Even as children encounter scientific perspectives about the world, their existing misunderstandings do not necessarily disappear. In fact, because early "knowledge" influences the interpretation of subsequent experiences, misconceptions are often quite resistant to change even in the face of blatantly contradictory information (Kuhn, 2001b; P. K. Murphy & Mason, 2006). Thus, teachers and other adults must make a concerted effort to help youngsters revise their early theories to incorporate more accurate and productive worldviews. In other words, they must help youngsters undergo **conceptual change**. Theorists and researchers have offered several strategies for promoting conceptual change:

- Ask children to articulate their current beliefs, either verbally or in pictures.
- Present phenomena that children cannot adequately explain within their existing perspectives—in other words, create *disequilibrium*.
- Engage children in discussions of the pros and cons of various explanations of observed phenomena.
- Explicitly point out what the differences between children's beliefs and "reality" are.
- Show how the scientifically accepted explanation of an event or phenomenon makes more sense than any alternative explanation children themselves can offer.
- Provide children with compelling evidence (e.g., video of the earth from outer space) that addresses particular misconceptions that children typically have (e.g., that the earth is flat).
- Arrange for children to gain hands-on experiences during experiments that address the underlying presuppositions children have about a topic.

- Have children study a topic for an extended period so that accurate explanations are thoroughly understood rather than learned in a superficial, rote manner.
- Teach a more thorough theoretical explanation than is the case with children's personal intuitive frameworks for a phenomenon, such as moving children from viewing nutrition as entailing simple consumption and excretion to it additionally consisting of extracting diverse nutrients from digested food and circulating these in the blood.
- Share historical cases with children in which there has been a significant progression of thought about a scientific topic (e.g., before and after discoveries of germs in human biology, plate tectonics in earth science, and planets revolving around the sun in astronomy). (D. B. Clark, 2006; Gripshover & Markman, 2013; P. K. Murphy & Alexander, 2008; P. K. Murphy & Mason, 2006; C. L. Smith, 2007; Vosniadou, 2009)

Summary

Some theorists propose that children gradually construct integrated belief systems (theories) about the physical world, the biological world, the social world, and mental events. Such integrated conceptual models are not always accurate, however. For example, children's theories about the physical world may include erroneous beliefs about the solar system and laws of motion. To the extent that children's theories include misconceptions, they may interfere with their ability to acquire more sophisticated understandings. Educators can use strategies known to facilitate conceptual change to overcome these misconceptions.

ENHANCEDetext *self-check*

AN INTEGRATIVE ACCOUNT OF COGNITIVE PROCESSES

The information processing and theory construction frameworks endorse the need for precise measurement of children's mental representations and events. In this regard, these two frameworks have extended our understanding of cognitive development beyond Piaget's and Vygotsky's pioneering ideas. Information processing research has made significant inroads into the question of how people process new information and how cognitive processes change over the course of childhood and adolescence. Theory theory helps us understand why children's naive beliefs (e.g., "The world is flat") persist even in the face of contradictory evidence.

Together these two approaches lead us to conclude that cognitive development involves more gradual changes and domain-specific reasoning capabilities than Piaget suggested. The Basic Developmental Issues table "Comparing Theories in Cognitive Science" compares the information processing framework and theory theory with respect to nature and nurture, universality and diversity, and qualitative and quantitative changes.

In their present forms, both frameworks have limitations. Even though theory theory researchers have begun to use mathematical and computer models of conceptual change, most descriptions are fairly general and restricted to a limited number of models (Gopnik, Wellman, Gelman, & Meltzoff, 2010; K. Nelson, 1996a; Siegler & Alibali, 2005). Individual differences about any domain can be sizable, making it difficult for educators to address the full range of concepts children may have (M. E. Martinez, 2010).

Information processing theories are more precise, but their exactness may not be a completely accurate description of how human memory works. People learn and remember many things that they don't consciously pay attention to or think about (Frensch & Rünger, 2003; Goujon, Didierjean, & Poulet, 2013). In addition, mounting research evidence indicates that working memory and long-term memory are closely interconnected and possibly overlapping entities, rather than the distinctly separate components depicted in Figure 7-1 (Kirschner, Sweller, & Clark, 2006; Ormrod, 2008). Finally, individuals' goals, motivations, and neurological underpinnings have yet to be adequately integrated into the information processing paradigm.

Perhaps the biggest challenge for today's developmental psychologists is to explain exactly how and why cognitive development occurs. Theorists have made progress on this

BASIC DEVELOPMENTAL ISSUES
Comparing Theories in Cognitive Science

ISSUE	INFORMATION PROCESSING	THEORY THEORY
Nature and Nurture	Nature endows children with brain mechanisms that enable them to direct attention to particular stimuli, assess an event or task at hand, and retain acquired knowledge and skills. Information processing difficulties (e.g., learning disabilities, attention-deficit hyperactivity disorder) often have biological origins. Nevertheless, the focus is primarily on environmental factors, in particular, on how environmental input is interpreted, stored, integrated, and remembered and on how formal instruction can facilitate learning.	Basic understandings of the physical world—or at least predispositions to divide up and interpret the world in particular ways—seem to be in place within the first few weeks or months after birth, and infants have biologically built-in abilities or perhaps subtle neurological preferences that evolve with experience. As children observe and interact with their physical and social environments, they construct increasingly elaborate and integrated understandings and beliefs about physical, social, and mental phenomena.
Universality and Diversity	The components of the information processing system (i.e., the sensory register, working memory, long-term memory, and the central executive) are universal. However, some children use their information processing capabilities more effectively than others, especially when instructed to do so. Children's prior knowledge and their mastery of cognitive strategies influence the degree to which they can learn new information and employ skills effectively.	Several biologically built-in knowledge and predisposition (e.g., for developing depth perception or being able to distinguish animate and inanimate things) are universal across cultures. Informal experiences, formal schooling, and community practices and beliefs—things that are apt to differ from one culture to the next—lead children to embellish on their initial understandings in culturally specific ways.
Qualitative and Quantitative Change	Over the course of development, children and adolescents acquire a variety of new cognitive strategies that are qualitatively different from earlier ones. Each strategy evolves gradually and becomes increasingly efficient and effective—a trend that reflects quantitative change. Children eventually select a few of the more powerful strategies to use when solving problems in a combination of qualitative and quantitative change.	As children gain more information about their world, they may add to their theories in a quantitative manner. Under certain conditions, including concerted instruction, new and compelling experiences spur children to overhaul their theories in a way that reflects qualitative change.

front, to be sure. Children have an innate need to adapt to their environment, and they almost certainly acquire more complex strategies when adults scaffold these competencies. But we do not yet have a detailed understanding of how various aspects of heredity and experience work in concert in the transformation of newborn infants into cognitively sophisticated adults.

To arrive at such an understanding, psychologists need to pull together the insights of multiple perspectives. What we might ultimately decide is that we need the information processing perspective to account for certain aspects of learning (e.g., growth in knowledge, patterns in memory), whereas the theory theory perspective is necessary for accounting for children's integrative models of casually rich matters (e.g., what makes people and animals act as they do). In the future, we can anticipate that the cognitive science framework will give more prominence to a person's goals, emotions, and social relationships, which, as fundamental parts of human life, invigorate thinking.

As we wait for further refinements in cognitive science, we can fruitfully apply the insights that have already been generated. Existing research findings tell us a great deal about what to look for in children's development and how to work effectively with various age groups (see the Observation Guidelines table "Observing Cognitive Ideas, Processes, and Metacognition").

Summary

Cognitive science significantly advances our understanding of children's cognitive development. How children attend to, think about, and remember perceptions, facts, and experiences has been the focus of the information processing framework. Children's understandings of physical properties, including naïve ideas about the laws of physics and the nature of living

OBSERVATION GUIDELINES
Observing Cognitive Ideas, Processes, and Metacognition

CHARACTERISTIC	LOOK FOR	EXAMPLE	IMPLICATION
Intersubjectivity	• Reciprocal interactions with caregivers • Attempts to coordinate personal actions toward an object with related actions from someone else • Social referencing (i.e., responding to an object or event based on how a trusted adult responds to it)	A teacher at a child care center is frightened when a large dog appears just outside the fenced-in play yard, and she yells at the dog to go away. Fifteen-month-old Owen observes her reaction and begins to cry.	Regularly engage infants in affectionate and playful interactions (smiles, coos, etc.). Remember that your own reactions will communicate messages about the value, appeal, and safety of objects and events.
Attention	• Orienting toward movement or noise • Sustained attention to human beings and inanimate objects • Ability to stay on task for an age-appropriate period • On-task behavior when distracting stimuli are present	During story time, a second-grade teacher has been reading Roald Dahl's (1964) *Charlie and the Chocolate Factory*. Most of the children are attentive, but Ben fidgets and soon finds a new form of entertainment: making silly faces at nearby classmates.	Monitor children's ability to pay attention. If children have exceptional difficulty staying on task, minimize distractions, teach them strategies for focusing their attention, and give them opportunities to release pent-up energy regularly.
Automatization of Basic Skills	• Retrieval of simple facts in a rapid, effortless fashion • Ability to use simple problem-solving strategies quickly and efficiently	Elena easily solves the problem $4/12 = x/36$ because she realizes almost immediately that it is the same as 1/3.	Give children numerous opportunities to use and practice essential facts and skills; whenever possible, do so within the context of interesting and motivating activities.
Learning Strategies	• Use of rehearsal in the elementary grades • Use of more integrative strategies (e.g., organization, elaboration) in the secondary grades • Flexible use of strategies for different learning tasks	Terri studies each new concept in her high school physics class by repeating the textbook definition aloud three or four times. Later she can barely remember the definitions she studied and is unable to apply the concepts when trying to solve physics problems.	Show struggling learners that their difficulties may be due to ineffective strategies, and teach them strategies that can help them learn more successfully.
Self-Regulated Learning Capabilities	• Initiative in identifying and seeking out needed information • Intentional efforts to keep attention focused on an assigned task • Establishment of goals for learning • Effective planning and time management	At wrestling practice one day, John tells his coach that he has just read several articles about the pros and cons of using steroids to increase muscle mass. "I'm confused about why experts advise against them," he says. "Can you help me understand their logic?"	When youngsters fail to complete independent assignments in a timely or thorough manner, provide more structure for subsequent tasks. Gradually remove the structure as they become better able to regulate their learning and performance.
Beliefs About Knowledge and Learning	• Optimism that knowledge improves when one focuses on understanding (rather than memorization) • Attempts to master interrelationships among ideas (e.g., cause and effect, similarities and differences) • Eagerness to compare and critique perspectives and theories	Several middle school students are studying for a test on westward migration in North America during the 1800s. Some students focus on cause-and-effect relationships among events. Others make a list of facts from the textbook and study them in a piecemeal fashion.	Convey the message that mastering any single domain is an ongoing task that requires effort in understanding. Communicate that knowledge about a topic includes an understanding of how concepts and ideas are interrelated. Suggest that competing perspectives may each have merit but must be critically evaluated with evidence and logic.
Children's Personal Theories About Academic Concepts	• Statements that reveal commitments to explanatory models of physical, social, biological, and mental causes • Resistance to accepting a new perspective due to commitment to existing views • Vacillations in beliefs about a particular topic, such as phases of the moon, while in transition from one theory to another	Second-grade children mention a variety of explanations about plant needs and growth. A few believe that plants absorb food directly from the soil or from fertilizer rather than making their own food during photosynthesis.	Before beginning a series of lessons, ask children a few simple questions about what they already know about the topic. Try to address their misconceptions by providing counter-evidence and showing them how an unfamiliar model is more scientifically accurate, comprehensive, and consistent with the evidence.

things, is the focus of the theory construction perspective. Both frameworks offer promising extensive applications for educators. Limitations include unclear origins of ideas, narrow array of topics, and neglect of goals and emotions.

ENHANCEDetext *self-check*

PRACTICING FOR YOUR LICENSURE EXAMINATION

Many teaching tests require students to use what they have learned about child development in responses to brief vignettes and multiple-choice questions. You can practice for your licensure examination by reading the following case study and answering a series of questions.

The Library Project

In the final year of her teacher education program, Jessica Jensen is a teacher intern in four eighth-grade social studies classes. She has recently assigned a month-long group project that involves considerable library research. Midway through the project, Jessica writes the following entry in her journal:

> Within each group, one student is studying culture of the region, one has religion, one has economy, and one government. The point is for the students to become "experts" on their topic in their region. There are a lot of requirements to this assignment. I'm collecting things as we go along because I think a project this long will be difficult for them to organize . . .?
>
> So we spent all week in the library. I collected a minimum of two pages of notes yesterday, which will be a small part of their grade. The one thing that surprised me in our work in the library was their lack of skills. They had such difficulty researching, finding the information they needed, deciding what was important, and organizing and taking notes. As they worked, I walked around helping and was shocked. The librarian had already gotten out all of the appropriate resources. Even after they had the books in front of them, most did not know what to do. For instance, if they were assigned "economy," most looked in the index for that particular word. If they didn't find it, they gave up on the book. After realizing this, I had to start the next day with a brief lesson on researching and cross-referencing. I explained how they could look up *commerce, imports, exports,* and how these would all help them. I was also shocked at how poor their note-taking skills were. I saw a few kids copying paragraphs word for word. Almost none of them understood that notes don't need to be in full sentences. So, it was a long week at the library.
>
> Next week is devoted to group work and time to help them work on their rough drafts. With the difficulty they had researching, I can imagine the problems that will arise out of turning their notes into papers. (journal entry courtesy of Jessica Jensen)

Constructed-Response Question

1. Initially, Jessica realizes that her students will need some structure to complete the project successfully. In what ways do she and the librarian structure the assignment for the students?

Multiple-Choice Questions

2. How does the students' prior knowledge influence the effectiveness of their strategies?

    a. Students' lack of knowledge about such terms as *economics* makes it difficult for them to use the index and to cross-reference terms.

    b. Students' limited knowledge about their topic makes it difficult for them to make sense of the material they read.

    c. Students' lack of exposure to the topics they are researching makes it difficult for them to paraphrase and summarize what they've read.

    d. All of the above.

3. Given the information on metacognition in this chapter, how might Jessica teach students about strategy usage?

    a. Jessica needs to realize that due to their age, the eighth-grade students are not yet capable of acquiring learning strategies.

    b. Jessica can model and give students practice in using such strategies as identifying the main point of a passage, paraphrasing the material they read, referring to an index in a book, and keeping notes organized.

    c. None, because with additional reflection, Jessica will come to the conclusion that students already know how to use learning strategies and simply need to be told to try harder.

    d. Jessica should teach students to memorize the assertions of experts and repeat these comments verbatim in their reports.

ENHANCEDetext *licensure exam*

Key Concepts

CHAPTER EIGHT

Intelligence

CASE STUDY: Gina

Seventeen-year-old Gina has always been an enthusiastic learner. As a toddler, she talked early and often. As a 4-year-old, she asked her mother to identify a few words in a reading primer, used these words to deduce letter–sound relationships, and deciphered additional words on her own. By the time she reached kindergarten, she was reading first- and second-grade-level storybooks.

In elementary school Gina consistently achieved straight As on her report cards until finally, in sixth grade, she broke the pattern by getting a B in history. Since then, she has earned a few more Bs, but As continue to dominate her record. Her performance has been highest in her advanced math courses, where she easily grasps the abstract concepts that many of her classmates find difficult to understand.

Now in her senior year in high school, Gina has other talents as well. She won her high school's creative writing contest 2 years in a row. She landed challenging roles in her school's drama productions. And as president of her school's National Honor Society, she is exhibiting impressive drive while coordinating a peer-tutoring program for struggling students.

Gina's teachers describe her as a "bright" young woman. Her friends affectionately call her a "brainiac." Test results in her school file bear out these appraisals: An intelligence test that she took in junior high school yielded a score of 140, and she recently performed at the 99th percentile on college aptitude tests.

This is not to say that Gina is strong in every arena. She shows little artistic ability in her paintings or clay sculptures. Her piano playing is mediocre despite 5 years of weekly lessons. In athletic events she has little stamina, strength, or flexibility. She is shy and unsure of herself at social events. And she hasn't earned an A in history since fifth grade, in large part because her idea of how best to learn history involves simply memorizing people, places, and dates.

- What evidence is there that Gina is intelligent?
- In which abilities does Gina exhibit her strongest talents?
- In which abilities is Gina apparently less advanced?

Every child is intelligent to a certain degree. Gina's performance reflects exceptional intelligence: She has earned high marks in many subjects throughout her school career. Yet intelligence is not a set-in-concrete characteristic that youngsters either have or don't have. Gina has definite talents as well as areas that are a challenge for her, with all of these abilities growing and changing with experience.

Among her assets are those in academic areas that rely on advanced verbal skills, organizational abilities, and mathematical reasoning. Gina also excels at dramatic self-expression. She does not show the same extraordinary potential in history, art, music, athletics, or informal social situations, yet she will certainly be able to advance in these competencies if she puts her mind to it and is assisted in her efforts. Like Gina, every child is poised to make the most of his or her unique abilities if given appropriate support at home, in school, and within the community.

THEORIES OF INTELLIGENCE

Theorists think of intelligence in a variety of ways, but most agree that it has several distinctive qualities:

- It is *adaptive*, such that abilities are used flexibly to meet a person's goals in particular situations.
- It involves a capacity for *learning*. People who are intelligent in particular areas (e.g., verbal reasoning) learn new information and procedures more quickly and easily than people who are less intelligent in those domains.

OBJECTIVES

8.1: Describe human abilities according to well-known theories of intelligence, alternative views of these capacities, and practical applications from key ideas about intelligence.

8.2: Outline methods for assessing children's intelligence and the implications of intelligence testing for children.

8.3: Review evidence of separate and interacting factors contributing to intellectual growth.

8.4: Explain key methods for nurturing the abilities of exceptional children at each end of the intelligence continuum.

- It involves the *use of prior knowledge* to analyze and understand new conditions effectively.
- It reflects the complex coordination of *many distinct mental processes*.
- It *develops* with age, such that specific mental processes and their orchestration become more efficient with use and maturation.
- It is *culture specific*. In different societies, being intelligent might mean reasoning about complex and abstract ideas, getting along with others, acquiring strong moral values, respecting one's elders, or exhibiting coordinated motor skills. (Crago, 1988; Greenfield, 1998; H. Keller, 2003; Laboratory of Comparative Human Cognition, 1982; J. Li, 2004; Neisser et al., 1996; Nisbett, 2009; Sternberg, Jarvin, & Grigorenko, 2011; Suzuki, Naqvi, & Hill, 2014)

With these qualities in mind, we offer one possible (but intentionally broad) definition of **intelligence**: the ability to apply past knowledge and experiences flexibly and in a culturally appropriate manner while accomplishing challenging new tasks.

Models of Intelligence

Views on intelligence have evolved considerably over the past two centuries. Inquiries into intelligence were initially based on the real-world concern for children who were not succeeding with standard educational methods. In the early 1900s, school officials in France asked psychologist **Alfred Binet** (1857–1911) to develop a method for identifying students who would have exceptional difficulty in regular classrooms without special educational services. To accomplish the task, Binet devised a test that measured general knowledge, vocabulary, perception, memory, and abstract thought (Binet & Simon, 1948). He found that students who performed poorly on his test tended to perform poorly in the classroom as well. Binet's test was the earliest version of what we now call an **intelligence test**.

Such down-to-earth concerns have since been supplemented with theoretical discussions on the essence of intelligence. Scholars have debated whether intelligence is one characteristic that a child has to a greater or lesser degree, or alternatively if it is a compilation of several distinct abilities, each of which represents a strength or weakness for the child. As you will find out, evidence is strong for both positions, and many theorists now conclude that children have more or less of a general ability that permits them to solve novel problems in a variety of situations, as well as a collection of specific abilities (e.g., understanding spoken words or holding a lot of information in memory) that they employ in circumscribed situations.

Another theoretical issue that has garnered interest has been the extent to which the capacity for intelligence is inherited or derived from experience. Originally, scholars were impressed with data indicating the genetic basis of intelligence, yet increasingly experts have found strong evidence for the effects of child rearing, schooling, nutrition, and other environmental factors. Currently, experts in intelligence are resoundingly optimistic that intelligence can be enhanced with appropriate conditions and, when necessary, intervention (Dweck, 2009; B. Roche, Cassidy, & Stewart, 2013; Nisbett, 2009). These themes—practical implications, underlying structures, and origins—are addressed to varying degrees in the following five theories of intelligence.

Spearman's *g*

In the early 1900s, British psychologist **Charles Spearman** (1863–1945) proposed that intelligence comprises both (a) a single, pervasive reasoning ability (a *general factor*) that is used in a wide variety of tasks and (b) a number of narrow abilities (*specific factors*) involved in executing a subset of related tasks (Spearman, 1904, 1927). From Spearman's perspective, children's performance on any given task depends both on how generally bright they are and on any specific skills that the task involves. Measures of various language skills (vocabulary, word recognition, reading comprehension, etc.) are all highly correlated, presumably because they each reflect general intelligence and the same specific factor, verbal ability. A score on language skills will correlate to a lesser extent with a score on mathematical problem solving because the two measures tap into different specific abilities.

Many contemporary psychologists have found sufficient evidence in the substantial positive correlations among diverse intellectual abilities to conclude that a general factor in intelligence exists (e.g., N. Brody, 2006; M. Reynolds, Floyd, & Niileksela, 2013). This factor is often known simply as Spearman's **g**. Some contemporary theorists suspect that the ability to process information quickly may be at the heart of *g*, speculation that is supported by the substantial correlations that exist between measures of children's general intelligence and information processing speed (e.g., as measured by rapidly pressing the *M* key every time the number *5* appears on the right side of a computer screen; Demetriou, Mouyi, & Spanoudis, 2008). Neurological evidence indicates that children who are especially intelligent have brains that efficiently process ideas using large numbers of healthy neurons and glial cells, especially in the front area of the brain where planning and decision making reside (Gläscher et al., 2010; Kievit et al., 2012; Menary et al., 2013; van den Heuvel, Stam, Kahn, & Hulshoff Pol, 2009).

Not all psychologists agree that a *g* factor exists, however. Some suggest that the evidence for a single general factor can be either strong or weak depending on the specific abilities measured and on the particular statistical methods used to analyze the data (Neisser, 1998a; Sternberg, 2003a; Sternberg & Grigorenko, 2000). Others argue that the appearance of a general factor is an artifact of test items having been taken from skills valued in a limited number of societies, especially mainstream cultures of Europe and North America (Gardner, 2006). Increasingly, experts point out that even if *g* exists, children possess specific abilities that would be preferable to address (Mather, 2009; McGrew, 2005). Hence it could be quite helpful for a teacher to learn that a child has trouble identifying sounds and matching them with letters because these skills can be practiced and improved. In contrast, knowing the child's most recent general intelligence score provides virtually no direction for instruction unless the score is exceptionally low or high (we address strategies for guiding children with intellectual gifts and disabilities later in this chapter).

Cattell-Horn-Carroll Theory of Cognitive Abilities

The Cattell-Horn-Carroll theory of cognitive abilities is a merger of views that expand on the conjectures of **Raymond Cattell** (1905–1998), a British psychologist who worked in the United States. Extending the ideas of Spearman, Cattell (1963, 1987) found evidence for two distinctly different components of general intelligence. First, Cattell proposed, children differ in **fluid intelligence**, the ability to acquire knowledge quickly and adapt to new situations effectively. Second, they differ in **crystallized intelligence**, the knowledge and skills accumulated from past experiences, schooling, and culture. These two components may be more or less relevant to different intellectual trials. Fluid intelligence relates more to novel tasks, especially those that require rapid decisions and are largely nonverbal in nature. Crystallized intelligence is more important for familiar tasks, especially those heavily dependent on language and prior knowledge.

According to Cattell, fluid intelligence is largely the result of inherited biological factors, whereas crystallized intelligence depends on fluid intelligence and experience and so is influenced by both heredity and environment (Cattell, 1980, 1987). Fluid intelligence peaks in late adolescence and begins to decline gradually in adulthood. In contrast, crystallized intelligence continues to increase throughout childhood, adolescence, and most of adulthood (Cattell, 1963).

More recent work has led to refinements in the abilities Cattell's identified. Psychologists John Horn and John Carroll obtained evidence indicating that the distinction between fluid and crystallized abilities held up, yet there were other abilities that emerged as well. Other scholars distinguished abilities from fluid and crystallized intelligence, and a new integrative framework emerged, the Cattell-Horn-Carroll (CHC) theory of cognitive abilities (P. L. Ackerman & Lohman, 2006; Carroll, 1993, 2003; D. Flanagan, Alfonso, & Reynolds, 2013; Golay & Lecerf, 2011; J. L. Horn, 2008; McGrew, 2005). In the CHC theory, intelligence has three layers, or *strata*. At the top layer (Stratum III) is general intelligence, or *g*. Emerging out of *g* are 10 broad abilities (in Stratum II), including *fluid intelligence* and *crystallized intelligence*, the two abilities originally identified by Cattell, as well as 8 additional broad abilities:

- *Quantitative knowledge* (applying knowledge about mathematical operations)
- *Reading/writing* (performing complex literacy skills)
- *Long-term storage and retrieval* (putting information into memory and remembering it)

FOR FURTHER EXPLORATION . . .

Read examples of narrow abilities in the Cattell-Horn-Carroll model.

ENHANCEDetext
content extension

- *Short term memory* (attending to and remembering a small number of items for a short time)[1]
- *Visual-spatial abilities* (generating visual images and identifying patterns in an incomplete visual display)
- *Auditory processing* (analyzing and synthesizing sound elements and auditory patterns)
- *Cognitive processing speed* (performing easy and familiar tasks efficiently)
- *Decision/reaction time* (making decisions quickly about simple stimuli).[2]

From out of these broad abilities, 70 to 100 very specific abilities (Stratum I) are differentiated—reading speed, mechanical knowledge, visual memory, and so on.

Considerable evidence supports the CHC model. Numerous investigations with large samples and statistical models validate the multidimensional and hierarchical structure of intelligence (M. Chang, Paulson, Finch, Mcintosh, & Rothlisberg, 2014; Flanagan et al., 2013; Golay & Lecerf, 2011). The model is also generally consistent with research on the brain, data on developmental changes in children's intelligence, and evidence of hereditary and environmental influences on intelligence (McGrew, 2005). In addition, many school psychologists suggest that the CHC model can productively guide services for individual children who achieve at exceptionally advanced or delayed levels in particular academic areas (Bergeron & Floyd, 2006; Claeys, 2013; Fiorello & Primerano, 2005; Floyd, Bergeron, & Alfonso, 2006; Volker, Lopata, & Cook-Cottone, 2006).

For example, when one teacher noticed that a sixth-grade girl appeared to be having trouble with short-term memory and basic reading skills, she consulted with a school psychologist who administered a battery of tests and found that most of the girl's abilities were strong (i.e., she had good language skills, vocabulary, long-term memory, and knowledge of letter–sound relationships), but a few others reflected difficulty remembering sequences of spoken words (i.e., a problem with working memory for auditory information; Fiorello & Primerano, 2005). The psychologist recommended that the girl receive drills in spelling and letter–sound combinations so that these operations could be enacted without major demands on memory. Other recommendations included allowing her to use a tape recorder during class, request notes from a classmate, and review assigned books on tape.

A disadvantage of the CHC model is that it is still evolving and obviously very complex, making the full range of implications unclear. In addition, although it has been informed by numerous kinds of data, the framework is based primarily on existing intelligence tests. The CHC theory needs to be elaborated in the future with nontraditional tasks and with more diverse populations, including children in non-Western cultures.

Gardner's Multiple Intelligences

American psychologist **Howard Gardner** argues that traditional definitions of intelligence are too narrow (Gardner, 1995, 2003, 2009, 2011). He concedes that a general factor of intelligence may exist but questions its usefulness in explaining people's performance across situations. In his view, children and adults have at least eight distinctly different abilities, or *multiple intelligences* (MI), which are illustrated in Table 8-1. Three of the intelligences—linguistic, logical-mathematical, and spatial abilities—resemble the kinds of abilities that are tapped by conventional intelligence tests. According to Gardner, the remaining intelligences—musical, bodily-kinesthetic, interpersonal, intrapersonal, and naturalist abilities—are legitimate intellectual domains that have been neglected by test developers. Gardner also speculates that there may be a ninth, "existential" intelligence dedicated to philosophical and spiritual issues (e.g., Who are we? Why do we exist?). Because Gardner is on the fence about whether sufficient data distinguish an existential ability as a separate intelligence, it is not included in the table (Gardner, 1999, 2003, 2009). From Gardner's vantage point, it is not as important to agree on a specific number of intelligences as it is to accept that abilities exist as a plurality across a range of domains.

[1]The CHC broad ability of short-term memory incorporates the idea of the limited capacity of working memory, which is explained in Chapters 6 and 7.
[2]Additional abilities (e.g., general knowledge, kinesthetic abilities, and general cognitive speed) are under investigation for possible inclusion as broad abilities in the middle stratum (McGrew, 2005).

TABLE 8-1 Gardner's Multiple Intelligences

TYPE OF INTELLIGENCE[a]	EXAMPLES OF RELEVANT BEHAVIORS
Linguistic Intelligence Ability to use language effectively	• Making persuasive arguments • Writing poetry • Identifying subtle nuances in word meanings
Logical-Mathematical Intelligence Ability to reason logically, especially in mathematics and science	• Solving mathematical problems quickly • Generating mathematical proofs • Formulating and testing hypotheses about observed phenomena[b]
Spatial Intelligence Ability to notice details in what one sees and imagine and manipulate visual objects in one's mind	• Conjuring up mental images • Drawing a visual likeness of an object • Making fine discriminations among very similar objects
Musical Intelligence Ability to create, comprehend, and appreciate music	• Playing a musical instrument • Composing a musical work • Showing a keen awareness of the underlying structure of music
Bodily-Kinesthetic Intelligence Ability to use one's body skillfully	• Dancing • Playing basketball • Performing pantomime
Interpersonal Intelligence Ability to notice subtle aspects of other people's behaviors	• Correctly perceiving another's mood • Detecting another's underlying intentions and desires • Using knowledge of others to influence their thoughts and behaviors
Intrapersonal Intelligence Awareness of one's own feelings, motives, and desires	• Identifying subtle differences in one's experiences of such similar emotions as sadness and regret • Identifying the motives guiding one's own behavior • Using self-knowledge to relate more effectively with others
Naturalist Intelligence Ability to recognize patterns in nature and differences among natural objects and life-forms	• Identifying members of particular plant or animal species • Classifying natural forms (e.g., rocks, types of mountains) • Applying one's knowledge of nature in such activities as farming, landscaping, or animal training

[a]Gardner has also suggested the possibility of an existential intelligence dedicated to philosophical and spiritual issues, but he acknowledges that evidence for it is weaker than is the case for the eight intelligences described here.
[b]This example may remind you of Piaget's theory of cognitive development. Many of the abilities that Piaget described fall within the realm of logical-mathematical intelligence.

Sources: J. Chen & Gardner, 2012; Gardner, 1983, 1993, 1999, 2000, 2009; Gardner & Hatch, 1990.

Gardner presents far-reaching evidence to back the existence of multiple intelligences. He describes people who are quite skilled in one area (perhaps in composing music) yet seemingly average in other areas. He points out that people who suffer brain damage sometimes lose abilities that are restricted to a single intelligence. One person might show deficits primarily in language, whereas another might have difficulty with tasks that require spatial reasoning. Furthermore, Gardner argues that each of the intelligences has its own symbolic operations and has played an important role over the millennia in people's adaptations to their environments. Thus, whereas Spearman's theory and the Cattell-Horn-Carroll model are based heavily on traditional test scores, Gardner and his colleagues claim that other kinds of data (e.g., studies of people with exceptional talents, documentation of people with brain injuries) must be seriously considered in accounts of human abilities (Gardner, 2008, 2009; Gardner & Moran, 2006).

Gardner and his colleagues have identified several implications of his theory. One important application is giving children choices in how they demonstrate knowledge. Gardner recommends that teachers help children refine their unique profiles of abilities, for example, by implementing computer programs that personalize training. Teachers can vary their instructional modalities, for example, by asking students to show their mastery of mathematics with written formulas (logical-mathematical abilities) on one occasion, self-reflections on learning (intrapersonal abilities) on another, and analyses of data collected from the local ecology (naturalistic abilities) at yet another time. Soliciting a range of intellectual abilities increases the chances that the special talents of every child will be exercised at one time or another and that children will develop well-rounded understandings of subject matter (J. Chen & Gardner, 2012; Gardner, 2009).

Many educators around the world wholeheartedly embrace the insight that students can accomplish a great deal when instructional methods elicit an assortment of abilities (Armstrong, 2009; L. Campbell, Campbell, & Dickinson, 1998; Rattanavich, 2013; Rizzo, 2009). You can learn how educators in China have integrated Gardner's theory in the Development in Culture feature, "Multiple Intelligences in China."

DEVELOPMENT IN CULTURE
Multiple Intelligences in China

Three aspects of Howard Gardner's theory of multiple intelligences (MI) have been endorsed around the world (Armstrong, 2009; Gardner, 2009). First, integral to Gardner's theory is the idea that each of the eight (or nine, or more) intelligences is represented in unique ways in virtually all cultures (Gardner, 1983). People in varied circumstances can recognize the uses that they make of language, mathematics, spatial images, movement, music, personal insights, interpersonal understandings, and knowledge of nature (Armstrong, 2009). Second, the theory's advocacy for the arts and physical education has been compelling to many educators who believe that joy of learning is important and can be fostered with an encompassing view on learning (Gardner, 2009). Finally, educators have appreciated Gardner's interest in reaching underserved students with inclusive methods.

Educators in China have been particularly enthusiastic about applying lessons from the theory of MI. In fact, hundreds of thousands of Chinese educators have received training in this framework (J.-Q Chen, 2009; Zhang & Kong, 2012). Chinese educators increasingly recognize that traditional methods of instruction, which have emphasized memorization of basic facts, yield proficiencies that are inadequate for a rapidly changing society. For modern Chinese teachers, active learning, respect for individual differences, and innovation make MI theory an ideal framework for optimizing human potential (J.-Q. Chen, 2009; H. H.-P. Cheung, 2009).

The theory's compatibility with cultural ideals about learning has also contributed to its embrace in China. Dating back to the days of Confucius, Chinese culture has admired the plurality of human abilities (J.-Q. Chen, 2009; Shen, 2009). Today, an appreciation for individual differences has helped teachers respond sympathetically to learners who do not perform well on traditional academic tasks. In reflecting on the MI framework, one Chinese teacher said, "Unlike before, when I look at my students now, they are all good students. Everyone has shining points to appreciate" (H. H.-P. Cheung, 2009, p. 45). Another teacher made a similar observation, "I noticed some of my students who did not have high scores in school turned out to be more successful. MI theory shows me the reason. Those students' interpersonal intelligences might be higher. Each of them is unique" (H. H.-P. Cheung, 2009, p. 45).

In the process of absorbing basic tenets of MI theory, Chinese educators have adapted the framework to fit two features of their culture. First, intelligence in young children is considered inseparable from the abilities of their families (J.-Q. Chen, 2009). In other words, intelligence is considered a property of the family, not a quality of the individual child. Each family has its

INTELLIGENCE IN THE FAMILY. In China, Gardner's theory of multiple intelligences has drawn attention to the growth of intellectual development within the family.

own profile of intellectual strengths, interests, and skills, and each member of the family complements and supports the intelligence of other members. In this spirit, educators trained in MI theory hold classes in the evening and on weekends for parents. At school, children are encouraged to learn about their parents' values, interests, and child-rearing strategies so as to increase children's receptivity to family lessons.

Second, the cultural ideal of harmony is integrated into interpretations of MI theory. Chinese educators view children's intellectual strengths as balancing their weaknesses. To be effective, teachers must take into account the entire package of abilities and limitations in children. The notion of harmony also applies to offering an array of lesson formats so that everyone has a chance to succeed (J.-Q. Chen, 2009; Jing, 2013).

Chinese educators wrestle with certain challenges in translating the principles of MI theory to instruction (H. H.-P. Cheung, 2009). Large class sizes make it difficult to individualize innovative instructional methods. Pressures to prepare high school students for college entrance examinations complicate the applications for older adolescents. Finally, some Chinese educators have the misconception that the framework directs them to train every child to a high level of accomplishment in each of the eight or nine intelligences, rather than allowing children freedom to excel with the talents of their choice.

In psychological circles, reviews of Gardner's theory are mixed. Some psychologists do not believe that Gardner's evidence is sufficiently convincing to accept the notion of eight or nine distinctly different abilities (N. Brody, 2006; A. R. Jensen, 2007; Sternberg, 2013). Others agree that people may have a variety of independent abilities but these are different intelligences than the ones Gardner described (e.g., D. Flanagan et al., 2013; J. L. Horn & Noll, 1997; Sternberg et al., 2000). Still others reject the idea that abilities in specific domains, such as in music or bodily movement, are really "intelligence" per se (Bracken, McCallum, & Shaughnessy, 1999; Sattler, 2001).

Sternberg's Theory of Successful Intelligence

American psychologist **Robert Sternberg** has developed a series of interrelated theories on how people use their cognitive abilities to achieve personal goals. Sternberg sees intelligence as a multifaceted capacity that allows an individual to adapt effectively to the environment (see Figure 8-1). He suggests that people may be more or less intelligent in three sets of abilities (Sternberg, 1985, 2005, 2009). *Analytical intelligence* involves making sense of, analyzing, contrasting, and evaluating the kinds of information seen in academic settings and on intelligence tests. *Creative intelligence* involves imagination, invention, and synthesis of ideas within new situations. *Practical intelligence* involves applying knowledge and skills effectively with everyday problems and social situations. Children blend these three types of intelligence in everyday tasks and gradually learn to recognize their personal strengths in each, use them to advantage, and correct or compensate for their individual weaknesses.

These three types of intelligence involve the interplay of three additional factors: (a) the environmental *context* in which the behavior occurs, (b) the way in which one's memory of prior *experience* is brought to bear on a particular task, and (c) the *cognitive processes* required by the task (Sternberg, 1985, 1997, 2003b).

> ### Successful Intelligence
>
> - Is comprised of analytical, creative, and practical abilities
> - Helps a person achieve personal goals
> - Requires a balancing among particular abilities
> - Draws from memory and engages specific cognitive processes
> - Allows a person to adapt, shape, and select their environments

FIGURE 8-1 **Sternberg's theory of successful intelligence.** According to Sternberg, a child uses a multifaceted collection of abilities to achieve personal goals.

Environmental Context. In Sternberg's view adjustment to the environment might take one of three forms: (a) modifying a response to deal successfully with specific conditions, (b) modifying the environment to better fit one's own strengths and needs, or (c) selecting an alternative environment conducive to success. Thus, a given action may be considered more or less intelligent depending on the demands of the setting. For example, learning to describe events in explicit detail is intelligent in some contexts (e.g., at school), whereas speaking in an informal manner with reference to shared experiences is smart in other settings (e.g., with friends).

Prior Experience. Intelligent behavior sometimes involves the ability to deal successfully with a brand-new situation. At other times, it involves the ability to respond to familiar situations rapidly and efficiently. In both cases, a child's prior experiences play a critical role. When children encounter a new task or problem, they must consider the kinds of reactions that have been effective in similar circumstances. When they deal with familiar tasks, basic skills are well practiced so that the necessary processes can be completed quickly and effortlessly.

Cognitive Processes. In addition to examining how context and prior experience affect behavior, we must also consider how a child thinks about a particular situation. Sternberg suggests that numerous cognitive processes are involved in intelligent behavior: interpreting a new situation in productive ways, sustaining concentration on a task, separating important information from irrelevant details, identifying possible problem-solving strategies, finding relationships among seemingly different ideas, and making effective use of external feedback. Different cognitive processes are likely to be relevant to different situations, and so a child may behave more or less "intelligently" depending on specific demands.

Sternberg and his colleagues recommend that teachers diversify the abilities they tap across lessons. Although it is not realistic to target the full gamut of abilities in any single lesson, teachers can diversify their repertoire over a period of time. In a science unit, students might get to conduct standard experiments on light, write a fantasy story about a light beam traveling around the world, identify patterns in astronomical data from knowledge of the speed with which light travels, etc. (Sternberg, Jarvin, & Grigorenko, 2009). In one investigation, students who took part in a well-balanced curriculum with exercises in analytical, practical, and creative intelligence performed at higher levels than did students who received conventional instruction (Sternberg, Torff, & Grigorenko, 1998).

A modest amount of research supports Sternberg's theory. Some evidence indicates that analytical, creative, and practical skills exist and are somewhat independent of one another and of general intelligence (Sternberg, 2009). Other results indicate that Sternberg's abilities are associated with later academic success, sometimes more strongly than is the case with conventional tests of ability. However, several scholars worry that certain aspects of Sternberg's theory (e.g., how various factors work together) are described in such general terms that they are difficult to test empirically (Sattler, 2001; Siegler & Alibali, 2005). A few intelligence specialists are not yet convinced that the practical abilities identified in Sternberg's theory are really different from general intelligence (N. Brody, 2006; Ekinci, 2014; Gottfredson, 2003). Despite these limitations, Sternberg's perspective draws attention to the cognitive processes that underlie a child's multifaceted abilities and reminds us that a child's ability to behave intelligently varies according to context, his or her goals, and the knowledge required by a task.

Distributed Intelligence

Implicit in our discussion so far has been the assumption that intelligent behavior is something that children engage in with little if any help from external resources. But some psychologists point out that youngsters are far more likely to behave intelligently when they have the support of their physical, social, and cultural environments (A. Bennett et al., 2007; Pea, 1993; Perkins, 1995; Sternberg, Grigorenko, & Bridglall, 2007). For example, it's easier for many adolescents to solve for x in the equation

$$\frac{7}{25} = \frac{x}{375}$$

if they have pencil and paper with which to work out the problem. And they are more likely to write a convincing persuasive essay if they brainstorm their ideas with peers before beginning to compose their notes.

This idea that intelligent behavior depends on physical, social, and cultural support mechanisms is referred to as **distributed intelligence**. Learning specialists **Roy Pea** and **David Perkins** have observed that children can "distribute" their thinking (and therefore think more intelligently) in at least three ways (Pea, 1993; Perkins, 1992, 1995). First, young people can use physical objects, especially technology (e.g., calculators, computers), to handle and manipulate large amounts of information. Second, they can work with others to explore ideas and solve problems. Third, they can represent the situations they encounter using symbolic tools—for instance, the words, diagrams, charts, mathematical equations, and so on—that help them simplify or make better sense of complex topics and problems.

The framework of distributed intelligence has considerable appeal to many educators who recognize that *all* children—not just those who have the advantage of "smart" genes or those whose families foster their academic skills at home—deserve to have their abilities nurtured by teachers and classmates (Barab & Plucker, 2002; Hoerr, 2003). In fact, children often develop more advanced skills when working together, pooling their knowledge, using new technologies, and tackling realistic problems (C. Alvarez, Salavati, Nussbaum & Milrad, 2013; Greeno, 2007; L. Xu & Clarke, 2012). Theorists have only begun to explore the implications of a "distributed" view of intelligence, however. Much work remains to be done, both in identifying the specific ways in which the environment can support intelligent behavior and in determining the effect such support is likely to have.

The five perspectives just presented provide diverging views of human intelligence. Differences with respect to three themes—nature and nurture, universality and diversity, and qualitative and quantitative change—are presented in the Basic Developmental Issues table "Contrasting Theories of Intelligence."

BASIC DEVELOPMENTAL ISSUES
Contrasting Theories of Intelligence

ISSUE	SPEARMAN'S GENERAL FACTOR (g)	CATTELL-HORN-CARROLL THEORY OF COGNITIVE ABILITIES	GARDNER'S THEORY OF MULTIPLE INTELLIGENCES	STERNBERG'S THEORY OF SUCCESSFUL INTELLIGENCE	THEORY OF DISTRIBUTED INTELLIGENCE
Nature and Nurture	Spearman did not focus on the issue of nature versus nurture. Researchers have subsequently found evidence that g is related to both heredity and environment.	Proponents of the Cattell-Horn-Carroll model claim that fluid intelligence is strongly determined by genetic factors. Crystallized intelligence is influenced by both heredity and environment such that educators can teach children how to improve their abilities.	Gardner believes that heredity contributes to individual differences in the various intelligences. Culture influences the form of each intelligence. Informal experiences and instruction determine the manifestation of intelligences.	Sternberg emphasizes the roles of environmental context (e.g., culture), prior experience, and the person's own goals and choices in particular settings. Thus his focus is primarily on nurture.	Generally, people act more intelligently when they have access to resources. Specific mechanisms for supporting thinking (e.g., social interaction and the symbolic representations of one's culture) vary among individuals and settings.
Universality and Diversity	Spearman assumed that the existence of g is universal across cultures. People vary both in general intellectual ability and in more specific abilities.	Substantial evidence suggests that the multidimensional structure of abilities is universal. Individual children differ in levels of general intelligence, broad abilities, and specific abilities.	The various intelligences are products of human evolution and are seen worldwide. However, any particular intelligence will manifest itself differently in separate settings and cultures.	Context, experience, and cognitive processes universally affect intelligent behavior. Different cultures place distinct demands on analytical, creative, and practical abilities.	The physical, social, and symbolic support mechanisms at one's disposal vary widely from situation to situation and from one cultural group to another.
Qualitative and Quantitative Change	Spearman derived his theory from various tests of cognitive abilities. Implicit in his tests is the assumption that abilities change quantitatively over time.	A quantitative increase occurs in fluid analytical abilities in childhood and is followed by a decline in later adulthood (Cattell, 1963). Abilities also change qualitatively as when a baby attends to interesting stimuli and later can verbalize observations.	Growth in intelligences reflects both quantitative and qualitative changes. In logical-mathematical intelligence, children gain skills in increments (quantitatively) but also acquire new (and qualitatively different) abilities.	The effects of prior experiences, more automatized knowledge and skills, and progressively efficient cognitive processes involve quantitative change. The acquisition of new strategies involves qualitative change.	Some resources enhance ability quantitatively (e.g., paper and pencil increase mathematical accuracy than mental calculations alone). Other instruction enhances intelligence qualitatively (e.g., enhancing comprehension by asking thought-provoking questions).

Alternative Perspective on Intelligence

Data on associations between specific abilities and other talents, school achievement, and real-world outcomes have guided the study of intelligence. A few emerging approaches are less firmly grounded in this research yet suggestive of new abilities not measured by existing intelligence tests. These additional competencies have been detected in various cultures, in settings that invite creative innovation, and in response to emotionally rich situations.

Cross-Cultural Views on Intelligence

As you have learned, intelligence is *culture specific*. The magnificent flexibility of the brain allows children to adapt their talents to the demands and opportunities of their society. In Western civilizations, intelligence is a means for analyzing information into categories and propositions for evidence, whereas in Eastern cultures people invest their intelligence in perceptions of complexity, contradiction, and social obligation (Nisbett, 2003). Social skills are recognized as attributes of intelligent people in the Chewa people of eastern Zambia, whose older children exercise their intellectual abilities in caring for younger siblings (Serpell, 2011).

In a diverse society, children vary in how their abilities are socialized. If there is a divergence between teachers and parents in fundamental beliefs related to intelligence, students will have abilities that are treasured at home yet unrecognized at school. In some cases students are unacquainted with specific intellectual abilities, for example, mathematical reasoning, that are foundations for academic success. These and other academic abilities may be exercised in different ways at home and school and sometimes with lesser emphasis than is assumed by educators. Languages and cultural knowledge acquired in the family and community also affect intellectual performance in the classroom. Test scores for children who are unfamiliar with the language and customs presumed by assessments have questionable usefulness in guiding instructional adjustments for children.

Creativity

Questions on intelligence tests generally have right or wrong answers, unlike many dilemmas in real life, whose remedies transcend known facts and existing technologies. How we promote job growth in the community, compose a story, invent a cure for cancer, and express personal feelings through artwork are complicated endeavors with indeterminate answers. Such endeavors require **creativity**, the valuable process of generating novel and worthwhile solutions to goals, needs, and problems.

Traditionally, creativity has been measured by a test that requires people to formulate original solutions to unfamiliar problems, such as by generating as many ways as possible to use a pencil, book, or brick (Guilford, 1967; Goff & Torrance, 2002; Torrance, 1981). Creativity scores are calculated from the number of different ways and the number of uniquely original ways (not proposed by others) that the person formulates. Fluency in formulating novel uses for objects is only part of creativity, however. Experts believe that the additional step of taking brainstormed ideas and pruning them down to a limited number of viable options is a key part of the creative process (Goodwin & Miller, 2013; C. S. Lee & Therriault, 2013).

When thinking creatively, a person uses familiar intellectual processes, such as searching memory, comparing possible ways of representing a problem, putting ideas together in new ways, and selecting final answers that have been carefully vetted (C. S. Lee & Therriault, 2013). Nevertheless, creativity is not the same as intelligence. The ability to act imaginatively appears to require distinct talents in applying mental processes fluidly and dynamically. Yet being original is not enough to be creative. One can formulate numerous ideas that are not necessarily appropriate for the task at hand. Thus a creative solution aptly addresses the constraints of the problem, such as building a fort in the classroom that can house five children out of existing materials.

Exercising inventive abilities changes with development, but perhaps not in the manner you might think. Unlike intelligence, creativity does not necessarily increase with development. Overall, children are more creative than adults, and younger children are more creative than older children, suggesting that this capacity *diminishes* as children progress through the school years (Goodwin & Miller, 2013; Land & Jarman, 1992). Part of the decline is due to children learning society's conventions for solving common problems. Instructional strategies may also stifle creativity by emphasizing facts and procedures over free expression.

Despite the prevailing decrease in creativity, teachers *can* nurture children's originality and inventiveness. Art teachers might provide open spaces with a wide range of resources, advise students that they are welcome to explore, encourage peer conversations, and use strategies that foster children's innovative work (D. Davies et al., 2012). A strong imagination benefits children who will become artists, of course, and children with other professional aspirations can benefit as well. In fact, many creative scientists find that an artistic mind-set, previously acquired at the piano, in a workshop, or with a camera, plays an integral role in their discoveries and inventions (Root-Bernstein & Root-Bernstein, 2013).

In certain types of lessons, children can be encouraged to envision multiple ways for approaching a task. An elementary teacher might ask children to brainstorm about funny things that farm animals do before selecting one animal to write a story about, and a middle school science teacher could encourage students to speculate about several hypotheses before pursuing one (S. Brookhart, 2013). Building a structurally sound bridge out of toothpicks, writing an essay on how life would be different in Europe if a major battle in World War II had resulted in a different outcome, and preparing a video discouraging bullying at school are all projects that could incorporate creative processes.

Emotional Intelligence

Just as some students have special talents that make it easy for them to learn to read or solve algebraic equations, other students have exceptional abilities in recognizing why they feel as they do, in brushing off disappointments, and in expressing empathy to friends in need. The former students have intellectual abilities that contribute to their academic success. Do the latter students have emotional capacities that contribute to their well-being? Surely they do. Emotional abilities, their development, and strategies for fostering them are sufficiently important that we devote an entire chapter to them later in the book.[3]

In the context of intelligence, the question arises as to whether skill with emotions is an actual intelligence. The answer is complex. Certainly the basic definition of intelligence—the ability to use prior knowledge flexibly in accomplishing new tasks—applies to coping with emotions. Furthermore, the ability to handle emotions has several qualities of intelligence we introduced previously. Emotional regulation is adaptive in that it helps a child maintain productive friendships and family relationships, improves with learning and experience, and is, to some degree, culture specific. For these reasons, several experts on emotions describe the ability to perceive, understand, and regulate affective feelings as **emotional intelligence** (Curci, Lanciano, Soleti, Zammuner, & Salovey, 2013; D. Goleman, 1995; Keefer, Holden, & Parker, 2013; Laborde, Lautenbach, Allen, Herbert, & Achtzehn, 2014). Mainstream intelligence theorists tend to disagree, however, not discounting the importance of emotional regulation, but questioning whether this capacity constitutes a coherent ability that is distinct from well-established dimensions of intelligence and personality (N. Brody, 2004; Brouzos, Misailidi, & Hadjimattheou, 2014; Waterhouse, 2006).

Real-World Insights from Theories of Intelligence

Although experts disagree about the exact nature of intelligence, sufficient consensus exists to derive a few applications. Consider these implications:

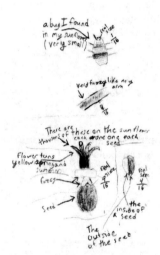

ARTIFACT 8-1 Examine 10-year-old Amaryth's sketches for use of several distinct abilities.

 • **Vary demands for specific intellectual abilities.** As you have learned, intelligence is a multifaceted cluster of abilities. Although traditional forms of education emphasize verbal and quantitative skills, students are capable of many other talents, including artistic and musical abilities, creative powers, and athletic skills. As we saw in recommendations by Howard Gardner and Robert Sternberg, lessons, projects, and assessments within a unit can elicit a healthy diversity of intellectual abilities. Oftentimes a single project exercises two or more distinct abilities, as you can infer in a drawing by 10-year-old Amaryth in Artifact 8-1. Amaryth applies Gardner's naturalist intelligence in detecting patterns in the sunflower seeds, spatial intelligence in measuring the insect and sunflower, and linguistic intelligence when describing the stem as "very fuzzy like my arm."

 • **Watch for children's personal strengths and weaknesses.** From the beginning of the school year, teachers gradually notice which children easily grasp concepts across the curriculum, and which others regularly run into trouble, patterns that arise in part due to varying levels of general intelligence. (Later in this chapter we examine strategies for children who are intellectually gifted and others with intellectual disabilities.) As the year progresses, teachers begin to observe nuances in individual children's proficiencies and struggles with specific abilities. One child may excel at all things mathematical and another may have trouble keeping lengthy instructions in mind.

 • **Document children's abilities.** Collect work samples that reveal students' strengths and difficulties, perhaps in visual-spatial abilities in geometry, auditory processing while learning to read, or mathematical competencies when calculating numerical equations. When children struggle with one or more of these skills, teachers can provide handouts with written

---

[3]Emotional development is the focus of Chapter 11.

OBSERVATION GUIDELINES
Seeing Intelligence in Children's Daily Behavior

CHARACTERISTIC	LOOK FOR	EXAMPLE	IMPLICATION
Oral Language Skills	• Sophisticated vocabulary • Colorful speech • Creative storytelling • Clever jokes and puns	Jerome entertains his friends with jokes and wild exaggerations about the characteristics and actions of other people.	Look for unusual creativity or advanced language development in children's everyday speech.
General Intelligence	• Ability to learn new information quickly • Exceptional knowledge about a variety of topics • Ability to find relationships among diverse ideas • Excellent memory	Four-year-old Gina teaches herself to read using several primers she finds at home. Initially, her mother identifies a few words for her. From these words she deduces many letter–sound correspondences that enable her to decipher additional words.	Make note of situations in which a child learns and comprehends new material far more quickly than peers. Look for creative analogies and interconnections in expressed ideas.
Problem-Solving Skills	• Ability to solve challenging problems • Flexibility in applying previously learned strategies to new kinds of problems • Ability to improvise with commonplace objects and materials	A fourth-grade class plans to perform a skit during an upcoming open house. Jeff suggests that they turn their desks to face the side of the classroom, allowing a sheet to be hung from a light fixture as a stage curtain.	Present unusual tasks and problems for which children have no ready-made strategies or solutions.
Cognitive and Metacognitive Strategies	• Use of sophisticated learning strategies • Desire to understand rather than memorize • Effective comprehension monitoring	Shannon, a sixth grader, explains that she learned the countries on South America's west coast (Colombia, Ecuador, Peru, Chile) by creating the sentence "Colin eats peas and chocolate."	Ask children to describe how they think about things they are trying to learn and remember.
Curiosity and Inquisitiveness	• Voracious appetite for knowledge • Tendency to ask a lot of questions • Intrinsic motivation to master challenging subject matter	Alfredo reads every book and article he can find about outer space. He has a particular interest in black holes.	Find out what children like to do in their free time and direct them to relevant resources.
Leadership and Social Skills	• Ability to persuade and motivate others • Exceptional sensitivity to other people's feelings and body language • Ability to mediate disagreements and help others reach reasonable compromises	As a high school student, Gina organizes and directs a peer-tutoring program.	Observe how children interact with their peers at play, in cooperative group work, and during extracurricular activities.

Sources: Blake & Giannangelo, 2012; B. Clark, 1997; A. W. Gottfried, Gottfried, Bathurst, & Guerin, 1994; Y. Huang, Hsu, Su, & Liu, 2014; Maker, 1993; Perkins, 1995; Sousa, 2009; Torrance, 1995; Turnbull, Turnbull, & Wehmeyer, 2010; Winner, 1997.

procedures, audiotaped books, or other resources that bolster overall accomplishments. Extraordinary accomplishments indicate the need for new challenges. School psychologists and other specialists are regularly available to offer advice on adapting lessons for children with unusual intellectual profiles.

• **Be open-minded about ways for demonstrating intelligence.** As we've seen, some experts believe that human intelligence isn't a single entity—that it is, instead, a collection of relatively separate abilities that children have to varying degrees depending on their individual characteristics, experiences, and cultural backgrounds. The Observation Guidelines table "Seeing Intelligence in Children's Daily Behavior" presents a variety of behaviors that reveal intelligence.

• **Encourage children to use technology, help one another, and pool their knowledge.** Although we generally think about talent as an individual matter, the reality is that children often achieve at higher levels in groups than alone and with access to various technologies than without such resources. The theory of distributed intelligences reminds us that children—like adults in the workplace—think more effectively when they can consult with others and use applicable tools.[4]

[4]In Chapter 15, we offer recommendations for facilitating children's peer relationships.

• **Encourage creativity.** Given the emphasis in most classrooms on basic skills and core knowledge, children realize that they are expected to learn procedures and concepts as presented by teachers. Yet there are occasions when real creativity enhances learning. Because children may not automatically identify circumstances in which they have freedom of expression, teachers need to signal when novel projects are welcome. Teachers can structure these lessons to be conducive to innovative accomplishment—for example, by providing an assortment of materials, communicating that objectives have no single procedures or solutions, and encouraging children to brainstorm about potential ideas at the beginning of the assignment.

• **Learn about talents that are cultivated at home and in the community.** Spending time in local communities is a valuable way to learn about the intellectual talents that are respected in the culture. Invitations to families to share their aspirations for children at school meetings are also useful. In the classroom, teachers can occasionally offer options, such as through a wide selection of themes in historical novels and multiple formats for demonstrating comprehension (e.g., oral presentations, posters, essays, or cartoons).

• **Promote "intelligent" cognitive strategies.** Look again at this chapter's opening case study. Gina's relative weakness in history is due largely to her ineffective study strategies. In fact, teachers and other professionals can endorse more effective learning, studying, and problem solving—and in doing so promote more intelligent behavior (Cornoldi, 2010; Perkins, 1995; Sternberg, 2002).[5]

Summary

Intelligence involves effective learning processes and adaptive behaviors in a particular setting. Some theorists believe that intelligence is a single entity (a general factor, or *g*) that influences children's learning and performance across a wide variety of tasks. This belief is reflected in the widespread use of IQ scores as general estimates of academic ability. Other theorists (e.g., Gardner and Sternberg) propose that intelligence consists of a number of somewhat independent abilities that cannot be accurately reflected in a single IQ score. Increasing evidence reveals that children are more likely to behave "intelligently" when they have physical, social, and symbolic support systems to ease their efforts. Emerging views suggest the existence of additional talents, including culture-specific abilities, creative knacks, and emotional sensitivities.

Adults can anticipate that individual children will be intelligent in distinct ways and capitalize on these unique strengths in lessons. Adults can also give children social support and the physical and symbolic tools that enhance intelligent thinking and performance. Significant limitations in core abilities can be effectively accommodated with professional guidance from school psychologists, counselors, and special education teachers.

ENHANCEDetext *self-check*

Assessing Children 8-1

Practice identifying intellectual abilities that are tapped in academic lessons.

ENHANCEDetext *application exercise*

Assessing Children 8-2

Practice assessing the distinct intellectual abilities required by an academic unit.

ENHANCEDetext *application exercise*

[5]Cognitive and metacognitive strategies are examined in Chapter 7.

MEASUREMENT OF INTELLIGENCE

Although psychologists have not been able to agree on exactly what intelligence is, they have been trying to measure it for more than a century. Most intelligence tests in use today have been developed to do the same thing that Alfred Binet's first test was intended to do: identify children with special needs who would benefit from customized educational services.

Tests of Intelligence

A diagnostic battery of intelligence tests is administered to determine why certain children are showing developmental delays or academic difficulties. In other instances, intelligence tests are used to identify children with exceptionally high abilities who require more in-depth instruction and advanced classwork to nurture their cognitive growth.

Intelligence tests typically include a wide variety of questions and problems for children to tackle. By and large, the focus is not on what children have specifically been taught at school, but rather on what they have learned and deduced from their everyday experiences. To give you a feel for the nature of intelligence tests, we briefly describe four of them.[6]

Wechsler Intelligence Scale for Children

One widely used intelligence test is the fourth edition of the *Wechsler Intelligence Scale for Children,* or WISC-IV, designed for children and adolescents ages 6 to 16 (Wahlstrom, Breaux, Zhu & Weiss, 2012; Wechsler, 2003). The WISC-IV consists of 15 subtests, with subtest scores being combined to obtain composite scores in Verbal Comprehension, Perceptual Reasoning, Working Memory, and Processing Speed. Subtest scores are also added to determine a total score, known as a Full Scale IQ. Illustrations of items like those on the WISC-IV are presented in Figure 8-2.

Stanford-Binet Intelligence Scales

A second commonly used instrument is the fifth edition of the *Stanford-Binet Intelligence Scales* (Roid, 2003; Roid & Pomplun, 2012). The Stanford-Binet can be used with children (as young as age 2), adolescents, and adults. The individual being assessed is asked to perform a wide variety of tasks, some involving verbal concepts (e.g., defining vocabulary words, finding logical inconsistencies in a story, or interpreting proverbs) and others involving objects or pictures (e.g., remembering a sequence of objects, copying geometric figures, or identifying absurdities in pictures). The Stanford-Binet yields an overall IQ score, and its most recent edition also yields Verbal and Nonverbal IQs, plus more specific scores in Fluid Reasoning, Knowledge, Working Memory, Visual-Spatial Processing, and Quantitative Reasoning.

Universal Nonverbal Intelligence Test

The WISC-IV and Stanford-Binet depend heavily on language: Even when tasks involve reasoning about strictly nonverbal, visual material, the child is usually given verbal instructions about how to complete them. In contrast, some measures of intelligence involve no language whatsoever. An example is the *Universal Nonverbal Intelligence Test,* or UNIT (Bracken & McCallum, 1998, 2009; McCallum & Bracken, 2012). Designed for children and adolescents ages 5 to 17, the UNIT consists of six subtests involving memory or reasoning regarding visual stimuli. Its content (e.g., people, mice, cheese) was chosen from objects and symbols presumed to be universal across all industrialized cultures. Instructions are given entirely through gestures, pantomime, and modeling, and the child responds by either pointing or manipulating objects. For example, the child may trace a path through a maze or construct a three-dimensional design using colored cubes.

Nonverbal tests such as the UNIT are especially useful for children who have hearing impairments or language-related learning disabilities, as well as for children for whom English is a second language. Children who are deaf and children who have been raised speaking a language other than English perform better on the UNIT than on more traditional

---

[6]You can find descriptions of several widely used standardized tests at www.ctb.com (for CTB and McGraw-Hill), www.riverpub.com (for Riverside Publishing), and www.pearsonassessments.com (for Pearson Assessments and PsychCorp tests).

Following are descriptions of 6 of the 15 subtests on the WISC-IV, along with items similar to those included in the subtests.

Similarities

This subtest is designed to assess a child's verbal reasoning and concept formation.

- In what way are a lion and a tiger alike?
- In what way are an hour and a week alike?
- In what way are a circle and a triangle alike?

Comprehension

This subtest is designed to assess a child's understanding of general principles and social situations.

- What should you do if you see someone forget his book when he leaves a restaurant?
- What is the advantage of keeping money in a bank?
- Why is copper often used in electrical wires?

Information

This subtest is designed to assess a child's general knowledge about a broad range of topics.

- How many wings does a bird have?
- What is steam made of?
- What is pepper?

Letter-Number Sequencing

This subtest is designed to assess a child's working memory capacity. In each item, a letter-number sequence is presented, and the child is asked to repeat first the numbers (in numerical order) and then the letters (in alphabetical order).

- Q-3 [Response:3-Q]
- M-3-P-6 [Response:3-6-M-P]
- 5-J-4-A-1-S [Response:1-4-5-A-J-S]

Arithmetic

This subtest is designed to assess a child's ability to solve orally presented arithmetic problems within a certain time limit, tapping into both working memory capacity and knowledge of arithmetic.

- Sam had three pieces of candy and Joe gave him four more. How many pieces of candy did Sam have altogether?
- Three women divided eighteen golf balls equally among themselves. How many golf balls did each person receive?
- If two buttons cost $0.15, what will be the cost of a dozen buttons?

Block Design

This subtest is designed to assess a child's ability to analyze and reproduce geometric designs, thus tapping into visual-spatial ability. The child looks at a series of designs, such as the one below, and is asked to re-create them using blocks that are solid red on two sides, solid white on two sides, and diagonally red and white on the remaining two sides.

FIGURE 8-2 **WISC-IV.** Items similar to those found on the *Wechsler Intelligence Scale for Children®*—Fourth Edition. *Copyright © 2003 by NCS Pearson, Inc. Reproduced with permission. All rights reserved.*

language-based intelligence tests (N. L. Bell, McConnell, Lassiter, & Matthews, 2013; Krivitski, McIntosh, Rothlisberg, & Finch, 2004; Maller, 2000; McCallum, 1999).

The Cognitive Assessment System

The *Cognitive Assessment System* (CAS) is a multidimensional measure of cognitive processes (Naglieri & Otero, 2012). The CAS was founded on the premise that cognitive processes identified in neurological research are the basis for intelligence. It includes four parts: an *Attention* scale (examines selective attention to a particular stimulus, e.g., finding particular numbers on a page despite many distracters); a *Simultaneous* scale (tests the ability to integrate separate stimuli into a single representation, e.g., after looking at a geometric figure, finding it embedded in a more complex pattern); a *Planning* scale (checks the ability to generate a plan for solving a novel problem, e.g., rapidly matching letters and numbers on separate pages, carrying out the plan, staying focused, and evaluating one's performance); and a *Successive Subtest* scale (assesses the ability to process information in a specific order, e.g., repeating words in the same sequence as the examiner states them).

Intelligence Scores

In the early 20th century, some psychologists began to calculate scores for intelligence tests by comparing a child's *mental age* (referring to the age-group of students whose performance is most similar to the child's performance) with his or her chronological age (W. Stern, 1912; Terman, 1916). The mathematical formula involved division, and so the resulting score was called an *intelligence quotient,* or **IQ score**.[7] Even though we still use the term *IQ,* intelligence test scores are no longer based on the old formula. Instead, they are determined by comparing a person's performance on the test with the performance of others in the same age-group. Scores near 100 indicate average performance: People with a score of 100 have performed better than half of their age-mates on the test and not as well as the other half. Scores well below 100 indicate below-average performance on the test, and scores well above 100 indicate above-average performance.

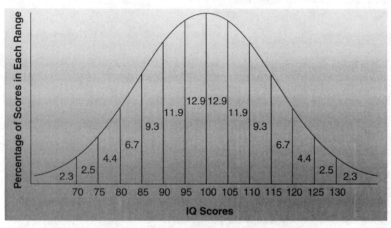

FIGURE 8-3   Percentage of IQ scores in different ranges.

Figure 8-3 shows the percentage of people getting scores at different points along the scale (e.g., 12.9 percent get scores between 100 and 105). Notice how the curve is high in the middle and low at both ends. This shape tells us that many more people obtain scores close to 100 than scores very much higher or lower than 100. If we add up the percentages in different parts of Figure 8-3, we find that approximately two-thirds (68 percent) of individuals in any particular age-group score within 15 points of 100 (i.e., between 85 and 115). In contrast, only 2 percent score as low as 70, and only 2 percent score as high as 130.[8] Figure 8-3 does not include scores below 70 or above 130. Such scores are possible but relatively rare. You might recall that Gina, in the opening case study, once obtained a score of 140 on an intelligence test. A score of 140 is equivalent to a percentile rank of 99.4. In other words, only 6 people out of every 1,000 would earn a score as high as or higher than Gina's.

Keep in mind that use of an IQ score rests on the validity of the notion of general intelligence. As you have learned, not everyone believes that *g* is a meaningful concept, and practically speaking, knowing a child's relative standing on an aggregate of varied items is arguably less informative than finding out the particular intellectual domains in which a child excels and struggles (Mather, 2009; Stanovich, 1999).

Consider the performance of an elementary student on the scales of the *Cognitive Assessment System* (Naglieri & Conway, 2009). Gary performed well below average but still in the normal range on the full-scale CAS, specifically at the 19th percentile, meaning that approximately 8 in 10 children outperformed him (CAS scales are defined on p. 289). What is more illuminating, however, is his uneven performance across the four scales and especially his score on the *Planning* scale. Gary performed better than 55 percent of peers on the *Attention* scale, 23 percent on the *Simultaneous* scale, 39 percent on the *Successive Subtest* scale; but only 5 percent on the *Planning scale*. After receiving test score results, Gary's teacher focused on the challenges that Gary faced in planning. His teacher moved him to a quiet corner where he was not likely to be distracted and taught him steps in selecting goals; carrying out a task carefully, for example, making sure he wrote digits into the proper column for subtraction problems; and checking his completed work. With support related to planning and evaluating his performance, Gary improved in his mathematics achievement, more than doubling the number of correct problems.

[7]Alfred Binet himself objected to the use of intelligence quotients, believing that his tests were too imprecise to warrant such scores. Lewis Terman, an American psychologist, was largely responsible for popularizing the term *IQ* (Montagu, 1999).

[8]If you have some knowledge of descriptive statistics, you probably recognize Figure 8-3 as a normal distribution. IQ scores are based on a normal distribution with a mean of 100 and, for most tests, a standard deviation of 15.

Validity and Reliability of Intelligence Tests

If tests are to be used to make decisions about services for children, scores need to be accurate. In general, the *validity* of an intelligence test is the extent to which it actually measures intelligence. The *reliability* of an intelligence test is the extent to which it yields consistent, dependable scores.[9]

Researchers take a variety of approaches to determine the validity of intelligence tests. For instance, they look for evidence that older children perform better on test items than do younger children—a result consistent with the assumption that children think more intelligently with age. Listen to how three children define the word *freedom* in the "Intelligence" videos for middle childhood, early adolescence, and late adolescence in Observing Children interviews:

Observing Children 8-1
Notice how children's definitions are increasingly sophisticated with age.

ENHANCEDetext *video example*

Kate (age 8):   You want to be free. Or you want to play something . . . and you got caught and they have to keep you like in jail or something like in a game and you want to get free.

Ryan (age 13):   It means that you can, like, do stuff that you want.

Paul (age 17):   Basically something that everyone has these days or should have. It's the right to be able to make your own decisions and choose for yourself what you want to do or want to be.

Notice how, with age, the responses are increasingly abstract and complex. Kate limits her definition to a specific behavior, getting out of "jail" in a game. Ryan defines the term more broadly, implying that it has relevance to a wide variety of situations. Paul offers an abstract definition as well, but his is more precise than Ryan's.

Researchers also examine the validity of intelligence tests by determining how closely IQ scores correlate with school achievement and other accepted indicators of intelligence. Many studies indicate that traditional measures of general intelligence, such as the WISC-IV, the Stanford-Binet, and the CAS, have considerable validity in this respect. On average, children and adolescents who earn higher scores on these tests have higher academic achievement and complete more years of education than their lower-scoring peers (N. Brody, 1997; Firkowska-Mankiewicz, 2011; Naglieri, De Lauder, Goldstein, & Schwebech, 2006). To a lesser degree, intelligence scores also predict income and occupation (Baum & Bird, 2010; Firkowska-Mankiewicz, 2011; Furnham & Cheng, 2013; Sternberg, 1996). We have less information about the UNIT, but emerging evidence indicates that it, too, has some validity as a measure of intelligence (N. L. Bell, McConnell, Lassiter, & Matthews, 2013; McCallum & Bracken, 1997, 2012).

It is obviously important that tests do not discriminate among groups. A test has **cultural bias** when one or more of its items either offend or unfairly penalize people of a particular ethnic background, gender, or socioeconomic status, to the point that the validity of test results is undermined. For example, a test could contain items that refer to Western sports, popular culture, or other content that does not directly assess intelligence and as a result confuse a child who would be able, with different content, to perform the relevant intellectual operations. Lack of familiarity with question format (e.g., multiple-choice items) may also hamper children's performance (Heath, 1989; Neisser et al., 1996). Facility with the English language is a factor as well. Children for whom English is a second language perform relatively poorly on tests administered in English that are primarily verbal in nature (E. C. Lopez, 1997). Publishers of intelligence tests routinely employ individuals from diverse backgrounds to ensure that test content is fair and appropriate for students of all races and ethnicities (R. L. Linn & Miller, 2005; L. A. Suzuki, Onoue, & Hill, 2013). Nevertheless, tests can be biased in ways that are not always anticipated by test developers.

To determine the reliability of intelligence tests, researchers look at various indications of consistency, especially the extent to which the same test yields similar scores on two different occasions. Other indicators of reliability include evidence that different forms of a test yield comparable results and that two different examiners score a child's performance in the same general way. Children's scores on the WISC-IV, Stanford-Binet, UNIT, and CAS are highly reliable in these respects. Nevertheless, measures of reliability are based on aggregate

---

[9]In Chapter 2 we introduce the concepts of validity and reliability.

Preparing for Your Licensure Examination
Your teaching test might ask you about the degree to which intelligence tests are valid and reliable.

data from groups, and an individual child's score can be inconsistent, perhaps due to being ill or distressed on one day of testing but feeling healthy, alert, and motivated the next time the test is administered.

Dynamic Assessments

The approaches described so far focus on what children can *currently* do with little or no assistance from anyone else. In contrast, **dynamic assessment** focuses on assessing children's ability to learn in new situations, usually with an adult's assistance (Camilleri & Botting, 2013; Feuerstein, 1979; Feuerstein, Feuerstein, & Gross, 1997; Haywood & Lidz, 2007). Typically, dynamic assessment involves (a) identifying one or more tasks that children cannot initially do independently, (b) providing in-depth instruction and practice in behaviors and cognitive processes related to the task(s), and then (c) determining the extent to which each child has benefitted from the instruction. Accordingly, dynamic assessment is sometimes called *assessment of learning potential*.

Dynamic assessment is compatible with several theoretical perspectives. As Sternberg has pointed out, intelligence involves adaptation to new situations (Sternberg, 2009). And as the concept of distributed intelligence reminds us, intelligent behavior is heavily context dependent. But Vygotsky's theory of cognitive development is probably most relevant here.[10] Vygotsky proposed that we get a more complete picture of children's cognitive development when we assess not only their *actual developmental level* (the upper limit of tasks they can successfully accomplish on their own), but also their *level of potential development* (the upper limit of tasks they can accomplish when they have the assistance of more competent individuals).

Dynamic assessment is a fairly new approach to assessing intelligence, so psychologists are only beginning to discover its strengths and weaknesses. On the plus side, it often yields more optimistic evaluations of children's abilities than are represented by traditional measures of intelligence (H. L. Swanson & Lussier, 2001; Tzuriel, 2000). In another important advantage, dynamic assessment can provide a wealth of qualitative information about children's approaches to learning, which can be helpful in guiding future instruction (Camilleri & Botting, 2013; Feuerstein, 1979; Hamers & Ruijssenaars, 1997). To illustrate, a boy named Justin was initially able to tell only a very simple story. After a brief period of instruction, Justin articulated complex ideas, expressed varied vocabulary, and used advanced grammar. In studying the boy's responses and records, his assessment team realized that his previous academic delays had probably been due to his frequent absences, tardiness, and weak educational foundation—not to limited intelligence. Accordingly, the team was optimistic that Justin could benefit from instruction that addressed his missing academic skills. In this manner, dynamic assessments can be especially effective in determining the academic concepts and learning strategies that children need to practice in order to progress academically (Lin, 2010; T.-H. Wang, 2010).

Yet disadvantages of dynamic assessment are also apparent. A dynamic assessment often involves considerable training before it can be used appropriately, and it typically requires a great deal of time to administer (Anastasi & Urbina, 1997; Tzuriel, 2000). Furthermore, questions have been raised about how best to determine the validity and reliability of dynamic assessment instruments, which have been evaluated as less strong than traditional measures of intelligence (H. L. Swanson & Lussier, 2001). Nevertheless, dynamic assessments can provide important information as to the child's abilities to benefit from particular kinds of instruction and are thus worth serious consideration (Haywood & Lidz, 2007; Olswang, Feuerstein, Pinder, & Dowden, 2013).

Developmental Assessments with Infants and Young Children

If an adult is to assess a child's cognitive abilities accurately, the child must, of course, be a cooperative participant in the process—for instance, by staying alert, paying attention, and maintaining interest in the assessment tasks. Yet infants and young children are not always able to cooperate. Infants may be sleepy, fussy, or afraid of the stranger conducting the assessment. Young children regularly have short attention spans, lose interest in test questions,

[10]You learned about Vygotsky's theory of cognitive development in Chapter 6.

or misinterpret instructions. Because of such factors, which can vary considerably from one occasion to the next, assessments for infants and young children are not highly reliable (Anastasi & Urbina, 1997; L. Ford & Dahinten, 2005; J. Müller et al., 2013; C. E. Snow & Van Hemel, 2008).

Nevertheless, teachers, child care providers, and other professionals sometimes need to monitor the cognitive development of infants and young children, perhaps to identify significant developmental delays that require intervention or perhaps to determine readiness for various kinds of educational experiences. Here we briefly describe the nature of tests available for infants, toddlers, and preschoolers.

Assessments with Infants and Toddlers

Infants born in hospital settings are typically assessed as soon as they are born. At both 1 minute and 5 minutes after birth, a doctor or nurse evaluates their color, heart rate, reflexes, muscle tone, and breathing, giving each characteristic a rating between 0 and 2. A perfect score on this *Apgar Scale* is 10. You can see an Apgar Scale being performed on a newborn child in the video "An Apgar Assessment" in an Observing Children video. A more in-depth assessment for young infants from birth until 2 months is the *Neonatal Behavioral Assessment Scale* (Brazelton, 2009; Nugent, 2013). Often used to identify significant neurological abnormalities, it assesses alertness and attention, the quality of visual and auditory processing, and a variety of reflexes and behaviors.

Observing Children 8-2
Watch an Apgar Scale being performed on a newborn baby.
ENHANCEDetext *video example*

Perhaps the most widely used test for older infants and toddlers is the third edition of the *Bayley Scales of Infant Development* (Bayley, 2006). Designed for children ages 1 month to 3½ years, it includes five scales. Three scales—for cognitive development (attention, memory, concept formation, etc.), language, and motor skills—are assessed through interactions with the child. Two additional scales—for social-emotional functioning and adaptive behavior—are assessed through parent questionnaires. The Bayley Scales would typically be administered only if an infant faced a risk in development, such as being born very early, and in such a situation the test score is moderately predictive of later cognitive abilities (dos Santos, de Kieviet, Königs, van Elburg, & Oosterlaan, 2013).

Developmental assessments appear to determine current abilities reasonably well. You can observe tasks similar to those used in infant assessments of cognitive abilities in an Observing Children video. Such assessments can be helpful in identifying significant cognitive disabilities if used in combination with other information. When combined with observations of a child, interviews with parents, and medical records, developmental assessments can help identify particular needs before they become serious problems. However, caregivers should keep in mind that measures of cognitive growth in the first few years of life are only modestly related to intelligence in later years (Fagan, Holland, & Wheeler, 2007; McCall, 1993; P. P. Yang, Jong, Hsu, & Lung, 2011). "Bright" babies do not necessarily become the smartest fourth graders, and toddlers who appear slow to learn may eventually catch up to, or even surpass, peers (more about this point in the discussion of IQ stability a bit later in the chapter).

Observing Children 8-3
Observe tasks similar to those used in infant tests of cognitive abilities.
ENHANCEDetext *video example*

Assessments with Preschoolers

As you've previously learned, the Stanford-Binet Intelligence Scales can be used for children as young as 2 years. Another commonly used test for young children is the third edition of the *Wechsler Preschool and Primary Scale of Intelligence,* or WPPSI-IV (M. W. Watkins & Beaujean, 2013; Wechsler, 2012). Suitable for children ages 2½ to 7½, the WPPSI-IV has 15 subtests (fewer for children under 4). In addition to an overall IQ, it yields a Verbal Comprehension Index, Visual Spatial Index, Working Memory Index, and, for children ages 4 and older, Fluid Reasoning and Processing Speed indices.

As measures of intelligence for young children, both the Stanford-Binet and WPPSI-IV correlate with other measures of intelligence and provide reasonable estimates of children's current cognitive functioning. In other words, their scores have some degree of validity and reliability (Roid & Tippin, 2009; Wechsler, 2012). Although young children's IQ scores correlate somewhat with their scores in later years, the correlations are modest at best—no doubt because many young children have high energy levels, short attention spans, and little interest in sitting still for more than a few minutes, and also because the content of tests for young and older children is somewhat different. Thus measures of IQ obtained in the preschool years should *not* be used to make firm predictions about children's academic performance over the long run.

Other tests for preschoolers, known as *school readiness tests*, are designed to determine whether children have acquired the cognitive skills that many kindergarten and first-grade teachers view as essential foundations for their curricula (e.g., abilities to pay attention; count and perform simple mathematical procedures; and identify letters, colors, and shapes). Although widely used in school districts, such tests have come under fire in recent years for two reasons. First, their scores correlate only moderately at best with children's academic performance even a year or so later (La Paro & Pianta, 2000; Stipek, 2002). Second, by age 5, most children are probably ready for some sort of structured educational program. Rather than determining whether children can adapt to a particular educational curriculum and environment, it is probably more beneficial to determine how instruction can be adapted to each child's needs (Lidz, 1991; Panter & Bracken, 2013; Stipek, 2002). In this manner, children who do not yet have basic numeracy and literacy skills need appropriate intervention—not just a test score that reveals their weaknesses.

Critiques of Intelligence Testing

The study of intelligence is at a crossroads, having shifted from the underlying premise that intelligence is a largely inherited, one-dimensional characteristic to the realization that it is a multifaceted core of abilities, each of which is influenced by experience. In the context of changes in thinking, several concerns about contemporary intelligence testing are compelling:

IQ scores are often interpreted without recognition of their fallibility. Over the years, the use of intelligence tests has been controversial. In earlier decades (as recently as the 1970s), IQ scores were frequently used as the sole criterion for identifying children with an intellectual disability. In part as a result of this practice, children from racial and ethnic minority groups were disproportionately represented in special education classes, where their potential for academic achievement was tragically underestimated and ineffectively nurtured.

Most clinical and school psychologists, counselors, and other specialists now have sufficient training in assessment to understand that a single IQ score should never warrant a diagnosis of intellectual disability. Decisions about special educational placement and services must always be based on multiple sources of information about a child. Yet many other people (including a few teachers) view IQ scores as indisputable records of permanent characteristics. We occasionally hear remarks such as "She has an IQ of such-and-such" spoken in much the same matter-of-fact manner as someone might say "She has brown eyes."

For most children, IQ scores are reasonably accurate reflections of their general learning potential. But for some children, IQ scores are poor summaries of what they can do at present or in the future. Teachers and other professionals must be extremely careful not to put too much stock in any single intelligence score. Furthermore, the use of global IQ scores obscures the differentiated profiles of intellectual strengths and abilities that most children have.

Assessment of intelligence focuses almost exclusively on skills valued in mainstream Western culture. The items found on traditional intelligence tests focus on cognitive skills (logical reasoning, abstract thought, etc.) that are valued primarily in middle-class societies (Sternberg, 2012). Such a bias enhances the tests' ability to predict students' achievement because schools in these societies emphasize the same skills. However, traditional intelligence tests do not do justice to the range of skills that many children apply in daily life.

Intelligence tests overlook dispositions and metacognitive strategies that are important contributors to intellectual functioning. Most descriptions and measures of intelligence focus on specific things that a child *can* do (abilities), with little consideration to what a child *wants* to do (motivations) or is *likely* to do (dispositions). Intelligence tests don't evaluate the extent to which children view a situation from multiple perspectives, examine data with a critical eye, regulate their own learning, or reflect on their thoughts and actions. Nor do they assess children's self-discipline or expectations on how they can improve their performance with renewed effort or a change in strategy. Yet such qualities are often just as important as intellectual abilities in determining success in academic and real-world tasks (Duckworth & Seligman, 2005; Dweck, 2010; Kuhn, 2001a; Nisbett, 2009; P. A. O'Keefe, 2013; Perkins, 1995).

Preparing for Your Licensure Examination

Your teaching test might ask you about appropriate cautions to follow when interpreting the results of intelligence tests.

Many theorists have placed higher priority on measuring intelligence than on developing it. Implicit in the practice of intelligence testing is the assumption that intelligence is a relatively fixed, and largely inherited, ability. Fortunately, some psychologists and educators are now calling for a shift from the assessment of intelligence to its enhancement (Boykin, 1994; Nisbett, 2009; Sternberg et al., 2000). As theorists and researchers gain a better understanding of the nature of intelligence and the environmental factors that promote it, schools can, we hope, adopt a more proactive approach, one in which all children are given the opportunities and resources they need to maximize their learning.

Intelligence tests have been used for questionable purposes. Existing intelligence tests have been designed primarily to identify individuals who require special educational services, and in this context they can be helpful if administered carefully, with due regard for other evidence. Yet researchers have used them in other ways as well—for instance, to make group comparisons, draw conclusions about the relative effects of heredity and environment in intellectual development, and evaluate the effectiveness of preschool programs for low-income children. Intelligence tests have been meticulously prepared yet have advantages and disadvantages when use for these secondary purposes. For example, if an early childhood intervention were designed to enhance children's general well-being and educational success, than an intelligence test alone would provide a narrow glimpse into the program's effects.

Educational Implications of Intelligence Testing

Teachers can help children by making recommendations for testing when a special need comes to light and by providing customized accommodations when test results corroborate other indications of this need. Consider the following advice:

• **Maintain a healthy skepticism about the accuracy of IQ scores.** Intelligence tests can, in many cases, provide a general idea of children's current cognitive functioning. Yet IQ scores are rarely dead-on measures of what children can do. As we have seen, the scores of young children can vary considerably from one testing to the next and are not always accurate predictors of children's future academic success. Furthermore, the scores of children are affected by their background experiences, motivation, and English proficiency. We cannot stress this point enough: IQ scores should *never* be used as the sole criterion in making diagnoses and decisions about children.

• **Foster growth in intellectual abilities.** Children whose test results suggest significant weaknesses in one or more domains are able to achieve successfully when families, educators, and other professionals communicate confidence in their capacity for growth and follow through with customized instruction. Individualized guidance should allow a child to improve in areas of weakness (e.g., with a child who has trouble perceiving sounds in words, an adult might use rhymes, clapping exercises, and word games) while arranging other lessons that leverage skills of relative strength (e.g., for a child with strong spatial-visual skills, an adult might present a maze, puzzle, or chart).

• **Explain the value of intelligence testing to parents.** As you have learned, obtaining intelligence test results can be advantageous for a child struggling in the classroom. It is not always possible to know why a child is having difficulty, or specifically whether or not an intellectual delay or exceptional gift contributes to adjustment and achievement problems. Profiles on intellectual tests are not definitive, as we have repeatedly underscored, yet results can inform which instructional goals are worth pursuing and which formats will improve the child's chances of achieving his or her potential.

• **Avoid interpreting test scores unless appropriately trained in tests and measurements.** As professionals, teachers understand their responsibilities as well as their limits. Ideally, teachers have basic information about the validity and reliability of intelligence tests, but they are not experts in intellectual assessments and should not portray themselves in this manner to parents. Where teachers do have expertise in is general pedagogy and instructional adaptations to various intellectual profiles—a critical piece of the equation for children.

• **When a child's schoolwork suggests significant difficulties or talents, document the child's daily performance.** By saving artifacts as a child completes particular tasks, the teacher compiles worthwhile signs of the child's talents and weaknesses, information that can illuminate intelligence test results. For example, a first-grade girl may exhibit significant delays in drawing, forming letters, and cutting, but be verbally facile and skilled in composing intricate stories orally. An intelligence test could yield information about advanced verbal skills that was not apparent in most daily assignments due to her neuromuscular delay.

• **Collaborate with parents and specialists when a child has been classified as needing special services.** The classroom teacher is a full participant in developing the individualized education program (IEP) for a child.[11] Parents, the classroom teacher, other professionals including school psychologists and special education experts, and often the child work together to determine individualized goals and instructional strategies that optimize personal educational gain. Teachers are in a uniquely informed position to confirm and occasionally refute test results given their experience with the child's performance in several subjects. Teachers can also guide the IEP planning process by describing the academic challenges the child faces on a daily basis, his or her regular achievements, and accommodations that have proven effective thus far.

Summary

Most intelligence tests have been developed primarily to identify individuals who have special needs (e.g., those who are gifted or have an intellectual disability). Contemporary intelligence tests include a variety of tasks designed to assess what people have learned from their everyday experiences. Performance on these tests is usually summarized by one or more IQ scores, which are determined by comparing an individual's performance with the results of others of the same age. In some instances dynamic assessments may be more useful for evaluating children's capabilities in specific areas or for predicting their ability to benefit from certain kinds of instruction. Developmental assessments for infants and young children are often helpful in identifying those who have significant delays; however, these tests should not be used to make long-term predictions about cognitive development.

Intelligence tests can provide a general idea of the child's current cognitive functioning—if the child has understood the instructions, is reasonably motivated, and shares general cultural views with the test's developers, and if the test results are supplemented by additional information about the child's abilities. Educators and other practitioners should remain optimistic about every child's potential for intellectual growth and play a crucial role in designing and implementing individualized accommodations.

ENHANCEDetext *self-check*

BIOECOLOGY OF INTELLIGENCE

A variety of factors determine children's intelligence. Children have unique genetic profiles, and they develop personal habits—playing football, doing crossword puzzles, or reading books—that allow them to exercise individual talents. Children further respond to distinct opportunities, pressures, and sometimes risks in family relationships, and they are further affected by diet and schooling. The bioecological model specifies that the influences of nature and nurture change with development, and we begin with evidence on how intelligence is transformed with age.

Development of Intelligence

In one sense, children definitely become more "intelligent" as they develop: They know more, think in more complex ways, and solve problems more effectively. However, IQ scores are based not on how much children develop over time, but rather on how well children perform in comparison with their age-mates. By definition, the average IQ score for any age-group is 100 and does not increase with age. Given that fact, a child would not be expected to increase significantly in IQ scores with age unless he or she were to be receiving especially outstanding instruction or other facilitating conditions.

IQ scores do change in two important ways over the course of development:

• *IQ scores become increasingly stable.* As noted previously, performance on infant assessments is not terribly predictive of later intelligence. One reason is that infants'

BIOECOLOGY OF DEVELOPMENT

As children develop their intellectual abilities, they are affected by an assortment of personal and environmental factors.

---

[11]You learned about the IEP in Chapter 4.

moods and priorities can be at odds with the demands of testing, making test scores somewhat unreliable. A second reason is that the types of items on assessments for young children are considerably different than items on tests for older children and adolescents. The Developmental Trends table "Intelligence at Different Age Levels" specifies common indicators of intelligence at various age levels, along with important considerations to keep in mind at each level.

DEVELOPMENTAL TRENDS
Intelligence at Different Age Levels

AGE	WHAT YOU MIGHT OBSERVE	DIVERSITY	IMPLICATIONS
Infancy (Birth–2 Years)	• Success on test items that involve recognition of previously seen objects, visual preferences, and eye–hand coordination • Distractibility and short attention span • Differentiated responses to familiar adults and strangers • Variability in performance from one assessment to the next • Performance dependent on examiner's ability to establish a positive relationship with the infant	• Temperamental differences (e.g., a tendency to be shy or cautious) affect infants' willingness to interact with the examiner and test materials. • Compared to full-term infants, infants born prematurely are less physically developed, more easily fatigued, and more prone to obtain comparatively low test scores. With responsive care, premature infants gradually develop into healthy, intelligent individuals. • Exposure to drugs or alcohol before birth may adversely affect test performance.	• Create a relaxed tone and comfortable examiner–child interaction before beginning an assessment. • Use results only to identify significant developmental delays requiring immediate intervention; refrain from making long-term predictions about intellectual growth. • Communicate honestly with parents about the child's performance, while also describing the assessment's strengths and weaknesses as a tool for learning about children's abilities.
Early Childhood (2–6 Years)	• Success on test items that involve naming objects, stacking blocks, drawing circles and squares, remembering short lists, and following simple directions • Short attention span, influencing test performance • Variability in test scores from one occasion to the next	• Significant developmental delays in the early years may indicate an intellectual disability. • On average, children from economically disadvantaged families perform at lower levels on measures of cognitive development than do children from middle-income families; however, enriching preschool experiences can narrow the gap.	• Use cognitive assessments primarily to identify significant delays in development; follow up by arranging intervention programs for children with delays. • Provide preschool experiences that foster language skills, knowledge of numbers and counting, and visual-spatial thinking.
Middle Childhood (6–10 Years)	• Success on test items that involve defining concrete words, remembering sentences and short sequences of digits, grasping concrete analogies, recognizing similarities among objects, and identifying absurdities in illogical statements • Some consistency in test scores from one occasion to the next • Noticeable differences among children in mastery of classroom subject matter	• For this age range, intelligence tests are heavily verbal in nature; thus proficiency with English can significantly affect test performance. • Children with learning disabilities are apt to perform poorly on some parts of an intelligence test. • Children may perform weakly in situations where the examiner has not established rapport.	• On some lessons, individualize instruction to capitalize on children's learning strengths. • Do *not* assume that poor performance in one domain (e.g., verbal tasks) indicates limited ability in other areas. • Take children's cultural and linguistic backgrounds into account when interpreting IQ scores.
Early Adolescence (10–14 Years)	• Success on test items that involve defining commonly used abstract words, drawing logical inferences from verbal descriptions, and identifying similarities between opposite concepts • Considerable individual differences in the ability to understand abstract material	• Some adolescents may not perceive a high score as personally advantageous and so may not be motivated to perform at their best. • Cultures that stress traditional gender roles may actively discourage girls from achieving in mathematics and science and boys from achieving in literacy.	• Expect considerable diversity in adolescents' ability to master abstract classroom material, and individualize instruction accordingly. • Make sure that school enrichment programs include students from all ethnic groups; do not rely exclusively on IQ scores to identify students as gifted.

(continued)

DEVELOPMENTAL TRENDS (continued)
Intelligence at Different Age Levels

AGE	WHAT YOU MIGHT OBSERVE	DIVERSITY	IMPLICATIONS
Late Adolescence (14–18 Years)	• Success on test items that involve defining infrequently encountered words, distinguishing overlapping abstract words, interpreting proverbs, and breaking down complex geometric figures into component parts • Relative stability in IQ scores • Increasing independence in arranging opportunities consistent with ability levels	• Concerns about appearing "too smart" may continue into the high school years. • Some adolescents may underperform due to the anxiety of being tested in a subject for which they and others of the same ethnicity are widely believed to be incapable (see upcoming discussion of stereotype threat on p. 305).	• Provide challenging activities for teenagers who are gifted. • Encourage bright adolescents from lower-income families to pursue a college education, and help them with the logistics of college applications (e.g., applying for financial aid).

Sources: Bayley, 2005; Bornstein, Hahn, & Wolke, 2013; Brooks-Gunn, 2003; Brooks-Gunn, Klebanov, & Duncan, 1996; Colombo, 1993; G. A. Davis & Rimm, 1998; S. I. Greenspan & Meisels, 1996; Luckasson et al., 2002; D. J. Matthews, 2009; L. C. Mayes & Bornstein, 1997; McLoyd, 1998b; Meisels, Wen, & Beachy-Quick, 2010; Mello, Mallett, Andretta, & Worrell, 2012; Natarajan et al., 2013; Ogbu, 1994; Steele, 1997; Terman & Merrill, 1972; A. Thomas & Chess, 1977; Thorndike, Hagen, & Sattler, 1986; Wechsler, 2002, 2003.

As children progress through the school years, their IQ scores hover within an increasingly narrow range. Although children continue to develop cognitively, each child's relative intelligence in comparison to peers changes less as time goes on (N. Brody, 1992; Neisser et al., 1996; van Soelen et al., 2011). As an example, look once again at the chapter's opening case study. Gina obtained an IQ score of 140 (equivalent to the 99th percentile) in junior high school and performed at a similar level on college aptitude tests several years later. Scores become more consistent with age because of maturation, that is, with the increasing activation of genes that affect intelligence (Briley & Tucker-Drob, 2013). Also contributing to stability is children's developing ability to select their own activities, which they increasingly make to be compatible with their intellectual abilities and personal interests.

Despite the increasing stability of IQ scores, each individual score reflects a youngster's performance on a particular test from only one occasion. Some degree of change (sometimes as much as 10 to 20 points' worth, and occasionally even more) can be expected over the years. The longer the time interval between two administrations of an intelligence test, the greater the change in IQ we are likely to see, especially when young children are involved (B. S. Bloom, 1964; McCall, 1993; Sattler, 2001). The magnitude and direction of major changes in scores—higher or lower or oscillations up and down—depend on children's access to nutrition, health status, and exposure to stimulating activities, as you will learn more about shortly.

• *IQ scores become increasingly accurate predictors of future academic achievement.* As IQ scores become more stable with age, their usefulness in predicting classroom performance increases. Yet educators should remember two things about the relationship between IQ and academic achievement. First, intelligence by itself does not *cause* achievement. Intelligence certainly plays an important role in school performance, but many other factors—motivation, quality of instruction, family resources and support, peer-group norms, and so on—are obviously involved. Second, the relationship between IQ scores and achievement is an imperfect one, with many exceptions. For a variety of reasons, some children with high IQ scores do not perform well in the classroom, and other children achieve at higher levels than would be predicted from their IQ scores.

Evidence for Hereditary Influences

Earlier we mentioned that measures of information processing speed correlate with IQ scores. Speed of processing depends on neurological efficiency, which in turn is largely genetically controlled. From this standpoint, we have support for a hereditary basis for intelligence. The fact that children with certain genetic defects (e.g., Down syndrome) have, on average, significantly lower IQ scores than their nondisabled peers provides further proof of heredity's influence (J. Carr, 2012; Keogh & MacMillan, 1996; Rihtman et al., 2010). But perhaps the most convincing evidence comes from twin studies and adoption studies.

Twin Studies

Numerous studies have compared monozygotic (identical) twins and dizygotic (fraternal) twins to get a sense of how strongly heredity affects IQ. Because monozygotic twins begin as a single fertilized egg, which then separates, their genetic makeup is virtually identical. In contrast, dizygotic twins are conceived as two separate fertilized eggs. Dizygotic twins share about 50 percent of their genes, with the other 50 percent being unique to each twin. Most twins of both types are raised together by the same parent(s) in the same home, so they share similar environments.

In one investigation, children were studied over several years to determine how their IQ scores correlated with siblings' scores (E. G. Bishop et al., 2003). If you take a look at the two columns for twins in Table 8-2, you will notice that the correlations for monozygotic twins are consistently higher than the correlations for dizygotic twins, non-twin siblings, and adopted siblings.[12] This pattern has been observed in many other investigations and suggests that intelligence has a sizable genetic basis. In fact, even when twins are raised separately (perhaps because they have been adopted by different parents), they generally have similar IQ scores (T. J. Bouchard & McGue, 1981; J. S. Kaplan, 2012; Plomin & Petrill, 1997; N. L. Segal, 2012). Twin studies also provide evidence for environmental effects, as we will see in a moment.

Adoption Studies

Another way to identify the effects of heredity is to compare adopted children with both their biological and adoptive parents. Adopted children tend to be more similar to their biological parents in genetic makeup. Their environment, of course, more closely matches that of their adoptive parents. Researchers have found that adopted children's IQ scores are more highly correlated with their biological parents' IQs than with their adoptive parents' IQs. In other words, in a group of people who place their infants up for adoption, those with the highest IQs tend to have offspring who, despite being raised by other people, also have the highest IQs. Furthermore, the IQ correlations between adopted children and their biological parents become stronger, and those between the children and their adoptive parents become weaker as children grow older (T. J. Bouchard, 1997; J. S. Kaplan, 2012; McGue, Bouchard, Iacono, & Lykken, 1993; Plomin, Fulker, Corley, & DeFries, 1997; Plomin & Petrill, 1997). (We will provide an explanation for this age-related increase in apparent genetic effects a little later.)

Researchers also compare correlations in the IQs of adopted siblings with associations in twins and nonadopted siblings (ordinary biological brothers and sisters). If you look again at Table 8-2, you can see that the correlations for dizygotic twins and nonadopted siblings are

TABLE 8-2 Correlations Between IQs of Sibling Pairs Living Together

AGE OF CHILDREN[a]	MONOZYGOTIC TWINS	DIZYGOTIC TWINS	NON-TWIN BIOLOGICAL SIBLINGS	ADOPTED SIBLINGS
Age 1	.59	.40	.38	.07
Age 3	.77	.51	.37	.26
Age 7	.76	.40	.47	.04
Age 9	.80	.21	.40	.24

[a]Tests of ability were administered to the same children repeatedly over several years in this longitudinal study.
Source: E. G. Bishop et al., 2003.

[12]In our teaching experiences, we have found that some students erroneously interpret the higher correlations as indicating that identical twins have higher intelligence. This is not the case. The size of each correlation indicates the *strength of the relationship* between twins' IQs, not the *level* of their intelligence—how generally smart they are.

generally higher than most of the correlations for adopted siblings. In other words, children who are genetically related resemble one another intellectually more than do children who are unrelated biologically. Although other factors are at work in such associations (which we will soon examine), twin and adoption studies point convincingly to a genetic component in intelligence (T. J. Bouchard, 1997; N. Brody, 1992; J. S. Kaplan, 2012).

Evidence for Environmental Influences

Considerable evidence indicates that the environment also has a significant impact on intelligence. We find some of this evidence in other analyses in twin and adoption studies. Investigations into the effects of nutrition, toxic substances, home environment, early intervention, and formal schooling provide additional support for the environment's significant impact. Also, a modest but steady increase in intelligence scores over the past several decades—known as the *Flynn effect*, to be discussed shortly—is probably at least partly attributable to environmental factors.

Twin Studies and Adoption Studies Revisited

Comparing across separate investigations, researchers have found an average correlation of .85 for monozygotic twins reared together and .74 for monozygotic twins reared apart (Devlin, Daniels, & Roeder, 1997; Nisbett, 2009). In other words, twins raised in different homes have less similar IQs than twins reared in the same home. Adoption studies, too, indicate that intelligence is affected by environmental experiences, especially during childhood (Capron & Duyme, 1989; J. S. Kaplan, 2012; Nisbett, 2009).

Consider also that twin and adoption studies do not fully disentangle environmental effects (J. S. Kaplan, 2012; Wahlsten & Gottlieb, 1997). An adopted child has shared a common environment for at least 9 months—the period of prenatal development—with his or her biological mother. Likewise, monozygotic twins who are separated at birth are often placed by adoption agencies in families that are similar in educational backgrounds and income levels. Furthermore, twin studies and adoption studies do not allow researchers to clarify how heredity and environment interact in their effects on intelligence. In genetic studies, interactive effects are included on the "heredity" side of the scoreboard (J. S. Kaplan, 2012; Nisbett, 2009; Turkheimer, 2000).

Despite the intertwined connections between the child's genes and his or her environment, other data suggest that environmental effects are stronger than they first appear. Twin studies are generally drawn from middle-income families because these individuals are most inclined to participate in longitudinal research (Nisbett, 2009). It is a well-documented trend that genetic effects are stronger in high-income families than in low-income families, probably because children in advantaged families have the experiences they need to express their full potential whereas children in less well-to-do families do not (T. C. Bates, Lewis, & Weiss, 2013; Turkheimer, Haley, Waldron, D'Onofrio, & Gottesman, 2003). Because IQ samples are over-represented with high-income families, figures for genetic effects are likely to be over-estimates.

Thus, in a range of comprehensive studies examining genetic contributions to intelligence, there is almost always an indication of strong effects from the environment. Let's look at some specific ways that the environment affects intelligence.

Early Nutrition

Severe malnutrition, either before birth or during the early years of life, can hinder neurological development (Lutter & Lutter, 2012; Protzko, Aronson, & Blair, 2013; Ricciuti, 1993). Attention, memory, abstract reasoning, intelligence, and general school achievement are all likely to suffer from inadequate nutrition. Children sometimes recover from short periods of poor nourishment (due, perhaps, to war or illness), but the adverse effects of long-term deprivation are apt to be enduring (Lutter & Lutter, 2012; Sigman & Whaley, 1998).

Aware of these long-term effects, some investigators have provided medically approved food supplements and vitamins to infants and young children who would not otherwise have adequate nutrition. Such interventions improve the development of motor skills and in some instances cognitive development (Geok Lin & Misra, 2012; Pollitt & Oh, 1994; Sigman & Whaley, 1998).

Toxic Substances

A variety of toxic substances, or *teratogens*, in children's prenatal environments—for instance, alcohol, drugs, radiation, and lead—affect neurological development and IQ scores (e.g., Betts, 2013; H. Eriksen et al., 2012; Streissguth, Barr, Sampson, & Bookstein, 1994). Children with fetal alcohol syndrome have mothers who consumed large amounts of alcohol during pregnancy; these children show poor motor coordination, delayed language, and intellectual disabilities.[13] Exposure to toxic substances can similarly threaten intelligence during infancy and early childhood because children's brains, which are growing rapidly, are vulnerable to harm.

Home Environment

Correlational studies indicate that stimulating home environments (e.g., those in which parents interact frequently with their children, make numerous reading materials available, encourage the development of new skills, and use complex sentence structures in conversation) are associated with higher IQ and achievement scores in children (R. H. Bradley & Caldwell, 1984; Keltikangas-Järvinen et al., 2010; Nisbett, 2009; Tong, Baghurst, Vimpani, & McMichael, 2007). The family's cultivation of the child's cognitive skills may be especially influential in lower-income backgrounds because there are few resources for the child outside the family.

We find additional evidence for the beneficial effects of stimulating home environments in Romania (Beckett, Castle, Rutter, & Sonuga-Barke, 2010; N. A. Fox, Almas, Degnan, Nelson, & Zeanah, 2011; C. A. Nelson, 2005). As a result of previous government policies, most Romanian orphans were at one time raised in large institutions. After a change in government and the intervention of a team of developmental psychologists, some institutionalized infants (randomly selected) were placed with adults willing to serve as foster parents. (Sadly, the intervention team could not find foster families for all of the infants.) As researchers periodically assessed the children's physical and cognitive development, they found dramatic differences between the two groups. Despite adequate nutrition, children remaining in an institution throughout infancy and the preschool years had smaller head circumferences and less brain activity than did foster children. When intelligence was assessed, the institutionalized children had an average IQ of 64, which is on par for a person with an intellectual disability, whereas the foster children, on average, had IQs in the normal range.

Early Intervention

When children live in impoverished home environments, enriching preschool programs and other forms of early intervention can make an appreciable difference. Children who participated in the Head Start preschool program in the United States have shown short-term IQ gains and other cognitive benefits (Bronfenbrenner, 1999; R. Lee, Zhai, Brooks-Gunn, Han, & Waldfogel, 2013; NICHD Early Child Care Research Network, 2002; Zigler, 2003). The intellectual effects of such programs don't continue indefinitely, however. Unless they receive follow-up interventions during the elementary school years, children lose some of the early cognitive advantages (Brooks-Gunn, 2003). Despite these fading benefits, children who attend Head Start programs exhibit other advantages later in life: They less often repeated grade levels, achieved at higher levels in school, more often attended college, enjoyed greater health, and exhibited less criminal behavior (Garces, Thomas, & Curry, 2002; Ludwig & Miller, 2007; Zigler & Styfco, 2010). Presumably, children in Head Start acquired curiosity, motivation, and critical skills, such as the self-regulatory abilities for sustaining attention and curbing impulses, that helped them apply their intellectual and social-emotional resources effectively at school, in interpersonal relationships, and eventually in employment settings (Fuhs & Day, 2011; A. J. Reynolds, Englund, Ou, Schweinhart, & Campbell, 2010).

Additional early interventions have shown long-term improvements in important areas, albeit not necessarily in IQ scores. In the Perry Preschool Program, children from economically disadvantaged families attended preschool and had teachers who coached mothers in how to interact with children in an educationally worthwhile manner. Other children from similar backgrounds had teacher visitors, and a third group received no intervention.

[13]You may recall reading about teratogens and fetal alcohol exposure in Chapter 4.

Participants in the program showed short-term gains in IQ and infrequent placements special education classes. At age 14 they scored higher on academic achievement tests, and at age 40 they had completed more schooling, had higher earnings, and were more likely to be in stable families than was the case with individuals who had not attended preschool or had home-visiting teachers (W. S. Barnett, 1992; Muennig, Schweinhart, Montie, & Neidell, 2009; A. J. Reynolds et al., 2010; Schweinhart & Weikart, 1993).

In the Abecedarian Program, children from disadvantaged backgrounds were assigned to one or more interventions. Children who received high-quality care beginning in infancy showed an IQ advantage in early childhood that persisted into the adult years (F. A. Campbell, Pungello, Miller-Johnson, Burchinal, & Ramey, 2001; F. A. Campbell & Ramey, 1995; F. A. Campbell et al., 2012; C. T. Ramey et'al., 2000; S. L. Ramey & Ramey, 1999). They also were less likely to be assigned to special education classes or to repeat a grade and were more likely to be accomplished readers, to graduate from high school, and to attend college than were individuals who had not received the intervention beginning in infancy. At age 30, Abecedarian graduates were more likely to have attended and graduated from college (F. A. Campbell et al., 2012).

Synthesizing across the various projects, early childhood interventions that begin in children's first years and offer intensive physical, social-emotional, and educational support foster children's intellectual abilities. Although intellectual gains fade slightly during the school years, some intellectual advantages persist, particularly when children attend high-quality elementary schools. Furthermore, other significant life benefits accrue, including higher achievements in secondary school and better life outcomes in adulthood.

Formal Schooling

The very act of attending school leads to small increases in IQ. In Western societies, children who begin their educational careers early and attend school regularly have higher IQ scores than children who do not. When children must start school later than is typical, their IQs are at least 5 points lower for every year of delay. In addition, children's IQ scores decline slightly (usually only temporarily) over the course of the summer months, if children are not attending school. Other things being equal, children who drop out of school have lower IQ scores than children who remain in school, losing an average of 2 to 3 IQ points for every year of high school not completed (Ceci & Williams, 1997; Falch & Sandgren Massih, 2011).

The intellectual benefits of schooling are seen in a wide variety of societies. As Vygotsky pointed out, schooling provides a systematic means through which children can acquire cultural tools, such as alphabets and mathematical systems. Participation in school also generally encourages the acquisition of advanced strategies that enrich students' learning of a broad range of concepts (M. Cole, 2006; Falch & Sandgren Massih, 2011; Nettelbeck & Wilson, 2005). Schooling is important not only because of its direct facilitation of intellectual skills, but also because teachers' warm, steady relationships with children instill an eagerness to acquire academic concepts (Nisbett, 2013).

The Flynn Effect

The last few decades have seen a slow, steady increase in average performance on IQ tests throughout the industrialized world (Flynn, 1987, 2007; D. F. Marks, 2011; Neisser, 1998b; R. L. Williams, 2013). This trend is commonly known as the **Flynn effect**.[14]

Why might populations of children become smarter? Conceivably some genetic factors are having an impact. Recent decreases in the numbers of children conceived by first cousins and other close relatives appear to have strengthened the health of the human gene pool (Mingroni, 2007). Genetic problems, including certain intellectual disabilities, are more prevalent in children of closely related parents than in children of unrelated parents. Yet most theorists believe that the Flynn effect is largely the result of changes in children's environments worldwide. Better nutrition, protection from infectious diseases, smaller family sizes, higher-quality home environments, better schooling, and more enriching and informative stimulation (access to television, reading materials, etc.) are all possible contributing

---

[14]The Flynn Effect was named in recognition of relevant research by James R. Flynn.

factors (Daley, Whaley, Sigman, Espinosa, & Neumann, 2003; Eppig, Fincher, & Thornhill, 2010; Neisser, 1998b; R. L. Williams, 2013).

Fusion of Nature and Nurture

The bioecological model of development suggests that factors inside and outside the child intermingle in development. What is less clear is *how much* power nature and nurture have on intelligence during various stages of life. Most psychologists now believe that it may ultimately be impossible to separate the relative effects of heredity and environment. Theorists are reasonably certain that nature and nurture interact in the following ways:

Heredity establishes a range rather than a precise figure. Heredity does not dictate that a child will have a particular IQ score. Instead, it appears to set a range of abilities that a child will eventually develop, with the actual level depending on his or her specific environmental experiences (Weinberg, 1989). Heredity may also affect how susceptible or resistant a child becomes to particular environmental influences (Rutter, 1997). In the opening case study, Gina learned how to read before she attended school and with only minimal help from her mother. Yet had she not had her mother to help her or grew up malnourished, Gina's intellectual gifts may have failed to blossom.

Genetic expression is influenced by environmental conditions. Genes, the basic units of heredity, are not self-contained, independent "carriers" of particular characteristics but rather flexible instructions that respond directly to conditions in the child's body and indirectly to features in the environment.[15] In an extremely impoverished setting—one with inadequate nutrition and little if any stimulation—heredity may have little to say about the extent to which children develop intellectually. In an ideal environment—one in which nutrition, parenting practices, and educational opportunities are optimal and age-appropriate—heredity can have a significant influence on children's intelligence (Ceci, 2003; Turkheimer et al., 2003).

Furthermore, intelligence is the result of many genes, each contributing a small amount to the efficiency of thinking processes (Bouchard, 2014; S. K. Loo et al., 2012; Sattler, 2001). Particular genes may "kick in" at different points in development, and their expression will be influenced by particular environmental conditions at those times. Thus we do not have a single heredity–environment interface, but rather a number of heredity–environment interactions, each contributing to intellectual growth (Simonton, 2001).

Especially as they get older, children choose their environments and experiences. Children actively seek out environmental conditions that match their inherited abilities—a phenomenon known as **niche-picking** (Benbow & Lubinski, 2009; Halpern & LaMay, 2000; Scarr & McCartney, 1983; Tucker-Drob & Harden, 2012). Children who, genetically speaking, have an exceptional quantitative reasoning ability may enroll in advanced mathematics courses, voluntarily tackle mathematical brainteasers, and in other ways nurture their own inherited talents. Children with average quantitative ability are less likely to take on these challenges and so have fewer opportunities to develop their mathematical skills. Given the ubiquity of such choices, the relative effects of heredity and environment are difficult to tease apart.

Earlier we mentioned that the IQ correlations between adopted children and their biological parents become stronger over time. We now have a possible explanation for this finding. Children gain increasing independence with growth. Especially as they reach adolescence, they spend less time in their home environments, and they make more of their own decisions about the kinds of opportunities to pursue—decisions undoubtedly based, in part, on their natural talents and tendencies (McGue et al., 1993; Petrill & Wilkerson, 2000). Similarly, correlations between the IQs of monozygotic twins increase in strength with age and presumably reflect a growing ability to act on the genetic tendencies they share (you can see an age-related increase in IQ correlations for monozygotic twins in Table 8-2; Hoekstra, Bartels, & Boomsma, 2007).

Demographic Factors

The bioecological model reminds us that children from different backgrounds are apt to have distinct intellectual opportunities and challenges. In fact, the experiences that children have

---

[15]Chapter 4 examines the physiological processes by which genes and environmental experiences interact.

as boys and girls, as recipients of steady resources or financial insecurity, and as members of ethnic and racial groups, affect their intellectual development. As you will find out, differences among groups tend to be small and due primarily to differential allotment of resources to children with particular characteristics.

Gender

Apart from a greater frequency of intellectual disabilities in boys than girls, there are rarely any significant gender differences in IQ scores (Halpern et al., 2007; D. Lai, Tseng, Hou, & Guo, 2012; Neisser et al., 1996). This finding is at least partly a function of how intelligence tests are developed: As a general rule, test constructors eliminate any test items on which one gender performs better than the other.

Average differences in specific cognitive abilities are sometimes found but are usually small. Girls are often slightly better at such verbal tasks as reading and writing (Calvin, Fernandes, Smith, Visscher, & Deary, 2010; Fearrington et al., 2014; Maccoby & Jacklin, 1974). Especially after puberty, boys perform somewhat better on tasks involving visual-spatial thinking (which require people to imagine two- or three-dimensional figures and mentally manipulate them), and adolescents with extremely high mathematical ability are more likely to be male than female (Calvin et al., 2010; Hegarty & Kozhevnikov, 1999; D. Reilly & Neumann, 2013). In verbal, visual-spatial, and mathematical domains, however, there is typically a great deal of overlap between the two genders.

These minor gender differences in particular intellectual abilities may be partly due to hormonal differences or subtle anatomical differences in the brain (Hahn, Jansen, & Heil, 2010; Halpern, 2004; D. Reilly & Neumann, 2013). Environmental factors appear to play a role as well. In many Western cultures boys are more likely to have toys that require physical manipulation in space (e.g., blocks, model airplanes, and footballs). In contrast, girls are more likely to have dolls, housekeeping items (e.g., dishes, plastic food), and board games—items that are apt to encourage verbal communication with peers (Auster & Mansbach, 2012; Halpern, 1992; Leaper & Friedman, 2007).

In recent years, perhaps because of the push for more equitable educational opportunities, males and females have become increasingly similar in their abilities (L. C. Ball, Cribbie, & Steele, 2013; Spelke, 2005). For all intents and purposes, educators should expect boys and girls to have similar potential in all subject areas.[16]

Socioeconomic Status

Intelligence test scores are correlated with socioeconomic status (SES).[17] On average, children from lower-SES families earn somewhat lower IQ scores, and they also perform at lower levels in school, than do children from middle-SES families (Brooks-Gunn, 2003; Linver, Brooks-Gunn, & Kohen 2002; H. Wong & Edwards, 2013). Children who grow up in persistently impoverished conditions are at greatest risk for poor performance, but children who endure only short-term poverty may also fall behind peers in intellectual skills (McLoyd, 1998b).

Several factors contribute to differences in IQ and school achievement among socioeconomic groups (Berliner, 2009; C. Fitzpatrick, McKinnon, Blair, & Willoughby, 2014). Poor nutrition, lack of health care, and greater-than-average exposure to environmental toxins can impede neurological development among economically impoverished children. Parents who work long hours (especially single parents) may have little time to spend with their children and may be unable to afford high-quality child care (Marshall, 2004). Some parents with limited educational backgrounds do not know how to help children acquire academic skills (Portes, 1996). Excessive hardships can undermine parents' ability to remain emotionally responsive to children, with children absorbing the family's stress to such an extent that they become overwhelmed, fail to acquire healthy coping skills, and develop weak pathways in the brain for memory and self-control (R. Grant, Gracy, Goldsmith, Shapiro, & Redlener, 2013; Pilyoung et al., 2013). Children's lower school attendance rates, due to health problems, family crises, and frequent changes of residence, further diminish opportunities for acquiring academic skills.

---

[16]Boys and girls don't always *believe* they have similar abilities, however, as you will discover in Chapter 12.
[17]Socioeconomic status is defined and described in Chapter 3.

Children with special needs are at heightened risk when they live in economic poverty. In low-income settings, children with intellectual disabilities may not have access to the customized instruction they need, either at home or in poorly funded schools, to buttress their limitations and exercise their talents (D. Torres, 2013). Conversely, children with intellectual gifts may not have access to the necessary resources to develop their full potential.

Ethnicity and Race

Every ethnic, racial, and cultural group has child-rearing practices that nurture the intellectual development of its young people. Yet not every group is given the same opportunities within the larger society. Minor variations in intelligence result from these differences in resources, privileges, and hardships. On average, Asian Americans and European Americans slightly outperform African Americans and Hispanic Americans (Ang, Rodgers, & Wänström, 2010; N. Brody, 1992; Neisser et al., 1996; Nisbett et al., 2012).

The primary reason for this small disadvantage in average IQ scores is that African American and Hispanic American children are apt to grow up in families and neighborhoods with more modest incomes than those of European American children (Brooks-Gunn et al., 1996; McLoyd, 1998b). Lower socioeconomic status can affect the quality of nutrition, availability of stimulating toys and books, and value of educational experiences. Even when different ethnic and racial groups have similar economic resources, long-term discrimination (e.g., exclusion from better schools and jobs, lower expectations for classroom performance) can limit children's opportunities for intellectual growth (Ogbu, 1994).

As they grow, children of color are apt to respond to other people's perceptions that they lack intelligence. Some children give minimal answers (e.g., "I don't know") while taking intelligence tests as a way of shortening an unsettling testing session (Zigler & Finn-Stevenson, 1992). Other children do not see the point of answering questions that contradict their own cultural perspectives on what intelligence is (Sternberg et al., 2007). Still others exhibit a phenomenon known as **stereotype threat**: They perform more poorly—unintentionally and perhaps as a result of excessive anxiety—if they believe that members of their group typically do not do well on particular kinds of tests (Guyll, Madon, Prieto, & Scherr, 2010; Heerboth & Mason, 2012; Steele, 1997).

An encouraging trend is that the IQ scores and other measures of cognitive ability have, in recent years, become increasingly similar among ethnic and racial groups. Such a trend can be attributed to more equitable environmental conditions across society (Ceci, Rosenblum, & Kumpf, 1998; Dickens & Flynn, 2001; Nisbett et al., 2012). Nevertheless, it remains a serious concern that not every child has a reasonable chance to fully develop his or her emerging intellectual skills.

Implications of Bioecological Models of Intelligence

Given existing knowledge about the bioecological development of intelligence, as well as our concerns about shortcomings in the field, we offer the following suggestions to teachers and other practitioners who work with children:

• **Support early intervention programs in your community.** Early intervention is especially important for infants and toddlers with developmental disabilities, as well as for young children living in low-income neighborhoods or unstable family settings. Interventions can take the form of regular checkups and nutritional support for pregnant women, stimulating infant care and preschool programs for young children, and education for parents. Interventions are most effective when they begin early, integrate a variety of services into a support network, and address children's physical, social, and emotional needs as well as their level of cognitive development (Loeb, Fuller, Kagan, & Carroll, 2004; Shonkoff & Phillips, 2000).

• **Downplay potential problems with being evaluated.** Earlier you learned that children can feel threatened by an upcoming test if they focus on being part of a group, perhaps as a member of a certain race, that is believed to achieve less favorably than other groups. As a result, these children may feel anxious and not able to concentrate on problems on the test. Teachers can try to head off this debilitating reaction by conveying their confidence in children's abilities, recasting the situation as a challenge rather than a danger, and emphasizing the utility of test results for guiding future learning (Alter, Aronson, Darley, Rodriguez, & Ruble, 2010).

> **• Cultivate youngsters' intellectual abilities throughout the school years.** Research evidence strongly supports the role that schools can play in fostering children's potential throughout the preschool, elementary, middle, and secondary school years (A. Bennett et al., 2007; Nisbett, 2009; Sternberg et al., 2007). In particular, youngsters from economically disadvantaged families are positively affected when teachers foster their curiosity and explicitly teach advanced intellectual abilities. Teachers can help fill in any gaps in children's knowledge, make sure children are familiar with basic mathematical concepts and reading processes, and scaffold children's ability to apply what they learn to new contexts (A. Bennett et al., 2007).

Summary

Performance on intelligence tests predicts school achievement to some degree, with IQ scores becoming increasingly stable and having greater predictive power with age. Nevertheless, some children's IQ scores change considerably over time, especially during the early years.

Studies with twins and adopted children indicate that intelligence may be partly an inherited characteristic. But environmental conditions, including nutrition, exposure to toxic substances, home environment, preschool programs, and formal schooling, can also have a significant impact on IQ scores. Heredity and environment interact in their influence, to the point where it is impossible to separate the relative effects of these two factors on children's intellectual development. Fortunately, educators can determine children's individual needs and tailor their instruction accordingly.

ENHANCEDetext *self-check*

EXCEPTIONALITIES IN INTELLIGENCE

No matter how we define or measure intelligence, we find that some children show exceptional talent and others exhibit sizable cognitive delays relative to peers. For the most part, educators can easily accommodate such variability within normal instructional practices. In a few situations, however, young learners have ability levels so different from those of agemates that they require special educational services in order to reach their full potential. We turn now to exceptionalities in intelligence. The two ends of the intelligence continuum are commonly known as *giftedness* and *intellectual disability*.[18]

Children Who Have Gifts and Talents

Gina, first introduced in the opening case study, is an example of someone who is gifted (you may also see the term *gifted and talented*). **Giftedness** is unusually high ability or aptitude in one or more areas (e.g., mathematics, science, creative writing, art, or music) to the point where special educational services are necessary to help a youngster meet his or her full potential (e.g., C. M. Ackerman & Fifield, 2005; U.S. Department of Education, 1993). Some school districts identify students as gifted primarily on the basis of general IQ scores, often using 125 or 130 as a minimum cutoff point. But many experts argue that IQ scores should not be the only criterion for selection into special services, and that such factors as creativity, motivation, and children's everyday accomplishments need to be considered. Examining multiple indicators, including a portfolio of the child's work, may be especially useful in identifying talented children from diverse backgrounds who, perhaps because of a language barrier, lack of confidence, or weak academic preparation, are not as likely to score at exceptionally high levels on intelligence tests (Council for Exceptional Children, 1995; S. Graham, 2009; F. O'Reilly & Matt, 2012).

Individual children who are gifted are very different from one another in their strengths and talents, but as a group they tend to share certain characteristics. Compared to children not identified as gifted, these youngsters process information more quickly and remember it more easily, have advanced reasoning and metacognitive skills, and use effective learning

---

[18]In the United States, different states may establish somewhat different criteria for these two categories, especially with regard to determining eligibility for special educational services. The needs of children with intellectual disabilities are more likely to be accommodated than those with exceptional intellectual gifts.

and problem-solving strategies (K. R. Carter & Ormrod, 1982; K. E. Snyder, Nietfeld, & Linnenbrink-Garcia, 2011). Often they have an abundant curiosity and an exceptional drive to learn, seek out new challenges, make their own discoveries, express themselves creatively, and master tasks independently (D. A. Greenspan, Solomon, & Gardner, 2004; Rakow, 2012; Winner, 2000). They tend to set extremely high standards for their performance, sometimes to the point of unrealistic perfectionism (W. D. Parker, 1997; Tsui & Mazzocco, 2007). Most have high self-esteem, good social skills, and above-average emotional adjustment, although a few extremely gifted children have social or emotional difficulties, such as being overly sensitive to criticism (Edmunds & Edmunds, 2005; Garces-Bacsal, 2011; A. E. Gottfried, Fleming, & Gottfried 1994; Sousa, 2009).

Giftedness may be partly an inherited characteristic, but the environment clearly plays a role as well (B. Clark, 1997; A. W. Gottfried, Gottfried, & Guerin, 2009; Shavinina & Ferrari, 2004). Children who are gifted are more likely to be firstborn or only-born children and thus generally have more attention from their parents than do other children. Children who are gifted generally have many opportunities to practice their abilities from an early age, long before they have been identified as being gifted. And they are more inclined to seek out enriching opportunities—an example of the *niche-picking* phenomenon described earlier.

As is true for Gina in the opening case study, a child's giftedness is often evident throughout childhood and adolescence. Some gifted children use unusually advanced language beginning in infancy, and others show signs of giftedness in early childhood, such as intense curiosity (Colombo, Shaddy, Blaga, Anderson, & Kannass, 2009; C. Harrison, 2004). Yet others are "late bloomers"; their talents become evident relatively late in the game, perhaps as environmental conditions bring talents to fruition.

Fostering the Development of Children with Gifts and Talents

Gifted students tend to be among our schools' greatest underachievers. When required to progress at the same rate as their nongifted peers, they achieve at levels far short of their capabilities (K. R. Carter, 1991; Rakow, 2012). Drawing on Vygotsky's theory of cognitive development, we could say that children who are gifted are unlikely to be working within their zone of proximal development when they are limited to the same tasks assigned to peers, diminishing their opportunities to develop advanced cognitive skills (Lubinski & Bleske-Rechek, 2008).

Children who are gifted often appreciate encouragement to take on demanding work in certain areas. Nine-year-old Elena reveals her desire for challenge in her description of PEAK, a program at her school for students who are gifted, in an Observing Children video:

Adult: What do you like best about school?
Elena: I like PEAK. . . . It's for smart kids who have, like, good ideas for stuff you could do. And so they make it more challenging for you in school. So instead of third-grade math, you get fourth-grade math.

Many students with special gifts and talents become bored or frustrated when their school experiences don't provide assignments that allow them to develop their unique abilities (Feldhusen, Van Winkle, & Ehle, 1996; Rakow, 2012; Winner, 2000). They may lose interest in school tasks and put in only the minimum effort they need to get by in the classroom.

Yet some young people try to hide their exceptional talents. They may fear that peers will ridicule them for their high academic abilities and enthusiasm for academic topics, especially in secondary school (Covington, 1992; DeLisle, 1984; J. O'Connor, 2012). Girls in particular are prone to hide their talents, especially if they have been raised in cultures that do not value high achievement in girls and women (G. A. Davis & Rimm, 1998; Nichols & Ganschow, 1992). Some children who are gifted also have a disability. Children with exceptional gifts and talents may have learning disabilities, ADHD, autism, emotional disorders, or physical or sensory challenges (e.g., Hettinger & Knapp, 2001; Lovett & Sparks, 2013). In such situations teachers and other practitioners must, when planning instruction, address disabilities as well as areas of giftedness. A few gifted children—for example, those with a limited English background or those who have specific learning disabilities—need training in basic skills. Several strategies for helping children with exceptional abilities maximize their potential are presented and illustrated in the Development and Practice feature "Addressing the Unique Needs of Children with Gifts and Talents."

Preparing for Your Licensure Examination
Your teaching test might ask you about the characteristics of children with intellectual gifts and creative talents.

Preparing for Your Licensure Examination
Your teaching test might ask you about strategies for fostering the intellectual skills of children with gifts and creative talents.

Observing Children 8-4
Listen to Elena's desire for a challenging curriculum.
ENHANCEDetext *video example*

DEVELOPMENT AND PRACTICE
Addressing the Unique Needs of Children with Gifts and Talents

Continually watch for unusual gifts and talents in children.

- A second-grade teacher, Mr. Evans, periodically takes notes on the strengths of each student. One student, Abrielle, was bossy, disruptive, and a challenge for Mr. Evans. After he looked at his notes, however, he realized that several of her characteristics suggested a potentially gifted intellect: she occasionally corrected him and classmates with highly detailed information, displayed an advanced sense of humor, wondered why certain rules were necessary, and examined advanced books about machines, inventions, and technology. Mr. Evans talked with her parents about having Abrielle tested to see if she qualified for the school's gifted and talented program. (Middle Childhood)

- A fifth-grade teacher notices that one of her students has unusual proficiency with spatial and mechanical tasks. The boy repairs the class's broken clock, navigates with a homemade map as he rides the bus, completes intricate mazes, and draws plans for robots. Although the boy achieves at only average grades in school, the teacher is impressed with his talents and mentions them to a school psychologist, who will follow-up on his eligibility for special services. In the meantime the teacher provides opportunities for him to exercise spatial and mechanical skills in a few classroom activities. (Middle Childhood)

Individualize instruction in accordance with students' specific talents.

- With help from the kindergarten teacher, the school librarian provides numerous nonfiction picture books about a variety of topics (e.g., with themes related to animal life, historical figures, astronomy, and airplanes). Children select one book of interest, examine its illustrations, and draw a few pictures of their own. With assistance from the teacher, they create their own booklets on what they have learned. (Early Childhood)

- Two mathematically gifted junior high school students study calculus with a retired mathematician who volunteers her time three mornings a week. A classmate with exceptional reading skills selects classic works of literature appropriate to his reading level. (Early Adolescence)

Form study groups of gifted students who have similar abilities and interests.

- A music teacher provides semiweekly practice sessions for a quintet of musically talented 10- and 11-year-olds. As group members polish skills, they enjoy themselves sufficiently that they begin meeting daily, on their own, and ask their teacher for guidance when they spot a problem. (Early Adolescence)

- A high school dramatic arts teacher arranges for students to write a brief play in their study groups. Several members of the school's theater club spend the entire weekend scripting the play and subsequently perform it enthusiastically for the class. (Late Adolescence)

Teach complex cognitive skills within the context of specific school topics.

- An elementary teacher has an advanced science group conduct a series of experiments. To promote critical thinking, she guides the students in establishing hypotheses and procedures and in considering rival explanations while conducting the experiments. (Middle Childhood)

- In an earth science class, a middle school teacher gives students a variety of projects related to weather. For students who have little background on the topic, the teacher provides basic information and asks students to prepare a public service announcement about an upcoming weather system (Sousa, 2009). For students who want more of a challenge, the teacher asks students to prepare and administer a survey about people's awareness of weather patterns. (Early Adolescence)

Provide opportunities for independent study.

- A second-grade teacher finds educational software through which a mathematically gifted 8-year-old can study decimals, exponents, square roots, and other advanced concepts. (Middle Childhood)

- A high school student who is exceptionally talented in the arts is encouraged by her advisor to offer recommendations about the kind of studios, stages, theatrical supplies, and musical instruments that the school needs to offer basic support for budding artists. (Late Adolescence)

Encourage students to set high goals for themselves, but without expecting perfection.

- A middle school literacy teacher encourages students to set increasingly high goals for themselves in reading and writing. She gives them their test score results and information on state standards in literacy so that students can select their own short-term goals for bridging the gap between their current levels of proficiency and the standards. (Early Adolescence)

- A high school counselor encourages a gifted student from a low-income, single-parent family to consider going to a prestigious college. He also helps the student find sources of financial assistance for higher education. (Late Adolescence)

Challenge children to express themselves creatively.

- An elementary teacher encourages children to express their knowledge creatively. The teacher asks children to compose poems, write speeches, detect patterns in mathematics, and design multimedia presentations. (Middle Childhood)

- In a high school lesson on romanticism, a teacher asks students to imagine that Ralph Waldo Emerson is coming to their school. For the assignment, the students write an essay on conditions in their community and speculate on how Emerson might respond to these situations. (Late Adolescence)

Seek outside resources to help students develop their exceptional talents.

- A high school student with an aptitude for learning foreign languages takes a Russian course at a local university. Through her new contacts in the class, she finds correspondence buddies in Russia and talks with them on *Skype*. (Late Adolescence)

- A high school requires students to complete a series of requirements across their 4 years of study—community service as freshmen, job shadowing as sophomores, an internship as juniors, and a major project during their senior year. In planning each activity, students are encouraged to obtain advice from teachers, parents, and experts in their community. (Late Adolescence)

Sources: Ambrose, Allen, & Huntley, 1994; Feldhusen, 1989; Fiedler, Lange, & Winebrenner, 1993; Harradine, Coleman, & Winn, 2014; Milner & Ford, 2007; S. M. Moon, Feldhusen, & Dillon, 1994; W. D. Parker, 1997; Piirto, 1999; Rakow, 2012; Smutny, von Fremd, & Artabasy, 2009; Spicker, 1992; Sternberg et al., 2009.

Children with Intellectual Disabilities

Children with an **intellectual disability** show developmental delays in several areas of life.[19] Two characteristics must be evident before the age of 18 in order for a person to be diagnosed with an intellectual disability (American Association on Intellectual and Developmental Disabilities, 2013):

- *Significantly below-average general intelligence.* Children with an intellectual disability perform poorly on traditional intelligence tests, with IQ scores being no higher than 70 or 75 (reflecting performance in roughly the bottom 2 percent of their age-group). Children learn slowly and perform poorly on school tasks in comparison with age-mates, and they show consistently low achievement across all or most academic areas.
- *Deficits in adaptive behavior.* An additional criterion is a deficit in **adaptive behavior**, which includes the application of abilities needed to be autonomous in everyday life, including conceptual understandings (e.g., about time, number, language, and literacy), social skills (e.g., getting along with others, being responsible, not being victimized), and practical skills (e.g., involving personal self-care, using public transportation, using a telephone, and spending money). In these areas children with an intellectual disability often exhibit understandings and behaviors typical of individuals much younger than themselves.

Children with intellectual disabilities show impairments in information processing. Some have weak attention and working memory skills (Schuchardt, Gebhardt, & Mäehler, 2010; A. Witt & Vinter, 2013). Others have trouble generalizing what they learn to new situations (Dempster & Corkill, 1999). Some find it difficult to understand how other people think and feel and to cope effectively with anger, frustration, and embarrassment (Baurain & Nader-Grosbois, 2013). The play activities of children with intellectual disabilities are kinds that would ordinarily be observed in much younger children, such as intruding into peers' activities, asking inappropriately personal questions, and failing to wait a turn during conversation (F. P. Hughes, 2010; Malone, Stoneham, & Langone, 1995; Matson & Fodstad, 2010).

Intellectual disabilities are often caused by abnormal genetic conditions (e.g., Down syndrome). Yet heredity is not always to blame. Some instances of intellectual disabilities are due to noninherited biological causes, such as severe malnutrition or substance abuse during the mother's pregnancy (e.g., recall our earlier discussion of fetal alcohol syndrome), oxygen deprivation associated with a difficult birth, or serious conditions such as meningitis or exposure to environmental toxins such as lead (National Dissemination Center for Children with Disabilities, 2013; Streissguth et al., 1994; Wodrich, Tarbox, Balles, & Gorin, 2010).

Fostering the Development of Children with Intellectual Disabilities

The great majority of children with intellectual disabilities attend school, and many of them are capable of mastering a wide range of academic and vocational skills. However, students with intellectual disabilities regularly require accommodations to instructional objectives and formats. Given that they have difficulty in learning and generalizing information, lessons that are clear, concrete, and inclusive of repetition and practice are necessary.

Children with intellectual disabilities are often described as developmentally delayed. Indeed, these children often resort to immature strategies in learning and relating to others (Goharpey, Crewther, & Crewther, 2013). However, children with intellectual disabilities are not simply "slow" learners. They acquire concepts and skills in distinct ways that vary by the nature of their disability and their personal profile of talents and limitations. For example, children with Down syndrome tend to have a limited working capacity for orally transmitted information, making it difficult for them to sound out long words when learning to read. Yet they also typically have a relatively strong visual working memory and acquire sight words fairly easily (Ratz, 2013). In that reading acquires a complex collection of abilities beyond sight reading, children with Down syndrome need practice in phonological awareness and sounding out words in order to advance in reading. Of course, every child with Down

Preparing for Your Licensure Examination
Your teaching test might ask you about the characteristics of children with intellectual disabilities.

Preparing for Your Licensure Examination
Your teaching test might ask you about instructional strategies for fostering the academic and life skills of children with intellectual disabilities.

---

[19]Although readers may be more familiar with the term *mental retardation* for the condition of low general intelligence, many advocates for children with special needs prefer the term *intellectual disability* because it has less of a social stigma (American Association on Intellectual and Developmental Disabilities, 2013).

DEVELOPMENT AND PRACTICE
Maximizing the Development of Children with Intellectual Disabilities

Encourage young children to use the strengths they have, and offer instruction in acquiring new knowledge and skills in delayed subjects.

- An 18-month-old boy who has intellectual and physical disabilities has recently begun attending an infant care center. His caregiver thinks creatively about how to help him interact in his physical environment. She glues Popsicle sticks to the pages of cardboard books so that he can easily grab them and turn the pages. To help him feel secure in his infant chair, she puts skid-proof material on the seat of the chair and cushions at the sides to keep him upright. (Infancy)

- A preschool teacher encourages 4-year-old Sierra, who is characteristically nonverbal, to articulate her desires. When Sierra points at a cabinet, her teacher anticipates that the little girl wants her favorite ball, which is typically stored there. The teacher prompts Sierra, "Do you want to play with the ball, Sierra?" Sierra smiles and nods affirmatively. The teacher asks her, "Can you say 'ball,' Sierra?" Sierra says, "Bah." The teacher replies, "Good job, Sierra, you asked for your ball. Let me get it for you now." (Early Childhood)

Introduce new material at a slower pace, and provide opportunities for practice.

- A fourth-grade teacher gives a student only two new addition facts a week, primarily because any more than two overwhelm him. Every day, the teacher has the student practice writing the new facts and review the addition facts learned in previous weeks. (Middle Childhood)

- A paraprofessional stands by as 13-year-old Yarah completes a mathematics worksheet with single-digit multiplication problems. Yarah completes the problems and occasionally asks for help. Yarah will work on a similar worksheet tomorrow and also a few days next week to solidify her memory of multiplication facts. (Early Adolescence)

Explain tasks concretely and with explicit attention to required steps.

- An elementary art teacher gives a student explicit training in the steps she needs to take at the end of each painting session: (1) Rinse the paintbrush at the sink, (2) put the brush and watercolor paints on the shelf in the back room, and (3) put the painting on the counter by the window to dry. Initially, the teacher needs to remind the student of every step in the process. With time and practice, the student eventually carries out the process independently. (Middle Childhood)

- In preparation for an internship, a teacher tells students about general requirements of jobs—being on time, following directions, using a quiet voice, and so forth. The teacher asks students to anticipate some potential problems and consider how they might respond—for example, how they will get to work if their parents are unable to drive them. (Late Adolescence)

Give explicit guidance about how to study.

- An elementary teacher tells a student, "When you study a new spelling word, it helps if you repeat the letters out loud while you practice writing the word. Let's try it with *house*. Watch how I repeat the letters—H . . . O . . . U . . . S . . . E—as I write the word. Now you try doing what I just did." (Middle Childhood)

- A high school teacher advises a student how to take a standardized test. The teacher tells the student that it's important to write your name at the top of the first page, fill in the bubbles, check when done to see that all the items have been answered, and do one's best without worrying about the result. (Late Adolescence)

Give feedback about specific behaviors rather than about general performance.

- A fourth-grade teacher notices that a student in his class is showing a lot of progress in library skills. He tells the student, "I saw how interested you have been in your progress at the library. You returned your two books from last week and checked out three books this week. I can't wait to hear about your new books." (Middle Childhood)

- A vocational educator tells a high school student, "You did a good job in wood shop this week. You followed the instructions correctly and put away the equipment when you were finished with it." (Late Adolescence)

Encourage self-determination.

- An elementary teacher shows a boy how to find a seat during lunchtime. The teacher encourages the boy to find a familiar face from class, ask politely if he can join the others, and listen to the conversation before making a relevant comment. In the future, the boy tries these procedures when entering a scout meeting. (Middle Childhood)

- A life skills instructor shows a high school student how to use her calculator to figure out her total lunch bill. The instructor also gives the student practice in identifying the correct bills and coins to use when paying various amounts. (Late Adolescence)

Sources: K. L. Fletcher & Bray, 1996; Patton, Blackbourn, & Fad, 1996; Perkins, 1995; Shogren, Kennedy, Dowsett, & Little, 2014; Turnbull et al., 2010.

syndrome is unique and such general information needs to be supplemented with insights into personal circumstances. The Development and Practice feature "Maximizing the Development of Children with Intellectual Disabilities" (above) illustrates several effective strategies that apply broadly but can be customized to the needs of individual learners.

Summary

Children and adolescents identified as having gifts and talents show exceptional achievement or promise in one or more domains. Giftedness may be manifested differently in different cultures, but in general, gifted individuals demonstrate rapid learning, advanced reasoning, and sophisticated cognitive strategies. In contrast, children with an intellectual disability exhibit low general intellectual functioning and deficits in adaptive behavior. In individual children, either kind of exceptionality may have genetic roots, environmental causes, or both. Children with unusually high or low intelligence maximize their cognitive development when instruction is geared to their unique strengths and weaknesses.

ENHANCEDetext *self-check*

PRACTICING FOR YOUR LICENSURE EXAMINATION

Many teaching tests require students to use what they have learned about child development in responses to brief vignettes and multiple-choice questions. You can practice for your licensure examination by reading the following case study and answering a series of questions.

Fresh Vegetables

Twelve-year-old Steven had no known genetic or other organic problems but had been officially labeled as having an intellectual disability (mental retardation) based on his low scores on a series of intelligence tests. His prior schooling had been limited to just part of one year in a first-grade classroom in inner-city Chicago. His mother had kept him home after a bullet grazed his leg while he was walking to school one morning. Fearing for her son's safety, she would not let him outside the apartment after that, not even to play, and certainly not to walk the six blocks to the local elementary school.

When a truant officer finally appeared at the door one evening 5 years later, Steven and his mother quickly packed their bags and moved to a small town in northern Colorado. They found residence with Steven's aunt, who persuaded Steven to go back to school. After considering Steven's intelligence and achievement test scores, the school psychologist recommended that he attend a summer school class for students with special needs.

Steven's summer school teacher soon began to suspect that Steven's main problem might simply be a lack of the background experiences necessary for academic success. One incident in particular stands out in her mind. The class had been studying nutrition, and so she had asked her students to bring in some fresh vegetables to make a large salad for their morning snack. Steven brought in a can of green beans. When a classmate objected that the beans weren't fresh, Steven replied, "The hell they ain't! Me and Momma got them off the shelf this morning!"

If Steven didn't know what *fresh* meant, the teacher reasoned, then he might also be lacking many of the other facts and skills on which any academic curriculum is inevitably based. She and the teachers who followed her worked hard to help Steven make up for all those years in Chicago during which he had experienced and learned so little. By the time Steven reached high school, he was enrolling in regular classes and maintaining a 3.5 grade point average.

"Fresh Vegetables" from CASE STUDIES: APPLYING EDUCATIONAL PSYCHOLOGY, 2nd Edition, by Jeanne Ellis Ormrod and Dinah McGuire. Copyright © 2007 by Jeanne Ellis Ormrod and Dinah McGuire. Reprinted by permission of Pearson Education, Inc., Upper Saddle River, NJ. Adapted by permission of the publisher.

Constructed-Response Question

1. Does Steven really seem to have an intellectual disability? Why or why not?

Multiple-Choice Questions

2. What factors have contributed to Steven's current abilities and intellectual weaknesses?

   a. Steven's intellectual limitations are primarily the result of genetic factors.

   b. Steven's profile of intellectual skills and limitations is exclusively from environmental experiences.

   c. Steven's skills and limitations derive from a blend of genetic and environmental factors.

   d. Steven's intellectual abilities are due to a series of developmental changes, with genetic factors contributing a lot during infancy and environmental experiences being influential in the childhood years.

3. Which of the following statements is the most accurate interpretation of Steven's academic performance?

   a. Steven's limited exposure to school made it unlikely that he would be able to succeed academically without intensive instruction.

   b. Given evidence of Steven's low intelligence, we can expect that he will never succeed in any school subject.

   c. Steven has low general intelligence but may have special abilities in focused areas, for example, a keen sensitivity to other people's needs or advanced coordination in athletics.

   d. If Steven's teacher offered him daily training in taking items similar to those on intelligence tests, his intellectual capacity would increase and allow for rapid improvements in academic achievement.

ENHANCEDetext *licensure exam*

Key Concepts

CHAPTER NINE

Language Development

CASE STUDY: Mario

As a young boy growing up in rural Vermont, Mario had the good fortune to learn two languages. At home, his parents spoke Spanish almost exclusively, communicating to one another in their shared native tongue and passing along their cultural heritage to their son. Most of Mario's early exposure to English was in the child care centers and preschools he attended off and on from the time he was 2 years old.

When Mario was 5, his dominant language was Spanish, but he was proficient in English as well. After his first 2 months in kindergarten, his teacher wrote the following in a report to Mario's parents:

> [Mario is] extremely sociable. He gets along fine with all the children, and enjoys school. He is quite vocal. He does not seem at all conscious of his speech. His slight accent has had no effect on his relations with the others. Whenever I ask the class a question, he is always one of the ones with his hand up.
>
> His greatest problem seems to be in the give and take of conversation. Since he always has something to say, he often finds it difficult to wait his turn when others are talking. When he talks, there are moments when you can see his little mind thinking through language—for he sometimes has to stop to recall a certain word in English which he might not have at his finger tips. (Fantini, 1985, p. 28)

The "slight accent" in Mario's English led a speech therapist to recommend speech therapy, which Mario's parents declined. In fact, all traces of an accent disappeared from Mario's speech by age 8, and his third-grade teacher was quite surprised to learn that he spoke a language other than English at home.

Standardized tests administered over the years attested to Mario's growing proficiency in English. Before he began kindergarten, his score on a standardized English vocabulary test was at the 29th percentile, reflecting performance that, although a little on the low side, was well within the average range. Later, when he took the California Achievement Test in the fourth, sixth, and eighth grades, he obtained scores at the 80th percentile or higher (and mostly above the 90th percentile) on the reading, writing, and spelling subtests. When Mario spent a semester of fifth grade at a Spanish-speaking school in Bolivia, he earned high marks in Spanish as well, with grades of 5 on a 7-point scale in reading, writing, and language usage.

As Mario grew older, his vocabulary and written language skills developed more rapidly in English than in Spanish, in large part because most of his instruction at school was in English. His father described the situation this way:

> [B]y about fifth grade (age ten), he had entered into realms of experience for which he had no counterpart in Spanish. A clear example was an attempt to prepare for a fifth grade test on the topic of "The Industrial Revolution in England and France." It soon became clear that it was an impossibility to try to constrain the child to review materials read and discussed at school—in English—through Spanish. With this incident, [use of English at home] became a fairly well established procedure when discussing other school topics, including science, mathematics, and the like. (Fantini, 1985, p. 73)[a]

- What language skills did Mario learn?
- How did Mario's experiences in his family and school affect his language development?

[a] Excerpts from "Case Study: Mario" from LANGUAGE ACQUISITION OF A BILINGUAL CHILD: A SOCIOLOGICAL PERSPECTIVE by A. E. Fantini. Copyright © 1985 by Alvino E. Fantini. Reprinted by permission of the author.

OBJECTIVES

9.1: Evaluate the merits and limitations of five theoretical frameworks of language development.

9.2: Trace the development of language in terms of changes in semantics, syntax, listening abilities, speaking skills, pragmatics, and metalinguistic awareness.

9.3: Summarize and apply research on second-language learning.

9.4: Examine diversity in language development that arises due to a wide range of factors, including individual characteristics and exceptionalities in language abilities.

Acquiring the language of one's culture is a challenging undertaking. To understand and use a language effectively, children must master its four components. First, they acquire **phonology**: They must know how words sound and produce the sequence of sounds that make up any given word. Second, they master **semantics**, the meanings of a large number of words. Third, they gain command of **syntax**, rules for how words can be legitimately combined to form understandable phrases and sentences. Finally, children learn the **pragmatics** of language, the use of social conventions that enable effective communication with others.

Mastering these four components of language is a remarkable achievement for any child. For children like Mario who acquire them in more than one language, the task is even more impressive. Given the multifaceted nature of human language, it is not surprising that Mario needed extra time to acquire basic skills in both English and Spanish. At age 5, he had minor difficulties with English phonology (the kindergarten teacher mentioned a "slight accent"), semantics (his score on a vocabulary test was a tad on the low side), and pragmatics (especially turn taking). Over the long run, however, Mario's bilingual upbringing clearly did *not* hinder his language development. The accent in his English disappeared by age 8, and test scores in the fourth and fifth grades were well above average.

In this chapter we revisit Mario as we explore the monumental achievements of language learning during childhood. We begin our discussion by looking at several theoretical perspectives on how children acquire their first language—that is, their **native language**.

THEORIES OF LANGUAGE DEVELOPMENT

By age 3 or 4, most children have acquired sufficient proficiency in language that they are able to carry on productive conversations with people around them. How they accomplish this task in such a short time is one of the great mysteries of child development. Theorists have offered numerous explanations of how children learn their native language. Here we describe an early framework based on modeling and reinforcement plus four contemporary perspectives: nativism, cognitive process theories, sociocultural theories, and functionalism.

Modeling and Reinforcement

Some early theorists suggested that language development is largely the result of modeling— that children simply imitate the speech of others. Observation and imitation of others are certainly involved in the acquisition of language (Arbib, 2005; R. Moore, 2013). Infants imitate the specific sounds and general vocal patterns that caregivers utter (Balog, 2010; Kokkinaki & Vitalaki, 2013; Tronick, Cohn, & Shea, 1986). Older children pick up other people's words and expressions. When Mario began attending an English-speaking preschool, he came home using such expressions as "Shut up!" and "Don't do dat!" which he had apparently acquired from classmates (Fantini, 1985, p. 97).[1]

The behaviorist B. F. Skinner (1957) suggested that *reinforcement* also plays a role, in that parents and other adults praise or in some other way reward increasingly mature language use. In Skinner's view, when infants make a variety of speech sounds in a seemingly random fashion, adults respond favorably to—and so encourage children to repeat—those sounds used in the local language. As children grow older, Skinner proposed, adults reinforce the use of actual words, then the use of multiword combinations, and eventually only word combinations that are, from an adult's perspective, grammatically correct.

Despite their intuitive appeal, theories of imitation and reinforcement have not withstood the scrutiny of research. The speech of young children includes many phrases (e.g., "Allgone milk") that people around them neither say nor reinforce (R. N. Aslin, 2014; N. Chomsky, 1959; V. Cook & Newson, 1996; D. Lightfoot, 1999). Moreover, parents usually reinforce their children's statements based on what is factually accurate rather than what is grammatically correct (R. Brown & Hanlon, 1970; Byrnes & Wasik, 2009). Even in the elementary and secondary school years, the great majority of grammatical errors in children's speech go uncorrected (Bohannon, MacWhinney, & Snow, 1990). And children continue to produce grammatically incorrect sentences despite feedback that the sentences need revision, as the following dialogue illustrates:

Child: Nobody don't like me.
Mother: No, say "nobody likes me."
Child: Nobody don't like me.

---

[1] Excerpt from "Case Study: Mario" from LANGUAGE ACQUISITION OF A BILINGUAL CHILD: A SOCIOLOGICAL PERSPECTIVE by A. E. Fantini. Copyright © 1985 by Alvino E. Fantini. Reprinted by permission of the author.

[Eight repetitions of this dialogue]

Mother: No, now listen carefully; say "nobody likes me."
Child: Oh! Nobody don't likes me. (McNeill, 1966, p. 68)

Clearly, neither modeling nor reinforcement alone—or even together—is sufficient to explain how children eventually acquire an adult-like form of their native language.

Nativism

In an approach known as **nativism**, theorists have turned to biology to explain language development.[2] One early pioneer, **Noam Chomsky** (1965, 1976, 2006), proposed that growing children have a biologically built-in mechanism—a **language acquisition device**—that enables them to learn complex aspects of language in a very short time. This mechanism provides certain "prewired" knowledge and skills that make the task of learning language much simpler than it would be if children had to start from scratch.

Many psychologists share Chomsky's belief that human beings inherit predilections—certain biases in the brain for processing language in particular ways—that assist with linguistic knowledge and skills. Beginning at a very early age, infants can detect subtle differences among similar speech sounds. They can divide a steady stream of sound into small segments (e.g., syllables) and identify common patterns in what they hear. They seem to have a few built-in concepts (e.g., colors such as red, pink, and yellow) that predispose them to categorize perceptions and experiences in certain ways.

According to Chomsky, children also have the basis of a *Universal Grammar*, a set of parameters that prompt them to form certain grammatical structures and not others (Boeckx, Fodor, Gleitman, & Rizzi, 2009; N. Chomsky, 2006; Guimarães, 2013). As long as children are regularly exposed to language in an interactive setting, they easily construct a working knowledge of their language's rules for placing particular types of words in sequence. They learn to distinguish basic structures, for example, a *noun* (a word that describes a person, place or thing) from a *verb* (a word that describes an action or state of being). This proficiency is largely unconscious but is shown in their comprehension and production of speech. The world's many languages have different specific rules, but they collectively are limited in the range of systems they encode, in synchrony with the abilities of the human mind.

Endorsement for nativism is found in evidence of common language patterns across discrepant circumstances. Children from diverse cultural and linguistic backgrounds reach milestones in language development at similar ages, indicative of maturational factors. Virtually all children, even those who are born deaf and have never heard a human voice, begin to produce speech-like syllables in the first year of life (S. Iyer & Oller, 2008; Lieven & Stoll, 2010; J. L. Locke, 1993). Subsequent growth depends on exposure and interaction. Children who have had contact with different languages—either spoken or manually signed—make similar progress in producing meaningful words and stringing them together into interpretable sequences (Crago, Allen, & Hough-Eyamie, 1997; Snedeker, Geren, & Shafto, 2007; Vohr, Topol, Watson, St. Pierre, & Tucker, 2014).

Additional support for the nativist view comes from evidence of *sensitive periods* in language development, that is, from research indicating that children must have certain experiences during particular windows of time in order to achieve full mastery of language. Children who have had very little exposure to speech in the early years, perhaps because of a parent's mental illness or an orphanage's understaffing, are apt to have trouble acquiring advanced grammatical structures even with later intensive language instruction (Curtiss, 1977; B. Huang, 2014; Merz, McCall, & Wright, 2013; Newport, 1990; Ramírez, Lieberman, & Mayberry, 2013). Also, youngsters typically learn how to pronounce a second language flawlessly only if they learn it before mid-adolescence, as did Mario in our introductory case study (Abrahamsson, 2012; Flege, Munro, & MacKay, 1995; Gluszek & Dovidio, 2010). Finally, young people have an easier time in mastering complex syntax when they are immersed in the language within the first 5 to 10 years of life (Abrahamsson, 2012; Bialystok, 1994b; J. S. Johnson & Newport, 1989).

---

[2]You have seen the influence of nativism in the discussion of *theory theory* in Chapter 7.

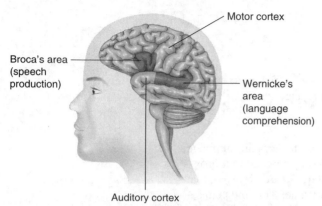

FIGURE 9-1 Primary language centers in the left hemisphere of the brain. Wernicke's area processes sounds and comprehends speech. Broca's area permits production of speech.

Neurological research further demonstrates the biological underpinnings of language. For most people, including the majority of right-handed children and deaf children who use a visual-manual sign system, the left hemisphere of the brain dominates in language processing (Lazard, Innes-Brown, & Barone, 2014; A. J. Newman, Supalla, Hauser, Newport, & Bavelier, 2010).[3] Within the left hemisphere, two specific regions specialize in language functions (see Figure 9-1). *Broca's area*, located near the forehead, plays a key role in producing speech. *Wernicke's area*, behind the left ear, is heavily involved in understanding speech. Areas in the right hemisphere offer corresponding support, sifting through multiple possible meanings of statements, perceiving humor and sarcasm, and keeping track of events in a story (Neville & Bavelier, 2001; A. J. Newman et al., 2010; R. Ornstein, 1997).

Despite such findings, researchers have yet to obtain clear evidence that human beings do, in fact, inherit a neurological mechanism—Chomsky's hypothesized *language acquisition device*—that is dedicated solely to learning language. Even if research eventually confirms the existence of such a mechanism, questions would remain about how that general capacity is translated into specific cognitive and motivational processes when a given child learns a particular language in a defined setting (Pinker, 1987). The theoretical perspectives that follow better address these factors.

Cognitive Process Theories

In contrast to Chomsky's position, cognitive process theorists assert that children are born not with a specialized language mechanism but rather with a host of perceptual abilities and thinking skills that allow them to make inferences about patterns in their native language. While taking part in interactions, infants mentally churn through the input they hear and infer statistical regularities in sequences of sounds, forms of speech, and use of words. For instance, they learn that Mommy regularly says "Daddy" when pointing at Daddy, and that the sound "D-a" occurs in speech but "R-t" does not. Subsequently, children adapt their own speech to conform to these observed patterns, and language skills improve accordingly.

The cognitive process model reveals the dynamic, ongoing learning that occurs as children process language input, exercise their maturing brains, and take initiative in conversation. In other words, language skills are not automatically achieved, but rather *emerge* out of children's activity as speakers and listeners. For this reason, many cognitive scholars take a dynamic systems perspective and advocate an *emergent* framework of language development (Gogate, & Hollich, 2010; Laks, 2013; McMurray, Horst, & Samuelson, 2012).

The cognitive process model shows exactly how children contribute to their own language learning. For example, they focus on the ends of words and word order (Slobin, 1985).[4] Children also rely on language they have already learned when trying to decipher an unknown feature, as when they use familiar word order and knowledge of other words when guessing an unfamiliar term's meaning (Gleitman, Cassidy, Nappa, Papafragou, & Trueswell, 2005; Pinker, 1987). In the sentence, "Dog owners *adore* their pets," a child may not have previously encountered the word "adore" but surmise from word order and experience with the family dog that the word probably refers to some kind of affectionate response.

In order to notice regularities in language, children must of course pay attention to them (M. Harris, 1992; Koenig & Woodward, 2010; Pruden, Hirsh-Pasek, Golinkoff, & Hennon, 2006). Within a few days after birth, infants show a preference for attending to human voices over other sounds, and they are able to distinguish between familiar and unfamiliar voices (DeCasper & Fifer, 1980; DeCasper & Prescott, 2009; J. L. Locke, 1993). At 6 months, infants closely watch the movements of a speaker's lips, inspections that presumably help them learn how to form particular sounds themselves (D. J. Lewkowicz & Hansen-Tift, 2012).

---

[3]The brain's two hemispheres have a few distinct responsibilities, as you might recall from Chapter 5.
[4]Cognitive process theories are examined in Chapter 7.

Reasoning is another integral part of language learning (M. Atkinson, 1992; Frazier, Gelman, & Wellman, 2009; S. A. Graham, Booth, & Waxman, 2012). Young children form hypotheses about the meanings of words based on the context in which the words are used. In one study (Au & Glusman, 1990), researchers showed preschoolers an unfamiliar animal and consistently called it a *mido*. Later they presented a collection of odd-looking animals (including some midos) and asked the children to find a *theri* in the set (see Figure 9-2). Although the children had no information to guide their selection, they always chose an animal other than a mido. Apparently, they deduced that because the midos already had a name, a theri had to be a different kind of animal.

Certain discoveries with language are easier to make than others, contributing to the order in which children attain specific milestones. Children generally learn nouns before verbs, probably because they find it easier to map a word onto an object (e.g., *ball*) than onto a continuous stream of action (e.g., *throwing* the ball; Gentner, 2006; Golinkoff & Hirsh-Pasek, 2008; Waxman et al., 2013). After the first verbs enter their speech, children find more and more words to label the conspicuous movements they notice, for example, describing the trajectory of an object as *coming out* of a box and the manner of movement as *walking* to school (Pulverman, Song, Hirsh-Pasek, Pruden &, Golinkoff, 2014). As you might expect, children learn verbs for actions they can see (e.g., *running*) before those for actions they cannot see (e.g., *thinking*; Golinkoff & Hirsh-Pasek, 2008).

Cultural customs influence mental processes in language learning. Adults have an intuitive sense of the challenges infants face and, depending on traditions in their society, may simplify their speech or explicitly teach particular verbal expressions. Many U.S. and European parents engage their infants in dyadic exchanges with short, simple, high-pitched language, long pauses, and gestures identifying the people or objects under discussion (M. Harris, 1992; Lieven & Stoll, 2010; B. McMurray, Kovack-Lesh, Goodwin, & McEchron, 2013). Young children find such **infant-directed speech** compelling; even hearing-impaired children are drawn to its animated features (S. Robertson, von Hapsburg, Hay, Champlin, & Werner, 2013). You can hear examples of infant-directed speech in Observing Children video clips.

These modifications apparently help with comprehension, for instance, by clarifying the parent's focus of attention, but are not crucial for language learning (G. A. Bryant, Liénard, & Barrett, 2012; B. McMurray et al., 2013). The neurological basis for language learning is sufficiently strong that infants acquire its intricate features regardless of adults' adjustments, provided they have plenty of occasions to hear speech and interact verbally. For example, among the Kaluli in Papua New Guinea, mothers carry their infants around all day and hold infants facing outward, not speaking to them directly but allowing them to listen in on conversations with older children and adults (Schieffelin, 1985, 1990). Kaluli mothers do not intentionally ease the task of language and instead infants use meticulous mental processes while eavesdropping. After children speak their first words, adults tell children what they should say in particular situations.

The cognitive process framework has become enormously influential in contemporary explanations of language learning. Evidence that children absorb regularities and use intelligent analytical strategies to determine language functions is compelling. Yet we are left with many fascinating questions: Do children acquire these regularities statistically, sorting through the speech they hear and identifying the most common patterns? Do they identify rules of grammar? Do they chunk information they hear? Or how do they possibly make sense of a complicated stream of speech? These unanswered questions do not reflect weaknesses in the cognitive process account but do suggest much work ahead for linguists, psychologists, anthropologists, and educators.

Sociocultural Theories

In reading about the cognitive process model, you learned that children apply painstaking mental processes in language development, some of which are adapted to the specific methods adults use to make language accessible. Here we examine an approach that puts

This is a *mido*.

Which one of these is a *theri*?

FIGURE 9-2 **Which one of these is a theri?** Children are more likely to attach new words to objects for which they don't already have labels. In this situation, a child is likely to choose either the purple crocodile-like creature or the yellow dinosaur-like creature as being a *theri*. *After Au & Glusman, 1990.*

Observing Children 9-1

Listen to infant-directed speech in three infancy clips.

ENHANCEDetext *video example*

Preparing for Your Licensure Examination

Your teaching test might ask you about cultural influences on language learning.

interactional traditions in the spotlight. Whereas cognitive process theorists emphasize the intellectual operations involved in acquiring language, sociocultural theorists examine how social interactions foster language development. From this perspective children are *socialized* to use language (Ochs & Schieffelin, 1995; Salomo & Liszkowski, 2013; Sterponi, 2010). Such **language socialization** involves both explicit instruction about language (e.g., when parents insist that children say "please" and "thank you") and indirect means for fostering appropriate linguistic behaviors (e.g., when parents wait for children to take a turn in speaking, allow them to interject a few words, and sensitize children to the rhythms of interaction). Furthermore, social interactions provide a mechanism through which children *internalize* language.[5] Consistent with Vygotsky's theory of cognitive development, children use words first in their interactions with others, and then, through the process of internalization, gradually incorporate words into thought processes (Hobson, 2004; Kuvalja, Verma, & Whitebread, 2013; K. Nelson, 1996a).

From a sociocultural perspective, an understanding critical for language acquisition is *intersubjectivity*, the mutual awareness that two or more people are thinking about the same thing simultaneously.[6] For children to learn new words while interacting with others, they must be aware of this mutual focus (Mundy & Newell, 2007; Tomasello, 1999; Vuksanovic & Bjekic, 2013). As an illustration, imagine that a father and his 3-year-old daughter are shopping at the local supermarket. "Oh good," the father exclaims, "a carambola. I love carambolas!" If the daughter has never heard the word *carambola* before, she will likely look at her father's face and then follow his gaze to the object in question (in this case, a yellow-green, star-shaped fruit). She is apt to do this only if she realizes that her father is looking at the object he is talking about.

As early as the second year, and quite possibly before that, children use what they infer about other people's thoughts to assist them in learning word meanings (Golinkoff & Hirsh-Pasek, 2006; Mundy & Newell, 2007; Tomasello, 1999). In one study, 18-month-olds were looking at one new toy while an adult looked at another (D. A. Baldwin, 1993). When the adult exclaimed, "A modi!" the children typically turned their attention to see what the adult was looking at. A short time later, when the children were asked to get the modi, they were most likely to choose the toy the adult had been looking at, even though they themselves had been looking at something different when they first heard the word.

A primary strength of the sociocultural framework is its clear commitment to the social dimensions of language acquisition. Language, after all, begins in every child's life as a social tool for communication. A second strength of the framework is the revelation of the many distinct routes of language development. Children are flexible in their approaches to language learning, adapting easily to various types of language input and conversational traditions. Yet the sociocultural framework is less informative in identifying the biological underpinnings of language or the full range of cognitive processes that children use.

Functionalism

Another important question involves motivation: What does language help children accomplish in daily life? Some psychologists argue that over the course of evolution, human beings developed language skills because language serves several useful functions—hence the term **functionalism**. Language helps children acquire knowledge, maintain productive relationships, control their own behavior, and influence the actions of others (L. Bloom & Tinker, 2001; Karniol, 2010; O'Connell & Kowal, 2008; Tamis-LeMonda & Song, 2013). When Mario attended preschool as a 3-year-old, he quickly learned such expressions as "No do dat no more!" and "Get outta here!" (Fantini, 1985, pp. 97–98).[7] We can reasonably infer that such phrases enabled Mario to assert his rights with classmates pursuing conflicting agendas.

---

[5]You might recall reading about Vygotsky's views on internalizing speech in Chapter 6.
[6]Intersubjectivity is introduced in Chapter 7.
[7]Excerpt from "Case Study: Mario" from LANGUAGE ACQUISITION OF A BILINGUAL CHILD: A SOCIOLOGICAL PERSPECTIVE by A. E. Fantini. Copyright © 1985 by Alvino E. Fantini. Reprinted by permission of the author.

Functionalists point out that language development is closely intertwined with—and, in fact, is critical for—development in other domains (L. Bloom & Tinker, 2001; Langacker, 1986). Language enhances cognitive development by providing symbols for representing events, exchanging information, and regulating personal behavior. Language is essential for moral development as well. Through conversations with adults and peers, children learn socially acceptable ways of behaving toward others.

Language is so important for the human species that children seem to have the ability not only to learn it but also to *create* it. We find an example in a study of children attending a school for the deaf in Nicaragua (Senghas & Coppola, 2001). Before coming to the school, the children had little or no exposure to sign language, and teachers at the school focused primarily on teaching them how to lip-read and speak Spanish. Although many of the children made little progress in Spanish, they became increasingly adept at communicating with one another through a variety of hand gestures, and they consistently passed their sign language on to newcomers. Over a period of 20 years, the children's language became more systematic and complex, with a variety of syntactic rules taking shape.

The principal merit of functionalism is its identifications of the purposes that language fulfills. The initial function of language is sharing experiences with others, with motivations gradually expanding and differentiating into such specific objectives as conveying respect, asserting personal rights, insulting others, expressing emotions, informing listeners, telling stories, and regulating personal behavior. Although the functionalist framework is not as strong in identifying biological underpinnings or precise cognitive processes, its core ideas complement rather than oppose the nativist, cognitive process, and sociocultural frameworks.

Evaluating Theories of Language Development

The Basic Developmental Issues table "Contrasting Contemporary Theories of Language Development" summarizes how nativism, cognitive process theories, sociocultural theories, and functionalism differ with respect to the themes of nature and nurture, universality and diversity, and qualitative and quantitative change. An important difference among various theoretical perspectives is one of focus: Nativism focuses largely on syntactic development, cognitive process and sociocultural theories look more closely at semantic development (with sociocultural theories also considering pragmatic skills), and functionalism considers how motivation fits into the picture.

Although theorists isolate single elements of children's language in order to make their analysis manageable, children embrace full complexity. They tackle the full gamut of phonological, semantic, syntactic, and pragmatic rules as they speak and rely on these patterns as they listen. Not only do children honor the full spectrum of language regularities as they communicate, they manage to improve their skills in the process. In the next section, we focus closely on the numerous developmental changes that occur in children's language.

Summary

Although modeling, reinforcement, and feedback play a modest role in language development, early theories based on such processes could not adequately account for the fact that most children acquire a native language in a very short period, with only limited guidance from adults. Several more recent theoretical perspectives have emerged, each focusing on a different aspect of language development. *Nativists* propose that young children have certain inherited abilities that facilitate language acquisition, especially syntactic growth. *Cognitive process theorists* apply general principles of cognition (e.g., the importance of attention, the detection of patterns in language input) to explain how language develops. *Sociocultural theorists* emphasize the role that social interactions play in language learning. *Functionalists* propose that children are motivated to acquire language primarily because it enhances their ability to satisfy personal needs. To account for the range of advancements that occur in children's language development, scholars are apt to draw from elements of two or more frameworks.

ENHANCEDetext *self-check*

BASIC DEVELOPMENTAL ISSUES
Contrasting Contemporary Theories of Language Development

ISSUE	NATIVISM	COGNITIVE PROCESS THEORIES	SOCIOCULTURAL THEORIES	FUNCTIONALISM
Nature and Nurture	By and large, children develop language only when they are exposed to it; thus, environmental input is essential. But children also rely on one or more biological mechanisms that provide predetermined "knowledge" about the nature of language.	Language acquisition is the interplay of inherited abilities and the child's detection of regularities in language input (e.g., sounds that occur regularly in the native language, clues in the context that enable inferences about word meaning).	Sociocultural theorists don't necessarily discount the role of heredity, but they prioritize the social contexts and the cultural legacy (e.g., culture-specific interpretations of phrases) that a society passes along from one generation to the next.	As their needs and desires become increasingly ambitious, children propel their own language development with efforts to communicate more effectively. Their needs and desires are the result of both heredity and environment, but personal experience in a specific environment is emphasized.
Universality and Diversity	Although human languages differ in many respects, most have certain things in common (e.g., they include both nouns and verbs). Furthermore, children speaking different languages reach milestones at similar ages. Diversity exists primarily in the specific phonological, semantic, syntactic, and pragmatic features of particular languages.	Cognitive mechanisms that enable language acquisition (e.g., attention, analysis of speech sounds) are universally employed across cultures. Children's unique experiences, which vary among communities, lead to differences in the language(s) that children speak, the pathways to proficiency, and the concepts they communicate.	Some mechanisms that promote language development, for example, intersubjectivity, are universal across cultures. At the same time, different societies support these general mechanisms in distinctive ways and cultivate culturally specific linguistic practices.	The drive to understand and be understood by others is universal. Different cultural groups may be more responsive to certain ways of communicating more than others. Specific cultures use unique traditions in communicating respect, telling stories, and performing other functions of language.
Qualitative and Quantitative Change	Children acquire syntactic structures in predictable stage-like changes. Young children have a neurological basis for learning language, and proceed through one-word to two-word phases and later more complex constructions with defined grammar. If not exposed to conversation by the end of early childhood, language growth takes a laborious path toward partial mastery.	Many changes in language development—for instance, children's growing vocabularies, ongoing refinement of word meanings, increasingly correct pronunciation, and expanding working memory capacities (enabling production of longer and more complex sentences)—come about in a quantitative fashion with particular advancements occurring before others based on the distinctions that children can more easily make.	The nature of adult–child relationships that foster language development may change both quantitatively and qualitatively over time. As a qualitative change, intersubjectivity intially involves only an interaction between an adult and a child but later involves a mutual focus on, as well as shared understandings of, an object. Trend-like increases occur in the absorption of language conventions from the community.	Children's expressions of needs and desires change in quality and intensity. Whereas a 2-year-old might simply be interested in getting "more cookie," a 15-year-old might ask, "When I'm old enough to drive, can I have my own car if I earn the money for it?" Thus, both qualitative changes (e.g., use of new grammatical structures, such as dependent clauses) and quantitative changes (e.g., increasing sentence length) occur.

DEVELOPMENTAL TRENDS IN LANGUAGE LEARNING

Preparing for Your Licensure Examination

Your teaching test might ask you to recognize key developmental milestones in learning language.

Developmental changes in language are intertwined with a growing ability to communicate. Children's first form of communication is crying. Soon thereafter, they communicate by making eye contact, smiling, and cooing and, a bit later, by pointing and gesturing, and ultimately, with verbal interaction (e.g., Goldin-Meadow, 2006; Kraljević, Cepanec, & Šimleša, 2014; Tamis-LeMonda & Song, 2013; Tomasello, Carpenter, & Liszkowski, 2007). In the following sections, we explore changes in language during infancy, childhood, and adolescence.

Semantic Development

Infants begin categorizing objects by 3 or 4 months of age, understand the meanings of a few words as early as 8 months of age, and typically say their first word at about 12 months (Byrnes & Wasik, 2009; Fenson et al., 1994; M. Harris, 1992; Oller, Oller, & Oller, 2014).

By the time children are 16 to 18 months old, many have 50 words in their expressive vocabularies (Byrnes & Wasik, 2009; O'Grady, 1997). There is considerable variability from child to child, however. Mario did not say his first word until he was 16 months old, and by his second birthday he was using only 21 words (Fantini, 1985).

At some point during the end of the second year or beginning of the third year, a virtual explosion in speaking vocabulary occurs, with children using 30 to 50 new words a month and, later, as many as 20 new words *each day* (M. Harris, 1992; O'Grady, 1997). In the preschool years, children also begin to organize their knowledge of various words into general categories (e.g., *juice, cereal,* and *morning* are all related to *breakfast*), hierarchies (e.g., *dogs* and *cats* are both *animals*), and other inter-word relationships (S. A. Gelman & Kalish, 2006; M. Harris, 1992).

At 6 years of age, children's semantic knowledge typically includes 8,000 to 14,000 words, of which 2,600 are included in speech (Byrnes & Wasik, 2009; Carey, 1978). By the sixth grade, they understand, on average, 50,000 words in what they hear and read, although they cannot necessarily produce all of these words themselves. By the end of high school, vocabulary includes approximately 80,000 words (Owens, 2012).

The dramatic increase in words that children understand and use is the most obvious aspect of semantic development. Yet several other principles characterize growth, as we now explain.

Young children divide the continuous stream of speech they hear into its individual word "pieces." Doing so is not as easy as you might think: Even in the simplified infant-directed speech described earlier, one word flows quickly into the next with barely a break in sound (Jusczyk, 1997). Despite nonstop verbal action, infants begin to identify separate words in speech by 7 or 8 months of age (Aslin, Saffran, & Newport, 1998; Bortfeld, Morgan, Golinkoff, & Rathbun, 2005). Exactly how they accomplish this feat remains a mystery, but they probably rely on the characteristic rhythm, stress patterns, and consistencies in sound sequences in their native language (K. G. Estes, Evans, Alibali, & Saffran, 2007; Gervain & Mehler, 2010; Gonzalez-Gomez, Nazzi, Kreiman, & Jacewicz, 2013). Children notice that some sound combinations regularly co-occur in sequence in a particular language, whereas other combinations do not (Jusczyk, 1997). Consider the English statement, "Call Peter for dinner" ("C" (*Cuh*), "a" (*ahh*), and "l" (*ahl*) flow easily together, but "l" (*luh*) and "p" (*puh*) do not, signaling to the listener that "call" is one word, and "cal_l_" and "_P_eter" are separate words. Similarly, "r"(*err*) and "f" (*fuh*) do not unfold fluently, providing a cue that "Pete_r_" and "_f_or" are also distinct words. As children learn which sounds can and cannot be bundled together, identify the stress on syllables, and notice other clues, they divide an ongoing stream of sounds into distinguishable words.

Children use a virtual toolkit of strategies for learning the meanings of words. As children are identifying the specific words in speech, they must also zero in on their meanings. In some cases adults provide instruction, perhaps by labeling objects or by asking questions ("Where is the _____?"), while looking at picture books with children (M. F. Collins, 2010; Dunham, Dunham, & Curwin, 1993; Manolitsis, Georgiou, & Parrila, 2011). More often, caregivers, teachers, and other individuals don't explicitly identify what they are referring to when they use new words. As a result, youngsters must infer the meaning from clues intrinsic to speech and from the contexts in which the words are used.

Infants and young toddlers sometimes need numerous repetitions of a word before they understand it (A. M. Peters, 1983; Pruden et al., 2006; Woodward, Markman, & Fitzsimmons, 1994). But by the time children are age 2 or 3, they often infer a word's general meaning after only one exposure—a process known as **fast mapping** (Carey & Bartlett, 1978; McKean, Letts, & Howard, 2013). Young children seem to use a number of general rules to fast-map word meanings. Here are some examples:

- If I see several objects and know labels for all of them except one, the new word is probably the name of the unlabeled object. (Recall the research study involving the words *mido* and *theri*.)
- If someone uses a word while pointing to a particular object, the word probably refers to the *whole* object rather than to just a part of it.
- When a word is used to refer to a particular object or action, it refers to *similar* objects or actions as well.

- If a word is preceded by an article (e.g., "This is a *ball*"), it refers to a category of objects. If it has no article in front of it (e.g., "This is *Tobey*"), it is the name of a *particular* object (i.e., it is a proper noun; Au & Glusman, 1990; K. W. Brady & Goodman, 2014; Choi & McDonough, 2007; S. A. Gelman & Raman, 2003; S. A. Gelman & Taylor, 1984; Golinkoff, Hirsh-Pasek, Bailey, & Wenger, 1992; M. Hansen & Markman, 2009; Jaswal & Markman, 2001; Markman, 1989; Spiegel & Halberda, 2011; E. A. Walker, McGregor, Bacon, & Tobey, 2013.)

As children get older, they continue to refine their understandings of words through repeated encounters in conversation, books, and explicit instruction (Byrnes & Wasik, 2009; Carey & Bartlett, 1978; Yildirim et al., 2014). As an example, consider how three children in the same family once defined the word *plant:*

Andrew (age 7):   Something that people plant in a garden or somewhere.
Amaryth (age 10): A growing thing that's sometimes beautiful.
Anthony (age 13): A life-form that uses sunlight and carbon dioxide to live.

Notice how Andrew's definition is concrete and limited to contexts in which his parents and other people might have used the word. Amaryth's definition is more general, in that it includes a characteristic of all plants: growth. Only Anthony's definition includes characteristics that a biologist might identify. Presumably Anthony had acquired this understanding of the word *plant* in a science class at school.

Comprehension usually, but by no means always, precedes production. Psychologists studying language development frequently make a distinction between receptive and expressive language skills. **Receptive language** is the ability to understand what one hears and reads. In other words, it involves language *comprehension*. In contrast, **expressive language** is the ability to communicate effectively either orally or in writing. In other words, it involves language *production*.

It would be quite reasonable to assume that receptive language skills must precede expressive language skills, that children must understand what words mean before using them in speech and writing. You can see that 16-month-old Corwin shows greater facility in understanding than producing words in an Observing Children video. Yet many theorists don't believe that the relationship between receptive and expressive language is clear-cut (Owens, 2012). As you have learned, children understand some words because of clues in the conversation, for example, parents looking and pointing at objects they are describing. In addition, children use some words whose meanings they don't completely understand. Teresa recalls a 3-year-old preschooler in her class who talked about the "accoutrements" in her toy purse, presumably after hearing others use the word in a similar context. Although the girl used the word appropriately in that situation, she presumably did not understand all of its connotations: in this situation, production exceeded comprehension. Essentially, receptive and expressive language skills develop hand in hand, with language comprehension facilitating language production, language production enhancing language comprehension, and both relying on cognitive abilities.

Children initially focus on lexical words; grammatical words come later. All languages have two main categories of words (Shi & Werker, 2001). **Lexical words** have some connection, either concrete or abstract, to objects, events, or circumstances in people's physical, social, and psychological worlds. They include nouns (e.g., *horse, freedom*), verbs (e.g., *swim, think*), adjectives (e.g., *handsome, ambiguous*), and adverbs (e.g., *quickly, intentionally*). **Grammatical words** (also known as *function words*) have little meaning by themselves but affect the meanings of other words or the interrelationships among words or phrases. They include articles (e.g., *a, the*), auxiliary verbs (e.g., the *have* in *I have swum*), prepositions (e.g., *before, after*), and conjunctions (e.g., *however, unless*). By the time children are 6 months old, they can distinguish between lexical and grammatical words and show a distinct preference for lexical words (Bornstein et al., 2004; Shi & Werker, 2001).

Over time, children refine their understandings of lexical words. Children initially have a general idea of what certain words mean but define them imprecisely and occasionally use them incorrectly. One common error is **underextension**, in which children attach overly restricted meanings to words, leaving out some situations to which the words apply. For example, Jeanne once asked her son Jeff, then 6, to tell her what an *animal* is. He gave this definition:

It has a head, tail, feet, paws, eyes, nose, ears, lots of hair.

Observing Children 9-2

Notice how Corwin appears to have greater facility in understanding words (receptive language) than in pronouncing them (expressive language).

ENHANCEDetext *video example*

Like Jeff, young elementary schoolchildren often restrict their meaning of *animal* primarily to nonhuman mammals, such as dogs and horses, and insist that fish, birds, insects, and people are *not* animals (Carey, 1985; Saltz, 1971). Another frequent error is **overextension**: Words are given meanings that are too broad and so are applied to inappropriate situations. For example, a child might say "I'm *barefoot* all over!" or "I'll get up so early that it will still be *late*" (Chukovsky, 1968, p. 3; italics added).

In addition to underextending and overextending word meanings, children sometimes confuse the meanings of similar words. The following conversation illustrates 5-year-old Christine's confusion between *ask* and *tell:*

Adult:	Ask Eric his last name. [Eric Handel is a classmate of Christine's.]
Christine:	Handel.
Adult:	Ask Eric this doll's name.
Christine:	I don't know.
Adult:	Ask Eric what time it is.
Christine:	I don't know how to tell time.
Adult:	Tell Eric what class is in the library.
Christine:	Kindergarten.
Adult:	Ask Eric who his teacher is.
Christine:	Miss Turner. (dialogue from C. S. Chomsky, 1969, p. 55; format adapted)

In a similar manner, young children often confuse comparative words, sometimes interpreting *less* as "more" or thinking that *shorter* means "longer" (Owens, 2012; Palermo, 1974).

Children have difficulty with grammatical words throughout the elementary and middle school years. Children's mastery of grammatical words typically evolves slowly over a period of several years. For instance, although 3-year-olds can distinguish between the articles *a* and *the*, children as old as 9 are occasionally confused about when to use each one (Owens, 2012; Reich, 1986). Children in the upper elementary and middle school grades, and occasionally at the high school level, have trouble with many conjunctions and adverbial phases, such as *but*, *although*, *yet*, *however*, *honestly*, and *unless* (Ebbels, Marić, Murphy, & Turner, 2014; E. W. Katz & Brent, 1968; Owens, 2012). As an illustration, consider the following two pairs of sentences:

Jimmie went to school, but he felt sick.
Jimmie went to school, but he felt fine.

The meal was good, although the pie was bad.
The meal was good, although the pie was good.

Even 12-year-olds have trouble identifying the correct sentence in pairs like these, reflecting only a vague understanding of the connectives *but* and *although* (E. W. Katz & Brent, 1968). (The first sentence is correct in both cases.)

Understanding of abstract words emerges later than understanding of concrete words. Children's increasing ability to think abstractly is reflected in their semantic development (Anglin, 1977; Haskill & Corts, 2010; Quinn, 2007).[8] Young children in particular are apt to define words (even fairly abstract ones) in terms of the obvious, concrete aspects of their world. For example, when Jeanne's son Jeff was 4, he defined *summer* as the time of year when school is out and it's hot outside. By the time he was 12, he knew that scientists define summer in terms of the earth's tilt relative to the sun—a much more abstract notion.

Fostering Semantic Development

Language experts have identified several strategies that teachers, parents, and other caregivers can use to help children learn word meanings:

• **Talk regularly to, with, and around infants, toddlers, and preschool children.** Even when infants have not yet begun to talk, they learn a great deal from hearing their native language. Initially, they learn its basic characteristics, such as its typical rhythms and stress patterns and the range of sounds it includes. Later, as they begin to mentally "divide" speech into individual words, they draw inferences about what words mean. Although the simple sentences and attention-grabbing tones some parents use may initially attract infants into conversation, it's

---

[8]Children's ability to think abstractly is examined in Chapter 6.

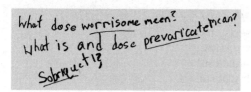

What dose worrisome mean?
What is and dose prevaricate mean?
Subrauct13

ARTIFACT 9-1 Worrisome. On a page from her fifth-grade journal, 10-year-old Amaryth jotted down unfamiliar words from a book she was reading.

the richness of language—the variety of words, complex syntactic structures, and so on—that facilitates children's vocabulary growth (B. Hart & Risley, 1995; Hoff & Naigles, 2002; Pan, Rowe, Singer, & Snow, 2005).

• **Invite children to listen to stories and later to read themselves.** Reading to young children expands their vocabularies, especially when the adult periodically pauses to talk about unfamiliar words (Brabham & Lynch-Brown, 2002; Lugo-Neris, Jackson, & Goldstein, 2010). When children begin reading themselves, they continue to encounter a rich corpus of language. Avid readers learn many more new words and develop larger vocabularies than do children who read infrequently (Fukkink & de Glopper, 1998; Stanovich, 2000; Swanborn & de Glopper, 1999; Zucker, Cabell, Justice, Pentimonti, & Kaderavek, 2013). As you can see in Artifact 9-1, 10-year-old Amaryth encountered several new words in her reading.

• **Define new words.** By the time children are school age, they often learn words more easily when told specifically what the words mean—in other words, when they are given definitions (Crevecoeur, Coyne, & McCoach, 2014; Tennyson & Cocchiarella, 1986). Definitions are especially helpful when the essential characteristics of a concept are abstract. Most children can learn what a *circle* is and what *red* means even without definitions, because roundness and redness are characteristics that are easily noticed. But the important characteristics of such conceptually based ideas as *polygon* and *fragile* are subtle, and for words like these, definitions can be useful.

• **Provide examples and nonexamples of new words.** Children often acquire a more accurate understanding of a word when they are shown several examples (Barringer & Gholson, 1979; Tennyson & Cocchiarella, 1986). Ideally, such examples should be as different from one another as possible so that they illustrate the word's entire range. If adults limit their examples of *animal* to dogs, cats, cows, and horses, children will understandably draw the conclusion that all animals have four legs and fur (a case of underextension). If instead adults also mention goldfish, robins, beetles, earthworms, and people as examples of *animal*, children are apt to realize that these creatures can differ considerably in physical appearance.

In addition to seeing examples, children benefit from learning non-examples of a word, especially those that are "near misses" (Winston, 1973). For instance, to learn what a *salamander* is, a child might be shown several salamanders and be told what the characteristic features are; next, the child could be shown such similar animals as a snake and a lizard and told that these critters are "*not* salamanders." By presenting both examples and nonexamples, adults minimize the extent to which children are likely to overextend their use of words.

• **Give feedback to children when they use words incorrectly.** Misconceptions about word meanings reveal themselves in children's speech. Astute teachers listen closely not only to what children say but also to how they say it, and they look at how children use words in their writing. A preschooler might mistakenly refer to a rhinoceros as a "hippo," an elementary school student might deny that a square is a rectangle, and a high school student might use the term *atom* when she is really talking about molecules. In such situations adults should gently correct the misconceptions, perhaps by saying something along these lines: "A lot of people get hippos and rhinoceroses confused, because both of them are large and gray. This animal has a large horn on its nose, so it's a rhinoceros. Let's find a picture of a hippo and see how we can tell the difference."

Syntactic Development

Which one of the following sentences is grammatically correct?

• Growing children need nutritious food and lots of exercise.
• Experience students find to be many junior high school an unsettling.

You undoubtedly realized that the first sentence is grammatically correct and the second is not. But *how* were you able to tell the difference? Can you describe the specific grammatical rules you used to make your decisions?

Rules of syntax—the rules we use to combine words into meaningful sentences—are incredibly complex (e.g., N. Chomsky, 2006). Yet much of our knowledge about syntax is unconscious. Although we can produce acceptable sentences and readily understand the syntactically correct sentences of others, we cannot always put our finger on exactly what it is we know about language that allows us to understand grammatical rules.

Despite the elusive nature of syntactic rules, children pick them up quickly. By the time they reach school age, children have mastered many of the basics of sentence construction (Christie, 2012; Haskill & Corts, 2010; McNeill, 1970). Grammar acquisition continues in school, with children filling in minor gaps in their syntactic knowledge throughout the elementary school years and, to a lesser extent, in the secondary school years as well. Following are noteworthy milestones in syntactic development over the course of childhood.

Early syntactic knowledge builds on an awareness of patterns in speech. In one study, 7-month-olds heard a series of "sentences," each comprised of three nonsense syllables (e.g., *ga*, *na*, *ti*, *li*). Infants in Group 1 consistently heard them in a predictable "ABA" pattern (e.g., "Ga ti ga," "Li na li"), whereas infants in Group 2 heard them consistently in an "ABB" pattern (e.g., "Ga ti ti," "Li na na"; Marcus, Vijayan, Bandi Rao, & Vishton, 1999). After losing interest in whichever sentences they were exposed to (reflecting *habituation*), they heard another series of "sentences" with new nonsense syllables.[9] Some of these sentences followed the ABA pattern (e.g., "Wo fe wo"), whereas others followed the ABB pattern (e.g., "Wo fe fe"). The infants paid greater attention when listening to the new pattern, showing their distinction between familiar and unfamiliar structures.

Some syntax appears in children's earliest word combinations. Initially, children use only single words to express their thoughts. At 18 months, Teresa's son Connor would simply say "mo" if he wanted more of whatever he was eating or playing with at the time. And like many toddlers, he would stretch out his arms and plead "Up!" when he wanted to be carried or cuddled. Developmental scientists sometimes use the word **holophrase** to refer to such one-word "sentences" (Byrnes & Wasik, 2009). As toddlers begin to combine words into two-word "sentences" in the latter half of their second year, using a limited number of grammatical forms (e.g., adjective + noun), their two-word combinations frequently reflect description ("Pillow dirty"), location ("Baby table"), or possession ("Adam hat"; R. Brown, 1973, p. 141). These early multiple-word sentences, known as **telegraphic speech**, include lexical words (rather than grammatical words) almost exclusively. By using such words, children maximize the meaning of their short sentences—they get "the most bang for the buck"—just as many adolescents and adults do when they send text messages. As children's sentences increase in length, they also increase in syntactic complexity—for instance, by including a subject, verb, and object (e.g., "I ride horsie") or describing both an action and a location ("Put truck window," "Adam put it box"; R. Brown, 1973, p. 205). Sometime before age 3 children begin to include grammatical words—*the, and, because,* and so on—in their sentences (O'Grady, 1997; Owens, 2012).

Young children rely heavily on word order when interpreting sentences. By the time they are 1½, children have a basic command of word order (Dove, 2012; Gertner, Fisher, & Eisengart, 2006; Hirsh-Pasek & Golinkoff, 1996). They know that "Big Bird is washing Cookie Monster" means something different from "Cookie Monster is washing Big Bird." Yet young children are sometimes misled by the order in which words appear (O'Grady, 1997). Many preschoolers apply a general rule that a pronoun refers to the noun that immediately precedes it. Consider the sentence "John said that Peter washed him." Many 4-year-olds think that *him* refers to *Peter,* and hence conclude that Peter washed himself. Similarly, kindergartners are apt to have trouble with the sentence "Because she was tired, Mommy was sleeping" because no noun appears before *she.*

Children use information about the prevalence of word combinations. Some theorists suggest that acquiring syntax involves discovering the probabilities with which various word combinations appear in sentences (Dove, 2012; MacWhinney & Chang, 1995; Sirois, Buckingham, & Shultz, 2000). Children may notice that *the* is usually followed by names of things or by "describing" words (e.g., they might hear "the dog," "the picnic," or "the pretty hat"). In contrast, *the* is rarely followed by words that identify specific actions (e.g., they never hear "the do" or "the went").

[9]Habituation is described in Chapter 2.

Children attend to word meaning when making inferences about syntactic rules. Children occasionally engage in **semantic bootstrapping**, the process of using word meanings as a basis for understanding syntactic categories (Bates & MacWhinney, 1987; S. A. Gelman & Kalish, 2006; Pinker, 1984, 1987; L. Wagner, 2010). They may notice that labels for people and concrete objects always serve particular functions in sentences, action words serve other functions, spatial-relationship and direction words serve still others, and so on. Through this process they gradually acquire an intuitive understanding of nouns, verbs, prepositions, and other parts of speech—an understanding that allows them to use words appropriately in sentences. For instance, when told that "The dog consumed his meal," children not familiar with the word *consumed* may correctly infer that the dog *did* something with his dinner, most likely eating it.

Children's questions increasingly incorporate multiple syntactic rules. In some languages it's easy to ask questions. In Chinese, for instance, a person can change a statement into a question simply by adding *ma* to the end of the sentence. In English, asking questions is more complicated, for one thing requiring a change to the order of the subject and verb (from "You are hungry" to "Are you hungry?"). When past tense is involved, asking a question requires putting the auxiliary verb but *not* the main verb first ("Have you eaten yet?"). And when something other than a yes or no answer is called for, a question word (e.g., *who, what, where, how*) must also appear at the beginning ("What did you eat?").

English-speaking children master these question-asking rules a step at a time. Initially, their questions may be nothing more than telegraphic sentences with a rise in pitch at the end (e.g., "Kitty go home?"; R. Brown, 1973, p. 141). At about age 2½, they attach question words to the beginning, and sometime in their third year, they add an auxiliary verb such as *is* or *does*. However, preschoolers often neglect one or more requirements for asking questions. For instance, they may ask "What you want?" (forgetting to add the auxiliary verb) or "What you will do?" (omitting the auxiliary verb before the subject; de Villiers, 1995, pp. 516, 518). By the time they are 5, most English-speaking children have mastered the correct syntax for questions (de Villiers, 1995).

Children learn general rules for word endings before they learn the many exceptions. Knowledge of syntax includes awareness of when to use word endings (suffixes) such as *-s*, *-er*, and *-ed*. When children first learn the rules for using suffixes (e.g., *-s* indicates plural, *-er* indicates a comparison, and *-ed* indicates past tense), they often apply these rules indiscriminately. Thus a child might say "I have two *foots*," "Chocolate is *gooder* than vanilla," and "I *goed* to Grandma's house." This phenomenon, known as **overregularization**, is especially common during the preschool and early elementary years. It gradually diminishes as children master the irregular forms of words: The plural of *foot* is *feet*, the comparative form of *good* is *better*, the past tense of *go* is *went*, and so on (Blom, Paradis, Oetting, & Bedore, 2013; Cazden, 1968). Yet most high school students (and many adults as well) haven't completely mastered the irregularities of the English language (Marcus, 1996).

The ability to comprehend passive sentences evolves gradually during the preschool and elementary school years. In a passive sentence, the subject of the sentence is the recipient, rather than the agent, of the action that the verb conveys. Passive sentences frequently confuse young children, who may incorrectly attribute the action to the subject. Consider these two sentences:

> The boy is pushed by the girl.
> The cup is washed by the girl.

Preschoolers are more likely to be confused by the first sentence—that is, to think that the boy is the one doing the pushing—than by the second sentence (Karmiloff-Smith, 1979). The first sentence has two possible "actors," but the second sentence has only one: Both boys and girls can push someone else, but cups can't wash girls. Complete mastery of passive sentences doesn't appear until the elementary school years (O'Grady, 1997; Perovic, Vuksanović, Petrović, & Avramović-Ilić, 2014; Sudhalter & Braine, 1985).

Children are confused by certain types of sentences with multiple clauses. At about age 4 children begin to produce simple subordinate clauses, such as those that follow and modify nouns (e.g., "This is the toy *that I want*"; Owens, 2012, p. 298). Yet throughout the elementary school years children struggle to understand certain kinds of multiple-clause sentences. Sentences with one clause embedded in the middle of another are especially difficult, particularly if the noun tying the clauses together has a different function in each clause. Consider the sentence "The dog *that was chased by the boy* is angry" (Owens, 2012, p. 348). The dog is the subject of the main clause ("The dog . . . is angry") but is the recipient of the action in the embedded clause (". . . [dog] was chased by the boy"). Seventh graders easily understand such sentences, but younger children over-rely on word order and conclude that the boy, rather than the dog, is angry.

Knowledge of syntactic rules continues to develop in the later elementary and secondary levels. Beginning in the upper elementary and middle school grades, children may be taught to identify the various parts of a sentence (e.g., subject, direct object, prepositional phrase, and subordinate clause) about which they previously acquired intuitive knowledge. They also study various verb tenses (e.g., present, past, present progressive) even though they have been using these tenses in everyday speech for quite some time. In middle school and high school, adolescents learn more subtle aspects of syntax, such as subject–verb and noun–pronoun agreement, correct uses of *that* versus *which* to introduce subordinate clauses, functions of punctuation marks such as colons and semicolons, and so on. They rarely develop such knowledge on their own, however. Instead, most of their syntactic development during this period probably occurs as the result of formal instruction, especially through courses in language arts, English composition, and foreign languages (e.g., Pence & Justice, 2008; Riches, 2013).

Fostering Syntactic Development

Especially as they are learning the more complex and subtle aspects of syntax, children and adolescents often benefit from ongoing instruction and practice with syntactic structures. Following are several examples of how caregivers and teachers can promote youngsters' syntactic development.

• **Expand on young children's telegraphic speech.** When young children speak in telegraphic sentences, caregivers can engage in **expansion** by repeating the sentences in a more mature form. When a toddler says, "Doggy eat," mother might respond by saying, "Yes, the doggy is eating his dinner." Expansion gives children gentle feedback about fleshing out their own utterances and encourages them to use more complex syntactic forms (C. Bouchard et al., 2010; N. Scherer & Olswang, 1984; Topping, Dekhinet, & Zeedyk, 2013).

• **Teach irregular forms of verbs and comparative adjectives.** Children do not always hear the irregular forms of verbs and adjectives in everyday speech. Playmates may talk about what's *badder* or *worser,* and many adults confuse the past tenses of the verbs *lay* and *lie* (which are *laid* and *lay,* respectively). In elementary school, some formal instruction in irregular forms is the only way that children discover the correct forms of certain words.

• **Classify various sentence structures for children.** Having children examine and practice common syntactic structures (active and passive voice, independent and dependent clauses, etc.) has at least two benefits. First, children should be better able to vary their sentence structure as they write—a strategy associated with more sophisticated writing (Beers & Nagy, 2009; Christie, 2012; Spivey, 1997). Second, learning the labels for such structures (e.g., *passive voice*) in English should help them acquire analogous structures in other languages at a later time.

• **Every now and then ask children to express their ideas formally.** In typical everyday conversation, adults and children alike often use incomplete sentences and are lax in their adherence to grammatical rules (V. Cook & Newson, 1996; D. Lightfoot, 1999; K. Miller, 2013). But what's common in casual speech is often frowned on in writing and public speaking. In official communications (e.g., a letter to the editor of a local newspaper or a presentation to a large group), correct grammar is, in many people's minds, an indication that the writer or speaker is educated and someone to take seriously (Purcell-Gates, 1995). Also important is that formal language allows the student to communicate abstract and theoretical ideas that are integral to advanced subject matter (Christie, 2012).

Development of Listening Skills

Children's ability to analyze discrete sounds is fundamental to progress in semantic and syntactic development. Other important listening skills include comprehending messages and determining how to respond when a misunderstanding becomes evident. The development of listening skills is characterized by several trends.

In the first year, infants learn to hone in on sounds in their native language. The basic elements of speech—all the consonants and vowels a language includes—are collectively known as **phonemes**. Phonemes are the smallest units of speech that indicate differences in meaning in a particular language. For instance, the word *bite* has three phonemes: a "buh" sound, an "eye" sound, and a "tuh" sound. If we change any one of these sounds—for instance, if we change *b* to *f (fight)*, long *i* to long *a (bait)*, or *t* to *k (bike)*—we get new words with entirely different meanings.

Children are active processors of sounds from day one. At birth, infants can discriminate among a wide variety of phonemes, including many that they don't hear in the speech around them (Jusczyk, 1995; Partanen, Pakarinen, Kujala, & Huotilainen, 2013; Werker & Lalonde, 1988). Yet newborn babies prefer to listen to their native language over other languages, suggesting that they have acquired language patterns from overhearing speech during prenatal development (Huotilainen, 2013; Mehler et al., 1988; Moon, Lagercrantz, & Kuhl, 2013). Furthermore, newborn infants prefer human speech to other sounds and regular speech to recordings of the same speech played backwards (Gervain & Mehler, 2010). Several months after birth, infants prefer words they hear frequently, including their own names (Mandel, Jusczyk, & Pisoni, 1995).

This early tuning-in to the native language gradually alters what infants "hear" and "don't hear" in speech. By the time children are a year old, they primarily specialize in differences that are important in their own language (Gervain & Mehler, 2010; Jusczyk, 1997; Werker & Tees, 1999). One-year-old infants in English-speaking countries continue to hear the difference between the "l" and "r" sounds, a distinction critical for making such discriminations as *lap* versus *rap* and *lice* versus *rice*. In contrast, Japanese children gradually lose the ability to make this distinction because the Japanese language treats the two sounds as a single phoneme. Similarly, babies in English-speaking societies lose the ability to distinguish among various "s" sounds that comprise two or more different phonemes in certain other languages.

As you can see, the first year of life is an important one for learning the sounds that are used in one's native language. Thereafter, children fine-tune their discriminative powers. For instance, they may have some difficulty distinguishing between words that differ by only one phoneme until they are 5 years old (Gerken, 1994; Rayner, Foorman, Perfetti, Pesetsky, & Seidenberg, 2001). Furthermore, they may continue to hear some sounds not used in their own language until they are 8 to 10 years old (Giannakopoulou, Uther, & Ylinen, 2013; Siegler & Alibali, 2005).

Young children rely more than older children on context, but youngsters of all ages take context into account. Children do not necessarily focus on every sound, or even every word, when they listen to what people say. Eighteen-month-olds often guess the word a speaker is going to say after hearing only the first two phonemes (Fernald, Swingley, & Pinto, 2001). Older children often realize from contextual cues that what a speaker says is different from what he or she actually means (M. Donaldson, 1978; Flavell et al., 2002; Paul, 1990). Hence, kindergartners may correctly conclude that a teacher who asks "Whose jacket do I see lying on the floor?" is actually requesting the jacket's owner to pick it up and put it where it belongs.

Older children and adolescents consider the context in comparing a message to the reality of the situation. Such a comparison enables them to detect sarcasm—to realize that the speaker actually means the exact opposite of what he or she is saying (Capelli, Nakagawa, & Madden, 1990; Glenwright & Pexman, 2010). They understand that someone who says "Oh, that's just *great!*" in dire circumstances doesn't think the situation is "great" at all.

Cognitive factors influence oral comprehension. Not only does children's ability to understand what they hear depend on their knowledge of word meanings and syntax, it also reflects their general knowledge about the world. Children can better understand a friend's story about a trip to a fast-food restaurant if they have a script for what such visits typically entail. Children's knowledge about the world enables them to draw inferences from the things they hear and fill in gaps in the information presented. For instance, when told that a father and daughter have gone to the beach and, after placing their towels, are testing the warmth of the water, children who have previously gone to the beach will assume that father and daughter are sticking their toes in the sea water rather than judging the warmth of water in their thermos.

Also influential to understanding oral language is working memory capacity (Anthony, Lonigan, & Dyer, 1996; Côté, Rouleau, & Macoir, 2014; Florit, Roch, Altoè, & Levorato, 2009). When information exceeds children's working memory capacity, it will, as the common expression puts it, "go in one ear and out the other."[10] Because young children can keep fewer words in mind than can older children, they are especially limited in their ability to understand what others tell them. Preschoolers, for instance, often have trouble remembering and following directions with multiple steps (L. French & Brown, 1977).

Older children become increasingly able to appreciate layers of meaning in words. As children move into the middle and secondary grades, they become better able to understand and explain **figurative speech**, a phrase whose meaning transcends literal interpretation. For instance, they understand that idioms, phrases that have nonliteral meanings, should not be taken at face value—that a person who "hits the roof" doesn't really hit the roof and that someone who is "tied up" isn't necessarily bound with rope. In Artifact 9-2, you can see 8-year-old Jeff's whimsical drawing of the statement that someone's eyes are bigger than his or her stomach.

Older children also become progressively more adept at interpreting similes and metaphors (e.g., "Her hands are like ice," "Eugene is the Rock of Gibraltar"). And in the late elementary years, they draw generalizations from such proverbs as "Look before you leap" and "Don't put the cart before the horse." In two Observing Children videos, you can see this developmental improvement in children's ability to understand proverbs. Whereas 10-year-old Kent seems baffled by the old adage "A rolling stone gathers no moss," 14-year-old Alicia offers a reasonable explanation: "Maybe when you go through things too fast, you don't collect anything from it."

Young children have definite ideas about what "good listening" is. Children listen to many explanations from teachers, parents, and other adults in situations where they are expected to remain quiet. Children who ask questions, especially those who talk out of turn or seem intentionally disruptive, are reminded to remain quiet until invited to speak (Bosacki, Rose-Krasnor, & Coplan, 2014). As a result of socialization and perceptions of required student roles, children in the early elementary grades believe they are being good listeners if they sit quietly without interrupting the speaker. Older children (e.g., 10- and 11-year-olds) are more likely to recognize that good listening additionally requires mental engagement and comprehension skills (T. M. McDevitt, Spivey, Sheehan, Lennon, & Story, 1990). In adolescence, many youngsters begin to realize that being a *socially effective* listener involves listening to others in an open-minded, nonjudgmental, and empathic manner (Imhof, 2001).

Preschool and elementary schoolchildren do not always listen critically. Children regularly ignore ambiguities and blatant inconsistencies in what they hear and read. Children's **comprehension monitoring**—the process of evaluating comprehension of oral and written material—develops slowly over childhood and well into the adolescent and adult years (Berkeley & Riccomini, 2013; Markman, 1979; Skarakis-Doyle & Dempsey, 2008). With cognitive development and encouragement, children learn to compare separate assertions as they listen, an ability that requires considerable memory capacity and attention.

Nor do they ask for clarification when confused. Children may fail to ask for assistance when confused. In a series of studies (T. M. McDevitt, 1990; T. M. McDevitt et al., 1990), children in grades 1, 3, and 5 responded to the following dilemma:

> This is a story about a girl named Mary. Mary is at school listening to her teacher, Ms. Brown. Ms. Brown explains how to use a new computer that she just got for their classroom. She tells the children in the classroom how to use the computer. Mary doesn't understand the teacher's directions. She's confused. What should Mary do? (T. M. McDevitt, 1990, p. 570)

ARTIFACT 9-2   Your eyes are bigger than your stomach. Eight-year-old Jeff drew this picture of a common idiom in English.

Observing Children 9-3
Observe a developmental progression in Kent's and Alicia's interpretations of proverbs.
ENHANCEDetext *video example*

---

[10]You can remind yourself of the characteristics of working memory by returning to Chapter 7.

DEVELOPMENT AND PRACTICE
Promoting Listening Skills in Children

Present only small amounts of information at one time.

- A preschool teacher helps the 3- and 4-year-olds in her class make "counting books." She has previously prepared nine sheets of paper (each with a different number from 1 to 9) for each child. She has also assembled a variety of objects that the children can paste onto the pages to depict the numbers (two buttons for the "2" page, five pieces of macaroni for the "5" page, etc.). As she engages the children in the project, she describes one or two steps at a time. (Early Childhood)

- As a kindergarten teacher reads aloud to children, she stops at the end of each page, allowing children time to absorb the segment. After a brief comments from the children, the teacher resumes with the story. (Early Childhood)

Expect children to listen attentively for only short periods.

- An infant caregiver notices that the babies in her care like to watch her face as she talks to them during diaper changes and bottle feedings. After a few moments of listening to her voice and looking at her facial expressions, however, babies are apt to look away. She continues to talk with them quietly but does not force interaction. (Infancy)

- A kindergarten teacher has learned that most of his students can listen quietly to books on tape for no more than 10 or 15 minutes at a stretch. He plans 10-minute sessions at the beginning of the school year and gradually lengthens the time over the first few months of school. (Early Childhood)

Discuss the components of good listening.

- A kindergarten teacher explains how children are to act during story time. After soliciting input from the children, the teacher posts several

guidelines: (1) Pay attention to the story, (2) stay seated, (3) keep your hands to yourself, and (4) take your turn in discussions. (Early Childhood)

- A second-grade teacher explains to students that "good listening" involves more than just sitting quietly; it requires paying attention and trying to understand what the speaker is saying. After a police officer briefly describes bicycle safety, she asks the children to summarize what they heard about safety precautions and ask any questions they might have. (Middle Childhood)

Encourage particular courses of action to take when confused by a speaker.

- A preschool teacher tells children it is time for "free choice." The children move around the room and select one activity or another. When a boy who has recently moved to the school walks around aimlessly, the teacher talks with him privately, explaining what free choice means and encouraging him to ask questions when he doesn't understand something. (Early Childhood)

- At the beginning of the year, a middle school teacher explains to students that he will try to be clear in his explanations but there will be times when he forgets to mention key steps. Students have several solutions they can try when unclear on what to do—they can figure it out themselves, ask for help from another student, or ask him to clarify. He tells the students that he would rather they ask for his help or question a friend rather than remaining confused. (Early Adolescence)

Some children responded that Mary should ask the teacher for further explanation. But others said that Mary should either listen more carefully or seek clarification from classmates. Many children, younger ones especially, believe it is inappropriate to ask a teacher for help, perhaps because they lack confidence or have previously been discouraged from asking questions at home or at school (Cluver, Heyman, & Carver, 2013; Marchand & Skinner, 2007; T. M. McDevitt, 1990; Puustinen, Lyyra, Metsäpelto, & Pulkkinen, 2008).

Promoting Listening Comprehension

During conversations and classroom lessons, adults can enhance children's capacity for effective listening. You can see examples of adults fostering relevant abilities in the Development and Practice feature "Promoting Listening Skills in Children" (above). In addition, consider these suggestions:

- **Informally assess children's understanding.** Although children profit from being exposed to rich and varied language, adults must be careful to use familiar language when it is important for children to understand something, for example, directions for a high-stakes test or steps to take in an emergency. In such a situation, adults need to assess children's understandings, perhaps—depending on their age—by having them restate what they have heard in their own words, draw a picture, or demonstrate steps to an action themselves (Jalongo, 2008).

- **Read to children on a regular basis.** Many parents tell young children stories, but some do not, perhaps because they have little free time, are not familiar with stories, or lack confidence in their reading abilities. Teachers can encourage parents to read to their children while also reading themselves to children in the classroom (M. Fox, 2013). Children can learn to love literature, develop new vocabulary, and understand complex syntax from listening to stories.

• **Adjust the length of verbal presentations to the attention span of the age-group.** People of all ages can understand a message only when they are paying attention, and even with full concentration they can handle only a limited amount of information on a single occasion. Given such limitations, children benefit from brief and occasionally repeated instructions (e.g., Wasik, Karweit, Burns, & Brodsky, 1998).

• **Encourage critical listening.** Sometime around ages 3 to 6, children realize that what people say is not necessarily true (e.g., Koenig, Clément, & Harris, 2004; K. Lee, Cameron, Doucette, & Talwar, 2002). Yet throughout the elementary and secondary school years, youngsters sometimes have difficulty separating fact from fiction (Rozendaal, Buijzen, & Valkenburg, 2012). Children who are taught not to believe everything they hear are more likely to evaluate messages for errors, falsehoods, and ambiguities. For example, when children are reminded that television commercials are designed to persuade them to buy something, they are less likely to be influenced by the appeals (Calvert, 2008; Halpern, 1998; D. F. Roberts, Christenson, Gibson, Mooser, & Goldberg, 1980).

• **Recommend strategies for children to use when they do not understand something.** Depending on their beliefs and practices with listening, children might rather sit in silence than ask a question of a teacher or classmate. If questions are okay in your classroom, let children know. If you prefer that they wait until you are finished talking, advise them of such. If you find that you must repeat instructions often, consider supplementing oral instructions with written steps in handouts or on the bulletin board or electronic whiteboard.

Development of Speaking Skills

As children become more adept in understanding what other people say, they also become more skilled at expressing their own thoughts, feelings, and wishes. Children's increasing proficiency in speech is the result of many things: better muscular control of the lips, tongue, and other parts of the vocal apparatus; more semantic and syntactic knowledge; increasing memory capacity; experience in formulating ideas; and growing awareness of what listeners are apt to know and believe. Following are several trends that characterize advancements in speech.

In the first year of life, children become increasingly proficient in making speech-like sounds. Between 1 and 2 months of age, infants begin **cooing**, making vowel sounds in an almost "singing" manner (e.g., "aaaaaaa," "ooooooo"). Sometime around 6 months, they start **babbling**, combining consonants and vowel sounds into repeated syllables (e.g., "mamamamama," "doodoodoo") without apparent meaning. With time, babbling becomes increasingly speech-like, as infants combine syllables into language-like utterances and drop the sounds not present in their native language (J. L. Locke, 1993). Thus, infants first babble in a universal "language" that includes a wide variety of phonemes; as they become more accustomed to their native tongue, they babble primarily with these sounds alone. Children who are deaf and whose parents communicate with sign language go through a similar phase of spirited experimentation with manual signs, playfully repeating gestures that with time resemble conventional signs (Oller et al., 2014).

Young children sometimes use gestures to communicate. During their first year of life, infants try to communicate through their actions. An infant might put his fingers in his mouth to indicate that he wants something to eat. A toddler might wrinkle her nose and sniff as a way of "talking" about flowers. To some degree, the use of such gestures paves the way for later language development (Esteve-Gibert & Prieto, 2014; Goodwyn & Acredolo, 1998; Volterra, Caselli, Capirci, & Pizzuto, 2005).[11] Youngsters don't entirely abandon gestures as they gain proficiency in spoken language, however. You can observe a young girl's effective use of gestures while speaking in an Observing Children video.

Pronunciation continues to improve in the early elementary years. As you've discovered, children say their first word sometime around their first birthday, and by age 2 or so most

Observing Children 9-4
Observe one girl's effective use of gestures during a conversation with an adult.
ENHANCEDetext *video example*

---

[11]Gestures also play a role in young children's reasoning (see Chapter 7).

children talk a great deal. Yet children typically do not master all the phonemes of the English language until age 8 or so (Hulit & Howard, 2006; Owens, 2012). During the preschool years, they are likely to have difficulty pronouncing *r* and *th* (they might say "wabbit" instead of "rabbit" and "dat" instead of "that"). Most children can make these sounds by the time they are 5 or 6, but at this age may still have trouble with such consonant blends as *spl* and *thr* (Byrnes & Wasik, 2009; Eriks-Brophy, Gibson, & Tucker, 2013; Pence & Justice, 2008). Recall the kindergarten teacher's reference to Mario's "slight accent." Mario mastered Spanish pronunciation by age 3. A few months later, he could produce many of the additional phonemes required for English. Nevertheless, Spanish sounds occasionally crept into Mario's English for several years after that (Fantini, 1985).

As children grow older, their conversations increase in length, coherence, and conceptual depth. Early conversations are brief. Most young children are quite willing and able to introduce new topics while talking with others, but they have difficulty sustaining a single topic during conversation (Brinton & Fujiki, 1984; Byrnes & Wasik, 2009; K. Nelson, 1996a). As they grow older, they can carry on lengthier discussions about one issue or event. In adolescence, the content of their conversations becomes more abstract (McAdams & McLean, 2013; Owens, 2012).

Children become progressively accomplished in adapting messages to the needs of their listeners. As early as age 3, preschoolers talk more while playing with others present than when alone, even though they don't always seem to expect a response (McGonigle-Chalmers, Slater, & Smith, 2013). Children of this age also use simpler language with toddlers than they do with adults and peers (Shatz & Gelman, 1973). Yet preschoolers and elementary schoolchildren don't consistently take their listeners' visual perspectives and prior knowledge into account and so may provide information that is inadequate to help listeners figure out what they are trying to communicate (Glucksberg & Krauss, 1967). To illustrate, a child might ask, "What's this?" without regard for whether the listener can see the object in question.

As children grow older, they become increasingly able to clarify their meanings for particular listeners (Aldrich, Tenenbaum, Brooks, Harrison, & Sines, 2011; T. M. McDevitt & Ford, 1987; Sonnenschein, 1988). They also become better able to read subtle nonverbal signals (e.g., puzzled brows, lengthy silences) that indicate others' confusion. Children who spend a lot of time interacting with different kinds of listeners become especially proficient in adapting to individual needs. For example, children of the Ituri Forest of the Democratic Republic of Congo regularly interact with children who are younger or older themselves, giving them considerable practice in adjusting speech to listeners with varied perspectives (Rogoff, Morelli, & Chavajay, 2010).

Over time, children gain competence in relaying events and imaginative stories. Beginning in the preschool years, children can tell a story, or **narrative**—an account of a sequence of events, either real or fictional, that are logically interconnected (McKeough, 1995; Sutton-Smith, 1986). Young children's narratives are quite brief and may simply link two events together, often about themselves, but by age 5 or 6, children recount the motivations and qualities of characters in their stories (K. Kelly & Bailey, 2013; Kemper, 1984; Nicolopoulou & Richner, 2007). You can listen to a 7-year-old boy's narrative about his changing home life in an Observing Children video.

During the elementary years, fictional stories are common, definite plot lines emerge, and descriptions of people's thoughts, motives, and emotions become increasingly sophisticated (Bauer, 2006; Kemper, 1984). In high school, students build on their skills in telling stories in other kinds of oral presentations, such as persuasive speeches and informative accounts of projects they have conducted.

In retelling personal experiences and imaginative renditions, children follow cultural practices. In her classic research, linguistic anthropologist **Shirley Brice Heath** (1983) identified two distinct styles of narrating events in working-class communities in the Piedmont Carolinas of the United States. In the predominantly European American community of Roadville, children relayed factual accounts of their personal experiences, whereas in the mostly African American community of Trackton, children told entertaining and far-fetched fictional stories. Children's narratives in many other cultures reflect particular styles for communicating personal imagination, experience, and values, including moral standards, gender roles, and political orientations (M. Mills, Watkins, Washington, Nippold, & Schneider, 2013; Sterponi, 2010).

Observing Children 9-5

Listen to a 7-year-old boy describe the origins of, and changes in, his early family life.

ENHANCEDetext *video example*

Preparing for Your Licensure Examination

Your teaching test might ask you about how culture affects a child's language development.

Creative and figurative expressions emerge in early childhood and develop further during middle childhood and adolescence. Many children enjoy "playing" with language (J. Thomas, 2012). Good friends might converse in "pig Latin" in which initial consonants are moved to the ends of words, and a long-*a* sound is added to each word. (As an illustration, the sentence *This sentence is written in pig Latin* would be "Is-thay entence-say is-ay itten-wray in-ay ig-pay atin-lay.") Children also take delight in jokes and riddles that play on the multiple meanings of words or similar-sounding phrases ("How much do pirates pay for their earrings?" "A buccaneer"). Creative wordplay is especially common in many African American communities (e.g., Smitherman, 2007). It sometimes takes the form of **playing the dozens**, playful teasing of one another through creative insults—for example, "Your mama's so fat she's got to sleep in the Grand Canyon" (Goodwin, 2006, p. 232; J. Lee, 2009).

Promoting Speaking Skills

To help children and adolescents develop their speaking skills, teachers and other adults should, of course, give them opportunities to talk to and in front of others. The following strategies can be beneficial:

• **Regularly invite infants to join you in "conversation."** In an Observing Children video, you can observe "conversations" that 16-month-old Corwin has with his mother. Although Corwin says few words distinctly enough to be understood, he knows how to take turns in the dialogue and understands enough of what his mother says to respond appropriately to her questions.

Infants respond most effectively to invitations to interact when adults gently encourage them without forcing exchanges. Young infants as early as 6 months of age are able to take turns in verbal interactions with adults, cooing or emitting a vocalizaton when the adults pause (de Barbaro, Johnson, & Deák, 2013; Masataka, 1992). When a caregiver mimics infants' vocalizations or responds affectionately to their gestures, infants generate even more speech-like sounds (K. Bloom, Russell, & Wassenberg, 1987; J. L. Miller & Lossia, 2013). Another effective strategy for encouraging infants' communication is to teach them signs and gestures. For instance, caregivers might teach signs for *more* and *please* (see Figure 9-3; Acredolo & Goodwyn, 1990; Góngora & Farkas, 2009; Vallotton, 2012). In this manner, infants learn to express their wishes before they can verbalize them.

• **Let children know when their messages are hard to understand.** People of all ages have trouble every now and then in communicating their thoughts clearly. Young children have particular difficulty because of their limited ability to consider the knowledge and perspectives of listeners. Asking questions or expressing confusion when children describe things ambiguously gradually helps them express their thoughts precisely (e.g., D. Matthews Lieven, & Tomasello, 2007).

Observing Children 9-6
Observe Corwin's turn-taking ability during interactions with his mother.

ENHANCEDetext *video example*

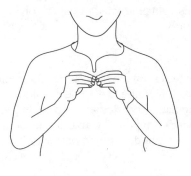

"More"

Place your fingertips together in front of your chest, as if adding something to the top of a pile.

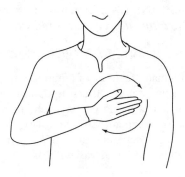

"Please"

Hold your hand close to your heart with palm facing toward your chest, and move it clockwise (from an observer's viewpoint).

FIGURE 9-3 More, please. Children as young as 6 months of age can communicate with gestures. Examples include signs for *more* and *please* in American Sign Language.

• **Ask children to recall real events and create fictional stories.** Adults often ask children to respond in narrative form. For instance, a teacher might ask, "What did you do this weekend?" or say, "Make up a story about a child bringing a cow to show-and-tell." Giving children opportunities to relate events, either actual or imaginary events, provides a context in which they can practice speaking (Hale-Benson, 1986; Hemphill & Snow, 1996; E. Levy & McNeill, 2013; McCarty & Watahomigie, 1998).

Storytelling ability can be enhanced by training and practice (Mandel, Osana, & Venkatesh, 2013; McKeough, 1995; J. R. Price, Roberts, & Jackson, 2006). Consider how 6-year-old Leanne's ability to tell a story improved over a 2-month period as a result of specific instruction in how to conceptualize and tell stories:

Before instruction:
A girl—and a boy—and a kind old horse. They got mad at each other. That the end. (McKeough, 1995, p. 170)

After instruction:
Once upon a time there was a girl. She was playing with her toys and—um—she asked her mom if she could go outside—to play in the snow. But her mom said no. And then she was very sad. And—and she had to play. So she she [sic] asked her mom if she could go outside and she said yes. She jumped in the snow and she was having fun and she had an idea and she jumped in the snow and she feeled happy. (McKeough, 1995, p. 170)

• **Encourage creativity in oral language.** Linguistic creativity can be expressed in many ways, including stories, poems, songs, rap, jokes, and puns. Such forms of language not only encourage inventive language use but also help children identify parallels between seemingly dissimilar objects or events. Recognizing commonalities enables children to construct similes, metaphors, and other analogies. Some children have experience in exaggeration and hyperbole, features of speech that can be integrated into stories. The playful use of language can help children discover general characteristics of language, as an incident in Mario's childhood illustrates:

Seven-year-old Mario tells his parents a joke that he has heard at school earlier in the day. He relates the joke in English: "What did the bird say when his cage got broken?" His parents have no idea what the bird said, so he tells them, "Cheap, cheap!"

Mario's parents find the joke amusing, so he later translates it for the family's Spanish-speaking nanny: *"¿Qué dijo el pájaro cuando se le rompió la jaula?"* He follows up with the bird's answer: *"Barato, barato."* Mario is surprised to discover that the nanny finds no humor in the joke. He knows that he has somehow failed to convey the point of the joke but cannot figure out where he went wrong. (Fantini, 1985, p. 72)[12]

The joke, of course, gets lost in translation. The Spanish word *barato* means "cheap" but has no resemblance to the sound that a bird makes. Only several years later did Mario understand that humor based in wordplay does not always translate from one language to another (Fantini, 1985). His eventual understanding of this principle was an aspect of his growing *metalinguistic awareness*, a topic we examine shortly.

Development of Pragmatics

The pragmatic features of language include verbal and nonverbal strategies for communicating effectively with others. Initiating conversations, changing the subject, asking for things politely, and arguing persuasively all require pragmatic knowledge. Also falling within the domain of pragmatics are **sociolinguistic behaviors**—types of verbal interactions that are considered acceptable for a speaker in a particular setting depending on his or her age, gender, status, and familiarity with others.

Conversational Rules

Most children acquire conversational skills (e.g., prefacing a request with "please" and responding courteously to other people's questions) long before they reach school age. By and large, sociolinguistic conventions are learned through socialization in families and cultural

[12]Excerpt from "Case Study: Mario" from LANGUAGE ACQUISITION OF A BILINGUAL CHILD: A SOCIOLOGICAL PERSPECTIVE by A. E. Fantini. Copyright © 1985 by Alvino E. Fantini. Reprinted by permission of the author.

groups (D. Friedman, 2010; Ochs, 2002; Rogoff, 2003). Children train one another informally, sometimes subtly and at other times bluntly, about what are and are not acceptable gestures for relating to one another. Adults occasionally teach sociolinguistic behaviors ("Say 'thank you' for the gift"). Modeling is also influential. Children mimic the way their parents answer the telephone, greet people on the street, and talk with relatives.

Classroom Rules for Communication

Classrooms have their own patterns of communication that children learn to follow. As you can see in an Observing Children video, children find out when and how they can ask for help and interact in groups. Mario once explained to his parents how his kindergarten teacher asked students to take turns when speaking in class (we present an English translation of Mario's Spanish):

> [A]t school, I have to raise my hand . . . and then wait a long, long time. And then the teacher says: "Now you can speak, Mario," and she makes the other children shut up, and she says, "Mario's speaking now." (Fantini, 1985, p. 83)[13]

Observing Children 9-7
Listen to a language expert talk about learning of pragmatic rules in the classroom.
ENHANCEDetext *video example*

Speech Register

Another part of language development is becoming familiar with one or more **speech registers**, the styles of spoken language that are used by people who interact in similar roles in a community. By communicating frequently, individuals come to share pronunciations, word choices, and other means for expressing their relationships (L. Wagner, Greene-Havas, & Gillespie, 2010). Teenagers talking on the basketball court and young people interviewing for a job use decidedly different registers. On the court, teenagers speak in a jocular fashion, interrupting one another often, using lingo, and relying on shared understandings. The same youngsters at a job interview enact a polite and restrained tempo, being explicit in their descriptions, and pronouncing words carefully. Young people use still other registers when talking with their parents, younger brothers and sisters, and religious leaders.

Like so many achievements in language development, learning to use the right speech register takes time and practice. Conversation on the playground allows for spontaneity and laughter. In the classroom, children are to be attentive to classroom rules as to how and when they ask a question and request help. The lunchroom is somewhere in between, allowing for children to take initiative while keeping their voices down. Most children distinguish these different demands fairly quickly, but some children, especially those with certain intellectual disabilities, have difficulties in adapting speech to the demands of particular settings (Hatton, 1998; Mervis, & Becerra, 2007).

Cultural Rules for Conversation

Conventions for communication—those unspoken rules about how conversations are supposed to take place—can seem obvious to teachers yet mysterious to students. As a result, a teacher might become irritated when a child violates these conventions, for example, making a request that is impolite (saying "Gimme a pencil" rather than "May I please have a pencil, Ms. Martinez?"). In reality, the child may simply not yet have acquired the polite form of making a request. Because conventions for communication are culturally specific, misunderstandings can occur at any age. It behooves teachers to learn about common variations in styles of communicating, as discussed next.

Talking Versus Being Silent. Relatively speaking, Western culture is a chatty one. People often say things to one another even when they have very little to communicate, making small talk as a way of maintaining interpersonal relationships and filling awkward silences (Irujo, 1988; Trawick-Smith, 2014). In some African American communities, people speak frequently and often with a great deal of energy and enthusiasm (Gay, 2006; Lein, 1975). In certain other cultures, silence is golden. Many Brazilians and Peruvians greet their guests silently, some Arabs stop talking to indicate a desire for privacy, and several Native American

---

[13]Excerpt from "Case Study: Mario" from LANGUAGE ACQUISITION OF A BILINGUAL CHILD: A SOCIOLOGICAL PERSPECTIVE by A. E. Fantini. Copyright © 1985 by Alvino E. Fantini. Reprinted by permission of the author.

communities value silence in certain circumstances (Basso, 1972; Menyuk & Menyuk, 1988; Trawick-Smith, 2014).

Interacting with Adults. In many European American families, children feel they can speak freely when they have comments or questions. Yet in many other communities, children learn very early that they should engage in conversation with adults only when their participation has been solicited. In such cultures, speaking directly to adults is seen as rude (Banks & Banks, 1995; Delgado-Gaitan, 1994; Paradise & Rogoff, 2009). In some parts of Mexico and Alaska, children are expected to learn primarily by quiet observation of adults. Accordingly, these children rarely ask questions or otherwise interrupt what adults are doing (García, 1994; Gutiérrez & Rogoff, 2003; Romero-Little, 2011).

Making Eye Contact. Among many people from European American backgrounds, looking someone in the eye is a way of indicating that they are trying to communicate or are listening intently. But for other people, especially some individuals in a number of African American, Hispanic, and Native American backgrounds, a child who looks an adult in the eye is showing disrespect. Children in such cultures may be taught to look down in the presence of adults (Torres-Guzmán, 1998; Trawick-Smith, 2014). The following anecdote shows how accommodation to this culturally learned behavior can make a difference:

> A teacher [described a Native American] student who would never say a word, nor even answer when she greeted him. Then one day when he came in she looked in the other direction and said, "Hello, Jimmy." He answered enthusiastically, "Why hello Miss Jacobs." She found that he would always talk if she looked at a book or at the wall, but when she looked at him, he appeared frightened. (Gilliland, 1988, p. 26)

Maintaining Personal Space. In some groups, such as in some African American and Turkish communities, people stand close together when they talk, and they touch one another frequently (Hale-Benson, 1986; A. Ozdemir, 2008). In contrast, numerous European Americans and Japanese Americans keep a fair distance from one another—they maintain **personal space**—especially if they don't know one another well (Trawick-Smith, 2014).

Responding Orally to Questions. A common interaction pattern in many Western classrooms is the **IRE cycle**: A teacher *initiates* an interaction by asking a question, a student *responds* to the question, and the teacher *evaluates* the response (Mehan, 1979). Similar interactions are frequently found in parent–child interactions in middle-income European American homes. These parents might ask their toddlers such questions as "Where's your nose?" and "What does a cow say?" and praise them for correct answers. But children from some other backgrounds are unfamiliar with such question-and-answer sessions when they first come to school (Losey, 1995; Rogoff, 2003).

A number of classrooms use another type of scripted response for students, in which students respond chorally. You can see an example of this instructional style in an Observing Children video. Although elementary-age schoolchildren are apt to be enthusiastic participants in such exchanges, especially after growing accustomed to their rhythms, such interactions are more effective for rote learning than for conceptual learning, and some children find them dull and stifling, as they cannot pose personal questions or articulate their own understandings of issues (Hargreaves, 2012; C. Harris, Phillips, & Penuel, 2012; McConney & Perry, 2011; Tarman & Tarman, 2011).

Observing Children 9-8

Watch a classroom of children responding orally in unison to a teacher's prompts.

ENHANCEDetext *video example*

Responding to Particular Types of Questions. Cultural groups also familiarize children with specific types of questions. European American parents frequently ask their children questions that they themselves know the answers to. Parents from a range of other cultures rarely ask such questions (Crago, Annahatak, & Ningiuruvik, 1993; Heath, 1989; Rogoff & Morelli, 1989). Parents in certain African American communities in the southeastern United States are more likely to ask questions involving comparisons and analogies. Rather than asking "What's that?" they may instead ask "What's that *like?*" (Heath, 1980). Also, children in these communities are specifically taught *not* to answer questions that strangers ask about personal situations and home life (e.g., "What's your name?" "Where do you live?").

Waiting and Interrupting. Teachers frequently ask their students questions and then wait for an answer. But exactly how long do they wait? The typical **wait time** for many teachers is a second or even less, at which point they either answer a question themselves or call on another student (M. B. Rowe, 1974, 1987). Yet people from some cultures leave lengthy pauses before responding as a way of indicating respect, as this statement by a Northern Cheyenne illustrates:

> Even if I had a quick answer to your question, I would never answer immediately. That would be saying that your question was not worth thinking about. (Gilliland, 1988, p. 27)

In many cultural groups, children are more likely to participate in class and answer questions when given several seconds to respond (C. A. Grant & Gomez, 2001; Mohatt & Erickson, 1981; Tharp, 1989; Worley, 2012).

Children from certain other backgrounds may interrupt adults or peers who haven't finished speaking—an action that some teachers interpret as rudeness. In some Australian Aboriginal, African American, Puerto Rican, and Jewish families, family discourse often consists of several people talking at once. In fact, people who wait for their turn might find themselves excluded from the discussion altogether (Condon & Yousef, 1975; Farber, Mindel, & Lazerwitz, 1988; Rendle-Short & Moses, 2010; Trawick-Smith, 2014).

Teaching Sociolinguistic Rules in the Classroom

Children need time to acquire new communication abilities at school, and in the meantime, teachers can try to identify and accept communication patterns children bring from home. With the Observation Guidelines table, "Identifying Cultural Differences in Sociolinguistic Conventions," you can practice identifying some styles of communicating that vary by society.

It also makes sense to directly teach the communication rules that you want children to follow. To help children to understand and be motivated to abide by classroom communication rules, teachers can follow these practices:

- **Explain and demonstrate communication rules.** Children may find certain customs odd, such as raising their hands to speak. Explanations, reminders, and rewards for following these rules can convince students to practice the desired behaviors. Teachers might also model an action, for example, listening politely to a student during a school announcement, pointing out the actions involved in respectful attention, and reminding students to practice these actions during show-and-tell activity. Teachers can also help children to distinguish the requirements of various settings—it's okay to laugh and shout during recess but not during a reading lesson.

- **Be flexible when children are adjusting to new communication rules.** Teachers can watch for children's use of communication conventions that are different from those typically used in the classroom. Ms. Miller exhibits this sensitivity when she realizes that one of her children, Ding Fang, seems to be abiding by the Chinese custom of remaining silent during a threatening social situation:

Ms. Miller:	What's going on over here? It seems like you two are having an argument.
Ding Fang:	(Looks down, says nothing)
Maura:	(In an angry tone) She took my car. (Now shouting at her peer) I was playing with that, you know!
Ding Fang:	(Says nothing, does not establish eye contact)
Ms. Miller:	Is that right, Ding Fang? Did you take Maura's car?
Ding Fang:	(Remains silent)
Ms. Miller:	Ding Fang? Can you tell me what happened?
Ding Fang:	(Still silent)
Ms. Miller:	Well, you don't seem to want to talk about it right now.
Ding Fang:	(Remains silent; looks as if she might cry)
Ms. Miller:	(Recognizes that Ding Fang is upset) You know, maybe this isn't such a good time to talk about it. Why don't we just go look at a book for a while. Would you like to do that? (Trawick-Smith, 2014, p. 297)[14]

Preparing for Your Licensure Examination
Your teaching test might ask you about how cultures determine conventions for speaking and listening.

[14]Excerpt from EARLY CHILDHOOD DEVELOPMENT: A MULTICULTURAL PERSPECTIVE, 6th Edition by Jeffrey Trawick-Smith. Copyright © 2014 by Jeffrey Trawick-Smith. Reprinted by permission of Pearson Education, Inc., Upper Saddle River, NJ.

OBSERVATION GUIDELINES
Identifying Cultural Differences in Sociolinguistic Conventions

CHARACTERISTIC	LOOK FOR	EXAMPLE	IMPLICATION
Talkativeness	• *Frequent talking*, even about trivial matters, or • *Silence* unless something important needs to be said	When Muhammed unexpectedly stops talking to his peers and turns to read his book, the other children are puzzled.	Don't interpret a child's sudden or lengthy silence as necessarily reflecting apathy or intentional rudeness.
Style of Interacting with Adults	• *Willingness to initiate conversations* with adults, or • *Speaking to adults only when spoken to*	Elena is exceptionally quiet in class and answers questions only when her teacher directs them specifically to her. At lunch and on the playground, however, she readily talks and laughs with her friends.	Keep in mind that children won't always tell you when they're confused. If you think they may not understand, take them aside and ask a few questions to assess what they have learned. Provide additional instruction to address gaps in understanding.
Eye Contact	• *Looking others in the eye* when speaking or listening to them, or • *Looking down* or away in the presence of adults	Herman always looks at his feet when an adult speaks to him.	Don't assume that children aren't paying attention just because they don't look you in the eye.
Personal Space	• *Standing quite close* to a conversation partner, perhaps touching that person frequently, or • *Keeping distance* between oneself and others when talking with them	Michelle is noticeably uncomfortable when other people touch her.	Give children some personal space during one-on-one interactions. To facilitate cross-cultural interactions, teach children that what constitutes personal space differs from culture to culture.
Responses to Questions	• *Answering questions readily*, or • *Failing to answer even very easy questions*	Leah never responds to "What is this?" questions, even when she knows the answers.	Be aware that some children are not accustomed to answering the types of questions that many Western adults ask during instruction. Respect children's privacy when they are reluctant to answer personal questions.
Wait Time	• *Waiting several seconds* before answering questions, or • *Not waiting at all*, and perhaps even interrupting others	Mario often interrupts his classmates during class discussions.	When addressing a question to an entire group, allow children to think before calling on a student to answer. To discourage interruptions, communicate a procedure (e.g., hand raising and waiting to be called by name).

Development of Metalinguistic Awareness

Metalinguistic awareness is the conscious understanding of the nature and functions of language. In the late preschool or early elementary school years, children become aware that words are the basic units of language, that spoken words are comprised of phonemes, and that different phonemes are associated with different letters or letter combinations (Lonigan, Burgess, Anthony, & Barker, 1998; T. A. Roberts, 2005; Tong, Deacon, & Cain, 2014; Tunmer, Pratt, & Herriman, 1984). As they move into the upper elementary and middle school grades, students begin to recognize and label parts of speech, to a large degree from formal instruction about nouns, verbs, and so on (e.g., Sipe, 2006; Vavra, 1987). Adolescents regularly grasp nonliteral references, and they show they are keeping track of intended meanings by repairing errors in speech (e.g., "I meant to say. . . ."; Haskill & Corts, 2010). More sophisticated aspects of metalinguistic awareness, such as interpreting phrases with multiple meanings, continue to advance throughout adolescence (Nippold & Taylor, 1995; Owens, 2012).

Analyses of metalinguistic development focus on the effects of particular experiences. Playing with language through rhymes, chants, jokes, and puns seems to be especially instructive. For example, rhymes help children discover the relationships between sounds and letters. Jokes and puns help children discover that words and phrases can have more than one meaning (L. Bradley & Bryant, 1991; Cazden, 1976; Nwokah, Burnette, & Graves, 2013; Yuill, 2009).

Listening to stories and reading books also promote metalinguistic awareness (Ravid & Geiger, 2009; Yaden & Templeton, 1986). The very process of reading to children helps them realize that printed language is related to spoken language. In addition, some children's books use words and phrases to accentuate rhymes, metaphorical statements, and multiple meanings. An example is *Amelia Bedelia Goes Camping* (Parish & Sweat, 2003), one in a series of books featuring an obtuse maid who takes everything her employers say quite literally. When they tell Amelia it's time to "hit the road" (an idiom in English), she hits the road with a stick—a response that our own children found amusing.

Formal language instruction augments a student's metalinguistic awareness. By exploring parts of speech, sentence structures, and the like, children gain a better grasp of the underlying structure of language. By reading and analyzing poetry and classic literature, they discover a variety of mechanisms (similes, metaphors, symbolism, and such transitional devices as "However, . . .," Equally important, . . .," and "In short, . . .") that a writer might use to convey connections between ideas. In an Observing Children video, you can listen to several literary techniques that a 13-year-old boy includes in his story.

Finally, research consistently demonstrates that knowledge of two or more languages (bilingualism) promotes metalinguistic awareness (X. Chen et al., 2004; Reyes & Azuara, 2008). By the time Mario was 5, he showed considerable awareness of the nature of language:

> Mario was well aware that things were called in one of several possible ways, that the same story could be retold in another language (he was capable of doing this himself), and he knew that thoughts were convertible or translatable through other forms of expression. . . . He knew that a [language] could be varied so as to make it sound funny or to render its messages less transparent, such as in Pig Spanish. . . .
>
> [As Mario grew older,] he became increasingly analytical about the medium which so many take for granted as their sole form of expression. He demonstrated interest, for example, in the multiple meaning of some words ("'right' means three things"); and in peculiar usages ("Why do you call the car 'she'?"); as well as intuitions about the origins of words ("'soufflé' sounds French"). (Fantini, 1985, pp. 53–54)[15]

Observing Children 9-9

Listen to the literary techniques that a 13-year-old boy uses in his narrative, including a classic beginning ("There once was a small monkey") and dramatic phrases ("It's a crisis, a phenomenon, a catastrophe!").

ENHANCEDetext *video example*

Promoting Metalinguistic Development

Factors that promote metalinguistic awareness—language play, reading experiences, formal instruction, and bilingualism—have several implications for teaching and working with children.

• **Explore multiple meanings through ambiguities, jokes, and riddles.** Having fun with language can be educational as well as entertaining. Teachers, parents, and other practitioners might ask children to identify the double meanings of such sentences as *He is drawing a gun* and *This restaurant even serves crabs* (Wiig, Gilbert, & Christian, 1978). Jokes and riddles provide another vehicle for exploring multiple meanings (Shultz, 1974; Shultz & Horibe, 1974; Yuill, 2009):

> Call me a cab.
> Okay, you're a cab.

> Tell me how long cows should be milked.
> They should be milked the same as short ones, of course.

• **Read literature that plays on the nature of language.** One of our favorite children's books is *The Phantom Tollbooth* (Juster, 1961), which has considerable fun with word meanings and common expressions. In one scene the main character (Milo) asks for a square meal and is served (you guessed it) a plate "heaped high with steaming squares of all

---

[15]Excerpt from "Case Study: Mario" from LANGUAGE ACQUISITION OF A BILINGUAL CHILD: A SOCIOLOGICAL PERSPECTIVE by A. E. Fantini. Copyright © 1985 by Alvino E. Fantini. Reprinted by permission of the author.

sizes and colors." Among the all-time classics in English wordplay are Lewis Carroll's *Alice's Adventures in Wonderland* and *Through the Looking Glass*. These books are packed with whimsical double word meanings, homonyms, and idioms, as the following excerpt from *Through the Looking Glass* illustrates:

> "But what could [a tree] do, if any danger came?" Alice asked.
> "It could bark," said the Rose.
> "It says, 'Boughwough!'" cried a Daisy. "That's why its branches are called boughs."

- **Encourage children to learn a second language.** Promoting metalinguistic awareness is just one of the benefits of learning a second language. In the next section we look more closely at second-language learning and bilingualism.

Summary

Linguistic knowledge and skills improve throughout childhood. School-age children add several thousand new words to their vocabulary each year. Over time, children rely less on word order and more on syntax to interpret other people's messages, and they comprehend and produce sentences with increasingly complex structures. Their conversations with others increase in length, they become better able to adapt the content of their speech to the characteristics of their listeners, and they become more aware of the unspoken social conventions that govern verbal interactions in their culture. They also acquire a growing understanding of the nature of language as an entity in and of itself.

ENHANCEDetext *self-check*

DEVELOPMENT OF A SECOND LANGUAGE

The majority of children around the world speak two or more languages (McCabe et al., 2013). Here we address two issues related to the development of a second language: the experiences of second-language learning and approaches to teaching a second language.

Experiences in Learning a Second Language in Childhood

Some children, like Mario, learn to speak two languages fluently. Like other **bilingual** individuals, Mario became accomplished in speaking both English and Spanish and learned to switch from one language to the other according to the languages spoken by his conversational partners.

School-age children who are proficient in their native language but not in English are referred to as **English language learners (ELLs)**. In the United States, English language learners represent a rapidly expanding group of K–12 students (C. B. Olson et al., 2012). Ten percent of children in U.S. public schools are English language learners, with California having the highest rate, at 29 percent (National Center for Education Statistics, 2014). U.S. children speak 350 different native languages, with Spanish being the most common (C. B. Olson et al., 2012).

English language learners have a diverse collection of abilities, backgrounds, and support systems. Some children have recently arrived in the country and speak little English, whereas others exhibit excellent oral communication skills in English and display only minor problems with reading and writing (Bunch, 2013). A small proportion of English language learners grow up with well-to-do parents who can afford to live in "good" neighborhoods, enroll them with well-equipped schools, hire tutors, and arrange enriching after-school activities. The majority of English language learners grow up in low-income families who must—due to their financial situations—rely on the schools for English instruction (C. B. Olson et al., 2012).

Advantages of Bilingualism

Being bilingual yields clear advantages. Foremost, it allows children to maintain interpersonal relationships with important people in their lives. In many Native American groups, for example, the ancestral language is used for conducting local business and communicating oral history and cultural traditions (McCarty & Watahomigie, 1998). Although most Puerto

FOR FURTHER EXPLORATION . . .

Read about effective instruction for English language learners from diverse backgrounds.

ENHANCEDetext
content extension

Rican children gain more valuable professional opportunities if they know English, they often speak Spanish at home and with peers, showing respect to their elders and maintaining their cultural identity (Nieto, 1995; Torres-Guzmán, 1998).

Acquiring a second language also benefits children intellectually and neurologically (Diaz, 1983; A. M. Padilla, 2006; Reich, 1986; Stocco, Yamasaki, Natalenko, & Prat, 2014). The process of learning two languages, using each in appropriate circumstances, and keeping two languages straight strengthens the brain's all-important *executive functions*, which allow the child to shift easily from one intellectual task to another in accordance with task demands (Bialystok & Viswanathan, 2009; Marzecová et al., 2013).[16] Bilingual children also become more metalinguistically sophisticated about the nature of language, as we mentioned previously (Bialystok, Peets, & Moreno, 2014).

Challenges Faced by Bilingual Children

Despite the advantages children enjoy while acquiring two languages, they encounter definite challenges. One is short-lived: Initial delays in language development, especially in vocabulary, sometimes occur, and words from one language can intrude as the child speaks in the other language. By elementary school, bilingual children generally catch up with monolingual peers and easily keep the two languages separate (C. Baker, 1993; Bialystok, 2001; Fennell, Byers-Heinlein, & Werker, 2007).

Yet many children have few opportunities to speak English outside of school, and even in school, may not have access to English-speaking peers with whom to communicate (Bunch, 2013). Even when they near fluency, bilingual students may lag behind native English speakers in understanding the nuances of English that are vital to grasping advanced academic lessons. Primarily because of these difficulties, English language learners on average obtain lower achievement test scores in elementary, middle, and high school, and they graduate from high school less often than do native-English-speaking classmates (J. Kim, 2011; National Center for Education Statistics, 2012).

Another potential problem for English language learners is achieving only partial mastery of each of their two languages. If enrolled in educational programs that emphasize English only, children may begin to speak increasingly in English and lose proficiency—or at least fail to make expected progress—in their first language (Austin, Blume, & Sánchez, 2013). Arrested development in the native language results in children's ineffectiveness in relating to their families, a definite risk factor.

Sadly, English language learners may also find that educators and other adults misunderstand their needs. One common misconception is that English language learners are confused or lazy when they slip back and forth between the two or more languages. A few teachers believe that these children do not belong in their classroom or should be exposed to only limited academic content until they are fully proficient in English, beliefs that if acted upon seriously restrict children's opportunities for learning (Polat & Mahalingappa, 2013).

Teaching a Second Language

Just as very young children learn their native language through daily exposure and interaction, so, too, can they learn a second language when given frequent chances to speak it. But when children begin to learn a second language at an older age, perhaps in the elementary grades or later, they often learn it more quickly if their language-learning experiences are structured (Strozer, 1994).

The particular model of instruction that a school selects depends on political pressures (how willing the community is to support second-language learning) and policy mandates (what the local authorities require). Cultural practices are also influential, as you can read more about in the Development in Culture feature, "Learning Second Languages in Cameroon."

Several approaches to second-language instruction have been used in schools, including bilingual education, submersion, structured English immersion programs, immersion, and foreign language instruction. The first three of these programs are typically used with

---

[16]*Executive functions* refer to deliberate thinking processes, such as planning and decision making, and are introduced in Chapter 5.

DEVELOPMENT IN CULTURE
Learning Second Languages in Cameroon

Educational anthropologist Leslie Moore spent several years in northern Cameroon, first as a Peace Corps volunteer and later as a researcher. During observations in Maroua, Cameroon, Moore observed children whose first language was Fulfulde and who were learning French at the local public school and Arabic during religious lessons (L. C. Moore, 2006, 2010, 2013).

Moore noticed similarities and differences in the ways that children were taught French and Arabic. In both cases, *guided repetition* was a primary way by which children learned the languages. Teachers would model a phrase and ask children to repeat it in unison. Children eagerly complied and gradually grew proficient in their pronunciation of both French and Arabic sounds, words, and phrases.

Yet the underlying purposes of learning French and Arabic were different and led to subtle distinctions in how instruction was implemented. The purpose of learning French was to become educated within modern society. Children were taught French as a second language and were also taught their basic subjects in French. Children needed to acquire sufficiently high levels of proficiency that they could understand a teacher's instructions and comprehend basic vocabulary in mathematics, civics, hygiene, and national culture.

The purpose of learning Arabic was more specific—it prepared children to recite the *Qur'an*, the Islamic book of sacred scriptures. Children did not learn to speak Arabic conversationally but rather memorized the particular phrases they needed to read along in the Qur'an. Children would recite verses from the Qur'an over and over, being careful to use appropriate intonations. Being able to recite the Qur'an prepared children to develop Muslim identities, including being reverent in matters of faith.

REPEAT AFTER ME. In Cameroon schools, imitation and rehearsal are primary means for learning second languages.

Moore identified advantages and disadvantages of guided repetition in the two contexts. Rote memorization appeared to work especially well in teaching children to recite the Qur'an because young children were expected to recite scripture as a matter of faith and not question its meaning. Guided repetition functioned reasonably well in the public school, yet had definite limitations in fostering advanced mastery of French. Many children did not develop the French expertise they needed to understand challenging material in the upper school grades, and a high proportion of children repeated grades and dropped out of elementary school.

Preparing for Your Licensure Examination
Your teaching test might ask you about principles of second-language learning.

English language learners, and the latter two programs are usually offered to help native English speakers learn a second language.[17] Let's examine the characteristics of each.

In **bilingual education**, English language learners receive intensive instruction in English while studying other academic subject areas in their native language. The sequence might be as follows:

1. Students join native English speakers for classes in subject areas that do not depend too heavily on language skills (e.g., art, music, physical education). They study other subject areas in their native language and also begin classes in *English as a Second Language* (ESL).
2. Once students have acquired some English proficiency, instruction in English begins for one or two additional subject areas (perhaps for math and science).
3. When it is clear that students can learn successfully in English in the subject areas identified in step 2, they join their English-speaking classmates in regular classes in these subjects.
4. Eventually students are sufficiently proficient in English to join the mainstream in all subject areas and no longer require their ESL classes. (Krashen, 1996; A. M. Padilla, 2006; Valdés, Bunch, Snow, & Lee, 2005)

These four steps are often carried out quickly and completed within 2 to 3 years. Yet rushing children's language learning is a concern because simple knowledge of basic conversational English is not enough for success in an English-only curriculum (A. M. Padilla, 2006).

[17]Similar models of second-language instruction are used in many other countries.

After all, students must have sufficient mastery of English vocabulary and grammar that they can readily understand and learn from English-based textbooks and lectures, and such mastery takes considerable time to achieve—often 5 to 7 years (Cummins, 1981, 2000). Moreover, concerns have been raised that children in transitional programs do not develop high levels of literacy in either their native language or in English (Estrada, Gómez, & Ruiz-Escalante, 2009). In one variant of this model, *transitional bilingual education*, the bilingual teacher instructs children in regular subjects in their first language and teaches English as a separate subject. English is gradually introduced for other subjects.

In another type of bilingual program, *developmental bilingual education*, both the native language and English are maintained. Developmental bilingual teachers instruct the children in both languages for an indefinite period. In a related model, *dual language instruction*, a mixed group of children who are native English speakers and others who are English language learners (and usually speak Spanish) receive instruction in both languages throughout their time in school (Estrada et al., 2009). Dual language programs have resulted in high levels of academic achievement, motivation, and student enthusiasm (Estrada et al., 2009).

Many schools have limited funds, relatively few children who speak the same native language, and an insufficient number of bilingual teachers. As a result, they may simply place English language learners in a regular classroom with other native English speakers. In the **submersion approach**, children are essentially left to their own devices in acquiring English. In **structured English immersion** programs, children receive intensive instruction in English over or year or so. Teachers offer instruction in English language as well as specially adapted instruction in English for the academic subjects (K. Clark, 2009). The main emphasis is on teaching in English, with educators hoping children will gain proficiency in English rapidly so that they can enter the regular classroom and catch up with classmates on academic subjects.

Two other programs are commonly used with native *English* speakers learning a second language. In **immersion** programs, children receive instruction in language arts in their first language and instruction in a second language in other subjects. Immersion programs begin as early as kindergarten and as late as sixth grade or after. For native English speakers, immersion in the second language for part or all of the school day helps students acquire basic proficiency in the language quickly, with any adverse effects on academic achievement being short lived (Collier, 1992; T. H. Cunningham & Graham, 2000; Genesee, 1985; A. M. Padilla, 2006).

In traditional **foreign language instruction**, children are taught a second language as a subject, occasionally as early as elementary school and regularly in middle school and high school. Children receive instruction in the foreign language for approximately 20 to 50 minutes daily or a couple of times weekly. Instruction that is based on drills and grammatical lessons is less effective than lessons that emphasize cultural awareness, oral communication, and community involvement (Otto, 2010).

Which models are most effective, and why? Non-native English speakers need to learn English so that they can master academic subjects and ultimately communicate with other English-speaking citizens, yet they also need to continue to communicate with family members, friends, and others in their neighborhoods. If English language learners are taught exclusively in English, they are at risk for losing expertise in their native language before developing adequate proficiency in English—a phenomenon known as **subtractive bilingualism**—and their cognitive development will suffer in the process. In this regard, bilingual programs may be superior to submersion and structured English immersion models. Because bilingual education is designed to foster growth in *both* English and a child's native language, it is apt to promote cognitive as well as linguistic growth (Estrada et al., 2009; McBrien, 2005b; Pérez, 1998; Tse, 2001; Winsler, Díaz, Espinosa, & Rodriguez, 1999). Furthermore, bilingual programs, and especially dual language instruction programs, tend not to isolate English language learners from their peers, which is a concern with English immersion models (Rios-Aguilar, González-Canche, & Moll, 2010).

For native English learners, immersion and foreign language instruction that permits conversation and fosters ties to the culture of the new language community seem beneficial. Native English speakers who live in an English-speaking country and are immersed in a different language at school still have many opportunities—at home, with friends, and in the local community—to continue using and developing English.

Second-language instruction is a controversial topic that will continue to inspire new instructional models and research. In the meantime, most English language learners are placed in regular classrooms without dedicated services, a condition that is due to several factors, including budget restrictions, the absence of qualified teachers, and the prevailing belief that children should learn English as quickly as possible (Goldenberg, 2008). Teachers in regular classrooms strive to support these children in learning English, acquiring knowledge of academic subjects, and adjusting in school, as you can see in the Development and Practice feature "Working with English Language Learners." Consider these additional recommendations:

• **Accept children's right to speak in their first language.** One of the fundamental rights children have is speaking freely in their home language (United Nations Children's Fund, n.d.). Speaking comfortably in their native tongue allows for allegiance to family and community (Hudley & Mallinson, 2011). Children should never be rebuked for using their mother tongue or for making mistakes when venturing to speak, write, and spell words in English.

• **Post the schedule for the day, instructional objectives, and definitions for key vocabulary in English.** You can help English language learners orient to the rhythms of the class and the intentions of the lessons by providing reference material in English (Goldenberg, 2008; Haynes & Zacarian, 2010). For nonreaders, teachers can communicate the focus of the day and lessons with verbal explanations, pantomime, videos, and, if possible, translations from other students in the class, classroom aides, or volunteers who speak the child's native language.

• **Be explicit about concepts and skills.** In learning their first language, children use a process by which they easily absorb the regularities in language. When learning a second language, the process is more deliberate, and teachers can assist in this regard by exposing children to English but also by overtly teaching them vocabulary, rules of grammar, and pragmatic conventions. This need is especially acute during academic learning—imagine the confusion an English language learner would have when introduced to the concept *Pythagorean Theorem* without a definition. Children also appreciate explanations of idioms ("That website is *over my head*," "Let me *sleep on it*," "I'm going to *call it a day*") when they pop up in literature or conversation.

• **Scaffold children's learning with handouts and instructions for assignments.** Handouts with structured words frames can provide assistance in English while focusing children's attention on core ideas (e.g., "The three types of camouflage we examined were _____, _____, and _____."). Written instructions that specify steps in completing a task focus everyone's attention and provide an especially useful tool for English language learners who might not otherwise understand the progression of the lesson.

• **Enlist the support of parents.** Bilingual parents may wonder whether they should speak English at home or alternatively continue to speak their native language. As you have learned, young children are well able to learn two languages, and parents can be advised that speaking their native language at home will not harm and can potentially benefit their children (Goldenberg, Hicks, & Lit, 2013). Given the distinct advantages to acquiring literacy skills in the native language, teachers can specifically encourage parents to read to children in the family's home language.

• **Teach native English speakers a second language.** Given the benefits of bilingualism, the fact that we live in global society, and strong evidence that young children have an amazing capacity to learn language, it makes sense to introduce second-language instruction for native English speakers in preschool or the elementary grades rather than waiting until middle or high school, which is currently common practice (Kalashnikova & Mattock, 2014; Roeper, 2012).

Summary

Individuals easily learn two languages during infancy and early childhood but, if they lack this early exposure, retain the ability to learn a second language later in childhood, during adolescence, and as adults. Research consistently indicates that knowing two or more languages fosters important brain functions and promotes metalinguistic awareness. Several

DEVELOPMENT AND PRACTICE
Working with English Language Learners

Ask children's parents about children's language backgrounds.

- A bilingual preschool teacher greets a family new to her Head Start center. As they get to know one another, she addresses the parents in their native Spanish language. She advises the parents about the activities and policies in the program and asks them about the child's interests, friendships, and family. She also asks about the child's routines in speaking English and Spanish—what language is spoken at home, with friends, with neighbors, and so forth. (Early Childhood)
- At an initial meeting with a mother and father who have recently moved into the neighborhood with their two teenagers, the principal greets the family with a few words in Spanish, warmly welcomes them to the school, and with help from the bilingual counselor, obtains information about who is in the family and the kinds of circumstances in which the students speak English and Spanish. (Late Adolescence)

Teach literacy skills in the student's native language.

- When working with students whose families have recently emigrated from Mexico, a first-grade teacher teaches basic letter–sound relationships and word decoding skills in Spanish (e.g., showing how the printed word *dos* can be broken up into the sounds "duh," "oh," and "sss"). (Middle Childhood)
- In a first-grade classroom, most of the children speak English but several speak Spanish or Vietnamese at home. The teacher makes read-along books available in English, Spanish, and Vietnamese and, with help of bilingual aides, posts the days of the week on the calendar and simple instructions on the board in the three languages. (Middle Childhood)

If you don't speak a student's native language, recruit parents, community volunteers, or other students to assist with communication.

- A high school has implemented a new Spanish Buddy program, in which bilingual high school students pair up with English language learners from Central America in a nearby elementary school. The high school students meet weekly with the children assigned to them. They talk informally with their elementary buddy at the beginning of each session and then read a story to him or her in Spanish. (Late Adolescence)
- A second-grade teacher invites the mother of a Salvadoran child to come to school and share traditions from her culture. The mother shares tamales with the class and talks about the different wrappers that people use to form the tamales, including corn husks, banana leaves, and paper. The children ask a lot of questions about Salvadoran customs. (Middle Childhood)

When using English to communicate, speak more slowly than you might otherwise, and clearly enunciate each word.

- A third-grade teacher is careful that he says "going to" rather than "gonna" and "want to" rather than "wanna." At the same time, the teacher does not correct children speaking informally in dialects that use such pronunciation. She politely points out the differences when children are preparing essays in formal English. (Middle Childhood)
- A high school speech teacher provides a rubric for presentations. In addition to including criteria for organization, persuasive appeal, and an animated delivery, the teacher includes standards that benefit English language learners, especially requirements that key terms are defined in a handout and words are pronounced clearly. (Late Adolescence)

Use visual aids to supplement verbal explanations.

- Before introducing a lesson on the desert habitat, a fifth-grade teacher draws a picture of a desert on a poster, labels a few common plants and animals that live there, prepares a list of key biological adaptations in harsh environments (e.g., conserving water, keeping predators away), and writes down vocabulary words (e.g., *desert, conserve, predator*). (Middle Childhood)
- A high school history teacher uses photographs she's downloaded from the Internet to illustrate a short lecture on ancient Egypt. She also includes key terms (e.g., *pyramid, sarcophagus*) on the electronic whiteboard. (Late Adolescence)

During small-group learning activities, periodically encourage same-language students to talk with one another in their native language.

- When a middle school science teacher assigns students into cooperative groups to study the effects of weight, length, and force onto a pendulum's oscillation rate, she puts three native Chinese speakers into a single group. She suggests that they can talk in either English or Chinese as they do their experiments. (Early Adolescence)
- A high school chemistry teacher asks a couple of Vietnamese students to brainstorm how chemistry is evident in contemporary Vietnamese society. The students then share their ideas with other groups, who have been asked to identify how chemistry is influential in other societies. (Late Adolescence)

Have students work in pairs to make sense of textbook material.

- As two middle school students study a section of their geography textbook, one reads aloud while the other listens and takes notes. They frequently stop to talk about what's been read, and then they switch roles. (Early Adolescence)
- A high school literature teacher guides a small group of English language learners by asking them a series of questions about a novel. Students answer the questions and then give their own perspectives on dilemmas raised in the story. (Late Adolescence)

Invite students to read, write, and report about their native countries.

- A second-grade teacher asks children to write a report about people who have made a difference in the community in which their parents grew up. The teacher encourages the children to talk with their parents as well as to find books about their parents' culture from the library. (Middle Childhood).
- A middle school social studies teacher has students conduct research on a country from which they or their ancestors have immigrated. The students create posters to show what they have learned, and they proudly talk about their posters at "International Day." (Early Adolescence)

Sources: Agirdag, 2009; Comeau, Cormier, Grandmaison, & Lacroix, 1999; Ernst-Slavit & Mason, 2012; Espinosa, 2007; García, 1995; Herrell & Jordan, 2004; Igoa, 1995; Krashen, 1996; McClelland, 2001; McClelland, Fiez, & McCandliss, 2002; National Center on Linguistic and Cultural Responsiveness, 2014; A. M. Padilla, 2006; Peregoy & Boyle, 2008; Ramirez & Soto-Hinman, 2009; Rothenberg & Fisher, 2007; Slavin & Cheung, 2005; Valdés et al., 2005.

instructional models exist for teaching English to English language learners. Research is still ongoing, but serious concerns are being raised about the effectiveness of academic instruction solely in English for English language learners. Nevertheless, it is common practice for English language learners to receive no assistance in their native-language learning at school, and thus the classroom teacher is advised to consider the needs of these children in classroom lessons. It is important for second-language learners to be encouraged to develop advanced skills in their native language so that they can continue to communicate with family and community members.

ENHANCEDetext *self-check*

Assessing Children 9-1

Describe how two languages are used for English language learners in Ms. Angelica Reynosa's history lesson.

ENHANCEDetext *application exercise*

Assessing Children 9-2

Identify the types of instructional strategies that a teacher uses with English language learners.

ENHANCEDetext *application exercise*

BIOECOLOGY OF DEVELOPMENT

Children bring individual qualities to experiences in familiar groups as they go about learning one or more languages.

INDIVIDUALITY IN LANGUAGE DEVELOPMENT

The bioecological framework captures the wide range of factors that converge in a child's language development. As you have learned, a baby is born with bundles of neurons that allow for identification of regularities in speech, connections between words and concepts, and inferences about grammatical relations. Stylistically, children develop methods of speaking based on their experiences as a boy or girl and as a member of one or more communities. In children with irregular neurological structures or hearing impairments, the course of language development depends on access to a signing community, treatment from a speech-language therapist, or other resources. In the remainder of this chapter, we examine features that contribute to children's individuality as language learners.

Gender

As infants and toddlers, girls are, on average, more verbally active than boys. Girls begin to speak about a month earlier, form longer sentences sooner, and have a larger vocabulary (M. Eriksson et al., 2012; Halpern & LaMay, 2000; Reznick & Goldfield, 1992). Once they reach the school years, girls outperform boys on tests of verbal ability. This gender difference in verbal ability is quite small, however, and plenty of boys have exemplary language skills that surpass those of most girls.

Qualitative gender differences in conversation exist as well. On average, boys see themselves as information providers and speak more directly and bluntly. Girls typically deepen relationships through their conversations and are more likely to be indirect, tactful, and well mannered (Kyratzis, & Tarım, 2010; Ladegaard & Bleses, 2003; C. M. Mehta &

Strough, 2009; Owens, 2012; Tannen, 1990). At least in European American middle-class families, girls tend to talk more than boys about emotions and relationships (Fivush, 1994; Fivush & Buckner, 2003).

Family Income

As mentioned in the earlier discussion of nativism, children from diverse backgrounds reach language milestones at similar ages. However, children from higher-income homes tend to have larger vocabularies (B. Hart & Risley, 1995; Thomas, Forrester, & Ronald, 2013; Wasik & Bond, 2001). This difference is largely due to the quantity and quality of language that parents use with their children. Although most mothers in Western societies interact frequently with their children, on average mothers with ample incomes talk with their young children for longer periods of time, ask more questions, elaborate to a greater extent on topics, and expose their children to a larger variety of words than do mothers with low incomes (B. Hart & Risley, 1995, 1999; Weisleder & Fernald, 2013). Stress is a major reason for diminished interaction in low-income families, as the numerous struggles of economic poverty, including worrying about finding food, clothing, shelter, transportation, and medical care for children, can be so overwhelming that parents lack energy at the end of the day to converse with children (Thomas et al., 2013).

Preparing for Your Licensure Examination Your teaching test might ask you how gender, family income, and ethnicity influence children's language development.

Of course, children from low-income families are a highly variable group. Some grandparents, aunts, and uncles regularly converse with children and help parents relax sufficiently such that they, too, are able to enjoy prolonged conversations with children and share stories at night. Other children from economically poor backgrounds receive little exposure to language at home but nevertheless gain literacy skills in high-quality preschools (Obradović et al., 2009).

Ethnicity

As you have already learned, sociolinguistic conventions, use of figurative language, and narrative styles differ from one group to another. Children from some groups use a form of English different from **Standard English** (sometimes known as Mainstream American English). For example, certain children living in the southern parts of the U.S. and some African American children speak in a **dialect**, a form of English (more generally, a form of any language) that includes unique pronunciations and syntactic structures. Dialects tend to be associated either with particular geographical regions or with particular ethnic and cultural groups. In Artifact 9-3, you can see evidence of the local dialect from the Northern Mariana Islands.

Southern English is a dialect prevalent in the southern part of the United States. This way of speaking has an infectious drawl. Although non-southerners may find this accent to be charming, they also are apt to underestimate the intelligence of southerners after hearing them speak (Hudley & Mallinson, 2011). Examples of distinctive pronunciations include:

> Yesterday I really have bad day. Because I break the window When I knock at the door. knowbody was there. Then I knock at the window very hard it break. My mom got

ARTIFACT 9-3 Yesterday. A local dialect is evident in this writing sample from a fifth grader who lives in the Northern Mariana Islands of the Pacific Ocean. The student blends present and past tenses in a description of an event. *Writing sample courtesy of the Commonwealth of the Northern Mariana Islands Public School System.*

- The *z* sound is pronounced as *d* before nasal consonants (e.g., *wasn't* is pronounced "wadn't").
- The *ai* sound at the end of a word is typically pronounced as *ah* (e.g., *time* is pronounced "tom," *mile* is "mall").
- *Ing* is spoken as *in* (e.g., *walking* sounds like "walkin"). (Hudley & Mallinson, 2011)

Another widely studied ethnic dialect is **African American English**. This dialect, which is actually a group of similar ways of speaking, is often used in informal settings throughout the United States but also in schools, churches, and other institutions that embrace African American culture. This dialect is characterized by certain unique pronunciations, idioms, and grammatical constructions. For example:

- The *th* sound at the beginning of a word is often pronounced as *d* (e.g., *that* is pronounced "dat").
- The *ng* sound at the end of a word is typically pronounced as *n* (e.g., *bringing* is pronounced "bringin").

- The *-ed* ending on past-tense verbs is often dropped (e.g., "We walk to the park last night").
- The present- and past-tense forms of the verb *to be* are consistently *is* and *was*, even if the subject of the sentence is the pronoun *I* or a plural noun or pronoun (e.g., "I is runnin'," "They was runnin'").
- The verb *is* is often dropped in simple descriptive sentences (e.g., "He a handsome man").
- The word *be* is used to indicate a constant or frequently occurring characteristic (e.g., "He be talking" describes someone who talks much of the time; Hudley & Mallinson, 2011; Hulit & Howard, 2006)

Obviously, not all African Americans speak an African American dialect, and individuals who do may restrict its use to certain settings. In addition, some people who do not identify as African Americans use language that has characteristics of African American English (Hudley, 2009).

At one time many people jumped to the conclusion that an African American dialect represented a less complex form of speech than Standard English. They urged educators to teach students to speak "properly" as quickly as possible. But psychologists, linguists, and many educators now realize that African American dialects, Southern English, and other dialects are complex versions of English with their own grammatical rules that promote communication and complex thought as readily as does Standard English (Fairchild & Edwards-Evans, 1990; D. Hill, 2013; Hulit & Howard, 2006; B. Z. Pearson, Velleman, Bryant, & Charko, 2009).

Children learn to see their native dialect as an integral part of their cultural identity (Agirdag, 2009; Ogbu, 2003; A. W. Tatum, 2008). Obviously, when a local dialect is the language most preferred by residents of a community, it is the most effective means through which youngsters can communicate in daily interactions. Unfortunately, some children are discouraged from using familiar dialects at school and made to feel that they (and their people) are not welcome there. In reality, it is important for children's welfare to speak freely in their dialect at least some of the time.

Yet learning to speak Standard English is important as well. Many of the textbooks, literature, and tests children read at school are written in Standard English; not surprisingly, then, children who have proficiency in Standard English have an easier time learning to read (Charity, Scarborough, & Griffin, 2004; Hudley, 2009; T. A. Roberts, 2005). Balancing expectations for use of dialects and Standard English seems the best way to go. Teachers may encourage Standard English in certain written reports and oral presentations, but they should be receptive to other dialects in creative writing, informal classroom discussions, and other educational lessons (DeBose, 2007; Hudley & Mallinson, 2011; Ogbu, 1999, 2003; D. Paris, 2009).

In addition, teachers can advise children that nonstandard dialects are, like Standard English, rule-governed codes, with appropriate uses in certain contexts (D. Hill, 2013; B. Pearson, Conner, & Jackson, 2013). For example, middle school students who have read Woodson's (2009) story *Peace, Locomotion*, might compose a letter to one of the characters in African American English and prepare a summary of the story's plot in Standard English (D. Hill, 2013).

Learning one or more dialects goes hand-in-hand with other aspects of language learning. In the Developmental Trends table "Language Skills at Different Age Levels," you can see the many aspects of language learning typically achieved during the childhood years.

Exceptionalities in Language Development

Preparing for Your Licensure Examination
Your teaching test might ask you to describe strategies for supporting children with exceptionalities in language development.

As you have seen, individual children vary in in the pace and style of language learning, depending on a host of bioecological factors. A few children have language impairments and sensory limitations that limit their communication and academic abilities but can be effectively guided with special accommodations.

Specific Language Impairments

Some children develop normally in all respects except for language. Children with **specific language impairments** have delays or abnormalities in spoken language or in language

DEVELOPMENTAL TRENDS
Language Skills at Different Age Levels

AGE	WHAT YOU MIGHT OBSERVE	DIVERSITY	IMPLICATIONS
Infancy (Birth–2 Years)	• Interest in listening to the human voice and exchanging vocalizations with adults • Repetition of vowel sounds (cooing) at age 1–2 months and consonant-vowel syllables (babbling) at about 6 months • Understanding of some common words at about 8 months • Use of single words at about 12 months • Use of two-word combinations at about 18 months • Rapid increase in vocabulary in the second year	• In the latter half of the first year, babbling reflects phonemes of the native language. • More cautious children may wait a bit before beginning to speak. • Chronic ear infections can interfere with early language development. • Infants with severe hearing impairments orally babble, but babbling does not progress to words. They may "babble" manually if their caregivers regularly sign to them. • Cultural patterns (e.g., verbal interaction or nonverbal contact) affect infants' language learning.	• Engage young infants in "conversations," using simplified and animated speech, and respond affectionately when they vocalize. • Label and describe the objects and events children observe. • Ask simple questions (e.g., "Is your diaper wet?" "What does a cow say?"). • Repeat and expand on children's early "sentences" (e.g., follow "Kitty eat" with "Yes, the kitty is eating his dinner"). • Teach simple hand signs that preverbal infants can use to communicate.
Early Childhood (2–6 Years)	• Rapid advances in vocabulary and syntax • Incomplete understandings of simple words (e.g., through underextension, overextension, and confusion between simple comparatives such as *more* vs. *less*) • Overregularization (e.g., *foots*, *gooder*, *goed*) • Focus on word order and context (instead of syntax) in interpretation • Understanding of "good listening" as being quiet • Beginning awareness of how words are divided up into separate sounds • Difficulty pronouncing some phonemes and blends (e.g., *r, th, spl*) • Increasing ability to construct narratives	• Children raised in bilingual environments may show slight delays in language development, particularly in vocabulary, but any delays are short-lived and rarely a cause for concern. • Major language impairments (e.g., abnormal syntactic constructions) reveal themselves in the preschool years and warrant referrals to a specialist. • The richness of parents' language affects children's vocabulary growth.	• Read age-appropriate storybooks as a way of enhancing vocabulary. • Give tactful corrective feedback when children's use of words indicates inaccurate understandings. • Work on simple listening skills (e.g., sitting quietly, paying attention, asking questions when confused). • Ask follow-up questions to make sure that children accurately understand important messages. • Ask children to construct narratives about recent events (e.g., "Tell me about your camping trip last weekend"). • Teach children communication rules at school.
Middle Childhood (6–10 Years)	• Increasing understanding of temporal words (e.g., *before*, *after*) and comparatives (e.g., *bigger*, *as big as*) • Incomplete knowledge of irregular word forms • Literal interpretation of messages (especially before age 9) • Pronunciation mastered by age 8 • Consideration of a listener's knowledge and perspective when speaking • Sustained conversations about concrete topics • Construction of narratives with plots and cause-and-effect relationships • Linguistic creativity and wordplay (e.g., rhymes, word games)	• Some minor language impairments (e.g., persistent articulation problems) are evident and can be addressed by specialists. • Children from certain groups (e.g., some children who are African American) show advanced ability to use figurative language (e.g., metaphor, hyperbole). • Bilingual children are apt to show advanced metalinguistic awareness. • Reading habits may affect children's metalinguistic awareness, vocabulary, and syntactic development. • Deaf children who sign exhibit metalinguistic awareness by identifying incorrectly formed or sequenced signs.	• Use group discussions as a way to explore academic subject matter. • Have children develop and present short stories. • Teach irregular word forms (e.g., the superlative form of *bad* is *worst*, the past tense of *bring* is *brought*). • Encourage jokes and rhymes that capitalize on double meanings and homonyms (sound-alike words). • When articulation problems are evident in the upper elementary grades, consult with a speech-language pathologist.

(continued)

DEVELOPMENTAL TRENDS (continued)

AGE	WHAT YOU MIGHT OBSERVE	DIVERSITY	IMPLICATIONS
Early Adolescence (10–14 Years)	• Increasing awareness of the terminology used in academic disciplines • Ability to understand complex, multiple-clause sentences • Emerging ability to look beyond literal interpretations; comprehension of simple proverbs • Growing capacity to carry on conversations about abstract topics • Significant growth in metalinguistic awareness	• Frequent readers tend to have large vocabularies. • Girls are more likely than boys to converse about intimate matters. • Certain adolescents (e.g., some African American teens) may bandy mock insults back and forth in an advanced creative manner. • Adolescents may prefer to use their native *dialects* even if they have mastered *Standard English*.	• Begin to use the terminology preferred by experts in academic disciplines (e.g., *simile* in language arts, *theory* in science). • Use classroom debates to explore controversial issues. • Ask adolescents to consider underlying meanings of proverbs. • Explore the nature of words and phrases as entities in and of themselves. • Teach students that formal English and nonstandard dialects are rule-governed language systems.
Late Adolescence (14–18 Years)	• Acquisition of terms related to specific academic disciplines • Subtle refinements in grammar, mostly as a result of formal instruction • Appropriate use of a variety of connectives (e.g., *although*, *however*, *nevertheless*) • General ability to understand figurative language (e.g., metaphors, proverbs, hyperbole)	• Boys are apt to communicate their thoughts in a direct and straightforward manner; girls are more likely to be indirect and tactful. • A preference for one's native dialect over Standard English continues into the high school years. • The kinds of slang vary depending on peer groups.	• Explain the terminology of academic disciplines. • Distinguish between similar abstract words (e.g., *weather* vs. *climate*, *velocity* vs. *acceleration*). • Explore complex syntactic structures (e.g., multiple embedded clauses). • Consider underlying meanings in poetry and fiction. • Encourage students to use nonstandard dialect in conversation and creative writing; teach Standard English in formal settings.

Sources: C. Baker, 1993; Bruer, 1999; Bruner, 1983; Byrnes & Wasik, 2009; N. Chomsky, 1972; Eilers & Oller, 1994; Elias & Broerse, 1996; Fantini, 1985; Fenson et al., 1994; Fifer & Moon, 1995; Goodwyn, Acredolo, & Brown, 2000; Hale-Benson, 1986; Imhof, 2001; Y.-S. Kim, Apel, & Al Otaiba, 2013; J. L. Locke, 1993; T. M. McDevitt, 1990; K. Nelson, 1973; Nicolopoulou & Richner, 2007; O'Grady, 1997; Ortony, Turner, & Larson-Shapiro, 1985; Owens, 2012; Pence & Justice, 2008; L. A. Petitto, 1997; A. Smith, Andrews, Ausbrooks, Gentry, & Jacobowitz, 2013; R. H. Thompson, Cotnoir-Bichelman, McKerchar, Tate, & Dancho, 2007.

comprehension that significantly interfere with their performance at school. Such impairments may involve problems in one or more of the following:

- Receptive language (e.g., inability to distinguish among different phonemes, difficulty understanding or remembering directions)
- Articulation (e.g., mispronunciations or omissions of certain speech sounds)
- Fluency (e.g., stuttering, an atypical rhythm in speech)
- Syntax (e.g., abnormal syntactic patterns, incorrect word order)
- Semantics (e.g., infrequent use of grammatical words, such as prepositions and conjunctions; frequent use of words with imprecise meanings, such as *thing* or *that*; difficulty interpreting words that have two or more meanings)
- Pragmatics (e.g., talking for long periods without letting others speak, failing to stick with the topic of conversation; American Speech-Language-Hearing Association, 1993; Claessen, Leitão, Kane, R., & Williams, 2013; Hulit & Howard, 2006; Joanisse, 2007)

Specific language impairments are also suspected when children don't demonstrate age-appropriate language. Speech patterns that reflect a regional or ethnic dialect and those that are due to a bilingual background do *not* fall within the realm of specific language impairments. (Recall the speech therapist who inappropriately recommended that Mario have speech therapy.)

In comparison with their nondisabled peers, children with specific language impairments have greater difficulty mentally processing particular aspects of spoken language—perhaps the quality, pitch, duration, or intensity of specific sounds in speech (Corriveau, Pasquini, & Goswami, 2007; P. R. Hill, Hogben, & Bishop, 2005; Thatcher, 2010). Some have problems with reading and writing (Catts, Adlof, Hogan, & Weismer, 2005; Deacon et al., 2014; J. R. Johnston, 1997; Leonard, 2009). Personal and social problems may also emerge. A few youngsters feel so self-conscious about their language disability that they are reluctant to speak with peers (Patton, Blackbourn, & Fad, 1996). Sadly, those that sound "odd" or are difficult to understand are sometimes ridiculed by thoughtless classmates (Durkin & Conti-Ramsden, 2007; Laws, Bates, Feuerstein, Mason-Apps, & White, 2012; Rice, Hadley, & Alexander, 1993).

In some cases specific language impairments are inherited (D. Bishop, 2010; J. Logan et al., 2011; M. L. Rice, 2013; F. M. Spinath, Price, Dale, & Plomin, 2004). In other instances struggles with language are associated with specific brain abnormalities that occur for unknown reasons (Basu, Krishnan, & Weber-Fox, 2010; Hellal & Lorch, 2013; J. L. Locke, 1993). Often the exact cause of the impairment is unknown (T. F. Campbell et al., 2003; Hulit & Howard, 2006; P. P. Wang & Baron, 1997).

Teachers and other school professionals can supplement the work of trained speech and language specialists by encouraging the language development of youngsters with specific language impairments. Several recommendations are presented in the Development and Practice feature "Working with Children Who Have Specific Language Impairments."

Sensory Impairments and Language Development

Children with visual impairments (e.g., blindness) typically have normal syntactic development but are apt to have more limited vocabularies than do sighted age-mates (M. Harris, 1992). Because they cannot always see objects and events around them, they simply don't have as many opportunities to make connections between words and the objects or concepts they represent (Hobson, 2004; M. B. Rowe, 1978).

Children with hearing impairments (e.g., deafness) are at risk for delays in both syntactic and semantic development, especially if an impairment is present at birth or emerges early in life (M. Harris, 1992). Children who have been completely deaf from birth or soon thereafter typically need special training to develop proficiency in speaking. Yet these children are apt to show normal language development in *sign language* if family members and others use it as the primary means of communicating with them (Lederberg, Schick, & Spencer, 2013; Mann, Marshall, Mason, & Morgan, 2010; Newport, 1990; L. A. Petitto, 1997). Deaf infants who are regularly exposed to sign language often begin to "babble" with their hands at 7 to 10 months, are apt to sign their first word at around 18 to 22 months, and use multiword phrases soon thereafter. Like hearing children, children who use sign language construct rules that guide their language use, and they gradually expand on and refine these rules over time (Goldin-Meadow, 2005; L. A. Petitto, 1997).

The case study of BoMee (Wilcox, 1994) illustrates just how much is possible when parents provide a linguistically rich environment through sign language. BoMee was born in Korea 8 weeks prematurely. Although she could hear at birth, early illnesses or medications caused profound hearing loss early in life. At age 2½, BoMee was adopted by American parents, who regularly used sign language with her. Within a few weeks after BoMee's arrival, her parents began to sign self-talk as a way of "thinking aloud." For instance, BoMee's mother might have signed "What goes next in this recipe?" or "Where are my shoes?" Within a week, BoMee began signing her own self-talk, such as "Where my shoes are?" Soon self-talk was a regular feature in BoMee's problem-solving activities. On one occasion, BoMee was trying to put a dress on her doll, but the dress was too small. She signed to herself:

> Hmmm, wrong me. This dress fit here? Think not. Hmmm. For other doll here. (Translation: *Hmmm, I'm wrong. Does this dress go on this doll? I don't think so. Hmmm. It goes on this other doll.*) (Wilcox, 1994, p. 119)

BoMee showed other normal linguistic behaviors as well. She adapted her language when she signed to her baby brother. And just as hearing children typically read aloud in the early stages of reading, BoMee signed "out loud" when she began to read.

DEVELOPMENT AND PRACTICE
Working with Children Who Have Specific Language Impairments

Be on the lookout for children who exhibit significant delays or other language problems unusual for their age.

- A caregiver is familiar with milestones in language development and watches for unusual delays in children (e.g., absence of babbling, pointing, and gestures by the end of the first year; no words by 16 months; and no two-word phrases by the second year). Without overreacting, the caregiver advises parents of children who show major delays that a speech-language therapist could help determine whether treatment might be helpful. (Infancy)
- A preschool teacher consults a speech-language pathologist about a 4-year-old girl who communicates only by pointing and gesturing. "She's certainly not shy," the teacher explains. "She often tries to get other children's attention by poking them, and she loves to sit on my lap during story time." The consulting professional encourages the teacher to model social gestures and praise the little girl when she uses verbal gestures. (Early Childhood)

Encourage children to speak.

- A fourth-grade teacher has a student who repeats himself a lot, hesitates while speaking, changes the topic during the middle of a sentence, and says "um . . ." frequently. The teacher offers several discussion guidelines to the entire class that are good practices for everyone and particularly helpful for the student with a speech disorder, including waiting patiently for the person who has the floor to finish a sentence, looking at the speaker and keeping still, and valuing everyone's contribution to the conversation. (Middle Childhood)
- An 11-year-old boy has trouble pronouncing several blends of consonants (e.g., he says "thpethial" for *special*) and is meeting regularly with a speech therapist to address the problem. His fifth-grade teacher encourages him to speak in class, especially in small-group settings. When he does so, she models acceptance of his disability, and if a classmate makes fun of his speech, she discreetly takes the classmate aside and explains that all children have strengths and weaknesses and that everyone in her class deserves respect. (Early Adolescence)

Listen patiently.

- Before children read their stories out loud for the class, an elementary teacher discusses expectations on how to listen. She tells the children that everyone is expected to listen quietly and respectfully and to make comments, give compliments, and offer tactful suggestions that will help their classmates become better writers. (Middle Childhood)
- A high school student stutters when she speaks and sometimes struggles for several seconds midway through a sentence in articulating a particular word. Her teachers know that she is able to complete her thoughts if given the time. (Late Adolescence)

Politely ask for clarification when a message is unclear.

- A preschool teacher sits down with a child who has a language delay and helps him formulate his thoughts. The teacher comments on his actions and expands on his simple phrases. When she is not clear on his meaning, she asks for clarification, providing him with options if she can guess what he might be trying to say. When he says "whenchit," she asks, "Are you pretending that you are fixing the clock with a special wrench?" (Early Childhood)
- An 8-year-old boy often says "this" or "that thing there" when referring to objects in the classroom. Suspecting that he may have an undiagnosed language disability, his third-grade teacher talks with his parents and then refers him to a school psychologist for evaluation. In the meantime, the teacher expands on the boy's speech with more complete references. (Middle Childhood)

Provide guidance on how to talk effectively with others.

- During storybook sharing, third-grade children form groups of two or three students and talk about the books they had read. Before the groups meet, their teacher suggests that the way to be a good listener is to offer a compliment to the person who gives a report or to make a comment on a feature of the book that seems interesting. A girl with a language delay contributes to her group and receives constructive feedback from classmates. (Middle Childhood)
- A middle school girl dominates conversations in small-group discussions, rambling on at such length that her classmates have trouble getting a word in edgewise. Her teacher meets with her during lunch one day to remind her of the importance of letting everyone participate. Together they identify a strategy that will help her restrict her comments: Whenever she starts to speak, she will look at the second hand on her watch and yield the floor after a maximum of 30 seconds. (Early Adolescence)

Sources: L. Bloom & Lahey, 1978; Otto, 2010; Patton et al., 1996; Smith-Lock, Leitao, Lambert, & Nickels, 2013; Turnbull, Turnbull, & Wehmeyer, 2010.

Like Mario, BoMee had an advantage in metalinguistic awareness. She was exposed to both English-based signs and American Sign Language (which have somewhat different vocabularies and syntactic structures) and quickly became bilingual in her knowledge of the two language systems. She also understood very early that some people talk and others use sign language. Furthermore, shortly after her third birthday, she appropriately signed "This Little Piggy" in two different ways—in English-based signs and in American Sign Language—depending on which of the two languages a listener understood. Clearly, children with

DEVELOPMENT AND PRACTICE
Working with Children Who Have Hearing Impairments

Intervene early to address correctable hearing impairments.

- Among the children in an infant room is a 2-year-old boy who is deaf. His mother expresses interest in a cochlear implant but cannot afford one. The boy's teacher and an audiologist locate a charitable organization that will pay for the cost of surgery. With the implant, the boy begins to hear the language around him, and his receptive and expressive language rapidly develop. (Infancy)
- A second-grade teacher wonders whether a boy in her class might have a hearing difficulty. She notices that he responds to her only when she is in face-to-face interaction with him. During large-group instruction, he does not follow directions without hearing them several times and seems to misunderstand a lot of what she and classmates say. The teacher talks with the boy's parents, and together they decide to have him referred to a speech-language pathologist for testing. (Middle Childhood)

Communicate instruction through multiple modalities.

- During a large-group meeting of the class, a fifth-grade teacher places a girl with a hearing impairment nearby so that she has a good view of the teacher and can see the pictures more clearly. (Middle Childhood)

- A 15-year-old who is deaf has a student aide who accompanies her to all of her classes and signs the content of teachers' lectures and explanations. Even so, her teachers make sure that they communicate as much as possible through sight as well as sound. They write important points on the chalkboard and illustrate key ideas with pictures and graphics. (Late Adolescence)

Learn a few elements of American Sign Language and finger spelling, and teach them to classmates of signing children.

- A teacher in a combined first- and second-grade class has several students who are deaf, and so she both speaks and signs to her class as she presents new information and describes assignments. All of her students know enough American Sign Language to converse using basic signs with one another. (Middle Childhood)
- An elementary school with a large population of children who have hearing impairments offers a weekly workshop in American Sign Language. Several parents and other family members of children who sign attend, as do a few parents of hearing children who volunteer in the classroom and want to be able to communicate with all of the children. (Middle Childhood)

Sources: Bruer, 1999; I. Cruz et al., 2013; Newport, 1990; Otto, 2010; Svirsky, Robbins, Kirk, Pisoni, & Miyamoto, 2000.

hearing loss can have very normal cognitive and linguistic development when their language environment is appropriate for them.

Many families now turn to cochlear implants with children who are deaf or seriously hard of hearing. When the hearing device is inserted when children are young, and when parents frequently include children in frequent verbal engagement and use expansions of children's simple speech (e.g., when the toddler says "me ookee," the father responds, "Do you want a cookie?"), language development proceeds normally (I. Cruz, Quittner, Marker, & DesJardin, 2013).

Teachers, parents, and other adults can help children who are deaf or hard of hearing with measures that address children's circumstances. Examples are presented in the Development and Practice feature "Working with Children Who Have Hearing Impairments" (above).

Summary

Children develop language in particular ways according to their personal characteristics and experiences. Subtle qualitative differences have been observed in the conversational styles of males and females. Children from higher-socioeconomic-status backgrounds tend to have larger vocabularies, probably because they are likely to be exposed to a wider variety of words. Ethnic groups may show differences in sociolinguistic behaviors, storytelling traditions, use of figurative language, and dialects. Numerous personal and environmental influences interact in highly individual ways in language development.

Some children have disabilities that affect their language development. Specific language impairments include abnormalities in receptive or expressive language that significantly interfere with children's performance and accomplishments in and out of school. Children with hearing impairments and, to a lesser extent, those with visual impairments may have more limited language proficiency because of reduced exposure to language or reduced awareness of the meaningful contexts in which it is used.

ENHANCEDetext *self-check*

PRACTICING FOR YOUR LICENSURE EXAMINATION

Many teaching tests require students to use what they have learned about child development in response to brief vignettes and multiple-choice questions. You can practice for your licensure examination by reading the following case study and answering a series of questions.

Boarding School

Some parts of Alaska are so sparsely settled that building local high schools is not economically feasible. So in certain Native Alaskan communities, older students are sent to boarding school for their high school education. A high priority for teachers is to help students master Standard English. With this information in mind, consider the following incident:

> Many of the students at the school spoke English with a native dialect and seemed unable to utter certain essential sounds in the English language. A new group of speech teachers was sent in to correct the problem. The teachers worked consistently with the students in an attempt to improve speech patterns and intonation, but found that their efforts were in vain.
>
> One night, the boys in the dormitory were seeming to have too much fun, and peals of laughter were rolling out from under the door. An investigating counselor approached cautiously and listened quietly outside the door to see if he could discover the source of the laughter. From behind the door he heard a voice, speaking in perfect English, giving instructions to the rest of the crowd. The others were finding the situation very amusing. When the counselor entered the room he found that one of the students was speaking. "Joseph," he said, "You've been cured! Your English is perfect." "No," said Joseph returning to his familiar dialect, "I was just doing an imitation of you." "But if you can speak in Standard English, why don't you do it all of the time?" the counselor queried. "I can," responded Joseph, "but it sounds funny, and I feel dumb doing it." (Garrison, 1989, p. 121)

Constructed-Response Question

1. Why might Joseph prefer his native dialect to Standard English?

Multiple-Choice Questions

2. The counselor told Joseph that he had "been cured." What belief about Joseph's native dialect does this statement reflect?

   a. The belief that Joseph's dialect was inferior to Standard English

   b. The belief that the dialect was a legitimate way of communicating if delivered with a Standard English accent

   c. The belief that the counselor could benefit from learning the Native American dialect

   d. The belief that acquiring a nonstandard dialect is the result of a physiological defect that can be treated medically

3. Considering the information in this chapter, how might teachers deal effectively with the language proficiencies of children in Joseph's school?

   a. Teachers can insist that children use only Standard English at school.

   b. Teachers can revert to teaching all subjects in the local dialect.

   c. Teachers can encourage Standard English in written work and in formal oral presentations but welcome the local dialect in creative writing and informal class discussions.

   d. Teachers can allow children to use the local dialect in formal communication and Standard English in letters home to families.

ENHANCEDetext *licensure exam*

Key Concepts

phonology (p. 313)
semantics (p. 313)
syntax (p. 313)
pragmatics (p. 313)
native language (p. 314)
nativism (p. 315)
language acquisition device (p. 315)
infant-directed speech (p. 317)
language socialization (p. 318)
functionalism (p. 318)
fast mapping (p. 321)
receptive language (p. 322)
expressive language (p. 322)

lexical word (p. 322)
grammatical word (p. 322)
underextension (p. 322)
overextension (p. 323)
holophrase (p. 325)
telegraphic speech (p. 325)
semantic bootstrapping (p. 326)
overregularization (p. 326)
expansion (p. 327)
phonemes (p. 328)
figurative speech (p. 329)
comprehension monitoring (p. 329)
cooing (p. 331)

babbling (p. 331)
narrative (p. 332)
playing the dozens (p. 333)
sociolinguistic behaviors (p. 334)
speech register (p. 335)
personal space (p. 336)
IRE cycle (p. 336)
wait time (p. 337)
metalinguistic awareness (p. 338)
bilingualism (p. 340)
English language learner (ELL)
   (p. 340)
bilingual education (p. 342)

submersion approach (p. 343)
structured English immersion
   (p. 343)
immersion (p. 343)
foreign language instruction (p. 343)
subtractive bilingualism (p. 343)
Standard English (p. 347)
dialect (p. 347)
African American English (p. 347)
specific language impairment
   (p. 348)

CHAPTER TEN

Development in the Academic Domains

> ## CASE STUDY: Osvaldo's Story
>
> Suzanne Peregoy, a specialist in language and literacy development, spent several days in a kindergarten classroom with English language learners. She observed the children's daily experiences in writing, listening to stories, and taking on defined roles in the dramatic play center (Peregoy & Boyle, 2008). During one language arts lesson, Suzanne asked the children if they might like to write a story in English that she would bring home to her husband. She handed out pieces of paper with blank spaces at the top for drawings and lines at the bottom for written text.
>
> The children took pen to paper. Lisa wrote, "I love my mom" and illustrated her story with a picture of herself, her mother, and several hearts (Peregoy & Boyle, 2008, p. 153). Rosa drew her family of seven and filled in a few lines with evenly spaced block letters. Osvaldo was last to finish. He first wrote a series of letters, which were unintelligible to Suzanne, and then drew a boy with a soccer ball. Suzanne asked him several times what he was writing. He replied that he didn't know and eventually, after her persistent questioning, responded, "I won't know what my story is about until I finish my picture!" (Peregoy & Boyle, 2008, p. 153).
>
> When Suzanne returned to the classroom at a later time, Osvaldo asked her, "How'd your daddy like the story?" (Peregoy & Boyle, 2008, p. 153). Osvaldo wanted to know how Suzanne's "daddy," meaning her husband, had interpreted his story.
>
> - What did Osvaldo understand about writing?
> - What kinds of writing skills will Osvaldo master in the years ahead?

Osvaldo is learning how to write. He realizes that stories communicate to an audience. He understands that readers have their own responses to stories. He appreciates that print and art can both be used to communicate. He sees his artwork as having the primary responsibility for telling his story.

In the years ahead, Osvaldo will learn more about writing. He will continue to illustrate his stories and find that he can communicate more of his thoughts with words. He will learn to use conventional spelling, follow the rules of grammar and punctuation, and represent a topic cohesively. With guidance from his teachers, the foundations Osvaldo has already achieved will help him tackle these and other challenges in writing.

As children enter preschool and kindergarten, they, like Osvaldo, bring relevant background knowledge for academic subjects—reading, writing, arithmetic, geography, music, and so on. Schools extend these early mental frameworks with experience, instruction, and encouragement. In this chapter, we look at development in the primary academic disciplines over the course of childhood.

CHILDREN'S ACADEMIC LEARNING

Children learn academic subjects according to developmental principles. Ideas such as *equivalence* in mathematics and *revolution* in social studies are first learned in concrete terms and later expanded into abstract concepts. Children recognize letters in the alphabet and make basic letter-sound connections before they recognize words by sight or decode unfamiliar words on the page (J. R. Kirby, Parrila, & Pfeiffer, 2003; McLachlan & Arrow, 2013; Pallante, & Kim, 2013). And children learn to count before they add and multiply (Camos, 2003; Price, Mazzocco, & Ansari, 2013).

As with other aspects of child development, both common trends and notable variations exist in the order in which children progress academically. In mathematics, diversity

OBJECTIVES

10.1: Demonstrate sensitivity to children's developmental needs while helping them achieve high academic standards.

10.2: Summarize and apply research on developmental trends in reading and writing skills.

10.3: Describe age-related advancements in children's mathematical and scientific competencies and instruction that inspires growth in these subjects.

10.4: Outline developmental changes in children's knowledge and skill in social studies and the arts, and summarize methods for fostering these proficiencies.

BIOECOLOGY OF DEVELOPMENT

Children's mastery of academic skills depends on their personal abilities and interests; experiences at home, in school, and in the community; prevailing practices and instructional methods in society; and particular standards imposed on them by education bodies and government officials.

Preparing for Your Licensure Examination

Your teaching test might ask you how to design instruction that addresses academic standards.

is especially pronounced at advanced levels of performance. Only some students learn advanced algebra, and fewer still acquire an understanding of how speed and motion are represented in calculus. A range of factors, including involvement of parents and caregivers, access to resources, quality of instruction, personal health, and genetic endowment, accounts for these variations (Asbury & Plomin, 2014; Burchinal, Lowe Vandell, & Belsky, 2014).

Institutions in society, especially school districts, policy groups, and state departments of education, exert powerful influences on academic learning by identifying elements of subjects that are to be taught over the grade levels. In many countries around the world, discipline-specific experts and government authorities compile comprehensive lists of topics and skills for different grades. Such content-area standards guide instruction beginning in kindergarten and extending through high school. In the United States, the *No Child Left Behind Act* (NCLB) of 2001 required that each of the 50 states establish standards for reading, mathematics, and science. In NCLB's wake, the National Governors Association and Council of Chief State School Officers produced standards in mathematics and English language arts. These expectations, included in the *Common Core Standards,* emphasize mature reasoning and applications to realistic problems needed in college and the workplace. The standards have now been adopted by 45 of the 50 states (National Governors Association and Council of Chief State School Officers, 2014).

The underlying value of the standards framework is persuasive. Children are educated according to a series of learning objectives and assessed regularly by tests aligned with these same aims. Ordinarily, when teachers establish instructional goals toward clearly defined standards, children make good progress (Hamre & Pianta, 2005). In the initial evaluation of Common Core in Kentucky, an early adopter of the standards in 2010, 47 percent of high school graduates were rated as being ready for college or careers, up from 38 percent the previous year (Kentucky Department of Education, 2012).

Yet not all research on the standards model has been favorable. Pressures on teachers to raise children's test scores have resulted in fixations on the particular skills examined on statewide achievement assessments. Thus teachers now spend more time on literacy, math, and science—and especially on rudimentary abilities they think will be on the tests—and less time on social studies, foreign language, the arts, and other subjects of interest to children (Liebtag, 2013; McCarty, 2009; Pianta, Belsky, Houts, & Morrison, 2007; R. M. Thomas, 2005). Moreover, students who consistently perform poorly on the tests (many of whom come from low-income families) are at risk for dropping out of school, a response that can seem a better option than wrestling with schoolwork perceived to be a lost cause (Hemelt & Marcotte, 2013; Hursh, 2007).

Every child has the right to a well-rounded education, one with effective instruction across a range of fields. Thus it behooves teachers to apply their developmental expertise in bridging what children already know with proficiencies that are specified in standards—and in other academic areas deemed important to lifelong success. Consider the following suggestions for implementing standards in a developmentally sensitive manner:

• **Help *all* children achieve high standards.** Proponents of the standards framework have espoused a commitment to provide all students with high-quality instruction. Nearly all teachers approach instruction with this same dedication, yet they are bound to find that some children fail to meet the yardsticks. Obviously, new methods must be tried when children struggle, and when difficulties persist, banding together with other professionals to determine conditions for improving students' learning is in order. Some educators are concluding that they must re-examine instructional strategies, expand their teaching skills, improve the school's climate for learning, and deepen their relationships with children and families (ASCD, n.d.).

• **Use age-appropriate methods for cultivating learning objectives.** Unless academic standards are translated thoughtfully, young children may be disadvantaged because their need to explore is not addressed (Alliance for Childhood, 2010; National Association for the Education of Young Children, 2012). Preschool and kindergarten children go about learning by searching, handling, inspecting, and discovering properties in their environment. These learning qualities beg for spontaneity, not an over-reliance on lecture and memorization, which restricts learning and hampers adjustment (Bonawitz et al., 2011; E. Miller & Carlsson-Paige, 2013).

When unsuitable methods are implemented in the context of traditional testing procedures, in which attention is drawn to right and wrong answers, young children are apt to withdraw or melt down (Alliance for Childhood, 2010; National Association for the Education of Young Children, 2012). Numerous early childhood teachers are rising to the challenge by addressing accountability in a manner that is developmentally attuned to young children's needs, which typically means integrating skills and assessments into hands-on activities.

• **Foster foundational skills children have not previously attained before progressing to more advanced skills.** When children begin elementary school, they encounter demands for basic skills—often before they have acquired the prerequisites. This emphasis is occurring because the Common Core Standards were developed with mature endpoints in mind—proficiencies necessary for young adults to be successful in college and the workforce. Operating backwards through the lifespan, designers successively simplified adult skills into learning outcomes, beginning with what high school students should be able to do and proceeding downward for youngsters in middle and elementary school. The reverse, a prospective developmental analysis beginning with what young children *are* able to understand and do, and continuing upwards through childhood and the adolescent years, was *not* conducted.

The result is that certain standards were articulated that are of questionable value for young children. For example, Common Core K.NBT.1 specifies that kindergarten children should be able to understand *place value*, the idea that digits reflect different quantities depending on the column: "Compose and decompose numbers from 11 to 19 into ten ones and some further ones, e.g., by using objects or drawings, and record each composition or decomposition by a drawing or equation (such as 18 = 10 + 8); understand that these numbers are composed of ten ones and one, two, three, four, five, six, seven, eight, or nine ones" (National Governors Association and Council of Chief State School Officers, 2014). Yet young children do not easily acquire *place value*, as we will see later in this chapter, and other objectives in mathematics are more suitable for them (L. F. Main, 2012). To make the best of a challenging mandate, many early childhood educators design instructional goals that consider the general spirit of the standards as well as children's actual abilities.

• **When necessary, adapt standards to students' needs.** When a boy with autism has trouble understanding the motivations of characters in literature, as specified in a standard, a teacher might create a storyboard that simplifies the plot and includes comments as to why characters act in a certain way. With an English language learner who achieves the essence of a mathematics standard but is not able to explain how she comes to solutions, also a requirement of the standard, her teacher encourages her to talk it through with a classmate who shares her native language. Fortunately, many schools have access to school psychologists, special education teachers, gifted and talented specialists, and other instructional leaders who advise teachers on adapting lessons for students with exceptional needs.

Nevertheless, the full collection of expectations is not realistic for all students with significant intellectual disabilities (K. Beals, 2014). Depending on children's individual abilities, standards may need to be revised dramatically or addressed over multiple lessons, with component skills taught directly rather than presumed to be in place (Wakeman, Karvonen, & Ahumada, 2013). In a few circumstances, as when a student with a significant intellectual disability nears high school completion, more practical skills might take priority, such as learning how to use public transportation and becoming punctual, reliable, and polite in a work setting (J. McDonnell, 2010).

• **Learn how children of various ages understand academic concepts and express relevant skills.** Standards are just that—lists of skills and concepts that students are expected to know. They are *not* lessons, strategies, courses, or curricula. Moreover, existing standards are typically based on topics and skills that are *typically taught* at grade levels, rather than on a developmental analysis of what youngsters of various ages can reasonably learn (e.g., VanSledright & Limón, 2006). By studying the remaining sections of this chapter, you will acquire an understanding of progressions in children's reading, writing, mathematics, science, social studies, and the arts. An appreciation for these developmental progressions and their many exceptions will help you design and modify instruction for students.

Summary

State departments of education, subject-matter specialists, policy makers, and local school districts have created standards to guide instruction, especially in reading, writing, math, and science. Such standards provide useful guidance for teachers as they plan lessons for their students. Teachers need to remember, however, that standards, voluminous as they are, are focused on a limited number of subjects and neglect accomplishments in other areas (e.g., work habits, social skills, emotional well-being) that are equally important for students' development.

Teachers can translate standards into successful lessons when they realize how students of a given age typically learn subject matter. The process of defining instruction that addresses standards *and* meets the needs of students draws from expertise and creativity on the part of teachers. Young children and students with serious intellectual disabilities require definite adjustments in standards-based instruction.

ENHANCEDetext *self-check*

READING AND WRITING

Children's literacy skills in reading and writing build on their knowledge of spoken language.[1] However, written language differs from spoken language in important ways. To learn to read and write, children must understand the relationships between how words sound and how they appear on paper. Children must also master the nuances of a written symbol system that have no obvious counterparts in spoken language, such as punctuation marks and correct uses of upper- and lowercase letters (Bolaños et al., 2013; S. G. Paris & Cunningham, 1996; C. Wood, Kemp, Waldron, & Hart, 2014).

Emergent Literacy

Through early exposure to reading and writing, young children learn many things about written language. For instance, they learn that:

- print conveys meaningful information.
- it is fun to read and listen to stories and books.
- different kinds of printed matter (storybooks, newspapers, grocery lists, greeting cards, etc.) serve different purposes.
- spoken language is transcribed according to certain rules (e.g., words are made up of discrete sounds that are represented with letters of the alphabet).
- written language includes predictable elements and conventions (e.g., fairy tales often begin with "Once upon a time," and in English, writing proceeds from left to right and from the top to the bottom of the page). (Cabell, Justice, Konold, & McGinty, 2010; W. Chong et al., 2014; Dougherty Stahl, 2014; Hilbert & Eis, 2014; S. G. Paris & Cunningham, 1996; Pérez, 1998; Serpell, Baker, & Sonnenschein, 2005)

Such knowledge about written language, known as **emergent literacy**, sets the groundwork for reading and writing development.

Teachers who provide easy access to reading and writing materials facilitate the acquisition of this foundational knowledge. They demonstrate reading and writing activities, take children on trips to the library, talk about the things they themselves have read and written, and show that reading and writing are useful and enjoyable activities. But perhaps most important, they read to children regularly (L. Baker, Scher, & Mackler, 1997; C. M. Edwards, 2014; Huebner & Payne, 2010). Reading to children is especially valuable when adults exhibit sensitivity to children's interests, ask questions, invite responses, and connect story concepts to events in children's lives (C. M. Edwards, 2014; Huebner & Payne, 2010).

Young children whose parents read to them frequently learn to read and write more quickly once they reach elementary school than do peers without this exposure (Aram, Korat, & Hassunah-Arafat, 2013; Myrberg & Rosén, 2009; Sénéchal & LeFevre, 2002). Partly this is

[1]Language development is described in depth in Chapter 9.

OBSERVATION GUIDELINES
Assessing Emergent Literacy in Young Children

CHARACTERISTICS	LOOK FOR	EXAMPLE	IMPLICATION
Attitudes Toward Books	• *Looking through books* • *Interest and attentiveness* when adults read storybooks • *Eagerness to talk about stories* that are read	Martina often mentions the *Berenstain Bears* books that her father reads to her at home.	Devote a regular time to reading aloud, choose books with colorful pictures and imaginative story lines, and stop occasionally to discuss events in the story. Make regular trips to the library.
Behaviors with Books	• *Careful handling of books* (e.g., holding them right-side up, turning pages in appropriate direction, not tearing pages) • *Pretend reading* by pointing at pages and talking about characters • *Referring to pictures* while constructing the sequence of events in a story • *Asking "What does this say?"* when coming across repeated phrases • *Imitation of sounds* by a caregiver reading to child	Rusty doesn't seem to know what to do with the books in his preschool classroom. He opens them haphazardly and sees nothing wrong with ripping out pages.	If children have had few experiences with books, occasionally read one-on-one with them. Let them hold the books and turn the pages. Gently show them how to take care of books so that pages don't tear.
Letter and Word Recognition	• *Recognition of product names* in logos and other familiar contexts • *Correct identification* of some alphabet letters • *Recognition of own name* in print	Katherine sees a take-out bag from a local fast-food restaurant and determines that it says "Burger King."	Prominently label coat hooks and other items that belong to children. Post the alphabet, and label major parts of the room (e.g., "sink," "art supplies," and "science area").
Writing Behaviors	• *Production of letter-like shapes* • *Writing in a left-to-right sequence* (in English and certain other languages) • *Ability to write some letters* correctly or almost correctly • *Ability to write own name*	Hank can write his name, but he frequently reverses the *N* and sometimes leaves it out altogether.	Give children numerous opportunities to experiment with writing implements (paper, crayons, markers, etc.). Invite children to trace and copy their names, and guide letter formation when children want help. Ask them to put their first names or initials on artwork.
Knowledge About the Nature and Purposes of Written Language	• *Awareness that specific words are always spelled in same way* • *Correct identification of reference materials*, perhaps calendars and computer manuals • *Pseudowriting* for particular purposes	When Shakira and Lucie pretend to shop, they create several squiggles on a piece of paper. They say that this is a list of items they need to get at the store.	Encourage play activities that involve pretend writing (e.g., writing and delivering "letters" to friends or classmates). Let children see you engaging in a variety of reading and writing activities.

Sources: Cabell et al., 2010; W. Chong et al., 2014; Hawkins, 1997; McLane & McNamee, 1990; S. G. Paris, Morrison, & Miller, 2006; D. W. Rowe & Harste, 1986; Serpell et al., 2005; Share & Gur, 1999; Sulzby, 1985.

due to the skills children learn in the process, but the pleasure children learn to associate with literacy activities is also a factor. Children who enjoy their early reading experiences often become enthusiastic readers themselves (L. Baker et al., 1997; Sukhram & Hsu, 2012; Vandermaas-Peeler, Nelson, Bumpass, & Sassine, 2009).

Teachers and other caregivers can spot emergent literacy in children's actions with books and writing implements. The Observation Guidelines table "Assessing Emergent Literacy in Young Children" (above) offers several ideas about what to watch for in the early childhood years.

Letter Recognition and Phonological Awareness

Knowing letters and the sounds that each one represents is an obvious prerequisite for learning to read (M. Harris & Giannouli, 1999; Reutzel, Child, Jones, & Clark, 2014). Another indispensable foundation is having a strong **phonological awareness**, that is, the ability to hear the distinct sounds that make up words (Boscardin, Muthén, Francis, & Baker, 2008; Reutzel et al., 2014). Phonological awareness includes specific skills such as these:

• Hearing distinct syllables within words (e.g., hearing "can" and "dee" as separate parts of *candy*)

- Dividing words into discrete word sounds, or *phonemes* (e.g., hearing the sounds "guh," "ay," and "tuh" in *gate*)[2]
- Blending separate phonemes into meaningful words (e.g., recognizing that, when put together, the sounds "wuh," "eye," and "duh" make *wide*)
- Identifying words that rhyme (e.g., realizing that *cat* and *hat* end with the same sound).

Phonological awareness develops gradually during the preschool and early elementary years (Byrnes & Wasik, 2009; Lonigan, Burgess, Anthony, & Barker, 1998; Shing, 2013). Most children can detect syllables within words by age 4, well before they begin school and start learning to read. Soon after, perhaps around age 5, they begin to realize that many syllables can be divided into two parts: an *onset* (one or more consonants that precede the vowel sound) and a *rime* (the vowel sound and any consonants that follow it). By the time they are 6 or 7, many children can identify the individual phonemes in spoken words. This last ability seems to emerge hand in hand with learning to read (Anthony & Francis, 2005; Goswami, 1999).

Children learn to distinguish speech sounds during repeated experiences in listening to conversation. Attending to stories and participating in various word games also promotes a discerning ear (Muter, 1998; Shing, 2013). The Development and Practice feature "Promoting Phonological Awareness and Letter Recognition in Young Children" (below) presents several useful strategies.

Word Recognition

Many preschool children can correctly identify words in familiar contexts. For example, numerous young children correctly identify the word *stop* when it appears on a red, octagonal sign beside the road. They might also "read" the word *Cheerios* on a cereal box. And they

DEVELOPMENT AND PRACTICE
Promoting Phonological Awareness and Letter Recognition in Young Children

Read alphabet books with colorful pictures, amusing poems, or entertaining stories.

- A teacher reads *The Ocean Alphabet Book* (Pallotta & Mazzola, 1986) to an 18-month-old boy. It is the boy's favorite book, and he points at the pictures as his teacher reads the words. (Infancy)
- A preschool teacher shares *Alphabet Adventure* (A. Wood & Wood, 2001) with her group of 3-year-olds. The children eagerly follow along as the main character, "Little i," looks for her lost dot, and they delight in finding various letters on each page. (Early Childhood)

Have children find words that rhyme.

- A grandmother reads Dr. Seuss's (1968) *The Foot Book* to her 3-year-old granddaughter, stopping at the end of familiar phrases to allow the little girl to chime in with anticipated rhyming words. (Early Childhood)
- A kindergarten teacher challenges his students to think of at least five words that rhyme with *break*. (Early Childhood)

Ask children to identify words that begin (or end) with a particular sound.

- A preschool teacher asks children to join her in finding words that end with an "oo" sound. She says, "'Zoo' and the number 'two' end with an 'oo' sound. Can you think of other words that end with an 'oo' sound?" Children volunteer, "Achoo!," "Do," and "True." (Early Childhood)

- A first-grade teacher says, "Listen to the 'str' sound at the beginning of *string*. What are some other words that begin with 'str'?" (Middle Childhood)

Say a few words and ask children which one begins (or ends) in these sounds.

- After reading Robert McCloskey's (1948) book *Blueberries for Sal*, a preschool teacher asks his children, "Do you hear the difference between *kuplink, kuplank,* and *kuplunk*?" (Early Childhood)
- A second-grade teacher asks, "Listen carefully to these four words: *end, dent, bend,* and *mend*. Which one ends in a different sound than the others? Listen to them again before you decide: *end, dent, bend,* and *mend*." (Middle Childhood)

Have children practice forming alphabet letters.

- A preschool teacher gives children pieces of paper with large letters she has prepared with glue and colored sand. Children trace the letters with their fingers. (Early Childhood)
- A kindergarten teacher has children make letters with their bodies. One child stands with his arms outstretched like a *Y*, and two others bend over and clasp hands to form an *M*. (Early Childhood)

[2]This aspect of logical awareness is sometimes called *phonemic awareness*.

know that a word at a fast-food restaurant is *McDonald's* when the *M* takes the form of the well-known golden arches (Ehri, 1994, 2014; Juel, 1991).

Sometime around age 5, children begin to look more closely at words. Initially, they are apt to focus on visually distinctive features, perhaps seeing the "tail" hanging down at the end of *dog* or the two "ears" sticking up in the middle of *rabbit*. Soon after, they begin to use some of a word's letters for phonetic clues about what the word must be. For instance, they might read *box* by looking at the *b* and *x* and ignoring the *o* (Ehri, 1991, 2014).

Once children have mastered letter-sound relationships, they initially rely heavily on these relationships as they read (Byrnes & Wasik, 2009; Ehri, 1994; Farrington-Flint & Wood, 2007). Doing so allows them to identify such simple words as *cat*, *bed*, and *Jane*. With such a strategy, they have difficulty when they encounter words that violate pronunciation rules. For instance, using the rule that *ea* is pronounced "ee" (as in *meat* and *treat*), they might read *head* as "heed" or *sweater* as "sweeter." Some languages, including English, have so many irregularities that children must use additional cues besides the sounds of similar syllables. If they come to "stomach" and sound it out as "stow-match," they will be puzzled unless other cues in suggest the meaning (e.g., "My *stomach* reminded me that I was hungry").

By the middle elementary grades, most children have a basic **sight vocabulary**, which allows them to recognize a sizable number of words with little effort. That is, a good deal of word recognition has become *automatized*.[3] When they encounter words that aren't in their sight vocabulary, they draw on letter-sound relationships, familiar prefixes and root words, common spelling patterns, and the meaning of other words in the passage (Ehri, 2014; Solity & Vousden, 2009).

Reading Comprehension

In its basic form, reading comprehension involves understanding the words and sentences on the page. But for advanced readers, it also means going *beyond* the page to make inferences and predictions, identify main ideas, and detect assumptions by the author (Perfetti, 1985). Thus reading comprehension is a very *constructive* process: Readers combine what they see on the printed page with their existing knowledge to derive meaning. Several general trends characterize the development of reading comprehension:

Children's growing knowledge base facilitates reading comprehension. As children grow older, they become better able to understand what they read, in part because they know more about the topics (Rayner, Foorman, Perfetti, Pesetsky, & Seidenberg, 2001). In fact, reading comprehension ability at *any* age is influenced by relevant knowledge (Lipson, 1983; Priebe, Keenan, & Miller, 2012; L. Snyder & Caccamise, 2010). For example, when second graders read about spiders, those who already know about their eight legs, fangs, and webs remember more and draw inferences more easily than peers who know less about the subject (P. D. Pearson, Hansen, & Gordon, 1979). Therefore, it is often helpful to assess students' working knowledge of basic terms before assigning an essay or chapter. You can watch a bilingual teacher in an Observing Children video review terms before asking three boys to read chapters from a nonfiction book.

Observing Children 10-1
Watch a teacher introduce key terms before students read nonfiction passages.

ENHANCEDetext *video example*

Children become familiar with common structures of fictional and nonfictional texts. Most 5- and 6-year-olds can distinguish between books that tell stories and those that provide information (S. L. Field, Labbo, & Ash, 1999). As children get older, they also learn how texts are organized, and such knowledge helps them make better sense of what they read. For example, they gradually acquire a **story schema** that represents components of fictional narratives (main characters, plot, problem resolution, etc.) and use this expectation in understanding a short story or novel (Graesser, Golding, & Long, 1991; Nwokah, Burnette, & Graves, 2013; N. L. Stein, 1982). With age, children also use common structures in nonfiction to enhance their comprehension. When reading a textbook, they may rely on headings and subheadings to help identify key ideas.

---

[3]In Chapter 7, *automatization* is defined as the process of becoming familiar and able to respond efficiently with certain tasks. When skills are automatized, working memory is freed up for other challenging processes.

Observing Children 10-2

Watch bilingual third graders learn about making inferences while reading.

ENHANCEDetext *video example*

FOR FURTHER EXPLORATION . . .

Read more about developmental changes in reading skill.

ENHANCEDetext
content extension

Preparing for Your Licensure Examination

Your teaching test might ask you how to support children's metacognitive strategies in reading.

BIOECOLOGY OF DEVELOPMENT

In the bioecological framework, children contribute to their own reading with personal abilities and interests. Experiences at home, in school, and with peers influence enthusiasm preferences for written materials.

Children become increasingly able to draw inferences from what they read. As they listen to stories, young children begin to draw inferences about why people act as they do and why events unfold in particular ways (Lepola, Lynch, Laakkonen, Silvén, & Niemi, 2012; Tompkins, Guo, & Justice, 2013). Such inferences are not automatic: In learning to read, children sometimes need to be encouraged to think about connections between ideas and events. You can listen to a bilingual teacher explain what *inferences* are in an Observing Children video. In the upper elementary grades, children find it easier to draw inferences and remember what they read (Bowyer-Crane & Snowling, 2010; S. G. Paris & Upton, 1976). At this point, however, they may continue to take the things they read at face value, make little attempt to evaluate the quality of ideas, and fail to notice blatant contradictions (Markman, 1979; Vorstius, Radach, Mayer, & Lonigan, 2013). As youngsters reach adolescence and move into the secondary grades, they read written material with a more critical eye (Chall, 1996).

Metacognition in Reading

Metacognition, a person's understandings of his or her own cognitive processes and efforts to control these processes while learning, is an important part of reading.[4] One of the first aspects of metacognition to emerge is the recognition that reading involves more than identifying the words on a page—that it involves making *sense* of text. This awareness depends in part on how adults portray the process of reading to young children. When a researcher asked a first grader named Marissa if something she had just read made sense to her, she responded, "What I read never makes sense. The teacher just gives us books so we can practice reading words—they don't have to make sense" (I. W. Gaskins, Satlow, & Pressley, 2007, pp. 196–197).

Successful readers obviously *do* realize that reading is a process of making sense (I. W. Gaskins et al., 2007; Snyder & Caccamise, 2010). As children gain more experience in reading, and especially interpreting textbooks and other informational text, they are able to develop such comprehension strategies as identifying the main idea of a passage (van den Broek, Lynch, Naslund, Ievers-Landis, & Verduin, 2003). Reading strategies, when supported, improve further in the upper elementary and middle school grades; trained high school students are more likely to monitor their comprehension and backtrack (i.e., reread) when they don't understand something (Garner, 1987; I. W. Gaskins et al., 2007). Not all adolescents use effective metacognitive reading strategies, however, and those who engage in little metacognition generally have difficulty in understanding and remembering what they read (Alvermann & Moore, 1991; Ortlieb, 2013).

As young people move through the school years, they generally read with greater fluency and flexibility and comprehend increasingly complex and challenging material. The Developmental Trends table "Reading at Different Age Levels" traces the development of reading over the course of childhood.

Bioecology of Reading Development

As you have learned, children's experiences at home affect their reading development. The kind of reader a child becomes also depends on support at school (e.g., the presence of age-appropriate books), behaviors by classmates (e.g., whether friends talk about books they've read), and practices within the broader society (e.g., the role that literacy plays in an ethnic community; S. A. Hart, Soden, Johnson, Schatschneider, & Taylor, 2013; A. B. Jordan, 2005). Connections between settings are equally important. A middle school boy may become a disinterested reader at school if not allowed to choose books that represent his interests, as developed at home.

Biological Factors

Exceptional talents and difficulties in reading are each found to have a genetic basis (Logan et al., 2013). Many (but not all) children who are later identified as intellectually gifted begin to read early, and some read voraciously (Piirto, 1999; E. Rowe, Miller, Ebenstein, & Thompson, 2012).

---

[4]Metacognition is described in Chapter 7.

DEVELOPMENTAL TRENDS
Reading at Different Age Levels

AGE	WHAT YOU MIGHT OBSERVE	DIVERSITY	IMPLICATIONS
Infancy (Birth–2 Years) 	• Manual exploration of cloth and cardboard books • Increasing enjoyment of stories • More attention to pictures than to story lines • Attention to and enjoyment of rhythm and rhymes in spoken language	• Individual infants vary in exposure to stories depending on habits of their families. • Some toddlers who are read to regularly participate actively in reading (e.g., by pointing to and labeling objects in pictures), whereas others listen quietly.	• Read books with catchy rhythms and rhymes that maintain attention and nurture phonological skills. • During story time, label and talk about pictures in books. Recognize that toddlers may not be able to sit still for an entire story.
Early Childhood (2–6 Years) 	• Attention focused largely on pictures rather than print during adult storybook reading (especially before age 6) • Incorporation of books and familiar story lines into play activities • Some knowledge of conventions of written language (e.g., left-to-right direction) by age 4 • Increasing knowledge of letters and letter-sound correspondences • Identification of a few words in well-known contexts (e.g., words on commercial products) • Use of a word's distinctive features (e.g., a single letter or overall shape) in attempts to identify it	• Children who have had little exposure to books are unfamiliar with sitting down for stories. • Some cultures emphasize oral language more than written language. • Parents who speak a language other than English may read to children in their native tongue, experiences that provide a good foundation for reading and writing in English. • Some children begin school knowing the alphabet and have a small sight vocabulary. Others need to start from scratch in learning letter-sound connections.	• Read to young children using colorful books with high-interest content. • Teach letters of the alphabet through engaging activities. • Teach letter-sound relationships through storybooks, games, rhymes, and enjoyable writing activities. • Point out clues in a book (e.g., pictures, words they already know) when readers encounter unfamiliar words. • Encourage parents to read regularly to children and visit the local library. • Send home literacy bags containing a school book and sheet with reading tips in each, asking parents to return the contents the following week.
Middle Childhood (6–10 Years) 	• Rapid growth in reading skills during this period • Ability to hear individual phonemes within words • Increasing proficiency in identifying unfamiliar words • Growing sight-word vocabulary, leading to greater reading fluency • Beginning of silent reading (at age 7 or 8) • Emerging ability to draw inferences • Tendency to take print at face value without critically evaluating the content or looking below the surface for underlying themes	• Children with deficits in phonological awareness have a difficult time learning to read. • Children with hearing impairments may be delayed in mastering letter-sound relationships. • On average, girls develop reading skills earlier than boys. • Children vary in use of comprehension strategies. • Children with strong vocabularies may learn to read more easily than children with limited vocabularies.	• Explore "families" of words (e.g., "fight," "sight," and "light") that share similar sounds and spelling. • Assign well-written trade books (e.g., children's paperback novels) as soon as children are able to read and understand them. • Engage children in discussions about books. Focus on interpretation, inferences, and speculation. • For delayed readers, teach phonological awareness, word identification skills, and basic comprehension strategies within the context of meaningful reading activities.
Early Adolescence (10–14 Years) 	• Automatized recognition of common words • Ability to learn new information through reading • Emerging ability to go beyond literal meaning • Developing metacognitive processes that aid comprehension (e.g., keeping track of emerging understandings, backtracking when confused, or becoming aware of gaps in comprehension)	• Adolescents with deficits in phonological awareness continue to lag behind peers in reading. • Individuals who were poor readers in elementary school often continue to be weak readers in adolescence. • Some individuals (e.g., students with intellectual disabilities) may identify single words yet not understand passages that they read. • Individuals with sensory challenges may lack certain understandings assumed by authors.	• Assign age-appropriate reading materials in academic areas while also providing scaffolding (e.g., questions to answer). • Explore classic works of poetry and fiction. • Seek advice and assistance from specialists to help promote the reading skills of youngsters who lag behind peers.

(continued)

DEVELOPMENTAL TRENDS (continued)

AGE	WHAT YOU MIGHT OBSERVE	DIVERSITY	IMPLICATIONS
Late Adolescence (14–18 Years)	• Automatized recognition of many abstract and discipline-specific words • Ability to consider multiple viewpoints about a single topic • Ability to critically evaluate text • Practice with new metacognitive reading strategies	• Poor readers draw few inferences from what they read and exert limited metacognitive control while reading. • Adolescents with reading disabilities may become frustrated when reading demanding text. • Girls are more likely than boys to enroll in advanced literature classes. • Many adolescents prefer to make their own choices rather than have books assigned to them.	• Encourage adolescents to draw inferences and make predictions from what they read. • Ask students to analyze classic works of poetry and fiction. • Modify reading materials and paper-and-pencil assessments for individuals with delayed reading abilities. • Scaffold reading assignments for weak readers, with learning objectives, comprehension questions, fill-in-the-blank outlines, and other guidelines.

Sources: Brand, Marchand, Lilly, & Child, 2014; K. Cain & Oakhill, 1998; Chall, 1996; Ehri, 1994; Felton, 1998; Hedges & Nowell, 1995; P. Johnston & Afflerbach, 1985; Y. Kim, Petscher, Schatschneider, & Foorman, 2010; Logan et al., 2013; McBride-Chang & Treiman, 2003; Orlieb, 2013; L. Reese, Garnier, Gallimore, & Goldenberg, 2000; T. A. Roberts, 2005; Treiman, Cohen, Mulqueeny, Kessler, & Schechtman, 2007; Trelease, 1982; Wigfield, Eccles, & Pintrich, 1996.

Children with intellectual disabilities learn to read more slowly than age-mates and are apt to develop fewer effective reading strategies. In some instances they develop excellent word identification skills yet understand little of what they read (Cossu, 1999).

Children with sensory disabilities face distinct challenges when learning to read. Youngsters who are visually impaired cannot see the printed page when caregivers read to them and so may develop strong listening skills but limited knowledge about such conventions of written language as the left-to-right progression of words, capitalization, and punctuation (M. Tobin & Hill, 2012; Tompkins & McGee, 1982). Yet the world of literacy is available to these children when appropriate accommodations are made and practice encouraged. Blind children who read in Braille, a form of written language encoded in raised dots and felt by the fingertips, have stronger comprehension skills when they have become proficient in Braille than when they are novices in reading in this manner (Ferrell, 2006). Children with hearing impairments who have learned a manual language (e.g., American Sign Language) cannot easily identify letter-sound relationships and may have limited knowledge of the idioms and other regularities in oral speech (J. F. Andrews & Mason, 1986). Nevertheless, young children with hearing loss are very responsive to listening to stories with their parents (e.g., when parents invite children to comment and expand on their verbal contributions), and those who are deaf and use manual sign language gain strong literacy skills when participating in comprehensive and balanced reading programs (DesJardin et al., 2014; van Staden, 2013).

Some children with learning disabilities have considerable difficulty learning to read. In its extreme form, this difficulty is known as **dyslexia**, a disability with a presumed biological basis that manifests itself in several ways (Galaburda & Rosen, 2001; Keenan & Meenan, 2014; R. L. Peterson & Pennington, 2010). Contrary to popular belief, dyslexia is typically *not* a problem of visual perception, such as reading words or letters backwards. Instead, most children with dyslexia have deficits in phonological awareness (Keenan, & Meenan, 2014; H. L. Swanson, Mink, & Bocian, 1999). A few have difficulty identifying visual stimuli quickly, which results in difficulty automatizing connections between printed words and their meanings (Menghini et al., 2010; Wolf & Bowers, 1999). A number of children with reading disabilities have other information-processing difficulties, such as a small working memory capacity or a tendency to process information slowly (Hulme & Snowling, 2013; Keenan & Meenan, 2014). Still others are not dyslexic but have one or more deficiencies, perhaps in decoding words or comprehending complex passages, due to lack of experience in reading, with these delays, if not remediated, evolving over time into more serious problems (Keenan & Meenan, 2014).

Gender Differences

On average, girls read with greater skill than do boys (Chia & Kee, 2013; Weaver-Hightower, 2003). In the high school grades, girls are more likely than boys to enroll in advanced literature classes (Wigfield et al., 1996). Boys tend to have less interest in reading, in part because they find fewer books at school that pique their curiosity but also because many of them prefer more physically active pastimes (Marinak & Gambrell, 2010; Senn, 2012). A 10th grader named Devin expressed the latter reason this way: "Why should I want to read about doing things when I can actually *do* them?" (Newkirk, 2002, p. 54). Many boys prefer nonfiction to fiction and, when they do read novels, like to read books focused on action and adventure, science fiction, fantasy, comedy, and horror (Hébert & Pagnani, 2010; Senn, 2012). Some boys are interested in reading materials on the Internet, for example, the content of websites and gaming manuals.

Socioeconomic Differences

On average, children from low-income families come to school with fewer literacy skills than is the case for children from middle- and upper-income families (Serpell et al., 2005). After they enter school, delayed children are typically guided in parsing the sounds of words and identifying letter-sound correspondences but tend not to receive as much help with comprehension (C. Fitzpatrick, McKinnon, Blair, & Willoughby, 2014). As they progress through school, this disparity in reading ability increases (Jimerson, Egeland, & Teo, 1999; Portes, 1996).

Of course, children from low-income families are well able to achieve high standards in reading when teachers address the full spectrum of their skills and limitations. Early intervention is sometimes worthwhile before delays escalate and become more difficult to treat (Y. Griffiths & Stuart, 2013). Teachers can also reach out to parents and suggest, if they are not already doing so, that they read regularly to children and cheer on early reading attempts (Dumont, Trautwein, Nagy, & Nagengast, 2014). For children who do not respond well to initial interventions, services need to be intensified and customized according to individual challenges, perhaps in phonological awareness, speech and language disorders, restricted exposure to language, or other issues (Y. Giffiths & Stuart, 2013).

Ethnic and Cultural Experiences

The interpretations that children make of what they read depend in large part on their upbringing in a specific cultural setting. As an example, Rosenna Bakari, a colleague of ours who specializes in African-centered education, describes an incident involving her 7-year-old daughter Nailah:

> [An event] that always stands out in my mind is a reading comprehension question that Nailah had in a workbook. The question asked why two brothers drew a line down the middle of a messy room to clean it. The answer was pretty obvious: The boys were dividing the room in half so that they could each clean their part. However, Nailah could not get to that answer no matter how I scaffolded her. When I told her the answer, she replied, "Why would they divide the room up? They should just both clean it together." I immediately realized that in her African-centered world, division rarely takes place. Most things in our house are communal. Each child is responsible for the other. So for her to get to that answer would have taken something beyond reasonable reading comprehension. She would have had to understand that there are people in the world who operate under different views about sharing and responsibility. That's a more difficult task for a seven-year-old. (R. Bakari, personal communication, 2002)

Young people from all backgrounds respond more favorably to literature that reflects their own customs than to cultural practices that are unfamiliar (Gollnick & Chinn, 2002; M. Stewart, 2013). In a literature class with immigrant adolescents, a teacher might include books that feature the courage of refugees, for example, Dia Cha's (1996) *Dia's Story Cloth: The Hmong People's Journey of Freedom.* Novels with similar themes, such as Julia Mercedes Castilla's (2009) *Strange Parents,* might likewise be of interest (M. Stewart, 2013). In working with African American high school boys, one educator found that accounts of personal struggles by African American men were especially inspiring (A. W. Tatum, 2008). One boy, Quincy, previously a nonreader, read all night after starting Anthony Davis and Jeffrey Jackson's (1998) book, "*Yo, Little Brother . . .": Basic Rules of Survival for Young African American Males.*

Promoting Reading Development

Traditionally, reading was taught primarily during the elementary grades. Teachers hoped that middle school and high school students read well enough to learn successfully from textbooks and other printed materials. Research indicates that this assumption is not warranted. Even at the high school level, many adolescents have not yet mastered all of the skills involved in reading effectively. Children with delayed emergent literacy skills face may struggle for several years, and those in elementary school with reading delays may continue to be poor readers in the secondary grades (Adlof, Catts, & Lee, 2010; Felton, 1998; Shaywitz, 2004). The Development and Practice feature "Promoting Effective Reading Comprehension Strategies" presents several suggestions for supporting literacy skills in elementary, middle, and high school. Also consider the following general strategies:

• **Foster emergent literacy in young children.** Reading aloud to young children is a crucial way to support comprehension and motivation. Pausing to ask questions while reading to children fosters active participation. Simple questions about what is happening in the story become stepping stones to inferences, such as thinking up a few reasons oneself as to why a character might have acted as he or she did (Dougherty Stahl, 2014). Brief videos of familiar stories and wordless picture books can provide additional opportunities for building comprehension skills.

• **Advise parents how to read to young children.** Infants and children can acquire a love of reading, an enriched vocabulary, an ear for grammatically correct language, and other literacy skills from being read to on a regular basis (C. M. Edwards, 2014). Consider the following interaction between a mother and her toddler son:

Mother:	Do you wanna see the cow? Would you like to read with Mama? You ready for the cow? Where is he? [turns the page] Huh! The cow says . . .
Child:	Mooo!
Mother:	What's that? [points to something in the book]
Child:	Boon.
Mother:	Balloon! We can count! One . . .
Child:	Two.
Mother:	Two! [reading book] This is my nose. Where's your nose?
Child:	[touches his nose]
Mother:	Nose! Where's your toes?
Child:	[grabs his toes]
Mother:	There's your toes!

Mother models enthusiasm for the book and uses its content to review object labels (*balloon*, *nose*, *toes*) and general world knowledge (numbers, what a cow says) with her son. When parents use such strategies as they read, their children acquire larger vocabularies, increased knowledge of written language, and an appreciation for literature (Colmar, 2014; E. Reese, Sparks, & Leyva, 2010; Whitehurst et al., 1994). Parents who are unaware of how children learn from storybook sessions may benefit from explicit instruction in labeling and describing pictures, asking questions that encourage inferences and predictions, and inviting children to make comments. A few parents mistakenly think they can teach infants to read using commercial packages, which, although enticing to them, turn out to be ineffective for children (S. B. Neuman, Kaefer, Pinkham, & Strouse, 2014). These parents might be advised of the many advantages of naturally paced shared reading.

• **Incorporate practice with basic skills into engrossing activities.** Explicit instruction in basic reading skills—relating letters to sounds, identifying simple words, finding main ideas, and so on—facilitates reading development (Ehri, 2014; Elbro & Petersen, 2004). To become truly effective readers, children must automatize the most basic aspects of reading, including letter-sound relationships and recognition of common words (McGeown & Medford, 2014; Stainthorp, Stuart, Powell, Quinlan, & Garwood, 2010). Automaticity of reading skills develops primarily through repetition.

One approach is to provide drill-and-practice activities—workbook exercises, flash cards, and so on—that help children automatize specific reading skills. Instruction in basic

DEVELOPMENT AND PRACTICE
Promoting Effective Reading Comprehension Strategies

Teach reading comprehension skills across subject areas.

- A middle school mathematics teacher demonstrates questions to ask oneself while reading narrative mathematical problems: Can I tell what this question is really asking? What other options are there to interpret the problem? What options do I have for solving it? How will I know if I have a good solution? (Early Adolescence)

- When a life skills instructor tells his students to read a section of the first aid manual, he suggests several strategies to help them remember the material. For instance, as students begin each section, they should look at the heading and ask a question they think the section will address. At the end of the section, they should stop and consider whether their question was answered. (Late Adolescence)

Model effective reading strategies.

- A girl in a seventh-grade history class reads aloud a passage describing how, during Columbus's first voyage across the Atlantic, many members of the crew wanted to turn around and return to Spain. Her teacher says, "Let's think of some reasons why the crew might have wanted to go home." One student responds, "Some of them might have been home-sick." Another suggests, "Maybe they thought they'd never find their way back if they went too far." (Early Adolescence)

- A high school literacy teacher advises students that it may be difficult for them to keep track of all the characters in the novel they will be reading. She says, "When I was reading it, I had to jot down a few notes on who everyone was so I could follow the plot." (Late Adolescence)

Encourage children to relate what they are reading to things they already know.

- Children in a third-grade classroom are reading books on outer space. Before they begin reading a book, their teacher asks them to write answers to three questions: (a) What do you already know about outer space? (b) What do you hope to learn? and (c) Do you think what you learn in your books will change what you already know? (Middle Childhood)

- While reading autobiographies, students answer questions on a worksheet about basic aspects of the writers' lives (e.g., who was in their family, where they grew up, what kind of education they had). Students also write about how the authors' upbringing was similar to, and different from, their own. (Early Adolescence)

Arrange for children to discuss readings with classmates.

- A third-grade teacher invites children to learn about mollusks by reading a passage together. Before beginning the passage, the children ask one another about what they already know about mollusks and then stop at the end of each section to talk about what they have read and anticipate what they will learn next. (Middle Childhood)

- A high school history teacher asks students to compare notes on what they have learned from reading letters from soldiers during the U.S. Civil War. The students form teams, with each side reading either letters from northern or southern soldiers, and then prepare skits that include excerpts from the letters. (Late Adolescence)

Ask children to identify key elements in stories.

- A fourth-grade teacher instructs students to ask themselves a series of questions as they read stories: (a) Who is the main character? (b) Where and when did the story take place? (c) What did the main characters do? (d) How did the story end? and (e) How did the main character feel? (Middle Childhood)

- A high school literature teacher asks students to reflect on how the various genres they have examined during the year—short stories, poetry, dramatic texts, and novels—use different strategies to convey mood and emotion. (Late Adolescence)

Suggest that children visualize what they are reading.

- A second-grade teacher asks children to come up with creative ways to represent challenges faced by characters in a story. Children draw characters with distressed facial expressions and also use various images, including a person falling off a cliff, a prison cell, and a fistfight, to show the turmoil in characters' lives. (Middle Childhood)

- When a high school English class reads Nathaniel Hawthorne's (1892) *The Scarlet Letter*, the teacher suggests that students envision what the two main characters, Arthur Dimmesdale and Hester Prynne, might look like. She then asks a few students to describe their mental images.

Scaffold children's early efforts to use complex strategies.

- A middle school science teacher asks her students to write summaries of short textbook passages. She gives them four rules to use as they develop their summaries: (a) Identify the most important ideas, (b) delete trivial details, (c) eliminate redundant information, and (d) identify relationships among the main ideas. (Early Adolescence)

- In a high school chemistry course, students use a computer program to structure their observations and notes. The program asks students to respond to questions such as these: What calculations are necessary? What data must be gathered? What steps are needed to gather the data? (Late Adolescence)

Sources: Dabarera, Renandya, & Zhang, 2014; Deeters, 2008; Gambrell & Bales, 1986; I. W. Gaskins et al., 2007; Pressley et al., 1994; Reutzel et al., 2014; Rinehart, Stahl, & Erickson, 1986; Sejnost & Thiese, 2010; Short & Ryan, 1984; Senn, 2012; M. Stewart, 2013.

skills does not *have* to be dull, however. With a little thought, teachers, parents, and other adults can develop enjoyable, meaningful activities to teach almost any basic reading skill. For instance, to promote phonological awareness in young children, adults might conduct a game of "20 Questions" (e.g., "I'm thinking of something in the room that begins with the letter *B*") or ask children to bring something from home that begins with the letter *T*. To foster greater automaticity in word recognition, teachers might encourage children to create

ARTIFACT 10-1 Long *o*, silent *e*. In this assignment, 7-year-old Meggie, a first grader, practices words with a long *o* sound and silent *e*.

Observing Children 10-3

Watch and listen to a teacher emphasize the beginning sounds of words.

ENHANCEDetext *video example*

"sound boards" (e.g., identifying and listing words that end in "ack," perhaps *black*, *slack*, and *track*; Bear, Invernizzi, Templeton, & Johnston, 2008).

Some children cannot easily parse words into separate sounds or associate sounds with letter combinations (in the case of alphabetic languages such as English). For these children, extra practice in phonemic awareness (e.g., the sounds in *cat* are *c-a-t*) and phonics, in which sounds are mapped onto letters, is generally needed. In Artifact 10-1, you can see 7-year-old Meggie's exercise with words that have a long *o* and silent *e*. You can also watch a teacher direct young children's attention to the beginning sounds of words in an Observing Children video.

• **Give children practice in reading aloud as well as silently.** When children learn to read orally with accuracy and expression, they are better able to comprehend the text they encounter. Teachers can model how to read fluently and give children plenty of guided practice (Reutzel et al., 2014). In order to be able to read fluently, of course, children need to have developed a basic sight vocabulary, so that they can quickly recognize words. Also part of their arsenal is proficiency in sounding out words, applying context in identifying unknown words, and watching for familiar sentence structures.

• **Identify and address reading problems early.** If children struggle with reading, they are apt to read as little as possible. As a result, the gap between them and their peers widens over time (Stanovich, 2000). To minimize delays, children should make up reading deficits, ideally with explicit training in basic skills early on, in first grade or even earlier. Many children with early reading difficulties benefit from intensive training in letter recognition, phonological awareness, word identification, and comprehension strategies (Bursuck & Blanks, 2010; Hulme & Snowling, 2013; D. C. Simmons et al., 2013).

• **Allow for choices in high-interest works of fiction and nonfiction.** Children and adolescents read more energetically and persistently, use more advanced metacognitive strategies, and remember more content when they are interested in what they are reading than when they are not (R. C. Anderson, Shirey, Wilson, & Fielding, 1987; E. Fox, 2009; Senn, 2012). As much as possible, then, teachers, parents, and other adults should make available reading materials that are likely to be relevant to young people's own lives and concerns, and, when appropriate, they should give youngsters some choices about what to read.

• **Conduct group discussions about novels.** Children often grasp text more effectively when they discuss what they read with peers. Adults can form "book clubs" in which trained children lead small groups of classmates in discussions about specific books (Bean Thompson, 2013; Kumasi, 2014; S. McMahon, 1992). Similarly, adults can hold "grand conversations" about a particular work of literature, asking youngsters to share their responses to open-ended questions, perhaps related to interpretations or critiques of various aspects of a novel (Eeds & Wells, 1989; E. H. Hiebert & Raphael, 1996). By tossing around interpretations of what they are reading, children model effective reading and listening comprehension strategies for one another (R. C. Anderson et al., 2001).

• **Make available a variety of media for children to express their interpretations.** Children might perform skits to illustrate stories, write personal letters that a character in a story might send to another, or create works of art that illustrate the setting of a novel or the underlying meaning of a poem. In Artifact 10-2, 16-year-old Jeff illustrates the meaning of a poem with two sides of a mask.

• **Encourage reading outside of school.** Reading beyond school walls—for instance, reading after school and during the summer months—accounts for a significant portion of young people's growth in comprehension (D. P. Hayes & Grether, 1983; Sheldon, Arbreton, Hopkins, & Grossman, 2010; Springen, 2014). Providing books that children can take home encourages outside reading and can significantly enhance comprehension skills (Koskinen et al., 2000). Visits to the local library can also encourage voluntary reading.

• **Elicit the transfer of literacy skills from one language to another.** Even in an English-speaking country, reading instruction doesn't necessarily need to begin in English. As bilingual children gain proficiency in English and begin to tackle English reading materials, they apply

We Wear the Mask
by Paul Laurence Dunbar

We wear the mask that grins and lies,
It hides our cheeks and shades our eyes,—
This debt we pay to human guile;
With torn and bleeding hearts we smile,
And mouth with myriad subtleties.

Why should the world be overwise,
In counting all our tears and sighs?
Nay, let them only see us, while
We wear the mask.

We smile, but, O great Christ, our cries
To thee from tortured souls arise.
We sing, but oh the clay is vile
Beneath our feet, and long the mile;
But let the world dream otherwise,
We wear the mask!

ARTIFACT 10-2   The mask. Sixteen-year-old Jeff illustrated the poem "We Wear the Mask" by Paul Laurence Dunbar for his American Literature class. Jeff's brightly colored painting (at left) is the cheerful face ("mask") that its African American owner presents in public. The black face (at right) is the flip side of the mask, as viewed by the person wearing it. Depicted in the holes of the mask are a lynching (left eye); a whipping (right eye); an African American woman and a white baby (nostrils), reflecting white men's rape of slaves; and a slave ship with someone being thrown overboard (mouth).

relevant knowledge from their native language—phonological awareness, vocabulary, and so on (Huennekens & Xu, 2010; L. López, 2012; C. P. Proctor, August, Carlo, & Snow, 2006).

Writing Development

Children must coordinate numerous abilities as they write. Let's examine age-related trends that occur as children gain experience in writing.

Early Childhood

Children write long before they reach school age, especially if they see people around them writing. By 18 months of age—sometimes even earlier—many toddlers scribble enthusiastically with crayons (McLane & McNamee, 1990; Winner, 2006). Children's early efforts with writing implements are largely exploratory, reflecting experimentation with different kinds of marks on paper and other surfaces.

With increasing motor coordination, preschool children better control their hand movements and produce recognizable shapes. By age 4, their writing is clearly different from drawing (S. Graham & Weintraub, 1996; Sulzby, 1986). It may consist of wavy lines or connected loops that loosely resemble adults' cursive writing. Children's early writing—or more accurately, *pseudowriting*—often reveals considerable knowledge about written language, including the orientation and spacing of letters. Perfecting one letter at a time, children eventually achieve a standard of legibility with the entire alphabet (Puranik, Petscher, & Lonigan, 2013).

Young children are generally more interested in representing and communicating a message than in getting letter shapes just right. They may include drawings and letters together, spontaneously shift from one literate form to another, and eagerly anticipate reactions from teachers and parents. As you may remember in our opening case study, Osvaldo combined print and art and was interested in how his audience responded to his story.

Middle Childhood and Adolescence

True writing is, of course, much more than simply putting letter-like forms on paper. To become proficient writers, children must not only master handwriting and spelling but also learn conventions for capitalization and punctuation. They must discover how to communicate

Observing Children 10-4
Observe fourth-grade children learning how to improve their writing.

ENHANCEDetext *video example*

thoughts clearly. They must regulate the entire writing effort using metacognitive skills. And they must polish their skills such that every decision in the writing process does not slow them down unnecessarily. Until basic processes are automatized, virtually any writing task exceeds the limits of a child's working memory capacity (Bourke, Davies, Sumner, & Green, 2014; S. Graham, 2006; Hoskyn & Tzoneva, 2008).

Progress in writing occurs on several fronts as youngsters gain experience in elementary, middle school, and high school. Children show improvements in spelling, syntax and grammar, and composition skills. By exposing children to good writing, pointing out ideal features, and giving feedback about their writing, teachers can help children make definite progress, as you can see in an Observing Children video (Jago, 2014).

Handwriting

During the elementary school years, children's handwriting gradually becomes smaller and more regular, and they shift from concentrating on forming each letter to writing entire words and sentences (S. Graham & Weintraub, 1996; Rumi, Toshihiro, & Kenryu, 2013). Little additional improvement in handwriting occurs after elementary school, although youngsters continue to simplify letters and write more efficiently (Olive, Favart, Beauvais, & Beauvais, 2009). Many educators now see keyboarding skills and proficient use of a word processor as necessary tools for writing (ASCD, 2014). Rapid, automatized handwriting and keyboarding are important factors in effective writing because they allow students to focus attention on their thoughts and not on transcribing them (S. Graham, Harris, & Fink, 2000; Medwell & Wray, 2014).

Spelling

As you might expect, phonological awareness is as important in spelling as it is in reading (Lennox & Siegel, 1998; Treiman & Kessler, 2013). Children learn proper spellings of a few words (such as their names) almost as soon as they learn how to write letters of the alphabet. But in their early writing they tend to engage in considerable guesswork about how words are spelled, creating **invented spellings** that correctly capture certain sounds but not others (N. H. Clemens, Oslund, Simmons, & Simmons, 2014; Treiman, 1998). Consider the invented spellings in this kindergartner's creation entitled "My Garden" (note that "HWS" is *house*):

> THIS IS A HWS
> THE SUN
> WL SHIN
> ND MI
> GRDN
> WL GRO
> *(Hemphill & Snow, 1996, p. 192)*

As children develop greater phonological awareness, their spellings increasingly represent most or all of the phonemes they hear (Awramiuk, 2014; Hemphill & Snow, 1996). Sometime around first or second grade, they incorporate common letter patterns (e.g., *-ight*, *-ound*, and *-ing* in English) into unfamiliar words (Critten, Pine, & Steffler, 2007; Nation & Hulme, 1998). Children's ability to spell improves steadily, especially if they read and write regularly. Most children eventually automatize the spelling of words they use often (Rittle-Johnson & Siegler, 1999). To make more difficult words accessible, some teachers expose children to selected word families (e.g., "fight" and "right," "team" and "beam"). Other teachers group children according to spelling proficiency and provide them with customized spelling lists and computer programs (B. McNeill & Kirk, 2014; Saine, Lerkkanen, Ahonen, Tolvanen, & Lyytinen, 2013).

Syntax and Grammar

As children grow older, they write in longer sentences and with more varied sentence structures. By the time they are 12 or 13 years old, the syntactic structures they use in written work are considerably more complex than those in their speech. With age, too, comes an increasing ability to follow punctuation and capitalization rules without reminders from adults

(Feifer, 2013; R. B. Gillam & Johnston, 1992; Ravid & Zilberbuch, 2003). Regular reading and writing contribute to refinements in the mechanics of writing and in the complexity and style of expressing ideas. Teachers can guide children by drawing attention to functions of parts of speech and rules of grammatical expression (J. Anderson, 2014).

Composition Skills

When preschool children engage in early writing activities at home, they often do so with a particular purpose in mind, such as labeling a possession or writing a letter to a grandparent. Only when children enter kindergarten or first grade do they write for writing's sake. Children's earliest compositions are usually narratives, such as recollections of personal experiences or short, fictional stories (Hemphill & Snow, 1996).

In previous years, acquisition of basic skills in expository writing (e.g., research reports, persuasive essays) occurred rather late in schooling, probably because teachers were not accustomed to asking for such written work until the upper elementary grades (Owens, 2008). Emerging views on writing instruction, including those guiding Common Core standards, give greater attention to writing across the curriculum, resulting in children in the early grades now being asked to write about their understandings in science, mathematics, and social studies. Students are also currently taught how to write clearly and defend their conclusions (Alberti, 2012).

The quality of compositions changes in many ways throughout the elementary and secondary school years, as reflected in the following trends:

Children write about topics in greater depth as they grow older. When children of various ages are asked to write about a particular topic, the older ones include more ideas (de Milliano, van Gelderen, & Sleegers, 2012; Zumbrunn & Bruning, 2013). Such growth continues throughout the school years. For instance, when writing persuasive essays, high school students include more arguments than do elementary and middle school students, and 12th graders include more arguments than do 9th graders (Knudson, 1992; McCann, 1989).

Children increasingly take their audience into account. Just as children become ever more capable in adapting speech to the characteristics of their listeners, they become more attentive to their readers' needs with age and experience.[5] Young children realize that an audience will need to interpret their drawings and writing, but as they grow, children become better able to envision their audience and tailor text accordingly (S. Graham, 2006; Leyva, Hopson, & Nichols, 2012; Perfetti & McCutchen, 1987).

During adolescence, a knowledge-telling approach gradually evolves into a knowledge-transforming approach. Young writers often compose a narrative or essay by writing down ideas in the order in which they come to mind. Such an approach is known as **knowledge telling** (Scardamalia & Bereiter, 1986; S. Graham, Harris, & Olinghouse, 2007; Whitehead & Murphy, 2014). With age, experience, and practice with basic writing skills, young people become better able to communicate a meaningful perspective on a topic, one that helps potential readers *understand* the material, an approach known as **knowledge transforming**.

With age and instruction comes a growing ability to write a cohesive composition. In the elementary grades, children use few if any devices to tieseparate pieces of their creation together. They may write a story by beginning with "Once upon a time" and list a sequence of events that connect only loosely to one another, ending with "They lived happily ever after" (Boyle & Charles, 2011; McLane & McNamee, 1990). Their nonfiction, too, may be little more than a list of facts or events. Older children, and especially adolescents, are more capable of analyzing and synthesizing their thoughts as they write, and so they compose more cohesive, integrated texts, in part because they are increasingly able to build text around causes for events and motivations of characters (Byrnes & Wasik, 2009; McCutchen, 1987; Sun & Nippold, 2012).

---

[5]We describe children's consideration of listeners' perspectives in Chapter 9.

Metacognition in Writing

Good writers think about a topic ahead of time and plan how they are going to render it. After preparing drafts, they critically evaluate their writing, looking not only for grammatical and spelling errors but also for omissions, ambiguities, logical flaws, and contradictions (Eunjyu, 2013; S. Graham, 2006; Tracy, Reid, & Graham, 2009). Such editing skills emerge slowly and are incomplete by the end of adolescence, in large part because youngsters' metacognitive capabilities in writing are still growing. In fact, young people typically remain challenged in identifying problems in their writing, particularly those related to clarity and cohesiveness (Berninger, Fuller, & Whitaker, 1996; Fitzgerald, 1987; Koutsoftas & Gray, 2013). They often don't revise their work unless an adult specifically urges them to do so. When they *do* rewrite, they tend to make only small, superficial changes. Yet with instruction in how to plan ahead and later revise stories and reports, students are generally able to improve their drafts (Tracy et al., 2009). Handouts and posters with strategies for generating ideas and revising preliminary versions can be useful; an example for fourth graders is included in Figure 10-1 (Babkie & Provost, 2002; Nguyen & Gu, 2013).

With appropriate support from adults, children gradually learn to express themselves effectively. The Developmental Trends table "Writing at Different Age Levels" identifies accomplishments in writing seen during infancy and the preschool, elementary school, and secondary school years.

Steps in Writing the Paper	Describe Your Steps
1. Planning the Paper Example: *I decided to write about wings of birds in a four-paragraph paper.*	Describe the focus and structure of your paper: _____ _____
2. Generating Ideas Example: *I used a concept map and then wrote an outline.*	Explain the strategy you used to develop your ideas: _____ _____
3. Organizing Thoughts Example: *I followed my outline.*	Identify your plan for organizing the sequence of ideas in your paper: _____ _____
4. Writing the First Draft Example: *I turned off my cell phone and took an hour to write down my thoughts.*	Summarize how you developed your first draft: _____ _____
5. Reviewing the Draft Example: *I needed to fix the conclusion because it didn't make sense.*	Tell what you decided to change when you re-read your first draft: _____ _____
5. Finalizing the Paper Example: *I corrected a few spelling errors and changed the conclusion.*	Describe the changes you made when finalizing your essay: _____ _____

FIGURE 10-1 Worksheet for Fourth Graders on Steps in Writing an Essay.

BIOECOLOGY OF DEVELOPMENT

Children learn to express themselves as writers through experiences at home, with peers, and at school.

Bioecology of Writing Development

As is true for reading development, a child's writing progress is influenced by his or her individual characteristics and experiences at home, with peers, at school, and in the community. Many parents invite their children to sit with them as they prepare shopping lists, letters, or notes on the computer, piquing their interest (Skibbe, Bindman, Hindman, Aram, & Morrison, 2013). Compatibility among environments is also influential. A boy who actively composes stories at home will not share his talent at school if he expects harsh judgment there.

DEVELOPMENTAL TRENDS
Writing at Different Age Levels

AGE	WHAT YOU MIGHT OBSERVE	DIVERSITY	IMPLICATIONS
Infancy (Birth–2 Years)	• Development of eye–hand coordination, including the *pincer grasp*, through which infants use a thumb and forefinger to pick up and hold objects • Appearance of scribbling at 18 to 24 months • Interest in mimicking "writing" by adults	• Individual differences appear in the advancement of fine motor skills. • Infants can imitate only what they see, so those who never see anyone writing are unlikely to use crayons and other writing implements to mark up paper.	• Allow toddlers to manipulate small objects that do not present choking hazards. • Demonstrate how to make lines and shapes with writing implements. • Have a variety of tools available for scribbling (e.g., with fat crayons and washable, nontoxic markers, butcher paper). • Tape writing paper to the table or floor to permit easy clean up.
Early Childhood (2–6 Years)	• Improving muscular control in writing and drawing • Pseudowriting (e.g., wavy lines, connected loops) in preschool play activities • Ability to write own name (perhaps at age 3) • Ability to write most letters of the alphabet (at age 4 or later) • Invented spellings (at ages 5 to 6)	• Some cultures place greater emphasis on writing than others. • Some children have little exposure to written materials or knowledge of letters. • Children with visual impairments are apt to have little awareness of print conventions (left-to-right progression, use of punctuation, etc.).	• Make writing implements (pencils, markers, paper) easily accessible. • Give children opportunities to write their names and a few other words. • Have children act out stories they have orally composed. • Ask children to dictate stories, letters, poems, or reports for you to transcribe, and that children can later illustrate.
Middle Childhood (6–10 Years)	• Steady improvement in smoothness of handwriting; gradual decrease in handwriting size • Increasing application of letter-sound relationships and common letter patterns when spelling words • Predominance of narratives in writing • Increasing length in stories and reports as handwriting and spelling improve • Difficulty identifying problems (especially lack of clarity) in own writing • Developing proficiency in keyboarding skill and use of word processing program	• Better readers tend to be better writers, presumably because general language ability provides a foundation for both competencies. • Children with deficits in phonological awareness have a more difficult time learning to spell. • Girls show higher achievement in writing and spelling beginning in the elementary years. • Children with dyslexia and other learning disabilities often have poor handwriting skills. • Children with certain learning impairments and learning disabilities have difficulty with spelling.	• Engage children in authentic writing activities (e.g., in writing letters to relatives or creating a newsletter). • Provide practice in spelling, grammar, and punctuation within authentic activities. • Explore how particular phonemes are spelled. • Introduce expository forms of writing (e.g., lab reports and social studies essays). • Include editing in the schedule; provide criteria for self-evaluation. • Use keyboards with large letters or tactile feedback for students with low vision, and use Braille writers with blind children.
Early Adolescence (10–14 Years)	• Automatized spelling of common words • Improvement in expository forms of writing • Use of longer and more complex syntactic structures • Tendency not to edit and revise unless encouraged to do so	• Some students (e.g., those with learning disabilities) may continue to have difficulty with spelling and sentence structure. • A few adolescents write in their spare time (e.g., keeping diaries, writing notes to friends), whereas others write only when required at school.	• Provide instruction in spelling, punctuation, and grammar, emphasizing functions in communicating meaning. • Teach persuasive and argumentative forms of writing. • Suggest a specific audience for whom to write. • Give feedback on first drafts, especially on clarity. • Encourage adolescents to use local dialects in creative writing projects.

(continued)

DEVELOPMENTAL TRENDS (continued)

AGE	WHAT YOU MIGHT OBSERVE	DIVERSITY	IMPLICATIONS
Late Adolescence (14–18 Years)	• Ability to write about a particular topic in depth • More organized, unified, and interconnected essays than in previous years • Increasing tendency to knowledge-transform rather than knowledge-tell • More revisions than at younger ages, but with a focus on superficial rather than substantive problems	• Individuals with learning disabilities may focus largely on mechanics (e.g., correct spelling and grammar) while composing, perhaps because such skills are not yet automatized. • Individuals from some cultural backgrounds (e.g., a few from East Asian countries) may be reluctant to put thoughts on paper unless certain that their thinking is acceptable.	• Assign and scaffold lengthy writing projects. • Teach specific strategies for organizing and synthesizing ideas. • Show examples of good writing (e.g., an essay that illustrates knowledge transforming). • For teens with language-based disabilities, downplay spelling and grammar in written work; teach strategies for overcoming weaknesses. • Encourage peers to evaluate one another's reports using prepared rubrics.

Sources: Beal, 1996; Berninger et al., 1996; Broc et al., 2013; Byrnes, 1996; Cameron, Hunt, & Linton, 1996; Dien, 1998; Donne, 2012; Duarte Ribeiro & Loução Martins, 2013; J. M. Fletcher, Lyon, Fuchs, & Barnes, 2007; Gentry, 1982; Glaser & Brunstein, 2007; S. Graham, 2014; S. Graham et al., 2007; Halpern, 2006; J. Hansen & Kissel, 2009; Hedges & Nowell, 1995; Hemphill & Snow, 1996; Kellogg, 1967; MacArthur & Graham, 1987; McLane & McNamee, 1990; Rochat & Bullinger, 1994; Shanahan & Tierney, 1990; Smitherman, 1994; Yaden & Templeton, 1986; Young-Suk, Al Otaiba, Folsom, Greulich, & Puranik, 2014.

The numerous intellectual demands that accompany writing affect children differently depending on their personal characteristics. Some children who are gifted exhibit extraordinary writing talent. Most children with intellectual disabilities and some with specific learning disabilities have problems in handwriting, spelling, and expressing themselves coherently (J. M. Fletcher et al., 2007). Children with writing delays typically focus their writing efforts on spelling, grammar, and punctuation (S. Graham, Schwartz, & MacArthur, 1993). The quality of their writing improves considerably when demands on the mechanical aspects of writing are minimized (e.g., when they can dictate their stories and other compositions) and when they are given specific steps to follow as they write (Hallenbeck, 1996; R. J. Sawyer, Graham, & Harris, 1992).

The bioecological framework reminds us that writing is learned over time in distinct social settings. Children observe their parents and other family members writing for particular purposes and later experiment with these actions, perhaps keeping a journal at night or regularly posting personal updates on a Facebook account. At school, children are guided in formal writing assignments, through instruction from teachers, and during interactions with peers.

In one study with fourth- and fifth-grade students, researchers focused on Juan, an English language learner who had previously failed to complete his written assignments. When an activity called for children to pair up for a writing assignment, Juan teamed up with his friend Ned and made much more progress than on his own. In the following excerpt, the boys speculate about why turtles are disappearing, and Juan is motivated to take notes for the assignment:

Ned: Another way he could get drown is a crab could get him.

Juan: He puts his head in his shell?

Ned: If he sticks his head in his shell, he can't get it out. Then it gets trapped. Then the crab will stick his claws inside it, and sometimes they eat turtles. They stick their claws inside and eat turtles. Sea turtles. He sticks his claws inside and gets the turtle's head and starts eating it. (Juan is writing.)

Juan: Or . . . putting . . . his . . . head . . . in . . . his . . . shell . . . can drown him, too?

Ned: What?

Juan: Putting his head in his shell can drown him too?

(Juan is writing. He continues his questioning to fill in the matrix where there are question marks.) (Bicais & Correia, 2008, p. 370)

Promoting Writing Development

Growth in writing requires a long-term effort. Psychologists and experienced educators have offered several suggestions for facilitating youngsters' writing development:

- **Provide tools for drawing and writing as soon as children are old enough to use them.** Quite early in life, children explore the outcomes of their hand movements in drawing, writing, and painting. For toddlers, the sensory experience of painting with wet fingertips is an obvious attraction, but gradually children attend to marks they make on the page. As fine motor skills, cognitive abilities, and knowledge of written symbols improve during the preschool years, children become increasingly able to produce recognizable shapes and letters.

As children grow older, other kinds of tools are helpful. Some children have the potential to be skilled writers but cannot form letters due to neuromuscular delays (McCarney, Peters, Jackson, Thomas, & Kirby, 2013). For these children, being able to type stories and reports allows them to share their knowledge (Ashburner, Ziviani, & Pennington, 2012). In fact, some schools now teach keyboarding in lieu of cursive, reasoning that there is not time for both and that facility on the computer is critical in our electronic age (Bauerlein, 2013). A few students with learning disabilities are not able to write or keyboard but dictate stories and essays and take advantage of voice-to-text conversion applications (I. Lee, 2013). Other students do not face a particular learning challenge but nevertheless find it motivating to use technologies such as *iBooks Author*, an application by Apple, Inc., that allows students to create interactive books (Encheff, 2013).

- **Present authentic writing tasks.** Youngsters write more frequently, and in a more organized and effective (e.g., knowledge-transforming) manner, when they can write for a "real" audience (not just for their teacher) and when they're interested in the topic (S. L. Benton, 1997; S. Peterson, 2014). When one high school English teacher noticed that several capable students weren't completing assigned writing tasks, he asked students to write about their personal experiences and share their work on the Internet. The students began writing regularly, presumably because they could write for a real audience and choose their topic (Garner, 1998). Current events and personal circumstances motivate the desire to communicate about hopes, aspirations, and injustices—topics of concern to many young people (Chandler-Olcott, 2013). By the same token, students who are participating in service learning or internships have experiences that beg to be documented (Perren, Grove, & Thornton, 2013). In the Development and Culture feature "Summer Camp in Bosnia," a group of girls wrote stories for younger children at camp.

- **Scaffold children's writing efforts.** Given the many challenges of writing, especially for beginners, it can help to guide certain steps. You can observe one high school teacher scaffold the writing skills of English language learners in an Observing Children video. In addition, consider the following forms of guidance:

  - Allow children with limited writing skills to dictate rather than write their stories.
  - Ask children to set specific goals for their writing.
  - Help students organize their thoughts before beginning to write, perhaps asking them to talk about their ideas with a classmate or draw a picture of the characters or concepts they will be describing.
  - Invite children to brainstorm ideas for communicating effectively (e.g., by using examples, analogies, and similes, as you can see in Artifact 10-3).
  - Post a *word wall,* a list of concepts being addressed in a particular unit (e.g., key terms in a social studies), as a poster or list on the bulletin board.
  - Ask children to keep a journal of their observations of a particular phenomenon (e.g., a record of plant growth for a science lesson).
  - Guide children with questions they should address when writing a story (e.g., Who are the main characters? When and where does the story take place? What are the main characters trying to accomplish? What happens to them? How does the story end?).

Like What...
hot like...
cold like...
sounds like...
tastes like...
feels like...
looks like...
smells like...
moves like...

Simile- comparison uses like or a:

SADNESS

Sadness is cold like an old empty house. It sounds like a cold winter wind. Sadness tastes like a glass of spoiled milk. It feels like an ice cub that been out of the refridgerator for two minutes. Sadness moves like a single leaf in the slow autumn wind. Sadness crawls across the floor hoping to go by unoticed.

ARTIFACT 10-3 **Similes of sadness.** Teachers can help children by providing structures that scaffold initial writing efforts. After her class brainstormed the kinds of similes a writer might use, 11-year-old Charlotte wrote similes of sadness.

DEVELOPMENT IN CULTURE
Summer Camp in Bosnia

Jacqueline Darvin, a college professor in literacy education, attended a conference one spring and became impressed with the work of the Global Children's Organization, a group of educators, professionals, and other volunteers who offer summer camps for children growing up with unrest, violence, and intolerance (GCO; Darvin, 2009). Jacqueline learned that GCO had implemented programs for children in Los Angeles and Northern Ireland and was planning a program in the former Yugoslavia. She joined the group and traveled to a summer camp in Bosnia.

Children at the Bosnian camp had grown up in communities afflicted with ethnic conflicts, high rates of unemployment, and political corruption. Children's families had strong allegiances as Bosnians, Bosnian Serbs, or Bosnian Croats, ethnic groups that had previously fought one another in a brutal war. Some of the children who attended camp had lost their parents in the war, and others had witnessed violence firsthand, sometimes at school.

At the camp, children were warmly welcomed in community-building exercises. Children also participated in numerous relaxing sports and leisure activities, including artwork, horseback riding, and hiking. Jacqueline's contribution to the activities was a literacy project. She invited the oldest girls at the camp (between 10 and 13 years old) to compose and illustrate books that they would share with younger children. Girls individually selected one of three themes to write about: peace and freedom, preservation of nature, or funny stories about horses. Children wrote their books in their native Serbo-Croatian language, and English-speaking native speakers translated the books for Jacqueline.

A few girls wrote about horses, but the majority focused on peace and friendship or the beauty of the natural world. An interest in developing new relationships with people from dissimilar backgrounds was evident in those who wrote about peace and friendship. Melita wrote about her desire to make friends with children from different backgrounds:

When I was small, I always thought about meeting many friends and wanted to be surrounded by many people. Always, I was thinking and dreaming about this. I was in the dark, but one day, my eyes were opened. The people I met were different religions, from different countries, had different feelings, but the one thing we had in common was friendship and love. . . . It didn't matter that we had different colour skin, that we prayed to God in a different way and talked to Him about our eminent departure (from camp) and the pain we would feel. But sure enough, it was time to leave. We were all sad. But in a way, we

These Bosnian children race on inflatable beach mattresses with new friends at summer camp.

were happy because we knew that we would see each other again and forever carry each other in our hearts.[a] (Darvin, 2009, p. 55)

Jacqueline had selected preservation of nature in Bosnia as a second option because of people's growing concern about pollution, water shortages, and illegal stripping of forests. Many children were aware of these concerns and appreciative of their time in a scenic rural setting. Children who selected this theme wrote about the natural beauty around them. One student, Anela, communicated her sense of awe in a poem:

One night,
A little star was shining in the sky.
In the morning,
The birds woke up from their nests.
The flowers bloomed from their green buds
To please the missing stars.[a] (Darvin, 2009, p. 54)

As they prepared books, the girls exchanged ideas and helped one another with illustrations. Local camp counselors assisted with spelling and grammar when asked. As final touches, the girls wrote brief autobiographies, added photographs of themselves on the back covers, and laminated the books. Having completed the stories, the girls hosted a story hour for the 6- to 8-year-old children at camp. The girls were pleased with their accomplishments, and the younger children were impressed with the books.

[a]"Make Books, Not War: Workshops at a Summer Camp in Bosnia" by Jacqueline Darvin, from LITERACY, March 17, 2009, Volume 43, Issue 1. Copyright © 2009 by Jacqueline Darvin. Reprinted with permission of LITERACY, a journal of the United Kingdom Literacy Association.

- Identify elements for children to include in their assignment (e.g., in a persuasive essay, include a thesis statement, supporting arguments, and rebuttals to possible counterarguments).
- Suggest that children initially focus on communicating clearly; postpone attention to writing mechanics (e.g., spelling, punctuation) until later drafts.
- Provide specific questions that children should ask themselves as they review their writing (e.g., "Are my ideas logically organized?" "Do I have a topic sentence in each paragraph?").

- Ask children to collaborate on writing projects, or to read and respond to one another's work.
- Encourage use of word processing programs while writing and editing.
  (ASCD, 2014; Benko, 2012; Benton, 1997; Boyle & Charles, 2011; Glaser & Brunstein, 2007; S. Graham & Perin, 2007; J. Hansen & Kissel, 2009; K. R. Harris & Graham, 1992; McLane & McNamee, 1990; Sitko, 1998; Sperling, 1996; Tracy et al., 2009; Zumbrunn & Bruning, 2013).

• **Include writing assignments in all areas of the curriculum.** Writing is an important form of communication for expressing insights about historical documents, scientific observations, artistic interpretations, and mathematical patterns. Because writing takes different forms in separate disciplines, students need to practice expressing their ideas in different fields, for example, with critiques of fiction, a science lab report, and an analysis of historical documents. Particularly at the secondary level, teachers need to teach writing skills for communicating knowledge in the disciplines (De La Paz, 2005; D. Gillam, 2014; Sejnost & Thiese, 2010).

Summary

When toddlers and preschoolers have multiple and varied experiences with reading materials, they learn a great deal about the nature of written language. They understand that spoken language is represented in consistent ways and that different kinds of printed materials serve distinct purposes. Such knowledge, known as *emergent literacy*, is an important foundation for the reading and writing skills children acquire in school.

Skilled reading involves knowing letter-sound correspondences, recognizing letters and words quickly, constructing meaning from the words on the page, and regulating the reading process. Phonological awareness (hearing the distinct sounds within spoken words), word identification skills, and the automatic recognition of common words typically emerge by the early and middle elementary school years. Reading comprehension and metacognitive strategies develop throughout childhood and adolescence.

Some children with sensory impairments or learning disabilities have more difficulty learning to read than do their nondisabled peers. Researchers have also found gender, socioeconomic, and cultural factors in reading development. Strategies for fostering reading development include teaching parents strategies for effective storybook reading, promoting children's phonological awareness, providing access to authentic literature, making culturally relevant reading materials available, and engaging children in discussions about what they have read.

To become skillful writers, children must master not only handwriting and spelling but also methods for communicating thoughts clearly; conventions for capitalization, punctuation, and syntax; and control of the entire writing effort. Handwriting and keyboarding are usually mastered in the elementary grades, but other aspects of writing continue to develop throughout the school years. In the middle school and high school years, many youngsters gradually abandon a *knowledge-telling* approach to writing (in which they write ideas in whatever order the ideas come to mind) in favor of a *knowledge-transforming* approach (in which they conscientiously communicate their ideas with the reader's needs in mind). Self-evaluation and editing skills improve somewhat during adolescence.

To a considerable degree, writing development depends on children's general intellectual development, but some children have difficulty writing despite normal cognitive development in other areas. Teachers and other adults can promote writing development by introducing preschoolers to simple writing activities (e.g., making alphabet letters, using pseudowriting in pretend play), assigning authentic writing tasks in the elementary and secondary grades, scaffolding everyone's writing efforts with age-appropriate structures, and, with older children and adolescents, requiring writing in all areas of the school curriculum.

ENHANCEDetext *self-check*

Observing Children 10-5

Observe a high school teacher scaffold the writing of students who are learning English as a second language. Notice how she makes the writing task manageable (by selecting the goal of writing an obituary), focused (with the 5 W's), and interactive (by having students work in pairs).

ENHANCEDetext *video example*

Assessing Children 10-1

Assess Rakie's understanding of reading and writing.

ENHANCEDetext *application exercise*

MATHEMATICS AND SCIENCE

Beginning in the first few years of life, children are intrinsically interested in the mathematical and scientific regularities of their world. At school, they extend their knowledge by counting, envisioning quantities on a number line, employing the scientific method, and identifying properties in living and nonanimate things. As students progress through the grade levels, mathematics and science become progressively more challenging, and if they stay in the game, students gain a wide range of career options in our technologically advancing society.

The Essence of Mathematics

Mathematics is a cluster of realms—arithmetic, algebra, geometry, statistics, and so on—with distinct methods for solving quantitative problems. Achievements across these related areas depend on the individual's abilities to perceive changes in volume, count items accurately, calculate mathematical formulas properly, and understand and regulate strategies for solving mathematical problems.

Number Sense and Counting

From birth, children are sensitive to variations in quantity, size, volume, and magnitude. This sensitivity, which has a neurological basis, matures with development (Cantrell & Smith, 2013; Mou & vanMarle, 2014). By 5 or 6 months of age, infants notice the difference between two collections of small, varying amounts (e.g., a set of two objects and a set of three objects), and they distinguish between two large collections with visibly different amounts (e.g., a set of 16 dots and a set of 32 dots; Wynn, 1995; F. Xu & Spelke, 2000). It is an impressive feat, although babies are probably noticing the perceptible difference before them rather than counting and comparing the items. As they approach their first birthday, infants exhibit an understanding of *more* versus *less*. For example, 9- to 11-month-olds notice the difference between sequences of pictures that reflect increases versus decreases in quantity (Brannon, 2002; McCrink & Wynn, 2009).

Except for small groupings, infants' awareness of quantity is imprecise. The ability to count is necessary to distinguish between larger, nearly comparable quantities—say, between collections of seven versus eight objects (Lipton & Spelke, 2005). Children in Western cultures typically begin counting before their third birthday, and many 3- and 4-year-olds can count to 10 (Ginsburg, Cannon, Eisenband, & Pappas, 2006; Manfra, Dinehart, & Sembiante, 2014). Five-year-olds can usually count far beyond 10 (perhaps to 50), although they may get confused about the order of such higher numbers as 70, 80, and 90 (Fuson & Hall, 1983). As children work with two- and three-digit written numbers in the elementary grades, they increasingly master the correct sequence of numbers well into the hundreds (Case & Okamoto, 1996; W. Chan, Au, & Tang, 2014).

As you know, there is more to counting than saying the numbers in proper sequence. When children first begin to count, they learn numbers by rote without understanding their connections to amounts of items (Geary, 2006; Träff, 2013; Wynn, 1990). As a result, they may say two successive numbers (e.g., ". . . three, four . . .") while pointing to a single object and so count it twice. Or, instead, they may point to two successive objects while saying only one number. But by the time they are age 4 or 5, most children have mastered several basic principles of counting, including the following:

- *One-to-one principle.* Each object in the set being counted must be assigned one and only one number word. You would say "one" while pointing to one object, "two" while pointing to another object, and so on until every object has been counted exactly once.

- *Cardinal principle.* The last number word counted indicates the number of objects in the set. In other words, if you count from one to five when counting objects, then there are five objects in the set.
- *Order-irrelevance principle.* A set of objects has the same number regardless of the order in which individual objects are counted. (Bryant & Nuñes, 2011; Gallistel & Gelman, 1992; Griffin, 2009; Sarnecka & Wright, 2013)

Initially children apply these principles primarily to small number sets (e.g., of 10 or fewer items), but within a few years they relate the principles to larger sets as well. Practice in counting with objects is an educationally worthwhile activity for numerous children in preschool and kindergarten, older children who have not had much practice in counting, and students with intellectual disabilities (W. Chan et al., 2014; Jimenez & Kemmery, 2013).

Mathematical Concepts

As children count, they gain insights into numbers. Some of these ideas facilitate their under-standing of rudimentary arithmetic yet later must be overcome due to their incompatibility with advanced mathematics. For example, children initially come to believe that:

- All numbers are whole numbers.
- The smallest number is either 0 or 1.
- Numbers always become larger as they move farther from zero.
- Addition to a number invariably makes it larger.
- Subtraction from a number consistently makes it smaller.

These ideas are consistent with positive whole numbers, of course, but lose accuracy when fractions, decimals, and negative numbers enter the mix (Bofferding, 2014; Vosniadou & Brewer, 1992). Until children realize that principles governing whole numbers do not gen-eralize to all other kinds of numbers, they have trouble accepting that multiplying a whole number by a fraction can yield a smaller number or that adding two negative numbers will result in a sum that is smaller than either of the numbers being added.

Other concepts are more robust across mathematical conditions, and when acquired, in-crease the chances that children grasp more advanced mathematical principles. An especially critical one in the early elementary grades is the *part-whole principle*, the ideas that any single number can be broken into two or more smaller numbers (e.g., 7 can be broken into 1, 2, and 4) and that any two or more numbers can be combined. These principles seem to be central to children's understanding of addition and subtraction (Baroody, Tiilikainen, & Tai, 2006; Z. Cheng, 2012; Sophian & Vong, 1995).

A more advanced concept in mathematical reasoning is the idea of *proportion*, the rela-tive part of a whole, a concept that is reflected in fractions, ratios, and decimals. Proportional reasoning emerges very gradually over the course of childhood.[6] As early as 6 months of age, infants show an intuitive awareness of proportions—for instance, in distinguishing visual dis-plays reflecting 2-to-1 and 4-to-1 ratios, and in noticing a difference between containers that are ¼ and ¾ full of liquid (Denison & Xu, 2014; Jeong, Levine, & Huttenlocher, 2007; McCrink & Wynn, 2007). By about age 3 children can distinguish smaller and larger proportions in fractions of circles. By the early elementary grades children can understand simple, specific fractions (e.g., ½ or ⅓) if they can relate these portions to everyday objects (Empson, 1999; M. B. Wood, Olson, Freiberg, & Vega, 2013).

Yet students are apt to continue to struggle with more complex fractions and other proportions until well into adolescence (Modestou & Gagatsis, 2010; Van Dooren, De Bock, Hessels, Janssens, & Verschaffel, 2005). It seems that they regularly misapply their knowledge of whole numbers (Ni & Zhou, 2005). For example, because 4 is greater than 3, students are apt to conclude that ¼ is greater than ⅓. And because 256 is greater than 7, they are apt to think that 0.256 must be greater than 0.7. Instruction is instrumental to overcoming these conceptual barriers. You can observe a secondary teacher introducing proportions in the context of familiar fractions in an Observing Children video.

Observing Children 10-6
Observe secondary students participate in a lesson about proportions.

ENHANCEDetext *video example*

---

[6]As you might recall from Chapter 6, Piaget suggested that children become capable of proportional reasoning when they enter the formal operations stage, sometime around ages 11 or 12. More recent research indicates that children exhibit glimmerings of proportional reasoning before Piaget expected but also take longer to solidify than Piaget anticipated.

Middle school and high school math classes increasingly focus on abstract concepts, such as *pi* (π), *irrational numbers*, and the *variable*. Mathematical principles, such as *the product of two negative numbers is a positive number* and *the angles of a triangle always have a total of 180°*, also become increasingly abstract. Because such concepts are intangible, formal instruction is usually necessary (Chazan, Brantlinger, Clark, & Edwards, 2013; Geary, 1994; R. S. Nickerson, 2010).

Mathematical Operations

Two of the most basic mathematical operations are addition and subtraction. Infants have a preliminary understanding of these processes well before their first birthday (McCrink & Wynn, 2009; Slater, Bremner, Johnson, & Hayes, 2011; Wynn, 1992). Imagine that two Mickey Mouse dolls are placed on a table in front of you. An experimenter lowers a screen to block your view of the dolls, and then you watch the experimenter take one of the dolls from behind the screen and put it away. You assume that only one doll remains on the table, but as the screen is raised, you still see *two* dolls there. Even 5-month-olds show surprise at this outcome, indicating an awareness that something isn't as it should be.

By 2½ or 3 years of age, children clearly understand that adding objects to a set increases quantity and that subtracting objects decreases quantity (J. Huttenlocher, Jordan, & Levine, 1994). By age 3 or 4, many begin to apply their knowledge of counting to simple addition and subtraction problems, typically using procedures they develop on their own, especially counting on fingers (Lafay, Thevenot, Castel, & Fayol, 2013; Siegler & Jenkins, 1989). Consider the problem *If I have 2 apples and you give me 3 more apples, how many apples do I have altogether?* A child might put up two fingers and then three more fingers and count all the fingers to reach the solution, "5 apples." Children also encounter simple division problems in the preschool years (e.g., when they must share food or toys with others), and even some 3-year-olds use counting to divide quantities equitably (K. Miller, 1989).

Somewhat later, children begin to use a *min* strategy in addition, in which they start with the larger of the two numbers (for the apple problem, they would start with 3) and then add on, one by one, the smaller number (e.g., counting "three apples . . . then four, five . . . five apples altogether"; Siegler & Jenkins, 1989). They might do something similar for subtraction, starting with the original number of objects and then counting down the number of objects removed: "Five . . . then four, three . . . three apples left." Children increasingly rely on memory of basic addition and subtraction facts (e.g., $2 + 3 = 5$, $5 - 3 = 2$), and with this advancement, depend less on fingers and other objects (Geary, Hoard, & Nugent, 2012; Siegler & Jenkins, 1989).[7]

In North America, formal instruction in multiplication usually begins in first or second grade. With multiplication, children typically learn and use a mixture of strategies (J. B. Cooney & Ladd, 1992; Geary, 2006). When working with small numbers, they may simply use addition (e.g., solving "$3 \times 3 = ?$" by adding $3 + 3$ and then adding another 3 to the sum). Sometimes they count by twos, fives, or some other number (e.g., solving "$5 \times 4 = ?$" by counting "5, 10, 15, 20"). At other times they apply certain rules, such as *anything times zero is zero* or *anything times 1 is itself*. Gradually, retrieval of basic multiplication facts replaces strategies and rule-based derivations (D. H. Bailey, Littlefield, & Geary, 2012; J. B. Cooney, Swanson, & Ladd, 1988; De Brauwer & Fias, 2009).

The same general principles hold with division, which is at first acquired slowly. With formal instruction and practice, processes become more accurate and efficient. As they tackle division problems, children often rely on their knowledge of other arithmetic facts, especially multiplication facts (e.g., if $5 \times 4 = 20$, then $20 \div 5 = 4$; Geary, 1994). Nevertheless, reliance on retrieval is not always possible with more complicated division problems (e.g., $1611 \div 3$),

---

[7]The changing frequency of addition strategies over time reflects the *overlapping waves* framework of strategy use, in which children initially use a few different methods for solving a problem, gradually prefer ones that are more adaptive, and also experiment with new techniques as they come to mind. Siegler's framework of learning, which demonstrates evidence for overlapping strategies, is presented in Chapter 7 (see Figure 7-3 on p. 260).

making it valuable for children to learn how to divide numbers with the help of a pencil and paper (Hickendorff, van Putten, Verhelst, & Heiser, 2010).

Blended Competencies in Mathematics

So far, we've described mathematical understandings and calculations as if they were separate abilities. In reality, the two capacities are intertwined. Being able to use mathematical procedures properly requires an understanding of notations and rules. For example, in completing arithmetic calculations, you must solve equations within parentheses before proceeding to other calculations, moving from left to right, and tackling multiplication and division before addition and subtraction. Thus, with $[5 \times 3] \times 2 + 4$, you would calculate 5×3 to get 15, multiply 15 by 2 to get 30, and add 4 to end up with 34. Also illustrating the blend between calculations and interpretations, children gain a sense of expected results when using familiar procedures. Consider the question: Is 250 or 2,500 a better estimate of 51×49.? If you apply your elementary school mathematics, you realize that in multiplying two 2-digit whole numbers you derive a number that has four digits. With a calculator, pen and paper, or exceptional working memory, you can find the answer of 2,499, making 2,500 the far better estimate.

A manifestation of the connection between understandings and procedures involves *place value*. When children encounter arithmetic problems involving two-digit or larger numbers, and especially when the problems involve "carrying" or "borrowing" across columns, they must apply their knowledge of place value. As we discussed earlier, the idea that digits reflect different quantities depending on their column (whether they are in the ones column, tens column, and so on) is a fairly abstract one that many elementary school children struggle to understand (Byrge, Smith, & Mix, 2014; Fuson & Kwon, 1992). When children do not understand place value, they are apt to make errors when tackling problems that require carrying or borrowing. In Artifact 10-4, you can see mistakes made by two children who retrieve basic math facts but make errors in carrying and borrowing procedures. Such mistakes are less frequent when children not only know *how* to carry and borrow but also know *why* carrying and borrowing make sense.

Also fundamental to mathematical progress is the tie between constructing a mental number line and performing numerical operations. According to Robbie Case and his colleagues, children's development of a mental number line is foundational to their thinking about numbers and to their success in adding, subtracting, and comparing numbers (S. Griffin & Case, 1997).[8] In Case's model, children develop a mental framework called a *central conceptual structure* of numbers that guides numerical representations and operations. In this developmental process, children integrate what they know about numbers, counting, addition, subtraction, and place value into a mental model that guides their calculations (Bofferding, 2014; Case & Okamoto, 1996; Case, Okamoto, Henderson, & McKeough, 1993; Griffin, 2009; Griffin, Case, & Siegler, 1994).

In Case's view, 4-year-olds understand the difference between "a little" and "a lot" and recognize that adding objects leads to more items and subtracting objects leads to fewer items. Also, many 4-year-olds can accurately count a small set of objects and readily conclude that the last number they say is the total number of objects in the set (the cardinal principle). Thus 4-year-olds can visually compare a group of five objects with a group of six objects and tell you that the latter group contains more objects. Yet they cannot easily answer a question such as "Which is more, five or six?" because the question involves knowledge of counting and a more-versus-less comparison.

By the time children are 6 years old, they can answer simple "Which is more?" questions. Case proposed that at the age of 6, children have integrated their understanding of *more* and *less* with counting. Children's knowledge and reasoning about numbers now include several key elements:

- Children understand and can say the verbal numbers "one," "two," "three," and so on.
- They recognize the written numerals 1, 2, 3, and so on.

$$\begin{array}{r} 26 \\ +47 \\ \hline 613 \end{array} \qquad \begin{array}{r} 603 \\ -305 \\ \hline 208 \end{array}$$

ARTIFACT 10-4 **Arithmetic errors.** The child who solved the addition problem on the left simply put the sums of $6 + 7$ (13) and $2 + 4$ (6) side by side at the bottom. The child who solved the subtraction problem on the right apparently knew that borrowing was necessary to perform the subtraction in the ones column. Finding only a zero in the tens column, she instead borrowed "10" from the hundreds column. Thus, she subtracted $13 - 5$ in the ones column and $5 - 3$ in the hundreds column.

---

[8]Robbie Case was introduced as a neo-Piagetian theorist in Chapter 6.

- They have a systematic process for counting objects: They say each consecutive number as they touch each successive object in a group. Eventually, children count by mentally "tagging" (rather than physically touching) each object.
- They also use their fingers for representing small quantities (e.g., three fingers equals three objects). Their use of fingers for both counting objects and representing quantities may be a key means through which they integrate the two processes into a single conceptual structure.
- They equate movement toward higher numbers with such concepts as "a lot," "more," and "bigger." Similarly, they equate movement toward lower numbers with such concepts as "a little," "less," and "smaller."
- They understand that movement from one number to the next is equivalent to either adding one unit to the set or subtracting one unit from it, depending on the direction of movement.

In essence, the more comprehensive conceptual structure at age 6 forms a mental number line that facilitates execution of such processes as addition, subtraction, and comparisons of quantities. At age 8, Case proposed, children have sufficiently mastered this central conceptual structure such that they can begin using two mental number lines simultaneously to solve mathematical problems. They can now answer such questions as "Which number is bigger, 32 or 28?" and "Which number is closer to 25, 21 or 18?" Such questions require them to compare digits in both the ones column and tens column, with each comparison taking place along separate number lines. In addition, 8-year-olds presumably have a better understanding of operations that require transformations across columns, such as "carrying 1" to the tens column during addition or "borrowing 1" from the tens column during subtraction.

Finally, at about age 10, children become capable of generalizing the relationships between two number lines to the entire number system. They now understand how the various columns (ones, tens, hundreds, etc.) relate to one another and can expertly move back and forth among the columns. They can also treat the answers to mathematical problems as mental entities in and of themselves and so can answer such questions as "Which number is bigger, the difference between 29 and 13 or the difference between 25 and 8?" You can see how a child of this age might make this comparison in Figure 10-2.

Case did not track the development of children's central conceptual structure for number after age 10. He acknowledged, however, that children's understanding of numbers continues to develop well into adolescence. He pointed out that teenagers often have trouble with questions such as "What is a half of a third?" and suggested that their difficulty results from an incomplete understanding of division and the results (e.g., fractions) that it can yield.

Other researchers have obtained data on these later advancements. By the time students reach middle school, most are relatively proficient in solving simple arithmetic problems with whole numbers (Byrnes, 1996; Carr, 2012). As they move through the middle school and high school grades, much of the math curriculum involves procedures for working with proportions, negative numbers, roots, exponents (e.g., $\sqrt{18}$, 4^3), and unknown variables (e.g., x, y). Students must shift their conception of the number line from discrete values into it being continuous, infinite, and inclusive of fractions, decimals, and negative numbers. This transition turns out to be quite challenging for some students, who fail to integrate rational numbers (fractions and decimals) into their concept of numbers. These struggling students have trouble envisioning where fractions and decimals belong on the number line and do not grasp why multiplying certain fractions produces a smaller number (Carr, 2012).

In middle school and high school, students encounter further challenges in algebra, trigonometry, and calculus. With algebra, continued difficulty in seeing fractions and numbers with decimals as points on the number line can interfere with progress, as can failure to grasp the meaning of variables and functions. Some students focus on solving a particular value for x when the formula in which x appears represents a succinct way for showing the slope and intercept in an array of data points (Carr, 2012). Yet plugging in one value for x provides only a glimpse into the pattern the formula represents.

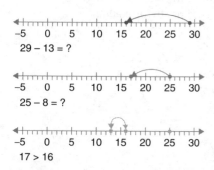

FIGURE 10-2 Which number is bigger, 29 − 13 or 25 − 8? In Robbie Case's theory, children need to solve the two subtraction problems separately and then compare the answers, a process that is facilitated by a mental representation of number lines and a mental capacity to keep the various components of the task in mind. Facility with mental number lines is especially helpful as the numbers being compared become larger and the calculations more complex. (The two subtraction problems yield answers of 16 and 13, respectively, which means the first equation yields the larger number.)

As you are learning, advanced proficiency in mathematics requires young people to *make sense of* procedures, rather than simply apply them in a rote fashion. In fact, understanding of advanced mathematical procedures is closely tied to comprehension of rudimentary mathematical principles, in much the same way that understanding of addition and subtraction is closely connected to mastery of numbers and counting (Geary, 1994; Hecht, Close, & Santisi, 2003; N. C. Jordan, Glutting, & Ramineni, 2010). When children *cannot* make sense of mathematical procedures—perhaps because they haven't yet mastered the abstract concepts on which the procedures are based or perhaps because no one has shown them why certain manipulations are mathematically logical—they are apt to use the procedures incorrectly and fail to see applications to real-world problems.

Metacognition in Mathematics

Metacognition is an essential element in mathematical accomplishment, especially as students progress to advanced material. Not only do youngsters need to understand what they're doing when they tackle mathematical problems, they also need to plan, monitor, and assess their problem-solving efforts.

Several different metacognitive abilities are worthwhile to learn. Checking the accuracy of basic calculations is an important step that children do not always think to follow unless urged to do so by teachers (Okita, 2014). Metacognitive oversight also includes setting goals for a problem-solving task, monitoring the effectiveness of problem-solving strategies, and evaluating a final solution to determine whether it's a logical one (Cardelle-Elawar, 1992; Desoete, 2009; L. S. Fuchs et al., 2003). Only a child who reflects on his or her problem-solving efforts will recognize that a sum of 613 is *not* a reasonable answer to the problem 26 + 47.

When students are asked to engage in metacognitive processes, they focus on how they know what they are doing and what their mathematical work really means (Carr, 2010). When approaching story problems, students can circle important phrases and graph relationships (Pennequin, Sorel, Nanty, & Fontaine, 2010). When explaining how and why they solved a problem, students gain insights into what they do and do not understand. For instance, as students articulate their rationales for solving double-digit additional problems in a particular way, they develop a greater appreciation for place value (Carr, 2012; J. Hiebert & Wearne, 1992).

Bioecology of Mathematics Development

Virtually all children are born with the capacity to detect variations in quantity. But youngsters differ considerably in the ways they go about learning mathematics, the specific purposes for which they see mathematics being used around them, and the kind of instruction they receive in this subject.

Some children grasp challenging mathematics principles in a seemingly effortless fashion. A few children have learning disabilities that impede their abilities to understand number concepts, automatize math facts, and solve simple arithmetic problems quickly—disabilities that in an extreme form are known as **dyscalculia** (R. Cowan & Powell, 2014; N. C. Jordan, Hanich, & Kaplan, 2003; Mussolin, Mejias, & Noël, 2010; Reigosa-Crespo et al., 2012). Dyscalculia is present in children who struggle to learn basic arithmetic and prefer to use finger counting of small numbers well into middle childhood. For most individuals with serious delays in mathematics, this condition is probably at least partly neurologically based.

Gender differences in mathematics exist but are smaller than many people believe. Some researchers find a slight advantage for one gender or the other depending on the age-group, cultural setting, and task in question (Else-Quest, Hyde, & Linn, 2010; A. M. Gallagher & Kaufman, 2005). However, boys show greater *variability* in math. More boys than girls have very high mathematical ability, especially in high school, and more boys than girls have significant disabilities in this subject (Else-Quest et al., 2010; Forgasz & Hill, 2013; Halpern et al., 2007; Reigosa-Crespo et al., 2012). The prevalence of adolescent males at the upper end of the math-ability continuum may be partly due to biology, and in particular to sex-related hormones (e.g., testosterone) that differentially affect brain development before and after puberty (Halpern, 1992; Hegarty & Kozhevnikov, 1999; Lippa, 2002). One area in which these hormones come into play is in the development of **visual-spatial ability**, the

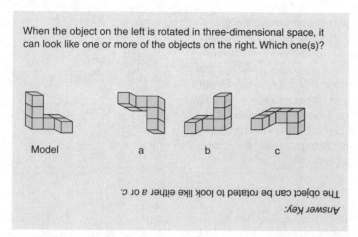

When the object on the left is rotated in three-dimensional space, it can look like one or more of the objects on the right. Which one(s)?

Model   a   b   c

Answer Key:
The object can be rotated to look like either *a* or *c*.

FIGURE 10-3 Example of a task requiring visual-spatial ability.
Task modeled after Shepard & Metzler, 1971.

capacity to imagine and mentally manipulate two- and three-dimensional figures (see Figure 10-3). On average, boys and men perform better than girls and women on such measures, which gives them an advantage in certain kinds of mathematical tasks (Bull, Cleland, & Mitchell, 2013; Halpern et al., 2007; Hoppe et al., 2012).

Yet environmental factors also play a part in gender differences in mathematics. In many Western societies, mathematics has historically been viewed as a "male" domain more suitable for boys than girls. Some parents and teachers absorb this stereotype and expect boys to do better than girls in mathematics and offer them more encouragement (Bleeker & Jacobs, 2004; Espinoza, Arêas da Luz Fontes, & Arms-Chavez, 2014; Robinson-Cimpian, Lubienski, Ganley, & Copur-Gencturk, 2014; Tiedemann, 2000). Perhaps partly as a result of such differential treatment, boys tend to express greater confidence about their mathematical ability, even when actual achievement levels for the two genders have been similar, with this difference emerging as early as first grade (Lindberg, Linkersdörfer, Ehm, Hasselhorn, & Lonnemann, 2013; Vermeer, Boekaerts, & Seegers, 2000).

Cultural practices and resources also determine certain experiences with mathematics. For instance, 10- to 12-year-old candy sellers in Brazil are able to solve arithmetic and ratio problems with large numerical values, presumably due to their many experiences in calculating change and determining profits and losses in the marketplace (Saxe, 1988). Cultural practices in schools also affect mathematical competencies. Asian teachers are apt to provide thorough explanations of mathematical concepts, focus classroom discussions on making sense of problem-solving procedures, foster the coherence of children's knowledge of mathematics, and assign a lot of math homework (Cai, Ding, & Wang, 2014; Schleppenbach, Perry, Miller, Sims, & Fang, 2007; J. Wang & Lin, 2005).

Curiously, even the terminology for numbers in a native language can influence mathematical development. Many theorists speculate that the structure of number words in Asian languages (Chinese, Japanese, Korean) facilitates children's mathematical development (Fuson & Kwon, 1992; K. F. Miller, Smith, Zhu, & Zhang, 1995; Miura & Okamoto, 2003). In these languages the base-10 number system is clearly reflected in number words. The word for 11 is literally "ten-one," the word for 12 is "ten-two," and the word for 21 is "two-ten-one." Furthermore, words for fractions reflect what a fraction *is*. For example, the word for ¼ is literally "of four parts, one." In contrast, English has many number words (e.g., *eleven, twelve, thirteen, twenty, thirty, one-half, one-fourth*) that don't reveal much about number structure.

With well-designed education, children around the world evolve from intuitive observers of simple mathematical patterns into disciplined thinkers who adeptly handle abstract mathematical relations. The Developmental Trends table "Mathematics at Different Age Levels" characterizes some of the mathematical abilities commonly seen in infants, children, and adolescents.

Promoting Development in Mathematics

Mathematical tools, many of which must be taught, help children make sense of numerical patterns. We offer the following suggestions for teachers to help children make steady progress in mathematics:

• **Teach preschool and kindergarten children to count and recognize numbers.** These basic competencies form the foundation of virtually every aspect of mathematics. Adults can arrange activities involving counting, comparing quantities, adding, and subtracting, especially for children who face delays or have not had relevant experiences at home (Bird, 2009; Ginsburg, Lee, & Boyd, 2008). In preschool, children can count small blocks, steps on a stairs, apple slices on the table, and the like. In kindergarten, children can count and compare numbers in well-designed board games and other structured tasks (Laski & Siegler, 2014).

DEVELOPMENTAL TRENDS
Mathematics at Different Age Levels

AGE	WHAT YOU MIGHT OBSERVE	DIVERSITY	IMPLICATIONS
Infancy (Birth–2 Years)	• Some awareness that adding or subtracting something affects quantity (appearing at around 5 months) • Rudimentary ability to discriminate among different proportions (by 6 months) • Discrimination between changing states that show increases versus decreases in amount	• Some toddlers are familiar with small-number words (e.g., *two*, *three*), usually because their parents use the words often. • Children with visual impairments may have fewer chances to make more-versus-less comparisons.	• Use small-number words (e.g., *two*, *three*) when talking with infants if doing so makes sense in the interaction. • Provide age-appropriate toys that encourage children to focus on size or quantity (e.g., nesting cups, stacking blocks). • Count objects in front of the infant and use comparative words for size (e.g., *small* and *big*).
Early Childhood (2–6 Years)	• Conscious understandings that adding objects results in an increase and removing objects results in a decrease (by age 2½ or 3) • Initial attempts at counting (at around age 3) • Increasing ability to count correctly (perhaps to 50 by age 5) • Emergence of self-constructed strategies for addition and subtraction (e.g., using fingers to count) • Some familiarity with division in everyday sharing tasks	• On average, children from middle-income families begin counting earlier than peers from low-income families. • On average, Chinese children learn to count at a younger age than children whose native language is English. The more "transparent" nature of Chinese number words is thought to be partly responsible for this difference. • At age 5, Chinese- and Japanese-speaking children typically have a better grasp of place value than do English-speaking children.	• Occasionally ask mathematical questions (e.g., "How many are there?" "Where's the triangle?"). • In storybook reading sessions, occasionally read books with counting activities (e.g., *The Icky Bug Counting Book*, Pallotta & Masiello, 1992). • Use concrete manipulatives to facilitate counting and simple addition and subtraction. • Count steps, leaves, apple slices, and other common actions and objects.
Middle Childhood (6–10 Years)	• Increasing ability to count correctly into the hundreds and beyond • Acquisition of more efficient addition and subtraction strategies, including retrieval of number facts • Increasing mastery of multiplication and division strategies • Growing understanding of place value and its relevance to carrying and borrowing • Some understanding of simple fractions • Increasing ability to solve word problems	• Children vary considerably in strategies. Some 8-year-olds have basic arithmetic facts automatized, whereas others rely heavily on fingers. • Children who speak certain Asian languages generally master multidigit addition and subtraction earlier than English-speaking children. • Some children have difficulty inhibiting ideas about whole numbers when multiplying fractions and decimals, expecting that multiplication will always generate larger numbers. • Some children dislike math, typically because they have become frustrated in efforts to understand it.	• Help children understand the logic underlying basic mathematical procedures (e.g., show the relevance of the concept of *place value* in carrying and borrowing). • Provide frequent practice in basic arithmetic as a way of promoting automaticity. • Use number lines as a way of helping children understand how numbers of various kinds relate to one another. • Have low-achieving fourth and fifth graders tutor first and second graders in basic arithmetic skills.
Early Adolescence (10–14 Years)	• Increasing ability to understand abstract concepts (e.g., π, *variable*) • Growing understanding of and facility with proportions • Some naive beliefs about mathematics (e.g., that it involves memorizing procedures without necessarily understanding them)	• Young adolescents who have not yet automatized basic arithmetic facts are apt to struggle when encountering challenging mathematical problems. • Some adolescents overgeneralize their knowledge about whole numbers to problems involving fractions and decimals. • Adolescents vary widely in their comprehension of abstract mathematical concepts.	• Conduct small-group activities in which students compare and explain multiple approaches to solving a single problem. • Teach metacognitive strategies for solving problems (e.g., identify the goal to be achieved, break a complex problem into smaller steps, consider whether the solution is reasonable).

(continued)

DEVELOPMENTAL TRENDS (continued)

AGE	WHAT YOU MIGHT OBSERVE	DIVERSITY	IMPLICATIONS
Late Adolescence (14–18 Years)	• Increasing facility with abstract concepts and principles (e.g., unknowns such as *x* and *y*) • Difficulty translating word problems into algebraic expressions • Tendency for teens to memorize and carelessly apply mathematical procedures, rather than reflecting on the procedures	• Individual differences in abilities increase in the high school years, due both to "tracking" according to students' past achievement and the prevalence of elective mathematics courses. • On average, girls have less confidence about their ability to do mathematics even when they achieve at the same level as boys.	• Ask teenagers to apply their math skills to real-life contexts and problems. • Allow teens to use calculators with complex mathematical operations so as to allow them to devote working memory capacity to the overall problem-solving effort. • Minimize competition for high grades (this strategy is especially important for girls).

Sources: C. Björklund, 2014; Brannon, 2002; Bull & Lee, 2014; Byrge et al., 2014; Byrne & Shavelson, 1986; Cardelle-Elawar, 1992; Carr & Biddlecomb, 1998; Case & Okamoto, 1996; J. B. Cooney & Ladd, 1992; Davenport et al., 1998; De Corte, Greer, & Verschaffel, 1996; Eccles, Freedman-Doan, Frome, Jacobs, & Yoon, 2000; Empson, 1999; Fuson & Kwon, 1992; Gallistel & Gelman, 1992; Geary, 2006; Ginsburg et al., 2006; Greeno, Collins, & Resnick, 1996; C. S. Ho & Fuson, 1998; Klibanoff, Levine, Huttenlocher, Vasilyeva, & Hedges, 2006; Krasa & Shunkwiler, 2009; McCrink & Wynn, 2004; K. Miller, 1989; Schoenfeld, 1988; Siegler & Jenkins, 1989; Van Dooren et al., 2005; Wynn, 1990; F. Xu & Spelke, 2000; Zamarian, Ischebeck, & Delazer 2009.

• **Use manipulatives and visual displays to connect mathematical concepts with concrete reality.** Manipulatives (beans, blocks, Cuisenaire rods, toothpicks bundled in groups of 10 and 100, etc.) can help children grasp the nature of addition, subtraction, place value, and fractions (C. Björklund, 2014; Fujimura, 2001; Fuson & Briars, 1990). Visual aids such as number lines and pictures of pizzas depicting fractions can be instructive in the early elementary grades, and graphs and diagrams of geometric figures can facilitate understanding for secondary students (J. L. Schwartz, Yarushalmy, & Wilson, 1993; Steenpaβ & Steinbring, 2014). For more advanced mathematics, such as calculus, teachers can explain how concepts are relevant in physics, engineering, and computer science and show graphs with rates of change. Because visual displays do not automatically instill understanding, an explanation of the underlying relationships is typically needed.

• **Encourage visual-spatial thinking.** Although boys may have a biological advantage in visual-spatial thinking, structured experiences that *encourage* such representations can help bring girls up to speed (Nuttall, Casey, & Pezaris, 2005; Sprafkin, Serbin, Denier, and Connor, 1983; Wilhelm, Jackson, Sullivan, & Wilhelm, 2013). In the preschool and early elementary grades, such experiences might involve blocks, Legos, puzzles, simple graphs, and basic measurement tools. As children move into the middle elementary grades and beyond, visual-spatial tasks might include analysis of complex graphs and three-dimensional geometry (Nuttall et al., 2005; Sandamas, Foreman, & Coulson, 2009; von Károlyi, 2013).

• **Provide the scaffolding children need to find successful solutions to challenging problems.** Complex mathematical tasks put a strain on the child's working memory, concentration, and ability to shift strategies as necessary (Bull & Lee, 2014; H. L. Swanson, Jerman, & Zheng, 2008). Fortunately, a variety of tools are available to ease the burden. For children in the early elementary grades, such tools include manipulatives and pencil and paper for keeping track of quantities, calculations, and other information. Once children have mastered basic mathematical facts and understand the logic behind arithmetic operations, they might use calculators or computers while working with large numbers or cumbersome data sets (Horowitz, Darling-Hammond, & Bransford, 2005). Cognitive scaffolds are valuable as well. A teacher might encourage students to brainstorm possible approaches to problems, model new problem-solving strategies, and teach techniques for checking progress (Calin-Jageman & Ratner, 2005; W. Chen, Rovegno, Cone, & Cone, 2012). When teaching algebra, a teacher might ask a student a conceptually focused question about how the *x* intercepts of a graph are related to factors in an equation instead of simply asking the student to solve the equation (Rakes, Valentine, McGatha, & Ronau, 2010).

• **Arrange for children to apply mathematical tools in service to the community.** Some students enjoy the pure elegance of mathematical patterns, but others find mathematical proficiencies to be motivating to the degree that they see them in use. In fact, many children find mathematics appealing when they can integrate data into reports that serve the public good. Children can be asked to chart survey responses, measure water quality, and do other things to better conditions for people, animals, or the environment. These activities may be particularly effective for groups that are typically under-represented in scientific, mathematical, and engineering fields (Bystydzienski & Brown, 2012; D. Cross et al., 2012).

• **Supplement teacher-led lessons and hands-on activities with interactive technologies.** Several features of mathematics make it an appealing subject to reinforce with educational technology: Practice is essential at all levels of expertise, several mathematical concepts can be portrayed with visual charts and demonstrations, concepts must be learned in a prescribed order, and individual differences of children's achievement are sizable. An increasing number of well-designed computer programs address these features with individualized instruction and lessons that include diagnostic assessments and ample visual displays (A. Cheung & Slavin, 2013).

• **Encourage children to invent, use, and defend their own strategies.** As you have seen, young children often invent approaches (e.g., the *min* strategy) for adding and subtracting objects well before they have formal instruction in addition and subtraction. Rather than ignore methods children have developed on their own, teachers can encourage those that seem to be effective. As children acquire more efficient strategies over time, they will gradually abandon more primitive ones (Geary, 1994; Siegler, 1989). Also beneficial is asking children to reflect on and explain in writing why they solved a problem as they did (Carr & Biddlecomb, 1998; Rittle-Johnson, 2006). In Artifact 10-5, you can see Noah's explanations as to how he solved a subtraction problem.

ARTIFACT 10-5 354 – 298. Children can often benefit by explaining their solutions. In this assignment, Noah explains what he did when he solved a subtraction problem.

The Nature of Science

Scientists use certain steps, for example, formulating questions, separating and controlling variables, testing hypotheses, making observations, and thinking through why certain results are obtained. With disciplined adherence to these procedures, scientists identify and explain regularities in the world. For children, learning about science involves being mentored into theory construction and scientific reasoning.

Children's Theories about Scientific Phenomena

In studying children's scientific knowledge, many developmental theorists take a *theory theory* approach, in which children are presumed to construct (rather than absorb) a body of information about physics, biology, or other domains (Gopnik & Meltzoff, 1997).[9] These intuitive understandings appear early in life and change systematically as children encounter new information. Definite ideas about properties of objects and motion are shown by infants between 2 and 5 months, in that they demonstrate expectations that an object maintains its existence and shape as it moves, that two objects cannot occupy the same space at the same time, and that one object can influence another object only when the two come into contact (Baillargeon, 2004; T. L. Hubbard, 2013; Spelke, 1994).

Such early understandings are consistent with classical principles of physics. As children get older and gain more experience with the physical world, they construct increasingly elaborate theories about physical entities. Many school-age children view all physical phenomena either as actual substances (i.e., touchable "things" that have specific locations) or as properties of those substances (e.g., being hot or cold; Reiner, Slotta, Chi, & Resnick, 2000). This **substance schema** can be quite useful in explaining everyday events (e.g., holding a ball, touching a stove). Yet children overgeneralize it to such phenomena as light, which scientists acknowledge can be thought of taking the form of waves of particles, but which does not have the same type of matter as tangible objects (Megalakaki, 2008; Reiner et al., 2000).

[9]See Chapter 7 if you need a refresher about *theory theory*.

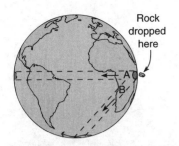

FIGURE 10-4 Which way? If a rock is dropped into a hole near the equator, into which of the two tunnels will it fall?

Another idea that children acquire quite early but eventually overapply is the concept of *gravity*. At three or four months of age, children have some understanding that objects fall down (never up) when there is nothing to support them (Baillargeon, 1994). This "downward" view of gravity works quite well on a small scale. But imagine the situation depicted in Figure 10-4. A rock is dropped at the equator, at the entrances to two tunnels that go through the earth. Tunnel A comes out at the equator on the opposite side of the earth. Tunnel B comes out at the South Pole. Into which tunnel will the rock fall? Many middle school students say that the rock will fall into Tunnel B, apparently thinking that gravity always pulls something "down." They respond in this way even if they have explicitly learned that gravity pulls objects toward the center of the earth (Pulos, 1997).

One important step in children's early theory building is making a distinction between biological and nonbiological entities. By the time infants are 6 months old, most are aware that people and other animals move in ways that nonliving things do not. By age 3 or 4, children know that humans and other animals, but not nonliving objects, can move *themselves,* and that living and nonliving entities change in different ways—living things grow, and nonliving things may increase in size but do not change with physiological processes (Jipson & Callanan, 2003; Massey & Gelman, 1988). At about age 4, children also realize that two living creatures in the same category, even if they look quite different, are apt to share characteristics—for instance, that a blackbird has more in common with a flamingo (because both are birds) than it does with a bat (S. A. Gelman & Markman, 1986). By the middle elementary school years, children understand that both plants and animals are defined largely by their genetic heritage and internal makeup—for instance, that round, reddish fruits that come from pear trees must be pears rather than apples.

With experience and instruction, children make further distinctions within domains. Many teachers are aware of children's naive theories and arrange lessons that challenge children to develop scientific insights into relevant phenomena. Instructional methods for facilitating conceptual change in science vary somewhat by students' ages. In the preschool years, children need a wide berth in exploring the sensory world. Young children watch water pouring through funnels and contrasting qualities with sand, which when carefully mounded and patted, forms hills and valleys, turrets and towers. Teachers extend children's scientific knowledge by providing age-appropriate materials, bringing nature into the classroom, asking children to sort and classify objects, and encouraging children to articulate their observations (Moomaw, 2013).

If carefully supported, young children merge, and sometimes replace, rudimentary scientific concepts with their intuitive understandings of physics and biology. What is needed in this transition is a lot of discussion, informal guidance, focused observations, and scientific themes integrated into materials over time (National Science Teachers Association, 2014). Children might study light and shadows, plants, magnetism, animals, or the seasons over a several-week period, making simple measures and looking for patterns (Piasta, Pelatti, & Miller, 2014). Adults can guide the observations that children make with systematic materials, forms for recording observations, discussions about evidence, and scientific explanations.

In the elementary school years, children continue to be interested in scientific phenomena, especially in the natural world. Living and nonliving things, first distinguished in infancy, are differentiated further. Living things are now seen to include plants, not just animals; nonliving things include rocks, swing sets, imaginary friends, dead animals, and all sorts of other things (Carey, 1988; Opfer & Siegler, 2004). At school, children are exposed to parts of the body and to some degree internal physiological structures and processes, life cycles, and basic needs (Elmesky, 2013). Children enjoy learning about astronomy (e.g., about phases of the moon, the structure of the earth, and the composition of the sun), especially when teachers organize meaningful observations accompanied by flashlights, three-dimensional glasses, miniature solar systems, posters, and the like (Isik-Ercan, Zeynep Inan, Nowak, & Kim, 2014). Classification skills are exercised in all sorts of lessons—from grouping similar birds by type of beak to distinguishing objects that are attracted to magnets from those that are not. Basic reasoning about evidence and couching observations in scientific terms is now possible and instructive (Elmesky, 2013).

In the secondary years, science is more technical, and topics in current affairs influence what adolescents want to learn. For example, reproductive technologies and climate change are regularly covered in the media and intrigue students, even though these topics may not be addressed at school (H. Morris, 2014). With the help of charts, pictures, microscopes, and other instruments, adolescents can learn about small structures, for example, cells, molecules, and atoms (Elmesky, 2013). With adequate explanations and supportive information, students can understand how complicated systems function (e.g., the circulatory system in the human body).

A major challenge for secondary science teachers is protecting sufficient time to incorporate demonstrations, compare rival explanations, and generate reflection in students in the context of the enormous volume of facts that awaits them. In fact, students generally forget the scientific facts, laws, and summaries of theories they studied unless given the chance to wrestle with relevant observations, data, and the implications of evidence for explanatory models (Akbaş & Gençtürk, 2011; Kaya & Geban, 2012; Kuhn, 2011).

Scientific Reasoning Skills

Even in the first year of life children are predisposed to identify cause-and-effect relationships in the world around them. But children's ability to think as scientists appears much later, and then only gradually. **Scientific reasoning** encompasses a number of cognitive processes, including posing a question, planning an investigation, analyzing evidence, and drawing appropriate conclusions (Kuhn & Franklin, 2006; D. Mayer, Sodian, Koerber, & Schwippert, 2014). Common to the steps of the scientific method is a conscious intention to acquire and evaluate new knowledge.

The capacities to formulate hypotheses and separate and control variables while testing these propositions emerge gradually over the course of middle childhood and adolescence. Formulating hypotheses depends on at least two things that change with age: (a) the ability to think about abstract and potentially contrary-to-fact ideas, and (b) a knowledge base that can help a person generate a *variety* of ideas. Elementary schoolchildren often distinguish between experiments that do and do not control variables appropriately, yet they are apt to have trouble controlling variables in their *own* experiments—a task that requires them to keep track of several things simultaneously (Kuhn, Pease, & Wirkala, 2009; Metz, 2004). With instruction and practice, children can begin to learn this crucial feature of the scientific method (Lazonder & Egberink, 2014; Lorch et al., 2014).

Although adolescents are more proficient than elementary schoolchildren in separating and controlling variables, they do have difficulty in identifying influential factors (Kuhn, Amsel, & O'Loughlin, 1988; Pei-Ying, Sufen, Huey-Por, & Wen-Hua Chang, 2013). Furthermore, in their hypothesis testing, adolescents tend to test hypotheses they think are correct and ignore hypotheses that, in their minds, are *in*correct (Byrnes, 1996). Such *try-to-prove-what-I-already-believe* thinking reflects a *confirmation bias*. A confirmation bias refers to the tendency of people to favor information that is consistent with what they already believe and appears not only when adolescents test hypotheses but also when they interpret their data (Klaczynski, 2000; Kuhn et al., 1988; Kyza, 2009). In general, adolescents tend to overlook results that conflict with their favorite hypotheses and explain away unexpected results that they *cannot* ignore. For example, when students in a high school science laboratory observe results that contradict what they expected to happen, they might complain that "Our equipment isn't working right" or "I can never do science anyway" (Minstrell & Stimpson, 1996, p. 192).

Metacognition in Science

Ultimately, children must discover that science is, like other disciplines, a dynamic body of ideas that evolve as new data come in. They must also be able to reflect on and critically evaluate their own beliefs. And, of course, they must be willing to change their views in the face of disconfirming evidence. Such understandings, abilities, and dispositions emerge gradually over childhood and adolescence (Gillies, Nichols, Burgh, & Haynes, 2014; Kuhn & Pearsall, 2000; C. Zimmerman, 2007). Giuliana, an eighth grader, reveals beliefs about the evolving nature of scientific views:

> When the atom was discovered, it was considered the smallest particle, but now the quark's been discovered. What we believed before, now we don't believe anymore because the quark is smaller. Perhaps in fifty years' time an even smaller particle will turn up and then we'll be told that what we believed in before was false. It's really something to do with progress. (Mason, 2003, p. 223)

Youngsters' beliefs about science affect the approaches they take when they study. Students who believe that "knowing" science means understanding the connections between concepts and related evidence are going to study and learn more effectively than students who think that learning science means acquiring isolated facts (M. C. Linn, Songer, & Eylon, 1996; Yang & Tsai, 2010). And students who recognize that scientific theories inevitably change over time are more likely to evaluate theories (including their own) with a critical eye (Bereiter, 1994; M. C. Linn et al., 1996).

As you have been learning, scientific development reflects transformations in reasoning skills, ideas about everyday phenomena, and reflections about the nature of science. The Developmental Trends table "Science at Different Age Levels" presents examples of the scientific knowledge and reasoning you are apt to see in infancy, childhood, and adolescence.

DEVELOPMENTAL TRENDS
Science at Different Age Levels

AGE	WHAT YOU MIGHT OBSERVE	DIVERSITY	IMPLICATIONS
Infancy (Birth–2 Years)	• Knowledge of a few basic principles of physics (e.g., two objects cannot occupy the same space at the same time) • Emerging awareness that humans and animals are fundamentally different from nonliving things • Emerging ability to infer cause-and-effect relationships	• Infants differ in the number and diversity of opportunities to explore objects and surroundings. • Infants with sensory impairments (e.g., blindness, hearing loss) are more limited in the scientific phenomena they can observe unless adults intervene with sensory-adapted materials.	• Put infants and toddlers in contexts in which they can safely explore and experiment with physical objects. • Let toddlers interact with small, gentle animals (e.g., rabbits, cocker spaniels) under your close supervision.
Early Childhood (2–6 Years)	• Increasing differentiation between living and nonliving things (e.g., awareness that living things grow due to intrinsic physiological processes and nonliving things change in other ways) • Increasing understanding that members of a biological category (e.g., *birds*) share characteristics despite differences in appearance • Naive beliefs about the solar system (e.g., the earth is flat)	• Children in some cultures (e.g., Japanese children) are more likely to think of plants and nonliving objects as having "minds." • Children who grow up in inner-city environments may have little exposure to life cycles (e.g., calves being born, trees losing leaves in the fall and growing blossoms in the spring).	• Read nonfiction picture books that depict wild and domesticated animals. • Take children to zoos, farms, arboretums, and other settings where they can see a variety of animals and plants. • Talk with children about natural phenomena, pointing out the physical properties of objects (e.g., some objects float and others sink). • Engage children in simple hands-on investigations of natural phenomena.
Middle Childhood (6–10 Years)	• Intuitive understanding that biological entities are defined by their genetic heritage and internal makeup • Tendency to think of all physical phenomena as having a physical and potentially touchable substance • Some ability to discriminate between valid and invalid tests of hypotheses	• Children differ in their early exposure to scientific concepts (e.g., through family visits to natural history museums and access to age-appropriate science books). • Some children are apt to view supernatural forces (e.g., God, the devil, witchcraft) as being responsible for natural disasters or illness.	• Have children conduct simple experiments with familiar materials; for example, have them raise sunflowers with varying amounts of light and water. • Obtain computer programs that let students "explore" human anatomy or "dissect" small animals in a virtual "laboratory." • Discuss scientific explanations for everyday observations.
Early Adolescence (10–14 Years)	• Some ability to think abstractly about scientific phenomena and to separate and control variables • Formulation and testing of hypotheses influenced by existing beliefs (confirmation bias) • Some tendency to misapply scientific concepts (e.g., thinking that gravity pulls objects toward the South Pole)	• Especially in adolescence, boys tend to have more positive attitudes toward science than do girls. Girls are more likely than boys to underestimate their scientific abilities. • Influences of religion on beliefs about natural phenomena (e.g., evolution) are noticeable in early adolescence.	• Have adolescents explore individual interests in science fair projects, scaffolding their efforts at forming hypotheses and controlling irrelevant variables. • Provide scientific explanations that are sufficiently concrete that young adolescents can understand and apply them.

DEVELOPMENTAL TRENDS (continued)

AGE	WHAT YOU MIGHT OBSERVE	DIVERSITY	IMPLICATIONS
Late Adolescence (14–18 Years)	• Growing ability to understand abstract scientific concepts • Increasing skill in separating and controlling variables • Confirmation bias in experimentation and interpretation of results • Increasing awareness that science is a dynamic and changing discipline	• On average, boys achieve at higher levels in the physical sciences, but the gender gap in science achievement has decreased in recent years. • Boys are more likely than girls to aspire to careers in science. • Cultures that place high value on honoring authority figures tend to promote the belief that scientific findings should not be questioned except insofar as they are disputed by religious doctrine.	• Gradually introduce abstract explanations for phenomena, such as the idea that heat results from molecules colliding. • To increase girls' interest and involvement in science, occasionally form same-gender groups in science labs and activities. • Arrange internships for students with scientists from diverse ethnic and cultural backgrounds.

Sources: Baillargeon, 1994; Bandura, Barbaranelli, Caprara, & Pastorelli, 2001; L. B. Cohen & Cashon, 2006; E. M. Evans, 2001; S. A. Gelman & Markman, 1986; Halpern et al., 2007; Hatano & Inagaki, 1996; Jipson & Callanan, 2003; Klaczynski, 2000; Kuhn et al., 2009; Larrain, Freire, & Howe, 2014; Leaper & Friedman, 2007; Lee-Pearce, Plowman, & Touchstone, 1998; M. C. Linn & Muilenburg, 1996; Massey & Gelman, 1988; Metz, 2004; Piasta, Pelatti, & Miller, 2014; Pomerantz, Altermatt, & Saxon, 2002; Pulos, 1997; Qian & Pan, 2002; Reiner et al., 2000; M. B. Rowe, 1978; Schauble, 1990; Spelke, 1994; Stanovich, West, & Toplak, 2012; Tamburrini, 1982; Ullman, 2010a; Vosniadou, 1991; B. Y. White & Frederiksen, 1998; Wigfield et al., 1996.

Bioecology of Science Development

The bioecological framework reveals that children contribute to their own science development by exploring the particular environments in which they live. Influential personal characteristics include interests, temperaments, abilities, and disabilities. Youngsters with sensory impairments have restricted experience in observing certain scientific phenomena firsthand, unless of course adults supplement their exposure. For example, when a reference is made to the color of burning wood, a perceptive teacher might tell a child who is blind how wood changes in appearance in fire (M. B. Rowe, 1978).

As is true with mathematics, science-related fields, especially physical science and engineering, have traditionally been regarded as "male" domains (Halpern et al., 2007; Marchand & Taasoobshirazi, 2013; Ullman, 2010a). Perhaps for this reason, boys tend to like science more than girls do, and they are more likely to aspire to careers in science (Bandura et al., 2001). On average, girls get higher grades in science than boys do, but boys tend to come out slightly ahead on national science achievement tests, especially in the physical sciences (Halpern et al., 2007; Leaper & Friedman, 2007). Yet with encouragement and exposure to women in scientific and technological fields and classes that build on their interests, girls are able and motivated to achieve in these areas (Ullman, 2010a).

The bioecological framework reminds us that ideas about scientific topics learned by the child in one context affect his or her interpretation of related views in another setting (Simpson & Parsons, 2008). In one school in northern California, teachers invited children and parents who came from a predominantly Mien (Laotian) background to plant a garden and build a garden house at the school (Hammond, 2001). Families had extensive technological expertise from previous experiences in hunting, farming, preserving food, building houses, producing fabrics, forging metals, and creating elaborate jewelry. The Mien parents and children applied many of their indigenous abilities in planting the garden and building the house, creating a basis for discussion about scientific matters and motivating their attendance at family science nights.

Cultural environments shape many other beliefs about the biological and physical worlds. Japanese children are more likely than European American children to think of plants (e.g., a tree, a blade of grass) and certain nonliving objects as having some sort of "mind" that thinks (M. Cole & Hatano, 2007; Hatano & Inagaki, 1996). In another example, schools in China encourage respect for authority figures and downplay differences of opinion among experts. Possibly as a result, high school students in China are more likely than U.S. students to believe that science involves simple, undisputed facts rather than evolving perspectives about unresolved issues (Qian & Pan, 2002).

Religion comes into play for some youngsters as they develop ideas about the origins of life, the universe, and the ultimate causes of events. In the elementary grades, some children think that supernatural forces (e.g., God, the devil, witchcraft) are largely responsible for illness or natural disasters (O. Lee, 1999; Legare, Evans, Rosengren, & Harris, 2012).

Young people's acceptance or rejection of Darwin's theory of evolution is closely connected to their religious and philosophical positions about how living creatures came into existence (E. M. Evans, 2001; Yasri & Mancy, 2014). Teachers of course should not challenge students' religious beliefs, but they can advise students about compelling evidence related to scientific theories (Hanley, Bennett, & Ratcliffe, 2014).

Promoting Development in Science

In the first few years of life, children's science "education" takes the form of informal experiences. At this point, the best strategy is to provide objects and experiences—blocks, water tables, sand piles, field trips to farms and zoos, and so on—that help children acquire general knowledge on which more formal science instruction can later build. As we discussed previously, scaffolding with observations, classification of objects, and preliminary discussions about scientific concepts can be instructive in early childhood.

Once children reach kindergarten or first grade, the curriculum includes a few science topics. As we've seen, children's scientific reasoning capabilities and their ability to separate and control variables are limited. Yet even at the elementary level, it is counterproductive to portray science as primarily a collection of facts. By having students engage in simple investigations almost from the very beginning of schooling, children gain experiences unraveling mysteries in the world (Forsey, 2014; Khalid, 2010; Kuhn, 2007). As they proceed through elementary, middle, and high school, students ideally encounter numerous chances to make observations, practice scientific skills, and update their understandings as they reflect on evidence and formal scientific theories. Several instructional strategies facilitate scientific advancements:

• **Show children the relevance of science to what they already know.** Students are more likely to understand scientific concepts when teachers create a bridge between the formal curriculum and what children already understand. Depending on the age of students, teachers might ask children to draw pictures of concepts (e.g., on plant growth); talk about what they *know*, *want* to learn, and ultimately learn *(KWL)*; or write about the topic in a pre-assessment (Israel, Maynard, & Williamson, 2013).

• **Engage students in scientific investigations.** As early as preschool, children can be immersed in scientific methods and encouraged to exercise their curiosity, make predictions, and observe patterns in their natural world (Gerde, Schachter, & Wasik, 2013). As children advance through the grades, investigations becomes more structured. Unfortunately, many laboratory activities are little more than cookbook recipes: Students are given specific materials and instructions to follow step by step. Such activities can help make scientific phenomena more concrete for students but are occasionally uninspiring and often insufficient to change students' ideas about the topic.

Laboratories activities by themselves are unlikely to foster scientific thinking processes (formulating and testing hypotheses, separating and controlling variables, and so on) (Keil & Silberstein, 1996; M. J. Padilla, 1991; J. Singer, Marx, Krajcik, & Chambers, 2000). So in addition, teachers should allow students to conduct experiments in which the procedures and outcomes are not always predetermined. For instance, teachers might ask students to address such questions as "Does one fast-food restaurant provide more meat in a hamburger than others?" or "Is the local drinking water really safe to drink?" (M. J. Padilla, 1991; J. Singer et al., 2000).

Youngsters typically need scaffolding for such activities. For instance, a teacher might do the following:

• Present situations in which only two or three variables need to be controlled.
• Provide regular guidance, hints, and feedback regarding the need to evaluate observations objectively.
• Ask questions that encourage students to make predictions and critically analyze their observations (e.g., "What do you think will happen?" "What is your evidence?" "Do you see things that are inconsistent with what you predicted?"). (Byrnes, 1996; Carey, Evans, Honda, Jay, & Unger, 1989; Kuhn et al., 1988; Kuhn & Dean, 2005; Legaspi & Straits, 2011; Lorch et al., 2014; Minstrell & Stimpson, 1996; Thatch, 2008)

• **Provide age-appropriate explanations for physical and biological phenomena.** Although youngsters can discover a great deal through experimentation, they also need to learn the concepts, principles, and theories that scientists use to make sense of the world (Vygotsky, 1934/1986). Ideally, they should pull the things they learn into integrated, meaningful bodies of knowledge. Often teachers can make interrelationships accessible for students by presenting diagrams, flowcharts, or two- or three-dimensional models (Glynn, Yeany, & Britton, 1991a; Schwarz & White, 2005). Students themselves can draw pictures of causal forces, as you can see in 9-year-old Trisha's representation of the water cycle in Artifact 10-6.

• **Actively promote conceptual change.** Thanks to confirmation bias, youngsters are apt to seek out information that endorses, rather than contradicts, what they currently believe.[10] Piquing students' interest about why the world works as it does is a factor in conceptual change, as is helping them feel relaxed enough to entertain alternative explanations (Hadjiachilleos, Valanides, & Angeli, 2013; Vosniadou & Mason, 2012). Perhaps one of the most effective approaches for facilitating conceptual change is to entertain competing perspectives within a classroom environment that communicates the message, "It's okay to make errors and change our minds" (Minstrell & Stimpson, 1996; C. L. Smith, 2007; Vosniadou, 2009).

ARTIFACT 10-6 **The water cycle.** Children regularly benefit from requests to identify cause-and-effect relationships. In this drawing, 9-year-old Trisha shows her understanding that various phenomena in nature are interrelated.

Several lessons may be needed when children resist the implications of compelling evidence that their former beliefs are wrong. Take the example of young children's initial notion that the earth is a flat surface, not a solid sphere. Children live on an apparently level plane, so when first exposed to the notion that the earth is a round ball, they try to protect their prior belief by supplementing it with subtle revisions that the earth is a hollow sphere with a flat surface inside or that the earth is a sphere with a flattened surface on its top (Vosniadou, 2009). It typically takes a series of discussions and exposures to spherical models before children can accept the scientific view that the earth is a solid ball floating in space.

• **Ask students to write about scientific topics.** The journey from basic scientific knowledge to advanced expertise is a long one. Assignments that require students to write up scientific reports with arguments for certain conclusions can help students improve their scientific thinking. Sophisticated reasoning is challenging in any setting and all the more difficult while writing about ideas in science; therefore, it is necessary to give students many occasions to write, exemplars of strong scientific reports, and constructive feedback (Sampson, Enderle, Grooms, & Witte, 2013).

Summary

Children are attentive to quantity in the first year of life, but they learn to count large numbers of objects only if their culture provides the cognitive tools (e.g., number words) that make counting possible. Often they create strategies for performing simple mathematical operations (e.g., adding and subtracting small numbers) on their own, but instruction is usually necessary for the construction of complex concepts and procedures. For optimal mathematical development, children should truly understand (rather than simply memorize) mathematical procedures and learn that there is more than one correct way to solve a problem.

Some children have learning disabilities that impede their ability to automatize arithmetic facts or solve simple math problems, and others have little exposure to numbers and

---

[10]Chapter 7 suggests several strategies for promoting conceptual change.

counting before they begin school. Gender and cultural differences in mathematics have been observed as well. Concrete manipulatives, encouragement to count and compare numbers of items, and visual aids facilitate children's mathematical development, especially in the preschool and elementary years. Also, once children have mastered and automatized basic facts and skills, they are able to advance in their mathematical problem-solving abilities, especially when provided with effective instruction and tools that reduce demands on working memory.

Although children are born with the ability to apprehend basic principles of physics, by and large they acquire scientific knowledge through their informal experiences and formal instruction. As early as the preschool years, they begin to form theories (sometimes accurate, sometimes not) about categories of living creatures and cause-and-effect relationships in their physical world. The ability to reason as scientists do (e.g., formulating and testing hypotheses, drawing conclusions from collected data) develops gradually during childhood and improves in adolescence, yet even many high school students have difficulty analyzing data objectively and communicating their scientific insights.

Children's individual abilities (e.g., visual-spatial skills) and disabilities (e.g., blindness) affect development in science, as do gender stereotypes and cultural beliefs. Authentic scientific investigations, age-appropriate explanations, and intentional efforts to bring about conceptual change can all enhance youngsters' scientific understandings and reasoning skills.

ENHANCEDetext *self-check*

SOCIAL STUDIES AND THE ARTS

In their studies of children's development in academic subject areas, researchers have focused largely on reading, writing, mathematics, and science. Yet they have also learned a few things about children's development in social studies, art, and music. We now look at trends in each of these areas.

Social Studies

The field of *social studies* examines a wide range of topics in history, political science, geography, anthropology, and government, whose collective mastery prepares a young person for informed and responsible citizenship. By school entry, children are well on their way to gaining foundational knowledge about their social world and, over the elementary, middle, and high school years, they expand on these ideas.

Preschool children have strong interests in the types of jobs and traditions that people have in their community. In elementary school, social studies lessons are generally taught in an interdisciplinary manner that shows similarities and differences between lives of ancestors, people in far away lands, and their own circumstances. When youngsters move to middle and secondary school, they frequently take courses focused on a specific aspect of a single discipline, such as U.S. History or Human Geography.

As with other subjects, children learn social studies most effectively when they can relate concepts to personal knowledge. As you might expect, children often need help in understanding why people remote in time and place acted as they did. Children are more likely to understand other people's livelihoods when teachers discuss natural resources and local climates (Brophy, Alleman, & Knighton, 2009). For example, although many children are interested in the kinds of houses that Native American communities have historically built, they may not realize *why* tribes designed particular kinds of dwellings—that tribes moving with migrating buffalo needed portable structures (and therefore created tipis), those in eastern states could count on an abundance of wood (and thus built longhouses), and groups in the southwest had a plentiful supply of mud and clay (and hence constructed pueblos) (Brophy et al., 2009).

Children's knowledge of social studies gradually shifts from simple and personal concerns to intricate understandings of how other people live their lives and how the social world can be represented with symbolic tools such as maps. Let's look at progressions in two specific domains of social studies: history and geography.

Preparing for Your Licensure Examination
Your teaching test might ask you about how to teach lessons as part of an interdisciplinary unit.

History

Children's first awareness of history typically involves their *own* history. Sometime between ages 2 and 4, children construct an *autobiographical self:* They recall past events in their own lives and realize that they exist *in time*, with a past and a future as well as a present.[11] When improving language skills enable an exchange of ideas with family members and playmates, children gradually expand their sense of history to include other people whom they know well.

Children's knowledge of history on a broader scale emerges largely as a result of formal instruction. In the elementary grades, awareness of history tends to be concrete and simplistic. Children may conceptualize the birth of the United States as resulting from a single, specific event (e.g., the Boston Tea Party) or as involving nothing more than constructing new buildings and towns (Ormrod, Jackson, Kirby, Davis, & Benson, 1999). Another difficulty for elementary schoolchildren is a limited ability to understand historical time. They might refer to events that happened "a long, long time ago" or "in the old days" but tell you that such events happened in 2010. They tend to lump historical events into two general categories: those that happened very recently and those that happened many years ago.

At around age 10, children acquire some ability to put historical events in sequence and attach them to particular time periods (Barton & Levstik, 1996). Accordingly, systematic history instruction usually begins in fourth or fifth grade. Yet when children first study the scope of history, they have little direct knowledge on which to build. They haven't lived in the time periods they study, nor have they seen most of the locations they learn about. What they *can* build on is their knowledge of human beings. Children can better understand historical events when they discover that figures from the past had particular goals, motives, and personalities—in other words, that people in history were, in many respects, just ordinary folks (Bickford III, 2013; Brophy et al., 2009; Yeager et al., 1997). Following are several strategies that help children gain a "human" understanding of history:

- Assign works of fiction that realistically depict people living in particular times and places.
- Role-play family discussions that focus on making decisions during critical times in history (e.g., deciding whether to send a teenage son off to war).
- Ask children to analyze historical documents that represent conflicting perspectives on a historical event, encouraging them to speculate about how the intent and experience of writers influenced their responses.
- Have "journalists" (two or three students) interview people (other students) who "participated" in a historical event.
- Assign readings from original documents, including diaries, letters, newspaper articles, and so on. (Bickford III, 2013; Brophy & Alleman, 1996; Brophy et al., 2009; Brophy & VanSledright, 1997; Nokes, Dole, & Hacker, 2007; M. B. W. Wolfe & Goldman, 2005)

Geography

The discipline of geography is concerned not only with where various natural features and cultural groups are located but also with why and how they got there. Geographers study how rivers and mountain ranges end up where they do, why people are more likely to settle in some locations than in others, and how people in various locations make a living.

Many children have a simple view of geography. They may conceive of it as being little more than the names and locations of various countries, capital cities, rivers, mountain ranges, and so on—especially when geography is presented in this way (Bochenhauer, 1990; VanSledright & Limón, 2006). Even in the high school years, students rarely reflect on why various locations have the features they do or on how the economic and cultural practices of various social groups might be partly the result of their physical environment.

[11]Chapter 7 introduces the concept of autobiographical self.

An essential tool in geography is, of course, the *map*. Central to geographical thinking is an understanding that maps depict the arrangement and characteristics of particular locations. By age three or four, children have some ability to recognize relationships between simple graphics and the physical locations that the graphics represent (J. Huttenlocher et al., 1999; Liben, Myers, Christensen, & Bower, 2013). During the next several years, children increasingly use maps to identify locations in their immediate, familiar surroundings (Blades & Spencer, 1987; C. Davies & Uttal, 2007). However, their ability to use maps to navigate through *un*familiar territory remains fairly limited until adolescence at the earliest (C. Davies & Uttal, 2007; Liben, Kastens, & Stevenson, 2002).

When children in the early elementary grades look at larger-scale maps—perhaps those depicting a state or country—they tend to take what they see literally (Gardner, Torff, & Hatch, 1996; Liben, 2009). They may think that lines separating states and countries are actually painted on the earth or that an airport denoted by a picture of an airplane has only one plane. Young children also have trouble maintaining a sense of proportion when interpreting maps. They might deny that a road could actually be a road because "it's not fat enough for two cars to go on" or insist that a mountain depicted on a three-dimensional relief map can't possibly be a mountain because "it's not high enough" (Liben & Downs, 1989b; Liben & Myers, 2007, p. 202). Students in middle childhood grasp nonliteral representations, but even so, in the early elementary years, large-scale aerial maps are much more interpretable than are smaller-scale aerial maps (M. Kim, Bednarz, & Kim, 2012).

As children get older, and especially as they reach adolescence, they become more proficient in dealing with the symbolic and proportional nature of maps (Forbes et al., 1999; Liben & Myers, 2007). Salt maps, made up of flour, salt, cream of tartar, and water, allow children to mold hills, valleys, and other geological textures and develop a sense of the terrain of a region. Direct instruction as to reading legends and other symbolic features rounds out children's knowledge base. Numerous electronic applications are also available to help children learn how to orient with a map (Olson, 2012).

Of course, geography is much more than maps. The field offers deep insights into the customs of inhabitants in various regions. Children are fascinated with the circumstances of other people in different areas, and current events intensify children's interests. Famines, earthquakes, tsunamis, mudslides, and floods can be analyzed from the perspectives of survivors. Children can examine who is affected, how the aftermath of the tragedy is managed, and the resources that are used to decrease risk for people living there (J. Riley, 2014). Regional clashes between separate cultures also trigger desires in children to learn more. Studying resources in the area, economic markets, historical struggles, and political systems can help students gain a deeper understanding of people living there (K. Cook, 2014).

Visual Art

As budding artists, children exercise a variety of skills. They imagine new worlds; express thoughts and emotions; interpret the meaning of pictures, sculptures, and performances; practice fine motor skills; reason spatially; explore perspective and dimensions; and analyze such compositional elements as shape, proportion, light, and color (Papandreou, 2014; Smutny & von Fremd, 2009).

The particular artistic skills children use depend on their age and experience. As early as age 2, children begin to represent their visions on paper—for instance, by making a series of dots to mimic how an animal hops (Willcock, Imuta, & Hayne, 2011; Winner, 2006). They also begin to experiment with geometric figures, especially lines and circles. At age 3, their repertoire of shapes expands to include squares, rectangles, triangles, crosses, and X's, and they soon begin combining such shapes to create pictures (Golomb, 2004; Kellogg, 1967). Many of their early drawings are of a person, which might initially consist of a circle (depicting either a head or a head plus body) with a few facial features (e.g., eyes, mouth) within it and four lines (two arms, two legs) extending from it. With age, preschoolers add features—perhaps hair, hands, fingers, and feet—to figures.

Sometime around age 4, children combine drawings of several objects to create pictures of groups or nature scenes. Initially, they may scatter things haphazardly around the page, but eventually they place objects on the page in an orientation that is consistent with everyday reality. In the elementary grades, children become capable of producing a wide variety of shapes and contours, and their drawings become more detailed, realistic, and appropriately proportional (N. R. Smith et al., 1998; Willcock et al., 2011; Winner, 2006). By the upper elementary grades, children portray depth in their drawings (Braine, Schauble, Kugelmass, & Winter, 1993). Demonstration and feedback hone skills with such artistic techniques as texturizing, as you can see in an Observing Children video.

Observing Children 10-7
Observe an art teacher demonstrating how to add definition and texture to drawings.
ENHANCEDetext *video example*

Some youngsters draw and paint very little once they reach adolescence, especially if art is not a regular part of the school curriculum, and so their artistic skills may progress little beyond this point (Cohn, 2014; S. Moran & Gardner, 2006; Winner, 2006). Young adolescents frequently hold themselves to a high expectation for representing images realistically and become disappointed when they cannot achieve the desired standard (Luehrman & Unrath, 2006). Those who continue to create art refine their abilities to show texture, depth, perspective, and spatial relationships (N. R. Smith et al., 1998; Willats, 1995). They may also try to convey mood and emotion by selectively using particular shapes, hues, and color intensities (N. R. Smith et al., 1998).

When a culture neither values nor encourages art, children's artistic skills evolve slowly if at all (Cohn, 2014; Gordon, 2004; Trawick-Smith, 2014). But when drawing implements are readily available to children—as they are in many societies—certain universals in artistic development appear in the preschool years (Case & Okamoto, 1996; Golomb, 2004; Kellogg, 1967). Children from diverse industrialized cultures are apt to draw houses as squares with smaller, internal squares depicting windows, doors, and perhaps chimneys. And they begin to compose complex pictures in the same sequence and at approximately the same ages regardless of their background.

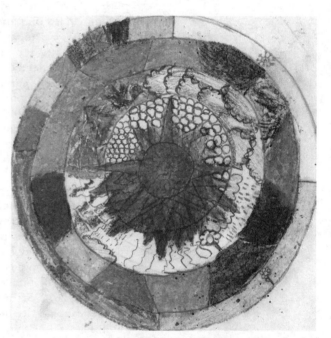

ARTIFACT 10-7 **Pre-Columbian calendar.** Fifteen-year-old Berlinda drew and colored this calendar after looking at Mayan artwork.

Artistic techniques are highly valued and cultivated in some societies. If children receive extensive instruction in artistic techniques, as many children do in Japan and China, their drawings are elaborate, detailed, and true-to-life (Alland, 1983; Case & Okamoto, 1996; Cohn, 2014). By the middle elementary grades, some children begin to mimic popular images in their local cultural environment, such as the drawings they see in comic books and children's magazines (B. Wilson, 1997; Winner, 2006). Images from history and social studies are also ripe for inspiration. In Artifact 10-7, you can see 15-year-old Berlinda's pencil and chalk drawing of pre-Columbian art.

Music

Human beings of all ages enjoy music. Six-month-olds pay more attention to their mothers when they are singing rather than talking to them (Nakata & Trehub, 2004; Vlismas, Malloch, & Burnham, 2013). Mother's lively songs help capture infants' attention and keep infants on an even keel, perking them up a bit if they seem low on energy and soothing them if they are overly aroused (Shenfield, Trehub, & Nakata, 2003). Five- to 24-month-old infants are more likely to sway, rock, and make other rhythmic movements to music than to speech (Zentner & Eerola, 2010).

Just as young infants hear subtle differences in spoken language that adults don't hear, so, too, do they pick up on subtle changes in music that adults don't notice.[12] When a melody changes slightly (say, by a note or two within the same key), 8-month-olds are more

---

[12]You can read more about this change in Chapter 9.

Observing Children 10-8
Watch preschool children singing and swaying to music.
ENHANCEDetext *video example*

likely than adults to notice the difference (Trainor & Trehub, 1992). But as youngsters grow older, and especially as they progress through the preschool and early elementary school years, they increasingly perceive patterns (melodies, keys, complex rhythms, etc.) rather than individual notes (Geist, Geist, & Kuznik, 2012; Gromko & Poorman, 1998).

Musical patterns incite children to dance and sing. With neuromuscular maturation and practice, children gain proficiency in singing during early and middle childhood (Persellin & Bateman, 2009; Winner, 2006). At around age 2, they begin to repeat some of the lyrics they hear. They soon add a rhythmic structure and up-and-down "melody" of sorts. Preschool children love to learn new songs, as you can see in an Observing Children video. By the time they are 5 or 6, most can sing a recognizable tune and keep it largely within the appropriate key and meter. For most youngsters, further development in singing comes primarily from training, as does proficiency with an instrument (D. J. Elliott, 1995; Miksza & Gault, 2014; Winner, 2006).

Another important aspect of musical development is **music literacy**, the ability to read and understand musical notation. As early as age 4, children can, when asked, invent original ways to represent musical sounds with objects—for instance, using large, heavy objects to represent loud notes and smaller objects to represent softer notes, and large or dark circles on paper as opposed to smaller and lighter-colored ones (Gromko, 1996; P. Lee, 2013). Standard musical notation is a cultural creation, and so children must be instructed in its interpretation. Youngsters' ability to read music can enhance their ability to hear and remember the subtle nuances of a musical piece (Gromko & Poorman, 1998).

Virtually all cultures have some form of music, and the types of music with which children grow up affect their musical sensitivities (Brittin, 2014; Hannon & Trehub, 2005; Werker & Tees, 1999). But within any single culture, individual children have varying abilities to hear and appreciate music. About 4 percent of children have **amusia** (or tone deafness), an inability to detect small changes in pitch that are common in melodies. These youngsters show little or no improvement in their perception of musical tones despite instruction and practice, suggesting that the ability to hear music *as* music may have a biological basis (Gardner et al., 1996; K. L. Hyde & Peretz, 2004; Lebrun, Moreau, McNally-Gagnon, Goulet, & Peretz, 2012). In contrast, some children not only hear, but also *remember*, subtle differences in pitch. Although most people can remember the relative pitches of notes in a melody, individuals with *absolute pitch* can also recall the *exact* pitch of a note they have heard in, say, a popular song (Shellenberg & Trehub, 2003). Absolute pitch is more common in infants and preschoolers than in older children or adults, thus it seems that children lose this ability if it is not exercised (Miyazaki, Makomaska, & Rakowski, 2012; Saffran & Griepentrog, 2001).

The ability to *produce* music also seems to draw from both nature and nurture (D. J. Elliott, 1995; Treffert & Wallace, 2002). Some children with autism have exceptional instrumental talent (Stanutz, Wapnick, & Burack, 2014). After watching a movie on television one evening, 14-year-old Leslie Lemke sat down at the family piano and played Tchaikovsky's Piano Concerto No. 1, which had been a soundtrack for portions of the movie. He had never heard the concerto before that night, yet his rendition was flawless. Lemke is now a world-renowned pianist, even though he has autism and an intellectual disability, is blind, and has never had a piano lesson (Treffert & Wallace, 2002).

Some policy makers view art and music as luxuries that are expendable when budgets are tight. In reality, formal instruction in these subjects has distinct benefits for growing children. For instance, creating paintings or collages that capture certain events or moods can help children enrich their short stories and poetry (Olshansky, O'Connor, & O'Byrne, 2006). Drawing illustrations of scientific phenomena or historical events can enhance children's understanding of these situations (J. H. Davis, 2008; Edens & Potter, 2001). Evidence is inconsistent about the broader role that music plays in cognition, with some investigations indicating benefits to intellectual pattern recognition, sustained attention, and executive control processes, and other investigations *not* demonstrating this impact (Mehr, Schachner, Katz, & Spelke, 2013; Schellenberg, 2006; Smutny & von Fremd, 2009). Regardless of the effects that may or may not happen with basic cognitive processes, art and music enrich the lives of students, acquaint them with their cultural heritage, strengthen their resilience, and motivate creative performance (Eerola & Eerola, 2014; Salmon & Rickaby, 2014).

Education in Social Studies and the Arts

The path to responsible citizenship is facilitated by knowledge of the diverse world in which we live; an awareness of the struggles and accomplishments of our ancestors; recognition for how culture and livelihood affect personal welfare; and an appreciation for music, arts, and other creative works in society. In our discussion, we have embedded good educational practices in our descriptions of social studies and the arts. We close with these additional recommendations:

• **Implement rousing social studies lessons.** As children grow older, they become increasingly interested in how the social world works, including jobs adults take on, the processes by which governments balance rights and interests, and the customs practiced locally and around the world. Although a recent tendency has been to downplay social studies due to rising concerns about basic literacies, children want to know about their social world, and social studies can be a motivating context for exercising literacy skills. Documents, experiences, data, and video clips on the Internet can provide intriguing material to read, analyze, and write about. Children acquire social studies effectively when materials are presented dynamically—for instance, with skits, letters to pen pals from a foreign land, visits from the mayor, analyses of conflicting perspectives in different historical documents, and practice in orienting around the local neighborhood with compass and map.

• **Teach and advocate for the arts.** Music, drama, dance, sculpture, film production, and the visual arts draw simultaneously from the three primary domains of development (physical, cognitive, and social-emotional areas), challenge children academically, help them refine motor skills, and allow their self-expression. Curiously, the arts (and physical education) are among the first areas placed on the cutting board when budgets are slashed. Despite the excruciating trade-offs that must be weighed during a recession, a long-term perspective on children's welfare indicates substantial value in the arts.

Children undergo similar progressions across academic domains, shifting from personal, concrete, and spontaneous approaches to use of abstract, comprehensive, and integrated conceptual frameworks and learning strategies. The Basic Developmental Issues table "Progressions in the Academic Domains" summarizes how three general themes— nature and nurture, universality and diversity, and qualitative and quantitative change—play out in academic subjects.

Summary

Social studies, history, geography, art, and music have received less attention in developmental research than have literacy, science, and mathematics, but researchers are finding age-related trends in these subject areas. Children in the early elementary grades are apt to struggle with historical time, and they may not appreciate that historical "knowledge" is a matter of perspective rather than fact. Geographical reasoning requires understanding of the symbolic and proportional nature of maps, which emerges gradually over childhood. Educators can help children to understand the traditions and motivations of other people by communicating the conditions of their lives.

Art and music are found in virtually all cultures, but the specific forms that they take differ considerably from one society to another. Infants around the world enjoy music, and children's early drawings of people are similar regardless of where they grow up. Advanced art and music abilities are largely dependent on instruction, available resources, and practice.

ENHANCEDetext *self-check*

Assessing Children 10-2

Listen to students' understanding of history.

ENHANCEDetext *application exercise*

BASIC DEVELOPMENTAL ISSUES
Progressions in the Academic Domains

ISSUE	READING AND WRITING	MATH AND SCIENCE	SOCIAL STUDIES	ART AND MUSIC
Nature and Nurture	Although children are biologically predisposed to learn spoken language, facility in reading and writing is largely the result of exposure to printed materials and education. Nature can interfere with normal literacy development, however: Some children with biologically based disabilities have unusual difficulty in learning to read and write.	Within the first few months of life, infants notice differences in quantity and, at some rudimentary level, understand basic principles of physics. Some theorists speculate that these early acquisitions reflect neurologically based knowledge. By and large, however, children's knowledge of numbers and scientific phenomena develops through experience and instruction.	The bodies of knowledge and cognitive tools that children acquire in social studies are primarily the result of instruction and informal experiences in the family (trips to historical sites, contact with other societies, use of maps on subway systems, etc.). Maturational processes partly determine the age at which children are able to think about historical time and understand symbolism in maps.	Hereditary and maturational factors play a role in artistic and musical development. Preschool children's ability to draw depends largely on maturation of fine motor skills. Most children have an inborn appreciation for music, and some show exceptional talent even without instruction. For the most part, advancements in art and music result from training and practice.
Universality and Diversity	Phonological awareness facilitates reading development even when written language is *not* based on how words are pronounced. However, children learn to read and write more easily when words have highly regular and predictable spelling patterns. Children's literacy development depends on the extent to which adults model and encourage reading and writing.	Although children worldwide are aware of quantity, precision in comparing quantities depends on cultural number concepts and operations. Certain basic scientific knowledge (e.g., knowing that animals are fundamentally different from inanimate objects) is similar worldwide, but several understandings (e.g., the origins of the human species) differ depending on upbringing.	Knowledge of social studies is largely the product of the environment, and universal acquisitions have not been identified. In industrialized societies, history is taught in school, and maps are used to aid navigation. In traditional societies, knowledge of history comes from hearing stories by elders, and people navigate largely by locating distinctive landmarks.	Virtually all cultures have art and music. Artistic styles and musical patterns differ considerably from culture to culture, and development in these areas varies accordingly. Although preschoolers' drawings tend to be quite similar across cultures, by middle childhood their artwork begins to mimic the styles and images they see in their environment.
Qualitative and Quantitative Change	Literacy shows many qualitative changes over time. Children shift their primary focus from word identification to comprehension (in reading), transition from knowledge telling to knowledge transforming (in writing), and increasingly incorporate metacognitive processes in literate activities (in both reading and writing). Literacy development is quantitative in that children become able to recognize and spell more and more words, and basic reading and writing skills become increasingly automatized.	As children get older, they acquire more knowledge about mathematical and scientific concepts and principles—a progression that reflects quantitative change. They also acquire new and qualitatively different ways of thinking about math and science. Elementary schoolchildren begin to rely on retrieval rather than counting fingers as they solve addition and subtraction problems, and adolescents gain new reasoning skills (e.g., separating and controlling variables) in scientific experimentation.	A good deal of development in social studies is quantitative, in that children gradually acquire more information about historical events and geographical locations. Qualitative changes are seen in how children *think* about history and geography. With appropriate instruction children realize that knowledge of history is comprised of available accounts of what happened, many of which reflect a particular opinion on events. As children gain proportional reasoning, they understand the scales with which maps are constructed.	Many qualitative changes are seen in art and music development. With growth and experience, children's drawings embody a sense of composition (e.g., creating an organized scene rather than a random collection of objects), perspective, and texture. In the preschool years, songs begin to reflect a consistent rhythm and key. Quantitative change is seen in children's increasing knowledge of musical notation and gradual improvement in a musical instrument.

PRACTICING FOR YOUR LICENSURE EXAMINATION

Many teaching tests require students to apply their knowledge of child development in analyzing brief vignettes and answering multiple-choice questions. You can practice for your licensure examination by reading the following case study and answering a series of questions.

AP Calculus

Galen liked math but lacked confidence in his ability to handle difficult material. He eventually decided he would try the Advanced Placement (AP) Calculus class because he had heard good things about the teacher, Mr. Wagner.

As Galen settled into the class, he grew to like the predictable format. For each lesson, Mr. Wagner began with a description of a specific concept in calculus and then asked students to complete a series of steps about it for homework. Homework took the form of an electronic journal entry, in which students prepared an overview of the concept (in an *Introduction*), explained its principles (in a *Research* section), clarified its meaning (in an *Interpretation*), and formulated relevant equations (in a final *Examples* section).

At the end of the year, students printed their homework assignments and bound them into a booklet with an essay they wrote about what they had learned from the class. Skim Galen's assignment (Figure A) and read an excerpt from his essay on the next page. Unless you're a calculus buff, ignore the math equations, and focus instead on how the various sections were used to solidify students' understandings of the concepts and their applications.

Introduction

This journal discusses derivatives and their rules. Derivatives are key to measuring a *rate of change*. We also look at the tangent of a secant line, and how to determine a tangent to a function with a point.

Research

A Derivative is the rate of change of an output as a function of some input. $\frac{\Delta y}{\Delta x} = slope\, of\, chord$

The derivative equals the tangent of the secant line. It has the following forms:

$\frac{dy}{dx} = slope$ of tangent $\quad \boxed{m_{tan} \lim_{h \to 0} \frac{f(x+h)-f(x)}{h}} = \boxed{\frac{dy}{dx} = \frac{df(x)}{dx}}$

The derivative can be shown graphically as well. After all it is a *rate of change*.

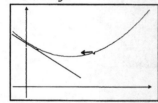

As these two point's distance gets closer to zero.

They start to form a tangent, and at zero there is a tangent to the secant line.

FIGURE A   Galen's homework. For every concept in calculus, Galen and his classmates followed a template for their homework. Notice the general structure of the homework, in which students examined a concept in terms of its essential meaning, principles, and implications.

Research(cont.)

Determining the equation of a line tangent to a curve at a point:

1. Determine f(c) if needed.
2. Determine the derivative function.
3. Determine m=f'(c)
4. Determine b. (b = y - mx)

$y = mx + b$

$m = f'(c) \qquad f(c)=y$

$b = y - mx$

$b = f(c) - f'(c)c$

Interpretation

The derivative is a *rate of change*. It is the tangent to the secant line, that is created as two points on the secant line, get close together, *as their distance goes to zero*. The derivative takes the form of $\frac{dy}{dx}$ or $\frac{df(x)}{dx}$. They are really important in high end math, can be applied to anything that is changing at a constant rate.

Examples

a) $y = x^2 - 4x + 4$

$\lim_{h \to 0} y' = \frac{((x+h)^2 - 4(x+h) + 4) - (x^2 - 4x + 4)}{h}$

$\lim_{h \to 0} y' = \frac{x^2 + 2xh + h^2 - 4x - 4h + 4 - x^2 + 4x - 4}{h}$

$\lim_{h \to 0} y' = \frac{2xh + h^2 - 4h}{h}$

$\lim_{h \to 0} y' = \frac{h(2x + h - 4)}{h}$

$\lim_{h \to 0} y' = 2x + h - 4$

$\boxed{\lim_{h \to 0} y' = 2x - 4}$

What can I say about this year of AP Calculus? Let me start by saying how much I have learned and that I actually enjoyed learning the material. It's been an excellent year and we covered a lot of ground. I feel prepared for college calculus, and depending on my test score, may go to Calculus II at college. We learned about preliminary concepts (the pre-calc), limits, the derivative, the integral, and practical applications of each of those. For each unit we created journals to help us further understand the content. Overall I found the journals helpful but for most material it was overkill for me.

Mr. Wagner has been a great teacher. He makes the material understandable and interesting to learn. I like the routine he has for teaching to which we have grown accustomed. Each unit is separated into sections and each sub-section follows a similar pattern. We get a sheet to take notes over the smart notebook lesson we have in class, a homework assignment, and a quiz. This system worked really well for me and other students because we knew what to expect, and it was a good way to separate the learning into three parts—each part further bettering our understanding of the unit. . . .

The material we covered throughout the year is complex stuff and math that is used at a high level. The main applications that paralleled with real life patterns were derivation and integration. The derivative is a rate of change, the slope of the tangent line following the graph of a function. This is really important for instantaneous velocity, as the derivative of the position function is the velocity function, and the derivative of the velocity function is the acceleration function. . . . Also we learned how to determine the volume of a 3D shape using cross-sections and the integral. A real-life example could be finding the volume of a pond with the use of semi-circle cross-sections . . .

It's been a fun year, and it's made me appreciate how lucky I am to be learning such incredible things like calculus. The math we're doing is really complex and interesting and it's definitely not something everyone can do. We've been lucky to have a great teacher to teach us about the study of change. We've explored some real-life applications, while used as a high-level, it is math that is very important and helpful in our world.

Constructed-Response Question

1. What did Galen like about calculus and the way he was taught?

Multiple-Choice Questions

2. Would Mr. Wagner have been able to achieve similar results in calculus achievement with preschool children if he used the same instructional strategies with them?

    a. No, because preschool children dislike mathematics.
    b. Yes, because young children have the same ability as adolescents in acquiring challenging mathematical concepts.
    c. No, because young children would rarely have the abstract reasoning abilities that are necessary for learning calculus.
    d. Yes, because young children would easily translate abstract mathematics concepts into ideas that have a tangible basis in reality.

3. Which of the following instructional strategies was *not* one of the techniques summarized by Galen as being used by Mr. Wagner?

    a. Encourage students to invent, use, and defend their own strategies.
    b. As youngsters work on new and challenging mathematical problems, provide the scaffolding they need to find successful solutions.
    c. Use visual displays to tie mathematical concepts and procedures to concrete reality.
    d. Use concrete manipulatives when instructing children in mathematics.

ENHANCEDetext *licensure exam*

Key Concepts

standards (p. 358)
emergent literacy (p. 360)
phonological awareness (p. 361)
sight vocabulary (p. 363)

story schema (p. 363)
dyslexia (p. 366)
invented spelling (p. 372)
knowledge telling (p. 373)

knowledge transforming (p. 373)
dyscalculia (p. 385)
visual-spatial ability (p. 385)
substance schema (p. 389)

scientific reasoning (p. 391)
music literacy (p. 400)
amusia (p. 400)

CHAPTER ELEVEN

Emotional Development

CASE STUDY: Merv

Merv had had a difficult childhood growing up in an economically poor family in Hawaii. Her father was an alcoholic, and her mother had been anxious, depressed, and preoccupied with her own troubles. Neither parent took adequate care of Merv or her six brothers and sisters. Merv's parents regularly fought and occasionally struck Merv and the other children. Food, shoes, clothing, and basic school supplies were scarce. Other parents in their neighborhood considered Merv and her siblings to be unworthy playmates for their own children (Werner & Smith, 2001).

Remarkably, Merv beat the odds. By the time she reached her 40s, Merv was a productive, well-adjusted woman who worked as a parent educator and had been married since age 16 to "a pretty neat guy . . . a schoolteacher" (Werner & Smith, 2001, pp. 100–101). Merv and her husband raised their seven children in a manner that was gentle, patient, and loving. Merv also remained close to her own brothers and sisters. She led a happy, fulfilled life.

Merv credited four childhood experiences with making her a strong, secure person. First of all, Merv had learned to work hard, as she described in this memory:

As children, we took care of the yard, the house, the clothes, each other, and the cars. We did everything. My father cooked when there was something to cook, and my mother simply coped. . . . When things got rough, I learned to dig in my heels and say, "How am I going to make this happen?" versus "This is too hard, I quit." (Werner & Smith, 2001, pp. 95–96)[a]

Second, Merv had "caring and supportive people" to guide and nurture her (Werner & Smith, 2001, p. 96). Merv thrived on care she received from her grandmother Kahaunaele. During Merv's visits to Kahaunaele's house, Kahaunaele showered Merv with love, bathed the girl, and combed the tangles out of her long hair. Love from her grandmother came to be supplemented with kindness from several teachers and school staff. Merv's principal once said to her, "You are Hawaiian and you can be anything you choose to be" (p. 98). Merv was forever grateful for these words of encouragement.

Third, Merv received a good education. When she was 12 years old, she accepted an invitation to attend a prestigious school on another Hawaiian island. At the Kamehameha School, Merv was well cared for, academically and socially. Her life changed dramatically at age 16, however, when she became pregnant and was expelled from school for becoming an unwed mother. Merv married the father of her baby and was soon allowed to return when a school counselor went "out on a major limb" for her, having realized that she was "not a bad student. She just made a mistake" (p. 100).

Finally, Merv learned to trust that there is goodness in the world. Merv saw hope as a vital quality for all young people, and noted that inspiration can be found in a variety of places:

Somewhere, someplace down the line, somebody had taught me, "There is somebody greater than us who loves you." And that is my hope and my belief. Whatever that translates for you—a belief in God, a belief in a religion, a goal, a dream, something that we can hang on to. As adults, we need to give our young people hope and something to hang on to. As young people, we need to find our own. (Werner & Smith, 2001, p. 101)

- What basic need did Merv have that was ultimately fulfilled by people outside her immediate family?
- What do Merv's childhood experiences suggest about how teachers and other practitioners can contribute to children's emotional development?

[a] Excerpts from JOURNEYS FROM CHILDHOOD TO MIDLIFE: RISK, RESILIENCE, AND RECOVERY by Emmy E. Werner and Ruth S. Smith. Copyright © 2001 by Cornell University. Used by permission of the publisher, Cornell University Press.

OBJECTIVES

11.1: Describe the central challenges in each of Erikson's eight stages of psychosocial development, and identify the strengths and limitations of Erikson's theory.

11.2: Summarize the developmental course of children's first attachments, distinguish the four primary attachment styles, and explain the tactics teachers and other practitioners can use to foster secure attachments in children.

11.3: Encapsulate developmental trends in children's emotional understanding and expression, and outline strategies for enhancing children's emotional health.

11.4: Define key dimensions of temperament and personality, and generate techniques for accepting children's individuality.

11.5: Describe ways to help children with emotional and behavioral problems be successful at school.

Every child needs to be loved. Merv's own parents neglected her, but her grandmother adored her, her brothers and sisters formed lasting bonds with her, and a few kind-hearted educators provided her personal encouragement and a high-quality education. In this chapter you will find that affectionate care is the mainstay of children's first relationships. When children are treated with sensitivity, they learn to trust other people, express their needs, and empathize with other people's feelings. You will learn that children do not always obtain adequate support for weathering life's challenges. When adversities outweigh children's **coping skills**, their personal mechanisms for managing distress, the unfortunate outcome can be anxiety, depression, and other problematic emotional conditions. Fortunately, teachers, counselors, and other practitioners can, as they nurture children, ease their troubles and steer them toward a healthy future.

ERIKSON'S THEORY OF PSYCHOSOCIAL DEVELOPMENT

Physical and cognitive abilities change dramatically during childhood. Learning to walk, run, talk, count, read, and write are important milestones. Yet equally momentous transformations occur in the social-emotional domain. To give you an overview of these significant social-emotional changes, we introduce Erikson's theory of psychosocial development.

Lessons Learned from Life's Challenges

Erik Erikson (1902–1994) was a *psychodynamic theorist* who believed that people grow from life's challenges.[1] In his own youth, Erikson had struggled with who he was as a person. He often felt different from others, having been born to a single Danish mother in Germany during an era when two-parent families were the norm. Adding to his sense of uniqueness, he was Jewish but had blond hair and blue eyes, a rare combination of characteristics that puzzled other people and made him feel strange (Crain, 2011). Erikson had little interest in school and failed to earn a college degree, yet he eventually became a well-known scholar of human development.

 In his theory, Erikson suggested that people undergo eight "crises," dilemmas addressed in the form of **psychosocial stages** between birth to old age (Erikson, 1963, 1966). Each crisis is a turning point, the resolution of which directs a person's future concerns. He called these eight predicaments *psychosocial* stages because the various challenges represent qualitatively different concerns about oneself *(psycho)* and relationships with other people *(social)*. Erikson observed that when individuals constructively address these challenges, they gain lasting personal assets. When their efforts fall short, people are apt to dwell on their problems. As they move from stage to stage, everyone builds on accumulated assets and deficits, occasionally revisiting unresolved crises.

 As they reflect on their life experiences, people navigate through each of the challenges. Let's look at the potential outcomes of the eight stages.

Trust versus Mistrust (Infancy)

According to Erikson, infants' primary task is to learn whether or not they can trust other people. When caregivers can be depended on to feed a hungry stomach, change an uncomfortable diaper, and provide affection at regular intervals, an infant learns *trust*—that others are dependable. When caregivers ignore an infant's needs, are inconsistent in attention, or are abusive, the infant learns *mistrust*—that the world is an unpredictable and dangerous place.

Autonomy versus Shame and Doubt (Toddler Years)

As toddlers gain better control of their bodies, they become capable of satisfying their own needs. Toddlers learn to feed, wash, dress, and use the toilet. When parents and other caregivers encourage self-sufficient behavior, toddlers develop *autonomy,* a sense of being

Preparing for Your Licensure Examination

Your teaching test might ask you about the basic principles and implications of Erikson's theory.

---

[1]Erik Erikson's theory is introduced in Chapter 1.

able to handle problems on their own. But when caregivers demand too much too soon, refuse to let children perform tasks of which they are capable, or ridicule early attempts at self-sufficiency, children instead develop *shame and doubt* about conducting themselves appropriately.

Initiative versus Guilt (Preschool Years)

If all goes well, children spend their infancy and toddler years learning that the world is a good place, people love them, and they can make things happen. With a growing drive toward independence, preschoolers develop their own ideas about activities they want to pursue. They undertake simple art projects, make houses and roadways in the sandbox, and share fantasies about being superheroes. When adults encourage such efforts, children develop *initiative,* the energy and motivation to undertake activities independently. When adults discourage such activities, children may instead develop *guilt* about acting improperly.

Industry versus Inferiority (Elementary School Years)

When children reach elementary school, they are expected to master many new skills, and they soon learn that they can gain recognition from adults through their academic, athletic, artistic, and civic-minded accomplishments. When children take pride in completed projects and are praised for achievements, they demonstrate *industry,* a pattern of working hard, gaining mastery in tool use, and persisting at lengthy tasks. But when children are ridiculed or punished for their efforts or when they find that they cannot meet adults' expectations, they may develop feelings of *inferiority* about their abilities.

Identity versus Role Confusion (Adolescence)

As they make the transition from childhood to adulthood, adolescents wrestle with questions about who they are and how they fit into the adult world. Values learned during childhood are now reassessed in light of a new sexual drive and the desire to be true to oneself. Initially, youth experience *role confusion*—mixed feelings about the specific ways in which they fit into society—and may experiment with actions and attitudes (e.g., affiliating with various peer groups, trying several sports and hobbies, and learning about the views of different political groups). In Erikson's view, most adolescents eventually achieve a sense of *identity* regarding who they are and where their lives are headed.

Intimacy versus Isolation (Young Adulthood)

Once people have established their identities, they are ready to make commitments to others. They become capable of *intimacy*—that is, they form close, reciprocal bonds (e.g., through marriage, other intimate relationships, or close friendships) and willingly make the sacrifices and compromises that such relationships require. When people cannot form mutually devoted relationships (perhaps because of their disregard for others' needs), a sense of *isolation* may result.

Generativity versus Stagnation (Middle Age)

During middle age, the primary developmental tasks are contributing to society and guiding future generations. When an individual makes a contribution, perhaps by raising a family or by working toward the betterment of society, a sense of *generativity,* or productivity, results. In contrast, an individual who is self-centered and unable or unwilling to help others experiences *stagnation*—dissatisfaction with lack of production.

Integrity versus Despair (Retirement Years)

According to Erikson, the final developmental task is a retrospective one. As individuals look back on their past experiences, they develop feelings of contentment and *integrity* if they believe they have led a happy, productive life. Alternatively, they may develop a sense of *despair* if they look back on a life of disappointments and unachieved goals.

   For Erikson, successful progress through each stage is not an absolute accomplishment but a matter of degree. In other words, people advance through each stage when they develop *more* of the positive tendency and *less* of the negative tendency. Erikson believed that having modest deficits, balanced with adequate assets, helps people respond sensibly to the opportunities and threats they face in daily life. A young boy who has learned to trust his parents is hopeful when meeting a new teacher, yet having also known a few short-tempered grown-ups, he will be cautious until he gets to know the teacher better. Because his optimism is tempered with restraint, the boy is ready to form healthy relationships. In contrast, with too much of a deficit (e.g., when uneasiness outweighs peace of mind), a tipping point is reached and the person becomes unhappy, isolated, and socially impaired.

Contemporary Perspectives on Erikson's Theory

Three strengths of Erikson's theory make it a compelling framework of human development. First, Erikson argued that important changes occur *throughout* the life span. Thanks in part to Erikson's theory, developmental scholars now accept that catalysts for growth surface at every age (e.g., with the need to be productive, define one's personal commitments, and become intimate). Second, Erikson focused on truly significant developments, including forming trusting relationships and establishing an identity (Marcia & Josselson, 2013; Vaughan & Rodriguez, 2013). Finally, Erikson's stages reflect the idea that development is a dynamic synthesis of nature, nurture, and a person's own motivation to make sense of life (Côté, 2005; Dunkel & Sefcek, 2009; Turns & Kimmes, 2014). Erikson's integrative model fits nicely with the prevalent contemporary view on human development that a person's changes are complex blends of his or her characteristics, maturation, adaptation to the environment, ongoing reflection, and opportunities and hardships

These theoretical strengths notwithstanding, Erikson's framework has limitations. For one thing, Erikson's observations of the human condition were largely anecdotal and his conclusions rather vague (Crain, 2011). The systematic research findings that have accumulated since Erikson formulated his theory indicate that his stages are probably not completely accurate descriptions of what happens at each age period. For instance, Erikson believed that most people achieve a sense of identity by the end of adolescence. In reality youth typically continue to wrestle with their personal commitments well into the young adult years (Bartoszuk & Pittman, 2010; J. Kroger, 2004). Also problematic for the theory is the fact that Erikson based his stages primarily on observations of men from a limited number of backgrounds. Women and individuals from non-Western cultures may face a different series of tasks than the ones Erikson identified. Although Erikson viewed the cultural context as influential in resolving age-related tasks, he probably underestimated just how differently various cultural groups think about particular assets. For example, many cultures intentionally discourage self-assertiveness *(autonomy)* in young children, sometimes as a way of protecting children from dangers in the environment and at other times as a means for strengthening ties to family members (Kağitçibaşi, 2007; Morelli & Rothbaum, 2007). You can see a summary of the research on Erikson's stages in Table 11-1.

Despite the holes in Erikson's theory, his framework does offer a valuable perspective on human life. As we mentioned, Erikson's framework has several strong points, and it offers the additional advantage of inspiring optimism about young people's potential for growth. Most educators agree with Erikson that youngsters can usually find the fortitude they need to transform life's challenges into such worthwhile assets as a healthy self-confidence, a commitment to productive social values, and a solid work ethic.

Although Erikson failed to provide detailed information about how to cultivate social-emotional skills in youngsters, other developmental scholars have taken up this cause. The focus of Erikson's first stage, a trusting relationship with caregivers, has been thoroughly examined by researchers, and we look at this topic shortly. Other key tasks that Erikson examined—reflecting on personal characteristics, having the motivation to complete challenging tasks, living up to moral obligations, and forming close relationships with people outside the family—build on this initial sense of security.[2]

---

[2]Children's sense of identity is examined in Chapter 12, motivation in Chapter 13, morality in Chapter 14, and peer relationships in Chapter 15.

TABLE 11-1 Developmental Research Related to Erikson's Stages

STAGE	AGE	RESEARCH
Trust vs. Mistrust	Birth to 1 year	Developmental investigations support Erikson's assertion that learning to trust others is a fundamental acquisition (Ainsworth, Blehar, Waters, & Wall, 1978; Bowlby, 1988; Klatzkin, Lieberman, & Van Horn, 2013). However, although Erikson indicated that infancy was a critical time for developing a first trusting relationship, recent research indicates that children often get second chances. For example, when children receive unresponsive care during early infancy, their first attachments are likely to be insecure, but if their later care is warm and sensitive, they can often develop secure relationships.
Autonomy vs. Shame and Doubt	1 to 3 years	Evidence supports Erikson's conclusion that toddlers have a strong will to practice emerging skills without restriction. Toddlers are motivated to handle objects, walk on their own, and explore a home's forbidden areas. Yet not every culture agrees with Erikson that autonomy is a virtue: Some groups see young children's drive for independence as an immature impulse (S. Griffith & Grolnick, 2014; Kağıtçıbaşı 2007).
Initiative vs. Guilt	3 to 5 years	Erikson aptly portrayed preschool-aged children as radiating a sense of purpose. Research confirms that young children show initiative in conversation and play. Erikson also paved the way for contemporary research on shame, double, and guilt. Developmental studies indicate that young children tend to feel distressed when they break a rule or fail to live up to a standard (Kagan, 1984; Kochanska, 1993; R. A. Thompson & Newton, 2010).
Industry vs. Inferiority	6 to 10 years	Erikson saw middle childhood as a period for completing demanding tasks proficiently. Cross-cultural research indicates that adults routinely assign chores to children in this age range, reflecting widespread recognition that school-aged children are capable of responsible behavior. Research also indicates that children compare their own abilities to those of peers and lose confidence when they come up short in domains that they value (J. S. Barnes & Spray, 2013; Harter, 2006; W. Wu, West, & Hughes, 2010).
Identity vs. Role Confusion	10 to 20 years	Erikson's focus on identity has spawned a lot of research. Studies generally confirm Erikson's assertion that young people actively engage in soul searching related to who they are, what they believe in, what it means to have a particular race and ethnicity, and where they are going in life (Marcia, 1980, 1988; M. B. Spencer, 2014). This preoccupation with identity issues extends for a longer period than Erikson proposed (Bartoszuk & Pittman, 2010).
Intimacy vs. Isolation	Young adulthood	Evidence confirms that taking part in intimate relationships is a common concern for young adults. However, some critics suggest that being closely connected with others is a human quality that transcends any single time period (Gilligan, 1982). Furthermore, the early adult years are more complex than Erikson suggested. Young adults are concerned not only with finding a mate but also with getting a good job and in many cases caring for their own small children.
Generativity vs. Stagnation	Middle age	During middle age, most adults organize their lives such that they contribute to the betterment of society, as Erikson proposed. One common critique of Erikson's theory is that he believed that men were primarily concerned with their careers and women with parenting their children. Yet in Western cultures today, both career and family are serious concerns for men and women alike (Livingston, 2014; B. E. Peterson & Stewart, 1996).
Integrity vs. Despair	Retirement years	Looking back on one's life is an important task for many older adults, just as Erikson thought (R. N. Butler, 1963; Torges, Stewart, & Duncan, 2009). However, older adults tackle many other developmental tasks, including finding ways to cope with losses and make the best of their later years (Baltes, 1997; Ramírez, Ortega, Chamorro, & Colmenero, 2014). In other words, older adults live in the present as well as the past.

Summary

Erikson proposed that psychosocial characteristics emerge over the course of eight stages, with the first beginning in infancy and the last occurring in old age. Erikson blazed many trails for later developmental scholars; the volumes of research inspired by his work have obtained general verification as well as a few inaccuracies. Despites its flaws, Erikson's theory is well regarded due to its hopeful portrayal that a person's initiative, warm relationships, and constructive responses to adversity can yield good outcomes across the life span.

ENHANCEDetext *self-check*

ATTACHMENT

Human beings of all ages have a fundamental need to feel socially connected to, and loved and respected by, other people. In other words, they have a **need for relatedness** (Park, Crocker, & Vohs, 2006; S. Ward & Parker, 2013). Across the life span, this need is fulfilled with social bonds of various types, including family relationships, friendships, and romantic ties.

The child's first bond, called an **attachment**, is an enduring emotional tie that unites the child to caregiver and has far-reaching effects on his or her development (Ainsworth, 1973). In the past few decades, the dominant framework on infant–caregiver relationships has been **ethological attachment theory**, a perspective originally proposed by British psychiatrist **John Bowlby** (1907–1990) and later fleshed out by Canadian-American psychologist **Mary Ainsworth** (1913–1999) (Ainsworth, 1963, 1973; Ainsworth et al., 1978; Bowlby, 1951, 1958).

Ethological attachment theory suggests that the human capacity for close relationships evolved over millions of years of human history. Severe environmental conditions in our ancestors' past made it necessary for small children to stay close to parents and for parents to watch over their children. These mutually close ties helped children survive their infancy, develop into productive members of society, and raise their own children in a nurturing manner. The capacity for attachment was presumably passed down from generation to generation.

In today's world, attachments are seen in infants' crying, clinging, and crawling toward parents when distressed. Under less demanding conditions, infants show affection with snuggles, smiles, and cooing. However, what develops in infants is not simply a collection of discrete behaviors, such as crying and smiling, but also an underlying system for relating to parents. This system has two important elements. First, infants learn to use their parents as a *safe haven*. Infants depend on parents for protection from harm and for comfort when feelings of hunger, fatigue, or fear escalate to unmanageable levels. Second, infants use parents as a *secure base*. They relax in the presence of affectionate parents and feel sufficiently safe that they can venture here and there, crawling away but glancing back now and then for reassuring looks from Mom and Dad.

Developmental Course of Children's Attachments

In the process of forming an attachment, infants learn a lot about themselves and other people. A baby slowly develops expectations about shared routines ("When Grandma says, 'Peekaboo,' I hide my eyes and laugh"), beliefs about other people ("Mommy takes care of me"), emotional connections ("I love my Daddy"), and sense of self ("I am lovable"). Children's emerging expectations are facilitated by maturation, cognitive development, and social experience. Bowlby believed that there are four phases in attachment development:

Preattachment. From birth until about 6 to 12 weeks, infants use social signals (e.g., smiling, crying, and making eye contact) that elicit care from others. Babies initially treat adults in an equal opportunity fashion, allowing anyone with the right touch to comfort them (Schaffer, 1996). Yet rudimentary attachments are being formed in these early weeks as infants begin to recognize selected caregivers who respond affectionately to them.

Attachment-in-the-Making. From 6 to 12 weeks through 6 to 8 months after birth, infants learn that they cannot count on just anyone for attention, but instead turn to the few special people who regularly care for them. By the second or third month, infants smile selectively at people they know best, and a month or so later, they laugh uproariously at good-humored antics (Bridgett, Laake, Gartstein, & Dorn, 2013; Camras, Malatesta, & Izard, 1991). In the early months, adults carry the burden for maintaining a social exchange, but infants, when in the right mood, participate eagerly (Saarni, Campos, Camras, & Witherington, 2006). Sensitive caregivers notice when baby is calm and alert, use the occasion to extend a greeting, and wait for baby to make a simple response. With experience, infants become familiar with the rhythms of interaction and playful exchange with caregivers.

Clear-Cut Attachment. Between 6 to 8 months until a year and a half after birth, infants show a full-fledged attachment to one person or a small number of people, including, perhaps, a mother, father, grandparent, employed caregiver, or some combination of these or other individuals. Attachments can be seen when infants reach out to be picked up by adored caregivers; protest when separated from them; and wriggle and coo when adored they walk into the room.

When distressed, infants calm to comforting gestures from responsive parents. Just in time to accompany crawling, nature activates an adaptive emotional reaction, fear of the unknown. Thus, rather than crawling off into the hinterlands, infants stick fairly close to familiar caregivers. When puzzling situations appear out of nowhere, such as a barking dog (woof!) or a jack-in-the-box's loud, unexpected effect (pop!), infants demand reassurance (now!).

Adults unknown to the baby also now trigger fearful reactions. In the latter half of the first year of life and well into the second year, an unfamiliar adult often incites fear in **stranger anxiety** (Hahn-Holbrook, Holbrook, & Bering, 2010; Mangelsdorf, Shapiro, & Marzolf, 1995). You can observe an infant's apprehension of an unfamiliar adult in an Observing Children video. If the stranger has an unusual appearance and moves intrusively, fear can intensify into a red-faced, tearful, arm-flapping demand for safe haven from a familiar caregiver.

Reciprocal Relationship. From about 1½ to 2 years of age, infants use their emerging cognitive and language abilities to make inferences about their parents' goals and plans. Toddlers now grasp some of the factors that determine the parent's coming and going, for example, the mother's schedule in going to work, and accordingly are less inclined to protest the separation. Children now take an active role in their relationships with parents, initiating interactions and taking turns in a conversation, the latter of which you can see in 16-month-old Corwin's interchange in an Observing Children video.

Early Childhood

Parents continue to react sympathetically to children's emotions but gradually shift from giving responsive hands-on care to guidance with rules and facilitation of their interests (Landry et al., 2014). Children who have been consistently treated with kindness, patience, and respect actively reciprocate with affectionate gestures. In Artifact 11-1, you can see "love notes" prepared by Ivy and Alex for their mothers.

Observing Children 11-1
Observe an infant's fear of an unfamiliar adult.
ENHANCEDetext *video example*

Observing Children 11-2
Observe Corwin's contributions to an interaction with his mother.
ENHANCEDetext *video example*

ARTIFACT 11-1   I love you, Mom. Three-year-old Ivy and 4-year-old Alex have chosen the same graphic device, a stacks of hearts, to represent the depth of their feelings for their mothers. Young children often choose other devices as well, such as drawing themselves holding hands with a loved one.

As they did in their infant days, young children rely on familiar caregivers to provide refuge when they are sick, scared, or distressed (S. F. Waters et al., 2010). Protests over separations are fewer now, and stranger anxiety becomes less intense, as children realize that other caregivers besides parents can be dependable (Pinquart, Feußner, & Ahnert, 2013). Affectionate teachers and relatives can be trusted to protect children on occasion (Main & Cassidy, 1988; Schaffer, 1996). Peers also become attachment figures. Children who have developed healthy attachments with parents are generally able to form friendships in which they balance looking after their own needs with compromising with age-mates (Groh et al., 2014; Howes, 1999; Kochanska & Kim, 2013).

Middle Childhood and Adolescence

During the school years, youngsters typically preserve their bonds with parents, all the while growing close to siblings, grandparents, extended family members, teachers, and classmates. Predictable separations (such as going to school each day or to summer camp for a week) worry only a small number of elementary schoolchildren. When relationships with parents are seriously disrupted, however, perhaps because of divorce or death, children may become alarmed, angry, aggressive, or physically ill (Pribilsky, 2001).

Although continuing to derive stability and support from bonds with parents, adolescents prefer to receive loving attention behind the scenes. They also become increasingly close to friends and romantic partners (Elmore & Huebner, 2010; Mayseless, 2005; Venta, Shmueli-Goetz, & Sharp, 2014). In their desire for autonomy and close bonds with peers, teens prepare (consciously or not) for the inevitable departure from the family nest.

Security in Attachment

The developmental course of attachments we have outlined is one that assumes a faithful relationship between caregiver and child. As you will learn, most adults responsible for children earn their trust, but in unfortunate exceptions, a few do not.

If you look around at a group of toddlers or preschool children, you may notice variations in responses to being afraid, hurt, or upset. Some children seek and find comfort in the reassuring arms of caregivers; a few are clingy and fretful; and one or two want to be left alone. To study such differences in the laboratory, Mary Ainsworth created a mildly stressful situation for 1-year-old infants. In a sequence of events, a mother and her infant were first brought to a playroom and left alone. A stranger (a research assistant) soon entered the room and attempted to play with the baby. After 3 minutes, the mother left, leaving the baby alone with the stranger. Subsequently, the mother returned and the stranger departed, leaving mother and baby together. Next, mother departed, with baby alone; the stranger returned at this point. Finally, the mother returned and the stranger departed (Ainsworth et al., 1978). This sequence, now known as the *Strange Situation,* has become a popular tool for assessing attachment in young children.

In the Strange Situation, attention is focused primarily on the child's behavior. Observers rate the child's attempts to seek contact with the caregiver, resistance to or avoidance of caregiver, exploration of toys in the room, and level of distress. From such ratings, the child is given one of several classifications:

Observing Children 11-3

Observe an infant's distress at his father's departure, followed by his relaxation at the father's return.

ENHANCEDetext *video example*

- Infants who exhibit **secure attachment** use caregivers as a secure base. When caregivers are present, infants actively explore new toys and surroundings. When caregivers return after leaving the room, infants smile and talk to them, move over to greet them, or in other ways seek their proximity. In an Observing Children video, you can see a securely attached infant show distress at his father's departure and relief at the father's return. About 60 to 70 percent of infants are classified as securely attached (Ainsworth et al., 1978; R. A. Thompson, 2006).
- Infants who exhibit **insecure-avoidant attachment** seem oblivious to a caregiver's presence. They fail to greet the caregiver and may even look away when reunited. Instead, they go about their business independently, and they are somewhat superficial in their interactions with toys. About 15 to 20 percent of children tested in Strange Situation studies are insecure-avoidant (Ainsworth et al., 1978; R. A. Thompson, 2006).
- Infants who exhibit **insecure-resistant attachment** seem preoccupied with their caregivers yet are not easily comforted when returned to them. When caregivers

come back, the infants remain distressed and angry. They may rush to parents and other caregivers yet quickly struggle to be released. Insecure-resistant infants comprise about 10 percent of participants in Strange Situation studies (Ainsworth et al., 1978; R. A. Thompson, 2006).

- More serious problems in attachment, which were not part of Ainsworth's original classification, have since been identified by other experts. A **disorganized and disoriented attachment** style has been documented, in which infants lack a coherent way of responding to worrisome events (Carlson, Hostinar, Mliner, & Gunnar, 2014; Main & Solomon, 1986, 1990; Zilberstein & Messer, 2010). Infants classified in this manner appear calm one moment, yet, without provocation, are scared or angry the next. Infants even interrupt their own actions midstream, for example, by crawling toward caregivers and then suddenly freezing with apprehension. In addition, a very few children show *no* attachment behaviors or exhibit other extremely serious problems, such as displaying fear of familiar caregivers rather than being comforted by them. Approximately 15 percent of children show a disorganized and disoriented attachment, no attachment, or another serious attachment problem (R. A. Thompson, 2006).

The Observation Guidelines table "Assessing Young Children's Attachment Security" summarizes how children with particular kinds of attachments might act. In observing children, teachers and caregivers should guard against taking any single response from a child as an undisputable indicator of attachment security; they should instead look for patterns of behavior over time.

The Bioecology of Attachment

In taking a bioecological perspective, we are reminded that the child contributes to his or her first relationships by relaxing when comforted, taking an active role in the interaction, and expressing positive regard for the caregiver. The types of attachments that emerge are affected by the quality of the caregiver–child relationship, the child's own behavior, and the cultural setting.

Quality of Caregiver–Child Relationship

The relationship between caregiver and child is the primary basis of attachment security. When caregivers are sensitive to young children, protect them from harm, respond sympathetically to their emotions, and provide for their needs, children are usually able to develop secure attachments (Farrow & Blissett, 2014; R. A. Thompson, 2006). Caregivers who are sensitively engaged show these qualities:

- *Consistent responses to infants' needs.* Caregivers establish routines for feeding, diapering, and holding infants. They do not run to every whimper, but they do notice and respond to infants' basic emotional reactions and are faithfully available when infants are in true anguish (M. Cassidy & Berlin, 1994; Farrow & Blissett, 2014; Morawska, Laws, Moretto, & Daniels, 2014; R. A. Thompson, Easterbrooks, & Padilla-Walker, 2003). When introducing a new food, sensitive parents observe infants' facial expressions and their tasting and swallowing. Caregivers who fail to be responsive are neglectful, intrusive, or erratically available; others are callous to infants' preferences and feelings.
- *Regular expressions of affection.* Caregivers dote on babies by caressing them, holding them gently, looking into their eyes, talking to them, and expressing tenderness. With these gestures, caregivers communicate pleasure in the mutual exchange (Posada, 2013). Caregivers who fail to show this quality may be withdrawn or even hostile and rejecting.
- *Openness to babies influencing the pace and direction of interaction.* Caregivers let infants take the lead on occasion. They carefully note where infants are looking, notice their body posture, look for emotional expressions, and recognize when infants want to interact (Farrow & Blissett, 2014; Isabella & Belsky, 1991; D. N. Stern, 1977). Adults also act in synchrony with infants, considering it a turn in the interaction when infants smile, move their hands, or babble. Caregivers who fail to show this quality may instead be intrusive, not respectful of infants' interests, and inclined to direct infants' attention and behavior, perhaps to the point that infants look away, cry, or try to go to sleep. Other unresponsive caregivers fail to notice infants' bids for affection—for example, by ignoring infants' attempts to make eye contact.

FOR FURTHER EXPLORATION . . .

Read more about serious problems in infants' attachments to their parents and other primary caregivers.

ENHANCEDetext
content extension

BIOECOLOGY OF DEVELOPMENT

Children play a role in their attachments by learning about family members and reciprocating with affectionate gestures. Children develop secure attachments when cared for by responsive family members who follow cultural traditions in expressing affection.

OBSERVATION GUIDELINES
Assessing Young Children's Attachment Security

CHARACTERISTIC	LOOK FOR	EXAMPLE	IMPLICATION
Secure Attachment	• *Active, intentional exploration* of the environment in the presence of caregiver • *Protest at being separated from a caregiver*; ability to be soothed when the caregiver returns • *Initial wariness of strangers*, with subsequent acceptance if reassured by a familiar caregiver	Luis cries when his father drops him off at the child care center in the morning. After a few minutes, he settles down and crawls to an affectionate teacher who is beginning to become an attachment figure for him.	It is natural for young children to resist separation from family members. Help little tykes establish a routine for saying good-bye in the morning, and give them extra attention during transitions. Reassure parents and describe the activities their children typically turn to after they relax.
Insecure-Avoidant Attachment	• *Superficial exploration* of the environment • *Indifference to a caregiver's departure*; failure to seek comfort upon the caregiver's return • *Apparent discomfort around strangers*, but without an active resistance to their social overtures	Jennifer walks around her new child care center with a frown on her face. She parts easily with her mother and willingly explores her new environment, albeit without much enthusiasm. Jennifer glances up when her mother comes at the end of the day but doesn't seem overjoyed with her mother's return.	Independence from parents is often a sign of children's familiarity with child care or preschool settings. For children who seem at ease with separation, support them throughout the day. When children appear indifferent to family members, form your own affectionate relationships with these children, knowing that such ties could become their first secure bonds.
Insecure-Resistant Attachment	• *Exceptional clinginess and anxiety* with caregiver • *Agitation and distress* at caregiver's departure; continued crying or fussing after caregiver returns • *Apparent fear of strangers*; tendency to stay close to caregiver in new situation	Irene tightly clutches her mother as the two enter the preschool room, and she stays close by as her mother signs her in for the morning. She is extremely upset when her mother leaves, seems to play with little enthusiasm during her mother's absence, and remains agitated for a long time after their reunion later in the day.	If children appear anxious when they enter a new child care or preschool setting, give them extra time to separate from parents. Sometimes a "comfort" object from home (a teddy bear or blanket) can help. Be patient as you interact with these children, knowing that they may eventually be able to form a secure attachment with you.
Disorganized and Disoriented Attachment or Other Serious Attachment Problem	• *Unpredictable emotions* • *Cautious approaches* to caregivers, possibly indicative of fright • *Failure to contact caregiver* when distressed (after age 1) • *Reckless exploration* and failure to seek reassurance from caregiver • *Reversed roles*, with excessive concern about caregiver • *No signs of attachment* to familiar caregivers; and possible fear of them • *Indiscriminately friendly behavior* and no preferential actions toward familiar caregivers • *Signs of overwhelming grief* after death of a primary caregiver	Myles seems lost at school. He arrives hungry, walks around aimlessly, and eventually sits and plays with blocks. He is aggressive with his peers, and his teacher sees bruises on his arms.	Provide special attention to and closely monitor children who seem to have serious attachment problems. Be on the lookout for signs of abuse, and be ready to consult authorities. Remember that these children are *not* doomed to serious lifelong problems, but you must work hard to establish positive, trusting relationships with them. Professional intervention may be necessary.

Sources: Ainsworth et al., 1978; J. Cassidy, Jones, & Shaver, 2013; Gervai, 2009; M. T. Greenberg, 1999; Lundahl, Bettmann, Hurtado, & Goldsmith, 2014; Main & Solomon, 1986, 1990; Schuengel et al., 2013; Svanberg, Mennet, & Spieker, 2010; R. A. Thompson, 2006; Zeanah, 2000.

Children's Characteristics

Children actively participate in their relationships with caregivers by making their needs known, relaxing when comforted, and reciprocating with affection. Through their moods, gestures, and behaviors, infants influence the manner in which caregivers interact with them. Whereas some fuss a lot when scared, others protest less adamantly. Infants who are exceptionally fearful and irritable can be difficult to care for, whereas those who are good natured and sociable invite positive interactions (Brumariu & Kerns, 2013; R. A. Thompson, 2006).

For most children with disabilities, their special circumstances play only a minor role in the security of their bonds to caregivers. Babies who are premature, delayed in developmental milestones, and unusually fussy tend to develop secure attachments as long as their individual needs are met with patience and compassion (van IJzendoorn, Goldberg, Kroonenberg, & Frenkel, 1992; Spangler, 2013). Likewise, babies with chromosomal or genetic disorders or other disabilities typically form secure attachments when parents provide responsive care (E. A. Carlson, Sampson, & Sroufe, 2003).

Yet attachment problems can arise in children with disabilities. Some parents find it taxing to meet the needs of a child with disabilities (Abubakar et al., 2013). Or they may struggle to identify infants' cues for distress and affection, with the infants in turn not easily understanding their parents' motives. Children with Down syndrome have been found to form close bonds with parents but, when distressed, request comfort using subtle gestures that are not easily recognized by parents (Schuengel, de Schipper, Sterkenburg, & Kef, 2013).

The bioecological framework reminds us that the relationships that parents develop with their children are affected by the broader settings in which they live. Although most parents are able to respond warmly to children's bids for affection, burdens can accumulate in parents' lives and spark their impatience, insensitivity, and withdrawal (J. Patterson & Vakili, 2014). When risks take multiple forms, perhaps a serious marital conflict, chronic illness, and economic poverty, parents may become too overwhelmed to offer sensitive care to infants, especially those who are exceptionally needy, irritable, or muted in their bids for affection.

Cultural Setting

Parents follow cultural practices in caring for infants, and infants in turn grow accustomed to the style of interaction. Many Japanese, Indonesian, and Korean infants become upset when their mothers leave the room and take a while to calm down after their return (Jin, Jacobvitz, Hazen, & Jung, 2012; Miyake, Chen, & Campos, 1985; Takahashi, 1990). This reaction probably occurs because infants in these societies rarely separate from mothers and when they do, it is in the care of close relatives (especially grandparents) rather than strangers (Saarni et al., 2006). In contrast, in Germany, many babies do not fret much when their mothers leave the room, nor do they move frantically toward mothers at their return (Grossmann, Grossmann, Huber, & Wartner, 1981; LeVine & Norman, 2008). German mothers regularly leave infants to do brief errands, and the infants grow used to being on their own for brief periods of time.

Cultures also prescribe appropriate methods for responding to infants' distress (Jin et al., 2012; Morelli & Rothbaum, 2007). Gusii mothers of Kenya continually hold, comfort, and watch their infants, who rarely cry (LeVine, 2004). Gusii mothers are alarmed when they watch videos of Western mothers allowing infants to cry, even for a few moments. In comparison, some Western mothers believe that they are cultivating self-reliance when they allow infants to comfort themselves. Consider the experience of a German aunt who is caring for Karl, almost 2 years of age, while his parents are away on a 2-week vacation:

> "Oh, he's a good boy, but a bit fussy," his aunt says. . . . The aunt tells of how early he wakes up in the morning, at six o'clock, "but I'm not to take him out of bed, Sigrid (Karl's mother) said, he's to stay there until nine or he'll just get used to it and she won't have it; she's done that from when he was a baby." So Karl is kept in bed, he stays quiet, she doesn't know what he does, hears him move about in his bed, babbling to himself. (LeVine & Norman, 2008, p. 134)

In North America and Western Europe, many parents tenderly respond to their infants' cooing and babbling (P. M. Cole & Tan, 2007; R. A. Thompson & Virmani, 2010). Consider an affectionate interaction between a U.S. father and his 3-month-old daughter Toto after a family event. In the following exchange, the father interacts good-naturedly with Toto, regularly waiting for, and then commenting on, her vocalizations:

Father: 5:30 p.m. Post-mortem on a party.
Toto: Eh.
Father: What was your reaction? What was your reaction? Did you like the food?
Toto: Ah! Ahaa ah.
Father: Yeah, that milk huh? It wasn't so bad, huh? And the guests—did you like the guests?
Toto: Eh.

Father:	No, not so interesting.
Toto:	Eh! Ah ah.
Father:	What about the host and hostess?
Toto:	Aha aaaaah!
Father:	Yeah! Uncle Jim and Auntie Ann!
Toto:	Aaah!
Father:	Yeah, they're very nice.
Toto:	Ha! Ha! Ha! Oh.
Father:	Yeah; and did you enjoy yourself?
Toto:	Aha! Aaah! Aaah!
Father:	Yeah you had a good time. Well that's nice.
Toto:	Ah haa!
Father:	Well that's really nice.
Toto:	Heheh! Ahh! Hehh!
Father:	Did you think so as well? Yeah, I think so. Hmm? Yes?
Toto:	Hah! Aaaah! Ah!
Father:	You didn't cry at all and you were very polite!
	(dialogue from Reissland, 2006, p. 44)

From this exchange and other similar interactions, Toto is learning that her father can be trusted to be warm, reliable, and respectful of her efforts at communication. Parents from different societies show their sensitivity through gentle touch and anticipation of infants' physical needs rather than through mutual vocalizations. Like Toto, infants in these cultures learn that their parents can be trusted to care for them.

Multiple Attachments

Early investigators focused on mothers as primary attachment figures, probably because women physically bear children and have historically done most of the feeding, bathing, and diapering (Ainsworth et al., 1978; Bowlby, 1969/1982). Increasingly, research has examined the significant roles that fathers, other caregivers, and siblings play as attachment figures.

When two parents are present in the home, infants frequently show an initial preference for one parent and soon welcome the second parent as a second attachment figure. Both parents are likely to instill secure attachments when they responsively attend to children's needs, express affection, and remain in children's lives for an extended time (Boldt, Kochanska, Yoon, & Koenig Nordling, 2014; Howes, 1999; R. A. Thompson et al., 2003). Nevertheless, mothers and fathers go about expressing their warmth in slightly different ways. Mothers tend to be more hands-on in caring for infants, enthusiastic while interacting with them, verbal in their interactions, and thoughtful about what their infants might be experiencing, whereas fathers tend to engage infants in physical play, handling of toys, and exploration of the environment (M. E. Lamb & Lewis, 2004; Malmberg et al., 2007; Nordahl, Janson, Manger, & Zachrisson, 2014). You can observe a father's playful style with his 7-month-old daughter in an Observing Children video.

Although attachment theorists initially suggested that an infant's early attachments to primary caregivers (especially the mother) set the tone for *all* future relationships (e.g., Bowlby, 1973), more recent research has shown otherwise. As Merv's experience in the opening case study reveals, the kinds of bonds children form with parents do not firmly dictate the quality of future relationships. Contemporary researchers have found that young children regularly form attachments with siblings, grandparents, and other caregivers (E. Farmer, Selwyn, & Meakings, 2013; M. Lewis, 2005; Seibert & Kerns, 2009). In fact, many children who have been maltreated by their parents during infancy are able to develop secure attachments to foster and adoptive parents within a brief period of time (Altenhofen, Clyman, Little, Baker, & Biringen, 2013).

Having a network of affectionate people at their disposal has valuable benefits for children (Easterbrooks et al., 2013; C. B. Fisher, Jackson, & Villarruel, 1998; Howes, 1999). The various attachment figures in the child's network can each take on distinct affectionate roles. A 1-year-old crawls to Grandma when a stranger enters the family home; at 6, the same child now seeks advice from his older sister as he faces bullies on the playground; and at 14, the

Observing Children 11-4

Observe 7-month-old Madison and her father interact playfully and affectionately.

ENHANCEDetext *video example*

youngster has heart-to-heart talks with an uncle about career options. Relationships with all of these family members remain steady, but the particular kinds of support are differentially helpful over time.

Attachments with teachers and employed caregivers serve a critical role for many children. Secure bonds with professionals, as is the case with parents, depend on responsive care, sustained relationships, and mutual emotional investment (Ahnert, Pinquart, & Lamb, 2006; Howes, 1999). During the preschool and elementary years, children often develop close bonds with teachers, thriving on teachers' affectionate care and gaining a sense of security in their presence (Cugmas, 2011; H. A. Davis, 2003). In fact, when children's relationships with parents are impaired, a close bond with a teacher can compensate for an insecure start on life (Sabol & Pianta, 2012).

In the middle school years, close relationships with teachers occur but are now less common because young adolescents spend only a small portion of time with any single teacher, are in classes with large groups of students, and may feel anonymous at school. When young adolescents have supportive relationships with their teachers, they tend to enjoy school, feel competent, and achieve at high levels academically (Al-Yagon, 2012; H. A. Davis, 2003; Roeser, Midgley, & Urdan, 1996).

Unfortunately, obstacles to close relationships with teachers intensify in high school. Adolescents often find relationships with teachers to be adversarial—it's "us" against "them"— possibly because many high school teachers view adolescents as rebellious, independent, and resistant to close relationships with them (H. A. Davis, 2003). Yet good relationships with teachers are possible and clearly beneficial for youth. High school students who have supportive relationships with teachers and other mentors are more likely to be well adjusted and to complete high school than are students without such support (Cotterell, 1992; Georgiou, Demetriou, & Stavrinides, 2008).

Attachment Security and Later Development

A secure attachment during infancy predicts positive long-term benefits. In Western cultures, children who have been securely attached as infants tend to become relatively independent, empathic, socially competent preschoolers (Sroufe, 1983; Sroufe, Egeland, Carlson, & Collins, 2005; Vaughn, Egeland, Sroufe, & Waters, 1979). In middle childhood and adolescence, they tend to be self-confident, adjust easily to school environments, establish productive relationships with teachers and peers, do well on classroom tasks, and graduate from high school (Groh et al., 2014; E. O'Connor & McCartney, 2006; Urban, Carlson, Egeland, & Sroufe, 1991). Security of attachment is also related to later relationships, general well-being, and parenting, with adults who had been securely attached as infants tending to look after their own children in a sensitive way (Berlin, Cassidy, & Appleyard, 2008; Mikulincer & Shaver, 2013). Of course, the full range benefits of secure relationships depend on cultural practices. For Japanese children, close and affectionate relationships with caregivers foster dependence on caregivers' benevolence and a desire to act harmoniously with others (Morelli & Rothbaum, 2007).

Attachment theorists believe that a secure bond helps children form positive, self-fulfilling expectations about other people. As children gain experience with primary caregivers, they form a mental representation of the degree to which their needs are met in primary relationships (Bowlby, 1969/1982, 1973; R. M. Ryan, Stiller, & Lynch, 1994). Especially when they are young, children's understanding of "typical" relationships is largely unconscious but nevertheless influential in directing relationships with other individuals, including teachers (S. C. Johnson et al., 2010; Maier, Bernier, Pekrun, Zimmermann, & Grossmann, 2004). Secure children expect other people to be trustworthy, and they give second chances to those who initially let them down—expectations and actions that sustain healthy interpersonal ties. In contrast, children with insecure attachments may form expectations of other people as untrustworthy and unworthy of second chances.

Early attachments also affect children through learned emotional responses. With secure relationships, children who become angry, hurt, and scared are typically soothed. Yet children whose caregivers are insensitive fail to help children settle down, and as a result, these children are prone to respond to pressure, strain, discomfort, and threat with maladaptive escalations of anger and fear (Borelli et al., 2010; Madigan, Atkinson, Laurin, & Benoit, 2013). Such emotional responses become habitual, in part because of their biological basis—the child responds in a certain way when angered, disappointed, frustrated, ashamed, or the like, triggering the release of certain hormones and a cascade of physiological reactions— possibly a nervous sensation in the stomach, sweating, or a headache. As these emotions unfold, children respond in an individually characteristic way, perhaps shouting and pushing, taking a deep breath, walking away from the situation, or seeking out a sympathetic friend or teacher who can listen and advise (B. Klein, Gorter, & Rosenbaum, 2013).

Despite the effects of attachment quality on expectations and emotions, many children with initially troubled attachments *are* able to rebound when later treated with kindness and respect, especially if the positive change comes by early childhood. In one investigation children whose parents were initially harsh and insensitive but later exhibited high-quality parenting were likely to develop increasingly productive social skills (NICHD Early Child Care Research Network, 2006b). Children who have been raised in stark orphanages with perfunctory care are often able to form secure bonds with responsive adoptive parents (Carlson et al., 2014). The reverse trend also occurs, although perhaps less often. Children who initially form secure attachments but later live through one or more traumatic events (perhaps a stormy divorce, a debilitating illness in the family, or their abuse) may have difficulty forming good relationships as adolescents or adults (M. Lewis, Feiring, & Rosenthal, 2000; Mikulincer & Shaver, 2007; E. Waters, Merrick, Treboux, Crowell, & Albersheim, 2000).

Thus, as youngsters grow older, relationships with teachers and friends and, eventually, romantic partners, provide opportunities for new types of attachments (M. W. Baldwin, Keelan, Fehr, Enns, & Koh-Rangarajoo, 1996; C. Chow & Ruhl, 2014). Children thus supplement their initial mental representation of what interpersonal relationships are like with new understandings of how relationships can unfold. Eventually, these various mental representations become integrated as a part of the child's personality (R. A. Thompson, 2006). In other words, children may initially develop trust in a parent and later become trusting people themselves.

Implications of Attachment Research

As we have seen, infants' attachments provide the foundation for later relationships. This foundation can be rebuilt if it's shaky, and it must occasionally be bolstered if, despite a solid beginning, it weakens in the face of adverse circumstances. Drawing from attachment literature, we offer these recommendations for teachers, counselors, and other professionals:

• **Care for young children in a warm and sensitive manner.** Although family members are usually the recipients of children's first attachments, young children additionally form close bonds with employed caregivers and teachers, especially those who are familiar, responsive, and trustworthy. The Development and Practice feature "Offering Warm and Sensitive Care to Infants and Toddlers" illustrates such high-quality care.

• **Give children time to adjust to you.** It takes time for young children to form bonds with new caregivers, although the particular difficulties they face depend to some degree on the quality of their relationships with parents. Infants who are securely attached to parents usually need several weeks to adjust to an unfamiliar caregiver's unique personality and style of interacting. In the meantime, new caregivers need to offer lots of comfort during separations from parents. Infants who have not yet experienced sensitive care may feel anxious or withdrawn for weeks or even months before they decide that a new adult can be trusted. While children are adjusting, practitioners can be affectionate, meet their needs, empathize with their feelings, and celebrate their accomplishments. In fact, children without prior secure attachments often benefit immensely when other caregivers act consistently, patiently, and lovingly (García Sierra, 2012; Howes & Ritchie, 1998).

Teachers who become the targets of young children's first attachments realize that children may initially protect themselves by being hostile, aloof, or superficially friendly (García Sierra, 2012). Sensitive teachers persist in showing consideration despite unusual or offensive behaviors that children exhibit. They also reassure children when negative feelings spin out of control—as you have learned, children with insecure and disorganized attachments to parents will generally not have learned how to calm down when threatened or angered.

DEVELOPMENT AND PRACTICE
Offering Warm and Sensitive Care to Infants and Toddlers

Meet infants' needs in a timely fashion.

- An infant program has one caregiver for every three infants, a ratio that helps ensure no child being left unattended for long. When it is impossible to tend immediately to the needs of individual children, a caregiver reassures them that their needs are important and she will be there as soon as possible. (Infancy)
- A mother is talking on her cell phone when her baby begins to cry. The mother tells her friend that she will call her back after she gives her baby a bottle and rocks him to sleep. (Infancy)

Respond positively to newly developed abilities.

- Caregivers in one center cheer on milestones, including advances in crawling, first steps, and first words. They share their delight with family members but are sensitive to the desire of parents to be among the first to witness the advancement: "Raj is getting ready to walk, isn't he!" (Infancy)
- A father notices that his 6-month-old son has begun to flip over from back to front. The father gets on the floor beside his son and imitates his roll over. Together they laugh as they move back and forth. (Infancy)

Be polite but matter-of-fact when referring to infants' bodies.

- The director of an infant program trains staff members to use neutral terms for body functions. She asks a new teacher not to use the term "stinky baby," but instead to make a simple statement that an infant's diaper needs to be changed. (Infancy)
- A grandfather notices that his grandson has diarrhea and is developing diaper rash. As he changes the baby's diaper, he tells him, "Your bottom is getting very sore. I'm going to put some ointment on you after I wipe your bottom." (Infancy)

Set limits and redirect unacceptable behavior in a firm, but gentle way.

- The director of an infant-toddler program reminds teachers that their role is one of a *nurturer* who helps children learn self-control rather than an *authority figure* who doles out punishments. He suggests, "Tell children what they *can* do instead of telling them what they *cannot* do. You might say, 'Walk inside, please. Run outside.'" (Infancy)
- A quick-moving toddler has managed to unplug a humidifier and spill water from the tank. Her caregiver removes her from the scene and inserts safety plugs into the socket. She tells the little girl, "I made a mistake by placing the humidifier where you could reach it. Let me put it somewhere else so you don't get hurt." (Infancy)

Structure group care so that infants can maintain stable relationships with caregivers.

- An infant-toddler program is arranged into separate rooms so that each caregiver has a small number of children with whom to interact. Toddler teachers make a point to visit the infant room occasionally, so that they get to know children who will soon be moving to their room. (Infancy)
- In one child care center, caregivers arrange children into groups that stay together; as the infants outgrow the "Infant Room," for example, they "graduate" together to the "Toddler Room," and their caregiver goes with them. (Infancy)

- **Nurture bonds in children of all ages.** The need for close attachments does not end with infancy. Children stand to gain immensely by having high-quality relationships with their teachers during the elementary, middle, and high school years. Generally, teachers and caregivers find it easier to become acquainted with individual children in elementary school than do practitioners working with adolescents in middle and high school. However, teachers of middle and high school students can express their concern for individual students and get to know adolescents they advise or see often (H. A. Davis, 2003). Adults can further promote ties among youngsters, giving them chances to become involved in clubs and sports teams, work together in projects, and so forth.

- **Model affectionate caregiving for family members.** Parents of infants who had insecure relationships themselves in their childhoods may lack confidence and enjoyment in their parenting (Mikulincer & Shaver, 2007). One of the most effective tactics family educators can take with insensitive parents is to *show* them (in person or through videotapes) how infants devour affectionate gestures, especially during such routine games as playing peekaboo and sharing simple nursery rhymes (Bakermans-Kranenburg, van IJzendoorn, & Juffer, 2003; Carr, 2014; Svanberg et al., 2010). Family educators can demonstrate how to hold a baby tenderly and return the baby's smiles, vocalizations, and eye contact. They also can point out the signals infants give that indicate they are not ready to play (e.g., averting a gaze) or have had enough (e.g., pouting).

- **Encourage parents to watch children's self-initiated actions.** Practitioners can encourage parents to watch for children's interests and preferences. Babies learn a great deal by performing such simple activities as looking at their fingers, sucking on their toes, and listening to voices. When parents appreciate the significance of infants' spontaneous learning, they are more inclined to affirm and extend it ("Look at that mirror, Abigail! Is it shiny? Do you see yourself?").

• **Encourage parents to think about how children understand events.** Parents do not always understand what makes their babies "tick" ("Why does Mike keep jumping out of his crib? Every time he does this, he gets hurt. What is he *thinking?*"). Professionals can share ideas about infants' motives, feelings, and understandings to help parents appreciate how babies might view the world ("Mike is one determined little guy, isn't he? He really wants to explore his environment!"). When parents learn to reflect on how infants feel and construe events, attachments tend to become more secure (Koren-Karie, Oppenheim, Dolev, Sher, & Etzion-Carasso, 2002).

• **Advise parents about the special needs of children with disabilities.** Some parents feel so overwhelmed by the challenge of caring for a child with a disability that they struggle to identify their child's unique perspective. Yet teachers and caregivers can help parents recognize their child's distinctive ways of expressing emotions. You might ask parents of a blind baby if the baby enjoys exploring their faces with her hands. Similarly, you could point out to parents of a child with Down syndrome that children with this condition sometimes express their discomfort in subtle, rather than insistent ways, and that they appreciate it when caregivers slow down during interactions and give them a chance to control the flow of the exchange (D. Howe, 2006; Schuengel et al., 2013).

• **When children are separated from a primary caregiver, determine the types of extra intercession they need.** Many divorced parents share custody of children, with their children invariably wanting to maintain contact with both parents. Teachers can help by sending home copies of newsletters to both parents' homes. Counselors can also talk with parents about ways in which children of different ages handle rotations between households (J. B. Kelly & Lamb, 2000). When a parent is deployed in the military, hospitalized after surgery, incarcerated, employed out of state, or recently deceased, teachers can offer children reassurance, watch for signs of a traumatic reaction (e.g., regressing in basic skills, such as losing bladder control or struggling to fall asleep at nap time), and recommend intervention if children are truly suffering (Lieberman & Van Horn, 2013; Shear & Shair, 2005). For example, a preschool child who begins to pull her hair out and to ingest it after her father's death may be responding with a self-injurious behavior that signifies her deep distress (Shumsky, 2013).

• **Advocate for stability in employed caregivers.** Children grow attached to teachers who devotedly meet their needs and encourage their initiative. Yet turn-over in early childhood teaching staff is substantial, probably because the position is compensated only modestly and widely misconceived to be an easy job. With teachers coming and going, young children can easily become bonded to a teacher who is present one day only to vanish the next. School and center leaders can promote a stable early childhood staff by paying a competitive wage, enforcing minimal education requirements (e.g., at least three college-level early childhood education courses or a bachelor's degree in the field), and investing in teachers' professional development (e.g., local conferences in which they can get advice on topics of concern, such as culturally sensitive feeding practices or methods for discouraging biting in toddlers) (Blank, 2010; J. Cassidy et al., 2013; Dennis & Horn, 2014; S. Wagner et al., 2013).

• **Encourage multiple attachments.** In the child care center and at school, children may talk about a variety of people in their lives (e.g., brothers and sisters, aunts and uncles, grandparents, and neighbors). Teachers and other practitioners can encourage children to invite these important individuals to school events and orientation meetings. Educators can further help children by establishing a productive classroom environment that fosters youngsters' relationships with one another.[3]

---

[3]We examine classroom climate and a sense of community in Chapter 15.

• **Offer a range of services when children are placed in new families.** When children are removed from families by social service authorities because of maltreatment or neglect, they usually find the transition traumatic but gradually bond to new caregivers (Chisholm, Carter, Ames, & Morison, 1995; Marcovitch et al., 1997; Zilberstein & Messer, 2010). However, professionals who work with children and their new families should not leave this adjustment to chance. Instead, they can prepare new families to recognize and meet children's individual needs. For example, a foster family might be advised to expect temper tantrums from an 8-year-old child who has recently joined the family. With coaching, new parent figures can communicate their expectations for controlled behavior, follow through with agreed-on consequences to violations of rules, and persist in showing love before the child is able to reciprocate with affection. Parents who are under excessive **stress**, the physiological response of feeling worried, tense, and pressured, may benefit from counseling and other therapies (J. Patterson & Vakili, 2014).

• **Encourage sympathetic dispositions in children.** Some children who have had few affectionate relationships develop poor social skills and so may, in many people's eyes, be difficult to like. These children may appear self-centered and unconcerned about others' distress; for example, they may hit a peer who has gotten hurt rather than offer sympathy (Volling, 2001). To help a child who seems uncaring, you can model appropriate reactions when someone is hurt, talk about the injured person's feelings, and encourage the child to offer help and show sympathy. (We examine the cultivation of empathy more thoroughly later in this chapter.)

• **Be especially sensitive with children who show insecurity or other attachment problems.** Children who have not yet developed secure attachments to parents may benefit from warm and consistent routines, especially during arrivals and departures. Without prior history of a mutually loving relationship, children need repeated experiences with the pleasant give-and-take of social interaction (C. S. Cain, 2006; Mercer, 2006). Depending on the age of the child, you might sit quietly with the child in a relaxing activity, such as building blocks together or tossing a ball back and forth. At the same time, children who are anxious in a group setting sometimes feel so insecure that they persistently ask for attention, and their teachers will wish to reassure them without fostering dependence. Professional intervention can be helpful when attachment behaviors become difficult to read or manage (Schuengel et al., 2013).

• **Address the needs of the family when parents struggle with unmet emotional needs.** When parents themselves are emotionally depressed, they may be unresponsive toward their infants, or even hostile and intrusive (Burrous, Crockenberg, & Leerkes, 2009; Teti, Gelfand, Messinger, & Isabella, 1995). Infants with depressed parents may themselves become chronically sad and withdrawn. Professional intervention that helps parents resolve their emotional needs may be a necessary step before they are able to use an involved, affectionate parenting style (Benoit & Parker, 1994; Main, Kaplan, & Cassidy, 1985). During the period in which a parent receives mental health treatment, the other parent or another family member may be able to pick up the slack with tender and responsive care.

• **Seek guidance when attachment problems seem serious.** Some attachment problems are so profoundly disruptive that families require intensive services from a counselor, psychologist, or social worker (C. S. Cain, 2006; Zilberstein & Messer, 2010). You should definitely seek professional guidance when you suspect a serious problem—for instance, when a distressed child never seeks comfort from a familiar caregiver, shows fear of family members, or displays some other highly unusual style of responding to parents (see indicators of serious attachment problems in the Observations Guidelines table "Assessing Young Children's Attachment Security" on p. 416). Fortunately, parents who are willing to learn new ways of interacting and coping have the potential to learn from therapy.

Summary

Ideally, children's first attachments are close and enduring bonds between themselves and their caregivers. Sensitive and responsive attention is the necessary ingredient for secure attachments, but children also contribute by returning affection. Secure attachments in the early years lead to positive social-emotional outcomes in later life. However, attachments manifest themselves somewhat differently in different cultures, and the nature of people's attachments can change over time.

Teachers and other professionals can strive to develop their own positive relationships with children. Sensitive and ongoing care of individual children is the backbone of high-quality relationships with children. Educators can also watch for significant social-emotional challenges faced by children and seek professional guidance if necessary.

ENHANCEDetext *self-check*

EMOTION

Emotions (sometimes referred to as *affective states*) are the feelings, both physiological and psychological, that people have in response to events that are personally relevant to their needs and goals (Campos, Frankel, & Camras, 2004). Emotions energize thinking and acting in ways that are often adaptive for the circumstances (Goleman, 1995; Muris & Meesters, 2014). *Sadness* leads a child to find comfort from others and reassess whether a goal is possible; *anger* spurs a child to try a new tactic or abandon an unrealistic goal; and *happiness* prompts a child to share positive feelings with others and repeat a pleasurable experience in the future (Saarni et al., 2006). These and other emotions are described in the Observation Guidelines table "Assessing Emotion in Children."

OBSERVATION GUIDELINES
Assessing Emotion in Children

CHARACTERISTIC	LOOK FOR	EXAMPLE	IMPLICATION
Happiness	• *Smiles* • *Laughter* • *Spontaneity*	Paul, age 17, relaxes with his friends during his school's end-of-year athletic field day. He is happy about having schoolwork over and looks forward to his summer job and paychecks.	Happiness helps people enjoy life and seek pleasurable experiences. Help children find appropriate outlets to express joy, and celebrate with them. Encourage them to talk about things they are happy about.
Anger	• *Frowns and angry expressions* • *Possible retaliation* toward the source of anger	Aranya, age 14, is furious that she wasn't admitted into an elective course, whereas her two closest friends were. Aranya is angry with the principal, whom she thinks dislikes her.	Anger helps people deal with obstacles to their goals, often spurring them to try new tactics. Help youngsters express their anger appropriately and redirect their energy toward reasonable solutions.
Fear	• *Frightened expression* • *Withdrawal* from circumstances • *Physiological responses*, such as sweating and nervous behavior	Tony, age 2½, sits on his mat, eyes wide, body tense. He stares at a new poster of a clown in his preschool classroom. He is downright scared, runs to his teacher, and buries his head in her lap.	Fear occurs when people feel threatened and believe that their safety and well-being are at stake. Fear motivates people to flee, seek reassurance, and perhaps fight back. Help children articulate their fears and offer them reassurance.
Sadness	• *Sad expression* • *Crying* • *Pouting* • *Being quiet* • *Possible withdrawal* from a situation	Greta, age 15, sits quietly on a bench near her locker. With her head hung low, she rereads the letter from a cheerleading organization. She has not been admitted to a prestigious cheerleading summer camp.	People are sad when they cannot attain a desired goal or when they experience a loss, such as a friend moving to a distant city. Sadness causes people to reassess their goals. Ask children how they are doing, let them regroup, and encourage them to join familiar activities.
Disgust	• *Wrinkled nose* • *Remarks such as "Phew!"* • *Withdrawal* from the source of displeasure	Norton, age 8, looks skeptically at the meal he has just received in the school cafeteria. He wrinkles his nose and averts his gaze from the "tuna melt" on his plate.	Disgust occurs when people encounter food, smells, and sights they find repulsive. Respect children's feelings of disgust, but also encourage them to reflect on why they might respond to particular substances in this way.

OBSERVATION GUIDELINES (continued)
Assessing Emotion in Children

CHARACTERISTIC	LOOK FOR	EXAMPLE	IMPLICATION
Anxiety	• *Frequent worrying* • *Excessive fidgeting*, hand wringing, or nail biting • *Avoidance* of source of anxiety	Tanesha, age 16, has to give an oral presentation to her class. She has spent a lot of time preparing but is worried that, when standing by herself in front of the group, she might get so nervous that she forgets what she needs to say.	As long as it is not excessive, anxiety can spur people to take steps to avoid problems and achieve valued goals. Teach youngsters strategies that keep anxiety at a manageable level, as well as tactics that help them achieve their goals.
Shame	• *Signs of embarrassment* • *Attempts to withdraw* from a situation • *Looking down and away* from other people	Luke, age 9, is stunned. He's just had an accident, urinating on the floor. He had felt a bit antsy beforehand but wasn't aware that he needed to use the toilet. Now 20 pairs of eyes are glued on him.	When children feel ashamed, they know they are not meeting a community's basic ideals. Shame is more motivating when it comes from within rather than stemming from ridicule. Help children redirect their behavior to meet desired standards.
Guilt	• *Sad expression* • *Self-conscious demeanor* • *Possible concern* for a person who has been harmed	A. J., age 12, regrets bad-mouthing his friend Pete. A. J. sinks down low in his chair, feeling remorse for what he said behind Pete's back and for Pete's sadness.	Guilt occurs when people do something that violates personal standards. It leads people to right a wrong and protect others from harm. Suggest to children that they can behave differently next time.
Pride	• *Happy expression* • *Desire to show off* work and accomplishments to other people	Jacinda, age 5, is beaming. For the last 20 minutes, she's painstakingly pasted sequins, stars, and feathers onto a mask. Her final product is a colorful, delicately adorned creation. She displays her happiness with an ear-to-ear grin.	People are proud when they earn others' respect and meet personal goals. Pride fosters continued commitment to achieving high standards and sharing accomplishments with others. Share in children's joy when they accomplish something meaningful for them.

Adaptive functions of emotions based on concepts in Saarni et al., 2006.

As children grow, they learn to recognize feelings in others and reflect on their own affective sensations. A major accomplishment in childhood is **emotional regulation**, the ability to moderate affective states such that feelings are experienced authentically and expressed according to both personal needs and social conventions (Campos et al., 2004; Laurent, 2014). Emotional regulation is a part of *self-regulation* in that it contributes to the child's ability to control behavior to meet personal standards.[4] Children who make healthy strides in emotional regulation accept—unconsciously, to begin with—that their affective states are valid reactions to everyday events but need to be managed rather than allowed to spin out of control (M. Lewis, 2014). Examples of emotional regulation for children include using words rather than fists when angry, seeking comfort from a loved one when upset, and recasting the disappointment of being rejected from a team as an opportunity for trying out a new sport.

Another component of emotional regulation is learning to cope effectively with daily *stressors*, events that overwhelm children, such as unrealistic demands from parents, heated conflicts in the family, low marks on tests, threats from bullies, ridicule from classmates, and uncertainty about being fed, housed, and clothed (Cummings, Braungart-Rieker, & Schudlich, 2013; Laurent, 2014; Muris & Meesters, 2014). Having previously formed secure attachments, in which children have learned to relax in the midst of distress, many children, like Merv in our opening case, overcome significant turmoil without too much trouble.

Emotional regulation is a critical part of a child's well-being. Let's look at the emergence of specific emotional skills, the emotional struggles that children sometimes face, and the kinds of assistance at school that help children meet emotional needs.

[4]Chapter 3 introduces self-regulation.

Developmental Changes in Emotions

How youngsters express, understand, and cope with emotions changes with age and experience. Emotional development is characterized by these trends:

Infants begin life with a few basic emotions and gradually add new feelings. *Contentment, interest,* and *distress* are felt within the first 6 months of life (Braungart-Rieker, Hill-Soderlund, & Karrass, 2010; Easterbrooks et al., 2013; Emde, Gaensbauer, & Harmon, 1976). Hungry babies most certainly feel pleasure when they begin to feed their hungry stomachs. A small smile may occur when infants are relaxed, happy, or enchanted with animated people. Infants show interest by watching objects carefully, inspecting their own body parts, mouthing fingers and toes, and tilting their heads to listen to the fine points of speech and music. Newborns exposed to a loud and sudden noise express distress, usually by crying, and they do the same when hungry and tired.

As they mature, infants add to these basic emotions. Simple distress can become true *anger* when desires are obstructed: Daddy does not come immediately to pick baby up, and Mommy does not indulge baby's desire to press buttons on her mobile phone. Infants show their anger by crying, thrashing, and looking directly, with accusation, at caregivers. Infants tend to show *fear* during the second half of the first year, as with the stranger anxiety we examined earlier. Animals and objects that move in unexpected ways also scare infants.

Infants respond to other people's emotions. The capacity to detect basic emotions in others is present in infancy (Bischof-Köhler, 2012; Haviland & Lelwica, 1987; Hutman & Dapretto, 2009). This ability is illustrated by the **emotional contagion** of babies: When one starts crying, others soon join in (Eisenberg, 1992; Hatfield, Cacioppo, & Rapson, 1994). Reflexive crying is not the same as a true empathic response, however, in which a person is aware of, and concerned with, another's distress. Rather, it is the primitive emotional response of sharing another's distress, much like your own experience in yawning after having witnessed another person in the same act.

Within the first few months of life, infants react to the emotional expressions of caregivers in meaningful ways. They prefer to look at their father smiling than frowning, and they learn to coordinate their expressions with those of familiar caregivers. While interacting with a parent, older sibling, or teacher, infants gradually synchronize their facial expressions with the appearances of their social partner. It takes a lot of practice to coordinate emotions, however, with babies recurrently looking away, appearing distressed, and falling out of synchrony, sometimes even more often than the times they share eye contact and smile in good-natured engagement (Easterbrooks et al., 2013).

When caregivers violate infants' expectations for a particular emotional expression (perhaps by showing no smiles after a period of social play), infants react. Between 3 and 9 months, they respond to a parent's deadpan face by crying, looking away, and using self-soothing behaviors such as sucking their thumbs (Conradt & Ablow, 2010; C. H. Liu, Yang, Fang, Snidman, & Tronick, 2013; G. A. Moore, Cohn, & Campbell, 2001; Tronick, Als, Adamson, Wise, & Brazelton, 1978). These reactions are sufficiently dramatic that they reveal infants' anticipation for how responsive caregivers typically act. They further suggest how difficult it must be when parents are depressed, impaired with drugs, or otherwise unable to engage with them—infants in these situations do not receive the responsive interaction for which they yearn.

Children learn to guide their actions on the basis of other people's facial expressions, mannerisms, and tone of voice. Toward the end of the first year, children monitor others' emotions, particularly of parents and trusted caregivers, when they are not sure of how to respond. Infants show *social referencing* early in their second year: They watch their parents' faces and body language and listen to emotional tones in their voices in a novel or puzzling situation (Boccia & Campos, 1989; Easterbrooks et al., 2013).[5] For instance, a 16-month-old girl may glance at Mommy's face when a new babysitter enters the house. By determining whether Mommy is smiling or frowning, the little girl gets a sense of how to respond to the babysitter.

---

[5]Social referencing is introduced in Chapter 7.

Children expand their repertoire of basic emotions to include self-conscious emotions. Simple feelings such as fear, anger, and pleasure in infancy are supplemented with **self-conscious emotions** in early childhood. These affective states reflect awareness of social standards (M. Lewis, 1993, 2014; R. A. Thompson & Newton, 2010). Self-conscious emotions include guilt, embarrassment, and pride. Teresa recalls early displays of guilt in both of her sons. As preschoolers, the boys would often respond angrily when misbehavior resulted in their being sent to their room or having a privilege taken away. Occasionally they'd swat at her or stomp out of the room. However, they'd often return a while later, looking at her face and affectionately rubbing her arm as they apologized.

Children increasingly reflect on emotions. As early as age 2 or 3, children talk about emotions that they and others experience ("Daniel got mad and pushed me"), and they realize that emotions are connected to people's desires ("Kurt loves to go down the slide and was really mad when he didn't get a turn") (Bretherton, Fritz, Zahn-Waxler, & Ridgeway, 1986; Easterbrooks et al., 2013). By middle childhood, they realize that their interpretations of a situation determine how they feel about it and that other people may have different views and, as a result, different feelings ("Arlene feels bad because she thinks I don't like her") (P. L. Harris, 1989). Children also learn to connect words for emotions (*happy, sad, angry,* etc.) with particular facial expressions and the conditions under which these emotions are elicited.

By middle childhood, children appreciate that emotional expressions do not always reflect people's true feelings (Saarni et al., 2006; Selman, 1980). A 9-year-old may observe his teacher's apparently cheerful demeanor and be aware that because she just lost her brother to cancer she is probably sad inside. During the end of middle childhood, children also understand that they and other people can have ambivalent feelings (S. K. Donaldson & Westerman, 1986; Zajdel, Bloom, Fireman, & Larsen, 2013). A 12-year-old girl may love her father but be angry with him for moving out of the house; she may like going to see him during custodial visits but not like the feelings of turmoil the visits evoke in her.

Children gradually learn to regulate their emotions. Children gradually acquire a constellation of strategies that help them cope with stressful situations (E. M. Brenner & Salovey, 1997; Cummings et al., 2013; P. M. Cole, Armstrong, & Pemberton, 2010). As newborns, infants need help when they feel hungry, scared, or hurt. Most can count on caregivers to help them find relief. As parents and other family members tend to infants' needs, offer a soothing touch, and reassure them verbally, infants calm down and learn that distress can be relieved under certain circumstances (P. M. Cole et al., 2010). Infants also soothe themselves to some extent: They may suck on a thumb, avert their gaze from a stranger, or crawl away from a scary toy (Cummings et al., 2013; Macklem, 2008; Mangelsdorf et al., 1995).

> **Preparing for Your Licensure Examination**
> Your teaching test might ask you about various aspects of self-regulation.

Guidance from parents continues to help young children expand on their coping strategies (Cummings et al., 2013; S. Meyer, Raikes, Virmani, Waters, & Thompson, 2014). Parents may reappraise the situation, reason through why events unfolded as they did, suggest that an alleged combatant is really a disgruntled friend, and recommend a few possible tactics to take. Here a mother suggests a few actions for her young child:

Child: [crying] Mommy!
Mother: Are you okay?
Mother: You want a tissue?
Mother: Can I kiss it and make it better?
Mother: You want to get your baby and make it better?
Mother: Hug your baby.
Mother: Wanna hug your baby? (P. M. Cole et al., 2010, pp. 67–68)

Emotional regulation skills expand dramatically during early childhood, assuming warm and responsive care from adults. Children identify their feelings using particular terms (e.g., being "annoyed") and talk themselves through challenging situations (e.g., reminding themselves to assert that it is *their* turn for the ball rather than shoving the boy currently in its possession; P. M. Cole et al., 2010). Parents serve an important role by expressing frustration verbally: "I'm angry that you promised to make dinner but didn't do it." Children may subsequently use a similar strategy with peers: "I'm angry that you said you'd give me a turn to play with the truck and gave it to Andy before I had a chance." By elementary school,

ARTIFACT 11-2 I try not to hit and shout. Seven-year-old Miguel commented on his efforts to express anger appropriately.

children have typically learned to talk comfortably about emotions, consider the perspectives of others (e.g., being polite when receiving an unwanted gift from a well-meaning relative), express their emotions in play, remain composed when angry, and anticipate the kind of situations that are likely to be enjoyable or upsetting (Macklem, 2008).

During the middle childhood and adolescent years, emotional regulation continues to evolve. Many young people realize that when they are upset they can substitute one activity for another (e.g., watching baseball on television after an injury rather than trying to play the game themselves), ask for support from peers or adults, try to be patient, or change the way they think about a troubling situation (e.g., by trying to forget about it, go to sleep, or reappraise the situation by focusing on its positive features; E. L. Davis, Levine, Lench, & Quas, 2010; P. M. Cole et al., 2011). Some children talk themselves through challenging situations as an adult might have done for them in the past, and in so doing curb aggressive impulses or persist on a difficult assignment despite obstacles (K. L. Day & Smith, 2013). In Artifact 11-2, 7-year-old Miguel reflects on how he controls his temper. Elementary and secondary school students also become more vigilant in hiding certain feelings, for example, when trying to project a nonchalant mood when in reality disappointed with a low test score.

Children develop personal styles of responding to stress. Children who have been raised by responsive caregivers typically adjust to occasional hardships with relative ease (Hibel, Granger, Blair, & Cox, 2011). Yet even a child who has had an affectionate upbringing is likely to falter if threatening events exceed his or her coping skills. Those who have developed insecure or disorganized attachments, without the advantages of later responsive relationships or informal coaching in coping skills, find it especially challenging to deal with the hassles of daily life.

Styles of responding to stress become engrained as circuits in the brain and body. Emotions are processed by a collection of interacting parts, most notably the *hypothalamic-pituitary-adrenocortical (HPA) axis*, a system for registering stress and mobilizing the body for protective action. This system develops during the prenatal period and matures in early childhood (R. Thompson, 2014). When a child encounters a threat in the environment (perhaps an unfamiliar adult entering the room), the *hypothalamus*—an almond-sized structure in the brain involved with basic physiological processes including eating, sleeping, and maintaining body temperature—is put on alert and galvanizes the *pituitary,* a pea-sized gland that sends instructions to other glands to produce hormones. Once stimulated, the pituitary releases a substance that triggers the *adrenocortical glands,* small organs near each kidney, to produce cortisol. Release of cortisol mobilizes the child's energy, suppresses immune response, and arouses the cardiovascular system, effects that collectively enable the child to focus intently on a threat and react quickly if necessary.

Activation of the HPA axis has the life-sustaining purpose of escaping danger. Yet when overloaded, the outcome is diminished health. Chronic stress undermines the immune function, elevates blood pressure, and increases inflammatory tendencies in the body. When confronted with excessive stress without ample reassurance from caregivers, children struggle physiologically. Those who are exposed to toxic stress have trouble relaxing and become hyper-vigilant, feeling that something is invariably wrong and remaining on constant alert for potential dangers (J. E. Carroll et al., 2013; S. B. Johnson, Riley, Granger, & Riis, 2013). Children with toxic stress are at risk for obesity and other health problems, and they have difficulty concentrating, remembering things, enjoying productive relationships with peers, and restraining impulsive behavior. Moreover, children exposed to toxic stress face serious long-term risks through wear and tear on the body, for example, by developing heart disease and succumbing to substance abuse.

Given the marvelous capacity for resilience in childhood, children retain the ability to acquire new coping strategies even after having solidified previous patterns. Interventions emphasizing warm, responsive, and stable care with infants, toddlers, and older children who exhibit abnormal stress reactions can generate improvements in their coping skills (P. A. Fisher Gunnar, Dozier, Bruce, & Pears, 2006; Samuels & Blitz, 2014). We examine anxiety and depressions later in the chapter but for now suggest the importance of remaining as unruffled in possible in the face of turmoil, so as to keep children relaxed, watching carefully for children's body language and facial expressions, and establishing pleasant routines, such as a warm afternoon meeting in which children sit in a circle and take turns telling about their day (Walkley & Cox, 2013).

Adolescents who have experienced toxic stress have the same needs as younger children, in that they require ongoing considerate care. New challenges arise as young people's failure to regulate emotions, intensified by the hormones of puberty, culminates in overblown reactions (Obadina, 2013). Specially trained counselors, foster parents, and teachers can help anxious, irritable, and distrustful adolescents distinguish situations that are truly threatening from those that are not. Adults can also coach adolescents in expressing emotions in open but controlled ways (Catania, Hetrick, Newman, & Purcell, 2011; Dozier & Fisher, 2014).

Concern for others' feelings develops with age. Empathy, the ability to recognize and share the feelings of another person, is essential for getting along in society (Eisenberg, Eggum, & Edwards, 2010; Hoffman, 1991). An empathic child draws from cognitive skills while inferring the perspective of another person and from emotional skills while the other person's feelings (Schwenck et al., 2014).

Empathy develops gradually. In their first months, infants cry reflexively at hearing others in distress, at 6 months, they gesture to someone in distress, and between 8 and 12 months appear uncomfortable and quizzical when another child is hurt (Davidov, Zahn-Waxler, Roth-Hanania, & Knafo, 2013). In the second year, toddlers show empathic concern by patting a distressed friend on the back (Zahn-Waxler, 1991). By the third year, children console injured friends by expressing sympathy through facial expressions and reassuring words. Empathy advances further during the elementary school years, with children gaining cognitive skills for identifying others' perspectives and inferring the kinds of support that would best alleviate the distress. Empathic concern continues to grow during the adolescent years, although it is occasionally superseded by less honorable motives, such as prioritizing one's own immediate needs at another's expense (Van der Graaff et al., 2014). You can listen to Brendan express empathic concern for injured birds in an Observing Children video.

Observing Children 11-5
Listen to Brendan express empathic concern for injured birds.
ENHANCEDetext *video example*

The developmental growth in empathy that we examined depends on reasonably sensitive parenting. As infants begin to synchronize facial expressions and vocalizations with those of parents, they gain a sense of parents' emotional states (Farrant, Devine, Maybery, & Fletcher, 2012; Feldman, 2007; Kochanska, 2002). Infants soon notice a parent becoming concerned when he or she is distressed and afterwards reciprocate with sympathetic gestures. With older children, parents regularly talk about the plights of other people and help children interpret these experiences. Such guidance enhances children's ability to engage in perspective taking and motivates them to assist others in need (Farrant et al., 2012).

As you have learned, some children lack the advantage of being in a mutually responsive relationship. This deprivation is problematic because it leaves children feeling bad about themselves and unprepared to focus on others' needs. Peer relationships suffer, as does the child's impetus to behave compliantly at school (A. Carr, 2014; Happé & Frith, 2013). In many cases, children who lack relevant socialization at home can gain access to the necessary support from concerned teachers, foster parents, extended family members, and counselors. For example, in the classroom and on the playground, teachers can gently remind a self-centered child to consider the feelings of a distressed classmate (Luke & Banerjee, 2012). With children who are downright callous of others' feelings, professional treatment is desirable (A. Carr, 2014; Happé & Frith, 2013).

The upper elementary and secondary years unleash new pressures. Concerns about fitting in at school, making mistakes in front of others, completing difficult homework, deciding on a career, and having an ideal body type intensify during adolescence (Bokhorst, Westenberg, Oosterlaan, & Heyne, 2008; Moksnes, Espnes, & Haugan, 2014; Phelan et al., 1994). Other pressures are felt at home. As youngsters grow more independent, they sometimes find themselves embroiled in disputes with parents (Arnett, 1999; Moksnes et al., 2010). Some young people encounter other worrying circumstances in their community, such as violence or prejudice (Conner-Warren, 2014). These and other

ARTIFACT 11-3 Under pressure. During his high school year, 17-year-old Jeff felt "locked in" by the combined pressures of a demanding course load, impending due dates for college applications, and his role as confidant for several troubled friends. Late one night, he put his schoolwork aside to create this picture. Because he had trouble drawing human figures, he combined two favorite things—a soft drink can and black-and-white cowhide—to represent himself. A cage and gigantic boulder hold him in, and so he cannot join his peers (represented by other soft drink cans) who frolic freely in the distance.

BIOECOLOGY OF DEVELOPMENT

Children's emotional development is influenced by their gender and experience in social settings.

pressures can provoke serious apprehension in adolescents. In Artifact 11-3, you can see 17-year-old Jeff's portrayal of the pressures he experienced during his senior year of high school.

Coping skills expand during childhood and into adolescence. You may recall that even infants cope with distress using such simple tactics as sucking on a thumb or calling for a parent. During early and middle childhood, distraught children continue to rely on parents and trustworthy teachers for consolation and advice. They also try such strategies as distracting themselves with a movie or electronic game, planning how to avoid the same problem in the future, and watching how peers solve similar dilemmas. Teenagers continue to add coping skills to their repertoire, for instance by talking through personal concerns with trusted friends (Zimmer-Gembeck & Skinner, 2008).

Obviously, not all responses to stress are adaptive. Instead of addressing concerns directly, some students hope problems will simply go away—sometimes they do, of course, but not always (Zimmer-Gembeck & Skinner, 2008). Other young people ruminate over difficulties, some to such an extent that they become extremely anxious or depressed. At other times young people complain, feel sorry for themselves, blame others, withdraw socially, deny that anything is wrong, or alter unpleasant moods with drugs and alcohol. Adolescents ideally learn how to carefully select methods for dealing with difficult situations and their own misery, drawing from productive coping skills more often than maladaptive responses.

Bioecology of Emotions

You've learned that experiences in families and at school are strongly influential in children's emotional welfare. Children's personal characteristics (some inherited) and experiences outside the family also contribute to emotional expression. Children are more inclined to become empathic when they inherit relevant dispositions and have parents who have been attentive to their and others' feelings (Brownell, Svetlova, Anderson, Nichols, & Drummond, 2013; Knafo & Uzefovsky, 2013; Zhou et al., 2002).[6] Other factors that strongly influence children's emotions include gender, culture, and socioeconomic status.

Gender

On average, male and female babies are similar in emotional states; any gender differences are subtle and situation dependent (J. E. O. Blakemore, Berenbaum, & Liben, 2009; Eisenberg, Martin, & Fabes, 1996). After the age of 2, consistent gender differences emerge. Boys show more anger than girls beginning in early childhood, and girls show more positive emotions overall but also more sadness, fear, and guilt from the elementary grades onward (Blakemore et al., 2009; Chaplin & Aldao, 2013; Eisenberg et al., 1996). Some girls are inclined to dwell on their problems rather than take action or distract themselves. Such a ruminating style is a risk factor for depression (Epkins, Gardner, & Scanlon, 2013; J. S. Hyde, Mezulis, & Abramson, 2008; Nolen-Hoeksema, Morrow, & Fredrickson, 1993). Boys are more apt to put on a self-confident front when they feel vulnerable (Blakemore et al., 2009; Chaplin & Aldao, 2013; Ruble, Martin, & Berenbaum, 2006). This style, too, has its disadvantages, especially when boys feel pressured to live up to unrealistic standards of strength.

Biology contributes to gender differences in emotions. Rising hormone levels at puberty are associated with intensified activity in emotional areas of the brain, increased moodiness and depression in girls, and aggressiveness and rebelliousness in boys (Buchanan, Eccles, & Becker, 1992; Goddings, Burnett Heyes, Bird, Viner, & Blakemore, 2012; Klapwijk et al., 2013). Yet socialization also determines gender differences in emotional responding. Parents are more likely to talk about fear and sadness with daughters and anger with sons (Kennedy

[6]In Chapter 14, we examine the connection between children's empathic responses and their helping behaviors.

Root & Denham, 2010; Malatesta & Haviland, 1982). Adolescent girls tend to respond to other girls' concerns with sympathy, whereas boys are more apt to respond to one another with disregard or ridicule, making boys less likely to share their personal worries in the future (Klimes-Dougan et al., 2014).

Culture

The language children speak defines aspects of emotion that are important in their culture. In English, words for emotions—for example, being anxious, happy, or excited—focus on internal, private states (Boiger, De Deyne, & Mesquita, 2013; Kagan, 2010). Some other languages emphasize the bodily sensations of emotions, such as being dizzy, having a headache, or feeling a racing heartbeat. A language also encodes nuances of emotion that are relevant in a culture. A child speaking English may hear about someone being "ashamed," whereas a child speaking Chinese encounters five distinct terms for shame, words that each communicate different causes of and responses to personal transgressions (H. Frank, Harvey, & Verdun, 2000).

Culture also guides children in sharing emotions in specific circumstances. Children in *individualistic* cultures are encouraged to express the full gamut of their emotions, including happiness, pride, frustration, and anger, as it is considered healthy to reveal one's innermost feelings (Boiger et al., 2013; Morelli & Rothbaum, 2007).[7] In contrast, *collectivistic* cultures disapprove of displays of anger, frustration, and pride because they reflect self-absorption and disrupt a group's harmony.

Yet families within any single culture differ markedly in how they socialize children's emotional expression. In a study with families in England, researchers listened to conversations among 3-year-old children, their mothers, and their older siblings; some children *never* mentioned emotions during an hour-long conversation at home, whereas one child mentioned emotions more than 27 times (J. Dunn, Brown, & Beardsall, 1991). On average, mothers were more likely to talk about feelings than were the children. When family "lessons" occur, children learn about how emotions operate.

Socioeconomic Status

Children living in families that face economic hardships are at heightened risk for emotional and behavioral problems. Children whose families have low incomes are more prone to anxiety, depression, and behavior problems (e.g., physical aggression) than are children from advantaged backgrounds (Kagan, 2010; Tolani & Brooks-Gunn, 2006). These children have more than their share of reasons to feel sad, fearful, and angry, including watching their parents struggle to meet ends and encountering violence and drug addiction in their neighborhoods. As we mentioned previously, educators, physicians, and mental health specialists are beginning to understand that reducing the detrimental effects of toxic stress is of great consequence for children's health and learning ability. Fortunately, carefully prepared early interventions are proving successful in fostering many young children's emotional development, and programs for older children can also be effective (Landry et al., 2014).

Obviously not every child who grows up in a low-income environment is emotionally burdened. Many children who face financial hardships receive stable, loving care from their immediate and extended families and in the process acquire good coping skills. In our opening case study, Merv was able to leverage loving care from her grandmother, siblings, and a few teachers as she built a happy and responsible life. In other situations, children from certain low-income backgrounds receive such loving, stable, and attentive care that they surpass their more advantaged peers in emotional skills. For instance, a group of children whose parents emigrated from Mexico to the United States with limited financial resources have shown fewer emotional and behavioral problems than is the case with American-born children (Espinosa, 2008). Similarly, close-knit ties in families, especially between children and their mothers, have been integral in the adjustment and high achievement of many African American students (J. Williams, & Bryan, 2013).

---

[7]Collectivistic and individualistic cultures are introduced in Chapter 3 and also examined earlier in this chapter in the context of attachment research.

Nor are children from middle- and high-income backgrounds immune to stress. Some middle-income parents project their own aspirations onto children, expecting children to follow unrealistic developmental timetables, such as cooperatively sharing toys with peers at 18 months or reading at 3 years. When children fail to meet these timetables, overzealous parents may become overly critical or institute new activities—perhaps sports, tutoring, or other after-school programs—that promise to increase skills (Hyson, Hirsh-Pasek, Rescorla, Cone, & Martell-Boinske, 1991; S. Wheeler, 2014). Certainly at least a few children from these backgrounds worry about parents' expectations, particularly when they think they are not measuring up (Hilt, Cha, & Nolen-Hoeksema, 2008; M. Levine, 2006).

Promoting Children's Emotional Development

Classrooms are emotionally rich settings that elicit children's joy, pride, and laughter but also their frustration, boredom, disappointment, embarrassment, shame, and anger. We offer these suggestions for promoting children's emotional well-being:

• **Help crying infants find comfort.** Caregivers can do several things to help infants in distress. First, they can strive to give timely reassurance—not always immediately, because they may have other demands, but not so delayed that infants' crying escalates into real suffering. Second, caregivers can allow actions that infants themselves use to reduce stress. Searching for a favorite blanket, putting a finger in the mouth, and tugging at an ear with a gentle hand are positive signs that infants are learning to soothe themselves. Third, caregivers can consciously invite a baby to join them in a calm state—by showing baby a smiling face, holding him or her close to the chest, and breathing in a shared rhythm (Gonzalez-Mena, 2002). Fourth, caregivers can investigate why an infant might be crying and try to meet the unfilled need or remove the source of pain. Finally, caregivers should try to stay calm and not take it personally—infants sometimes cry despite the most sensitive care.

• **Watch children's facial expressions, label their feelings, and coach them in expressing themselves.** Adults who respond sympathetically to upset children essentially tell them that feelings matter and can be dealt with constructively. Beginning in early childhood, children can learn the labels and implications of particular feelings: "I know you were angry with Davis for pulling your hair. You did a good job with using your words to tell him how you felt. Are you feeling a little better now?" As children grow, adults can coach children in fine-tuning emotional displays to the requirements of the particular social situation. Blowing up about a low test score will not be well received by classmates or the teacher, but expressing disappointment privately with the teacher can lead to productive problem solving as to how to prepare for the next examination.

• **Create a warm and accepting atmosphere.** Children learn most effectively when they are calm, happy, or excited about an activity (Bauminger & Kimhi-Kind, 2008; Linnenbrink & Pintrich, 2004; M. Rasmussen & Laumann, 2013). The classroom itself, with attractive decorations, age-appropriate furniture, and areas with pillows and rugs, can help children relax and engage. Traditions that begin and end the day and greeting students by their proper names enhance a sense of belonging. Teachers can post and enforce the school code of conduct and any additional classroom rules, which generally prohibit name calling. Occasional class meetings can clear the air and reaffirm commitments to desired behaviors. A school's mutually respectful climate facilitates a sense of safety. During lessons, teachers can communicate expectations about asking questions and responding to one another's ideas, advising students that everyone has valid perspectives and no one should be teased or mocked.

• **Pay attention to your own emotions.** Practitioners who work with children and families often find themselves frustrated by the people they serve (Button, 2007; B. Davis, 2001). Teachers may become angry with rude children, harried parents, unrealistic external mandates, and inadequate resources for schools. Frustration is a natural emotion but must be handled with care. Exploding at the nearest bystander or retreating into personal despair are *not* good ideas; counting to 10 and finding another professional to talk with *can* be helpful in preserving one's mental health.

• **Model appropriate ways for dealing with negative emotions.** Youngsters often struggle with how to deal with anger, fear, and sadness; they can benefit from seeing adults express these emotions appropriately (Delaney, 2006; W. S. Pollack, 2010). Teresa remembers how her fifth-grade teacher expressed anger: Rather than raising her voice, she lowered it to a whisper. The teacher's approach worked well: Students sensed her disappointment, responded with concern, and tried to make amends. Educators can boost the benefits of modeling controlled, honest emotions by offering an explanation: "I'm really angry now. Let's talk this out when we've all calmed down."

• **Offer age-appropriate outlets for emotional expression.** When children are young, they usually find safe outlets in play to communicate their feelings. Through fantasies with peers, children work out fears and conflicts, perhaps as monsters, superheroes, or bad guys (Kohlberg & Fein, 1987; Mathieson & Banerjee, 2010; Mooney, 2014). For older children, writing about feelings, perhaps in essays or journals, or expressing emotions in artwork, dance, or music, can be therapeutic. In Artifact 11-4, 8-year-old Noah acknowledges his sadness in a journal entry, and in Artifact 11-5, 10-year-old Shea reflects on the range of her recent emotions.

• **Discuss emotions of characters in literature and ancestors in history.** Stories provide occasions to live vicariously through a character's emotions (Fleer & Hammer, 2013; Mar & Oatley, 2008). As young children become familiar with fairy tales, fables, and short stories, for example, in *The Empty Pot*, they share fear, anger, love, and other strong feelings with classmates and with the adult telling the story; in the process they grow accustomed to embracing emotions in social situations (Fleer & Hammer, 2013). In *Frog and Toad Are Friends* (Lobel, 1979), a book suitable for 4- to 8-year-olds, Frog waits impatiently to play with his hibernating friend, Toad, and plays a trick on him to get him up early. The story provides a forum for discussions about feelings that may arise between friends, such as resentment at being teased or misled (Solomon, Watson, Battistich, Schaps, & Delucchi, 1992). Meanwhile, older children and adolescents might read firsthand accounts of historical events and talk through how people in various contexts have responded emotionally to hostilities and inequities.

• **Ask children to guess how people might feel in particular scenarios.** Children can practice analyzing particular situations and considering how those involved might feel. In Figure 11-1, you can see one situation that an elementary school counselor asks children to pretend they face. Adults can assure children that anger, fear, guilt, and other feelings are reasonable reactions in certain situations. In addition, they can ask children to think about how they should act when they have uncomfortable feelings of their own.

• **Accept cultural variations in emotional displays.** Some cultures encourage open communication about feelings, whereas others actively discourage emotional expressiveness. Adults working with children from diverse cultures must be mindful of such differences when interpreting children's emotional expressions (or lack thereof) (Trommsdorff & Heikamp, 2013). A girl who is pokerfaced when she has been eliminated from the final round of a school spelling bee may choose not to show her disappointment, reflecting self-restraint she has acquired at home. A sympathetic teacher who notices her stiff reaction will not insist that she talk about her feelings but will find a moment later in the day to speak privately with her, congratulate her on her good performance, and give her a few tips if she would like to advance further in her spelling skill.

• **Encourage boys and girls to cope with their feelings.** Obviously, both boys and girls have emotional needs. Being careful not to stereotype the sexes, concerned educators can look for occasions when children use gender-typical methods of emotional regulation that worsen matters for them. Adults might watch for occasions when girls are ruminating over problems and help them work through their feelings, actively tackle the problems, and get on with life. Similarly, when boys seem to be trying hard to brush off a significant personal loss, adults can acknowledge that the event is, in fact, likely to be upsetting but can be

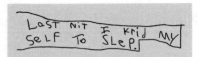

ARTIFACT 11-4 Last night. In this journal entry, 8-year-old Noah reveals his sadness about his parents' recent divorce.

ARTIFACT 11-5 What hits me. In this essay, 10-year-old Shea describes her recent emotions.

FIGURE 11-1 Respecting others' privacy. Counselors can ask children to pretend they are characters in particular situations and help them talk about how they might feel and respond.

tackled with active coping skills, for example, confiding in friends and teachers or writing about the situation.

• **Help children limit stress levels.** When stress is long-lasting, anxiety easily results. **Anxiety** is an emotional condition characterized by worry and apprehension, often about future events with unknown outcomes. Children who are anxious may experience such physiological symptoms as muscle tension and headaches and have trouble concentrating. Educators can do a variety of things to help keep anxiety at a manageable level. Deep breathing, stretching, outdoor recess, and mentally retreating with a good book are all tactics that teachers can establish as routines. When teachers assign oral reports, they can encourage students to create index cards or other memory "crutches." Before giving an important test (such as end-of-year state examinations), teachers can administer practice tests that give students a general idea of what to expect. In general, teachers should communicate realistic expectations for classroom performance and provide the support students need to *meet* those expectations.

• **Recognize and address the special needs of children in toxic stress.** Children who live in constant anguish cannot easily focus on school subjects (Ursache & Raver, 2014). Yet a strong education is vital for their future. If jittery children are to derive maximum benefit from their education, classrooms must be warm settings. Teachers can encourage concentration, acknowledge improvements in attention, and give students plenty of brief breaks. Should the opportunity arise, teachers can advise parents of educationally worthwhile activities that reduce stress. Sharing a bedtime routine, especially with a good-night story, has pay-offs in young children's literacy development and also reduces stress in children—and parents (Zajicek-Farber, Mayer, & Daughtery, 2012).

• **Consider using a research-based curriculum for fostering emotional development.** To have a significant impact on children's emotional expression, school personnel can implement a systematic program for educating children in an environment that is warm, open, and instructive on handling feelings (Case-Smith, 2013; S. H. Landry et al., 2014). One illustration of a comprehensive emotional education program is the *Promoting Alternative Thinking Strategies (PATHS)* curriculum (Domitrovich, Cortes, & Greenberg, 2007). Second- and third-grade children are taught that all feelings are okay, some feelings are comfortable and others uncomfortable, feelings can help children learn what to do in certain situations, and some ways of dealing with emotions are better than others. Children keep a record of their feelings and use a poster showing a traffic signal as a guide to regulating their responses to feelings. Teachers encourage children to refer to the steps on a poster: to stop and calm down (red), slow down and consider their options (yellow), and try a plan (green). This program has been shown to increase emotional understanding and decrease problem behaviors in children with diverse ability levels.

The Basic Developmental Issues table "Attachment and Emotional Development" shows how attachments and emotions draw from nature and nurture, show universality and diversity, and exhibit qualitative and quantitative change. As you have learned, nature furnishes children with inclinations to form attachments and express emotions, and nurture translates these abstract capacities into real-life relationships and abilities.

Summary

Emotions have adaptive functions for young people, helping them decide how to direct their attention and activity. Children become increasingly able to regulate their emotions in ways that are both socially acceptable and personally satisfying. Individual differences in emotional functioning are the result of both biology (e.g., genetic instructions for neurotransmitters and gender-specific hormones) and environment (e.g., socialization by parents, peers, and culture).

Classrooms are fertile environments for emotions. Children arrive at school with certain coping skills and stress responses that affect their ability to concentrate, remember information, and make friends. Teachers, counselors, and other school leaders can teach children

BASIC DEVELOPMENTAL ISSUES
Attachment and Emotional Development

ISSUE	ATTACHMENT	EMOTIONAL DEVELOPMENT
Nature and Nurture	Children are biologically predisposed to form close bonds with their parents and other primary caregivers (reflecting nature), but they are more likely to form secure bonds with adults who have showered them with love (nurture). Parents, in turn, are by nature predisposed to care for their offspring, but they learn specific ways of interacting with children from other family members and from the community and culture in which they live.	The full range of emotions is made possible by human genetic instructions; the brain is wired to experience anger, pleasure, fear, and so on. Genetic factors also affect individual differences in temperament (e.g., activity level and ways of responding to new stimuli). Nurture affects how emotions are expressed. Children learn to control expression of negative emotions by observing other people and practicing various ways of dealing with these feelings.
Universality and Diversity	The predisposition to form close social-emotional bonds is universal. Sensitive care is the common route to healthy attachments. However, not every child receives this responsive attention and thus not all children form secure attachments. Being clingy and demanding may help infants who live in an environment with scarce resources. Similarly, being able to form multiple relationships enhances adjustment when numerous caregivers are present during the early years.	All children experience such basic emotions as happiness, sadness, anger, and fear. The tendency for emotional states to energize particular responses (e.g., fleeing in response to fear) is also universal. But substantial diversity is present in how children regulate their emotions (e.g., when trying to relax or conceal their true feelings). Some children are more likely than others to respond to social situations in a positive, upbeat fashion.
Qualitative and Quantitative Change	The development of attachments largely reflects quantitative change: Children gradually become more active as social partners, initiating conversations and other exchanges, taking turns to keep interactions going, and so on. Qualitative change occurs when young children, who have previously leapt into the arms of strangers, suddenly display stranger anxiety.	Children gradually gain the knowledge and skills needed to assess others' emotions. By watching facial expressions, listening to tones of voice, and drawing inferences from behaviors, children learn how others express and control emotions. The emergence of self-conscious emotions (pride, guilt, etc.) represents a qualitative change that reflects a new awareness of social standards.

how to express themselves according to cultural practices and personal needs. School personnel can emphasize that all emotions are okay and that what needs to be learned is how to manage them.

ENHANCEDetext *self-check*

Assessing Children 11-1

Listen to and compare a young girl's and an adolescent boy's descriptions of emotions and coping strategies.

ENHANCEDetext *application exercise*

Assessing Children 11-2

Listen to strategies for fostering emotional development in young children.

ENHANCEDetext *application exercise*

TEMPERAMENT AND PERSONALITY

Visit any group of children—perhaps at a local child care center, a school, or an after-school program—and you are bound to notice dramatic differences in individual children's energy, mood, spontaneity, and attention to academic tasks. Such variations reflect differences in children's *temperaments* and *personalities*.

Temperament refers to a child's typical and somewhat stable ways of responding to events, novel stimulation, and personal impulses (Cummings et al., 2013; Kagan & Fox, 2006; Rothbart, Sheese, & Conradt, 2009).[8] Individual differences in temperament are present even in infancy. Some infants are fussy and demanding; others are cheerful and easily pacified. Temperament has a genetic basis, as we shall see, but it also is very much affected by children's relationships and experiences.

As children grow older, they develop distinctive ways of behaving, thinking, and feeling. That is, they develop unique **personalities**. Temperament affects personality: A child who is timid relates to people and events differently than one who is socially confident (Cummings et al., 2013). But personality includes more than temperament. Personality is affected by children's intellectual interests and the many habits they acquire while growing up—for example, their traditions for fulfilling family obligations, strategies for dealing with stressful situations, style of interacting with others, methods for managing personal belongings, and preferences for spending leisure time.

Both temperament and personality help us understand how individual children respond to emotions, form relationships, and act within schools and other group settings. Temperament may be especially helpful to consider when children are infants and toddlers; personality may be more relevant as youngsters move into their later childhood and adolescent years. Let's look more closely at both concepts and consider their implications for educators.

Elements of Temperament and Personality

Temperament and personality are each made up of constellations of relatively independent dimensions. Individual children may have a lot, a little, or an in-between amount of each attribute.

Temperament

Much of the initial work on temperament was done using parents' reports and researchers' observations of infants' typical behaviors. Parents and researchers judged the extent to which the infants were active and adaptable to change. In considering the dramatic individual differences that emerged from this analysis, experts realized that infants' temperaments partly determine the types of care that are most effective for them as individuals (A. Thomas & Chess, 1977).

Infants who exhibit a high activity level (squirming a lot, wiggling while having a diaper change) may benefit from many opportunities for safe exploration around the environment. For children with low activity levels, adults might need to slow down their pace, enjoy quiet interaction with them, and only then invite more active play. Thus, children's well-being depends to some extent on the *goodness of fit* between their temperament and the particular environment in which they are raised (Chess & Thomas, 1992). Having a good fit does not mean that the adult shares the same temperament with the child but rather that the adult warmly accepts and accommodates the child's personal rhythms and dispositions.

More recent research has focused on the neurological basis of temperament. American psychologist **Mary Rothbart** and her colleagues suggest that particular temperaments emerge as children's brains develop distinctive capacities for responding to impulses and regulating attention, emotion, and activity (Rothbart, 2007, 2012; Rothbart & Bates, 2006; Rothbart et al., 2009). At birth, children react rather automatically to changes in stimuli by crying, thrashing their limbs, and looking away. As they grow, they develop new ways to deal

---

[8]Temperament is introduced in Chapter 1.

with sensations and environmental demands. Fear prompts children to be wary of potentially dangerous things, whereas a sense of initiative incites children to explore the world. Restraint emerges gradually, as children learn to direct their attention and actions flexibly, according to social rules and requirements and anticipated consequences for possible decisions. These distinctive ways of responding to stimuli (i.e., reacting automatically, withdrawing out of fear, exploring with enthusiasm, and directing activity intentionally) are housed in different parts of the brain. As these various systems develop, they may be weak or strong in separate children and collectively determine individual temperaments.

According to Rothbart and her colleagues, children may be low or high, or somewhere in between, on three dimensions of temperament:

- Children who score high on *extraversion/surgency* show high levels of optimistic anticipation, impulsivity, activity, and sensation seeking, and they smile and laugh often.
- Children who score high on *negative affectivity* are shy and often fearful, frustrated, sad, uncomfortable, and not easily soothed.
- Children who show high levels of *effortful control* are proficient in strategically focusing and shifting their attention. They effectively plan for the future, suppress inappropriate responses, and take pleasure in complex and novel stimuli.

These three temperamental dimensions are fairly stable, partly due to genetic factors, and shown by identical twins reared in different homes having similar temperaments (N. D. Henderson, 1982; J. J. Li, & Lee, 2014; Tellegren, Lykken, Bouchard, & Wilcox, 1988). Children's genetic makeup apparently affects their temperaments through its effects on brain chemistry, such as the efficiency of certain neurotransmitters, the levels of cortisol released during stressful situations, and the comparative level of activity between the two sides of the brain (Cummings et al., 2013; Kagan, Snidman, Vahn, & Towsley, 2007; Rothbart et al., 2009).

Stability in temperament is further enabled by persistent characteristics in children's environments. The typical ways in which parents express or withhold affection and respond to children's displays of emotions influence the manner in which children deal with conflict, stressful circumstances, and novel events. Thus, children who live in a family that offers relatively little support tend to become irritable and aggressive as they grow (Fanti & Henrich, 2010). Young children with overly directive and intrusive parents tend to become emotionally reserved and impulsive (Clincy & Mills-Koonce, 2013).

Yet environments can also modify a child's temperament. Separate societies encourage certain personal characteristics more so than others. In Western cultures, children are expected to be reasonably outgoing with peers. When parents encourage children who are shy to interact with peers and develop independent problem-solving skills, these reserved children are apt to become socially confident (Arcus, 2001; Feng, Shaw, & Moilanen, 2011; N. A. Fox, Henderson, Rubin, Calkins, & Schmidt, 2001). In China, acting in a socially restrained manner is valued, as you can learn more about in the Development in Culture feature "Temperament in China."

Personality

Over time, a child integrates biologically based emotional tendencies with his or her experiences, relationships, and intellectual interests. The result is a distinctive and somewhat stable personality. A child who is passionate about finding order in the material world may, as a 4-year-old, have an insatiable curiosity for dinosaurs; as an 8-year-old, be fascinated with space and aeronautics; as a 12-year-old, learn all he can about bridges and buildings; as a 16-year-old, become an expert in computers; and as a young man, prepare for a career in environmental engineering.

Despite their relative stability, children's personalities can change slightly (and sometimes dramatically) in response to the demands of particular situations. A 12-year-old girl may be highly sociable (e.g., talking frequently, smiling at others, and befriending numerous peers) but find it difficult to make new friends when her family moves across the country and encounters unfamiliar customs and values. The demands of particular settings within a community can likewise affect which aspects of complex personalities children reveal. An 8-year-old boy may be spontaneous and cheerful on the playground but distracted and agitated in the classroom.

DEVELOPMENT IN CULTURE
Temperament in China

China has a population of over 1.3 billion people, 265 million of whom are children ranging in age from infancy through 14 years (X. Chen & Wang, 2010). Fifty-six separate ethnic groups exist in China, and the country is rapidly shifting from reliance on a centrally planned financial system to a market economy with strong international ties.

Obviously, children throughout China are exposed to distinct customs. Yet several cultural beliefs and practices pervade family and community life across China. Confucianism offers especially prominent guidelines (X. Chen & Wang, 2010). Confucius (551–479 B.C.) was a highly influential philosopher who lived during a time of significant social upheaval, when China was making the transition from slavery to a feudal society, and he espoused practices for restoring a harmonious social order. Moral standards in Confucianism include benevolence, righteousness, propriety, and wisdom. Children are expected to pledge obedience and respect to their parents, and parents in turn must guide and discipline their children. Children are similarly expected to respect their teachers and other authority figures and be considerate of peers as well.

Taoism is another prevalent belief system in China. Taoism advocates internal harmony by being soft and tender (X. Chen & Wang, 2010). People are advised to be flexible, adjust to life circumstances, and refrain from struggles over material wealth. In the ideologies of both Confucianism and Taoism, children are directed to be calm, honorable, and attentive to the needs of the group.

SERENITY. This young boy walks quietly with his grandmother in Shaxi Village in the Yunnan Province of China.

Confucian and Taoist ideals prescribe that children remain relatively quiet, compliant, and emotionally restrained in family, classroom, and peer settings so as to maintain mutual support in the group. As you might anticipate, children require a lot of guidance from adults before they reliably overcome their own impulses and defer to the needs of others. This socialization begins early. Chinese parents regularly encourage young children to tone down emotional expressions into muted, socially acceptable levels. In one experimental study, Chinese infants produced less facial movement, fewer smiles, and less crying than did European American infants (Camras et al., 1998).

Chinese parents also encourage children to temper their independent exploratory behaviors. In an observational study, 2-year-old Chinese children were more likely than Canadian children of the same age to stay close to mothers in the presence of a stranger or unfamiliar toys (X. Chen et al., 1998). In addition, Chinese children are expected to abide by basic rules even when parents are not present to oversee their conduct. In another experimental study, Chinese toddlers more willingly put away toys without their mother's intervention than did Canadian toddlers (X. Chen, Rubin, et al., 2003).

As they grow older, Chinese children prefer controlled behavior in peers. Shy Chinese preschool children are more likely to be accepted by peers than are shy Canadian children by theirs (X. Chen, DeSouza, Chen, & Wang, 2006). However, it appears that shyness is manifested in several distinct ways in China (Y. Xu, Farver, Chang, Zhang, & Yu, 2007). Children who exhibit *regulated shyness* show social restraint that is consistent with Chinese customs. They do not draw attention to themselves, are modest and unassuming, and are considerate of peers. In comparison, children who exhibit *anxious shyness* are overwhelmed with negative emotions such that they find it difficult to behave appropriately in social settings. These children find it too stressful to enter peer groups and instead stay on the periphery. Regulated-shy children have an advantage over anxious-shy children in China, probably because children with the former characteristics are able to insinuate themselves into groups whereas the latter are not (Y. Xu et al., 2007).

Curiously, biological factors also play a small role in Chinese children being emotionally controlled. Genetic factors appear partly responsible for Chinese infants displaying fewer smiles and more vigorously withdrawing from stressful circumstances than is the case with Caucasian infants (Kagan, 2010). Thus, it seems that Chinese society enhances a modest biologically based temperament for emotional restraint with cultural values for social harmony and personal serenity.

Recognizing that a child's personality changes somewhat over time and across situations, psychologists have found five relatively stable dimensions of personality:

- *Extraversion*—extent of being socially outgoing
- *Agreeableness*—extent of being warm and sympathetic
- *Conscientiousness*—extent of being persistent and organized
- *Neuroticism*—extent of being anxious and fearful
- *Openness*—extent of being curious and imaginative

These five dimensions were originally identified with adults, but they also characterize children to some degree (A. D. Haan, Deković, den Akker, Stoltz, & Prinzie, 2013; John, Caspi, Robins, Moffitt, & Stouthamer-Loeber, 1994). As with constancy in temperament, the stability of personality dimensions is due partly to genetics and partly to consistency in children's environments.

Helping Children Be Themselves

Teachers can plan lessons and activities that address the varied temperaments and personalities of youngsters in their care. Here are some suggestions:

• **Identify the kinds of temperaments that you naturally prefer, as well as those that push your buttons.** Many teachers prefer to work with children who are curious, happy, obedient, hard working, cooperative, intelligent, cautious, and efficient (Keogh, 2003; S. McClowry et al., 2013; Wentzel, 2000). Teachers tend to find it less rewarding to work with children who are easily distracted, angry or irritable, disruptive, and exceptionally assertive. Teachers also are less proficient in managing the misbehavior of children they perceive to be difficult. When teachers come to realize that they automatically (and often unconsciously) respond in certain ways to particular temperaments, they can take the first steps toward holding their biases in check and developing their professional skills in managing irritable and noncompliant children. Coming to see these children as being sensitive and lacking in self-regulation can help you develop a valuable mindset for teaching the missing skills instead of doling out punishment.

• **Adjust to young children's stylistic ways of responding to the world.** Warmly accepting children's personal ways of regulating their attention is an important service that adults can provide to children (Rudasill, Gallagher, & White, 2010). To meet the needs of active infants, caregivers might permit them to explore and move often. In contrast, infants who show a lower activity level may sit contentedly and let the world come to them (A. Thomas & Chess, 1977; Zero to Three, 2002). With infants who have a lower activity level, caregivers might sit quietly with them, talk softly about pictures in a book, and acknowledge their interests in toys. With older children, teachers can observe children's focus of attention, affectionately remind distractible children to stay engaged in lessons, and offer other opportunities for free choice.

• **Consider children's temperaments when forming groups.** Teachers can help children who are shy or impulsive by pairing them with peers who might compensate for their natural inclinations. A first-grade teacher might plan a Halloween activity of making "dirt" cake, knowing she can count on one boy to be methodical in measuring cocoa and other ingredients and pair him with another boy who will attack the project enthusiastically but without restraint. Together, they might make a good team. Because there is never any guarantee that temperamentally dissimilar children will work effectively together, you need to monitor the evolving dynamics of groups once you form them.

• **Allow children to apply their natural strengths, but encourage them to try out new strategies for learning.** Permitting children to choose from among a few specified options is an important way to respect children's individuality. When children are asked to report on a book they have read, they might choose from an array of formats, such as a written analysis, poster, or oral presentation. However, children are naturally inclined to remain in their comfort zone and can benefit from practice with less developed talents. Hence a child who has trouble concentrating may be taught to use attention-focusing strategies, and a child who chooses books impulsively might be asked to prepare a checklist of desirable topics to refer to when selecting a new book at the library.

• **Communicate your expectations about acceptable behaviors.** When adults make expectations explicit and consistently enforce compliance, children with many kinds of temperaments and personalities thrive (Denno, Carr, & Bell, 2010; Keogh, 2003). Those who are apprehensive about doing the right thing can be assured that they *are* acting in an acceptable manner. Others who are inclined to act impulsively can be reminded of rules, consequences for misbehavior, and strategies they can use to keep track of their behaviors.

- **Set up reasonable routines.** Most children prefer a schedule that is somewhat predictable (H. A. Davis, 2003). Children adjust to activities more easily when they know what to expect, for example, when they know that after they arrive at school in the morning, they are to place their backpacks and jackets in designated places, go straight to their desks, and begin writing a new entry in their class journals. Children also need to be advised of the procedures of a classroom, such as how to line up or disperse for lunch, and the circumstances under which they can sharpen their pencils, use the restroom, and ask for assistance.

- **Help children cope with changes in routines.** Children with certain temperaments and personalities (for instance, those who are timid or irritable) may find alterations to routines to be difficult (Keogh, 2003). To help these children, educators can tell them ahead of time about anticipated modifications in school personnel, schedules, or rules. Elementary schoolchildren can be introduced to a substitute teacher the week before their regular teacher departs for a family leave. Middle school adolescents can be shown the blueprints for a new auditorium before the existing structure is leveled, and high school students should receive a copy of a new code of conduct for their school before it is instituted. When changes *cannot* be anticipated ahead of time, children appreciate hearing as soon as possible about these alterations, especially those changes that affect them personally.

- **Physically arrange the classroom to minimize disruptions and noise.** Defined pathways between desks, protected spaces in high-traffic areas, and separate areas for relaxation can minimize tussles among children who are easily frustrated, lacking in social skills, or simply tired (Emmer, Evertson, & Worsham, 2000; Tassoni, 2013). Children who are easily distracted by noise might occasionally be allowed to complete assignments in the school library.

- **Make appropriate adjustments for children who show unusually high or low levels on one or more personality dimensions.** Children with exceptional personality dimensions stand out from other children. These children need to be accepted for who they are but also need accommodations that guide their learning, peer relationships, emotional expression, and motivation to follow rules. Let's consider how educators might adjust to some unusually high or low levels of the personality dimensions we introduced earlier:

  - *Extraversion.* Extraverted children are active, assertive, emotionally expressive, talkative, enthusiastic, and socially outgoing. These children often appreciate opportunities to work on projects with peers. Teachers might occasionally offer a public forum (such as a dramatic performance) for self-expression. Teachers can intersperse opportunities for physical movement around quiet activities to give these children needed exercise. Some exuberant children need gentle reminders from teachers to stay focused and listen to others (Rimm-Kaufman et al., 2002). Children who are shy may benefit from private conversations with teachers and friendly invitations from peers and adults to join in an activity.
  - *Agreeableness.* Agreeable children are warm, responsive, generous, kind, sympathetic, and trusting. They may be pleased when adults and other children notice and comment on their cooperative spirit. Children who are less prone to be agreeable and socially sensitive may benefit if teachers encourage them to compliment peers, share toys, offer comfort to others in distress, and voice opinions without insulting people. Extremely irritable children are at risk for developing behavior problems but have the ability to adjust well when assisted by knowledgeable teachers, counselors, psychologists, and doctors (Aman et al., 2009; Ehrler, Evans, & McGhee, 1999; A. E. West & Weinstein, 2012).
  - *Conscientiousness.* Conscientious children are attentive, persistent in activities, organized, and responsible. Teachers can admire the persistence and organization shown by these children and point out how their style pays off in well-designed work products. Children who follow lower standards can be taught to set appropriate goals, resist counterproductive urges, and monitor their own progress toward goals (Muris, Meesters, & Rompelberg, 2006).
  - *Neuroticism.* Neurotic children are anxious, fearful, lacking in confidence, and self-pitying. These children need support in dealing with negative feelings (Kwok, Hughes, & Luo, 2007). They also need encouragement to try challenging tasks they might otherwise avoid. Children who are relaxed and confident thrive when given continuous support from adults. No one is self-assured all the time, however, and adults can express

extra support when normally confident children face momentous losses, personal failures, or traumatic events.

- *Openness*. Children who are open are curious, eager to explore their world, and imaginative. They can be encouraged to exercise their budding skills in many contexts. However, curious children are not always motivated to achieve in school and may need encouragement from teachers to tackle conventional academic assignments (Abe, 2005). Those who are less driven to explore art, literature, history, and the scientific world may need to be shown the intrigue and beauty of these and other fields.

- **Recognize the complexity of children's personalities.** The various dimensions of temperament and personality combine in a myriad of creative ways that can both delight and tax adults. A teacher may have one child who is socially outgoing but a bit anxious and not terribly agreeable; another child who is self-confident and conscientious, but somewhat conforming and slow to exercise her imagination; another who worries constantly and craves approval from adults and is quietly curious and thoughtful; and many other children, each with an individual profile. *Every* child has special needs when it comes to temperament and personality.

The Developmental Trends table "Emotional and Personal Characteristics at Different Age Levels" captures what you have learned about children's attachment, emotional qualities, and temperaments and personalities. By now it should be abundantly clear that children are well served when adults appreciate their individual qualities, assistance that is all the more crucial when children have serious emotional problems, a theme we explore in the final section.

DEVELOPMENTAL TRENDS
Emotional and Personal Characteristics at Different Age Levels

AGE	WHAT YOU MIGHT OBSERVE	DIVERSITY	IMPLICATIONS
Infancy (Birth–2 Years)	• Attachment behaviors (seeking contact with caregiver when afraid, hurt, or hungry; being sufficiently relaxed in the presence of caregiver to explore the environment) • Distress at separation from caregiver • Crying and smiling gradually supplemented with laughter, hand gestures, and words • Beginning ability to soothe self by sucking thumb, hugging favorite blankets, pulling on ear, and so on	• Some children have multiple attachments and move easily from one caregiver to another, whereas others have a single close attachment and strongly protest separation from this person. • Some cultures encourage small children to express all their feelings, including anger and sadness. Other cultures place group harmony above self-expression and discourage expression of certain feelings; instead, they teach restraint and attention to the harmonious functioning of the group.	• Try to remain calm when infants and toddlers cry and shout. • Be responsive and sensitive to the needs of infants—they are learning to trust you while you satisfy their needs. • Seek professional guidance when you encounter infants who appear to have serious attachment problems. • Provide infants with lots of reassurance during separation distress. • Tell parents what you do to comfort their child and how long it takes for him or her to settle down after their departure.
Early Childhood (2–6 Years)	• Desire to be close to parents when afraid, hurt, or uncertain • Ability to talk about and accept where parents go during a temporary separation from them • Attachments to multiple people, including mother, father, siblings, extended family members, and teachers • Wide variety of emotions (e.g., happiness, sadness, fear, anger, disgust) • Familiarity with and use of labels for basic emotions • Emergence of self-conscious emotions (e.g., pride, embarrassment, guilt)	• Children vary in the number of close attachments they form, the extent to which they are reassured by these individuals, and their responses to strangers. Some cling tightly to caregivers; others venture confidently to explore new environments and strangers. • Children vary in how they express their emotions. Some are controlled, especially in masking anger and sadness. Others are more expressive. • Children with chronically stressed families may find it challenging to concentrate.	• Realize that young children may initially be cautious or fearful in a new classroom and become more confident as they form secure attachments with teachers. • Be patient in establishing relationships with young children; some form attachments quickly, but others take several weeks or months before bonding with adults outside the home. • Teach appropriate ways of handling negative emotions. Encourage children to "use their words" rather than push or hit when angry.

(Continued)

DEVELOPMENTAL TRENDS (continued)
Emotional and Personal Characteristics at Different Age Levels

AGE	WHAT YOU MIGHT OBSERVE	DIVERSITY	IMPLICATIONS
Middle Childhood (6–10 Years)	• Continued close relationships with family members • Increasing number of bonds with people outside the family, including peers, teachers, and other adults • Increasing ability to regulate emotions • Broadening of coping skills to include seeking guidance from peers and teachers	• Children are emotionally affected by major family disruptions (e.g., divorce of parents, death or illness of a family member). Changes in family membership may undermine children's security, usually temporarily but sometimes for a longer period. • Some children have strong role models for emotional regulation. Others see parents exploding and even getting violent.	• Incorporate discussions of emotions into the curriculum; for example, address the feelings of characters in literature and history. • Model appropriate ways of expressing feelings. • Respect cultural differences in regulating emotions. • Try to form good relationships with all children in your care.
Early Adolescence (10–14 Years)	• Frequent fluctuations in mood, partly as a result of hormonal changes and an increasing number of stressful experiences at home and in school • Careful regulation of emotions in public (e.g., hiding excitement about a good grade in order to appear "cool" to peers) • Shift in confiding in parents to using a wider support system, which continues to include parents but now also has friends and teachers	• Individual adolescents differ in the extent to which they conform to typical gender roles in expressing emotions. • Most adolescents expand coping skills in middle and high school, but some internalize their stresses (e.g., with depression or anxiety). • Others respond with overt behaviors (e.g., being violent, breaking the law, bullying others).	• Be a supportive listener when young people want to share their anxieties. • Keep in mind that some moodiness is normal in the middle school grades. Talk with parents or the school counselor about the emotional well-being of youngsters who seem especially troubled. • Give young people the chance to express their empathy through service learning in their community.
Late Adolescence (14–18 Years)	• Seeking emotional intimacy with same-sex and opposite-sex peers • Continued attachments to parents, but with strong preferences for parental affection to be demonstrated in private rather than in public • Increasing ability to be comforted by peers when distressed • Development of new strategies for coping with stress • Occasionally intense stress as adolescents strive to meet high school graduation requirements, maintain good relationships with peers, and stay in good standing with parents.	• For some adolescents, relationships with parents are full of conflict and offer little emotional support. • Some adolescents use drugs and alcohol to deal with negative emotions. • Some adolescents (girls especially) ruminate over small setbacks and disappointments. • Some adolescents (boys especially) hide their feelings and project the impression that losses, disappointments, and embarrassments do not bother them.	• When adolescents are in minor conflicts with parents, help them see that most parents want the best for them even though they may forget to express affection and use discipline that seems unfair. • Refer youngsters to a school counselor when family relationships deteriorate significantly or youngsters show signs of depression. • Ask adolescents to reflect on the emotional experiences of fictional characters and historical figures. • Teach new coping skills to anxious teens.

Summary

Children are born with individual dispositions to respond to the world and express their emotions in certain ways. These constitutional inclinations, called temperaments, are affected by experience and social relationships. Children exercise their temperamental dimensions, integrating their stylistic behaviors into their intellectual interests and social habits, gradually emerging as distinctive personalities. Teachers and other practitioners help children when they effectively accommodate children's unique temperaments and personalities.

ENHANCEDetext *self-check*

CARING FOR CHILDREN WITH EMOTIONAL PROBLEMS

Some children have more than their share of negative experiences, to the point where their ability to tackle everyday problems is disrupted. As you saw with Merv's experience in the opening case study, many children overcome, or at least learn to cope effectively with, such significant problems, especially when they receive steady support at home, in school, and in the community. Let's look at some of the serious emotional and behavioral problems children face as well as strategies for supporting their resilience.

Common Emotional and Behavioral Disorders

Problems in children's mental health are more common than many adults realize. Approximately 25 percent of children in the United States are affected by an emotional or behavioral problem, for one or more periods during childhood (Braaten, 2011; Tolani & Brooks-Gunn, 2006). At school, children with **emotional and behavioral disorders** have one or more of the following difficulties:

- In learning, not due to any known intellectual, sensory, health, or other physiological factors
- In connecting with others, such that satisfactory relationships with peers and teachers are not maintained
- In controlling personal behavior, to the extent that self-harm, harm to others, and expressions of low self-worth occur regularly
- In regulating mood, as reflected in significant anxiety or depression
- Being afraid, angry or otherwise distressed at school, with resulting headaches, stomach pain, or other physiological complaints (U.S. Department of Education, 2004).

Children with an emotional or behavioral disorder may receive services through special education programs at school to ease their adjustment. Here we look at three relatively common conditions—depression, anxiety, and conduct disorder—which, in children, reflect the need for understanding and informed care.

Depression

People with **depression** feel exceptionally sad, discouraged, and hopeless; they may also feel restless, sluggish, helpless, worthless, or unusually guilty. Children with depression may be unresponsive to caregivers, withdraw from social interactions with peers, report such physical complaints as headaches and stomach pain, and appear consistently sad or irritable (Allison, Nativio, Mitchell, Ren, & Yuhasz, 2014; Braaten, 2011; A. Carr, 2014). Depressed youngsters may have trouble concentrating, keeping up with usual activities, eating, and sleeping (American Psychiatric Association, 1994). A variation of depression, *bipolar disorder,* occurs when individuals experience periods of extreme elation and hyperactivity as well as periods of deep depression.

The specific symptoms of depression vary somewhat from culture to culture. The American Psychiatric Association (APA) provides several examples of how depression might manifest itself in different cultures:

> Complaints of "nerves" and headaches (in Latino and Mediterranean cultures), of weakness, tiredness, or "imbalance" (in Chinese and Asian cultures), of problems of the "heart" (in Middle Eastern cultures), or of being "heartbroken" (among Hopi). (APA, 1994, p. 324)

Many instances of depression and bipolar disorder probably have genetic roots (Cicchetti, Rogosch, & Toth, 1997; Hankin et al., 2009). These conditions run in families, are often foreshadowed by temperamental moodiness, and may reflect chemical imbalances in the brain. Environmental factors also play a role in depression. For instance, the death of a loved one, mental illness in or marital conflict between parents, child maltreatment, poverty, and inadequate schools may bring about or worsen depressive symptoms (Buchmann et al.,

Preparing for Your Licensure Examination
Your teaching test might ask you about how you can help children with emotional and behavioral disorders.

2014; Vrijsen et al., 2014). Children who have certain genes and grow up in a stressful environment are at significant risk (J. Chen, Li, & McGue, 2013). When children do succumb to extreme stress with a depressive episode, the event may alter their neurological chemistry, making it more likely that they will suffer another depressive episode in the future (Akiskal & McKinney, 1973; Luby, 2010).

Depression rates in children vary by age and gender. Before adolescence, depression and bipolar disorder are rare. Their prevalence increases dramatically during adolescence. By the age of 19, approximately one in three girls and one in five boys has been seriously depressed one or more times (Oltmanns & Emery, 2007). Higher rates of depression occur in girls beginning in adolescence because of hormone changes and the tendency of girls to dwell on their problems (Hilt & Nolen-Hoeksema, 2009).

Youth with serious depression or bipolar disorder are at risk for considering or committing suicide (M. G. Sawyer et al., 2010; Shilubane et al., 2014). The overwhelming despair and high frequency of suicide that accompany depression make it a condition that educators must take seriously. Through their daily contact with youngsters, teachers have numerous opportunities to observe children's moods and so may become concerned about their possible depression. (Friends and family, though they have closer ties to youngsters, may not comprehend or accept how serious the problem is.) Educators will want to offer emotional reassurance to young people who appear troubled, but they should also consult with principals and counselors if they suspect severe depression or another serious emotional disturbance.

Anxiety Disorder

In its milder forms, anxiety is a common and very "normal" emotion. But some people, including some children and adolescents, fuss and fret excessively and find it difficult to control their worrisome thoughts and feelings; in other words, they have an **anxiety disorder** (APA, 2000; A. Carr, 2014). Children with a *generalized anxiety disorder* worry unreasonably about a wide variety of things, including their academic achievement and potential catastrophic events such as wars or hurricanes. Other individuals have more specific anxiety disorders, perhaps stewing constantly about gaining weight, having a serious illness, being away from family and home, feeling embarrassed in public, or being scared to go to school (A. Carr, 2014; Ollendick, Costa, & Benoit, 2010).

As you might expect, nature and nurture both contribute to anxiety disorders. These disorders have a genetic basis and run in families (Hudson et al., 2013; Last, Hersen, Kazdin, Francis, & Grubb, 1987; Ogliari et al., 2010). Family environment also plays a role in their onset. Some evidence suggests that a number of anxious children have had insecure attachments to their parents and have been exposed to aloof and critical parenting and also to exceedingly controlling and intrusive parenting (Cooper-Vince, Pincus, & Comer, 2014; Luijk et al., 2010; P. S. Moore, Whaley, & Sigman, 2004). With these types of care, children worry about their ability to make independent decisions and to handle uncertain and threatening situations.

Conduct Disorder

When children display a chronic pattern of misbehavior and show little shame or guilt about their wrongdoings, they are sometimes identified as having a **conduct disorder**. Youngsters who display a conduct disorder ignore the rights of others in ways that are unusual for their age. Common symptoms include aggression toward people and animals (e.g., initiating physical fights, forcing someone into sexual activity, torturing animals), destruction of property (e.g., setting fires, painting graffiti), theft and deceitfulness (e.g., breaking into cars, lying about shoplifting so as not to be caught), and serious violations of rules (e.g., ignoring reasonable curfews, being truant from school; APA, 2000; A. Carr, 2014; Gelhorn et al., 2009). Approximately 2 to 6 percent of school-age youths could be classified as having a conduct disorder, with rates being three or four times higher for boys than for girls (Kazdin, 1997).

One or two antisocial acts do not make a conduct problem. Conduct disorders are more than a matter of "kids being kids" or "sowing wild oats." Instead, they represent deep-seated and persistent disregard for the rights and feelings of others. Youth with conduct disorders tend to see the world through conflict-colored glasses, for example, by assuming that others have hostile intentions toward them (Dodge et al., 2003).

Conduct disorder is especially serious (and likely to foreshadow adjustment problems in the adult years) when it begins prior to adolescence (J. G. Barrett, 2005; D. Shaw, 2013). Youngsters who exhibit conduct disorders beginning in childhood are likely to have many problems in adulthood, including antisocial and criminal behavior, frequent changes in employment, high divorce rates, little participation in families and community groups, and early death. In contrast, conduct disorders that don't emerge until adolescence are often the result of affiliation with peers who engage in delinquent behavior; as these late-onset offenders mature and find new social contacts, they tend to stop engaging in destructive acts.

As is true for the emotional disorders we've previously considered, biology may be *partly* to blame for conduct disorders. Children with conduct disorders have difficulty inhibiting aggressive impulses, perhaps as a result of brain damage or other neurological conditions (Fishbein et al., 2006; S. White et al., 2013). Families are influential as well: Conduct disorders are relatively common when children's parents provide little affection, abuse children, and are highly critical and harsh in their physical punishment (G. R. Patterson, DeBaryshe, & Ramsey, 1989; Tuvblad, Bezdjian, Raine, & Baker, 2013). Neighborhoods can also be a factor in conduct disorders, as when children witness violence in their communities and later become physically aggressive themselves (Ridenour, Clark, & Cottler, 2009; Shahinfar, Kupersmidt, & Matza, 2001).

Supporting Youngsters with Emotional and Behavioral Problems

Young people with mental health conditions gain a better outlook on life when they receive counseling and other mental health treatments. In an Observing Children video, you can watch an adolescent girl learning to express uncomfortable emotions to her mother with help from a counselor. Sensitive attention from teachers and other school staff can also be helpful. Educators can implement these strategies:

Observing Children 11-6
Listen to an adolescent girl being coached in expressing her disappointment, embarrassment, and hurt to her mother during a counseling session.

ENHANCEDetext *video example*

• **Communicate your interest in and concern for troubled children.** Having a supportive relationship with a teacher protects a child from everyday stresses and increases the chances that the child adjusts well at school (Rueger, Chen, Jenkins, & Choe, 2014; Valiente, Lemery-Chalfant, Swanson, & Reiser, 2008). Many youngsters with emotional disorders have few positive ties with individuals outside of school, and so their relationships with caring teachers, school counselors, and other skilled professionals are all the more critical. The many "little things" educators and other practitioners do each day, including greeting youngsters warmly, expressing concern when they seem worried, and lending a ready ear when they want to share ideas or frustrations, can make a world of difference for children (S. C. Diamond, 1991).

• **Teach social skills.** Many children with emotional problems have difficulty maintaining friendships (Asher & Coie, 1990; Kingery, Erdley, Marshall, Whitaker, & Reuter, 2010). You can support these youngsters by encouraging them to practice particular social skills, such as saying something friendly to a peer and resolving conflicts by talking openly about the problem (Gillham, Reivich, Jaycox, & Seligman, 1995; Marquez et al., 2014).[9]

• **Provide extra structure for youngsters who have high levels of anxiety.** One especially effective strategy is to communicate expectations for performance in clear and concrete terms. Highly anxious youngsters perform better in well-structured environments, such as classrooms in which expectations for academic achievement and social behavior are communicated directly (Sieber, O'Neil, & Tobias, 1977; Stipek, 1993). When they know what to expect and how they will be evaluated, these young people are more inclined to relax, enjoy themselves, and learn. Of course, prevention of excessive anxiety before children develop an anxiety disorder is also a valuable investment. In a preschool program designed to help children manage their anxiety, called FRIENDS, children learn to attend to their *Feelings*, *Relax*, think about their *Inner* feelings, *Explore* plans, motivate themselves with comments about having done *Nice* work, remind themselves "*Don't* forget to practice," and *Stay* calm (Anticich, Barrett, Silverman, Lacherez, & Gillies, 2013).

[9]We offer additional recommendations for fostering children's social skills in Chapters 12, 14, and 15.

• **Respect children's autonomy.** Every child needs to be able to make choices. Some young people, especially those who consistently defy authority figures, often behave even less appropriately when adults try to control them. With these youngsters, it is important that practitioners not get into power struggles, situations where only one person wins and the other loses (S. C. Diamond, 1991). Instead, adults might create situations in which children conform to expectations yet also know they have some control over what happens to them.

• **Advise parents about your concerns.** Parents whose children have emotional and behavioral problems may appreciate advice on meeting children's needs. Depending on the particular challenges that children face, parents may need guidance in establishing clear rules, recognizing children's good behaviors, disciplining children, helping children to understand and manage their feelings, or regulating their own emotions (Garland, Augustyn, & Stein, 2007; Rosenblum & Muzik, 2014). Family educators play a special role in the community in coaching parents to try new childrearing methods.

• **Be alert for signs that an adolescent may be contemplating suicide.** Seriously depressed youngsters may fail to reach out for help when they believe that no one cares about them or that they should be able to solve their problems on their own. A few are worried that people would think less of them if they were to disclose their mental anguish (Freedenthal & Stiffman, 2007). Informed professionals keep alert to the signs troubled students give off (consciously or not) that they may be thinking about taking their own lives. Warning signs include the following:

- Signs of depression, hopelessness, and helplessness
- Abrupt withdrawal from social relationships (possibly after being rejected by peers or breaking up with a boyfriend or girlfriend)
- Disregard for personal appearance
- Serious health problems (e.g., a debilitating injury from an accident or a chronic condition resulting from an eating disorder)
- A dramatic personality change
- A sudden elevation in mood
- A preoccupation with death and morbid themes
- Serious problems at school, home, or in the community (e.g., expulsion from school, death of a friend, pregnancy, or arrest for illegal behavior)
- Overt or veiled threats (e.g., "I won't be around much longer")
- Actions that indicate "putting one's affairs in order" (e.g., giving away prized possessions)
- Substance abuse
- Repeated self-injury
- Preference for certain kinds of music (e.g., heavy metal rock music with morbid themes)
- Efforts to obtain suicidal means (e.g., medications, ropes, or guns)
- In some cases, impulsive personality

(M. M. Jensen, 2005; L. L. Kerns & Lieberman, 1993; Taliaferro & Muehlenkamp, 2014)

Adults must take these behaviors seriously, particularly if they see more than one of the signs on the list. Educators should show genuine concern for potentially suicidal youngsters and seek trained help from a school psychologist or counselor *immediately* (McCoy, 1994; Spirito, Valeri, Boergers, & Donaldson, 2003).

Summary

Some youngsters face serious emotional and behavioral problems that require thoughtful accommodation from adults. Youngsters with depression, an anxiety disorder, or a conduct disorder often benefit from professional intervention. In addition, teachers and other adults can offer reassurance, communicate expectations for appropriate behavior, and address children's personal concerns, such as getting along with peers and having some control over everyday decisions.

ENHANCEDetext *self-check*

PRACTICING FOR YOUR LICENSURE EXAMINATION

Many teaching tests require students to apply their knowledge of child development in analyzing brief vignettes and answering multiple-choice questions. You can practice for your licensure examination by reading the following case study and answering a series of questions.

The Girly Shirt

Eight-year-old Tim caused quite a disruption in class this morning. His teacher, Amy Fox, isn't quite sure why things got out of hand, and so she is meeting with Tim while the rest of the class is at lunch to learn what happened.

Ms. Fox: Things got out of control in class this morning, didn't they, Tim?

Tim: I guess they did.

Ms. Fox: Tell me what happened.

Tim: John and Steven were teasing me about my shirt. They really made me mad.

Ms. Fox: They were teasing you about your shirt? What did they say?

Tim: That it's too pink. That it's a "girly" color.

Ms. Fox: Really? I don't think it's too "girly" at all. In fact, I rather like that color on you. But anyway, you say the boys teased you about it. What did you do then?

Tim: I yelled at them. Then when you gave me that dirty look, they kept on laughing, and so I kept on yelling.

Ms. Fox: I see. John and Steven were certainly wrong to tease you about your clothes. I'll speak to them later. But right now I'm concerned about how you reacted to the situation. You were so loud that the class couldn't possibly continue with the lesson.

Tim: I know. I'm sorry.

Ms. Fox: I appreciate your apology, Tim. And I'd like to make sure that the next time someone hurts your feelings—maybe intentionally, maybe not—you don't blow up the way you did today. Let's come up with a plan for how you might keep your temper under better control.

Constructed-Response Question

1. What type of plan might be effective in helping Tim control his anger?

Multiple-Choice Questions

2. What aspect of emotional development is Tim struggling with in this incident?
    a. Emotional regulation, because he is having trouble controlling his temper
    b. Emotional contagion, because he is absorbing the feelings of the other boys
    c. Empathy, because he, like the other boys, disliked his shirt
    d. Insecure attachment, because he is not able to use his peers as a safe haven

3. Let's assume that Tim has been somewhat irritable since infancy. What factors might account for this temperament?
    a. Tim's temperament is the outgrowth of his unique genetic profile.
    b. Tim's temperament is the result of harsh and punitive parenting.
    c. Tim's temperament is the complex result of his genetic disposition, his family relationships, and his own choices and experiences.
    d. Temperament changes dramatically from day to day and week to week; therefore, it is not possible to identify any factors that account for consistency in his irritability.

ENHANCEDetext *licensure exam*

Key Concepts

coping skills (p. 408)

psychosocial stages (p. 408)

need for relatedness (p. 412)

attachment (p. 412)

ethological attachment theory (p. 412)

stranger anxiety (p. 413)

secure attachment (p. 414)

insecure-avoidant attachment (p. 414)

insecure-resistant attachment (p. 414)

disorganized and disoriented attachment (p. 415)

stress (p. 423)

emotion (p. 424)

emotional regulation (p. 425)

emotional contagion (p. 426)

self-conscious emotion (p. 427)

toxic stress (p. 428)

empathy (p. 429)

anxiety (p. 434)

personality (p. 436)

emotional and behavioral disorder (p. 443)

depression (p. 443)

anxiety disorder (p. 444)

conduct disorder (p. 444)

CHAPTER TWELVE

Development of Self and Social Understandings

CASE STUDY: Theodore

At age 16, Theodore had an assignment to write about who he was as a person. Following is his response:

Hello. I'm Theodore. I am 16 years old and come from America. I'm a very happy person and have an optimistic view on life. Although life can be very challenging and confusing at times, I always think to myself it will be all right later on. I think everybody is equal and everybody should be treated the same, even though this is close to impossible.

I love to hang out with my friends and family. I think family is one of the most important things in life. I love my family and feel very lucky, and I am very appreciative for all they have done for me. Not everybody can have such a loving family though, and that makes me very sad. Occasionally I get great urges to go out and try to help people all around the world who are in need of support. But also at times I feel very helpless, and I feel like I can't do much to help, which makes me upset. Living in a small city in America is very great, but I know there is more out there in the world, and I wish I could experience living in a developing country. I have been able to travel to several countries and have friends around the world that I keep in contact with on Facebook.

I am just a sort-of average kid who is medium in height and underweight. I have longish brown hair and big feet. I like girls and some like me back. I love to play video games and watch movies. I also like to play any kind of sports with my friends, especially Ultimate Frisbee.

I have no idea what I will be when I grow up. I am interested in SO many things, and it seems I will never be able to narrow it down. I am interested in computers/engineering, being a medical doctor of sorts, being an airplane pilot, and more. My biggest dream in life is to travel around the world as much as I can and learn about people, culture, food, history, language, religions, everything else I can learn about, everywhere in the world.

Throughout my life I have changed a lot physically and mentally. I look at the world very differently than I did even a few months ago, and I will probably think differently a couple months down the road. I grow more and more patient and less egocentric every day. I think I am going in the right direction except for a few things. Although I am smart and get good grades, I could work a lot harder in school and on other academic things. I could do extra homework. I find it hard to muster the gumption to work harder and do more academic things such as enter a spelling bee or science contest or something.

Well that's who I am today. Ask me again in a couple of years and see what I say!

- What does Theodore say about himself?
- How does Theodore think about his social world?

OBJECTIVES

12.1: Trace key developments in children's ideas about themselves and the strategies by which teachers foster healthy self-perceptions.

12.2: Discuss changes in social cognition during childhood, and identify ways in which teachers support social understandings in children.

Theodore, like all young people, has developed insights about himself and his social world. These insights are made possible by having a social brain and interacting with other people.

Each child is born with a starter kit for interpersonal interactions—a preference for looking at faces (especially the eyes and mouth), listening to voices, distinguishing one person from the next, and joining in an interaction (Happé & Frith, 2014). These rudimentary abilities are exercised during social contact; in the process, the child gains awareness of the self as an agent in the social world. Early perceptions are simple and concrete, such as recognizing another person by physical features, but they evolve into abstract reflections, as in Theodore's gratitude for the blessings he has in his family and community.

In addition to thinking about themselves, children become perceptive in understanding what makes other people tick. Theodore mentions that he is becoming less and less egocentric. He uses his perspective-taking skills with family and friends and also with people in other societies. He feels a commitment to helping others in need. Having a sense of self and an inclination to consider the needs of others helps Theodore, and other young people, get along in society.

In this chapter, you will learn that a few children face challenges in developing a positive self-concept. In absorbing messages that other people communicate about their value as human beings, they conclude that they are incapable, unattractive, and unwanted. Other children have difficulty grasping the viewpoints of other people. Fortunately, teachers and other professionals can help children see their worth and develop their ability to consider other people's perspectives.

SENSE OF SELF

Children develop knowledge, beliefs, judgments, and feelings about themselves, sentiments collectively known as a **sense of self**. Particular elements of self-perceptions go by a variety of names, including self-concept, self-esteem, and self-worth. In general, one's *self-concept* addresses the question "Who am I?" Self-concept includes understandings of one's own characteristics, strengths, and weaknesses ("I am a Puerto Rican American," "My nose is crooked"). The terms *self-esteem* and *self-worth* are synonyms that address the question "How good am I as a person?" They include judgments and feelings about one's value and worth (e.g., "I am proud to be Puerto Rican and American," "I hate my crooked nose!").

Children's self-concept and self-worth are closely related (Byrne, 2002; Harter, 2012; Richman, Hope, & Mihalas, 2010). Children who focus largely on their negative features tend to believe they are undeserving human beings. Those who hold favorable impressions of their characteristics tend to have high self-esteem. In this chapter, we examine self-concept and self-esteem together, often calling them self-perceptions but occasionally using one or another when distinctions in the research merit their separation.

Purpose of the Self

Children's sense of self serves several functions. It helps children understand things that happen to them ("Other kids ask me to join their teams, so I must be good at sports"). It motivates them to engage in behaviors to which others might respond approvingly ("If I'm nice to Russ, maybe he'll ask me to play with him"). It influences their reactions to events ("I'm upset that I'm not reading as well as my classmates"). And once they begin to look seriously at a particular *future self*, it helps them make choices appropriate for their goals ("To become a veterinarian, I need to take a biology class").

Perhaps most important, a sense of self helps a person find a comfortable niche in a complex world, a place in which the individual feels capable, cared for, and respected. Many psychologists believe that human beings have a basic need to think of themselves as competent, likable, and worthy individuals, thereby achieving a positive sense of self-worth (Covington, 1992; Marshall, Parker, Ciarrochi, & Heaven, 2014). Although children cannot always feel good about themselves, they usually can protect themselves. To maintain a strong self-worth, children use a variety of tactics, including affiliating with other individuals who treat them kindly and with respect, and putting themselves in situations where they can be successful.

Factors Influencing Self-Perceptions

Self-concept emerges in the arms of parents. When caregivers regularly nurture infants with affection and responsive care, infants learn not only that their caregivers love them but that they themselves are worthy of being loved (Bretherton, 1991). As children grow, parents enhance children's sense of self by treating them warmly and communicating expectations for mature behavior. Parents who accept children as they are—applauding children's abilities and taking *in*abilities in stride—are likely to have offspring with high self-esteem. Parents who punish children for things they do not or cannot do, without also praising them for things done well, are apt to have offspring with low self-esteem (Ahmann, 2014; Harter, 1999).

Adults outside the family are increasingly influential with age. Teachers, school nurses, and other practitioners foster a positive sense of self when they have high yet realistic expectations for children's performance; empathize with children who are lonely, anxious, and depressed; and offer needed support to succeed on difficult tasks (M. J. Harris & Rosenthal, 1985; Olowokere & Okanlawon, 2014).

Meanwhile, peers communicate information about children's social and athletic competence, perhaps by seeking out a child's companionship or ridiculing the child in front of others (Bogart et al., 2014; Dweck, 2000). Age-mates contribute to a child's sense of self in a second way as well: They provide information about what he or she "should" be able to do. As you will learn, by the elementary school years, how children evaluate themselves often depends on how their own performance compares to that of peers (Ehm, Lindberg, & Hasselhorn, 2014; Guay, Boivin, & Hodges, 1999). Children who see themselves achieving at higher levels than age-mates usually develop a more positive sense of self than do those who consistently find themselves falling short.

Membership in one or more peer groups can also influence children's sense of self, especially in adolescence (Birkeland, Breivik, & Wold, 2014; Lave & Wenger, 1991). If you think back to your own school years, you might recall taking pride in a regional championship earned by your school's athletic team or feeling good about a community service project completed by your club. Some young people affiliate with others on Facebook and other social networking sites and in the process gain a sense of being part of a circle of friends (Best, Manktelow, & Taylor, 2014; R. K. Baker & White, 2010). Being a member of an ethnic group similarly affects a youngster's sense of self, as we show later in this chapter in our analysis of identity.

School provides a context in which children make sense of their academic abilities and accomplishments. Academically, children base their self-perceptions on their growing record of performance (Damon, 1991; M. Seaton, Parker, Marsh, Craven, & Yeung, 2014). Children are more likely to believe they will succeed in school and later in college if they have been successful in their previous work. Conversely, those children who struggle recurrently see their abilities as limited and their academic futures as bleak. As we suggested earlier, peer comparison becomes integral to this evaluation, but personal accomplishments and struggles are also strikingly important. In the minds of children, their own performance in meeting expected standards and their impressions of how classmates judge their abilities become intertwined. A second grader named Tom, who had dyslexia, once described how he felt when struggling with reading in first grade:

> I falt like a losr. Like nobad likde me. I was afrad then kais wod tec me. Becacz I wased larning wale . . . I dan not whet to raed. I whoe whte to troe a book it my mom.
> *(I felt like a loser. Like nobody liked me. I was afraid that kids would tease me. Because I wasn't learning well . . . I did not want to read. I would want to throw a book at my mom.)*
> (N. F. Knapp, 2002, p. 74)

Most young children focus more on what they do well than on what they do poorly, and so they are inclined to think rather highly of themselves (Jacobs, Lanza, Osgood, Eccles, & Wigfield, 2002; Salley, Vannatta, Gerhardt, & Noll, 2010). Often they downplay areas that give them trouble (e.g., "Math is dumb"). They may also explain their shortcomings in ways that enable them to maintain a positive sense of self. In an Observing Children video, you can see 10-year-old David give a healthy, upbeat spin on why he doesn't recall as many words as

Observing Children 12-1

Listen to David put a positive spin on why he didn't remember as many words as he had predicted.

ENHANCEDetext *video example*

he expects to. He predicts that he might recall 12 out of 12 words but actually recalls only 3. Here is David's positive interpretation:

David: Okay, shirt, carrot, bed. I'm sorry, I can't remember the rest of it. It's just, I don't know. My brain was turned off right now. I use it a lot during school hours so then I just like to relax. . . .

Interviewer: What did you do to remember the ones that you remembered?

David: Even though I said 12, I was just trying to challenge myself a little.

The need to protect one's self-worth is so strong that it sometimes leads children to create obstacles that give them an excuse for failing. In other words, youngsters occasionally do things that actually *undermine* their chances of success—a phenomenon known as **self-handicapping**. Self-handicapping takes a variety of forms, including the following:

- *Reducing effort.* Putting forth an obviously insufficient amount of effort to succeed
- *Setting unattainably high goals.* Working toward goals that even the most capable individuals couldn't achieve
- *Taking on too much.* Assuming so many responsibilities that no one could possibly accomplish them all
- *Procrastinating.* Putting off a task until success is virtually impossible
- *Cheating.* Presenting others' work as one's own
- *Using alcohol or drugs.* Taking substances that will inevitably reduce performance (Covington, 1992; Shih, 2009; K. Snyder, Malin, Dent, & Linnenbrink-Garcia, 2014; Urdan, Ryan, Anderman, & Gheen, 2002)

It might seem paradoxical that youngsters who want to be successful would actually undermine their own accomplishments. But if they believe they are unlikely to succeed no matter what they do—and especially if failure will reflect poorly on their intelligence—they increase their chances of *justifying* failure. Self-handicapping is seen as early as elementary school and becomes increasingly common in the high school and college years (Alesi, Rappo, & Pepi, 2012; Urdan, 2004).

So far our discussion has focused primarily on the effects of experience on self-perception—that is, on children's processing of their encounters in the social and school environment. Biology has an impact as well. Self-esteem has a hereditary basis in that people who share many genes tend to view themselves in a similarly positive or negative way (H. Chen et al., 2013; Raevuori et al., 2007). Genes probably affect self-esteem indirectly through their effects on partially inherited characteristics (e.g., temperaments, motor skills, and cognitive abilities and disabilities) that contribute to successes and failures in social, athletic, and academic pursuits. Physical appearance also makes a difference: Adults and peers alike respond more favorably to children who are physically attractive (R. A. Gordon, Crosnoe, & Wang, 2013; S. H. W. Mares, de Leeuw, Scholte, & Engels, 2010).

Developmental Trends in the Self

Children's physical, cognitive, and social abilities change with age, and their perceptions of themselves shift accordingly. Researchers have observed the following developmental trends in sense of self:

Children construct increasingly abstract, integrated, and multifaceted understandings of who they are. Young children define themselves with a few specific, concrete, easily observable characteristics and behaviors. Children in the preschool and early elementary grades can distinguish between a few general aspects of themselves, for example, how competent they are in daily activities and how much family and friends like them (Davis-Kean & Sandler, 2001; E. Reese, Yan, Jack, & Hayne, 2010). As they grow older, they make finer and finer discriminations (Harter, 2012; Kuzucu, Bontempo, Hofer, Stallings, & Piccinin, 2014). By the upper elementary grades, they realize that they may be more or less advanced in their academic work, athletic activities, classroom behavior, likability among peers, and physical attractiveness. By adolescence, they have self-perceptions about their competence at adult-like tasks and their romantic appeal. Adolescents begin to describe their characteristics and behaviors as reflecting such intangible qualities as being "tech savvy" or "moody" (D. Hart, 1988; Meadows, 2010).

Most youngsters adopt criteria that others use in evaluating behavior and characteristics. Psychologists specializing in the self suggest that children internalize some of other people's ideas about desirable characteristics and behaviors (Burton & Mitchell, 2003; J. L. Williams & Smalls-Glover, 2014). As youngsters acquire such criteria, their self-esteem is increasingly based on *self*-judgments rather than others' judgments. A boy whose parents regularly praise him for his high grades is likely to begin judging *himself* by the grades he earns. You can see such internalization in an interview with 15-year-old Greg in an Observing Children video:

Observing Children 12-2
Observe how Greg has acquired standards for academic performance similar to those of his parents.

ENHANCEDetext *video example*

Interviewer:	What are the things that make you want to do well in school?
Greg:	My parents. [*Both laugh.*]
Interviewer:	Okay.
Greg:	My parents mostly. . . . And myself . . . sometimes.
Interviewer:	Okay. How do your parents influence you wanting to do well in school?
Greg:	I don't know. They did well so they want me to. . . .
Interviewer:	You said that sometimes you also want to do well for you. Can you tell me more about that?
Greg:	'Cause, I mean, you feel better if you get all As than Cs or Fs.

Yet the standards that youngsters internalize are not always realistic or productive. A girl whose friends place a premium on fashion-magazine standards for thinness may think she is "fat" even when she is dangerously underweight—a misperception commonly seen in youngsters who have eating disorders (Attie, Brooks-Gunn, & Petersen, 1990; Nanu, Tăut, & Băban, 2013).

Children become increasingly committed to particular standards. Youngsters generally have high self-esteem when they evaluate themselves as being strong in domains that are important to them. For some, academic achievement may be the overriding factor, whereas for others popularity with peers may be more influential. Some children invest in athletic accomplishments, and others may value their contributions to the family or community. And for many youngsters around the world, physical attractiveness contributes heavily to self-esteem (D. Hart, 1988; Harter, 2012).

Despite experiencing a general trend toward becoming progressively more certain of their own personal standards, some youngsters remain heavily dependent on others' opinions well into adolescence. They may be so preoccupied with approval from peers and adults that they base their own sense of self-worth largely on what others think—or at least on what *they think* others think—of them (Dweck, 2000; Ghoul, Niwa, & Boxer, 2013; Harter, Stocker, & Robinson, 1996). Teenagers who have such **contingent self-worth** are often on an emotional roller coaster, feeling elated one day and devastated the next, depending on how classmates, parents, and teachers have recently treated them.

As children grow older, their feelings of self-worth depend more on peers' behaviors and opinions. In the early years, parents and other family members are key players in shaping children's sense of self. As children spend more time away from home, however, they become more aware of and concerned about what nonfamily members—and especially peers—think of them (Birkeland et al., 2014; Richman et al., 2010). Whereas parents often express approval for good behavior and high academic achievement, peers tend to prefer physical attractiveness, athleticism, and being a fun playmate. Peers by no means replace the influence of parents, however. Well into the adolescent years, youngsters' self-perceptions continue to be strongly affected by interactions with parents (S. M. Cooper & Smalls, 2010; Harter, 2012).

Children increasingly behave in ways that mirror their self-perceptions. Those who see themselves as "good students" are more apt to pay attention in class, use effective learning strategies, and tackle challenging tasks, whereas those who believe they are "poor students" are apt to misbehave in class, study infrequently, and avoid difficult subject matter. Children who see themselves as friendly and likable are apt to seek the company of classmates and perhaps ask for help when needed or run for student council, whereas those who believe they are disliked may keep to themselves or behave aggressively toward age-mates. As you might guess, children who routinely *under*estimate their ability avoid the many challenges necessary for cognitive, social, and physical growth (Assor & Connell, 1992; D. Phillips & Zimmerman, 1990). These children are at risk for developing depression and other mental health problems (Nuijens, Teglasi, & Hancock, 2009; van Tuijl, de Jong, Sportel, de Hullu, & Nauta, 2014).

Children's sense of worth becomes more stable over time. Beginning in middle childhood and continuing into adolescence and beyond, self-esteem becomes fairly stable, such that those with positive self-perceptions tend to continue to see themselves in favorable terms (J. Kim & Cicchetti, 2009; R. W. Robins & Trzesniewski, 2005). Conversely, children who think poorly of themselves in elementary school generally have relatively low self-esteem in high school and adulthood. Several factors contribute to the increasing stability of self-perceptions:

- Children usually behave in ways consistent with what they believe about themselves, and their behaviors are apt to produce reactions from others that confirm their self-concepts.
- Children tend to seek out information that confirms what they already believe. Those with positive self-perceptions are more likely to seek out feedback about their strengths, whereas others with negative self-perceptions focus on their weaknesses (S. Epstein & Morling, 1995; R. T. Liu, Kraines, Massing-Schaffer, & Alloy, 2014).
- Children seldom put themselves in situations where they believe they won't succeed, thus minimizing the chances of discovering that they *can* perform well in a domain about which they've been pessimistic. If a middle school student believes he is a poor athlete and so refuses to go out for the baseball team, he may never learn that, in fact, he has the potential to become a good player.
- Many factors affecting self-esteem—inherited abilities and disabilities, parents' encouragement, physical attractiveness, and so on—remain relatively stable throughout childhood (Goleniowska, 2014; O'Malley & Bachman, 1983; Raevuori et al., 2007).

Preparing for Your Licensure Examination
Your teaching test might ask you about basic ways in which children's self-perceptions change with age.

This is *not* to say that once children acquire an unfavorable sense of self, they will always think poorly of themselves. Quite the contrary can be true, especially with new circumstances—including being put in situations where they are shown how to succeed and coaxed into taking risks (Marsh & Craven, 1997; Rönnau-Böse & Fröhlich-Gildhoff, 2009).

Characteristics of the Self During the Developmental Periods

The developmental trends just listed reflect gradual changes in sense of self over time. We now look at unique aspects of self-perceptions during the five age periods.

Infancy (Birth–Age 2)

The first elements of children's sense of self emerge during infancy. Through repeated physical experiences, babies discover that they have bodies that bring them discomfort (through hunger, fatigue, and injury) and pleasure (through feeding, sucking thumbs, and snuggling in the arms of caregivers) (R. A. Thompson, 2006). As we suggested earlier, children form impressions of themselves as being lovable (or not) from their relationships with parents and caregivers. Infants who form secure bonds with caregivers are apt to develop positive self-perceptions, whereas infants who form insecure attachments are less likely to view themselves as favorably.[1]

In the first year, infants develop a sense of self-awareness. As they drop a ball, kick a mobile, and engage a parent with a cry or smile, infants realize that their behavior elicits particular effects (R. A. Thompson & Virmani, 2010). Imitations of other people's facial expressions nourish their early sense of self; likewise, they notice and appreciate when adults imitate their behavior (Langfur, 2013; Meltzoff, 2007). As they improvise in mimicking others' expressions (e.g., opening and closing their mouths more quickly than their older brother

---

[1]In Chapter 11, you can find more information about how children develop perceptions about themselves and others while forming close bonds with parents.

does), it dawns on them that they and other people are separate entities. Late in the first year, activities involving joint attention come into play as well. When Mommy and baby examine a toy together, baby shifts her gaze between toy and Mommy's face. Baby begins to learn that she has a sense of "we-ness" with her mother (Emde & Buchsbaum, 1990). Thus, infants integrate rudimentary perceptions of separateness *and* interpersonal connection into their sense of who they are.

In the second year, infants begin to recognize themselves in the mirror. In a clever study of self-recognition, babies 9 to 24 months were placed in front of a mirror (M. Lewis & Brooks-Gunn, 1979; R. A. Thompson & Virmani, 2010). Their mothers wiped their faces, leaving a red mark on their noses. Older infants, especially those 15 months or older, touched their noses when they saw their reflections, as if they understood that the reflected images belonged to them. Of course, this sense of self is spontaneous and fleeting—reflecting a dawning awareness of the self in action, not an introspective this-is-me-and-I-have-these-qualities self-image. Relevant to their emerging sense of self, infants gain a feeling of mastery—confidence in action—as they exert desired effects on objects by releasing levers, bouncing balls, and activating music.

Early Childhood (Ages 2–6)

In early childhood, language acquisition and other cognitive developments permit advancements in the self. Once children begin to talk, their self-awareness becomes more obvious. Children begin to refer to themselves by the pronouns *I* and *me,* and at ages 2 and 3 commonly exclaim "Mine!" during tussles with siblings and peers (Brownell, Iesue, Nichols, & Svetlova, 2013; L. Levine, 1983). Learning about what is *mine* is a natural part of development and is probably a precursor to sharing. Young children also increasingly assert their competence and independence (e.g., by refusing assistance with putting on their jackets) and articulate their self-awareness by labeling emotions (e.g., "Happy me").[2]

Another acquisition that depends on cognitive development is the *autobiographical self,* the child's memory of important events in his or her life.[3] Children's early recollections take the form of sparse and fragmented snippets that don't hang together in a meaningful way. On average, children remember few if any events that occurred before age 3½, and their recall of events before age 2 is virtually nonexistent. Memories for events become increasingly detailed and integrated during the preschool years as children talk about their experiences with other people (Fivush & Nelson, 2004; Q. Wang, 2013).

With language and an autobiographical memory, young children now have means to reflect on themselves as human beings, with words and memories. Initially, they see themselves largely in terms of obvious physical characteristics and simple psychological traits (Damon & Hart, 1988; Harter, 2012). As they learn from caregivers what things are "good" and "bad," they begin to apply these standards in evaluating themselves (Eisenberg, Spinrad, Valiente, & Duckworth, 2014; Kagan, 1981). Often they feel sad or angry when they don't measure up. Hence, a 4-year-old boy may become quite frustrated when he has set the goal of being a tall-tower-builder and inadvertently knocks over his blocks.

By and large, however, most young children have upbeat self-concepts and high self-esteem. Often they believe that they are more capable than they really are (Harter, 2012; Lockhart, Chang, & Story, 2002). Such optimism is perhaps due to their tendency to base self-assessments on continuing improvements in "big boy" and "big girl" activities. Their overconfidence is mostly beneficial for their development in that it motivates them to persist at challenging tasks (Bjorklund & Green, 1992; Pintrich & Schunk, 2002).

Middle Childhood (Ages 6–10)

During middle childhood, children see themselves in complex physical and psychological terms. Elementary school children remain fairly optimistic but become aware that they do some

FOR FURTHER EXPLORATION . . .

Learn how a sense of self in early childhood contributes to productive peer relations.

ENHANCEDetext
content extension

---

[2]Children's ability to label emotions is a milestone in their social-emotional development and is examined in Chapter 11.
[3]The *autobiographical self* is defined in Chapter 7.

Song of Myself

I am Shea
Above me are the bright colored leaves on the trees
Below me are seeds waiting to become flowers next spring
Before me are years to come full of new things to be learned
Behind me are memories I've forgotten
All around me are my friends lending me a helping hand
I see children having fun
I smell the sweet scent of flowers
I hear the birds talking to each other
I feel the fur of a helpless baby bunny
I move like wind as I run through the grass
I am old like the planets who have been here from the beginning
I am young like a seed waiting to sprout
I am the black of a panda's patches
I am the gold of the sun
I am the green of a cat's eye
I am the many colors of the sunset
I am a parrot, kangaroo, tiger, turtle
I am kind, responsible, pretty, smart
I think, plan, help, research
I give ideas to people that need them
I fear lightning
I believe that we all are equal
I remember my dreams
I dream of bad things as well as the good
I do not understand why some people pollute the Earth
I am Shea, a child of honesty
May I walk in peace

ARTIFACT 12-1 **Song of Myself.** During middle childhood, children see themselves as complex beings with characteristics in numerous domains. Shea wrote this poem about herself using "stems" provided by her teacher (e.g., "Above me . . .," "I feel . . .," "I am . . .," and "I dream . . .").

things well and other things poorly (Bong, Cho, Ahn, & Kim, 2012; Marsh & Craven, 1997; Wigfield, 1994). In Artifact 12-1, Shea's poem reveals her multifaceted view of herself.

As children progress through the elementary grades, they have many opportunities to compare themselves with others and become more cognitively able to *make* such comparisons. Most youngsters now receive doses of critical feedback from teachers and also observe some of their peers outshining them some of the time, and so their self-assessments typically decline from the overconfidence of the preschool years to the realistic levels of middle childhood (Bong et al., 2012; Marsh & Hau, 2003). Becoming more sensible about their talents and limitations probably helps children choose age-appropriate activities and work toward achievable goals (Baumeister, Campbell, Krueger, & Vohs, 2003; Harter, 2012).

Early Adolescence (Ages 10–14)

By the time they enter middle school, at around age 10, young students have had many chances to reflect on who they are as individuals. They have learned to apply standards of importance to them—perhaps being academically strong, attractive in physical appearance, popular with peers, and honorable in serving the community. Yet life does not stand still. The many transformations they now face as young adolescents challenge their self-image, and they must form new ideals.

Puberty heightens introspection in young people, who respond to the momentous changes in their lives with images of themselves as emerging adults. To achieve this new sense of self, they must reassess their direction in life. This journey from child to adult is a long one, and requires imagination as to what the future holds, as you can see in 10-year-old Alex's drawings about a range of occupations he could pursue, some fanciful and others serious (see Artifact 12-2). Given the inherent difficulty in finding a career pathway, adolescents appreciate assignments that allow them to explore a range of fields, jobs, and practical duties, for example, through visits to work sites, job shadows, and internships (J. M. Holland, 2011; J. Newman & Hubner, 2012).

A drop in self-esteem often occurs at about the time that youngsters move from elementary school to middle school or junior high school; this drop is sometimes more pronounced for girls (Cai, Wu, Luo, & Yang, 2014; Marsh, 1990b; Santo et al., 2013). The physiological changes of puberty are one factor in the decline. Self-evaluations depend increasingly on perceptions of appearance and popularity, and boys and girls alike tend to think of themselves as being less attractive once they reach adolescence (Gatti, Ionio, Traficante, & Confalonieri, 2014; Harter, Whitesell, & Junkin, 1998). Changes in the school environment, such as disrupted friendships, more superficial teacher–student relationships, and more rigorous academic standards, also have a negative impact (Eccles & Midgley, 1989; Morin, Maïano, Marsh, Nagengast, & Janosz, 2013).

Self-examination in early adolescence takes two additional forms. First, youngsters become more concerned with how others see them (Harter, 2012). They may initially go to extremes, thinking that everyone

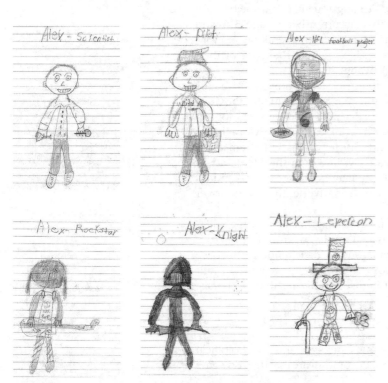

ARTIFACT 12-2 **Future selves.** In these spontaneously created drawings, 10-year-old Alex envisions a variety of possible roles he might take on, some realistic and others far-fetched.

else's attention is focused squarely on them (Alberts, Elkind, & Ginsberg, 2007; J. Martin & Sokol, 2011). This self-centered quality of adolescence is sometimes called the **imaginary audience**. Because they believe they are the center of attention, teenagers (girls especially) are often preoccupied with their physical appearance and can be quite self-critical. Many adolescents change the way they speak and act according to who they are with at the time, increasing the chances they will gain others' approval. Yet young adolescents are generally not fully aware of their different styles with different people.

A second noteworthy phenomenon in early adolescence is the **personal fable**. Young teenagers can feel as if they are completely unlike anyone else (Bester, 2013; Elkind, 1981a; P. L. Hill & Lapsley, 2011). They are apt to think their own feelings are unique—that the people around them have never had such experiences. Hence they may insist that no one else, least of all parents and teachers, can possibly know how they feel. They may also believe that they have special powers and are invulnerable to harm.

Adults should keep in mind that modest levels of the personal fable and the imaginary audience serve valuable functions for adolescents. Being somewhat—but not excessively—self-centered may help adolescents navigate their many challenges with physical, social, and academic changes and with preparing for adult roles (C. T. Barry & Kauten, 2014). The personal fable—in particular, the sense of invulnerability—may encourage young people to venture out and try new things (Bjorklund & Green, 1992; Lapsley, 1993). The imaginary audience keeps youngsters "connected" to their larger social context. Because they continually attend to how others might judge their actions, they are more apt to behave in ways that their society views favorably (Lapsley, 1993; R. M. Ryan & Kuczkowski, 1994). At some point, both the imaginary audience and personal fable apparently outlive their purposes for most teens, because these tendencies slowly diminish in late adolescence and early adulthood (Lapsley, 1993; P. D. Schwartz, Maynard, & Uzelac, 2008).

Late Adolescence (Ages 14–18)

As their worlds expand, teenagers have a greater variety of social experiences with people from diverse backgrounds. With their increasing ability to reflect on their own behaviors, they become consciously aware that they take on different personalities when interacting with parents, teachers, friends, and romantic partners. Teens may also discover parts of themselves that they do not like. Furthermore, their sense of self may include multiple qualities that they perceive to be somewhat contradictory (Garn, McCaughtry, Martin, Shen, & Fahlman, 2012; D. Hart, 1988). The inconsistencies can be a source of confusion, as a ninth grader revealed:

> I really don't understand how I can switch so fast from being cheerful with my friends, then coming home and feeling anxious, and then getting frustrated and sarcastic with my parents. Which one is the *real* me? (Harter, 1999, p. 67)

As high school students wrestle with the question *Who is the real me?*, they gradually broaden their sense of self to accommodate the range of personas in which they find themselves (Harter, 2012). For instance, they may resolve self-perceptions of being both "cheerful" and "depressed" by concluding that they are "moody" or explain inconsistent behaviors by deciding they are "flexible" or "open minded."

In the process of reconciling their "multiple selves," older adolescents make progress toward establishing a sense of **identity**, a self-constructed definition of who they are, what they find important, what they believe, and what they should do in life. In Erik Erikson's historically significant theory of human development, adolescents' search for identity is a pivotal challenge.[4] Contemporary research indicates that before youngsters achieve a true sense of their adult identity, most need considerable time to explore career options, political views, religious convictions, and so on. Canadian psychologist **James Marcia** (1980, 1991; Marcia & Josselson, 2013) identified four distinct patterns of behavior that characterize the search for identity:

- *Identity diffusion*. The adolescent has made no commitment to a particular career path or ideological belief system. Possibly there has been some haphazard experimentation with particular roles or beliefs, but the adolescent has not yet embarked on a serious exploration of issues related to self-definition.

---

[4] Erikson's stage of *identity vs. role confusion* is described in Chapter 11.

- *Foreclosure*. The adolescent has made a commitment to an occupation and a particular set of beliefs. The choices have been made without much deliberation or exploration of other possibilities; rather, they have been based largely on what others (especially parents) have prescribed.
- *Moratorium*. The adolescent has no strong commitment to a particular career or set of beliefs but is actively exploring a variety of values and career tracks.
- *Identity achievement*. The adolescent has previously gone through a period of moratorium and emerged with a clear choice regarding a small range of occupations as well as a commitment to particular political and religious beliefs.

Marcia's framework presumes that some exploration is necessary. Foreclosure—identity choice without prior exploration—rules out potentially more productive alternatives, and identity diffusion leaves young people without a clear sense of direction. Being in moratorium can be an uncomfortable experience for adolescents (consider the uneasiness that Theodore in the introductory case study, expressed with not yet having decided on a career path), but it is often an important step in achieving a healthy identity (Marcia 1988; Marcia & Josselson, 2013).

In fact, for most older high school students, the search for identity is hardly complete. Even so, their self-esteem has largely recuperated from the unsettling experiences of the middle school and early high school years (Harter, 2012). Several developmental advancements contribute to this rebound in sense of self. Most older adolescents have acquired the social skills they need to get along well with others. They have accepted the apparent inconsistencies in their self-perceptions and have considerable autonomy in choosing activities at which they are likely to be successful. And they increasingly judge themselves based on their *own* (rather than other people's) standards. When adolescents find others who share their passion for a particular direction, pastime, or field of study, they gain of sense of camaraderie, as you can see in 17-year-old Kiley's reflections on her affiliations with the music department in Artifact 12-3.

It was during high school that I discovered who I was. Freshman and sophomore year I was a hermit crab, slowly trying to change to a new shell. I was eager to make the process yet I was yearning for something to hold on to help ease the way. For me my path of stepping stones was the — High School music department.

When I walked into chorus my freshman year, I was petrified. I felt like I was involved in a cult of some sort. Everyone either seemed extremely friendly or in love with the music department. I have to admit that at first I thought that the music department was pretty lame. Everyday I would walk in and see everyone hugging their friends or people crying on each other's shoulders, what was this? Everyone seemed so dependent on each other. I had my thoughts of quitting; I didn't know a lot of people and wasn't excited at the thought of making friends with them either, but I stuck it out, singing has always been my passion and I wasn't about to never perform again. This is who I was, I wasn't about to let some crazy group of people intimidate me.

By the middle of my sophomore year I was a full time band geek; besides the fact that I wasn't even in the band. I finally let my walls cave in and let the music department be my second home. I loved it. I could come in during the middle of a bad school day and always find a friend, always have someone their for me. The seniors in the rest of the school always seemed so big, so intimidating, but when I walked through the doors of the music department everyone was equal; there were no judgments and everyone felt welcome.

The music department changed me. I am no longer shy or timid but I am me to the fullest extent of the word. I now have the ability to walk into a group of people and make friends instantly. The music department helped me realize that performing is my passion, it's what I love; it's who I am. I am now ready to go audition, to go out and show the world what I am made of. Throughout high school nothing else has made such a lasting impression on me, I am not going to sit back one day as a mother and tell my children about my freshman PE class; my only eventful memories are contained within the walls of the music department. . . .

The music department has given me the strength to move on. When I am nervous I know I can always think back to my — years, and the confidence that slowly grew with the help of loving arms. I may be unsure about the future but I am excited. I will always remember the friends I made, the confidence I earned, and the love I shared within the four years; or better yet the four solid walls of the — High School music department

---

ARTIFACT 12-3 Hermit crab. As an assignment for one of her 11th-grade classes, 17-year-old "Kiley" (a pseudonym) wrote the essay shown here. (We have blanked out the name of Kiley's school but have left spelling and grammar errors intact.)

Even as older adolescents move toward independence, their attachments to family members, especially parents, continue to play a significant role in their adjustment. Adolescents who have strong emotional bonds with sensitive parents tend to have high self-esteem (R. M. Ryan & Lynch, 1989; Wouters, Doumen, Germeijs, Colpin, & Verschueren, 2013). This emotional support gives adolescents needed license to explore various aspects of their developing identities (Mullis, Graf, & Mullis, 2009). Other parenting styles (e.g., uninvolved, controlling, or rejecting parenting) can cause adolescents to feel alienated from parents and susceptible to the opinions of others; these adolescents are more likely to have the *contingent self-worth* you read about earlier (Josselson, 1988; Wouters et al., 2013).

As you have learned, self-perceptions change dramatically by age. The Developmental Trends table "Sense of Self at Different Age Levels" encapsulates the self-perceptions you might see, and the responses you might make, with children in each developmental period.

DEVELOPMENTAL TRENDS
Sense of Self at Different Age Levels

AGE	WHAT YOU MIGHT OBSERVE	DIVERSITY	IMPLICATIONS
Infancy (Birth–2 Years)	• Increasing awareness of being separate from caregivers (in the first year) • Emerging self-awareness of having an impact on other people and the environment (especially at the end of the first year) • Increasing recognition of self in mirror (in the second year) • A few first-person pronouns, such as *I, me, mine* (late in the second year)	• The quality of child–caregiver relationships influences infants' belief that they are worthy of love. • The regularity with which adults comment on infants' images in a mirror and refer to their facial features (e.g., "We'd better wipe your runny nose") may affect self-recognition.	• Communicate affection by cuddling and talking to infants and by attending to their physical needs in a timely and consistent manner. • Talk with infants and toddlers about their bodily features and possessions ("Where's your nose?" "Here's your teddy bear!").
Early Childhood (2–6 Years)	• Frequent use of *I, me,* and *mine,* especially at ages 2 and 3 • Emergence of an autobiographical self (beginning at age 3 or 4) • Concrete self-descriptions (e.g., "I'm a boy," "I'm pretty") • Overconfidence about what tasks can be accomplished	• Children whom others treat affectionately tend to develop a positive sense of self. Those who are rejected, ridiculed, or ignored have a harder time seeing themselves in favorable terms. • Some children gain an emerging awareness that they belong to a particular racial or ethnic group (by about age 5).	• Acknowledge children's possessions, but encourage sharing. • Engage children in joint retellings of recent events. • Don't disparage children's lofty ambitions ("I'm going to be president!"), but focus their efforts on accomplishing short-term goals.
Middle Childhood (6–10 Years)	• Increasing distinction among various aspects of oneself (e.g., among academic performance, athletic ability, and personal likability) • Increasing tendency to base sense of self on how one's own performance compares with that of peers • Increasing internalization of others' standards for performance (continues into adolescence) • Generally good self-esteem in most children	• Different children place greater or lesser importance on various domains (e.g., on academic performance vs. athletic prowess) in deriving their overall sense of self-worth. • In middle childhood, girls begin to evaluate their physical appearance less favorably than boys do.	• Praise children for their talents and accomplishments in numerous areas (e.g., in physical activities, social relationships, and specific academic subjects). • Help children find arenas in which they can be especially successful. • If necessary, teach hygiene and personal grooming habits that enhance children's acceptance by peers.

(continued)

DEVELOPMENTAL TRENDS (continued)

AGE	WHAT YOU MIGHT OBSERVE	DIVERSITY	IMPLICATIONS
Early Adolescence (10–14 Years)	• Increasing tendency to define oneself in abstract rather than concrete characteristics • Possible drop in self-esteem after the transition to middle school or junior high • Heightened sensitivity to what others think of oneself *(imaginary audience)*, leading to a preoccupation with physical appearance • Belief in oneself as overly unique *(personal fable)*, occasionally leading to feeling of invulnerability	• Drops in self-esteem, when sizable and not followed by a gradual rebound, can signal a problem. • On average, youngsters increasingly base their self-perceived strengths on gender stereotypes (e.g., boys see themselves as good in mathematics and science, girls see themselves as good in reading) even when actual achievement levels are similar. • Members of ethnic groups vary in the extent to which their ethnicity plays a role in their core identity.	• When students are making the transition to middle school or junior high, be especially supportive and optimistic about their potential for success. • Be patient when adolescents show exceptional self-consciousness; give them strategies for presenting themselves well to others (e.g., how they might introduce themselves to unfamiliar peers).
Late Adolescence (14–18 Years)	• Decrease in the self-consciousness that was evident in early adolescence • Reconciliation of many apparent contradictions in oneself • Concern with identity issues: Who am I? What do I believe? What course should my life take?	• Adolescents whose sense of self-worth continues to depend heavily on others' behaviors and opinions (those who have *contingent self-worth*) are more susceptible to mood swings and peer pressure. • Some adolescents willingly accept the professional goals and ideologies that parents offer. Others engage in more soul-searching as they piece together their own identity. • Gender non-conforming youth defy traditional gender roles through clothing, hairstyle, and actions.	• Provide opportunities for adolescents to explore diverse belief systems and try on a variety of occupational "hats." • Be on the lookout for teens whose self-worth seems especially dependent on peers' opinions; help them discover areas of talent that can contribute to a more stable sense of self-worth.

BIOECOLOGY OF DEVELOPMENT

Children develop a sense of self while reflecting on their experiences in complex social environments.

Self in a Bioecological Context

The individual self-perceptions change with age in ways we have just examined but also are affected by children's personal characteristics and affiliations in groups. American psychologist **Margaret Beale Spencer** has developed an informative framework, the *Phenomenological Variant of Ecological Systems Theory* (PVEST), which examines processes in defining a sense of self as children interact with social partners, use resources afforded to them by society, build on their assets and confront their risks, develop coping skills, and achieve certain outcomes (see Figure 12-1).[5]

Spencer views her theory as a *bioecological* framework because it extends Urie Bronfenbrenner's (Bronfenbrenner, 1979; Bronfenbrenner & Morris, 2006) conceptualization that children are profoundly influenced by their biological dispositions as well as by their relationships, including with families, friends, and others in society.[6] According to Spencer, children encounter both *risk factors* (e.g., growing up in poverty and dealing with discrimination) and *protective factors* (e.g., being intelligent and having involved parents and dedicated teachers). A few of these threats and safeguards are based in part on experiences in ethnic groups. For example, many African American children regularly confront prejudice and discrimination. Yet as a group, African American children also enjoy numerous advantages, in many cases strong extended family support, an active spiritual life, good coping skills, and supportive neighbors (E. McGee & Spencer, 2014; M. B. Spencer, 2006). In comparison, many European American children benefit from access to a high-quality education and ample family income yet struggle with life's challenges, stresses that are evident in the comparatively high suicide rates in white youth (National Institute of Mental Health, 2008b; M. B. Spencer, 2006).

[5]Margaret Beale Spencer's work is introduced in Chapter 3.
[6]Urie Bronfenbrenner's bioecological systems theory is described in Chapters 1 and 3.

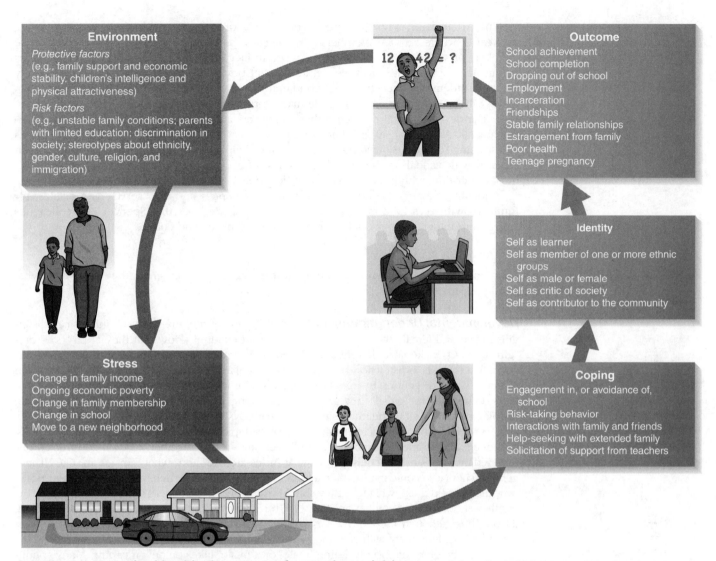

FIGURE 12-1 Emerging identities in contexts of protection and risk. *Based on information in M. B. Spencer, 2006; Spencer & Swanson, 2013. In the example, 8-year-old Jerry has a close relationship with his grandfather, his primary guardian. When the two move to a new city, Jerry experiences stress when he enrolls in a new school but learns to cope with help from a new friend and teacher. Jerry begins to identify as a good student and becomes an active participant at school.*

In the PVEST model, children do not passively succumb to pressures in their environment. Instead, they actively interpret the implications of events and relationships for themselves. One boy welcomes the addition of a new father figure into the family, as he perceives his mother's new husband as an affectionate provider who is concerned with his welfare. Another boy feels threatened by the presence of his new stepfather, whom he sees as trying to displace his birth father. Thus individual children facing the same objective circumstances can show distinctly different responses.

To address the environmental forces they experience, children develop an array of *coping skills*, behavioral strategies for overcoming the stresses of everyday life. Children regularly develop adaptive coping skills that allow them to make the best of a difficult situation, but in some situations they adopt maladaptive habits that actually hinder their adjustment. One adolescent girl may respond to decreased attention from her parents (perhaps due to a parent's new job or a family crisis) by spending more time with grandparents and asking for help from her school adviser. A second girl may respond to the same circumstance by staying away from home, associating with deviant peers, and getting into trouble.

As children exercise coping skills, they build and rebuild their personal *identity*. How children respond to difficulties, perhaps low achievement or exposure to community violence, reflects on who they are becoming. Children come to see themselves as strong or weak learners; as vital members of families or as rejected children; and as productive members of society or as rebels who engage in illegal activities. These and other identities culminate in important outcomes. An adolescent boy who sees himself as an academically talented student will likely try to get good grades and eventually earn a high school diploma. A boy who sees himself as a renegade may drop out of school.

The developmental outcomes that youngsters attain, in turn, determine their new environments. An adolescent girl who is on track to earn her high school diploma now thinks about going to college or working in her aunt's hair salon next year. Her cousin has been charged with vandalism, burglary, and assault of a classmate, and the cousin now spends most of her time with peers who commit delinquent acts.

Identity, then, is the outcome of many experiences and also serves as a catalyst for future growth. Let's look more closely at three characteristics that Spencer and colleagues suggest are integral to personal identity: gender, ethnicity, and culture.

Gender

From an early age, children show an interest in gender. As they grow, they determine what gender means for them.

Developmental Understanding of Gender. By the end of the first year, infants can distinguish male and female faces, and by age 2½, most children know that they are a "boy" or a "girl" (J. E. O. Blakemore, Berenbaum, & Liben, 2009; Kohlberg, 1966). After children understand that there is a distinction between males and females, they undertake a diligent search to figure out their gender. By age 4 or 5, children understand that gender is permanent—that boys do not become girls if they grow their hair long and wear ribbons, and that girls do not become boys if they cut their hair short and wear boys' clothes (Bem, 1989; Ruble et al., 2007).

As children become increasingly aware of the typical characteristics and behaviors of boys, girls, men, and women, they begin to pull their knowledge together into self-constructed understandings, or **gender schemas**, of "what males are like" and "what females are like." These gender schemas become part of their self-concept and guide their behavior and characteristics—how they should dress, what toys they should play with, what interests and academic subject areas they should pursue, and so on (Bem, 1981; Halim et al., 2014; Ruble, Martin, & Berenbaum, 2006). Thus, although they know it is biology that determines gender, they accentuate their masculinity or femininity with clothing, pastimes, and mannerisms (Halim et al., 2014).

With the onset of puberty, being "male" or "female" takes on new meaning. Many youngsters show a surge in gender-specific interests at this time (Ruble et al., 2006; Steensma, Kreukels, de Vries, & Cohen-Kettenis, 2013). Girls may show a newfound interest in their appearance, and boys may develop a heightened fascination with sports. To affirm their masculinity or femininity, many adolescents shy away from behaviors more closely associated with the opposite sex. Girls in general show less interest and confidence in subject areas that have been historically preferred by boys—for instance, in mathematics, science, and sports (Barkatsas, Kasimatis, & Gialamas, 2009; Kessels, Heyder, Latsch, & Hannover, 2014; E. M. Evans, Schweingruber, & Stevenson, 2002; Leaper & Friedman, 2007). As a result of aligning their behavior and interests with others of their same gender, adolescents firm up their gender identity with an embracement of themselves as being male or female (Steensma et al., 2013).

Origins of Differences in Interests and Actions in Boys and Girls. The consistency of psychological differences between the sexes raises questions about how these patterns originate. Biology clearly has a strong influence on how boys and girls behave. The brain is first marked "male" or "female" by subtle differences in anatomy during prenatal development (J. E. O. Blakemore et al., 2009; Steensma et al., 2013). At puberty, gender differences in the brain are amplified as hormones intensify gender characteristics. In a few cases these hormones increase the likelihood of problem behaviors and emotional responses. In boys, these rising hormones are associated with increased aggression—a stereotypically male characteristic.[7]

---

[7]Aggression is examined in Chapter 14.

Other people play an influencial role by encouraging children to think about males and females in particular ways. Family and peers often model gender-typical behavior, reinforce children for "staying within bounds," and punish them (e.g., by ridicule or exclusion) when they violate accepted gender roles (Cassano & Zeman, 2010; Pipher, 1994). A boy who cries after breaking his arm may be called a "sissy," and a girl who excels in mathematics might be teased for being a "math geek." Society influences children's roles through gender typical jobs (backhoe operators are almost always men) and differences in priorities ("Why don't you gals go shopping and let us guys watch the game?"; Halim, Ruble, & Tamis-Lemonda, 2013; Tennenbaum & Leaper, 2002).

Yet much of the pressure to act "appropriately" for one's gender comes from within rather than from others (Bem, 1981). This tendency for children and adolescents to conform to their own ideas about appropriate behaviors is known as **self-socialization**. For example, when teachers actively encourage children to engage in non-gender-stereotypical activities (boys playing with dolls, girls playing with toy cars, etc.), children may experiment with new activities for a brief while but soon revert to their earlier, more gender-stereotypical ways (Lippa, 2002).

Variations on Gender Identity. Thus far we have spoken of gender identity as an either-or proposition, but as you undoubtedly know, not every young person identifies with only one gender or develops the gender identity that is typical of those born biologically male or female.

Hormones, genetic factors, and other unknown circumstances influence the self-perceptions that the child develops related to gender (Steensma et al., 2013). For example, during prenatal development, an error in genes can lead to deficiencies in receptivity to male and female hormones, with direct effects on the developing brain of the baby. In one case, a girl baby is exposed to an unusual dosage of male hormones in utero and as a child progressively feels more male than female. In another pregnancy, a boy baby is exposed to a preponderance of female hormones; although he has male genitalia, he later develops definite feminine characteristics in clothing preferences, mannerisms, and interests. A very small number of children are born with ambiguous genitalia; for example, a girl who has female chromosomes and internal female organs is born with what appears to be a male penis. Depending on how astute doctors and nurses are, the child might be declared a boy at birth.

In these and other situations, some children come to feel that they are a different gender than that assumed by parents and defined by their chromosomes. *Gender nonconforming children* identify with a gender role that is not typical of others with the same chromosomal sex. Some youth invent their own gender role, perhaps taking on an appearance and behavior that is characteristic of the opposite sex or, alternatively, exhibiting features of both sexes (Janssen & Erickson-Schroth, 2013).

It is important to realize that gender identity is independent of sexual orientation. A *transgendered adult*, a person who develops a gender identity different from his or her biological sex, might be attracted to men, women, or both men and women. Adolescents who are trying to figure out the essence of their gender must eventually determine the type of individuals to whom they are intimately attracted.

Educators, counselors, and other professionals increasingly recognize that variations exist in gender identity. Adding to the challenges of wrestling with complicated feelings about gender and having few friends who understand their identity search, gender nonconforming youth may encounter peers who are downright rude. Teachers and other practitioners can accept gender nonconforming children for whom they are, young people driven to explore their personal identity. Adults can also enforce prohibitions on harassment and consult with school counselors and psychologists when gender nonconforming students struggle in peer relationships (Singh, Meng, & Hansen, 2014).

Ethnicity

Ethnic identity, an awareness and pride in one's ethnic heritage and willingness to adopt many of the behaviors of one's ethnic group, is another feature of the self (Adams-Bass et al., 2014; Phinney, 1989). The gradual development of ethnic identity has elements that we discussed previously when examining James Marcia's stages of identity formation.[8] Children begin by absorbing the messages that parents and other trusted caregivers offer about their ethnic affiliation, in much the same way that they might accept their parents' religious faith or job advice (leading to a foreclosure in ethnic identity; S. J. Schwartz et al., 2014). Initially, children are unconcerned with the meaning of ethnicity but receptive to their parents' views and only later, during adolescence, keenly attentive to its meaning for themselves (reflecting a moratorium in ethnic identity). Ultimately adolescents resolve what their ethnicity means for their personal identity (in ethnic identity achievement; Phinney, 1989).

Research with children backs up this general trend. By the time children reach kindergarten or first grade, they may be aware that they belong to a different "group" than some of their age-mates. A variety of characteristics make them ethnically identifiable in a crowd, including their skin color, facial features, and language. Already at this age, many children accurately classify themselves as being African, Mexican, Laotian, and so on and can describe some of the traditions of their group (Adams-Bass et al., 2014; R. D. Parke & Clarke-Stewart, 2011; Sheets, 1999). Parents and other family members give them labels (*Black, Chinese,* etc.) that communicate that they are special in an important way. By early adolescence, youngsters actively consider how their lives are affected by being a member of a particular ethnic group. By late adolescence, large numbers of youngsters achieve a strong ethnic identity.

Youngsters who develop a strong ethnic identity are likely to have experienced gestures by parents that encourage loyalty to their group. Many African American parents speak with pride about their heritage, inform children about the valiant struggles of their ancestors, and teach children how to cope with racial prejudice (Adams-Bass et al., 2014; D. Hughes, 2003). Many Puerto Rican and Dominican families transmit cultural pride by posting flags, inviting extended family over for traditional meals, speaking Spanish, and celebrating the religious and political holidays of their native lands (Csizmadia, Kaneakua, Miller, & Halgunseth, 2013; Pahl & Way, 2006).

Yet not all the messages that children with a non-white background receive are positive ones. Unfortunately, numerous children from ethnic minority and immigrant families are victims of prejudicial remarks. Sozan, an adolescent girl whose family members were Kurdish refugees to the United States, regularly heard classmates criticize her thick eyebrows and the scarf she wore out of respect for her religion, suggesting that she had a "unibrow" (i.e., one long eyebrow extending across her forehead) and was bald (McBrien, 2005a, p. 66). These were deeply hurtful comments, but Sozan held onto her faith and customs, as you can see in her self-portrait in Artifact 12-4.

Children from ethnic minority backgrounds typically consider their cultural background to be a more central feature of their self-concept than do children from majority backgrounds (Aboud, 1988; Kiang & Fuligni, 2010; K. L. Turner & Brown, 2007). European American children tend to see their ethnicity as the norm and are usually not strongly motivated to learn more about it. In contrast, children from other ethnicities realize that they are different from peers and are interested in learning about family origins. In the process of exploring their ancestry, children of color regularly develop more positive self-perceptions overall than do children from majority groups, possibly because they benefit from overtures by familiar adults that portray their heritage in a positive light (Adams-Bass et al., 2014; H. Cooper & Dorr, 1995).

Some young people respond to discrimination by taking proactive steps to learn about the strengths of their ethnic group and common tactics that combat negative race relations and inequities. Being victimized repeatedly by prejudiced individuals can overwhelm young people, however. In fact, exposure to discrimination creates a risk for low academic achievement and depression (Perreira, Kiang, & Potochnick, 2013; Scrimin, Moscardino, & Natour, 2014).

Children who have more than one ancestry, perhaps because of growing up in an immigrant or *multiethnic* family, are especially keen to explore their various heritages. The special tasks that children with multiethnic backgrounds have include learning about their two or more ethnic or racial heritages, determining how they are different and alike from others, synthesizing their separate heritages into a self-concept, and calling on distinct parts of their backgrounds when they want to or when the occasion requires this knowledge (Manzi, Ferrari,

---

[8] We introduce the concept of *ethnic identity* in Chapter 3.

ARTIFACT 12-4 Blending heritages. Sozan sees herself as a young Muslim woman who is committed to her cultural heritage and also wants to take advantage of the customs and opportunities in the United States.

"Sozan Self-Portrait from Dissertation" from DISCRIMINATION AND ACADEMIC MOTIVATION IN ADOLESCENT REFUGEE GIRLS by J. L. McBrien (Unpublished doctoral dissertation, Emory University, Atlanta, GA) DISSERTATION ABSTRACTS INTERNATIONAL SECTION A: HUMANITIES AND SOCIAL SCIENCES, 66 95-4). Copyright © 2005 by J. Lynn McBrien. Reprinted with permission.

Rosnati, & Benet-Martinez, 2014). Youngsters who are the beneficiaries of multiple heritages may fluctuate back and forth between allegiances to one ethnic identity or another, especially depending on circumstances (A. M. Lopez, 2003; B. D. Tatum, 1997). Consider Alice, who migrated from China to the United States at age 8. Although she gained fluency in English fairly quickly, for several years she had trouble reconciling the Chinese and American aspects of herself:

> [A]t home my parents expect me to be not a traditional Chinese daughter . . . but they expect things because I was born in China and I am Chinese. And at school, that's a totally different story because you're expected to behave as an American. You know, you speak English in your school; all your friends speak English. You try to be as much of an American as you can. So I feel I'm caught somewhere in between. . . . I feel I can no longer be fully Chinese or fully American anymore. (Igoa, 1995, p. 85)

After exploring numerous options for self-expression, many teens with multiethnic backgrounds ultimately construct a strong, multifaceted ethnic identity.

For the most part, students with a positive ethnic identity (including those with a strong multiethnic identity) perform well academically (Chavous et al., 2003; Costigan, Hua, & Su, 2010). Having a clear ethnic identity is linked to high self-esteem, a willingness to help other people, and few acts of violence (Corenblum, 2014; Phinney, Cantu, & Kurtz, 1997). Other findings indicate that young people with a clear ethnic identity are less likely to partake in drugs and other risky behaviors (Brook, Chenshu, Finch, & Brook, 2010; Umaña-Taylor & Alfaro, 2006). Apparently, pride in one's ethnic heritage serves as an emotional "buffer" against insults and discrimination (Romero & Roberts, 2003).

Occasionally, people outside the family (and rarely, other family members) communicate that aspects of a child's ethnic heritage are undesirable, a destructive message that obviously upsets the child (C. Brown & Brown, 2014; C. R. Cooper, Jackson, Azmitia, Lopez, & Dunbar, 1995). For example, a light-skinned girl with an African American mother and European American father might be told that she can "pass" as white, reflecting a denigration of her mother's background. Teachers, of course, must insist that children not ridicule class-mates about any aspect of their ethnic heritage. By establishing an inclusive environment wherein children from all backgrounds are valued, teachers lessen negative pressures on children with diverse and multidimensional ethnicities (Perreira et al., 2013).

Culture

Cultures tell children what they should think about, how they should relate to other people, and what it means to be a good person.[9] These core lessons are integrated into children's sense of self (Morelli & Rothbaum, 2007; R. A. Thompson & Virmani, 2010).

Particular cultures differ in the extent to which they encourage children to attend to personal needs (those of the individual self) or other people's needs (those of the collective group). Some societies (e.g., many groups in North America) place a lot of emphasis on personal needs. In *individualistic societies*, parents, teachers, and other adults encourage children to focus on their own wishes, motivations, and emotions (Markus & Hamedani, 2007; Rudy, Carlo, Lambert, & Awong, 2014).[10] Children are encouraged to become person-ally confident in their initiatives and self-worth. In comparison, children in *collectivistic soci-eties* place more emphasis on fitting into an esteemed group. Adults in these latter cultures encourage children to take pride in the accomplishments of their families and communities (Banks & Banks, 1995; A. O. Harrison, Wilson, Pine, Chan, & Buriel, 1990). Children in these societies are more willing to acknowledge their weaknesses than is true for individualistic groups, perhaps because for them, admitting personal limitations is a sign of humility (a desirable quality) rather than an indication of poor self-esteem (Brophy, 2004).

As a result of being socialized in any society, children learn to think of themselves as having personal qualities and as being an integral part of a community—with the relative emphasis on each depending on the orientation of the culture. A 6-year-old European Ameri-can girl describes herself primarily in individual terms, perhaps being smart and athletic but also as a member of a sports team, whereas a Chinese boy of the same age mentions some of his own qualities but emphasizes his ties to family (Q. Wang, 2006). Thus, children from both individualistic and collectivistic societies are likely to embrace both personal qualities and interpersonal connections, even though the emphasis varies. In our opening case study, Theodore described himself as having certain individual qualities (e.g., being smart, not as academically motivated as he might be) and as being closely connected with family and friends.

The earlier anecdote about Sozan reveals that for many children, the process of incor-porating cultural beliefs into a sense of self is enriched by, and occasionally complicated by, exposure to two or more cultures. Around the world, many children of immigrant families are exposed to their family's native customs as well as to the new community's way of life (Hernandez, 2010). Hence children may encounter one or more cultures at home and others in the community. When children are exposed to two or more backgrounds at home, they generally take an approach that is adaptive and resourceful, drawing here and there from the various traditions they have encountered, depending on the demands of the situation. You can read about how children actively acquire the customs of a new society in the Development and Culture feature "At Home in Ireland."

Enhancing Children's Sense of Self

As with all areas of development, adults are more effective in nurturing children's sense of self when they understand how children think, feel, and express themselves in that domain. In the Observations Guidelines table "Observing Indicators of Children's Self-Perceptions," you can see some of the ways that children reveal how they see themselves. As you develop an awareness for how children view themselves, you will also find occasions to affirm their sense of self-worth. Consider trying one or more of the following strategies:

• **Communicate a genuine interest in children's well-being.** As children hear what adults say about them, they wonder, "What do these things mean about me?" Youngsters often

---

[9]The characteristics and influences of culture are introduced in Chapter 3.
[10]Individualistic and collectivist societies are examined in Chapters 3 and 11.

DEVELOPMENT IN CULTURE
At Home in Ireland

In the 19th and 20th centuries, millions of Irish citizens, including Teresa's four grandparents, emigrated from Ireland to other countries in search of employment. Decades later, and with a strong educational system, the economic environment had changed dramatically. By the early 1990s, Ireland boasted low unemployment, modest corporate tax rates, and a well-educated workforce. Not only did many Irish emigrants return home, but the "Celtic Tiger," as Ireland came to be called, took in a record-breaking number of immigrants, with a large proportion coming from Eastern Europe, especially Poland.

A previously homogenous country comprised primarily of fair-skinned individuals of Roman Catholic faith, Ireland welcomed the newcomers with interest and sympathy, but also trepidation. To learn about people's adjustment to the changes, two researchers conducted interviews with native Irish, immigrants, and asylum seekers living in refugee hostels in Cork, a large city in the southwest of the country (O'Sullivan-Lago & de Abreu, 2010).

Many of those interviewed expressed uncertainty about rapid changes in Ireland. One native Irishman, Dermot, lamented the break from a traditional past, worrying that longstanding Irish customs would be replaced by practices from other European countries. Alejandro, an immigrant from Galicia, an autonomous community in northern Spain, was torn between his allegiance to Galicia and his increasingly strong recognition that he felt at home in his adopted city of Cork. Alike, an asylum seeker, was apprehensive about her personal future, specifically worried as to whether she would be able to make Ireland her permanent home.

Schools were commonly seen as a place of integration for children from different backgrounds. Irishman Dermot observed that children from different backgrounds were easily integrated in the classroom. Asylum seekers were eager to see their children attend school and acquire Irish accents and customs. Jumoke was enthusiastic that her daughter, who could already speak Arabic and English, would acquire an Irish accent.

IRRESISTIBLE FUN. These Irish children are members of a neighborhood hockey club and participants in St. Patrick's Day festivities. Their enjoyable antics would likely be appealing to immigrant children.

Some of the immigrants and asylum seekers believed that in order for their children to fit in, their families would need to give up at least some of their own traditions. Children in immigrant families eagerly practiced new customs, such as Irish sports, as they interacted with peers. Their parents were slower and more hesitant in acquiring new customs. Thus, children essentially led the way in the family's assimilation, with parents marveling at the speed with which their children acquired an Irish accent, made friends, and became proficient in local sports. Despite a dramatic downturn in the Irish economy in the late 2000s, many immigrants and refugees decided to remain in Ireland, in large part due to their children having made good adjustments there.

OBSERVATION GUIDELINES
Observing Indicators of Children's Self-Perceptions

CHARACTERISTIC	LOOK FOR	EXAMPLE	IMPLICATION
Self-Concept	• *Increased time spent looking in mirror* and inspecting one's image (in infancy) • *Verbal references to self* (e.g., "I," "mine") (in infancy and early childhood) • *Self-assessments in areas of proficiency and weakness* (e.g., "I'm good at math but bad at reading") (in middle childhood and adolescence)	Eighteen-month-old Sierra stands at the full-length mirror. She looks up and down at her reflection, smiles, and, after noticing a scrape on her knee in the mirror, bends down to touch her leg and says "Ouch."	Express a genuine interest in every individual child. Encourage young children's emerging insights into their sense of self (e.g., "Look who's in the mirror!" and "I see you copying me! Can you make your hands do this?"). As children grow, compliment them on special accomplishments, extra effort on tasks, and unusual talents.

(continued)

OBSERVATION GUIDELINES (continued)
Observing Indicators of Children's Self-Perceptions

CHARACTERISTIC	LOOK FOR	EXAMPLE	IMPLICATION
Self-Worth	• *Comments on the self's inherent goodness or capability* (e.g., "I'm a good boy") • *Attempts to protect the self from threatening information* (e.g., anger at hearing critical comments after a flawed high-jump attempt, or self-handicapping gestures such as not studying for a challenging test) • *Changes in mood* depending on most recent treatment by peers (reflecting *contingent self-worth*)	After receiving his mathematics score, 13-year-old Emmett crumples up the paper, and throws it in the trash. The next time he has a mathematics test, he does not study at all, even though he knows he's confused about the math concepts his class has been studying.	Encourage children to take disappointments in stride, suggesting that although they may not have done as well on particular tasks as they would have liked, with renewed effort, a change in tactics, and perhaps a little assistance, they have the ability to progress. Provide a range of activities so that everyone has a chance to excel in one or more domains.
Autobiographical Self	• *Conversations with parents about past family events* in which the child participated • *Recollections about personally significant events* or family celebrations	Five-year-old Jeremiah draws a picture of himself with his parents, two sisters, and the family dog in front of a farm. He explains that his family used to live in rural Idaho and then moved to the Oregon coast when his parents changed jobs.	Create assignments that allow children to reflect on their family origins and early experiences. Have kindergarten children bring in photographs of themselves as babies and preschoolers. Ask older children to write essays about their early years.
Gender Schema	• *Insistence that boys must act one way and girls another* (especially in early childhood) • *Selection of toys that are stereotypical for one's gender*, for example, toy cars, blocks, and action figures by boys and dolls and board games by girls • *Heightened interest in same-sex role models* in magazines and other media during adolescence	In her spare time, 13-year-old Janice likes to browse through her mother's fashion magazines, looking for tips on how to apply cosmetics, meet boys, and interact in groups. Her older brother Reggie reads his father's automotive mechanics magazines.	Recognize that during various points in their development, children may go through phases of rigidly endorsing traditional gender roles, but also point out that both men and women have many opportunities in life and that few individuals can live up to the media's standards of attractiveness. Be aware of the special needs of gender nonconforming children.
Identity	• *Early in identity formation, varied levels of concern about the future*: —Questions about jobs —Noncritical acceptance of career goals suggested by parents —Expression of a desire to define lifelong goals • *During late adolescence, serious attempts to form an identity*: —Active search of careers, political viewpoints, and religious faiths —Occasional well-justified political beliefs and detailed plans to prepare for future occupations	Mr. Decker asks the ninth graders in his advisee group to write a brief essay about the kinds of jobs they find appealing. Some of the students write about jobs their parents currently have, and others write little, having apparently not given the matter much thought. A few of the students ask Mr. Decker if they can learn more about different jobs as part of their homeroom class.	Give children opportunities to examine and try out a variety of adult roles. With young children, rotate various props through a housekeeping area (e.g., dress-up clothes and equipment that might be found in a police station, gas station, or doctor's office). With older children, ask parents to come to school to talk about their jobs. With adolescents, arrange internships in local businesses, community agencies, and other institutions.
Ethnic Identity	• *Comments about being a member of a particular ethnic group* • *Growing preference for customs of one's own ethnic group* (e.g., meal practices, holiday celebrations, tastes in music and art) • *Frustration* with discrimination toward one's ethnic group	Fourteen-year-old Diego is proud of his Latino heritage. He follows many of his parents' Mexican traditions, loves Mexican food, and regularly watches Spanish-speaking programs on television. Diego is incensed by the derogatory names for Hispanics used by a few students at his high school.	Foster pride by welcoming ethnic traditions at school. Encourage youngsters to write about ethnic customs in assignments, and infuse multicultural material into instruction. Establish cooperative groups that cross ethnic lines and ensure that children from different backgrounds take on equally responsible positions. Adamantly discourage ethnic slurs.

interpret harsh words and thoughtless actions as indications that adults do not like them, possibly because they are not worthy of being liked. We urge all adults, but especially teachers, school nurses, and other personnel to think carefully about what they say and do to children. Messages of affection and high regard come in a variety of forms, including the following:

- Giving children a smile and warm greeting at the beginning of the day
- Complimenting children on a special talent, new skill, or exceptional effort
- Asking children to talk about important events in their lives
- Being a good listener when children appear angry or upset
- Being well prepared for lessons and other activities with children
- Including children in decision making and in evaluations of their performance
- Expressing sensitivity to the stressful circumstances children may experience in daily life
- Acknowledging that children can occasionally have an "off" day and not holding it against them. (L. H. Anderman, Patrick, Hruda, & Linnenbrink, 2002; Cushman & Cowan, 2010; H. A. Davis, 2003; Olowokere & Okanlawon, 2014)

• **Hone in on age-related developments.** Adults are most likely to help children when they cherish the qualities children are in the midst of acquiring—perhaps a sense of mastery in inserting blocks into slots during infancy ("Look what you can do!"), self-possession and cooperation during early childhood ("You are so nice to share your car!"), a multifaceted self-concept during middle childhood ("Keyboarding seems to be easier for you than writing out your story"), adjustment to a new school in early adolescence ("You seem to be settling in well to the new school. Anything I can help with?"), and exploration of career goals in late adolescence ("One of your options for the senior project is to do an internship in a field of your interest").

• **Promote success on academic, social, and physical tasks.** Experiences with success are powerful catalysts for the development of positive self-perceptions, especially within particular domains, such as mathematics or music (Bong et al., 2012; Damon, 1991; Marsh & Craven, 1997). Thus teachers should gear assignments to youngsters' capabilities, for instance, by making sure that they have already mastered any necessary prerequisite concepts and skills. However, success at very easy activities is unlikely to have much of an impact. Mastering the significant challenges in life—earning the hard-won successes that come only with effort and persistence—brings more resilient self-perceptions (Dweck, 2000; Winne, 1995a). Thus teachers are most likely to bolster youngsters' sense of self when they assign challenging tasks and provide the structure youngsters need to accomplish them successfully. They should also help young people keep the little "failures" along the way in stride: Mistakes are an inevitable part of learning something new.

• **Focus children's attention on their personal improvement rather than on how well they perform in comparison to classmates.** Youngsters are likely to be optimistic about their chance for success if they see they are making regular progress—if they continually make gains through effort and practice. They are *un*likely to be optimistic if they focus their attention on how their age-mates are surpassing them (Deci & Ryan, 1992; Duijnhouwer, Prins, & Stokking, 2012; Stipek, 1996).

• **Be honest about children's shortcomings, but provide ample guidance for overcoming them.** Youngsters are likely to be successful over the long run if they come to grips with their areas of weakness. If adults give only positive feedback—and especially if they provide inflated evaluations of children's performance—children may be unaware of areas that need improvement (Dweck, 2000; Paris & Cunningham, 1996). And when adults praise children for successes on very easy tasks, children may conclude that they are not capable of handling anything more difficult, or, alternatively, may come to believe that they must always achieve at high levels (Brummelman, Thomaes, Orobio de Castro, Overbeek, & Bushman, 2014; Pintrich & Schunk, 2002).

Realistically, adults need to give children negative as well as positive feedback. When feedback must include information about children's shortcomings, the best approach is to give it within the context of high (yet achievable) expectations for future performance (Deci & Ryan, 1985; Pintrich & Schunk, 2002). Following are examples of how a teacher might put a positive spin on negative feedback:

- "You're generally a very kind person, but you hurt Jenny's feelings by making fun of her new outfit. Perhaps you can think of a good way to make her feel better."
- "In the first draft of your research paper, many of your paragraphs don't lead logically to the ones that follow. A few headings and transitional sentences would make a world of difference. Let's find a time to discuss how you might use these techniques to improve the flow of your paper."

When children have long-standing difficulties in certain domains, discovering that their failures are due to a previously undiagnosed disability, such as dyslexia or ADHD, sometimes helps repair damage to self-esteem. Such a realization helps some children make sense of *why* they can't perform certain tasks as well as their peers. It can also spur children and their teachers to identify coping strategies. In the following reflection, one young adolescent boy reveals how, in coming to terms with his dyslexia, he's acquired a healthy sense of self despite his disability:

> Dyslexia is your brain's wired differently and there's brick walls for some things and you just have to work either around it or break it. I'm dyslexic at reading that means I need a little bit more help. If you have dyslexia the thing you have to find is how to get over the hump, the wall. Basically you either go around it and just don't read and get along in life without it or you break down the wall. (Zambo, 2003, p. 10)

Obviously, it can be detrimental if children are given labels for their conditions without simultaneously learning about strategies that will help them overcome their difficulties.

• Provide opportunities to explore a wide variety of activities. Not all students can achieve at superior levels in the classroom, nor can they all be superstars on the playing field. Youngsters are more likely to have a positive sense of self if they find an activity—perhaps singing, gardening, student government, or competitive jump-roping—in which they shine (Harter, 1999; Ruiz-Gallardo, Verde, & Valdés, 2013). By exploring many different fields and beginning to zero in on a few possible career paths, young people take an important step toward forming a sense of their adult identity.

• Consider the unique needs of girls and boys. Many youngsters place little value on characteristics and abilities that they think are more "appropriate" for members of the opposite sex. In addition, they may place high value on qualities they think they need to be "feminine" or "manly." Some teenage girls strive for impossible standards of physical beauty. And some teenage boys worry that they are maturing too slowly and lack the height and build of their classmates.

With these points in mind, adults might occasionally use somewhat different tactics in nurturing the self-esteem of girls and boys. They might help girls identify realistic standards by which to judge their physical appearance. And given girls' tendency to react more negatively to failures, adults might encourage them to pat themselves on the back for their many successes, even those (and perhaps *especially* those) in traditionally male domains such as science and mathematics. But boys, too, have special needs. Many boys are often brought up to believe they should be "tough" and hide any feelings of self-doubt or inadequacy. Adults may want to take special pains to acknowledge a boy's "softer" sides—for instance, his compassion and skill in interacting with small children.

• Communicate respect for diverse ethnic and cultural backgrounds. Although most educators are aware of the need to respect diversity in children's backgrounds, they do not always know how best to show such regard. An important first step, of course, is understanding the traditions, values, and priorities of ethnic and cultural groups. In addition to showing appreciation for children's native languages and dialects, educators can communicate respect for diverse groups through strategies such as these:

- Treat all children as full-fledged members of the classroom and community, rather than as exotic "curiosities" who come from a strange and separate world.

- Call children by given names unless they specifically request otherwise (see Artifact 12-5).
- Look at historical and current events from diverse cultural perspectives—for instance, by considering American, European, African, and Arabic perspectives on recent events in the Middle East.
- Make assignments in which children can explore their family heritage.
- Expose children to the accomplishments of numerous ancestral cultures in readings and activities.
- Visit the communities in which children live, and invite their families to school to share their talents, origins, and traditions.
- Create situations in which youngsters from diverse backgrounds must collaborate to achieve success—for example, through cooperative group activities or community service projects. (Banks & Banks, 1995; Branch, 1999; Fantino & Colak, 2001; García, Arias, Murri, & Serna, 2010; Howard, 2007; Ladson-Billings, 1994; A. Romero, Edwards, Fryberg, & Orduña, 2014; Villegas & Lucas, 2007; S. C. Wong, 1993)

> I had lots of friends back home, and I remember all of them, we used to play soccer together. I have also friends here now, well … mostly classmates.
>
> School is OK but there is one thing that bothers me. My name is Mohammed, no other. Here, my teacher calls me Mo, because there are five other kids with the same name. My friends sometimes call me M J, which is not too bad, but I wish they will call me by my real name. I like what my grandma called me: "Mamet." I like how she used to say it. One thing makes me really mad. I have a pen pal called Rudy. He lives in Toronto. Once I showed his letter to my teacher and she said: "That is nice name." Now, all my friends call me Rudy. I hate it, because that's not me, that's not my name. My name is "MO-HA-MMED." Do you understand me?

ARTIFACT 12-5   My name is Mohammed. For many children, their given name is an important part of their identity, as this reflection by a refugee child in Canada illustrates.

Excerpt from "Refugee Children in Canada: Searching for Identity," by A. M. Fantino and A. Colak, 2001, Child Welfare, 80, pp. 591–592, a publication of the Child Welfare League of America.

In their efforts to be sensitive to children's cultural backgrounds, some well-meaning practitioners make the mistake of thinking of children as belonging exclusively to a single ethnic or cultural group. Yet in this age of increasing multiracial ethnicities and multicultural families, youngsters do not want to be pigeonholed. Teachers must keep in mind that some of their students have a multifaceted ethnic, racial, cultural, and religious heritage, and many students want to be integral parts of the multiple groups in which they spend time, including the dominant society (Borrero & Yeh, 2011; Csizmadia, Kaneakua, Miller, & Halgunseth, 2013; A. M. Lopez, 2003). It also is worth bearing in mind that children of any ethnic heritage, however simple or complex, may or may not exhibit typical characteristics of people whose ancestry they share, an additional reason to accept that children personally meaningful choices, some of which will change over time and with circumstances, in how they represent themselves.

- **Cultivate gratitude and hope.** Students can become more optimistic when they take a moment to count their blessings (Shoshani & Steinmetz, 2013). Students can be encouraged to keep journals in which they regularly describe good things in their lives. They might also be encouraged to write about their strengths and how they have applied them recently to overcome a problem. Or, they could reflect on a couple of tactics they might try to address a challenge they are currently facing.

- **Give youngsters second chances to develop healthy self-perceptions.** Adolescents who struggle academically or have friendships with antisocial peers tend to see themselves as disconnected from school. These self-perceptions are not easily changed, but concerted efforts from a teacher sometimes have desirable effects. In one instance a group of adolescents with learning disabilities were moved from one school (Piney Ridge), where they were failing, to another school in which teachers got to know them individually and encouraged their success (Youngblood & Spencer, 2002). With time the adolescents came to see themselves as capable academically and socially, as one boy explains:

Interviewer: What makes you. . . . Why do you think there's a difference between the student helping each other in this program and not helping each other at Piney?

Rashae: Because they're. . . . Well half of them over there criminal. They're like they just got out of jail or whatever. I mean, they just. . . . I think Piney Ridge like a school for bad kids.

Interviewer: So why do you think they're more likely to help you over here?

Rashae: Because everybody over here nice. They don't think about just they self. Think about other people in the class. . . . Well we help one another in the class work or out of class. (dialogue from Youngblood & Spencer, 2002, p. 103)

• **Put self-esteem in its proper perspective.** The popular educational literature often overrates self-esteem as a target for intervention, sometimes to the point where it becomes the primary target (Dweck, 2000). Certainly we want children to feel good about themselves, but increasing evidence suggests that efforts to enhance self-esteem as *the* ultimate goal for children are ineffective, and for several reasons (Baumeister et al., 2003; Meadows, 2010). First, children appreciate optimistic evaluations from adults but are more likely to be convinced of their own capabilities when they see themselves reaching high standards. Thus, rather than telling children that they are smart and good, it makes more sense to create conditions where children are likely to achieve success, with instruction that builds on prior knowledge. Second, self-esteem seems to be closely linked to personal happiness and resilience yet, counter to society's expectations, it does *not* protect young people from numerous risks in life. Thus, self-esteem is a resource that helps students weather adversity, yet youngsters with high self-esteem do not avoid drugs and other risks any more than youngsters with low self-esteem do (Baumeister et al., 2003; Lewandowski et al., 2014). Hence, other developmental outcomes must receive equal billing. Third, a few children with an inflated sense of self are aggressive and callous to the feelings of others (Baumeister et al., 2003). Rather than simply being told how good they are, these children need to encounter expectations for respecting the needs of other people. Finally, not every culture aspires to high self-esteem in its children, at least as self-esteem is typically conceptualized in Western cultures. Instead, some communities socialize children to focus more on being humble and courteous to friends, family members, and adults in authority.

Summary

Children's *sense of self* includes their beliefs about who they are as people (self-concept) and their judgments about their value (self-esteem or self-worth). Most children interpret events in ways that allow them to maintain a positive self-image. Realistic self-perceptions, or perhaps self-perceptions that are just slightly inflated, are optimal, in that they encourage children to set their sights on potentially achievable challenges.

To a considerable degree, children's sense of self is based on their own prior successes and failures. Yet other people also play a role, either by treating children in ways that communicate high or low regard, or (in the case of peers) by demonstrating the kinds of things children "should" be able to do at a certain age. Membership in various groups (e.g., athletic teams, ethnic groups, friends through social media) also has an impact, as do gender, culture, physical appearance, disabilities, and inherited characteristics.

With age, children construct increasingly complex and multifaceted understandings of who they are as people. In the early years, their self-perceptions are fairly simplistic, concrete, and categorical (e.g., "I have brown eyes," "I'm a boy"). But as they acquire the capacity for abstract thought, their self-descriptions increasingly include general, abstract qualities (e.g., "thoughtful," dependable"). In adolescence they also begin to wrestle with who they ultimately want to become as human beings.

ENHANCEDetext *self-check*

Assessing Children 12-1

Listen to how a teacher helps seventh and eighth graders reflect on their ethnic identity.

ENHANCEDetext *application exercise*

SOCIAL COGNITION

As you have learned, children regularly think about who they are and what they are becoming. As they gain a sense of their own thoughts, feelings, and other characteristics, children realize that other people have qualities and perspectives that differ from their own. Most children devote a lot of mental energy to **social cognition**, their speculations and reasoning about what other people are thinking and feeling.

As you might expect, social cognition has many facets. We begin our discussion with an analysis of children's understanding of what other people think and their ability to consider others' perspectives during social interactions. We next examine biases in children's thinking that can lead to prejudice. We finally consider bioecological variations that exist in children's social-cognitive abilities and outline the many things adults can do to foster children's social cognition.

Understanding What Others Think

Just as children construct theories about their physical and biological surroundings, so, too, do they construct theories about their psychological world. More specifically, they develop a **theory of mind** that eventually encompasses complex understandings of people's mental and emotional states—thoughts, beliefs, feelings, motives, intentions, and so on.

Children put these general understandings to work in social interactions, stepping into others' shoes and looking at events from others' perspectives. Such **social perspective taking** helps children make sense of actions that might otherwise be puzzling. As children gain practice in inferring others' people points of view, they are apt to become increasingly skilled interpersonally, especially when they are able to strike a healthy balance between pursuing their own needs and helping others meet theirs (Caputi, Lecce, Pagnin, & Banerjee, 2012; R. D. Parke & Clarke-Stewart, 2011).

Infancy (Birth–Age 2)

Infants quickly discover that, unlike inanimate objects, people are active, expressive, and responsive (Mandler, 2007a; Poulin-Dubois, Frenkiel-Fishman, Nayer, & Johnson, 2006). In the latter part of their first year, they also begin to realize that people have an "inner life" that objects do not have. By about 9 or 10 months, infants achieve *intersubjectivity*, an awareness that they share a focus of attention with their social partners.[11] At about the same time or shortly thereafter, they acquire an awareness of **intentionality**. That is, they know that other people behave in order to accomplish certain goals, and they begin to draw inferences about people's intentions from such actions as reaching for, pointing at, and gazing at objects (Beier & Carey, 2014; Carruthers, 2013).

In the second year, infants become increasingly mindful of other people's mental states. Infants as young as 12 months engage in *social referencing*, the tendency to watch an adult react to an unfamiliar person, object, or event in a particular way and then show the same kind of response.[12] By 18 months, children know that their own actions influence other people's emotions and behaviors. Infants are likely to offer an adult a food item to which the adult has previously reacted favorably, even though they themselves dislike that kind of food (Repacholi & Gopnik, 1997).[13] Early comforting gestures may reflect an attempt to consider another person's perspective, although a child may also help a social partner for other reasons besides wishing to alleviate that person's distress, for example, because helping that person allows him or her to better engage with the child (P. L. Harris, 2006; Paulus, 2014). Conversely, in other situations in some case, toddlers may use information about someone's perspective to annoy him or her (J. Dunn & Munn, 1985; Flavell, Miller, & Miller, 2002). As a toddler, Jeanne's daughter Tina occasionally ran into the street and then looked tauntingly back at Mom as if to say, "Look at what I'm doing! I know this upsets you! Catch me if you can!"

[11]*Intersubjectivity* is introduced in Chapter 7.
[12]Social referencing is described in Chapter 7.
[13]In Chapter 6 we saw evidence that preschoolers are not as egocentric as Piaget said they were. Here we see evidence that even toddlers can occasionally take another person's perspective.

Early Childhood (Ages 2–6)

In the preschool years, children become increasingly aware of other people's mental states. Beginning at age 2 (sometimes even earlier), children spontaneously use words that refer to desires and emotions (e.g., *want, feel, sad*), and by age 3, mental state words such as *think, know,* and *remember* (Bartsch & Wellman, 1995; Lagattuta, 2014). By the time children are 3, they also realize that the mind is distinct from the physical world—that *thoughts, memories,* and *dreams* are not tangible entities (J. A. Baird & Astington, 2005; Wellman & Estes, 1986; Woolley, 1995).

In trying to understand why other people act as they do, young children are initially attentive to what others want—perhaps to eat another cookie, finish up the ironing, or watch a video on a mobile device. In the third and fourth year, children develop an appreciation that others have *desires* that differ from their own (P. L. Harris, 2006). Preschoolers are often eager to learn why people do the things they do, as this conversation between 2½-year-old Adam and his mother illustrates:

Adam:	Why she write dat name?
Mother:	Because she wanted to.
Adam:	Why she wanted to?
Mother:	Because she thought you'd like it.
Adam:	I don't want to like it. (Wellman, Phillips, & Rodriguez, 2000, p. 908)

Inherent in Adam's question *Why she write dat name?* is an advancement in theory of mind: Preschoolers become increasingly aware of connections between other people's desires and behaviors.

After gaining an appreciation that they and other people have *desires,* young children gradually gain an understanding of other people's *knowledge* (P. L. Harris, 2006; Saracho, 2014). Initially, preschoolers have trouble looking inward and describing their own thoughts. Furthermore, they may mistakenly assume that what *they* know is what other people know as well. Consider the following situation:

> Max puts a piece of chocolate in the kitchen cupboard and then goes out to play. While he is gone, his mother discovers the chocolate and moves it to a drawer. When Max returns later, where will he look for his chocolate? (based on Wimmer & Perner, 1983)

Max will look in the cupboard, of course, because that's where he thinks the chocolate is. However, 3-year-olds are quite certain he will look in the drawer, where the chocolate is actually located. Not until age 4 or 5 do children appreciate a *false belief:* They realize that circumstances may reasonably lead people to believe something different from what they know to be true (Laranjo, Bernier, Meins, & Carlson, 2014; M. Rhodes & Wellman, 2013; Wimmer & Perner, 1983).

Gradually children become increasingly adept at inferring people's intentions and other mental states from their behavior in a certain circumstance (Astington & Pelletier, 1996; Fireman & Kose, 2010; Saracho, 2014). Look at the two scenarios in Figure 12-2. *Which boy would like to swing?* Obviously the boy in the lower picture is the one who has an *intention* of using the swing. Most 5-year-olds correctly answer the question we've just asked you, but few 3-year-olds do (Astington, 1991).

FIGURE 12-2 Which boy would like to swing? Children who can correctly answer this question can distinguish between intention and behavior. *"Which Boy Wants to Swing" by J W. Astington, from "Intention in the Child Theory of Mind" from CHILDREN'S THEORIES OF MIND: MENTAL STATES AND SOCIAL UNDERSTANDING by D. Frye. Illustration copyright © 2009 by J. W. Astington. Reprinted with permission via Copyright Clearance Center.*

Middle Childhood (Ages 6–10)

As children reach the elementary grades, they become capable of more sophisticated inferences about people's mental states. They realize that people's facial expressions, statements, and actions do not always reflect their true thoughts and feelings (Flavell et al., 2002; Gnepp, 1989; Spritz, Fergusson, & Bankoff, 2010). A person may intentionally lie about a situation to mislead someone else, and another person who appears happy may actually be sad.

Middle childhood heralds deeper understandings of the nature of thinking as well. In particular, children understand that people *interpret* an event, rather than simply "record" it, a phenomenon that allows for differences in perspectives among people (Chandler & Boyes, 1982; P. L. Harris, 2006). Finally, children recognize that people's thoughts and feelings are often closely intertwined. Thus different thoughts about a situation lead to different feelings about it (P. L. Harris, 1989). A 9-year-old might say, "Arlene feels bad because she thinks I don't like her. I *do* like her, though."

Middle childhood brings another change in theory of mind. Children at this age sometimes use information they have gleaned about peers, siblings', and adults' needs and vulnerabilities to outwit, tease, and manipulate them (Lonigro, Laghi, Baiocco, & Baumgartner, 2014). Thus, theory of mind is a tool that allows children to understand and accommodate the needs of their social partners, yet it can be—and is—occasionally applied with harmful intent.

Early Adolescence (Ages 10–14)

Fueled by maturation of the brain, perspective taking continues to develop during the adolescent years (Blakemore & Mills, 2014; Smetana & Villalobos, 2009). Several social networks in the brain are put into overdrive, enabling a heightened sensitivity to social interaction. Young people find intensified pleasure in contact with peers and become even more interested than previously in figuring out what makes other people think and feel as they do.

Adolescents also appreciate that people can have mixed feelings about events and other individuals (Harter & Whitesell, 1989; Rostad & Pexman, 2014). They realize that a person may simultaneously have multiple, and possibly conflicting, intentions (Chandler, 1987). They become increasingly thoughtful about the divergent perspectives that people may have about a single event, as you can see in Artifact 12-6. In general, young adolescents find it easier to think about the perspectives of people they know and like, presumably because these individuals have shared their views in the past (T. G. O'Connor & Hirsch, 1999; Smetana & Villalobos, 2009).

Courtesy of their expanding reasoning abilities, working memory capacity, social awareness, and neurological maturation, young adolescents begin to engage in **recursive thinking** (Müeller & Overton, 2010; Perner & Wimmer, 1985). That is, they now contemplate what other people might be thinking about them and eventually reflect on their own and other people's thoughts through multiple iterations (e.g., "You think that I think that you think . . ."). This is not to say that adolescents always use this capacity. In fact, thinking only about one's own perspective, without regard for the perspectives of others, is a common phenomenon in the early adolescent years (recall our earlier discussion of the *imaginary audience*).

Late Adolescence (Ages 14–18)

Older adolescents can draw on a rich knowledge base derived from numerous social experiences, and so they become ever more skillful at identifying people's psychological characteristics, intentions, and needs (Eisenberg, Carlo, Murphy, & Van Court, 1995; Paget, Kritt, & Bergemann, 1984). More challenging social situations involving conflicts among friends, alliances and betrayals, and assurances and broken promises demand sophisticated perspective-taking skills. High school students become increasingly attuned to the complex dynamics—the combination of thoughts, feelings, present circumstances, and past experiences—that influence behavior (Fett et al., 2014; Selman, 1980; Tynes, 2007). What we see emerging in the high school years, then, is a budding psychologist: an individual who can be quite astute in deciphering and explaining the motives and actions of others.

Social Perspective Taking in Action

As you have been learning, taking the perspective of another person is not simply an intellectual exercise. Drawing inferences about other people's thoughts, desires, and intentions

We were playing freeze tag one day at recess. Leslie got tagged and asked me to step on her shadow before anyone else. I stepped on Becca's shadow before I stepped on Leslie's and she got mad. I told Leslie to stop being so selfish and bratty. She took it extremely personally and stormed off, told a teacher, and called her mom.

I later apologized and we became friends again. I invited her to my birthday and she came but I could tell she felt uncomfortable. So, I decided to do makeovers. I was playing around with lipsticks and accidentally messed up on Leslie's makeover, but laughed because I knew it could be fixed. She ran to see the "damage" in the mirror, started to cry, and called her mom and left.

From then on, I've never really understood her and we've never been close. We see eachother and say "hi" in the halls, but that's it.

ARTIFACT 12-6 I've never really understood her. Young adolescents exert a lot of effort in deciphering the perspectives of other people but are most effective in identifying the viewpoints of individuals they know well. In this reflective essay, 13-year-old Georgia expresses dismay over an acquaintance's interpretation of events.

allows children to better meet such personal goals as comforting a friend in distress, outsmarting an opponent in a game, and pleasing a demanding teacher. Let's look more closely at this critical human capacity through the lens of American psychologist **Robert Selman**'s theory of social perspective which portrays developmental trends in children's thinking during social exchanges.

Selman asked children to think about the various perspectives that different people have about a situation. Consider the following situation:

> Holly is an 8 year old girl who likes to climb trees. She is the best tree climber in the neighborhood. One day while climbing down from a tall tree she falls off the bottom branch but does not hurt herself. Her father sees her fall. He is upset and asks her to promise not to climb the trees any more. Holly promises.
>
> Later that day, Holly and her friends meet Sean. Sean's kitten is caught up in a tree and cannot get down. Something has to be done right away or the kitten may fall. Holly is the only one who climbs trees well enough to reach the kitten and get it down, but she remembers her promise to her father. (Selman & Byrne, 1974, p. 805)

Children are asked if Holly understands Sean's feelings about the kitten, if Sean realizes why it will be difficult for Holly to decide whether or not to climb up the tree, and what Holly believes her father will think if he learns she eventually does climb the tree. To answer these questions, you must look at the situation from the perspectives of three different people: Sean, Holly, and Holly's father. By presenting situations like this one and asking children to view them from various perspectives, Robert Selman (1980; Selman & Schultz, 1990) found that with age, children show an increasing ability to take and act on the perspective of others. He described a series of five levels that characterize the development of perspective taking:

- *Level 0: Egocentric perspective taking.* Children are aware of physical differences among people but have little awareness of psychological differences. They are incapable of looking at a situation from anyone's perspective but their own (hence the reference to Level 0). As an example, 3-year-old Andrea assumes that her preschool friends know how scared she is about climbing on the jungle gym. Hence she expresses indignation when Rose and Sue Ann ask her to climb with them.
- *Level 1: Subjective perspective taking.* Children realize that people have different thoughts and feelings as well as different physical features. However, they view someone else's perspective in a relatively simplistic, one-dimensional fashion (e.g., a person is simply happy, sad, or angry) and tend to equate behavior with feelings (e.g., a happy person will smile, and a sad person will pout or cry). For instance, 8-year-old Li-Wen realizes that her friend Tony is sad about his grandfather's recent death but does not understand that he also feels relief that his grandfather's suffering is over.
- *Level 2: Second-person, reciprocal perspective taking.* Children realize that people occasionally have mixed feelings about an event—for instance, that Holly might feel both compassion for the kitten and uneasiness about breaking her promise to her father. At this level, children also understand that people may feel differently than their behaviors indicate and that others may sometimes do things they didn't really want or intend to do. In this manner, 11-year-old Peter understands that his friend Mark has misgivings about his decision to experiment with inhalants. Peter perceives reservation in Mark's voice and body language as he tells about his escapades.
- *Level 3: Third-person, mutual perspective taking.* Youngsters can take an outsider's perspective of interpersonal relationships: They can look at their own interactions with another person as a third individual might. They appreciate the need to satisfy both their own and another's needs simultaneously and therefore readily grasp the advantages of cooperation, compromise, and trust. To illustrate, two high school freshmen, Jasmine and Alethea, discover that they've each arranged a homecoming party for the same night. They learn that they've both sent invitations to mutual friends. Because they were both looking forward to hosting a party, they discuss options for rescheduling one of the parties or co-hosting the event.

- *Level 4: Societal, symbolic perspective taking.* Adolescents begin to realize that people are affected by the many factors in their environments and, furthermore, that people are not always aware of why they act as they do. In their psychology course, high school seniors Kent and Joaquin are preparing a joint oral report on strategies of social persuasion. They find magazine advertisements that are geared toward teens and discuss images and feelings that advertisers are trying to invoke.

Selman aptly captures general trends in perspective taking, but his original work seems to have underestimated young children's capabilities. Convincing evidence by other theorists reveals perspective-taking abilities by preschool age, and you might recall our illustration earlier of when an infant offers food to an adult consistent with that adult's preferences. Even young preschoolers realize that another person can see an object only if he or she is looking in the object's direction and has a clear, unobstructed view. Older preschoolers also grasp that the same object may look different to people viewing it from separate angles—for example, that a book that is right-side-up to one person will be upside-down to someone sitting across the table (Flavell, 2000). Furthermore, in their daily communication, children appear to be truly other-oriented a lot of the time; that is, they listen to what other people say, respond appropriately, and take into account how their listeners might be thinking and feeling (Garvey & Hogan, 1973; Rozendaal & Baker, 2010).

Selman's original theory is limited in another way. The early versions of his theory imply that progress through levels is almost inevitable. In more recent work, Selman has indicated that children's social awareness is not guaranteed by basic maturational processes and instead is highly dependent on personal experience (Selman, 2003). For example, Selman and his colleagues have found that children use their experiences in teasing when understanding others' motives (Dray, Selman, & Schultz, 2009; S. L. Katz, Selman, & Mason, 2008).

All things considered, Selman's work suggests that adults can gradually nudge young people toward more advanced ways of thinking about the people around them—perhaps "one level up" in perspective taking. Therefore, preschool teachers might point out how classmates' feelings might differ from children's own feelings (Level 1). Adults who work with students in the elementary grades can discuss situations in which people may have mixed feelings or want to hide their feelings—situations such as going to a new school, trying a difficult but enjoyable sport for the first time, or celebrating a holiday without a favorite family member present (Level 2). Adults who work with adolescents might, either informally (e.g., in free-flowing conversations) or formally (e.g., in a high school psychology class), explore the many ways in which people are affected by their past experiences and present understandings (Level 4).

The progressions in social cognition we've examined suggest that it's a long road from infants' initial flickers of social awareness to adolescents' far-reaching insights into how minds coordinate a broad array of mental states. In the Developmental Trends table "Social Cognition at Different Age Levels," you can see some of the primary social-cognitive accomplishments and common manifestations of diversity at each age level.

Social-Cognitive Bias and Prejudice

By now you understand just how much mental work is involved in thinking about social situations. Yet, people often take shortcuts to ease the load on their memory and make their dealings with others more efficient (K. L. Mosier, 2013; Tversky & Kahneman, 1990). Many of these shortcuts reflect **social-cognitive biases**, predispositions to interpret or respond to social situations in particular ways. For example, in various situations a child might assume that a single action reflects a person's typical behavior (Seiver, Gopnik, & Goodman, 2013). Eight-year-old Dwight observes a new boy arguing with his friend on the playground and jumps to the conclusion that the boy is a bully.

Most social-cognitive biases are a minor nuisance; they lead to small distortions in thinking but don't cause grave harm. A few, however, have serious consequences. Children occasionally jump to hasty conclusions about others based on group membership (e.g., gender, ethnicity, sexual orientation, religious affiliation). In other words, they respond on the basis of a **stereotype**, a rigid, simplistic, and erroneous characterization of a particular

DEVELOPMENTAL TRENDS
Social Cognition at Different Age Levels

AGE	WHAT YOU MIGHT OBSERVE	DIVERSITY	IMPLICATIONS
Infancy **(Birth–2 Years)** 	• Awareness of one's ability to share a focus of attention with caregiver (*intersubjectivity*) • Observation of other people's emotional reactions, followed by the child having a similar response (*social referencing*) • Emerging realization that other people have desires, goals, and intentions different from one's own	• Infants who receive inadequate care at home may be delayed in acquiring intersubjectivity and social referencing. • Infants who are autistic may avoid eye contact with caregivers and not understand the connection between where others are pointing and what they are thinking about.	• Get to know infants as individuals and the kinds of social interactions that each of them enjoys. • Use words such as *like, want,* and *think* in descriptions of yourself and children. • Patiently explain why you must prohibit tempting yet dangerous activities to help children begin to understand your perspective.
Early Childhood **(2–6 Years)** 	• Increasing use of "feeling" and "thinking" words (e.g., *want, sad, know*) • Growing realization that the mind does not always represent events accurately (e.g., that a person may have a false belief) • Growing ability to take others' perspectives	• Children whose parents talk frequently about thoughts and feelings tend to have a more advanced theory of mind. • Children with certain cognitive impairments (e.g., autism) and those with reduced exposure to language as a result of hearing impairments tend to have a delayed theory of mind.	• Talk about various people's thoughts, feelings, perspectives, and needs. • Establish fun routines (e.g., tossing a ball, turning the pages of a book together) with children who find it difficult to synchronize their behavior with others. • Recognize that territorial behaviors are common in early childhood, but encourage sharing.
Middle Childhood **(6–10 Years)** 	• Recognition that people's actions do not always reflect their true thoughts and feelings • Growing realization that other people interpret (rather than simply remember) their experiences • Softening of rigid stereotypes of particular groups of people (for most children)	• Compared to peers, children with certain disabilities (e.g., attention-deficit hyperactivity disorder [ADHD], autism, general intellectual disability) are more apt to have difficulty in making accurate inferences about people's motives and intentions. • Children whose families or communities consistently promote unflattering images of particular groups may continue to have strong prejudices.	• Assist children in their attempts to discern the viewpoints of characters in stories and of public figures during historical events. • When addressing the experiences of a particular ethnic group (perhaps their literary accomplishments or struggles during historical events), make a point to expose children to individuals within the group who hold distinctly different perspectives.
Early Adolescence **(10–14 Years)** 	• Recognition that people may have multiple and possibly conflicting feelings and motives • Emerging ability to think recursively about one's own and others' thoughts	• Some adolescents become so concerned about how other people see them that they succumb to peer pressure and take extreme measures to please other people. • Intellectual disabilities may hinder adolescents' abilities to consider multiple points of view.	• Conduct discussions that require adolescents to look at controversial issues from multiple perspectives. • Do not tolerate ethnic jokes or other remarks that show prejudice toward a particular group.
Late Adolescence **(14–18 Years)** 	• Recognition that people are products of their environment and that past events and present circumstances influence personality and behavior • Use of a peer group as a forum for self-exploration and self-understanding • Increasing awareness that members of any single category of people (e.g., women, people with disabilities) can be very different from one another	• Most high school students use their social perspective-taking abilities constructively, but a few students use their knowledge of other people's vulnerabilities to inflict harm on them. • Adolescents who are familiar with people from diverse cultures may find it relatively easy to infer the perspectives of individuals from different backgrounds.	• Talk about other people's complex (and sometimes conflicting) motives, perhaps while discussing contemporary issues, historical events, or works of fiction. • Assign autobiographies and other readings that depict individuals who have actively worked for the greater good of society, asking students to write about the motivations, beliefs, and ideas of these individuals.

group. Often a stereotype encompasses a host of negative attributes (e.g., "stingy," "lazy," "promiscuous") and leads children to exhibit negative attitudes, feelings, and behaviors—that is, **prejudice**—toward the group in question.

The roots of stereotypes and prejudice lie in the natural tendency of human beings to categorize their experiences. In their first few years, children learn that people belong to different groups, such as boys and girls, and "blacks" and "whites." Many preschoolers can distinguish members of various ethnic groups (Aboud, 1988). As children form these social categories, they are apt to favor their own group and expect less desirable characteristics from individuals in other groups, especially if the groups are in conflict (Aboud, 2005; Aboud & Spears Brown, 2013; R. D. Parke & Clarke-Stewart, 2011). By age 4, children show definite biases about social groups, expecting that members of their own community are better in some way than individuals from other groups (Aboud & Spears Brown, 2013).

On average, stereotypes and prejudice decrease as children move through the elementary grades (D. E. Carter, Detine-Carter, & Benson, 1995; F. H. Davidson, 1976). This decline is probably due to children's increasing realization that social categories have their limits. Many children slowly realize that individuals who share membership in a category (e.g., "girls") are similar in some ways but very different in others. Other individual factors strengthen stereotypes, and so some children show an increase in prejudice as they reach early adolescence (Aboud, 2005; J. H. Pfeifer, Brown, & Juvonen, 2007). Parents may incite prejudice through words and deeds—for instance, by telling ethnic jokes, restricting playmates to same-race peers, expressing negative attitudes about other races, affiliating with individuals only from their own ingroup, and enrolling their children in schools with as little diversity as possible (Allport, 1954; Ashmore & DelBoca, 1976; Degner & Dalege, 2013; Meeusen, 2014). Popular images in television and other media—where males are depicted as strong and aggressive, females weak and passive, and members of certain ethnic groups unimportant characters or "bad guys"—also have an impact (Durkin, Nesdale, Dempsey, & McLean, 2012; Huston et al., 1992).

By adolescence and probably before, children who are victims of prejudice are well aware that others' treatment of them is unfair (Phinney & Tarver, 1988; E. Seaton, Yip, Morgan-Lopez, & Sellers, 2012). Over time they acquire a variety of strategies—seeking the support and companionship of other group members, forming a positive ethnic identity, and so on—for coping with prejudice and discrimination (Forsyth & Carter, 2012; Swim & Stangor, 1998). Even so, young people who are victims of prejudice are more likely than peers to become ill or depressed and at risk for achieving at lower levels in school (English, Lambert, & Ialongo, 2014; B. D. Tatum, 1997).

Bioecology of Social Cognition

The bioecological framework suggests that the personal characteristics of children and their experiences in complex environments contribute to emerging social understandings. Let's look at two qualities affecting social cognition: having certain exceptionalities and growing up in a particular social setting.

Exceptionalities Affecting Social Cognition

Some children with disabilities are disadvantaged in their understanding of other people, in large part because their brains do not allow them to easily recognize faces, think about other people's perspectives, and detect emotions. Children with *Fragile X syndrome*, who typically have intellectual disabilities and are socially anxious, perform at relatively low levels on theory-of-mind tasks (P. Lewis et al., 2006; Losh, Martin, Klusek, Hogan-Brown, & Sideris, 2012).[14] When children have significant hearing impairments from birth and do not have a way to communicate early in life (e.g., with hearing parents after an early cochlear implantation or with signing parents), they miss out on discussions about "thinking," "feeling," "wanting," and the like, and their theory of mind develops slowly (C. C. Peterson, 2002; Sundqvist, Lyxell, Jönsson, & Heimann, 2014). Some children with ADHD find it difficult to take the perspective of other people, possibly because of having impaired brain circuits for social reasoning, finding it difficult to control disruptive behaviors, and being perceived as undesirable social partners by peers (Maoz et al., 2014; Stormont, 2001).

[14]*Fragile X syndrome* is described in Chapter 4.

BIOECOLOGY OF DEVELOPMENT

Children's own characteristics and their experiences in social groups affect how they understand other people.

Preparing for Your Licensure Examination

Your teaching test might ask you about the characteristics of children with autism and Asperger's syndrome.

One group of children with disabilities has an especially significant deficit in social cognition. Children with **autism spectrum disorders** have one of several conditions characterized by a serious impairment in social communication and restricted, repetitive behaviors (e.g., repeatedly flipping through the pages of a book or running water over one's hands). Children with these disorders vary considerably in the severity of their symptoms, hence the reference to being somewhere on the *spectrum* (American Psychiatric Association, 2013; Waterhouse & Gillberg, 2014). Children with *autistic disorder* (also known simply as *autism*) by age 3 show deficits in reciprocal social interactions, communication, and language; limitations in imitation or imaginative play; preoccupations with parts of objects; unusual sensory aversions or preferences; restricted concerns; and frequently, an intellectual disability. Children with *Asperger's syndrome* are similar to their peers with autism in that they have problems with social abilities and exhibit repetitive behaviors, but unlike children with autism have normal intelligence and language. Children with *Rett syndrome* have a significant intellectual disability, an unsteady gait, repetitive hand movements (e.g., wringing hands), and problems with social interactions.

Common to autism spectrum disorders are marked deficits in social cognition (e.g., self-awareness, theory of mind, and perspective taking) and in social skills (e.g., gaining entry into a peer group, interacting appropriately with others; Baron-Cohen, Tager-Flusberg, & Cohen, 1993; A. Samson et al., 2014). Although children with autism spectrum disorders typically form close attachments to their caregivers, they often prefer to be alone and have difficulty in making friends (Bauminger-Zviely & Agam-Ben-Artzi, 2014; Hobson, 2004). Children with these conditions may also have trouble regulating their emotions and are under- or oversensitive to sensory stimulation (Ashburner, Bennett, Rodger, & Ziviani, 2013; Samson et al., 2014; R. C. Sullivan, 1994). Temple Grandin, a brilliant woman who has gained international prominence as a designer of livestock facilities, recalls what it was like to be a child with autism:

> From as far back as I can remember, I always hated to be hugged. I wanted to experience the good feeling of being hugged, but it was just too overwhelming. It was like a great, all-engulfing tidal wave of stimulation, and I reacted like a wild animal. . . .
>
> When I was little, loud noises were also a problem, often feeling like a dentist's drill hitting a nerve. They actually caused pain. I was scared to death of balloons popping, because the sound was like an explosion in my ear. Minor noises that most people can tune out drove me to distraction. (Grandin, 1995, pp. 63, 67)

Given the variability of characteristics in children with a diagnosis of autism spectrum disorder, it should be no surprise that numerous irregularities in the brain seem to occur. The activation of brain waves and connectivity among neurons in social areas of the brain have been found to be unusual in autistic children (Strzelecka, 2014; Vanderwert & Nelson, 2014). A particular type of brain cell, the *mirror neuron,* is irregular in their case (Rizzolatti & Fabbri-Destro, 2010). **Mirror neurons** are specialized brain cells that grow in social regions of the brain and are activated when a person performs a certain act, perhaps reaching for a cup or clapping his or her hands, and also when the person observes someone else carrying out the same behavior.[15] Mirror neurons play a role in imitation and also allow an individual to draw reasonable inferences about what another person is doing, thinking, and feeling. Other irregularities have also been found. In addition, at least some children with autism have larger-than-usual brains by the first year of life (suggesting excessive growth of neurons and failure of normal synaptic pruning mechanisms[16]); they may also develop abnormal structures in the cerebellum (which modulates controlled movements), brainstem (which controls automatic functions necessary for survival, including breathing, digestion, and circulation of blood), and the front part of the cortex (which controls planning, inhibiting of automatic responses, and coordinating of complex, multistep actions; Fan, Decety, Yang, Liu, & Cheng, 2010; Minshew & Williams, 2007; Ozonoff, 2010).

Despite their unusual brain structures and activities, and perhaps in part because of them, children with autism have distinct strengths. Many children with this condition are able to resist distractions and focus intently on visual details in objects (Gernsbacher, Stevenson, Khandakar, & Goldsmith, 2008; Rondan & Deruelle, 2007). Autistic children sometimes connect deeply to certain animals, such as horses or dogs, are quite capable of learning new skills, solve mathematical problems with unique strategies, and have families that become

---

[15]Mirror neurons are discussed in Chapter 7.
[16]The brain's process of *pruning* back on an overabundance of *synapses* is explained in Chapter 4.

their strong advocates (B. L. Hawkins, Ryan, Cory, & Donaldson, 2014; Iuculano et al., 2014; Sarahan & Copas, 2014; J. J. Xue, Ooh, & Magiati, 2014). Occasionally, children with autism exhibit *savant syndrome*, in that they possess an extraordinary talent that stands in sharp contrast to their other mental abilities (Treffert, 2014; Winner, 2000).[17] Quite possibly, having weak connections across separate areas of the brain enables individuals with autism to concentrate in specific domains that do not require much cross-talk (Casanova, 2008).

In many societies, children with one of the autism spectrum disorders are in the regular classroom for all or part of the school day. Teachers can help these children feel secure by keeping the classroom layout and schedule fairly consistent. When working with young autistic children, teachers can strive to establish one-on-one relationships with them, initially getting to know them by sitting beside them, expressing an interest in their activities with objects, and encouraging (but not demanding) give-and-take in interactions (Schreibman, 2008; Wieder, Greenspan, & Kalmanson, 2008). To help facilitate their limited theory of mind, teachers can teach vocabulary for such internal mental processes as "thinking," "wishing," and "remembering." Given that these children may have difficulties with planning, using certain learning strategies, and evaluating their learning performance, teachers can explicitly scaffold these skills and help them generalize to new tasks (Cote et al., 2014; El Zein, Solis, Vaughn, & McCulley, 2014). Such strategies can help children with autism not only achieve at higher levels but also have a stronger sense of self-determination (Seo, 2014).

As children with autism spectrum disorders grow older, they continue to need guidance in interpreting what other people are doing and how to interact with peers. Teachers can advise youngsters about what to expect during upcoming social events, such as sitting with peers during a school play or holding hands with another child during a field trip. They can discourage actions that other youngsters find disturbing, such as repetitive behaviors, so as to increase their social acceptance by peers (Turnbull, Turnbull, & Wehmeyer, 2010). They can also teach appropriate ways to secure peers' attention, take turns in conversation, refrain from dominating the discussion, ask for something politely, and participate in pretend play with friends (Y. Chang, et al., 2014; K. Chung et al., 2007; Meadan, Angell, Stoner, & Daczewitz, 2014). Some teachers set up buddy arrangements, in which a child without a serious disability is trained to interact with the child with autism and adjust to his or her needs, for example, by maintaining mutual attention with him or her and by commenting on ongoing activities (Kohler, Greteman, Raschke, & Highnam, 2007). School counselors may provide helpful resources for prompting targeted behaviors, such as handheld tablets with reminders and video-recordings of the child practicing particular social skills (Auger, 2013).

Social Setting

The people with whom children spend time, and the practices they follow, are potentially influential in social cognitive development. Discussions with adults about what people think, feel, want, and so on enhance children's awareness of thoughts and emotions (J. M. Jenkins, Turrell, Kogushi, Lollis, & Ross, 2003; Ziv, Smadja, & Aram, 2013). Parents who openly consider differing points of view during family discussions help children realize that multiple perspectives legitimately exist (Astington & Pelletier, 1996; Taumoepeau & Ruffman, 2008). In the early years, sociodramatic play activities, in which children take on a variety of roles ("mommy," "doctor," etc.), can help children imagine what people might think and feel in different contexts (Lillard, 1998; Saracho, 2014). Discussions and conflicts with siblings provide an especially motivating context in which to use perspective-taking skills (McAlister & Peterson, 2013; Randell & Peterson, 2009).

Children exposed to a wide range of cultural customs acquire a theory of mind, often at similar ages (D. Liu, Wellman, Tardif, & Sabbagh, 2008; Shahaeian, Nielsen, Peterson, & Slaughter, 2014). Children around the world first learn about other people's desires and then develop other specific abilities in social cognition depending on priorities in their culture. After grasping that other people are motivated to fulfill their desires, Chinese children next develop an appreciation that people can be either knowledgeable or ignorant, whereas children in the United States and Australia next come to realize that different people have varying beliefs (Wellman, Fang, Liu, Zhu, & Zhu, 2006).

---

[17]One example of such a talent is the astonishing artistic ability of a few children, as Nadia revealed in her drawings of horses (see p. 150 in Chapter 4).

Cultures also influence *how much* children think about other people's thoughts and feelings (Lillard, 1999). Some cultures frequently explain people's behaviors in terms of mental events, whereas others are more likely to focus on external circumstances. In the United States, children who live in urban areas regularly refer to people's psychological states when explaining good and bad behaviors (e.g., "He helped me catch bugs, because he and I like to catch bugs"). In contrast, children in rural areas are more likely to attribute people's behaviors to situational factors (e.g., "She helped me pick up my books, because if she didn't I would have missed the bus"). The latter approach is also common in many Southeast Asian cultures (J. G. Miller, 1987).

As you have learned in this chapter, a sense of self and basic social understandings about other people derive from both nature *and* nurture. In the Basic Developmental Issues table "Comparing Sense of Self and Social Cognition," you can see other ways that the two characteristics reflect developmental dimensions.

Fostering the Development of Social Cognition

The research findings just reviewed have several implications for teachers and other adults who work with children:

• **Talk about mental concepts in age-appropriate ways.** Adults can talk with children about thoughts and feelings, and together they might speculate about what other people (e.g., peers, figures in historical events, fictional characters) were thinking and feeling. Adults should, of course, try to gear such discussions to children's cognitive capabilities. Preschoolers understand such straightforward feelings as being *sad, disappointed,* and *angry* (Saarni, Campos, Camras, & Witherington, 2006). Adolescents have sufficiently advanced cognitive and social reasoning capabilities that they can consider abstract and complex psychological qualities (e.g., being *passive aggressive* or having an inner *moral compass*).

BASIC DEVELOPMENTAL ISSUES
Comparing Sense of Self and Social Cognition

ISSUE	SENSE OF SELF	SOCIAL COGNITION
Nature and Nurture	Human beings appear to have an inborn need to think of themselves as competent, likable, and worthy individuals. A positive sense of self is fostered in environments wherein adults encourage children's attainment of mature standards for behavior and arrange for them to make steady progress.	The ability to consider other people's perspectives (their intentions, desires, and thoughts) depends on having a normally maturing human brain. The capacities of theory of mind and social perspective taking are nurtured by social experiences with other people and, in particular, with exposure to different viewpoints.
Universality and Diversity	General developmental trends in self-perceptions are fairly universal. Most children first develop simple views of the self and then see the self in more complex terms. For example, children progressively integrate their many discrete self-perceptions into general abstractions of their qualities as persons. Diversity emerges due to unique experiences in families and peer groups. Variations are also reflected in the self-perceptions of boys and girls from different cultures and distinct ethnic groups.	Theory of mind appears to be a nearly universal capacity. A few children (e.g., some with autism or serious intellectual disabilities) exhibit delays in understanding other people's desires, intentions, thoughts, and feelings. Diversity is present in the age at which children acquire specific elements of theory of mind and is tied to opportunities to hear about other people's ideas, desires, and feelings and cultural practices that foster thinking about other people's perspectives.
Qualitative and Quantitative Change	Infants' basic awareness of themselves, arising from experiences with bodily sensations and shared focus of attention with caregivers, is transformed qualitatively when they begin to speak about thoughts and feelings with others. Qualitative changes also occur when adolescents fold separate selves into unified abstract models of their psychological characteristics. Quantitative changes occur as children increase their knowledge about things that they are good at and activities for which they lack proficiency.	A series of qualitative changes, for example, in the acquisition of *intersubjectivity* and *social referencing*, sets the stage for an emerging awareness that other people have their own perspectives. Qualitative changes also occur in abilities to coordinate multiple perspectives and meet their own needs in a complex social environment. Quantitative changes are evident in increasingly sophisticated understandings of other people's thoughts, intentions, and feelings.

DEVELOPMENT AND PRACTICE
Encouraging Social Perspective Taking

Ask children to share their interpretations with one another.

- A first-grade teacher finds several children arguing over why Serena fell during a game of tag. The teacher comforts Serena and then asks the children about what happened. Some believe she stumbled over her loose shoelaces, others argue that one of the other girls got in her way, and one boy thinks Serena wasn't looking where she was going. The teacher suggests that each of them may be partly right. He also urges them to be more careful when they play running games, because it is easy to bump into one another by accident. (Middle Childhood)

- After a field trip to a local museum, a high school art teacher asks her students to share their interpretations of how the artists have combined colors in their paintings. The students learn that some of them thought the color combinations were aesthetically vibrant and appealing, whereas others thought the color palettes were garish. (Late Adolescence)

Encourage children to speculate about characters' thoughts, emotions, and motives literature.

- As a teacher in a child care center reads a story to a group of young children, she occasionally stops to ask questions about what the different characters might be thinking and feeling. While reading *The Berenstain Bears' Trouble with Pets* (Berenstain & Berenstain, 1990), she asks, "Why does the Bear family let Little Bird fly away?" and "How do you think Mama and Papa Bear feel when Lady makes a mess in the living room?" (Early Childhood)

- In *The Corn Grows Ripe* by Dorothy Rhoads (1956), Tigre, a 12-year-old Mayan boy living in the Yucatán, must take on new responsibilities when his father is injured. Mr. Torres assigns the book to his middle school students and leads a discussion about Tigre's new responsibilities. The students express a variety of opinions about how they would feel about taking on these new duties. (Early Adolescence)

Ask children to consider the perspectives of people they don't know very well.

- A preschool teacher makes a batch of cookies for senior citizens who regularly come to their class to read to children. The children prepare a basket for each of their senior friends, place a few cookies in it, and insert thank-you notes. She says to the children, "Imagine how surprised our senior friends are going to be! I bet they're going to be really happy when they see the baskets." (Early Childhood)

- During a discussion of a recent earthquake in South America, an eighth-grade social studies teacher asks students to imagine how people must feel when they lose their home and possessions and don't know whether their loved ones are dead or alive. (Early Adolescence)

- **Encourage children to look at situations from other people's perspectives.** Classrooms and other group settings provide many opportunities for children to look at the world as others do, and over time such opportunities enhance children's theory of mind and perspective-taking capabilities. The Development and Practice feature "Encouraging Social Perspective Taking" illustrates effective strategies.

- **Help children tune in to the nonverbal cues that can help them "read people's minds."** Some children readily pick up on the body language that reveals companions' thoughts and feelings. Other children are less perceptive. The latter group can benefit from explicit instruction in signals they might look for—the furrowed brow that indicates confusion, the agitation that indicates frustration or impatience, the "silent treatment" that suggests anger, and so on (e.g., Franco, Davis, & Davis, 2013; Minskoff, 1980).

- **Coach children who face substantial delays with psychological concepts.** Children who are obstructed in theory of mind may need systematic exposure to psychological words (e.g., *wanting, thinking,* and *believing*). Paula, a 9-year-old girl with fetal alcohol syndrome, was delayed in her cognitive and language development, had trouble interacting with other children, and rarely used terms for her own or others' mental states (Timler, Olswang, & Coggins, 2005). An intervention was designed to foster Paula's awareness of these characteristics. Paula and two other children met with a speech-language specialist over several weeks and considered how characters in hypothetical scenarios might have thought about the events. After a few weeks, Paula regularly used mental state terms in her speech:

> "I *know* Marco didn't let me play soccer unless I gave him one dollar bill."
> "The teacher *thought* I was making this story up and I'm trying to get him in trouble because he told her a lie."
> "I *know* because I saw the toilet paper in the boy's hand."
> "She *knows* that we got the wrong pizza because we were arguing about where we wanted to go and we went to Dominoes."
> (Timler et al., 2005, p. 81)

Preparing for Your Licensure Examination

Your teaching test might ask you about fostering productive social relationships among children from diverse backgrounds.

• **Promote an inclusive setting.** Creating a warm and respectful climate for children from diverse backgrounds takes ongoing work (Andreouli, Howarth, & Sonn, 2014). Certain procedures are essential, especially having a code of conduct that prohibits name-calling on the basis of ethnicity, race, gender, religion, socioeconomic status, abilities and disabilities, and other social categories. Also worthwhile is establishing affirmative values, such as respecting people regardless of their backgrounds, a quality that can be infused into resources and curricula (e.g., by screening books for ethnic stereotypes), outreach to families (e.g., by inviting parents and guardians to share their upbringings, jobs, and special talents in the classroom), and classroom traditions (e.g., by morning greetings and afternoon farewells and regular class meetings).

• **Actively work to break down stereotypes and reduce prejudice.** One effective strategy is to encourage children to see people as *individuals*—as human beings with their own unique strengths and weaknesses—rather than as members of particular groups (C. D. Lee & Slaughter-Defoe, 1995; Spencer & Markstrom-Adams, 1990). Another strategy is to increase interpersonal contacts among people from diverse groups (and ideally to create a sense that "we are all in this together") through cooperative group activities, multischool community service projects, or pen pal relationships with oeers in distant locations (Koeppel & Mulrooney, 1992; Rutland, Killen, & Abrams, 2010). As children gain contact with people from unfamiliar groups, they tend to see one another as being more similar than they previously thought, and prejudices often dissipate (Stathi, Cameron, Hartley, & Bradford, 2014). Cross-racial friendships are fostered when children notice one another's talents, hear about one another's individual characteristics, and find that they can depend on one another during collaborative projects.

Adults should challenge any stereotypes and prejudicial attitudes they encounter in children's speech or actions. If a teenager talks about "lazy migrant workers," a teacher might respond by saying, "I wonder where that idea came from. Migrant workers are often up before dawn and pick produce until dusk. Many take other demanding jobs when the growing season is over." Notice how the teacher confronts the "lazy migrant worker" stereotype tactfully and matter-of-factly and does not assume that the teen's remark has malicious intent. Playing on their interest to appear tolerant and open minded may be more effective than chastising them for attitudes they have not carefully thought through (Dovidio & Gaertner, 1999). Some educators have found it effective to train children to intervene as bystanders when they hear prejudicial remarks themselves (Aboud & Fenwick, 1999; Dessel, 2010).

Summary

As children grow older, they become more attuned to and interested in the mental lives of those around them. In the process of developing a *theory of mind,* they gradually learn that people have thoughts, feelings, and motives different from their own and that these internal states can be complex and at times contradictory. Children also become increasingly skilled in taking the perspectives of others. Unfortunately, youngsters' growing beliefs about other people may also include rigid stereotypes about certain groups, leading them to act toward members of those groups in prejudicial ways.

Classrooms and other group settings are important contexts in which children and adolescents develop awareness of other people's needs and perspectives. Teachers and other adults can foster greater knowledge in numerous ways—for instance, by talking frequently about people's thoughts and feelings, exposing youngsters to multiple and equally legitimate perspectives about particular topics and events, and confronting inaccurate and counterproductive stereotypes.

ENHANCEDetext *self-check*

Assessing Children 12-2

Listen to a teenage girl talk about her ethnic identity.

ENHANCEDetext *application exercise*

PRACTICING FOR YOUR LICENSURE EXAMINATION

Many teaching tests require students to apply their knowledge of child development in analyzing brief vignettes and answering multiple-choice questions. You can practice for your licensure examination by reading the following case study and answering a series of questions.

Two Histories

Rachel Stephanie Bolden-Kramer is an adolescent from San Francisco, California. In her poem, *Two Histories*, Rachel tells her experience of having a dual ethnic heritage:

> Daddy wanted to name me Wilhemina after his mother.
> You know you're supposed to name your baby after someone who's gone.
> Not alive.
> But then my mother protested.
> I should carry her mother's name, Anne.
> "Rachel" kept me from the arguments and sour family disputes.
> But did it compromise or anger both sides?
> And that's what I'm stuck with,
> Every day
> Every move
> I'm a compromise
> Light skin
> But thick bone structure
> Half 'n half Jewish girl who fights for BSU[a]
> Latke and greens
> The horah and the butterfly
> Act White
> Won't date Black men
> Think she's better
> Has good hair
> Looks more Latina than half-breed
> But that boy always called me mixed in such an ugly way
> Some say, "Nigga get off the swing"
> Others say, "You're really not like those other Black people"
> And I get told it's better to pretend I'm White
> But I got two histories in me
> Both enslaved
> And both warriors.
>
> Rachel Stephanie Bolden-Kramer[a]
>   (WritersCorps, 2003, pp. 39–40)

Constructed-Response Question

1. What challenges and assets did Rachel have in forming an ethnic identity?

Multiple-Choice Questions

2. How might the developmental theorist James Marcia describe Rachel's ethnic identity formation?
   a. Rachel is in a state of *diffusion*, in which she has failed to embark on serious exploration of her ethnic identity.
   b. Rachel is in *foreclosure*, a state of committing to a vision of her ethnicity established for her by her parents.
   c. Rachel spent several years in *identity achievement*, embracing clear commitments to her ethnic identity, before entering *foreclosure*, the condition of committing to particular ideals and ways of life established for her by her parents.
   d. Rachel went through a period of *moratorium*, in which she actively searched for the meaning of her ethnic identity and now seems to be in *identity achievement*.

3. How would you describe Rachel's development from the perspective of Margaret Beale Spencer's framework of identity development?
   a. Rachel had *protective factors*, supportive parents who shared their cultural values and traditions with her and her own personal insight and resolve. Rachel also faced the *risk factor* of having bigoted and insensitive peers.
   b. As Rachel reflected on her ethnic identity and relationships with peers and family members, she developed *coping skills*.
   c. In the process of developing coping skills, Rachel gained a sense of her own *ethnic identity*.
   d. All of the above.

ENHANCEDetext *licensure exam*

[a]"Two Histories" by Rachel Stephanie Bolden-Kramer from PAINT ME LIKE I AM: TEEN POEMS FROM WRITERSCORPS. Copyright © 2003 by WritersCorps. Reprinted with permission from WritersCorps.

Key Concepts

sense of self (p. 450)
self-handicapping (p. 452)
contingent self-worth (p. 453)
imaginary audience (p. 457)
personal fable (p. 457)

identity (p. 457)
gender schema (p. 462)
self-socialization (p. 463)
social cognition (p. 473)
theory of mind (p. 473)

social perspective taking (p. 473)
intentionality (p. 473)
recursive thinking (p. 475)
social-cognitive bias (p. 477)
stereotype (p. 477)

prejudice (p. 479)
autism spectrum
    disorders (p. 480)
mirror neuron (p. 480)

CHAPTER THIRTEEN

Self-Regulation and Motivation

CASE STUDY: Making Kites

Janet Keany teaches a mathematics class for fifth and sixth graders who have a history of poor performance in mathematics.[a] She has recently shown her class how concepts in geometry relate to aerodynamics, emphasizing that the size and shape of an object affect the ease with which it can fly. As a follow-up to the lesson, she asks her students to experiment with a variety of sizes and shapes as they each design a kite.

The kite project lasts several days. A researcher observes the class throughout the project and interviews the students afterward. She finds that different students take very different approaches to the task and have widely varying perspectives about it. A girl named Sara approaches the task as a scientist might: She is keenly interested in creating an aerodynamic kite design and realizes that doing so will take time and patience. She re-designs her kite three times to make it as aerodynamic as possible. After the project, she summarizes her results:

> ... I wasn't completely successful, because I had a few problems. But I realized that most scientists, when they try experiments, well, they're not always right. . . . [I]f I can correct myself on [errors] then I don't re-ally mind them that much. I mean, everybody learns from their mistakes. I know I do. . . . I think mistakes are actually good, to tell you the truth. . . .
>
> When I had my test flights, the shape flew really, really well, and I was going to stick with that shape. . . . I had no doubts because I knew that I could really do it; I knew I could put this together really well, 'cause I had a lot of confidence in myself. . . . (D. K. Meyer, Turner, & Spencer, 1997, pp. 511–512)

Unlike Sara, Amy sticks with a single kite design throughout the project even though she has trouble getting her kite to fly. Later, Amy tells the researcher:

> I knew from the start what shape I wanted. Once I had the materials it was very easy to make the kite. . . . [T]here wasn't enough wind for the kites to fly. (pp. 510, 513)

The researcher asks Amy how important the project was to her and whether she ever takes risks at school. She responds:

> I feel lazy because I don't like to make challenges for myself, to make goals. I just like to do it as I go along, not make goals or challenges. . . . I like to do well for [the teacher] and my parents, and myself, I guess. . . . [I]f it doesn't affect my grade, whether I do this or not, if I totally fail and do everything wrong, if it doesn't affect my grade, then I'll [take risks]. (pp. 510, 512)

Had her kite flown, how might Amy have explained it? Amy tells the researcher that it would probably have been "beginner's luck" (D. K. Meyer, Turner, & Spencer, 1994, 1997).

- What differences do you notice in how the two girls approach the kite-making activity?
- What goals do Sara and Amy pursue as they create their kites? What challenges do they each overcome?
- How does Sara explain her success? How does Amy explain her failure?

[a]Although the case is real, "Janet Keany" is a pseudonym.

OBJECTIVES

13.1: Identify developmental trends in, and practical applications of, self-regulation.

13.2: Differentiate between extrinsic and intrinsic motivation, and identify factors influencing the manifestations of each.

13.3: Describe the kinds of goals children set and the attributions they make for how well they achieve their goals.

13.4: Summarize strategies for motivating children at school.

Sara and Amy exhibit *self-regulation*, the ability to guide personal actions and emotions, while producing their kites. The project takes several days, and the girls must keep their focus on designing and creating the kites and making adjustments as necessary. In their distinctive ways, the girls also show **motivation**, the driving force for energizing, directing, and sustaining behavior toward particular ends. The girls reveal motivation through the effort they invest in the activity, which for Sara means producing an operational kite, and for Amy means achieving a passing grade.

The particular efforts that people invest in while completing activities depend on how they think about the projects. Sara is willing to experiment and make mistakes so that she can construct the best kite possible, whereas Amy prefers an easier and less successful course of action that meets minimum expectations for the assignment. Sara overcomes her mistakes by interpreting them as clues to aerodynamics. Amy perseveres to complete the design she started with and has no real commitment to producing an operational kite. Sara attributes her successful kite to her own effort and ability, whereas Amy concludes that her failure was due to poor weather conditions specifically, not enough wind.

In this chapter, we examine the development of self-regulation and motivation two inter-related concepts. Self-regulation is the broader notion, consisting of intentional actions that are energized by motivation. Thus children implement self-regulatory abilities (e.g., setting goals, keeping track of progress, and altering tactics as necessary) when they are proficient in these skills *and* sufficiently motivated. As you will learn in this chapter, teachers and other adults can foster children's self-regulation and their motivation, and in so doing enhance children's education, interpersonal relationships, and general well-being.

SELF-REGULATION

Children use self-regulation skills throughout the day. A 3-year-old boy arrives at his new preschool in the morning, bites his fingernails, and holds back tears as he waves good-bye to his mother. Children in a kindergarten class fold their arms as they stand in line for outdoor play, not touching one another as they wait. Fourth-grade students concentrate on a teacher's explanations despite the noise of younger children playing outside. And adolescents in a composition class begin a writing project, adding the interim deadlines onto their calendars and reviewing the rubric to see what standards they must achieve.

The essence of self-regulation is an ability to resist an impulse.[1] As children use one or more capacities related to self-regulation, they intentionally inhibit a strongly felt desire, instead mobilizing actions to meet an acquired standard (Heatherton, 2011; Mittal, Russell, Britner, & Peake, 2013; Nash, Schiller, Gianotti, Baumgartner, & Knoch, 2013). Children use this capacity when waiting for a desired reward, persevering in the face of challenges, and resisting temptations.

The neurological networks that permit self-regulation are known as *executive functions* because a person who uses them is managing mental processes in a top-down manner, with a particular goal in mind, much as a business executive exerts control over operations in a company. Several self-regulatory capabilities rely on executive functions:

- *Setting goals:* identifying and striving for self-chosen goals and standards
- *Controlling impulses:* resisting sudden urges to engage in forbidden or counterproductive behaviors
- *Socializing oneself:* striving to act in accordance with society's standards for behavior
- *Managing emotions:* modulating the expression of affective states so that demonstrated feelings are personally adaptive and socially acceptable
- *Motivating oneself:* creating conditions that make a task more engaging or rewarding
- *Deploying mental processes:* directing and monitoring one's attention and learning strategies in ways that achieve personal goals
- *Tracking progress:* keeping tabs on the results of one's efforts and making adjustments as necessary

Developmental Trends in Self-Regulation

A few signs of self-regulation are evident in infancy. In the first year, infants exert control over their own attention and look away from things they don't want to see (Eisenberg, Spinrad, Valiente, & Duckworth, 2014). In the second year, they speed up or slow down

---

[1]Self-regulation is introduced as a quality influenced by parents in Chapter 3, as a characteristic that varies among children due to neurological characteristics in Chapter 5, as an outcome of guidance from adults in Chapter 6, in the context of strategic learning in Chapter 7, and with reference to emotional regulation in Chapter 11.

their locomotion depending on interests and circumstances. Also in the first year, children exhibit self-soothing actions, such as pulling at an ear or snuggling into a favorite blanket when distressed.

As children grow, they develop an intensified motivation to make their own choices. Some parents in Western cultures complain about the "terrible twos," a period between the second and third birthdays when children are fussy when not allowed free reign in forbidden territory. The immature brain makes it difficult for children to inhibit certain behaviors, especially those that result in immediate rewards. Young children further lack sufficient working memory to think through what they want to do, how they might do it, and perhaps why they *shouldn't* do it.

This strengthening of intentions is an essential part of self-regulation, and most children gradually learn to control when and where they pursue their desires. One essential skill that emerges beginning in early childhood is the ability to **delay gratification**, the forgoing of small, immediate rewards for more substantial consequences down the road (Green, Fry, & Myerson, 1994; Mittal et al., 2013; C. Moore, 2010; Vaughn, Kopp, & Krakow, 1984). A 3-year-old is apt to choose a small toy she can have *now* over a larger and more attractive toy she can have tomorrow. In contrast, an 8-year-old is usually willing to wait a day or two for the more appealing item.

With maturation and relevant experience, children gradually develop the ability to delay gratification and use other self-regulatory skills. Researchers have identified several age-related trends:

Self-regulation advances simultaneously along three fronts. *Behaviorally*, children must learn to sit when required to do so and inhibit such actions as shouting out an answer when the classroom rule is to raise your hand and wait to be called on. Children must refrain from hitting irksome classmates and take turns and share toys with friends. *Emotionally*, children learn to express their feelings in a balanced and culturally acceptable manner, neither keeping them bottled up nor exploding disruptively. *Cognitively*, children must attend to academic lessons, including ones that they do not enjoy, and set specific learning goals, monitor progress, and make adjustments as warranted. Self-regulation in each of these domains is essential for successful adjustment at school (Williford, Whittaker, Vitiello, & Downer, 2013).

Children become better able to direct their actions in light of future consequences. The young child is incited by an immediate reward: A single cookie received right now is infinitely preferable to two cookies obtained in an hour. By early elementary school, children can imagine more than one way to handle many situations and now compare the merits and disadvantages of each (C. Moore, 2010). Children begin to conceive of themselves in the present as well as in the future and consider both conditions when choosing a response. Children also learn to inhibit tempting acts, perhaps grabbing a toy out of the hands of another child.

Children increasingly talk their way, and eventually think their way, through situations. The *inner speech* that **Lev Vygotsky** (1896–1934) described is a key mechanism by which children regulate their behavior.[2] As children acquire language skills, they talk themselves through new challenges (in tying shoes: "Put one lace over and then under the other; then make a loop . . ."). Children internalize their self-talk, first whispering to themselves and eventually *mentally* telling themselves what they should do. Children also repeat the advice they have heard from others, either verbally or mentally (in putting on a cardigan: "Put one arm in first, then the next, now button it up from the bottom upward"). Such self-talk helps children complete simple physical tasks and later achieve difficult interpersonal and academic goals, for instance, resolving conflicts and keeping attention focused during a classroom test (Alarcón-Rubio, Sánchez-Medina, & Prieto-García, 2014; Berk, 1994; Landry & Smith, 2010).

External rules are gradually internalized. Developing a **conscience**—an internalized sense of right and wrong—is an important part of the process by which children act in socially appropriate ways. Having a close relationship with parents sets the stage for children

---

[2]Vygotsky's theory of cognitive development is introduced in Chapter 6.

in complying with parents' guidance and eventually accepting family rules as their own (Hoffman, 1979; Kochanska, Koenig, Barry, Kim, & Yoon, 2010; I. W. Silverman, 2012).

Given children's strong wills, the process of internalization takes time. Children comply with simple requests and restrictions by the time they are 12 to 18 months old (Kopp, 1982). As they become increasingly verbal, they use self-talk to prevent themselves from engaging in prohibited behaviors even when caregivers are absent—for instance, saying "no" or "can't" to themselves as they reach for an electric outlet (Kochanska, 1993). By age 3 or 4, many children practice flexible strategies in following adult rules and prohibitions. If they are asked to wait for a short time (e.g., 15 minutes), they might invent games or sing to themselves to pass the time more quickly (Mischel & Ebbesen, 1970). If a playmate has an enticing toy, they may turn away and engage in an alternative activity as a way of lessening the temptation to grab the toy (Kopp, 1982).

As children grow, they live up to progressively complex principles—table etiquette, proper ways to address unfamiliar adults, tactics for saying "no" to drugs, and so forth. Children increasingly take ownership of society's rules and regulations through the process of internalization (Kochanska, Coy, & Murray, 2001; R. M. Ryan & Deci, 2009). The first sign of internalization (the *introjection* phase) is evident when children feel internal pressure (e.g., guilt) to comply with rules and regulations. Later (at the *identification* phase), children perceive rules and other desired behaviors to be valuable to them personally. Finally (at the *integration* phase), following basic standards becomes an integral part of children's sense of self. At this point, a teenage girl might define herself as being "law abiding" or "concerned about others' welfare" and behave in ways consistent with her self-perception.

Children's judgments about how well they are doing on a particular task become more frequent. Infants do not evaluate their own behavior, nor do they show much concern about how others assess it. In contrast, 2-year-olds often seek adults' approval for their actions (Stipek, Recchia, & McClintic, 1992). Sometime around age 3, children show signs of judging their own performance. For instance, they look happy when they're successful and sad when they fail (Heckenhausen, 1984).

As children move through the preschool, elementary, and middle school years, they show a marked increase in self-assessment (A. D. Elder, 2010; van Kraayenoord & Paris, 1997). Previously their parents praised certain behaviors and criticized others, teachers evaluated their academic performance as having certain strengths and limitations, and peers let them know in no uncertain terms about the effectiveness of their social skills. Children reflect on these comments, internalize many criteria, and direct their own behavior accordingly.

Willpower gradually builds during early and middle childhood and then takes a temporary dip during adolescence. Although neurological circuits for self-regulation develop throughout infancy and childhood, the teenage brain undergoes a dramatic re-wiring that initially weakens self-control (R. C. Lorenz et al., 2014). Maturation in the brain intensifies the pleasure the young person experiences when taking risks, especially in the presence of peers. In this state, youngsters are at risk for acting rashly. Many adolescents succumb to temptations, sometimes frequently. Yet with further maturation, coaching from adults, support from peers, and resolve, they are able to double up in their willpower and stay focused on long-term goals.

Bioecology of Self-Regulation

The many facets of self-regulation draw on both nature and nurture. Although virtually all children develop an infrastructure for executive functions, significant individual differences arise in how robust these brain circuits become (Eisenberg et al., 2014; Hrabok & Kerns, 2010). Partly as a result of genetic factors, children with impulsive temperaments as toddlers or preschoolers have trouble inhibiting inappropriate behaviors when they move into elementary, middle, and high school (Eigsti et al., 2006; Leve et al., 2013). Some children with disabilities—for instance, certain brain injuries, learning disabilities, or mental illness—need to be taught how to resist impulses and plan ahead (Gligorović & Đurović, 2014; Meltzer, 2007).

Environmental factors—especially socialization practices—also play a strong role in the development of self-regulation. Infants are spontaneous, inattentive to any long-term goals, and deficient in managing their changeable states and moods. Parents assume the role of baby-regulator, keeping him or her safe, teaching standards of self-care, and moderating

BIOECOLOGY OF DEVELOPMENT

Self-regulation is made possible by brain circuits for guiding behavior, which are fostered by practice in self-control and encouragement from adults to plan ahead and ignore distractions and other impulses.

out-of-control reactions to fear, hunger, and pain. Contrary to a common belief, sensitive comforting does not make infants dependent. Instead, infants who receive responsive care are likely to become securely attached to their parents and gain the foundation for self-regulation skills (Eisenberg et al., 2014).

As children grow, caregiver sensitivity remains a catalyst for self-regulation but now is most successful when accompanied by expectations for staying focused, acting appropriately, and managing emotions. During the preschool years, most parents socialize children to follow rules of basic safety and standards for proper social behaviors (Gralinski & Kopp, 1993; Hrabok & Kerns, 2010). When parents, teachers, and other adults have warm and supportive relationships with children, set reasonable boundaries for behavior, and take everyone's needs into consideration, they create optimal conditions for making appropriate choices (Eisenberg et al., 2014; Reeve, Bolt, & Cai, 1999; B. J. Zimmerman, 2004). Caregivers provide valuable rules for proper behavior (e.g., "Eat your vegetables," "Honor your father and mother") that children recall—and may act on—when later faced with relevant choices (Hrabok & Kerns, 2010; Landry & Smith, 2010). Adults can also be helpful in self-regulation of emotions. In one study, parents who persuaded their children that an undesirable prize was not a concern tended to have children who expressed little disappointment with the prize (A. S. Morris et al., 2011).

As you might expect, the particular lessons children have in self-regulation are embedded within cultural traditions. By way of example, some Asian cultural groups place a high priority on self-discipline (P. M. Cole & Tamang, 2001; Trommsdorff, 2012). Even as toddlers, children are strongly encouraged to control their feelings, minimizing the "terrible twos" phenomenon mentioned earlier (D. Y. F. Ho, 1994). Preschoolers are expected to work diligently and persistently on assigned tasks. Children in other societies learn other lessons in self-regulation, perhaps that they should interact cooperatively with peers, play imaginatively with toys, or complete chores for the benefit of their family.

Finally, some children living in economically poor families have difficulty with some aspects of self-regulation skills (A. L. Roy & Raver, 2014). Pressures on low-income parents—long work hours, challenges in feeding and clothing children, and struggles in finding transportation and affordable medical care—make it difficult for them to remain sensitive, reassuring, and engaged. Ongoing anxiety makes it difficult for children to concentrate on complex information at school and keep their impulses in check when frustrated or angered. Fortunately, many children from low-income families manage to develop strong self-regulatory skills despite these difficult circumstances, often with support from extended family members and others with guidance by teachers in preschool, kindergarten, and the early elementary grades (G. W. Evans & Fuller-Rowell, 2013; Raver, 2012).

Promoting Self-Regulation

To appreciate why self-regulation is so important, consider the following situation. A group of 4-year-old children are individually given a choice of having one marshmallow now or several marshmallows in 15 minutes. Most children choose to wait for the larger reward but several ask for the one marshmallow *now* (Mischel, Shoda, & Rodriguez, 1989). It is a simple task, but children's ability to delay gratification on it is associated with their literacy and mathematics skills and productive peer relationships. It is also predictive of adjustment years later—in adolescence, with dealing with frustration, getting along with others, and achieving in school, and in adulthood, with their health (Eigsti et al., 2006; Mischel et al., 1989; Montroy, Bowles, Skibbe, & Foster, 2014; Schlam, Wilson, Shoda, Mischel, & Ayduk, 2013; Shoda, Mischel, & Peake, 1990). Other evidence corroborates the connection between childhood self-control and adult outcomes related to financial security, low rates of criminal offending, and little drug dependence (Moffitt et al., 2011). Fortunately, self-control, the ability to plan for the future, and other aspects of self-regulation are responsive to adult intervention. We offer the following recommendations:

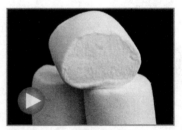

Observing Children 13-1
Watch children participate in the classic marshmallow task and listen to psychologist Walter Mischel explain its significance.[3]
ENHANCEDetext *video example*

• **Structure the preschool curriculum such that young children are invited to plan ahead for an activity and then, during it, evaluate how well they are achieving their intentions.** As you have learned, delay of gratification and related executive functions are under way by

---

[3]Should this YouTube video not work for you, which might be the case in certain countries, try searching for one of the many other videos that are available on the marshmallow task.

the preschool years. Having this basic capacity is in fact crucial to be able to fulfill demands for goal-directed activity in preschool, kindergarten, and beyond—listening to teachers and resisting distractions; persisting on artwork, puzzles, and other learning tasks; and squelching impulses to bop annoying classmates (Ursache, Blair, & Raver, 2012). Those who enter preschool without these skills easily get off on the wrong track. They are at risk for struggling socially, becoming disruptive, letting stresses escalate to unmanageable levels, and not acquiring the basic literacies they need to progress in elementary school.

Inadequacies in early executive functions need not be a lifelong impairment, of course. Young children are well able to strengthen emerging self-regulatory skills with structured opportunities for practice. Several programs illustrate the receptivity of children to setting goals, persisting on tasks, and inhibiting automatic responses (Ursache et al., 2012). For example, in the *Research-Based Developmentally Informed (REDI) Head Start* project, children encounter a comprehensive preschool curriculum that focuses on fostering self-control in behavior and emotions (Bierman et al., 2014). Children are taught the meaning of emotions, how they can express certain feelings, how they are to resolve disagreements with peers, and how to stop and think before acting. Compared to peers from similar backgrounds enrolled in another preschool program, REDI children were more engaged with the curriculum and less aggressive in peer interactions.

In the *Tools of the Mind* program, preschool children participate in a play-based curriculum in which they plan their make-believe play and later evaluate how well it went (Bodrova & Leong, 2009; Leong & Bodrova, 2012). When forming their plans, children are encouraged to anticipate difficulties, such as having another child competing for the same role. Before beginning to play, they conjure up potential solutions, such as changing the script slightly so that two characters with the same role are needed. Teachers ask children to elaborate on their anticipated plan and specify the various steps, so as to increase the complexity and length of their social interactions. Children are encouraged to cooperate, take turns, and take one another's perspectives. Preliminary evidence indicates that children who experienced the Tools program were more likely to ignore distractions and less likely to exhibit problematic behaviors than were children in other preschools (W. Barnett et al., 2008; A. Diamond, Barnett, Thomas, & Munro, 2007).

In the *Kids in Transition to School* (KITS) program, children getting ready for kindergarten who are in foster care and have typically experienced multiple caregiver arrangements are trained in self-regulation, early literacy, and prosocial skills, all important components of school readiness (Pears et al., 2013). Young children in foster care tend to enter school with low academic skills and significant emotional and behavioral needs. With regard to self-regulation, children in the KITS program are taught how to concentrate, sit still, and wait their turn. For literacy, they are taught letter naming, phonological skills, conventions in print, and comprehension abilities. In the prosocial domain, children are educated about sharing and other valuable interpersonal skills. Children who participated in the KITS program have acquired stronger self-regulatory and early literacy skills (but did not differ in prosocial skills) compared to other children in foster care who received regular services through the child welfare system.

Long-term follow-ups on children who attended experimental preschools in the United States during the 1960s and 1970s affirm that high-quality preschools that nurture children intellectually, socially, emotionally, and behaviorally can exert a significant and lasting impact on their welfare. At least part of the reason seems to be that these carefully designed preschools fostered children's self-regulation, which precipitated all sorts of advantages in their lives (Goodwin & Miller, 2013). For example, in the *High/Scope* program in Ypsilanti, Michigan, preschool children from low-income families acquired language and cognitive abilities as well as reasoning skills, and they learned how to conduct themselves in the classroom and, for parts of the day, to select and plan their activities (Belfield, Nores, Barnett, & Schweinhart, 2008; Schweinhart, 2006). Although initial effects on intelligence faded after a few years, more of the High/Scope students went on to graduate from high school than did similar individuals without this early childhood intervention. Furthermore, as adults, High/Scope graduates were more likely to be employed, to earn more, to be arrested less, and to require less government service (e.g., with public financial assistance).

Although the particular curricula of these early childhood interventions have varied, they commonly fostered high-quality relationships between children, teachers, and peers; supported children's ability to make choices among several age-appropriate options; and addressed the full gamut of skill domains—cognitive, behavioral, and social-emotional abilities. In the process, educators from these programs were able to prepare children for the many self-regulatory demands that they would later encounter in school and in life.

• **With older students, demonstrate desired behaviors and arrange for routines that encourage them.** Children are in a better position to make wise choices when they know what to expect and can reasonably anticipate that certain behaviors will yield desired outcomes (Bronson, 2000; Holler & Greene, 2010; Meltzer, Pollica, & Barzillai, 2007). Communicating general guidelines for behavior, establishing regular routines for completing tasks and assignments, and identifying the locations of items that children need during the day (pencils, hole punchers, dictionaries, etc.) help children work productively with minimal adult supervision. As children grow accustomed to classroom routines, they become adept at meeting expectations (Ursache et al., 2012). Boredom, frustration, disappointment, and other unpleasant emotions are more easily tolerated when the customs are well practiced. In fact, as children gain experience in staying on task despite distracting circumstances, they actually strengthen their resolve for the future. Thus, exercise of self-control begets advances in self-control (Ursache et al., 2012).

• **Provide children of all ages with choices.** Although young children inevitably require adult supervision to keep them safe, they clearly benefit from making choices (Holler & Greene, 2010; Perry, VandeKamp, Mercer, & Nordby, 2002). Young children might be invited to select an activity from the puzzle area, dramatic play center, sensory table, or block zone during a free play period. At the same time, caregivers and teachers can foresee and preempt problems when children make their own decisions. Preschool and kindergarten teachers might create a few rules for taking turns and sharing materials, designate certain areas of the classroom for messy undertakings (e.g., painting, working with clay), and put potentially dangerous objects out of reach (Bronson, 2000).

Elementary school children similarly need frequent opportunities to make their own decisions. Independent assignments, computer-based instructional programs, group projects, homework, and the like help students, especially when activities are structured so that they know how to proceed and understand expectations for performance (H. Cooper, Robinson, & Patall, 2006; Corno & Mandinach, 2004; Landry & Smith, 2010). When children make poor choices, adults should offer constructive feedback that will scaffold, rather than dampen, enthusiasm for exercising independence.

• **Create checklists for guiding children's completion of a task.** Some middle and high school students lose track of their class materials and assignments, not because they are lazy or unmotivated, but because they have poor organizational skills. For these students, mechanisms for keeping track of homework and due dates can be helpful (Belfiore & Hornyak, 1998). In one intervention, students asked the teacher for assistance when they needed it and also learned to reward themselves (e.g., allowing themselves to play a board game or spend time on a computer) when they finished a task. Initially, the teacher needed to monitor whether checklists accurately reflected what they had accomplished, but eventually monitoring was no longer necessary. In Figure 13-1, you can see a checklist for elementary

Student's Name _____		Date _____	
Step	Yes	No	Teacher's Comment
1. I took my homework out of my backpack and put it in the basket			
2. I took out my journal and pen and placed them on the table.			
3. I hung up my sweater or jacket on the coat rack.			
4. I took a deep breath and sat down.			
5. I said good morning to classmates at my table.			
6. I looked at the bulletin board to find out which topic I should write about in my journal.			

FIGURE 13-1 Daily Checklist for Elementary Students at Beginning of Day

children focused on being prepared for the first lesson of the day. In other contexts, teachers can use checklists for steps for completing lengthy projects, for example, in dividing up a lengthy writing assignment into brainstorming ideas, identifying key concepts, writing topic sentences, adding evidence, filling in the gaps, and editing (Meltzer, 2010).

• **Provide guidance when, and only when, children really need it.** Being self-regulating doesn't necessarily always mean doing something independently. It also involves knowing when assistance is needed and seeking it out (Karabenick & Sharma, 1994; Kaya & Kablan, 2013). Accordingly, teachers might welcome any reasonable requests for help and not convey the message that children are "dumb" or bothersome for asking (R. S. Newman & Schwager, 1992). Sometimes, however, children ask for help when they really just want attention or companionship. If a 4-year-old asks for help on a puzzle, an astute preschool teacher might, after watching the child at work, say, "I don't think you need help with this. But I can keep you company for a few minutes if you'd like" (Bronson, 2000).

• **Use suggestions rather than direct commands as much as possible.** Children are more likely to internalize guidelines for behavior when adults make recommendations on how to accomplish goals, elicit children's perspectives, and provide a rationale for why some behaviors are unacceptable (Baraldi & Iervese, 2010; Hoffman, 1975). Younger children respond more favorably to suggestions that are concrete rather than abstract. To avoid incidents of bumping and pushing in the cafeteria, for example, teachers at one school asked students to imagine they had "magic bubbles" around them. The students could keep their bubbles from "popping" if they kept a safe distance between themselves and others. This simple strategy resulted in fewer behavior problems at lunchtime (Sullivan-DeCarlo, DeFalco, & Roberts, 1998).

• **Teach specific self-regulation skills.** Children become more self-regulating when they learn methods for directing their behavior. Particular strategies can be taught as follows:

Self-monitoring. Children aren't always aware of how frequently they do something wrong or how infrequently they do something right. To help them become aware of their actions, adults can ask them to observe and record their own behavior. Such self-focused observation and record keeping often bring about significant improvements in children's academic and social behaviors (Roebers, Krebs, & Roderer, 2014; J. R. Sullivan & Conoley, 2004; Webber, Scheuermann, McCall, & Coleman, 1993). Initially some children may need assistance in monitoring their behavior, for example, whether they have stayed on task during a lesson (DuPaul & Hoff, 1998). You can see a boy monitoring his school behavior with the help of an electronic gadget in an Observing Children video.

Observing Children 13-2
Observe young Brandon being supported in his self-regulation with a gadget that buzzes periodically so that he can assess his attention and register his progress.

ENHANCEDetext *video example*

Self-instructions. Sometimes children need a reminder about how to respond in particular situations. By teaching specific ways of talking themselves through an endeavor, adults give them a means through which they remind *themselves* about appropriate actions. Such a strategy is often effective with young children and especially those with poor impulse control (Ennis & Jolivette, 2014; Meichenbaum, 1985). Educators can try such simple methods as giving a child a line drawing of an ear as a reminder to listen quietly during storybook reading (A. Diamond et al., 2007). Checklists, assessment rubrics (with defined standards), and lists of steps can be worthwhile for older students.

Self-motivation. Children may appreciate strategies to keep themselves motivated during dull but important tasks. For example, they might identify several reasons why completing an activity will help them over the long run. They might embellish a task in some way to make it more interesting. Or they might learn how to divide a lengthy task into a number of small pieces and then reward themselves after completing each part (Wery & Thomson, 2013; B. J. Zimmerman & Cleary, 2009).

Self-evaluation. To become truly self-regulating, children must acquire reasonable criteria by which to guide and judge their accomplishments. For instance, teachers might ask students to reflect on improvement ("What can we do that we didn't do before?") or complete self-assessment instruments that show them what to look for in their own performance (Panadero, Tapia, & Huertas, 2012; S. G. Paris & Ayres, 1994). At the secondary school level (and perhaps even sooner), students might play a role in identifying the criteria by which their performance might reasonably be evaluated.

- **Tailor levels of support to the characteristics of children with disabilities.** Independence is a major concern for children with disabilities, especially because adults are apt to monitor their behavior closely (Sands & Wehmeyer, 1996; Wu & Chu, 2012). Adults can help by taking a long-term perspective on the self-regulation of these children, arranging independent activity that protects them from harm yet exercises their initiative. For instance, one teacher asks a student with an intellectual disability to take the daily attendance sheet to the office but reminds her that as soon as she has done so, she should return immediately to class (Patton, Blackbourn, & Fad, 1996). Another teacher gives a student who is blind a chance to explore the classroom before other students have arrived, locating objects in the classroom (wastebasket, pencil sharpener, etc.) and identifying distinctive sounds (e.g., the buzz of a wall clock) that help the student get his bearings (J. W. Wood, 1998).

- **Be a good role model in demonstrating your own willpower.** Adults promote self-regulation by modeling controlled and strategic behaviors (M. R. Sanders & Mazzucchelli, 2013; B. J. Zimmerman & Cleary, 2009). In a variant on the classic marshmallow task introduced previously, fourth and fifth graders watched adult models make a series of choices between small, immediate rewards and more valuable, postponed ones (e.g., plastic chess pieces available on that day versus wooden ones that they could have in 2 weeks). Some children observed a model choosing the immediate rewards (e.g., saying, "Chess figures are chess figures. I can get much use out of the plastic ones right away," p. 701; Bandura & Mischel, 1965). Others observed a model choosing the deferred rewards (e.g., saying, "The wooden chess figures are of much better quality, more attractive, and will last longer. I'll wait 2 weeks for the better ones," p. 701). Immediately after they observed the models, and also on a second occasion several weeks later, the children were asked to choose between small, immediate rewards and larger, deferred ones (e.g., a small plastic ball now or a much larger one in 2 weeks). The children were more likely to delay gratification if they had seen the model do likewise. In other contexts, an adult might make remarks such as the following:

  - "That was a delicious cookie! I'd like another but I won't take it because I want to be healthy."
  - "Let's talk about it later. I'm angry now and need to cool down first."
  - "I know those word problems take a while to finish. One thing I do with a big project is break it up and take a quick break when I'm half-way through; I also reward myself when I'm all finished."

- **Protect adolescents from their distinct vulnerabilities.** Adolescents have more advanced cognitive skills than do younger children but face definite challenges in resisting certain temptations. Particular areas in the brain mature unevenly during adolescence, causing some vexing problems with self-regulation (A. A. Baird, 2010; Ernst & Hardin, 2010; Van Leijenhorst & Crone, 2010). During adolescence, neurological circuits for emotions, sensitivity to rewards, and social interests outpace networks for judgment and restraint. As a result, adolescents find it difficult to stay focused on academic tasks when peers entice them with high-spirited adventures. Many secondary teachers provide outlets for social needs by arranging for students to work together in teams (Dyson & Plunkett, 2012; Slavin, Lake, & Groff, 2009). On school grounds, risky activities need to be discouraged and group activities supervised, as even compliant and conscientious students can easily succumb to temptation.

Teachers and other practitioners can mention occasions when they are prioritizing a long-term goal over a short-term reward (e.g., "I'd love to go to that concert this weekend but I'm almost done with my master's thesis and need to work on the discussion section"). When learning a new computer application, they could suggest how they'll be able to be more facile with it if they browse through the tutorial first.

The Development and Practice feature "Teaching Self-Regulation Skills" includes several illustrations of the strategies just described. Adults play a crucial role in fostering keep tabs on children's ability to take charge of their own learning and changing tactics when persisting with faulty techniques.

DEVELOPMENT AND PRACTICE
Teaching Self-Regulation Skills

Have children observe and record their own activities.

- When a third-grade student has trouble staying on task, her teacher asks her to stop and reflect on her behavior every 10 minutes (with aid of an egg timer) and determine whether she has been on task at the time. The student uses the following checklist to record her observations. Within a couple of weeks, the student's on-task behavior has noticeably improved. (Middle Childhood)

Self-Observation Record for _____ Karen _____

Every ten minutes, put a mark to show how well you have been staying on task.

+   means you were almost always on task
1/2 means you were on task about half the time
−   means you were hardly ever on task

9:00-9:10	9:10-9:20	9:20-9:30	9:30-9:40	9:40-9:50	9:50-10:00
+	+	−	+	1/2	−
10:00-10:10	10:10-10:20	10:20-10:30	10:30-10:40	10:40-10:50	10:50-11:00
1/2	−	recess		+	1/2
11:00-11:10	11:10-11:20	11:20-11:30	11:30-11:40	11:40-11:50	11:50-12:00

- A high school adviser notices that one of his students is getting low grades. After a discussion with him the adviser finds that the young man often forgets to do his homework and at other times forgets to check his backpack for finished homework. The teacher develops a weekly calendar for the boy and checks with him to see that he has written his due dates on the calendar and crossed off assignments as he gives them to his teachers. (Late Adolescence)

Teach children instructions they can apply themselves.

- A counselor helps a fifth grader control his impulsive behavior on multiple-choice tests by having him mentally say to himself as he reads each question: "Read the entire question. Then look at each answer carefully and decide whether it is correct or incorrect. Then choose the answer that seems *most* correct." (Middle Childhood)
- A high school history teacher advises his students of what they can do to begin their homework. She tells them, "Remind yourself to use the **POM** strategy: **P**repare your learning space, **O**rganize your materials by taking out your history book and a pen and paper for taking notes, and **M**inimize your distractions by turning the television off, silencing your cell phone, and getting to work." (Late Adolescence)

Help children identify ways to make tedious tasks more rewarding.

- A third-grade teacher suggests that students practice writing the week's new spelling words at home every night. "That might not sound like much fun," she says, "but it's an important thing to do. Who can think of a way to make spelling practice more fun?" One student suggests writing out words in rainbow colors or spelling them out in crossword puzzles. Another suggests trying to think of sentences that spell the words with first letters—for example, *"Eighty-nine overweight unicorns get hiccups"* spells *enough.* (Middle Childhood)
- A high school chemistry explains the order of elements in the periodic table and encourages students to attend to atomic number (across) and chemical characteristics (down). He demonstrates how sodium and lithium in the first group react vigorously when dropped in water to help students visualize a basic common property of these two elements. When students study the table, they remember the properties of elements that they have observed. (Late Adolescence)

Teach children to reward themselves for appropriate behavior.

- A middle school teacher suggests that her students are more likely to develop regular study habits if they make a favorite activity—for example, shooting baskets or watching television—contingent on completing homework first. (Early Adolescence)
- A high school geography class has been fascinated with recent lessons on cultural exchanges among people who have migrated from one country to another. After moving to a unit on properties of maps, the teacher finds that students have lost their enthusiasm. The teacher acknowledges that students may find certain geography topics more interesting than others. To help them stay engaged, he encourages them to identify a reward (perhaps a pizza party, free period, or choice for an upcoming topic) that they can earn when everyone has completed the project on mapping. (Late Adolescence)

Encourage children to evaluate their own performance.

- A middle school mathematics teacher has students grade their own mathematics homework. After totaling up their points, students enter their scores in an electronic assignment log. Students also enter a few narrative comments on how they are doing and whether or not they need help with any concepts. Those who need assistance see the teacher during the last 10 minutes of class. (Early Adolescence)
- Early in baseball season, the coach of a boys' baseball team videotapes each athlete as he practices batting, pitching, and fielding ground balls. The coach then models good form for each of these activities and lists several things the boys should look for as they watch themselves on tape. (Late Adolescence)

Summary

With age and experience, most children become increasingly able to control their own behavior. They more effectively restrain their impulses and emotional reactions, gradually internalize adults' rules and restrictions, and evaluate their own actions using appropriate criteria. Yet even at the high school level, some youngsters don't regulate their behaviors effectively. Adults promote self-regulation by establishing definite guidelines for behavior while also attending to children's needs, listening to their perspectives, and providing a reasonable rationale for restrictions. Adults can also model self-regulating behaviors, give children age-appropriate opportunities for independence, and teach such specific skills as self-monitoring, self-instructions, self-motivation, and self-evaluation.

ENHANCEDetext *self-check*

Assessing Children 13-1

Listen to second-grader Keenan's comments about her self-regulation of reading and writing skills.

ENHANCEDetext *application exercise*

Extrinsic and Intrinsic Motivation

Virtually all children and adolescents are motivated in one way or another. Achilles expresses interest in science and seeks out challenging coursework. Ethan is more concerned with social affairs, interacting with peers, and texting friends. Mia is focused on athletics, excels in physical education classes, and works out daily in hopes of making the varsity soccer team.

Sometimes youngsters have strong **extrinsic motivation**: They are motivated to attain or avoid certain consequences in the outside world. They may complete a classroom assignment in order to get adult approval (as Amy did in the opening case), or they may try to earn passing grades to avoid punishment from their family. At other times youngsters have deep **intrinsic motivation**: They are motivated by factors within themselves or inherent in a task they are performing. They might read a book simply for the pleasure it brings, experiment with various kite shapes to find out which one flies best (as Sara did), or return a wallet to its owner as a way of being true to an internal moral code.

Both extrinsic and intrinsic motivation can spur children to acquire new knowledge and skills and engage in productive behaviors. But intrinsic motivation has numerous advantages over extrinsic motivation. Intrinsically motivated children are eager to learn classroom material, willingly tackle assigned tasks, use effective learning strategies, and achieve at high levels. In contrast, extrinsically motivated children may have to be enticed or prodded, are apt to study classroom topics only superficially, and are often interested in performing only easy tasks and meeting minimal classroom requirements (Froiland & Oros, 2014; A. E. Gottfried, Fleming, & Gottfried, 2001; R. M. Ryan & Deci, 2009). Extrinsic motivation has its own advantages, though. Knowing that children will work hard to achieve certain rewards, teachers and other practitioners can motivate them with incentives for exhibiting mature behavior. We examine that issue now.

Factors Affecting Extrinsic Motivation

Human beings of all ages usually behave in ways that bring desired results. In an early theory of learning known as *operant conditioning*, the American behaviorist **B. F. Skinner** (1904–1990) proposed that children engage in behaviors that lead to pleasant consequences, which he called **reinforcers** (e.g., Skinner, 1953, 1968).[4] From Skinner's

Preparing for Your Licensure Examination
Your teaching test might ask you to distinguish between extrinsic and intrinsic motivation.

perspective, people voluntarily choose behaviors that are currently being reinforced or have often been reinforced in the past. Miguel might practice the piano regularly if his parents continually compliment his efforts. Brigita might throw frequent temper tantrums if she's learned that these fits are the only way she can get special toys or privileges. Peter might misbehave in class if doing so gains him the attention of his teacher and classmates. The last of these examples illustrates an important point: Reinforcers are not always what we would typically think of as "rewards." The attention Peter gets for his misbehavior may seem unpleasant to others: Peter's teacher may scold him for acting out, or his classmates might shake their heads in disapproval. But if Peter's misbehaviors increase as a result, then the attention is indeed a reinforcer.

Concepts in behavioral learning. In early infancy, children are largely concerned with **primary reinforcers**, those rewards that satisfy built-in needs or desires. Some primary re-inforcers, such as food and drinks, are essential for health. Others, such as physical affection, cuddling, and smiles, are more social in nature. Human beings seem to have evolved to ap-preciate social reinforcers as ways of enhancing their connections to others and so, indirectly, enhancing their chances of survival (Harlow & Zimmerman, 1959; Vollmer & Hackenberg, 2001).

Over time, children begin to associate other consequences with primary reinforcers. A child might discover that approval from Mother often comes with a candy treat or that a good grade frequently leads to a hug from Father. Through such associations, consequences such as praise, money, good grades, and attention (sometimes even attention in the form of a scolding) become reinforcing in their own right. That is, they become **secondary reinforcers**. Because secondary reinforcers are consequences that children *learn* to appreciate, and be-cause children have widely different upbringings, the effectiveness of any one of them will differ considerably from one child to the next.

Although Skinner argued that direct reinforcement to children was necessary to influ-ence their behavior, as social learning theorists have found that children's motivation is af-fected not only by children's own experiences but also by the consequences they see *other people* receive (Bandura, 1965, 1977). In other words, observed consequences may affect children vicariously. In **vicarious reinforcement**, a child who observes a peer being rein-forced for doing something is likely to behave similarly. Psychologists and educators today are inclined to take advantage of children's self-regulatory and social learning skills rather than taking the hard line that Skinner did, asserting that children's mental lives—their goals, expectations, and strategic abilities—are irrelevant to the acquisition of mature behaviors. As you will recall from our earlier discussion of self-regulation, children use their abilities to plan ahead and inhibit their impulses in order to achieve the rewards they want.

Reinforcement in the classroom. Principles of reinforcement are an invaluable part of any teacher's toolkit especially when children's long-term needs to be self-regulating are part of the plan (Austin & Bevan, 2011; DeLeon, Bullock, & Catania, 2013; Kamps, 2002). In order to use reinforcement effectively, teachers and other practitioners need to identify the type of behavior they would like children to achieve—perhaps sitting in their seat and paying atten-tion (rather than continually getting up and wandering around the room). To give children a realistic chance for achieving progress toward that goal, teachers must establish interim targets whose mastery gets them closer to mature behavior. Thus, although Ms. Owens might prefer for her first-grade students to be on task for the entire school day, she would select a briefer time frame, say, a 15-minute interval, to begin with and advise her students of the expected standard of behavior in working quietly. She then might walk around the room and put a gold star on the papers of children who have been on task, praising them, and saying for example, "Tom, I like the way you are working so quietly and carefully on your assignment. Good job!"

These techniques have become an especially valuable resource for children with special needs. Educator Ann Turnbull and her colleagues illustrate the process with Jane, an adolescent girl with autism who needs assistance in acquiring adaptive behaviors for everyday life.[5] Jane wants approval from her teacher, and thus praise is used as a reinforcer (Turnbull, Turnbull, & Wehmeyer, 2010). In the process of learning to sort silverware, Jane

---

[5]Autism and the autism spectrum disorders are examined in Chapter 12.

is first shown a *discriminative stimulus*, a reminder that a particular response is necessary. Next, she emits the desired *response* of placing the utensils in their proper places and finally receives *reinforcement*, verbal praise. Here's how Jane is coached in sorting silverware:

> You lay a spoon, a fork, and a knife in front of her and provide a discriminative stimulus by saying, "Jane, show me the spoon." Most likely, Jane will point to or touch one of the utensils, or, if she is not certain, not respond at all. If she points to the spoon, you immediately praise her, saying, "Great job, Jane! That's right, that's the spoon." Your praise constitutes the reinforcing stimulus. If she points to a different utensil or to none of them, she does not get your reinforcer (verbal praise); instead, you prompt her again to identify the spoon. Eventually, if you reinforce ("Great job!"), her correct response (pointing to the spoon) to your discriminative stimulus ("Show me the spoon"), while ignoring or not reinforcing Jane's other responses, she will respond more consistently to the stimulus with the appropriate response. (Turnbull et al., 2010, p. 322)

The characteristics of children shape how reinforcement is implemented. For young children, immediate reinforcement is most effective in managing behavior, given their limited ability to delay gratification (J. C. Coleman et al., 2012). Desires for types of rewards vary by age and individual preference, making it worthwhile for teachers to ask students about preferences. Some teachers administer simple surveys to students to get feedback on options—would they like puzzles, 15 minutes of free time with classmates, popcorn, or something else (Panahon & Martens, 2013)? With students who are seriously disruptive, the teacher usually consults a psychologist or special educator, sometimes with help from parents, and designs a customized plan that reinforces appropriate actions.

Punishment at school. Once in a while children are neither intrinsically motivated to acquire important skills nor responsive to simple reinforcement. In rare cases when children persist with a particular misbehavior despite adults' best efforts, punishment is sometimes used. Psychologists define **punishment** as a consequence that *decreases* the frequency of the response it follows.[6] Whereas children are likely to behave in ways that lead to reinforcement, they are *un*likely to behave in ways that lead to punishment. Punishment of undesirable responses (e.g., engaging in off-task behaviors during a lesson), especially when combined with reinforcement of more productive responses (e.g., sitting attentively during the lesson), can bring about improvements in children's behavior (Minshawi et al., 2014; Walters & Grusec, 1977).

In working with children with serious behavioral problems, teachers may award points (reinforcement) for appropriate behaviors and take away points (punishment) for misbehaviors. After a certain time interval (perhaps at the end of the day or week), children can exchange the points they've accumulated for small toys or privileges. Taking away previously earned points for unacceptable behavior (a strategy called *response cost*) can be effective in bringing about behavior change (Landrum & Kauffman, 2006; K. D. O'Leary & O'Leary, 1972).

However, punishment is a tool of last resort. Punishment does not by itself teach a more productive behavior and can have unwanted effects. Punishment that takes the form of aggression, inflicts physical or psychological harm, or involves suspension or expulsion from school has been shown to be ineffective (S. A. Hemphill & Schneider, 2013; Luiselli, 2009; Skiba, 2014). After such punishment, students may reduce the targeted behavior temporarily but become angry and humiliated and exhibit increases in antagonistic behavior. Suspensions and expulsions are also problematic because students are deprived of valuable educational experiences.

Children sometimes reduce a certain behavior after observing others being punished for it. In **vicarious punishment**, a child who sees a peer being punished for a particular behavior is unlikely to behave in that way. For example, children might learn that exhibiting unsportsman-like conduct on the playing field results in being benched during the next game. As a result, they make an effort to control their temper on the field.

---

[6]Be aware that the term *negative reinforcement* is *not* a synonym for punishment. Negative reinforcement increases rather than decreases the behavior it follows by removing an unpleasant stimulus and causing a sense of relief in the person. Punishment decreases the behavior it follows.

Preparing for Your Licensure Examination
Your teaching test might ask you how reinforcement can be implemented in the classroom.

Observing Children 13-3
Observe children explain a program of reinforcement used in their class.
ENHANCEDetext *video example*

FOR FURTHER EXPLORATION . . .
Learn more about types, effects, and uses of punishment.
ENHANCEDetext *content extension*

Factors Affecting Intrinsic Motivation

Although children actively select behaviors that maximize rewards and minimize punishments, they also manage their conduct according to internal factors—especially, their personal interests. As the following principles reveal, some of the factors underlying intrinsic motivation are at work early in life, whereas others emerge over time as children learn more about themselves and the environment.

Observing Children 13-4

Observe a young child exploring a toy with intrinsic motivation.

ENHANCEDetext *video example*

Children have a natural predisposition to explore their environment. Following in **Jean Piaget's** (1896–1980) footsteps, many developmental theorists believe that children are naturally curious about their world and actively seek out information to make sense of it (Alvarez & Booth, 2014; R. M. Ryan & Deci, 2009; Taffoni et al., 2014).[7] Infants constantly experiment with objects to discover their properties and with actions to determine their effects. Later, as children gain proficiency in their native language, they also ask questions (e.g., "How do they make statues?" "Why does it rain sometimes?") to satisfy their curiosity (Callanan & Oakes, 1992, p. 218; Kemler Nelson, Egan, & Holt, 2004). You can observe a young child's intrinsic motivation to explore her physical world in an Observing Children video.

Children strive for consistency in understanding the world. Jean Piaget suggested that another key factor driving a child's learning is *disequilibrium*, an inconsistency between new information and what the child believes to be true. According to Piaget, disequilibrium causes mental discomfort and spurs the child to integrate, reorganize, and in some cases replace existing schemes with new ideas and procedures that better align with the new information. Like Piaget, many contemporary developmental theorists believe that beginning early in life, human beings have an innate need to see the world in a coherent manner (Bronson, 2000; B. Hayes & Rehder, 2012; Keil, 2010).

Children choose activities at which they think they can be successful. Some psychologists propose that an important source of intrinsic motivation is an innate need to feel *competent*—to believe that one can deal effectively with the environment (K. Richards & Levesque-Bristol, 2014; R. M. Ryan & Deci, 2009). A need for competence pushes children to acquire increasingly effective ways for dealing with their surroundings. It may be one important reason why we human beings have, over the course of time, been able to adapt successfully to many different habitats (R. White, 1959). As you can see in an Observing Children video, 9-year-old Elena expresses interest and confidence in her mathematics, her favorite subject:

Observing Children 13-5

Notice the importance of challenge at school to 9-year-old Elena.

ENHANCEDetext *video example*

Interviewer: What do you like best about school?
Elena: I like PEAK [a program for students identified as gifted]. It's this thing where you go to this program. It's for smart kids who have, like, good ideas for stuff you could do. And so they make it more challenging for you in school. So instead of third-grade math, you get fourth-grade math.
Interviewer: What do teachers do that encourage you to do well at school?
Greg: [S]ome of them kind of make it a competition, like class rank and stuff. . . . And that makes you want to. . . . And the challenge. If it's a really hard class, then I . . . will usually try harder in harder classes.

To maintain and enhance their sense of competence, children are apt to choose and persist at activities for which they have high **self-efficacy**—that is, on activities at which they believe they can be successful (Bandura, 1997, 2012; Schunk & Pajares, 2009). In the opening case study, Sara reveals a high sense of self-efficacy about building a kite: "I had no doubts because I knew that I could really do it; I knew I could put this together really well" (D. K. Meyer et al., 1997, p. 512). Once youngsters have high self-efficacy for a task or activity, they eagerly seek out challenges that will enhance their skills and knowledge.

When children have *low* self-efficacy for an activity or content domain, they may try to avoid it as much as possible. A student with a reading disability reveals one strategy:

When it comes time for reading I do everything under the sun I can to get out of it because it's my worst nightmare to read. I'll say I have to go to the bathroom or that I'm sick and I have

[7]Piaget's theory of cognitive development is examined in depth in Chapter 6.

to go to the nurse right now. My teacher doesn't know that I'll be walking around campus. She thinks I am going to the bathroom or whatever my lame excuse is. All I really want to do is get out of having to read. (Zambo & Brem, 2004, p. 5)

Children prefer activities for which they have autonomy. As early as 6 months of age, infants become frustrated when a parent stops them from moving their arms freely or when a device they've learned to operate successfully unexpectedly stops playing music (Braungart-Rieker, Hill-Soderlund, & Karrass, 2010; M. W. Sullivan & Lewis, 2003). By 14 months, infants actively resist parents' requests that would prevent them from reaching their immediate goal (e.g., "Put the cookie down") (Dix, Stewart, Gershoff, & Day, 2007). In general, children are more intrinsically motivated when they have a **sense of self-determination** (R. M. Ryan & Deci, 2009; Sebire, Jago, Fox, Edwards, & Thompson, 2013). A child who thinks "I *want* to do this" or "I'd *like* to learn more about that" has a high sense of self-determination. A child who thinks "I *must* do this" or "*My teacher wants* me to learn that" thinks that someone is directing the course of events. You can listen to Alicia articulate her need for self-determination in selecting literature in an Observing Children video.

Observing Children 13-6
Observe Alicia's need for self-determination in selecting her own literature.

ENHANCEDetext *video example*

Developmental Trends in Intrinsic Motivation

As you are learning, a child's intrinsic motivation is a vital capacity that evolves with age and experience. Let's consider the major changes.

As children grow older, their interests become increasingly stable. When we say that children have an *interest* in a topic or activity, we mean that they find it intriguing or rewarding in and of itself. Interest, then, is one form of intrinsic motivation. Psychologists distinguish between two general types of *interest* (Hidi, Renninger, & Krapp, 2004; Middleton, 2013; Schiefele, 2009). **Situational interest** is evoked by something in the environment—something that is perhaps new, unusual, or surprising. In contrast, **personal interest** comes from within the child and is largely unrelated to immediate circumstances.

In infancy and early childhood, interests are mostly situational and short lived: Young children are readily attracted to novel, attention-getting stimuli and events for, say, a few seconds or minutes (Courage, Reynolds, & Richards, 2006; Elkins, 2013). Sometimes these encounters plant the seeds from which longer-term personal interests grow (Hidi & Renninger, 2006). By the middle to upper elementary grades—sometimes even earlier—children acquire longstanding personal interests, perhaps in animal life or mechanical movements, which persist over a period of time and ultimately become important parts of children's identities (J. M. Alexander, Johnson, Leibham, & Kelley, 2008; Hidi et al., 2004; Middleton, 2013). Joey displayed an exceptional interest in art beginning at age 3. As you can see in Artifact 13-1, he had a long-term interest in drawing the human form and, later, in fashion design.

Age 8　　　　　　　Age 11　　　　　　　Age 17

ARTIFACT 13-1　Joey's portraits. In these drawings, Joey shows his personal interest in drawing the human form.

Children increasingly pursue activities that they perceive to be of instrumental value. A task or activity has **value** when children believe there are benefits in performing it (Dweck & Elliott, 1983; M. Wang & Eccles, 2013; Wigfield & Eccles, 2000). Some activities are valued because they are associated with certain personal qualities. A boy who wants to be smart and thinks that smart people do well in school will place a premium on academic success. Other activities have high value because they are means to desired goals. Much as she disliked mathematics, Jeanne's daughter Tina struggled through math classes throughout high school because many colleges require 4 years of math. Still other activities are valued simply because they bring enjoyment (Eccles & Wigfield, 1985; Zhu, Sun, Chen, & Ennis, 2012). An adolescent may value watching movies or reading novels for the sheer pleasure of the activities.

The type of value that children place in schoolwork changes developmentally. In the elementary grades, children primarily choose activities they perceive to be interesting and enjoyable. As they reach adolescence and proceed through the secondary grades, they increasingly choose activities that, in their minds at least, will be instrumental to their achievement of personal goals (Eccles, Wigfield, & Schiefele, 1998; Wigfield, Tonks, & Eccles, 2004).

As children develop, children tend *not* to value activities that require more effort than they're worth. A teenager who would ideally like to get straight As in school may downplay the importance of As if she finds that they cut into her social life (e.g., Otis, Grouzet, & Pelletier, 2005). Children also *de*value activities that they associate with frustration and failure ("I don't see why I need to do these stupid geometry proofs!") and that lessen their sense of competence ("I've never been good at math. It's dumb anyway") (Lawanto, Santoso, & Yang Liu, 2012; Wigfield & Eccles, 2000).

Over time, children internalize the motivation to engage in certain activities. As children grow older, most adopt at least some of the values and priorities of the people around them. Such **internalized motivation** typically develops gradually, perhaps in the sequence depicted in Figure 13-2 (R. M. Ryan & Deci, 2009). Initially, children may engage in some activities primarily because of the external consequences that result. Students may do schoolwork to earn praise or avoid being punished for poor grades. With time other people's approval becomes increasingly important to children. Eventually children internalize the "pressure" to perform certain activities and see these activities as important in their own right. Such internalization of values is most likely to occur if adults who espouse those values (parents, teachers, etc.) do the following:

- Engage in valued activities themselves.
- Provide a warm, supportive, and somewhat structured environment for children.
- Offer enough autonomy that children have a sense of self-determination about their actions.

(Jacobs, Davis-Kean, Bleeker, Eccles, & Malanchuk, 2005; R. M. Ryan, Connell, & Grolnick, 1992; R. M. Ryan & Deci, 2000; K. M. Sheldon, 2013)

Some of our readers may think that internalized motivation is essentially the same as intrinsic motivation. Certainly internalized motivation is a *form* of intrinsic motivation, in that it comes from inside the child rather than from things in the here-and-now environment. But in one important way it is quite different from other forms of intrinsic motivation. Intrinsic motivation that arises spontaneously within the child (e.g., curiosity about an intriguing object) can increase or decrease somewhat unpredictably. In contrast, because internalized motivation eventually becomes an integral part of their beliefs about who they are as human beings, it remains fairly stable and dependable over time (Otis et al., 2005; Reeve, Deci, & Ryan, 2004; R. M. Ryan & Deci, 2009).

Intrinsic motivation for learning school subject matter declines during the school years. Young children are often eager to learn new things at school. But sometime in elementary school, children become less intrinsically motivated to learn classroom topics (Corpus, McClintic-Gilbert, & Hayenga, 2009; Gillet, Vallerand, & Lafrenière, 2012; Spinath & Steinmayr, 2008, 2012). Their

1. External regulation. Children may initially be motivated to behave (or not to behave) in certain ways based primarily on the external consequences that follow behaviors; that is, children are extrinsically motivated.

2. Introjection. Children begin to behave in ways that gain the approval of others, partly as a way of protecting and enhancing their sense of self. They feel guilty when they violate certain standards for behavior but do not fully understand the rationale behind these standards.

3. Identification. Children begin to regard certain behaviors as being personally important or valuable to themselves.

4. Integration. Children integrate certain behaviors into their overall system of motives and values. In essence, these behaviors become a central part of their sense of self.

FIGURE 13-2   Emergence of internalized motivation. *Based on R. M. Ryan & Deci, 2009.*

intrinsic motivation may be especially low when youngsters are anxious, such as during the transition from elementary to secondary-school (Eccles & Roeser, 2009; Wigfield, Byrnes, & Eccles, 2006).

The decline in intrinsic motivation for academic subject matter is probably due to several factors. As children move through the grade levels, evidence mounts that they are not necessarily as competent as some of their peers, and with this awareness they may shy away from activities for which they have low self-efficacy (Harter, 1992, 1996; Wigfield et al., 2006). Frequent reminders of the importance of good grades for promotion, graduation, and college admission may undermine students' intrinsic motivation and sense of self-determination (Deci & Ryan, 1992; Eccles & Roeser, 2009). In addition, as youngsters grow older, they may become increasingly bored and impatient with highly structured, repetitive activities, especially those delivered in a take-it-or-leave-it fashion (Battistich, Solomon, Kim, Watson, & Schaps, 1995; Headden, 2013). The following interview with a high school student named Alfredo illustrates this last point:

Adult:	Do you think your classes are interesting?
Alfredo:	Some of them are. But some of them are boring. You go to the same class every day and you just do the same type of work every day. Like biology, I like [the teacher of this] class. She's about the only one I like. And last year I had the same problem. The only class I liked last year was science. . . . We used to do different things every day . . . but like classes like Reading, you go inside, read a story with the same person every day. That's boring.
Adult:	That's boring? So will you just not show up?
Alfredo:	No, I'll go but I won't do nothing sometimes. (dialogue from Way, 1998, p. 198)

Despite the typical downward trend in intrinsic motivation, some youngsters remain interested in academic subjects throughout the school years, especially if they have internalized the importance of school learning, encounter optimal levels of challenge, and are shown the relevance of academic concepts to students' interests (Eccles & Roeser, 2009; Froiland & Oros, 2014; Otis et al., 2005). Virtually all children have intrinsic motivation for *some* activities—perhaps for skateboarding, dancing, and playing electronic games. The Observation Guidelines table "Recognizing Intrinsic Motivation in Children's Behaviors" lists characteristics and behaviors to look for.

OBSERVATION GUIDELINES
Recognizing Intrinsic Motivation in Children's Behaviors

CHARACTERISTIC	LOOK FOR	EXAMPLE	IMPLICATION
Inquisitiveness	• *Eagerness to explore and learn* • *Fascination with objects, other people, or both* • *Frequent and thoughtful questions* • *Lack of concern about external rewards for learning*	Jamie often takes great interest in the new toys he finds at preschool. He is especially drawn to objects that come apart and can be reassembled.	Pique children's curiosity with puzzling situations, unusual phenomena, and opportunities to explore. Make sure the environment is safe for exploration.
High Self-Efficacy	• *Obvious pleasure during learning* • *Eagerness to tackle challenging topics and activities* • *Willingness to make mistakes*	Luana delights in tackling the brainteasers that her math teacher occasionally assigns for extra credit.	Give children the support they need to succeed at challenging tasks. Use evaluation procedures that do not penalize mistakes.
Autonomy	• *Pursuit of self-chosen activities* • *Willingness to engage in minimally structured tasks* • *Sensitivity to issues with control*	Mark, Reggie, and Cynthia form a rock band and practice together every chance they get. They actively seek out "gigs" at school and in the community.	Provide opportunities for children to pursue self-chosen activities. Give them only as much structure as they need to achieve instructional goals.

(continued)

OBSERVATION GUIDELINES (continued)
Recognizing Intrinsic Motivation in Children's Behaviors

CHARACTERISTIC	LOOK FOR	EXAMPLE	IMPLICATION
Effective Learning Strategies	• *Focus on making sense of subject matter*, rather than on rote memorization of facts • *Persistence* in trying to solve difficult problems and understand complex ideas	Lenesia reads an assigned chapter in her geography textbook. Despite reading the section on mountain formation several times, she is confused about how folded mountains form. The following day she asks her teacher to explain the process.	In instruction and assessment activities, emphasize genuine understanding and integration of the subject matter, rather than rote memorization of isolated facts. Explicitly teach learning strategies and methods for monitoring their use.
Long-Term Interests	• *Consistent selection of a particular topic* when choices are given • *Frequent initiation of activities* in a particular domain	Whenever his after-school group goes to the local library, Connor looks for books about military battleships and aircraft.	Relate subject matter to children's interests and needs. Give them occasional choices regarding topics they study and write about.
Priorities	• *Consistent pursuit of certain activities* and disregard of alternatives • *Apparent adoption of other people's values* (e.g., a strong work ethic) as one's own, reflecting internalized motivation	Audrey is clearly frustrated when unexpected events at home prevent her from doing an assignment as thoroughly as she'd like. "Even though I got an A," she says later, "I didn't do as well as I *could* have if I'd had more time."	Encourage activities that will be in youngsters' best interest over the long run. Do so in a warm, supportive environment in which youngsters have input into decision making.

Intrinsic and extrinsic motivations develop hand in hand and occasionally interact such that one or the other takes precedence. A girl who originally likes to dance for the challenge and pleasure of the movement may become increasingly motivated by accolades from her parents and instructor. A boy who is at first dependent on reinforcement for good behavior may ultimately decide that he likes to cooperate on his own accord. The Basic Developmental Issues table "Contrasting Extrinsic and Intrinsic Motivation" explains how these two types of motivation relate to recurrent themes in children's growth.

BASIC DEVELOPMENTAL ISSUES
Contrasting Extrinsic and Intrinsic Motivation

ISSUE	EXTRINSIC MOTIVATION	INTRINSIC MOTIVATION
Nature and Nurture	Primary reinforcers satisfy inborn and presumably inherited needs (e.g., hunger, thirst). Secondary reinforcers acquire their reinforcing effects through regular association with primary reinforcers.	Children have a natural curiosity about the world. Their needs to feel competent and resolve inconsistencies may be inborn. Other factors that contribute to intrinsic motivation, such as confidence in an ability, depend on experience.
Universality and Diversity	By and large, primary reinforcers are universal. Secondary reinforcers (e.g., praise) are *learned* reinforcers; thus, their effectiveness differs from child to child. Individual differences also exist in the types of rewards that children find desirable.	Innate sources of motivation, such as curiosity and a need to feel competent, are universal, as is the goal-directed nature of human behavior. Yet individuals have diverse interests, values, and goals, and they attribute their successes and failures to different factors.
Qualitative and Quantitative Change	Children increasingly delay gratification, a trend that reflects quantitative change. Occasionally children respond differently to awards over time with a qualitative change. A child who appreciates a teacher's praise in elementary school may later, as an adolescent, *avoid* compliments due to fear of peer ridicule.	Children shift from exclusively pursuing their own interests to internalizing some of the priorities and values of people around them, reflecting qualitative change. But for many youngsters, intrinsic motivation for learning subject matter declines over the school years, as a quantitative trend.

Summary

Motivation energizes, directs, and sustains behavior. It can be either extrinsic (evoked largely by the external consequences that certain behaviors bring) or intrinsic (emanating from characteristics within a person or inherent in a task being performed). On average, children who are intrinsically motivated use more effective learning strategies and achieve at higher levels than those who are extrinsically motivated.

One key source of extrinsic motivation is the extent to which either primary reinforcers (things that satisfy built-in biological needs) or secondary reinforcers (things that have become reinforcing through frequent association with other reinforcing consequences) follow various behaviors. With age, children become increasingly able to forgo small, immediate rewards in favor of larger, delayed ones. An additional source of extrinsic motivation is punishment: Children tend to avoid behaviors that have previously led to unpleasant consequences either for themselves or for others.

Research on intrinsic motivation has implications for fostering children's sense of competence and control. The principles of reinforcement are invaluable to professionals, especially in managing classrooms and other group environments. In the process of this work, adults should strive to maintain an orderly environment that is conducive to learning, but in which the long-term goal of making progress toward self-regulation is a priority.

ENHANCEDetext *self-check*

Assessing Children 13-2

Examine Mr. Wimberley's tactics in managing his sixth-grade classroom and intervening with two disputing boys.

ENHANCEDetext *application exercise*

GOALS AND ATTRIBUTIONS

Many psychologists believe that human beings are purposeful in their nature. Children set goals for themselves and choose behaviors to achieve them (Boekaerts, 2009; Dweck & Elliott, 1983; E. Higgins & Scholer, 2015). Some goals ("I want to finish reading my dinosaur book") are transitory. Others ("I want to be a paleontologist") can be enduring. Seeing purpose in activity also extends to explanations for performance and achievement. Children are prompted to explain to themselves why they accomplished a goal and why, in other circumstances, they struggled without meeting a standard.

Development of Goals

Short-term goals emerge in infancy. As infants develop their motor skills (reaching, grabbing, crawling, etc.), they become capable of getting things they want. When one end of a string is attached to a 2-month-old baby's foot and the other end is attached to a mobile, at some point the baby realizes that foot motion makes the mobile move (Mash, Bornstein, & Banerjee, 2014; Rovee-Collier, 1999; Rovee-Collier & Cuevas, 2009). The infant begins to shake his or her foot vigorously, apparently as a way to accomplish the objective of attaining the interesting visual display. Later, with the onset of crawling and reaching, the world is theirs for the taking.

As children grow and mature neurologically, they pursue longer-term and more broadly based goals. Being happy and healthy, doing well in school, learning about the world, getting along with peers, bringing honor to the family, and having a romantic partner are just a few of the many possibilities (M. E. Ford, 1996; Schutz, 1994; Taffoni et al., 2014). Of course, individual children differ in their foremost goals. Those who attain high levels of academic achievement typically make classroom learning a high priority. Those who achieve at lower levels are often more concerned with maintaining social relationships (Wentzel & Wigfield, 1998; Wigfield, Eccles, & Pintrich 1996).

Achievement Goals

Let's return to the opening case study. Sara is primarily concerned with constructing a kite that flies well, and she redesigns it three times to make it more aerodynamic. She doesn't mind the occasional stumbling blocks she encounters: "I mean everybody learns from their mistakes. I know I do" (D. K. Meyer et al., 1997, p. 511). In contrast, Amy sticks with her initial design, one that is easy to make but never gets off the ground. She says that she is primarily concerned with pleasing her teacher and parents, acknowledges that she rarely takes risks at school if a good grade is at stake, and then adds, "I feel lazy because I don't like to make challenges for myself, to make goals. I just like to . . . do it as I go along, not make goals or challenges" (p. 510).

Both girls want to do well in school; that is, they both have *achievement goals*. However, their reasons for wanting to do well are quite different. Sara has a **mastery goal**: She wants to acquire new knowledge and skills related to kites and their construction, and to do so she must inevitably make a few mistakes. Amy has a **performance goal**: She wants to present herself as competent in the eyes of others and so tries to avoid making mistakes (Dweck & Master, 2009; Mega, Ronconi, & De Beni, 2014; Nicholls, 1984).[8]

Researchers have found it helpful to distinguish between two kinds of performance goals. In a **performance-approach goal**, the focus is on achieving positive outcomes, such as good grades, adult approval, or respect from classmates. In a **performance-avoidance goal**, the focus is more on *avoiding undesirable* outcomes, such as exhibiting poor performance in public or being the subject of peer ridicule. Performance goals sometimes have an element of social comparison, in that children are concerned with how their accomplishments compare to those of their peers (A. J. Elliot & McGregor, 2000; Maehr & Zusho, 2009).

In most instances, mastery goals are the optimal situation. To the extent that children and adolescents have mastery goals, they engage in the very activities that will help them learn: They pay attention at school, study hard, and learn from their mistakes. Furthermore, they have a healthy perspective about learning, effort, and failure: They realize that learning is a process of trying hard and persevering even after temporary setbacks (E. M. Anderman & Maehr, 1994; Lüftenegger, van de Schoot, Schober, Finsterwald, & Spiel, 2014).

In contrast, children with performance goals—especially those with performance-*avoidance* goals—may be so concerned about how others evaluate them that they stay away from challenging tasks that might help them master new skills (Dweck, 1986; Schweinle, Berg, & Sorenson, 2013; Urdan, 1997). Performance-*approach* goals are a mixed bag: They sometimes have very positive effects, spurring children on to achieve at high levels, especially in combination with mastery goals (Linnenbrink, 2005; Maehr & Zusho, 2009). Yet by themselves, performance-approach goals may be less beneficial than mastery goals: To accomplish them, children may exert only the minimal effort required and use relatively superficial learning strategies such as rote memorization. Performance-approach goals appear to be most detrimental when children are fairly young (e.g., in the elementary grades) and have low self-efficacy for classroom tasks (Kaplan & Midgley, 1997; Midgley, Kaplan, & Middleton, 2001).

Mastery goals, performance-approach goals, and performance-avoidance goals are not necessarily mutually exclusive. On many occasions children have two kinds, or even all three (Covington & Müeller, 2001; Meece & Holt, 1993). However, the relative prevalence of different achievement goals changes with age. Most young children seem to be primarily concerned with mastery goals. But by the time they reach second grade, they begin to show signs of having performance goals as well, and such goals become increasingly prevalent as they move into middle and high school (Eccles & Midgley, 1989; A. J. Elliot & McGregor, 2000; Nicholls, Cobb, Yackel, Wood, & Wheatley, 1990). The greater emphasis on performance goals at older ages is due partly to youngsters' growing awareness of how

---

[8]You may sometimes see the term *learning goal* or *task involvement* instead of *mastery goal* and the term *ego involvement* instead of *performance goal* (e.g., Dweck & Elliott, 1983).

their performance compares with that of peers and also to an increasing focus on grades and other evaluations at the upper grade levels (Duchesne & Ratelle, 2010; Nicholls et al., 1990).

Social Goals

Human beings have a basic *need for relatedness*—that is, they want to feel socially connected with, and secure the love and respect of, other people. For infants and toddlers, this need is reflected in early efforts to engage other people through crying, smiling, eye contact, and imitation, and social exchanges. For many school-age children and adolescents, it may be reflected in the high priority they put on interacting with friends, sometimes at the expense of finishing chores, schoolwork, or other assigned tasks (Rodkin, Ryan, Jamison, & Wilson, 2013; Wigfield, Eccles, Mac Iver, Reuman, & Midgley, 1991). In an Observing Children video, 15-year-old Greg reveals the importance of social relationships in his life at school:

Observing Children 13-7
Observe how social connections are a priority for Greg.
ENHANCEDetext *video example*

Interviewer:	What do you like best about school?
Greg:	Lunch.
Interviewer:	Lunch?
Greg:	All the social aspects. . . . Just friends and cliques. . . .

Like Greg, many high school students find the nonacademic aspects of school to be the most enjoyable parts of the day (Otis et al., 2005).

Consistent with their need for relatedness, children are apt to have a variety of **social goals**, perhaps including the following:

- Forming and maintaining friendly or intimate relationships with other people
- Gaining other people's approval
- Helping one another achieve their goals
- Becoming part of a cohesive, mutually supportive group
- Achieving status and prestige within a peer group
- Meeting social obligations and keeping interpersonal commitments
- Assisting and supporting others, and ensuring their welfare (Beier, Over, & Carpenter, 2014; Berndt & Keefe, 1996; Dowson & McInerney, 2001; M. E. Ford & Smith, 2009)

Young people's social goals affect their behavior and performance in the classroom and in other group settings. If they are seeking friendly relationships with peers or are concerned about others' welfare, they may eagerly engage in such activities as cooperative learning and peer tutoring (Allodi, 2010; Dowson & McInerney, 2001; R. King, McInerney, & Watkins, 2012). If they want to gain adults' attention and approval, they are apt to strive for good grades and in other ways shoot for performance goals (Hinkley, McInerney, & Marsh, 2001). Those concerned with looking good in front of peers might study hard or not, depending on their academic goals and those of peers they wish to impress.

Future Aspirations

As you have learned, early goals are transitory. Young children regularly change their minds, perhaps wanting to be a firefighter one week and professional basketball player the next. In the later elementary school years, many children begin to formulate a few long-term goals (Harter, 1999; Oyserman & Markus, 1993; Usinger & Smith, 2010). They may want to go to college or pursue a career in a certain field.

Thus, career development takes a developmental course. In learning about jobs, children initially absorb information about typical jobs held by men and women in their society (R. B. Miller & Brickman, 2004). A little later, perhaps in middle childhood and early adolescence, children speculate about careers that seem feasible for them (Bandura, 1986). These initial interests are by no means firm commitments but rather general judgments of potentially desirable jobs. Their selections are based on perceptions of what they are capable of in specific domains (e.g., whether they like working with people and have an appetite for science). Young people also consider obstacles to working in these fields (possibly financial impediments, reactions from peers, their level of academic achievement) (Beal & Crockett, 2013). By middle to late adolescence, many (although by no means all) young people settle on a narrower range of careers (Marcia, 1980). Such preferences set the stage for more definite steps in career exploration, such as selecting high school classes necessary for college admission or vocational training.

For some young people, career exploration is difficult. Many young people do not have much insight into their own talents, as when an adolescent holds onto a dream of becoming a professional basketball player long after it becomes obvious to parents and the high school coach that the boy's short stature, slight build, and uncoordinated motor skills make it unlikely he will achieve this goal. Other youngsters are hampered because they have gained little exposure to the world of work, never having had a part-time job or been exposed to adults in challenging professions (S. L. Turner & Conkel, 2010).

Given the obstacles they face, along with challenges inherent in choosing a career, many young people need support in defining realistic goals. Being exposed to men and women in the community with a wide range of occupations is valuable exposure for youngsters, especially for those who lack such contacts. Adolescents may find it helpful to participate in career-exploration activities, for example, in completing surveys about their interests and values, reading about the requirements for jobs of interest, and selecting some preliminary fields to explore (S. L. Turner & Conkel, 2010). Some high schools require students to complete internships and other practical assignments in which students spend time in a job setting and observe the daily activities of employees (E. Levine, 2010; Xie & Reider, 2014). It is especially important for professionals to provide foundational experiences for young people from low-income backgrounds, perhaps introducing them to a person who holds a desirable job. Educators can also help high school students complete a college application, a daunting task, especially for those whose are not able to find guidance. Internships are particularly valuable for students from low-income backgrounds and those who do not have access to role models or practical experiences in career settings of interest.

Coordinating Multiple Goals

Most children have numerous goals that they juggle. Sometimes they find activities that allow them to achieve several goals simultaneously. They might satisfy both achievement goals and social goals by forming a study group to prepare for an exam. But at other times they may believe they have to abandon one goal to satisfy another (Boekaerts, 2009; Phelan, Yu, & Davidson, 1994). Youngsters who want to do well in school may choose not to perform at their best so that they can maintain relationships with peers who don't value academic achievement.

Students with mastery goals may find that the demands of school lead them to focus on performance goals (e.g., getting good grades) rather than studying the subject matter as thoroughly as they'd like. Brian, a junior high school student, expresses his ambivalence about striving for performance goals over mastery goals:

> I sit here and I say, "Hey, I did this assignment in five minutes and I still got an A on it." I still have a feeling that I could do better, and it was kind of cheap that I didn't do my best and I still got this A. . . . I think probably it might lower my standards eventually, which I'm not looking forward to at all. . . . I'll always know, though, that I have it in me. It's just that I won't express it that much. (S. Thomas & Oldfather, 1997, p. 119)

Teachers' instructional strategies and grading practices influence the extent to which students successfully juggle mastery goals with social and performance goals (Midgley, 2002). Students are more likely to invest their effort when assignments entice them to learn new skills (thus encouraging a focus on mastery), when they have occasional group projects (thus helping them also meet their social goals), and when evaluation criteria allow for mistakes (thus helping them meet their performance goals). Students are unlikely to strive for mastery goals when assignments ask little of them (consider Brian's concern about low standards), when teachers insist that they compete with one another for resources or strive for high test scores, and when any single failure has a significant impact on final grades.

Attributions

In the opening case study, Amy has not gotten her kite to fly. Even though she has put little effort into designing and constructing the kite, she chalks up her failure to insufficient wind and speculates that a successful kite would have been a matter of luck. In contrast, Sara, who has created a more aerodynamic kite, takes ownership of both her success ("I knew that I could really do it") and her little failures along the way ("I mean, everybody learns from their mistakes" [Meyer et al., 1997, p. 511]).

The various explanations people have for their successes and failures—or in some cases for the successes and failures of others—are called **attributions**. Children form a variety of attributions about the causes of events in their lives. They develop beliefs about why they do well or poorly on classroom assignments, why they are popular or have trouble making friends, why they are skilled athletes or total klutzes, and so on. They may attribute their successes and failures to such factors as aptitude or ability (how smart or proficient they are), effort (how hard they're trying), other people (how well an instructor teaches or likes them), task difficulty (how easy or hard something is), luck, mood, illness, fatigue, or physical appearance. Such attributions differ from one another in three general ways (Pasta, Mendola, Longobardi, Prino, & Gastaldi, 2013; Weiner, 1986, 2000, 2004):

- *Internal versus external.* Children may attribute the causes of events to factors within themselves (*internal* things) or to factors outside themselves (*external* things). In the opening case study, Sara's attributions are clearly internal, whereas Amy's are mostly external.
- *Stable versus unstable.* Children may believe either that events are due to *stable* factors, which probably won't change much in the near future, or to *unstable* factors, which do vary from one occasion to the next. Sara attributes her success to her own, relatively stable ability ("I knew that I could really do it"). In contrast, Amy's explanations of "not enough wind" and "beginner's luck" are based on unstable factors that change unpredictably.
- *Controllable versus uncontrollable.* Children may attribute events to *controllable* factors, which they can influence and change, or to *uncontrollable* factors, which they cannot influence. Sara clearly sees herself in control of her success ("I knew I could put this together really well, 'cause I had a lot of confidence in myself"), whereas Amy has no control over weather conditions or a lucky break.

Children's attributions are self-constructed *interpretations* that don't always match reality. In general, children tend to attribute their successes to internal causes (e.g., high ability, hard work) and their failures to external causes (e.g., bad luck, other people's behaviors; Marsh, 1990a; Whitley & Frieze, 1985). By patting themselves on the back for the things they do well and putting the blame elsewhere for poor performance, they can maintain a sense of competence (Clifford, 1990; S. G. Paris & Byrnes, 1989). Yet youngsters are most likely to be successful over the long run when they attribute successes and failures alike to *internal and controllable factors*—that is, to things they are doing or might do differently.

Researchers have observed several developmental trends in children's attributions:

Children increasingly distinguish among various attributions. Up until age 5 or 6, children don't discriminate among the possible causes of their successes and failures—effort, ability, luck, task difficulty, and so on (S. Graham & Williams, 2009; Nicholls, 1990). Especially troublesome for young children is the distinction between effort and ability:

- At about age 6, children begin to recognize that effort and ability are separate qualities. At this point they believe that people who try hardest are those who have the greatest ability and that effort is the primary determiner of successful outcomes.
- At about age 9, they begin to understand that effort and ability can compensate for each other: Students with less ability may have to exert greater effort to achieve the same outcomes as their more able peers.
- By about age 13, children clearly differentiate between effort and ability. They realize that people differ both in their capacity to perform a task and in the amount of effort they exert. They also realize that a lack of ability sometimes precludes success no matter how much effort a person puts forth—that some people simply don't have what it takes to accomplish certain things.

Preparing for Your Licensure Examination
Your teaching test might ask you about the role that attributions play in children's achievement.

Many children increasingly attribute their successes and failures to stable, uncontrollable characteristics rather than to effort. Children have varying ideas of what *ability* is. Some have an **incremental view** of ability, thinking that they will almost certainly become proficient in an activity if they try hard and persevere. Others have an **entity view**, believing that their capacity to perform various tasks is an inherited trait or is in some other way beyond their control (Dweck, 2000; Dweck & Master, 2009; Throndsen, 2011).

In the elementary grades, children tend to attribute their successes to effort and hard work, and so they are usually optimistic about their chances for success and may work harder when they fail. By adolescence, they are apt to attribute success and failure more to a fairly stable ability that is beyond their control. To some degree, then, children move from an incremental view of ability in the elementary years to an entity view in adolescence (Dweck, 2000; Nicholls, 1990; Throndsen, 2011). Probably for this reason, adolescents are more discouraged by temporary setbacks than is the case with elementary school children (Eccles & Wigfield, 1985; Pressley, Borkowski, & Schneider, 1987).

Yet there are individual differences here: Some young people continue to hold an incremental view throughout high school. Others gradually discover the impact of hard work and effective learning strategies as they move through the high school grades. Adolescents who have an incremental view of ability are more likely to have mastery goals, seek out challenges that will enhance their competence, take reasonable risks with new strategies, try new approaches, persist in the face of difficulty, and achieve at high levels (Blackwell, Trzesniewski, & Dweck, 2007; Dweck, Mangels, & Good, 2004; Revelle, 2013).

As they get older, children become more aware of reactions that different attributions elicit. Adults are often sympathetic and forgiving when children fail because of something beyond their control (illness, lack of ability, etc.) but frequently get angry when children fail because they didn't try very hard. By the time children reach the upper elementary grades, most are aware of this fact and apt to express attributions that elicit favorable reactions (S. Graham & Williams, 2009; Juvonen, 2000). A child who knows very well that she did poorly on a school assignment because she didn't put forth her best effort may distort the truth, telling her teacher that she doesn't "understand this stuff" or "wasn't feeling well."

Children also learn to adjust their attributions for peers. Generally speaking, fourth graders believe that their peers value diligence and hard work. Thus, they are likely to say that they did well on an assignment because they worked hard. In contrast, many eighth graders believe that their peers disapprove of those who exert much effort on academic tasks. Thus, older students often convey the impression that they aren't working very hard—for instance, that they didn't study very much for an important exam (S. Graham & Williams, 2009; Howie, 2002; Juvonen, 2000).

Children gradually develop predictable patterns of attributions. When young people have frequent success in new endeavors, they gain confidence that they can master a variety of tasks. They attribute their accomplishments to their own ability and effort and have an *I can do it* attitude known as a **mastery orientation**. Yet other youngsters, especially those who encounter a consistent string of failures, become increasingly pessimistic about their chances for future success. They develop an *I can't do it* attitude known as **learned helplessness**.

Even when children with a mastery orientation and those with learned helplessness initially have equal ability, those with a mastery orientation behave in ways that lead to higher achievement over the long run. In particular, they set ambitious goals, seek out new challenges, and persist in the face of obstacles. Children with learned helplessness behave quite differently. Because they underestimate their ability, they set goals they can easily accomplish, avoid challenges that might actually enhance their learning, and respond to failure in counterproductive ways (e.g., giving up quickly) that almost guarantee future failure (Altermatt & Broady, 2009; Seligman, 1991; Ulusoy & Duy, 2013).

Occasionally preschoolers develop learned helplessness about a particular activity if they consistently fail at it, and they may conclude that they are basically "bad" or "dumb" children (Altermatt & Broady, 2009; Burhans & Dweck, 1995). By age 5 or 6, a few children begin to show a general inclination toward learned helplessness. These children express little confidence about tackling challenging tasks and quickly abandon activities at which they initially struggle (McMillan & Jarvis, 2013; D. I. Ziegert, Kistner, Castro, & Robertson, 2001). By and large, however, children rarely exhibit extreme forms of learned helplessness before age 8, perhaps because they still believe that success is due largely to their own efforts (Eccles et al., 1998; Lockhart, Chang, & Story, 2002; S. G. Paris & Cunningham, 1996). Feelings of helplessness are more common in adolescence. Some adolescents believe they have no control over things that happen to them and are at a loss for how to achieve (Ciarrochi & Heaven, 2008; C. Peterson, Maier, & Seligman, 1993).

Origins of Attributions

To a significant degree, children's attributions are the result of their previous successes and failures (Covington, 1987; Hornstra, van der Veen, Peetsma, & Volman, 2013; Pasta, Mendola, Longobardi, Prino, & Gastaldi, 2013). Those who usually succeed when they give a task their best shot are likely to believe that success is due to internal factors such as effort or high ability. Those who frequently fail despite considerable effort are likely to believe that success is due to something beyond their control—perhaps to a lack of genetic potential or to such external factors as bad luck or a teacher's arbitrary judgments.

But children also pick up on other people's beliefs about why they have done well or poorly (Cimpian, Arce, Markman, & Dweck, 2007; S. Graham & Williams, 2009; Hareli & Weiner, 2002). Sometimes others' attributions are quite explicit, as the following statements illustrate:

- "That's wonderful. Your hard work has really paid off, hasn't it?" *(effort)*
- "You did it! You're so smart!" *(fairly stable ability)*
- "Hmmm, maybe this just isn't something you're good at." *(ability once again)*
- "Maybe you're just having a bad day." *(luck)*

A combination of observing chronic failure in oneself and hearing unflattering attributions from others can be devastating, as a journal entry by a high school student with an undiagnosed learning disability reveals:

> When I told one teacher in jr. high that I thought I had dyslexia, he told me that I was just lazy. Yeah, right! Me, lazy? I would end up with the same routine before every vocabulary test or important assignment. I would spend a week trying to memorize words that, no matter what I did, I couldn't spell right. On test days, I would turn in the test, and get an F. All I could do was hope that I'd do better on the next one.
>
> It only got worse in high school, where there were more spelling and essay tests, with more complicated words that seemed too impossible to memorize. Finally, I just started to think, "Why should I even try? I am just going to end up with an 'F' anyway." It seems that an "F" was going to symbolize what I would end up in the future. (The Freedom Writers, 1999, p. 147)

In some instances adults communicate attributions indirectly. When adults criticize and express anger about children's poor performance, they imply that children have the ability to master the task and simply aren't trying hard enough. When they instead express pity, they imply that low ability is the reason for the failure (Vlachou, Eleftheriadou, & Metallidou, 2014; Weiner, 1984). Adults communicate low ability, too, when they praise easy successes, provide unneeded assistance on easy tasks, or encourage children to abandon challenging ones (Droe, 2013; Hokoda & Fincham, 1995; Schunk & Pajares, 2004).

Bioecology of Motivation

Children's personal characteristics and experiences affect their goals, attributions, and other aspects of motivation. Maturational states and developmental abilities affect the tangible

BIOECOLOGY OF DEVELOPMENT

Children's individual characteristics and experiences at home and in the community affect their motivational states, goals, and attributions.

rewards and activities that children find reinforcing. Temperament partly determines inclinations to act on curiosity or, alternatively, to stay on the sidelines of activities (Keogh, 2003). Children with attention-deficit hyperactivity disorder (many of whom have poor impulse control) are apt to have difficulty in delaying gratification (Chelonis et al., 2011; Curchack-Lichtin, Chacko, & Halperin, 2014). Some children with significant physical disabilities have a reduced sense of self-determination because other people play a prominent role in meeting their needs (Luckner & Sebald, 2013; Sands & Wehmeyer, 1996). Children with intellectual disabilities or learning disabilities may show signs of learned helplessness if their past efforts at school have met with failure (E. Carter, Weir, Cooney, Walter, & Moss, 2012; Hersh, Stone, & Ford, 1996).

Children also have unique motivations associated with being boys or girls and as members of particular cultural and ethnic groups. Let's examine these trends.

Gender

Boys and girls have somewhat distinct motivational patterns. On average, young boys are more likely to develop interests that involve a specific topic (e.g., about frogs, dinosaurs, or a particular sport). In contrast, young girls show more interest in literacy and creative activities such as drawing and painting (J. M. Alexander et al., 2008; Baroody & Diamond, 2013; K. E. Johnson, Alexander, Spencer, Leibham, & Neitzel, 2004). In the elementary grades, boys and girls find greater or lesser value in academic domains depending, in part, on whether they view particular subjects as appropriate for their gender. Many children (but certainly not all) perceive some subjects (e.g., writing, music) to be for girls and others (e.g., math, science) to be for boys (Eccles et al., 1998; C. L. Martin & Ruble, 2010).

Generally girls are more concerned with doing well in school: They are more engaged in classroom activities, work more diligently on school assignments, and are more likely to graduate from high school (Duckworth & Seligman, 2006; Halpern, 2006). Furthermore, women currently enroll at higher rates in college than do men, and in North American and European countries more women than men earn college degrees (J. E. O. Blakemore, Berenbaum, & Liben, 2009; R. E. Dwyer, Hodson, & McCloud, 2013; Halpern et al., 2007). Boys suffer to some degree from negative stereotypes about their abilities, especially in literacy (Latsch & Hannover, 2014). Nevertheless, young men are more likely to pursue graduate degrees, especially in mathematics, engineering, and the physical sciences (J. E. O. Blakemore et al., 2009).

Despite girls' eagerness to achieve academically, they tend to have less confidence about their abilities. When researchers compare girls and boys who have equal achievement levels, they find that girls typically have higher self-efficacy in stereotypically feminine domains (e.g., reading, writing, the arts) and boys have higher self-efficacy in stereotypically masculine domains (e.g., science and mathematics; Andrade, Wang, Du, & Akawi, 2009; Wigfield et al., 2006). In addition, girls (especially high-achieving girls) are more easily discouraged by failure than are boys (Dweck, 2000). We can explain this difference, at least in part, by looking at gender differences in attributions. Researchers have observed a tendency for boys to attribute their successes to ability and their failures to lack of effort, thus displaying the attitude that *I know I can do this if I work at it*. Girls tend to show the reverse pattern: They attribute their successes to effort and their failures to lack of ability, believing that *I don't know whether I can keep on doing it, because I'm not very good at this type of thing*. When encountering failure, boys are apt to have an incremental view of ability (they can grow their skills) and girls an entity view (they are stuck with what they have). Gender differences in attributions, which can appear even when youngsters' previous achievement levels have been equal, are most often observed in stereotypically male domains such as mathematics and sports (Chedzoy & Burden, 2009; Dweck, 2000).

Historically, boys had more ambitious career aspirations than was the case for girls (Deaux, 1984; Lueptow, 1984). In recent years, many girls—especially those in Western countries—have also begun to set their sights on challenging professions (Bandura,

Preparing for Your Licensure Examination

Your teaching test might ask you about gender differences in motivation.

Barbaranelli, Caprara, & Pastorelli, 2001; Lapan, Tucker, Kim, & Kosciulek, 2003). But even as traditional boundaries delineating "appropriate" professions for men and for women have begun to dissolve, many adolescents continue to limit themselves to gender-stereotypical careers (Lippa, 2002; Weisgram, Bigler, & Liben, 2010). Gender patterns in career choices are also partly due to differences in confidence in achieving in various academic domains (Bandura et al., 2001; Heilbronner, 2013; Jacobs, Lanza, Osgood, Eccles, & Wigfield, 2002). Also, girls are more likely than boys to be attracted to helping professions (e.g., teaching, counseling) and to be concerned about balancing a career with family life (Cinamon & Rich, 2014; Mahaffy & Ward, 2002).

Culture and Ethnicity

Children everywhere are naturally curious about the physical world and the society in which they live. Similarly, all children want to make at least some of their own choices. And of course, all children are motivated to accomplish something—perhaps succeeding in school, learning a second or third language, helping their family, or preparing for a future career path.

Yet each culture fosters motivational qualities in ways that fit with prevailing practices in that society. As a result, the amount and forms of self-determination differ considerably from group to group (d'Ailly, 2003; J. Kim, Schallert, & Kim, 2010). Adults in some Native American communities express confidence in young children by giving them a lot of freedom to make choices (Deyhle & LeCompte, 1999). Some African American parents believe that young children should be closely supervised out of concern for their safety (Hale-Benson, 1986; Richman & Mandara, 2013). And in some Asian cultures, young people prefer that trusted adults make important choices for them (Iyengar & Lepper, 1999; N. Zhou, Lam, & Chan, 2012).

Children from many—probably most—cultural groups place high value on getting a good education (Gallimore & Goldenberg, 2001; K. Griffin, del Pilar, McIntosh, & Griffin, 2012; Okagaki, 2001). But to some degree, different groups encourage distinct values related to school learning. Many people in China, Japan, and Russia emphasize learning for learning's sake: With knowledge comes personal growth, better understanding of the world, and greater potential to contribute to society. Important for these cultures, too, are hard work and persistence in academic studies (Hess & Azuma, 1991; Hufton, Elliott, & Illushin, 2002; J. Li, 2006). Some students from American backgrounds are less likely to be diligent when classroom topics have little intrinsic appeal, but they often find value in academic assignments that pique their curiosity and require creativity, independent thinking, and critical analysis (Hess & Azuma, 1991; Kuhn & Park, 2005).

Attributions for academic tasks are also socialized during everyday tasks, for example, when adults offer explanations about why children might not have succeeded at a task. Students from Asian cultures are more likely to attribute classroom success and failure to controllable factors (e.g., effort) than are students brought up in Western cultures (Muramoto, Yamaguchi, & Kim, 2009; Weiner, 2004). Thus, children are urged to try harder and be more careful.

Finally, children's cultural experiences inform them of the kinds of goals that are realistic to pursue. A girl in one community may envision herself as an astronaut, computer programmer, or civil engineer, whereas a girl in another community looks forward to becoming a weaver or midwife. In the Development in Culture feature "Achievement Orientation in Tanzania," you can read about areas of achievement perceived by a group of rural Tanzanian children.

As you have learned, motivation changes with age but also responds systematically to individual experience. The Developmental Trends table "Motivation at Different Age Levels" identifies motivational characteristics and the types of diversity you are likely to see in children of different age groups.

Preparing for Your Licensure Examination
Your teaching test might ask about how children learn to be motivated in a cultural context.

DEVELOPMENT IN CULTURE
Achievement Orientation in Tanzania

How can an adult determine what a child wants to accomplish in life? Simply asking children to describe their goals is an option, but doing so has disadvantages. Many children feel uncomfortable sharing their private dreams and fears with a stranger. Others cannot easily respond to abstract questions about events that have not yet taken place.

Priya Nalkur, an expert in human development, was aware of methodological difficulties in assessing children's ideas about achievement yet committed to examining these ideas in children from the Kilimanjaro region of Tanzania, Africa (Nalkur, 2009). She needed a strategy that would put children at ease, give them something concrete to respond to, and allow them to use a familiar means of expression. She decided to interact individually with children, show them pictures of people engaged in a task, and ask them to make up stories about what was going on in the pictures.

In her research, Nalkur invited children to examine three cards drawn of human figures with east African features and clothing. Picture 1 had a boy sitting at his desk and staring at a violin; Picture 2 showed a young woman carrying books and looking off into a field; and Picture 3 had a man hanging onto a suspended rope with his hand. Nalkur selected these pictures because they typically elicit motivational themes. Young people are apt to project their own desires into their interpretations of the drawings.

Nalkur encouraged children to develop stories that explained what the person in the card was doing before, during, and after the scene in the picture. She believed that the method would provide a comfortable context for children, who could focus on meaningful stimuli and create stories, a tradition that is celebrated in their culture. To further create a relaxing atmosphere, Nalkur enlisted the help of a small group of cooperating children who led warm-up games before child participants looked at pictures and told their stories.

LIVING IN THE PRESENT, PREPARING FOR THE FUTURE. This Masai boy proudly wears the traditional clothing of his tribe. He is developing an outlook on the future that is infused with his cultural values and practices.

Nalkur drew from three groups of research participants. "Street children" lived primarily on the streets, in some cases having lost their parents to acquired immunodeficiency syndrome (AIDS) or having left home due to parents' abandonment or abuse. "Former street children" were those who had previously slept on the streets but had been in a shelter for at least 1 year at the time of the interview. "Schoolchildren" lived with families and attended school. Nalkur decided to include only boys in her sample because street children in Tanzania are mainly boys. One hundred and eighty-three boys from ages 11 to 18 participated, with roughly a third in each of the groups.

Children's stories regularly included the theme of *maisha magumu*, a feeling of having a "difficult life"[a] (Nalkur, 2009, p. 1013). Children were affected by widespread frustration from adults concerning the local economy being weak and offering inadequate access to employment, health care, or education. Yet children also conveyed resilience. They demonstrated a faith in their own self-reliance and communicated a belief that they could overcome a host of difficult challenges in life.

As you might expect, the particular achievement orientations that children expressed varied somewhat by group. Street children expressed hope in the future and in other people's obligation for making life better for children. Although their aspirations were for a bright future, the street children did not seem to know how to achieve their goals. They often described troubled characters who were unaware of how to make progress in life. Former street children told stories about taking charge of their lives. Friends and adults outside the family played an important role for former street children that was not fulfilled by parents. Schoolchildren told stories that linked hard work in school to academic achievement. They talked about jobs, performance in school, and effort in studying. The schoolchildren were aware of temptations around them but also articulated strategies for taking control of their lives, as shown by one student:

> There was once a young man who was a thief. Together with his friends, he made others join their behavior. He lived a very difficult life, and eventually decided to join adult education to avoid getting a bad name in the community. He became very keen in studying to have a better future. He in turn motivated his friends who were thieves to not continue with that lifestyle. He told them to continue with education so as not to have a bad reputation. Eventually, they too got educated and worked to improve the community as a whole. (12 years, Picture 3)[a] (p. 1023).

In her interpretations of the responses, Nalkur suggested that children's achievement orientations arose from their experiences. Street children expressed hope for protection from harm, yet did not seem to know how to achieve their goals. Former street children's emphasis on friendship may have derived from their recognition that it was primarily other children who could be counted on for affection. Finally, the schoolchildren saw a clear connection between being well educated and having a good life.

DEVELOPMENTAL TRENDS
Motivation at Different Age Levels

AGE	WHAT YOU MIGHT OBSERVE	DIVERSITY	IMPLICATIONS
Infancy (Birth–2 Years)	• Curiosity about objects and people • Enthusiasm for moving body parts, handling objects, and exploring the environment through locomotion • Some goal-directed behavior as early as 3 months • Little or no interest in praise, especially in the first year; greater appreciation of praise after age 1	• Temperament and culture influence children's willingness to explore and experiment with the physical environment. • Attachment security influences children's willingness to explore. • Children with significant disabilities may show less interest in exploration than do their nondisabled peers.	• Create a predictable, affectionate environment in which children feel comfortable exploring. • Provide new and unusual objects that pique children's curiosity. • Identify and provide objects and events that can capture the interest of children with disabilities.
Early Childhood (2–6 Years)	• Preference for small and immediate rewards over larger and delayed ones • Overconfidence about one's ability to perform new tasks • Strong motivation to learn the causal properties of objects and events • Rapidly changing, situation-dependent interests; emergence of stable interests in some children • Focus on obtaining the approval of adults more than that of peers • Focus on mastery (rather than performance) goals • Little understanding of reasons for successes and failures	• Differences in desire for social interaction are evident as early as age 3 or 4. • Children who begin school without basic knowledge of colors, shapes, letters, or numbers may notice differences between their own abilities and those of peers—differences that may set the stage for poor self-efficacy down the road if the missing knowledge is not soon acquired. • Learned helplessness in a particular domain occasionally appears as early as age 4 or 5 after a history of failure.	• Provide a wide variety of potentially interesting toys, storybooks, props for dramatic play, and other equipment. • Praise (or in some other way reinforce) desired behaviors as they occur. • Provide the guidance children need in order to experience success more often than failure. • Address delays in literacy, numeracy, self-regulation, and other school-readiness skills.
Middle Childhood (6–10 Years)	• Increasing ability to delay gratification • Emerging awareness of how one's own performance compares with that of peers; more realistic assessment of abilities • Increasing prevalence of performance goals • Increasing distinction between effort and ability as possible causes of success and failure; tendency to attribute successes to hard work	• As a result of low self-efficacy, children with a history of learning problems have less intrinsic motivation to learn academic subject matter. • Some very bright, talented girls may be reluctant to do their best because of concerns about appearing unfeminine or surpassing peers. • Children with certain disabilities are more likely to develop learned helplessness about achieving academic success.	• Communicate the message that with appropriate effort, strategy, and support, virtually *all* children can master knowledge and skills in academic areas. • Focus children's attention on the progress they are making, rather than on how their performance compares to that of peers. • Stress the importance of learning for the intrinsic pleasure it brings; downplay the importance of grades.
Early Adolescence (10–14 Years)	• Increasing interest in social activities; intensified concern with approval from peers • Declining sense of competence, often accompanying transition to middle school or junior high • Decline in intrinsic motivation to learn school subject matter; stronger performance goals • Increasing belief that skill is the result of stable factors (e.g., inherited ability) rather than effort and practice • Growing motivation to achieve in stereotypically gender-appropriate domains	• Students who are gifted may show passions for learning in areas of interest, for example, making films or doing mathematical puzzles. • Some adolescents believe that demonstrating high achievement can interfere with popularity. • Adolescents from a few ethnic groups (e.g., some from a few Asian societies) place high value on adult approval. • Some individuals develop a sense of learned helplessness about achieving academic success.	• Evaluate adolescents on the basis of how well they are achieving instructional objectives, not on how well their performance compares with that of classmates. • Assign cooperative group projects that allow adolescents to interact with one another, display their unique talents, and contribute to the success of their group. • When youngsters exhibit a pattern of failure, provide needed support for them to become successful in their endeavors.

(continued)

DEVELOPMENTAL TRENDS (continued)

AGE	WHAT YOU MIGHT OBSERVE	DIVERSITY	IMPLICATIONS
Late Adolescence (14–18 Years)	• Ability to postpone immediate pleasures in order to gain long-term rewards • Increasing stability of interests and priorities • Increasing focus on the utilitarian value of activities • Tendency to attribute performance levels more to ability than to effort • Tentative decisions about career areas	• Girls work harder on school assignments and are more likely to graduate from high school than are boys. • Adolescents from some Asian cultures often attribute their successes and failures to effort rather than ability. • Many teens have career aspirations that are stereotypically gender appropriate.	• Point out the relevance of various academic domains (e.g., mathematics) for long-term goals. • Design assignments in which adolescents apply academic content to real-world adult tasks. • Allow teens to pursue personal interests within the context of academic domains.

Sources: Alvarez & Booth, 2014; Atun-Einy, Berger, & Scher, 2013; Bandura et al., 2001; L. A. Bell, 1989; Burhans & Dweck, 1995; L. Coleman & Guo, 2013; H. Cooper & Dorr, 1995; Corpus et al., 2009; Deshler & Schumaker, 1988; Dweck & Master, 2009; Eccles & Midgley, 1989; Eccles & Roeser, 2009; Fewell & Sandall, 1983; S. Graham, 1989; L. Green et al., 1994; Halpern, 2006; Harter, 1996; Jacobs et al., 2002; Jacobsen, Lowery, & DuCette, 1986; K. E. Johnson et al., 2004; Juvonen, 2000; Leaper & Friedman, 2007; Legare, 2014; Lillard, 1997; Lockhart et al., 2002; Nicholls, 1990; Otis et al., 2005; S. G. Paris & Cunningham, 1996; Portes, 1996; Rovee-Collier, 1999; R. M. Ryan & Deci, 2009; Schultz & Switzky, 1990; Schunk & Pajares, 2009; Seligman, 1991; Vaughn et al., 1984; Wigfield et al., 2006; Ziegert et al., 2001.

Summary

Children direct their behavior toward personal objectives from the beginning of life and increasingly pursue long-term goals. When they enter school, most children want to do well in school but significant individual differences exist in how they go about achieving academic goals. Some children want to acquire new knowledge and skills (i.e., they have *mastery goals*) whereas others want to look good or avoid looking bad in front of classmates and teachers (i.e., they have *performance goals*). Children's social goals are also important and can be accommodated by thoughtful teachers.

Among factors influencing children's motivation are the attributions children make regarding their successes and failures in particular activities. Children are most optimistic when they attribute both successes and failures to internal factors that they can control (e.g., amount of effort and use of good strategies). Ultimately, some children acquire a general *I can do it* attitude (a *mastery orientation*), whereas others acquire an *I can't do it even if I try* attitude (*learned helplessness*).

Children's motivational goals and beliefs are affected by personal characteristics and experiences in particular environments. Children's temperaments and any disabilities they might have affect how they display their curiosity as well as their ability to delay gratification, self-determination, and learned helplessness. Boys and girls exhibit a few differences in motivation, particularly in their interests, academic aspirations, and confidence in their abilities. Cultural values partly determine how children express their autonomy, persist with tasks, make attributions, and form aspirations for the future.

ENHANCEDetext *self-check*

MOTIVATING CHILDREN AT SCHOOL

A common misconception about motivation is that it is something children "carry around" inside of them—for instance, that some students are consistently motivated to learn at school and others are not. As you learned with intrinsic motivation, it is true that some sources of motivation come from within. However, it's equally true that youngsters' immediate environments have dramatic effects on their motivation to learn. Such environment-dependent motivation is known as **situated motivation** (D. T. Hickey & Granade, 2004; Järvelä, Järvenoja, & Malmberg, 2012; S. G. Paris & Turner, 1994). Yet simple pep talks ("I know you can do it if you try!") are not terribly helpful, especially over the long run (Brophy, 2004). Far more effective is providing scaffolding for challenging activities and enticing children to tackle those tasks largely for the pleasure and sense of competence they bring (Eccles, 2007; Hidi & Renninger, 2006). The following strategies are also widely recommended:

• **Focus on promoting intrinsic (rather than extrinsic) motivation.** Externally imposed consequences—praise, money, good grades, and so on—often bring about desired changes in children's behavior. Such reinforcers have disadvantages, however. Although they provide a source of extrinsic motivation, they can undermine children's *intrinsic* motivation if children perceive them to be controlling, manipulative, or in some other way limiting of their self-determination (R. M. Ryan & Deci, 2009; Vansteenkiste, Lens, & Deci, 2006). Furthermore, externally imposed reinforcers may communicate the message that assigned tasks are unpleasant chores (why else would a reinforcer be necessary?), rather than activities to be carried out for their own sake (B. A. Hennessey, 1995; Stipek, 1993).

Ideally, teachers, parents, and other adults focus children's attention *not* on the external consequences of their efforts but on the internal pleasures (enjoyment, satisfaction, pride, etc.) that accompany certain tasks and activities. Adults can also increase children's intrinsic motivation for learning important topics and skills using strategies such as these:

- Communicating enthusiasm for a topic
- Piquing curiosity with new and intriguing objects and phenomena
- Incorporating fantasy, adventure, or suspense into activities
- Creating disequilibrium by presenting puzzling phenomena
- Getting children physically involved with a topic (e.g., through role-playing or hands-on experimentation)
- Relating important skills and subject matter to children's interests and goals
- Offering choices when several alternatives will be equally effective in helping children acquire desired skills
- Accentuating children's choice in studying material (e.g., "You've selected some interesting books to read.")
- Identifying areas in which each child can be especially successful.
- Encouraging children to set personal goals for learning more about subjects in which they are interested (Brophy, 2004; Froiland, Oros, Smith, & Hirchert, 2012; Martens, de Brabander, Rozendaal, Boekaerts, & van der Leeden, 2010; Patall, Cooper, & Wynn, 2008; R. M. Ryan & Deci, 2009; Schraw, Flowerday, & Lehman, 2001)

• **Enhance children's self-efficacy for mastering important knowledge and skills.** One critical way to enhance children's self-efficacy in reading, mathematics, or another academic domain is, of course, to help them achieve success in that realm—for instance, by tailoring instruction to their existing ability levels, scaffolding their efforts, and so on (Lodewyk & Winne, 2005; Schunk & Pajares, 2009). Another effective approach is to show them *other people's* successes. When children see peers of similar age and ability accomplish a task, they are more likely to believe that they, too, can accomplish it (Schunk & Hanson, 1985).

• **Maintain children's sense of self-determination when giving instructions.** Every group needs a few rules and procedures to ensure that children act appropriately and activities run smoothly. Furthermore, teachers and other professionals must often impose restrictions about how children carry out assigned tasks. The trick is to present rules, procedures, guidelines, and structure without communicating an intention to *control* children's behavior. Instead, adults should present these things as *information*—for instance, as conditions that help children accomplish important goals (Froiland et al., 2012; Hagger, Chatzisarantis, Barkoukis, Wang, & Baranowski, 2005; R. M. Ryan & Deci, 2009). Following are examples:

- "We can make sure everyone has an equal chance to speak if we listen without interrupting."
- "I'm giving you a particular format to follow when you do your math homework. If you use this format, it will be easier for me to figure out which concepts you understand and which ones you need more help with—and I'll be able to give you better guidance."
- "Let's remember that other children will be using the same paints and brushes later today, so we need to make sure everything we use now is still in tip-top shape when we're done. It's important, then, that we clean the brushes thoroughly when we're done painting."

Preparing for Your Licensure Examination

Your teaching test might ask you about educational strategies for supporting children's self-determination.

• "I'm available to give you a few hints if you need it, but see if you can work through the problems on your own before coming to me."

• **Encourage children to shoot for objectives that they can reasonably attain.** Children often respond more favorably to goals they set for themselves than those set by others (Boekaerts, 2009; Lens, 2001; Wentzel, 1999). Yet many children have trouble conceptualizing a "future" that is abstract (e.g., getting a good education) and perhaps many years down the road (e.g., going to medical school; Bandura, 1997; Husman & Freeman, 1999; Usinger & Smith, 2010). They may initially respond more favorably to short-term, concrete goals—perhaps learning a certain number of math facts in a given week, getting the next belt in karate, or earning a merit badge in a scout troop (R. B. Miller & Brickman, 2004; Schunk & Rice, 1989). By working toward a series of short-term goals, youngsters get regular feedback about the progress they are making, acquire a greater sense of self-efficacy that they can master new skills, and achieve at demonstrably higher levels (Iselin, Mulvey, Loughran, Chung, & Schubert, 2012; Schunk, 1996). In other words, children's achievement of short-term goals puts them closer to realization of the long-term goals they have set for their future selves. In Artifact 13-2, 10-year-old Amaryth outlines her goals in sports and science.

As students reach adolescence, their increasing capacity for abstract thought allows them to envision long-term goals (e.g., winning a spot on a varsity sports team or having a career in journalism). Yet perhaps as a result of low self-efficacy or limited financial resources, some of them set their sights quite low. Teachers and other practitioners should not only encourage these young people to think ambitiously but also convince them that high goals are achievable. When encouraging girls to consider stereotypically masculine career paths, adults might provide examples of women who have led successful and happy lives in those careers. When encouraging teens from low-income families to think about going to college, adults might assist them with filling out scholarship applications and scheduling appointments with college financial aid officers.

• **Encourage mastery goals as well as (ideally even more than) performance goals.** To some degree, performance goals are inevitable in today's schools. Students invariably look to their peers' performance when evaluating their own accomplishments, and many aspects of the adult world (gaining admission to college, seeking employment, working in private industry, etc.) are competitive. Yet adults do youngsters a disservice when they focus too much attention on "looking good" and surpassing peers. When adults instead explain how certain knowledge is useful, highlight ongoing progress, and acknowledge that learning entails effort and mistakes, they are emphasizing mastery goals that will enhance achievement over the long run (Bong, 2001; Brophy, 2004; Tas & Cakir, 2014).

• **Downplay the seriousness of failures.** Children and adolescents are more apt to accept responsibility for their failures—and therefore to learn from them—if adults don't make a big deal of mistakes and instead give them numerous opportunities to improve assignments (Ames, 1992; Dweck & Master, 2009; Katkovsky, Crandall, & Good, 1967). In some instances adults may also find it appropriate to focus children's attention on the *processes* they use to tackle problems rather than on the final outcome of their efforts. A teacher may occasionally give an assignment with instructions like these:

> It doesn't matter at all how many you get right. In fact, these problems are kind of hard. I'm just interested in learning more about what [you] think about while [you're] working on problems like these. I want you to focus on the problem and just say out loud whatever you're thinking while you're working—whatever comes into your head. (Stipek & Kowalski, 1989, p. 387)

• **Help youngsters meet their social goals.** One of the reasons adolescents focus so much on performance goals is that making a good impression helps them gain acceptance from peers. Adolescents encounter most of their peers at school and naturally make social goals

ARTIFACT 13-2 **Amaryth's goals.** Ten-year-old Amaryth describes how she worked toward goals on the soccer field and in the classroom. Her teacher had encouraged her to articulate her goals and acknowledged her accomplishments.

DEVELOPMENT AND PRACTICE
Helping Children Meet Their Social Goals

Continually communicate the message that you like and respect the young people with whom you are working.

- A second-grade teacher tells a student that she saw his karate exhibition at the local mall over the weekend. "You were great!" she says. "How many years have you been studying karate?" (Middle Childhood)
- A high school teacher reads about a group of students at school who produce informal movies in their free time and post them on YouTube. "I watched some of your movies," he says to one of the students. "Very clever. Let me know about any new videos that you post." (Late Adolescence)

Plan learning tasks that involve social interaction.

- A sixth-grade social studies teacher incorporates classroom debates, small-group discussions, and cooperative learning tasks into each month's lesson plans. (Early Adolescence)
- A high school chemistry teacher forms cooperative groups for conducting experiments. Every student is assigned a role essential to the functioning of the group—manager of equipment, recorder of notes, checker of observations, or spokesperson to the class. Students rotate through each of the roles during the span of the trimester. (Late Adolescence)

Get youngsters involved in large projects in which they must work toward common objectives.

- The eighth graders at one middle school are sharply divided into informal groups, and some students are routinely excluded from interaction. The school music teacher suggests that a production of the musical *You're a Good Man, Charlie Brown* become a project for the entire class. All 92 eighth graders are either in the cast or working on costumes, scenery, or lighting. The ambitious scope of the project and the fact that the class's efforts will eventually be on public display instill a cohesive class spirit among students, with formerly popular and unpopular students working respectfully with one another. (Early Adolescence)
- An environmental studies club organizes a Green Day for the school. Students in the club post flyers and Facebook requests for everyone to bring in objects that can be recycled, repurposed, or safely disposed. Students, teachers, and staff bring in used batteries, printer cartridges, eyeglasses, and cell phones. (Late Adolescence)

Teach strategies that enable youngsters to present themselves well to others.

- A preschool teacher welcomes a new boy, Fernando, to the classroom and introduces him to the other children. After noticing that he seems to be shy, the teacher observes him carefully and spots his exceptional skill in building intricate block structures. She encourages a few other children who also like to build to admire his work, "Look at the amazing space station Fernando is making. I bet he could use help from some other engineers." (Early Childhood)
- As fourth graders prepare for upcoming oral reports on their small-group science projects, their teacher offers suggestions for capturing their audience's interest. "You might present a puzzling question your classmates would really like to know the answer to," she says. "Or you might show them something that will surprise them. Perhaps you can think of a short, simple experiment they might conduct to arrive at the same conclusion *you* did." (Middle Childhood)

Give praise in private when a student appears sensitive about peers' reactions.

- Laura, a girl in middle school, has worked hard as student body president. Her adviser, Mr. Gomez, has observed the results of her efforts in inspiring all of the officers to work together for the betterment of the school. Realizing that Laura would want to give credit to others in her group, Mr. Gomez takes her aside to compliment her on her leadership skills. (Early Adolescence)
- A high school English teacher reads a particularly creative story written by a young man who, she knows, is concerned about maintaining his "cool" image. On the second page of his story (which the student's classmates are unlikely to see), she writes, "This is great work, Tony! I think it's good enough to enter into the state writing contest. Can we meet before or after school to talk about the contest?" (Late Adolescence)

Respect individual differences.

- A preschool teacher notices that some of his students have a greater need for social contact than others. Some enjoy cooperative play activities, whereas others are more interested in experimenting with physical objects. Although he interacts with all children regularly, he is careful not to interrupt those happily engrossed in play. (Early Childhood)
- An elementary student whose parents recently divorced is getting accustomed to the new pickup routine. His father picks him up on Mondays through Wednesdays and his mother picks him up Thursdays and Fridays. The boy places great importance on his social life and wants to continue to see friends after school. When he is going home with a friend for a couple of hours, his teacher watches to make sure he takes his overnight bag if it's a day when he is shifting between his mother's and father's homes. (Middle Childhood)

Sources: M. E. Ford & Smith, 2007; Hamre & Pianta, 2005; Harter, 1999; Juvonen, 2000, 2006; Ladd, Herald-Brown, & Kochel, 2009; Ormrod, 2008; Stevens & Slavin, 1995; M. Thompson & Grace, 2001 (school play example); Rodkin et al., 2013; Wentzel & Wigfield, 1998; Wigfield et al., 1996.

a high priority there (B. B. Brown, Eicher, & Petrie, 1986; Rodkin, Ryan, Jamison, & Wilson, 2013; Wentzel & Wigfield, 1998). The Development and Practice feature "Helping Children Meet Their Social Goals" (above) suggests several ways in which educators can address youngsters' social needs within the context of academic instruction.

• **Give encouraging messages about the causes of a performance level.** When commenting on children's successes, probably the best approach is to mention such controllable factors as effort and learning strategies (Dweck & Master, 2009; Gunderson et al., 2013; Weiner, 1984).

In this way, adults provide assurance that children are certainly capable of succeeding with hard work and perseverance. A teacher might say:

- "You've done very well. I can see that you've been trying very hard to get better."
- "Your project shows good strategies and a lot of hard work."

When identifying possible causes for failures, however, adults can focus primarily on increasing effort and improving strategies and give such feedback privately (Brophy, 2004; Cimpian et al., 2007; Dweck, 2000). Following are examples:

- "The more you practice, the better you will get."
- "Perhaps you need to study a little each night rather than waiting until the night before. And let's talk about how you might also study *differently* than you did last time."

When children's failures are consistently attributed to controllable factors such as lack of effort or ineffective strategies and when increased effort or new techniques do, in fact, produce success, children often work harder, persist longer in the face of failure, and seek help when they need it (Dweck & Master, 2009; Eccles & Wigfield, 1985).

The most effective feedback—no matter whether it commends successes or identifies weaknesses—also maintains children's sense of self-determination. More specifically, it provides information about children's performance but doesn't convey a desire to control their behavior (Deci, 1992; Standage, Cumming, & Gillison, 2013). In complimenting a student who has written a good persuasive essay, a teacher might say, "Your arguments are well organized and quite convincing" (emphasis on what the student has done well), rather than saying, "Good job in following my guidelines" (emphasis on following the teacher's instructions). And in admonishing students for off-task behavior during a cooperative learning activity, a teacher might ask, "Are you guys going to have time to work on your project tonight if you don't finish it during class?" (emphasis on students' own time management concerns), rather than saying, "How many times do I have to remind this group to *get to work?*" (emphasis on keeping the students under control).

- **Teach children to give themselves encouraging attribution messages as well.** Numerous investigations have shown that children can be taught more productive attributions for their successes and failures, with higher achievement and more persistence in the face of failure often being the result (e.g., Chodkiewicz & Boyle, 2014; Dweck, 1975). In these *attribution retraining* studies, children are asked to engage in a particular task (e.g., reading challenging text, solving arithmetic problems, constructing geometric puzzles), with occasional failures interspersed among more frequent successes. Within this context, one viable approach for changing attributions is for an adult to interpret each success in terms of high effort or good strategies and each failure in terms of insufficient effort or ineffective strategies. But even more effective is teaching children to explicitly attribute their *own* successes and failures to amount of effort or specific strategies (Dweck & Master, 2009; Fowler & Peterson, 1981).

- **Use extrinsic reinforcers when necessary.** Despite adults' best efforts, children sometimes have little interest in acquiring knowledge or skills critical for their later success in life. To encourage learning or desired behaviors in such situations, adults may have to provide extrinsic reinforcers—not only praise but perhaps also free time, grades, special privileges, or points toward a small prize. How can adults use such reinforcers without undermining children's intrinsic motivation? One effective strategy is to reinforce children not simply for doing something but for doing it *well*. Another is to communicate that an extrinsic reinforcer is merely a concrete acknowledgment of significant progress or achievement—an accomplishment about which children should feel very proud (Brophy, 2004; J. Cameron, 2001). Especially when working with youngsters from cultures that place high priority on family or community ties, adults might point out the positive impact that children's actions have on other people (Abi-Nader, 1993; Dien, 1998; Suina & Smolkin, 1994). A teacher might say, "Think how proud your family will be!" or "Everyone in school will appreciate the beautiful wall murals you have painted in the hallway."

A more controversial use of extrinsic reinforcers is to pay students for earning advanced test scores or high grades or attending tutoring sessions (Wright, 2009). Cash incentives have been tried in school districts in schools serving predominantly low-income students in several large U.S. cities, including New York City, Chicago, and Washington, D.C. Proponents of cash incentives have argued that low-income students need financial support so that they can afford to study after school rather than working long hours in part-time jobs. Others suggest that students from low-income families do not receive the same financial advantages of students from wealthier backgrounds and appreciate the opportunity to be awarded with financial incentives. So far the evidence on the impact has been mixed, with some studies indicating higher performance among those receiving incentives and others not finding this advantage (Bettinger, 2012; J. Henderson, 2009). Many educators are concerned about such initiatives, however, warning that if funding for these programs dries up, students will probably decrease their efforts.

• **Use praise that validates students' hard work and successful strategies.** Some students with weak academic skills have special educational needs. Extensive research on praise has found that children are sensitive to the implications of adults' compliments. Adults should generally try to avoid praise for children's intelligence, as in "You're such a smart kid!" This flattering remark, however well intentioned, is interpreted as intelligence being fixed, which in turn decreases children's confidence in their abilities in the future. In comparison, telling children that they must have tried hard or used a particularly effective problem-solving strategy helps them focus in on factors that they can control in the future (Esparza, Shumow, & Schmidt, 2014; Gunderson et al., 2013). Adults should also try to be specific in describing the child's accomplishment. Telling a sixth grader that his essay conscientiously addressed the major qualities of the rubric and was particularly convincing in its vivid details is more informative than telling him, "Good job!"

• **Be attentive to the needs of students who are behind classmates in academic skills.** Some students with weak academic skills have learning disabilities or other special educational needs. Others have limited proficiency in English or a cultural background that is not enthusiastically embraced at school. Still others may encounter serious personal problems (e.g., a pregnancy, an arrest, a parent's incarceration), not have friends at school, or come from home environments in which academic success is not encouraged (Behnke, Gonzalez, & Cox, 2010; Hirschfield, 2009; Makarova & Herzog, 2013; Steinberg, Blinde, & Chan, 1984). Regardless of the reasons for delayed progress, students who fail to acquire minimum academic skills are at risk for dropping out of school (Boling & Evans, 2008; Fortin, Marcotte, Diallo, Potvin, & Royer, 2013).

Low-achieving students come from all socioeconomic levels, but youngsters from low-income families are especially likely to leave school before high school graduation (Rumberger, 1995; Suh, Suh, & Houston, 2007). Boys are more likely to drop out than girls, and African Americans, Hispanic Americans, and Native Americans have higher dropout rates than other groups (A. Edwards, 2014; Oguntoyinbo, 2009; Roderick & Camburn, 1999).

Of course, low-achieving students almost always have the ability to succeed if given appropriate support from concerned adults. In a study with Canadian adolescents who were at risk for dropping out of high school but instead went on to earn their high school diploma, young people had established relationships with concerned adults outside the family (in many cases teachers), responded to challenges by reminding themselves of their own strong abilities, and made strategic choices for keeping themselves on track (e.g., distancing themselves from peers who took drugs; Lessard, Fortin, Marcotte, Potvin, & Royer, 2009). One of the students, Aubrey, reported her experience:

> My father left when he learned that my mother was pregnant with me. I never knew him. My mother raised me on her own until she met my brother and sister's father, who lived with us until my sister was three years old. Then, it took a few years until my mother met another man. She never lived with him, though. We moved often, but we always stayed in the same town. I changed schools three times while in primary school. Being shy, it took me some time to make new friends each time.
>
> All went well in primary school. Teachers were really nice to me. They would come see me when they thought I did not understand. I loved English but had a really hard time with math. In class, I always paid attention. I never let others get me sidetracked. I did what was asked of me. In high school, math was still hard, but French was worse. I just couldn't handle it. I was failing. I saw the final exams coming and I kept telling myself that I had to succeed. I might have gone to ask for help, but I really did not get along with my French teacher. He was a dictator. I kept telling myself that I can do it. I did it, I passed my final exam and I got my high school diploma.[9] (Lessard et al., 2009, pp. 22–23)

[9]Excerpt from "Why Did They Not Drop Out? Narratives from Resilient Students" by A. Lessard, L. Fortin, D. Marcotte, P. Potvin, & É Royer from THE PREVENTION RESEARCHER, Volume 16, Issue 3, pp. 22–23. Copyright © 2009 Integrated Research Services, Inc., Eugene, OR. Reprinted with permission.

DEVELOPMENT AND PRACTICE
Encouraging Students Who Are Achieving at Low Levels

Make the curriculum relevant to students' lives.

- In a unit on the physics of sound, a junior high school science teacher shows students how basic principles reveal themselves in rock music. On one occasion the teacher brings in a guitar and explains why holding down a string at different points along its neck creates different frequencies and therefore higher and lower notes. (Early Adolescence)

- A middle school social studies teacher invites students to select an autobiography from an assortment of books written by authors from a range of backgrounds. Students regularly choose books written by individuals who share their own cultural experiences. (Early Adolescence)

Use students' strengths to promote high self-efficacy in certain domains.

- An elementary school serving predominantly families from low-income backgrounds forms a singing group (the "Jazz Cats") for which students must try out. The group performs at a variety of community events, and the students are recognized for their talent. Group members exhibit confidence in their musical abilities, improvement in other school subjects, and greater teamwork and leadership skills. (Middle Childhood)

- A middle school science teacher encourages her students to enter a local science fair. Several students participate, and they design innovative projects such as ones focused on chemical analyses of water from local estuaries or migration patterns of bees during periods of restricted access to pollen. After participating in the fair, students become more motivated in science. (Early Adolescence)

Provide extra support for academic success.

- At the beginning of class each day, a middle school teacher distributes a general outline that can guide students' note taking. She also writes two or three questions on the board that students should be able to answer at the end of the lesson. (Early Adolescence)

- A high school algebra teacher arranges with his principal to hire a tutor for students who are struggling in mathematics. The tutor works over the lunch hour and after school to offer help with homework. A local electronics company sponsors snacks for the students to munch on during the drop-in tutoring sessions. (Late Adolescence)

Communicate optimism about students' chances for career success.

- A kindergarten teacher equips the dramatic play area in her classroom with supplies and clothing from a wide array of professions—an airplane pilot's cap, a doctor's stethoscope, a beautician's hairbrush and rollers, a cash register with play money, and so forth. "What will you pretend to be today?" she asks the children. After they make their selections, she comments, "Isn't it wonderful to think about jobs you could have when you grow up?" (Early Childhood)

- A mathematics teacher in a low-income, inner-city high school recruits students to participate in an intensive math program. The teacher and students work evenings, Saturdays, and vacations, and all of them later pass the Advanced Placement calculus exam. (Late Adolescence).

Show students that they are personally responsible for their successes.

- A high school teacher says to a student, "Your essay about recent hate crimes is powerful. You've given the topic a lot of thought, and you've clearly mastered several of techniques of persuasive writing. I'd like you to think seriously about submitting your essay to the local paper for its editorial page. Can we spend some time during lunch tomorrow fine-tuning the grammar and spelling?" (Late Adolescence)

- "Every single student in my advisee group is capable of going to college or a vocational program," an adviser tells his high school students at the beginning of the year. "But getting into college and choosing a major will be easier for you if you start planning now." During the year, students take a career inventory of interests; arrange for a 3-day internship with a professional in a job of personal interest; and search through catalogs from local colleges, universities, and vocational programs. (Late Adolescence)

Get students involved in extracurricular activities.

- A middle school encourages its students to get involved in at least one of its many extracurricular activities. Students can choose from various athletic teams as well as an astronomy club, band, color guard, hip-hop dance group, honor societies, science club, student council, school yearbook group, Peers for Peace group, school newspaper club, gay–straight alliance, and Ultimate Frisbee team. Each of the groups actively recruits members at the beginning of the year and conducts an additional membership drive halfway through the year. (Early Adolescence)

- A high school adviser encourages a student with a strong throwing arm to go out for the school baseball team and introduces the student to the baseball coach. The coach, in turn, expresses his enthusiasm for having the student join the team and asks several current team members to welcome him. (Late Adolescence)

Involve students in school policy and management decisions.

- A teacher in a third-grade classroom encourages children to organize a Valentine's Day party. With a little guidance from their teacher, children form several small groups, each of which is tasked with a particular job—bringing in decorations, asking parents to send in a drink or snack, creating bags for each child to store goodies, and typing up a list of children's names for those preparing Valentine's Day cards. (Middle Childhood)

- Students and teachers at one high school hold regular "town meetings" to discuss how the groups are operating and how disputes can be resolved. Meetings are democratic, with students and teachers alike having one vote apiece, and the will of the majority being binding. (Late Adolescence)

Sources: Alderman, 1990; L. W. Anderson & Pellicer, 1998; Behnke et al., 2010; Christenson & Thurlow, 2004; Cosden, Morrison, Albanese, & Macias, 2001; Fredricks, Blumenfeld, & Paris, 2004; S. Goldstein & Brooks, 2006; Hamre & Pianta, 2005; A. Higgins, 1995 (town meetings example); Jenlink, 1994 (Jazz Cats example); M. S. Knapp, Turnbull, & Shields, 1990; Lee-Pearce, Plowman, & Touchstone, 1998; Milner, 2006; A. Smith & Thomson, 2014; Towne, 2009.

The motivational strategies we've listed in the preceding pages are critical for most students who are low achieving. The Development and Practice feature "Encouraging Students Who Are Achieving at Low Levels" (above) offers additional suggestions.

Summary

To some degree, children's intrinsic motivation to tackle an activity depends on factors that develop gradually over time (e.g., self-efficacy, sense of self-determination, a mastery orientation) and is affected by experience. Piquing youngsters' curiosity and interest, helping them be successful in their efforts to master new skills, enhancing their sense of autonomy, and encouraging the formation of specific goals are just a few of the many things adults can do to enhance youngsters' motivation to engage in productive activities.

ENHANCEDetext *self-check*

PRACTICING FOR YOUR LICENSURE EXAMINATION

Many teaching tests require students to apply their knowledge of child development in analyzing brief vignettes and answering multiple-choice questions. You can practice for your licensure examination by reading the following case study and answering a series of questions.

Tears of Pearls

When students in a sixth-grade class don't turn in homework assignments, a teacher intern insists that they write a 200-word essay explaining the missing homework and describing how they plan to be more diligent next time. In an essay shown on this page, 11-year-old Andrea explains why she didn't turn in her analysis of the lyrics to the song "Tears of Pearls," by the Australian singing duo Savage Garden. Read Andrea's essay and then answer the questions that follow it.

---

200 word essay

I am very sorry this happened. I feel guilty that I forgot to pass the assignment Tears of Pearls in. Every time in social studies I will make sure I passed in <u>all</u> my assignments so that this will not happen again. I understand how hard it is for you to keep track of two classes work and I think it is a good idea you are doing this. I wish I wasn't so forgetful. Hopefully this will not happen to me again. Every night I will check my social studies folder to make sure the homework is complete. Now all I have to do is get it to school and put it in the pass in box. It was complete but I just forgot to pass it in. Every night I do my homework and my mom checks it and it goes in my back pack but sometimes I just forget to give it to you. I'm sorry. I really am. It is sometimes hard for us kids sometimes too. It is sometimes hard for us kids to be prepared but I guess that's just something we'll have to learn before middle school! Oh and sometimes we're packed with homework and the next day its hard to get it back together and into your and Mrs. Copeland's hands as soon as possible (A.S.A.P.). Like I said it's hard for you too and I can understand, but sometimes things (other) things are hard for us too. For the third time im really am sorry
sincerly,
Andrea

Constructed-Response Question

1. What kinds of benefits might Andrea gain from preparing this essay?

Multiple-Choice Questions

2. What does Andrea say that indicates she is developing self-regulatory skills in completing her school assignments?
   a. Andrea reported that she completed the assignment (reflecting her desire to be conscientious) but forgot to turn it in.
   b. Andrea felt guilty about not getting her homework in on time.
   c. Andrea reports that her mother checks her homework and they put it in her backpack.
   d. All of the above.

3. What evidence is there that Andrea still needs help in regulating her learning at school?
   a. Andrea forgets to turn in her homework.
   b. Andrea relies on her mother to check her homework.
   c. Andrea expresses uncertainty as to how to proceed.
   d. All of the above.

ENHANCEDetext *licensure exam*

Key Concepts

motivation (p. 487)

delay of gratification (p. 489)

conscience (p. 489)

self-monitoring (p. 494)

self-instructions (p. 494)

self-motivation (p. 494)

self-evaluation (p. 494)

extrinsic motivation (p. 497)

intrinsic motivation (p. 497)

reinforcer (p. 497)

primary reinforcer (p. 498)

secondary reinforcer (p. 498)

vicarious reinforcement (p. 498)

punishment (p. 499)

vicarious punishment (p. 499)

self-efficacy (p. 500)

sense of self-determination (p. 501)

situational interest (p. 501)

personal interest (p. 501)

value (p. 502)

internalized motivation (p. 502)

mastery goal (p. 506)

performance goal (p. 506)

performance-approach goal (p. 506)

performance-avoidance goal (p. 506)

social goal (p. 507)

attribution (p. 509)

incremental view (of ability) (p. 510)

entity view (of ability) (p. 510)

mastery orientation (p. 510)

learned helplessness (p. 510)

situated motivation (p. 516)

CHAPTER FOURTEEN

Moral Development

CASE STUDY: Changing the World, One City at a Time

Alice Terry had worked as a middle school teacher with gifted and talented students in a rural area of Georgia. Over the years, Alice had given her students a chance to work on projects addressing pressing needs in their community, including restoring buildings, preparing a waste management plan for their county, and designing a walking tour past historic buildings and monuments (A. W. Terry, 2000, 2001, 2003, 2008; A. W. Terry & Panter, 2010).

After her middle students completed the projects, they talked with Alice about what they had learned. Students reported that they acquired numerous benefits from participating in the projects, often gaining a sense of purpose in their work. Now in high school, several adolescents who had renovated a theater as middle school students described their accomplishments:

"Makes you feel like you have a—" Trina interrupted.

"A place in life," Kevin continued. "We, like, have our—we have, like, a place. No, not a place, but we have a a—a mark."

Anna blurted out, "We left our mark, yeah!"

"Our mark. When we were eighth graders," Kevin added, "we really made a difference."

"We'll go back," Ann responded, "and probably find some of our signatures somewhere."

"Our footprints are in there," Kevin mused. "Our breath will still be there."[a] (A. W. Terry, 2000, p. 126)

Along with gaining a sense of purpose, the adolescents acquired valuable social insights about relationships with peers. For example, students realized that they had to consider how their moods affected others:

"You can't be in a grouchy mood and do stuff like this," Anna began, "'cause folks are just gonna get mad at you—you can't do that . . . . You got to have a good attitude about it."

Kevin interjected, "Everybody has to have a good attitude."

Anna added, "Or nothing will get done." (A. W. Terry, 2000, p. 124)

A related social lesson was that cooperation was imperative to the group's progress. When asked to advise other adolescents who would be working on community service projects, the students emphasized teamwork:

"Learn to . . . work together," Kevin advised.

Anna added, "Work hard."

"Get along. To just, um, use their time wisely so they can get the most out of the project," Trina remarked. (A. W. Terry, 2000, p. 126)

In addition, students learned about themselves. Kat, now a young woman, had been impatient with her teammates and recalled lessons in self-control and tolerance:

I used to just blow up at people. . . . I guess we were working in such close quarters that, you know, if somebody that you didn't like was there, they were going to breathe on you at some point. You were going to have to put up with it. (A. Terry, 2000, pp. 126–127)

- What did Alice Terry understand about the moral needs of young people?
- What skills did the adolescents learn as they participated in community service projects?

[a]Excerpts from "An Early Glimpse: Service Learning from an Adolescent Perspective" by A. W. Terry, from JOURNAL OF SECONDARY GIFTED EDUCATION, Vol. 11, Issue 3, pp. 124, 126–128, 303–304. Copyright © 2000 by Prufrock Press, Inc. Reprinted with permission of Prufrock Press, Inc. http://www.prufrock.com

OBJECTIVES

14.1: Describe developmental trends in children's moral reasoning and factors that facilitate these progressions.

14.2: Identify key influences on the development of prosocial and aggressive behaviors, including methods at school that promote good behavior and safe school environments.

Children readily acquire moral values, but now and again they need guidance in treating one another humanely. In the introductory case study, Alice Terry understood that adolescents could benefit from an opportunity to work together and serve their community. As a result of their experiences, these young people learned important lessons—that their community needed them, that they had to compromise and act considerately in order to achieve common goals, and that they could derive considerable satisfaction from their collective accomplishments.

In this chapter, we examine children's moral development. We look specifically at children's reasoning about right and wrong and their tendencies to help and occasionally to hurt others. As you have discovered to be true about other aspects of development, teachers and other professionals play a vital role in children's ability to act decently, responsibly, and honorably.

MORAL REASONING

Moral development involves acquiring standards about right and wrong and acting in accordance with these standards. Three influential theories, from Piaget, Kohlberg, and a band of social domain scholars, explain regularities in children's moral reasoning.

Piaget's Theory of Moral Development

After conducting observations of children's social games (e.g., playing with marbles) and interviews with children about people's wrongdoings, the pioneering developmental theorist **Jean Piaget** (1896–1980) proposed that, over time, children construct increasingly mature understandings of "good" and "bad" behavior (Piaget, 1960b).[1] In the early elementary years, children believe that behaviors that are "bad" or "naughty" are those that cause serious damage or harm. Thus, a young child might say that a person who accidentally broke 15 dishes was more badly behaved than a person who intentionally broke just one dish. By the upper elementary grades, children consider people's motives when evaluating behaviors. At this age, they would see the person who intentionally broke one dish as the guiltier party.

Piaget noticed other changes in the ideas that children formed about moral issues. For preschoolers, "good" behavior consists of obeying adults and other authority figures. Around age 5, children begin to judge what is good and appropriate based on established *rules* for behavior. At this point, they see regulations as firm dictates to be obeyed without question. Piaget called this rule-based morality *moral realism*. Sometime around age 8 or 9, children begin to recognize that rules are created primarily to help people get along and can be changed if everyone agrees to the change.

Many developmental scholars find value in Piaget's notion that children construct their own ideas about moral behavior—often as a result of having discussions with adults and peers—rather than simply adopt the moral guidelines of those around them (Hoffman, 2000; Kohlberg, 1984; Vozzola, 2014). Furthermore, theorists agree that development of children's moral understandings depends on advancing cognitive capabilities, such as social perspective taking and abstract thought (Eisenberg, 1995; Kohlberg, 1969).

Nevertheless, researchers have found that Piaget was not always accurate about when various aspects of moral reasoning emerge; for instance, many preschoolers recognize that certain behaviors (e.g., pushing others or damaging their property) are wrong even if an adult tells them that such behaviors are acceptable (Nucci, 2009; Tisak, 1993; Turiel, 1983). And as you will learn in the next section, another prominent theorist, Lawrence Kohlberg, found significant developmental changes in moral thinking in adolescence and adulthood, periods that were not examined by Piaget.

Kohlberg's Theory of Moral Development

When the groundbreaking cognitive-developmental psychologist **Lawrence Kohlberg** (1927–1987) first began to examine early theorists' descriptions of children's moral development,

Preparing for Your Licensure Examination

Your teaching test might ask you to describe how moral development is a constructive process that depends on experience and reflection.

[1]Piaget's theory of cognitive development is described in detail in Chapter 6.

he was disappointed with much of what he read (Kohlberg, 1963, 1964).[2] At the time, several outspoken theorists (e.g., Sigmund Freud, B. F. Skinner) argued that people behave morally only in response to pressure from others. Kohlberg rejected this idea, siding instead with Piaget's view that individuals develop their own ideas about proper courses of action. Yet whereas Piaget studied moral development as one of several distinct topics he examined, Kohlberg made moral thinking his life's work and was therefore able to provide a detailed account of youngsters' moral thinking.

Kohlberg was the first researcher to look in depth at the age-related ways in which people analyze hypothetical conflicts. Consider the following situation:

> In Europe, a woman was near death from a rare form of cancer. There was one drug that the doctors thought might save her, a form of radium that a druggist in the same town had recently discovered. The druggist was charging $2,000, ten times what the drug cost him to make. The sick woman's husband, Heinz, went to everyone he knew to borrow the money, but he could only get together about half of what the drug cost. He told the druggist that his wife was dying and asked him to sell it cheaper or let him pay later. But the druggist said no. So Heinz got desperate and broke into the man's store to steal the drug for his wife. (Kohlberg, 1984, p. 186)

Should Heinz have stolen the drug? What would you have done if you were Heinz? Which is worse, stealing something that belongs to someone else or letting another person die a preventable death, and why?

The story of Heinz and his dying wife is an example of a **moral dilemma**, a situation in which two or more people's rights or needs are at odds and for which there is no clear-cut right or wrong solution. Following are three boys' responses to Heinz's dilemma. We have given the boys fictitious names so that we can talk about them afterward.

> *Andrew (a fifth grader):* Maybe his wife is an important person and runs a store, and the man buys stuff from her and can't get it any other place. The police would blame the owner that he didn't save the wife. He didn't save an important person, and that's just like killing with a gun or a knife. You can get the electric chair for that. (Kohlberg, 1981, pp. 265–266)
>
> *Vlad (a high school student):* If he cares enough for her to steal for her, he should steal it. If not he should let her die. It's up to him. (Kohlberg, 1981, p. 132)
>
> *Hector (a high school student):* In that particular situation Heinz was right to do it. In the eyes of the law he would not be doing the right thing, but in the eyes of the moral law he would. If he had exhausted every other alternative I think it would be worth it to save a life. (Kohlberg, 1984, pp. 446–447)

Each boy offers a different reason to justify why Heinz should steal the lifesaving drug. Andrew suggests that the druggist (whom he calls the owner) needs to be punished for not saving a life. Vlad takes a self-serving view, proposing that the decision to either steal or not steal the drug depends on how much Heinz loves his wife. Only Hector considers the value of human life in justifying why Heinz should break the law.

After obtaining hundreds of responses to moral dilemmas, Kohlberg proposed that the development of moral reasoning is characterized by a sequence of six stages grouped into three general *levels* of morality: preconventional, conventional, and postconventional (Colby, Kohlberg, Gibbs, & Lieberman, 1983; Kohlberg, 1963, 1976, 1984) (see Table 14-1). **Preconventional morality** is the earliest and least mature form of moral reasoning, in that a child has not yet adopted or internalized society's conventions regarding what is right or wrong—hence the label *preconventional*. Andrew's response to the Heinz dilemma is a good example of preconventional, Stage 1 thinking, in that he focuses on the consequences (death in the electric chair) of not providing the medicine. Kohlberg also classified Vlad's response as preconventional, in this case as a Stage 2 response. Vlad is beginning to recognize the importance of saving someone else's life, but the decision to do so ultimately depends on whether or not Heinz loves his wife. In other words, his decision depends on *his* feelings alone.

Conventional morality is characterized by an acceptance of society's conventions regarding right and wrong. At this level, an individual obeys rules even when there are no consequences for obedience or disobedience. Adherence to rules is somewhat rigid, however, and its appropriateness or fairness is seldom questioned. In contrast, people

---

[2]Kohlberg's theory is introduced in Chapter 1.

TABLE 14-1 Kohlberg's Three Levels and Six Stages of Moral Reasoning

LEVEL	AGE RANGE	STAGE	NATURE OF MORAL REASONING
Level I: Preconventional Morality	Seen in preschool children, most elementary school students, some junior high school students, and a few high school students	Stage 1: Punishment-avoidance and obedience	People make decisions based on what is best for themselves, without regard for others' needs or feelings. They obey rules only if established by more powerful individuals; they may disobey if they aren't likely to get caught. "Wrong" behaviors are those that will be punished.
		Stage 2: Exchange of favors	People recognize that others also have needs. They may try to satisfy others' needs if their own needs are also met ("You scratch my back, I'll scratch yours"). They continue to define right and wrong primarily in terms of consequences to themselves.
Level II: Conventional Morality	Seen in a few older elementary school students, some junior high school students, and many high school students (Stage 4 typically does not appear until the high school years.)	Stage 3: Good boy/good girl	People make decisions based on what actions will please others, especially authority figures and others with high status (e.g., teachers, popular peers). They are concerned about maintaining relationships through sharing, trusting, and being loyal, and they take other people's perspectives into account when making decisions.
		Stage 4: Law and order	People look to society for guidelines about right or wrong. They know rules are necessary for keeping things running smoothly and believe it is their "duty" to obey them. However, they perceive rules to be inflexible; they don't necessarily recognize that as society's needs change, rules should change as well.
Level III: Postconventional Morality	Rarely seen before college (Stage 6 is extremely rare even in adults.)	Stage 5: Social contract	People recognize that rules represent agreements among many individuals about appropriate behavior. Rules are seen as potentially useful mechanisms that can maintain the general social order and protect individual rights, rather than as absolute dictates that must be obeyed simply because they are "the law." People also recognize the flexibility of rules, with those that no longer serve society's best interests needing to be changed.
		Stage 6: Universal ethical principles	Stage 6 is a hypothetical, "ideal" stage that few people ever reach. People in this stage adhere to a few abstract, universal principles (e.g., equality of all people, respect for human dignity, commitment to justice) that transcend specific norms and rules. They answer to a strong inner conscience and willingly disobey laws that violate their own ethical principles.

Sources: Colby & Kohlberg, 1984; Colby et al., 1983; Kohlberg, 1976, 1984, 1986.

Observing Children 14-1

Listen to three young people give reasons for not spending money found in a lost wallet.

ENHANCEDetext *video example*

who exhibit **postconventional morality** view rules as useful but changeable mechanisms created to maintain the social order and protect human rights, rather than as absolute dictates that must be obeyed without question. Postconventional individuals live by their own abstract principles about right and wrong—principles that typically include such basic human rights as life, liberty, and justice. They may disobey rules inconsistent with their principles, as we see in Hector's Stage 5 response to the Heinz dilemma: "In the eyes of the law he would not be doing the right thing, but in the eyes of the moral law he would."

Kohlberg recognized that ranges in moral reasoning can be significant at a given age. Younger children will reason primarily from within a preconventional framework but in the high school classroom, each of the three levels of reasoning may be evident at one time or another. You can listen to three young people give reasons for not spending money found in a lost wallet in Observing Children videos.

A great deal of research on moral development has followed on the heels of Kohlberg's work. Some of it supports Kohlberg's sequence of moral reasoning: Generally speaking, children and adolescents make advancements in the order that Kohlberg proposed (Colby & Kohlberg, 1984; Nucci, 2009; Stewart & Pascual-Leone, 1992). Furthermore, Kohlberg's basic idea that moral development is a constructive process has stood the test of time—theorists remain intrigued with children's need to analyze behaviors as right or wrong (Nucci, 2006; Thornberg, 2010; Turiel, 2008a). Nevertheless, psychologists have identified several weaknesses in Kohlberg's theory.

One set of problems is related to how Kohlberg defined morality. For one thing, Kohlberg included both *moral issues* (e.g., causing harm) and *social conventions* (e.g., having rules to help society run smoothly) into his views of morality, but as you will see, children view these two domains differently. In addition, he largely overlooked one very important aspect of morality: that of helping others and showing them compassion (Gilligan, 1982, 1987). Furthermore, although Kohlberg acknowledged that moral thinking is intertwined with emotions, he emphasized cognitive factors. Contemporary researchers have shown just how strongly emotions (e.g., empathy and guilt) are related to moral thought and action (Arsenio & Lemerise, 2010; Laible, Murphy, & Augustine, 2014; Turiel & Killen, 2010). In fact, it now appears that emotions, not cognitive insights, provide the initial gateway into morality. By the second year of life, children respond to emotional cues of another's distress and often provide simple gestures of comfort (A. Dahl, Campos, & Witherington, 2011; R. A. Thompson, 2012).

Another limitation of Kohlberg's theory is his proposal that environmental factors have only a modest impact on moral development. Kohlberg assumed that children's moral thinking is guided by their own introspection, largely without adult assistance. Yet recent research indicates that children are very much influenced by parents and other adults as well as by their many cultural experiences (Grusec, 2006; Malti, Eisenberg, Kim, & Buchmann, 2013; Recchia, Wainryb, Bourne, & Pasupathi, 2014; R. A. Thompson, 2012).

Finally, Kohlberg discounted situational factors that youngsters actually do take into account when deciding what's morally right and wrong in specific contexts (Rest, Narváez, Bebeau, & Thoma, 1999; Minnameier & Schmidt, 2013). For example, children are more apt to think of lying as immoral if it causes someone else harm than if it has no adverse effect—that is, if it is just a "white lie" (Turiel, Smetana, & Killen, 1991).

> **Preparing for Your Licensure Examination**
>
> Your teaching test might ask you about the basic tenets and educational implications of Kohlberg's theory of moral development.

Social Domain Theory of Moral Development

American psychologist **Elliott Turiel** and his colleagues have followed the leads of Jean Piaget and Lawrence Kohlberg in examining children's beliefs about the appropriateness of people's actions (Jambon & Smetana, 2014; Turiel, 2008b; Turiel & Killen, 2010). The unique contribution that Turiel and his collaborators have made has been to demonstrate that young children easily distinguish issues about morality from concerns about society's conventions—an ability that was largely overlooked by Kohlberg. By comparing children's responses to carefully defined moral and social-conventional violations, Turiel and his colleagues have been able to demonstrate capabilities in reasoning that were not evident in Kohlberg's data.

Children identify important issues in three social domains. Young children understand that **moral transgressions** (e.g., hitting others, stealing their belongings, and calling them nasty names) are wrong because they cause damage, violate human rights, and run counter to basic principles of equality, freedom, or justice (J. G. Miller, 2007; Nucci, 2009; Recchia et al., 2014). Preschool and kindergarten children also realize that **conventional transgressions** (e.g., talking back to adults or burping at meals) violate widely held understandings about how one should act and are wrong but not as serious as moral transgressions. Conventional transgressions are usually specific to a particular culture. Although burping is frowned on in mainstream Western culture, people in some cultures burp as a compliment to the cook. Moreover, young children see some choices, such as selecting a friend, as a **personal matter**; therefore, determining what is a right or wrong choice is up to the individual. The ability to distinguish moral violations, conventional transgressions, and personal choices appears to be universal, as you can learn more about in the Development in Culture feature "Moral Development in Colombia."

DEVELOPMENT IN CULTURE
Moral Development in Colombia

Children around the world develop several common ideas about social responsibility as well as some divergent views. Evidence of universality is present in the widespread ability of children to distinguish between moral, social, and personal actions (Jambon & Smetana, 2014; Turiel, 2006b; Wainryb, 2006). By the preschool years, children realize that moral violations (e.g., hitting and pushing, or taking another's belongings) are hurtful acts that are rarely justified. Young children consider violations of social conventions (e.g., failing to say "please" or "thank you," or ignoring table etiquette) to be disrespectful but not as reprehensible as moral violations. With reference to the personal domain (e.g., selecting a friend or choosing a hairstyle), children typically say that individuals themselves should make their own decisions.

Research by Alicia Ardila-Rey and her colleagues in Colombia, South America, examines these understandings in children. As with children in many other cultures, Colombian children differentiate separate domains of social action. In one study, interviewers read stories to 3- to 7-year-old Colombian children from middle-class families (Ardila-Rey & Killen, 2001). Stories portrayed hypothetical children who were at odds with teachers over moral issues (e.g., hitting another child), social-conventional conflicts (e.g., drinking milk standing up rather than following the classroom's custom of sitting down while consuming beverages), and personal disagreements (e.g., choosing to sit next to another classmate during a story other than the one chosen for the child by the teacher). Interviewers asked children about the proper course of action for teachers to take when the hypothetical children failed to live up to the teachers' expectations.

LEARNING RIGHT FROM WRONG. These Colombian children have daily experiences that help them acquire important moral and social understandings.

Children stated that teachers should offer explanations when the hypothetical children violated moral rules. They believed that children in the stories had misbehaved because they were young and uninformed, not because they were being malevolent or intentionally disobedient. Therefore, the imaginary children were thought to need guidance, not punishment. In comparison, the interviewed children believed teachers should negotiate with the fictional children who violated social-conventional rules or insisted on pursuing personal actions disapproved of by teachers. From the children's perspective, teachers should advise students about social-conventional and personal domains and then allow students to make their own decisions. In the following responses, children defended the rights of peers to exercise their independence in personal matters:

> "Children have their own rights, they have the right to choose what to play with" *("Los niños tienen sus propios derechos; ellos tienen derecho de jugar a lo que quieran jugar")*. "It is the child's play, not the teacher's play. The child can do whatever she wants to do" *("Es el juego de la niña, no es el juego de la profesora. La niña puede jugar a lo que ella quiera")*. "They can't force you to sit with a friend who is not your friend" *("A uno no lo pueden obligar a sentarse con un amigo que no es su amigo")*. (Ardila-Rey & Killen, 2001, p. 253)

Other research with Colombian children shows diversity in views about social conduct. In one investigation of children's evaluations of moral transgressions, 6- to 12-year-old Colombian children were recruited from two towns: Chía, a small and peaceful rural community with an educated population, and Soacha, a densely populated and economically impoverished community with high rates of crime and violence (Ardila-Rey, Killen, & Brenick, 2009). The vast majority of children from both groups evaluated the moral transgressions of hitting and refusing to share toys as being wrong. But children in the two groups differed in views about the acceptability of hitting or not sharing when another person had been aggressive ("Would it be okay to do it if they had teased or hurt her first? Why?" "Would it be okay to hit her back? Why?" [Ardila-Rey et al., 2009, p. 189]). Compared to children in Chía, who had grown up in a relatively peaceful setting, children from Soacha, who had been exposed to a lot of violence, more often responded that hitting and not sharing would be acceptable if the other person had acted aggressively or selfishly.

These and other studies indicate that Colombian children from very different backgrounds believe that children should be given considerable latitude in making their own social decisions, but should try to abide by moral rules that protect the welfare of other people. Subtle variations exist, however, in children's beliefs about the circumstances in which moral rules are legitimately ignored. Children who have been exposed to excessive levels of violence are more inclined than peers who have grown up in peaceful communities to excuse a person's aggressive and selfish acts when that individual's own rights have been violated.

Research in support of the social domain theory indicates that children construct understandings of rules as they think about everyday experiences. When they or another person hurts someone else, the person who has been hurt tends to express anger, pain, or sadness, and adults may point out the negative outcomes of inappropriate acts for victims (Dunn, 2006; Parke & Clarke-Stewart, 2011; Recchia et al., 2014). Conversely, children notice that when someone violates a social convention, everyone's responses tend to be less strident and focus instead on the rules that have been broken.

Children's reflections on their social experiences are reflected in their ever-growing appreciation for responsibilities in the various domains. During early childhood, children describe violations in the moral domain in concrete terms, as causing physical harm to others, whereas older children additionally express concerns with inequality, social exclusion, and other more abstract concepts (Smetana, 2006). Similarly, children's awareness of social conventions is rudimentary in early childhood but increases throughout the elementary and secondary school years (Helwig & Jasiobedzka, 2001; Mullins & Tisak, 2006; Turiel, 2006b). A young child may suggest that it is wrong to call a teacher by his or her first name because of the school's custom of using the title "Mr.," "Miss," "Mrs.," or "Ms.," whereas an older child may be able to explain further that failing to use the proper title is disrespectful to the authority figure (Turiel, 1983). Concerns about the personal domain, initially focusing on such concrete issues as choosing one's own friends and clothing, expand to include reflections on psychological issues, for example, matters affecting one's own safety, comfort, and health (Tisak & Turiel, 1984; Thornberg, 2010).

In the process of learning about specific domains, children gradually notice that particular actions have repercussions in several domains. For example, adolescents may realize that a teacher's decision to place boys and girls into separate groups can be evaluated from several different perspectives (Killen, Margie, & Sinno, 2006). Morally, it might be considered unfair because one gender or the other could be denied an equal opportunity for learning. In conventional terms, the decision might be considered acceptable because separating boys and girls is a common practice that sometimes increases attention and learning within groups. In the personal domain, the decision might be considered an imposition that violates students' right to select their own groups.

Children also develop an increasingly thorough understanding of cultural practices in the various domains. Previously, you learned that children around the world distinguish moral, conventional, and personal violations, but it is also the case that children learn culture-*specific* ways of classifying rules and violations. Social conventions in some areas of India include women wearing a sari (traditional apparel draped around the body) and a bindi (a forehead decoration), whereas some Mennonite and Amish women in the United States and Canada wear long dresses and bonnets (Parke & Clarke-Stewart, 2011). Such variations in dress are not simply fashion statements; they uphold the social order in traditional cultures. Moral rules also vary somewhat across culture. In Hindu society, fish is considered a "hot" food that would stimulate sexual desire and is not to be consumed by widows who are seeking salvation for their deceased husbands (Shweder, Mahapatra, & Miller, 1987). Widows in Western cultures historically did not refrain from eating fish but instead wore black for a period of time and followed other customs showing their grief.

In summary, social domain theory offers a viable framework for understanding children's moral reasoning. It has inspired an impressive volume of studies that portrays children as perceptive evaluators of social action. As a limitation, this perspective has not yet inspired much research about the links among moral thinking, emotions, and behavior, but scholars in the field have begun to make strides in analyzing these important connections (Arsenio & Lemerise, 2010; Dahl, Sherlock, Campos, & Theunissen, 2014; Smetana & Killen, 2008; Turiel & Killen, 2010).

Developmental Trends in Morality

Many contemporary developmental psychologists believe that moral development involves general *trends* rather than hard-and-fast stages. Contemporary psychologists have identified the following developmental changes in children's moral reasoning and behavior:

Children begin using internal standards to evaluate behavior at a very early age. Indeed, toddlers apply standards for right and wrong before age 2 (Kochanska, Casey, & Fukumoto,

Observing Children 14-2

See evidence that Corwin has emerging internal standards in an Observing Children video.

ENHANCEDetext *video example*

1995; Kochanska & Kim, 2014; R. A. Thompson & Newton, 2010). Toddlers may wince, cover their eyes or ears, or cry when they witness an aggressive interaction. Many toddlers distinguish between what's "good" and "bad," for example looking at a broken object and saying "uh-oh!" (Kagan, 1984; S. Lamb & Feeny, 1995). You can see 16-month-old Corwin's concern when his block tower falls down in an Observing Children video. Sometime around age 3 or 4, children understand that causing physical harm to another person is wrong regardless of what authority figures might tell them and irrespective of what consequences behaviors bring (Helwig, Zelazo, & Wilson, 2001; Smetana, 1981; Turiel, 2006b). A little later they understand that causing another person psychological harm through teasing or calling him or her names is also wrong (Jambon & Smetana, 2014).

Children's capacity to respond emotionally to others' distress increases over the school years. Certain emotions accompany and evoke moral actions, and these emotions emerge gradually as children grow older. Children begin to show signs of **guilt**—a feeling of discomfort when they know that they have inflicted damage or caused someone else suffering—as early as 22 months (Kochanska, Gross, Lin, & Nichols, 2002).[3] Children's capacity for guilt increases over the childhood years and seems to be an essential part of a conscience. Feeling guilty deters future wrongdoing; children especially prone to feeling guilt tend to refrain from serious misbehaviors (Kochanska et al., 2002; W. Roberts, Strayer, & Denham, 2014; Tangney & Dearing, 2002). Excessive levels of guilt can be detrimental, however, leading children to become self-berating and depressed (Luby et al., 2009; Zahn-Waxler & Kochanska, 1990).

Children also develop a capacity for **shame**, the feeling of being embarrassed or humiliated when they realize that they are failing to meet basic standards of moral behavior. Precursors to shame emerge during early childhood and then evolve into conscious emotions in middle childhood. Toddlers sometimes avoid adults or appear anxious when they have done something wrong, but children generally are in the middle elementary grades before they reliably exhibit shame (Barrett, 2005; Damon, 1988; Hoffman, 1991). Feeling shame does not seem to inhibit wrongdoing as effectively as does guilt. In fact, some children who are ashamed act out disruptively, aggressively, and even criminally (MacDermott, Gullone, Allen, King, & Tonge, 2010; Muris & Meesters, 2014).

Guilt and shame occur when children believe they have done something wrong. In contrast, *empathy,* the capacity to experience the same feelings as another person, and **sympathy**, a genuine feeling of sorrow and concern about another person's problems or distress, motivate moral behavior even in the absence of wrongdoing.[4] These emotions emerge in early childhood and continue to develop throughout middle childhood and adolescence (Ongley & Malti, 2014; Zahn-Waxler, Radke-Yarrow, Wagner, & Chapman, 1992). In the primary grades, children show empathy mostly for people they know, including friends and classmates. But by the upper elementary and secondary school grades, youngsters also feel empathy for people they *don't* know—perhaps for the economically poor, homeless, or individuals in catastrophic circumstances (Eisenberg, 1982; Hoffman, 1991; Markstrom, Huey, Stiles, & Krause, 2010). In the opening case study, adolescents felt empathic for unfamiliar people in their community, wishing to preserve historical landmarks and natural resources for everyone's benefit. Also during adolescence, young people become better able to disregard their own personal distress, and by this means become able to attend helpfully to another's misfortune (Eisenberg, Spinrad, & Sadovsky, 2006).

Children's understanding of fairness evolves throughout early and middle childhood. The ability to share with others depends on a sense of **distributive justice**, the commitment to a certain model for sharing a valued commodity (food, toys, playground equipment, etc.). Children's notions of distributive justice change with age and accompanying levels of moral reasoning (Damon, 1977; Gummerum, Keller, Takezawa, & Mata, 2008; Gunzburger, 1977; Kienbaum & Wilkening, 2009). In the preschool years, beliefs about what is fair are based primarily on *self-interest*; for instance, it would be perfectly "fair" to give oneself a large handful of candy and smaller amounts to others. By the early elementary grades, children believe in *parity*: They base their judgments about fairness on strict equality (a desired commodity

[3]The developmental course of guilt is examined in Chapter 11.
[4]Empathy is introduced in Chapter 11.

is divided into equal portions). Sometime around age 8, children begin to take merit and special needs into account consistently. They may think that people who contribute more to a group's efforts should reap a greater portion of the group's rewards and that people who are economically poor might be given more resources than others. Children show glimmers of concerns with *equity*, such that they take into account how much everyone puts into the project. For example, those who helped from start to finish in making a batch of cookies would get more than those who only helped assemble the ingredients.

As children get older, they increasingly make moral decisions that reflect a combination of distinct factors. Children's behaviors are correlated with their moral reasoning (Eisenberg, Zhou, & Koller, 2001; Hinnant, Nelson, O'Brien, Keane, & Calkins, 2013; Turiel, 2008b). Those who, from Kohlberg's perspective, reason at higher stages are less likely to cheat, insult others, or engage in delinquent activities and more likely to help people in need and disregard orders that put others in harm's way (Kohlberg, 1975; Kohlberg & Candee, 1984).

Yet as children act in particular circumstances, other factors besides moral reasoning come into play. Children's perspective-taking ability and emotions (in particular, their guilt, empathy, and sympathy) influence their decisions to behave morally (Batson, 1991; Damon, 1988; Lonigro, Laghi, Baiocco, & Baumgartner, 2014). Personal goals affect moral behavior as well. Although children may want to do the right thing, they may also be concerned with whether others will approve of their actions and what positive or negative consequences might result. Children are more apt to behave in accordance with moral standards if the benefits are high ("Will other people like me better?") and the personal costs are low ("How much will I be inconvenienced?") (Batson & Thompson, 2001; Narváez & Rest, 1995; Nunner-Winkler, 2007). In the opening case study, group solidarity and shared pride partly compensated students for their hard work and discomfort in resolving interpersonal differences.

As you have learned, a constellation of moral understandings, emotions, and skills emerges gradually in children. The Developmental Trends table "Moral Reasoning and Behavior at Different Age Levels" describes advancements you are likely to see in infancy, childhood, and adolescence.

DEVELOPMENTAL TRENDS
Moral Reasoning and Behavior at Different Age Levels

AGE	WHAT YOU MIGHT OBSERVE	DIVERSITY	IMPLICATIONS
Infancy (Birth–2 Years)	• Acquisition of basic standards for behavior (e.g., saying "uh-oh!" after knocking over and breaking an object) • Careful inspection of adults' responses to broken objects, spilled drinks, and injured people • Reactions of distress when witnessing aggressive behavior	• In the second year, children label objects and events in ways that reflect cultural standards (e.g., *good, bad, dirty, boo boo*). • Toddlers who are fearful and inhibited experience considerable distress when parents respond harshly to their wrongdoings.	• Consistently discourage behaviors that cause harm or distress to others (e.g., hitting or biting peers). • Acknowledge undesirable events (e.g., spilled milk or a broken object), but don't overreact or communicate that children are inadequate for having caused them.
Early Childhood (2–6 Years)	• Some awareness that behaviors causing physical or psychological harm are morally wrong • Guilt for certain misbehaviors (e.g., damaging a valuable object) • Greater concern for one's own needs than those of others; complaining "It's not fair" when resources are not distributed equally • Realization that some violations of social practices reflect moral transgressions, whereas others are conventional violations or personal decisions	• Some cultures emphasize early training in moral values; for example, in many Hispanic communities, a child who is *bien educado* (literally, "well educated") knows right from wrong and behaves accordingly. • Children who show greater evidence of guilt about transgressions are more likely to adhere to rules for behavior. • At ages 2 and 3, girls are more likely to show guilt than are boys; boys catch up around age 4.	• Make standards for behavior very clear. • Have a discussion with children about how they interpret and follow general rules. • Invite children to have input into classroom rules. • When children misbehave, give reasons why such behaviors are unacceptable, focusing on the harm and distress they have caused others (see discussion on parents' use of *induction*) on pages 537–538.

(continued)

DEVELOPMENTAL TRENDS (continued)

AGE	WHAT YOU MIGHT OBSERVE	DIVERSITY	IMPLICATIONS
Middle Childhood (6–10 Years)	• Sense of distributive justice increasingly taking into account people's differing contributions, needs, and circumstances (e.g., people with disabilities might get a larger share) • Increasing empathy for unknown individuals who are suffering or needy • Feelings of shame as well as guilt for moral wrongdoings	• Some cultures place greater emphasis on ensuring people's individual rights, whereas others place greater value on the welfare of the community as a whole. • Children whose parents explain *why* certain behaviors are unacceptable show more advanced moral development.	• Talk about how rules enable classrooms and other groups to run more smoothly. • Present simple moral dilemmas similar to circumstances children might encounter themselves (e.g., "What should a girl do when she has forgotten her lunch money and finds a dollar bill on the floor under a classmate's desk?").
Early Adolescence (10–14 Years)	• Some tendency to think of moral rules as standards that should be followed for their own sake • New inclination to disobey classroom rules but ability to appreciate how disruptions affect other people when these are pointed out • Tendency to believe that distressed individuals (e.g., the homeless) are entirely responsible for their own fate	• Sometime around puberty, some youngsters begin to incorporate moral traits into their overall sense of self. • Youngsters' religious faith (e.g., their beliefs in an afterlife) influences their judgments about what behaviors are morally right and wrong.	• Involve adolescents in group projects that will benefit their school or community. • Encourage adolescents to think about how society's laws and practices affect people in need (e.g., individuals who are economically disadvantaged). • When imposing discipline for moral transgressions, point out harm caused to others. • Talk about moral issues, for example, a school-wide increase in acts of disrespect.
Late Adolescence (14–18 Years)	• Understanding that rules and conventions help society run smoothly • Increasing concern about doing one's duty and abiding by the rules of society as a whole rather than simply pleasing authority figures • Genuine empathy for people in distress • Belief that society has an obligation to help those in need	• For some older adolescents, high moral values are a central part of their overall identity; these individuals often show a strong commitment to helping those less fortunate than themselves. • Adolescents who focus on their own needs almost exclusively are more likely to engage in antisocial activities.	• Explore moral issues in social studies, science, and literature. • Give teenagers a political voice in decision making about rules at school and elsewhere. • Explain why it is necessary to maintain academic integrity, monitor test-taking, and offer to help students with their work so as to decrease cheating.

Sources: Chandler & Moran, 1990; Damon, 1988; DeVries & Zan, 2003; Eisenberg & Fabes, 1998; Farver & Branstetter, 1994; Flanagan & Faison, 2001; D. Hart & Fegley, 1995; Helwig & Jasiobedzka, 2001; Hoffman, 1975, 1991; Kochanska et al., 1995, 2002; Kohlberg, 1984; D. L. Krebs & Van Hesteren, 1994; Kurtines, Berman, Ittel, & Williamson, 1995; S. Lamb & Feeny, 1995; Lapsley & Carlo, 2014; Laupa & Turiel, 1995; Nucci, 2009; Nucci & Weber, 1995; Rizzo & Bosacki, 2013; Schonert-Reichl, 1993; Smetana & Braeges, 1990; R. A. Thompson & Newton, 2010; Triandis, 1995; Turiel, 2006a; Vozzola, 2014; Yates & Youniss, 1996; Yau & Smetana, 2003; Zahn-Waxler et al., 1992.

Bioecology of Moral Development

A child is born with a brain that guides moral development. Empathy has neurological precursors at birth—networks of neurons that enable sharing of another person's emotions (de Souza, 2014; Missana, Grigutsch, & Grossmann, 2014). The ability to distinguish moral and social conventional events also has a neurological basis, with moral transgressions, as intrinsically objectionable events, being relatively straightforward for the brain to detect, whereas violations of social conventions, which require a mental search through acquired social rules, take longer for the brain to identify (Lahat, Helwig, & Zelazo, 2013).

Yet having a healthy brain with robust networks for moral reasoning, feeling, and responding does not guarantee a disposition to do the right thing. Nor are all children born with strong circuits for social and moral abilities. Specific areas (e.g., those that support thoughts about other people's perspectives) tend to be weak in children with certain disabilities, for example, those with autism, a developmental disorder that appears early in life and is characterized by deficits in communication, social relationships, and repetitive behaviors (Happé & Frith, 2014). Other evidence indicates that moral capacities must be nurtured, even in children with intact brains, with empathy and related abilities failing to develop normally when parents are callous, indifferent, or harsh (de Souza, 2014; Frick, Ray, Thornton, & Kahn, 2014). Those children who are born with a genetic vulnerability to stress *and* who are maltreated by parents are especially prone to moral problems. They may become conduct disordered, such that they exhibit chronic disobedience and a long-standing disregard for the feelings of others (Happé & Frith, 2014).

Of course, children do not grow into morally responsible or irresponsible citizens based solely on the robustness of their brain networks and treatment by adults. According to the bioecological framework, children contribute to their own moral development through a number of processes—for example, by complying with adults' rules; misbehaving and evaluating why the transgression was wrong; reflecting on bystanders' reactions to their good manners and misdeeds; and classifying violations of practices as moral, conventional, or personal matters. Children's own characteristics and experiences also influence their moral reasoning and behavior, as we now examine.

BIOECOLOGY OF DEVELOPMENT
Children's personal characteristics and environmental experiences influence their moral development.

Level of Intellectual Abilities

Let's return once again to Hector's response to the Heinz dilemma: "In the eyes of the law he would not be doing the right thing, but in the eyes of the moral law he would." Advanced moral reasoning, involving thoughtful consideration of moral standards and such ideals as equality, justice, and basic human rights, requires reflection about multidimensional ideas (Kohlberg, 1976; Turiel, 2002). Children who are intellectually gifted are, on average, more likely than peers to thoughtfully analyze moral issues and address injustices (Schwenck et al., 2014; Silverman, 1994). In comparison, those with an intellectual disability tend to reason at lower levels regarding moral issues (Langdon, Clare, & Murphy, 2010).

Yet intellectual skills do not *guarantee* moral development. It is quite possible to think abstractly about academic subject matter and yet reason in a self-centered, "preconventional" manner (Kohlberg, 1976). In other words, having a basic intellectual capacity is a necessary but insufficient condition for moral development.

Sense of Self

Gaining a sense of oneself as a person who is caring, honest, and respectful of others' rights is an important achievement in moral development. Children are more likely to engage in compassionate action when they think of themselves as capable of helping other people—in other words, when they are confident about their ability to make a difference (Narváez & Rest, 1995). This capacity begins in early childhood when children see themselves doing the right thing—even when no one is looking. In adolescence youngsters may integrate a commitment to moral values into their personal goals and identity (Arnold, 2000; S. A. Hardy, Walker, Olsen, Woodbury, & Hickman, 2014). Those who think of themselves as moral, caring individuals generally place a high priority on acting in accordance with these self-perceptions. Their acts of compassion are not limited to friends and acquaintances but also extend to the community at large, as was the case with the young people in the opening case study.

Parenting

The nature of the parent–child relationship and the type of discipline a parent uses affect moral development. Having a warm relationship with parents motivates the child to learn and follow rules (Kochanska & Kim, 2014; R. A. Thompson & Newton, 2010). But no child adheres to a stringent moral code all of the time, and the way that a parent responds to misbehavior influences his or her subsequent moral development. Certainly it is necessary to impose consequences for harmful actions. However, punishment, especially physical punishment, can focus children's attention on their own distress rather than why they should improve their behavior next time (Hoffman, 1975; Nucci, 2001). Children are more likely to make gains in moral development when they think about the harm that certain behaviors have caused for *others*. Giving children reasons why certain behaviors are unacceptable, with a focus on other people's perspectives, is known as **induction** (Hoffman, 1975). Consider these examples:

- "Having your hair pulled the way you just pulled Mai's can be really painful."
- "You probably hurt John's feelings when you call him names like that."
- "This science project you've just ridiculed may not be as fancy as yours, but I know that Michael spent many hours working on it and was quite proud of what he'd done."

Consistent use of induction in disciplining children, especially when accompanied by *mild* punishment for misbehavior—for instance, insisting that children make amends for their wrongdoings—promotes compliance with rules and fosters empathy, compassion, and altruism (Hoffman, 1975; Patrick & Gibbs, 2012; R. A. Thompson & Newton, 2010). In contrast, power-assertive techniques, in which parents impose their will through spanking, making threats, expressing anger, and issuing commands (e.g., "Do this because I say so!"), are relatively *in*effective in promoting moral development (Damon, 1988; Kochanska et al., 2002; Zhou et al., 2002).

Parents also help their children to understand their moral responsibilities by talking about recent events in which children acted in consideration of, or with disregard for, the needs of another person. These conversations are not strictly disciplinary but rather occasions for making sense of a morally charged event. When parents draw attention to how other people were helped or hurt by something the child did, the child is apt to develop a strong conscience (Laible & Thompson, 2000; Recchia et al., 2014; R. A. Thompson & Newton, 2010).

Interactions with Peers

Children learn many moral lessons during interactions with age-mates. As infants play with other children at home or in child care settings, they may notice others' reactions when they grab a toy or push someone away. Beginning in the preschool years and continuing through adolescence, issues related to sharing, cooperation, and negotiation emerge during group activities (Damon, 1981; Galliger, Tisak, & Tisak, 2009; K. McDonald, Malti, Killen, & Rubin, 2014). Conflicts frequently arise as a result of physical harm, disregard for one another's feelings, mistreatment of possessions, concerns about betrayal, and exclusion from social groups (Feigenberg, King, Barr, & Selman, 2008; Killen & Nucci, 1995; K. McDonald et al., 2014). To learn to resolve interpersonal conflicts successfully, children must engage in social perspective taking, show consideration for others' feelings and rights, refrain from jumping to conclusions, and respect everyone's needs (Killen & Nucci, 1995; Raikes, Virmani, Thompson, & Hatton, 2013; E. Singer & Doornenbal, 2006).

Gender

On average, girls are somewhat more likely than boys to express guilt, shame, empathy, and sympathy—emotions associated with moral behavior (Alessandri & Lewis, 1993; Apavaloaie, Page, & Marks, 2014; Mestre, Samper, Frías, & Tur, 2009; Roos, Hodges, & Salmivalli, 2014; Zahn-Waxler & Robinson, 1995). Girls' greater tendency to communicate guilt and shame may be related to their general inclination to attribute personal failures to internal qualities. In other words, girls are more likely than boys to take personal responsibility for their misdeeds.

Although girls and boys may communicate somewhat differently about moral situations, do they also *reason* differently? In presenting a variety of moral dilemmas to young adults of both genders, Kohlberg found that females reasoned, on average, at Stage 3, whereas males were more likely to reason at Stage 4 (Kohlberg & Kramer, 1969). Yet psychologist **Carol Gilligan** has argued that Kohlberg's stages do not adequately describe female moral development (Gilligan, 1982, 1987; Gilligan & Attanucci, 1988). In particular, Gilligan has suggested that Kohlberg's stages reflect a **justice orientation**—an emphasis on fairness and equal rights—that better characterizes males' moral reasoning. In contrast, she has proposed, girls are socialized to take a **care orientation** toward moral issues—that is, to focus on interpersonal relationships and responsibility for others' well-being. The following dilemma can elicit either a justice orientation or a care orientation:

The Porcupine Dilemma
A group of industrious, prudent moles have spent the summer digging a burrow where they will spend the winter. A lazy, improvident porcupine who has not prepared a winter shelter approaches the moles and pleads to share their burrow. The moles take pity on the porcupine and agree to let him in. Unfortunately, the moles did not anticipate the problem the porcupine's sharp quills would pose in close quarters. Once the porcupine has moved in, the moles are constantly being stabbed. The question is, what should the moles do? (Meyers, 1987, p. 141, adapted from Gilligan, 1985)

People with a justice orientation are apt to look at this situation in terms of someone's rights being violated. They might point out that the burrow belongs to the moles, and so the moles can legitimately throw the porcupine out. If the porcupine refuses to leave, the moles might harm or perhaps even kill him. In contrast, people with a care orientation are likely to show compassion when dealing with the porcupine. They might suggest that the moles cover the porcupine with a blanket so his quills won't annoy anyone (Meyers, 1987).

Gilligan has raised a good point: There is more to moral thinking than justice. By including compassion for other human beings as well as respect for others' rights, she has broadened our conception of what morality encompasses (Milanowicz & Bokus, 2013; L. J. Walker, 1995). However, most research studies do not find major gender differences in moral reasoning (Leman & Björnberg, 2010; Nunner-Winkler, 1984; L. J. Walker, 1991, 2006). Minor differences (usually favoring females) sometimes emerge in early adolescence but disappear by late adolescence (Basinger, Gibbs, & Fuller, 1995). Furthermore, males and females typically incorporate both justice and care into their moral reasoning, applying different orientations (sometimes one, sometimes the other, sometimes both) to different moral problems (Rothbart, Hanley, & Albert, 1986; Smetana, Killen, & Turiel, 1991; L. J. Walker, 2006). Such findings are sufficiently compelling that Gilligan herself has acknowledged that both justice and care orientations are frequently seen in males and females alike (L. M. Brown, Tappan, & Gilligan, 1995; Gilligan & Attanucci, 1988).

Participation in Discussions About Moral, Conventional, and Personal Issues

Kohlberg proposed that children are guided in moral reasoning when challenged by moral dilemmas that are not easily reconciled with their current stage of moral reasoning—in other words, when they encounter situations that create disequilibrium. Discussions of moral issues do appear to promote moral reasoning, especially when children are exposed to an analysis that's slightly more advanced than their present viewpoint (DeVries & Zan, 1996; Power, Higgins, & Kohlberg, 1989; Schlaefli, Rest, & Thoma, 1985). Teachers can integrate dilemmas into the curriculum, for example, asking children whether it is right to steal food from a store to feed a hungry person (a moral issue), wear casual clothing to a formal event (a conventional issue), or wear a shirt with a rock band logo (a personal issue) (Nucci, 2009).

Religious Doctrine

Having a religious faith or other clear philosophical position plays an integral role in the moral development of many children. Even though religious beliefs do not typically enhance moral reasoning as Kohlberg defined it, perhaps most of the time, these beliefs *do* contribute to moral development by providing a compelling rationale for acting humanely (Needham-Penrose & Friedman, 2012; L. J. Walker & Reimer, 2006). Kohlberg's decision that justice, equality, and freedom must be espoused independently of a religious position in order to be considered advanced moral reasoning has been interpreted by some religious scholars as an unwarranted bias (Cullen, 1998; Moroney, 2006).

Despite the prevalent role of religion in justifying moral positions, having a religious faith has not been found to be crucial to moral advancement. Many children raised without a religious faith develop age-typical moral standards (McGowan, 2007; Norenzayan, 2014). Nor does religion ensure a moral orientation in serious matters. In a few unfortunate cases, children are taught to use their faith as a justification for mistreating others, as has occurred in some white supremacy groups and terrorist organizations (P. E. King & Benson, 2006; J. Miller, 2013). Thus, the connection between religion and moral reasoning is complex and understood through the filter of the theorist's own faith or non-belief.

Culture

Each cultural group has unique standards for distinguishing between behaviors that are "right" or "wrong." Consequently, there are differences by culture in moral behavior and reasoning.

In many cultures, lying to avoid punishment for inappropriate behavior is considered wrong, but in some societies it is a legitimate way of saving face (Triandis, 1995). Likewise, many cultures emphasize the importance of being considerate of other people (e.g., "Please

FOR FURTHER EXPLORATION . . .

Learn more about Gilligan's justice and care orientations.

ENHANCEDetext
content extension

Preparing for Your Licensure Examination
Your teaching test might ask you about the breadth of variables that influence children's moral development

be quiet so that your sister can study"), whereas others emphasize the importance of tolerating another's annoying behavior (e.g., "Please try not to let your brother's radio bother you when you study") (M. L. Fuller, 2001; H. L. Grossman, 1994). Some societies teach children to emphasize the rights of individuals, whereas others promote a sense of duty to family and society, and still others stress adherence to a sacred order (Haidt, 2008; J. G. Miller, 2007; Turiel, 2006a). Although many people in mainstream Western societies believe that males and females should have equal rights and opportunities, many Hindu people in India believe that a woman's obedience to her husband is integral to the moral order (Nucci, 2001; Shweder et al., 1987).

Despite these variations, separate cultures encourage a few common principles. Protecting others from harm is a universal value. Most cultures value both individual rights and concern for others (Turiel, 2006a; Turiel, Killen, & Helwig, 1987). And as you learned previously, children around the world learn to distinguish moral, conventional, and personal issues. Moreover, children universally attend to the demands of situations, focusing on justice in some circumstances, compassion in other interactions, and a balance between the two in still others (Lapsley & Carlo, 2014; J. G. Miller, 2007; Turiel, 1998; Turiel et al., 1987).

Promoting Moral Development

Several disciplinary strategies have been shown to promote advanced moral reasoning and behavior. Research findings point to the following recommendations for teachers and other adults who interact with children:

• **Ask children for input on classroom rules.** Children can gain insight into how to show respect for one another and what it means to live in a democracy when they are given a chance to reason about the rules for which they are held accountable (DeVries & Zan, 2003). Teachers, of course, need to guide the wording of rules, and children can continue to give input into how to resolve sticky situations that arise due to accidents, disputes, and distractions. Even young children can offer pragmatic solutions to realistic problems. When one educator asked preschoolers what it meant to abide by their classroom rule of not hurting their newly hatched chicks, the children came up with a combination of reasonable procedures, including picking up chicks carefully, not squeezing them, and not dropping them (DeVries & Zan, 2003) Being invited by teachers to give their ideas about ways to run the classroom smoothly, in this case protecting fragile chicks, helps children feel invested in the governance of the classroom. A second benefit is that children tend to use descriptions that are concrete and easily grasped by classmates, even if (humorously) obvious to adults.

• **Explain why certain behaviors are acceptable and others are not.** Adults must make it crystal clear that some behaviors (e.g., shoving, making racist remarks, bringing weapons to school) are not acceptable under any circumstances. Schools generally have written codes of conduct that specify prohibited behaviors, and classroom teachers can, as we have suggested, invite children to help generate classroom rules at the beginning of the year. Adults also need to explain that some behaviors are appropriate in certain situations yet restricted in others. For example, copying a classmate's work may be permissible when a student is in the process of learning but is unacceptable (constituting fraud) during tests of what a student has learned (Thorkildsen, 1995).

Adults can accompany disciplinary actions and discussions of rules with explanations about *why* certain behaviors cannot be tolerated, with an emphasis on harm to others (recall our earlier discussion of *induction*). A preschool teacher might say, "If we throw the blocks, someone may get hurt" (Bronson, 2000, p. 206). An elementary school teacher might remind students, "We walk when we are in line so nobody gets bumped or tripped" (Bronson, 2000, p. 205). Adults might also ask children to describe how they feel when they're victims of certain misbehaviors and speculate about how they would feel in a situation were they to be victimized in a certain way (Doescher & Sugawara, 1989; Hoffman, 1991). In addition, adults can encourage children to make amends for misdeeds (Nucci, 2001). A middle school teacher might say, "I'm sure you didn't mean to hurt Jamal's feelings, but he's pretty upset about what you said. What might you do or say to make him feel better?"

• **Discuss moral dilemmas with children.** Moral dilemmas often arise in conjunction with inappropriate behaviors (e.g., aggression, theft) at school. One effective approach is to form a *just community*, in which students and their teachers hold regular "town meetings" to discuss recent interpersonal conflicts and establish rules that help students become more productive and socially responsible (e.g., A. Higgins, 1995; Oser, Althof, & Higgins-D'Alessandro, 2008; Power et al., 1989).

Teachers and other professionals can do several things to ensure that discussions facilitate children's moral development (Nucci, 2001; Reimer, Paolitto, & Hersh, 1983; Thornberg, 2010). First, they should create a trusting and nonthreatening atmosphere in which children feel free to express their ideas without censure or embarrassment. Second, they can help children identify all aspects of a dilemma, including the perspectives of the individuals involved. Third, they can encourage children to explore the underlying basis of their thinking. For example, adults might encourage children to look at an infraction from the extent to which moral concerns, conventions, and personal choice are all involved (Nucci & Weber, 1991). Although classmates who deface their school building with graffiti might believe they are engaging in creative self-expression (personal choice), they are also breaking a rule (convention), disregarding other students' rights to study and learn in a clean and attractive setting (the dimension of justice), and thumbing their noses at the needs of those around them (the dimension of care).

• **Identify moral issues in the curriculum.** An English class studying works of Shakespeare might debate whether Hamlet was justified in killing Claudius to avenge the murder of his father (Nucci, 2009). A science class might discuss the ethical issues involved in using laboratory rats to study the effects of cancer-producing agents. Classroom discussions can also help young people distinguish among moral, conventional, and personal matters within the context of historical events. In American history a teacher might ask students to reflect on why George Washington refused to accept a letter from King George II of England. In Washington's mind, the letter violated an important social convention because it was addressed to "Mr. George Washington" rather than "President George Washington," thereby failing to recognize his status as leader of a legitimate nation (Nucci, 2001, 2006). Likewise, students might discuss moral dimensions in John Brown's 19th-century violent campaigns against slavery in the United States by considering the suffering inflicted on freedom fighters and oppressors. (Nucci, 2001, 2006).

• **Challenge children's moral reasoning with slightly more advanced reasoning.** Kohlberg's stages (see Table 14-1 on page 530) provide a useful framework for identifying moral arguments likely to provoke disequilibrium in youngsters. In particular, Kohlberg suggested that teachers offer reasoning that is one stage above a child's current thinking. Imagine that a teenage boy who is concerned primarily with gaining peer approval (Stage 3) often lets a popular cheerleader copy his homework. His teacher might present law-and-order logic (Stage 4), suggesting that a homework assignment has been designed to help students learn more effectively, especially when completed with minimal assistance. If adults present arguments at a level that is too much higher than that of children's current reasoning, however, children will have trouble understanding the logic and will typically disregard the argument. (Boom, Brugman, & van der Heijden, 2001; Narváez, 1998).

• **Encourage children to invite excluded classmates to participate in activities.** In almost every school, some children are excluded from social groups. Such rejection can occur as a result of prejudice and discrimination, with students occasionally perceiving peers with disabilities, those from low-income backgrounds, and individuals from different ethnic groups as undesirable playmates or incompetent learners (Killen, Mulvey, & Hitti, 2013; Killen & Smetana, 2010). Complicating matters, many children view the issue of selecting peers to eat lunch with or sit next to on the bus as their personal choice. Thus, they may feel justified when banning certain peers from their play. Yet teachers can appeal to children's sense of fairness by pointing out that they collectively want to have a classroom where *all* children feel that they belong. Teachers might also explain that rejected classmates are likely to feel hurt. In addition, teachers can make some assignments that require children to work together.

Preparing for Your Licensure Examination
Your teaching test might ask how you would facilitate discussions with children about social issues.

• **Get children actively involved in community service.** As you've learned, youngsters are more likely to adhere to strong moral principles when they have high self-efficacy for helping others and have integrated a commitment to moral ideals into their general sense of identity. Such self-perceptions don't appear out of the blue, of course, as the teacher in our opening case study, Alice Terry, understood. Children are more likely to have high confidence in helping others when they have the guidance, support, and feedback they need to carry out relevant behaviors successfully. Through ongoing **service learning**—food and clothing drives, visits to homes for the elderly, community cleanup efforts, and so on—children can learn that they have the skills to help those less fortunate than themselves and in other ways make the world a better place in which to live. In the process, they also begin to think of themselves as concerned, compassionate, and moral citizens (O'Flaherty, Liddy, Tansey, Roche, 2011; Nucci, 2001; Youniss & Yates, 1999). To gain full advantage from such experiences, students need to have some choice in the projects they take on, reflect on what they have accomplished, consider how they can extend their accomplishments in future work, and either write about or discuss their experiences with other participants (T. Gross, 2010; D. Hart, Atkins, & Donnelly, 2006; Morimoto & Friedland, 2013; Nucci, 2006; J. Terry, Smith, & McQuillin 2014).

• **Foster a climate of religious tolerance.** In the United States, the First Amendment to the Constitution requires that matters of church and state be kept separate. Many other nations offer similar protections. Public school teachers can certainly discuss religion within the context of social studies or other appropriate academic topics. But teachers in U.S. public schools cannot incorporate religious ideas or practices into classroom activities or community events in any way that shows preference for one religion over another, or even express a preference for religion over atheism. Just as professionals foster respect for diverse cultural backgrounds, so, too, should they cultivate acceptance of diverse religious beliefs. Many school districts and other institutions for youngsters have specific policies that prohibit any name-calling related to religious beliefs, practices, and affiliations.

Teaching respect for diverse religious perspectives does not communicate the message that all customs justified by religious beliefs are equally acceptable. Adults will certainly want to question practices that blatantly violate people's basic human rights. It *does* mean, however, that everyone needs to work hard to understand other groups' behaviors within the context of their religious beliefs.

• **Appeal to children's emotional understandings.** Kohlberg's theory of moral development has been enormously influential, as you have learned, but its historical focus on cognition has eclipsed our appreciation for how emotions are intertwined with reasoning about right and wrong (Lapsley & Carlo, 2014). Virtually all children are born with neurologically based emotional capacities that, with responsive and affectionate care, become connected up with cognitive abilities for reflecting on, and habits of behavior for acting on, moral principles. To become strong, these neurological connections must be nurtured at a parent's knee, and later at a teacher's side. Thus, teachers can remind children not only of rules but, especially for moral infractions, their implications for the welfare of other people.

• **Discourage cheating.** *Cheating* refers to the deliberate act of breaking a rule and misrepresenting oneself as having actually abided by it in order to gain an unfair advantage. Academic cheating, in which children falsely pass off work on a test or paper as their own, runs rampant through our schools, especially in the middle and high school grades (X. Ding et al., 2014; Muñoz-García & Aviles-Herrera, 2014). Students cheat with the help of technology (e.g., by getting answers on the Internet, paying for essays written by other people, and bringing formulas and other contraband information on calculators and under labels of water bottles) and classmates (e.g., by sharing answers and homework). Students may also fabricate reasons as to why an assignment is being turned in late.

Cheating is inherently wrong. It also typically violates codes of conduct from schools serving elementary through secondary students and thus can lead to punishment. Cheating undermines the integrity of the educational system because the validity of assessment results, the equality of grading schemes, and the justice of selection decisions (e.g., who receives a high school diploma) are put into question (Muñoz-García & Aviles-Herrera, 2014). Finally, students are harmed by their own cheating, in that they may cheat again in the future, become less disposed to embrace personal integrity, and invest reduced effort in their academic studies.

Yet according to many children, cheating is not a moral violation. It does not harm other people in the same way as pushing classmates off a swing or stealing their lunch does. For them, it may be a reasonable tactic to complete difficult assignments (F. Power & Power, 2006). Thus, children need to learn why cheating is wrong and not tolerated. We recommend the following tactics:

- *Develop an honor code.* Present in many universities, honor codes, which are statements that assert positive academic and behavioral characteristics, increasingly appear in a K-12 school's code of conduct because they delineate the virtues—and not just the actions to avoid—that students are expected to exhibit. Teachers can talk about the honor code with children, describing its intentions but also helping them connect abstract values with relevant behaviors, for example, respecting other people's creativity by not copying their statements word for word, and giving proper credit with citations and references.
- *Establish a climate of learning that is conducive to academic integrity.* Academic integrity means being honest and responsible in school assignments and other educational activities. These virtues are more likely to develop when adults encourage and model them and when teachers specifically motivate students with interesting and relevant material (Sorenson & Goldsmith, 2012). In other words, children are less likely to cheat when they are motivated to learn the material.
- *Describe different forms of cheating, the range of tactics that school personnel take to identify them, and the penalties that students suffer when caught.* Students need to learn what plagiarism is, why it is wrong, and how they can avoid it. In many situations it is fine for children to share ideas with one another, and therefore they need to know why and when they must work on their own.
- *Empathize with students about the pressures they experience in their schoolwork.* A primary reason children cheat is that they want to do well on their assignments, do not know how to study, and are worried about their performance. Answering their questions about schoolwork and reassuring them that they can talk with you is an important step in taking the desperation out of their school endeavors.
- *Supervise tests, watch for plagiarism, and be vigilant for other types of cheating.* Students are less likely to cheat when they think they might be caught, and therefore teachers are advised to monitor tests, walk around the room, and look for banned resources, such as cell phones, that are common devices for accessing prohibited information.
- *Follow through with penalties.* Given how prevalent cheating is, penalties should be serious but not severe. Students might be asked to re-do assignments they have plagiarized for their first offense, for example, and receive a zero on a second offense. Students who persist with dishonest behaviors after being consistently chastised may require counseling and other interventions, as this type of behavior cannot be tolerated and is associated with later problems in adjustment as adults (G. E. Miller, 1987).

Summary

An ability to distinguish between right and wrong emerges early in life and continues to develop over time. Infants are clearly uncomfortable when they witness others being hurt. Most preschoolers are aware that actions that cause significant physical or psychological harm are wrong even if an authority figure tells them otherwise. Children of this age are able to distinguish transgressions that violate moral rules from conventional social practices and from other decisions that might be considered a matter of personal choice. As children get older, they progress in their understanding of fairness and develop an increasing capacity to feel guilt, shame, and empathy about moral wrongdoings. As they advance in cognitive skills, and especially as they become capable of abstract thought, young people reason about moral issues in more sophisticated ways, and they are more likely to behave in accordance with basic moral principles. Even at the high school level, however, youngsters do not always take the moral high road, because personal needs and self-interests enter into moral decisions.

To some degree, different cultures foster distinct moral values, but virtually all societies recognize the importance of fairness, justice, and concern for others. Adults can promote young people's moral development by explaining why certain behaviors are unacceptable (in that they cause harm to another or jeopardize that person's rights), engaging youngsters in discussions about moral dilemmas, exposing them to diverse and slightly more advanced moral perspectives, and getting them actively involved in service to others.

ENHANCEDetext *self-check*

PROSOCIAL BEHAVIOR AND AGGRESSION

Children's helping and hurting behaviors have an impact on other people's physical and psychological well-being and therefore have moral implications. **Prosocial behavior** is an action intended to promote the welfare of another person, perhaps by sharing, teaching, or comforting. **Aggression** is an action intentionally taken to hurt another person either physically (e.g., hitting, shoving, or fighting) or psychologically (e.g., embarrassing, insulting, or ostracizing). Let's consider the typical developmental course of these behaviors and then examine their origins and educational implications.

Development of Prosocial Behavior

Even young infants are attuned to others' distress, in that they may start to cry when they hear other babies crying (Eisenberg, 1992; Hatfield, Cacioppo, & Rapson, 1994).[5] True prosocial behaviors—actions intended to help someone else—appear early in the second year (M. Carpenter, Uebel, & Tomasello, 2013; Farver & Branstetter, 1994; Kärtner, Keller, & Chaudhary, 2010; Zahn-Waxler et al., 1992). Toddlers spontaneously give adults or peers assistance with everyday tasks, and they are apt to offer their favorite blanket or teddy bear to someone who appears unhappy or in pain. As a general rule, children behave more prosocially—for instance, they become increasingly generous—as they grow older, especially when parents encourage them to be helpful to others (Brownell, Svetlova, Anderson, Nichols, & Drummond, 2013; Eisenberg, 1982; Eisenberg, Eggum, & Edwards, 2010).

Children engage in prosocial behaviors for a variety of reasons. Some motivations are self-serving. A 3-year-old boy may bring a toy to a distressed peer, hoping the other child will stop his annoying crying. A 7-year-old girl may help a classmate with schoolwork in order to gain her teacher's approval. At other times, children engage in prosocial behavior because they are genuinely concerned about the welfare of others. In the process of putting themselves in someone else's shoes, children experience the other person's feelings—that is, they have *empathy*. Many children who behave prosocially feel *sympathy*, a concern for another that does not necessarily involve sharing the same feeling as that person (Batson, 1991; A. Edwards et al., 2014; Eisenberg et al., 2010).

Empathy and sympathy both motivate prosocial behavior, but the relationships among these characteristics are complex. As you have learned, a child can engage in prosocial behavior for self-serving motives that have nothing to do with an understanding of the other person's feelings and that are not motivated by concern for his or her well-being. In addition, children can be empathic toward another's distress yet become so consumed by personal distress that they are unable to act helpfully (Eisenberg et al., 2010). Furthermore, children who are sympathetic toward the plight of others may provide needed assistance, but only if they are sufficiently confident about *how* to lend a hand.

As they grow older, children increasingly help others at least in part as a result of feelings of empathy and sympathy. American psychologist **Nancy Eisenberg** and her colleagues have identified five different levels, or *orientations*, to prosocial behavior, through which youngsters are apt to proceed over the course of childhood and adolescence. These orientations are described and illustrated in the Observation Guidelines table "Assessing Children's Prosocial Development." Children do not march through the orientations in a lock-step manner, however. Their behavior is apt to reflect two or more orientations in any particular time period, even as they increasingly exhibit more advanced orientations (Eisenberg, Carlo, Murphy, & Van Court, 1995; Eisenberg, Fabes, & Spinrad, 2006; Eisenberg, Miller, Shell, McNalley, & Shea, 1991).

[5]The infant's tendency to respond to others' emotions is explained in Chapter 11.

In particular circumstances that might elicit prosocial behavior, children are more likely to help another individual if they themselves have been the cause of the person's pain or distress (Eisenberg, 1995). Thus, feeling guilty is also closely related to prosocial behavior (Eisenberg et al., 2010). Children are likewise more likely to behave prosocially if others' misfortunes are the result of an accident, disability, or other uncontrollable circumstance, rather than the result of something the distressed people might be construed as having brought upon themselves (Eisenberg & Fabes, 1998; S. Graham, 1997).

Finally, prosocial behaviors are more common when benefits outweigh the costs—for instance, when children think the beneficiary might eventually do them a favor in return (Eisenberg, Fabes, Schaller, Carlo, & Miller, 1991; L. Peterson, 1980). For some youngsters, however, the benefits of prosocial actions are strictly internal: A feeling of personal satisfaction about helping someone else more than makes up for any loss of time or convenience (see the "empathic" and "internalized values" orientations in the Observation Guidelines table that follows). Unfortunately, some children believe that *aggression* yields more benefits than prosocial actions, as we shall see now.

OBSERVATION GUIDELINES
Assessing Children's Prosocial Development

CHARACTERISTIC	LOOK FOR	EXAMPLE	IMPLICATION
Hedonistic Orientation *(common in preschool and the early elementary grades)*	• Tendency to help others only when one can simultaneously address one's own needs with the same gesture • Prosocial behaviors directed primarily toward familiar adults and peers	Several preschoolers are at a table drawing pictures. Peter is using the only black crayon at the table. Alaina asks him for the crayon so she can color her dog black, telling him, "I just need it for a second." Ignoring her, Peter continues to use the black crayon for several more minutes and then puts it on the table.	Point out that other people have legitimate needs, and emphasize the importance of fairness and the value in helping others. For example, ask children to be "reading buddies" for younger children, explaining that doing so will help them become better readers themselves.
Superficial Needs-of-Others Orientation *(common in the elementary grades)*	• Some willingness to help others even at personal sacrifice • Only superficial understanding of others' perspectives	During an annual holiday toy drive, many children in a third-grade class contribute toys they have outgrown. They seem happy to do so, commenting that "Poor kids need toys too" and "This doll will be fun for somebody else to play with."	Commend youngsters for altruistic behaviors, and ask them to speculate on how their actions help recipients (e.g., "Can you imagine how the children will feel when they get your toys? Most of them escaped with only the clothes on their backs.").
Stereotyped, Approval-Focused Orientation *(seen in some elementary and secondary students)*	• Tendency to behave prosocially as a means to gain others' approval • Simplistic, stereotypical views of what "good" and "bad" people do	When walking to school, Cari sees Stanley stumble and accidentally drop his backpack in a puddle. She stops, asks if he's okay, and helps him wipe off his backpack. As she describes the incident to her teacher later that morning, she says, "Maybe he'll be my friend now. Anyway, it's nice to help someone."	Provide opportunities for youngsters to engage in prosocial activities. Choose activities that are apt to be enjoyable and in other ways rewarding in and of themselves.
Empathic Orientation *(common in the secondary grades)*	• Genuine empathy for other people's distress, even when one does not know the people personally • Willingness to help without regard for consequences to oneself	Members of a high school service club coordinate a schoolwide garage sale, with all proceeds going to help pay the medical expenses of a classmate with a rare form of cancer. Students spend several weekends collecting contributions, using their own money for the supplies they need to make the fund-raiser a success.	Alert youngsters to circumstances in which people's basic needs are not being met or in which human rights are being violated. Ask youngsters to brainstorm ways in which they might, in some small way, make a difference for people living in these circumstances.
Internalized-Values Orientation *(seen in a small minority of high school students)*	• Generalized concern for equality, dignity, human rights, and the welfare of society as a whole • Commitment to helping others integrated into one's overall sense of self	Franklin spends much of his free time working with Habitat for Humanity, an organization of volunteers who build houses for low-income families. "This is as important as my schoolwork," he says. "It's everyone's responsibility to help one another."	Create assignments—public service projects, fund-raisers, and so on—in which youngsters with an internalized-values orientation can share their enthusiasm for prosocial activities with peers.

Sources: First two columns based on Eisenberg, 1982; Eisenberg et al., 1995; and Eisenberg, Lennon, & Pasternack, 1986.

Development of Aggression

Aggression takes a range of forms. **Physical aggression** is an action that can potentially cause bodily injury. Examples are hitting, pushing, fighting, and using weapons. **Relational aggression** is an action that can adversely affect friendships and other interpersonal relationships. Examples are name-calling, spreading unflattering rumors, and ostracizing a peer from a desirable social group. You can observe a spontaneous act of relational aggression at recess in a combined second- and third-grade class in an Observing Children video,.

Observing Children 14-3

Observe an age-typical exclusionary gesture in girls at play, in which a girl who is not successful in persuading her friend to be on a certain team slights her by running off with another girl.

ENHANCEDetext *video example*

The capacity for aggression emerges early. By the latter half of the first year, infants show anger toward caregivers who prevent them from reaching desired objects (Hay et al., 2010; Lorber, Del Vecchio, & Smith Slep, 2014; C. R. Stenberg & Campos, 1990). As they approach their first birthday, infants swat at age-mates who take their toys or parents who obstruct their actions (Caplan, Vespo, Pedersen, & Hay, 1991; Dodge, Coie, & Lynam, 2006). By 18 months, children regularly hit, kick, push, and bite others (Nærde, Ogden, Janson, & Daae Zachrisson, 2014; Tremblay et al., 2004). Physical aggression peaks between 20 and 22 months and decreases thereafter. You can observe a young boy diverted from physical aggression in an Observing Children video.

Conflicts over possessions remain common during the preschool years, even when they are not expressed with hitting, shoving, or other physical means (S. Jenkins, Bax, & Hart, 1980). For most children, physical aggression declines after early childhood, for several reasons: Children learn to control their impulses, acquire better strategies for resolving conflicts, and become increasingly skillful at relational aggression (Dodge et al., 2006; Flanders et al., 2010; Mischel, 1974).

Observing Children 14-4

Observe a young boy start to engage in aggression before being asked by a teacher to use his words instead.

ENHANCEDetext *video example*

The developmental decline in physical aggression is not universal, however. When children remain physically aggressive after the transition into kindergarten, they are at risk for problems in social adjustment, peer acceptance, and relationships with teachers (Gower, Lingras, Mathieson, Kawabata, & Crick, 2014). Children who fail to show the expected pattern of diminished fighting generally exhibit one of two profiles, although extremely aggressive children may blend both. Children who exhibit **reactive aggression** hit, push, and shove primarily in response to frustration, anger, or provocation (Crick & Dodge, 1996; Hubbard, Morrow, Romano, & McAuliffe, 2010; Poulin & Boivin, 1999). When an age-mate teases a child for losing a game, the child may impulsively punch the teaser. In comparison, children who engage primarily in **proactive aggression** deliberately initiate aggressive behaviors—physical aggression, relational aggression, or both—as a means of obtaining desired goals. For example, a child may callously push an age-mate out of the way at a vending machine when he hears that there is only one remaining can of soda in the dispenser. Of the two groups, children who exhibit proactive aggression are more likely to have difficulty maintaining friendships with others (Poulin & Boivin, 1999). They may direct considerable aggression toward particular peers, and those who do are known as **bullies**.

Bullies, like other aggressive children, have problems handling emotions, especially anger, have weak social skills, and are less empathic than age-mates. Yet bullies have unique characteristics not shared with other aggressive children. Whereas aggressive children who are not bullies may bother a wide range of individuals, bullies are selective. They develop a peculiar relationship with their victims, whom they repeatedly humiliate, threaten, and intimidate. Many children who pick on other children were previously victimized themselves by peers or older children (and are sometimes called bully-victims). Bullies also can become victims later on, as a result of weak social skills. Finally, children who affiliate with and defend bullies are at risk for being bullied themselves at a later point in time (Cicchetti, Murray-Close, Huitsing, et al., 2014).

Bullies and other aggressive children are apt to exhibit one or more of the following problems in social cognition:[6]

- *Misinterpretation of social cues.* Children who are either physically or relationally aggressive toward peers tend to interpret others' behaviors as reflecting hostile intentions,

---

[6] Social cognitive abilities are examined in detail in Chapter 12.

especially when such behaviors are ambiguous in intent. This **hostile attributional bias** is especially prevalent in children who are prone to *reactive* aggression (Cicchetti, Murray-Close, Cillessen, Lansu, & Van Den Berg, 2014; Crick & Dodge, 1996; Dodge et al., 2003; A. Law & Fung, 2013). Thus, if a clumsy peer bumps gently into a reactively aggressive child, the aggressive child is prone to assume that the act was deliberately hurtful and retaliate with a push.

- *Prevalence of self-serving goals.* For most young people, establishing and maintaining interpersonal relationships are high priorities. For aggressive children, however, self-serving goals—perhaps maintaining an inflated self-image, seeking revenge, or gaining power and prestige—often take precedence (Crick & Dodge, 1996; K. L. McDonald, Baden, & Lochman, 2013).
- *Ineffective social problem-solving skills.* Aggressive children often have little knowledge of how to persuade, negotiate, or compromise, and so they resort to hitting, shoving, and barging into play (Priddis, Landy, Moroney, & Kane, 2014).
- *Beliefs about the appropriateness of aggression.* Many aggressive children believe that violence and other forms of aggression are acceptable ways of resolving conflicts and retaliating for others' misdeeds. They may believe they need to teach someone a "lesson." Those who display high rates of *proactive* aggression are apt to believe that aggressive action will yield positive results—for instance, that it will enhance their social status (Hubbard et al., 2010).

Bullies and other aggressive children have many venues for harassing peers besides face-to-face irritation and behind-the-scenes ostracism. A good number of children spread malicious gossip and inappropriate images of a classmate through text messages and social media (Bauman, 2011; Compton, Campbell, & Mergler, 2014). *Cyber-bullies* provoke considerable anguish in their victims, who may find themselves overnight—or even within the span of an hour—publicly exposed with sensitive images, embarrassing accusations, and even hateful messages.

We'd be remiss if we did not consider the special needs of children who are routinely victimized by bullies. Any child can be victimized at one time or another, but there are some common characteristics of children who are regular targets of bullies: Compared to their peers, they may be shy, immature, anxious, friendless, lacking in self-confidence, and not accustomed to defending themselves (Bierman, 2004; Marsh, Parada, Yeung, & Healey, 2001; Pellegrini, Bartini, & Brooks, 1999). Some have disabilities, are overweight, or are gay, lesbian, bisexual, or transgendered (Juvonen & Graham, 2014). You can listen to a girl talk about what it is like to be the target of a bully's aggression in an Observing Children video.

Children who are victimized benefit from guidance, sympathy, and reassurance that the bully will not be allowed to continue to intimidate them. Educators exert therapeutic effects by comforting victims and, when necessary, teaching them skills in self-defense, negotiation, and self-assertion. Intervention is important because children who have been bullied are at risk for later anxiety, depression, other mental health problems, chronic health conditions, and strains in intimate relationships (W. E. Copeland et al., 2014; Sigurdson, Wallander, & Sund, 2014; Wolke, Lereya, Fisher, Lewis, & Zammit, 2014).

As you have learned, helping and hurting behaviors change steadily over the childhood years. In the Developmental Trends table "Prosocial and Aggressive Behavior at Different Age Levels," we present characteristics that teachers and other practitioners are likely to see in infants, children, and adolescents, as well as common forms of diversity in the age-groups.

Observing Children 14-5
Listen to a girl talk about what it is like to be the target of a bully's aggression.

ENHANCEDetext *video example*

Bioecology of Prosocial Behavior and Aggression

Children's helping and hurting behaviors draw from an amalgamation of heredity, personal activity, and environmental experience. In this section we look at biological foundations of these behaviors, the experiences children have in social environments, experiences as boys or girls, and the impact of temperament.

BIOECOLOGY OF DEVELOPMENT
Children's prosocial development and aggression are affected by nature, nurture, and children's experiences.

DEVELOPMENTAL TRENDS
Prosocial and Aggressive Behavior at Different Age Levels

AGE	WHAT YOU MIGHT OBSERVE	DIVERSITY	IMPLICATIONS
Infancy **(Birth–2 Years)** 	• Appearance of simple prosocial behaviors (e.g., offering a teddy bear to a crying child) in second year • Anger at caregivers who prevent reaching toward desired objects • Conflicts with peers about toys and other objects • Occasional biting, hitting, or scratching of peers	• Infants may be more inclined to show prosocial actions when caregivers model these behaviors. • Some children have "difficult" temperaments; they may be especially contrary in the second year, biting others or exhibiting frequent temper tantrums.	• Allow infants to interact with one another under your supervision. • Verbalize sympathy toward an injured child within earshot of other children. • Warmly acknowledge infants' helping. • Set up the environment to reduce frustration by providing duplicates of favorite toys and creating separate areas for quiet play and active movement. • Tell aggressive toddlers that hitting is hurtful and receives a consequence (e.g., brief time-out). Demonstrate gentle touch instead.
Early Childhood **(2–6 Years)**	• Basic signs of empathy for people in distress • Rudimentary sharing and coordination of play activities • Attempts to comfort people in distress, especially those whom children know well; comforting strategies not always effective • Occasional aggressive struggles with peers over possessions • Emerging ability to inhibit aggressive impulses	• Children who are impulsive may use more physical aggression than those who are more patient and self-controlled. • Children are more apt to behave prosocially if they are reinforced for such behavior. • On average, boys are more physically aggressive than are girls.	• Recognize that selfish and territorial behaviors are common in early childhood. • Model sympathetic responses; explain how you are expressing concern and why you are doing it. • Encourage children to comfort a distressed peer. • Praise controlled and constructive responses to frustration. • Comfort the victims of aggression, and administer punishment to perpetrators. Explain why aggressive behavior is not tolerated.
Middle Childhood **(6–10 Years)**	• Growing repertoire of conflict resolution skills • Increasing empathy for unknown individuals who are suffering or needy • Deepening desire to help others as an objective in and of itself • Decrease in overt physical aggression, accompanied by rise in relational aggression and covert antisocial behaviors (e.g., lying, stealing)	• Children whose parents value prosocial behavior are more likely to exhibit cooperative gestures and to exhibit concern for others. • Some children consistently misinterpret peers' thoughts and motives (e.g., by interpreting accidents as deliberate attempts to cause harm). • A few children become increasingly aggressive in the elementary grades. • Some children are bullies who regularly victimize vulnerable peers (e.g., those without friends or with disabilities).	• Assist children in handling a conflict by asking them to consider their opponent's perspective, and together generate solutions that address everyone's needs. • Draw attention to a consoled child's relief ("Look how much better Sally feels now that you've apologized for hurting her feelings"). • Do not tolerate physical aggression or intimidation. Make sure children understand rules for behavior, and respond to aggression with appropriate consequences. • Be on the lookout for children who are frequent victims of aggression; coach them in self-assertion and social skills.
Early Adolescence **(10–14 Years)** 	• Decline in physical aggression • Frequent teasing and taunting of peers; occasional sexual harassment • Teasing and bullying using social network sites and cell phones • Occasional name-calling of teachers and other adults	• Beginning at puberty, a higher testosterone level in boys can intensify aggressive tendencies. • Some adolescents with social-emotional problems (e.g., those with conduct disorders) show deficits in empathy. • Bullying behavior in some youngsters may temporarily increase after transition to middle school or junior high.	• Communicate that giving, sharing, and caring for others are high priorities. • Keep a watchful eye on students' between-class and after-school activities; make it clear that aggression is *not* acceptable on school grounds. • Talk with adolescents about their peer relationships and the pressures they feel to conform.

DEVELOPMENTAL TRENDS (continued)

AGE	WHAT YOU MIGHT OBSERVE	DIVERSITY	IMPLICATIONS
Late Adolescence (14–18 Years)	• For many, decreasing aggressive behavior, often as a result of forming more intimate and rewarding relationships with others • Some acts of relational aggression in the form of teasing, excluding others, or cyber-bullying • Ability to offer constructive help to others as individuals or members of volunteer groups	• Some high school students are exceptionally committed to making the world a better place. • On average, youngsters who live in violent neighborhoods are more apt to become aggressive than are peers in safer neighborhoods. • Violence-prone adolescents often believe that socking another person is reasonable retribution for unjust actions. • Substance abuse and sexual activity increase the probability of aggression.	• Encourage community service work and commitment to helping others. Ask adolescents to reflect on their experiences through group discussions or written essays. • Enforce prohibitions against bringing weapons to school. • Provide intensive treatment to young people who exhibit especially aggressive tendencies.

Hereditary and Other Biological Influences

From an evolutionary perspective, both prosocial and aggressive inclinations have enabled human beings to survive (Hoffman, 1981; McCullough, Kurzban, & Tabak, 2011; Meloni, 2013). Prosocial behavior provides the basis for close relationships, promotes group cohesion, and helps people pull together in harsh conditions. Squabbling and warfare cause people to spread apart (thereby improving their chances of finding food and other essential resources) and, in times of battle, to compete such that only the strongest members survive, later giving birth to sturdy offspring.

An evolutionary perspective of such behaviors is, of course, speculative. Twin studies provide more convincing evidence that both prosocial and aggressive behaviors have biological origins. Monozygotic (identical) twins tend to be more similar than dizygotic (fraternal) twins with respect to altruistic behavior, empathy for others, and aggression (Brendgen, 2014; Eisenberg, Fabes et al., 2006; Lacourse et al., 2014; Rushton, Fulkner, Neal, Nias, & Eysenck, 1986).

Precisely how heredity affects children's tendencies to be especially helpful or hurtful is unknown, but genes probably determine aspects of the brain's physiology that affect emotions and interpretations of social cues. Specific areas of the brain become active when people listen to sad stories or witness another person's distress, indicating that these regions are devoted to empathic responses (S. Light et al., 2009; Ruby & Decety, 2001; Swain, Konrath, Dayton, Finegood, & Ho, 2013).

A similar picture emerges with the biological bases of aggression. Chemical substances in the brain affect children's aggressive tendencies, perhaps by influencing children's dispositions for seeking out certain kinds of stimulation or inhibiting aggressive impulses (E. Baker, Shelton, Baibazarova, Hay, & van Goozen, 2013; Gorodetsky et al., 2014). Aggressive behavior also appears to be triggered partly by the male hormone testosterone. On average, males are more aggressive than females, and after puberty, males with high testosterone levels tend to be more aggressive than males with lower levels (Carney & Mason, 2010; Susman et al., 1987). Finally, children and adults with irregularities to certain areas of the brain, especially damage to an area in the front of the cortex involved in planning and behavior control, display heightened aggression (Bertsch et al., 2013; Pennington & Bennetto, 1993; Raine & Scerbo, 1991).

Environmental Influences

The solid evidence of biological influences on empathy, prosocial behavior, and aggression does not mean that the environment is unimportant. On the contrary, parents, brothers and sisters, friends, neighbors, and others are enormously influential in how helping and hurting behaviors are manifested. Thus, a boy may be genetically vulnerable to being irritable and impulsive but learn self-control from parents, who calm his reactive biochemistry and teach him restraint.

A variety of mechanisms are at work. Close relationships are especially powerful in providing children with emotional foundations for helping and hurting behaviors. Children whose parents are sensitive, compassionate, and responsive tend to become empathic, cooperative, and helpful to others (Healy, Sanders, & Iyer, 2014; R. A. Thompson & Newton, 2010). Conversely, those whose parents are harsh or neglectful are at definite risk for becoming aggressive and developing other mental health problems. Affectionate parents typically guide children in coping effectively with anger and disappointment, whereas hostile parents inadvertently cultivate aggression, particularly reactive aggression, because children grow accustomed to letting their frustrations escalate and lashing out at others (Fite et al., 2010).

Another way that families are influential is by serving as role models. Children who observe sympathetic and generous models tend to be more helpful than those without such exposure (R. Elliott & Vasta, 1970; M. Mares, Palmer, & Sullivan, 2008). In this manner, a child notices and later emulates a parent's charitable acts in the community. Through similar processes, children who observe aggressive models show a greater-than-average number of antagonistic acts (C. A. Anderson et al., 2003; Febres et al., 2014; Huesmann, Dubow, & Boxer, 2011).

Parents' styles of interacting with and disciplining children also influence prosocial and aggressive tendencies. Children are more likely to adopt a prosocial demeanor when parents exhibit an *authoritative* parenting style—that is, when parents are warm and loving, hold high standards for behavior, and explain why certain behaviors are unacceptable (Baumrind, Larzelere, & Owens, 2010; Hoffman, 1988; Padilla-Walker, Carlo, Christensen, & Yorgason, 2012).[7] Children also tend to be more prosocial when parents enlist their help in caring for any younger siblings and in keeping the household going (Carlo, Koller, Raffaelli, & de Guzman, 2007; Whiting & Whiting, 1975). By way of contrast, other family environments are virtual breeding grounds for aggression. *Authoritarian* (rather than authorita*tive*) parenting, especially when accompanied by frequent physical punishment or abuse, encourages aggression, but so occasionally does very *permissive* parenting, presumably because children are left to their own devices in dealing with negative urges (Ehrenreich, Beron, Brinkley, & Underwood, 2014; Straus, 2000).

Another mechanism for prompting prosocial and aggressive behavior is reinforcement. Over the short run, children engage in more prosocial behavior if they are rewarded (e.g., with candy or praise) for such behavior (Eisenberg, Fabes, Carlo, & Karbon, 1992; Ramaswamy & Bergin, 2009). However, tangible rewards appear counterproductive over the long run, perhaps because children begin to perform prosocial actions primarily to benefit themselves ("I gave her my candy because I knew Dad would give me an even bigger treat for sharing") rather than to gain personal satisfaction from helping others (Eisenberg & Fabes, 1998; Szynal-Brown & Morgan, 1983). Aggressive behavior is often reinforced by its outcomes: It may enable children to gain desired objects or get revenge (Crick & Dodge, 1996; Lochman, Wayland, & White, 1993).

Age-mates and adults at school and in other institutions also promote prosocial and aggressive behaviors. Children are more likely to engage in prosocial behaviors, as well as integrate compassion into their overall sense of self, if teachers and other adults encourage empathic concern for one another and for others in the community (Krishnakumar, Narine, Roopnarine, & Logie, 2014; Youniss & Yates, 1999). Violent aggression at schools is rare, but milder forms—racial and sexual harassment, bullying, vandalization, and so on—are common (Bibou-Nakou, Asimopoulos, Hatzipemou, Soumaki, & Tsiantis, 2014; Frey, Newman, & Onyewuenyi, 2014; Garbarino, Bradshaw, & Vorrasi, 2002). Unfortunately, domestic disputes and criminal assaults are common in many neighborhoods, providing vivid models for dealing with conflict (Su, Mrug, & Windle, 2010). Community violence is strongly associated with proactive aggression, presumably because certain children exposed to vicious role models in their neighborhoods may eventually imitate violent acts (Fite et al., 2010).

---

[7]Authoritative, authoritarian, and permissive parenting styles are examined in Chapter 3.

Exposure to high rates of violence on television and in electronic games can also increase children's aggression. Decades of evidence from all sorts of methodologies indicate that witnessing a lot of violence on electronic formats makes viewers more aggressive (Hartmann, Krakowiak, & Tsay-Vogel, 2014). Plenty of qualifications moderate this conclusion, however: Children's own temperament, motivations, prior history of aggressive behavior, and child rearing experiences affect whether and how much they are affected by violent content. Regardless of their influence on actual behavior, children also acquire a range of understandings from these sources, including that aggression can be accompanied by a sense of power, as 6-year-old Myron shows in his drawing of Batman in Artifact 14-1.

Other aspects of society offer another constellation of influences. A child's culture determines typical targets of, and circumstances for, compassion. The routines that parents encourage are especially influential. For instance, the Murik mothers in Papua New Guinea frequently express compassion for children during mealtime rituals (Barlow, 2010). In immigrant families, young people with bilingual skills exhibit prosocial behavior when they translate communications for their parents and for others in the community who do not speak the language used in schools, banks, and clinics (Guan, Greenfield, & Orellana, 2014).

A culture also justifies particular kinds of aggression, prohibits others, and offers interpretations for individuals who regularly hit, ridicule, and ostracize others. In a study comparing peer relationships in American and Japanese fourth graders, both groups of children exhibited relational aggression (e.g., excluding other children from their play groups), but Japanese children who were prone to use a lot of relational aggression tended to feel depressed, whereas comparable American children did not, presumably because of the stronger emphasis on intimacy, exclusivity, and harmony in Japanese relationships (Kawabata, Crick, & Hamaguchi, 2010).

ARTIFACT 14-1 Batman. In his drawing of a superhero, 6-year-old Myron shows his understanding that aggression is a way of gaining power.

Gender

Beginning in the preschool years, boys are more physically aggressive than girls (Dodge et al., 2006; Eagly, 1987; Hay et al., 2011). Boys' greater inclination toward physical aggression is probably the result of both biological factors (recall the link between testosterone and aggression) and socialization (parents are more likely to allow aggression in sons than in daughters) (J. E. O. Blakemore, Berenbaum, & Liben, 2009; Condry & Ross, 1985). Some evidence indicates that boys engage in more name-calling and exclusionary behavior than do girls (Artz, Kassis, & Moldenhauer, 2013).

Boys also tend to be more assertive than girls. In mixed-sex groups, boys sometimes dominate activities and take charge of needed equipment, and they are more likely to get their way when group members disagree (Jovanovic & King, 1998). Such assertiveness may be nurtured in same-sex groups because boys' friendships typically involve more conflict and competition than girls' friendships do (Eisenberg, Martin, & Fabes, 1996; Leaper & Smith, 2004). In contrast, girls make frequent small concessions to keep the peace (P. M. Miller, Danaher, & Forbes, 1986; Rudolph, Caldwell, & Conley, 2005).

Individual Profiles

As you have learned, children's characteristics interact with environmental experiences in emerging approaches to helping and hurting others. Earlier you saw that authoritative parenting, a style in which mothers and fathers firmly but gently socialize children to act maturely, is associated with prosocial behavior in children. Yet now consider that children who are especially prone to be fearful are most likely to develop a strong conscience when exposed to this kind of parenting (Kochanska & Aksan, 2006). It appears that constitutionally anxious children easily find the direction they need in gentle induction. Other children who are relatively fearless are less responsive to authoritative discipline and instead develop a strong conscience when they have a close and secure bond with parents. Aggression, too, shows interactive effects, with children who have inherited a somewhat irritable and impulsive temperament being vulnerable to using violent behavior when reared in a harsh environment (Huesmann et al., 2011).

The many separate and blended effects on children's social behaviors mount over time, crystallizing into unique and stable patterns of helping and hurting behaviors (Knafo, Zahn-Waxler, Van Hulle, Robinson, & Rhee, 2008; Lacourse et al., 2014). Thus, the child's choices in expressing compassion or injuring others become ingrained as habits. A given child may regularly comfort peers in distress or frequently harass classmates.

The stability of prosocial and aggressive habits becomes a concern when children are seriously delayed in empathic responses or exceptionally aggressive. Impairments in empathy and aggressive behavior are associated with long-term problems in adjustment, peer relationships, and academic achievement (Eisenberg et al., 2010; S. Kim, Kim, & Kamphaus, 2010; Priddis et al., 2014). Children who are unusually aggressive when they are young (e.g., regularly hitting others, bullying) are also at risk for becoming violent in adolescence and adulthood (e.g., participating in gang fights and physical assaults; C. A. Anderson et al., 2003; Di Giunta et al., 2010; Ladd & Burgess, 1999).

As you might expect, it is much easier to intervene with aggressive children when they are young, but older children and adolescents typically do retain the capacity to acquire productive emotional and social capacities (Maldonado-Molina, Reingle, Tobler, Jennings, & Komro, 2010). In fact, some chronically aggressive individuals do not reduce their aggressive behaviors until the early adult years, when they find a reason—perhaps a job or intimate partner—to shape up their behavior.

Both prosocial behavior and aggression can be seen at one time or another in young-sters of various ages and backgrounds. You can read about other similarities between these two types of behavior in the Basic Developmental Issues table "Comparing Prosocial Behavior and Aggression."

BASIC DEVELOPMENTAL ISSUES
Comparing Prosocial Behavior and Aggression

ISSUE	PROSOCIAL BEHAVIOR	AGGRESSION
Nature and Nurture	The capacity for prosocial behavior is a natural, inborn human characteristic, but individual children have unique genetically based dispositions that predispose them to varying degrees of altruism. Affectionate caregiving, prosocial role modeling, and explicit requests for children to consider the needs of others are effective ways to encourage prosocial behavior in children.	The capacity for aggression has a biological basis. Temperamental dispositions, hormone levels, and neurological structures in the brain influence aggressiveness in individual children. Families, peers, neighbors, the media, and social institutions (e.g., schools) foster aggression (or restraint) through modeling, reinforcement, and discipline.
Universality and Diversity	The capacity for prosocial behavior is universal in the human species. Furthermore, people in most cultures become increasingly prosocial as they mature. Significant diversity exists in the extent to which cultural groups encourage prosocial activities (e.g., sharing, nurturing) and expose children to prosocial behavior and advice about how to care for people in need.	Aggressive behavior is universal in human beings. Some developmental sequences in aggressive expression, such as a gradual shift from physical aggression to verbal aggression, are ubiquitous. Diversity is present in the ways that children express aggression, in the amount of aggression they encounter in the environment, and in the extent to which aggression is condoned.
Qualitative and Quantitative Change	Qualitative changes occur in children's understanding of why helping others is valuable. Young children often give help to gain rewards or approval, whereas older children and adolescents are more likely to assist out of a genuine concern for others in need. Quantitative increases occur in children's knowledge of, and ability to carry out, effective prosocial strategies.	A gradual shift from physical aggression in early childhood to more verbal and relational forms of aggression in later years reflects a qualitative change. The shift from being a victim of bullying to becoming a perpetrator occurs rarely and reflects a qualitative change. The gradual decline in physical aggression in most children later in childhood reveals a quantitative reduction.

Sources: Dodge et al., 2006; Eisenberg et al., 2010; Eisenberg & Fabes, 1998.

DEVELOPMENT AND PRACTICE
Promoting Prosocial Skills and Discouraging Aggression

Talk about other people's feelings and needs in a sympathetic manner.

- A kindergarten teacher notices that Farai is standing next to Ivan in the block area. The teacher says to Ivan, "It looks like Farai would like to help you build your tower. What do you think?" (Early Childhood)
- When reading a story about a homeless child, Lia, a second-grade teacher, pauses and asks children to reflect on the girl's needs: "Lia is trying to figure out how her new classroom operates—who she can play with and what the rules are. How do you think she feels on her first day of school?" (Middle Childhood)

Communicate your concern for others who are hurt, and enlist children's support in caring for these individuals.

- A preschool teacher sympathizes with a boy who has skinned his knee. She brings out the first-aid kit and asks another child to get a bandage as she applies the antiseptic. (Early Childhood)
- A high school English teacher walks over to Abril and another student, Maddie, who has recently broken her leg. "Good morning, young ladies. Today we're going to be doing a few activities that involve moving around the room. Abril, would you mind helping Maddie carry her belongings when we shift seats?" (Late Adolescence)

Acknowledge children's good deeds.

- When a third-grade teacher notices a child helping a classmate who doesn't understand an assignment, she comments, "Thank you for helping Amanda, Jack. You're always ready to lend a hand." (Middle Childhood)
- In an advising session with Jerald, a middle school teacher asks him about his goals for the year. The teacher is delighted to hear about Jerald's volunteer work as a swim instructor for children with physical disabilities. The teacher encourages him, "Jerald, that's good work. Can you write a story for the school newspaper? You can talk about how rewarding your service is." (Early Adolescence)

Ask children to brainstorm approaches to solving moral dilemmas.

- A middle school teacher presents this situation to his class: "Imagine that one of your classmates comes up to you and asks if she can copy your homework. You don't want to let her copy it. But you don't want to make her angry. How might you refuse her request while keeping her friendship?" (Early Adolescence)

- A boy in a middle school literature class is doing a class project on a book he recently read. He downloads a pirated copy of the movie that was based on the book. His teacher comments that showing a scene from the movie could inspire a lot of interesting discussion, but the clip cannot be shown because doing so would be illegal and would violate the rights of people who made the movie. The boy says he will look into finding a non-pirated source for the clip. (Early Adolescence)

Give concrete feedback about appropriate and inappropriate social behaviors.

- A fifth-grade teacher takes Marshall aside after he exercises good self-restraint during a difficult social interaction. Previously impulsive and aggressive, Marshall counted to 10 and walked away after Tanner called him a "douchebag." The teacher acknowledged his self-control: "Way to go, Marshall. What Tanner did was wrong, and you handled the situation well." (Middle Childhood)
- During a cooperative learning activity, a high school teacher notices that the members of one group are getting angry. After briefly listening to their discussion, the teacher reminds them, "As we agreed yesterday, it's okay to criticize ideas, but it's *not* okay to criticize people." (Late Adolescence)

Encourage children to think carefully before acting in difficult social situations.

- A soccer coach finds that several of her 9-year-old players respond rashly to any physical contact. They might hit or yell at another player who unintentionally bumps into them on the playing field. The coach teaches the athletes four steps to follow in such situations: (a) Think about what just happened, (b) list three different ways to respond, (c) predict what might happen with each response, and (d) choose the best tactic. (Middle Childhood)
- With a rise in bullying in their school, teachers talk with children about what bullying is and how to handle being a victim of, or bystander to, harassment. One teacher tells her class, "No one needs to put up with bullying. If someone is picking on you, you can tell that person to stop it, but it's also important to step in when you see *someone else* being bullied. Say something. Tell the bully to stop it." (Middle Childhood)

Encouraging Children to Act Prosocially and Curb Aggressive Impulses

Teachers and other practitioners who work with young people have many opportunities to foster prosocial skills and discourage aggressive behaviors. You can see illustrations of educators fostering productive social capacities in the Development and Practice feature "Promoting Prosocial Skills and Discouraging Aggression" (see above). In addition, consider the following strategies that experts and experienced educators have found to be effective:

• **Treat children compassionately.** The root of empathy is love, and children are especially inclined to express their concern about others' welfare when they themselves have been treated warmly, gently, and with sensitivity. Infant caregivers can set the stage for productive social behaviors by interacting responsively with babies in their care, tending patiently to their needs, and comforting them when in distress (Gonzalez-Mena, 2010). As children grow older, adults can show compassion by asking them about their activities, encouraging their progress, and forgiving rather than shaming those who make mistakes (Sanders, 2010).

• **Expose children to models of prosocial behavior.** When educators model consideration for others, children are likely to respond with kindheartedness. Teachers might invite public servants or members of charitable organizations to talk with students about the many rewards of doing community service (Honig, 2009). Teachers can also provide literature with prosocial models (Nucci, 2009). One example is Harper Lee's (1960) *To Kill a Mockingbird*, set in segregated and racially charged Alabama of the 1930s, in which a lawyer defends an African American man falsely accused of raping a white woman, exemplifying a willingness to fight for social justice.

• **Give concrete guidelines for behavior.** Children should consistently hear the message that they must handle conflicts nonviolently. An important first step is to establish firm rules that prohibit physical aggression and possession of weapons. Behaviors that cause psychological harm—malicious gossip, prejudicial remarks, sexual harassment, intimidation, ostracism, and so on—must also be off-limits. And adults must consistently enforce these rules in the classroom, on the playground, in extracurricular activities, and elsewhere (Grumm & Hein, 2013; Juvonen, Nishina, & Graham, 2000; Learning First Alliance, 2001).

• **Label appropriate behaviors as they occur.** Teachers can heighten children's awareness of effective social skills by validating behaviors that embody those skills (Sanders, 2010; Vorrath, 1985; Wittmer & Honig, 1994). A teacher might say, "Thank you for *sharing* your art materials" or "I think that you two were able to write a more imaginative short story by *cooperating* on the project." Experts have found, too, that describing children as having desirable characteristics (generosity, empathy, etc.) has beneficial effects (Dunsmore, 2014; Grusec & Redler, 1980; R. S. L. Mills & Grusec, 1989). Eight-year-olds who are told "You're the kind of person who likes to help others whenever you can" or "You are a very helpful person" are more likely to share their belongings later on.

• **Create occasions for caring for others.** A preschool teacher might set up the pretend play area as an animal shelter, doctor's office, baby's room, grocery store, or other setting that elicits compassionate behavior. A teacher might offer subtle suggestions with prosocial themes: "My Grandma is preparing food baskets to take to people in need. I think I'll help her by buying some canned goods at your grocery store" (Sanders, 2010, p. 51). A school might sponsor an annual clothing drive for individuals in the community who are homeless or abused, and a teacher might take a field trip with his class to bring cookies to senior citizens at a local retirement home.

Preparing for Your Licensure Examination
Your teaching test might ask you about fostering prosocial behavior and discouraging aggressive behavior as part of a positive learning environment.

• **Plan cooperative group activities.** In cooperative learning activities, youngsters can practice help-giving, help-seeking, and conflict resolution skills (Choi, Johnson, & Johnson, 2011; Webb & Farivar, 1994). Furthermore, cooperative tasks that require a number of different skills can foster an appreciation for the strengths that children with diverse backgrounds contribute (E. G. Cohen, 1994; Lotan, 2006). Cooperative activities are most successful when children have a structure to follow (e.g., when each group member is given a specific role to perform) and are given guidelines about desirable behavior (E. G. Cohen, 1994; Pescarmona, 2014). For example, children could be told that everyone is expected to participate and that disagreement is permissible but hitting, shoving, and calling one another derogatory names are not.

• **Document the circumstances of an aggressive child's improper behavior.** If a child regularly exhibits hurtful behaviors, an adult should record their form (e.g., Is the child biting, pushing, or name-calling?) and the kinds of situations in which they occur (e.g., Has the child planned the aggressive act in order to gain resources or prestige, or alternatively does the child seem to be reacting out of frustration? Does he or she choose the same or different victim each time? Is there a particular time of day or setting in which the child is prone to act out?). This information can be used to formulate a plan that discourages the child's aggression and teaches him or her missing skills. For example, a teacher might make extra efforts to calm a child who gets unsettled during transitions. Another teacher might coach a boy in the skill of compromise because he is seen to grab toys rather than taking turns or sharing.

• **Implement an anti-bullying program that has been proven efficacious in reducing intimidation of vulnerable students.** Several school programs have been designed to reduce the frequency of bullying (Menard & Grotpeter, 2014; Morgan, 2012). Yet many of these programs have not had intended effects and in a few cases have actually led to increases in aggressive incidents. In programs that have been successful, clear expectations and sanctions are established for bullying, consequences are given as soon as possible to instigators of aggressive acts, and victims are reassured and offered counseling (Morgan, 2012). Anti-bullying programs also educate children on the need to step forward as a bystander and tell the perpetrator to stop.

• **Develop a peer mediation program.** Children often benefit from **peer mediation** training that teaches them how to intervene effectively in peers' interpersonal disputes (Daunic & Smith, 2010; Deutsch, 1993; Linnemeier, 2012). In such training, youngsters learn how to help peers resolve conflicts by asking opposing sides to express their points of view and work together to devise a reasonable resolution. In one study (D. W. Johnson, Johnson, Dudley, Ward, & Magnuson, 1995), students in grades 2 through 5 were trained to help peers resolve interpersonal conflicts by asking opposing sides to do the following:

1. Define the conflict (the problem).
2. Explain their own perspectives and needs.
3. Explain the *other* side's perspectives and needs.
4. Identify at least three possible solutions to the conflict.
5. Reach an agreement that addresses the needs of both parties.

Students took turns serving as mediator for their classmates, such that everyone had experience resolving the conflicts of others. As a result, students more frequently resolved their *own* interpersonal conflicts in ways that addressed the needs of both parties, and they were less likely to ask for adult intervention, than were students who had not had mediation training.

Peer mediation is most effective when youngsters of diverse ethnic backgrounds, socioeconomic groups, and achievement levels serve as mediators. Furthermore, it is typically most useful for relatively small, short-term interpersonal problems (hurt feelings, conflicts over use of limited academic resources, etc.). Yet it requires a lengthy training program, which entails a commitment from the students and financial investment from the schools. As another limitation, even the most proficient of peer mediators is likely to be ill prepared to handle conflicts that reflect deep-seated and emotionally charged behaviors, such as interactions that involve sexual harassment or homophobia (Casella, 2001; K. M. Williams, 2001).

• **Intervene at all ages but especially when children are young.** Children who display reactive aggression need practice in coping effectively with anger, in identifying others' perspective and motivations, and in dealing with conflict before it escalates (Hubbard et al., 2010). Children who exhibit reactive aggression also need to practice productive social skills, including negotiation. Because proactively aggressive children tend to be somewhat callous and unemotional in interactions with others, adults can encourage them to act with consideration for the feelings of others. Children who have more serious problems, including the potential to become violent, require more intensive support, as we see in the next section.

Creating a Safe School Environment

Students can achieve at optimal levels at school only if they know they are physically and psychologically safe. To be truly effective in combating aggression at school, teachers and administrators must ensure students' safety by addressing hurtful behavior comprehensively. The three-tier model depicted graphically in Figure 14-1 has been instrumental

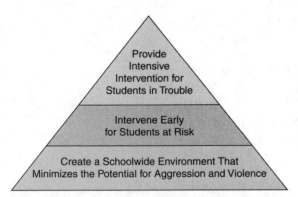

FIGURE 14-1 A three-level approach to preventing aggression and violence in schools. *Based on a figure in Safeguarding Our Children: An Action Guide (p. 3) by K. Dwyer and D. Osher, 2000, Washington, DC: U.S. Departments of Education and Justice, American Institutes for Research.*

in dealing with a range of needs related to aggression and mental health (Dwyer & Osher, 2000; B. B. Nelson et al., 2013; H. M. Walker et al., 1996).

Level I: Creating a Nonviolent School Environment

All children need to be able to interact in a school in which they feel safe, see good behaviors recognized, and find hurtful behaviors discouraged. Creating a peaceful, nonviolent school environment must be a long-term effort with the following strategies:

- Make a joint, schoolwide commitment to supporting *all* students' academic and social success.
- Provide a challenging and engaging curriculum.
- Form caring, trusting faculty–student relationships.
- Insist on genuine respect—among students as well as faculty—for people of diverse backgrounds, races, and ethnicities.
- Establish schoolwide policies and practices that foster appropriate behavior (e.g., give clear guidelines for behavior, consistently enforce penalties for infractions, and deliver instruction in productive social and problem-solving skills).
- Involve students in decision making about school policies and procedures.
- Provide mechanisms through which students can communicate their concerns openly and without fear of reprisal.
- Model, recognize, and teach prosocial behaviors (e.g., sharing, helping, cooperation).
- Establish close working relationships with community agencies and families.
- Reach out to families, advise them of services in their community, and offer workshops in identifying anxiety in children and setting age-appropriate limits on disruptive behavior.
- Openly discuss safety issues. (Burstyn & Stevens, 2001; Dwyer & Osher, 2000; Dwyer, Osher, & Warger, 1998; Gregory et al., 2010; Meehan, Hughes, & Cavell, 2003; Mendez, Ogg, Loker, & Fefer, 2013; Morrison, Furlong, D'Incau, & Morrison, 2004; Pellegrini, 2002)

The final strategy on the list—an open discussion of safety issues—encompasses a variety of specific techniques. For example, school faculty members can:

- Explain what bullying is (i.e., that it involves harassing or intimidating peers who cannot easily defend themselves) and why it is unacceptable.
- Solicit students' input on potentially unsafe areas (e.g., an infrequently used restroom or back stairwell) that require faculty supervision.
- Convey willingness to hear students' complaints about troublesome classmates (such concerns can provide important clues about which students are most in need of assistance and intervention).

Communication with students should be a two-way street so that students' misconceptions about bullying can be cleared up and students are given a chance to tell adults about what is happening to them. In one study, a student alerted adults to areas they should be watching more carefully, " . . . some of the bullying happens near the portables [portable classrooms] because they're out of sight and there's not really any teachers usually on the grass for duty, they're usually on the pavement" (C. E. Cunningham, Cunningham, Ratcliffe, & Vaillancourt, 2010, p. 325). Another student revealed that students did not interpret anti-bullying policies as pertaining to relational aggression as was intended by adults, "I think we need to like really put it out there that like gossiping and all that stuff is like bullying. Like it's a form of bullying. Like I just learned that this year, that gossiping and I'm like really trying to stop. But you know, girls, it's really hard" (C. E. Cunningham et al., 2010, p. 328).

Level II: Intervening Early for Students at Risk

Students who fail to develop productive social skills for interacting with peers and controlling anger are at risk for developing more serious problems. These students can develop skills when their individual needs are addressed. Effective interventions cannot be a one-size-fits-all approach, however, and must instead be tailored to students' individual strengths and needs. For some students intervention might take the form of social skills training. Others will benefit from counseling. In still other cases it might mean getting students actively involved in school clubs or extracurricular activities. And a few others require well-planned, systematic efforts to encourage and reinforce productive behaviors. But regardless of their nature, interventions are more effective when they occur *early* in the game—before students go too far down the path of antisocial behavior—and when they are delivered by a multidisciplinary team of teachers and other professionals (Dryfoos, 1997; Dwyer & Osher, 2000; Priddis et al., 2014).

Level III: Providing Intensive Intervention for Students in Trouble

In a few situations, intensive professional intervention is mandated. When left unchecked, aggressive tendencies can escalate, sometimes into serious violence. Children who are exceptionally and persistently aggressive do not always acquire the empathic capacity, desire to follow school rules, social skills with peers, and self-control that are crucial for healthy interpersonal interactions. They may have been brutally victimized themselves, sometimes repeatedly, and later act out the aggressive overtures they have seen others use. Violent behaviors can be used by youth initially out of lapses of self-control and later as part of a learned habit and with intention to hurt others. A few students will have developed an explosive temper or deep-seated disregard for others' welfare, probably due to serious problems at home and an emerging mental illness.

These young people are apt to remain delayed in coping and social skills, and not able to implement these capacities even in a warm and safe school environment. Nor do they respond to short-term interventions from Level II programs. In such situations, schools must work closely and collaboratively with mental health clinics, police and probation officers, and social services to help students at high risk for violence and protect others from harm (M. T. Greenberg et al., 2003; Hyman et al., 2006; Rollison et al., 2013).

Through their daily interactions with students, teachers may notice certain characteristics that suggest a need for intervention. Teachers should consult with their principals and other professionals if they notice several of these warning signs:

- *Social withdrawal.* Over time, a student interacts less and less frequently with teachers and peers. A student may directly or indirectly express the belief that he or she is friendless, disliked, or unfairly picked on.
- *Rapid decline in academic performance.* A student shows a dramatic change in academic performance and seems unconcerned about doing well. Cognitive and physical factors (e.g., learning disabilities, ineffective study strategies, brain injury) have been ruled out as causes of the decline.
- *Poor coping skills.* A student has little ability to deal effectively with frustration, takes the smallest affront personally, and has trouble bouncing back after minor disappointments. He or she frequently responds with uncontrolled anger to even the slightest injustice and may misdirect anger at innocent bystanders.
- *Sense of superiority, self-centeredness, and lack of empathy.* A student depicts himself or herself as smarter or otherwise better than peers, is preoccupied with his or her own needs, and has little regard for the needs of others.
- *Lengthy grudges.* A student is unforgiving of others' transgressions, even after considerable time has elapsed.
- *Violent themes in drawings and written work.* Violence predominates in a student's artwork, stories, and journal entries, with certain individuals (e.g., a parent or particular classmate) being regularly targeted in these fantasies. (Keep in mind that *occasional* violence in writing and art is not unusual, especially for boys.)
- *Intolerance for individual and group differences.* A student shows intense disdain for and prejudice toward people of a certain race, ethnicity, gender, sexual orientation, religion, or disability.
- *History of violence, aggression, and other discipline problems.* A student has a long record of destructive or cruel behaviors extending over several years.

Preparing for Your Licensure Examination
Your teaching test might ask you about enlisting the support of counselors, school psychologists, other school personnel, law enforcement officials, and professionals in the community for potentially violent youth.

- *Association with violent peers.* A student associates regularly with a gang or other anti-social peer group.
- *Violent role models.* A student may speak with admiration about Satan or Hitler, or another malevolent figure.
- *Frequent alcohol or drug use.* A student who abuses alcohol or drugs may have reduced self-control; in some cases substance abuse signals significant mental illness.
- *Access to firearms.* A student has easy access to guns and ammunition and may regularly practice using them.
- *Threats of violence.* A student has openly expressed the intent to harm someone else. ***This warning sign alone requires immediate action.***

(Dwyer et al., 1998; M. L. Mitchell & Brendtro, 2013; Ormrod, 2011; O'Toole, 2000; U.S. Secret Service National Threat Assessment Center, 2000)

By themselves, most of the signs are unlikely to signal a violent attack, but several of them in combination necessitates consultation with specially trained professionals. As noted, a child's stated intention to harm someone should *always* be considered seriously.

Although teachers must be vigilant about signs that a student may be planning to cause harm to others, it is essential that they keep several points in mind. First, despite tragic school shootings, in which lives of children, teachers, and other staff have been lost, extreme violence in schools is relatively rare (CQ Researcher, 2014; DeVoe et al., 2003; Garbarino et al., 2002). Second, the great majority of students who exhibit one or a few of the warning signs we've just examined will *not* become violent. Third, many teachers do not have sufficient training to make reliable judgments about certain aspects of children's personality (e.g., whether children hold grudges) and the nature of their home life (e.g., whether children have access to firearms) (Warnick, Johnson, & Rocha, 2010). And most important, a teacher must *never* use the warning signs as a reason to unfairly accuse, isolate, or punish a student (Dwyer et al., 1998; Mayworm & Sharkey, 2014). These signs provide a means for getting youngsters help if they need it, not for excluding them from the education that all young people deserve.

Gang-Related Problems

A frequent source of aggression at schools is gang-related hostilities. Although gangs are more prevalent in low-income, inner-city schools, they are found in suburban and rural schools as well (M. E. Buckle & Walsh 2013; Howell & Lynch, 2000; Sharkey, Shekhtmeyster, Chavez-Lopez, Norris, & Sass, 2010).

The three-level approach to combating school violence just described goes a long way toward suppressing gang activities. Level I activities that ensure children have good relationships at school and access to an engaging curriculum discourage children from joining gangs in the first place (Sharkey et al., 2010). The Level II strategy of encouraging students to take part in extracurricular activities of personal appeal may preempt gang initiation for those beginning to be at risk (Sharkey et al., 2010). As suggested in our discussion of Level III, students who are already exhibiting violent behavior need intensive intervention to acquire productive coping skills, reduce aggressive acts, and stay away from gang leaders.

It is also important to limit the influence of gangs already present within the school setting. Educators can take measures to communicate that schools are neutral territories that do not favor one gang or another and, in fact, prohibit all signs of gang affiliation. Recommended strategies include the following:

- Develop, communicate, and enforce clear-cut policies regarding potential threats to school safety.
- Identify the specific nature and scope of gang activity in the student population.
- Forbid clothing, jewelry, and behaviors that signify membership in a particular gang (e.g., bandanas, shoelaces in gang colors, certain hand signs).[8]
- Actively mediate between-gang and within-gang disputes. (Kodluboy, 2004; Sharkey et al., 2010)

[8]A potential problem with this strategy is that it may violate students' civil liberties. For guidance on how to walk the line between ensuring students' safety and giving them reasonable freedom of expression, see Kodluboy (2004) and Rozalski and Yell (2004).

In the last of these strategies—mediation—either adults or peers might serve as mediators, provided that they are familiar with the cultures and issues of the gang(s) involved (Kodluboy, 2004). But young people in gangs also need to see that they belong at school, can have decent relationships with teachers, and find academic learning relevant to their interests and aspirations (Kronholz, 2011).

Summary

Most children become increasingly prosocial and less aggressive over the years, with such changes being partly the result of their growing capacity for perspective taking, empathy, and sympathy. However, some children display troublesome levels of physical or relational aggression, perhaps partly as a result of temperamental characteristics, aggressive role models at home or in the community, or counterproductive social cognitive processes. These youngsters often need planned interventions to get them on the road to more productive relationships with others.

ENHANCEDetext *self-check*

Assessing Children 14-1

Listen to middle school students and their teacher talking about recent incidents of bullying and what they can do about them.

ENHANCEDetext *application exercise*

Assessing Children 14-2

Listen to fourth-grade students talk through the causes and effects in a story about a girl being bullied.

ENHANCEDetext *application exercise*

PRACTICING FOR YOUR LICENSURE EXAMINATION

Many teaching tests require students to apply their knowledge of child development in analyzing brief vignettes and answering multiple-choice questions. You can practice for your licensure examination by reading the following case study and answering a series of questions.

Gang Mediation

At Washington Middle School, many students belonged to one of several gangs that seemed to "rule the school." Fights among rival gangs were common, and non-gang members were frequent victims of harassment. School officials tried a variety of strategies to keep the gang-related behavior in check—mandating dress codes, conducting weapon searches, counseling or suspending chronic trouble makers, and so on—but without success.

In desperation, two school counselors suggested that the school implement a peer mediation program. The program began by focusing on the three largest gangs, which were responsible for most of the trouble on school grounds. Interpersonal problems involving two or more gangs would be brought to a mediation team, comprised of five school faculty members and three representatives from each of the three gangs. The team would abide by the following rules:

1. Really try to solve the problem.
2. No name-calling or put-downs.
3. No interrupting.
4. Be as honest as possible.
5. No weapons or acts of intimidation.
6. All sessions to be confidential until an agreement is reached or mediation is called off. (Sanchez & Anderson, 1990, p. 54)

All team members would have to agree to and sign off on any decisions that the team reached. However, participation in the process was voluntary, and students could withdraw at any time.

To lay the groundwork for productive discussions, faculty members of the mediation team met separately with each of the three gangs to establish feelings of rapport and trust and to explain how the mediation process would work. After considerable discussion and venting of hostile intergroup feelings, many gang members agreed to try the new approach. Meanwhile, the buzz throughout the student body was that "something unusual and special was happening" at Washington.

Mediation sessions were held in a conference room, with team members sitting around a large table so that they could maintain eye contact with one another. In the first session, common grievances were aired. Students agreed that they didn't like being put down or intimidated, that they worried about their physical safety, and that they all wanted one another's respect. Curiously, each gang also complained that the school administration showed preferential treatment for the *other* gangs. Through all of this, the students got one message loud and clear: They could speak freely and honestly at the meeting, without fear of reprisal from faculty members or other students.

In several additional meetings during the next 2 weeks, the team reached agreement that a number of behaviors would be unacceptable at school: There would be no put-downs, name-calling, hateful stares, threats, shoving, or gang graffiti. After the final meeting, each gang was separately called into the conference room. Its representatives on the mediation team explained the agreement, and other members of the gang were asked to sign it. Despite some skepticism, most members of all three gangs signed the agreement.

A month later, it was clear that the process had been successful, at least in improving the school's social climate over the short term. Members of rival gangs nodded pleasantly to one another or gave one another a "high five" sign as they passed in the hall. Gang members no longer felt compelled to hang out in groups for safety's sake. Members of two of the gangs were seen playing soccer together one afternoon. And there had been no gang-related fights all month. (case described in Sanchez & Anderson, 1990)[a]

Constructed-Response Question

1. Why do you think the mediation approach was successful when other approaches had failed? Draw on what you've learned about moral development, and identify at least three possible reasons.

Multiple-Choice Questions

2. Considering the recommendations in this chapter on creating a safe school environment, which of the following strategies might reasonably supplement the mediation program used in this school?
   a. Look carefully at the curriculum to make sure it is engaging for students.
   b. Advise students individually about extracurricular activities that might be of personal interest to them.
   c. Provide individual counseling for students who have previously exhibited violent behavior.
   d. All of the above

3. Given what you learned about aggression, which of the following explanations most accurately accounts for the reasons that children in the gangs might have become aggressive?
   a. As is the case with all children, gang members can be persuaded to do anything that adults want them to do.
   b. The children were probably affected by a combination of factors, perhaps including exposure to parents and peers who handled their conflicts aggressively, dispositions that put them at risk for responding impulsively, and their own habits and interpretations of social events.
   c. The children's genes, which made them irritable and impulsive, can be considered fully responsible for their aggressive style of interacting.
   d. None of the above

ENHANCEDetext *licensure exam*

Key Concepts

moral development (p. 528)	personal matter (p. 531)	care orientation (p. 538)	proactive aggression (p. 546)
moral dilemma (p. 529)	guilt (p. 534)	service learning (p. 542)	bully (p. 546)
preconventional morality (p. 529)	shame (p. 534)	prosocial behavior (p. 544)	hostile attributional bias (p. 547)
conventional morality (p. 529)	sympathy (p. 534)	aggression (p. 544)	peer mediation (p. 555)
postconventional morality (p. 530)	distributive justice (p. 534)	physical aggression (p. 546)	
moral transgression (p. 531)	induction (p. 537)	relational aggression (p. 546)	
conventional transgression (p. 531)	justice orientation (p. 538)	reactive aggression (p. 546)	

CHAPTER FIFTEEN

Peers, Schools, and Society

CASE STUDY: One Girl, Three High Schools

When I [Teresa] sat down with 17-year-old Catherine[1] and asked her to describe high school, Catherine smiled and asked, "Which one?"

I smiled back. "How many were there?"

She laughed: "I'm on my third one. Third one's a charm, right?"

"Definitely," I answered. "You've made it this far. Can you start with school number one?"

"My first high school was okay," Catherine explained. "I liked algebra . . . quadratic equations, all that. My teacher sent me to represent the school at a state contest. I liked art as well. I got to design a book and illustrate a poem. Shakespeare was dull. The teacher focused on symbols and ignored the stories—the characters and their relationships. But I basically liked the school. I had good friends. Teachers cared about us. Unfortunately, the school closed at the end of my freshman year." Her tone lowered, and she looked down, "Enter school number two. . . ."

"A tough time?" I asked.

"Yeah," Catherine answered. "The second school was a hard place. Not socially, because many of my friends went with me. But the atmosphere was bad. Classes were boring. Students goofed off. I read novels in class. Teachers did nothing. In Geometry [class] I drew pictures. Our history teacher shouldn't have been teaching. He'd been a missionary in Chile for 30 years and became a teacher because he needed a job and knew the principal. He was . . . weird . . . disturbed. And the principal was a real . . ."

I waited. She gathered her thoughts and continued, "The principal used some of the kids to tell on the others. Yeah . . . and one teacher was really depraved. He pretended to be Hitler, and got students to salute him . . . The principal did. . . . nothing . . ." her voice trailed off.

I absorbed what she was saying.

Catherine sighed. "I told my parents I wanted to leave. They weren't happy. But they figured out it was better for me to finish school *somewhere* than to drop out. They eventually let me leave."

"And school number three? What's it like?" I asked.

"It's really big. No one knows me here. . . . My real friends are in other schools, or have already graduated. The teachers give us a lot of choices, but I can't tell if that's because they like us [the students] or just can't be bothered. In my P.E. class, I'm allowed to run instead of join in dorky games. I run around the track, the fields, local neighborhoods. I like the freedom. The only personal contact I've had is in my writing class. We keep a journal, and our teacher reads it. My teacher wrote to me that she saves my journal for last because I write about real things. She and I have never talked, though."

"Do you have an advisor?" I asked.

"I don't think so," she answered quietly.

"A counselor?" I followed up.

"Well, yeah, I saw him once, took some kind of career inventory, and found out that my interest in mechanical things is at the one percentile," Catherine laughed. "So I guess I won't be an engineer."

"And now what?" I wondered.

"I've been accepted into college," Catherine answered. "It must have been my SATs[2]—not my grades." She laughed. "After my freshman year, I stopped studying. I read a lot, though, things that are not required. That helps me with the stuff tests measure. College will be different, I hope. At least I can learn about things I care about." She looked up and smiled.

- How did Catherine perceive her three schools?
- What challenges did she face?

[1]Catherine is a pseudonym.
[2]The SAT is a college admission test published by the College Board.

In the opening case study, 17-year-old Catherine, a bright young woman, was at risk for dropping out of high school. In her travails through secondary school, she experienced three distinct settings, which she found to be more or less interesting, engaging, and supportive Fortunately, her algebra teacher recognized her talent, as did her writing teacher, both validating her intelligence. Friends were an important part of her life and a source of support as she moved between schools.

Students are deeply affected by their school's atmosphere, relationships, and opportunities for a relevant, challenging, and engaging education. Schools successfully support students to the extent that they connect to their interests, effectively teach academic skills, build their confidence, foster a warm and safe climate for peer interaction, and ensure that each individual has an advocate each. In this chapter you will find that educational settings can be positive catalysts for growth, and that other elements of society, including peers, the media, interactive technologies, and after-school programs, also have the potential to promote healthy development.

PEERS

Peers, people of approximately the same age and position within a social group, make unique contributions to children's development—contributions that supplement rather than duplicate relationships they have with family and adults. In the next few pages, we examine various aspects of peer relationships, including their functions, constituent social skills, and forms.

Functions of Peer Relationships

Companionship with peers is one of children's top priorities. When peer relationships are warm and cordial, they serve several beneficial functions:

ARTIFACT 15-1   I had Katherine over yesterday. Seven-year-old Madison has a strong emotional bond with her friend, Katherine.

Peers offer emotional support. The presence of familiar peers helps children relax in new environments and cope with mild aggression and other stresses (Asher & Parker, 1989; K. Snow & Mann-Feder, 2013; Wentzel, 1999). In our opening case study, Catherine felt supported through school transitions by having close friends. Although some youngsters adjust quite successfully to troubling situations on their own, as a general rule children who have peers to turn to have higher self-esteem, fewer emotional problems (such as depression), and higher engagement with, and achievement in, school (Buhrmester, 1992; Cappella, Kim, Neal, & Jackson, 2013; Erath, Flanagan, Bierman, & Tu, 2010). In Artifact 15-1, 7-year-old Madison represents her close friendship with friend Katherine.

Peers serve as partners for practicing social skills. When children interact with peers, they enter social exchanges on a more or less equal footing. Friendships are by choice, and no individual has absolute power over another. Equality does not mean that friends have the same abilities or roles within the relationship, but true friends care for one another and accept each other's inherent goodness, motives, and talents. By satisfying their own needs while also maintaining productive relationships with others, children acquire such fundamental skills as social perspective taking and constructive conflict resolution skills (K. L. McDonald, Malti, Killen, & Rubin, 2014; Selman, 2003; Sutton-Smith, 1979).[3]

Peers train one another for a social life. Children socialize one another in several ways (Hartup, 2009; Rubin, Bukowski, & Parker, 2006; Shi & Xie, 2014). Peers stipulate options

[3]Social perspective taking is examined in Chapter 12.

for leisure time, perhaps jumping rope in a vacant lot, getting together in a study group, or smoking cigarettes on the street corner. They offer new ideas, presenting arguments for becoming a vegetarian or helping out in an animal rescue center. They serve as role models, showing what is possible and what is admirable. Peers reinforce one another for acting in ways deemed appropriate for their age, gender, ethnic group, and cultural background. And they sanction one another, through ridicule, gossip, or ostracism for stepping beyond acceptable bounds.

Peers contribute to a sense of identity. Association with peers helps children decide who they are and what they want to become (Clemens, Shipp, & Pisarik, 2008; Zosuls, Field, Martin, Andrews, & England, 2014). Young people learn a lot about themselves and their identity in peer groups, and, especially in adolescence, gain a sense of affinity with like-minded individuals. For instance, when Jeanne's son Alex was in middle school, he and his friends were avid skateboarders and spent long hours at a local skateboard ramp practicing and refining their technique. Alex proudly labeled himself a "skater" and wore the extra-large T-shirts and wide-legged pants that conveyed this identity.

Children help one another make sense of their lives. During conversations with peers, children share ideas that help one another interpret confusing and troubling events. Children may talk about similar experiences in getting along with a classmate, dealing with a difficult teacher, or being punished by parents. Such informally instructive conversations occur throughout childhood but take on special significance during adolescence, when teenagers are changing rapidly and long for reassurance from peers facing similar challenges (Richard & Schneider, 2005; H. S. Sullivan, 1953).

Peers achieve common ways of looking at the world. As an outcome of interactions over time, children come to share views on the world. A long-standing group of children works out rules, often unspoken expectations and interpretations—a **peer culture**—that influence how group members behave (P. Davidson & Youniss, 1995; A. Lynch, Lerner, & Leventhal, 2013; C. Simmons, 2014). You can read more about this aspect of children's lives in the Development and Culture feature "Peer Culture in the United States and Italy."

Social Skills

Children are most likely to develop productive relationships when they have acquired age-typical **social skills**, strategies that facilitate effective interaction with others. Children who are adept in social skills are generally perceptive of other people's needs, able to establish and maintain high-quality relationships, and inclined to curb their own aggression. In other words, they are *socially competent* (Vaughn et al., 2009). Compared to children who are deficient in social skills, socially competent children achieve at higher levels academically, have higher self-esteem, are happier at school, are better able to deal with anger and frustration, exhibit fewer problem behaviors, and have better attendance at school (Berkovits & Baker, 2014; Bornstein, Hahn, & Haynes, 2010).

Developmental Trends in Social Skills

Socially competent children acquire particular skills as they interact with peers during each of the developmental periods:

Infancy (birth–2 years). Infants acquire basic social skills while interacting with parents. They are gradually able to coordinate their focus of attention with adults in the form of eye contact, smiles, and utterances. In the latter half of the first year, infants who spend time with other small children may babble and smile at one another or look where others point (Eckerman, 1979; S. Wittmer, 2012). As toddlers, children imitate one another, offer each other toys, and cooperate in simple tasks and play activities (P. L. Harris, 2006; Howes & Matheson, 1992; Meadows, 2010). These are not simply friendly behaviors—instead, infants and toddlers are actually forming relationships with familiar peers—seeking out one another

Preparing for Your Licensure Examination
Your teaching test might ask about developmental trends in peer relationships.

DEVELOPMENT IN CULTURE
Peer Culture in the United States and Italy

William Corsaro is a sociologist, a scientist who studies people's interactions in groups. Corsaro's specific interest is in how children relate to one another at school. In a series of *ethnographies* in the United States and Italy, he spent several months becoming familiar with preschool children's routines, the subtleties in their exchanges, and the purpose of their customs.[a] He gained children's confidence by sitting down beside them, quietly watching and listening, and letting them react to him. Occasionally, he joined in their play, always following their leads.

Children in both societies gradually accepted Corsaro. In the U.S. preschools, the children came to think of Corsaro as "Big Bill," whom they readily welcomed into their playgroups (Corsaro, 2003, p. 7).[b] The children eventually insisted that he sit with them during birthday parties and that their parents include him in plans for cookies, cupcakes, and Valentine cards. In the Italian preschools, children initially treated Corsaro as "an incompetent adult" because of his lack of fluency with the Italian language (Corsaro, 2003, p. 15).[b] Children teased Corsaro when he made mistakes in speaking Italian but also regularly taught him new phrases. Corsaro recalled an early triumph in winning the children over:

> I was sitting on the floor with two boys (Felice and Roberto) and we were racing some toy cars around in circles. Felice was talking about an Italian race car driver as we played, but because he was talking so fast I could understand only part of what he was saying. At one point, however, he raced his car into a wall and it flipped over. Then I clearly heard him say "*Luis è morto*," and I knew this meant, "He's dead." I guessed that Felix must be recounting a tragic accident in some past Grand Prix event. At that moment I remembered and used a phrase that I had learned in my first Italian course: "*Che peccato!*" ("What a pity!"). Looking up in amazement Felice said, "Bill! Bill! *Ha ragione! Bravo Bill!*" ("Bill! Bill! He's right! Way to go, Bill!"). "*Bravo, Bill!*" Roberto chimed in. (Corsaro, 2003, pp. 17–18)[b]

As a result of his extended time with children in both settings, Corsaro gained an insider's perspective on children's *peer cultures* (Corsaro, 2003; Corsaro & Eder, 1990). During their time together, children in the two societies developed their own informal routines. For example, in one American preschool, children became excited when they heard the characteristic noises of trash collectors attaching the dumpster to a lift. The truck was visible from the top of the jungle gym, and whichever child noticed it coming shouted to the others that the "garbage man" had arrived (Corsaro, 2003, p. 49).[b] Others quickly climbed the bars to get a good look, and the children cheered in unison and made sound effects as the driver grabbed the container and emptied its contents. Every day the routine was the same, as

PEER CULTURE IN ITALY. These Italian children are exchanging secrets, perhaps built on their shared understandings and customs.

it was a year later when Corsaro observed a new group of children at the school.

Other themes that regularly guided children's play were those of being scared and finding protection. Children would take turns pretending to be monsters; others would chase or flee from the monsters and find safe haven in a home base. Another dynamic that pervaded children's play was making friends and protecting existing friendships. Concerns with loyalty and rivalry were also regularly borne out in interactions among young children.

Finally, children conspired in acts of mischief. For example, children tried to convince teachers that it was acceptable to run inside because they were pretending to be police chasing robbers. Toy weapons were not allowed in school, yet children pretended to shoot one another by pointing and cocking their fingers. A couple of children brought in contraband toys and candy and shared these items with one another out of sight of teachers. Other children shirked their responsibilities at cleanup time by surreptitiously moving from an area that they had messed up to another tidier location in the classroom, where they would be absolved from housework.

Many aspects of children's peer culture were unknown to teachers. Although some of children's routines, such as sharing contraband toys, might have been considered objectionable had they been identified, peer culture overall was a constructive way for children to learn how to act in a group.

---

[a]Ethnographies are introduced in Chapter 2.
[b]Excerpts from WE'RE FRIENDS, RIGHT?: INSIDE KIDS' CULTURE by William A. Corsaro. Copyright © 2003 by William A. Corsaro. Reprinted with permission by the National Academy of Sciences, Courtesy of the National Academies Press, Washington, D.C.

and even finding comfort from a well known peer when adjusting to a new room at the child care center (Recchia & Dvorakova, 2012).

Early Childhood (2–6 years). Having capacities for language and for coordinating attention with others established, young children are prepared to interact more effectively with age-mates, especially within the context of play. One early researcher identified six different kinds of behaviors in children age 2 to 5 (Parten, 1932). These categories, which globally reflect increasing social interaction, are described in the Observation Guidelines table "Observing the Social Aspects of Young Children's Play." You can also see children engaged in parallel play in an Observing Children video.

Developmental trends can be seen in the prevalence of types of play. Across the early childhood years, children typically become more interactive and cooperative in their play activities (Gottman, 1983; Howes & Matheson, 1992; Meadows, 2010). The imagination and

Observing Children 15-1

Observe children in parallel play.

ENHANCEDetext *video example*

OBSERVATION GUIDELINES
Observing the Social Aspects of Young Children's Play

CHARACTERISTIC	LOOK FOR	EXAMPLE	IMPLICATION
Unoccupied Behavior	• *Failure to engage in any activity*, either with or without another individual • *Aimless wandering* • *Quiet sitting and staring*	During free-play time, Donald often retreats to a corner of the play yard, where he sits quietly either running his fingers through the dirt or staring off into space.	Try to engage the child with intriguing toys or in a small-group activity. Consult with a specialist if unoccupied behavior is persistent despite multiple attempts to engage the child.
Solitary Play	• *Absorption* in one's own playthings • *Apparent lack of awareness* of other children's presence	Although Laura and Erika are sitting next to each other in the sandbox, they are facing in opposite directions. Laura is digging a large hole for her pond, and Erika is making roads with a toy bulldozer.	Keep in mind that children's independent play has value for them. Occasionally present new toys or games that encourage participation by several children.
Onlooker Behavior	• *Unobtrusive observation* of other children's play activities	As three of his classmates play "store," Jason quietly watches them from the side of the room.	Ask the child if he or she would like to play with the other children. If so, ask the others quietly if the onlooker might join in.
Parallel Play	• *Playing next to another child*, but with little or no interaction • *Similarities in the behaviors of two or more children* who are playing near each other	Naticia and Leo are both making "sky-scrapers" with wooden blocks. Sometimes one child looks at what the other is doing, and occasionally one child makes a tower similar to the other's construction.	Comment that both children are doing something similar. Gently suggest an enjoyable activity that incorporates what both children are doing, but don't force interaction.
Associative Play	• *Some talking and sharing* of objects with another child • *Occasional comments* about what another child is doing	Several children are working at the same table creating different animals from Play-Doh. They occasionally ask for a particular color ("Gimme the red") or make remarks about others' creations ("You made a kitty just like I did").	Keep in mind that associative play is often a productive way for children to get to know one another. Once children feel comfortable together, you can suggest an activity that would encourage cooperative behaviors.
Cooperative Play	• *Active sharing* of toys and coordination of activities • *Taking on specific roles* related to a common theme	Sheldon sets up a "doctor's office" and Jan comes to visit him with her teddy bear, who has a "sore throat." Sheldon puts a tongue depressor to the bear's mouth and instructs it to "Say 'aahh.'"	Provide a variety of toys and other objects that are best used in group play—balls, props for playing "house" and "store," and so on.

First two columns based on Parten, 1932.

Observing Children 15-2

Watch two young boys in cooperative play while two other boys take a primarily onlooker role.

ENHANCEDetext *video example*

Observing Children 15-3

Observe Acadia and Cody coordinating their activities and resolving their differences as they play at the park.

ENHANCEDetext *video example*

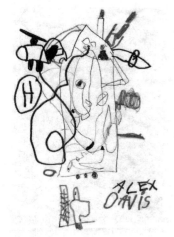

ARTIFACT 15-2 Our robot. Alex (age 5) and Davis (age 6) shared fantasies that guided them in drawing this picture together. As they worked on the picture, the boys continually listened to one another and built on each other's ideas.

social coordination that characterize cooperative play make it an especially important activity of early childhood. You can see an episode of cooperative play with two young boys who build a house of blocks in an Observing Children video.

In one form of cooperative play, *sociodramatic play*, children assume complementary imagined roles and carry out a logical sequence of actions. In the following scenario, we see Eric and Naomi, long-time friends, assuming the roles of husband and wife. Naomi is making plans to go shopping:

N: I'm buying it at a toy store, to buy Eric Fisher a record 'cause he doesn't have a. . . .
E: What happened to his old one?
N: It's all broken.
E: How did it get all broken?
N: Ah, a robber stealed it, I think. That's what he said, a robber stealed it.
E: Did he see what the action was? You know my gun is in here, so could you go get my gun? It's right over there, back there, back there, not paper . . . did you get it?
N: Yes, I found the robbers right in the closet.
E: Good, kill 'em.
N: I killed 'em.
E: Already?
N: Yes, so quick they can't believe it. (Gottman, 1986, p. 191)

Sociodramatic play activities contribute to children's growing social competence. In this kind of play children coordinate their perspectives, share fantasies, and take turns (Meadows, 2010; Rubin et al., 2006; C. Simmons, 2014). They must agree on individual roles ("I'll be the warrior"; "Okay, I'll be the chief"), props ("The log can be our base"), and rules and guidelines that govern actions ("We'll let Frances play, but she has to be the horse").

In the process of playing, children exercise skills in assertiveness, negotiation, conflict resolution, and self-regulation (G. Anderson, Spainhower, & Sharp, 2014; Göncü, 1993). Many learn to become progressively more polite in making requests. Whereas a 3-year-old is apt to be a bit bossy ("Give me the red one"; "You hafta . . ."), 5- and 6-year-olds are more likely to use hints and suggestions ("Would you like. . .?" "Let's . . .") (Parkhurst & Gottman, 1986, p. 329). Through negotiating roles and story lines, they discover the advantages of compromise ("I want to be the Mommy, you're the baby"; "No, you were the Mommy last time, so it's *my* turn"; "Okay, but next time I get to be the Mommy"). Moreover, children learn how to give one another emotional support, perhaps by voicing approval for one another's actions and creations ("That's pretty") or expressing sympathy for a playmate's distress ("Don't worry about that, it'll come off") (Gottman, 1983, p. 58; Rubin et al., 2006).

In an Observing Children video, you can watch two 4-year-olds, Acadia and Cody, use a variety of strategies to nourish their relationship and prevent any disagreements from escalating. They make explicit reference to their friendship ("Let's go, Cody, my best friend"). They encourage one another to climb ("This is gonna be cool!"). They admit when they're wrong ("Silly me, I forget everything"). And eventually they come to agreement about which slide to go down ("Yeah. Let's do it"). Another illustration of close coordination in activities is found in Artifact 15-2, a drawing created by two young boys during afternoon play.

Overall, the active, imaginative interactions of cooperative pretend play seem to exercise significant social, cognitive, and physical skills, even though this type of play may not be crucial for a child's healthy development (Lillard et al., 2013). Furthermore, the other kinds of play also serve important functions for children, especially at the younger ages. Parallel play, although seemingly nonsocial, has a definite value: Children use it to learn more about peers' interests and find common ground for social interactions (Bakeman & Brownlee, 1980; Rubin et al., 2006). Solitary play is not only used by very young children but sometimes preferred by older children who are less social than peers (Coplan, Ooi, Rose-Krasnor, & Nocita, 2014). Other children often play with peers but also prefer to spend time alone discovering the properties of objects and improving their proficiency with tools, natural specimens, and toys (A. D. Pellegrini, 2013).

Middle Childhood (6–10 years). Once children begin elementary school, about 30 percent of their social interactions are with peers (Rubin et al., 2006). Many of their interactions at school are in activities in which they are learning academic skills together. As a result of their many social experiences, children become aware that some ways of behaving are acceptable to peers, whereas others are not. With a growing awareness of other people's opinions, most children become eager to behave in socially acceptable ways.

Children also become concerned with rights within the group. Agreements are common, but conflicts inevitably arise. It can be easier said than done to resolve disagreements equitably (Frederickson & Simmonds, 2008; Newcomb & Bagwell, 1995; Salvas et al., 2014). Most children discover that such strategies as sulking ("I'm going home!"), threatening ("I'm never gonna play with you again!"), and hitting ("Take that!") rarely work. Through experimentation with a variety of strategies and through their growing capacity for social perspective taking, most children become proficient at maintaining amicable relationships with age-mates. You can see a 10-year-old boy's representation of the emotional difficulties and relief related to settling an argument with a good friend in Artifact 15-3.

Whereas younger children are apt to get together in groups of two or three and engage in free-flowing fantasy, elementary school children convene in larger groups. Children get together in these peer networks, perhaps at recess, in the neighborhood, or as part of an after-school team or activity. Various roles emerge as children interact repeatedly, with one or more children dominating, and a few unhealthy associations occasionally emerging, such as social exclusions and bully–victim relationships, in which one child has more power than another and repeatedly picks on him or her.

In informal settings, such as on the playground or at one another's homes, children of this age regularly play games with established rules. Verbal contests (e.g., "Twenty Questions," "I Spy"), board games, computer games, and team sports are common (Hartup, 1984; Knowles, Parnell, Stratton, & Ridgers, 2013). By participating in such activities, children discover how to use rules to their own advantage ("If I put another house on Boardwalk, you have to pay me double the next time you land on it"). They learn how to form alliances ("I'll run behind him, and then you pass me the ball over his head"). And they develop strategies for dealing with ambiguous situations ("It was *in!*" "Are you kidding? It was *out!*" "Okay, we'll say it's out, but next time *I* get to decide!"). Children also play electronic games together, especially when discouraged from going outside by parents worried about their safety (K. Clarke, 2013; Sherry, Lucas, Greenberg, & Holmstrom, 2013).

ARTIFACT 15-3 **Making peace.** Ten-year-old Jacob drew a child getting into an argument with a friend and then coming to a mutually acceptable solution. In his, artwork Jacob reveals his awareness that arguing with friends can be unpleasant, and that disputes can be resolved to everyone's satisfaction.

Early Adolescence (10–14 years). A major task during young adolescence is identifying peers at school with whom to affiliate. Young people tend to attract social partners who are similar to them in key ways—in their academic achievement, ethnicity, appearance (e.g., how much they weigh), and behavior (e.g., how altruistic and aggressive they are) (Echols & Graham, 2013). As students get to know one another and gel as a group, they come to see others outside their group as different from themselves. Young adolescents have a tendency to pigeonhole classmates with such labels as "brains," "jocks," "skaters," and "geeks" (B. B. Brown & Dietz, 2009; Wölfer & Scheithauer, 2014). Naturally they prefer to affiliate with young people who are similar to themselves who, in their eyes, better understand them (B. D. Tatum, 1997).

Once students reach puberty, they increasingly rely on peers for emotional support (G. H. Brody et al., 2014; Levitt, Guacci-Franco, & Levitt, 1993). Many begin to reveal their innermost thoughts to others, especially to familiar peers during face-to-face conversations and electronically mediated communications (e.g., over the Internet) (Dolev-Cohen & Barak, 2013;

Levitt et al., 1993). But even as their tendency for self-disclosure expands, young adolescents become self-conscious about what others think of them.

Age-mates frequently exert **peer pressure** by encouraging adolescents to behave in certain ways and not others. Youngsters who have poor relationships with their families, live in economically disadvantaged neighborhoods, and base their self-esteem on other people's opinions seem to be especially vulnerable to negative peer pressure (Erwin, 1993; Matjasko, Needham, Grunden, & Farb, 2010). Yet young people obviously make their own choices and imitate peers' behavior selectively, as this reflection by a youngster reveals:

> There's all this crap about being accepted into a group and struggling and making an effort to make friends and not being comfortable about your own self-worth as a human being. You're trying very hard to show everyone what a great person you are, and the best way to do that is if everyone else is drinking therefore they think that's the thing to do, then you might do the same thing to prove to them that you have the same values that they do and therefore you're okay. At the same time, the idea of peer pressure is a lot of bunk. What I heard about peer pressure all the way through school is that someone is going to walk up to me and say, "Here, drink this and you'll be cool." It wasn't like that at all. You go somewhere and everyone else would be doing it and you'd think, "Hey, everyone else is doing it and they seem to be having a good time—now why wouldn't I do this?" In that sense, the preparation of the powers that be, the lessons that they tried to drill into me, they were completely off. They had no idea what we are up against. (C. Lightfoot, 1992, p. 240)

Because much of the motivation to conform to peers' standards comes from within rather than from others, young people who have a firm sense of their own identity are better able than insecure peers to resist the urge to imitate others' characteristics (Buck, Kretsch, & Harden, 2013; Hartup, 1983).

Late Adolescence (14–18 years).

Late Adolescence (14–18 years). Older adolescents spend almost a third of their waking hours interacting with peers (Rubin et al., 2006). Teenagers spend little time with adults and very little time *exclusively* with an adult, such as a parent or teacher (Csikszentmihalyi, 1995; Csikszentmihalyi & Larson, 1984).

Adolescents help one another in their quest to define who they are as individuals. They talk through their values and aspirations and use peers as a forum for self-exploration (Gottman & Mettetal, 1986; Meadows, 2010). Because adolescents choose their confidantes, intimate conversations tend to be reciprocally supportive. Adolescents continue to provide one another with temptations to engage in risky behaviors, but they also encourage sharing, cooperation, ethical decisions, and community involvement (Wentzel, 2014).

A greater capacity for abstract thought allows older adolescents to think of other people as unique individuals rather than as members of specific groups. Older teens become increasingly aware of the characteristics they share with people from diverse backgrounds. Perhaps as a result, ties to sharply divided groups dissipate, hostilities soften, and youngsters become more flexible about the people with whom they associate (B. B. Brown & Dietz, 2009; Shrum & Cheek, 1987). One graduate of a racially mixed high school put it this way:

> Senior year was wonderful, when the black kids and the white kids got to be friends again, and the graduation parties where everyone mixed. . . . It was so much better. (T. Lewin, 2000, p. 20)

The Bioecology of Social Skills

The particular social skills that children use depend not only on their age but also on their individual features. Social skills are especially influenced by personal characteristics, gender, family experiences, and culture.

Personal Characteristics.

Personal Characteristics. Children's biological predispositions play a definite role in their peer relationships. Children who are born with a tendency to be impulsive and irritable are at risk for becoming disruptive, insensitive, and aggressive in their peer relationships (Berdan, Keane, & Calkins, 2008; Boivin et al., 2013). Those who are especially shy and withdrawn may also have trouble because they fail to initiate contact with peers. Of course, with support, virtually all children are capable of forming close peer relationships.

BIOECOLOGY OF DEVELOPMENT

Personal characteristics, gender, family experience, and culture collectively influence children's social skills.

On average, children with high intelligence (e.g., youngsters whom school personnel have identified as gifted) have good social skills. Youngsters with highly advanced intellectual abilities have trouble establishing and maintaining effective interpersonal relationships with age-mates when they feel *very* different from their peers, have parents who have not been accepting of them, or are in an educational setting where they are outcasts (Olszewski-Kubilius, Lee, & Thomson, 2014; Winner, 1997).

Many children with disabilities, too, have good interpersonal skills, but some others do not. Children with significant sensory or physical disabilities may have few opportunities to interact with peers. And children who have impaired social cognition—for instance, those with a significant intellectual disability or one of the autism spectrum disorders—often have deficiencies in social skills as well (E. W. Carter et al., 2014; S. Greenspan & Granfield, 1992).[4] For instance, a child who is autistic may fail to express empathy to distressed peers, carry on a one-sided conversation, or exhibit tantrums when frustrated. Youngsters with chronic emotional and behavioral problems (e.g., conduct disorders) are apt to have difficulty making and keeping friends, usually because of having poor social problem-solving skills (Asher & Coie, 1990; Renk, White, Scott, & Middleton, 2009).

Gender. Beginning in preschool, boys and girls tend to segregate into same-gender groups (Paley, 1984; Parke & Clarke-Stewart, 2011; Sallquist, DiDonato, Hanish, Martin, & Fabes, 2012). In sociodramatic play, girls enact scenarios that are relatively calm and sedate (e.g., playing house or school). In contrast, boys introduce elements of adventure and danger (e.g., playing cops and robbers or fighting intergalactic battles).

As boys grow older they continue to place high priority on physical action. Girls spend much more time simply talking—sharing personal concerns, telling secrets, offering emotional support, and so on (Berndt, 1992; Rose & Smith, 2009). Girls feel more attached to peers than do boys and are also more sensitive to subtle, nonverbal messages (body language) (J. H. Block, 1983; Gorrese & Ruggieri, 2012). On average, girls are slightly more kind and considerate, but boys regularly show their "softer" sides, displaying affection and sympathy appropriate for the occasion (Baillargeon et al., 2011; Eisenberg & Fabes, 1998).

Family and Community Experiences. Many families promote their children's peer relationships by encouraging get-togethers with peers who live close by. Parents commonly coach children in social skills, for example, encouraging them to take turns instead of fighting over toys (Healy, Sanders, & Iyer, 2014; Russell & Finnie, 1990). Contact with peers is also influenced by local circumstances. Generally, children in working-class and middle-class neighborhoods have numerous peers who live in nearby homes (Ladd, 2005). Some parents living in economically disadvantaged communities restrict their children's free time with peers due to concerns about dangers in the neighborhood. In affluent communities, few families with children are apt to live nearby, and parents may or may not have time to chauffeur children around to social events (Medrich, 1981). Numerous parents from all kinds of backgrounds manage to overcome barriers to social contact for their children but certain others do not.

Culture. Earlier we indicated that long-standing groups of children develop their own customs and shared understandings, which become their peer culture. Such groups of familiar children are embedded in broader settings, societies that have the encompassing rules, traditions, languages, symbols, and tools that saturate all aspects of their lives, and from which children draw as they develop local pastimes and common ground. For example, in North America most children come into frequent contact with age-mates from an early age. Parents value the ability of their children to get along with peers, and they encourage children's friendships with "play dates," appointments for their children to get together at one house or another. Japanese children have less free time than do U.S. children and thus fewer chances to interact with peers in informal settings, but they acquire valuable skills at school, where teachers cultivate their commitment to kind and sensitive treatment of classmates, including those with disabilities (Kayama & Haight, 2013; Rothbaum, Pott, Azuma, Miyake, & Weisz, 2000).

[4]The autism spectrum disorders are examined in Chapter 12.

To some degree, cultural groups model particular styles of relating to other people. For example, children in China, especially in the rural areas, are encouraged to be shy, whereas those in Israel are encouraged to be assertive (X. Chen, Wang, & Wang, 2009; Krispin, Sternberg, & Lamb, 1992).

Types of Connections with Peers

Children affiliate with one another in four distinct ways. First, they select social partners with whom to affiliate informally, often on a short-term basis, for example, by choosing whom to sit next to at lunchtime, with the result that some children are regularly accepted as buddies and others are not. Second, young people form friends with whom they share secrets and pastimes. Third, young people form larger social groups, especially during the older childhood and adolescent years. Finally, they become partners in romance, principally during the adolescent period.

Selection of Partners for Informal Interactions

Children make many choices every day as to which age-mates to affiliate with—with whom to walk home after school, ask for help with homework, and invite to their birthday parties. Socially skilled children—those who are trusting, cooperative, sensitive, and responsive with others—are frequently approached by peers and given valuable opportunities for social learning (Blandon, Calkins, Grimm, Keane, & O'Brien, 2010; J. Chin, 2014; Santos, Vaughn, Peceguina, & Daniel, 2014).

Developmental researchers examine *peer acceptance* by asking children in a classroom to confidentially nominate individual classmates with whom they would like to interact and others whom they would prefer to avoid. Researchers then collect these nominations and classify each child into one of five groups: *popular, rejected, neglected, controversial,* and *average* (Coie, Dodge, & Coppotelli, 1982; Dishion, Kim, Stormshak, & O'Neill, 2014; Rubin et al., 2006). Researchers subsequently compare the typical social features of children in the five groups.

Children who are well liked by numerous peers are considered **popular**. When researchers ask children to identify classmates they would most like to do something with, children don't necessarily choose those whom they and their teachers perceive to be the most admired members of the student body (Lafontana & Cillessen, 1998; Parkhurst & Hopmeyer, 1998). When we talk about *popular children* in terms of peer acceptance, we are describing young people who are well liked, kind, and trustworthy, rather than those who hold obvious high-status positions such as head cheerleader or football quarterback. Children who are well accepted by peers typically have good social skills. They know how to initiate and sustain conversations, refrain from talking only about their own needs, detect the subtle social cues that others give off, adjust their behaviors to changing circumstances, and act prosocially, often sharing, cooperating, and empathizing with others (Oortwijn, Boekaerts, Vedder, & Fortuin, 2008; Santos et al., 2014).

Children who are frequently excluded by peers are known as **rejected children**. Rejected children generally have poor social skills—for example, they may persistently draw attention to themselves and be impulsive, aggressive, and disruptive in the classroom (Asher & Renshaw, 1981; Ladd, Ettekal, Kochenderfer-Ladd, Rudolph, & Andrews, 2014; Putallaz & Heflin, 1986). Some rejected children are aggressive, placing a higher priority on acquiring objects and gaining power over others than on maintaining congenial interpersonal relationships (Dodge, Bates, & Pettit, 1990; Parke & Clarke-Stewart, 2011). Other rejected children appear immature, insensitive, inattentive, strange, or exceptionally timid (Bierman, 2004). Rejected children's tendency to alienate others leaves them few opportunities to develop the social skills they so desperately need, and many consequently feel lonely and distressed and sometimes become targets of bullying behaviors (Beeri & Lev-Wiesel, 2012; Coie & Cillessen, 1993).

A third group of children consists of **neglected children**, those whom age-mates rarely select as peers they would either most like or least like to do something with (Asher & Renshaw, 1981). Many neglected children are quiet and keep to themselves. Some prefer to be alone, others do not know how to go about making friends, and still others may be quite content with one or two close friends (Parke & Clarke-Stewart, 2011). Neglected status is often only a temporary situation; children categorized as neglected at one time are not always so categorized in follow-up assessments (Rubin et al., 2006; S. Walker, 2009).

A fourth category, **controversial children**, includes youngsters who are very well liked by some peers and intensely disliked by others. Controversial children are apt to have characteristics of both popular and rejected children. For example, they may be aggressive on some occasions and cooperative at other times (Coie & Dodge, 1988). The fifth group consists of children who, for lack of a better term, are known simply as *average:* Some peers like them and others don't, but without the intensity of feelings shown for popular, rejected, or controversial children and also without the invisibility of neglected children.

Because of its apparent effects on children, peer acceptance is an important quality for adults to monitor. In the Observation Guidelines table "Noticing Children's Level of Peer Acceptance," we present common characteristics of popular, rejected, neglected, controversial, and average children and suggest basic strategies for supporting students with these varying levels of peer acceptance.

OBSERVATION GUIDELINES
Noticing Children's Level of Peer Acceptance

CHARACTERISTIC	LOOK FOR	EXAMPLE	IMPLICATION
Popular Children	• *Good communication skills* • *Sensitivity and responsiveness* to others' wishes and needs • *Willingness to assimilate* into ongoing activities • *Signs of leadership potential*	On the playground, 8-year-old Daequan moves easily from one group to another. Before joining a conversation, he listens to what others are saying and adds a relevant comment. He doesn't draw much attention to himself but is well liked by most of his classmates.	Use popular children as leaders when trying to change other children's behavior. For example, when starting a recycling program, ask a well-regarded student to help get the program off the ground.
Rejected Children	• *For some, high rates of aggression* • *For others, immature, anxious, or impulsive behavior, including disruptions in class* • *For still others, unusually shy and withdrawn behavior* • *Unwillingness of other children* to play or work with them • *In some cases, appearance to other children of being strange and annoying*	Most children dislike 10-year-old Terra. She frequently calls classmates insulting nicknames, threatens to beat them up, and noisily intrudes into their private conversations.	Help rejected children learn basic social skills, such as how to initiate a conversation. Place them in cooperative groups with classmates who are likely to be accepting. With aggressive children, give appropriate consequences and teach strategies for controlling impulses. Publicly compliment rejected children on things they do well. Consult counselors when rejected children fail to respond to interventions.
Neglected Children	• *Tendency to be relatively quiet;* little or no disruptive behavior • *Fewer-than-average interactions* with age-mates but possible friendships with one or two peers • *For some, anxiety about interacting with others* • *Possible temporary* neglected status	Fourteen-year-old Sedna is initially reserved at her new school. She eats her lunch and walks home alone. Later in the year, however, she seems happier and more involved in school activities.	Identify group activities in which neglected children might feel comfortable. Arrange situations in which shy children with similar interests can get to know one another.
Controversial Children	• *Acceptance by some peers, rejection by others* • *Possible aggression and disruptive behavior in some situations, yet helpfulness, cooperation and sensitivity in others*	Thirteen-year-old Marcus is usually charming and cheerful, but occasionally he makes jokes at someone else's expense. His sunny personality impresses many classmates, yet his biting humor offends a few others.	Let controversial children know in no uncertain terms when their behaviors are inappropriate, but acknowledge their effective social skills as well.
Average Children	• *Tendency to be liked by some peers but disliked by others* • *Average interpersonal skills* (e.g., typical levels of prosocial behavior and aggression) • *Ability to find a comfortable social niche*	Five-year-old Joachim doesn't attract much attention to himself. He's made a few friends in kindergarten and seems to get along fairly well with them, but he sometimes has trouble handling disagreements.	Help average children refine their emerging social skills. Encourage them to be tactful, honest, and kind with peers. Acknowledge sensitivity, cooperation, and leadership, and teach alternatives to aggression and self-centered behavior.

Sources: Bierman, 2004; Coie & Dodge, 1988; Coie & Kupersmidt, 1983; Dodge, 1983; Ladd et al., 2014; Parke & Clarke-Stewart, 2011; Putallaz & Gottman, 1981; Rubin et al., 2006; Santos et al., 2014; S. Walker, 2009.

Friendships

In addition to wanting to be accepted by peers, children invariably hope to have one or more friends. Some of children's friendships are brief liaisons; others last a lifetime. Many are relatively casual; a few are deep and intimate. Some children have a large number of friends; others invest steadfastly in one or two close ones. Despite their varied types, friendships have four common qualities that distinguish them from other kinds of peer relationships:

My best friend is brian and we have had many fun times together with my other friends (anthony and arthur) too. We have been friends since 1ST grade, He has always been in my class those years, so has arthur and anthony, We have had sad and happy times/adventures, We sometimes argued. We would play hide and seek and get soda and other things at the Moble home park, We both enjoyed hamsters as pets, Sometimes he came to my house to play

ARTIFACT 15-4 My best friend. Ten-year-old Joseph explains that he has shared many experiences with his friend Brian.

• **Friendships are voluntary relationships.** Children often spend time with peers through happenstance: Perhaps they ride the same school bus, are members of a single class, or join a given sports team. In contrast, children *choose* their friends. Children make active efforts to affiliate with friends, and two or more youngsters typically remain pals as long as they continue to enjoy one another's company and successfully resolve their differences.

• **Friendships are powered by shared routines.** Friends establish traditions that are meaningful and mutually enjoyable. Over time, friends talk through their likes and dislikes, establishing common ground about many topics (Sorsana, Guizard, & Trognon, 2013; Suttles, 1970). Children talk, smile, and laugh more often with friends than with nonfriends; they also engage in more complex fantasy play with friends (J. G. Parker, 1986). In Artifact 15-4, 10-year-old Joseph writes about the fun activities he and his friend Brian have enjoyed together.

• **Friendships are reciprocal relationships.** In the time they spend together, friends address one another's needs (J. L. Epstein, 1986; J. Neal, Neal, & Cappella, 2014). Although friends take on slightly different roles in their relationship, generally they are equal partners. One friend may instigate fun activities, and the other may be an especially sympathetic listener, with both styles reflecting personal characteristics, perceptions of the partner's needs, and mutual regard.

• **Friendships offer ongoing, dependable support.** Friends help each other cope with stressful events by providing reassurance (Berndt & Keefe, 1995; Cranley Gallagher, 2013). Because friends have an emotional investment in their relationship, they work hard to look at situations from each other's point of view and resolve disputes that threaten to be divisive. As a result, they practice perspective taking and conflict resolution (Basinger, Gibbs, & Fuller, 1995; Calder, Hill, & Pellicano, 2013; DeVries, 1997).

The particular benefits that friendships have for children depend somewhat on their current developmental abilities. As we look at the nature of friendship across the five developmental periods, we see that friendships begin with mutual enjoyment and gradually add such characteristics as loyalty, trust, compromise, and intimacy.

Infancy (birth–2 years). Primitive relationships among peers emerge during infancy. In the beginning, social interests are fleeting and exploratory, and infants are as likely to crawl over one another as to pass a toy back and forth. Yet as infants grow, develop basic cognitive and language skills, and become familiar with one another, they smile, watch one another's faces and actions, and coordinate their play (Gonzalez-Mena, 2012; Rubin et al., 2006). When Teresa's son Connor was 9 months old, he became friendly with Patrick, another boy of the same age at his child care center. The two boys established familiar play routines, often laughing and chasing one another as they crawled around the room. Although they weren't yet speaking, and they certainly didn't swap secrets, they were clearly attuned to each other's behaviors. Such social interests solidify, and in their second year, toddlers make social overtures regularly, carry on complex interactions, and display positive emotions with peers whom they know and like (Howes, 1988).

Early Childhood (2–6 years). In the preschool years children infuse language, fantasy, and play into social interactions with familiar peers. When 3- and 4-year-olds interact with friends rather than with nonfriends, they are more likely to offer social greetings, share materials, carry on a conversation, engage in complex play, and exhibit good social skills (Charlesworth & LaFreniere, 1983; Hoyte, Torr, & Degotardi, 2014). These bonds are important to children, as you can see Dana's drawing in Artifact 15-5. In addition to exchanging affection, young friends work through disagreements (Hartup & Laursen, 1991). In the process of resolving these conflicts, children learn to assert themselves while also showing their regard for friends.

Middle Childhood (6–10 years). During the elementary school years, children continue to act differently with friends than with nonfriends. With friends they are more likely to express their feelings and speculate about one another's emotional states (Newcomb & Bagwell, 1995; Newcomb & Brady, 1982). At this age friends develop trust and loyalty, and many, girls especially, use self-disclosure as a strategy for maintaining a friendship (Diaz & Berndt, 1982; Rotenberg, & Boulton, 2013; Swenson & Rose, 2009). Friendships are more stable in middle childhood than in earlier years, and children are more deliberate in selecting playmates with qualities similar to their own (Berndt & Hoyle, 1985; Rubin, Lynch, Coplan, Rose-Krasnor, & Booth, 1994).

Children in this age range typically choose friends of their own gender, perhaps in part because same-gender peers are more likely to share interests and pastimes (Gottman, 1986; Zosuls, Field, Martin, Andrews, & England, 2014). Ten-year-old Andres shows his affection for buddies in his drawing in Artifact 15-6. A few children at this age make friends with children of the opposite gender, and such relationships are valuable in promoting social perspective taking and flexible communication skills (McDougall & Hymel, 2007).

ARTIFACT 15-5 Friends. Four-year-old Dana drew a picture of herself and her friend Dina. The two girls met in child care and became close companions. Afterward, they moved to separate towns but happily renewed their friendship when given a chance at summer camp.

Early Adolescence (10–14 years). Differences in relationships between friends and nonfriends intensify during early adolescence (Basinger et al., 1995; J. G. Parker & Gottman, 1989). Many young adolescents let down their guard and reveal their vulnerabilities to close friends, even as they may try to maintain self-confidence in front of other age-mates. Adolescents also confront feelings of possessiveness and jealousy over friends (J. G. Parker, Kruse, & Aikins, 2010). Gradually, young adolescents learn that friendships don't have to be exclusive, and friendship pairs converge into larger groups.

Late Adolescence (14–18 years). Older adolescents tend to be quite selective in their choice of friends (J. L. Epstein, 1986). Gone are the days when they run out of fingers as they count off their "close" friends, except, of course, on social media. In face-to-face relationships, older teenagers tend to nurture connections with a few friends that they keep for some time, in some cases over a lifetime. They frequently turn to friends for emotional support in times of trouble or confusion and are likely to engage in lengthy discussions about personal problems and possible solutions (Asher & Parker, 1989; Weeks & Pasupathi, 2010). When young people cannot easily turn to parents to reason through personal problems, friends can be a great source of comfort (Espinoza, Gillen-O'Neel, Gonzales, & Fuligni, 2013).

ARTIFACT 15-6 Good buddies. Ten-year-old Andres drew a picture of himself with two of his buddies. Many close friendships in the elementary and middle school years occur among children of the same gender.

Social Groups

Another kind of peer relationship occurs with social groups in middle childhood and adolescence. As a result of their expanding social contacts, youngsters form large social groups that regularly fraternize (Knifsend & Juvonen, 2014; Rubin et al., 2006). Initially, these groups are comprised of collections of single-gender friendships, but in adolescence they often include both boys and girls.

Youngsters' social groups vary considerably in size, function, and character. However, many have the following attributes:

Group members develop a common culture. As you have learned, children who choose to affiliate with one another develop common routines and ways of thinking about their lives. This shared culture gives group members a sense of community, belonging, and identity. Identification with a group also prompts young people to notice that they and members of their same group have certain characteristics in common that differ from other groups.

Group members socialize one another to follow group norms. Group members encourage conformity by reinforcing behaviors that are appropriate in the eyes of the group and discouraging behaviors that are not (Clasen & Brown, 1985; Deutsch, Steinley, & Slutske, 2014). Fortunately, many peer groups embrace productive characteristics, such as honesty, fairness, cooperation, academic achievement, and a sense of humor (Damon, 1988; Padilla-Walker & Carlo, 2014). Others, however, encourage unproductive behaviors, such as threatening classmates, making fun of classmates who are "brainy" or have disabilities, and endorsing cheating and drug use (B. B. Brown, 1993; Deutsch et al., 2014). Of course, young people do not passively become what fellow group members want them to be. In fact, youngsters generally affiliate with peers who have similar characteristics and then pressure themselves to adopt the group's norms (Gottman & Mettetal, 1986; Kwon & Lease, 2009).

Group members influence youngsters more strongly in some areas of life than others. Young people rarely accept a peer's suggestions without question (B. B. Brown, 1990; Padilla-Walker & Carlo, 2007). Instead, they typically evaluate what peers ask them to do, often with memories of advice they previously received from family members, teachers, and others outside the peer group. Peer groups are particularly influential in matters of style—for example, in dress, music, and social activities. In contrast, parents, teachers, and other adults continue to be influential in views about education, morality, religion, and careers (E. C. Cook, Buehler, & Henson, 2009; Hartup, 1983).

Group members have a sense of unity. Once youngsters gel as a group, they prefer members to nonmembers, and they develop feelings of loyalty to individuals within the group. In some cases they also feel hostility toward members of other groups and view their competitors as unfriendly and incompetent (Sherif, Harvey, White, Hood, & Sherif, 1961; L. K. Taylor et al., 2014). Such feelings toward *out-groups* are particularly intense when two or more groups actively compete for status or resources, as rival athletic teams and adolescent gangs often do.

Dominance hierarchies emerge within the group. When children's groups continue for any length of time, a pecking order, or **dominance hierarchy**, gradually evolves (J. L. Martin, 2009; Strayer, 1991). Some group members rise to the top, leading the way and making decisions for everyone. Other group members are followers: They look to those around them for guidance on how to behave and assume lesser roles in the group's activities. Sometimes less dominant individuals find unique positions within the group, perhaps the proverbial clown, daredevil, nursemaid, or brainiac. Although dominance hierarchies are common in any group, when interactions become tightly controlled by position, those lower in the pecking order are at risk for being ignored, ostracized, or even bullied (Garandeau, Lee, & Salmivalli, 2014).

Once youngsters reach puberty, social groups become a particularly prominent feature of their social worlds. Developmental researchers have described several kinds of groups that are significant during the adolescent years: cliques and crowds, subcultures, and gangs.

Cliques and Crowds. **Cliques** are moderately stable friendship groups of s three to nine individuals, often of the same gender. Cliques provide the basis for many voluntary social interactions during childhood and adolescence (X. Chen, Chang, & He, 2003; Kwon, Lease, & Hoffman, 2012). Clique boundaries tend to be fairly rigid and exclusive (some people are in, others are out), and membership affects social status and level of influence with other peers.

Children begin to form cliques as early as first grade as dyads of friends begin to affiliate with other small friendship groups and together evolve as cliques (Witvliet, van Lier, Cuijpers, & Koot., 2010). Cliques remain moderately stable, with individual children often affiliating with the same group for a year or more but also entering and exiting at will and allowing others to join in occasionally. As children grow, they may become increasingly concerned with being accepted into a particular clique. Young adolescents wonder about their social standing: "Who likes me?" "Will I be popular at my new school?" "Why didn't Sal invite

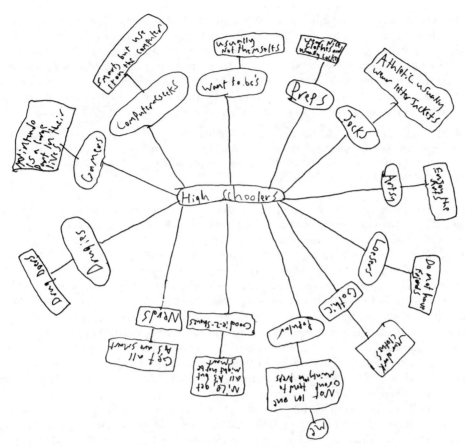

ARTIFACT 15-7   Social networks. Fourteen-year-old Connor diagrammed the complex collection of student groupings he observed during his freshman year in high school. In his inner circle he labeled the different groups (e.g., *preps, jocks, gamers*), and in the outer circle he described each one (e.g., "wear nice clothes and usually cocky," "athletic, usually wear letter jackets," "Nintendo is a large part in their lives").

me to his party?" (Gavin & Furman, 1989). When they leave one clique to join another, they are apt to engender feelings of betrayal, hurt, and jealousy in the friends they leave behind (Kanner, Feldman, Weinberger, & Ford, 1987).

Cliques decline in prevalence during the adolescent years and are replaced by **crowds**, larger collections of peers who are defined by others according to their reputation (B. B. Brown & Dietz, 2009). Like cliques, crowds provide support to young people and opportunities to practice social skills, although not all lessons are favorable. Some young people affiliate with crowds that reinforce negative behaviors. In Artifact 15-7, Connor diagrams the types of crowds he noticed his first year of high school. Crowds tend to disband during the final 2 years of high school, when young people feel freer to act as individuals and intermingle with people from different backgrounds.

Subcultures. A large number of adolescents affiliate with a well-defined **subculture**, a group that resists the dominant culture by adopting a significantly different way of life (Czymoniewicz-Klippel, 2013; J. S. Epstein, 1998). Some subcultures are tightly knit groups, and others are loosely configured, with members coming and going. Some subcultures are relatively benign; for instance, a middle school skateboarders' subculture may simply espouse a particular mode of dress and recreational pastime. Other subcultures, such as those that promote drug use, endorse racist and anti-Semitic behaviors (e.g., skinheads), or practice Satanic rituals, are obviously worrisome (C. C. Clark, 1992; Intravia, Wolff, Stewart, & Simons, 2014).

Adolescents are apt to affiliate with subcultures when they feel alienated from society (perhaps from their school or their community generally), uncomfortable about fitting in with peers at school, pessimistic about the future, and motivated to exercise their autonomy (C. C. Clark, 1992; Czymoniewicz-Klippel, 2013). Some young people feel not only disenfranchised from community life but also rejected by their families, heightening their need for intimacy. For example, "street families" of homeless youth offer one another protection and emotional support. One 16-year-old girl described her street family:

> Well, it's like we all just put what we have together and share. In our family, we all work together to make sure we are all taken care of. It's like someone will panhandle one day and someone else will do it the next. And whatever people get they will bring it back and share with everyone. (H. Smith, 2008, p. 764)

Gangs. A **gang** is a cohesive group characterized by initiation rites, distinctive colors and symbols, alleged ownership of a territory, feuds with one or more rival groups, and criminal activity (A. Campbell, 1984; Gover, Jennings, & Tewksbury, 2009). Gangs have well-defined dominance hierarchies, strict rules, and stiff penalties for breaking them.

Once confined to a few neighborhoods in inner cities, gangs have now become widespread, especially in lower-income inner-city areas, but increasingly in suburbs and rural areas (National Drug Intelligence Center, 2008; Rojek, Petrocelli, & Oberweis, 2010). Young people who join gangs often live in low-income neighborhoods with high rates of community violence and few opportunities for steady employment (Gilman, Hill, Hawkins, Howell, & Kosterman, 2014; J. S. Hong, 2010). Joining a gang enables young people to receive emotional support, demonstrate loyalty to friends and family, gain recognition for accomplishments, and obtain financial rewards (through criminal activities) (A. Campbell, 1984; Kodluboy, 2004; Melde, Taylor, & Esbensen, 2009).

In some instances gang members endorse prosocial behaviors, including caring for one another (Moje, 2000). But generally speaking, gangs do more harm than good. High rates of using and selling drugs, carrying destructive weapons, and intimidating peers make gangs a serious concern for law enforcement officers and community leaders (Gilman et al., 2014; Parks, 1995). Although many gang members report joining gangs to escape violence in their community, the reality is that they face a greater risk of being victimized if they join a gang. Young people are targeted inside of the gang during initiation, as a result of punishment for violating a gang rule, or as part of a sexual assault; they also become hurt during disputes with other gangs, for example, in fights involving weapons (Melde et al., 2009).

Many educators recognize gangs as a serious problem. Youth in gangs often intimidate classmates, defend the school as their territory, and recruit new members from the student body. Ideally, educators try to address children's needs long before children are tempted to join gangs.[5] When youngsters feel cared for by teachers and are confident in their own academic abilities, they are more likely to remain in school and avoid criminal activity (M. M. Jensen, 2005).

Valuable *prevention strategies* include early childhood curricula that prepare young children with literacy skills and a healthy dose of self-confidence, and after-school programs, such as the Boys and Girls Clubs of America, that give older children productive outlets for their time (Grekul & Sanderson, 2011). *Interventions* entice youths to leave gangs by offering job training, adult mentoring, gang mediation, and counseling (Winterdyk & Ruddell, 2010; Zaff, Ginsberg, Boyd, & Kakli, 2014). *Suppression programs* reduce gang activities through weapon seizures and arrests for gang-related incidents near schools.

Romantic Liaisons and Relationships

Starry-eyed desires create an entirely different kind of peer connection. Awareness of romantic intimacy emerges in early childhood. Many children, especially those living in traditional two-parent families, believe that getting married and having children is a normal and

---

[5]Multitiered educational strategies that discourage young people from joining gangs and intervene with those who have already joined gangs are described in Chapter 14.

inevitable part of growing up. In Artifact 15-8, 5-year-old Alex draws his image of his parents on their wedding day. Children sometimes act out their fantasies in play, as this episode involving Eric and Naomi illustrates:

E: Hey, Naomi, I know what we can play today.
N: What?
E: How about, um, the marry game. You like that.
N: Marry?
E: How about baker or something? How about this. Marry you? OK, Naomi, you want to pretend that?
N: Yes.
E: OK, Naomi, do you want to marry me?
N: Yeah.
E: Good, just a minute, Naomi, we don't have any marry place.
N: We could pretend this is the marry place.
E: Oh, well, pretend this, ah, there'll have to be a cake.
N: The wedding is here first.
E: OK, but listen to this, we have to have a baby, oh, and a pet.
N: This is our baby. (Gottman, 1986, p. 157)

Consistent with what we have learned about cognitive abilities at this age, young children's understandings of courtship and marriage are simple and concrete. In the preceding scenario, Naomi and Eric focus on having a "marry place" and wedding cake. Such fantasies help young children anticipate their eventual entry into romantic relationships.

Dating. As children grow, they gradually expand on their ideas about what it means to participate in romantic relationships, and many date. Prior to puberty, some children practice courtship behaviors, with girls vying for the attention of boys by using cosmetics and choosing clothing and hairstyles that make them look older and (they think) prettier, and with boys flaunting whatever manly airs they can muster (Elkind, 1981b; Giordano, 2003). The early romances of late middle childhood and early adolescence often exist more in youngsters' minds than in reality, as the following conversation between two young teenage girls illustrates:

A: How's Lance [*giggle*]? Has he taken you to a movie yet?
B: No. Saw him today but I don't care.
A: Didn't he say anything to you?
B: Oh . . .
A: Lovers!
B: Shut up!
A: Lovers at first sight! [*Giggle*.]
B: [*Giggle*.] Quit it! (Gottman & Mettetal, 1986, p. 210; reprinted with the permission of Cambridge University Press)

As young people reach adolescence, subsets form as couples. Relationships may become serious and involve emotional intimacy (Connolly & McIsaac, 2009; Rubin et al., 2006). In determining how to act in romantic relationships, young people apply the social skills and understandings that they have gained in close relationships. Adolescents with secure attachments to family members are likely to have successful dating experiences, probably because they have greater self-confidence, better social skills, and more experience being in trusting relationships (W. A. Collins & Sroufe, 1999; Rauer, Pettit, Lansford, Bates, & Dodge, 2013). Adolescents who are accustomed to balanced give-and-take at home are apt to use this same method of decision making with romantic partners, negotiating what movie to see, which party to attend, and so on. In contrast, teenagers who have seen family violence may hit and push partners or, conversely, tolerate partners' aggressive behavior ("He didn't mean it"; "She was drunk"; "He'll outgrow it") (D. A. Wolfe & Wekerle, 1997). Young people also select from among patterns they have absorbed related to intimacy, perhaps being loyal to a partner, "hooking up" (being intimate on a one-time basis) with a stranger, or having a "friendship with benefits" (a casual relationship in which partners are sexually active but not committed to one another) (Connolly & McIsaac, 2009).

ARTIFACT 15-8 **Wedding day.** Most preschoolers are curious about courtship and marriage. Here Teresa's son Alex (age 5) depicts his image of his parents getting married.

Adolescents' first romantic relationships offer young people definite advantages. Being in a relationship fulfills needs for companionship, affection, and security and may significantly enhance social status with peers (W. A. Collins & Sroufe, 1999; Connolly & McIsaac, 2009). Such relationships also provide opportunities for young people to experiment with new interpersonal behaviors and examine previously unexplored aspects of their identity.

At the same time, romantic relationships can wreak havoc on adolescents' emotions (W. A. Collins & van Dulmen, 2006; Ha, Dishion, Overbeek, Burk, & Engels, 2014). They may find it exciting and frustrating to enter (and exit) romantic liaisons with one another. In some cases the emotional highs and lows that come with romance—the roller-coaster ride between exhilaration and disappointment—cloud judgment, trigger depression, and distract young people from schoolwork (Ha et al., 2014; Larson, Clore, & Wood, 1999).

Sexual Intimacy. Both genders have some capacity for sexual arousal even before puberty (Conn & Kanner, 1940; de Graaf & Rademakers, 2006). Children and preadolescents occasionally look at or touch one another in private places and play games with sexual overtones (e.g., strip poker; Dornbusch et al., 1981; A. Montgomery, 2009). However, sexual contact before adolescence typically lacks the erotic features present in later development, by which time young people have developed the physical structures and physiological impetus to become sexually active.

As they mature, adolescents try to come to terms with their emerging sexuality. They must learn to accept their changing bodies, cope with unanticipated feelings of desire, and reconcile the conflicting messages they get from home, peers, religious groups, and the media as to the circumstances in which varying degrees of sexual intimacy are appropriate (Brooks-Gunn & Paikoff, 1993). For many adolescents sexual intimacy goes hand in hand with, and is a natural outgrowth of, long-term romantic relationships (Graber, Britto, & Brooks-Gunn, 1999). For others, it is something that should be saved for the "right moment," perhaps for marriage. And for a few, sexual intimacy is an activity completely separate from romantic involvement. For these individuals, it may be a means of enhancing social standings with peers, experimenting with a risky activity, exploring sexual orientations, gaining others' approval and affection, or simply experiencing physical pleasure (W. A. Collins & Sroufe, 1999; Peltzer, 2010; Woody, D'Souza, & Russel, 2003).

In a few cases, young people progress to sexual intercourse during their first intimate encounter but more commonly follow a developmental sequence over time. For example, young people typically begin with hand-holding and a simple kiss and then add more personal contacts. Despite increases in casual sex, adolescents usually initiate sexual intercourse only after several years of sexually intimate exploration (Connolly & McIsaac, 2009; DeLamater & MacCorquodale, 1979; Victor, 2012).[6]

Although sexual maturation is a natural process, it is not a simple matter to address. With young children, parents mention sexuality, especially, where babies come from—in general terms—in the context of love and marriage, the names of body parts, and restrictions to which a child's private parts can be touched (K. A. Martin & Torres, 2014). No one knows how best to handle adolescent sexuality—not parents or teachers, and certainly not adolescents themselves. Many adults ignore the topic, assuming (or perhaps hoping) it's not yet relevant for adolescents in their care. Even teenagers who have good and open relationships with their parents have few chances to talk about sex (Brooks-Gunn & Furstenberg, 1990; Farringdon, Holgate, McIntyre, & Bulsara, 2014). And when parents and teachers do broach the topic of sexuality with adolescents, they often raise it in conjunction with problems, such as irresponsible behavior, substance abuse, disease, and unwanted pregnancy.

Sexual Orientation and Gender Identity. By **sexual orientation**, we mean the particular sex(es) to whom an individual is romantically and sexually attracted. A small but significant percentage of adolescents find themselves sexually attracted to their own gender either instead of or in addition to the opposite gender. Although it has been difficult to establish precise figures, researchers have estimated that 2 to 3 percent of young people report

---

[6]See Chapter 5 for a discussion of adolescents' unsafe sexual behaviors.

being gay, lesbian, or bisexual, with an additional few percent either having some degree of same-sex attractions while continuing to identify primarily as heterosexual or realizing later in adulthood that they are homosexual or bisexual (Bailey, Dunne, & Martin, 2000; Savin-Williams, 2005).

Gender identity refers to the commitment a person has of having masculine or feminine characteristics. A few youngsters are *transgendered*, in that they have a different *gender identity* than is apparent from their physiological sex apparent at birth. A young person may identify as male, female, both, neither, or none, or the adolescent's image of personal gender may take yet another form or change with circumstances. Teachers have occasion to recognize transgendered youth due to their preferences in clothing, hairstyles, and behavior. Gender identity is *not* the same as sexual orientation. A person who is transgendered may have any sexual orientation.

It has become increasingly clear that sexual orientation and gender identity are at least partly caused by biological factors (Savin-Williams & Diamond, 1997; VanderLaan, Blanchard, Wood, & Zucker, 2014). Some evidence for a genetic component comes from twin studies: Monozygotic (identical) twins are more similar in their sexual orientation and gender identity than are dizygotic (fraternal) twins (Dawood et al., 2009; Gabard, 1999). Other research has revealed that unusually high levels of steroids and hormones circulating in the prenatal environment initiate a cascade of physiological effects, including subtle changes to brain circuits, which later influence sexual orientation and gender identity (LeVay, 2011; Rahman & Wilson, 2003). Certain aspects of the mother's physiology may also play a role. For example, boys who have numerous older brothers are more likely to become homosexual, presumably because their mothers' bodies became reactive to circulating male hormones with later pregnancies and produced substances that diminished the masculinity of the fetus's developing brain (VanderLaan et al., 2014).

Regardless of the exact factors determining sexual orientation and gender identity, it seems clear that these important aspects of human development are not casual decisions or perhaps decisions at all. Many homosexual, bisexual, and transgendered young people recall feeling "different" from peers since childhood (D. A. Anderson, 1994; Carver, Egan, & Perry, 2004; Kenneady & Oswalt, 2014). Adolescence can be a particularly confusing time for them, as they struggle to form an identity while feeling different and isolated from peers (Needham & Austin, 2010; C. J. Patterson, 1995). When their attractions to same-gender peers become stronger, they may initially work hard to discount such sentiments. At an older age, they may begin to accept some aspects of their homosexuality and gender identity, and later still they may "come out" and identify fully and openly with other gay, lesbian, or transgendered individuals.

When the topic of homosexuality comes up in the school curriculum, it is usually within the context of acquired immunodeficiency syndrome (AIDS) and other risks (Gowen & Winges-Yanez, 2014; Malinsky, 1997). Unfortunately, adolescents with a homosexual, bisexual, or transgender orientation are often harassed by peers and occasionally victimized in hate crimes (Elze, 2003; McGuire, Anderson, Toomey, & Russell, 2010). Under such circumstances some gay, lesbian, bisexual, and transgendered youth become "silent, invisible, and fearful" (M. B. Harris, 1997, p. xxi). Feeling that school is not a safe place for them to be, these youth may stay home or even decide to drop out of school (C. Burton, Marshal, & Chisolm, 2014; Elia, 1994).

Despite these social hardships, most gay, lesbian, and transgendered youths have good mental health and find the support they need, especially when they tell others about their orientation (Kosciw, Palmer, & Kull, 2014; Savin-Williams, 1989). In Artifact 15-9, 19-year-old Michael describes his journey to self-acceptance. Rates of depression and anxiety are higher than usual in transgendered youth than in other young people, and much of this adjustment problem is due to the heartache of ostracism from peers and family (K. Richmond, Carroll, & Denboske, 2010).

Fostering Productive Peer Relationships

Group environments for children—classrooms, schools, after-school programs, and so forth—are excellent settings for fostering children's social skills, peer acceptance, and

As long as I can remember, I always felt a little different when it came to having crushes on other people. When I was in elementary school I never had crushes on girls, and when I look back on that time now, I was probably most attracted to my male friends. I participated in some of the typical "boy" activities, like trading baseball cards and playing video games, but I was never very interested in rough sports. I often preferred to play with the girls in more role-playing and cooperative games. Of course, I didn't understand much about sex or gender roles at the time. I just figured I would become more masculine and develop feelings for the opposite sex after going through puberty.

To my dismay, middle school and the onset of puberty only brought more attention to my lack of interest in girls. The first time I thought about being gay was when I was in 6th grade, so I was probably 11 or 12 years old at the time. But in my mind, being gay was not an option and I began to expend an incredible amount of energy repressing my developing homosexual urges. In 7th grade, I had my first experience with major depression. Looking back on it, I am almost positive that being gay was the immediate cause of the depression. . . . When I finally recovered from the episode a few months later, I did my best to move on with my life and forget about my problems with sexuality. I continued to repress my feelings through high school, a task that became more and more difficult as the years went by. I never really dated any girls and my group of friends in high school was highly female. When I was 16, a junior in high school, I had another more severe bout of

depression. . . . I continued to be ashamed of my feelings and refused to even tell my psychologist about concerns over my sexuality. After finally emerging from my depression, I came to somewhat of an agreement with myself. I decided that I would simply put my conflict on hold, hoping it would resolve itself. Unfortunately, I still held on to the hope that it would resolve itself in heterosexuality and I remained distraught by my feelings. I finally came out during my freshman year at [college] with the support of my friends and an extremely accepting social environment.

Having exposure to the homosexual lifestyle in college is what finally made me realize that I could have a normal life and that I would not have to compromise my dreams because of it. Even though my high school was relatively liberal and very supportive of different backgrounds, there was very little discussion about homosexuality, even in health class. We had visibly gay teachers, but it was rarely openly talked about. I think the reason it took me so long to accept my sexuality was simply because I had no exposure to it while growing up. It angers me that people refer to homosexuality as a lifestyle choice because I had no choice over my sexuality. I spent seven years of my life denying my homosexuality, and believe me, if there had ever been a choice between gay or straight during that time, I would have chosen straight in a second. Today I can't imagine my life without being gay and I would never choose to be straight.

Essay used with permission.

ARTIFACT 15-9 **This Is Who I Am.** After a year of college, 19-year-old Michael wrote this essay.

friendships. Thoughtful guidance is particularly important for youngsters who are socially isolated or rejected by their peers. We offer the following suggestions:

Preparing for Your Licensure Examination
Your teaching test might ask about what teachers and other practitioners can do to facilitate productive peer interactions.

• **Set up situations in which youngsters can enjoy friendly interactions with one another.** Teachers can arrange structured cooperative learning activities that require all group members to share equal responsibility, and they can provide play equipment such as balls and climbing structures that lend themselves to coordinated interaction (Slavin, 1990; Stanton-Chapman, 2014). Adults might also ask youngsters to read to a peer with a visual impairment, sign to a child with hearing loss, provide tutoring to a classmate with a learning disability, or take notes for a child with a physical impairment. In addition, adults can acknowledge the mutual benefits of children's helpful gestures ("Thanks, Jamie, for helping Branson—he really appreciates your assistance, and you seemed to have learned a lot by explaining concepts to him").

• **Help young children ease into social groups.** Young children who are shy or new to a community can benefit from intercession by educators. In the following anecdote, Mrs. Kusumoto, a Japanese preschool teacher, skillfully models desired behaviors and helps one child, Fumiko, enter a group of peers:

Mrs. Kusumoto helps Fumiko put a cha-cha-cha tape in the portable cassette player, and calls a second girl to come over and join them on a small stage made of blocks. The two girls and Mrs. Kusumoto stand on the stage, singing and shaking their maracas. Then Mrs. Kusumoto steps down and faces them, singing along and encouraging them to continue. After a few minutes she attempts to melt away. The girls continue singing briefly, but when the song ends the second girl runs off, leaving Fumiko alone and unoccupied. She looks for Mrs. Kusumoto and begins following her around again. Mrs. Kusumoto approaches a small group of girls who are playing house, asking them: "Would you like to invite this girl over for dinner? After giving the concert, she is very hungry." One of the girls nods silently. Fumiko smiles and enters the "house." She stands there uncertainly, saying nothing. Mrs. Kusumoto inquires, "Fumiko-chan. Have you had your dinner? Why don't you join us? Don't you want something to eat? It looks good." Fumiko nods and the girls bring her a couple [of] dishes of clay "food." Mrs. Kusumoto looks on briefly, then moves quietly out of the scene. (Holloway, 2000, pp. 100–101)

As Mrs. Kusumoto's gestures suggest, teachers can sometimes gently nudge children into cooperative play, although children naturally insist on choosing their own friends to affiliate with on special occasions such as their birthdays (Hollingsworth & Buysse, 2009; Stanton-Chapman, 2014).

• **Teach social skills and problem-solving strategies.** By participating in and reflecting on interactions with adults and peers, many youngsters acquire proficient social behaviors. But some—perhaps because of limited opportunities to interact with age-mates, poor role models at home, or a cognitive disability—know little about how to initiate conversations, exchange compliments, offer emotional support, or in other ways establish and maintain rewarding interpersonal relationships. Some also lack productive strategies for solving social problems. They may barge into a game without asking to join in or respond to teasing with aggression. Teachers and counselors can coach social skills, perhaps advising a child, "To join a conversation, stand for a moment next to the other students who are talking and then watch for a time when you might say something relevant to their topic. You can also offer a compliment or ask the students about their opinion on something."

• **Minimize barriers to social interaction.** Children are less likely to interact with peers when physical, linguistic, or social barriers stand in the way (Anaby et al., 2013; Bobzien et al., 2013; Matheson, Olsen, & Weisner, 2007). Jeanne recalls a junior high school student who could not negotiate the cafeteria steps with her wheelchair and frequently ended up eating lunch alone. Educators can be on the lookout for such impediments and campaign for their removal. They can also teach groups of youngsters who speak different languages (including American Sign Language) some basic vocabulary and simple phrases in one another's native tongues.

• **Cultivate empathy for peers with special needs.** Some children feel resentment or anger because of their belief that peers with special needs should be able to control inappropriate behaviors (Juvonen, 1991). In fact, classmates are less tolerant of peers with cognitive difficulties or emotional and behavioral disorders than they are of peers with obvious physical disabilities (Madden & Slavin, 1983; Ysseldyke & Algozzine, 1984). Through paired or small-group activities, adults can show nondisabled students that peers with disabilities have many of the same talents, thoughts, feelings, and desires that they themselves have (E. W. Carter, Asmus, & Moss, 2013; Staub, 1998).

• **Recruit a student to serve as a buddy to a child with special needs.** A teacher might train one or more students to tutor a peer with a disability, showing them how to explain concepts, review his or her understanding of a concept, and encourage participation (E. W. Carter et al., 2013). Other strategies are to ask a student to invite a peer with a disability to have lunch with during one or more days during the week or check on his or her activities during particular times of the day. Students with disabilities can benefit from this assistance educationally as well as socially, and their buddies without disabilities can acquire a deeper commitment to inclusion and a broader view of friendship (E. W. Carter et al., 2013).

• **Encourage a general feeling of respect for others.** Adults who successfully promote friendships among diverse groups of children are often those who consistently communicate that all members of their community are welcome and respected (Allodi, 2010; Battistich, Solomon, Kim, Watson, & Schaps, 1995). Fernando Arias, a high school vocational education teacher, put it this way:

> In our school, our philosophy is that we treat everybody the way we'd like to be treated. . . . Our school is a unique situation where we have pregnant young ladies who go to our school. We have special education children. We have the regular kids, and we have the drop-out recovery program . . . we're all equal. We all have an equal chance. And we have members of every gang at our school, and we hardly have any fights, and there are close to about 300 gangs in our city. We all get along. It's one big family unit it seems like. (Turnbull, Pereira, & Blue-Banning, 2000, p. 67)

FOR FURTHER EXPLORATION . . .

Learn more about how to help children with disabilities be included in social interaction with peers.

ENHANCEDetext
content extension

• **Be a backup system when relationships with peers aren't going well.** Disruptions in peer relationships—perhaps because of interpersonal conflicts or a friend's relocation to a distant city—can trigger emotional distress in youngsters (Wentzel, 2009). Warm, supportive adults can lessen the pain in such circumstances and when a child has no close friends (Guay et al., 1999; Wentzel, 1999). Such sympathetic overtures are especially important for children who have little support at home and might otherwise turn to deviant peer groups for attention (Parks, 1995). Good relationships with teachers often have the effect of putting children at ease; as a result, children who have previously had difficulties in making friends may reach out to peers after gaining support from a teacher (De Laet et al., 2014.). It's important to keep in mind, however, that students are aware of a peer becoming dependent on a teacher, and therefore teachers need to balance their gestures of kindness to a neglected child with subtle efforts at inclusion in social activities. In other words, positive peer relationships should remain a long-term goal even as a teacher reaches out to a student who has been ignored or rejected by peers.

• **Be aware of family influences on children's peer relationships.** Family practices strongly influence children's interactions with peers. Some parents are quite protective, rarely allowing their children to play with peers outside the family, whereas others actively arrange for children to affiliate with friends (A. C. Fletcher, Bridges, & Hunter, 2007). Children who have not had much experience with peers at home or in the neighborhood can gain valuable experience in groups at school, particularly when teachers imperceptibly nudge them in to existing groups. For example, a teacher might sit with a few children at lunch and, when noticing a child eating alone, ask him or her to join them (e.g., "Sasha, we're talking about our pets. Would you like to tell us about your new puppy").

• **Provide the specific kinds of support that rejected children need most.** An important first step in helping rejected children is to determine the reasons why other children find them unpleasant to be around (Bierman, & Powers, 2009). As you have learned, some rejected children are aggressive, have limited social skills, and use coercive behaviors to get their way. Other rejected children have trouble asserting their desires and opinions. Once educators understand exactly what is missing from a rejected child's skill set, they can take steps to help him or her acquire the missing competencies.

Having a reputation as being aggressive or socially odd is a risk factor for becoming excluded or victimized (Hoglund & Chisholm, 2014). Even after children show improvements in social behavior, peers may continue to dislike and reject them (Bierman, Miller, & Staub, 1987; Prinstein, Rancourt, Guerry, & Browne, 2009). When encountering formerly aggressive children, many peers assume "once a bully, always a bully." To improve children's reputations, adults can create structured cooperative learning groups in which formerly ostracized children can use their newly developed social skills to show peers that they are now able to be good companions.

• **Accept the preoccupations adolescents develop in one another.** When young people reach puberty, they become preoccupied with who harbors secret yearnings for whom, whether the targets of desire reciprocate with affection, and which friends are sexually active. As a practitioner working with young people, you may find this undercurrent of romantic desire to be a distraction. While endeavoring to keep young people focused on their academic learning, you can nevertheless try to accept that these preoccupations are a natural, healthy part of coming-of-age.

• **Expect diversity in adolescents' romantic relationships.** Some young people attract a series of steady admirers, whereas others are inexperienced in, possibly even indifferent to, the world of romance. And, as mentioned earlier, a small percentage of adolescents will have yearnings for members of their own gender. Thus, adults should not presume that an adolescent girl wants to have a boyfriend, a boy wants to have a girlfriend, or even that the young person sees dating as a culturally appropriate option.

• **Be supportive when young people are struggling with dissolutions of romantic relationships.** To some adults the romantic bonds and breakups of adolescents seem trivial, but they sometimes cause considerable stress in teenagers. Adolescents may feel deep humiliation after rejection by a desired romantic partner or a profound sense of loss as a long-term relationship ends. In such situations teachers and counselors can help adolescents sort through their feelings and look forward with optimism to new relationships (Bannister, Jakubec, & Stein, 2003; Larson et al., 1999). In such situations, students might benefit from therapy from the counselor, supportive and nonjudgmental conversations with another adult, formal education about healthy relationships, and informal occasions to express their feelings in diaries, journals, music, or other avenues (Boniel-Nissim & Barak, 2013; A. Sparks, Lee, & Spjeldnes, 2012).

• **Describe sexual harassment and indicate why it is prohibited.** **Sexual harassment** is any action that a targeted person can reasonably construe as hostile, humiliating, or sexually offensive (Sjostrom & Stein, 1996). It is a form of discrimination and therefore prohibited by the laws of many nations, including U.S. laws. Sexual harassment can be a problem at the late elementary, middle school, and high school levels, when youngsters are maturing and developing an interest in sexual matters. Youngsters must be advised that sexual harassment will not be tolerated. They should be informed that under no circumstances may they degrade one another—by words, gestures, or actions—with regard to physical traits or sexual orientation. An example of a description of sexual harassment, appropriate for students at varying grade levels, appears in Figure 15-1.

• **Protect the rights of gay, lesbian, bisexual, and transgender youth.** Teachers and other adults sometimes overhear peers teasing students who violate traditional gender roles or speak openly about attraction to same-sex individuals. Unfortunately, some educators tolerate these remarks and contribute to an environment that is hostile to gay, lesbian, bisexual, and transgender youth. As one transgendered adolescent advised, "[teachers] should actually speak up, because I've been in a lot of classrooms where stuff is said, and the teachers don't do [anything]. And if they did, it would stop right there" (McGuire, Anderson, Toomey, &

SEXUAL HARASSMENT: IT'S NO JOKE!

- **Sexual harassment is unwanted and unwelcomed sexual behavior** which interferes with your right to get an education or to participate in school activities. In school, sexual harassment may result from someone's words, gestures or actions (of a sexual nature) that make you feel uncomfortable, embarrassed, offended, demeaned, frightened, helpless or threatened. If you are the target of sexual harassment, it may be very scary to go to school or hard to concentrate on your school work.

- **Sexual harassment can happen once, several times, or on a daily basis.**

- **Sexual harassment can happen any time and anywhere** in school—in hallways or in the lunchroom, on the playground or the bus, at dances or on field trips.

- **Sexual harassment can happen to anyone!** Girls and boys both get sexually harassed by other students in school.

- **Agreement isn't needed.** The target of sexual harassment and the harasser do not have to agree about what is happening; sexual harassment is defined by the girl or boy who is targeted. The harasser may tell you that he or she is only joking, but if their words, gestures or actions (of a sexual nature) are making you uncomfortable or afraid, then you're

being sexually harassed. You do not have to get others, either your friends, teachers or school officials, to agree with you.

- **No one has the right to sexually harass another person!** School officials are legally responsible to guarantee that all students, you included, can learn in a safe environment which is free from sexual harassment and sex discrimination. If you are being sexually harassed, your student rights are being violated. Find an adult you trust and tell them what's happening, so that something can be done to stop the harassment.

- **Examples of sexual harassment in school:**
  - touching, pinching, and grabbing body parts
  - being cornered
  - sending sexual notes or pictures
  - writing sexual graffiti on desks, bathroom walls or buildings
  - making suggestive or sexual gestures, looks, jokes, or verbal comments (including "mooing," "barking" and other noises)
  - spreading sexual rumors or making sexual propositions
  - pulling off someone's clothes
  - pulling off your own clothes
  - being forced to kiss someone or do something sexual
  - attempted rape and rape

REMEMBER: SEXUAL HARASSMENT IS SERIOUS AND AGAINST THE LAW!

FIGURE 15-1 **It's no joke.** Example of how teachers and school counselors might describe sexual harassment in language that children and adolescents understand. *Excerpt from "Stop Sexual Harassment in Schools" by Nan Stein, from USA TODAY, May 18, 1993. Copyright © 1993 by Nan Stein, Ed.D. Used with permission of the author.*

Russell, 2010, p. 1183). Students who are transgendered, homosexual, or different in some other ways from peers adjust more easily when teachers create a welcome environment for all youth, accept young people for who they are, and intervene when they hear a young person being teased or harassed.

• **Keep information about human sexuality on hand.** A conventional belief has held that education about human sexuality is the prerogative of parents and has no place in schools. Typically, if sex education is a part of the school curriculum at all, it focuses on the biological aspects of sexual intercourse and offers little information to help teens make sense of their conflicting feelings about physical intimacy. Adolescents' participation in a sex education curriculum usually requires parents' approval, and many parents are loath to give it. Less controversial alternatives include making developmentally appropriate literature about relevant issues accessible in school libraries and letting adolescents know that school counselors and nurses are always willing to talk with them about matters of health and intimacy. Adults need to be prepared to answer a range of questions, including how young people can protect themselves during intimate contact, rebound from a hurtful relationship, and tell parents about being gay.

• **Make appropriate referrals or contact authorities when necessary.** Teachers occasionally learn unexpectedly about youngsters' personal lives. Students may tell teachers they are pregnant, have a pregnant girlfriend, have been raped or sexually abused, or suspect they've contracted a sexually transmitted infection. Educators need to be prepared to fulfill any legal obligation they have to contact law enforcement or community agencies about a possible crime. Some situations, such as questions about a sexually transmitted infection, do not require contact with parents or authorities, depending on regional requirements, and instead merit giving referrals for the young person. Although students may feel embarrassed or ashamed about their health circumstances, it usually also makes sense to advise them to talk with family members.

As you have learned, adults can do many things to foster productive peer relationships. In the Developmental Trends table "Peer Relationships at Different Age Levels," you can review typical features and variations in affiliations among children of different ages and consider their implication.

DEVELOPMENTAL TRENDS
Peer Relationships at Different Age Levels

AGE	WHAT YOU MIGHT OBSERVE	DIVERSITY	IMPLICATIONS
Infancy (Birth–2 Years)	• Growing interest in other infants in the same child care setting • Beginning attempts to make contact with familiar infants, such as looking at their faces and smiling at them • Occasional laughing, chasing, and passing of toys back and forth • In second year, side-by-side play and awareness of one another's actions	• Some infants have not had social experiences with siblings or other children; they may need time to adjust to the presence of other children in a child care center. • Security of attachment to caregivers may affect children's interaction with peers. • Infants who are temperamentally shy, fearful, or inhibited may be wary of other children.	• Place small babies side by side when they are calm and alert. • Talk about what other children are doing (e.g., "Look at Willonda shaking that toy; let's go watch how she makes the beads spin"). • Supervise small children to prevent them from hurting one another. When they accidentally bother others, redirect them (e.g., "Come this way, Tammy. Chloe doesn't like it when you bump into her").
Early Childhood (2–6 Years)	• Increasing frequency and complexity of interactions with familiar peers • Developing preference for play activities with particular peers • Formation of rudimentary friendships based on proximity and easy access (e.g., formation of friendships with neighbors and preschool classmates) • Involved conversations and imaginative fantasies with friends	• Children who have had pleasant experiences with peers find it easier to make friends in a new setting. • Children who have sociable and easygoing temperaments tend to form and keep friends more easily than those who are shy, aggressive, anxious, or high-strung.	• Help shy children gain entry into groups, especially if they have had limited social experience. • When necessary, help children resolve conflicts with friends, but encourage them to identify solutions that benefit everyone, and let them do as much of the negotiation as possible.

DEVELOPMENTAL TRENDS (continued)

AGE	WHAT YOU MIGHT OBSERVE	DIVERSITY	IMPLICATIONS
Middle Childhood (6–10 Years)	• Concern about being accepted by peers • Tendency to assemble in larger groups than in early childhood • Less need for adult supervision than previously • Outdoor peer groups structured with games and sports • Increase in gossip as children show concern over friends and enemies • Some social exclusiveness, with friends being reluctant to allow outsiders to join in their activities • Predominance of same-gender friendships	• Boys tend to play in larger groups than girls do. • Some children are temperamentally cautious and timid; they may stand at the periphery of a group. • Some children are actively rejected by peers, perhaps because they are perceived as odd, immature, or socially unskilled.	• Supervise children's peer relationships from a distance; intervene when a situation escalates. • Tactfully facilitate the entry of isolated children into ongoing games, cooperative learning groups, and informal lunch gatherings. • Teach rejected children how to interact appropriately with peers.
Early Adolescence (10–14 Years)	• Variety of contexts (e.g., competitive sports, extracurricular activities, parties) in which interactions with peers take place • Heightened concern about acceptance and popularity among peers • Fads and conformity in dress and communication styles in groups • Same-gender cliques, often restricted to members of a single ethnic group • Increasing intimacy, self-disclosure, and loyalty among friends • New interest in members of opposite gender; for gay and lesbian youths, in same gender • For some, initiation of dating, often within the context of larger group activities	• Some young adolescents are very socially minded; others are more quiet and reserved. • Gossiping and social exclusion may continue in some groups. • A few young adolescents become involved in gangs or other delinquent social groups. • A small number of young adolescents are sexually active. • A minority of adolescents begin to construct an identity as gay, lesbian, bisexual (attracted to both genders), or transgendered.	• Make classrooms, schools, and other settings affirming places for all adolescents. Create an atmosphere of respect for students with all sorts of backgrounds. • Do not tolerate name calling, insensitive remarks, or sexual harassment. • Provide appropriate places for adolescents to hang out before and after school. • Identify mechanisms (e.g., cooperative learning groups, public service projects) through which teenagers can work toward productive goals. • On some occasions, decide which students will fraternize; on others, let them choose their work partners. • Sponsor after-school activities (e.g., in sports, music, or interest areas).
Late Adolescence (14–18 Years)	• Emerging understanding that relationships with numerous peers do not necessarily threaten close friendships • Increasing dependence on friends for advice and emotional support, with adults remaining important in such matters as educational choices and career goals • Less cliquishness toward the end of high school; greater tendency to affiliate in large and less exclusive crowds • Increasing amount of time in mixed-gender groups • Many social activities unsupervised by adults • Emergence of long-standing romantic couples, especially in final 2 years of high school	• Some teenagers have parents who continue to monitor their whereabouts; others have little adult supervision. • Adolescents' choices of friends affect their leisure activities, risk-taking behaviors, and attitudes toward schoolwork. • Teens who find themselves attracted to same-gender peers face unique challenges in constructing adult identities, especially if others are not accepting of their sexual orientation.	• In literature and history, assign readings with themes of psychological interest to adolescents (e.g., loyalty among friends and self-disclosure of vulnerability). • Encourage adolescents to join extracurricular activities that make them feel an integral part of their school. • Sponsor dances and other supervised social events that give adolescents opportunities to socialize.

Summary

Peers serve important functions in social-emotional development. Not only do they offer companionship, but they also create contexts for practicing social skills, making sense of social experiences, and acquiring certain values. Peer relationships change systematically throughout childhood; activities tend to shift from simple gestures and imitation (infancy), to pretend play (early childhood), to structured group games (middle childhood), to social activities within cliques and crowds (early adolescence), and finally to larger, mixed-gender groups (late adolescence). Friendships are especially important peer relationships that provide emotional support and venues to resolve conflicts in mutually satisfying ways.

Although preschoolers and elementary school children have an interest in romantic relationships, young people do not understand the multifaceted nature of intimacy until they reach adolescence. As they go through puberty, they must come to terms with their changing bodies, sexual drives, and sexual attraction to peers. Romances, either actual or imagined, can delight youngsters but also put emotions in turmoil. Some adolescents experiment with sexual intimacy with only limited information about potential risks. Others wrestle with sexual feelings for same-gender peers. As adolescents experience a range of new feelings, they are apt to appreciate adults' sensitivity.

ENHANCEDetext *self-check*

SCHOOLS

Schools are entrusted with the education of children of course, but also with their welfare. Three characteristics of schools make them enriching environments for children: having a strong sense of community; issuing clear, age-appropriate, and affirming socialization messages, and sensitivity to developmental transitions.

The School as a Community

Educators foster a **sense of community** in schools when students, teachers, and other staff share goals, validate one another's efforts, and believe that everyone makes an important contribution (Garcia-Reid, Peterson, Reid, & Peterson, 2013; D. Kim, Solomon, & Roberts, 1995; Sayer, Beaven, Stringer, & Hermena, 2013). When schools cultivate a sense of community, students are more likely to exhibit prosocial behavior, positive attitudes about school, intrinsic motivation to learn, and high achievement. A sense of community is associated with lower rates of disruptive classroom behavior, emotional distress, truancy, violence, drug use, and dropping out of school (D. Kim et al., 1995; O'Brennan & Furlong, 2010; Sayer et al., 2013).

A sense of community is the outgrowth of hard work by teachers, other school staff, families, and students. Teachers set the tone by addressing three factors: (a) the climate of the classroom, (b) instructional methods, and (c) school traditions.

Classroom Climate

Teachers foster a productive climate when they establish a warm, affectionate atmosphere in the classroom, show that they care for children individually, and express their interest in children's learning. Students are apt to thrive when their classrooms exhibit the following features:

Observing Children 15-4

This poster in a middle school corridor illustrates one important element of classroom climate: being safe.

ENHANCEDetext *video example*

- Teachers let students know that they care about them.
- Students feel safe; for instance, they know that they can make mistakes without being ridiculed by their teacher or classmates and that they can seek help from others when they need it. Nor will they be physically hurt by classmates. You can examine a poster that communicates that school is intended to be a safe place in an Observing Children video.
- Teachers adopt an *authoritative* approach to instruction and classroom management, setting clear guidelines for behavior but, in the process, also considering students' needs and involving them in decision making.

- Teachers provide sufficient order and structure to guide classroom assignments while also giving students opportunities to engage in appropriate self-chosen and self-directed activities.
- Teachers encourage children to pursue common goals, giving them the sense that they are a bonded group.
- Teachers implement fun routines, perhaps arranging for enjoyable games during recess or classroom activities.

Preparing for Your Licensure Examination
Your teaching test might ask about strategies for establishing a productive classroom environment.

Classrooms that reflect these principles are, in general, productive ones: Students are motivated to learn new skills, perceive themselves as being reasonably capable, achieve at high academic levels, and act in a socially competent manner (G. A. Davis & Thomas, 1989; Scott-Little & Holloway, 1992; H. K. Wilson, Pianta, & Stuhlman, 2007).

When other aspects of children's lives are troubled—for instance, when children have strained family relationships, live in dangerous neighborhoods, or are confronted with a natural disaster—perceived support from teachers is important in helping youngsters feel safe, competent, and understood (Loukas, Roalson, & Herrera, 2010; E. P. Smith, Boutte, Zigler, & Finn-Stevenson, 2004). Positive relationships with teachers are also associated with high levels of achievement in students (Maulana, Opdenakker, & Bosker, 2014).

Instructional Methods

Teachers can foster a sense of community by using instructional methods that are active, engaging, and cooperative. In one instructional model, children form a **community of learners**, a classroom arrangement in which students help one another achieve common learning goals. A community of learners has characteristics such as these:

- All students are active participants in classroom activities.
- Collaboration among two or more students is a common occurrence and plays a key role in learning.
- Diversity in students' interests and progress is expected and respected.
- Students and teacher coordinate their efforts at helping one another learn; no one has exclusive responsibility for teaching others.
- Everyone is a potential resource for the others; different individuals are likely to serve as resident experts on different occasions, depending on the topics and tasks at hand.
- The teacher provides guidance for classroom activities, but students may also contribute to the course of activities.
- Students regularly critique one another's work, giving feedback in such a way that recipients feel affirmed and encouraged to improve their performance.
- The process of learning is emphasized as much as, and sometimes more than, the finished product. (A. L. Brown & Campione, 1994; Campione, Shapiro, & Brown, 1995; Rogoff, 1994; Sewell, 2011)

Preparing for Your Licensure Examination
Your teaching test might ask about instructional methods that facilitate children's engagement with learning.

The outcomes of community-of-learner groups are often quite positive, especially when teachers encourage children to abide by age-appropriate rules for interaction. Communities of learners tend to promote fairly complex thinking processes and are highly motivating for students (A. L. Brown & Campione, 1994; Sewell, St George, & Cullen, 2013; Turkanis, 2001). For instance, students in these groups occasionally insist on going to school even when they are ill, and they become disappointed when the school year ends (Rogoff, 1994).

School Traditions

Teachers can foster a sense of community by encouraging children to participate actively in school activities and day-to-day operations. Schools that operate as true communities encourage everyone to work together as considerate and productive citizens (Battistich et al., 1995; Battistich, Solomon, Watson, & Schaps, 1997; Cemalcilar, 2010; Rothstein-Fisch & Trumbull, 2008). Several strategies are helpful in creating this positive school spirit:

- Soliciting students' ideas about school activities, such as how Valentine's Day might be observed
- Creating mechanisms through which students can help make the school run smoothly and efficiently (e.g., assigning various helper roles to students on a rotating basis)

- Emphasizing prosocial values in school codes of conduct, in newsletters, and on bulletin boards
- Providing public recognition of students' contributions to the overall success of the classroom and school
- Creating schoolwide traditions that are fun for youngsters and their families, such as carnivals and field days (D. Kim et al., 1995; Lickona, 1991; Osterman, 2000)

Ideally, the various instructional practices and traditions of an educational environment combine to help fulfill children's many needs. Early childhood educator **Robert Pianta** and his colleagues have found that children at the elementary level often have good relationships at school, but do not receive the instructional support they need to make adequate academic progress (Downer, Booren, Lima, Luckner, & Pianta, 2010; Hamre, Hatfield, Pianta, & Jamil, 2014; Jerome, Hamre, & Pianta, 2009). Although children are resilient to a certain number of less-than-optimal conditions in their lives, educators can optimize children's development by providing for their full range of needs, including children's desires for warm relationships, effective instruction, and an affectionate school environment.

Socialization in Schools

Teachers extend the work that parents have begun in asking children to follow certain behaviors (e.g., showing politeness by saying "please" and "thank you") and avoid others (e.g., hitting other children). Teachers and other practitioners also transmit information about values specific to the school environment and their expectations about children's abilities to achieve in school.

School Values

Teachers begin to socialize children the moment that children enter school. Teachers typically expect and encourage behaviors such as these:

- Showing respect for authority figures
- Controlling impulses
- Following instructions
- Completing assigned tasks in a timely manner
- Working independently
- Cooperating with classmates
- Striving for academic excellence

Children seem to cope most effectively in a new classroom when teachers openly communicate such expectations. However, much of the time teachers do not remember to articulate their standards. Teachers' unstated expectations for behavior are sometimes known as the *hidden curriculum* (Anyon, 1988; Rahman, 2013).

A teacher's hidden curriculum may or may not be consistent with sound developmental principles. A teacher may emphasize the importance of always getting the right answer, doing tasks in only one way, or, as the following dialogue between a teacher and several students illustrates, getting things done as quickly as possible:

Teacher:	I will put some problems on the board. You are to divide.
Child:	We got to divide?
Teacher:	Yes.
Several children:	[*Groan*] Not again, Mr. B., we done this yesterday.
Child:	Do we put the date?
Teacher:	Yes. I hope we remember we work in silence. You're supposed to do it on white paper. I'll explain it later.
Child:	Somebody broke my pencil. [*Crash*—a child falls out of his chair.]
Child:	[*repeats*] Mr. B., somebody broke my *pencil!*
Child:	Are we going to be here all morning? (Anyon, 1988, p. 367)

In this situation the teacher presents math problems merely as things that need to be done—not as tasks that might actually have some benefit—and the children clearly have little interest in the assignment.

Children may or may not find it easy to live up to teachers' expectations, but they are more likely to be successful in the classroom if they are at least *aware* of the standards. Teachers can do three things:

• **Tell children about desirable behavior.** Children come to school with their own styles of acting and do not easily decipher teachers' expectations for how students are supposed to communicate in groups, ask for help, express their confusion, and so forth. In general, children find it easier to act in acceptable ways when teachers explain their expectations, post important rules for behavior on a bulletin board, or disseminate rules in simple handouts (Gettinger & Kohler, 2006).

• **Ask children about their perceptions of classroom rules.** Children actively interpret classroom events and, when asked, can offer informative points of view about classroom operations. In one study in Sweden, children viewed teachers as being hypocritical by asking children not to chew gum but then surreptitiously chewing gum themselves (Thornberg, 2008). In one conversation with a researcher, three 11-year-old boys complained about having to go outside during breaks, saying that they did not get headaches when they stayed inside even though this was the reason for outside activities given by teachers. A more thorough discussion between the teachers and children might have led to a mutually respectful understanding and perhaps even a plan that everyone found reasonable.

• **Offer extra help to students who find it difficult to decipher expectations at school.** Some youngsters, perhaps due to a cognitive or social-emotional disability, find it particularly challenging to determine which behaviors are appropriate and which are unacceptable in various situations. A particular child with Asperger syndrome, a type of autism spectrum disorder, might need to be told that although squealing on the playground is considered fun, shouting inside the classroom will annoy others (Myles & Simpson, 2001). Strategies that appear effective in making the hidden curriculum transparent for children with disabilities include role playing, asking children to speculate about proper courses of action in various situations, and conducting "social autopsies"—conversations with the child about social mistakes and better courses of action for the future (Myles & Simpson, 2001).

Teachers' Expectations About the Abilities of Students

As we have seen, teachers have expectations for how students should behave in the classroom. But teachers also form expectations about how individual students are *likely* to perform. In many instances teachers size up their students fairly accurately: They know which ones need help with reading skills, which other ones have trouble working together in a cooperative group, and so on, and they adapt their instruction accordingly (Alber-Morgan, 2010; Goldenberg, 1992).

But teachers occasionally make inaccurate assessments. They are apt to underestimate the abilities of students who

- Are overweight or physically unattractive
- Misbehave frequently in class
- Speak in dialects other than Standard English
- Are members of ethnic minority groups
- Are recent immigrants
- Come from low-income backgrounds
- Have a disability

  (R. E. Bennett, Gottesman, Rock, & Cerullo, 1993; Licona, 2013; J. Oakes & Guiton, 1995; J. Peterson, Puhl, & Luedicke, 2012; Ritts, Patterson, & Tubbs, 1992; Speybroeck et al., 2012)

Teachers with low expectations for students are apt to offer these individuals few opportunities for speaking in class, and they generally ask them easy questions, give little feedback about their responses, and present them with few, if any, challenging assignments (Rosenthal, 1994; Straehler-Pohl, Fernández, Gellert, & Figueiras, 2014). In contrast, teachers with high expectations for students generally create a warmer classroom climate, interact with students frequently, provide more opportunities for students to respond, and give positive feedback (Rubie-Davies, 2007).

Most children are well aware of their teachers' differential treatment of individual students within the classroom and use these observations to draw inferences about their own and classmates' abilities (R. Butler, 1994; Good & Nichols, 2001; Weinstein, 1993). Children also make inferences about their own abilities from the kind of remarks teachers make to them. Children who routinely receive low-ability messages from teachers begin to see themselves as their teachers see them. Furthermore, students may exert little effort on academic tasks, or they may frequently misbehave in class (Murdock, 1999; Rattan, Good, & Dweck, 2012). In some cases, teachers' expectations lead to a **self-fulfilling prophecy**: What teachers expect students to achieve becomes what students actually do achieve.

Communicating High Expectations

A characteristic consistently found in effective schools is high expectations for student performance (M. Phillips, 1997; Roderick & Camburn, 1999). Even if students' initial academic performance is low, educators and other professionals must remember that cognitive abilities can and do change over time, especially when the environment is conducive to growth. We suggest two strategies to help teachers maintain a realistic yet optimistic outlook on what young people can accomplish:

• **Learn more about students' backgrounds.** Adults are most likely to develop low expectations for students' performance when they have rigid biases about certain ethnic or socioeconomic groups (J. Leonard & Martin, 2013; Reyna, 2000). Such biases are often the result of ignorance about students' home environments (K. Alexander, Entwisle, & Thompson, 1987; J. Leonard & Martin, 2013). Education is the key here: Teachers and other school personnel can learn about students' backgrounds and local communities. With a clear picture of students' families, activities, and values, educators are far more likely to think of students as *individuals*—each with a unique set of talents and skills—rather than as members of a stereotyped group.

• **Collaborate with colleagues to maximize children's success.** Educators are more likely to have high expectations for students when they are confident in their own ability to help students achieve academic and social success (Ashton, 1985; L. Wilson, 2007). Consider the case of one inner-city high school. For many years, teachers at the school believed that their low-achieving students were unmotivated to learn. Teachers also saw themselves, their colleagues, and school administrators as ineffective in helping these students succeed. To counteract such tendencies, the school faculty began holding regular 2-hour meetings in which they

- Read research related to low-achieving and at-risk students
- Explored hypotheses about why their students were having difficulty
- Developed, refined, and evaluated innovative strategies for helping students succeed
- Established a collaborative atmosphere in which, working together, they could take positive action

Such meetings helped the teachers form higher expectations for their students' achievement and gain a better understanding of what they themselves could do to help the students achieve (Weinstein, Madison, & Kuklinski, 1995).

Transitions to New Schools

Entering any new school requires youngsters to adjust to unfamiliar peers and teachers, new academic expectations, and novel activities in a new building. The experiences in adjusting to particular environments present distinct challenges to youngsters depending on their age and the fit between their developmental abilities and arrangements in the school related to social relationships, self-control, personal decision making, and academic achievement (Krampen, 2013).

Elementary Schools

In most Western societies, children typically begin elementary school at the age of 5 or 6, when society declares them "ready" for serious learning. Children generally find it easier to adjust to school when they enter with certain academic skills. Those who have been encouraged to listen to stories and use complex language at home usually adapt without difficulty to a school's literacy curriculum. Likewise, children who have had many constructive experiences with peers easily adjust to the social environment. In part because of having had scaffolded experiences with peers, children who have been in preschool tend to make better social adjustments and achieve at higher levels in first grade compared to children from similar backgrounds who have not enrolled in preschool (Chen, Claessens, & Msall, 2014; Consortium of Longitudinal Studies, 1983; Temple, Reynolds, & Arteaga, 2010).

In the process of adapting to a school's academic challenges, children get used to its regulatory atmosphere. Elementary classrooms tend to be more regimented than the cozy settings of family, child care, and preschool. As a result, when children first enter elementary school, one of their challenges is learning the procedures of the "big kids" school (Corsaro & Molinari, 2005). Here's how first grader Sofia described school rules to her mother and an interviewer:

Mother:	Do you know the rules? What are the rules in first grade?
Sofia:	You cannot run in the corridors, you cannot hurt anyone, you have to raise your hand before talking, you cannot lose toys.
Interviewer:	You know all the rules!
Sofia:	Then you cannot walk around, you cannot shout in the bathroom.
Interviewer:	You know everything.
Mother:	And then? Perhaps you must wait your turn.
Sofia:	And then, you have to be silent, write the date. That's all. (Corsaro & Molinari, 2005, pp. 74–75)

Of course, there is more to school than restrictions. To help children adjust to new classrooms, teachers generally offer lots of structure and reassurance during those initial weeks and months when children feel uneasy. Many schools offer orientations and encourage children and families to visit the classrooms before school begins. We authors recall that our children had elementary teachers who invited them to visit school in the spring or summer when student placements were announced and sent the children friendly letters before the school year began.

The relationships that children develop with their teacher are an important factor in children's adjustment to school. Teachers can help children by reaching out to them individually, getting to know their names, noticing what they do well, and generally encouraging them. In the elementary grades, each child is one of 15 to 30 students whom a teacher usually gets to know fairly well. Also easing children's adjustment is the teacher's attention to individual needs. Especially important are efforts to help children who begin the year lacking age-typical intellectual or social skills. Children with delays most certainly *are* ready to learn but may require individualized services.

Secondary Schools

Young people make two major transitions at the secondary level. First, beginning at grade 5, 6, or 7, many students move from elementary to either middle school or junior high school. Second, at grade 9 or 10, students move from middle or junior high school to high school. As they progress through these upper grade levels, students attend separate classes, each with its own teacher. The three secondary configurations—middle, junior high, and high school—have distinctive features but share qualities that distinguish them from elementary schools. A typical secondary school is unlike an elementary school in these ways:

- The school is larger and has more students.
- Teacher–student relationships are more superficial and less personal than they were in elementary school.
- There is more whole-class instruction, with less individualized instruction that takes into account each student's particular needs.
- Classes are less socially cohesive; students may not know their classmates well and be reluctant to call on them for assistance.
- Competition among students (e.g., for popular classes or spots on an athletic team) is more common, especially in high school.

- Students have more independence and responsibility for their own learning; for instance, they sometimes have relatively unstructured assignments to be accomplished over a 2- or 3-week period and must take the initiative to seek help if they are struggling.
- Standards for assigning grades are more rigorous, so students may earn lower grades than they did in elementary school. Grades are often assigned on a comparative basis, with only the highest-achieving students getting As and Bs. (Brewin & Statham, 2011; A. J. Davidson, Gest, & Welsh, 2010; Eccles & Midgley, 1989; Raccanello, Brondino, & Bernardi, 2013; Roderick & Camburn, 1999; Véronneau & Dishion, 2011; Wigfield, Eccles, & Pintrich, 1996)

Many educators lament the mismatch between the secondary environment and the needs of adolescents. At a time when adolescents are self-conscious, uncertain, driven to make their own decisions, and confronted with tumultuous changes in their bodies and social relationships, their contact with teachers is superficial and sometimes adversarial. To combat potential feelings of anonymity and disengagement, some high schools arrange for every teacher to take responsibility for a small group of students whom he or she gets to know individually. Advisors can orient students to the layout and customs of the school and talk regularly with them about how they are doing in classes, what study skills they are using, their progress with graduation requirements, and how they are relating to peers (Patel, 2014; Uvaas, 2010).

Fortunately, many schools are finding ways to welcome entering students and personalize learning environments as students settle into classes. The Development and Practice feature "Easing School Transitions" illustrates several strategies for helping youngsters adjust to new schools.

DEVELOPMENT AND PRACTICE

Easing School Transitions

Make contact with children before the beginning of school.

- In April a kindergarten teacher invites prospective students and their parents to come to an orientation in her classroom. The teacher arranges for snacks to be served and reserves time for a brief presentation and independent exploration of the room. (Early Childhood)
- Late in the summer, a high school teacher sends students in his homeroom a letter introducing himself and welcoming them to his room. He talks about the fun things he has done over the summer, including traveling, camping, reading, and volunteering in a community garden. He mentions his academic interests and tells students he looks forward to hearing about their summer. (Late Adolescence)

Provide a means through which every student can feel a part of a small, close-knit group.

- A physical education teacher arranges for students to work on motor skills in small groups. Students stay in the groups for several weeks and learn how to coach one another. During each lesson, students compliment one another on a particular aspect of the skill (e.g., dribbling or throwing a ball) that they are doing well and offer a suggestion on one feature that could be improved. (Middle Childhood)
- In September a middle school math teacher establishes *base groups* of three or four students, who provide assistance to one another throughout the school year. At the beginning or end of every class period, the teacher gives students in the base groups 5 minutes to help one another with homework assignments. (Early Adolescence)

Find time to meet one on one with every student.

- An elementary teacher holds individual conferences with children twice a year. The teacher looks through representative works that the children have created but also makes a point to ask the children how they feel about school and relationships with peers. (Middle Childhood)
- Early in the school year, a middle school social studies teacher holds individual meetings with each of his students. In these meetings he searches for common interests that he and his students share and encourages students to talk with him whenever they need help with academic or personal problems. Throughout the semester he continues to touch base with students individually (often during lunch or before or after school) to see how they are doing. (Early Adolescence)

Give young people the extra support they may need to master subject matter and study skills.

- An after-school program offers a comprehensive array of services to middle school students. Students receive tutoring in core subjects as well as opportunities to participate in leisure activities. Professionals in the community routinely visit the group and serve as mentors, and students discuss goals for the future and strategies for resisting negative temptations (T. E. Hanlon, Simon, O'Grady, Carswell, & Callaman, 2009). (Early Adolescence)
- A high school implements a homework hotline staffed by a teacher and a group of honor students. Teachers in the school make a point of encouraging students periodically to evaluate how well they are keeping up with their work and to ask for help when necessary (McCarthy & Kuh, 2005). (Late Adolescence)

Summary

Schools are influential contexts for children and adolescents. Schools not only prepare youngsters with essential academic skills but also serve as complex social environments that communicate to youngsters how welcome they are and how likely they are to succeed. Ideally, schools offer children a sense of community, deliver affirming messages about learning in general and individual abilities in particular, and support children as they transition into new academic environments.

ENHANCEDetext *self-check*

Assessing Children 15-1

Observe students being mentored in giving one another compliments about their presentations.

ENHANCEDetext *application exercise*

SOCIETY

As you have learned, youngsters acquire many skills, beliefs, and attitudes during ongoing interactions in the family, at school, and with peers. Children also learn from others in **society**—an enduring group of people who are socially and economically organized into collective institutions. We now examine the effects on children of society's services, the media, and interactive technologies.

Services for Children and Adolescents

The time that children spend outside of school is critical to their development. Child care and after-school activities are especially important outlets for children's time.

Child Care

Many young children are in the care of adults other than their parents for a significant portion of the week. Children are attended to in a range of settings, from family homes to commercial buildings, and by caregivers who differ in experience, education, and level of dedication. Such variations raise concerns about the degree to which all children are cared for in a manner that is affectionate, safe, and age-appropriate (Brauner, Gordic, & Zigler, 2004; H. F. Ladd et al., 2014).

Advocates for high standards in child care have two primary ways of defining quality. *Structural measures* include such objective indicators as caregivers' training and experience, child-to-caregiver ratios, staff turnover, and number and complexity of toys and equipment (Ghazvini & Mullis, 2002; Jeon, Buettner, & Hur, 2014). Early childhood specialists recommend that the child-to-caregiver ratio be no more than three infants or six toddlers for each adult (Bredekamp & Copple, 1997). *Process measures* of quality include sensitive care of children, affectionate child–caregiver relationships, productive child–peer interactions, and developmentally appropriate activities (Jeon et al., 2014; NICHD Early Child Care Research Network, 2006a). As an indication of high-quality processes, the schedules of activities in a toddler room might be fairly predictable from day to day but also flexible enough to be guided by children's individual and changing needs (Bredekamp & Copple, 1997). Thus, toddlers might be offered two snacks over the span of the morning, even though only a few choose to eat twice.

In reality, indicators of structure and process are related. For instance, low child-to-staff ratios, small group sizes, and advanced levels of caregiver education tend to be associated with responsive interactions with children (Bigras et al., 2010; Howes, Smith, & Galinsky,

1995). When caregivers have too many children to care for, their style of interacting with individuals tends to become rushed and mechanical.

In general, research confirms that high-quality child care yields advantages in children. Infants and small children typically develop secure attachments to employed caregivers who are warm, sensitive, and consistently involved in their care (Altenhofen, Clyman, Little, Baker, & Biringen, 2013; Barnas & Cummings, 1994). Children advance developmentally in cognitive, linguistic, literacy, and social skills while in good care, with the greatest benefits occurring in children whose caregivers have been inattentive, suggesting that the early environment has served as a valuable intervention (Jeon et al., 2014; Sylva, Melhuish, Sammons, Siraj-Blatchford, & Taggart, 2004).

In certain circumstances, child care creates risks if not actual harm. Exposure to child care at a young age and for long hours on average increases children's aggression and noncompliance slightly (Belsky & Eggebeen, 1991; M. E. Lamb & Ahnert, 2006; NICHD Early Child Care Research Network, 2002). These effects are not always seen and, when they are, are smaller for high-quality than for low-quality care (Rusby, Jones, Crowley, & Smolkowski, 2013). Enrollment in low-quality care, in which adults are brusque, nonresponsive, or overly critical, and in which the environment is developmentally inappropriate or dangerous, fail to foster the child's potential and instead causes distress, injuries, and physical harm.

After-School Programs and Extracurricular Activities

Depending on children's age and interests, family income, parents' work schedules, school programs, community resources, and other factors, children may have safe, educational, and challenging outlets or dangerous and destructive options for before and after school. Recreation, sports, and leisure—especially with peers—are a strong draw for young people but not always available.

Not every parent has access to affordable care, and as youngsters grow, they naturally want to care for themselves (Ceglowski, Shears, & Furman, 2010). Frequent *self-care* is a concern during the preschool and elementary years because children do not always anticipate or avoid hazardous situations. They may open the door when a stranger rings the doorbell and forget that they have left on the stove. They may become worried and lonely and, without supervision, fail to do homework or complete chores (Venter & Rambau, 2011). Beginning in the early adolescent years, lack of supervision in the after-school hours is associated with risky behaviors (Greenberg, 2014).

Observing Children 15-5

Listen to 12-year-old Colin describe what he does outside school.

ENHANCEDetext *video example*

Self-care arrangements are generally more effective when parents explain safety procedures, convey clear and firm expectations for behavior, and monitor children's activities by calling them on the telephone or by having another family member, such as a grandparent, check on them (Mahoney & Parente, 2009; Steinberg, 1986). Communities can help by providing safe, fun, and supervised activities. Young people who have productive outlets for their free time—perhaps in clubs, sports leagues, dance and martial arts lessons, scout troops, and so on—are apt to acquire valuable skills and avoid serious trouble. Twelve-year-old Colin gives a sense of his rich learning experiences in an Observing Children video:

Interviewer:	So you play basketball?
Colin:	Yeah. Yeah.
Interviewer:	What other . . . is that your favorite sport?
Colin:	I like basketball and track about the same.
Interviewer:	Do you play any other sports?
Colin:	Yeah. I play, basically, I play football, baseball, hockey. . . .
Interviewer:	Wow. What do you like about sports?
Colin:	Well, they're fun and just something to do.
Interviewer:	What kinds of hobbies do you have?
Colin:	I like coin collecting and . . . I garden and I try to take sign language and really do sign language. Yeah.
Interviewer:	So what kinds of clubs do you belong to?
Colin:	I belong to . . . well, I used to belong to 4-H. And I'm in the chess club, Boy Scouts, and sign language club.

The effects of after-school and extracurricular programs are difficult to investigate because comparison groups are not always available and the most influential features of specific programs are difficult to identify. Does an elementary school boy like his after-school program because of the kindness of the teacher, its access to digital technologies, the afternoon snacks, help with homework, or some other feature? (Maynard, Peters, Vaughn, & Sarteschi, 2013). It is not always possible to tell.

Despite lack of certainty about causal effects, a growing body of research suggests that participation in well-designed after-school and summer activities fosters children's cognitive and social-emotional development. Academically oriented programs appear to cultivate positive feelings about school, better school attendance, higher grades and achievement, superior classroom behavior, greater conflict resolution skills, and decreased tension with family members (Dryfoos, 1999; Granger, 2008; Téllez & Waxman, 2010). After-school programs focusing on mental health needs (e.g., on developing close relationships with adults, social skills with peers, sustained attention, and personal decision making) have been shown to enhance the academic, social, and personal adjustment of young people living in economic poverty (S. L. Frazier, Mehta, Atkins, Hur, & Rusch, 2013). High school students who participate in their school's extracurricular activities are more likely than nonparticipants to achieve at high levels and graduate from high school. They are also less likely to smoke cigarettes, use alcohol or drugs, exhibit anxiety, join gangs, engage in criminal activities, or become teenage parents (Biddle, 1993; H. Cooper, Valentine, Nye, & Lindsay, 1999; Dimech & Seiler, 2010; L. L. Myers, 2013).

After-school and summer programs vary in their focus and services, yet most espouse a commitment to strong relationships with each young person. In addition, effective programs include these features:

- Breadth of activities, including recreation, academic and cultural enrichment, and opportunities for pursuit of individual interests
- Chances for meaningful participation in authentic activities, such as building a fort, reading to younger children, or registering voters
- Opportunities for success, perhaps in domains in which youngsters have previously unrecognized talents
- Access to areas of enrichment, such as advanced technologies, that help build valuable skills
- Positive interactions and relationships with both adults and peers
- Clear limits, with youngsters actively participating in establishment of rules
- High regard and respect for young people's diverse cultural beliefs and practices
- Options for physical activity (C. R. Cooper, Denner, & Lopez, 1999; Durlak, Mahoney, Bohnert, & Parente, 2010; Gesell et al., 2013; Kerewsky & Lefstein, 1982; Lefstein & Lipsitz, 1995; Noam, & Bernstein-Yamashiro, 2013; Vickery, 2014).

Many adolescents spend some of their free time in part-time jobs. Work experience allows for practice in getting to work on time, adhering to the requirements of a position, being courteous in a business setting, and managing money. With limited work hours (e.g., 10 to 15 hours per week), adolescents usually have adequate time to study and remain involved in school activities (Mortimer, Shanahan, & Ryu, 1994; Staff, Messersmith, & Schulenberg, 2009; Steinberg, Brown, Cider, Kaczmarek, & Lazzaro, 1988). However, many adolescents work long hours in tedious jobs that fail to inculcate them with a motivation to work hard. Excessively long work hours put young people at risk for poor school achievement, limited participation in extracurricular activities, and drug and alcohol use (Staff et al., 2009).

As with after-school activities, we cannot be definite about the specific effects of extracurricular programs because youngsters who choose to participate in these services may be different from classmates who decide not to take advantage of them. Nonetheless, with the potential—and, we suggest, likely—benefits of extracurricular activities and after-school programs, these services merit investment. The Development and Practice feature "Enhancing Students' Before- and After-School Experiences" suggests strategies for educators and other practitioners to help young people make good use of their non-school time.

DEVELOPMENT AND PRACTICE
Enhancing Students' Before- and After-School Experiences

Help children navigate transitions between school and out-of-school care.

- After school a kindergarten teacher walks outside to make sure that each child connects with family members or car pool drivers, gets on the appropriate bus or van, or begins walking home. (Early Childhood)
- A teacher in an after-school elementary program asks arriving children to unpack their homework and put it in a special folder. After children have eaten, rested, and gotten a chance to play for a half hour or so, the teacher pulls out assignments and helps the children get started with their homework. (Middle Childhood)

Sponsor after-school clubs at your school.

- A middle school offers several clubs for students to participate in after school. Popular options include a Hispanic cultures club, several athletic teams, an honor society, a band, a community service group, and the yearbook staff. (Early Adolescence)
- Most of the teachers in a high school serve as sponsors for one or more after-school activities. The school offers traditional high school clubs, such as band, a theater group, competitive sports, and a debate society, and also invites students to help initiate new activities, for example, ultimate Frisbee and a community service organization. (Late Adolescence)

Inform parents and guardians about youth initiatives in their area.

- At a parent–teacher–student conference, a middle school teacher describes clubs and sports programs available at the school, as well as recreational and service opportunities in the local community. (Early Adolescence)
- A high school includes a page on its website with links to various clubs, leisure activities, and extracurricular options at school and in the community. During an advising session early in the year, teachers invite students to check out the various options they might consider trying. (Late Adolescence)

Establish a team of school personnel and after-school providers to ensure that programs meet children's physical, social-emotional, and academic needs.

- Two teachers, the principal, and the director of an after-school program meet regularly to discuss space, resources, and ways that the after-school program can give children needed rest, relaxation, snacks, and tutoring. (Middle Childhood)
- A middle school principal invites community leaders to offer a brief presentation to students and parents. The community leaders inform everyone about the various youth centers and leisure activities that are available in the area. (Early Adolescence)

Interactive Technologies

Around the world, children use a growing collection of **interactive technologies**—computers, video games, mobile devices, tablets, and cell phones (also known as cellular phones or mobile phones). Children use electronic technologies for several purposes, especially communication, information seeking, and entertainment.

Personal and Social Uses of Technology

Preparing for Your Licensure Examination

Your teaching test might ask about using the Internet and other digital tools to enrich the learning environment for students.

Young people today have access to a wide range of technologies. Especially beginning in middle school, teachers are apt to notice children sending *texts*, brief written messages that appear alone or are accompanied by photos or videos. Other regular pastimes are watching video clips, playing electronic games, and accessing *social network services* (websites that permit individuals to communicate with selected individuals, share photographs and update information about their activities, and participate in focused interest groups; examples include Facebook, MySpace, Big Tent, and WeChat). Many students additionally contribute to *blogs* (personalized websites that allow documentation of a person's ideas, images, and events, and that permit comments from visitors), Twitter (blogs with characters up to 140 characters in length), and *wikis* (interlinked websites that are created and edited with simple programming languages) (F. W. Baker, 2010).

Technologies play an important role in personal expression and identity formation. Young people use the Internet, particularly blogs and social media pages, to express their innermost thoughts and experiences. By describing daily events and reflections, adolescents learn about themselves—who they are and what they stand for (K. Davis, 2010). Frequently they project one or more *personas* (perhaps changing their age, gender, or interests), thus enabling them to develop insights into other people, discover new parts of themselves, and determine who they are becoming.

Social uses are also prevalent. To a large degree, computers and their progeny have changed the way youngsters relate to one another. For example, young people gain a sense of friendship with other youth they have never met but frequently team up with in online games (Leung & McBride-Chang, 2013). An 18-year-old senior, Natalie, expressed the value of communicating with her friends on LiveJournal:

> I mean it's great because I love being able to, I guess, empathize with stuff that [my friends are] going through, and then they get to read stuff that I'm going through and give—like commenting—"hey, do you want to talk through this?" or something, and that's really helpful. (K. Davis, 2010, p. 157).

Yet being able to send texts and post messages on a website adds a measure of distance, such that young people write things that they would rarely say in face-to-face communication or over the phone. Social media prompt a larger range of contacts than is possible in interpersonal interactions. Children may number their social media "friends" in the hundreds, even though they have only four or five close friends in their daily, nonelectronic lives (S. Quinn & Oldmeadow, 2013).

With so many peers to communicate with online, a young person has to parse out time for interaction and typically communicates in a more superficial manner than is the case with face-to-face conversation. Nevertheless, young people obtain experience in disclosing their thoughts and expressing sympathy to others in distress (K. Davis, 2010). Furthermore, young people tend to use social media in ways that are consistent with their personality (Hollenbaugh & Ferris, 2014). Those who are socially outgoing may create an active community on social media, whereas those who are introverted or insecure may be more selective and post somewhat more negative information about themselves. In a few situations, young people spend so much time interacting online that there is little time remaining for play or other exchanges with peers.

Some negative consequences are also possible. A teenager may withdraw from family and peers in favor of friends known only electronically. And the desire to stay connected electronically may lead to excessively long hours on the computer. A few youngsters develop bad habits in communication, such as *flaming* (i.e., verbally ridiculing someone in a public electronic site), *trolling* (i.e., making an inflammatory remark to provoke an argument), *hacking* into secured sites to disrupt services or spread computer viruses, and *plagiarizing* the work of others (Hellenga, 2002). Furthermore, adolescents who are regular users of the Internet are relatively more likely be sexually harassed or solicited (Clifton, Goodall, Ban, & Birks, 2013; Finkelhor, Mitchell, & Wolak, 2000).

Watching Television, Movies, and Video Clips

Many developmental experts conclude that television is detrimental for infants, whose foremost needs are for close bonds with caregivers and active exploration of the environment, requirements that cannot be met by watching TV (Courage & Setliff, 2010). Heavy viewing by older children is also a concern, especially when it interferes with physical activity and peer interaction (Caroli, Argentieri, Cardone, & Masi, 2004).

The content that children watch is an additional influence on them. Fortunately, many programs aired on television have educationally worthwhile content. *The Magic School Bus, Sesame Street, Reading Rainbow, Between the Lions*, and *Bill Nye the Science Guy* teach children vocabulary, word recognition, reading concepts, problem-solving skills, and scientific principles (D. R. Anderson, 2003; Kirkorian, Wartella, & Anderson, 2008; J. Sherry, 2013). Programs that model prosocial behaviors, for example, *Mister Rogers' Neighborhood, Sesame Street, Saved by the Bell*, and *Smurfs*, teach children valuable social skills (D. R. Anderson, 2003; C. G. Christensen & Myford, 2014; C. F. Cole, Labin, & del Rocio Galarza, 2008).

Unfortunately, counterproductive content coexists with, and potentially overshadows, socially responsible material in the media. Television programs, movies, and video games show ethnic minorities infrequently and when they do with grossly stereotypical characters—for instance, women as airheads, men as brutes, and people with dark skin as thugs (Eisenberg, Martin, & Fabes, 1996; Kahlenberg & Hein, 2010). Such offensive portrayals can easily instill impressionable children with misconceptions.

Furthermore, when youngsters repeatedly view slender and athletically toned actors, actresses, and rock stars, they may develop a standard of physical attractiveness that is not realistic for their own body frame (Anschutz, Engels, Van Leeuwe, & Van Strien, 2009).

ARTIFACT 15-10 Game gadget. Gene drew this picture of his video game equipment from memory, showing his familiarity with the apparatus and a game's combat theme.

Observing Children 15-6

Listen to Brent talk about his enjoyment of video games.

ENHANCEDetext *video example*

Observing Children 15-7

Observe children using the Internet to learn about worms.

ENHANCEDetext *video example*

Moreover, advertisements on television and Internet websites cultivate desires for particular cereals, fast food, clothing, toys, and digital devices—items that may or may not be in children's best interests (Buijzen & Valkenburg, 2003; S. Reese, 1996; D. M. Thomson, 2010).

Excessively violent and gruesomely graphic scenes are another concern. In fact, violence can be found in a large percentage of television programs and video games (C. A. Anderson et al., 2003; Comstock & Scharrer, 2006; Holtz & Appel, 2011). Repeated exposure to violent acts on television seems to make children more aggressive and may be particularly harmful to those already predisposed to be combative (Comstock & Scharrer, 2006; Eron, 1980; Holtz & Appel, 2011). In other words, children inclined to solve conflicts in physically aggressive ways are prone to choose programs with violent content and to become *more aggressive* after viewing them. In addition, heavy viewing of televised violence and excessive use of violent video games may *desensitize* children to acts of violence; that is, children's repeated viewing of violence seems to erode their empathy for victims of real aggressive acts (Lemmens, Valkenburg, & Peter, 2011; B. J. Wilson, 2008).

Playing Interactive Games

Interactive games played on consoles, computers, and handheld devices are an especially popular source of entertainment among Western youth, especially among boys in middle childhood and adolescence (Hamlen, 2011; D. F. Roberts & Foehr, 2008). Youngsters with access to video games spend numerous hours clutching controllers as they engage in virtual punching matches, motorcycle races, and explorations of mythical environments. In Artifact 15-10, Gene drew a picture of his video game controller with a character reaching out to punch someone. Six-year-old Brent shows his enthusiasm for video games in an Observing Children video. He says:

> I usually play video games. There's this army game and snowboard game and . . . and a game called "Smash Brothers." . . . They're cool.

The appeal of video games derives largely from their strikingly effective instructional principles. Video games allow children to pursue a tangible goal, implement continually evolving strategies, make steady progress, experience success, use increasingly advanced tools, and obtain personalized feedback at every step (Gentile & Gentile, 2008; Hamlen, 2011). Numerous nonviolent and creative video games are available, and youngsters can improve spatial and visual-attention skills as they play games (Greenfield, DeWinstanley, Kilpatrick, & Kaye, 1996; Griffiths, 2010). Children themselves report a variety of benefits from playing video games, including having fun, enjoying the challenge, cooperating with peers, making friends, expressing creativity, and trying out new identities (Giffiths, 2010; Granic, Lobel, & Engels, 2014; C. K. Olson, 2010). Particular games, such as those with health-promotion themes, can teach children valuable skills in caring for themselves, eating healthfully, and managing health conditions (Baranowski et al., 2011; D. A. Lieberman, 1997).

Nevertheless, playing video games can become a time-consuming habit, and overuse is a concern when it leads children to curtail healthful physical activity. Also, youngsters who play video games are likely to select at least some games that contain violent content and inappropriate social stereotypes.

Using Computers and the Internet at School

Personal computers and other electronic devices have many applications in the classroom. Through such mechanisms as e-mail, Web-based chat rooms, and electronic bulletin boards, students communicate with peers, teachers, and other adults to analyze data, exchange perspectives, build on one another's ideas, and solve problems (McCombs & Vakili, 2005; M. Scherer, 2011; Subrahmanyam & Greenfield, 2012). A class itself can have a website, allowing students to monitor announcements, turn in assignments, and make comments on a shared bulletin board (L. S. Dunn, 2011). You can observe children using the Internet to learn about worms in an Observing Children video.

Well-constructed software and interactive systems give students a carefully structured curriculum with personalized lessons and steady feedback. Serious educational games, for example, *The Great Entomologist Escape*, expose users to worthwhile scientific information.

In *The Great Entomologist Escape*, created by a high school science teacher, students pretend to be the lead scientist who must learn about ants and solve various practical problems (Annetta, 2010). Examples of dynamic, interactive websites include those of the National Library of Virtual Manipulatives,[7] Cells Alive,[8] National Geographic Creature Feature,[9] and Math in Daily Life[10] (Coiro & Fogleman, 2011). *Epistemic games*, electronic games that allow users to learn the thinking skills of experts in one or more fields, are becoming increasingly popular. In Sim City 4, students function as urban planners in designing simulated residential areas, commercial areas of cities, railways, airports, power plants, and other infrastructures for the locality. As they gain experience on the game, students solve complex real-world problems and learn about science, technology, and society (Salmani Nodoushan, 2009). Examples of other epistemic games are Age of Empires (focusing on history); Microsoft Flight Simulator (drawing from knowledge of aircraft flight, airports, and climatic conditions); and Digital Zoo (using principles of biomechanical engineering and animal physiology).

Implications of Technology

If utilized properly, electronic media and technologies contribute immensely to the education of children. We offer the following suggestions:

• **Encourage children to express themselves creatively.** Many young people like to reveal their thoughts, feelings, and imagination to one another through social media. Teachers can enlist this motivation for educational purposes. For example, students might interpret a poem in the context of their own lives, articulate opinions about a community issue, or become pen pals with students in another country. In the classroom, students can be quite inventive while using flexible applications, for example, representing themselves and their ideas with creative blends of photographs, videos, icons, text, and art. In the process of projecting themselves in an original manner, students gain personal satisfaction, communicate who they are to others, and acquire sophisticated technology skills.

• **Select technologies that meet instructional objectives.** Countless educational resources are available on the Internet and in commercial software to address a range of instructional objectives. Many educational packages, especially in reading and mathematics, allow children to practice skills that they are ready to learn and for which they need more practice. Yet teachers can also use the Internet much more innovatively by having children conduct research, collaborate with one another, and analyze data and information on a particular topic.

• **Use video segments that illustrate elusive concepts.** Some television programs and videos can make abstract concepts more understandable. For instance, when Teresa and a coleader guided a group of sixth and seventh graders in a discussion of George Bernard Shaw's (1915) play *Pygmalion*, everyone struggled to make sense of characters' dialects. Afterward, the group watched segments of *My Fair Lady*, a movie based on the play, and found the dialects much easier to understand.

• **Identify and accommodate students' age-typical abilities and interests with interactive technologies.** Young children are curious about what they can do on cell phones, tablets, laptops, and desktops—on virtually any interactive devices for which they are given access. During preschool and kindergarten, children are able to practice basic skills in recognizing the alphabet, counting, and even simple programming. Yet children in this age range learn by exploring the environment, interacting with adults and peers, and asking questions while listening to stories. Thus, despite their keen interest in tablets and computers, young children generally need restrictions on amount of time for use. As children grow older, and certainly into adolescence, they have much more capacity to benefit from interactive technologies but even then need guidance with educational purposes.

[7] http://nlvm.usu.edu/en/nav/vlibrary.html
[8] http://www.cellsalive.com
[9] http://kids.nationalgeographic.com/kids/animals/creaturefeature
[10] http://www.learner.org/interactives/dailymath

- **Teach critical analysis of information on the Internet, television, and film.** Educators can teach youngsters how to watch television with a critical eye (Calvert, 2008). For example, teachers can help young children understand that television commercials aim to persuade them to buy something, perhaps toys, cereal, or hamburgers. Teachers can also point out subtle advertising ploys for older children, such as the use of color, images (e.g., sexual symbols), and endorsements by famous actors and athletes. Adults can help young people become more aware of stereotypes and negative portrayals of men and women, certain ethnic groups, and various professions in videos.

Young people also need to learn how to navigate through countless electronic sites on the Internet. As they use the Internet for classroom assignments, they can learn that data provided by government agencies and well-respected nonprofit organizations are fairly reliable, but opinion pieces on someone's personal Web page may not be (Ostenson, 2014). With information expanding exponentially on the Internet, youngsters can also be taught how to find, retrieve, organize, synthesize, and evaluate information they find.

- **Teach children etiquette, civic mindedness, and safety on the Internet.** Educators can help students learn to be polite and restrained in their postings. Teachers can likewise talk with students about the kinds of information that is appropriate and risky to share. Of course, many students also need to be advised about the possible long-term harm that can befall individuals who portray themselves too candidly. To make these issues concrete, teachers might show how other people can track their images in tagged photographs and explain how employers perform electronic searches on job applicants (Richardson, 2011; Van Ouytsel, Walrave, & Ponnet, 2014).

- **Make advanced technology available to children with limited access.** Although children from middle- and upper-income families are apt to have access to personal computers at home, similar access is less common for children from low-income families. But computer expertise, including being able to find, comprehend, and evaluate information on the Internet, is increasingly critical for everyone's success. Fortunately, digital technologies are becoming more and more affordable, and school districts can sometimes make available laptops and hand-held devices and offer instruction in technology applications (Scherer, 2011). A preschool teacher might teach children how to play computer games that give practice in emergent literacy skills, and an after-school tutor might show young people how to use the Internet while completing homework.

- **Discourage youngsters from using technologies for aggressive purposes.** Educators and social scientists have had some success in persuading children that the glamorous, humorous, and pervasive manner in which violence is shown on television is misleading (Rosenkoetter, Rosenkoetter, Ozretich, & Acock, 2004). Thus, you might point out that, contrary to typical television scenes, violence is usually *not* an effective way to handle disagreements and often creates additional problems. You could also explain to children that violence is an eye-catching and unrealistic element that television producers use to attract audiences and make money.

Teachers and other adults must advise young people to refrain from *cyberbullying*, the sending or posting of harmful messages over the Internet or with other interactive technologies (Hinduja & Patchin, 2011; Willard, 2007). Adults should also discourage young people from posting racist messages or profanity in their blogs and from sending unflattering photographs of others or demeaning messages over cell phones. Some young people also need to be reminded to refrain from sending mocking or threatening statements as text messages or instant messages (Willard, 2007).

- **Encourage parents to regulate children's use of the Internet and television viewing.** At meetings and school events and in newsletters, educators can encourage parents to set specific television-viewing limits for their children. For instance, if parents find their children watching television many hours a day, they might want to set a 2-hour limit. Parents may find it informative to watch a few television programs with their children. In the process parents can discover how their children interpret what they watch and can provide a reality check when characters consistently violate norms for appropriate behavior ("Do you think people should really insult one another like that?").

Preparing for Your Licensure Examination
Your teaching test might ask about fostering critical thinking in children.

BASIC DEVELOPMENTAL ISSUES
Social Contexts of Child Development

ISSUE	INFLUENCES OF PEERS, SCHOOL, AND SOCIETY
Nature and Nurture 	In ideal circumstances, peers offer children emotional support, a safe forum for polishing social skills, and reassurance during shared transitions. Teachers communicate expectations about children's abilities, implement classroom traditions, organize learning groups, and cultivate a sense of belonging at school. Society has institutions that care for children, technological systems that enable widespread communication, and media that transmit messages about expected behaviors. *Nature* provides a necessary foundation for children's social development with a biologically based desire to interact with other people. Maturational changes are evident in children's evolving peer relationships. For example, increases in language and the ability to take the perspective of others enhance children's ability to resolve differences with peers. Individual differences that derive partly from genes (e.g., temperaments, appearance, and some disabilities) affect children's peer relationships and social acceptance.
Universality and Diversity 	*Universality* is present in the benefits children experience from being liked by peers, having relationships with caring adults outside the family (e.g., teachers and child care providers), participating in a school setting where they are encouraged to achieve and feel that they belong, and having safe and interesting options for free time. *Diversity* occurs in the particular social skills children develop, the extent to which peers find them likable social partners, the suitability of children's environments (e.g., the quality of child care centers), and the degree to which young people engage in risky behaviors (e.g., committing crimes with fellow gang members, engaging in unprotected sexual contact).
Qualitative and Quantitative Change 	Children undergo several *qualitative* transformations in their social relationships. Children form associations with peers that are fleeting exchanges during infancy, but these ties evolve into rich language-based and stable relationships during early and middle childhood and then into close friendships, cliques, and romantic relationships during adolescence. Other qualitative overhauls occur in the onset of sexual feelings for peers of opposite gender (or in some instances, same gender) and in youngsters' uses of particular technologies (e.g., initially preferring television and video games and later choosing e-mail and chat rooms). Children also exhibit gradual, *quantitative* changes in peer relationships, styles of behaving in schools, and uses of society's institutions and services. Children gradually refine their skills for interacting with peers, and once they adjust to a new school, slowly learn to follow its rules and expectations.

Parents can also familiarize themselves with websites their children visit and consider using Internet filters or blocks. They can be advised to talk with their children about who is on their buddy list and discourage any meetings with online acquaintances. In addition, parents can learn common acronyms in contemporary use—for example, LOL, laugh out loud; PAW, parents are watching; A/S/L, age, sex, and location; and WTGP, want to go private? (National Center for Missing and Exploited Children, 2004).

As you have learned, children grow up in a complex social world. The Basic Developmental issues table "Social Contexts of Child Development" (above) synthesizes the effects of peers, schools, and society on children from the perspective of nature and nurture, universality and diversity, and qualitative and quantitative change.

Summary

Society plays an important role through its provision of services to children. Groups of children spend time in child care settings that vary in quality—from those that are well staffed and properly trained with responsive and developmentally appropriate interactions to those that are overcrowded, neglectful, and harsh in their caregiving. Child care has the potential to be a beneficial experience in high-quality settings. After-school programs and extracurricular activities can bolster the development of youngsters when they include stable, affectionate relationships with adults and peers and options for productive pastimes.

Children spend many hours watching television and using computers of various kinds. Televisions, computers, tablets, cell phones, and other media have considerable potential to foster children's cognitive development, but their benefits have not yet been fully realized, and they are accompanied by risks. Violent and stereotypical content in the media can be a minor or serious problem for young people, depending on their pre-existing characteristics. Young people enjoy games and self-expression on social media sites but sometimes acquire bad habits on the Internet, saying things that are rude to others, leaving themselves open to others' cruel remarks or exploitation, and spending so much time on the Internet that they neglect their sleep, homework, physical activity, and face-to-face friendships.

ENHANCEDetext *self-check*

Assessing Children 15-2

Watch students in a middle school social studies classroom become actively engaged in interactive projects.

ENHANCEDetext *application exercise*

PRACTICING FOR YOUR LICENSURE EXAMINATION

Many teaching tests require students to apply their knowledge of child development in analyzing brief vignettes and answering multiple-choice questions. You can practice for your licensure examination by reading the following case study and answering a series of questions.

Aaron and Cole

Aaron and Cole became friends when they were both students in Mr. Howard's fifth-grade class. Although Aaron was in most respects a typical fifth grader, Cole had significant developmental delays. Special educator Debbie Staub (1998) described Cole's special educational needs and his strengths as follows:

> Cole has limited expressive vocabulary and uses one- or two-word sentences. He does not participate in traditional academic tasks, although he is included with his typically developing schoolmates for the entire school day. Cole has a history of behavioral problems that have ranged from mild noncompliance to adult requests to serious aggressive and destructive behavior such as throwing furniture at others. In spite of his occasional outbursts, however, it is hard not to like him. Cole is like an eager toddler who finds wonder in the world around him. The boys he has befriended in Mr. Howard's class bring him great joy. He appreciates their jokes and harmless teasing. Cole would like nothing better than to hang out with his friends all day, but if he had to choose just one friend, it would be Aaron. (D. Staub, 1998, p. 76)[a]

Throughout their fifth- and sixth-grade years, Aaron was both a good friend and a caring mentor to Cole.

> Without prompting from adults, Aaron helped Cole with his work, included him in games at recess, and generally watched out for him.

Aaron also assumed responsibility for Cole's behavior by explaining to Cole how his actions affected others. The following excerpt from a classroom observation illustrates Aaron's gentle way with Cole:

> Cole was taking Nelle's [a classmate's] things out of her bag and throwing them on the floor. As soon as Aaron saw, he walked right over to Cole and started talking to him. He said, "We're making a new rule—no being mean." Then he walked with Cole to the front of the room and told him to tell another boy what the new rule was. Cole tapped the boy's shoulder to tell him but the boy walked away. Cole looked confused. Aaron smiled and put his hand on Cole's shoulder and told him, "It's okay. Just remember the rule." Then he walked Cole back to Nelle's stuff and quietly asked Cole to put everything back. (pp. 77–78)

Aaron, too, benefited from the friendship, as his mother explained: "Our family has recently gone through a tough divorce and there are a lot of hurt feelings out there for everyone. But at least when Aaron is at school he feels good about being there and I think a big reason is because he has Cole and he knows that he is an important person in Cole's life" (pp. 90–91).

Dr. Staub observed that, despite their developmental differences, the boys' relationship was in many respects a normal one:

> I asked Mr. Howard once, "Do you think Cole's and Aaron's friendship looks different from others' in your class?" Mr. Howard thought for a moment before responding: "No, I don't think it looks that different. Well, I was going to say one of the differences is that Aaron sometimes tells Cole to be quiet, or 'Hey Cole, I gotta do my work!' But I don't know if that is any different than what he might say to Ben leaning over and interrupting him. I think I would say that Aaron honestly likes Cole and it's not because he's a special-needs kid." (p. 78)

Aaron and Cole remained close until Cole moved 30 miles away at the beginning of seventh grade.

Constructed-Response Question

1. In what ways did Aaron and Cole's friendship promote each boy's social-emotional development?

[a] Excerpts from "Case Study: Aaron and Cole" from DELICATE THREADS: FRIENDSHIPS BETWEEN CHILDREN WITH AND WITHOUT SPECIAL NEEDS IN INCLUSIVE SETTINGS by Debbie Staub. Copyright © 1998 by Debbie Staub Reprinted by permission of the author.

Multiple-Choice Questions

2. What did Aaron do that helped Cole become more socially competent with other peers?
   a. Aaron helped Cole to be accepted by peers by convincing Cole to join him in some risky behaviors.
   b. Aaron did Cole's homework so that Cole looked more capable in front of peers.
   c. Aaron encouraged Cole to avoid other children and remain his friend exclusively.
   d. Aaron coached Cole in such social skills as controlling his temper and remaining friendly with peers.

3. Aaron's and Cole's teacher, Mr. Howard, seemed to be supportive of the boys' friendship. Considering the perspectives in this chapter, what might Mr. Howard have done if he were committed to establishing an effective classroom climate?
   a. Communicate genuine caring and respect for all students.
   b. Encourage students to pursue common goals.
   c. Implement some fun routines on a regular basis.
   d. All of the above

ENHANCEDetext   *licensure exam*

Key Concepts

peer culture (p. 565)
social skills (p. 565)
peer pressure (p. 570)
popular children (p. 572)
rejected children (p. 572)

neglected children (p. 572)
controversial children (p. 573)
dominance hierarchy (p. 576)
clique (p. 576)
crowd (p. 577)

subculture (p. 577)
gang (p. 578)
sexual orientation (p. 580)
sexual harassment (p. 585)
sense of community (p. 588)

community of learners (p. 589)
self-fulfilling prophecy (p. 592)
society (p. 595)
interactive technology (p. 598)

Glossary

accommodation Process of responding to a new event by either modifying an existing scheme or forming a new one.

acculturation Process of taking on the customs and values of a new culture.

action research Systematic study of an issue or problem by a teacher or other practitioner, with the goal of bringing about more productive outcomes for children.

adaptive behavior Behavior related to daily living skills and appropriate conduct in social situations.

addiction Physical and psychological dependence on a substance, such that increasing quantities must be taken to produce the desired effect and withdrawal produces adverse physiological and psychological effects.

African American English Dialect of some African American communities that includes pronunciations, idioms, and grammatical constructions different from those of Standard English.

aggression Action intentionally taken to hurt another either physically or psychologically.

alleles Genes located at the same point on corresponding (paired) chromosomes and related to the same physical characteristic.

amusia Inability to detect the small changes in pitch that are common in melodies; an extreme form of tone deafness.

anorexia nervosa Eating disorder in which a person eats little or nothing for weeks or months and seriously jeopardizes health.

anxiety disorder Chronic emotional condition characterized by excessive, debilitating worry.

anxiety Emotional state characterized by worry and apprehension.

apprenticeship Mentorship in which a novice works intensively with an expert to learn how to accomplish complex tasks in a particular domain.

appropriation Gradual adoption of (and perhaps also adaptation of) other people's ways of thinking and behaving for one's own purposes.

assessment Task that children complete and adults use to make judgments of children's knowledge, abilities, and other characteristics.

assimilation Form of acculturation in which a person totally embraces a culture, abandoning a previous culture in the process.

assimilation In Piaget's theory, process of responding (either physically or mentally) to a new event in a way that is consistent with an existing scheme.

astrocyte Glial cell that regulates blood flow in the brain, brings nutrients to and metabolizes chemicals for neurons, and communicates with other similar cells and with neurons.

attachment An enduring emotional tie uniting one person with another.

attention-deficit hyperactivity disorder (ADHD) Disability characterized by inattention, hyperactivity, or impulsive behavior, or by all of these characteristics.

attribution Belief about the cause of one's own or another person's success or failure.

authentic activity Instructional activity similar to one that a child might eventually encounter in the outside world.

authentic assessment Task in which students apply their knowledge and skills in a real-life context.

authoritarian parenting style Parenting style characterized by strict expectations for behavior and rigid rules that children are required to obey without question.

authoritative parenting style Parenting style characterized by emotional warmth, high expectations and standards for behavior, consistent enforcement of rules, explanations regarding the reasons behind these rules, and the inclusion of children in decision making.

autism spectrum disorders Disorders marked by impaired social cognition, social skills, and social interaction, as well as by repetitive behaviors; extreme forms are often associated with significant cognitive and linguistic delays and highly unusual behaviors.

autobiographical self Mental "history" of important events in one's life.

automatization Process of becoming able to respond quickly and efficiently while mentally processing or physically performing certain tasks.

axon Arm-like part of a neuron that sends information to other neurons.

babbling Repeating certain consonant-vowel syllables over and over (e.g., "mamamama"); common in the latter half of the first year.

behaviorism Theoretical perspective in which children's behavioral and emotional responses change as a direct result of particular environmental stimuli.

bicultural orientation Form of acculturation in which a person is familiar with two cultures and selectively draws from the values and traditions of one or both cultures depending on the context.

bilingual education Approach to second-language instruction in which students are instructed in academic subject areas in their native language while simultaneously being taught to speak, read, and write in a second language.

bilingualism Knowing and speaking two languages fluently.

biological theory Theoretical perspective that focuses on inherited physiological structures of the body and brain that support survival, growth, and learning.

bulimia Eating disorder in which a person, in an attempt to be thin, eats a large amount of food and then purposefully purges it from the body by vomiting or taking laxatives.

bully Child or adolescent who frequently threatens, harasses, or causes physical or psychological injury to particular peers.

canalization Tight genetic control of a particular aspect of development.

care orientation Focus on nurturance and concern for others in moral decision making.

case study Naturalistic research study in which investigators document a single person's or a small group's experiences in depth over a period of time.

central conceptual structure Integrated network of concepts and cognitive processes that forms the basis for much of one's thinking, reasoning, and learning in a specific content domain.

central executive Component of the human information processing system that oversees the flow of information throughout the system and enacts cognitive strategies.

cephalocaudal trend Vertical ordering of motor skills and physical development; order is head first to feet last.

child development Study of the persistent, cumulative, and progressive changes in the physical, cognitive, and social-emotional development of children and adolescents.

child maltreatment Adverse treatment of a child in the form of neglect, physical abuse, sexual abuse, or emotional abuse.

chromosome Rod-like structure that resides in the nucleus of every cell of the body and contains genes that guide growth and development; each chromosome is made up of DNA and other biological instructions.

class inclusion Recognition that an object simultaneously belongs to a particular category and to one of its subcategories.

clinical method Procedure in which an adult probes a child's reasoning about a task or problem, tailoring questions to what the child has previously said or done in the interview.

clique Moderately stable friendship group of perhaps three to nine members.

codominance Situation in which the two genes of an allele pair, although not identical, both have some influence on a characteristic.

cognitive apprenticeship Mentorship in which an expert and a novice work together on a challenging task and the expert suggests ways to think about the task.

cognitive development Systematic changes in reasoning, concepts, memory, language, and intellectual skills.

cognitive process theory Theoretical perspective that focuses on the precise nature of human mental representations and operations.

cognitive science An interdisciplinary field, drawing from research in psychology, neuroscience, linguistics, anthropology, artificial intelligence, and philosophy, and examining the representations and operations of the human mind.

cognitive strategy Specific mental process that people intentionally use to acquire or manipulate information.

cognitive tool Concept, symbol, strategy, or other culturally constructed mechanism that helps people think more effectively.

cognitive-developmental theory Theoretical perspective that focuses on major transformations to the underlying structures of thinking over the course of development.

collectivistic culture Cultural group that encourages obedience to and dependence on authority figures and being honorable, cooperative, and invested in group accomplishments.

community of learners A classroom in which teacher(s) and students actively and collaboratively work to help one another learn.

community The neighborhood in which a child and his or her family live and the surrounding vicinity.

comprehension monitoring The process of evaluating one's comprehension of oral messages or written material.

conceptual change Revision of one's knowledge and understanding of a topic in response to new information about the topic.

conduct disorder Chronic emotional condition characterized by lack of concern for the rights of others.

conscience An internalized sense of right and wrong for guiding and evaluating one's behavior.

conservation Realization that if nothing is added or taken away, an amount stays the same regardless of any alterations in shape or arrangement.

constructivism Theoretical perspective proposing that learners construct a body of knowledge and beliefs, rather than absorbing information exactly as it is received.

context The broad social environments, including family, schools, neighborhoods, community organizations, culture, ethnicity, and society at large, that influence children's development.

contingent self-worth Overall sense of self that is highly dependent on others' opinions.

control group Group of participants in a research study who do not receive the treatment under investigation; often used in an experimental study.

controversial children Children whom some peers really like and other peers strongly dislike.

conventional morality In Kohlberg's theory, acceptance of society's conventions regarding right and wrong; behaving to please others or to live up to society's expectations for appropriate behavior.

conventional transgression In social domain theory, action that violates society's general guidelines (often unspoken) for socially acceptable behavior.

cooing Making and repeating vowel sounds (e.g., "oooooo"); common in early infancy.

coparents The two (or more) parents who share responsibility for rearing their children.

coping skills Personal mechanisms for managing distress

correlation Extent to which two variables are related to each other, such that when one variable increases, the other either increases or decreases in a somewhat predictable fashion.

correlational study Research study that explores relationships among variables.

cortex Part of the forebrain that enables conscious thinking processes, including executive functions.

creativity The valuable process of generating novel and worthwhile solutions to a person's goals, needs, and problems.

criterion-referenced test Task that reveals what students know and can do related to a specific standard.

cross-sectional study Research study in which the performance of individuals at different ages is compared at a single point in time.

crowd Large collection of adolescents who share certain characteristics, tend to affiliate together, and are defined by others according to their reputations.

crystallized intelligence Knowledge and skills accumulated from one's prior experience, schooling, and culture.

cultural bias Extent to which an assessment instrument offends or unfairly penalizes some individuals because of their ethnicity, gender, or socioeconomic status.

culturally responsive teaching A teacher's use of particular instructional strategies based on knowledge of children's cultural backgrounds and individual characteristics.

culture The values, traditions, and symbol systems of a long-standing social group that give purpose and meaning to children's daily activities and interpersonal relationships.

delay of gratification Forgoing small immediate rewards for larger ones at a future time.

dendrite Branchlike part of a neuron that receives information from other neurons.

depression Emotional condition characterized by significant sadness, discouragement, hopelessness, and, in children, irritability.

developmental milestone A physical, cognitive, or social-emotional skill that appears as part of a predictable sequence of emerging abilities in an age-related timetable.

developmental systems theory Theoretical perspective that focuses on the multiple factors, including the child's activity and systems inside and outside the child, that combine to influence development.

developmentally appropriate practice Instruction and other services adapted to the age, characteristics, and developmental progress of individual children.

dialect Form of a language characteristic of a particular geographic region or ethnic group.

differentiation A gradual transition from general possibility to specialized functioning over the course of development.

disequilibrium State of being unable to address new events with existing schemes.

disorganized and disoriented attachment Attachment classification in which children lack a single coherent way of responding to attachment figures.

distributed intelligence Thinking facilitated by physical objects and technology, social support, and concepts and symbols of one's culture.

distributive justice Beliefs about what constitutes people's fair share of a valued commodity.

diversity In a particular aspect of human development, the varied ways in which individuals progress.

dizygotic twins Twins that began as two separate zygotes and so are as genetically similar as two siblings conceived and born at different times.

DNA A spiral-staircase–shaped molecule that guides the production of proteins needed by the body for growth and development; short for *deoxyribonucleic acid*.

dominance hierarchy Relative standing of group members in terms of such qualities as leadership and social influence.

dominant gene Gene that overrides any competing instructions in an allele pair.

dynamic assessment Systematic examination of how a child's knowledge or reasoning may change as a result of learning a specific task or performing it with adult guidance.

dyscalculia Inability to master basic numerical concepts and operations in a developmentally typical time frame despite normal instruction.

dyslexia Inability to master basic reading skills in a developmentally typical time frame despite normal reading instruction.

egocentrism Inability of a child in Piaget's preoperational stage to view situations from another person's perspective.

elaboration Process of using prior knowledge to embellish new information and learn it more effectively.

embryo During prenatal weeks 2 through 8, the developing offspring that is in the process of forming major body structures and organs.

emergent literacy Knowledge and skills that lay a foundation for reading and writing; typically develops in the preschool years from early experiences with written language.

emotion Affective response to an event that is personally relevant to one's needs and goals.

emotional and behavioral disorder Disturbance in a child reflected in significant difficulties in emotions and behavior at school.

emotional contagion Tendency for infants to cry spontaneously when they hear other infants crying.

emotional intelligence The ability to perceive, understand, and regulate affective feelings.

emotional regulation The ability to moderate affective states such that feelings are experienced authentically and expressed according to personal needs and social conventions.

empathy Capacity to experience the same feelings as another person, especially when the feeling is pain or distress.

English language learner (ELL) School-age child who is not fully fluent in English because his or her family speaks a language other than English at home.

entity view (of ability) Belief that ability is a "thing" that is relatively permanent and unchangeable.

equilibration Movement from equilibrium to disequilibrium and back to equilibrium; a process that promotes the development of increasingly complex forms of thought and knowledge.

equilibrium State of being able to address new events using existing schemes.

ethnic identity Awareness of being a member of one or more ethnic groups, a sense of being like others with the same origins, and willingness to adopt certain values and behaviors characteristic of that group or groups.

ethnicity State of being in a group of people with a common heritage, geographical origin, language, religious faith, or combination of characteristics.

ethnography Naturalistic research study in which investigators spend an extensive period of time documenting the cultural patterns of a group of people in everyday settings.

ethological attachment theory Theoretical perspective that emphasizes the benefits to children derived from close bonds with caregivers, particularly protection from harm and a secure base from which to explore the environment.

executive functions Purposeful and goal-directed intellectual processes (e.g., planning, decision making) made possible by higher brain structures.

expansion Repetition of a child's short utterances in more complete and grammatically correct forms.

experimental study Research study in which a researcher manipulates one aspect of the environment (a treatment), controls other aspects of the environment, and assesses the treatment's effects on participants' behavior.

expressive language Ability to communicate effectively through speaking and writing.

extrinsic motivation Motivation provoked by the external consequences that certain behaviors bring.

family structure In a family with children, the family's makeup; specifically, the children in a family home and the adults who live with and care for the children.

family Two or more people who live together and are related by such enduring factors as birth, marriage, adoption, or long-term mutual commitment.

fast mapping Inferring a word's general meaning after a single exposure.

fetus During prenatal week 9 until birth, the developing offspring that grows in size and weight and in sensory abilities, brain structures, and organs needed for survival.

figurative speech Speech that communicates meaning beyond a literal interpretation of its words.

fine motor skills Small, precise movements of particular parts of the body, especially the hands.

fluid intelligence Ability to acquire knowledge quickly and thereby adapt effectively to new situations.

Flynn effect Gradual increase in intelligence test performance observed in many countries during the past several decades.

forebrain Part of the brain responsible for complex thinking, emotions, and motivation.

foreign language instruction Approach to second-language instruction in which native English speakers receive lessons in a new language for less than an hour once or twice a week or occasionally more often.

formal assessment Task planned and implemented by teachers to determine what students understand and can do.

formative assessment Task that is implemented before or during instruction to determine what children know and can do so as to fine-tune the instruction.

functionalism Theoretical perspective of language development that emphasizes the purposes language serves for human beings.

g General factor in intelligence that influences performance in a wide variety of tasks and content domains.

gamete Reproductive cell that, in humans, contains 23 chromosomes rather than the 46 chromosomes present in other cells in the body; a male gamete (sperm) and a female gamete (ovum) join at conception.

gang Cohesive social group characterized by initiation rites, distinctive colors and symbols, territorial orientation, feuds with rival groups, and criminal activity.

gender schema Self-constructed body of beliefs about the traits and behaviors of males or females.

gene Basic unit of heredity in a living cell; genes are made up of DNA and contained on chromosomes.

giftedness Unusually high ability in one or more areas, to the point where children require special educational services to help them meet their full potential.

glial cell Cell in the brain that provides structural or functional support for, and in some cases direction to, one or more neurons.

goal-directed behavior Intentional behavior aimed at bringing about an anticipated outcome.

grammatical word Nonlexical word that affects the meanings of other words or the interrelationships among words in a sentence.

gross motor skills Large movements of the body that permit locomotion through and within the environment.

grounded theory study Naturalistic research study in which investigators develop and elaborate new theories while comparing data (such as interview statements from participants) to the researchers' emerging interpretations.

growth spurt Rapid increase in height and weight during puberty.

guided participation Active engagement in adult activities, typically with considerable direction and structure from an adult or other more advanced individual; children are given increasing responsibility and independence as they gain experience and proficiency.

guilt Feeling of discomfort when one inflicts damage or causes someone else pain or distress.

habituation Changes in children's physiological responses to repeated displays of the same stimulus, reflecting loss of interest.

hindbrain Part of the brain controlling the basic physiological processes that sustain survival.

holophrase A single word used to express a complete thought; commonly observed in children's earliest speech.

hostile attributional bias Tendency to interpret others' behaviors as reflecting hostile or aggressive intentions.

identity Self-constructed definition of who one is, what things one finds important, what one believes, and what goals one wants to accomplish in life.

imaginary audience Belief that one is the center of attention in any social situation.

immersion Approach to second-language instruction in which native English speakers hear and speak the second language almost exclusively in the classroom.

inclusion Practice of educating all students, including those with severe and multiple disabilities,

in neighborhood schools and general education classrooms.

incremental view (of ability) Belief that ability can and does improve with effort and practice.

individual constructivism Theoretical perspective that focuses on how people independently construct meaning from their experiences.

individualistic culture Cultural group that encourages independence, self-assertion, competition, and expression of personal needs.

individualized education program (IEP) The goals and educational strategies established for a child with special needs based on evidence of the child's abilities and needs as interpreted by the child's parents, teachers, other specialists, and sometimes the child him- or herself.

induction Act of explaining why a certain behavior is unacceptable, usually with a focus on the pain or distress that someone has caused another.

infant-directed speech Short, simple, high-pitched speech often used when talking to young children.

infantile amnesia General inability to recall events that have occurred in the early years of life.

informal assessment Spontaneous observations made by teachers of what children do or say, resulting in inferences about children's characteristics.

information processing theory A family of related theoretical perspectives that focus on the specific ways in which people mentally acquire, interpret, and remember information.

inner speech "Talking" to oneself mentally rather than aloud as a way of guiding oneself through a task.

insecure-avoidant attachment Attachment classification in which children appear somewhat indifferent to attachment figures.

insecure-resistant attachment Attachment classification in which children are preoccupied with their attachment figures but gain little comfort from them when distressed.

integration An increasing coordination of body parts over the course of development.

intellectual disability Disability marked by significantly below-average general intelligence and deficits in adaptive behavior.

intelligence test General measure of current cognitive functioning, used primarily to predict academic achievement over the short run.

intelligence Ability to apply past knowledge and experiences flexibly to accomplish challenging new tasks.

intentionality Engagement in an action congruent with one's purpose or goal.

interactive technology Array of electronic, digitally based machines that are operated dynamically by a person whose commands determine emerging program sequences.

internalization In Vygotsky's theory, the gradual evolution of external, social activities into internal, mental activities.

internalized motivation Adoption of behaviors that others value, whether or not one's immediate environment reinforces those behaviors.

intersubjectivity Awareness of shared perceptions and understandings that provide the foundation for social interaction.

interview Data-collection technique that obtains self-report data through face-to-face conversation.

intrinsic motivation Motivation resulting from personal characteristics or from factors inherent in the task being performed.

invented spelling A child's early, self-constructed word spelling, which may reflect only some of the word's phonemes.

IQ score Score on an intelligence test, determined by comparing one's performance with the performance of same-age peers.

IRE cycle Adult–child interaction pattern marked by adult *initiation*, child *response*, and adult *evaluation*; in Western cultures, such a pattern is often seen in instructional settings.

joint attention Phenomenon in which two people (e.g., a child and caregiver) simultaneously focus on the same object or event, monitor each other's attention, and coordinate their responses.

justice orientation Focus on individual rights in moral decision making.

knowledge base One's knowledge about specific topics and the world in general.

knowledge telling Writing down ideas in whatever order they come to mind, with little regard for communicating the ideas effectively.

knowledge transforming Writing about ideas in such a way as to intentionally help the reader understand them.

language acquisition device Biologically built-in mechanism hypothesized to facilitate language learning.

language socialization Direct and indirect means through which other people teach children the language and verbal behaviors deemed to be appropriate in their culture.

learned helplessness General belief that one is incapable of accomplishing tasks and has little or no control of the environment.

learning disability Significant deficit in one or more cognitive processes, to the point where special educational services are required.

left hemisphere Left side of the cortex; largely responsible for sequential reasoning and analysis, especially in right-handed people.

lexical word Word that in some way represents an aspect of one's physical, social, or psychological world.

long-term memory Component of memory that holds knowledge and skills for a relatively long period of time.

longitudinal study Research study in which the performance of a single group of people is tracked over a period of time.

mastery goal Desire to acquire additional knowledge or master new skills (also known as a *learning goal*).

mastery orientation General belief that one is capable of accomplishing challenging tasks, accompanied by an intent to master such tasks.

maturation Genetically guided changes that occur over the course of development.

mediated learning experience Discussion between an adult and a child in which the adult helps the child make sense of an event they have mutually experienced.

mediation In Vygotsky's theory, a process through which adults help children make culturally appropriate sense of experiences, perhaps by attaching labels to objects or explaining the nature of certain phenomena.

meiosis The process of cell division and reproduction by which gametes are formed.

menarche First menstrual period in an adolescent female.

metacognition Knowledge and beliefs about one's own cognitive processes, as well as efforts to regulate those cognitive processes to maximize learning and memory.

metacognitive awareness Extent to which one is able to reflect on the nature of one's own thinking processes.

metalinguistic awareness Extent to which one consciously understands and thinks about the nature and functions of language.

midbrain Part of the brain that coordinates communication between the hindbrain and forebrain.

mirror neuron Specialized cell in the brain that fires either when the person performs a particular act or observes another individual performing the same act.

mitosis The process of cell duplication by which chromosomes are preserved and a human being or other biological organism can grow.

monozygotic twins Twins that began as a single zygote and so share the same genetic makeup.

moral development Advancements in reasoning and behaving in accordance with culturally prescribed or self-constructed standards of right and wrong.

moral dilemma Situation in which there is no clear-cut answer regarding the morally right thing to do.

moral transgression In social domain theory, action that causes damage or harm or in some other way infringes on the needs and rights of others.

motivation State that energizes, directs, and sustains behavior.

multifactorial trait Particular characteristic determined by many separate genes combining in influence with environmental experiences.

music literacy Ability to read and understand musical notation.

myelination The growth of a fatty sheath around neurons that allows them to transmit messages quickly.

narrative Verbal account of a temporal sequence of logically interconnected events; a story.

native language The first language a child learns.

nativism Theoretical perspective proposing that some knowledge is biologically built in and available at birth or soon thereafter.

nature Inherited characteristics that affect development.

need for relatedness Fundamental need to feel socially connected to, and loved and respected by, other people.

neglected children Children whom peers rarely select as someone they would either most like or least like to do something with.

neo-Piagetian theory Theoretical perspective that combines elements of Piaget's theory with more contemporary research findings and suggests that development in specific content domains is often stage-like in nature.

neuron Cell that transmits information to other cells; also called a *nerve cell*.

niche construction A child's active shaping of the environment through behaviors, activities, and choices, often in accordance with personal genetically based tendencies.

niche-picking Tendency to actively seek out environments that match one's inherited abilities.

norm-referenced test Task that shows how well an individual student performs in one or more subjects compared to a large and carefully defined peer group.

nurture Environmental conditions that affect development.

obesity Condition in which a person's body mass index, a measure of weight in relation to height, is at or above the 95th percentile for someone of the same age and gender.

object permanence Realization that objects continue to exist even when they are out of sight.

observation Data-collection technique whereby a researcher carefully observes and documents the behaviors of participants in a research study.

operation In Piaget's theory, an organized and integrated system of logical thought processes.

organization Process of identifying interrelationships among pieces of information as a way of learning them more effectively.

overextension Overly broad meaning for a word, such that it is used in situations to which it does not apply.

overregularization Use of a syntactic rule in situations where an exception to the rule applies.

paper-and-pencil assessment Task in which students answer questions or solve problems on worksheets or other prepared forms.

parenting style General pattern of behaviors that a parent uses to nurture and discipline his or her children.

peer culture General set of rules, expectations, and interpretations that influence how members of a particular peer group behave.

peer mediation Approach to conflict resolution in which one child or adolescent (the mediator) asks peers in conflict to express their differing viewpoints and then work together to identify an appropriate compromise.

peer pressure Tactics used to encourage some behaviors and discourage others in age-mates.

perception Interpretation of stimuli that the body has sensed.

performance assessment Task in which students demonstrate skills in the process of completing a project.

performance goal Desire to demonstrate high ability and make a good impression.

performance-approach goal Desire to look good and receive favorable judgments from others.

performance-avoidance goal Desire not to look bad or receive unfavorable judgments from others.

permissive parenting style Parenting style characterized by emotional warmth but few expectations or standards for children's behavior.

personal fable Belief held by many adolescents that they are unique beings invulnerable to normal risks and dangers.

personal interest Long-term, relatively stable interest in a particular topic or activity.

personal matter In social domain theory, action that is considered a choice that an individual can make without consulting others.

personal space A child's personally and culturally preferred distance from other people during social interaction.

personality Characteristic way a person behaves, thinks, and feels.

phonemes Smallest units of a spoken language that signify differences in meaning.

phonological awareness Ability to hear the distinct sounds of which spoken words are comprised.

phonology The sound system of a language; how words sound and are produced.

physical aggression Action that can potentially cause bodily injury (for example, hitting or scratching another person).

physical development Systematic changes of the body and brain and age-related changes in motor skills and health behaviors.

physiological measure Direct assessment of physical development or physiological functioning.

playing the dozens Friendly, playful exchange of insults, common in some African American communities; also called *joaning* or *sounding*.

popular children Children whom many peers like and perceive to be kind and trustworthy.

postconventional morality In Kohlberg's theory, behaving in accordance with self-developed abstract principles regarding right and wrong.

pragmatics Conventions and strategies used in effective and socially acceptable verbal interactions.

preconventional morality In Kohlberg's theory, a lack of internalized standards about right and wrong; making decisions based on what is best for oneself, without regard for others' needs and feelings.

prejudice Display of negative attitudes, feelings, and behaviors toward particular individuals because of their membership in a specific group.

premature infant Infant born early (before 37 weeks of prenatal growth) and sometimes with serious medical problems.

prenatal development Growth that takes place between conception and birth.

primary reinforcer Stimulus or event that satisfies a built-in biological need.

proactive aggression Deliberate aggression against another as a means of obtaining a desired goal.

prosocial behavior Action intended to benefit another person (for example, sharing with or helping another person).

proximodistal trend Inside-outside ordering of motor skills and physical development; order is inside first and outside last.

psychodynamic theory Theoretical perspective that focuses on how early experiences and internal conflicts affect social and personality development.

psychosocial stages In Erikson's theory, eight periods of life that involve age-related challenges.

puberty Physiological changes that occur during adolescence and lead to reproductive maturation.

punishment Consequence of a response that leads to a decrease in the frequency of that response.

qualitative change Relatively dramatic developmental change that reflects considerable reorganization in functioning.

quantitative change Developmental change that involves a series of minor, trendlike modifications.

quasi-experimental study Research study in which one or more experimental treatments are administered but in which random assignment to groups is not possible.

questionnaire Data-collection technique that obtains self-report data through a paper-and-pencil inventory.

race State of being in a group of people with shared physical features such as skin color, eye hair texture, and facial bone structure.

racial identity Awareness of being a member of a particular racial group or groups, sense of connection to individuals with the same classification, and willingness to be like others with a similar background.

reactive aggression Aggressive response to frustration or provocation.

reasoning The ability to think logically and weigh evidence reasonably when drawing conclusions.

receptive language Ability to understand the language one hears or reads.

recessive gene Gene that influences growth and development primarily when the other gene in the allele pair is identical to it.

reciprocal teaching Approach to teaching reading comprehension in which students take turns asking teacher-like questions of their classmates.

recursive thinking Thinking about what other people may be thinking about oneself, possibly through multiple iterations.

reflex Automatic motor response to a particular kind of stimulus.

rehearsal Attempt to learn and remember information by repeating it over and over.

reinforcer Consequence of a response that leads to an increase in the frequency of that response.

rejected children Children whom many peers identify as being unfavorable social partners.

relational aggression Action that can adversely affect interpersonal relationships (for example, calling another person names or socially excluding the person).

reliability Extent to which a data-collection technique yields consistent, dependable results—results that are only minimally affected by temporary and irrelevant influences.

resilience Ability of some youngsters (often enhanced with environmental support) to thrive despite adverse environmental conditions.

right hemisphere Right side of the cortex; largely responsible for simultaneous processing and synthesis, especially in right-handed people.

rough-and-tumble play Playful physical "fighting" common in early and middle childhood.

rubric A list of the ideal features of an assessment, often used by students in completing a task and by teachers in evaluating students' performance.

sample The specific participants in a research study; their performance is often assumed to indicate how a larger population of individuals would perform.

scaffolding Support mechanism, provided by a more competent individual, that helps a child successfully perform a task within his or her zone of proximal development.

schema Tightly integrated set of ideas about a specific object or situation.

scheme In Piaget's theory, an organized group of similar actions or thoughts that are used repeatedly in response to the environment.

schizophrenia A psychiatric condition characterized by irrational ideas and disorganized thinking.

scientific method Multistep process of carefully defining and addressing a research question using critical thinking and analysis of the evidence.

scientific reasoning Cognitive processes central to conducting scientific research and interpreting findings appropriately.

script Schema that involves a predictable sequence of events related to a common activity.

secondary reinforcer Stimulus or event that becomes reinforcing over time through its association with one or more other reinforcers.

secure attachment Attachment classification in which children use attachment figures as a source of comfort in times of distress and as a secure base from which to explore.

selective adoption Form of acculturation in which a person assumes some customs of a new culture while also retaining some customs of a previous culture.

self-conscious emotion Affective state that reflects awareness of a community's social standards (e.g., pride, guilt, shame).

self-efficacy Belief that one is capable of executing certain behaviors or reaching certain goals.

self-evaluation Judging one's own performance in accordance with predetermined criteria.

self-fulfilling prophecy Phenomenon in which an adult's expectations for a child's performance bring about that level of performance.

self-handicapping Action that undermines one's own success as a way of protecting self-worth during difficult tasks.

self-instruction Specific directions that one gives oneself while performing a complex behavior; a form of *self-talk*.

self-monitoring Process of observing and recording one's own behavior.

self-motivation Intentionally using certain strategies to keep oneself on task during a dull but important activity.

self-regulated learning Directing and controlling one's own cognitive processes in order to learn successfully.

self-regulation The processes by which children direct their actions, learning, and emotions in accordance with their personal goals and standards.

self-report Data-collection technique whereby participants are asked to describe their own characteristics and performance.

self-socialization Tendency to integrate personal observations and others' input into self-constructed standards for behavior and to choose actions consistent with those standards.

self-talk Talking to oneself as a way of guiding oneself through a task.

semantic bootstrapping Using knowledge of word meanings to derive knowledge about syntactic categories and structures.

semantics The meanings of words and word combinations.

sensation Physiological detection of stimuli in the environment.

sense of community In a classroom or school, a collection of widely shared beliefs that students, teachers, and other staff have common goals, support one another's efforts, and make important contributions to everyone's success.

sense of self-determination Belief that one has some choice and control regarding the future course of one's life.

sense of self Knowledge, beliefs, judgments, and feelings about oneself as a person.

sensitive period A period in development when certain environmental experiences have a more pronounced influence than is true at other times.

sensory register Component of memory that holds incoming information in an unanalyzed form for a very brief time (2 to 3 seconds or less).

separation Form of acculturation in which a person fails to learn or accept any customs and values from a new cultural environment.

service learning Activity that promotes learning and skill development through volunteerism or community service.

sexual harassment Form of discrimination in which a target individual perceives another's actions or statements to be hostile, humiliating, or offensive, especially pertaining to physical appearance or sexual matters.

sexual orientation Particular genders to which an individual is romantically and sexually attracted.

shame Feeling of embarrassment or humiliation after failing to meet certain standards for moral behavior.

sight vocabulary Words that a child can immediately recognize while reading.

situated motivation Phenomenon in which aspects of the immediate environment enhance motivation to learn particular things or behave in particular ways.

situational interest Interest evoked temporarily by something in the environment.

social cognition Process of thinking about how other people are likely to think, act, and react and choosing one's own interpersonal behaviors accordingly.

social constructivism Theoretical perspective that focuses on people's collective efforts to impose meaning on the world.

social desirability Tendency of children to give answers that will be perceived favorably by others.

social goal Goal related to establishing or maintaining relationships with other people.

social learning theory Theoretical perspective that focuses on how children's beliefs and goals influence their actions and how they often learn by observing others.

social perspective taking Imagining what someone else might be thinking or feeling.

social referencing Looking at someone else (e.g., a caregiver) for clues about how to respond to a particular object or event.

social skills Strategies used to interact effectively with others.

social-cognitive bias Mental shortcut used when thinking about other people or social events.

social-emotional development Systematic changes in emotions, self-concept, motivation, social relationships, and moral reasoning and behavior.

socialization Systematic efforts by other people and institutions to prepare youngsters to act in ways deemed by society to be appropriate and responsible.

society Large, enduring group of people that is socially and economically organized and has collective institutions and activities.

sociocognitive conflict Situation in which one encounters and has to wrestle with ideas and viewpoints of others different from one's own.

sociocultural theory Theoretical perspective that focuses on children's learning of tools, thinking processes, and communication systems through practice in meaningful tasks with other people.

sociodramatic play Play in which children take on specific roles and act out a scenario of imaginary events.

socioeconomic status (SES) One's general standing in an economically stratified society, encompassing family income, type of job, and education level.

sociolinguistic behaviors Types of verbal interactions that are considered socially acceptable in society for a speaker in a particular setting depending on his or her age, gender, status, and familiarity with others.

specific language impairment Disability characterized by abnormalities in producing or understanding spoken language, to the point where special educational services are required.

speech register The style of spoken language used by people who are in similar roles in a community.

spermarche First ejaculation in an adolescent male.

stage theory Theory that describes development as involving a series of qualitatively distinct changes.

stage A period of development characterized by a qualitatively distinct way of behaving or thinking.

Standard English Form of English generally considered acceptable in school (as reflected in textbooks, grammar instruction, etc.) and in other formal institutions by teachers and others.

standardized achievement test Formal assessment of knowledge and skills in carefully defined academic areas that is administered under controlled conditions.

standards Knowledge and skills in academic subjects that are established by public officials as expected targets for achievement by children in a particular grade level.

state of arousal Physiological condition of sleepiness or wakefulness.

stepfamily Family created when one parent–child(ren) group combines with another parent figure and any children in his or her custody.

stereotype threat Reduction in performance (often unintentional) as a result of a belief that one's group typically performs poorly.

stereotype Rigid, simplistic, and erroneous characterization of a particular group.

story schema Knowledge of the typical elements and sequence of a narrative.

stranger anxiety Fear of unfamiliar adults in the latter half of the first year and into the second year of life.

stress Physiological response that is experienced as being worried, tense, and pressured.

structured English immersion Approach to second-language instruction for English language learners in which the children receive intensive lessons in English for a year or so and are then placed in the regular classroom.

subculture Group that resists the ways of the dominant culture and adopts its own norms for behavior.

submersion approach Approach to second-language instruction in which English language learners are placed in the regular classroom and expected to acquire the new language simply through exposure.

substance schema General view of all physical phenomena as being either touchable substances or properties of those substances.

subtractive bilingualism Phenomenon in which immersion in a new-language environment leads to deficits in one's native language.

sudden infant death syndrome (SIDS) Death of an infant in the first year of life, typically during sleep, that cannot be explained by a thorough medical examination; the risk of SIDS is highest between 2 and 4 months of age.

summative assessment Task that is implemented after a unit of instruction or period of time to determine what children have learned.

symbol Mental entity that represents an external object or event, typically without reflecting its perceptual and behavioral qualities.

symbolic thought Ability to mentally represent and think about external objects and events.

sympathy Feeling of sorrow and concern about another's problems or distress.

synapse Junction between two neurons.

synaptic pruning A process in brain development whereby many previously formed synapses wither away, especially if they have not been used frequently.

synaptogenesis A process in brain development whereby many new synapses appear during the first few years of life.

syntax Rules consistently used to put words together into sentences.

telegraphic speech Short, grammatically incomplete sentences that include lexical (rather than grammatical) words almost exclusively; common in toddlers.

temperament A child's characteristic ways of responding to emotional events, novel stimuli, and personal impulses.

teratogen Potentially harmful substance that can cause damaging effects during prenatal development.

test Instrument designed to assess knowledge, abilities, or skills in a consistent fashion across individuals.

theory of mind Awareness that people have an inner, psychological life (thoughts, beliefs, feelings, etc.).

theory theory Theoretical perspective proposing that children construct increasingly integrated and complex understandings of physical and mental phenomena.

theory Integrated collection of principles and explanations regarding a particular phenomenon.

toxic stress Prolonged, elevated stress response to ongoing adversities in the absence of adequate reassurance from caregivers, resulting in diminished abilities to concentrate, remember, and restrain impulses, and culminating in risks for alcohol and substance abuse, cardiovascular disease, and other serious health problems.

traumatic brain injury (TBI) hits or jolts to the head that cause physiological damage, ranging rom a mild concussion to severe head wound, and, depending on severity, affect health and such psychological processes as attention, memory, emotions, learning, and other psychological processes.

underextension Overly restricted meaning for a word that excludes some situations to which the word applies.

uninvolved parenting style Parenting style characterized by a lack of emotional support and a lack of standards regarding appropriate behavior.

universality In a particular aspect of human development, the commonalities seen in the way virtually all individuals progress.

validity Extent to which a data-collection technique actually assesses what the researcher intends for it to assess.

value Belief that a particular activity has direct or indirect benefits.

vicarious punishment Phenomenon in which a child decreases a certain response after seeing someone else punished for that response.

vicarious reinforcement Phenomenon in which a child increases a certain response after seeing someone else reinforced for that response.

visual-spatial ability Ability to imagine and mentally manipulate two- and three-dimensional figures.

wait time The length of time a teacher pauses, after either asking a question or hearing a student's comment, before saying something.

working memory Component of memory that enables people to actively think about and process a small amount of information.

zone of proximal development (ZPD) Range of tasks that one cannot yet perform independently but can perform with the help and guidance of others.

zygote Cell formed when a male sperm fertilizes a female ovum; with reasonably healthy genes and nurturing conditions in the uterus, it may develop into a fetus and be born as a live infant.

Abe, J. A. A. (2005). The predictive validity of the five-factor model of personality with preschool age children: A nine year follow-up study. *Journal of Research in Personality, 39*, 423–442.

Abelev, M. S. (2009). Advancing out of poverty: Social class worldview and its relation to resilience. *Journal of Adolescent Research, 24*(1), 114–141.

Abi-Nader, J. (1993). Meeting the needs of multicultural classrooms: Family values and the motivation of minority students. In M. J. O'Hair & S. J. Odell (Eds.), *Diversity and teaching: Teacher education yearbook I (pp. 212–236)*. Fort Worth, TX: Harcourt Brace Jovanovich.

Abikoff, H., Gallagher, R., Wells, K. C., Murray, D. W., Huang, L., Lu, F., & Petkova, E. (2013). Remediating organizational functioning in children with ADHD: Immediate and long-term effects from a randomized controlled trial. *Journal of Consulting and Clinical Psychology, 81*(1), 113–128. doi:10.1037/a0029648

Abitbol Avtzon, S. (2013). Effect of neuroscience-based cognitive skill training on growth of cognitive deficits associated with learning disabilities in children grades 2–4. *Dissertation Abstracts International Section A, 73.*

Aboud, F. E. (1988). *Children and prejudice.* New York, NY: Basil Blackwell.

Aboud, F. E. (2005). The development of prejudice in childhood and adolescence. In J. F. Dovidio, P. Glick, & L. A. Rudman (Eds.), *On the nature of prejudice: Fifty years after Allport* (pp. 310–326). Malden, MA: Blackwell.

Aboud, F. E., & Fenwick, V. (1999). Exploring and evaluating school-based interventions to reduce prejudice. *Journal of Social Issues, 55*(4), 767–785. doi:10.1111/0022-4537.00146

Aboud, F. E., & Spears Brown, C. (2013). Positive and negative intergroup contact among children and its effect on attitudes. In G. Hodson, M. Hewstone (Eds.), *Advances in intergroup contact* (pp. 176–199). New York, NY: Psychology Press.

Abrahamsson, N. (2012). Age of onset and native-like L2 ultimate attainment of morphosyntactic and phonetic intuition. *Studies in Second Language Acquisition, 34*(2), 187–214. doi:10.1017/S0272263112000022

Abubakar, A., Alonso-Arbiol, I., Van de Vijver, F., Murugami, M., Mazrui, L., & Arasa, J. (2013). Attachment and psychological well-being among adolescents with and without disabilities in Kenya: The mediating role of identity formation. *Journal of Adolescence, 36*(5), 849–857.

Abushaikha, L., & Massah, R. (2013). Perceptions of barriers to paternal presence and contribution during childbirth: An exploratory study from Syria. *Birth: Issues in Perinatal Care, 40*(1), 61–66. doi:10.1111/birt.12030

Acevedo-Polakovich, I., Cousineau, J., Quirk, K., Gerhart, J., Bell, K., & Adomako, M. (2014). Toward an Asset Orientation in the Study of U.S. Latina/o Youth: Biculturalism, Ethnic Identity, and Positive Youth Development Ψ. *Counseling Psychologist, 42*(2), 201-229.

Ackerman, C. M., & Fifield, A. (2005). *Education policy brief: Gifted and talented education.* Retrieved from http://www.rdc.udel.edu/policy_briefs/v19_May.pdf

Ackerman, P. L., & Lohman, D. F. (2006). Individual differences in cognitive functions. In P. A. Alexander & P. H. Winne (Eds.), *Handbook of educational psychology* (2nd ed., pp. 139–161). Mahwah, NJ: Erlbaum.

Ackesjö, H. (2013). Children crossing borders: School visits as initial incorporation rites in transition to preschool class. *International Journal of Early Childhood.* doi:10.1007/s13158-013-0080-7

Acredolo, L. P., & Goodwyn, S. W. (1990). Sign language in babies: The significance of symbolic gesturing for understanding language development. In R. Vasta (Ed.), *Annals of child development: A research annual* (Vol. 7, pp. 1–42). London, England: Jessica Kingsley Publisher.

Adam, E. K. (2004). Beyond quality: Parental and residential stability and children's adjustment. *Current Directions in Psychological Science, 13,* 210–213.

Adam, E. K., Snell, E. K., & Pendry, P. (2007). Sleep timing and quantity in ecological and family context: A nationally representative time-diary study. *Journal of Family Psychology, 21,* 4–19.

Adamović, T. T., Sovilj, M. M., Ribarić-Jankes, K. K., Ljubić, A. A., & Antonović, O. O. (2013). 30. Comparative analysis of reflexes tested in babies immediately after birth. *Clinical Neurophysiology, 124*(7), e16. doi:10.1016/j.clinph.2012.12.039

Adams, B. (2008). Here comes the sun. *Science and Children, 46*(1), 56–58.

Adams-Bass, V., Stevenson, H., & Kotzin, D. (2014). Measuring the meaning of black media stereotypes and their relationship to the racial identity, black history knowledge, and racial socialization of African American youth. *Journal of Black Studies, 45*(5), 367–395.

Adamson, L. B., & McArthur, D. (1995). Joint attention, affect, and culture. In C. Moore & P. J. Dunham (Eds.), *Joint attention: Its origins and role in development* (pp. 205–221). Hillsdale, NJ: Erlbaum.

Adlof, S. M., Catts, H. W., & Lee, J. (2010). Kindergarten predictors of second versus eighth grade reading comprehension impairments. *Journal of Learning Disabilities, 43*(4), 332–345.

Adolph, K. E., & Berger, S. E. (2011). Physical and motor development. In M. H. Bornstein & M. E. Lamb (Eds.), *Cognitive development: An advanced textbook* (pp. 257–318). New York, NY: Psychology Press.

Affenito, S., Thompson, D., Dorazio, A., Albertson, A., Loew, A., & Holschuh, N. (2013). Ready-to-eat cereal consumption and the school breakfast program: Relationship to nutrient intake and weight. *Journal of School Health, 83*(1), 28-35.

Afflerbach, P., Cho, B., Kim, J., Crassas, M., & Doyle, B. (2013). Reading: What else matters besides strategies and skills? *Reading Teacher, 66*(6), 440–448. doi:10.1002/TRTR.1146

Agirdag, O. (2009). All languages welcomed here. *Educational Leadership, 66*(7), 20–25.

Agostino, A., Johnson, J., & Pascual-Leone, J. (2010). Executive functions underlying multiplicative reasoning: Problem type matters. *Journal of Experimental Child Psychology, 105*(4), 286–305.

Ahamed, Y., Macdonald, H., Reed, K., Naylor, P. J., Liu-Ambrose, T., & McKay, H. (2007). School-based physical activity does not compromise children's academic performance. *Medicine and Science in Sports and Exercise, 39*(2), 371–376.

Ahern, A. L., & Hetherington, M. M. (2006). The thin ideal and body image: An experimental study of implicit attitudes. *Psychology of Addictive Behaviors, 20,* 338–342.

Ahmann, E. (2014). Encouraging positive behavior in "challenging" children: The Nurtured Heart Approach™. *Pediatric Nursing, 40*(1), 38–42.

Ahnert, L., Pinquart, M., & Lamb, M. E. (2006). Security of children's relationships with nonparental care providers: A meta-analysis. *Child Development, 74,* 664–679.

Aigner, S., Heckel, T., Zhang, J., Andreae, L., & Jagasia, R. (2014). Human pluripotent stem cell models of autism spectrum disorder: emerging frontiers, opportunities, and challenges towards neuronal networks in a dish. *Psychopharmacology, 231*(6), 1089-1104. doi:10.1007/s00213-013-3332-1

Ainsworth, M. D. S. (1963). The development of infant–mother interaction among the Ganda. In B. M. Foss (Ed.), *Determinants of infant behavior* (Vol. 2, pp. 67–104). New York, NY: Wiley.

Ainsworth, M. D. S. (1973). The development of infant–mother attachment. In B. Caldwell & H. Ricciuti (Eds.), *Review of child development research* (Vol. 3, pp. 1–94). Chicago, IL: University of Chicago Press.

Ainsworth, M. D. S., Blehar, M. C., Waters, E., & Wall, S. (1978). *Patterns of attachment.* Hillsdale, NJ: Erlbaum.

Akbaş, Y., & Gençtürk, E. (2011). The effect of conceptual change approach to eliminate 9th grade high school students' misconceptions about air pressure. *Educational Sciences: Theory & Practice, 11*(4), 2217–2222.

Akiba, D., & García Coll, C. (2003). Effective interventions with children of color and their families: A contextual developmental approach. In T. B. Smith (Ed.), *Practicing multiculturalism: Internalizing and affirming diversity in counseling and psychology* (pp. 148–177). Boston, MA: Allyn & Bacon.

Akiskal, H. S., & McKinney, W. T. (1973). Depressive disorders: Toward a unified hypothesis. *Science, 162,* 20–29.

Al-Yagon, M. (2012). Adolescents with learning disabilities: Socioemotional and behavioral functioning and attachment relationships with fathers, mothers, and teachers. *Journal of Youth and Adolescence, 41*(10), 1294–1311. doi:10.1007/s10964-012-9767-6

Alan Guttmacher Institute (2001). *Can more progress be made? Teenage sexual and reproductive behavior in developed countries.* Retrieved from http://www.guttmacher.org/pubs/summaries/euroteens_summ.pdf

Alanís, I. (2013). Where's your partner? Pairing bilingual learners in preschool and primary grade dual language classrooms. *Young Children, 68*(1), 42-46.

Alarcón-Rubio, D., Sánchez-Medina, J. A., & Prieto-García, J. R. (2014). Executive function and verbal self-regulation in childhood: Developmental linkages between partially internalized private speech and cognitive flexibility. *Early Childhood Research Quarterly, 29*(2), 95–105. doi:10.1016/j.ecresq.2013.11.002

Alber-Morgan, S. (2010). *Using RTI to teach literacy to diverse learners, K–8: Strategies for the inclusive classroom.* Thousand Oaks, CA: Corwin Press.

Alberti, S. (2012). Making the shifts. *Educational Leadership, 70*(4), 24–27.

Alberts, A., Elkind, D., & Ginsberg, S. (2007). The personal fable and risk-taking in early adolescence. *Journal of Youth and Adolescence, 36,* 71–76.

Alderman, M. K. (1990). Motivation for at-risk students. *Educational Leadership, 48*(1), 27–30.

Aldrich, N. J., Tenenbaum, H. R., Brooks, P. J., Harrison, K., & Sines, J. (2011). Perspective taking in children's narratives about jealousy. *British Journal of Developmental Psychology, 29*(1), 86–109. doi:10.1348/026151010X533238

Alesi, M., Rappo, G., & Pepi, A. (2012). Self-esteem at school and self-handicapping in childhood: Comparison of groups with learning disabilities. *Psychological Reports, 111*(3), 952–962. doi:10.2466/15.10 .PR0.111.6.952-962

Alessandri, S. M., & Lewis, M. (1993). Parental evaluation and its relation to shame and pride in young children. *Sex Roles, 29,* 335–343.

Alexander, J. M., Johnson, K. E., Leibham, M. E., & Kelley, K. (2008). The development of conceptual interests in young children. *Cognitive Development, 23,* 324–334.

Alexander, K., Entwisle, D., & Thompson, M. (1987). School performance, status relations, and the structure of sentiment: Bringing the teacher back in. *American Sociological Review, 52,* 665–682.

Alexander, P. A., Graham, S., & Harris, K. R. (1998). A perspective on strategy research: Progress and prospects. *Educational Psychology Review, 10,* 129–154.

Alfassi, M., Weiss, I., & Lifshitz, H. (2009). The efficacy of reciprocal teaching in fostering the reading literacy of students with intellectual disabilities. *European Journal of Special Needs Education, 24*(3), 291–305.

Alferink, L. A., & Farmer-Dougan, V. (2010). Brain-(not) based education: Dangers of misunderstanding and misapplication of neuroscience research. *Exceptionality, 18*(1), 42-52. doi:10.1080/09362830903462573

Algood, C. L., Harris, C., & Hong, J. (2013). Parenting success and challenges for families of children with disabilities: An ecological systems analysis. *Journal of Human Behavior in the Social Environment, 23*(2), 126–136.

Algozzine, B., Babb, J., Algozzine, K., Mraz, M., Kissel, B., Spano, S., & Foxworth, K. (2011). Classroom effects of an Early Childhood Educator Professional Development Partnership. *NHSA Dialog, 14*(4), 246–262.

Alhaqbani, A., & Riazi, M. (2012). Metacognitive awareness of reading strategy use in Arabic as a second language. *Reading in a Foreign Language, 24*(2), 231–255.

Alison, J., Negley, S., & Sibthorp, J. (2013). Assessing the social effect of therapeutic recreation summer camp for adolescents with chronic illness. *Therapeutic Recreation Journal, 47*(1), 35-46.

Alland, A. (1983). *Playing with form.* New York, NY: Columbia University Press.

Alliance for Childhood. (2010). *Alliance warning: Core standards may lead to a plague of kindergarten tests.* Retrieved from http://www.allianceforchildhood.org/sites/allianceforchildhood.org/files/file/Core_Standards_06_08.pdf

Allison, V., Nativio, D., Mitchell, A., Ren, D., & Yuhasz, J. (2014). Identifying symptoms of depression and anxiety in students in the school setting. *Journal of School Nursing (Sage Publications Inc.), 30*(3), 165–172. doi:10.1177/1059840513500076

Allodi, M. W. (2010). Goals and values in school: A model developed for describing, evaluating and changing the social climate of learning environments. *Social Psychology of Education, 13*(2), 207–235. doi:10.1007/s11218-009-9110-6

Allport, G. W. (1954). *The nature of prejudice.* Reading, MA: Addison-Wesley.

Altenhofen, S., Clyman, R., Little, C., Baker, M., & Biringen, Z. (2013). Attachment security in three-year-olds who entered substitute care in infancy. *Infant Mental Health Journal, 34*(5), 435–445. doi:10.1002/imhj.21401

Altenhofen, S., Clyman, R., Little, C., Baker, M., & Biringen, Z. (2013). Attachment security in three-year-olds who entered substitute care in infancy. *Infant Mental Health Journal, 34*(5), 435–445. doi:10.1002/imhj.21401

Alter, A. L., Aronson, J., Darley, J. M., Rodriguez, C., & Ruble, D. N. (2010). Rising to the threat: Reducing stereotype threat by reframing the threat as a challenge. *Journal of Experimental Social Psychology, 46*(1), 166–171. doi:10.1016/j.jesp.2009.09.014

Altermatt, E. R., & Broady, E. F. (2009). Coping with achievement-related failure: An examination of conversations between friends. *Merrill-Palmer Quarterly 55*(4), 454–487.

Alvarez, A. L., & Booth, A. E. (2014). Motivated by meaning: Testing the effect of knowledge-infused rewards on preschoolers' persistence. *Child Development, 85*(2), 783–791. doi:10.1111/cdev.12151

Alvarez, C., Salavati, S., Nussbaum, M., & Milrad, M. (2013). Collboard: Fostering new media literacies in the classroom through collaborative problem solving supported by digital pens and interactive whiteboards. *Computers & Education, 63,* 368–379. doi:10.1016/j.compedu.2012.12.019

Alvermann, D. E., & Moore, D. W. (1991). Secondary school reading. In R. Barr, M. L. Kamil, P. B. Mosenthal, & P. D. Pearson (Eds.), *Handbook of reading research* (Vol. II, pp. 951–983). New York, NY: Longman.

Aman, M. G., McDougle, C. J., Scahill, L., Handen, B., Arnold, L. E. A., Johnson, C., et al. (2009). Medication and parent training in children with pervasive developmental disorders and serious behavior problems: Results from a randomized clinical trial. *Journal of the American Academy of Child & Adolescent Psychiatry, 48*(12), 1143–1154.

Ambrose, D., Allen, J., & Huntley, S. B. (1994). Mentorship of the highly creative. *Roeper Review, 17,* 131–133.

American Academy of Pediatrics Committee on Pediatric AIDS and Committee on Infectious Diseases. (1999). Issues related to human immunodeficiency virus transmission in schools, child care, medical settings, home, and community. *Pediatrics, 104,* 318–324.

American Academy of Pediatrics Committee on Sports Medicine and Fitness. (2000). Intensive training and sports specialization in young athletes. *Pediatrics, 106,* 154–157.

American Academy of Pediatrics Task Force on Infant Sleep Position and Sudden Infant Death Syndrome. (2000). Changing concepts of sudden infant death syndrome: Implications for infant sleeping environment and sleep position. *Pediatrics, 105,* 650–656.

American Association on Intellectual and Developmental Disabilities. (2013). *Definition of intellectual disability.* Retrieved from http://aaidd.org/intellectual-disability/definition#.UsEC9mRDtsg

American Educational Research Association. (2000). *Position on high-stakes testing.* Retrieved from http://www.aera.net/AboutAERA/AERARulesPolicies/AERAPolicyStatements/PositionStatementonHighStakesTesting/tabid/11083/Default.aspx

AmericanPregnancyAssociation.(2013a).*Ultrasound: Sonogram.* Retrieved from http://americanpregnancy.org/prenataltesting/ultrasound.html

American Pregnancy Association. (2013b). Childbirth education classes. Retrieved from http://americanpregnancy.org/labornbirth/childbirtheducation.html

American Psychiatric Association, DSM-5 Task Force. (2013). *Diagnostic and statistical manual of mental disorders: DSM-5™* (5th ed.). Arlington, VA: American Psychiatric Publishing, Inc.

American Psychiatric Association. (1994). *Diagnostic and statistical manual of mental disorders* (4th ed.). Washington, DC: Author.

American Psychiatric Association. (2000). *Diagnostic and statistical manual of mental disorders* (4th ed., text rev.). Washington, DC: Author.

American Psychiatric Association. (2013). *Desk reference to the diagnostic criteria from DSM-5.* Arlington, VA: American Psychiatric Publishers Inc.

American Psychological Association. (2002). Ethical principles of psychologists and code of conduct. *American Psychologist, 57,* 1060–1073.

American Speech-Language-Hearing Association. (1993). Definitions of communication disorders and variations. *ASHA, 35*(Suppl. 10), 40–41.

American Teacher. (2012). Testing integrity policy points to "a system problem." *American Teacher, 96*(3), 6.

Ames, C. (1984). Competitive, cooperative, and individualistic goal structures: A cognitive-motivational analysis. In R. Ames & C. Ames (Eds.), *Research on motivation in education: Vol. 1. Student motivation* (pp. 177–207). San Diego, CA: Academic Press.

Ames, C. (1992). Classrooms: Goals, structures, and student motivation. *Journal of Educational Psychology, 84,* 261–271.

Anaby, D., Hand, C., Bradley, L., DiRezze, B., Forhan, M., DiGiacomo, A., & Law, M. (2013). The effect of the environment on participation of children and youth with disabilities: A scoping review. *Disability and Rehabilitation: An International, Multidisciplinary Journal, 35*(19), 1589–1598. doi: 10.3109/09638288.2012.748840

Anastasi, A., & Urbina, S. (1997). *Psychological testing* (7th ed.). Upper Saddle River, NJ: Prentice Hall.

Anderman, E. M. (2012). Adolescence. In K. R. Harris, S. Graham, T. Urdan, A. G. Bus, S. Major, & H. L. Swanson (Eds.), *APA educational psychology handbook, Vol. 3: Application to teaching and learning* (pp. 43–61). Washington, DC: American Psychological Association. doi:10.1037/13275-003

Anderman, E. M., & Maehr, M. L. (1994). Motivation and schooling in the middle grades. *Review of Educational Research, 64,* 287–309.

Anderman, L. H., Patrick, H., Hruda, L. Z., & Linnenbrink, E. A. (2002). Observing classroom goal structures to clarify and expand goal theory. In C. Midgley (Ed.), *Goals, goal structures, and patterns of adaptive learning* (pp. 243–278). Mahwah, NJ: Erlbaum.

Anderson, C. A., Berkowitz, L., Donnerstein, E., Huesmann, L. R., Johnson, J. D., Linz, D., et al. (2003). The influence of media violence on youth. *Psychological Science in the Public Interest, 4,* 81–110.

Anderson, C. A., Berkowitz, L., Donnerstein, E., Huesmann, L. R., Johnson, J. D., Linz, D., et al. (2003). The influence of media violence on youth. *Psychological Science in the Public Interest, 4,* 81–110.

Anderson, C. L., & Brown, C. E. L. (2009). Fetal abnormalities: Antenatal screening and diagnosis. *American Family Physician, 79*(2), 117–123.

Anderson, D. A. (1994). Lesbian and gay adolescents: Social and developmental considerations. *The High School Journal, 77* (1,2), 13–19.

Anderson, D. R. (2003). The Children's Television Act: A public policy that benefits children. *Applied Developmental Psychology, 24,* 337–340.

Anderson, E. K. Jr. (2013). The experiences of teachers serving learning disabled students in special education: A phenomenological study. *Dissertation Abstracts International, 73.*

Anderson, E. R., & Greene, S. M. (2013). Beyond divorce: Research on children in repartnered and remarried families. *Family Court Review, 51*(1), 119–130. doi:10.1111/fcre.12013

Anderson, G., Spainhower, A., & Sharp, A. (2014). "Where do the bears go?" The value of child-directed play. *Young Children, 69*(2), 8–14.

Anderson, J. (2014). What writing is & isn't. *Educational Leadership, 71*(7), 10–14.

Anderson, J. C. (1983). *The architecture of cognition.* Cambridge, MA: Harvard University Press.

Anderson, J., Ellefson, J., Lashley, J., Miller, A., Olinger, S., Russell, A., Stouffer, J. & Weigman, J. (2010). The Cornerhouse forensic interview protocol: RATAC. *Thomas M. Cooley Journal of Practical & Clinical Law, 12*(2), 193–331.

Anderson, K. E., Lytton, H., & Romney, D. M. (1986). Mothers' interactions with normal and conduct-disordered boys: Who affects whom? *Developmental Psychology, 22,* 604–609.

Anderson, L. W., & Pellicer, L. O. (1998). Toward an understanding of unusually successful programs for economically disadvantaged students. *Journal of Education for Students Placed at Risk, 3,* 237–263.

Anderson, R. C., Nguyen-Jahiel, K., McNurlen, B., Archodidou, A., Kim, S.-Y., Reznitskaya, A., et al. (2001). The snowball phenomenon: Spread of ways of talking and ways of thinking across groups of children. *Cognition and Instruction, 19,* 1–46.

Anderson, R. C., Shirey, L., Wilson, P., & Fielding, L. (1987). Interestingness of children's reading materials. In R. Snow & M. Farr (Eds.), *Aptitude, learning, and instruction: III. Cognitive and affective process analyses* (pp. 287–299). Hillsdale, NJ: Erlbaum.

Andrade, H. L., Wang, X., Du, Y., & Akawi, R. L. (2009). Rubric-referenced self-assessment and self-efficacy for writing. *Journal of Educational Research, 102*(4), 287–301. doi:10.3200/JOER.102.4.287-302

Andreouli, E., Howarth, C., & Sonn, C. (2014). The role of schools in promoting inclusive communities in contexts of diversity. *Journal of Health Psychology, 19*(1), 16–21.

Andrews, J. F., & Mason, J. M. (1986). Childhood deafness and the acquisition of print concepts. In D. B. Yaden, Jr., & S. Templeton (Eds.), *Metalinguistic awareness and beginning literacy: Conceptualizing what it means to read and write* (pp. 277–290). Portsmouth, NH: Heinemann.

Andriessen, J. (2006). Arguing to learn. In R. K. Sawyer (Ed.), *The Cambridge handbook of the learning sciences* (pp. 443–459). Cambridge, England: Cambridge University Press.

Aneni, E. C., Hamer, D. H., & Gill, C. J. (2013). Systematic review of current and emerging strategies for reducing morbidity from malaria in sickle cell disease. *Tropical Medicine & International Health, 18*(3), 313–327. doi:10.1111/tmi.12056

Ang, S., Rodgers, J., & Wänström, L. (2010). The Flynn effect within subgroups in the U.S.: Gender, race, income, education, and urbanization differences in the NLSY-Children data. *Intelligence, 38*(4), 367–384.

Anglin, J. M. (1977). *Word, object, and conceptual development.* New York, NY: Norton.

Anjum, A., Gait, P., Cullen, K. R., & White, T. (2010). Schizophrenia in adolescents and young adults. In J. E. Grant & M. N. Potenza (Eds.), *Young adult mental health* (pp. 362–378). New York, NY: Oxford University Press.

Annetta, L. A. (2010). The "I's" have it: A framework for serious educational game design. Review of General Psychology, 14(2), 105–112. doi:10.1037/a0018985

Ansalone, G. (2006). Perceptions of ability and equity in the U.S. and Japan: Understanding the pervasiveness of tracking. *Radical Pedagogy, 8*(1), 1-1.

Anschutz, D., Engels, R., Van Leeuwe, J., & Van Strien, T. (2009). Watching your weight? The relations between watching soaps & music television and body dissatisfaction and restrained eating in young girls. *Psychology & Health, 24*(9), 1035–1050. doi:10.1080/08870440802192268

Anthony, J. L., & Francis, D. J. (2005). Development of phonological awareness. *Current Directions in Psychological Science, 14,* 255–259.

Anthony, J. L., Lonigan, C. J., & Dyer, S. M. (1996, April). *The development of reading comprehension: Listening comprehension or basic language processes?* Paper presented at the annual meeting of the American Educational Research Association, New York.

Anticich, S. J., Barrett, P. M., Silverman, W., Lacherez, P., & Gillies, R. (2013). The prevention of childhood anxiety and promotion of resilience among preschool-aged children: A universal school based trial. *Advances in School Mental Health Promotion, 6*(2), 93–121. doi:10.1080/1754730X.2013.784616

Anyon, J. (1988). Social class and the hidden curriculum of work. In G. Handel (Ed.), *Childhood socialization* (pp. 357–382). New York, NY: Aldine de Gruyter.

Apavaloaie, L., Page, T., & Marks, L. D. (2014). Romanian children's representations of negative and self-conscious emotions in a narrative story. *Europe's Journal of Psychology, 10*(2), 318–335. doi:10.5964/ejop.v10i2.704

Aram, D., Korat, O., & Hassunah-Arafat, S. (2013). The contribution of early home literacy activities to first grade reading and writing achievements in Arabic. *Reading & Writing, 26*(9), 1517–1536. doi:10.1007/s11145-013-9430-y

Arbib, M. (Ed.). (2005). *Action to language via the mirror neuron system.* New York, NY: Cambridge University Press.

Archer, S. L., & Curtin, S. (2011). Perceiving onset clusters in infancy. *Infant Behavior & Development, 34*(4), 534–540. doi:10.1016/j.infbeh.2011.07.001

Arcus, D. M. (1991). *Experiential modification of temperamental bias in inhibited and uninhibited children.* Unpublished doctoral dissertation, Harvard University, Cambridge, MA.

Arcus, D. M. (2001). Inhibited and uninhibited children: Biology in the social context. In T. D. Wachs & G. A. Kohnstamm (Eds.), *Temperament in context* (pp. 43–60). Mahwah, NJ: Erlbaum.

Ardila-Rey, A., & Killen, M. (2001). Middle class Colombian children's evaluations of personal, moral, and social-conventional interactions in the classroom. *International Journal of Behavioral Development, 25*(3), 246–255. doi:10.1080/01650250042000221

Ardila-Rey, A., Killen, M., & Brenick, A. (2009). Moral reasoning in violent contexts: Displaced and non-displaced Colombian children's evaluations of moral transgressions, retaliation, and reconciliation. *Social Development, 18*(1), 181–209. doi:10.1111/j.1467-9507.2008.00483.x

Armstrong, T. (2009). *Multiple intelligences in the classroom.* Alexandria, VA: Association for Supervision and Curriculum Development.

Arndt, T. L., Stodgell, C. J., & Rodier, P. M. (2005). The teratology of autism. *International Journal of Developmental Neuroscience, 23,* 189–199.

Arnett, J. J. (1999). Adolescent storm and stress, reconsidered. *American Psychologist, 54,* 317–326.

Arnold, M. L. (2000). Stage, sequence, and sequels: Changing conceptions of morality, post-Kohlberg. *Educational Psychology Review, 12,* 365–383.

Aronson, S. R., & Huston, A. C. (2004). The mother-infant relationship in single, cohabiting, and married families: A case for marriage? *Journal of Family Psychology, 18,* 5–18.

Arsenio, W. F., & Lemerise, E. A. (2010). Introduction. In W. F. Arsenio & E. A. Lemerise (Eds.), *Emotions, aggression, and morality in children: Bridging development and psychopathology* (pp. 3–9). Washington, DC: American Psychological Association.

Artman, L., & Cahan, S. (1993). Schooling and the development of transitive inference. *Developmental Psychology, 29,* 753–759.

Artz, S., Kassis, W., & Moldenhauer, S. (2013). Rethinking indirect aggression: The end of the mean girl myth. *Victims & Offenders, 8*(3), 308–328. doi:10.1080/15564886.2012.756842

Asai, S. (1993). In search of Asia through music: Guidelines and ideas for teaching Asian music. In T. Perry & J. W. Fraser (Eds.), *Freedom's plow: Teaching in the multicultural classroom.* New York, NY: Routledge.

Asbury, K., & Plomin, R. (2014). *G is for genes: the impact of genetics on education and achievement.* Chichester, West Sussex, England: John Wiley & Sons.

ASCD. (2014). Double take: The writing standards—and evidence-based practices. *Educational Leadership, 71*(7), 8.

ASCD. (n.d). *A whole child approach to education and the Common Core State Standards initiative.* Retrieved from http://www.ascd.org/ASCD/pdf/siteASCD/policy/CCSS-and-Whole-Child-one-pager.pdf

Ashburner, J., Bennett, L., Rodger, S., & Ziviani, J. (2013). Understanding the sensory experiences of young people with autism spectrum disorder: A preliminary investigation. *Australian Occupational Therapy Journal, 60*(3), 171–180. doi:10.1111/1440-1630.12025

Ashburner, J., Ziviani, J., & Pennington, A. (2012). The Introduction of keyboarding to children with autism spectrum disorders with handwriting difficulties: A help or a hindrance? *Australasian Journal of Special Education, 36*(1), 32–61. doi:10.1017/jse.2012.6

Asher, S. R., & Coie, J. D. (Eds.). (1990). *Peer rejection in childhood.* Cambridge, England: Cambridge University Press.

Asher, S. R., & Parker, J. G. (1989). Significance of peer relationship problems in childhood. In B. H. Schneider, G. Attili, J. Nadel, & R. P. Weissberg (Eds.), *Social competence in developmental perspective.* Dordrecht, The Netherlands: Kluwer.

Asher, S. R., & Renshaw, P. D. (1981). Children without friends: Social knowledge and social skill training. In S. R. Asher & J. M. Gottman (Eds.), *The development of children's friendships* (pp. 273–296). Cambridge, England: Cambridge University Press.

Ashkenazi, S., Black, J. M., Abrams, D. A., Hoeft, F., & Menon, V. (2013). Neurobiological underpinnings of math and reading learning disabilities. *Journal of Learning Disabilities, 46*(6), 549–569.

Ashmore, R., & DelBoca, F. (1976). Psychological approaches. In P. A. Katz (Ed.), *Elimination of racism (pp. 73–123).* New York, NY: Pergamon.

Ashton, P. (1985). Motivation and the teacher's sense of efficacy. In C. Ames & R. Ames (Eds.), *Research on motivation in education: Vol. 2. The classroom milieu (pp. 141-174).* Orlando, FL: Academic Press.

Aslin, R. N. (2014). Infant learning: Historical, conceptual, and methodological challenges. *Infancy, 19*(1), 2–27. doi:10.1111/infa.12036

Aslin, R. N., Saffran, J. R., & Newport, E. L. (1998). Computation of conditional probability statistics by 8-month-old infants. *Psychological Science, 9,* 321–324.

Association for Childhood Education International. (2009). *Preparation of elementary teachers.* ACEI position paper. Retrieved from http://www.acei.org/prepel.htm

Association for Middle Level Education. (2011). *Study guide for This We Believe: Keys to educating young adolescents.* Retrieved from http://www.amle.org/AboutAMLE/ThisWeBelieve/tabid/1273/Default.aspx

Association for Supervision and Curriculum Development. (2013). *The whole child.* Retrieved from http://www.ascd.org/whole-child.aspx

Assor, A., & Connell, J. P. (1992). The validity of students' self-reports as measures of performance affecting self-appraisals. In D. H. Schunk & J. L. Meece (Eds.), *Student perceptions in the classroom (pp. 25–47).* Hillsdale, NJ: Erlbaum.

Astington, J. W. (1991). Intention in the child's theory of mind. In C. Moore & D. Frye (Eds.), *Children's theories of mind* (pp. 157–172). Hillsdale, NJ: Erlbaum.

Astington, J. W., & Pelletier, J. (1996). The language of mind: Its role in teaching and learning. In D. R. Olson & N. Torrance (Eds.), *The handbook of education and human development: New models of learning, teaching and schooling* (pp. 593–619). Cambridge, MA: Blackwell.

Atkinson, J., & Braddick, O. (2012). Visual attention in the first years: Typical development and developmental disorders. *Developmental Medicine & Child Neurology, 54*(7), 589–595. doi:10.1111/j.1469-8749.2012.04294.x

Atkinson, M. (1992). *Children's syntax: An introduction to principles and parameters theory.* Oxford, England: Blackwell.

Atkinson, R. C., & Shiffrin, R. M. (1968). Human memory: A proposed system and its control processes. In K. Spence & J. Spence (Eds.), *The psychology of learning and motivation* (Vol. 2, pp. 89–195). New York, NY: Academic Press.

Attie, I., Brooks-Gunn, J., & Petersen, A. (1990). A developmental perspective on eating disorders and eating problems. In M. Lewis & S. M. Miller (Eds.), *Handbook of developmental psychopathology* (pp. 409–420). New York, NY: Plenum Press.

Atun-Einy, O., Berger, S., & Scher, A. (2013). Assessing motivation to move and its relationship to motor development in infancy. *Infant Behavior & Development, 36*(3), 457–469. doi:10.1016/j.infbeh.2013.03.006

Au, T. K., & Glusman, M. (1990). The principle of mutual exclusivity in word learning: To honor or not to honor? *Child Development, 61,* 1474–1490.

Au, T. K.-F., Chan, C. K. K., Chan, T.-K., Cheung, M. W. L., Ho, J. Y. S., & Ip, G. W. M. (2008). Folkbiology meets microbiology: A study of conceptual and behavioral change. *Cognitive Psychology, 57,* 1–19.

Auger, R. W. (2013). Autism spectrum disorders: A research review for school counselors. *Professional School Counseling, 16*(4), 256–268.

Augustine, E., Smith, L. B., & Jones, S. S. (2011). Parts and relations in young children's shape-based object recognition. *Journal of Cognition & Development, 12*(4), 556–572. doi:10.1080/15248372.2011.560586

Austeng, M., Akre, H., Falkenberg, E., Øverland, B., Abdelnoor, M., & Kværner, K. (2013). Hearing level in children with Down syndrome at the age of eight. *Research In Developmental Disabilities, 34*(7), 2251–2256. doi:10.1016/j.ridd.2013.04.006

Auster, C. J., & Mansbach, C. S. (2012). The gender marketing of toys: An analysis of color and type of toy on the Disney store website. *Sex Roles, 67*(7–8), 375–388. doi:10.1007/s11199-012-0177-8

Austin, J. L., & Bevan, D. (2011). Using differential reinforcement of low rates to reduce children's requests for teacher attention. *Journal of Applied Behavior Analysis, 44*(3), 451–461. PsycINFO, EBSCO*host.*

Austin, J., Blume, M., & Sánchez, L. (2013). Syntactic development in the L1 of Spanish-English bilingual children. *Hispania, 96*(3), 542–561. doi:10.1353/hpn.2013.0091

Austin, S. B., Ziyadeh, N. J., Forman, S., Prokop, L. A., Keliher, A., & Jacobs, D. (2008). Screening high school students for eating disorders: Results of a national initiative. *Preventing Chronic Disease, 5*(4). Retrieved from http://www.cdc.gov/pcd/issues/2008/oct/07_0164.htm

Austin, W. G. (2012). Relocation, research, and child custody disputes. In K. Kuehnle & L. Drozd (Eds.), *Parenting plan evaluations: Applied research for the family court* (pp. 540-559). New York, NY: Oxford University Press.

Averill, R., Anderson, D., Easton, H., Te Maro, P., Smith, D., & Hynds, A. (2009). Culturally responsive teaching of mathematics: Three models from

linked studies. *Journal for Research in Mathematics Education, 40*(2), 157–186.

Awramiuk, E. (2014). Invented spelling—a window on early literacy. *EDUKACJA Quarterly, 130*(5), 112–123.

Ayoub, C. C. (2006). Adaptive and maladaptive parenting: Influence on child development. In H. E. Fitzgerald, R. Zucker, & K. Freeark (Eds. in Chief), & N. F. Watt, C. Ayoub, R. H. Bradley, J. E. Puma, & W. A. LeBouef (Vol. Eds.), *The crisis in youth mental health: Critical issues and effective programs: Vol. 1. Early intervention programs and policies* (pp. 121–413). Westport, CT: Praeger.

Azzam, A. M. (2009/2010). Finding our way back to healthy eating: A conversation with David A. Kessler. *Educational Leadership, 67*(4), 6–10.

Bøttcher, L., & Dammeyer, J. (2012). Disability as a dialectical concept: Building on Vygotsky defectology. *European Journal of Special Needs Education, 27*(4), 433–446. doi:10.1080/08856257.2012.711958

Babkie, A. M., & Provost, M. C. (2002). 20 ways to—select, write, and use metacognitive strategies in the classroom. *Intervention in School & Clinic, 37*(3), 173-177. doi:10.1177/105345120203700307

Baddeley, A. (1981). The concept of working memory: A view of its current state and probable future development. *Cognition, 10*(1–3), 17–23.

Bagnato, S. J., McLean, M., Macy, M., & Neisworth, J. T. (2011). Identifying instructional targets for early childhood via authentic assessment: Alignment of professional standards and practice-based evidence. *Journal of Early Intervention, 33*(4), 243–253. doi:10.1177/1053815111427565

Bailey, D. H., Littlefield, A., & Geary, D. C. (2012). The codevelopment of skill at and preference for use of retrieval-based processes for solving addition problems: Individual and sex differences from first to sixth grades. *Journal of Experimental Child Psychology, 113*(1), 78–92. doi:10.1016/j.jecp.2012.04.014

Bailey, J. A., Hill, K. G., Guttmannova, K., Oesterle, S., Hawkins, J., Catalano, R. F., & McMahon, R. J. (2013). The association between parent early adult drug use disorder and later observed parenting practices and child behavior problems: Testing alternate models. *Developmental Psychology, 49*(5), 887–899. doi:10.1037/a0029235

Bailey, J. M., Dunne, M. P., & Martin, N. G. (2000). Genetic and environmental influences on sexual orientation and its correlates in an Australian twin sample. *Journal of Personality and Social Psychology, 78,* 524–536.

Baillargeon, R. (1994). How do infants learn about the physical world? *Current Directions in Psychological Science, 3,* 133–140.

Baillargeon, R. (2004). Infants' physical worlds. *Current Directions in Psychological Science, 13,* 89–94.

Baillargeon, R. H., Morisset, A., Keenan, K., Normand, C. L., Jeyaganth, S., Boivin, M., & Tremblay, R. E. (2011). The development of prosocial behaviors in young children: A prospective population-based cohort study. *The Journal of Genetic Psychology: Research and Theory on Human Development, 172*(3), 221–251. doi:10.1080/00221325.2010.533719

Baird, A. A. (2010). The terrible twelves. In P. D. Zelazo, M. Chandler, & E. Crone (Eds.), *Developmental social cognitive neuroscience. The Jean Piaget symposium series* (pp. 191–207). New York, NY: Psychology Press.

Baird, J. A., & Astington, J. W. (2005). The development of the intention concept: From the observable world to the unobservable mind. In R. R. Hassin, J. S. Uleman, & J. A. Bargh (Eds.), *The new unconscious* (pp. 256–276). New York, NY: Oxford University Press.

Bakari, R. (2000). *The development and validation of an instrument to measure preservice teachers'*

attitudes toward teaching African American students. Unpublished doctoral dissertation, University of Northern Colorado, Greeley.

Bakeman, R., & Brownlee, J. R. (1980). The strategic use of parallel play: A sequential analysis. *Child Development, 51,* 873–878.

Baker, C. (1993). *Foundations of bilingual education and bilingualism.* Clevedon, England: Multilingual Matters.

Baker, E., Shelton, K. H., Baibazarova, E., Hay, D. F., & van Goozen, S. M. (2013). Low skin conductance activity in infancy predicts aggression in toddlers 2 years later. *Psychological Science (Sage Publications Inc.), 24*(6), 1051–1056. doi:10.1177/0956797612465198

Baker, F. S. (2013). Making the quiet population of internationally adopted children heard through well-informed teacher preparation. *Early Child Development and Care, 183*(2), 223–246. doi:10.1080/03004430.2012.669757

Baker, F. W. (2010). Media literacy: 21st century literacy skills. In H. H. Jacobs (Ed.), *Curriculum 21: Essential education for a changing world* (pp. 133–152). Alexandria, VA: Association for Supervision and Curriculum Development.

Baker, L., Scher, D., & Mackler, K. (1997). Home and family influences on motivations for reading. *Educational Psychologist, 32,* 69–82.

Baker, R. K., & White, K. M. (2010). Predicting adolescents' use of social networking sites from an extended theory of planned behaviour perspective. *Computers in Human Behavior, 26*(6), 1591–1597.

Bakermans-Kranenburg, M. J., van IJzendoorn, M. H., & Juffer, F. (2003). Less is more: Meta-analyses of sensitivity and attachment interventions in early childhood. *Psychological Bulletin, 129,* 195–215.

Baldwin, D. A. (1993). Early referential understanding: Infants' ability to recognize referential acts for what they are. *Developmental Psychology, 29,* 832–843.

Baldwin, M. W., Keelan, J. P. R., Fehr, B., Enns, V., & Koh-Rangarajoo, E. (1996). Social-cognitive conceptualization of attachment working models: Availability and accessibility effects. *Journal of Personality and Social Psychology, 71,* 94–109.

Bale, C., & Archer, J. (2013). Self-perceived attractiveness, romantic desirability and self-esteem: A mating sociometer perspective. *Evolutionary Psychology, 11*(1), 68–84.

Balkan, M., Kalkanli, S., Akbas, H., Yalinkaya, A., Alp, M., & Budak, T. (2010). Parental decisions regarding a prenatally detected fetal chromosomal abnormality and the impact of genetic counseling: An analysis of 38 cases with aneuploidy in Southeast Turkey. *Journal of Genetic Counseling, 19*(3), 241–246. doi:10.1007/s10897-009-9275-3

Ball, J. W., Bindler, R. C., & Cowen, K. J. (2010). *Child health nursing: Partnering with children and families* (2nd ed.). Upper Saddle River, NJ: Pearson Education.

Ball, L. C., Cribbie, R. A., & Steele, J. R. (2013). Beyond gender differences: Using tests of equivalence to evaluate gender similarities. *Psychology of Women Quarterly, 37*(2), 147–154. doi:10.1177/0361684313480483

Balog, H. (2010). A comparison of maternal and child intonation: Does adult input support child production? *Infant Behavior & Development, 33*(3), 337–345.

Baltes, P. B. (1997). On the incomplete architecture of human ontogeny: Selection, optimization, and compensation as a foundation of developmental theory. *American Psychologist, 52,* 366–380.

Baltes, P. B., Lindenberger, U., & Staudinger, U. M. (2006). Life span theory in developmental psychology. In W. Damon & R. M. Lerner (Eds. in Chief) & R. M. Lerner (Vol. Ed.), *Handbook of child psychology: Vol. 1. Theoretical models of human development* (6th ed., pp. 569–664). Hoboken, NJ: Wiley.

Bandura, A. (1965). Influence of models' reinforcement contingencies on the acquisition of imitative responses. *Journal of Personality and Social Psychology, 1,* 589–595.

Bandura, A. (1977). *Social learning theory.* Englewood Cliffs, NJ: Prentice Hall.

Bandura, A. (1986). *Social foundations of thought and action: A social cognitive theory.* Englewood Cliffs, NJ: Prentice-Hall, Inc.

Bandura, A. (1997). *Self-efficacy: The exercise of control.* New York, NY: Freeman.

Bandura, A. (2006). Toward a psychology of human agency. *Perspectives on Psychological Science, 1,* 164–180.

Bandura, A. (2012). On the functional properties of perceived self-efficacy revisited. *Journal of Management, 38*(1), 9–44. doi:10.1177/0149206311410606

Bandura, A. (2012). Social cognitive theory. In P. M. Van Lange, A. W. Kruglanski, & E. Higgins (Eds.), *Handbook of theories of social psychology* (Vol. 1, pp. 349–373). Thousand Oaks, CA: Sage Publications Ltd.

Bandura, A., & Mischel, W. (1965). Modification of self-imposed delay of reward through exposure to live and symbolic models. *Journal of Personality and Social Psychology, 2,* 698–705.

Bandura, A., Barbaranelli, C., Caprara, G. V., & Pastorelli, C. (2001). Self-efficacy beliefs as shapers of children's aspirations and career trajectories. *Child Development, 72,* 187–206.

Banich, M. (2010, April). *The development of executive function during adolescence: Empirical findings and implications for the law.* Paper presented at the annual meeting of the Rocky Mountain Psychological Association, Denver.

Banks, J. A. (1994). *An introduction to multicultural education.* Needham Heights, MA: Allyn & Bacon.

Banks, J. A., & Banks, C. A. M. (Eds.). (1995). *Handbook of research on multicultural education.* New York, NY: Macmillan.

Bannister, E. M., Jakubec, S. L., & Stein, J. A. (2003). "Like, what am I supposed to do?": Adolescents' health concerns in their dating relationships. *Canadian Journal of Nursing Research, 35*(2), 16–33.

Barab, S. A., & Plucker, J. A. (2002). Smart people or smart contexts? Cognition, ability, and talent development in an age of situated approaches to knowing and learning. *Educational Psychologist, 37,* 165–182.

Baraldi, C., & Iervese, V. (2010). Dialogic mediation in conflict resolution education. *Conflict Resolution Quarterly, 27*(4), 423–445. doi:10.1002/crq.20005

Baranowski, T., Baranowski, J., Thompson, D., Buday, R., Jago, R., Griffith, M. J., et al. (2011). Video game play, child diet, and physical activity behavior change: A randomized clinical trial. *American Journal of Preventive Medicine, 40*(1), 33–38. doi:10.1016/j.amepre.2010.09.029

Barber, J. G., & Delfabbro, P. H. (2004). *Children in foster care.* New York, NY: Routledge.

Barga, N. K. (1996). Students with learning disabilities in education: Managing a disability. *Journal of Learning Disabilities, 29,* 413–421.

Barkatsas, A., Kasimatis, K., & Gialamas, V. (2009). Learning secondary mathematics with technology: Exploring the complex interrelationship between students' attitudes, engagement, gender and achievement. *Computers & Education, 52*(3), 562–570.

Barker, C. E., Bird, C. E., Pradhan, A., & Shakya, G. (2007). Support to the Safe Motherhood Programme in Nepal: An integrated approach. *Reproductive Health Matters, 15*(30), 1–10.

Barkley, R. A. (1998). *Attention-deficit hyperactivity disorder: A handbook for diagnosis and treatment* (2nd ed.). New York, NY: Guilford Press.

Barlow, K. (2010). Sharing food, sharing values: Mothering and empathy in Murik society. *Ethos, 38*(4), 339–353. doi:10.1111/j.1548-1352.2010.01154.x

Barnas, M. V., & Cummings, E. M. (1994). Caregiver stability and toddlers' attachment-related behaviors towards caregivers in day care. *Infant Behavior and Development, 17,* 141–147.

Barnes, J. S., & Spray, C. M. (2013). Social comparison in physical education: An examination of the relationship between two frames of reference and engagement, disaffection, and physical self-concept. *Psychology in the Schools, 50*(10), 1060–1072. doi:10.1002/pits.21726'

Barnett, J. E. (2001, April). *Study strategies and preparing for exams: A survey of middle and high school students.* Paper presented at the annual meeting of the American Educational Research Association, Seattle, WA.

Barnett, W. S. (1992). Benefits of compensatory preschool education. *Journal of Human Resources, 27,* 279–312.

Barnett, W., Jung, K., Yarosz, D. J., Thomas, J., Hornbeck, A., Stechuk, R., & Burns, S. (2008). Educational effects of the Tools of the Mind curriculum: A randomized trial. *Early Childhood Research Quarterly, 23*(3), 299–313. doi:10.1016/j.ecresq.2008.03.001

Baron-Cohen, S., Tager-Flusberg, H., & Cohen, D. J. (1993). *Understanding other minds: Perspectives from autism.* Oxford, England: Oxford University Press.

Baroody, A. E., & Diamond, K. E. (2013). Measures of preschool children's interest and engagement in literacy activities: Examining gender differences and construct dimensions. *Early Childhood Research Quarterly, 28*(2), 291–301. doi:10.1016/j.ecresq.2012.07.002

Baroody, A. J., Tiilikainen, S. H., & Tai, Y.-C. (2006). The application and development of an addition goal sketch. *Cognition and Instruction, 24,* 123–170.

Barrett, J. G. (2005). Conduct disorders. In C. B. Fisher & R. M. Lerner (Eds.), *Encyclopedia of applied developmental science* (Vol. 1, pp. 294–295). Thousand Oaks, CA: Sage.

Barringer, C., & Gholson, B. (1979). Effects of type and combination of feedback upon conceptual learning by children: Implications for research in academic learning. *Review of Educational Research, 49,* 459–478.

Barrouillet, P., Gavens, N., Vergauwe, E., Gaillard, V., & Camos, V. (2009). Working memory span development: A time-based resource-sharing model account. *Developmental Psychology, 45*(2), 477–490.

Barry, C. T., & Kauten, R. L. (2014). Nonpathological and pathological narcissism: Which self-reported characteristics are most problematic in adolescents? *Journal of Personality Assessment, 96*(2), 212–219. doi:10.1080/00223891.2013.830264

Barth, R. P. (2009). Preventing child abuse and neglect with parent training: Evidence and opportunities. *Future of Children, 19*(2), 95–118.

Barton, K. C., & Levstik, L. S. (1996). "Back when God was around and everything": Elementary children's understanding of historical time. *American Educational Research Journal, 33,* 419–454.

Bartoszuk, K., & Pittman, J. F. (2010). Profiles of identity exploration and commitment across domains. *Journal of Child and Family Studies, 19*(4), 444–450.

Bartsch, K., & Wellman, H. M. (1995). *Children talk about the mind.* New York, NY: Oxford University Press.

Basinger, K. S., Gibbs, J. C., & Fuller, D. (1995). Context and the measurement of moral judgment. *International Journal of Behavioral Development, 18,* 537–556.

Basinger, K. S., Gibbs, J. C., & Fuller, D. (1995). Context and the measurement of moral judgment.

International Journal of Behavioral Development, 18, 537–556.

Bassett, D. S., & Gazzaniga, M. S. (2011). Understanding complexity in the human brain. *Trends in Cognitive Sciences, 15*(5), 200–209. doi:10.1016/j.tics.2011.03.006

Basso, K. (1972). To give up on words: Silence in western Apache culture. In P. Giglioli (Ed.), *Language and social context.* New York, NY: Penguin Books.

Basso, K. H. (1984). Stalking with stories: Names, places, and moral narratives among the Western Apache. In E. M. Bruner & S. Plattner (Eds.), *Text, play and story: The construction and reconstruction of self and society* (pp. 19–55). Washington, DC: American Ethnological Society.

Basu, M., Krishnan, A., & Weber-Fox, C. (2010). Brainstem correlates of temporal auditory processing in children with specific language impairment. *Developmental Science, 13*(1), 77–91.

Bates, E., & MacWhinney, B. (1987). Competition, variation, and language learning. In B. MacWhinney (Ed.), *Mechanisms of language acquisition.* Hillsdale, NJ: Erlbaum.

Bates, T. C., Lewis, G. J., & Weiss, A. (2013). Childhood socioeconomic status amplifies genetic effects on adult intelligence. *Psychological Science, 24*(10), 2111–2116.

Batson, C. D. (1991). *The altruism question: Toward a social-psychological answer.* Hillsdale, NJ: Erlbaum.

Batson, C. D., & Thompson, E. R. (2001). Why don't moral people act morally? Motivational considerations. *Current Directions in Psychological Science, 10,* 54–57.

Battistich, V., Solomon, D., Kim, D., Watson, M., & Schaps, E. (1995). Schools as communities, poverty levels of student populations, and students' attitudes, motives, and performance: A multilevel analysis. *American Educational Research Journal, 32,* 627–658.

Battistich, V., Solomon, D., Watson, M., & Schaps, E. (1997). Caring school communities. *Educational Psychologist, 32,* 137–151.

Bauer, K. W., Hearst, M. O., Escoto, K., Berge, J. M., & Neumark-Sztainer, D. (2012). Parental employment and work-family stress: Associations with family food environments. *Social Science & Medicine, 75*(3), 496–504. doi:10.1016/j.socscimed.2012.03.026

Bauer, P. J. (2006). Event memory. In W. Damon & R. M. Lerner (Series Eds.), & D. Kuhn & R. Siegler (Vol. Eds.), *Handbook of child psychology: Vol. 2. Cognition, perception, and language* (6th ed., pp. 373–425). New York, NY: Wiley.

Bauer, P. J., & Dow, G. A. (1994). Episodic memory in 16- and 20-month-old children: Specifics not generalized, but not forgotten. *Developmental Psychology, 30,* 403–417.

Bauer, P. J., DeBoer, T., & Lukowski, A. F. (2007). In the language of multiple memory systems: Defining and describing developments in long-term declarative memory. In L. M. Oakes & P. J. Bauer (Eds.), *Short- and long-term memory in infancy and early childhood: Taking the first steps toward remembering* (pp. 240–270). New York, NY: Oxford University Press.

Bauerlein, V. (2013, January 31). The new scripts for teaching handwriting is no script at all. *Wall Street Journal—Eastern Edition,* A1–A12.

Baum, J., & Bird, B. (2010). The successful intelligence of high-growth entrepreneurs: Links to new venture growth. *Organization Science, 21*(2), 397–412. doi:10.1287/orsc.1090.0445

Bauman, S. (2011). *Cyberbullying: What counselors need to know.* Alexandria, VA: American Counseling Association.

Baumeister, R. F., Campbell, J. D., Krueger, J. I., & Vohs, K. D. (2003). Does high self-esteem cause better performance, interpersonal success, happiness, or healthier lifestyles? *Psychological Science in the Public Interest, 4*(1), 1–44.

Bauminger, N., & Kimhi-Kind, I. (2008). Social information processing, security of attachment, and emotion regulation in children with learning disabilities. *Journal of Learning Disabilities, 41*(4), 315–332.

Bauminger-Zviely, N., & Agam-Ben-Artzi, G. (2014). Young friendship in HFASD and typical development: Friend versus non-friend comparisons. *Journal of Autism & Developmental Disorders, 44*(7), 1733–1748. doi:10.1007/s10803-014-2052-7

Baumrind, D. (1967). Child care practices anteceding three patterns of preschool behavior. *Genetic Psychology Monographs, 75,* 43–88.

Baumrind, D. (1971). Current patterns of parental authority. *Developmental Psychology Monographs, 4*(1, Pt. 2).

Baumrind, D. (1980). New directions in socialization research. *American Psychologist, 35,* 639–652.

Baumrind, D. (1989). Rearing competent children. In W. Damon (Ed.), *Child development today and tomorrow* (pp. 349-378). San Francisco: Jossey-Bass.

Baumrind, D. (1991). Parenting styles and adolescent development. In R. Lerner, A. C. Petersen, & J. Brooks-Gunn (Eds.), *The encyclopedia of adolescence.* New York, NY: Garland Press.

Baumrind, D. (2013). Authoritative parenting revisited: History and current status. In R. E. Larzelere, A. Morris, A. W. Harrist (Eds.), *Authoritative parenting: Synthesizing nurturance and discipline for optimal child development* (pp. 11–34). Washington, DC: American Psychological Association. doi:10.1037/13948-002

Baumrind, D., Larzelere, R. E., & Owens, E. B. (2010). Effects of preschool parents' power assertive patterns and practices on adolescent development. *Parenting: Science and Practice, 10*(3), 157–201. doi:10.1080/15295190903290790

Baurain, C., & Nader-Grosbois, N. (2013). Theory of mind, socio-emotional problem-solving, socio-emotional regulation in children with intellectual disability and in typically developing children. *Journal of Autism and Developmental Disorders, 43*(5), 1080–1097. doi:10.1007/s10803-012-1651-4

Bayazit, I. (2013). An investigation of problem solving approaches, strategies, and models used by the 7th and 8th grade students when solving real-world problems. *Educational Sciences: Theory & Practice, 13*(3), 1920–1927. doi:10.12738/estp.2013.3.1419

Bayley, N. (2005). *Bayley Scales of Infant Development* (3rd ed.). San Antonio, TX: Psychological Corporation.

Bayley, N. (2006). *Bayley Scales of Infant and Toddler Development—Third edition: Administration manual.* San Antonio, TX: Harcourt Assessment.

Beal, C. R. (1996). The role of comprehension monitoring in children's revision. *Educational Psychology Review, 8,* 219–238.

Beal, S., & Crockett, L. (2013). Adolescents' occupational and educational goals: A test of reciprocal relations. *Journal of Applied Developmental Psychology, 34*(5), 219–229. doi:10.1016/j.appdev.2013.04.005

Beals, K. (2014, February 21). The Common Core is tough on kids with special needs. *The Atlantic.* Retrieved from http://www.theatlantic.com/education/archive/2014/02/the-common-core-is-tough-on-kids-with-special-needs/283973/

Bean Thompson, S. (2013). Don't forget the tweens. *Public Libraries, 52*(6), 29–30.

Bear, D. R., Invernizzi, M., Templeton, S., & Johnston, F. (2008). *Words their way: Word study for phonics, vocabulary, and spelling instruction* (4th ed.). Upper Saddle River, NJ: Pearson Prentice Hall.

Bearison, D. J. (1998). Pediatric psychology and children's medical problems. In W. Damon (Series Ed.), & I. E. Sigel, & K. A. Renninger (Vol. Eds.), *Handbook of child psychology: Vol. 4. Child psychology in practice* (5th ed., pp. 635–711). New York, NY: Wiley.

Beauchaine, T. P., Gatzke-Kopp, L., Neuhaus, E., Chipman, J., Reid, M., & Webster-Stratton, C. (2013). Sympathetic- and parasympathetic-linked cardiac function and prediction of externalizing behavior, emotion regulation, and prosocial behavior among preschoolers treated for ADHD. *Journal of Consulting and Clinical Psychology, 81*(3), 481–493. doi:10.1037/a0032302

Beckert, T. E., Strom, P. S., Strom, R. D., Darre, K., & Weed, A. (2008). Single mothers of early adolescents: Perceptions of competence. *Adolescence, 43*(170), 275–290.

Beckett, C., Castle, J., Rutter, M., & Sonuga-Barke, E. J. (2010). VI. Institutional deprivation, specific cognitive functions, and scholastic achievement: English and Romanian adoptee (era) study findings. *Monographs of the Society for Research In Child Development, 75*(1), 125–142. doi:10.1111/j.1540-5834.2010.00553.x

Beeri, A., & Lev-Wiesel, R. (2012). Social rejection by peers: A risk factor for psychological distress. *Child and Adolescent Mental Health, 17*(4), 216–221. doi:10.1111/j.1475-3588.2011.00637.x

Beers, S. F., & Nagy, W. E. (2009). Syntactic complexity as a predictor of adolescent writing quality: Which measures? Which genre? *Reading and Writing, 22*(2), 185–200.

Behnke, A. O., Gonzalez, L. M., & Cox, R. B. (2010). Latino students in new arrival states: Factors and services to prevent youth from dropping out. *Hispanic Journal of Behavioral Sciences, 32*(3), 385–409. doi:10.1177/0739986310374025

Bei, B., Byrne, M. L., Ivens, C., Waloszek, J., Woods, M. J., Dudgeon, P., Murray, G., Nicholas, C. L., Trinder, J., & Allen, N. B. (2013). Pilot study of a mindfulness-based, multi-component, in-school group sleep intervention in adolescent girls. *Early Intervention in Psychiatry, 7*(2), 213–220.

Beier, J. S., & Carey, S. (2014). Contingency is not enough: Social context guides third-party attributions of intentional agency. *Developmental Psychology, 50*(3), 889–902. doi:10.1037/a0034171

Beier, J. S., Over, H., & Carpenter, M. (2014). Young children help others to achieve their social goals. *Developmental Psychology, 50*(3), 934–940. doi:10.1037/a0033886

Bekkhus, M., Rutter, M., Barker, E. D., & Borge, A. I. H. (2011). The role of pre- and postnatal-timing of family risk factors on child behavior at 36 months. *Journal of Abnormal Child Psychology, 39*(4), 611–621. doi:10.1007/s10802-010-9477-z

Belenky, M. F., Bond, L. A., & Weinstock, J. S. (1997). *A tradition that has no name: Nurturing the development of people, families, and communities.* New York, NY: Basic Books.

Belfield, C. R., Nores, M., Barnett, S., & Schweinhart, L. (2008). The High/Scope Perry Preschool Program: Cost-Benefit analysis using data from the age-40 followup. In A. Schmitz & R. R. Zerbe (Eds.), *Applied benefit-cost analysis* (pp. 103–131). Elgar Reference Collection. International Library of Critical Writings in Economics, vol. 231. Cheltenham, U.K. and Northampton, MA: Elgar.

Belfiore, P. J., & Hornyak, R. S. (1998). Operant theory and application to self-monitoring in adolescents. In D. H. Schunk & B. J. Zimmerman (Eds.), *Self-regulated learning: From teaching to self-reflective practice.* New York, NY: Guilford Press.

Bell, L. A. (1989). Something's wrong here and it's not me: Challenging the dilemmas that block girls' success. *Journal for the Education of the Gifted, 12,* 118–130.

Bell, N. L., McConnell, J. E., Lassiter, K. S., & Matthews, T. (2013). The validity of the Universal Nonverbal Intelligence Test with the Woodcock-Johnson III Tests of Achievement. *North American Journal of Psychology, 15*(2), 243-256.

Bell, R. Q. (1988). Contributions of human infants to caregiving and social interaction. In G. Handel (Ed.), *Childhood socialization* (pp. 103–122). New York, NY: Aldine de Gruyter.

Belluscio, L. M., Berardino, B. G., Ferroni, N. M., Ceruti, J. M., & Cánepa, E. T. (2014). Early protein malnutrition negatively impacts physical growth and neurological reflexes and evokes anxiety and depressive-like behaviors. *Physiology & Behavior, 129*237-254. doi:10.1016/j.physbeh.2014.02.051

Belsky, J., & Eggebeen, D. (1991). Early and extensive maternal employment and young children's socio-emotional development: Children of the National Longitudinal Survey of Youth. *Journal of Marriage and Family, 53*(4), 1083–1098.

Belsky, J., Gilstrap, B., & Rovine, M. (1984). The Pennsylvania Infant and Family Development Project, I: Stability and change in mother–infant and father–infant interaction in a family setting at one, three, and nine months. *Child Development, 55,* 692–705.

Bem, S. L. (1981). Gender schema theory: A cognitive account of sex typing. *Psychological Review, 88,* 354–364.

Bem, S. L. (1989). Genital knowledge and gender constancy in preschool children. *Child Development, 60,* 649–662.

Benbenishty, R., & Schmid, H. (2013). Public attitudes toward the identification and reporting of alleged maltreatment cases among social groups in Israel. *Children and Youth Services Review, 35*(2), 332–339. doi:10.1016/j.childyouth.2012.11.013

Benbow, C. P., & Lubinski, D. (2009). Extending Sandra Scarr's ideas about development to the longitudinal study of intellectually precocious youth. In K. McCartney, & R. A. Weinberg (Eds.), *Annual meeting of the Association for Psychological Science (APS), 19th, May 2007, Washington, DC, US; This festschrift for Sandra Scarr was organized and presented at the aforementioned conference* (pp. 231–252). New York, NY: Psychology Press.

Benko, S. (2012). Scaffolding: An ongoing process to support adolescent writing development. *Journal of Adolescent & Adult Literacy, 56*(4), 291–300. doi:10.1002/JAAL.00142

Benko, S. L. (2012). Scaffolding: An ongoing process to support adolescent writing development. *Journal of Adolescent & Adult Literacy, 56*(4), 291–300. doi:10.1002/JAAL.00142

Bennett, A., Bridglall, B. L., Cauce, A. M., Everson, H. T., Gordon, E. W., Lee, C. D., et al. (2007). Task force report on the affirmative development of academic ability: All students reaching the top: Strategies for closing academic achievement gaps. In E. W. Gordon & B. L. Bridglall (Eds.), *Affirmative development: Cultivating academic ability* (pp. 239–275). Lanham, MD: Rowman.

Bennett, R. E., Gottesman, R. L., Rock, D. A., & Cerullo, F. (1993). Influence of behavior perceptions and gender on teachers' judgments of students' academic skill. *Journal of Educational Psychology, 85,* 347–356.

Benoit, A., Lacourse, E., & Claes, M. (2013). Pubertal timing and depressive symptoms in late adolescence: The moderating role of individual, peer, and parental factors. *Development and Psychopathology, 25*(2), 455–471.

Benoit, D., & Parker, K. C. (1994). Stability and transmission of attachment across three generations. *Child Development, 65,* 1444–1456.

Benton, S. L. (1997). Psychological foundations of elementary writing instruction. In G. D. Phye (Ed.), *Handbook of academic learning: Construction of knowledge* (pp. 235–264). San Diego, CA: Academic Press.

Berdan, L. E., Keane, S. P., & Calkins, S. D. (2008). Temperament and externalizing behavior: Social preference and perceived acceptance as protective factors. *Developmental Psychology, 44*(4), 957–968. doi:10.1037/0012-1649.44.4.957

Bereiter, C. (1994). Implications of postmodernism for science, or, science as progressive discourse. *Educational Psychologist, 29*, 3–12.

Berenstain, S., & Berenstain, J. (1990). *The Berenstain bears' trouble with pets.* New York, NY: Random House.

Bergen, D., & Fromberg, D. P. (2009). Play and social interaction in middle childhood. *Phi Delta Kappan, 90*(6), 426–430.

Berger, L. M., Paxson, C., & Waldfogel, J. (2009). Income and child development. *Children and Youth Services Review, 31,* 978–989.

Berger, R. (2000). Remarried families of 2000: Definitions, descriptions, and interventions. In W. C. Nichols, M. A. Pace-Nichols, D. S. Becvar, & A. Y. Napier (Eds.), *Handbook of family development* (pp. 371–390). New York, NY: Wiley.

Bergeron, R., & Floyd, R. G. (2006). Broad cognitive abilities of children with mental retardation: An analysis of group and individual profiles. *American Journal on Mental Retardation, 111,* 417–432.

Bergin, C. A., & Bergin, D. A. (2009/2010). Sleep: The E-zzz intervention. *Educational Leadership, 67*(4), 44–47.

Berk, L. E. (1994). Why children talk to themselves. *Scientific American, 271,* 78–83.

Berk, L. E. (1994). Why children talk to themselves. *Scientific American, 271,* 78–83.

Berkeley, S., & Riccomini, P. J. (2013). QRAC-the-code: A comprehension monitoring strategy for middle school social studies textbooks. *Journal of Learning Disabilities, 46*(2), 154–165. doi:10.1177/0022219411409412

Berkovits, L., & Baker, B. (2014). Emotion dysregulation and social competence: Stability, change and predictive power. *Journal of Intellectual Disability Research, 58*(8), 765–776. doi:10.1111/jir.12088

Berlin, L. J., Cassidy, J., & Appleyard, K. (2008). The influence of early attachments on other relationships. In J. Cassidy & P. R. Shaver (Eds.), *Handbook of attachment: Theory, research, and clinical applications* (2nd ed., pp. 333–347). New York, NY: Guilford Press.

Berliner, D. (2009). *Poverty and potential: Out-of-school factors and school success.* Boulder, CO, and Tempe, AZ: Education and the Public Interest Center & Education Policy Research. Retrieved from http://epicpolicy.org/publication/poverty-and-potential

Bernard, M., & Popard Newell, E. (2013). Students affected by neglect. In E. Rossen & R. Hull (Eds.), *Supporting and educating traumatized students: A guide for school-based professionals* (pp. 203–217). New York, NY: Oxford University Press.

Bernard, R. S., Cohen, L. L., & Moffet, K. (2009). A token economy for exercise adherence in pediatric cystic fibrosis: A single-subject analysis. *Journal of Pediatric Psychology, 34*(4), 354–365.

Berndt, T. J. (1992). Friendship and friends' influence in adolescence. *Current Directions in Psychological Science, 1,* 156–159.

Berndt, T. J., & Hoyle, S. G. (1985). Stability and change in childhood and adolescent friendships. *Developmental Psychology, 21,* 1007–1015.

Berndt, T. J., & Keefe, K. (1995). Friends' influence on adolescents' adjustment to school. *Child Development, 66,* 1312–1329.

Berndt, T. J., & Keefe, K. (1996). Friends' influence on school adjustment: A motivational analysis. In J. Juvonen & K. R. Wentzel (Eds.), *Social motivation: Understanding children's school adjustment* (pp. 248–278). Cambridge, England: Cambridge University Press.

Berninger, V. W., Fuller, F., & Whitaker, D. (1996). A process model of writing development across the life span. *Educational Psychology Review, 8,* 193–218.

Bertenthal, B. I., Campos, J. J., & Kermoian, R. (1994). An epigenetic perspective on the development of self-produced locomotion and its consequences. *Current Directions in Psychological Science, 3,* 140–145.

Bertera, E. M., & Crewe, S. (2013). Parenthood in the twenty-first century: African American grandparents as surrogate parents. *Journal of Human Behavior in the Social Environment, 23*(2), 178-192. doi:10.1080/10911359.2013.747348

Berthold, K., & Renkl, A. (2009). Instructional aids to support a conceptual understanding of multiple representations. *Journal of Educational Psychology, 101*(1), 70–87.

Bertsch, K., Grothe, M., Prehn, K., Vohs, K., Berger, C., Hauenstein, K., Keiper, P., Domes, G., Teipel, S., & Herpertz, S. C. (2013). Brain volumes differ between diagnostic groups of violent criminal offenders. *European Archives of Psychiatry and Clinical Neuroscience, 263*(7), 593–606. doi:10.1007/s00406-013-0391-6

Best, P., Manktelow, R., & Taylor, B. (2014). Online communication, social media and adolescent wellbeing: A systematic narrative review. *Children & Youth Services Review, 41,* 27–36.

Bester, G. (2013). Adolescent egocentrism in a learning context. *Africa Education Review, 10*(3), 393–409.

Bettinger, E. (2012). Paying to learn: The effect of financial incentives on elementary school test scores. *Review of Economics & Statistics, 94*(3), 686–698.

Betts, K. S. (2013). Lasting Impacts: Pre- and Postnatal PBDE Exposures Linked to IQ Deficits. *Environmental Health Perspectives, 121*(2), A58.

Bhatia, V. K., & Ebooks, C. (2014). *The Routledge Handbook of Language and Professional Communication.* New York, NY: Routledge.

Bialystok, E. (1994b). Towards an explanation of second language acquisition. In G. Brown, K. Malmkjær, A. Pollitt, & J. Williams (Eds.), *Language and understanding* (pp. 115-139). Oxford, England: Oxford University Press.

Bialystok, E. (2001). *Bilingualism in development: Language, literacy, and cognition.* Cambridge, England: Cambridge University Press.

Bialystok, E., & Viswanathan, M. (2009). Components of executive control with advantages for bilingual children in two cultures. *Cognition, 112*(3), 494–500.

Bialystok, E., Peets, K., & Moreno, S. (2014). Producing bilinguals through immersion education: Development of metalinguistic awareness. *Applied Psycholinguistics, 35*(1), 177–191. doi:10.1017/S0142716412000288

Bibace, R., & Walsh, M. E. (1981). Children's conceptions of illness. In R. Bibace & M. E. Walsh (Eds.), *New directions for child development: Children's conceptions of health, illness, and bodily functions* (pp. 31–48). San Francisco, CA: Jossey-Bass.

Bibou-Nakou, I. I., Asimopoulos, C. H., Hatzipemou, T. H., Soumaki, E. E., & Tsiantis, J. J. (2014). Bullying in Greek secondary schools: Prevalence and profile of bullying practices. *International Journal of Mental Health Promotion, 16*(1), 3-18. doi:10.1080/14623730.2013.857824

Bicais, J., & Correia, M. G. (2008). Peer-learning spaces: A staple in English language learners' tool kit for developing language and literacy. *Journal of Research in Childhood Education, 22*(4), 363–375.

Bickford III, J. (2013). Initiating historical thinking in elementary schools. *Social Studies Research & Practice, 8*(3), 60–77.

Biddle, S. J. (1993). Children, exercise and mental health. *International Journal of Sport Psychology, 24,* 200–216.

Bierman, K. L. (2004). *Peer rejection: Developmental processes and intervention strategies.* New York, NY: Guilford Press.

Bierman, K. L. (2004). *Peer rejection: Developmental processes and intervention strategies.* New York, NY: Guilford Press.

Bierman, K. L., & Powers, C. J. (2009). Social skills training to improve peer relations. In K. H. Rubin, W. M. Bukowski, & B. Laursen (Eds.), *Handbook of peer interactions, relationships, and groups* (pp. 603–621). New York, NY: Guilford Press.

Bierman, K. L., Miller, C. L., & Staub, S. D. (1987). Improving the social behavior and peer acceptance of rejected boys: Effect of social skill training with instructions and prohibitions. *Journal of Consulting and Clinical Psychology, 55,* 194–200.

Bierman, K. L., Nix, R. L., Heinrichs, B. S., Domitrovich, C. E., Gest, S. D., Welsh, J. A., & Gill, S. (2014). Effects of Head Start REDI on children's outcomes 1 year later in different kindergarten contexts. *Child Development, 85*(1), 140–159. doi:10.1111/cdev.12117

Bigelow, A. E., & Best, C. (2013). Peek-a-what? Infants' response to the still-face task after normal and interrupted peek-a-boo. *Infancy, 18*(3), 400–413. doi:10.1111/j.1532-7078.2012.00124.x

Bigner, B. J. (2006). *Parent–child relations: An introduction to parenting* (7th ed.). Upper Saddle River, NJ: Pearson Merrill Prentice Hall.

Bigras, N., Bouchard, C., Cantin, G., Brunson, L., Coutu, S., Lemay, L., et al. (2010). A comparative study of structural and process quality in center-based and family-based child care services. *Child & Youth Care Forum, 39*(3), 129–150. doi:10.1007/s10566-009-9088-4

Binet, A., & Simon, T. (1948). The development of the Binet-Simon Scale, 1905–1908. In W. Dennis (Ed.), *Readings in the history of psychology* (pp. 412–424). East Norwalk, CT US: Appleton-Century-Crofts. doi:10.1037/11304-047

Bird, R. (2009). *Overcoming difficulties with number: Supporting dyscalculia and students who struggle with math.* Los Angeles, CA: Sage.

Birkeland, M., Breivik, K., & Wold, B. (2014). Peer acceptance protects global self-esteem from negative effects of low closeness to parents during adolescence and early adulthood. *Journal of Youth & Adolescence, 43*(1), 70–80.

Bischof-Köhler, D. (2012). Empathy and self-recognition in phylogenetic and ontogenetic perspective. *Emotion Review, 4*(1), 40–48. doi:10.1177/1754073911421377

Bishop, D. (2010). Specific language impairment. In C. L. Cooper, J. Field, U. Goswami, R. Jenkins, & B. Sahakian (Eds.), *Mental capital and well-being* (pp. 767–773). Ames, IA: Wiley-Blackwell.

Bishop, E. G., Cherny, S. S., Corley, R., Plomin, R., DeFries, J. C., & Hewitt, J. K. (2003). Development genetic analysis of general cognitive ability from 1 to 12 years in a sample of adoptees, biological siblings, and twins. *Intelligence, 31,* 31–49.

Bivens, J. A., & Berk, L. E. (1990). A longitudinal study of the development of elementary school children's private speech. *Merrill-Palmer Quarterly, 36,* 443–463.

Björklund, C. (2014). Less is more—mathematical manipulatives in early childhood education. *Early Child Development & Care, 184*(3), 469–485. doi: 10.1080/03004430.2013.799154

Bjorklund, D. F. (1987). How age changes in knowledge base contribute to the development of children's memory: An interpretive review. *Developmental Review, 7,* 93–130.

Bjorklund, D. F. (2003). Evolutionary psychology from a developmental systems perspective: Comment on Lickliter and Honeycutt (2003). *Psychological Bulletin, 129,* 836–841.

Bjorklund, D. F., & Green, B. L. (1992). The adaptive nature of cognitive immaturity. *American Psychologist, 47,* 46–54.

Bjorklund, D. F., Dukes, C., & Brown, R. D. (2009). The development of memory strategies. In M. L. Courage & N. Cowan (Eds.), *The development of memory in infancy and childhood* (pp. 145–175). New York, NY: Psychology Press.

Bjorklund, D. F., Periss, V., & Causey, K. (2009). The benefits of youth. *European Journal of Developmental Psychology, 6*(1), 120–137.

Blachford, S. L. (2002). *The Gale encyclopedia of genetic disorders*. Detroit, MI: Gale Group.

Blackwell, L. S., Trzesniewski, K. H., & Dweck, C. S. (2007). Implicit theories of intelligence predict achievement across an adolescent transition: A longitudinal study and an intervention. *Child Development, 78*, 246–263.

Blades, M., & Spencer, C. (1987). Young children's strategies when using maps with landmarks. *Journal of Environmental Psychology, 7*, 201–217.

Blain-Brière, B., Bouchard, C., Bigras, N., & Cadoret, G. (2014). Development of active control within working memory: Active retrieval versus monitoring in children. *International Journal of Behavioral Development, 38*(3), 239-246. doi:10.1177/0165025413513202

Blair, C. (2002). School readiness: Integrating cognition and emotion in a neurobiological conceptualization of children's functioning at school entry. *American Psychologist, 57*, 111–127.

Blair, C., & Razza, R. P. (2007). Relating effortful control, executive function, and false belief understanding to emerging math and literacy ability in kindergarten. *Child Development, 78*, 647–663.

Blake, S., & Giannangelo, D. M. (2012). Creativity and young children: Review of literature and connections to thinking processes. In O. N. Saracho (Ed.), *Contemporary perspectives on research in creativity in early childhood education* (pp. 293–315). Charlotte, NC US: IAP Information Age Publishing.

Blakemore, C. (1976). The conditions required for the maintenance of binocularity in the kitten's visual cortex. *Journal of Physiology, 261*, 423–444.

Blakemore, J. E. O., Berenbaum, S. A., & Liben, L. S. (2009). *Gender development*. New York, NY: Psychology Press.

Blakemore, J. E. O., Berenbaum, S. A., & Liben, L. S. (2009). *Gender development*. New York, NY: Psychology Press.

Blakemore, S., & Mills, K. L. (2014). Is adolescence a sensitive period for sociocultural processing? *Annual Review of Psychology, 65*, 187–207. doi:10.1146/annurev-psych-010213-115202

Blandon, A. Y., Calkins, S. D., Grimm, K. J., Keane, S. P., & O'Brien, M. (2010). Testing a developmental cascade model of emotional and social competence and early peer acceptance. *Development and Psychopathology, 22*(4), 737–748. doi:10.1017/S0954579410000428

Blank, J. (2010). Early childhood teacher education: Historical themes and contemporary issues. *Journal of Early Childhood Teacher Education, 31*(4), 391–405. doi:10.1080/10901027.2010.523772

Blatchford, P., Baines, E., & Pellegrini, A. (2003). The social context of school playground games: Sex and ethnic differences, and changes over time after entry to junior school. *British Journal of Developmental Psychology, 21*, 481–505.

Bleeker, M. M., & Jacobs, J. E. (2004). Achievement in math and science: Do mothers' beliefs matter 12 years later? *Journal of Educational Psychology, 96*, 97–109.

Blevins, C. (2010). *Math lesson plan*. Retrieved from http://www.athens.edu/vinsobm/lesson_5.html

Blissett, J., & Fogel, A. (2013). Intrinsic and extrinsic influences on children's acceptance of new foods. *Physiology & Behavior.* doi:10.1016/j.physbeh.2013.02.013

Bloch, J. (2014). Reciprocity in a securely attached mother-infant dyad. *Journal of Infant, Child & Adolescent Psychotherapy, 13*(1), 11-23. doi:10.1080/15289168.2014.880298

Block, J. H. (1983). Differential premises arising from differential socialization of the sexes: Some conjectures. *Child Development, 54*, 1335–1354.

Blom, E., Paradis, J., Oetting, J., & Bedore, L. (2013). Past tense production by English second language learners with and without language impairment. *Journal of Speech, Language & Hearing Research, 56*(1), 281–294. doi:10.1044/1092-4388(2012/11-0112)

Bloom, B. S. (1964). *Stability and change in human characteristics*. New York, NY: Wiley.

Bloom, K., Russell, A., & Wassenberg, K. (1987). Turn taking affects the quality of infant vocalizations. *Journal of Child Language, 14*, 211–227.

Bloom, L., & Lahey, M. (1978). *Language development and language disorders*. New York, NY: Wiley.

Bloom, L., & Tinker, E. (2001). The intentionality model and language acquisition. *Monographs of the Society for Research in Child Development, 66*(4, Serial No. 267).

Bobzien, J., Richels, C., Raver, S. A., Hester, P., Browning, E., & Morin, L. (2013). An observational study of social communication skills in eight preschoolers with and without hearing loss during cooperative play. *Early Childhood Education Journal, 41*(5), 339–346. doi:10.1007/s10643-012-0561-6

Boccia, M., & Campos, J. J. (1989). Maternal emotional signals, social referencing, and infants' reactions to strangers. In N. Eisenberg (Ed.), *New directions for child development* (Vol. 44, pp. 25–49). San Francisco, CA: Jossey-Bass.

Bochenhauer, M. H. (1990, April). *Connections: Geographic education and the National Geographic Society*. Paper presented at the annual meeting of the American Educational Research Association, Boston.

Bock, J., & Johnson, S. E. (2004). Subsistence ecology and play among the Okavango Delta peoples of Botswana. *Human Nature, 15*, 63–81.

Bodrova, E., & Leong, D. J. (1996). *Tools of the mind: The Vygotskian approach to early childhood education*. Upper Saddle River, NJ: Merrill/Prentice Hall.

Bodrova, E., & Leong, D. J. (2009). Tools of the mind: A Vygotskian-based early childhood curriculum. *Early Childhood Services: An Interdisciplinary Journal of Effectiveness, 3*(3), 245–262.

Bodrova, E., Leong, D., & Akhutina, T. (2011). When everything new is well-forgotten old: Vygotsky/Luria insights in the development of executive functions. *New Directions for Child & Adolescent Development, 2011*(133), 11–28. doi:10.1002/cd.301

Bodrow, W., & Magalashvili, V. (2009). Knowledge visualization in IT-based discovery learning. *Communication and Cognition, 42*(1 & 2), 101–112.

Boeckx, C., Fodor, J. D., Gleitman, L., & Rizzi, L. (2009). Round table: Language universals: Yesterday, today, and tomorrow. In M. Piattelli-Palmarini, J. Uriagereka, & P. Salaburu (Eds.), *Of minds and language: A dialogue with Noam Chomsky in the Basque country* (pp. 195–220). New York, NY: Oxford University Press.

Boekaerts, M. (2006). Self-regulation and effort investment. In W. Damon & R. M. Lerner (Eds. in Chief), & K. A. Renninger & I. E. Sigel (Vol. Eds.), *Handbook of child psychology. Vol. 4: Child psychology in practice* (pp. 345–377). New York, NY: Wiley.

Boekaerts, M. (2009). Goal-directed behavior in the classroom. In K. R. Wenzel, & A. Wigfield (Eds.), *Handbook of motivation at school. Educational psychology handbook series* (pp. 105–122). New York, NY: Routledge/Taylor & Francis Group.

Bofferding, L. (2014). Negative Integer Understanding: Characterizing First Graders' Mental Models.

Journal for Research in Mathematics Education, 45(2), 194–245.

Bogart, L. M., Elliott, M. N., Klein, D. J., Tortolero, S. R., Mrug, S., Peskin, M. F., et al. (2014). Peer victimization in fifth grade and health in tenth grade. *Pediatrics, 133*(3), 440–447. doi:10.1542/peds.2013-3510

Bohannon, J. N., MacWhinney, B., & Snow, C. (1990). No negative evidence revisited: Beyond learnability, or who has to prove what to whom. *Developmental Psychology, 26*, 221–226.

Boiger, M., De Deyne, S., & Mesquita, B. (2013). Emotions in "the world": Cultural practices, products, and meanings of anger and shame in two individualist cultures. *Frontiers in Psychology, 4*, 1–14.

Boivin, M., Brendgen, M., Vitaro, F., Dionne, G., Girard, A., Pérusse, D., & Tremblay, R. (2013). Strong genetic contribution to peer relationship difficulties at school entry: Findings from a longitudinal twin study. *Child Development, 84*(3), 1098–1114. doi:10.1111/cdev.12019

Bokhorst, C. L., Westenberg, P. M., Oosterlaan, J., & Heyne, D. A. (2008). Changes in social fears across childhood and adolescence: Age-related differences in the factor structure of the Fear Survey Schedule for Children—Revised. *Journal of Anxiety Disorders, 22*, 135–142.

Bolaños, D., Cole, R. A., Ward, W. H., Tindal, G. A., Schwanenflugel, P. J., & Kuhn, M. R. (2013). Automatic assessment of expressive oral reading. *Speech Communication, 55*(2), 221–236. doi:10.1016/j.specom.2012.08.002

Boldt, L. J., Kochanska, G., Yoon, J., & Koenig Nordling, J. (2014). Children's attachment to both parents from toddler age to middle childhood: Links to adaptive and maladaptive outcomes. *Attachment & Human Development, 16*(3), 211–229. doi:10.1080/14616734.2014.889181

Boling, C. J., & Evans, W. H. (2008). Reading success in the secondary classroom. *Preventing School Failure, 52*(2), 59–66. doi:10.3200/PSFL.52.2.59-66

Bonawitz, E., Shafto, P., Gweon, H., Goodman, N. D., Spelke, E., & Schulz, L. (2011). The double-edged sword of pedagogy: Instruction limits spontaneous exploration and discovery. *Cognition, 120*(3), 322–330. doi:10.1016/j.cognition.2010.10.001

Boncoddo, R., Dixon, J. A., & Kelley, E. (2010). The emergence of a novel representation from action: Evidence from preschoolers. *Developmental Science, 13*(2), 370–377. doi:10.1111/j.1467-7687.2009.00905.x

Bong, M. (2001). Between- and within-domain relations of academic motivation among middle and high school students: Self-efficacy, task-value, and achievement goals. *Journal of Educational Psychology, 93*, 23–34.

Bong, M., Cho, C., Ahn, H., & Kim, H. (2012). Comparison of self-beliefs for predicting student motivation and achievement. *Journal of Educational Research, 105*(5), 336–352. doi:10.1080/00220671.2011.627401

Boniel-Nissim, M., & Barak, A. (2013). The therapeutic value of adolescents' blogging about social–emotional difficulties. *Psychological Services, 10*(3), 333–341. doi:10.1037/a0026664

Bonta, B. D. (1997). Cooperation and competition in peaceful societies. *Psychological Bulletin, 121*(2), 299–320.

Boom, J., Brugman, D., & van der Heijden, P. G. M. (2001). Hierarchical structure of moral stages assessed by a sorting task. *Child Development, 72*, 535–548.

Booth-LaForce, C., & Kerns, K. A. (2009). Child-parent attachment relationships, peer relationships, and peer-group functioning. In K. H. Rubin, W. M. Bukowski, & B. Laursen (Eds.), *Handbook* of peer interactions, relationships, and groups (pp. 490–507). New York, NY: Guilford Press.

Borelli, J. L., Crowley, M. J., David, D. H., Sbarra, D. A., Anderson, G. M., & Mayes, L. C. (2010). Attachment and emotion in school-aged children. Emotion, 10(4), 475–485.

Borgen, W., & Hiebert, B. (2014). Orienting educators to contemporary ideas for career counseling: An illustrative example. In G. Arulmani, A. J. Bakshi, F. L. Leong, A. G. Watts (Eds.), Handbook of career development: International perspectives (pp. 709-726). New York, NY: Springer Science + Business Media. doi:10.1007/978-1-4614-9460-7_40

Borkowski, J. G., Bisconti, T., Willard, C. C., Keogh, D. A., Whitman, T. L., & Weed, K. (2002). The adolescent as parent: Influences on children's intellectual, academic, and socioemotional development. In J. G. Borkowski, S. L. Ramey, & M. Bristol-Power (Eds.), Parenting and the child's world: Influences on academic, intellectual, and social-emotional development (pp. 161–184). Mahwah, NJ: Erlbaum.

Bornovalova, M. A., Cummings, J. R., Hunt, E. E., Blazei, R. R., Malone, S. S., & Iacono, W. G. (2014). Understanding the relative contributions of direct environmental effects and passive genotype–environment correlations in the association between familial risk factors and child disruptive behavior disorders. Psychological Medicine, 44(4), 831-844. doi:10.1017/S0033291713001086

Bornstein, M. H. (2009). Toward a model of culture⊠parent⊠child transactions. In A. Sameroff (Ed.), The transactional model of development: How children and contexts shape each other (pp. 139–161). Washington, DC: American Psychological Association.

Bornstein, M. H., & Lansford, J. E. (2010). Parenting. In M. H. Bornstein (Ed.), Handbook of cultural developmental science (pp. 259–277). New York, NY: Psychology Press.

Bornstein, M. H., Cote, L. R., Maital, S., Painter, K., Sung-Yun, P., Pascual, L., et al. (2004). Cross-linguistic analysis of vocabulary in young children: Spanish, Dutch, French, Hebrew, Italian, Korean, and American English. Child Development, 75(4), 1115–1139. doi:10.1111/j.1467-8624.2004.00729.x

Bornstein, M. H., Hahn, C., & Haynes, O. M. (2010). Social competence, externalizing, and internalizing behavioral adjustment from early childhood through early adolescence: Developmental cascades. Development and Psychopathology, 22(4), 717–735. doi:10.1017/S0954579410000416

Bornstein, M. H., Jager, J., & Putnick, D. L. (2013). Sampling in developmental science: Situations, shortcomings, solutions, and standards. Developmental Review, 33(4), 357-370. doi:10.1016/j.dr.2013.08.003

Bornstein, M., Hahn, C., & Wolke, D. (2013). Systems and Cascades in Cognitive Development and Academic Achievement. Child Development, 84(1), 154–162. doi:10.1111/j.1467-8624.2012.01849.x

Borrero, N. E., & Yeh, C. J. (2011). The multidimensionality of ethnic identity among urban high school youth. Identity, 11(2), 114–135. doi:10.1080/15283488.2011.555978

Borst, G. G., Poirel, N. N., Pineau, A. A., Cassotti, M. M., & Houdé, O. O. (2013). Inhibitory control efficiency in a Piaget-like class-inclusion task in school-age children and adults: A developmental negative priming study. Developmental Psychology, 49(7), 1366–1374. doi:10.1037/a0029622

Bortfeld, H., Morgan, J. L., Golinkoff, R. M., & Rathbun, K. (2005). Mommy and me: Familiar names help launch babies into speech-stream segmentation. Psychological Science, 16, 298–304.

Bos, H. (2013). Lesbian-mother families formed through donor insemination. In A. E. Goldberg & K. R. Allen (Eds.), LGBT-parent families: Innovations in

research and implications for practice (pp. 21–37). New York, NY: Springer Science + Business Media. doi:10.1007/978-1-4614-4556-2_2

Bosacki, S., Rose-Krasnor, L., & Coplan, R. (2014). Children's talking and listening within the classroom: teachers' insights. Early Child Development & Care, 184(2), 247–265. doi:10.1080/03004430.2013.781165

Boscardin, C. K., Muthén, B., Francis, D. J., & Baker, E. L. (2008). Early identification of reading difficulties using heterogeneous developmental trajectories. Journal of Educational Psychology, 100, 192–208.

Botsoglou, K., Hrisikou, S., & Kakana, D. (2011). Measuring safety levels in playgrounds using environment assessment scales: The issue of playground safety in Greece. Early Child Development and Care, 181(6), 749–760.

Bouchard, C., Bigras, N., Cantin, G., Coutu, S., Blain-Brière, B., Eryasa, J., et al. (2010). Early childhood educators' use of language-support practices with 4-year-old children in child care centers. Early Childhood Education Journal, 37(5), 371–379.

Bouchard, T. J. (2014). Genes, evolution and intelligence. Behavior Genetics, doi:10.1007/s10519-014-9646-x

Bouchard, T. J., & McGue, M. (1981). Familial studies of intelligence: A review. Science, 212, 1056.

Bouchard, T. J., Jr. (1997). IQ similarity in twins reared apart: Findings and responses to critics. In R. J. Sternberg & E. L. Grigorenko (Eds.), Intelligence, heredity, and environment (pp. 126–160). Cambridge, England: Cambridge University Press.

Boucher, O., Muckle, G., Jacobson, J. L., Carter, R., Kaplan-Estrin, M., Ayotte, P., Dewailly, Ã., & Jacobson, S. W. (2014). Domain-specific effects of prenatal exposure to PCBs, mercury, and lead on infant cognition: Results from the environmental contaminants and child development study in Nunavik. Environmental Health Perspectives, 122(3), 310-316. doi:10.1289/ehp.1206323

Bourke, L., Davies, S., Sumner, E., & Green, C. (2014). Individual differences in the development of early writing skills: Testing the unique contribution of visuo-spatial working memory. Reading & Writing, 27(2), 315–335. doi:10.1007/s11145-013-9446-3

Bouta, H., & Retalis, S. (2013). Enhancing primary school children collaborative learning experiences in maths via a 3D virtual environment. Education & Information Technologies, 18(4), 571–596. doi:10.1007/s10639-012-9198-8

Boutte, G. S., & McCormick, C. B. (1992). Authentic multicultural activities: Avoiding pseudomulticulturalism. Childhood Education, 68(3), 140–144.

Bowlby, J. (1951). Maternal care and mental health. Geneva, Switzerland: World Health Organization.

Bowlby, J. (1958). The nature of the child's tie to his mother. International Journal of Psycho-Analysis, 39, 350–373.

Bowlby, J. (1969/1982). Attachment and loss: Vol. 1. Attachment (2nd ed.). New York, NY: Basic Books.

Bowlby, J. (1973). Attachment and loss: Vol. 2. Separation: Anxiety and anger. New York, NY: Basic Books.

Bowlby, J. (1988). A secure base: Parent–child attachment and healthy human development. New York, NY: Basic Books.

Bowman, D., & Popp, P. A. (2013). Students experiencing homelessness. In E. Rossen & R. Hull (Eds.), Supporting and educating traumatized students: A guide for school-based professionals (pp. 73–92). New York, NY: Oxford University Press.

Bowman-Perrott, L., Davis, H., Vannest, K., Williams, L., Greenwood, C., & Parker, R. (2013). Academic benefits of peer tutoring: A meta-analytic review of single-case research. School Psychology Review, 42(1), 39–55.

Bowyer-Crane, C., & Snowling, M. J. (2010). Turning frogs into princes: Can children make inferences from fairy tales? Reading and Writing, 23(1), 19–29.

Boykin, A. W. (1994). Harvesting talent and culture: African-American children and educational reform. In R. J. Rossi (Ed.), Schools and students at risk: Context and framework for positive change. New York, NY: Teachers College Press.

Boyle, B., & Charles, M. (2011). "The three hags and Pocohantas": How collaboration develops early years writing skills. Literacy, 45(1), 10–18. doi:10.1111/j.1741-4369.2011.00576.x

Braaten, E. B. (2011). How to find mental health care for your child. Washington, DC: American Psychological Association.

Brabham, E. G., & Lynch-Brown, C. (2002). Effects of teachers' reading-aloud styles on vocabulary acquisition and comprehension of students in the early elementary grades. Journal of Educational Psychology, 94, 465–473.

Bracken, B. A., & McCallum, R. S. (1998). Universal Nonverbal Intelligence Test. Itasca, IL: Riverside.

Bracken, B. A., & McCallum, R. S. (2009). Universal Nonverbal Intelligence Test (UNIT). In J. A. Naglieri & S. Goldstein (Eds.), Practitioner's guide to assessing intelligence and achievement (pp. 291–313). Hoboken, NJ: Wiley.

Bracken, B. A., McCallum, R. S., & Shaughnessy, M. F. (1999). An interview with Bruce A. Bracken and R. Steve McCallum, authors of the Universal Nonverbal Intelligence Test (UNIT). North American Journal of Psychology, 1, 277–288.

Bradley, L., & Bryant, P. (1991). Phonological skills before and after learning to read. In S. A. Brady & D. P. Shankweiler (Eds.), Phonological processes in literacy (pp. 47-45). Hillsdale, NJ: Erlbaum.

Bradley, R. H., & Caldwell, B. M. (1984). The relation of infants' home environments to achievement test performance in first grade: A follow-up study. Child Development, 55, 803–809.

Bradley, R. H., Corwyn, R. F., McAdoo, H., & Coll, C. (2001). The home environments of children in the United States: Part I. Variations by age, ethnicity, and poverty status. Child Development, 72, 1844–1867.

Brady, K. W., & Goodman, J. C. (2014). The type, but not the amount, of information available influences toddlers' fast mapping and retention of new words. American Journal of Speech-Language Pathology, 23(2), 120-133. doi:10.1044/2013

Braine, L. G., Schauble, L., Kugelmass, S., & Winter, A. (1993). Representation of depth by children: Spatial strategies and lateral biases. Developmental Psychology, 29, 466–479.

Brainerd, C. J. (2003). Jean Piaget, learning research, and American education. In B. J. Zimmerman & D. H. Schunk (Eds.), Educational psychology: A century of contributions (pp. 251–287). Mahwah, NJ: Erlbaum.

Branch, C. (1999). Race and human development. In R. H. Sheets & E. R. Hollins (Eds.), Racial and ethnic identity in school practices: Aspects of human development (pp. 7–28). Mahwah, NJ: Erlbaum.

Brand, S., Marchand, J., Lilly, E., & Child, M. (2014). Home-school literacy bags for twenty-first century preschoolers. Early Childhood Education Journal, 42(3), 163–170. doi:10.1007/s10643-013-0603-8

Brannon, M. E. (2002). The development of ordinal numerical knowledge in infancy. Cognition, 83, 223–240.

Branstetter, S. A., & Furman, W. (2013). Buffering effect of parental monitoring knowledge and parent-adolescent relationships on consequences of adolescent substance use. Journal of Child and Family Studies, 22(2), 192–198. doi:10.1007/s10826-012-9568-2

Brant, A. M., Haberstick, B. C., Corley, R. P., Wadsworth, S. J., DeFries, J. C., & Hewitt, J. K. (2009).

The developmental etiology of high IQ. *Behavior Genetics, 39*(4), 393–405.

Braswell, G. S., & Callanan, M. A. (2003). Learning to draw recognizable graphic representations during mother–child interactions. *Merrill-Palmer Quarterly, 49,* 471–494.

Brauner, J., Gordic, B., & Zigler, E. (2004). Putting the child back into child care: Combining care and education for children ages 3–5. *Social Policy Report, 18.* Ann Arbor, MI: Society for Research in Child Development.

Braungart-Rieker, J. M., Hill-Soderlund, A. L., & Karrass, J. (2010). Fear and anger reactivity trajectories from 4 to 16 months: The roles of temperament, regulation, and maternal sensitivity. *Developmental Psychology, 46*(4), 791–804. doi:10.1037/a0019673

Braungart-Rieker, J. M., Hill-Soderlund, A. L., & Karrass, J. (2010). Fear and anger reactivity trajectories from 4 to 16 months: The roles of temperament, regulation, and maternal sensitivity. *Developmental Psychology, 46*(4), 791–804. doi:10.1037/a0019673

Brazelton, T. B. (2009). The role of the Neonatal Behavioral Assessment Scale: Personal reflections. In J. K. Nugent, B. J. Petrauskas, & T. B. Brazelton (Eds.), *The newborn as a person* (pp. 278–286). Hoboken, NJ: Wiley.

Breckenridge, K., Braddick, O., & Atkinson, J. (2013). The organization of attention in typical development: A new preschool attention test battery. *British Journal of Developmental Psychology, 31*(3), 271–288. doi:10.1111/bjdp.12004

Bredekamp, S. (2011). *Effective practices in early childhood education: Building a foundation.* Upper Saddle River, NJ: Pearson Education.

Bredekamp, S. (2011). *Effective practices in early childhood education: Building a foundation.* Upper Saddle River, NJ: Pearson Education.

Bredekamp, S., & Copple, C. (Eds.). (1997). *Developmentally appropriate practice in early childhood programs* (3rd ed.). Washington, DC: National Association for the Education of Young Children.

Bredekamp, S., & Copple, C. (Eds.). (1997). *Developmentally appropriate practice in early childhood programs* (3rd ed.). Washington, DC: National Association for the Education of Young Children.

Brendgen, M. (2014). The interplay between genetic factors and the peer environment in explaining children's social adjustment. *Merrill-Palmer Quarterly, 60*(2), 101–109.

Brener, N. D., Eaton, D. K., Kann, L. K., McManus, T. S., Lee, S. M., Scanlon, K. S., Fulton, J. E., & O'Toole, T. P. (2013). Behaviors related to physical activity and nutrition among U.S. High school students. *Journal of Adolescent Health.* doi:10.1016/j.jadohealth.2013.05.006

Brenner, E. M., & Salovey, P. (1997). Emotion regulation during childhood: Developmental, interpersonal, and individual considerations. In P. Salovey & D. J. Sluyter (Eds.), *Emotional development and emotional intelligence: Educational implications* (pp. 168–195). New York, NY: Basic Books.

Bretherton, I. (1991). Pouring new wine into old bottles: The social self as internal working model. In M. R. Gunnar & L. A. Sroufe (Eds.), *Self processes and development: The Minnesota Symposia on Child Development* (Vol. 23, pp. 1–42). Hillsdale, NJ: Erlbaum.

Bretherton, I., Fritz, J., Zahn-Waxler, C., & Ridgeway, D. (1986). Learning to talk about emotions: A functionalist perspective. *Child Development, 57,* 529–548.

Brewin, M., & Statham, J. (2011). Supporting the transition from primary school to secondary school for children who are looked after. *Educational Psychology in Practice, 27*(4), 365–381. doi:10.1080/02667363.2011.624301

Bridgett, D. J., Laake, L. M., Gartstein, M. A., & Dorn, D. (2013). Development of infant positive emotionality: The contribution of maternal characteristics and effects on subsequent parenting. *Infant & Child Development, 22*(4), 362–382. doi:10.1002/icd.1795

Brietzke, E., Moreira, C. L. R., Toniolo, R. A., & Lafer, B. (2011). Clinical correlates of eating disorder comorbidity in women with bipolar disorder type I. *Journal of Affective Disorders, 130*(1–2), 162–165. doi:10.1016/j.jad.2010.10.020

Briggs, N. C., Lambert, E. W., Goldzweig, I. A., Levine, R. S., & Warren, R. C. (2008). Driver and passenger seatbelt use among U.S. high school students. *American Journal of Preventive Medicine, 35*(3), 224–229.

Briley, D. A., & Tucker-Drob, E. M. (2013). Explaining the increasing heritability of cognitive ability across development: A meta-analysis of longitudinal twin and adoption studies. *Psychological Science, 24*(9), 1704–1713. doi:10.1177/0956797613478618

Brinton, B., & Fujiki, M. (1984). Development of topic manipulation skills in discourse. *Journal of Speech and Hearing Research, 27,* 350–358.

Brintworth, K., & Sandall, J. (2013). What makes a successful home birth service: An examination of the influential elements by review of one service. Midwifery, 29(6), 713–721. doi:10.1016/j.midw.2012.06.016

Brittian, A., O'Donnell, M., Knight, G., Carlo, G., Umaña-Taylor, A., & Roosa, M. (2013). Associations between adolescents' perceived discrimination and prosocial tendencies: The mediating role of Mexican American values. *Journal of Youth & Adolescence, 42*(3), 328–341. doi:10.1007/s10964-012-9856-6

Brittin, R. V. (2014). Young listeners' music style preferences: Patterns related to cultural identification and language use. *Journal of Research in Music Education, 61*(4), 415–430. doi:10.1177/0022429413509108

Broc, L., Bernicot, J., Olive, T., Favart, M., Reilly, J., Quémart, P., & Uzé, J. (2013). Lexical spelling in children and adolescents with specific language impairment: Variations with the writing situation. *Research In Developmental Disabilities, 34*(10), 3253–3266. doi:10.1016/j.ridd.2013.06.025

Brody, G. H., Chen, Y.-F., Murry, V. M., Ge, X., Simons, R. L., Gibbons, F. X., et al. (2006). Perceived discrimination and the adjustment of African American youths: A five-year longitudinal analysis with contextual moderation effects. *Child Development, 77,* 1170–1189.

Brody, G. H., Lei, M., Chae, D. H., Yu, T., Kogan, S. M., & Beach, S. H. (2014). Perceived discrimination among African American adolescents and allostatic load: A longitudinal analysis with buffering effects. *Child Development, 85*(3), 989–1002. doi:10.1111/cdev.12213

Brody, G. H., Stoneman, Z., & McCoy, J. K. (1994). Forecasting sibling relationships in early adolescence from child temperament and family processes in middle childhood. *Child Development, 65,* 771–784.

Brody, G. H., Yu, T., Beach, S. H., Kogan, S. M., Windle, M., & Philibert, R. A. (2013). Harsh parenting and adolescent health: A longitudinal analysis with genetic moderation. *Health Psychology.* doi:10.1037/a0032686

Brody, N. (1992). *Intelligence.* New York, NY: Academic Press.

Brody, N. (1997). Intelligence, schooling, and society. *American Psychologist, 52,* 1046–1050.

Brody, N. (2004). Review of "Emotional Intelligence: Science and Myth." *Intelligence, 32*(1), 109–111. doi:10.1016/S0160-2896(03)00059-X

Brody, N. (2006). Geocentric theory: A valid interpretation of Gardner's theory of intelligence. In

J. A. Schaler (Ed.), *Howard Gardner under fire: The rebel psychologist faces his critics* (pp. 73–94). Chicago, IL: Open Court.

Brodzinsky, D. M. (2006). Family structural openness and communication openness as predictors in the adjustment of adopted children. *Adoption Quarterly, 9*(4), 1–19.

Bronfenbrenner, U. (1979). *The ecology of human development: Experiments by nature and design.* Cambridge, MA: Harvard University Press.

Bronfenbrenner, U. (1999). Is early intervention effective? Some studies of early education in familial and extra-familial settings. In A. Montagu (Ed.), *Race and IQ* (expanded ed., pp. 343–378). New York, NY: Oxford University Press.

Bronfenbrenner, U. (2001). The bioecological theory of human development. In N. J. Smelser & P. B. Baltes (Eds.), *International encyclopedia of the social and behavioral sciences* (Vol. 10, pp. 6963–6970). New York, NY: Elsevier.

Bronfenbrenner, U. (2005). *Making human beings human: Bioecological perspectives on human development.* Thousand Oaks, CA: Sage.

Bronfenbrenner, U., & Morris, P. A. (2006). The bioecological model of human development. In W. Damon & R. M. Lerner (Eds. in Chief) & R. M. Lerner (Vol. Ed.), *Handbook of child psychology: Vol. 1. Theoretical models of human development* (6th ed., pp. 793–828). Hoboken, NJ: Wiley.

Bronfenbrenner, U., Alvarez, W. F., & Henderson, C. R., Jr. (1984). Working and watching: Maternal employment status and parents' perceptions of their three-year-old children. *Child Development, 55,* 1362–1379.

Bronson, M. B. (2000). *Self-regulation in early childhood: Nature and nurture.* New York, NY: Guilford Press.

Brook, J., Chenshu, Z., Finch, S., & Brook, D. (2010). Adolescent pathways to adult smoking: Ethnic identity, peer substance use, and antisocial behavior. *American Journal on Addictions, 19*(2), 178–186.

Brookhart, S. (2013). Assessing Creativity. *Educational Leadership, 70*(5), 28–34.

Brooks, R., & Meltzoff, A. N. (2014). Gaze following: A mechanism for building social connections between infants and adults. In M. Mikulincer & P. R. Shaver (Eds.), *Mechanisms of social connection: From brain to group* (pp. 167–183). Washington, DC: American Psychological Association. doi:10.1037/14250-010

Brooks-Gunn, J. (2003). Do you believe in magic? What we can expect from early childhood intervention programs. *Social Policy Report, 17*(1). Ann Arbor, MI: Society for Research in Child Development.

Brooks-Gunn, J., & Furstenberg, F. F. (1990). Coming of age in the era of AIDS: Puberty, sexuality, and contraception. *Milbrank Quarterly, 68*(Suppl. 1), 59–84.

Brooks-Gunn, J., & Paikoff, R. L. (1992). Changes in self-feelings during the transition toward adolescence. In H. R. McGurk (Ed.), *Childhood social development: Contemporary perspectives* (pp. 63–97). Hillsdale, NJ: Erlbaum.

Brooks-Gunn, J., & Paikoff, R. L. (1993). "Sex is a gamble, kissing is a game": Adolescent sexuality and health promotion. In S. G. Millstein, A. C. Petersen, & E. O. Nightingale (Eds.), *Promoting the health of adolescents: New directions for the twenty-first century* (pp. 180–208). New York, NY: Oxford University Press.

Brooks-Gunn, J., Klebanov, P. K., & Duncan, G. J. (1996). Ethnic differences in children's intelligence test scores: Role of economic deprivation, home environment, and maternal characteristics. *Child Development, 67,* 396–408.

Brophy, J. E. (2004). *Motivating students to learn* (2nd ed.). Mahwah, NJ: Erlbaum.

Brophy, J. E. (2004). *Motivating students to learn* (2nd ed.). Mahwah, NJ: Erlbaum.

Brophy, J. E., & Alleman, J. (1996). *Powerful social studies for elementary students.* Fort Worth, TX: Harcourt Brace.

Brophy, J. E., & VanSledright, B. (1997). *Teaching and learning history in elementary schools.* New York, NY: Teachers College Press.

Brophy, J. E., Alleman, J., & Knighton, B. (2009). *Inside the social studies classroom.* New York, NY: Routledge.

Brouzos, A., Misailidi, P., & Hadjimattheou, A. (2014). Associations between emotional intelligence, socio-emotional adjustment, and academic achievement in childhood: The influence of age. *Canadian Journal of School Psychology, 29*(2), 83-99. doi:10.1177/0829573514521976

Brown, A. L., & Campione, J. C. (1994). Guided discovery in a community of learners. In K. McGilly (Ed.), *Classroom lessons: Integrating cognitive theory and classroom practice.* Cambridge, MA: MIT Press.

Brown, A. L., & Palincsar, A. S. (1987). Reciprocal teaching of comprehension strategies: A natural history of one program for enhancing learning. In J. Borkowski & J. D. Day (Eds.), *Cognition in special education: Comparative approaches to retardation, learning disabilities, and giftedness (pp. 81-132).* Norwood, NJ: Ablex.

Brown, B. B. (1990). Peer groups and peer culture. In S. S. Feldman & G. R. Elliott (Eds.), *At the threshold: The developing adolescent* (pp. 171–196). Cambridge, MA: Harvard University Press.

Brown, B. B. (1993). School culture, social politics, and the academic motivation of U.S. citizens. In T. M. Tomlinson (Ed.), *Motivating students to learn: Overcoming barriers to high achievement.* Berkeley, CA: McCutchan.

Brown, B. B., & Dietz, E. L. (2009). Informal peer groups in middle childhood and adolescence. In K. H. Rubin, W. M. Bukowski, & B. Laursen (Eds.), *Handbook of peer interactions, relationships, and groups* (pp. 361–376). New York, NY: Guilford Press.

Brown, B. B., Eicher, S. A., & Petrie, S. (1986). The importance of peer group ("crowd") affiliation in adolescence. *Journal of Adolescence, 9,* 73–96.

Brown, C., & Brown, B. (2014). On passing (or not): Developing under multicultural heritages. *Journal of The American Academy of Child & Adolescent Psychiatry, 53*(6), 603–605. doi:10.1016/j.jaac.2014.02.011

Brown, C., & Chu, H. (2012). Discrimination, ethnic identity, and academic outcomes of Mexican immigrant children: The importance of school context. *Child Development, 83*(5), 1477–1485. doi:10.1111/j.1467-8624.2012.01786.x

Brown, J. V., Bakeman, R., Coles, C. D., Platzman, K. A., & Lynch, M. E. (2004). Prenatal cocaine exposure: A comparison of 2-year-old children in parental and nonparental care. *Child Development, 75,* 1282–1295.

Brown, L. F., Pridham, K. A., & Brown, R. (2014). Sequential observation of infant regulated and dysregulated behavior following soothing and stimulating maternal behavior during feeding. *Journal for Specialists In Pediatric Nursing, 19*(2), 139-148. doi:10.1111/jspn.12062

Brown, L. M., Tappan, M. B., & Gilligan, C. (1995). Listening to different voices. In W. M. Kurtines & J. L. Gewirtz (Eds.), *Moral development: An introduction (pp. 311–335).* Boston, MA: Allyn & Bacon.

Brown, R. (1973). *A first language: The early stages.* Cambridge, MA: Harvard University Press.

Brown, R., & Hanlon, C. (1970). Derivational complexity and order of acquisition in child speech.

In J. R. Hayes (Ed.), *Cognition and the development of language (pp. 11-54).* New York, NY: Wiley.

Browne, J., O'Brien, M., Taylor, J., Bowman, R., & Davis, D. (2014). 'You've got it within you': The political act of keeping a wellness focus in the antenatal time. *Midwifery, 30*(4), 420-426. doi:10.1016/j.midw.2013.04.003

Brownell, C. A., Iesue, S. S., Nichols, S. R., & Svetlova, M. (2013). Mine or yours? Development of sharing in toddlers in relation to ownership understanding. *Child Development, 84*(3), 906–920. doi:10.1111/cdev.12009

Brownell, C. A., Svetlova, M., Anderson, R., Nichols, S. R., & Drummond, J. (2013). Socialization of early prosocial behavior: Parents' talk about emotions is associated with sharing and helping in toddlers. *Infancy, 18*(1), 91–119. doi:10.1111/j.1532-7078.2012.00125.x

Brownell, C. A., Svetlova, M., Anderson, R., Nichols, S. R., & Drummond, J. (2013). Socialization of early prosocial behavior: Parents' talk about emotions is associated with sharing and helping in toddlers. *Infancy, 18*(1), 91–119. doi:10.1111/j.1532-7078.2012.00125.x

Brownell, M. T., Mellard, D. F., & Deshler, D. D. (1993). Differences in the learning and transfer performance between students with learning disabilities and other low-achieving students on problem-solving tasks. *Learning Disabilities Quarterly, 16,* 138–156.

Bruer, J. T. (1999). *The myth of the first three years: A new understanding of early brain development and lifelong learning.* New York, NY: Free Press.

Brumariu, L., & Kerns, K. (2013). Pathways to anxiety: Contributions of attachment history, temperament, peer competence, and ability to manage intense emotions. *Child Psychiatry & Human Development, 44*(4), 504–515.

Brummelman, E., Thomaes, S., Orobio de Castro, B., Overbeek, G., & Bushman, B. (2014). "That's not just beautiful—That's incredibly beautiful!" The adverse impact of inflated praise on children with low self-esteem. *Psychological Science, 25*(3), 728–735.

Bruner, J. S. (1966). *Toward a theory of instruction.* Cambridge, MA: Harvard University Press.

Bruner, J. S. (1972). The nature and uses of immaturity. *American Psychologist, 27,* 687–708.

Bruner, J. S. (1983). The acquisition of pragmatic commitments. In R. M. Golinkoff (Ed.), *The transition from prelinguistic to linguistic communication (pp. 27–42).* Hillsdale, NJ: Erlbaum.

Bruner, J. S., & Sherwood, V. (1976). Early rule structure: The case of "peekaboo." In R. Harre (Ed.), *Life sentences* (pp. 55–62). London, England: Wiley.

Bryan, J., & Henry, L. (2008). Strengths-based partnerships: A school-family-community partnership approach to empowering students. *Professional School Counseling, 12*(2), 149–156.

Bryan, T., Burstein, K., & Bryan, J. (2001). Students with learning disabilities: Homework problems and promising practices. *Educational Psychologist, 36,* 167–180.

Bryant, G. A., Liénard, P., & Barrett, H. (2012). Recognizing infant-directed speech across distant cultures: Evidence from Africa. *Journal of Evolutionary Psychology, 10*(2), 47–59. doi:10.1556/JEP.10.2012.2.1

Bryant, P., & Nuñes, T. (2011). Children's understanding of mathematics. In U. Goswami (Ed.), *The Wiley-Blackwell handbook of childhood cognitive development* (2nd ed., pp. 549–573). Malden, MA: Wiley-Blackwell.

Buchanan, C. M., Eccles, J. S., & Becker, J. B. (1992). Are adolescents the victims of raging hormones: Evidence for activational effects of hormones on

moods and behaviors at adolescence. *Psychological Bulletin, 111,* 62–107.

Buchmann, A. F., Holz, N., Boecker, R., Blomeyer, D., Rietschel, M., Witt, S. H., Schmidt, M., Esser, G., Banaschewski, T., Brandeis, D., Zimmermann, U., & Laucht, M. (2014). Moderating role of FKBP5 genotype in the impact of childhood adversity on cortisol stress response during adulthood. *European Neuropsychopharmacology, 24*(6), 837–845. doi:10.1016/j.euroneuro.2013.12.001

Buchoff, T. (1990). Attention deficit disorder: Help for the classroom teacher. *Childhood Education, 67*(2), 86–90.

Buck, G. A., Cook, K. L., Quigley, C. F., Prince, P., & Lucas, Y. (2014). Seeking to improve African American girls' attitudes toward science. *Elementary School Journal, 114*(3), 431–453.

Buck, K. A., Kretsch, N., & Harden, K. (2013). Positive attentional bias, attachment style, and susceptibility to peer influence. *Journal of Research on Adolescence, 23*(4), 605–613. doi:10.1111/jora.12026

Buckle, M. E., & Walsh, D. S. (2013). Teaching responsibility to gang-affiliated Youths. *JOPERD: The Journal of Physical Education, Recreation & Dance, 84*(2), 53–58.

Budd, G. M., & Volpe, S. L. (2006). School-based obesity prevention: Research, challenges, and recommendations. *Journal of School Health, 76,* 485–495.

Bugental, D. (2009). Predicting and preventing child maltreatment: A biocognitive transactional approach. In A. Sameroff (Ed.), *The transactional model of development: How children and contexts shape each other* (pp. 97–115). Washington, DC: American Psychological Association.

Buhrmester, D. (1992). The developmental courses of sibling and peer relationships. In F. Boer & J. Dunn (Eds.), *Children's sibling relationships: Developmental and clinical issues.* Hillsdale, NJ: Erlbaum.

Buijzen, M., & Valkenburg, P. M. (2003). The effects of television advertising on materialism, parent–child conflict, and unhappiness: A review of research. *Applied Developmental Psychology, 24,* 437–456.

Buka, S. L., Cannon, T. D., Torrey, E. F., Yolken, R. H., and the Collaborative Study Group on the Perinatal Origins of Severe Psychiatric Disorders (2008). Maternal exposure to herpes simplex virus and risk of psychosis among adult offspring. *Biological Psychiatry, 63*(8), 809–815.

Bukstein, O. C., & Deas, D. (2010). Substance abuse and addictions. In M. K. Dulcan (Eds.), *Dulcan's textbook of child and adolescent psychiatry* (pp. 241–258). Arlington, VA: American Psychiatric Publishing.

Bull, R., & Lee, K. (2014). Executive functioning and mathematics achievement. *Child Development Perspectives, 8*(1), 36–41. doi:10.1111/cdep.12059

Bull, R., Cleland, A. A., & Mitchell, T. (2013). Sex differences in the spatial representation of number. *Journal of Experimental Psychology, 142*(1), 181–192. doi:10.1037/a0028387

Bunch, G. (2013). Pedagogical language knowledge: Preparing mainstream teachers for English learners in the new standards era. *Review of Research in Education, 37*(1), 298–341. doi:10.3102/0091732X12461772

Burchinal, M. R., Lowe Vandell, D., & Belsky, J. (2014). Is the prediction of adolescent outcomes from early child care moderated by later maternal sensitivity? Results from the NICHD Study of Early Child Care and Youth Development. *Developmental Psychology, 50*(2), 542–553. doi:10.1037/a0033709

Burhans, K. K., & Dweck, C. S. (1995). Helplessness in early childhood: The role of contingent worth. *Child Development, 66,* 1719–1738.

Burns, C. E., Brady, M. A., Dunn, A. M., & Starr, N. B. (2000). *Pediatric primary care: A handbook for nurse practitioners*, (2nd ed.). Philadelphia, PA: Saunders.

Burny, E., Valcke, M., Desoete, A., & Van Luit, J. (2013). Curriculum sequencing and the acquisition of clock-reading skills among Chinese and Flemish children. *International Journal of Science & Mathematics Education, 11*(3), 761–785. doi:10.1007/s10763-012-9362-z

Burrous, C. E., Crockenberg, S. C., & Leerkes, E. M. (2009). Developmental history of care and control, depression and anger: Correlates of maternal sensitivity in toddlerhood. *Infant Mental Health Journal, 30*(2), 103–123.

Burstyn, J. N., & Stevens, R. (2001). Involving the whole school in violence prevention. In J. N. Burstyn, G. Bender, R. Casella, H. W. Gordon, D. P. Guerra, K. V. Luschen, et al. (Eds.), *Preventing violence in schools: A challenge to American democracy* (pp. 139–158). Mahwah, NJ: Erlbaum.

Bursuck, B., & Blanks, B. (2010). Evidence-based early reading practices within a response to intervention system. *Psychology in the Schools. Special Issue: Literacy and Disabilities, 47*(5), 421–431.

Burton, C., Marshal, M., & Chisolm, D. (2014). School absenteeism and mental health among sexual minority youth and heterosexual youth. *Journal of School Psychology, 52*(1), 37–47. doi:10.1016/j.jsp.2013.12.001

Burton, S., & Mitchell, P. (2003). Judging who knows best about yourself: Developmental change in citing the self across middle childhood. *Child Development, 74*, 426–443.

Bussi, M. G. B., & Boni, M. (2009). The early construction of mathematical meanings: Learning positional representation of numbers. In O. A. Barbarin & B. H. Wasik (Eds.), *Handbook of early child development and early education: Research to practice* (pp. 455–477). New York, NY: Guilford Press.

Butler, R. (1994). Teacher communication and student interpretations: Effects of teacher responses to failing students on attributional inferences in two age groups. *British Journal of Educational Psychology, 64*, 277–294.

Butler, R. N. (1963). The life review: An interpretation of reminiscence in the aged. *Psychiatry, 26*, 65–76.

Button, R. E. (2007). Teachers' anger, frustration, and self-regulation. In P. A. Schutz, & R. Pekrun (Eds.), *Emotion in education. Educational psychology series* (pp. 259–274). San Diego, CA: Elsevier Academic Press.

Byard, E., Kosciw, J., & Bartkiewicz, M. (2013). Schools and LGBT-parent families: Creating change through programming and advocacy. In A. E. Goldberg, K. R. Allen (Eds.), *LGBT-parent families: Innovations in research and implications for practice* (pp. 275–290). New York, NY: Springer Science + Business Media. doi:10.1007/978-1-4614-4556-2_18

Byrge, L., Smith, L. B., & Mix, K. S. (2014). Beginnings of place value: How preschoolers write three-digit numbers. *Child Development, 85*(2), 437–443. doi:10.1111/cdev.12162

Byrne, B. M. (2002). Validating the measurement and structure of self-concept: Snapshots of past, present, and future research. *American Psychologist, 57*, 897–909.

Byrne, B. M., & Shavelson, R. J. (1986, April). *On gender differences in the structure of adolescent self-concept.* Paper presented at the annual meeting of the American Educational Research Association, San Francisco.

Byrne, J., Hauck, Y., Fisher, C., Bayes, S., & Schutze, R. (2014). Effectiveness of a mindfulness-based childbirth education pilot study on maternal self-efficacy and fear of childbirth. *Journal of Midwifery & Women's Health, 59*(2), 192-197.

Byrnes, J. P. (1996). *Cognitive development and learning in instructional contexts.* Boston, MA: Allyn & Bacon.

Byrnes, J. P., & Wasik, B. A. (2009). *Language and literacy development: What educators need to know.* New York, NY: Guilford Press.

Bystydzienski, J., & Brown, A. (2012). "I just want to help people": Young women's gendered engagement with engineering. *Feminist Formations, 24*(3), 1–21. doi:10.1353/ff.2012.0027

Côté, I., Rouleau, N., & Macoir, J. (2014). New word acquisition in children: Examining the contribution of verbal short-term memory to lexical and semantic levels of learning. *Applied Cognitive Psychology, 28*(1), 104–114. doi:10.1002/acp.2961

Côté, J. E. (2005). Erikson's theory. In C. B. Fisher & R. M. Lerner (Eds.), *Encyclopedia of applied developmental science* (Vol. 1, pp. 406–409). Thousand Oaks, CA: Sage.

Cabell, S. Q., Justice, L. M., Konold, T. R., & McGinty, A. S. (2010). Profiles of emergent literacy skills among preschool children who are at risk for academic difficulties. *Early Childhood Research Quarterly, 26*(1), 1–14.

Cacchione, T. (2013). The foundations of object permanence: Does perceived cohesion determine infants' appreciation of the continuous existence of material objects? *Cognition, 128*(3), 397–406. doi:10.1016/j.cognition.2013.05.006

Cacchione, T., Schaub, S., & Rakoczy, H. (2013). Fourteen-month-old infants infer the continuous identity of objects on the basis of nonvisible causal properties. *Developmental Psychology, 49*(7), 1325–1329. doi:10.1037/a0029746

Cai, H., Wu, M., Luo, Y. L., & Yang, J. (2014). Implicit self-esteem decreases in adolescence: A cross-sectional study. *Plos ONE, 9*(2), 1–5. doi:10.1371/journal.pone.0089988

Cai, J., Ding, M., & Wang, T. (2014). How do exemplary Chinese and U.S. mathematics teachers view instructional coherence? *Educational Studies in Mathematics, 85*(2), 265–280. doi:10.1007/s10649-013-9513-3

Cain, C. S. (2006). *Attachment disorders: Treatment strategies for traumatized children.* Lantham, MD: Jason Aronson Publishing.

Cain, K., & Oakhill, J. (1998). Comprehension skill and inference-making ability: Issues of causality. In C. Hulme & R. M. Joshi (Eds.), *Reading and spelling: Development and disorders (pp. 329-342)).* Mahwah, NJ: Erlbaum.

Calder, L., Hill, V., & Pellicano, E. (2013). "Sometimes I want to play by myself": Understanding what friendship means to children with autism in mainstream primary schools. *Autism: The International Journal of Research & Practice, 17*(3), 296–316. doi:10.1177/1362361312467866

Calin-Jageman, R. J., & Ratner, H. H. (2005). The role of encoding in the self-explanation effect. *Cognition and Instruction, 23*, 523–543.

Calkins, S. D., & Marcovitch, S. (2010). Emotion regulation and executive functioning in early development: Integrated mechanisms of control supporting adaptive functioning. In S. D. Calkins & M. A. Bell (Eds.), *Child development at the intersection of emotion and cognition* (pp. 37–57). Washington, DC: American Psychological Association.

Callanan, M. A., & Oakes, L. M. (1992). Preschoolers' questions and parents' explanations: Causal thinking in everyday activity. *Cognitive Development, 7*, 213–233.

Callister, L., Corbett, C., Reed, S., Tomao, C., & Thornton, K. G. (2010). Giving birth: The voices of Ecuadorian women. Journal of Perinatal & Neonatal Nursing, 24(2), 146–154.

Callister, L., Eads, M., & See Yeung, P. (2011). Perceptions of giving birth and adherence to cultural practices in Chinese women. MCN: American Journal of Maternal Child Nursing, 36(6), 387–394.

Calvert, S. L. (2008). Children as consumers: Advertising and marketing. *Future of Children, 18*(1), 205–234.

Calvin, C. M., Deary, I. J., Webbink, D., Smith, P., Fernandes, C., Lee, S., et al. (2012). Multivariate genetic analyses of cognition and academic achievement from two population samples of 174,000 and 166,000 school children. *Behavior Genetics, 42*(5), 699–710. doi:10.1007/s10519-012-9549-7

Calvin, C. M., Fernandes, C., Smith, P., Visscher, P. M., & Deary, I. J. (2010). Sex, intelligence and educational achievement in a national cohort of over 175,000 11-year-old schoolchildren in England. *Intelligence, 38*, 424–432.

Cameron, C. A., Hunt, A. K., & Linton, M. J. (1996). Written expression as recontextualization: Children write in social time. *Educational Psychology Review, 8*, 125–150.

Cameron, J. (2001). Negative effects of reward on intrinsic motivation—a limited phenomenon: Comment on Deci, Koestner, and Ryan (2001). *Review of Educational Research, 71*, 29–42.

Camilleri, B., & Botting, N. (2013). Beyond static assessment of children's receptive vocabulary: The dynamic assessment of word learning (DAWL). *International Journal of Language & Communication Disorders, 48*(5), 565–581. doi:10.1111/1460-6984.12033

Camos, V. (2003). Counting strategies from 5 years to adulthood: Adaptation to structural features. *European Journal of Psychology of Education—EJPE (Instituto Superior De Psicologia Aplicada), 18*(3), 251–265.

Campbell, A. (1984). *The girls in the gang: A report from New York City.* New York, NY: Basil Blackwell.

Campbell, D. T., & Stanley, J. C. (1963). Experimental and quasi-experimental designs for research on teaching. In N. L. Gage (Ed.), *Handbook of research on teaching* (pp. 171–246). Chicago, IL: Rand McNally.

Campbell, F. A., & Ramey, C. T. (1995). Cognitive and school outcomes for high-risk African-American students at middle adolescence: Positive effects of early intervention. *American Educational Research Journal, 32*(4), 743–772.

Campbell, F. A., Pungello, E. P., Burchinal, M., Kainz, K., Pan, Y., Wasik, B. H., Barbarin, O. A., et al. (2012). Adult outcomes as a function of an early childhood educational program: An Abecedarian Project follow-up. *Developmental Psychology, 48*(4), 1033–1043. doi:10.1037/a0026644

Campbell, F. A., Pungello, E. P., Miller-Johnson, S., Burchinal, M., & Ramey, C. T. (2001). The development of cognitive and academic abilities: Growth curves from an early childhood educational experiment. *Developmental Psychology, 37*(2), 231–242.

Campbell, F. A., Ramey, C. T., Pungello, E., Sparling, J., & Miller-Johnson, S. (2002). Early childhood education: Young adult outcomes from the Abecedarian Project. *Applied Developmental Science, 6,* 42–57.

Campbell, F., Pungello, E., Burchinal, M., Kainz, K., Yi, P., Wasik, B., Barbarin, O, Sparling, J., & Ramey, C. (2012). Adult outcomes as a function of an early childhood educational program: An Abecedarian Project follow-up. *Developmental Psychology, 48*(4), 1033–1043. doi:10.1037/a0026644

Campbell, L., Campbell, B., & Dickinson, D. (1998). *Teaching and learning through multiple intelligences* (2nd ed.). Boston, MA: Allyn & Bacon.

Campbell, T. F., Dollaghan, C. A., Rockette, H. E., Paradise, J. L., Feldman, H. M., Shriberg, L. D., et al. (2003). Risk factors for speech delay of unknown origin in 3-year-old children. *Child Development, 74*, 346–357.

Campione, J. C., Shapiro, A. M., & Brown, A. L. (1995). Forms of transfer in a community of learners: Flexible learning and understanding. In A. McKeough, J. Lupart, & A. Marini (Eds.), *Teaching for transfer: Fostering generalization in learning (pp. 35–68).* Mahwah, NJ: Erlbaum.

Campos, J. J., Frankel, C. B., & Camras, L. (2004). On the nature of emotion regulation. *Child Development, 75,* 377–394.

Camras, L. A., Malatesta, C., & Izard, C. (1991). The development of facial expressions in infancy. In R. S. Feldman & B. Rime (Eds.), *Fundamentals of nonverbal behavior: Studies in emotion and social interaction* (pp. 73–105). New York, NY: Cambridge University Press.

Camras, L. A., Oster, H., Campos, J., Campos, R., Ujiie, T., Miyake, K., et al. (1998). Production of emotional facial expressions in European American, Japanese, and Chinese infants. *Developmental Psychology, 34*(4), 616–628.

Cangialose, A., & Allen, P. (2014). Screening for Autism spectrum disorders in infants before 18 months of age. *Pediatric Nursing, 40*(1), 33–37.

Cano, F., García, Á., Berbén, A. G., & Justicia, F. (2014). Science Learning: A path analysis of its links with reading comprehension, question-asking in class and science achievement. *International Journal of Science Education, 36*(10), 1710-1732. doi:10.1080/09500693.2013.876678

Cantrell, L., & Smith, L. B. (2013). Open questions and a proposal: A critical review of the evidence on infant numerical abilities. *Cognition, 128*(3), 331–352. doi:10.1016/j.cognition.2013.04.008

Capelli, C. A., Nakagawa, N., & Madden, C. M. (1990). How children understand sarcasm: The role of context and intonation. *Child Development, 61,* 1824–1841.

Caplan, M., Vespo, J. E., Pedersen, J., & Hay, D. F. (1991). Conflict over resources in small groups of 1- and 2-year-olds. *Child Development, 62,* 1513–1524.

Cappella, E., Kim, H., Neal, J. W., & Jackson, D. R. (2013). Classroom peer relationships and behavioral engagement in elementary school: The role of social network equity. *American Journal of Community Psychology, 52*(3–4), 367–379. doi:10.1007/s10464-013-9603-5

Capron, C., & Duyme, M. (1989). Assessment of effects of socio-economic status on IQ in a full cross-fostering study. *Nature, 340*(6234), 552–554.

Caputi, M., Lecce, S., Pagnin, A., & Banerjee, R. (2012). Longitudinal effects of theory of mind on later peer relations: The role of prosocial behavior. *Developmental Psychology, 48*(1), 257–270. doi:10.1037/a0025402

Cardelle-Elawar, M. (1992). Effects of teaching metacognitive skills to students with low mathematics ability. *Teaching and Teacher Education, 8,* 109–121.

Carey, S. (1978). The child as word learner. In M. Halle, J. Bresnan, & G. Miller (Eds.), *Linguistic theory and psychological reality.* Cambridge, MA: MIT Press.

Carey, S. (1985). *Conceptual change in childhood.* Cambridge, MA: MIT Press.

Carey, S. (1988). Are children fundamentally different kinds of thinkers and learners than adults? In K. Richardson, S. Sheldon (Eds.), *Cognitive development to adolescence: A reader* (pp. 105–138). Hillsdale, NJ: Erlbaum.

Carey, S., & Bartlett, E. (1978). Acquiring a single new word. *Papers and Reports on Child Language Development, 15,* 17–29.

Carey, S., Evans, R., Honda, M., Jay, E., & Unger, C. (1989). "An experiment is when you try it and see if it works": A study of grade 7 students' understanding of the construction of scientific knowledge. *International Journal of Science Education, 11,* 514–529.

Carla, B. (2003). Natural birthing lessons from Nepal. *British Journal of Midwifery, 11*(8), 492–495.

Carlisi, C. O., Pavletic, N. N., & Ernst, M. M. (2013). New perspectives on neural systems models of adolescent behavior: Functional brain connectivity. *Neuropsychiatrie De L'enfance Et De L'adolescence, 61*(4), 209–218. doi:10.1016/j.neurenf.2013.02.003

Carlo, G., Koller, S., Raffaelli, M., & de Guzman, M. R. T. (2007). Culture-related strengths among Latin American families: A case study of Brazil. *Marriage and Family Review, 41*(3/4), 335–360.

Carlson, E. A., Hostinar, C. E., Mliner, S. B., & Gunnar, M. R. (2014). The emergence of attachment following early social deprivation. *Development & Psychopathology, 26*(2), 479–489. doi:10.1017/S0954579414000078

Carlson, E. A., Sampson, M. C., & Sroufe, L. A. (2003). Implications of attachment theory and research for developmental-behavioral pediatrics. *Journal of Developmental and Behavioral Pediatrics, 24,* 364–379.

Carlson, N. R. (2014). *Foundations of behavioral neuroscience* (9th ed.). Boston, MA: Pearson.

Carlson, S. A., Fulton, J. E., Lee, S. M., Maynard, M., Brown, D. R., Kohl, H. W. III, et al. (2008). Physical education and academic achievement in elementary school: Data from the early childhood longitudinal study. *American Journal of Public Health, 98*(4), 721–727.

Carlson, S. M., White, R. E., & Davis-Unger, A. C. (2014). Evidence for a relation between executive function and pretense representation in preschool children. *Cognitive Development, 29*1-16. doi:10.1016/j.cogdev.2013.09.001

Carmona, S., Proal, E., Hoekzema, E. A., Gispert, J., Picado, M., Moreno, I., et al. (2009). Ventro-striatal reductions underpin symptoms of hyperactivity and impulsivity in attention-deficit/hyperactivity disorder. *Biological Psychiatry, 66*(10), 972–977.

Carnell, S., Kim, Y., & Pryor, K. (2012). Fat brains, greedy genes, and parent power: A biobehavioural risk model of child and adult obesity. *International Review of Psychiatry, 24*(3), 189–199. doi:10.3109/09540261.2012.676988

Carney, D. R., & Mason, M. F. (2010). Decision making and testosterone: When the ends justify the means. *Journal of Experimental Social Psychology, 46*(4), 668–671. doi:10.1016/j.jesp.2010.02.003

Caroli, M., Argentieri, L., Cardone, M., & Masi, A. (2004). Role of television in childhood obesity prevention. *International Journal of Obesity, 28,* S105–S108.

Carpenter, M., Uebel, J., & Tomasello, M. (2013). Being mimicked increases prosocial behavior in 18-month-old infants. *Child Development, 84*(5), 1511–1518. doi:10.1111/cdev.12083

Carpenter, S., Cepeda, N., Rohrer, D., Kang, S., & Pashler, H. (2012). Using spacing to enhance diverse forms of learning: Review of recent research and implications for instruction. *Educational Psychology Review, 24*(3), 369–378. doi:10.1007/s10648-012-9205-z

Carr, A. (2014). The evidence base for family therapy and systemic interventions for child-focused problems. *Journal of Family Therapy, 36*(2), 107–157. doi:10.1111/1467-6427.12032

Carr, J. (2012). Six weeks to 45 years: A longitudinal study of a population with Down syndrome. *Journal of Applied Research in Intellectual Disabilities, 25*(5), 414–422. doi:10.1111/j.1468-3148.2011.00676.x

Carr, M. (2010). The importance of metacognition for conceptual change and strategy use in mathematics. In H. S. Waters & W. Schneider (Eds.), *Metacognition, strategy use, and instruction* (pp. 176–197). New York, NY: Guilford Press.

Carr, M. (2012). Critical transitions: Arithmetic to algebra. In K. R. Harris, S. Graham, T. Urdan, A. G. Bus, S. Major, & H. L. Swanson (Eds.), *APA educational psychology handbook, Vol. 3: Application to teaching and learning* (pp. 229–255).

Washington, DC: American Psychological Association. doi:10.1037/13275-010

Carr, M., & Biddlecomb, B. (1998). Metacognition in mathematics from a constructivist perspective. In D. J. Hacker, J. Dunlosky, & A. C. Graesser (Eds.), *Metacognition in educational theory and practice* (pp. 69–91). Mahwah, NJ: Erlbaum.

Carr, M., & Schneider, W. (1991). Long-term maintenance of organizational strategies in kindergarten children. *Contemporary Educational Psychology, 16,* 61–72.

Carroll, J. B. (1993). *Human cognitive abilities: A survey of factor-analytic studies.* New York, NY: Cambridge University Press.

Carroll, J. B. (2003). The higher stratum structure of cognitive abilities: Current evidence supports g and about ten broad factors. *The scientific study of general intelligence: Tribute to Arthur Jensen* (pp. 5–21). Oxford, England: Elsevier.

Carroll, J. E., Gruenewald, T. L., Taylor, S. E., Janicki-Deverts, D., Matthews, K. A., & Seeman, T. E. (2013). Childhood abuse, parental warmth, and adult multisystem biological risk in the Coronary Artery Risk Development in Young Adults study. *PNAS—Proceedings of the National Academy of Sciences of the United States of America, 110*(42), 17149–17153. doi:10.1073/pnas.1315458110

Carruthers, P. (2013). Mindreading in infancy. *Mind & Language, 28*(2), 141–172. doi:10.1111/mila.12014

Carter, D. E., Detine-Carter, S. L., & Benson, F. W. (1995). Interracial acceptance in the classroom. In H. C. Foot, A. J. Chapman, & J. R. Smith (Eds.), *Friendship and social relations in children* (pp. 117–143). New Brunswick, NJ: Transaction.

Carter, E. W., Common, E. A., Sreckovic, M. A., Huber, H. B., Bottema-Beutel, K., Gustafson, J., Dykstra, J., & Hume, K. (2014). Promoting social competence and peer relationships for adolescents with autism spectrum disorders. *Remedial & Special Education, 35*(2), 91–101. doi:10.1177/0741932513514618

Carter, E. W., Weir, K., Cooney, M., Walter, M. J., & Moss, C. (2012). Fostering self-determination among children and youth with disabilities: Learning from parents. *Exceptional Parent, 42*(3), 13–17.

Carter, E., Asmus, J., & Moss, C. (2013). Fostering friendships: Supporting relationships among youth with and without developmental disabilities. *Prevention Researcher, 20*(2), 14–17.

Carter, K. R. (1991). Evaluation of gifted programs. In N. Buchanan & J. Feldhusen (Eds.), *Conducting research and evaluation in gifted education: A handbook of methods and applications.* New York, NY: Teachers College Press.

Carter, K. R., & Ormrod, J. E. (1982). Acquisition of formal operations by intellectually gifted children. *Gifted Child Quarterly, 26,* 110–115.

Carter, R., Jaccard, J., Silverman, W. K., & Pina, A. A. (2009). Pubertal timing and its link to behavioral and emotional problems among "at risk" African American adolescent girls. *Journal of Adolescence, 32,* 467–481.

Carver, P. R., Egan, S. K., & Perry, D. G. (2004). Children who question their heterosexuality. *Developmental Psychology, 40*(1), 43–53.

Casanova, M. F. (2008). The significance of minicolumnar size variability in autism: A perspective from comparative anatomy. In A. W. Zimmerman (Ed.), *Autism: Current theories and evidence* (pp. 349–360). Totowa, NJ: Humana Press. doi:10.1007/978-1-60327-489-0_16

Case, R. (1980). Implications of a neo-Piagetian theory for improving the design of instruction. In J. R. Kirby & J. B. Biggs (Eds.), *Cognition, development, and instruction* (pp. 161–186). New York, NY: Academic Press.

Case, R. (1985). *Intellectual development: Birth to adulthood.* Orlando, FL: Academic Press.

Case, R. (1991). *The mind's staircase: Exploring the conceptual underpinnings of children's thought ad knowledge*. Hillsdale, NJ: Erlbaum.

Case, R., & Okamoto, Y., in collaboration with Griffin, S., McKeough, A., Bleiker, C., Henderson, B., & Stephenson, K. M. (1996). The role of central conceptual structures in the development of children's thought. *Monographs of the Society for Research in Child Development, 61*(1–2, Serial No. 246).

Case, R., Okamoto, Y., Henderson, B., & McKeough, A. (1993). Individual variability and consistency in cognitive development: New evidence for the existence of central conceptual structures. In R. Case & W. Edelstein (Eds.), *The new structuralism in cognitive development: Theory and research on individual pathways* (pp. 71–100). Basel, Switzerland: Karger.

Case-Smith, J. (1996). Fine motor outcomes in preschool children who receive occupational therapy services. *American Journal of Occupational Therapy, 50*, 52–61.

Case-Smith, J. (2013). Systematic review of interventions to promote social-emotional development in young children with or at risk for disability. *American Journal of Occupational Therapy, 67*(4), 395–404. doi:10.5014/ajot.2013.004713

Casella, R. (2001). The cultural foundations of peer mediation: Beyond a behaviorist model of urban school conflict. In J. N. Burstyn, G. Bender, R. Casella, H. W. Gordon, D. P. Guerra, K. V. Luschen, et al. (Eds.), *Preventing violence in schools: A challenge to American democracy* (pp. 159–179). Mahwah, NJ: Erlbaum.

Casey, B. J., Giedd, J. N., & Thomas, K. M. (2000). Structural and functional brain development and its relation to cognitive development. *Biological Psychology, 54*, 241–257.

Caspi, A., Sugden, K., Moffitt, T. E., Taylor, A., Craig, I. W., Harrington, J., et al. (2003). Influence of life stress on depression: Moderation by the polymorphism in the 5-HTT gene. *Science, 30*, 1386–1389.

Cassano, M. C., & Zeman, J. L. (2010). Parental socialization of sadness regulation in middle childhood: The role of expectations and gender. *Developmental Psychology, 46*(5), 1214–1226.

Cassidy, J., Jones, J. D., & Shaver, P. R. (2013). Contributions of attachment theory and research: A framework for future research, translation, and policy. *Development & Psychopathology, 25*(4pt2), 1415–1434. doi:10.1017/S0954579413000692

Cassidy, M., & Berlin, L. J. (1994). The insecure-ambivalent pattern of attachment: Theory and research. *Child Development, 65*, 971–991.

Castilla, J. M. (2009) *Strange parents*. Houston, TX: Arte Público Press.

Catania, L. S., Hetrick, S. E., Newman, L. K., & Purcell, R. (2011). Prevention and early intervention for mental health problems in 0–25 year olds: Are there evidence-based models of care? *Advances in Mental Health, 10*(1), 6–19. doi:10.5172/jamh.2011.10.1.6

Cates, J. A., & Weber, C. (2012). A substance use survey with old order Amish early adolescents: Perceptions of peer alcohol and drug use. *Journal of Child & Adolescent Substance Abuse, 21*(3), 193–203. doi:10.1080/1067828X.2012.689935

Cattell, R. B. (1963). Theory of fluid and crystallized intelligence: A critical experiment. *Journal of Educational Psychology, 54*, 1–22.

Cattell, R. B. (1980). The heritability of fluid, *gf,* and crystallised, *gc,* intelligence, estimated by a least squares use of the MAVA method. *British Journal of Educational Psychology, 50*, 253–265.

Cattell, R. B. (1987). *Intelligence: Its structure, growth, and action*. Amsterdam, the Netherlands: North-Holland.

Catts, H. W., Adlof, S. M., Hogan, T. P., & Weismer, S. E. (2005). Are specific language impairments and dyslexia distinct disorders? *Journal of Speech, Language and Hearing Research, 48*, 1378–1396.

Cauffman, E., Shulman, E. P., Steinberg, L., Claus, E., Banich, M. T., Graham, S., et al. (2010). Age differences in affective decision making as indexed by performance on the Iowa Gambling Task. *Developmental Psychology, 46*(1), 193–207.

Cazden, C. B. (1968). The acquisition of noun and verb inflections. *Child Development, 39*, 433–448.

Cazden, C. B. (1976). Play with language and metalinguistic awareness: One dimension of language experience. In J. Bruner, A. Jolly, & K. Sylva (Eds.), *Play: Its role in development and evolution*. New York, NY: Basic Books.

Ceci, S. J. (2003). Cast in six ponds and you'll reel in something: Looking back on 25 years of research. *American Psychologist, 58*, 855–864.

Ceci, S. J., & Roazzi, A. (1994). The effects of context on cognition: Postcards from Brazil. In R. J. Sternberg & R. K. Wagner (Eds.), *Mind in context: Interactionist perspectives on human intelligence* (pp. 74–101). Cambridge, England: Cambridge University Press.

Ceci, S. J., & Williams, W. M. (1997). Schooling, intelligence, and income. *American Psychologist, 52*, 1051–1058.

Ceci, S. J., Rosenblum, T. B., & Kumpf, M. (1998). The shrinking gap between high- and low-scoring groups: Current trends and possible causes. In U. Neisser (Ed.), *The rising curve: Long-term gains in IQ and related measures* (pp. 287–302). Washington, DC: American Psychological Association.

Ceglowski, D., Shears, J., & Furman, R. (2010). "I want child care he's gonna be happy in": A case study of a father's child care experiences. *Early Education and Development, 21*(1), 1–20. doi:10.1080/10409280902783467

Cemalcilar, Z. (2010). Schools as socialisation contexts: Understanding the impact of school climate factors on students' sense of school belonging. *Applied Psychology, 59*(2), 243–272. doi:10.1111/j.1464-0597.2009.00389.x

Center for Children and Families. (2013). *How to establish a daily report card*. Retrieved from http://ccf.buffalo.edu/pdf/school_daily_report_card.pdf

Center for History and New Media. (2006). *Teaching American history: Conflict and consensus. Key moments in U.S. history*. Retrieved from http://chnm.gmu.edu/mcpstah/lesson-plans/1950-to-present/?planid26

Centers for Disease Control and Prevention (2002). *Planning for physical activity* (a BAM! Body and Mind Teacher's Corner resource). Retrieved from http://www.bam.gov/teachers/activities/planning.htm

Centers for Disease Control and Prevention (2013e). *HIV among women*. Retrieved from http://www.cdc.gov/hiv/risk/gender/women/facts/index.html

Centers for Disease Control and Prevention (2013h). *Injury prevention and control*. Retrieved from http://www.cdc.gov/traumaticbraininjury/prevention.html

Centers for Disease Control and Prevention. (2005a). *Nutrition and the health of young people*. Atlanta, GA: Author.

Centers for Disease Control and Prevention. (2007). Autism spectrum disorder fact sheet. Retrieved from http://www.cdc.gov/ncbddd/autism/ActEarly/autism.html

Centers for Disease Control and Prevention. (2009b). *Understanding child maltreatment*. Retrieved from http://www.cdc.gov/violenceprevention/pdf/CM-FactSheet-a.pdf

Centers for Disease Control and Prevention. (2010). *Heads up: Concussion in high school sports guide for coaches*. Retrieved from http://www.cdc.gov/concussion/pdf/Coach_Guide-a.pdf

Centers for Disease Control and Prevention. (2011). School health guidelines to promote healthy eating and physical activity. *Morbidity and Mortality Weekly Report, 60*(5). Retrieved from http://www.cdc.gov/mmwr/pdf/rr/rr6005.pdf

Centers for Disease Control and Prevention. (2012). Youth risk behavior surveillance—United States, 2011. *Morbidity and Mortality Weekly Report, 61*(4). Retrieved from http://www.cdc.gov/mmwr/pdf/ss/ss6104.pdf

Centers for Disease Control and Prevention. (2013). *Child maltreatment: Consequences*. Retrieved from http://www.cdc.gov/violenceprevention/childmaltreatment/consequences.html

Centers for Disease Control and Prevention. (2013). *Facts about birth defects*. Retrieved from http://www.cdc.gov/ncbddd/birthdefects/facts.html

Centers for Disease Control and Prevention. (2013a). *Adolescent and school health standard 6*. Retrieved from http://www.cdc.gov/healthyyouth/sher/standards/6.htm

Centers for Disease Control and Prevention. (2013b). *About BMI for children and teens*. Retrieved from http://www.cdc.gov/healthyweight/assessing/bmi/childrens_bmi/about_childrens_bmi.html

Centers for Disease Control and Prevention. (2013c). *Overweight and obesity: Childhood obesity facts*. Retrieved from http://www.cdc.gov/obesity/data/childhood.html

Centers for Disease Control and Prevention. (2013d). *Progress on childhood obesity: Many states show declines*. Retrieved from http://www.cdc.gov/VitalSigns/ChildhoodObesity/

Centers for Disease Control and Prevention. (2013f). *Injury prevention and control: Data and statistics*. Retrieved from http://www.cdc.gov/injury/wisqars/LeadingCauses.html

Centers for Disease Control and Prevention. (2013g). *Injury prevention and control: Traumatic brain injury*. Retrieved from http://www.cdc.gov/traumaticBrainInjury/causes.html

Central Intelligence Agency. (2010, January 15). *The world factbook. South Asia: Nepal*. Retrieved from https://www.cia.gov/library/publications/the-world-factbook/geos/np.html

Cermak, L. S., & Craik, F. I. M. (Eds.). (1979). *Levels of processing in human memory*. Hillsdale, NJ: Erlbaum.

Chall, J. S. (1996). *Stages of reading development* (2nd ed.) Fort Worth, TX: Harcourt, Brace.

Champagne, F. A. (2009). Beyond nature vs. nurture: Philosophical insights from molecular biology. *Observer, 22*(4), 4, 27–28.

Champion, J. (2013). Stories from a Mexican American Partera: Life on the Texas–Mexico border. Journal of Transcultural Nursing, 24(1), 94–102. doi:10.1177/1043659612452003

Chan, W., Au, T. K., & Tang, J. (2014). Strategic counting: A novel assessment of place-value understanding. *Learning & Instruction, 29*, 78–94. doi:10.1016/j.learninstruc.2013.09.001

Chandler, M. J. (1987). The Othello effect: Essay on the emergence and eclipse of skeptical doubt. *Human Development, 30*, 137–159.

Chandler, M., & Boyes, M. (1982). Social-cognitive development. In B. Wolman (Ed.), *Handbook of developmental psychology*. Upper Saddle River, NJ: Prentice Hall.

Chandler, M., & Moran, T. (1990). Psychopathy and moral development: A comparative study of delinquent and nondelinquent youth. *Development and Psychopathology, 2*, 227–246.

Chandler-Olcott, K. (2013). Expanding what it means to make evidence-based claims. *Journal of Adolescent & Adult Literacy, 57*(4), 280–288. doi:10.1002/jaal.252

Chang, M., Paulson, S. E., Finch, W., Mcintosh, D. E., & Rothlisberg, B. A. (2014). Joint confirmatory factor analysis of the Woodcock-Johnson Tests of

Cognitive Abilities, Third Edition, and the Stanford-Binet Intelligence Scales, Fifth Edition, with a preschool population. *Psychology in the Schools*, *51*(1), 32–57. doi:10.1002/pits.21734

Chang, N. (2012). What are the roles that children's drawings play in inquiry of science concepts? *Early Child Development and Care*, *182*(5), 621–637. doi:10.1080/03004430.2011.569542

Chang, S., & Yu, N. (2014). The effect of computer-assisted therapeutic practice for children with handwriting deficit: A comparison with the effect of the traditional sensorimotor approach. *Research in Developmental Disabilities*, *35*(7), 1648-1657. doi:10.1016/j.ridd.2014.03.024

Chang, Y., Laugeson, E., Gantman, A., Ellingsen, R., Frankel, F., & Dillon, A. (2014). Predicting treatment success in social skills training for adolescents with autism spectrum disorders: The UCLA Program for the Education and Enrichment of Relational Skills. *Autism: The International Journal of Research & Practice*, *18*(4), 467–470. doi:10.1177/1362361313478995

Chant, R. H. (2009). Developing involved and active citizens: The role of personal practical theories and action research in a standards-based social studies classroom. *Teacher Education Quarterly*, *36*(1), 181–190.

Chao, R. K. (1994). Beyond parental control and authoritarian parenting style: Understanding Chinese parenting through the cultural notion of training. *Child Development*, *65*, 1111–1119.

Chao, R. K. (2000). Cultural explanations for the role of parenting in the school success of Asian-American children. In R. D. Taylor & M. C. Wang (Eds.), *Resilience across contexts: Family, work, culture, and community* (pp. 333–363). Mahwah, NJ: Erlbaum.

Chaplin, T. M., & Aldao, A. (2013). Gender differences in emotion expression in children: A meta-analytic review. *Psychological Bulletin*, *139*(4), 735–765. doi:10.1037/a0030737

Chapman, M. (1988). *Constructive evolution: Origins and development of Piaget's thought*. Cambridge, England: Cambridge University Press.

Charity, A. H., Scarborough, H. S., & Griffin, D. M. (2004). Familiarity with school English in African American children and its relation to early reading achievement. *Child Development*, *75*, 1340–1356.

Charkaluk, M., Marchand-Martin, L., Ego, A., Zeitlin, J., Arnaud, C., Burguet, A., Marret, S., Rozé, J.-C., Vieux, R., Kaminski, Ancel, P.-Y., & Pierrat, V. (2012). The influence of fetal growth reference standards on assessment of cognitive and academic outcomes of very preterm children. *Journal of Pediatrics*, *161*(6), 1053–1058. doi:10.1016/j.jpeds.2012.05.037

Charles, E. P., & Rivera, S. M. (2009). Object permanence and method of disappearance: Looking measures further contradict reaching measures. *Developmental Science*, *12*(6), 991–1006.

Charlesworth, W. R., & LaFreniere, P. (1983). Dominance, friendship, and resource utilization in preschool children's groups. *Ethology and Sociobiology*, *4*, 175–186.

Chaudhary, M., & Gupta, A. (2012). Children's influence in family buying process in India. *Young Consumers*, *13*(2), 161–175. doi:10.1108/17473611211233512

Chavous, T. M., Bernat, D. H., Schmeelk-Cone, K., Caldwell, C. H., Kohn-Wood, L., et al. (2003). Racial identity and academic attainment among African American adolescents. *Child Development*, *74*, 1076–1090.

Chazan, D., Brantlinger, A., Clark, L. M., & Edwards, A. R. (2013). What mathematics education might learn from the work of well-respected African American mathematics teachers in urban schools. *Teachers College Record*, *115*(2), 1–40.

Chazan-Cohen, R., Jerald, J., & Stark, D. R. (2001). A commitment to supporting the mental health of our youngest children. *Zero to Three*, *22*(1), 4–12.

Chedzoy, S., & Burden, R. (2009). Primary school children's reflections on physical education lessons: An attributional analysis and possible implications for teacher action. *Thinking Skills and Creativity*, *4*(3), 185–193. doi:10.1016/j.tsc.2009.09.008

Chelonis, J. J., Johnson, T. A., Ferguson, S. A., Berry, K. J., Kubacak, B., Edwards, M. C., et al. (2011). Effect of methylphenidate on motivation in children with attention-deficit/hyperactivity disorder. *Experimental and Clinical Psychopharmacology*, *19*(2), 145–153. doi:10.1037/a0022794

Chen, H., Pine, D. S., Ernst, M., Gorodetsky, E., Kasen, S., Gordon, K., Goldman, D., & Cohen, P. (2013). The MAOA gene predicts happiness in women. *Progress in Neuro-Psychopharmacology & Biological Psychiatry*, *40*,122–125. doi:10.1016/j.pnpbp.2012.07.018

Chen, J., & Gardner, H. (2012). Assessment of intellectual profile: A perspective from multiple-intelligences theory. In D. P. Flanagan & P. L. Harrison (Eds.), *Contemporary intellectual assessment: Theories, tests, and issues* (3rd ed., pp. 145–155). New York, NY: Guilford Press.

Chen, J., Claessens, A., & Msall, M. E. (2014). Prematurity and school readiness in a nationally representative sample of Australian children: Does typically occurring preschool moderate the relationship? *Early Human Development*, *90*(2), 73–79. doi:10.1016/j.earlhumdev.2013.09.015

Chen, J., Li, X., & McGue, M. (2013). The interacting effect of the BDNF Val66Met polymorphism and stressful life events on adolescent depression is not an artifact of gene-environment correlation: evidence from a longitudinal twin study. *Journal of Child Psychology & Psychiatry*, *54*(10), 1066–1073.

Chen, J.-Q. (2009). China's assimilation of MI theory in education: Accent on the family and harmony. In J.-Q. Chen, S. Moran, & H. Gardner (Eds.), *Multiple intelligences around the world* (pp. 29–42). San Francisco, CA: Jossey-Bass.

Chen, L.-L., Su, Y.-C., Su, C.-H., Lin, H.-C., & Kuo, H.-W. (2008). Acupressure and meridian massage: Combined effects on increasing body weight in premature infants. *Journal of Clinical Nursing*, *17*(9), 1174–1181.

Chen, M. J., Gruenewald, P. J., & Remer, L. G. (2009). Does alcohol outlet density affect youth access to alcohol? *Journal of Adolescent Health*, *44*, 582–589.

Chen, W., Rovegno, I., Cone, S., & Cone, T. (2012). An accomplished teacher's use of scaffolding during a second-grade unit on designing games. *Research Quarterly for Exercise & Sport*, *83*(2), 221–234.

Chen, X., & Wang, L. (2010). China. In M. H. Bornstein (Ed.), *Handbook of cultural developmental science* (pp. 429–444). New York, NY: Psychology Press.

Chen, X., Anderson, R. C., Li, W., Hao, M., Wu, X., & Shu, H. (2004). Phonological awareness of bilingual and monolingual Chinese children. *Journal of Educational Psychology*, *96*, 142–151.

Chen, X., Chang, L., & He, Y. (2003). The peer group as a context: Mediating and moderating effects on the relations between academic achievement and social functioning in Chinese children. *Child Development*, *74*, 710–727.

Chen, X., DeSouza, A. T., Chen, H., & Wang, L. (2006). Reticent behavior and experiences in peer interactions in Chinese and Canadian children. *Developmental Psychology*, *42*(4), 656–665.

Chen, X., Hastings, P. D., Rubin, K. H., Chen, H., Cen, G., & Stewart, S. L. (1998). Child-rearing attitudes and behavioral inhibition in Chinese and Canadian toddlers: A cross-cultural study. *Developmental Psychology*, *34*(4), 677–686.

Chen, X., Rubin, K. H., Liu, M., Chen, H., Wang, L., Li, D., et al. (2003). Compliance in Chinese and Canadian toddlers: A cross-cultural study. *International Journal of Behavioral Development*, *27*(5), 428–436.

Chen, X., Wang, L., & Wang, Z. (2009). Shyness-sensitivity and social, school, and psychological adjustment in rural migrant and urban children in china. *Child Development*, *80*(5), 1499–1513. doi:10.1111/j.1467-8624.2009.01347.x

Chen, Y., McAnally, H., & Reese, E. (2013). Development in the organization of episodic memories in middle childhood and adolescence. *Frontiers in Behavioral Neuroscience*, 7.

Chen, Z., Sanchez, R. P., & Campbell, T. (1997). From beyond to within their grasp: The rudiments of analogical problem solving in 10- and 13-month-olds. *Developmental Psychology*, *33*, 790–801.

Cheng, Z. (2012). Teaching young children decomposition strategies to solve addition problems: An experimental study. *Journal of Mathematical Behavior*, *31*(1), 29–47. doi:10.1016/j.jmathb.2011.09.002

Chess, S., & Thomas, A. (1992). Interactions between offspring and parents in development. In B. Tizard & V. P. Varma (Eds.), *Vulnerability and resilience in human development: A festschrift for Ann and Alan Clarke* (pp. 72–87). London, England: Jessica Kingsley Publishers.

Chetland, E., & Fluck, M. (2007). Children's performance on the "give x" task: A microgenetic analysis of 'counting' and 'grabbing' behavior. *Infant and Child Development. Special Issue: Using the Microgenetic Method to Investigate Cognitive Development*, *16*(1), 35–51.

Cheung, A., & Slavin, R. (2013). The effectiveness of educational technology applications for enhancing mathematics achievement in K–12 classrooms: A meta-analysis. *Educational Research Review*, *9*, 88–113. doi:10.1016/j.edurev.2013.01.001

Cheung, H. H.-P. (2009). Multiple intelligences in China: Challenges and hopes. In J.-Q. Chen, S. Moran & H. Gardner (Eds.), *Multiple intelligences around the world* (pp. 43–54). San Francisco, CA: Jossey-Bass.

Cheyney, M., Burcher, P., & Vedam, S. (2014). A Crusade Against Home Birth. *Birth: Issues In Perinatal Care*, *41*(1), 1-4. doi:10.1111/birt.12099

Chi, M. T. H. (1978). Knowledge structures and memory development. In R. S. Siegler (Ed.), *Children's thinking: What develops?* Hillsdale, NJ: Erlbaum.

Chia, N., & Kee, N. (2013). Gender differences in the reading process of six-year-olds in Singapore. *Early Child Development & Care*, *183*(10), 1432–1448. doi:10.1080/03004430.2013.788812

Chin, J. (2014). Young children's trust beliefs in peers: Relations to social competence and interactive behaviors in a peer group. *Early Education And Development*, *25*(5), 601-618. doi:10.1080/10409289.2013.836698

Chisholm, K., Carter, M. C., Ames, E. W., & Morison, S. J. (1995). Attachment security and indiscriminately friendly behavior in children adopted from Romanian orphanages. *Development and Psychopathology*, *7*, 283–297.

Chiu, M. M. (2007). Families, economies, cultures, and science achievement in 41 countries: Country-, school-, and student-level analyses. *Journal of Family Psychology*, *21*, 510–519.

Chodkiewicz, A., & Boyle, C. (2014). Exploring the contribution of attribution retraining to student perceptions and the learning process. *Educational Psychology in Practice*, *30*(1), 78–87. doi:10.1080/02667363.2014.880048

Choi, J., Johnson, D. W., & Johnson, R. (2011). Relationships among cooperative learning experiences, social interdependence, children's aggression, victimization, and prosocial behaviors. *Journal of Applied Social Psychology*, *41*(4), 976–1003. doi:10.1111/j.1559-1816.2011.00744.x

Choi, S., & McDonough, L. (2007). Adapting spatial concepts for different languages: From preverbal event schemas to semantic categories. In J. M. Plumert & J. P. Spencer (Eds.), *The emerging spatial mind* (pp. 142–167). New York, NY: Oxford University Press.

Chomsky, C. S. (1969). *The acquisition of syntax in children from 5 to 10*. Cambridge, MA: MIT Press.

Chomsky, N. (1959). Review of B. F. Skinner's *Verbal Behavior*. *Language, 35,* 26–58.

Chomsky, N. (1965). *Aspects of the theory of syntax*. Cambridge, MA: MIT Press.

Chomsky, N. (1972). *Language and mind* (enlarged ed.). San Diego, CA: Harcourt Brace Jovanovich.

Chomsky, N. (1976). *Reflections on language*. London, England: Temple Smith.

Chomsky, N. (2006). *Language and mind* (3rd ed.). Cambridge, England: Cambridge University Press.

Chong, W., Moore, D. W., Nonis, K. P., Tang, H., Koh, P., & Wee, S. (2014). Mission I'm possible: Effects of a community-based project on the basic literacy skills of at-risk kindergarteners. *Infants & Young Children, 27*(1), 60–73. doi:10.1097/IYC.0b013e3182a60281

Chow, C., & Ruhl, H. (2014). Friendship and romantic stressors and depression in emerging adulthood: Mediating and moderating roles of attachment representations. *Journal of Adult Development, 21*(2), 106–115. doi:10.1007/s10804-014-9184-z

Christensen, C. G., & Myford, C. M. (2014). Measuring social and emotional content in children's television: An instrument development study. *Journal of Broadcasting & Electronic Media, 58*(1), 21–41. doi:10.1080/08838151.2013.875024

Christenson, S. L., & Thurlow, M. L. (2004). School dropouts: Prevention, considerations, interventions, and challenges. *Current Directions in Psychological Science, 13,* 36–39.

Christenson, S., Palan, R., & Scullin, S. (2009). Family–school partnerships: An essential component of student achievement. *Principal Leadership, 9*(9), 10–16.

Christie, F. (2012) The overall trajectory in language learning in school. *Language Learning, 62,* 187–224. doi:10.1111/j.1467-9922.2011.00683.x

Christie, J. F., & Johnsen, E. P. (1983). The role of play in social-intellectual development. *Review of Educational Research, 53,* 93–115.

Christoffersen, M. (2012). A study of adopted children, their environment, and development: A systematic review. *Adoption Quarterly, 15*(3), 220–237. doi:10.1080/10926755.2012.700002

Christopher, C., Saunders, R., Jacobvitz, D., Burton, R., & Hazen, N. (2013). Maternal empathy and changes in mothers' permissiveness as predictors of toddlers' early social competence with peers: A parenting intervention study. *Journal of Child & Family Studies, 22*(6), 769–778. doi:10.1007/s10826-012-9631-z

Chukovsky, K. (1968). *From two to five* (M. Morton, Trans.). Berkeley, CA: University of California Press.

Chung, K., Reavis, S., Mosconi, M., Drewry, J., Matthews, T., & Tassé, M. J. (2007). Peer-mediated social skills training program for young children with high-functioning autism. *Research in Developmental Disabilities, 28*(4), 423–436. doi:10.1016/j.ridd.2006.05.002

Ciarrochi, J., & Heaven, P. C. L. (2008). Learned social hopelessness: The role of explanatory style in predicting social support during adolescence. *Journal of Child Psychology and Psychiatry, 49*(12), 1279–1286. doi:10.1111/j.1469-7610.2008.01950.x

Cicchetti, D., Murray-Close, D., Cillessen, A. N., Lansu, T. M., & Van Den Berg, Y. M. (2014). Aggression, hostile attributions, status, and gender: A continued quest. *Development & Psychopathology, 26*(3), 635–644. doi:10.1017/S0954579414000285

Cicchetti, D., Murray-Close, D., Huitsing, G., Snijders, T. B., Van Duijn, M. J., & Veenstra, R. (2014). Victims, bullies, and their defenders: A longitudinal study of the coevolution of positive and negative networks. *Development & Psychopathology, 26*(3), 645–659. doi:10.1017/S0954579414000297

Cicchetti, D., Rogosch, F. A., & Toth, S. L. (1997). Ontogenesis, depressotypic organization, and the depressive spectrum. In S. S. Luthar, J. A. Burack, D. Cicchetti, & J. R. Weisz (Eds.), *Developmental psychopathology: Perspectives on adjustment, risk, and disorder* (pp. 273–313). Cambridge, England: Cambridge University Press.

Cicchetti, D., Spencer, M., & Swanson, D. (2013). Opportunities and challenges to the development of healthy children and youth living in diverse communities. *Development & Psychopathology, 25*(4pt2), 1551-1566. doi:10.1017/S095457941300076X

Cimpian, A., Arce, H.-M. C., Markman, E. M., & Dweck, C. S. (2007). Subtle linguistic cues affect children's motivation. *Psychological Science, 18,* 314–316.

Cinamon, R., & Rich, Y. (2014). Work and family plans among at-risk Israeli adolescents: A mixed-methods study. *Journal of Career Development, 41*(3), 163–184. doi:10.1177/0894845313507748

Claessen, M., Leitão, S., Kane, R., & Williams, C. (2013). Phonological processing skills in specific language impairment. *International Journal of Speech-Language Pathology, 15*(5), 471–483. doi:10.3109/17549507.2012.753110

Claeys, J. (2013). Theory and research: The nexus of clinical inference. *Journal of Psychoeducational Assessment, 31*(2), 170–174. doi:10.1177/0734282913478037

Clair, L., Jackson, B., & Zweiback, R. (2012). Six years later: Effect of family involvement training on the language skills of children from migrant families. *School Community Journal, 22*(1), 9–19.

Clark, B. (1997). *Growing up gifted* (5th ed.). Upper Saddle River, NJ: Merrill/Prentice Hall.

Clark,. C. C. (1992). Deviant adolescent subcultures: Assessment strategies and clinical interventions. *Adolescence, 27*(106), 283–293.

Clark, D. B. (2006). Longitudinal conceptual change in students' understanding of thermal equilibrium: An examination of the process of conceptual restructuring. *Cognition and Instruction, 24,* 467–563.

Clark, I. (2012). Formative assessment: Assessment is for self-regulated learning. *Educational Psychology Review, 24*(2), 205–249. doi:10.1007/s10648-011-9191-6

Clark, K. (2009). The case for structured English immersion. *Educational Leadership, 66*(7), 42–46.

Clarke, K. (2013). Guerilla fort construction: Activism for outdoor play. *Pathways: The Ontario Journal of Outdoor Education, 25*(4), 6–10.

Clasen, D. R., & Brown, B. B. (1985). The multidimensionality of peer pressure in adolescence. *Journal of Youth and Adolescence, 14,* 451–468.

Clemens, E. V., Shipp, A. E., & Pisarik, C. T. (2008). MySpace as a tool for mental health professionals. *Child and Adolescent Mental Health, 13*(2), 97–98.

Clemens, N. H., Oslund, E. L., Simmons, L. E., & Simmons, D. (2014). Assessing spelling in kindergarten: Further comparison of scoring metrics and their relation to reading skills. *Journal of School Psychology, 52*(1), 49–61. doi:10.1016/j.jsp.2013.12.005

Clifford, M. M. (1990). Students need challenge, not easy success. *Educational Leadership, 48*(1), 22–26.

Clifton, A., Goodall, D., Ban, S., & Birks, E. (2013). New perspectives on the contribution of digital technology and social media use to improve the mental wellbeing of children and young people: A state-of-the art review. *Neonatal, Paediatric & Child Health Nursing, 16*(1), 19–26.

Clincy, A. R., & Mills-Koonce, W. (2013). Trajectories of intrusive parenting during infancy and toddlerhood as predictors of rural, low-income African American boys' school-related outcomes. *American Journal of Orthopsychiatry, 83*(2–3), 194–206. doi:10.1111/ajop.12028

Cluss, P. A., Fee, L., Culyba, R. J., Bhat, K. B., & Owen, K. (2014). Effect of food service nutrition improvements on elementary school cafeteria lunch purchase patterns. *Journal of School Health, 84*(6), 355-362. doi:10.1111/josh.12157

Cluver, A., Heyman, G., & Carver, L. J. (2013). Young children selectively seek help when solving problems. *Journal of Experimental Child Psychology, 115*(3), 570–578. doi:10.1016/j.jecp.2012.12.011

Cochran-Smith, M., & Lytle, S. (1993). *Inside out: Teacher research and knowledge*. New York, NY: Teachers College Press.

Cody, H., & Kamphaus, R. W. (1999). Down syndrome. In S. Goldstein & C. R. Reynolds (Eds.), *Handbook of neurodevelopmental and genetic disorders* (pp. 385–405). New York, NY: Guilford Press.

Cohen, E. G. (1994). Restructuring the classroom: Conditions for productive small groups. *Review of Educational Research, 64,* 1–35.

Cohen, L. B., & Cashon, C. H. (2006). Infant cognition. In W. Damon & R. M. Lerner (Eds. in Chief) & D. Kuhn & R. S. Siegler (Vol. Eds.), *Handbook of child psychology: Vol. 2. Cognition, perception, and language* (6th ed., pp. 214–251). Hoboken, NJ: Wiley.

Cohen, L. B., & Cashon, C. H. (2006). Infant cognition. In W. Damon & R. M. Lerner (Eds. in Chief) & D. Kuhn & R. S. Siegler (Vol. Eds.), *Handbook of child psychology: Vol. 2. Cognition, perception, and language* (6th ed., pp. 214–251). Hoboken, NJ: Wiley.

Cohen, M. N. (1998, April 17). Culture, not race, explains human diversity. *The Chronicle of Higher Education*, p. B4.

Cohn, N. (2014). Framing "I can't draw": The influence of cultural frames on the development of drawing. *Culture & Psychology, 20*(1), 102–117. doi:10.1177/1354067X13515936

Coie, J. D., & Cillessen, A. H. N. (1993). Peer rejection: Origins and effects on children's development. *Current Directions in Psychological Science, 2,* 89–92.

Coie, J. D., & Dodge, K. A. (1988). Multiple sources of data on social behavior and social status. *Child Development, 59,* 815–829.

Coie, J. D., & Kupersmidt, J. (1983). A behavioral analysis of emerging social status in boys' groups. *Child Development, 54,* 1400–1416.

Coie, J. D., Dodge, K. A., & Coppotelli, H. (1982). Dimensions and types of social status: A cross-age perspective. *Developmental Psychology, 18,* 557–570.

Coie, J. D., Dodge, K. A., Terry, R., & Wright, V. (1991). The role of aggression in peer relations: An analysis of aggression episodes in boys' play groups. *Child Development, 62,* 812–826.

Coiro, J., & Fogleman, J. (2011, February). Using websites wisely. *Educational Leadership, 68*(5), 34–38.

Coker, T. R., Elliott, M. N., Kanouse, D. E., Grunbaum, J. A., Schwebel, D. C., Gilliland, M. J., et al. (2009). Perceived racial/ethnic discrimination among fifth-grade students and its association with mental health. *American Journal of Public Health, 99*(5), 878–884.

Colby, A., & Kohlberg, L. (1984). Invariant sequence and internal consistency in moral judgment stages. In W. M. Kurtines & J. L. Gewirtz (Eds.), *Morality, moral behavior, and moral development*. New York, NY: Wiley.

Colby, A., Kohlberg, L., Gibbs, J., & Lieberman, M. (1983). A longitudinal study of moral judgment.

Monographs of the Society for Research in Child Development, 48(1–2, Serial No. 200).

Cole, C. F., Labin, D. B., & del Rocio Galarza, M. (2008). Begin with the children: What research on *Sesame Street's* international coproductions reveals about using media to promote a new more peaceful world. *International Journal of Behavioral Development, 32*(4), 359–365. doi:10.1177/0165025408090977

Cole, C., & Winsler, A. (2010). Protecting children from exposure to lead: Old problem, new data, and new policy needs. *Social Policy Report, 24*(1). Ann Arbor, MI: Society for Research in Child Development.

Cole, M. (2006). Culture and cognitive development in phylogenetic, historical and ontogenetic perspective. In W. Damon & R. M. Lerner (Series Eds.) & D. Kuhn & R. Siegler (Vol. Eds.), *Handbook of child psychology: Vol. 2. Cognition, perception, and language* (6th ed., pp. 636–683). New York, NY: Wiley.

Cole, M., & Hatano, G. (2007). Cultural-historical activity theory: Integrating phylogeny, cultural history, and ontogenesis in cultural psychology. In S. Kitayama & D. Cohen (Eds.), *Handbook of cultural psychology* (pp. 109–135). New York, NY: Guilford Press.

Cole, P. M., & Tamang, B. L. (2001). Nepali children's ideas about emotional displays in hypothetical challenges. *Developmental Psychology, 34,* 640–646.

Cole, P. M., & Tan, P. Z. (2007). Emotion socialization from a cultural perspective. In J. E. Grusec & P. D. Hastings (Eds.), *Handbook of socialization: Theory and research* (pp. 516–542). New York, NY: Guilford Press.

Cole, P. M., Armstrong, L. M., & Pemberton, C. K. (2010). The role of language in the development of emotion regulation. In S. D. Calkins & M. A. Bell (Eds.), *Child development at the intersection of emotion and cognition* (pp. 59–77). Washington, DC: American Psychological Association.

Cole, P. M., Tan, P. Z., Hall, S. E., Zhang, Y., Crnic, K. A., Blair, C. B., & Li, R. (2011). Developmental changes in anger expression and attention focus: Learning to wait. *Developmental Psychology, 47*(4), 1078–1089. doi:10.1037/a0023813

Coleman, J. C., Crosby, M. G., Irwin, H. K., Dennis, L. R., Simpson, C. G., & Rose, C. A. (2013). Preventing challenging behaviors in preschool: Effective strategies for classroom teachers. *Young Exceptional Children, 16*(3), 3–10. doi:10.1177/1096250612464641

Coleman, L., & Guo, A. (2013). Exploring children's passion for learning in six domains. *Journal for the Education of The Gifted, 36*(2), 155–175. doi:10.1177/0162353213480432

Coles, R. L. (2006). *Race and family: A structural approach.* Thousand Oaks, CA: Sage.

Coley, R. L., & Chase-Lansdale, P. L. (1998). Adolescent pregnancy and parenthood. *American Psychologist, 53,* 152–166.

Collier, V. P. (1992). The Canadian bilingual immersion debate: A synthesis of research findings. *Studies in Second Language Acquisition, 14,* 87–97.

Collin-Vézina, D. (2013). Students affected by sexual abuse. In E. Rossen & R. Hull (Eds.), *Supporting and educating traumatized students: A guide for school-based professionals* (pp. 187–202). New York, NY: Oxford University Press.

Collins, A. (2006). Cognitive apprenticeship. In R. K. Sawyer (Ed.), *The Cambridge handbook of the learning sciences* (pp. 47–60). Cambridge, England: Cambridge University Press.

Collins, A., Brown, J. S., & Newman, S. E. (1989). Cognitive apprenticeship: Teaching the crafts of reading, writing, and mathematics. In L. B. Resnick (Ed.), *Knowing, learning, and instruction: Essays in honor of Robert Glaser.* Hillsdale, NJ: Erlbaum.

Collins, M. F. (2010). ELL preschoolers' English vocabulary acquisition from storybook reading. *Early Childhood Research Quarterly, 25*(1), 84–97.

Collins, W. A. (1990). Parent–child relationships in the transition to adolescence: Continuity and change in interaction, affects, and cognition. In R. Montemayor, G. Adams, & T. Gullota (Eds.), *Advances in adolescent development* (Vol. 2). Beverly Hills, CA: Sage.

Collins, W. A., & Sroufe, L. A. (1999). Capacity for intimate relationships: A developmental construction. In W. Furman, B. B. Brown, & C. Feiring (Eds.), *The development of romantic relationships in adolescence* (pp. 125–147). Cambridge, England: Cambridge University Press.

Collins, W. A., & van Dulmen, M. (2006). "The course of true love(s)?": Origins and pathways in the development of romantic relationships. In A. C. Crouter & A. Booth (Eds.), *Romance and sex in adolescence and emerging adulthood: Risks and opportunities* (pp. 53–86). Mahwah, NJ: Erlbaum.

Colmar, S. (2014). A parent-based book-reading intervention for disadvantaged children with language difficulties. *Child Language Teaching & Therapy, 30*(1), 79–90. doi:10.1177/0265659013507296

Colombo, J. (1993). *Infant cognition: Predicting later intellectual functioning.* Newbury Park, CA: Sage.

Colombo, J., Brez, C. C., & Curtindale, L. M. (2013). Infant perception and cognition. In R. M. Lerner, M. Easterbrooks, J. Mistry, & I. B. Weiner (Eds.), *Handbook of psychology, Vol. 6: Developmental psychology* (2nd ed., pp. 61–89). Hoboken, NJ: Wiley.

Colombo, J., Shaddy, D. J., Blaga, O. M., Anderson, C. J., & Kannass, K. N. (2009). High cognitive ability in infancy and early childhood. In F. D. Horowitz, R. F. Subotnik, & D. J. Matthews (Eds.), *The development of giftedness and talent across the life span* (pp. 23–42). Washington, DC: American Psychological Association.

Comeau, L., Cormier, P., Grandmaison, É., & Lacroix, D. (1999). A longitudinal study of phonological processing skills in children learning to read in a second language. *Journal of Educational Psychology, 91,* 29–43.

Compton, L., Campbell, M. A., & Mergler, A. (2014). Teacher, parent and student perceptions of the motives of cyberbullies. *Social Psychology of Education.* doi:10.1007/s11218-014-9254-x

Comstock, G., & Scharrer, E. (2006). Media and popular culture. In W. Damon & R. M. Lerner (Series Eds.) & K. A. Renninger & I. E. Sigel (Vol. Eds.), *Handbook of child psychology: Vol. 3. Social, emotional, and personality development* (6th ed., pp. 817–863). New York, NY: Wiley.

Condon, J. C., & Yousef, F. S. (1975). *An introduction to intercultural communication.* Indianapolis, IN: Bobbs-Merrill.

Condry, J. C., & Ross, D. F. (1985). Sex and aggression: The influence of gender label on the perception of aggression in children. *Child Development, 56,* 225–233.

Conn, J., & Kanner, L. (1940). Spontaneous erections in childhood. *Journal of Pediatrics, 16,* 237–240.

Conner, B. T., Hellemann, G. S., Ritchie, T. L., & Noble, E. P. (2010). Genetic, personality, and environmental predictors of drug use in adolescents. *Journal of Substance Abuse Treatment, 38,* 178–190.

Conner-Warren, R. (2014). Effects of cumulative trauma load on perceptions of health, blood pressure, and resting heart rate in urban African American youth. *Journal for Specialists in Pediatric Nursing, 19*(2), 127–138. doi:10.1111/jspn.12063

Conners, G. P., Veenema, T. G., Kavanagh, C. A., Ricci, J., & Callahan, C. M. (2002). Still falling: A community-wide infant walker injury prevention initiative. *Patient Education and Counseling, 46*(3), 169–173. doi:10.1016/S0738-3991(01)00210-5

Connolly, J. A., & McIsaac, C. (2009). Romantic relationships in adolescence. In R. M. Lerner, & L. Steinberg (Eds.), *Handbook of adolescent psychology, Vol. 2: Contextual influences on adolescent development* (3rd ed., pp. 104–151). Hoboken, NJ: Wiley.

Connor, P. D., Sampson, P. D., Streissguth, A. P., Bookstein, F. L., & Barr, H. M. (2006). Effects of prenatal alcohol exposure on fine motor coordination and balance: A study of two adult samples. *Neuropsychologia, 44,* 744–751.

Conradt, E., & Ablow, J. (2010). Infant physiological response to the still-face paradigm: Contributions of maternal sensitivity and infants' early regulatory behavior. *Infant Behavior & Development, 33*(3), 251–265.

Consortium of Longitudinal Studies. (Ed.). (1983). *As the twig is bent: Lasting effects of preschool programs.* Mahwah, NJ: Erlbaum.

Cook, C., Goodman, N. D., & Schulz, L. E. (2011). Where science starts: Spontaneous experiments in preschoolers' exploratory play. *Cognition, 120*(3), 341–349. doi:10.1016/j.cognition.2011.03.003

Cook, E. C., Buehler, C., & Henson, R. (2009). Parents and peers as social influences to deter antisocial behavior. *Journal of Youth and Adolescence, 38*(9), 1240–1252. doi:10.1007/s10964-008-9348-x

Cook, K. (2014). Planning a new key stage 3. *Teaching Geography, 39*(1), 16–17.

Cook, V., & Newson, M. (1996). *Chomsky's universal grammar: An introduction* (2nd ed.). Oxford, England: Blackwell.

Cook-Cottone, C. P., Tribole, E., & Tylka, T. L. (2013). Pillar II: Healthy physical activity. In *Healthy eating in schools: Evidence-based interventions to help kids thrive* (pp. 107–122). Washington, DC US: American Psychological Association. doi:10.1037/14180-006

Cooney, J. B., & Ladd, S. F. (1992). The influence of verbal protocol methods on children's mental computation. *Learning and Individual Differences, 4,* 237–257.

Cooney, J. B., Swanson, H. L., & Ladd, S. F. (1988). Acquisition of mental multiplication skill: Evidence for the transition between counting and retrieval strategies. *Cognition and Instruction, 5,* 323–345.

Cooper, C. R., Denner, J., & Lopez, E. M. (1999, Fall). Cultural brokers: Helping Latino children on pathways toward success. *The Future of Children: When School Is Out, 9,* 51–57.

Cooper, C. R., Jackson, J. F., Azmitia, M., Lopez, E., & Dunbar, N. (1995). Bridging students' multiple worlds: African American and Latino youth in academic outreach programs. In R. F. Macias & R. G. Garcia-Ramos (Eds.), *Changing schools for changing students: An anthology of research on language minorities* (pp. 211–234). Santa Barbara, CA: University of California Linguistic Minority Research Institute.

Cooper, H., & Dorr, N. (1995). Race comparisons on need for achievement: A meta-analytic alternative to Graham's narrative review. *Review of Educational Research, 65,* 483–508.

Cooper, H., Robinson, J. C., & Patall, E. A. (2006). Does homework improve academic achievement? A synthesis of research, 1987–2003. *Review of Educational Research, 76,* 1–62.

Cooper, H., Valentine, J. C., Nye, B., & Lindsay, J. J. (1999). Relationships between five after-school activities and academic achievement. *Journal of Educational Psychology, 91,* 369–378.

Cooper, S. M., & Smalls, C. (2010). Culturally distinctive and academic socialization: Direct and interactive relationships with African American adolescents' academic adjustment. *Journal of Youth and Adolescence, 39*(2), 199–212.

Cooper-Vince, C., Pincus, D., & Comer, J. (2014). Maternal intrusiveness, family financial means, and anxiety across childhood in a large multiphase sample of community youth. *Journal of Abnormal Child Psychology, 42*(3), 429–438.

Coopersmith, S. (1967). *The antecedents of self-esteem.* San Francisco: Freeman.

Copeland, W. E., Wolke, D., Lereya, S., Shanahan, L., Worthman, C., & Costello, E. (2014). Childhood bullying involvement predicts low-grade systemic inflammation into adulthood. *PNAS Proceedings Of The National Academy of Sciences of the United States of America, 111*(21), 7570–7575. doi:10.1073/pnas.1323641111

Coplan, R. J., Ooi, L. L., Rose-Krasnor, L., & Nocita, G. (2014). "I want to play alone": Assessment and correlates of self-reported preference for solitary play in young children. *Infant & Child Development, 23*(3), 229-238. doi:10.1002/icd.1854

Corbin, J. M., & Strauss, A. (2008). *Basics of qualitative research: Techniques and procedures for developing grounded theory* (3rd ed.). Los Angeles, CA: Sage.

Corenblum, B. (2014). Relationships between racial-ethnic identity, self-esteem and in-group attitudes among First Nation children. *Journal of Youth & Adolescence, 43*(3), 387–404. doi:10.1007/s10964-013-0081-8

Corno, L., & Mandinach, E. B. (2004). What we have learned about student engagement in the past twenty years. In D. M. McNerney & S. Van Etten (Eds.), *Big theories revisited* (pp. 299–328). Greenwich, CT: Information Age.

Cornoldi, C. (2010). Metacognition, intelligence, and academic performance. In H. S. Waters, & W. Schneider (Eds.), *Metacognition, strategy use, and instruction* (pp. 257–277). New York, NY: Guilford Press.

Corpus, J., McClintic-Gilbert, M., & Hayenga, A. (2009). Within-year changes in children's intrinsic and extrinsic motivational orientations: Contextual predictors and academic outcomes. *Contemporary Educational Psychology, 34*(2), 154–166. doi:10.1016/j.cedpsych.2009.01.001

Corriveau, K., Pasquini, E., & Goswami, U. (2007). Basic auditory processing skills and specific language impairment: A new look at an old hypothesis. *Journal of Speech, Language, and Hearing Research, 50,* 647–666.

Corsaro, W. A. (2003). *We're friends, right? Inside kids' culture.* Washington, DC: Joseph Henry Press.

Corsaro, W. A., & Eder, D. (1990). Children's peer cultures. *Annual Review of Sociology, 16,* 197–220.

Corsaro, W. A., & Molinari, L. (2005). *I compagni: Understanding children's transition from preschool to elementary school.* New York, NY: Teachers College Press.

Cortese, S. (2013). Gym for the attention-deficit/hyperactivity disorder brain? Still a long run ahead. . . . *Journal of the American Academy of Child & Adolescent Psychiatry, 52*(9), 894–896. doi:10.1016/j.jaac.2013.06.011

Cosden, M., Morrison, G., Albanese, A. L., & Macias, S. (2001). When homework is not home work: After-school programs for homework assistance. *Educational Psychologist, 36,* 211–221.

Cossu, G. (1999). The acquisition of Italian orthography. In M. Harris & G. Hatano (Eds.), *Learning to read and write: A cross-linguistic perspective* (pp. 10–33). Cambridge, England: Cambridge University Press.

Costigan, C. L., Hua, J. M., & Su, T. F. (2010). Living up to expectations: The strengths and challenges experienced by Chinese Canadian students. *Canadian Journal of School Psychology, 25*(3), 223–245.

Cote, D., Jones, V., Barnett, C., Pavelek, K., Nguyen, H., & Sparks, S. (2014). Teaching problem solving

skills to elementary age students with autism. *Education & Training in Autism & Developmental Disabilities, 49*(2), 189–199.

Cotterell, J. L. (1992). The relation of attachments and supports to adolescent well-being and school adjustment. *Journal of Adolescent Research, 7,* 28–42.

Cotton, S. M., & Richdale, A. L. (2010). Sleep patterns and behavior in typically developing children with autism, Down syndrome, Prader-Willi syndrome and intellectual disability. *Research in Autism Spectrum Disorders, 4,* 490–500.

Council for Exceptional Children. (1995). *Toward a common agenda: Linking gifted education and school reform.* Reston, VA: Author.

Courage, M. L., & Adams, R. J. (1990). Visual acuity assessment from birth to three years using the acuity card procedures: Cross-sectional and longitudinal samples. *Optometry and Vision Science, 67,* 713–718.

Courage, M. L., & Setliff, A. E. (2010). When babies watch television: Attention-getting, attention-holding, and the implications for learning from video material. *Developmental Review, 30*(2), 220–238. doi:10.1016/j.dr.2010.03.003

Courage, M. L., Reynolds, G. D., & Richards, J. E. (2006). Infants' attention to patterned stimuli: Developmental change from 3 to 12 months of age. *Child Development, 77,* 680–695.

Courtney, M. E., Piliavin, I., Grogan-Kaylor, A., & Nesmith, A. (2001). Foster youth transitions to adulthood: A longitudinal view of youth leaving care. *Child Welfare: Journal of Policy, Practice, and Program, 80*(6), 685–717.

Covington, M. V. (1987). Achievement motivation, self-attributions, and the exceptional learner. In J. D. Day & J. G. Borkowski (Eds.), *Intelligence and exceptionality* (pp. 355–389). Norwood, NJ: Ablex.

Covington, M. V. (1992). *Making the grade: A self-worth perspective on motivation and school reform.* Cambridge, England: Cambridge University Press.

Covington, M. V. (1992). *Making the grade: A self-worth perspective on motivation and school reform.* Cambridge, England: Cambridge University Press.

Covington, M. V., & Müeller, K. J. (2001). Intrinsic versus extrinsic motivation: An approach/avoidance reformulation. *Educational Psychology Review, 13,* 157–176.

Cowan, N. (2014). Working memory underpins cognitive development, learning, and education. *Educational Psychology Review, 26*(2), 197-223. doi:10.1007/s10648-013-9246-y

Cowan, R., & Powell, D. (2014). The contributions of domain-general and numerical factors to third-grade arithmetic skills and mathematical learning disability. *Journal of Educational Psychology, 106*(1), 214–229. doi:10.1037/a0034097

Cox, C. B. (2000). *Empowering grandparents raising grandchildren.* New York, NY: Springer.

Cox, M. E., Orme, J. G., & Rhoades, K. W. (2003). Willingness to foster children with emotional or behavioral problems. *Journal of Social Service Research, 29,* 23–51.

CQ Researcher (2014). Shootings and bullying. *CQ Researcher, 24*(18), 418–419.

Crago, M. B. (1988). *Cultural context in the communicative interaction of young Inuit children.* Unpublished doctoral dissertation, McGill University, Montreal, Canada.

Crago, M. B., Allen, S. E. M., & Hough-Eyamie, W. P. (1997). Exploring innateness through cultural and linguistic variation. In M. Gopnik (Ed.), *The inheritance and innateness of grammars (pp. 70-90).* New York, NY: Oxford University Press.

Crago, M. B., Annahatak, B., & Ningiuruvik, L. (1993). Changing patterns of language socialization in Inuit homes. *Anthropology and Education Quarterly, 24,* 205–223.

Craig, L., & Powell, A. (2013). Non-parental childcare, time pressure and the gendered division of paid work, domestic work and parental childcare. *Community, Work & Family, 16*(1), 100–119. doi:10.1080/13668803.2012.722013

Crain, W. (2011). *Theories of development: Concepts and applications* (6th ed.). Upper Saddle River, NJ: Pearson Prentice Hall.

Cranley Gallagher, K. (2013). Guiding children's friendship development. *Young Children, 68*(5), 26–32.

Crevecoeur, Y. C., Coyne, M. D., & McCoach, D. (2014). English language learners and English-Only learners' response to direct vocabulary instruction. *Reading & Writing Quarterly, 30*(1), 51–78. doi:10.1080/10573569.2013.758943

Crick, N. R., & Dodge, K. A. (1996). Social information-processing mechanisms in reactive and proactive aggression. *Child Development, 67,* 993–1002.

Criss, M. M., Pettit, G. S., Bates, J. E., Dodge, K. A., & Lapp, A. L. (1992). Family adversity, positive peer relationships, and children's externalizing behavior: A longitudinal perspective on risk and resilience. *Child Development, 73,* 1220–1237.

Critten, S., Pine, K., & Steffler, D. (2007). Spelling development in young children: A case of representational redescription? *Journal of Educational Psychology, 99,* 207–220. .

Croker, S., & Buchanan, H. (2011). Scientific reasoning in a real-world context: The effect of prior belief and outcome on children's hypothesis-testing strategies. *British Journal of Developmental Psychology, 29*(3), 409–424. doi:10.1348/026151010X496906

Cronin, D. (2003). *Diary of a worm.* New York, NY: Harper Collins.

Crosnoe, R. (2009). Family–school connections and the transitions of low-income youths and English language learners from middle school to high school. *Developmental Psychology, 45*(4), 1061–1076.

Crosnoe, R., & Elder, G. H., Jr. (2004). Family dynamics, supportive relationships, and educational resilience during adolescence. *Journal of Family Issues, 25*(5), 571–602.

Crosnoe, R., & Huston, A. C. (2007). Socioeconomic status, schooling, and the developmental trajectories of adolescents. *Developmental Psychology, 43,* 1097–1110.

Cross, D., Adefope, O., Rapacki, L., Hudson, R., Mi Yeon Lee1, m., & Perez, A. (2012). Success made probable: Creating equitable mathematical experiences through project-based learning. *Journal of Urban Mathematics Education, 5*(2), 55–86.

Crowl, A., Ahn, S., & Baker, J. (2008). A meta-analysis of developmental outcomes for children of same-sex and heterosexual parents. *Journal of GLBT Family Studies, 4*(3), 385–407. doi:10.1080/15504280802177615

Crowley, K., & Jacobs, M. (2002). Building islands of expertise in everyday family activity. In G. Leinhardt, K. Crowley, & K. Knutson (Eds.), *Learning conversations in museums* (pp. 333–356). Mahwah, NJ: Erlbaum.

Crum, W. (2010). Foster parent parenting characteristics that lead to increased placement stability or disruption. *Children and Youth Services Review, 32*(2), 185–190. doi:10.1016/j.childyouth.2009.08.022

Cruz, I., Quittner, A. L., Marker, C., & DesJardin, J. L. (2013). Identification of effective strategies to promote language in deaf children with cochlear implants. *Child Development, 84*(2), 543–559. doi:10.1111/j.1467-8624.2012.01863.x

Csikszentmihalyi, M. (1995). Education for the twenty-first century. *Daedalus, 124*(4), 107–114.

Csikszentmihalyi, M., & Larson, R. (1984). *Being adolescent: Conflict and growth in the teenage years.* New York, NY: Basic Books.

Csizmadia, A., Kaneakua, J. P., Miller, M., & Halgunseth, L. C. (2013). Ethnic-racial socialization and its implications for ethnic minority children's adjustment in middle childhood. *Journal of Communications Research, 5*(2), 227–242.

Cuevas, K., & Bell, M. (2014). Infant attention and early childhood executive function. *Child Development, 85*(2), 397-404. doi:10.1111/cdev.12126

Cugmas, Z. (2011). Relation between children's attachment to kindergarten teachers, personality characteristics and play activities. *Early Child Development & Care, 181*(9), 1271–1289. doi:10.1080/03004430.2010.523993

Cullen, B. (1998). Teaching the faith with humility: Indoctrination versus education. *Lutheran Education, 134*(2), 77-89.

Cummings, E. M., & Merrilees, C. E. (2010). Identifying the dynamic processes underlying links between marital conflict and child adjustment. In M. S. Schulz, M. K. Pruett, P. K. Kerig, & R. D. Parke (Eds.), *Strengthening couple relationships for optimal child development: Lessons from research and intervention* (pp. 27–40). Washington, DC: American Psychological Association.

Cummings, E., Braungart-Rieker, J. M., & Schudlich, T. (2013). Emotion and personality development. In R. M. Lerner, M. Easterbrooks, J. Mistry, & I. B. Weiner (Eds.), *Handbook of psychology, Vol. 6: Developmental psychology* (2nd ed., pp. 215–241). Hoboken, NJ: Wiley.

Cummins, J. (1981). Age on arrival and immigrant second language learning in Canada: A reassessment. *Applied Linguistics, 2*, 132–149.

Cummins, J. (2000). *Language, power, and pedagogy: Bilingual children in the crossfire.* Clevedon, England: Multilingual Matters.

Cunningham, C. E., Cunningham, L. J., Ratcliffe, J., & Vaillancourt, T. (2010). A qualitative analysis of the bullying prevention and intervention recommendations of students in grades 5 to 8. *Journal of School Violence, 9*(4), 321–338. doi:10.1080/15388220.2010.507146

Cunningham, T. H., & Graham, C. R. (2000). Increasing native English vocabulary recognition through Spanish immersion: Cognate transfer from foreign to first language. *Journal of Educational Psychology, 92*, 37–49.

Cunningham, W. A., & Zelazo, P. D. (2010). The development of iterative reprocessing: Implications for affect and its regulation. In P. D. Zelazo, M. Chandler, & E. Crone (Eds.), *Developmental social cognitive neuroscience* (pp. 81–98). New York, NY: Psychology Press.

Curchack-Lichtin, J., Chacko, A., & Halperin, J. (2014). Changes in ADHD symptom endorsement: Preschool to school age. *Journal of Abnormal Child Psychology, 42*(6), 993–eg1004. doi:10.1007/s10802-013-9834-9s

Curci, A., Lanciano, T., Soleti, E., Zammuner, V., & Salovey, P. (2013). Construct validity of the Italian version of the Mayer–Salovey–Caruso Emotional Intelligence Test (MSCEIT) v2.0. *Journal of Personality Assessment, 95*(5), 486–494. doi:10.1080/00223891.2013.778272

Curtiss, S. (1977). *Genie: A psycholinguistic study of a modern-day "wild child."* New York, NY: Academic Press.

Curwood, J., Magnified, A., & Lammers, J. C. (2013). Writing in the wild: Writers' motivation in fan-based affinity spaces. *Journal of Adolescent &*

Adult Literacy, 56(8), 677-685. doi:10.1002/JAAL.192

Cushman, P., & Cowan, J. (2010). Enhancing student self-worth in the primary school learning environment: Teachers' views and students' views. *Pastoral Care in Education, 28*(2), 81–95.

Czymoniewicz-Klippel, M. T. (2013). Bad boys, big trouble: Subcultural formation and resistance in a Cambodian village. *Youth & Society, 45*(4), 480–499. doi:10.1177/0044118X11422545

d'Ailly, H. (2003). Children's autonomy and perceived control in learning: A model of motivation and achievement in Taiwan. *Journal of Educational Psychology, 95*, 84–96.

Dabarera, C., Renandya, W. A., & Zhang, L. (2014). The impact of metacognitive scaffolding and monitoring on reading comprehension. *System, 42*, 462–473. doi:10.1016/j.system.2013.12.020

Dahl, A., Campos, J. J., & Witherington, D. C. (2011). Emotional action and communication in early moral development. *Emotion Review, 3*(2), 147–157. doi:10.1177/1754073910387948

Dahl, A., Campos, J. J., Anderson, D. I., Uchiyama, I., Witherington, D. C., Ueno, M., Poutrain-Lejeune, L., & Barbu-Roth, M. (2013). The epigenesis of wariness of heights. *Psychological Science, 24*(7), 1361–1367. doi:10.1177/0956797613476047

Dahl, A., Sherlock, B. R., Campos, J. J., & Theunissen, F. E. (2014). Mothers' tone of voice depends on the nature of infants' transgressions. *Emotion, 14*(4), 651–665. doi:10.1037/a0036608

Dahl, R. (1964). *Charlie and the chocolate factory* (Illustrated by Joseph Schindelman). New York, NY: Knopf.

Dahl, R. E., & Lewin, D. S. (2002). Pathways to adolescent health: Sleep regulation and behavior. *Journal of Adolescent Health, 31*(6 Suppl.), 175–184.

Dahlin, B., & Watkins, D. (2000). The role of repetition in the processes of memorizing and understanding: A comparison of the views of Western and Chinese secondary students in Hong Kong. *British Journal of Educational Psychology, 70*, 65–84.

Daley, R., Hill, M., Lewis, C., & Chitty, L. (2014). Non-invasive prenatal testing for Down's syndrome--Where are we now?. *British Journal Of Midwifery, 22*(2), 85-93.

Daley, T. C., Whaley, S. E., Sigman, M. D., Espinosa, M. P., & Neumann, C. (2003). IQ on the rise: The Flynn effect in rural Kenyan children. *Psychological Science, 14*, 215–219.

Dallaire, D. H., & Wilson, L. C. (2010). The relation of exposure to parental criminal activity, arrest, and sentencing to children's maladjustment. *Journal of Child and Family Studies, 19*(4), 404–418. doi:10.1007/s10826-009-9311-9

Dalli, C., & One, S. (2012). Involving children in educational research: Researcher reflections on challenges. *International Journal of Early Years Education, 20*(3), 224–233. doi:10.1080/09669760.2012.715408

Damon, W. (1977). *The social world of the child.* San Francisco, CA: Jossey-Bass.

Damon, W. (1981). Exploring children's social cognitions on two fronts. In J. M. Flavell & L. Ross (Eds.), *Social cognitive development: Frontiers and possible futures* (pp. 154–175). Cambridge, England: Cambridge University Press.

Damon, W. (1984). Peer education: The untapped potential. *Journal of Applied Developmental Psychology, 5*, 331–343.

Damon, W. (1988). *The moral child: Nurturing children's natural moral growth.* New York, NY: Free Press.

Damon, W. (1991). Putting substance into self-esteem: A focus on academic and moral values. *Educational Horizons, 70*(1), 12–18.

Damon, W., & Hart, D. (1988). *Self-understanding in childhood and adolescence.* New York, NY: Cambridge University Press.

DanceSafe. (2000a). *What is LSD?* Retrieved from http://www.dancesafe.org/documents/druginfo/lsd.php

DanceSafe. (2000b). *What is speed?* Retrieved from http://www.dancesafe.org/documents/druginfo/speed.php

Daniel, J. (2009). Intentionally thoughtful family engagement in early childhood education. *Young Children, 64*(5), 10–14.

Danner, F. W., & Day, M. C. (1977). Eliciting formal operations. *Child Development, 48*, 1600–1606.

Darling, S., Parker, M., Goodall, K. E., Havelka, J., & Allen, R. J. (2014). Visuospatial bootstrapping: Implicit binding of verbal working memory to visuospatial representations in children and adults. *Journal of Experimental Child Psychology, 119*112-119. doi:10.1016/j.jecp.2013.10.004

Darling-Hammond, L., & Bransford, J. (Eds.). (2005). *Preparing teachers for a changing world: What teachers should learn and be able to do.* San Francisco: Jossey-Bass/Wiley.

Darvin, J. (2009). Make books, not war: workshops at a summer camp in Bosnia. *Literacy, 43*(1), 50–59. doi:10.1111/j.1741-4369.2009.00483.x

Daunic, A. P., & Smith, S. W. (2010). Conflict resolution, peer mediation, and bullying prevention. In B. Algozzine, A. P. Daunic, & S. W. Smith (Eds.), *Preventing problem behaviors: Schoolwide programs and classroom practices* (2nd ed., pp. 113–132). Thousand Oaks, CA: Corwin Press.

Dauvier, B., Bailleux, C., & Perret, P. (2014). The development of relational integration during childhood. *Developmental Psychology, 50*(6), 1687-1697. doi:10.1037/a0036655

Davenport, E. C., Jr., Davison, M. L., Kuang, H., Ding, S., Kim, S., & Kwak, N. (1998). High school mathematics course-taking by gender and ethnicity. *American Educational Research Journal, 35*, 497–514.

Davidov, M., Zahn-Waxler, C., Roth-Hanania, R., & Knafo, A. (2013). Concern for others in the first year of life: Theory, evidence, and avenues for research. *Child Development Perspectives, 7*(2), 126–131. doi:10.1111/cdep.12028

Davidse, N., de Jong, M., Bus, A., Huijbregts, S., & Swaab, H. (2011). Cognitive and environmental predictors of early literacy skills. *Reading and Writing, 24*(4), 395–412. doi:10.1007/s11145-010-9233-3

Davidson, A. J., Gest, S. D., & Welsh, J. A. (2010). Relatedness with teachers and peers during early adolescence: An integrated variable-oriented and person-oriented approach. *Journal of School Psychology, 48*(6), 483–510. doi:10.1016/j.jsp.2010.08.002

Davidson, F. H. (1976). Ability to respect persons compared to ethnic prejudice in childhood. *Journal of Personality and Social Psychology, 34*, 1256–1267.

Davidson, M. R., London, M. L., & Ladewig, P. A. W. (2008). *Olds' maternal-newborn nursing and women's health across the lifespan.* Upper Saddle River, NJ: Pearson Prentice Hall.

Davidson, P., & Youniss, J. (1995). Moral development and social construction. In W. M. Kurtines & J. L. Gewirtz (Eds.), *Moral development: An introduction.* Boston, MA: Allyn & Bacon.

Davies, C., & Uttal, D. H. (2007). Map use and the development of spatial cognition. In J. M. Plumert & J. P. Spencer (Eds.), *The emerging spatial mind* (pp. 219–247). New York, NY: Oxford University Press.

Davies, D., Jindal-Snape, D., Collier, C., Digby, R., Hay, P., & Howe, A. (2013). Creative learning environments in education—A systematic literature review. *Thinking Skills & Creativity, 8,* 80–91. doi:10.1016/j.tsc.2012.07.004

Davies, P. T., Cicchetti, D., Hentges, R. F., & Sturge-Apple, M. L. (2013). The genetic precursors and the advantageous and disadvantageous sequelae of inhibited temperament: An evolutionary perspective. Developmental Psychology. doi:10.1037/a0032312

Davis, A. C., & Jackson, J. W. (1998). *"Yo, little brother--": Basic rules of survival for young African American males.* Chicago, IL: African American Images.

Davis, B. (2001). The restorative power of emotions in Child Protective Services. *Child and Adolescent Social Work Journal, 18,* 437–454.

Davis, D. A., & Davis, S. (2012). Morocco. In J. Arnett (Ed.), *Adolescent psychology around the world* (pp. 47–59). New York, NY: Psychology Press.

Davis, E. L., Levine, L. J., Lench, H. C., & Quas, J. A. (2010). Metacognitive emotion regulation: Children's awareness that changing thoughts and goals can alleviate negative emotions. *Emotion, 10*(4), 498–510.

Davis, G. A., & Rimm, S. B. (1998). *Education of the gifted and talented* (4th ed.). Boston, MA: Allyn & Bacon.

Davis, G. A., & Thomas, M. A. (1989). *Effective schools and effective teachers.* Needham Heights, MA: Allyn & Bacon.

Davis, H. A. (2003). Conceptualizing the role and influence of student–teacher relationships on children's social and cognitive development. *Educational Psychologist, 38,* 207–234.

Davis, H. A. (2003). Conceptualizing the role and influence of student–teacher relationships on children's social and cognitive development. *Educational Psychologist, 38,* 207–234.

Davis, J. H. (2008). *Why our schools need the arts.* New York, NY: Teachers College Press.

Davis, K. (2010). Coming of age online: The developmental underpinnings of girls' blogs. *Journal of Adolescent Research, 25*(1), 145–171. doi:10.1177/0743558409350503

Davis, M. (2013). Educators' perceptions of assistive technology for students with severe or multiple disabilities. *Dissertation Abstracts International Section A, 73.*

Davis, V. (2012). Interconnected but underprotected? Parents' methods and motivations for information seeking on digital safety issues. *Cyberpsychology, Behavior, and Social Networking, 15*(12), 669–674. doi:10.1089/cyber.2012.0179

Davis-Kean, P. E., & Sandler, H. M. (2001). A meta-analysis of measures of self-esteem for young children: A framework for future measures. *Child Development, 72,* 887–906.

Dawood, K., Bailey, J. M., & Martin, N. G. (2009). Genetic and environmental influences on sexual orientation. In Y. Kim (Ed.), *Handbook of behavior genetics* (pp. 269–279). New York, NY: Springer Science + Business Media. doi:10.1007/978-0-387-76727-7_19

Dawson-McClure, S., Calzada, E., Huang, K., Kamboukos, D., Rhule, D., Kolawole, B., Petkova, E., &Brotman, L. (2014). A population-level approach to promoting healthy child development and school success in low-income, urban neighborhoods: Impact on parenting and child conduct problems. *Prevention Science,* doi:10.1007/s11121-014-0473-3

Day, K. L., & Smith, C. L. (2013). Understanding the role of private speech in children's emotion regulation. *Early Childhood Research Quarterly, 28*(2), 405–414. doi:10.1016/j.ecresq.2012.10.003

de Barbaro, K., Johnson, C. M., & Deák, G. O. (2013). Twelve-month 'social revolution' emerges from mother-infant sensorimotor coordination: A longitudinal investigation. *Human Development, 56*(4), 223–248. doi:10.1159/000351313

De Brauwer, J., & Fias, W. (2009). A longitudinal study of children's performance on simple multiplication and division problems. *Developmental Psychology, 45*(5), 1480–1496.

De Corte, E., Greer, B., & Verschaffel, L. (1996). Mathematics teaching and learning. In D. C. Berliner & R. C. Calfee (Eds.), *Handbook of educational psychology* (pp. 491–549). New York, NY: Macmillan.

de Graaf, H., & Rademakers, J. (2006). Sexual behavior of prepubertal children. *Journal of Psychology and Human Sexuality, 18*(1), 1–21.

de Heering, A., Turati, C., Rossion, B., Bulf, H., Goffaux, V., & Simion, F. (2008). Newborns' face recognition is based on spatial frequencies below 0.5 cycles per degree. *Cognition, 106*(1), 444–454.

de Jong, T., & van Joolingen, W. R. (1998). Scientific discovery learning with computer simulations of conceptual domains. *Review of Educational Research, 68,* 179–201.

De La Paz, S. (2005). Effects of historical reasoning instruction and writing strategy mastery in culturally and academically diverse middle school classrooms. *Journal of Educational Psychology, 97,* 139–156.

De Laet, S., Doumen, S., Vervoort, E., Colpin, H., Van Leeuwen, K., Goossens, L., & Verschueren, K. (2014). Transactional links between teacher–child relationship quality and perceived versus sociometric popularity: A three-wave longitudinal study. *Child Development, 85*(4), 1647–1662.

De Lisi, R., & Golbeck, S. L. (1999). Implications of Piagetian theory for peer learning. In A. M. O'Donnell & A. King (Eds.), *Cognitive perspectives on peer learning* (pp. 3–37). Mahwah, NJ: Erlbaum.

de Milliano, I., van Gelderen, A., & Sleegers, P. (2012). Patterns of cognitive self-regulation of adolescent struggling writers. *Written Communication, 29*(3), 303–325. doi:10.1177/0741088312450275

De Pedro, K., Astor, R., Benbenishty, R., Estrada, J. r., Smith, G., & Esqueda, M. (2011). The children of military service members: Challenges, supports, and future educational research. *Review of Educational Research, 81*(4), 566–618.

de Souza, M. (2014). The empathetic mind: The essence of human spirituality. *International Journal of Children's Spirituality, 19*(1), 45–54. doi:10.1080/1364436X.2014.897221

de Villiers, J. (1995). Empty categories and complex sentences: The case of wh- questions. In P. Fletcher & B. MacWhinney (Eds.), *The handbook of child language* (pp. 508–540). Oxford, England: Blackwell.

de Weerdt, F., Desoete, A., & Roeyers, H. (2013). Behavioral inhibition in children with learning disabilities. *Research in Developmental Disabilities, 34*(6), 1998–2007. doi:10.1016/j.ridd.2013.02.020

de Wit, C. C., Sas, T. J., Wit, J. M., & Cutfield, W. S. (2013). Patterns of catch-up growth. Journal of Pediatrics, 162(2), 415–420. doi:10.1016/j.jpeds.2012.10.014

Deák, G. O., Triesch, J., Krasno, A., de Barbaro, K., & Robledo, M. (2013). Learning to share: The emergence of joint attention in human infancy. In B. Kar (Ed.), *Cognition and brain development: Converging evidence from various methodologies* (pp. 173–210). Washington, DC: American Psychological Association. doi:10.1037/14043-010

Deacon, S., Cleave, P. L., Baylis, J., Fraser, J., Ingram, E., & Perlmutter, S. (2014). The representation of roots in the spelling of children with specific language impairment. *Journal of Learning Disabilities, 47*(1), 13–21.

Deater-Deckard, K. (2009). Parenting the genotype. In K. McCartney & R. A. Weinberg (Eds.), *Experience and development: A festschrift in honor of Sandra Wood Scarr* (pp. 141–161). New York, NY: Psychology Press.

Deater-Deckard, K., Dodge, K., Bates, J., & Pettit, G. (1996). Physical discipline among African American and European American mothers: Links to children's externalizing behaviors. *Developmental Psychology, 32,* 1065–1072.

Deaux, K. (1984). From individual differences to social categories: Analysis of a decade's research on gender. *American Psychologist, 39,* 105–116.

DeBose, C. E. (2007). The Ebonics phenomenon, language planning, and the hegemony of Standard English. In H. S. Alim & J. Baugh (Eds.), *Talkin Black talk: Language, education, and social change* (pp. 30–42). New York, NY: Teachers College Press.

DeCasper, A. J., & Fifer, W. P. (1980). Of human bonding: Newborns prefer their mothers' voices. *Science, 208,* 1174–1176.

DeCasper, A. J., & Prescott, P. (2009). Lateralized processes constrain auditory reinforcement in human newborns. *Hearing Research, 255*(1–2), 135–141.

Deci, E. L. (1992). The relation of interest to the motivation of behavior: A self-determination theory perspective. In K. A. Renninger, S. Hidi, & A. Krapp (Eds.), *The role of interest in learning and development* (pp. 43–70). Hillsdale, NJ: Erlbaum.

Deci, E. L., & Ryan, R. M. (1985). *Intrinsic motivation and self-determination in human behavior.* New York, NY: Plenum Press.

Deci, E. L., & Ryan, R. M. (1992). The initiation and regulation of intrinsically motivated learning and achievement. In A. K. Boggiano & T. S. Pittman (Eds.), *Achievement and motivation: A social-developmental perspective* (pp. 3–36). Cambridge, England: Cambridge University Press.

Deeters, K. M. (2008). *Investigating a computerized scaffolding software for student designed science investigations.* (Doctoral dissertation, University of Nebraska, Lincoln). Available from ProQuest Dissertations and Theses database. (UMI Microform 3352767)

Degner, J., & Dalege, J. (2013). The apple does not fall far from the tree, or does it? A meta-analysis of parent–child similarity in intergroup attitudes. *Psychological Bulletin, 139*(6), 1270–1304. doi:10.1037/a0031436

Deitrick, L. M., & Draves, P. R. (2008). Attitudes toward doula support during pregnancy by clients, doulas, and labor-and-delivery nurses: A case study from Tampa, Florida. *Human Organization, 67*(4), 397–406.

DeLamater, J., & MacCorquodale, P. (1979). *Premarital sexuality: Attitudes, relationships, behavior.* Madison, WI: University of Wisconsin Press.

Delaney, K. R. (2006). Following the affect: Learning to observe emotional regulation. *Journal of Child and Adolescent Psychiatric Nursing, 19*(4), 175–181.

DeLeon, I. G., Bullock, C. E., & Catania, A. (2013). Arranging reinforcement contingencies in applied settings: Fundamentals and implications of recent basic and applied research. In G. J. Madden, W. V. Dube, T. D. Hackenberg, G. P. Hanley, & K. A. Lattal (Eds.), *APA handbook of behavior analysis, Vol. 2: Translating principles into practice* (pp. 47–75). Washington, DC: American Psychological Association. doi:10.1037/13938-003

Delgado-Gaitan, C. (1994). Socializing young children in Mexican-American families: An intergenerational perspective. In P. M. Greenfield & R. R. Cocking (Eds.), *Cross-cultural roots of minority child development* (pp. 55–86). Hillsdale, NJ: Erlbaum.

DeLisle, J. R. (1984). *Gifted children speak out.* New York, NY: Walker.

DeLoache, J. S. (2011). Early development of the understanding and use of symbolic artifacts. In U. Goswami (Ed.), *The Wiley-Blackwell handbook of childhood cognitive development* (2nd ed., pp. 312–336). Malden, MA: Wiley-Blackwell.

DeLoache, J. S., & Todd, C. M. (1988). Young children's use of spatial categorization as a mnemonic strategy. *Journal of Experimental Child Psychology, 46,* 1–20.

DeLoache, J. S., Cassidy, D. J., & Brown, A. L. (1985). Precursors of mnemonic strategies in very young children's memory. *Child Development, 56,* 125–137.

DeLoache, J. S., Miller, K. F., & Rosengren, K. S. (1997). The credible shrinking room: Very young children's performance with symbolic and nonsymbolic relations. *Psychological Science, 8,* 308–313.

Demarest, R. J., & Charon, R. (1996). *An illustrated guide to human reproduction and fertility control.* New York, NY: Parthenon.

Demetriou, A. (2000). Organization and development of self-understanding and self-regulation. In M. Boekaerts, P. Pintrich, & M. Zeidner (Eds.), *Handbook of self-regulation* (pp. 209–251). San Diego, CA: Academic Press.

Demetriou, A., Mouyi, A., & Spanoudis, G. (2008). Modelling the structure and development of g. *Intelligence, 36*(5), 437–454.

Dempster, F. N. (1991). Synthesis of research on reviews and tests. *Educational Leadership, 48,* 71–76.

Dempster, F. N., & Corkill, A. J. (1999). Interference and inhibition in cognition and behavior: Unifying themes for educational psychology. *Educational Psychology Review, 11,* 1–88.

Denckla, M. B. (2007). Executive function: Binding together the definitions of attention-deficit/-hyperactivity disorder and learning disabilities. In L. Meltzer (Ed.), *Executive function in education: From theory to practice* (pp. 5–18). New York, NY: Guilford Press.

Denison, S., & Xu, F. (2014). The origins of probabilistic inference in human infants. *Cognition, 130*(3), 335–347. doi:10.1016/j.cognition.2013.12.001

Denison, S., Reed, C., & Xu, F. (2013). The emergence of probabilistic reasoning in very young infants: Evidence from 4.5- and 6-month-olds. *Developmental Psychology, 49*(2), 243–249. doi:10.1037/a0028278

Denmark, N., & Harden, B. (2012). Un día en la vida: The everyday activities of young children from Central American immigrant families. *Early Child Development and Care, 182*(11), 1523–1543. doi:10.1080/03004430.2011.630073

Dennis, L., & Horn, E. (2014). The effects of professional development on preschool teachers' instructional behaviours during storybook reading. *Early Child Development & Care, 184*(8), 1160–1177. doi:10.1080/03004430.2013.853055

Denno, D. M., Carr, V., & Bell, S. H. (2010). *Addressing challenging behaviors in early childhood settings: A teacher's guide.* Baltimore, MD: Paul H. Brookes.

Deshler, D. D., & Schumaker, J. B. (1988). An instructional model for teaching students how to learn. In J. L. Graden, J. E. Zins, & M. J. Curtis (Eds.), *Alternative educational delivery systems: Enhancing instructional options for all students* (pp. 391–411). Washington, DC: National Association of School Psychologists.

DesJardin, J. L., Doll, E. R., Stika, C. J., Eisenberg, L. S., Johnson, K. J., Ganguly, D., et al. (2014). Parental support for language development during joint book reading for young children with hearing loss. *Communication Disorders Quarterly, 35*(3), 167–181. doi:10.1177/1525740113518062

Desoete, A. (2009). Metacognitive prediction and evaluation skills and mathematical learning in third-grade students. *Educational Research and Evaluation, 15*(5), 435–446.

Desrosiers, T., Herring, A., Shapira, S., Hooiveld, M., Luben, T., Herdt-Losavio, M., Lin, S., & Olshan, A. (2012). Paternal occupation and birth defects: findings from the National Birth Defects Prevention Study. *Occupational & Environmental Medicine, 69*(8), 534–542.

Dessel, A. (2010). Prejudice in schools: Promotion of an inclusive culture and climate. *Education and Urban Society, 42*(4), 407–429. doi:10.1177/0013124510361852

Deutsch, A. R., Steinley, D., & Slutske, W. S. (2014). The role of gender and friends' gender on peer socialization of adolescent drinking: A prospective multilevel social network analysis. *Journal of Youth and Adolescence, 43*(9), 1421–1435. doi:10.1007/s10964-013-0048-9

Deutsch, M. (1993). Educating for a peaceful world. *American Psychologist, 48,* 510–517.

Devereaux, Y., & Sullivan, H. (2013). Doula support while laboring: Does it help achieve a more natural birth? International Journal of Childbirth Education, 28(2), 54–61.

Devlin, B., Daniels, M., & Roeder, K. (1997). The heritability of IQ. *Nature, 388*(6641), 468–471.

DeVoe, J. F., Peter, K., Kaufman, P., Ruddy, S. A., Miller, A. K., Planty, M., et al. (2003). *Indicators of school crime and safety: 2002* (NCES 2003-009/ NCJ 196753). Washington, DC: U.S. Departments of Education and Justice.

DeVries, R. (1997). Piaget's social theory. *Educational Researcher, 26*(2), 4–17.

DeVries, R., & Zan, B. (1996). A constructivist perspective on the role of the sociomoral atmosphere in promoting children's development. In C. T. Fosnot (Ed.), *Constructivism: Theory, perspectives, and practice (pp. 103–119).* New York, NY: Teachers College Press.

DeVries, R., & Zan, B. (2003). When children make rules. *Educational Leadership, 61*(1), 64–67.

Deyhle, D., & LeCompte, M. (1999). Cultural differences in child development: Navajo adolescents in middle schools. In R. H. Sheets & E. R. Hollins (Eds.), *Racial and ethnic identity in school practices: Aspects of human development* (pp. 123–139). Mahwah, NJ: Erlbaum.

Di Carlo, M. (2012). How to use value-added measures right. *Educational Leadership, 70*(3), 38–42.

Di Giunta, L., Pastorelli, C., Eisenberg, N., Gerbino, M., Castellani, V., & Bombi, A. S. (2010). Developmental trajectories of physical aggression: Prediction of overt and covert antisocial behaviors from self and mothers' reports. *European Child & Adolescent Psychiatry, 19*(12), 873–882. doi:10.1007/s00787-010-0134-4

Dia Cha's (1996). *Dia's story cloth: The Hmong people's journey of freedom.* New York, NY: Lee & Low Books.

Diamond, A., Barnett, W. S., Thomas, J., & Munro, S. (2007). Preschool program improves cognitive control. *Science, 318*(5855), 1387–1388. doi:10.1126/science.1151148

Diamond, M., & Hopson, J. (1998). *Magic trees of the mind.* New York, NY: Dutton.

Diamond, S. C. (1991). What to do when you can't do anything: Working with disturbed adolescents. *Clearing House, 64,* 232–234.

Diaz, R. M. (1983). Thought and two languages: The impact of bilingualism on cognitive development. In E. W. Gordon (Ed.), *Review of research in education* (Vol. 10, pp. 23-54). Washington, DC: American Educational Research Association.

Diaz, R. M., & Berndt, T. J. (1982). Children's knowledge of best friend: Fact or fancy? *Developmental Psychology, 18,* 787–794.

Dibbens, L. M., Heron, S. E., & Mulley, J. C. (2007). A polygenic heterogeneity model for common epilepsies with complex genetics. *Genes, Brain & Behavior, 6,* 593–597.

Dick-Read, G. (1944). *Childbirth without fear.* New York, NY: Harper & Brothers.

Dickens, W. T., & Flynn, J. R. (2001). Heritability estimates versus large environmental effects: The IQ paradox resolved. *Psychological Review, 108,* 346–369.

Dien, T. (1998). Language and literacy in Vietnamese American communities. In B. Pérez (Ed.), *Sociocultural contexts of language and literacy (pp. 137–177).* Mahwah, NJ: Erlbaum.

Dien, T. (1998). Language and literacy in Vietnamese American communities. In B. Pérez (Ed.), *Sociocultural contexts of language and literacy.* Mahwah, NJ: Erlbaum.

Dierssen, M. (2012). Down syndrome: The brain in trisomic mode. *Nature Reviews Neuroscience, 13*(3), 844–858. doi:10.1038/nrn3314

Dimech, A. S., & Seiler, R. (2010). The association between extra-curricular sport participation and social anxiety symptoms in children. *Journal of Clinical Sport Psychology, 4*(3), 191–203.

Dimmitt, C., & McCormick, C. B. (2012). Metacognition in education. In K. R. Harris, S. Graham, T. Urdan, C. B. McCormick, G. M. Sinatra, & J. Sweller (Eds.), *APA educational psychology handbook, Vol. 1: Theories, constructs, and critical issues* (pp. 157–187). Washington, DC: American Psychological Association. doi:10.1037/13273-007

Ding, X., Omrin, D., Evans, A., Fu, G., Chen, G., & Lee, K. (2014). Elementary school children's cheating behavior and its cognitive correlates. *Journal of Experimental Child Psychology, 121,* 85–95.

DiPietro, J. A. (2004). The role of prenatal maternal stress in child development. *Current Directions in Psychological Science, 13,* 71–74.

diSessa, A. A. (1996). What do 'just plain folk' know about physics?. In D. R. Olson, N. Torrance (Eds.) *The handbook of education and human development: New models of learning, teaching and schooling* (pp. 709-730). Malden, MA: Blackwell.

diSessa, A. A. (2007). An interactional analysis of clinical interviewing. *Cognition and Instruction, 25,* 523–565.

diSessa, A. A., Gillespie, N. M., & Esterly, J. B. (2004). Coherence versus fragmentation in the development in the concept of force. *Cognitive Science, 28,* 843–900.

Dishion, T. J., Kim, H., Stormshak, E. A., & O'Neill, M. (2014). A brief measure of peer affiliation and social acceptance (PASA): Validity in an ethnically diverse sample of early adolescents. *Journal of Clinical Child and Adolescent Psychology, 43*(4), 601–612. doi:10.1080/15374416.2013.876641

Dix, T., Stewart, A. D., Gershoff, E. T., & Day, W. H. (2007). Autonomy and children's reactions to being controlled: Evidence that both compliance and defiance may be positive markers in early development. *Child Development, 78,* 1204–1221.

Dixon, J. A., & Kelley, E. (2007). Theory revision and redescription. *Current Directions in Psychological Science, 16,* 111–115.

Dixon, L., Skinner, J., & Foureur, M. (2013a). The emotional and hormonal pathways of labour and birth: integrating mind, body and behaviour. *New Zealand College of Midwives Journal,* 4815-23.

Dixon, L., Skinner, J., & Foureur, M. (2013b). Women's perspectives of the stages and phases of labour. *Midwifery, 29*(1), 10–17. doi:10.1016/j.midw.2012.07.001

Dodge, K. A. (1983). Behavioral antecedents of peer social status. *Child Development, 54,* 1386–1399.

Dodge, K. A., Bates, J. E., & Pettit, G. S. (1990). Mechanisms in the cycle of violence. *Science, 250,* 1678–1683.

Dodge, K. A., Coie, J., & Lynam, D. (2006). Aggression and antisocial behavior in youth. In W. Damon & R. M. Lerner (Series Eds.) & N. Eisenberg (Vol. Ed.), *Handbook of child psychology: Vol. 3. Social, emotional, and personality development* (6th ed., pp. 719–788). New York, NY: Wiley.

Dodge, K. A., Lansford, J. E., Burks, V. S., Bates, J. E., Pettit, G. S., Fontaine, R., & Price, J. (2003). Peer rejection and social information-processing factors in the development of aggressive behavior problems in children. *Child Development, 74,* 374–393.

Dodge, K. A., Lansford, J. E., Burks, V. S., Bates, J. E., Pettit, G. S., Fontaine, R., et al. (2003). Peer rejection and social information-processing factors in the development of aggressive behavior problems in children. *Child Development, 74,* 374–393.

Doescher, S. M., & Sugawara, A. I. (1989). Encouraging prosocial behavior in young children. *Childhood Education, 65,* 213–216.

Dohnt, H., & Tiggemann, M. (2006). The contribution of peer and media influences to the development of body satisfaction and self-esteem in young girls: A prospective study. *Developmental Psychology, 42,* 929–936.

Dolan, M. M., Casanueva, C., Smith, K. R., & Bradley, R. H. (2009). Parenting and the home environment provided by grandmothers of children in the child welfare system. *Children and Youth Services Review, 31,* 784–796.

Dolev-Cohen, M., & Barak, A. (2013). Adolescents' use of instant messaging as a means of emotional relief. *Computers in Human Behavior, 29*(1), 58–63.

Domellöf, M., & Szymlek-Gay, E. A. (2012). Iron nutrition and neurodevelopment in young children. In L. Riby, M. Smith, J. Foster (Eds.), *Nutrition and mental performance: A lifespan perspective* (pp. 13–28). New York, NY: Palgrave Macmillan.

Dominé, F., Berchtold, A., Akré, C., Michaud, P.-A., & Suris, J.-C. (2009). Disordered eating behaviors: What about boys? *Journal of Adolescent Health, 44,* 111–117.

Domitrovich, C. E., Cortes, R. C., & Greenberg, M. T. (2007). Improving young children's social and emotional competence: A randomized trial of the preschool "PATHS" curriculum. *Journal of Primary Prevention, 28,* 67–91.

Donaldson, M. (1978). *Children's minds.* New York, NY: Norton.

Donaldson, S. K., & Westerman, M. A. (1986). Development of children's understanding of ambivalence and causal theories of emotion. *Developmental Psychology, 22,* 655–662.

Donne, V. (2012). Keyboard instruction for students with a disability. *Clearing House, 85*(5), 201–206. doi:10.1080/00098655.2012.689784

Dornbusch, S. M., Carlsmith, J. M., Gross, R. T., Martin, J. A., Jennings, D., Rosenberg, A., et al. (1981). Sexual development, age, and dating: A comparison of biological and social influences upon one set of behaviors. *Child Development, 52,* 179–185.

Dornbusch, S. M., Ritter, P. L., Leiderman, P. H., Roberts, D. F., & Fraleigh, M. J. (1987). The relation of parenting style to adolescent school performance. *Child Development, 58,* 1244–1257.

dos Santos, E., de Kieviet, J. F., Königs, M., van Elburg, R. M., & Oosterlaan, J. (2013). Predictive value of the Bayley Scales of Infant Development on development of very preterm/very low birth weight children: A meta-analysis. *Early Human Development, 89*(7), 487–496. doi:10.1016/j.earlhumdev.2013.03.008

Dougherty Stahl, K. A. (2014). Fostering inference generation with emergent and novice readers. *Reading Teacher, 67*(5), 384–388. doi:10.1002/trtr.1230

Dove, G. (2012). Grammar as a developmental phenomenon. *Biology & Philosophy, 27*(5), 615–637. doi:10.1007/s10539-012-9324-4

Dovidio, J. F., & Gaertner, S. L. (1999). Reducing prejudice: Combating intergroup biases. *Current Directions in Psychological Science, 8,* 101–105.

Downer, J. T., Booren, L. M., Lima, O. K., Luckner, A. E., & Pianta, R. C. (2010). The individualized classroom assessment scoring system (inCLASS): Preliminary reliability and validity of a system for observing preschoolers' competence in classroom interactions. *Early Childhood Research Quarterly, 25*(1), 1–16. doi:10.1016/j.ecresq.2009.08.004

Downey, J. (2000, March). *The role of schools in adolescent resilience: Recommendations from the literature.* Paper presented at the International Association of Adolescent Health, Washington, DC.

Dowson, M., & McInerney, D. M. (2001). Psychological parameters of students' social and work avoidance goals: A qualitative investigation. *Journal of Educational Psychology, 93,* 35–42.

Doyle, P. A., Bird, B. C., Appel, S., Parisi, D., Rogers, P., Glarso, R., et al. (2006). Developing an effective communications campaign to reach pregnant women at high risk of late or no prenatal care. *Social Marketing Quarterly, 12*(4), 35–50.

Dozier, M., & Fisher, P. (2014). Neuroscience enhanced child maltreatment interventions to improve outcomes. *Social Policy Report, 28*(1), 25–27.

Dray, A. J., & Selman, R. L., & Schultz, L. H. (2009). Communicating with intent: A study of social awareness and children's writing. *Journal of Applied Developmental Psychology, 30,* 116–128.

Dreweke, J., & Wind, R. (2007, May). *Strong evidence favors comprehensive approach to sex ed.* Guttmacher Institute Media Center. Retrieved from http://www.guttmacher.org/media/nr/2007/05/23/index.html

Droe, K. (2013). Effect of verbal praise on achievement goal orientation, motivation, and performance attribution. *Journal of Music Teacher Education, 23*(1), 63–78. doi:10.1177/1057083712458592

Dryfoos, J. G. (1997). The prevalence of problem behaviors: Implications for programs. In R. P. Weissberg, T. P. Gullotta, R. L. Hamptom, B. A. Ryan, & G. R. Adams (Eds.), *Enhancing children's wellness* (Vol. 8, pp. 17–46). Thousand Oaks, CA: Sage.

Dryfoos, J. G. (1999, Fall). The role of the school in children's out-of-school time. *The Future of Children: When School Is Out, 9,* 117–134.

Duarte Ribeiro, L., & Loução Martins, A. (2013). Specific learning disabilities: Evidence from third grade students' handwriting performance. *Special Education, 2,* 158–163.

Duchesne, S., & Ratelle, C. (2010). Parental behaviors and adolescents' achievement goals at the beginning of middle school: Emotional problems as potential mediators. *Journal of Educational Psychology, 102*(2), 497–507. doi:10.1037/a0019320

Duckworth, A. L., & Seligman, M. E. P. (2005). Self-discipline outdoes IQ in predicting academic performance of adolescents. *Psychological Science, 16,* 939–944.

Duckworth, A. L., & Seligman, M. E. P. (2006). Self-discipline gives girls the edge: Gender in self-discipline, grades, and achievement test scores. *Journal of Educational Psychology, 98,* 198–208.

Duijnhouwer, H., Prins, F., & Stokking, K. (2012). Feedback providing improvement strategies and reflection on feedback use: Effects on students' writing motivation, process, and performance. *Learning & Instruction, 22*(3), 171–184. doi:10.1016/j.learninstruc.2011.10.003

Dumont, H., Trautwein, U., Nagy, G., & Nagengast, B. (2014). Quality of parental homework involvement: Predictors and reciprocal relations with academic functioning in the reading domain. *Journal of Educational Psychology, 106*(1), 144–161. doi:10.1037/a0034100

Duncan, G. (2013, April). Enhancing well-being of children and youth living in poverty. Paper presented at the annual meeting of the American Educational Research Association, San Francisco, CA.

Dunham, P. J., Dunham, F., & Curwin, A. (1993). Joint-attentional states and lexical acquisition at 18 months. *Developmental Psychology, 29,* 827–831.

Dunkel, C. S., & Sefcek, J. A. (2009). Eriksonian lifespan theory and life history theory: An integration using the example of identity formation. *Review of General Psychology, 13*(1), 13–23.

Dunn, J. (1984). *Sisters and brothers.* Cambridge, MA: Harvard University Press.

Dunn, J. (2006). Moral development in early childhood and social interaction in the family. In M. Killen & J. G. Smetana (Eds.), *Handbook of moral development* (pp. 331–350). Mahwah, NJ: Erlbaum.

Dunn, J. (2007). Siblings and socialization. In J. E. Grusec & P. D. Hastings (Eds.), *Handbook of socialization: Theory and research* (pp. 309–327). New York, NY: Guilford Press.

Dunn, J., & Munn, P. (1985). Becoming a family member: Family conflict and the development of social understanding in the second year. *Child Development, 56,* 480–492.

Dunn, J., Brown, J., & Beardsall, L. (1991). Family talk about feeling states and children's later understanding of others' emotions. *Developmental Psychology, 27,* 448–455.

Dunn, L. S. (2011, February). Making the most of your class website. *Educational Leadership, 68*(5), 60–62.

Dunsmore, J. C. (2014). Effects of person- and process-focused feedback on prosocial behavior in middle childhood. *Social Development.* doi:10.1111/sode.12082

DuPaul, G., & Hoff, K. (1998). Reducing disruptive behavior in general education classrooms: The use of self-management strategies. *School Psychology Review, 27,* 290–304.

Durand, V. M. (1998). *Sleep better: A guide to improving sleep for children with special needs.* Baltimore, MD: Paul H. Brookes.

Durkin, K., & Conti-Ramsden, G. (2007). Language, social behavior, and the quality of friendships in adolescents with and without a history of specific language impairment. *Child Development, 78,* 1441–1457.

Durkin, K., Nesdale, D., Dempsey, G., & McLean, A. (2012). Young children's responses to media representations of intergroup threat and ethnicity. *British Journal of Developmental Psychology, 30*(3), 459–476. doi:10.1111/j.2044-835X.2011.02056.x

Durlak, J. A., Mahoney, J. L., Bohnert, A. M., & Parente, M. E. (2010). Developing and improving after-school programs to enhance youth's personal growth and adjustment: A special issue of AJCP. *American Journal of Community Psychology, 45*(3–4), 285–293. doi:10.1007/s10464-010-9298-9

Dush, C. (2013). Marital and cohabitation dissolution and parental depressive symptoms in fragile families. *Journal of Marriage and Family, 75*(1), 91–109.

Dutt-Doner, K., Cook-Cottone, C., & Allen, S. (2007). Improving classroom instruction: Understanding the developmental nature of analyzing primary sources. *Research in Middle Level Education Online, 30*(6), 1-12.

Dwairy, M., Achoui, M., Abouserie, R., Farah, A., Sakhleh, A. A., Fayad, M., et al. (2006). Parenting styles in Arab societies: A first cross-regional research study. *Journal of Cross Cultural Psychology, 37,* 230–247.

Dweck, C. S. (1975). The role of expectations and attributions in the alleviation of learned helplessness. *Journal of Personality and Social Psychology, 31,* 674–685.

Dweck, C. S. (1986). Motivational processes affecting learning. *American Psychologist, 41,* 1040–1048.

Dweck, C. S. (2000). *Self-theories: Their role in motivation, personality, and development.* Philadelphia, PA: Psychology Press.

Dweck, C. S. (2008). Brainology: Transforming students' motivation to learn. *Independent School, 67*(2), 110–119.

Dweck, C. S. (2009). Foreword. In F. D. Horowitz, R. F. Subotnik & D. J. Matthews (Eds.), *The development* of giftedness and talent across the life span (pp. xi–xiv). Washington, DC: American Psychological Association.

Dweck, C. S. (2010). Even geniuses work hard. *Educational Leadership, 68*(2), 16–20.

Dweck, C. S. (2012). Mindsets and human nature: Promoting change in the Middle East, the schoolyard, the racial divide, and willpower. *American Psychologist, 67*(8), 614–622. doi:10.1037/a0029783

Dweck, C. S., & Elliott, E. S. (1983). Achievement motivation. In E. M. Hetherington (Ed.), *Handbook of child psychology: Vol. 4. Socialization, personality, and social development* (4th ed., pp. 643–691). New York, NY: Wiley.

Dweck, C. S., & Master, A. (2009). Self-theories and motivation: Students' beliefs about intelligence. K. R. Wentzel & A. Wigfield (Eds.), *Handbook of motivation at school* (pp. 123–140). New York, NY: Routledge/Taylor & Francis Group.

Dweck, C. S., Mangels, J. A., & Good, C. (2004). Motivational effects on attention, cognition, and performance. In D. Y. Dai & R. J. Sternberg (Eds.), *Motivation, emotion, and cognition: Integrative perspectives on intellectual functioning and development* (pp. 41–55). Mahwah, NJ: Erlbaum.

Dwyer, K., & Osher, D. (2000). *Safeguarding our children: An action guide*. Washington, DC: U.S. Departments of Education and Justice, American Institutes for Research. Retrieved from http://www.ed.gov/pubs/edpubs.html

Dwyer, K., Osher, D., & Warger, C. (1998). *Early warning, timely response: A guide to safe schools*. Washington, DC: U.S. Department of Education. Retrieved from http://www.ed.gov/offices/OSERS/OSEP/earlywrn.html

Dwyer, R. E., Hodson, R., & McCloud, L. (2013). Gender, debt, and dropping out of college. *Gender & Society, 27*(1), 30–55. doi:10.1177/0891243212464906

Dykens, E. M., & Cassidy, S. B. (1999). Prader-Willi syndrome. In S. Goldstein & C. R. Reynolds (Eds.), *Handbook of neurodevelopmental and genetic disorders* (pp. 525–554). New York, NY: Guilford Press.

Dyson, M., & Plunkett, M. (2012). Making a difference by embracing cooperative learning practices in an alternate setting: An exciting combination to incite the educational imagination. *Journal of Classroom Interaction, 47*(2), 13–24.

Eagly, A. H. (1987). *Sex differences in social behavior: A social-role interpretation*. Hillsdale, NJ: Erlbaum.

Eamon, M. K., & Mulder, C. (2005). Predicting antisocial behavior among Latino young adolescents: An ecological systems analysis. *American Journal of Orthopsychiatry, 75*, 117–127.

Early, D. M., Maxwell, K. L., Burchinal M., Alva, S., Bender, R. H., Bryant, D., et al. (2007). Teachers' education, classroom quality, and young children's academic skills: Results from seven studies of preschool programs. *Child Development, 78*, 558–580.

Easterbrooks, M., Bartlett, J., Beeghly, M., & Thompson, R. A. (2013). Social and emotional development in infancy. In R. M. Lerner, M. Easterbrooks, J. Mistry, & I. B. Weiner (Eds.), *Handbook of psychology, Vol. 6: Developmental psychology* (2nd ed., pp. 91–120). Hoboken, NJ: Wiley.

Ebbels, S. H., Mari☒, N., Murphy, A., & Turner, G. (2014). Improving comprehension in adolescents with severe receptive language impairments: a randomized control trial of intervention for coordinating conjunctions. *International Journal of Language & Communication Disorders, 49*(1), 30–48. doi:10.1111/1460-6984.12047

Eccles, J. S. (2007). Families, schools, and developing achievement-related motivations and engagement. In J. E. Grusec & P. D. Hastings (Eds.), *Handbook of socialization: Theory and research* (pp. 665–691). New York, NY: Guilford Press.

Eccles, J. S. (2007). Families, schools, and developing achievement-related motivations and engagement. In J. E. Grusec & P. D. Hastings (Eds.), *Handbook of socialization: Theory and research* (pp. 665–691). New York, NY: Guilford Press.

Eccles, J. S., & Midgley, C. (1989). Stage-environment fit: Developmentally appropriate classrooms for young adolescents. In C. Ames & R. Ames (Eds.), *Research on motivation in education: Vol. 3. Goals and cognition (pp. 13–44)*. San Diego, CA: Academic Press.

Eccles, J. S., & Roeser, R. W. (2009). Schools, academic motivation, and stage-environment fit. In R. M. Lerner & L. Steinberg (Eds.), *Handbook of adolescent psychology, Vol. 1: Individual bases of adolescent development* (3rd ed., pp. 404–434). Hoboken, NJ: Wiley.

Eccles, J. S., & Wigfield, A. (1985). Teacher expectations and student motivation. In J. B. Dusek (Ed.), *Teacher expectancies (pp. 185–226)*. Hillsdale, NJ: Erlbaum.

Eccles, J. S., Freedman-Doan, C., Frome, P., Jacobs, J., & Yoon, K. S. (2000). Gender-role socialization in the family: A longitudinal approach. In T. Eckes & H. M. Trautner (Eds.), *The developmental social psychology of gender* (pp. 333–360). Mahwah, NH: Erlbaum.

Eccles, J. S., Wigfield, A., & Schiefele, U. (1998). Motivation to succeed. In W. Damon (Series Ed.) & N. Eisenberg (Vol. Ed.), *Handbook of child psychology: Vol .3. Social, emotional, and personality development* (5th ed., pp. 1017–1095). New York, NY: Wiley.

Echols, L., & Graham, S. (2013). Birds of a different feather: How do cross-ethnic friends flock together? *Merrill-Palmer Quarterly, 59*(4), 461–488.

Eckerman, C. O. (1979). The human infant in social interaction. In R. Cairns (Ed.), *The analysis of social interactions: Methods, issues, and illustrations* (pp. 163–178). Hillsdale, NJ: Erlbaum.

Edens, K. M., & Potter, E. F. (2001). Promoting conceptual understanding through pictorial representation. *Studies in Art Education, 42*, 214–233.

Edmunds, A. L., & Edmunds, G. A. (2005). Sensitivity: A double-edged sword for the pre-adolescent and adolescent gifted child. *Roeper Review, 27*(2), 69–77.

Edwards, A. (2014). African-American male student perceptions about factors related to why black boys drop out of secondary school. *Dissertation Abstracts International Section A, 74.*

Edwards, A., Eisenberg, N., Spinrad, T. L., Reiser, M., Eggum-Wilkens, N. D., & Liew, J. (2014). Predicting sympathy and prosocial behavior from young children's dispositional sadness. *Social Development.* doi:10.1111/sode.12084

Edwards, C. (2014). Maternal literacy practices and toddlers' emergent literacy skills. *Journal of Early Childhood Literacy, 14*(1), 53–79. doi:10.1177/1468798412451590

Edwards, O. W., & Taub, G. E. (2009). A conceptual pathways model to promote positive youth development in children raised by their grandparents. *School Psychology Quarterly, 24*, 160–172.

Edwards, S., & Cutter-Mackenzie, A. (2013). Pedagogical play types: What do they suggest for learning about sustainability in early childhood education? *International Journal of Early Childhood.* doi:10.1007/s13158-013-0082-5

Eeds, M., & Wells, D. (1989). Grand conversations: An explanation of meaning construction in literature study groups. *Research in the Teaching of English, 23,* 4–29.

Eerola, P., & Eerola, T. (2014). Extended music education enhances the quality of school life. *Music Education Research, 16*(1), 88–104. doi:10.1080/14613808.2013.829428

Egeland, B. (2009). Taking stock: Childhood emotional maltreatment and developmental psychopathology. *Child Abuse and Neglect, 33,* 22–26.

Ehm, J., Lindberg, S., & Hasselhorn, M. (2014). Reading, writing, and math self-concept in elementary school children: influence of dimensional comparison processes. *European Journal of Psychology of Education—EJPE (Springer Science & Business Media B.V.), 29*(2), 277–294. doi:10.1007/s10212-013-0198-x

Ehrenberg, M., Regev, R., Lazinski, M., Behrman, L. J., & Zimmerman, J. (2014). Adjustment to divorce for children. In L. Grossman, S. Walfish (Eds.), *Translating psychological research into practice* (pp. 1-7). New York, NY: Springer Publishing Co.

Ehrenreich, S. E., Beron, K. J., Brinkley, D. Y., & Underwood, M. K. (2014). Family predictors of continuity and change in social and physical aggression from ages 9 to 18. *Aggressive Behavior.* doi:10.1002/ab.21535

Ehri, L. (2014). Orthographic mapping in the acquisition of sight word reading, spelling memory, and vocabulary learning. *Scientific Studies of Reading, 18*(1), 5–21. doi:10.1080/10888438.2013.819356

Ehri, L. C. (1991). Development of the ability to read words. In P. D. Pearson (Ed.), *Handbook of reading research* (Vol. II, pp. 383-417). White Plains, NY: Longman.

Ehri, L. C. (1994). Development of the ability to read words: Update. In R. B. Ruddell, M. R. Ruddell, & H. Singer (Eds.), *Theoretical models and processes of reading* (4th ed., pp. 323-358). Newark, DE: International Reading Association.

Ehrler, D. J., Evans, J. G., & McGhee, R. L. (1999). Extending big-five theory into childhood: A preliminary investigation into the relationship between big-five personality traits and behavior problems in children. *Psychology in the Schools, 36,* 451–458.

Eigsti, I., Zayas, V., Mischel, W., Shoda, Y., Ayduk, O., Dadlani, M. B., et al. (2006). Predicting cognitive control from preschool to late adolescence and young adulthood. *Psychological Science, 17*(6), 478–484. doi:10.1111/j.1467-9280.2006.01732.x

Eilers, R. E., & Oller, D. K. (1994). Infant vocalizations and early diagnosis of severe hearing impairment. *Journal of Pediatrics, 124,* 199–203.

Eisenberg, N. (1982). The development of reasoning regarding prosocial behavior. In N. Eisenberg (Ed.), *The development of prosocial behavior (pp. 219–249)*. New York, NY: Academic Press.

Eisenberg, N. (1992). *The caring child*. Cambridge, MA: Harvard University Press.

Eisenberg, N. (1995). Prosocial development: A multifaceted model. In W. M. Kurtines & J. L. Gewirtz (Eds.), *Moral development: An introduction*. Boston, MA: Allyn & Bacon.

Eisenberg, N. (2006). Emotion-related regulation. In H. E. Fitzgerald, B. M. Lester, & B. Zuckerman (Vol. Eds.), & H. E. Fitzgerald, R. Zucker, & K. Freeark (Eds. in Chief), *The crisis in youth mental health: Critical issues and effective programs. Vol. 1: Childhood disorders* (pp. 133–155). Westport, CT: Praeger.

Eisenberg, N., & Fabes, R. A. (1998). Prosocial development. In W. Damon (Series Ed.) & N. Eisenberg (Vol. Ed.), *Handbook of child psychology: Vol. 3. Social, emotional, and personality development* (pp. 701–778). New York, NY: Wiley.

Eisenberg, N., Carlo, G., Murphy, B., & Van Court, N. (1995). Prosocial development in late adolescence: A longitudinal study. *Child Development, 66,* 1179–1197.

Eisenberg, N., Eggum, N. D., & Edwards, A. (2010). Empathy-related responding and moral development. In W. F. Arsenio & E. A. Lemerise (Eds.), *Emotions, aggression, and morality in children:*

Bridging development and psychopathology (pp. 115–135). Washington, DC: American Psychological Association.

Eisenberg, N., Fabes, R. A., & Spinrad, T. L. (2006). Prosocial development. In N. Eisenberg, W. Damon, R. M. Lerner (Eds.), *Handbook of child psychology: Vol. 3, Social, emotional, and personality development* (6th ed., pp. 646–718). Hoboken, NJ: Wiley.

Eisenberg, N., Fabes, R. A., Carlo, G., & Karbon, M. (1992). Emotional responsivity to others: Behavioral correlates and socialization antecedents. In N. Eisenberg & R. A. Fabes (Eds.), *New directions in child development* (No. 55, pp. 57–73). San Francisco, CA: Jossey-Bass.

Eisenberg, N., Fabes, R. A., Schaller, M., Carlo, G., & Miller, P. A. (1991). The relations of parental characteristics and practices to children's vicarious emotional responding. *Child Development, 62*, 1393–1408.

Eisenberg, N., Lennon, R., & Pasternack, J. F. (1986). Altruistic values and moral judgment. In N. Eisenberg (Ed.), *Altruistic emotion, cognition, and behavior.* Hillsdale, NJ: Erlbaum.

Eisenberg, N., Martin, C. L., & Fabes, R. A. (1996). Gender development and gender effects. In D. C. Berliner & R. C. Calfee (Eds.), *Handbook of educational psychology (pp. 358–396).* New York, NY: Macmillan.

Eisenberg, N., Miller, P. A., Shell, R., McNalley, S., & Shea, C. (1991). Prosocial development in adolescence: A longitudinal study. *Developmental Psychology, 27*, 849–857.

Eisenberg, N., Spinrad, T. L., & Sadovsky, A. (2006). Empathy-related responding in children. In M. Killen & J. G. Smetana (Eds.), *Handbook of moral development* (pp. 517–549). Mahwah, NJ: Erlbaum.

Eisenberg, N., Spinrad, T. L., Valiente, C., & Duckworth, A. L. (2014). Conscientiousness: Origins in childhood? *Developmental Psychology, 50*(5), 1331–1349. doi:10.1037/a0030977

Eisenberg, N., Zhou, Q., & Koller, S. (2001). Brazilian adolescents' prosocial moral judgment and behavior: Relations to sympathy, perspective-taking, gender-role orientation, and demographic characteristics. *Child Development, 72*, 518–534.

Ekelin, M., Crang-Svalenius, E., & Dykes, A. K. (2004). A qualitative study of mothers' and fathers' experiences of routine ultrasound examination in Sweden. *Midwifery, 20*, 335–344.

Ekinci, B. (2014). The relationships among Sternberg's triarchic abilities, Gardner's multiple intelligences, and academic achievement. *Social Behavior & Personality: An International Journal, 42*(4), 625-633. doi:10.2224/sbp.2014.42.4.625

El Zein, F., Solis, M., Vaughn, S., & McCulley, L. (2014). Reading comprehension interventions for students with autism spectrum disorders: A synthesis of research. *Journal of Autism & Developmental Disorders, 44*(6), 1303–1322. doi:10.1007/s10803-013-1989-2

Elbro, C., & Petersen, D. K. (2004). Long-term effects of phoneme awareness and letter sound training: An intervention study with children at risk for dyslexia. *Journal of Educational Psychology, 96*, 660–670.

Elder, A. D. (2010). Children's self-assessment of their school work in elementary school. *Education 3–13, 38*(1), 5–11. doi:10.1080/03004270802602044

Elia, J. P. (1994). Homophobia in the high school: A problem in need of a resolution. *Journal of Homosexuality, 77*(1), 177–185.

Elias, G., & Broerse, J. (1996). Developmental changes in the incidence and likelihood of simultaneous talk during the first two years: A question of function. *Journal of Child Language, 23*, 201–217.

Elish-Piper, L., Matthews, M., & Risko, V. (2013). Invisibility: An unintended consequence of standards, tests, and mandates. *Journal of Language & Literacy Education / Ankara Universitesi SBF Dergisi, 9*(2), 4–23.

Elkind, D. (1981a). *Children and adolescents: Interpretive essays on Jean Piaget* (3rd ed.). New York, NY: Oxford University Press.

Elkind, D. (1981b). *The hurried child: Growing up too fast too soon.* Reading, MA: Addison-Wesley.

Elkins, A. (2013). Environments that inspire. *Teaching Young Children, 6*(5), 14–17.

Elliot, A. J., & McGregor, H. A. (2000, April). Approach and avoidance goals and autonomy-controlled regulation: Empirical and conceptual relations. In A. Assor (Chair), *Self-determination theory and achievement goal theory: Convergences, divergences, and educational implications.* Symposium conducted at the annual meeting of the American Educational Research Association, New Orleans, LA.

Elliott, D. J. (1995). *Music matters: A new philosophy of music education.* New York, NY: Oxford University Press.

Elliott, R., & Vasta, R. (1970). The modeling of sharing: Effects associated with vicarious reinforcement, symbolization, age, and generalization. *Journal of Experimental Child Psychology, 10*, 8–15.

Elliott, S. N., Kurz, A., & Neergaard, L. (2012). Large-scale assessment for educational accountability. In K. R. Harris, S. Graham, T. Urdan, A. G. Bus, S. Major, & H. Swanson (Eds.), *APA educational psychology handbook, Vol. 3: Application to teaching and learning* (pp. 111–138). Washington, DC US: American Psychological Association. doi:10.1037/13275-006

Elliott, S., & Elliott, G. (2014). Chess, contest, and English. *English Journal, 103*(3), 87-93.

Elmesky, R. (2013). Building capacity in understanding foundational biology concepts: A K-12 learning progression in genetics informed by research on children's thinking and learning. *Research In Science Education, 43*(3), 1155–1175. doi:10.1007/s11165-012-9286-1

Elmore, C. A., & Gaylord-Harden, N. K. (2013). The influence of supportive parenting and racial socialization messages on African American youth behavioral outcomes. *Journal of Child and Family Studies, 22*(1), 63–75. doi:10.1007/s10826-012-9653-6

Elmore, G. M., & Huebner, E. S. (2010). Adolescents' satisfaction with school experiences: Relationships with demographics, attachment relationships, and school engagement behavior. *Psychology in the Schools, 47*(6), 525–537.

Else-Quest, N. M., Hyde, J. S., & Linn, M. C. (2010). Cross-national patterns of gender differences in mathematics: A meta-analysis. *Psychological Bulletin, 136*(1), 103–127.

Elze, D. E. (2003). Gay, lesbian, and bisexual youths' perceptions of their high school environments and comfort in school. *Children and Schools, 25*(4), 225–239.

Emde, R. N., & Buchsbaum, H. (1990). "Didn't you hear my mommy?" Autonomy with connectedness in moral self-emergence. In D. Cicchetti & M. Beeghly (Eds.), *The self in transition: Infancy to adulthood* (pp. 35–60). Chicago, IL: University of Chicago Press.

Emde, R., Gaensbauer, T., & Harmon, R. (1976). *Emotional expression in infancy: A biobehavioral study* (Psychological Issues, Vol. 10, No. 37). New York, NY: International Universities Press.

Emmer, E. T., Evertson, C. M., & Worsham, M. E. (2000). *Classroom management for secondary teachers* (5th ed.). Boston, MA: Allyn & Bacon.

Empson, S. B. (1999). Equal sharing and shared meaning: The development of fraction concepts in a first-grade classroom. *Cognition and Instruction, 17*, 283–342.

Encheff, D. (2013). Creating a science e-book with fifth grade students. *Techtrends: Linking Research & Practice to Improve Learning, 57*(6), 61–72. doi:10.1007/s11528-013-0703-8

Engel, S. (2011). Children's need to know: Curiosity in schools. *Harvard Educational Review, 81*(4), 625–645.

Engeland, A., Bjørge, T., Daltveit, A., Skurtveit, S., Vangen, S., Vollset, S., & Furu, K. (2013). Effects of preconceptional paternal drug exposure on birth outcomes: cohort study of 340 000 pregnancies using Norwegian population-based databases. *British Journal of Clinical Pharmacology, 75*(4), 1134-1141. doi:10.1111/j.1365-2125.2012.04426.x

English, D. J. (1998). The extent and consequences of child maltreatment. *The Future of Children: Protecting Children from Abuse and Neglect, 8*(1), 39–53.

English, D., Lambert, S., & Ialongo, N. (2014). Longitudinal associations between experienced racial discrimination and depressive symptoms in African American adolescents. *Developmental Psychology, 50*(4), 1190–1196.

Ennis, R., & Jolivette, K. (2014). Existing research and future directions for self-regulated strategy development with students with and at risk for emotional and behavioral disorders. *Journal of Special Education, 48*(1), 32–45. doi:10.1177/0022466912454682

Epkins, C. C., Gardner, C., & Scanlon, N. (2013). Rumination and anxiety sensitivity in preadolescent girls: Independent, combined, and specific associations with depressive and anxiety symptoms. *Journal of Psychopathology and Behavioral Assessment, 35*(4), 540–551. doi:10.1007/s10862-013-9360-7

Eppig, C., Fincher, C. L., & Thornhill, R. (2010). Parasite prevalence and the worldwide distribution of cognitive ability. *Proceedings of the Royal Society,* 1–8.

Epstein, J. L. (1986). Friendship selection: Developmental and environmental influences. In E. Mueller & C. Cooper (Eds.), *Process and outcome in peer relationships* (pp. 129–160). New York, NY: Academic Press.

Epstein, J. L. (1996). Perspectives and previews on research and policy for school, family, and community partnerships. In A. Booth & J. F. Dunn (Eds.), *Family–school links: How do they affect educational outcomes?* Mahwah, NJ: Erlbaum.

Epstein, J. L., Galindo, C. L., & Sheldon, S. B. (2011). Levels of leadership: Effects of district and school leaders on the quality of school programs of family and community involvement. *Educational Administration Quarterly, 47*(3), 462–495. doi:10.1177/0013161X10396929

Epstein, J. L., Sanders, M. G., Salinas, K., Jansorn, N., Van Voorhis, F. L., Martin, C. S, Thomas, B. G., Greenfield, M. D., Hutchins, D. J., & Williams, K. J. (2009). *School, family, and community partnerships: Your handbook for action* (3rd ed.). Thousand Oaks, CA US: Corwin Press.

Epstein, J. S. (1998). Introduction: Generation X, youth culture, and identity. In J. S. Epstein (Ed.), *Youth culture: Identity in a postmodern world* (pp. 1–23). Malden, MA: Blackwell.

Epstein, S., & Morling, B. (1995). Is the self motivated to do more than enhance and/or verify itself? In M. H. Kernis (Ed.), *Efficacy, agency, and self-esteem.* New York, NY: Plenum Press.

Erath, S. A., Flanagan, K. S., Bierman, K. L., & Tu, K. M. (2010). Friendships moderate psychosocial maladjustment in socially anxious early adolescents. *Journal of Applied Developmental Psychology, 31*(1), 15–26. doi:10.1016/j.appdev.2009.05.005

Erickson, J. E., Keil, F. C., & Lockhart, K. L. (2010). Sensing the coherence of biology in contrast to psychology: Young children's use of causal relations to distinguish two foundational domains. *Child Development, 81*(1), 390–409.

Eriks-Brophy, A., Gibson, S., & Tucker, S. (2013). Articulatory error patterns and phonological process use of preschool children with and without hearing loss. *Volta Review, 113*(2), 87–125.

Eriksen, H., Kesmodel, U., Wimberley, T., Underbjerg, M., Kilburn, T., & Mortensen, E. (2012). Effects of tobacco smoking in pregnancy on offspring intelligence at the age of 5. *Journal of Pregnancy*, 1–9. doi:10.1155/2012/945196

Erikson, E. H. (1963). *Childhood and society* (2nd ed.). New York, NY: Norton.

Erikson, E. H. (1966). *Eight ages of man. International Journal of Psychiatry, 2*(3), 281–300.

Eriksson, M., Marschik, P. B., Tulviste, T., Almgren, M., Pérez Pereira, M., Wehberg, S., et al. (2012). Differences between girls and boys in emerging language skills: Evidence from 10 language communities. *British Journal of Developmental Psychology, 30*(2), 326–343. doi:10.1111/j.2044-835X.2011.02042.x

Ernst, M., & Hardin, M. (2010). Neurodevelopment underlying adolescent behavior. In P. D. Zelazo, M. Chandler, & E. Crone (Eds.), *Developmental social cognitive neuroscience. The Jean Piaget symposium series* (pp. 165–189). New York, NY: Psychology Press.

Ernst-Slavit, G. & Mason, M. (2012). *Making your first ELL home visit: A guide for classroom teachers.* Retrieved from http://www.colorincolorado.org/article/59138/

Eron, L. D. (1980). Prescription for reduction of aggression. *American Psychologist, 35,* 244–252.

Eron, L. D. (1987). The development of aggressive behavior from the perspective of a developing behaviorism. *American Psychologist, 42,* 435–442.

Erwin, P. (1993). *Friendship and peer relations in children.* Chichester, England: Wiley.

Esparza, J., Shumow, L., & Schmidt, J. (2014). Growth mindset of gifted seventh grade students in science. *NCSSSMST Journal, 19*(1), 6–13.

Espinosa, L. (2007). English-language learners as they enter school. In R. Pianta, M. Cox, & K. Snow (Eds.), *School readiness and the transition to kindergarten in the era of accountability* (pp. 175–196). Baltimore, MD: Paul H. Brookes.

Espinosa, L. (2008). *Challenging common myths about young English language learners.* FCD Policy Brief: Advancing PK–3 (No. 8). New York, NY: Foundation for Child Development.

Espinoza, G., Gillen-O'Neel, C., Gonzales, N. A., & Fuligni, A. J. (2013). Friend affiliations and school adjustment among Mexican-American adolescents: The moderating role of peer and parent support. *Journal of Youth and Adolescence.* doi:10.1007/s10964-013-0023-5

Espinoza, P., Arêas da Luz Fontes, A., & Arms-Chavez, C. (2014). Attributional gender bias: teachers' ability and effort explanations for students' math performance. *Social Psychology Of Education, 17*(1), 105–126. doi:10.1007/s11218-013-9226-6

Estes, K. G., Evans, J. L., Alibali, M. W., & Saffran, J. R. (2007). Can infants map meaning to newly segmented words? Statistical segmentation and word learning. *Psychological Science, 18,* 254–260.

Esteve-Gibert, N., & Prieto, P. (2014). Infants temporally coordinate gesture-speech combinations before they produce their first words. *Speech Communication, 57,* 301–316. doi:10.1016/j.specom.2013.06.006

Estrada, V. L., Gómez, L., & Ruiz-Escalante, J. A. (2009). Let's make dual language the norm. *Educational Leadership, 66*(7), 54–58.

Eunjyu, Y. (2013). Empowering at-risk students as autonomous learners: Toward a metacognitive approach. *Research & Teaching in Developmental Education, 30*(1), 35–45.

Evans, E. M. (2001). Cognitive and contextual factors in the emergence of diverse belief systems: Creation versus evolution. *Cognitive Psychology, 42,* 217–266.

Evans, E. M., Schweingruber, H., & Stevenson, H. W. (2002). Gender differences in interest and knowledge acquisition: The United States, Taiwan, and Japan. *Sex Roles, 47,* 153–167.

Evans, G. W., & Fuller-Rowell, T. E. (2013). Childhood poverty, chronic stress, and young adult working memory: The protective role of self-regulatory capacity. *Developmental Science, 16*(5), 688–696. doi:10.1111/desc.12082

Evans, G. W., & Kim, P. (2007). Childhood poverty and health: Cumulative risk exposure and stress dysregulation. *Psychological Science, 18,* 953–957.

Evans, G. W., & Schamberg, M. A. (2009). Childhood poverty, chronic stress, and adult working memory. *PNAS Proceedings of the National Academy of the United States, 106*(16), 6545–6549.

Evans, G. W., Li, D., & Sepanski Whipple, S. (2013). Cumulative risk and child development. *Psychological Bulletin.* doi:10.1037/a0031808

Evans, J. L., Hahn, J. A., Lum, P. J., Stein, E. S., & Page, K. (2009). Predictors of injection drug use cessation and relapse in a prospective cohort of young injection drug users in San Francisco, CA (UFO Study). *Drug and Alcohol Dependence, 101,* 152–157.

Fadiman, A. (1997). *The spirit catches you and you fall down: The Hmong child, her American doctors, and the collision of two cultures.* New York, NY: Noonday Press/Farrar,

Fagan, J. F., Holland, C. R., & Wheeler, K. (2007). The prediction, from infancy, of adult IQ and achievement. *Intelligence, 35,* 225–231.

Fahrmeier, E. D. (1978). The development of concrete operations among the Hausa. *Journal of Cross-Cultural Psychology, 9,* 23–44.

Fairchild, H. H., & Edwards-Evans, S. (1990). African American dialects and schooling: A review. In A. M. Padilla, H. H. Fairchild, & C. M. Valadez (Eds.), *Bilingual education: Issues and strategies* (pp. 75-86). Newbury Park, CA: Sage.

Fais, L., Kajikawa, S., Shigeaki, A., & Werker, J. F. (2009). Infant discrimination of a morphologically relevant word-final contrast. *Infancy, 14*(4), 488–499.

Falbo, T., & Polit, D. (1986). A quantitative review of the only child literature: Research evidence and theory development. *Psychological Bulletin, 100,* 176–189.

Falch, T., & Sandgren Massih, S. (2011). The effect of education on cognitive ability. *Economic Inquiry, 49*(3), 838–856. doi:10.1111/j.1465-7295.2010.00312.x

Fan, Y., Decety, J., Yang, C., Liu, J., & Cheng, Y. (2010). Unbroken mirror neurons in autism spectrum disorders. *Journal of Child Psychology and Psychiatry, 51*(9), 981–988. doi:10.1111/j.1469-7610.2010.02269.x

Fanti, K. A., & Henrich, C. C. (2010). Trajectories of pure and co-occurring internalizing and externalizing problems from age 2 to age 12: Findings from the National Institute of Child Health and Human Development Study of Early Child Care. *Developmental Psychology, 46*(5), 1159–1175.

Fantini, A. E. (1985). *Language acquisition of a bilingual child: A sociolinguistic perspective.* Clevedon, England: Multilingual Matters. (Available from the SIT Bookstore, School for International Training, Kipling Road, Brattleboro, VT 05302)

Fantino, A. M., & Colak, A. (2001). Refugee children in Canada: Searching for identity. *Child Welfare, 80,* 587–596.

Farber, B., Mindel, C. H., & Lazerwitz, B. (1988). The Jewish American family. In C. H. Mindel, R. W. Habenstein, & R. Wright (Eds.), *Ethnic families in America: Patterns and variations (pp. 400-437).* New York, NY: Elsevier.

Farmer, E., Selwyn, J., & Meakings, S. (2013). "Other children say you're not normal because you don't live with your parents." Children's views of living with informal kinship carers: Social networks, stigma and attachment to carers. *Child & Family Social Work, 18*(1), 25–34. doi:10.1111/cfs.12030

Farmer-Hinton R., Lewis, J., Patton, L., & Rivers, I. (2013). Dear Mr. Kozol. . . . Four African American women scholars and the re-authoring of *Savage Inequalities. Teachers College Record, 115*(5), 1–38.

Farr, R. H., & Patterson, C. J. (2013). Lesbian and gay adoptive parents and their children. In A. E. Goldberg & K. R. Allen (Eds.), *LGBT-parent families: Innovations in research and implications for practice* (pp. 39–55). New York, NY: Springer Science + Business Media. doi:10.1007/978-1-4614-4556-2_3

Farrant, B. M., Devine, T. J., Maybery, M. T., & Fletcher, J. (2012). Empathy, perspective taking and prosocial behaviour: The importance of parenting practices. *Infant & Child Development, 21*(2), 175–188. doi:10.1002/icd.740

Farrell, A. D., Erwin, E. H., Bettencourt, A., Mays, S., Vulin-Reynolds, M., Sullivan, T., et al. (2008). Individual factors influencing effective nonviolent behavior and fighting in peer situations: A qualitative study with urban African American adolescents. *Journal of Clinical Child and Adolescent Psychology, 37*(2), 397–411.

Farrelly, E., Cho, M. K., Erby, L., Roter, D., Stenzel, A., & Ormond, K. (2012). Genetic counseling for prenatal testing: Where is the discussion about disability? *Journal of Genetic Counseling, 21*(6), 814-824. doi:10.1007/s10897-012-9484-z

Farringdon, F., Holgate, C., McIntyre, F., & Bulsara, M. (2014). A level of discomfort! Exploring the relationship between maternal sexual health knowledge, religiosity and comfort discussing sexual health issues with adolescents. *Sexuality Research & Social Policy: A Journal Of The NSRC, 11*(2), 95–103. doi:10.1007/s13178-013-0122-9

Farrington-Flint, L., & Wood, C. (2007). The role of lexical analogies in beginning reading: Insights from children's self-reports. *Journal of Educational Psychology, 99,* 326–338.

Farrow, C., & Blissett, J. (2014). Maternal mind-mindedness during infancy, general parenting sensitivity and observed child feeding behavior: a longitudinal study. *Attachment & Human Development, 16*(3), 230–241. doi:10.1080/14616734.2014.898158

Farver, J. A. M., & Branstetter, W. H. (1994). Preschoolers' prosocial responses to their peers' distress. *Developmental Psychology, 30,* 334–341.

Farver, J. M., & Shin, Y. L. (1997). Social pretend play in Korean- and Anglo-American pre-schoolers. *Child Development, 68*(3), 544–556.

Farver, J. M., Xu, Y., Lonigan, C. J., & Eppe, S. (2013). The home literacy environment and Latino head start children's emergent literacy skills. *Developmental Psychology, 49*(4), 775–791. doi:10.1037/a0028766

Fausel, D. F. (1986). Loss after divorce: Helping children grieve. *Journal of Independent Social Work, 1*(1), 39–47.

Fearrington, J. Y., Parker, P. D., Kidder-Ashley, P., Gagnon, S. G., McCane-Bowling, S., & Sorrell, C. A. (2014). Gender differences in written expression curriculum-based measurement in third- through eighth-grade students. *Psychology in The Schools, 51*(1), 85–96. doi:10.1002/pits.21733

Febres, J., Shorey, R., Zucosky, H., Brasfield, H., Vitulano, M., Elmquist, J., et al. (2014). The relationship between male-perpetrated interparental aggression, paternal characteristics, and child psychosocial functioning. *Journal of Child & Family Studies, 23*(5), 907–916. doi:10.1007/s10826-013-9748-8

Federal Interagency Forum on Child and Family Statistics. (2013). *America's children in brief: Key national indicators of well-being, 2013.* Washington, DC: U.S. Government Printing Office.

Retrieved from http://www.childstats.gov/pdf/ac2013/ac_13.pdf

Federal Interagency Forum on Child and Family Statistics. (2013a). *Table FAM1.A Family structure and children's living arrangements: Percentage of children ages 0–17 by presence of parents in household and race and Hispanic origin, 1980–2011*. Retrieved from http://www.childstats.gov/americaschildren/tables/fam1a.asp

Federal Interagency Forum on Child and Family Statistics. (2013b). *Table FAM1.B Family structure and children's living arrangements: Detailed living arrangements of children by gender, race and Hispanic origin, age, parent's education, and poverty status, 2011*. Retrieved from http://www.childstats.gov/americaschildren/tables/fam1b.asp

Federal Interagency Forum on Child and Family Statistics. (2013c). *Special 1.A/C Adoption: Number and percentage of children ages 0–17 who are adopted and percentage of adopted children ages 0–17 who are of a different race than their adoptive parent by region and state, 2008*. Retrieved from http://www.childstats.gov/americaschildren11/tables/special1ac.asp

Federal Interagency Forum on Child and Family Statistics. (2013d). *America's children in brief: Key national indicators of well-being, 2012*. Washington, DC: U.S. Government Printing Office.

Federal Interagency Forum on Child and Family Statistics. (2013e). *Pop3 race and Hispanic Origin composition: Percentage of U.S. children ages 0–17 by race and Hispanic origin, 1980–2011 and projected 2012–2050*. Retrieved from http://www.childstats.gov/americaschildren/tables/pop3.asp

Feifer, S. G. (2013). Psychopathology of disorders of written expression and dysgraphia. In A. S. Davis (Ed.), *Psychopathology of childhood and adolescence: A neuropsychological approach* (pp. 145–157). New York, NY: Springer Publishing Co.

Feigenberg, L., King, M., Barr, D., & Selman, R. (2008). Belonging to and exclusion from the peer group in schools: influences on adolescents' moral choices. *Journal of Moral Education, 37*(2), 165–184. doi:10.1080/03057240802009306

Feinberg, M. E., Kan, M. L., & Goslin, M. C. (2009). Enhancing coparenting, parenting, and child self-regulation: Effects of family foundations 1 year after birth. *Prevention Science, 10*(3), 276–285.

Feinberg, M. E., Kan, M. L., & Hetherington, E. M. (2007). The longitudinal influence of coparenting conflict on parental negativity and adolescent adjustment. *Journal of Marriage and Family, 69*, 687–702.

Feinman, S. (1992). *Social referencing and the social construction of reality in infancy*. New York, NY: Plenum Press.

Feldhusen, J. F. (1989). Synthesis of research on gifted youth. *Educational Leadership, 26*(1), 6–11.

Feldhusen, J. F., Van Winkle, L., & Ehle, D. A. (1996). Is it acceleration or simply appropriate instruction for precocious youth? *Teaching Exceptional Children, 28*(3), 48–51.

Feldman, D. H. (2004). Piaget's stages: The unfinished symphony of cognitive development. *New Ideas in Psychology, 22*, 175–231.

Feldman, R. (2007). Mother-infant synchrony and the development of moral orientation in childhood and adolescence: Direct and indirect mechanisms of developmental continuity. *American Journal of Orthopsychiatry, 77*(4), 582–597. doi:10.1037/0002-9432.77.4.582

Felner, R. D., & DeVries, M. (2013). Poverty in childhood and adolescence: A transactional-ecological approach to understanding and enhancing resilience in contexts of disadvantage and developmental risk. In S. Goldstein, R. B. Brooks (Eds.), *Handbook of resilience in children* (2nd ed., pp. 105–126).

New York, NY: Springer Science + Business Media. doi:10.1007/978-1-4614-3661-4_7

Felton, R. H. (1998). The development of reading skills in poor readers: Educational implications. In C. Hulme & R. M. Joshi (Eds.), *Reading and spelling: Development and disorders* (pp. 329–342). Mahwah, NJ: Erlbaum.

Feng, X., Shaw, D., & Moilanen, K. (2011). Parental negative control moderates the shyness-emotion regulation pathway to school-age internalizing symptoms. *Journal of Abnormal Child Psychology, 39*(3), 425–436.

Fennell, C. T., Byers-Heinlein, K., & Werker, J. F. (2007). Using speech sounds to guide word learning: The case of bilingual infants. *Child Development, 78*, 1510–1525.

Fennimore, B. S. (2013). Honoring women who must raise their children alone. In J. Pattnaik (Ed.), *Father involvement in young children's lives: A global analysis* (pp. 169–179). New York, NY: Springer Science + Business Media. doi:10.1007/978-94-007-5155-2_10

Fenson, L., Dale, P., Reznick, J., Bates, E., Thal, D., & Pethick, S. (1994). Variability in early communicative development. *Monographs of the Society for Research in Child Development, 59*(5, Serial No. 242), 1–173.

Fernald, A., Swingley, D., & Pinto, J. P. (2001). When half a word is enough: Infants can recognize spoken words using partial phonetic information. *Child Development, 72*, 1003–1015.

Ferrell, K. (2006). Evidence-based practices for students with visual disabilities. *Communication Disorders Quarterly, 28*(1), 42–48.

Fetro, J. V., Givens, C., & Carroll, K. (2009/2010). Coordinated school health: Getting it all together. *Educational Leadership, 67*(4), 32–37.

Fett, A. J., Shergill, S. S., Gromann, P. M., Dumontheil, I., Blakemore, S., Yakub, F., & Krabbendam, L. (2014). Trust and social reciprocity in adolescence—A matter of perspective-taking. *Journal of Adolescence, 37*(2), 175–184. doi:10.1016/j.adolescence.2013.11.011

Feuerstein, R. (1979). *The dynamic assessment of retarded performers: The Learning Potential Assessment Device, theory, instruments, and techniques*. Baltimore, MD: University Park Press.

Feuerstein, R. (1990). The theory of structural cognitive modifiability. In B. Z. Presseisen (Ed.), *Learning and thinking styles: Classroom interaction*. Washington, DC: National Education Association.

Feuerstein, R., Feuerstein, R., & Gross, S. (1997). The Learning Potential Assessment Device. In D. P. Flanagan, J. L. Genshaft, & P. L. Harrison (Eds.), *Contemporary intellectual assessment: Theories, tests, and issues* (pp. 297–313). New York, NY: Guilford Press.

Fewell, R. R., & Sandall, S. R. (1983). Curricula adaptations for young children: Visually impaired, hearing impaired, and physically impaired. *Curricula in Early Childhood Special Education, 2*(4), 51–66.

Fiedler, E. D., Lange, R. E., & Winebrenner, S. (1993). In search of reality: Unraveling the myths about tracking, ability grouping and the gifted. *Roeper Review, 16*(1), 4–7.

Field, S. L., Labbo, L. D., & Ash, G. E. (1999, April). *Investigating young children's construction of social studies concepts and the intersection of literacy learning*. Paper presented at the annual meeting of the American Educational Research Association, Montreal, Canada.

Field, T. (2001). Massage therapy facilitates weight gain in preterm infants. *Current Directions in Psychological Science, 10*, 51–54.

Field, T., Woodson, R., Greenberg, R., & Cohen, D. (1982). Discrimination and imitation of facial expressions by neonates. *Science, 218*, 179–181.

Fields, R. D. (2009). *The other brain: From dementia to schizophrenia, how new discoveries are revolutionizing medicine and science*. New York, NY: Simon & Schuster.

Fifer, W. P., & Moon, C. M. (1995). The effects of fetal experience with sound. In J. P. Lecanuet, W. P. Fifer, N. A. Krasnegor, & W. P. Smotherman (Eds.), *Fetal development: A psychobiological perspective* (pp. 351-366). Hillsdale, NJ: Erlbaum.

Finders, M., & Lewis, C. (1994). Why some parents don't come to school. *Educational Leadership, 51*(8), 50–54.

Finger, B., Hans, S. L., Bernstein, V. J., & Cox, S. M. (2009). Parent relationship quality and infant-mother attachment. *Attachment and Human Development, 11*(3), 285–306.

Finkelhor, D., Mitchell, K. J., & Wolak, J. (2000). *Online victimization: A report on the nation's youth*. Durham, NH: Crimes Against Children Research Center. Retrieved from http://www.unh.edu/ccrc/pdf/Victimization_Online_Survey.pdf

Finkelhor, D., Ormrod, R., Turner, H., & Hamby, S. L. (2005). The victimization of children and youth: A comprehensive, national study. *Child Maltreatment, 10*(1), 5–25.

Fiorello, C. A., & Primerano, D. (2005). Research into practice: Cattell-Horn-Carroll cognitive assessment in practice: Eligibility and program development issues. *Psychology in the Schools, 42*(5), 525–536.

Fireman, G. D., & Kose, G. (2010). Perspective taking. In E. H. Sandberg & B. L. Spritz (Eds.), *A clinician's guide to normal cognitive development in childhood* (pp. 85–100). New York, NY: Routledge/Taylor & Francis Group.

Firkowska-Mankiewicz, A. (2011). Adult Careers: Does Childhood IQ Predict Later Life Outcome? *Journal of Policy & Practice in Intellectual Disabilities, 8*(1), 1–9. doi:10.1111/j.1741-1130.2011.00281.x

Fischer, K. W. (2008). Dynamic cycles of cognitive and brain development: Measuring growth in mind, brain, and education. In A. M. Battro, K. W. Fischer, & P. J. Lena (Eds.), *The educated brain* (pp. 127–150). New York, NY: Cambridge University Press.

Fischer, K. W., & Bidell, T. R. (2006). Dynamic development of action and thought. In W. Damon & R. M. Lerner (Eds. in Chief) & R. M. Lerner (Vol. Ed.), *Handbook of child psychology: Vol. 1. Theoretical models of human development* (6th ed., pp. 313–399). Hoboken, NJ: Wiley.

Fischer, K. W., & Immordino-Yang, M. H. (2002). Cognitive development and education: From dynamic general structure to specific learning and teaching. In E. Lagemann (Ed.), *Traditions of scholarship in education* (pp. 1–55). Chicago: Spencer Foundation.

Fischer, K. W., Stein, Z., & Heikkinen, K. (2009). Narrow assessments misrepresent development and misguide policy: Comment on Steinberg, Cauffman, Woolard, Graham, and Banich (2009). *American Psychologist, 64*(7), 595–600.

Fishbein, D. H., Hyde, C., Eldreth, D., Paschall, M. J., Hubal, R., Das, A., et al. (2006). Neurocognitive skills moderate urban male adolescents' responses to preventive intervention materials. *Drug and Alcohol Dependence, 82*(1), 47–60.

Fisher, C. B., & Vacanti-Shova, K. (2012). The responsible conduct of psychological research: An overview of ethical principles, APA Ethics Code standards, and federal regulations. In S. J. Knapp, M. C. Gottlieb, M. M. Handelsman, & L. D. VandeCreek (Eds.), *APA handbook of ethics in psychology, Vol. 2: Practice, teaching, and research* (pp. 335–369). Washington, DC: American Psychological Association. doi:10.1037/13272-016

Fisher, C. B., Jackson, J. F., & Villarruel, F. A. (1998). The study of African American and Latin

American children and youth. In W. Damon (Series Ed.) & R. M. Lerner (Vol. Ed.), *Handbook of child psychology: Vol. 1. Theoretical models of human development* (5th ed., pp. 1145–1207). New York, NY: Wiley.

Fisher, D., & Frey, N. (2007). *Checking for understanding: Formative assessment techniques for your classroom.* Alexandria, VA: Association for Super-vision and Curriculum Development.

Fisher, P. A., Gunnar, M. R., Dozier, M., Bruce, J., & Pears, K. C. (2006). Effects of therapeutic interventions for foster children on behavioral problems, caregiver attachment, and stress regulatory neural systems. *Annals of The New York Academy of Sciences, 1094*(1), 215–225. doi:10.1196/annals.1376.023

Fisher, P. A., Kim, H. K., & Pears, K. C. (2009). Effects of Multidimensional Treatment Foster Care for Preschoolers (MTFC-P) on reducing permanent placement failures among children with placement instability. *Children and Youth Services Review, 31*, 541–546.

Fite, P. J., Vitulano, M., Wynn, P., Wimsatt, A., Gaertner, A., & Rathert, J. (2010). Influence of perceived neighborhood safety on proactive and reactive aggression. *Journal of Community Psychology, 38*(6), 757–768. doi:10.1002/jcop.20393

Fitzgerald, J. (1987). Research on revision in writing. *Review of Educational Research, 57,* 481–506.

Fitzpatrick, C., McKinnon, R. D., Blair, C. B., & Willoughby, M. T. (2014). Do preschool executive function skills explain the school readiness gap between advantaged and disadvantaged children? *Learning & Instruction, 30,* 25–31. doi:10.1016/j.learninstruc.2013.11.003

Fitzpatrick, C., McKinnon, R., Blair, C., & Willoughby, M. (2014). Do preschool executive function skills explain the school readiness gap between advantaged and disadvantaged children? *Learning & Instruction, 30,* 25–31. doi:10.1016/j.learninstruc.2013.11.003

Fitzsimmons, P., Leddy, D., Johnson, L., Biggam, S., & Locke, S. (2013). The moon challenge. *Science & Children, 51*(1), 36–41.

Fivush, R. (1994). Constructing narrative, emotion, and self in parent-child conversations about the past. In U. Neisser & R. Fivush (Eds.), *The remembering self: Construction and accuracy in the self-narrative* (pp. 136–157). Cambridge, England: Cambridge University Press.

Fivush, R. (2009). Sociocultural perspectives on autobiographical memory. In M. L. Courage & N. Cowan (Eds.), *The development of memory in infancy and childhood* (pp. 283–301). New York, NY: Psychology Press.

Fivush, R., & Buckner, J. P. (2003). Creating gender and identity through autobiographical narratives. In R. Fivush & C. A. Haden (Eds.), *Autobiographical memory and the construction of a narrative self* (pp. 149–167). Mahwah, NJ: Erlbaum.

Fivush, R., & Nelson, K. (2004). Culture and language in the emergence of autobiographical memory. *Psychological Science, 15,* 573–577.

Fivush, R., Haden, C., & Adam, S. (1995). Structure and coherence of preschoolers' personal narratives over time: Implications for childhood amnesia. *Journal of Experimental Child Psychology, 60,* 32–56.

Flanagan, C. A., & Faison, N. (2001). Youth civic development: Implications of research for social policy and programs. *Social Policy Report, 15*(1), 1–14. Ann Arbor, MI: Society for Research in Child Development.

Flanagan, D., Alfonso, V., & Reynolds, M. (2013). Broad and narrow CHC Abilities measured and not measured by the Wechsler Scales: Moving beyond within-battery factor analysis. *Journal of Psychoeducational Assessment, 31*(2), 202–223. doi:10.1177/0734282913478047

Flanders, J. L., Simard, M., Paquette, D., Parent, S., Vitaro, F., Pihl, R. O., et al. (2010). Rough-and-tumble play and the development of physical aggression and emotion regulation: A five-year follow-up study. *Journal of Family Violence, 25*(4), 357–367. doi:10.1007/s10896-009-9297-5

Flannery, L. P., & Bers, M. (2013). Let's Dance the "Robot Hokey-Pokey"!: Children's programming approaches and achievement throughout early cognitive development. *Journal of Research on Technology in Education, 46*(1), 81–101.

Flavell, J. H. (2000). Development of children's knowledge about the mental world. *International Journal of Behavioral Development, 24*(1), 15–23.

Flavell, J. H., Friedrichs, A. G., & Hoyt, J. D. (1970). Developmental changes in memorization processes. *Cognitive Psychology, 1,* 324–340.

Flavell, J. H., Green, F. L., & Flavell, E. R. (1995). Young children's knowledge about thinking. *Monographs of the Society for Research in Child Development, 60*(1, Serial No. 243).

Flavell, J. H., Miller, P. H., & Miller, S. A. (2002). *Cognitive development* (4th ed.). Upper Saddle River, NJ: Prentice Hall.

Flay, B. R., & Allred, C. G. (2003). Long-term effects of the Positive Action program. *American Journal of Health Behavior, 27*(1), 6–21.

Fleer, M., & Hammer, M. (2013). Emotions in imaginative situations: The valued place of fairytales for supporting emotion regulation. *Mind, Culture & Activity, 20*(3), 240–259. doi:10.1080/10749039.2013.781652

Flege, J. E., Munro, M. J., & MacKay, I. R. A. (1995). Effects of age of second-language learning on the production of English consonants. *Speech Communication, 16,* 1–26.

Fleming, D. (2002). *Alphabet under construction.* New York, NY: Henry Holt.

Fletcher, A. C., Bridges, T. H., & Hunter, A. G. (2007). Managing children's friendships through interparental relationships: Roles of ethnicity and friendship context. *Journal of Marriage and Family, 69,* 1135–1149.

Fletcher, A. C., Hunter, A. G., & Eanes, A. Y. (2006). Links between social network closure and child well-being: The organizing role of friendship context. *Developmental Psychology, 42,* 1057–1068.

Fletcher, J. M., Lyon, G. R., Fuchs, L. S., & Barnes, M. A. (2007). *Learning disabilities: From identification to intervention.* New York: Guilford Press.

Fletcher, K. L., & Bray, N. W. (1996). External memory strategy use in preschool children. *Merrill-Palmer Quarterly, 42,* 379–396.

Florit, E., Roch, M., Altoè, G., & Levorato, M. C. (2009). Listening comprehension in preschoolers: The role of memory. *British Journal of Developmental Psychology, 27*(4), 935–951.

Floyd, R. G., Bergeron, R., & Alfonso, V. C. (2006). Cattell-Horn-Carroll cognitive ability profiles of poor comprehenders. *Reading and Writing, 19,* 427–456.

Flynn, E. G., Laland, K. N., Kendal, R. L., & Kendal, J. R. (2013). Developmental niche construction. *Developmental Science, 16*(2), 296–313. doi:10.1111/desc.12030

Flynn, J. R. (1987). Massive IQ gains in 14 nations: What IQ tests really measure. *Psychological Bulletin, 101,* 171–191.

Flynn, J. R. (2007). *What is intelligence? Beyond the Flynn effect.* New York: Cambridge University Press.

Fodor, J. A. (2000). *The mind doesn't work that way: The scope and limits of computational psychology.* Cambridge, MA: The MIT Press.

Follan, M., & McNamara, M. (2014). A fragile bond: adoptive parents' experiences of caring for children with a diagnosis of reactive attachment disorder. *Journal of Clinical Nursing, 23*(7/8), 1076–1085. doi:10.1111/jocn.12341

Fonner, V. A., Armstrong, K. S., Kennedy, C. E., O'Reilly, K. R., & Sweat, M. D. (2014). School based sex education and HIV prevention in low- and middle-income countries: A systematic review and meta-analysis. *Plos ONE, 9*(3), 1-18. doi:10.1371/journal.pone.0089692

Fontaine, K. L. (2011). *Complementary and alternative therapies for nursing practice* (3rd ed.). Upper Saddle River, NJ: Pearson Education.

Forbes, M. L., Ormrod, J. E., Bernardi, J. D., Taylor, S. L., & Jackson, D. L. (1999, April). *Children's conceptions of space, as reflected in maps of their hometown.* Paper presented at the annual meeting of the American Educational Research Association, Montreal, Canada.

Ford, L., & Dahinten, V. S. (2005). Use of intelligence tests in the assessment of preschoolers. In D. P. Flanagan & P. L. Harrison (Eds.), *Contemporary intellectual assessment: Theories, tests, and issues* (2nd ed., pp. 487–503). New York, NY: Guilford Press.

Ford, M. E. (1996). Motivational opportunities and obstacles associated with social responsibility and caring behavior in school contexts. In J. Juvonen & K. R. Wentzel (Eds.), *Social motivation: Understanding children's school adjustment* (pp. 126–153). Cambridge, England: Cambridge University Press.

Ford, M. E., & Smith, P. R. (2007). Thriving with social purpose: An integrative approach to the development of optimal human functioning. *Educational Psychologist, 42,* 153–171.

Ford, M. E., & Smith, P. R. (2009). Commentary: Building on a strong foundation: Five pathways to the next level of motivational theorizing. K. R. Wentzel & A. Wigfield (Eds.), *Handbook of motivation at school* (pp. 265–275). New York, NY: Routledge/Taylor & Francis Group.

Forgasz, H., & Hill, J. (2013). Factors implicated in high mathematics achievement. *International Journal of Science & Mathematics Education, 11*(2), 481–499. doi:10.1007/s10763-012-9348-x

Forsey, K. (2014). Taking the new curriculum outdoors. *Primary Science, 132,* 9–11.

Forsyth, J., & Carter, R. (2012). The relationship between racial identity status attitudes, racism-related coping, and mental health among black Americans. *Cultural Diversity & Ethnic Minority Psychology, 18*(2), 128–140.

Fortin, L., Marcotte, D., Diallo, T., Potvin, P., & Royer, É. (2013). A multidimensional model of school dropout from an 8-year longitudinal study in a general high school population. *European Journal of Psychology of Education EJPE (Springer Science & Business Media B.V.), 28*(2), 563–583. doi:10.1007/s10212-012-0129-2

Fowler, J. W., & Peterson, P. L. (1981). Increasing reading persistence and altering attributional style of learned helpless children. *Journal of Educational Psychology, 73,* 251–260.

Fox, E. (2009). The role of reader characteristics in processing and learning from informational text. *Review of Educational Research, 79*(1), 197–261.

Fox, M. (2013). What next in the read-aloud battle?: Win or lose? *Reading Teacher, 67*(1), 4–8. doi:10.1002/TRTR.1185

Fox, N. A., Almas, A. N., Degnan, K. A., Nelson, C. A., & Zeanah, C. H. (2011). The effects of severe psychosocial deprivation and foster care intervention on cognitive development at 8 years of age: findings from the Bucharest Early Intervention Project. *Journal of Child Psychology & Psychiatry, 52*(9), 919–928. doi:10.1111/j.1469-7610.2010.02355.x

Fox, N. A., Almas, A. N., Degnan, K. A., Nelson, C. A., & Zeanah, C. H. (2011). The effects of severe psychosocial deprivation and foster care intervention on cognitive development at 8 years of age: Findings from the Bucharest Early Intervention Project. *Journal of Child Psychology and Psychiatry, 52*(9), 919-928. doi:10.1111/j.1469-7610.2010.02355.x

Fox, N. A., Henderson, H. A., Rubin, K. H., Calkins, S. D., & Schmidt, L. A. (2001). Continuity and discontinuity of behavioral inhibition and exuberance: Psychophysiological and behavioral influences across the first 4 years of life. *Child Development, 72*(1), 1–21.

Franco, J. H., Davis, B. L., & Davis, J. L. (2013). Increasing social interaction using prelinguistic milieu teaching with nonverbal school-age children with autism. *American Journal of Speech-Language Pathology, 22*(3), 489–502. doi:10.1044/1058-0360(2012/10-0103)

Frank, C. (1999). *Ethnographic eyes: A teacher's guide to classroom observation.* Portsmouth, NH: Heinemann.

Frank, H., Harvey, O. J., & Verdun, K. (2000). American responses to five categories of shame in Chinese culture: A preliminary cross-cultural construct validation. *Personality and Individual Differences, 28*(5), 887–896.

Frazier, B. N., Gelman, S. A., & Wellman, H. M. (2009). Preschoolers' search for explanatory information within adult-child conversation. *Child Development, 80*(6), 1592–1611.

Frazier, S. L., Mehta, T. G., Atkins, M. S., Hur, K., & Rusch, D. (2013). Not just a walk in the park: Efficacy to effectiveness for after school programs in communities of concentrated urban poverty. *Administration and Policy In Mental Health And Mental Health Services Research, 40*(5), 406–418. doi:10.1007/s10488-012-0432-x

Frederickson, N. L., & Simmonds, E. A. (2008). Special needs, relationship type and distributive justice norms in early and later years of middle childhood. *Social Development, 17*(4), 1056–1073. doi:10.1111/j.1467-9507.2008.00477.x

Frederiksen, N. (1984). Implications of cognitive theory for instruction in problem-solving. *Review of Educational Research, 54,* 363–407.

Fredricks, J. A., Blumenfeld, P. C., & Paris, A. H. (2004). School engagement: Potential of the concept, state of the evidence. *Review of Educational Research, 74,* 59–109.

Freeark, K. (2006). Adoption and youth: Critical issues and strengths-based programming to address them. In K. Freeark & W. S. Davidson (Eds.), *The crisis in youth mental health: Critical issues and effective programs: Vol. 3. Issues for families, schools, and communities* (pp. 121–146). Westport, CT: Praeger/Greenwood.

Freedenthal, S., & Stiffman, A. R. (2007). "They might think I was crazy": Young American Indians' reasons for not seeking help when suicidal. *Journal of Adolescent Research, 22,* 58–77.

Freitag, C. M. (2007). The genetics of autistic disorders and its clinical relevance: A review of the literature. *Molecular Psychiatry, 12,* 2–22.

French, L., & Brown, A. (1977). Comprehension of "before" and "after" in logical and arbitrary sequences. *Journal of Child Language, 4,* 247–256.

Frensch, P. A., & Rünger, D. (2003). Implicit learning. *Current Directions in Psychological Science, 12,* 13–18.

Freud, S. (1905). *Three contributions to the theory of sex. The basic writings of Sigmund Freud* (A. A. Brill, Trans.). New York, NY: The Modern Library.

Freud, S. (1910). *The origin and development of psychoanalysis.* New York, NY: Henry Regnery (Gateway Editions), 1965.

Freud, S. (1923). *The ego and the id* (J. Riviere, Trans.). New York, NY: Norton, 1960.

Frey, K. S., Newman, J., & Onyewuenyi, A. C. (2014). Aggressive forms and functions on school playgrounds: Profile variations in interaction

styles, bystander actions, and victimization. *The Journal of Early Adolescence, 34*(3), 285–310. doi:10.1177/0272431613496638

Frick, P. J., Ray, J. V., Thornton, L. C., & Kahn, R. E. (2014). Annual research review: A developmental psychopathology approach to understanding callous-unemotional traits in children and adolescents with serious conduct problems. *Journal of Child Psychology and Psychiatry, 55*(6), 532–548. doi:10.1111/jcpp.12152

Friedman, D. (2010). Speaking correctly: Error correction as a language socialization practice in a Ukrainian classroom. *Applied Linguistics, 31*(3), 346–367. doi:10.1093/applin/amp037

Froiland, J., & Oros, E. (2014). Intrinsic motivation, perceived competence and classroom engagement as longitudinal predictors of adolescent reading achievement. *Educational Psychology, 34*(2), 119–132. doi:10.1080/01443410.2013.822964

Froiland, J., Oros, E., Smith, L., & Hirchert, T. (2012). Intrinsic motivation to learn: The nexus between psychological health and academic success. *Contemporary School Psychology, 16,* 91–100.

Frost, J. L., Shin, D., & Jacobs, P. J. (1998). Physical environments and children's play. In O. N. Saracho & B. Spodek (Eds.), *Multiple perspectives on play in early childhood education* (pp. 255-294). Albany: State University of New York Press.

Fruchter, N. (2007). *Urban schools, public will: Making education work for all our children.* New York, NY: Teachers College Press.

Fry, A. F., & Hale, S. (1996). Processing speed, working memory, and fluid intelligence. *Psychological Science, 7,* 237–241.

Fuchs, L. S., Fuchs, D., Prentice, K., Burch, M., Hamlett, C. L., Owen, R., et al. (2003). Enhancing third-grade students' mathematical problem solving with self-regulated learning strategies. *Journal of Educational Psychology, 95,* 306–315.

Fuhs, M., & Day, J. D. (2011). Verbal ability and executive functioning development in preschoolers at Head Start. *Developmental Psychology, 47*(2), 404–416. doi:10.1037/a0021065

Fujimura, N. (2001). Facilitating children's proportional reasoning: A model of reasoning processes and effects of intervention on strategy change. *Journal of Educational Psychology, 93,* 589–603.

Fujioka, T., Mourad, N., & Trainor, L. J. (2011). Development of auditory-specific brain rhythm in infants. *European Journal of Neuroscience, 33*(3), 521–529. doi:10.1111/j.1460-9568.2010.07544.x

Fukkink, R. G., & de Glopper, K. (1998). Effects of instruction in deriving word meanings from context: A meta-analysis. *Review of Educational Research, 68,* 450–469.

Fuller, M. L. (2001). Multicultural concerns and classroom management. In C. A. Grant & M. L. Gomez (Eds.), *Campus and classroom: Making schooling multicultural* (pp. 109–134). Upper Saddle River, NJ: Merrill/Prentice Hall.

Fuller, R. G., Campbell, T. C., Dykstra, D. I. Jr., & Stevens, S. M. (2009). The learning cycle: College teaching and the development of reasoning. In R. G. Fuller, T. C. Campbell, D. I. Dykstra Jr., & S. M. Stevens (Eds.), *College teaching and the development of reasoning: Science and engineering education sources* (pp. 115–133). Charlotte, NC: Information Age Publishing.

Furnham, A., & Cheng, H. (2013). Factors influencing adult earnings: Findings from a nationally representative sample. *The Journal of Socio-Economics, 44,* 120–125. doi:10.1016/j.socec.2013.02.008

Fusaro, M., & Nelson, C. A. III. (2009). Developmental cognitive neuroscience and education practice. In O. A. Barbarin & B. H. Wasik (Eds.), *Handbook of child development and early education: Research to practice* (pp. 57–77). New York, NY: Guilford Press.

Fuson, K. C., & Briars, D. J. (1990). Using a base-ten blocks learning/teaching approach for first- and second-grade place-value and multidigit addition and subtraction. *Journal for Research in Mathematics Education, 21,* 180–206.

Fuson, K. C., & Hall, J. W. (1983). The acquisition of early word meanings: A conceptual analysis and review. In H. P. Ginsburg (Ed.), *Children's mathematical thinking* (pp.49-107). New York, NY: Academic Press.

Fuson, K. C., & Kwon, Y. (1992). Korean children's understanding of multidigit addition and subtraction. *Child Development, 63,* 491–506.

Góngora, X., & Farkas, C. (2009). Infant sign language program effects on synchronic mother-infant interactions. *Infant Behavior & Development, 32*(2), 216–225.

Göncü, A. (1993). Development of intersubjectivity in the dyadic play of preschoolers. *Early Childhood Research Quarterly, 8,* 99–116.

Göncü, A., & Gauvain, M. (2012). Sociocultural approaches to educational psychology: Theory, research, and application. In K. R. Harris, S. Graham, T. Urdan, C. B. McCormick, G. M. Sinatra, & J. Sweller (Eds.), *APA educational psychology handbook, Vol. 1: Theories, constructs, and critical issues* (pp. 125–154). Washington, DC: American Psychological Association. doi:10.1037/13273-006

Gabard, D. L. (1999). Homosexuality and the Human Genome Project: Private and public choices. *Journal of Homosexuality, 37,* 25–51.

Gagnon, S. G., Huelsman, T. J., Kidder-Ashley, P., & Ballard, M. (2009). Student–teacher relationships matter: Moderating influences between temperament and preschool social competence. *Psychology in the Schools, 46*(6), 553–567.

Gainotti, G. (2007). Face familiarity feelings, the right temporal lobe and the possible underlying neural mechanisms. *Brain Research Reviews, 56*(1), 214–235.

Galaburda, A. M., & Rosen, G. D. (2001). Neural plasticity in dyslexia: A window to mechanisms of learning disabilities. In J. L. McClelland & R. S. Siegler (Eds.), *Mechanisms of cognitive development: Behavioral and neural perspectives* (pp. 307–323). Mahwah, NJ: Erlbaum.

Gallagher, A. M., & Kaufman, J. C. (Eds.) (2005). *Gender differences in mathematics: An integrative psychological approach.* Cambridge, England: Cambridge University Press.

Gallahue, D. L., & Ozmun, J. C. (1998). *Understanding motor development: Infants, children, adolescents, adults.* Boston: McGraw-Hill.

Galliger, C., Tisak, M., & Tisak, J. (2009). When the wheels on the bus go round: Social interactions on the school bus. *Social Psychology of Education, 12*(1), 43–62. doi:10.1007/s11218-008-9072-0

Gallimore, R., & Goldenberg, C. (2001). Analyzing cultural models and settings to connect minority achievement and school improvement research. *Educational Psychologist, 36,* 45–56.

Gallimore, R., & Tharp, R. (1992). Teaching mind in society: Teaching, schooling, and literate discourse. In L. C. Moll (Ed.), *Vygotsky and education: Instructional implications and applications of sociohistorical psychology* (pp. 175-205). New York, NY: Cambridge University Press.

Gallistel, C. R., & Gelman, R. (1992). Preverbal and verbal counting and computation. *Cognition, 44,* 43–74.

Gallistel, C. R., Brown, A. L., Carey, S., Gelman, R., & Keil, F. C. (1991). Lessons from animal learning for the study of cognitive development. In S. Carey & R. Gelman (Eds.), *Epigenesis of mind: Essays on biology and cognition* (p. 3–36). Hillsdale, NJ: Erlbaum.

Gallo, A. M., Hadley, E. K., Angst, D. B., Knafl, K. A., & Smith, C. A. M. (2008). Parents' concerns about issues related to their children's genetic conditions. *Journal for Specialists in Pediatric Nursing, 13*(1), 4–14.

Galotti, K. M., Komatsu, L. K., & Voelz, S. (1997). Children's differential performance on deductive and inductive syllogisms. *Developmental Psychology, 33,* 70–78.

Galupo, M., Cartwright, K. B., & Savage, L. S. (2010). Cross-category friendships and postformal thought among college students. *Journal of Adult Development 17*(4), 208–214. doi:10.1007/s10804-009-9089-4

Gambrell, L. B., & Bales, R. J. (1986). Mental imagery and the comprehension-monitoring performance of fourth- and fifth-grade poor readers. *Reading Research Quarterly, 21,* 454–464.

Ganiban, J. M., Ulbricht, J., Saudino, K. J., Reiss, D., & Neiderhiser, J. M. (2011). Understanding child-based effects on parenting: Temperament as a moderator of genetic and environmental contributions to parenting. *Developmental Psychology, 47*(3), 676–692.

Garandeau, C. F., Lee, I. A., & Salmivalli, C. (2014). Inequality matters: Classroom status hierarchy and adolescents' bullying. *Journal of Youth and Adolescence, 43*(7), 1123–1133. doi:10.1007/s10964-013-0040-4

Garbarino, J., & Abramowitz, R. H. (1992). Sociocultural risk and opportunity. In J. Garbarino (Ed.), *Children and families in the social environment* (pp. 35–70). New York, NY: Aldine de Gruyter.

Garbarino, J., Bradshaw, C. P., & Vorrasi, J. A. (2002). Mitigating the effects of gun violence on children and youth. *The Future of Children, 12*(2), 73–85.

García Coll, C. G., & Marks, A. K. (2009). *Immigrant stories: Ethnicity and academics in middle childhood.* New York, NY: Oxford University Press.

García Coll, C., Lamberty, G., Jenkins, R., McAdoo, H. P., Crnic, K., Wasik, B. H., et al. (1996). An integrative model for the study of developmental competencies in minority children. *Child Development, 67,* 1891–1914.

García Coll, C., Lamberty, G., Jenkins, R., McAdoo, H. P., Crnic, K., Wasik, B. H., et al. (1996). An integrative model for the study of developmental competencies in minority children. *Child Development, 67,* 1891–1914.

García Sierra, P. (2012). Attachment and preschool teacher: An opportunity to develop a secure base. *International Journal of Early Childhood Special Education, 4*(1), 1–16.

García, E. E. (1994). *Understanding and meeting the challenge of student cultural diversity.* Boston, MA: Houghton Mifflin.

García, E. E. (1995). Educating Mexican American students: Past treatment and recent developments in theory, research, policy, and practice. In J. A. Banks & C. A. M. Banks (Eds.), *Handbook of research on multicultural education (pp.372-387).* New York, NY: Macmillan.

García, E. E., & Jensen, B. (2007). Helping young Hispanic learners. *Educational Leadership, 64*(6), 34–39.

García, E., Arias, M., Murri, N., & Serna, C. (2010). Developing responsive teachers: A challenge for a demographic reality. *Journal of Teacher Education, 61*(1/2), 132–142.

Garces, E., Thomas, D., & Currie, J. (2002). Longer-term effects of Head Start. *American Economic Review, 92*(4), 999–1012.

Garces-Bacsal, R. (2011). Socioaffective issues and concerns among gifted Filipino children. *Roeper Review: A Journal on Gifted Education, 33*(4), 239–251. doi:10.1080/02783193.2011.603112

Garcia-Reid, P., Peterson, C., Reid, R. J., & Peterson, N. (2013). The protective effects of sense of community, multigroup ethnic identity, and self-esteem against internalizing problems among Dominican youth: Implications for social workers. *Social Work in Mental Health, 11*(3), 199–222. doi:10.1080/15332985.2013.774923

Gardiner, H. W., & Kosmitzki, C. (2008). *Lives across cultures: Cross-cultural human development* (4th ed.). Boston, MA: Pearson Allyn & Bacon.

Gardner, H. (1983). *Frames of mind: The theory of multiple intelligences.* New York: Basic Books.

Gardner, H. (1993). *Multiple intelligences: The theory in practice.* New York: Basic Books.

Gardner, H. (1995). Reflections on multiple intelligences: Myths and messages. *Phi Delta Kappan, 77,* 200–209.

Gardner, H. (1999). *Intelligence reframed: Multiple intelligences for the 21st century.* New York, NY: Basic Books.

Gardner, H. (2000). A case against spiritual intelligence. *International Journal of the Psychology of Religion, 10*(1), 27–34.

Gardner, H. (2003). *Multiple intelligences after twenty years.* Paper presented at the annual meeting of the American Educational Research Association, Chicago, IL. Retrieved from http://www.pz.harvard.edu/PIs/HG_MI_after_20_years.pdf

Gardner, H. (2006). Replies to my critics. In J. A. Schaler (Ed.), *Howard Gardner under fire: The rebel psychologist faces his critics* (pp. 277–344). Chicago, IL: Open Court.

Gardner, H. (2008). *The 25th anniversary of the publication of Howard Gardner's* Frames of mind: The theory of multiple intelligences. Retrieved from http://www.howardgardner.com

Gardner, H. (2009). Birth and the spreading of a "meme." In J.-Q. Chen, S. Moran, & H. Gardner (Eds.), *Multiple intelligences around the world* (pp. 3–16). San Francisco, CA: Jossey-Bass.

Gardner, H. (2011). The theory of multiple intelligences. In M. Gernsbacher, R. W. Pew, L. M. Hough, & J. R. Pomerantz (Eds.), *Psychology and the real world: Essays illustrating fundamental contributions to society* (pp. 122–130). New York, NY: Worth Publishers.

Gardner, H., & Hatch, T. (1990). Multiple intelligences go to school: Educational implications of the theory of multiple intelligences. *Educational Researcher, 18*(8), 4–10.

Gardner, H., & Moran, S. (2006). The science of multiple intelligences theory: A response to Lynn Waterhouse. *Educational Psychologist, 41*(4), 227–232.

Gardner, H., Torff, B., & Hatch, T. (1996). The age of innocence reconsidered: Preserving the best of the progressive traditions in psychology and education. In D. R. Olson & N. Torrance (Eds.), *The handbook of education and human development: New models of learning, teaching and schooling* (pp. 28–55). Cambridge, MA: Blackwell.

Garland, A., Augustyn, M., & Stein, M. T. (2007). Disruptive and oppositional behavior in an 11-year-old boy. *Journal of Developmental and Behavioral Pediatrics, 28,* 406–408.

Garn, A., McCaughtry, N., Martin, J., Shen, B., & Fahlman, M. (2012). A Basic Needs Theory investigation of adolescents' physical self-concept and global self-esteem. *International Journal of Sport & Exercise Psychology, 10*(4), 314–328.

Garner, A. S., Shonkoff, J. P., Siegel, B. S., Dobbins, M. I., Earls, M. F., McGuinn, L., Pascoe, J., & Wood, D. L. (2012). Early childhood adversity, toxic stress, and the role of the pediatrician: Translating developmental science into lifelong health. *Pediatrics, 129*(1), e224–e231. doi:10.1542/peds.2011-2662

Garner, R. (1987). Strategies for reading and studying expository texts. *Educational Psychologist, 22,* 299–312.

Garner, R. (1998). Epilogue: Choosing to learn or not-learn in school. *Educational Psychology Review, 10,* 227–237.

Garon, N., Bryson, S. E., & Smith, I. M. (2008). Executive function in preschoolers: A review using an integrative framework. *Psychological Bulletin, 134*(1), 31–60. doi:10.1037/0033-2909.134.1.31

Garrison, L. (1989). Programming for the gifted American Indian student. In C. J. Maker & S. W. Schiever (Eds.), *Critical issues in gifted education: Vol. 2. Defensible programs for cultural and ethnic minorities (pp. 79-90).* Austin, TX: Pro-Ed.

Garrison, L. (1989). Programming for the gifted American Indian student. In C. J. Maker & S. W. Schiever (Eds.), *Critical issues in gifted education: Vol. 2. Defensible programs for cultural and ethnic minorities.* Austin, TX: Pro-Ed.

Garvey, C., & Hogan, R. (1973). Social speech and social interaction: Egocentrism revisited. *Child Development, 44*(3), 562–568. doi:10.2307/1128013

Gaskins, I. W., Satlow, E., & Pressley, M. (2007). Executive control of reading comprehension in the elementary school. In L. Meltzer (Ed.), *Executive function in education: From theory to practice* (pp. 194–215). New York, NY: Guilford Press.

Gaskins, S. (1999). Children's daily lives in a Mayan village: A case study of culturally constructed roles and activities. In A. Göncü (Ed.), *Children's engagement in the world: Sociocultural perspectives* (pp. 25–61). Cambridge, England: Cambridge University Press.

Gatti, E., Ionio, C., Traficante, D., & Confalonieri, E. (2014). "I like my body; therefore, I like myself": How body image influences self-esteem—A cross-sectional study on Italian adolescents. *Europe's Journal of Psychology, 10*(2), 301–317. doi:10.5964/ejop.v10i2.703

Gaunt, K. D. (2006). *The games Black girls play: Learning the ropes from double-dutch to hip-hop.* New York, NY: New York University Press.

Gauvain, M. (2001). *The social context of cognitive development.* New York, NY: Guilford Press.

Gauvain, M. (2009). Social and cultural transactions in cognitive development: A cross-generational view. In A. Sameroff (Ed.), *The transactional model of development: How children and contexts shape each other* (pp. 163–182). Washington, DC: American Psychological Association.

Gauvain, M., & Munroe, R. L. (2009). Contributions of societal modernity to cognitive development: A comparison of four cultures. *Child Development, 80*(6), 1628–1642.

Gauvain, M., & Parke, R. D. (2010). Socialization. In M. H. Bornstein (Ed.), *Handbook of cultural developmental science* (pp. 239–258). New York, NY: Psychology Press.

Gauvain, M., & Perez, S. M. (2005). Parent–child participation in planning children's activities outside of school in European American and Latino families. *Child Development, 76,* 371–383.

Gauvain, M., Perez, S. M., & Beebe, H. (2013). Authoritative parenting and parental support for children's cognitive development. In R. E. Larzelere, A. Morris, A. W. Harrist (Eds.), *Authoritative parenting: Synthesizing nurturance and discipline for optimal child development* (pp. 211–233). Washington, DC: American Psychological Association. doi:10.1037/13948-010

Gavin, L. A., & Fuhrman, W. (1989). Age differences in adolescents' perceptions of their peer groups. *Developmental Psychology, 25,* 827–834.

Gay, G. (2006). Connections between classroom management and culturally responsive teaching. In C. M. Evertson & C. S. Weinstein (Eds.), *Handbook of classroom management: Research, practice, and contemporary issues* (pp. 343–370). Mahwah, NJ: Erlbaum.

Gaylord-Harden, N. K., Burrow, A. L., & Cunningham, J. A. (2012). A cultural asset framework for investigating successful adaptation to stress in African American youth. *Child*

Development Perspectives, 6(3), 264–271. doi:10.1111/j.1750-8606.2012.00236.x

Geary, D. C. (1994). *Children's mathematical development: Research and practical applications.* Washington, DC: American Psychological Association.

Geary, D. C. (2005). Folk knowledge and academic learning. In B. J. Ellis & D. F. Bjorklund (Eds.), *Origins of the social mind: Evolutionary psychology and child development* (pp. 493–519). New York, NY: Guilford Press.

Geary, D. C. (2006). Development of mathematical understanding. In W. Damon & R. M. Lerner (Series Eds.), & D. Kuhn & R. Siegler (Vol. Eds.), *Handbook of child psychology: Vol. 1. Cognition, perception, and language* (6th ed., 777–810). New York: Wiley.

Geary, D. C., Hoard, M. K., & Nugent, L. (2012). Independent contributions of the central executive, intelligence, and in-class attentive behavior to developmental change in the strategies used to solve addition problems. *Journal of Experimental Child Psychology, 113*(1), 49–65. doi:10.1016/j.jecp.2012.03.003

Geist, K., Geist, E., & Kuznik, K. (2012). The patterns of music. *Young Children, 67*(1), 74–79.

Gelhorn, H., Hartman, C., Sakai, J., Mikulich-Gilbertson, S., Stallings, M., Young, S., et al. (2009). An item response theory analysis of conduct disorder. *Journal of the American Academy of Child & Adolescent Psychiatry, 48*(1), 42–50.

Gelman, R., & Baillargeon, R. (1983). A review of some Piagetian concepts. In J. H. Flavell & E. M. Markman (Eds.), *Handbook of child psychology: Vol. 3. Cognitive development (pp. 167–230).* New York, NY: Wiley.

Gelman, S. A. (2003). *The essential child: Origins of essentialism in everyday thought.* New York, NY: Oxford University Press.

Gelman, S. A., & Kalish, C. W. (2006). Conceptual development. In W. Damon & R. M. Lerner (Series Eds.), & D. Kuhn & R. Siegler (Vol. Eds.), *Handbook of child psychology: Vol. 1. Cognition, perception, and language* (6th ed., pp. 687-733). New York, NY: Wiley.

Gelman, S. A., & Markman, E. M. (1986). Categories and induction in young children. *Cognition, 23,* 183–209.

Gelman, S. A., & Raman, L. (2003). Preschool children use linguistic form class and pragmatic cues to interpret generics. *Child Development, 74,* 308–325.

Gelman, S. A., & Taylor, M. (1984). How two-year-old children interpret proper and common names for unfamiliar objects. *Child Development, 55,* 1535–1540.

Gelman, S. A., Ware, E. A., Manczak, E. M., & Graham, S. A. (2013). Children's sensitivity to the knowledge expressed in pedagogical and non-pedagogical contexts. *Developmental Psychology, 49*(3), 491–504. doi:10.1037/a0027901

Genesee, F. (1985). Second language learning through immersion: A review of U.S. programs. *Review of Educational Research, 55,* 541–561.

Genesoni, L., & Tallandini, M. A. (2009). Men's psychological transition to fatherhood: An analysis of the literature, 1989–2008. *Birth, 36*(4), 305–317.

Gentile, D. A., & Gentile, J. R. (2008). Violent video games as exemplary teachers: A conceptual analysis. *Journal of Youth and Adolescence, 37,* 127–141.

Gentner, D. (2006). Why verbs are hard to learn. In K. Hirsh-Pasek, & R. M. Golinkoff (Eds.), *Action meets word: How children learn verbs* (pp. 544–564). New York, NY: Oxford University Press.

Gentry, R. (1982). An analysis of the developmental spellings in *Gnys at Wrk. The Reading Teacher, 36,* 192–200.

Genzuk, M. (1999). Tapping into community funds of knowledge. In *Effective strategies for English language acquisition: Curriculum guide for the professional development of teachers grades kindergarten through eight* (pp. 9–21). Los Angeles, CA: Los Angeles Annenberg Metropolitan Project, ARCO Foundation. Retrieved from http://www-bcf.usc.edu/~genzuk/Genzuk_ARCO_Funds_of_Knowledge.pdf

Geok Lin, K., & Misra, S. (2012). Micronutrient interventions on cognitive performance of children aged 5–15 years in developing countries. *Asia Pacific Journal of Clinical Nutrition, 21*(4), 476–486.

George, L. (2005). Lack of preparedness: Experiences of first-time mothers. *American Journal of Maternal/Child Nursing, 30*(4), 251–255.

Georgiou, S., Demetriou, A., & Stavrinides, P. (2008). Attachment style and mentoring relationships in adolescence. *Educational Psychology, 28*(6), 603–614.

Geraci, A. (2009/2010). Good food in the city. *Educational Leadership, 67*(4), 12–16.

Gerde, H., Schachter, R., & Wasik, B. (2013). Using the scientific method to guide learning: An integrated approach to early childhood curriculum. *Early Childhood Education Journal, 41*(5), 315–323. doi:10.1007/s10643-013-0579-4

Gerken, L. (1994). Child phonology: Past research, present questions, future directions. In M. A. Gernsbacher (Ed.), *Handbook of psycholinguistics* (pp. 781–820). San Diego, CA: Academic Press.

Gernsbacher, M. A., Stevenson, J. L., Khandakar, S., & Goldsmith, H. H. (2008). Why does joint attention look atypical in autism? *Child Development Perspectives, 2*(1), 38–45.

Gershoff, E. T., Aber, J. L., & Raver, C. C. (2005). Child poverty in the United States: An evidence-based conceptual framework for programs and policies. In R. M. Lerner, F. Jacobs, & D. Wertlieb (Eds.), *Applied developmental science: An advanced textbook* (pp. 269–324). Thousand Oaks, CA: Sage.

Gerson, S. A., & Woodward, A. L. (2013). The goal trumps the means: Highlighting goals is more beneficial than highlighting means in means-end training. *Infancy, 18*(2), 289–302. doi:10.1111/j.1532-7078.2012.00112.x

Gertner, Y., Fisher, C., & Eisengart, J. (2006). Learning words and rules: Abstract knowledge of word order in early sentence comprehension. *Psychological Science, 17,* 684–691.

Gervai, J. (2009). Environmental and genetic influences on early attachment. *Child and Adolescent Psychiatry and Mental Health, 3*(Sep 4).

Gervain, J., & Mehler, J. (2010). Speech perception and language acquisition in the first year of life. *Annual Review of Psychology, 61,* 191–218.

Gesell, A. (1928). *Infancy and human growth.* New York, NY: Macmillan.

Gesell, S. B., Sommer, E. C., Lambert, E., de Andrade, A., Whitaker, L., Davis, L., Beech, B., Mitchell, S., Arinze, N., Neloms, S., Ryan, C., & Barkin, S. L. (2013). Comparative effectiveness of after-school programs to increase physical activity. *Journal of Obesity*, 1–8. doi:10.1155/2013/576821

Gettinger, M., & Kohler, K. M. (2006). Process-outcome approaches to classroom management and effective teaching. In C. M. Evertson & C. S. Weinstein (Eds.), *Handbook of classroom management: Research, practice, and contemporary issues* (pp. 73–95). Mahwah, NJ: Erlbaum.

Ghazvini, A., & Mullis, R. L. (2002). Center-based care for young children: Examining predictors of quality. *Journal of Genetic Psychology, 163,* 112–125.

Ghoul, A., Niwa, E. Y., & Boxer, P. (2013). The role of contingent self-worth in the relation between victimization and internalizing problems in adolescents. *Journal of Adolescence, 36*(3), 457–464. doi:10.1016/j.adolescence.2013.01.007

Giallo, R., Cooklin, A., Wade, C., D'Esposito, F., & Nicholson, J. (2014). Maternal postnatal mental health and later emotional-behavioural development of children: the mediating role of parenting behaviour. *Child: Care, Health & Development, 40*(3), 327–336. doi:10.1111/cch.12028

Giannakopoulou, A., Uther, M., & Ylinen, S. (2013). Enhanced plasticity in spoken language acquisition for child learners: Evidence from phonetic training studies in child and adult learners of English. *Child Language Teaching and Therapy, 29*(2), 201–218. doi:10.1177/0265659012467473

Gibson, C. P., Jones, S. J., & Patrick, T. N. (2010). Conducting informal developmental assessments. *Exchange, 32*(3), 36–40.

Gibson, E. J., & Walk, R. D. (1960). The "visual cliff." *Scientific American, 202*(4), 64–71.

Gillam, D. (2014). Strategies for writing in the science classroom. *Science & Children,* 51(7), 95–96.

Gillam, R. B., & Johnston, J. R. (1992). Spoken and written language relationships in language/learning-impaired and normal achieving school-age children. *Journal of Speech and Hearing Research, 35,* 1303–1315.

Gillet, N., Vallerand, R., & Lafrenière, M. (2012). Intrinsic and extrinsic school motivation as a function of age: the mediating role of autonomy support. *Social Psychology of Education, 15*(1), 77–95. doi:10.1007/s11218-011-9170-2

Gillham, J. E., Reivich, K. J., Jaycox, L. H., & Seligman, M. E. P. (1995). Prevention of depressive symptoms in schoolchildren: Two-year follow-up. *Psychological Science, 6,* 343–351.

Gillies, R. M., Nichols, K., Burgh, G., & Haynes, M. (2014). Primary students' scientific reasoning and discourse during cooperative inquiry-based science activities. *International Journal of Educational Research, 63,* 127–140. doi:10.1016/j.ijer.2013.01.001

Gilligan, C. (1982). *In a different voice: Psychological theory and women's development.* Cambridge, MA: Harvard University Press.

Gilligan, C. F. (1985, March). *Keynote address at the Conference on Women and Moral Theory,* Stony Brook, NY.

Gilligan, C. F. (1987). Moral orientation and moral development. In E. F. Kittay & D. T. Meyers (Eds.), *Women and moral theory.* Totowa, NJ: Rowman & Littlefield.

Gilligan, C. F., & Attanucci, J. (1988). Two moral orientations. In C. F. Gilligan, J. V. Ward, & J. M. Taylor (Eds.), *Mapping the moral domain: A contribution of women's thinking to psychological theory and education.* Cambridge, MA: Center for the Study of Gender, Education, and Human Development (distributed by Harvard University Press).

Gilliland, H. (1988). Discovering and emphasizing the positive aspects of the culture. In H. Gilliland & J. Reyhner (Eds.), *Teaching the Native American (pp. 21-36).* Dubuque, IA: Kendall/Hunt.

Gilman, A. B., Hill, K. G., Hawkins, J., Howell, J. C., & Kosterman, R. (2014). The developmental dynamics of joining a gang in adolescence: Patterns and predictors of gang membership. *Journal of Research on Adolescence, 24*(2), 204–219. doi:10.1111/jora.12121

Ginsburg, H. P. (2009). The challenge of formative assessment in mathematics education: Children's minds, teachers' minds. *Human Development, 52,* 109–128.

Ginsburg, H. P., Cannon, J., Eisenband, J., & Pappas, S. (2006). Mathematical thinking and learning. In K. McCartney & D. Phillips (Eds.), *Blackwell handbook of early childhood development* (pp. 208–229). Malden, MA: Blackwell.

Ginsburg, H. P., Lee, J. S., & Boyd, J. S. (2008). Mathematics education for young children: What it is and how to promote it. *Social Policy Report, 22*(1). Ann Arbor, MI: Society for Research in Child Development.

Giordano, P. C. (2003). Relationships in adolescence. *Annual Review of Sociology, 29,* 257–281.

Gläscher, J., Rudrauf, D., Colom, R., Paul, L. K., Tranel, D., Damasio, H., & Adolphs, R. (2010). Distributed neural system for general intelligence revealed by lesion mapping. *Proceedings of the National Academy of Sciences of the United States of America, 107*(10), 4705–4709.

Glahn, D. C., & Burdick, K. E. (2011). Clinical endophenotypes for bipolar disorder. In H. K. Manji & C. A. Zarate Jr. (Eds.), *Behavioral neurobiology of bipolar disorder and its treatment* (pp. 51–67). New York, NY: Springer Science.

Glaser, C., & Brunstein, J. C. (2007). Improving fourth-grade students' composition skills: Effects of strategy instruction and self-regulation procedures. *Journal of Educational Psychology, 99,* 297–310.

Glasgow, J. N. (1994). Action research changes cultural attitudes. *Teaching Education, 6,* 41–48.

Gleitman, L. R., Cassidy, K., Nappa, R., Papafragou, A., & Trueswell, J. C. (2005). Hard words. *Language Learning and Development, 1*(1), 23–64.

Glenwright, M., & Pexman, P. M. (2010). Development of children's ability to distinguish sarcasm and verbal irony. *Journal of Child Language, 37*(2), 429–451.

Glick, J. E., & Bates, L. (2010). Diversity in academic achievement: Children of immigrants in U.S. schools. In E. L. Grigorenko & R. Takanishi (Eds.), *Immigration, diversity, and education* (pp. 112–129). New York, NY: Routledge.

Gligorović, M. M., & Durović, N. (2014). Inhibitory control and adaptive behaviour in children with mild intellectual disability. *Journal of Intellectual Disability Research, 58*(3), 233–242. doi:10.1111/jir.12000

Glucksberg, S., & Krauss, R. M. (1967). What do people say after they have learned to talk? Studies of the development of referential communication. *Merrill-Palmer Quarterly, 13,* 309–316.

Gluszek, A., & Dovidio, J. F. (2010). The way they speak: A social psychological perspective on the stigma of nonnative accents in communication. *Personality and Social Psychology Review, 14*(2), 214–237.

Glynn, S. M., Yeany, R. H., & Britton, B. K. (1991a). A constructive view of learning science. In S. M. Glynn, R. H. Yeany, & B. K. Britton (Eds.), *The psychology of learning science* (pp. 3–19). Mahwah, NJ: Erlbaum.

Glynn, S. M., Yeany, R. H., & Britton, B. K. (Eds.) (1991b). *The psychology of learning science.* Hillsdale, NJ: Erlbaum.

Gnepp, J. (1989). Children's use of personal information to understand other people's feelings. In C. Saarni & P. L. Harris (Eds.), *Children's understanding of emotion.* Cambridge, England: Cambridge University Press.

Goddings, A., Burnett Heyes, S., Bird, G., Viner, R. M., & Blakemore, S. (2012). The relationship between puberty and social emotion processing. *Developmental Science, 15*(6), 801–811. doi:10.1111/j.1467-7687.2012.01174.x

Goeke-Morey, M. C., Papp, L. M., & Cummings, E. (2013). Changes in marital conflict and youths' responses across childhood and adolescence: A test of sensitization. *Development and Psychopathology, 25*(1), 241–251. doi:10.1017/S0954579412000995

Goff, K., & Torrance, E. (2002). *Abbreviated Torrance Test for Adults Manual.* Bensenville, IL: Scholastic Testing Service.

Gogate, L. J., & Hollich, G. (2010). Invariance detection within an interactive system: A perceptual gateway to language development. *Psychological Review, 117*(2), 496–516. doi:10.1037/a0019049

Goharpey, N., Crowther, D. P., & Crewther, S. G. (2013). Problem solving ability in children with intellectual disability as measured by the Raven's Colored Progressive Matrices. *Research in Developmental Disabilities, 34*(12), 4366–4374. doi:10.1016/j.ridd.2013.09.013

Golay, P., & Lecerf, T. (2011). Orthogonal higher order structure and confirmatory factor analysis of the French Wechsler Adult Intelligence Scale (WAIS-III). *Psychological Assessment, 23*(1), 143–152. doi:10.1037/a0021230

Goldberg, A. E. (2007). (How) does it make a difference? Perspectives of adults with lesbian, gay, and bisexual parents. *American Journal of Orthopsychiatry, 77*(4), 550–562. doi:10.1037/0002-9432.77.4.550

Goldenberg, C. (1992). The limits of expectations: A case for case knowledge about teacher expectancy effects. *American Educational Research Journal, 29,* 517–544.

Goldenberg, C. (2008). Teaching English language learners: What the research does—and does not—say. *American Educator, 2*(2), 8–23, 42–44.

Goldenberg, C., Hicks, J., & Lit, I. (2013). Dual language learners effective instruction in early childhood. *American Educator, 37*(2), 26–29.

Goldin-Meadow, S, (2005). What language creation in the manual modality tells us about the foundations of language. *Linguistic Review, 22,* 199-225.

Goldin-Meadow, S. (1997). When gestures and words speak differently. *Current Directions in Psychological Science, 6,* 138–143.

Goldin-Meadow, S. (2006). Talking and thinking with our hands. *Current Directions in Psychological Science, 15,* 34–39.

Goldin-Meadow, S., Shield, A., Lenzen, D., Herzig, M., & Padden, C. (2012). The gestures ASL signers use tell us when they are ready to learn math. *Cognition, 123*(3), 448–453. doi:10.1016/j.cognition.2012.02.006

Goldstein, S., & Brooks, R. B. (Eds.) (2006). *Handbook of resilience in children.* New York, NY: Springer.

Goleman, D. (1995). *Emotional intelligence.* New York, NY: Bantam Books.

Goleniowska, H. (2014). The importance of developing confidence and self-esteem in children with a learning disability. *Advances in Mental Health & Intellectual Disabilities, 8*(3), 188–191. doi:10.1108/AMHID-09-2013-0059

Golinkoff, R. M., & Hirsh-Pasek, K. (2006). Baby wordsmith: From associationistic to social sophisticate. *Current Directions in Psychological Science, 15,* 30–33.

Golinkoff, R. M., & Hirsh-Pasek, K. (2008). How toddlers begin to learn verbs. *Trends in Cognitive Sciences, 12*(10), 397–403.

Golinkoff, R. M., Hirsh-Pasek, K., Bailey, L., & Wenger, N. (1992). Young children and adults use lexical principles to learn new nouns. *Developmental Psychology, 28,* 99–108.

Golinkoff, R., Ma, W., Song, L., & Hirsh-Pasek, K. (2013). Twenty-five years using the intermodal preferential looking paradigm to study language acquisition: What have we learned? *Perspectives on Psychological Science, 8*(3), 316–339. doi:10.1177/1745691613484936

Gollnick, D. M., & Chinn, P. C. (2002). *Multicultural education in a pluralistic society* (6th ed.). Upper Saddle River, NJ: Merrill/Prentice Hall.

Golomb, C. (2004). *The child's creation of a pictorial world* (2nd ed.). Mahwah, NJ: Erlbaum.

Golombok, S., Mellish, L., Jennings, S., Casey, P., Tasker, F., & Lamb, M. E. (2014). Adoptive gay father families: Parent-child relationships and children's psychological adjustment. *Child Development, 85*(2), 456-468. doi:10.1111/cdev.12155

Gomby, D. S., Culross, P. L., & Behrman, R. E. (1999). Home visiting: Recent program evaluations—Analysis and recommendations. *The Future of Children. Home Visiting: Recent Program Evaluations, 9*(1), 4–26.

González, N., Moll, L. C., & Amanti, C. (2005). Introduction: Theorizing practices. *Funds of knowledge: Theorizing practices in households, communities, and classrooms* (pp. 1–24). Mahwah, NJ: Erlbaum.

Gonzales-Backen, M. A. (2013). An application of ecological theory to ethnic identity formation among biethnic adolescents. *Family Relations, 62*(1), 92–108. doi:10.1111/j.1741-3729.2012.00749.x

Gonzalez, A.-L., & Wolters, C. A. (2006). The relation between perceived parenting practices and achievement motivation in mathematics. *Journal of Research in Childhood Education, 21,* 203–217.

Gonzalez, L. (2011). Class placement and academic and behavioral variables as predictors of graduation for students with disabilities. *Dissertation Abstracts International Section A, 71.*

Gonzalez-Gomez, N., Nazzi, T., Kreiman, J., & Jacewicz, E. (2013). Effects of prior phonotactic knowledge on infant word segmentation: The case of nonadjacent dependencies. *Journal of Speech, Language & Hearing Research, 56*(3), 840–849. doi:10.1044/1092-4388(2012/12-0138)

Gonzalez-Mena, J. (2010). Compassionate roots begin with babies. *Exchange, 32*(3), 46–49.

Gonzalez-Mena, J. (2012). On the way to friendship: Growing peer relationships among infants and toddlers. *Exchange (19460406), (205),* 48–50.

Good, T. L., & Nichols, S. L. (2001). Expectancy effects in the classroom: A special focus on improving the reading performance of minority students in first-grade classrooms. *Educational Psychologist, 36,* 113–126.

Good, T. L., McCaslin, M. M., & Reys, B. J. (1992). Investigating work groups to promote problem solving in mathematics. In J. Brophy (Ed.), *Advances in research on teaching: Vol. 3. Planning and managing learning tasks and activities* (pp. 115-160). Greenwich, CT: JAI Press.

Goodman, R. D., Miller, M., & West-Olatunji, C. A. (2012). Traumatic stress, socioeconomic status, and academic achievement among primary school students. *Psychological Trauma: Theory, Research, Practice, And Policy, 4*(3), 252–259. doi:10.1037/a0024912

Goodnow, J. J. (2010). Culture. In M. H. Bornstein (Ed.), *Handbook of cultural developmental science* (pp. 3–19). New York, NY: Psychology Press.

Goodwin, B., & Miller, K. (2013). Creativity requires a mix of skills. *Educational Leadership, 70*(5), 80–83.

Goodwin, B., & Miller, K. (2013). Teaching self-regulation has long-term benefits. *Educational Leadership, 70*(8), 80–81.

Goodwin, M. H. (2006). *The hidden life of girls: Games of stance, status, and exclusion.* Malden, MA: Blackwell.

Goodwyn, S. W., & Acredolo, L. P. (1998). Encouraging symbolic gestures: A new perspective on the relationship between gesture and speech. In J. M. Iverson & S. Goldin-Meadow (Eds.), *Nature and functions of gesture in children's communication (pp. 61-73).* San Francisco, CA: Jossey-Bass.

Goodwyn, S. W., Acredolo, L. P., & Brown, C. A. (2000). Impact of symbolic gesturing on early language development. *Journal of Nonverbal Behavior, 24,* 81–103.

Gopnik, A. (2009a, August 1). Babies rule! *New Scientist, 203*(2719), 44-45.

Gopnik, A. (2009b). Rational constructivism: A new way to bridge rationalism and empiricism. *Behavioral and Brain Sciences, 32*(2), 208–209.

Gopnik, A. (2009c, August 16). Your baby is smarter than you think. *New York Times.*

Gopnik, A., & Meltzoff, A. N. (1997). *Words, thoughts, and theories.* Cambridge, MA: MIT Press.

Gopnik, A., & Wellman, H. M. (2012). Reconstructing constructivism: Causal models, Bayesian learning mechanisms, and the theory theory. *Psychological Bulletin, 138*(6), 1085–1108. doi:10.1037/a0028044

Gopnik, A., Wellman, H. M., Gelman, S. A., & Meltzoff, A. N. (2010). A computational foundation for cognitive development: Comment on Griffths et al. and McLelland et al. *Trends in Cognitive Sciences, 14*(8), 342–343. doi:10.1016/j.tics.2010.05.012

Gordon, P. (2004). Numerical cognition without words: Evidence from Amazonia. *Science, 306,* 496–499.

Gordon, R. A., Crosnoe, R., & Wang, X. (2013). Physical attractiveness and the accumulation of social and human capital in adolescence and young adulthood: Assets and distractions. *Monographs of the Society for Research in Child Development, 78*(6), 1-137.

Gorodetsky, E. E., Bevilacqua, L. L., Carli, V. V., Sarchiapone, M. M., Roy, A. A., Goldman, D. D., & Enoch, M. A. (2014). The interactive effect of MAOA-LPR genotype and childhood physical neglect on aggressive behaviors in Italian male prisoners. *Genes, Brain & Behavior, 13*(6), 543–549. doi:10.1111/gbb.12140

Gorrese, A., & Ruggieri, R. (2012). Peer attachment: A meta-analytic review of gender and age differences and associations with parent attachment. *Journal of Youth and Adolescence, 41*(5), 650–672. doi:10.1007/s10964-012-9759-6

Goswami, U. (1999). The relationship between phonological awareness and orthographic representation in different orthographies. In M. Harris & G. Hatano (Eds.), *Learning to read and write: A cross-linguistic perspective (pp. 134-156).* Cambridge, England: Cambridge University Press.

Goswami, U. (2011). *Inductive and deductive reasoning.* In U. Goswami (Ed.), *The Wiley-Blackwell handbook of childhood cognitive development* (2nd ed., pp. 399–419). Malden, MA: Wiley-Blackwell.

Gottfredson, L. (2003). Dissecting practical intelligence theory: Its claims and evidence. *Intelligence, 31,* 343–397.

Gottfried, A. E., Fleming, J. S., & Gottfried, A. W. (1994). Role of parental motivational practices in children's academic intrinsic motivation and achievement. *Journal of Educational Psychology, 86,* 104–113.

Gottfried, A. W., Gottfried, A. E., & Guerin, D. W. (2009). Issues in early prediction and identification of intellectual giftedness. In F. D. Horowitz, R. F. Subotnik, & D. J. Matthews (Eds.), *The development of giftedness and talent across the life span* (pp. 43–56). Washington, DC: American Psychological Association.

Gottfried, A. W., Gottfried, A. E., Bathurst, K., & Guerin, D. W. (1994). *Gifted IQ: Early developmental aspects.* New York, NY: Plenum Press.

Gottlieb, G. (1991). Experiential canalization of behavioral development: Theory. *Developmental Psychology, 27,* 4–13.

Gottlieb, G., Wahlsten, D., & Lickliter, R. (2006). The significance of biology for human development: A developmental psychobiological systems view. In W. Damon & R. M. Lerner (Eds. in Chief) & R. M. Lerner (Vol. Ed.), *Handbook of child psychology: Vol. 1. Theoretical models of human development* (6th ed., pp. 210–257). Hoboken, NJ: Wiley.

Gottman, J. M. (1983). How children become friends. *Monographs of the Society for Research in Child Development, 48*(3, Serial No. 201).

Gottman, J. M. (1986). The world of coordinated play: Same- and cross-sex friendship in young children. In J. M. Gottman & J. G. Parker (Eds.), *Conversations of friends: Speculations on affective development* (pp. 139–191). Cambridge, England: Cambridge University Press.

Gottman, J. M., & Mettetal, G. (1986). Speculations about social and affective development: Friendship and acquaintanceship through adolescence. In J. M. Gottman & J. G. Parker (Eds.), *Conversations of friends: Speculations on affective*

development (pp. 192–237). Cambridge, England: Cambridge University Press.

Goujon, A., Didierjean, A., & Poulet, S. (2013). The emergence of explicit knowledge from implicit learning. *Memory & Cognition.* doi:10.3758/s13421-013-0355-0

Gover, A. R., Jennings, W. G., & Tewksbury, R. (2009). Adolescent male and female gang members' experiences with violent victimization, dating violence, and sexual assault. *American Journal of Criminal Justice, 34*(1–2), 103–115. doi:10.1007/s12103-008-9053-z

Gowen, L., & Winges-Yanez, N. (2014). Lesbian, gay, bisexual, transgender, queer, and questioning youths' perspectives of inclusive school-based sexuality education. *Journal of Sex Research, 51*(7), 788–800. doi:10.1080/00224499.2013.806648

Gower, A. L., Lingras, K. A., Mathieson, L. C., Kawabata, Y., & Crick, N. R. (2014). The role of preschool relational and physical aggression in the transition to kindergarten: Links with social-psychological adjustment. *Early Education and Development, 25*(5), 619–640. doi:10.1080/10409289.2014.844058

Graber, J. A., Britto, P. R., & Brooks-Gunn, J. (1999). What's love got to do with it? Adolescents' and young adults' beliefs about sexual and romantic relationships. In W. Furman, B. B. Brown, & C. Feiring (Eds.), *The development of romantic relationships in adolescence* (pp. 364–395). Cambridge, England: Cambridge University Press.

Graesch, A. P. (2009). Material indicators of family busyness. *Social Indicators Research, 93,* 85–94.

Graesser, A., Golding, J. M., & Long, D. L. (1991). Narrative representation and comprehension. In R. Barr, M. L. Kamil, P. B. Mosenthal, P. Pearson (Eds.), *Handbook of reading research* (Vol. 2, pp. 171–205). Hillsdale, NJ: Lawrence Erlbaum.

Graff, G. (2014). The intergenerational trauma of slavery and its aftermath. *The Journal Of Psychohistory, 41*(3), 181-197.

Graham, S. (1989). Motivation in Afro-Americans. In G. L. Berry & J. K. Asamen (Eds.), *Black students: Psychosocial issues and academic achievement.* Newbury Park, CA: Sage.

Graham, S. (1997). Using attribution theory to understand social and academic motivation in African American youth. *Educational Psychologist, 32,* 21–34.

Graham, S. (2006). Writing. In P. A. Alexander & P. H. Winne (Eds.), *Handbook of educational psychology* (2nd ed., pp. 457–478). Mahwah, NJ: Erlbaum.

Graham, S. (2009). Giftedness in adolescence: African American gifted youth and their challenges from a motivational perspective. In F. D. Horowitz, R. F. Subotnik, & D. J. Matthews (Eds.), *The development of giftedness and talent across the life span* (pp. 109–129). Washington, DC: American Psychological Association.

Graham, S. (2014). The use of multiple forms of assessment in the service of writing. *Literacy Research & Instruction, 53*(2), 96–100. doi:10.1080/19388071.2014.868249

Graham, S. A., Booth, A. E., & Waxman, S. R. (2012). Words are not merely features: Only consistently applied nouns guide 4-year-olds' inferences about object categories. *Language Learning and Development, 8*(2), 136–145. doi:10.1080/15475441.2011.599304

Graham, S., & Perin, D. (2007). A meta-analysis of writing instruction for adolescent students. *Journal of Educational Psychology, 99,* 445–476.

Graham, S., & Weintraub, N. (1996). A review of handwriting research: Progress and prospects from 1980 to 1994. *Educational Psychology Review, 8,* 7–87.

Graham, S., & Williams, C. (2009). An attributional approach to motivation in school. In K. R. Wentzel & A. Wigfield (Eds.), *Handbook of motivation at school* (pp. 11–33). New York, NY: Routledge.

Graham, S., Harris, K. R., & Fink, B. (2000). Is handwriting causally related to learning to write? Treatment of handwriting problems in beginning writers. *Journal of Educational Psychology, 92,* 620–633.

Graham, S., Harris, K. R., & Olinghouse, N. (2007). Addressing executive function problems in writing: An example from the self-regulated strategy development model. In L. Meltzer (Ed.), *Executive function in education: From theory to practice* (pp. 216–236). New York, NY: Guilford Press.

Graham, S., Schwartz, S. S., & MacArthur, C. A. (1993). Knowledge of writing and the composing process, attitude toward writing, and self-efficacy for students with and without learning disabilities. *Journal of Learning Disabilities, 26,* 237–249.

Gralinski, J. H., & Kopp, C. B. (1993). Everyday rules for behavior: Mothers' requests to young children. *Developmental Psychology, 29*(3), 573–584. doi:10.1037/0012-1649.29.3.573

Grammer, J. K., Purtell, K. M., Coffman, J. L., & Ornstein, P. A. (2011). Relations between children's metamemory and strategic performance: Time-varying covariates in early elementary school. *Journal of Experimental Child Psychology, 108*(1), 139–155. doi:10.1016/j.jecp.2010.08.001

Grammer, J., Coffman, J., & Ornstein, P. (2013). The effect of teachers' memory-relevant language on children's strategy use and knowledge. *Child Development, 84*(6), 1989–2002. doi:10.1111/cdev.12100

Grandin, T. (1995). *Thinking in pictures and other reports of my life with autism.* New York, NY: Random House.

Granger, R. C. (2008). After-school programs and academics: Implications for policy, practice, and research. *Social Policy Report, 22*(2). Ann Arbor, MI: Society for Research in Child Development.

Granic, I., Lobel, A., & Engels, R. E. (2014). The benefits of playing video games. *American Psychologist, 69*(1), 66–78. doi:10.1037/a0034857

Granrud, C. E. (2006). Size constancy in infants: 4-month-olds' responses to physical versus retinal image size. *Journal of Experimental Psychology: Human Perception and Performance, 32,* 1398–1404.

Grant, C. A., & Gomez, M. L. (2001). *Campus and classroom: Making schooling multicultural* (2nd ed.). Upper Saddle River, NJ: Merrill/Prentice Hall.

Grant, C. A., & Gomez, M. L. (2001). *Campus and classroom: Making schooling multicultural* (2nd ed.). Upper Saddle River, NJ: Merrill/Prentice Hall.

Grant, H., & Dweck, C. (2001). Cross-cultural response to failure: Considering outcome attributions with different goals. In F. Salili & C. Chiu (Eds.), *Student motivation: The culture and context of learning* (pp. 203–219). Dordrecht, The Netherlands: Kluwer Academic.

Grant, R., Gracy, D., Goldsmith, G., Shapiro, A., & Redlener, I. E. (2013). Twenty-five years of child and family homelessness: Where are we now? *American Journal of Public Health, 103*(S2), e1–e10. doi:10.2105/AJPH. 2013.301618

Graue, M. E., & Walsh, D. J. (1998). *Studying children in context.* Thousand Oaks, CA: Sage.

Gredler, M. E., & Shields, C. C. (2008). *Vygotsky's legacy: A foundation for research and practice.* New York, NY: Guilford Press.

Green, C. (2012). Listening to children: Exploring intuitive strategies and interactive methods in a study of children's special places. *International Journal of Early Childhood, 44*(3), 269–285. doi:10.1007/s13158-012-0075-9

Green, L., Fry, A. F., & Myerson, J. (1994). Discounting of delayed rewards: A life-span comparison. *Psychological Science, 5,* 33–36.

Green, Y. R., & Gray, M. (2013). Lessons learned from the Kinship Education and Support Program (KEPS): Developing effective support groups for formal kinship caregivers. *Social Work With Groups: A Journal of Community and Clinical Practice, 36*(1), 27–42. doi:10.1080/01609513.2012.698384

Greenberg, J. (2014). Significance of after-school programming for immigrant children during middle childhood: Opportunities for school social work. *Social Work, 59*(3), 243–251.

Greenberg, M. T. (1999). Attachment and psychopathology in childhood. In J. Cassidy & P. R. Shaver (Eds.), *Handbook of attachment: Theory, research, and clinical applications* (pp. 469–496). New York, NY: Guilford Press.

Greenberg, M. T., Weissberg, R. P., O'Brien, M. U., Zins, J. E., Fredericks, L., Resnik, H., et al. (2003). Enhancing school-based prevention and youth development through coordinated social, emotional, and academic learning. *American Psychologist, 58,* 466–474.

Greene, J. P., & Forster, G. (2004). *Sex, drugs, and delinquency in urban and suburban public schools* (Education Working Paper). Manhattan Institute for Policy Research. Retrieved from http://www.manhattan-institute.org/html/ewp_04.htm

Greene, K. (2014). History Maker. *Instructor, 123*(4), 10-11

Greenfield, P. M. (1998). The cultural evolution of IQ. In U. Neisser (Ed.), *The rising curve: Long-term gains in IQ and related measures* (pp. 81–123). Washington, DC: American Psychological Association.

Greenfield, P. M., & Quiroz, B. (2013). Context and culture in the socialization and development of personal achievement values: Comparing Latino immigrant families, European American families, and elementary school teachers. *Journal of Applied Developmental Psychology, 34*(2), 108–118. doi:10.1016/j.appdev.2012.11.002

Greenfield, P. M., DeWinstanley, P., Kilpatrick, H., & Kaye, D. (1996). Action video games and informal education: Effects on strategies for dividing visual attention. In P. M. Greenfield & R. R. Cocking (Eds.), *Advances in applied developmental psychology: Vol. 11. Interacting with video* (pp. 187–205). Westport, CT: Ablex.

Greeno, J. G. (2007). Toward the development of intellective character. In E. W. Gordon & B. L. Bridglall (Eds.), *Affirmative development: Cultivating academic ability* (pp. 17–47). Lanham, MD: Rowman.

Greeno, J. G., Collins, A. M., & Resnick, L. B. (1996). Cognition and learning. In D. C. Berliner & R. C. Calfee (Eds.), *Handbook of educational psychology (pp. 15-46).* New York, NY: Macmillan.

Greenough, W. T., Black, J. E., & Wallace, C. S. (1987). Experience and brain development. *Child Development, 58,* 539–559.

Greenspan, D. A., Solomon, B., & Gardner, H. (2004). The development of talent in different domains. In L. V. Shavinina & M. Ferrari (Eds.), *Beyond knowledge: Extracognitive aspects of developing high ability* (pp. 119–135). Mahwah, NJ: Erlbaum.

Greenspan, S. I., & Meisels, S. (1996). Toward a new vision for the developmental assessment of infants and young children. In S. J. Meisels & E. Fenichel (Eds.), *New visions for the developmental assessment of infants and young children.* Washington, DC: Zero to Three.

Greenspan, S., & Granfield, J. M. (1992). Reconsidering the construct of mental retardation: Implications of a model of social competence. *American Journal of Mental Retardation, 96,* 442–453.

Gregg, M., & Leinhardt, G. (1994a, April). *Constructing geography.* Paper presented at the annual meeting of the American Educational Research Association, New Orleans, LA.

Gregory, A., Cornell, D., Fan, X., Sheras, P., Shih, T., & Huang, F. (2010). Authoritative school discipline: High school practices associated with lower bullying and victimization. *Journal of Educational Psychology, 102*(2), 483–496. doi:10.1037/a0018562

Gregory, E., Choudhury, H., Ilankuberan, A., Kwapong, A., & Woodham, M. (2013). Practice, performance and perfection: Learning sacred texts in four faith communities in London. *International Journal of The Sociology of Language,* (220), 27-48. doi:10.1515/ijsl-2013-0012

Greif, M. L., Kemler Nelson, D. G., Keil, F. C., & Gutierrez, F. (2006). What do children want to know about artifacts? Domain-specific requests for information. *Psychological Science, 17,* 455–459.

Grekul, J., & Sanderson, K. (2011). "I thought people would be mean and shout." Introducing the Hobbema Community Cadet Corps: A response to youth gang involvement? *Journal of Youth Studies, 14*(1), 41–57. doi:10.1080/13676261.2010.489602

Griedler, M. E., & Shields, C. C. (2008). *Vygotsky's legacy: A foundation for research and practice.* New York, NY: Guilford Press.

Griffin, K., del Pilar, W., McIntosh, K., & Griffin, A. (2012). "Oh, of course I'm going to go to college": Understanding how habitus shapes the college choice process of black immigrant students. *Journal of Diversity in Higher Education, 5*(2), 96–111. doi:10.1037/a0028393

Griffin, S. (2009). Learning sequences in the acquisition of mathematical knowledge: Using cognitive developmental theory to inform curriculum design for pre-K–6 mathematics education. *Mind, Brain, and Education, 3*(2), 96–107.

Griffin, S. A., Case, R., & Siegler, R. S. (1994). Rightstart: Providing the central conceptual prerequisites for first formal learning of arithmetic to students at risk for school failure. In K. McGilly (Ed.), *Classroom lessons: Integrating cognitive theory and classroom practice.* Cambridge, MA: MIT Press.

Griffin, S., & Case, R. (1997). Re-thinking the primary school math curriculum: An approach based on cognitive science. *Issues in Education, 3*(1), 1.

Griffin, S., & Green, R. (2012). Transforming high poverty, underperforming schools: Practices, processes, and procedures. *National Forum of Applied Educational Research Journal, 26*(1/2), 77–93.

Griffith, S., & Grolnick, W. (2014). Parenting in Caribbean families: A look at parental control, structure, and autonomy support. *Journal of Black Psychology, 40*(2), 166–190.

Griffiths, M. (2010). Online video gaming: What should educational psychologists know? *Educational Psychology in Practice, 26*(1), 35–40. doi:10.1080/02667360903522769

Griffiths, Y., & Stuart, M. (2013). Reviewing evidence-based practice for pupils with dyslexia and literacy difficulties. *Journal of Research in Reading, 36*(1), 96–116. doi:10.1111/j.1467-9817.2011.01495.x

Gripshover, S. J., & Markman, E. M. (2013). Teaching young children a theory of nutrition: Conceptual change and the potential for increased vegetable consumption. *Psychological Science, 24*(8), 1541–1553.

Groh, A. M., Fearon, R., Bakermans-Kranenburg, M. J., van IJzendoorn, M. H., Steele, R. D., & Roisman, G. I. (2014). The significance of attachment security for children's social competence with peers: A meta-analytic study. *Attachment & Human Development, 16*(2), 103–136. doi:10.1080/14616734.2014.883636

Grolnick, W. S., & Pomerantz, E. M. (2009). Issues and challenges in studying parental control: Toward a new conceptualization. *Child Development Perspectives, 3*(3), 165–170.

Gromko, J. E. (1996, April). *Theorizing symbolic development in music: Interpretive interactions with preschool children.* Paper presented at the Music Educators National Conference, Kansas City, MO.

Gromko, J. E., & Poorman, A. S. (1998). Developmental trends and relationships in children's aural perception and symbol use. *Journal of Research in Music Education, 46,* 16–23.

Grosche, M., & Volpe, R. (2013). Response-to-intervention (RTI) as a model to facilitate inclusion for students with learning and behaviour problems. European Journal of Special Needs Education, 28(3), 254–269. doi:10.1080/08856257.2013.768452

Gross, D., Garvey, C., Julion, W., Fogg, L., Tucker, S., & Mokros, H. (2009). Efficacy of the Chicago Parent Program with low-income African American and Latino parents of young children. *Prevention Science, 10,* 54–65.

Gross, R. H. (2004). Sports medicine in youth athletes. *Southern Medical Journal, 97,* 880.

Gross, T. (2010). Service learning builds bonds to school for young learners. *Phi Delta Kappan, 91*(5), 24–26.

Grossman, H. L. (1994). *Classroom behavior management in a diverse society.* Mountain View, CA: Mayfield.

Grossmann, K. E., Grossmann, K., Huber, F., & Wartner, U. (1981). German children's behavior toward their mothers at 12 months and their fathers at 18 months in Ainsworth's Strange Situation. *International Journal of Behavioral Development, 4,* 157–181.

Grumm, M., & Hein, S. (2013). Correlates of teachers' ways of handling bullying. *School Psychology International, 34*(3), 299–312.

Grusec, J. (2006). The development of moral behavior and conscience from a socialization perspective. In M. Killen & J. G. Smetana (Eds.), *Handbook of moral development* (pp. 243–265). Mahwah, NJ: Erlbaum.

Grusec, J. E., & Davidov, M. (2007). Socialization in the family: The roles of parents. In J. E. Grusec & P. D. Hastings (Eds.), *Handbook of socialization: Theory and research* (pp. 284–308). New York, NY: Guilford Press.

Grusec, J. E., & Redler, E. (1980). Attribution, reinforcement, and altruism. *Developmental Psychology, 16,* 525–534.

Guan, S. A., Greenfield, P. M., & Orellana, M. F. (2014). Translating into understanding: Language brokering and prosocial development in emerging adults from immigrant families. *Journal of Adolescent Research, 29*(3), 331–355. doi:10.1177/0743558413520223

Guardino, C. M., & Dunkel Schetter, C. (2014). Coping during pregnancy: a systematic review and recommendations. Health Psychology Review, 8(1), 70-94. doi:10.1080/17437199.2012.752659

Guay, F., Boivin, M., & Hodges, E. V. E. (1999). Social comparison processes and academic achievement: The dependence of the development of self-evaluations on friends' performance. *Journal of Educational Psychology, 91,* 564–568.

Guilford, J. P. (1967). *The nature of human intelligence.* New York, NY: McGraw-Hill.

Guimarães, M. (2013). Does prosodic bootstrapping play any role in the acquisition of auxiliary fronting in English? *Syntax, 16*(2), 148–175. doi:10.1111/synt.12002

Gummerum, M., Keller, M., Takezawa, M., & Mata, J. (2008). To give or not to give: Children's and adolescents' sharing and moral negotiations in economic decision situations. *Child Development, 79,* 562–576.

Gunderson, E. A., Gripshover, S. J., Romero, C., Dweck, C. S., Goldin-Meadow, S., & Levine, S. C. (2013). Parent praise to 1- to 3-year-olds predicts children's motivational frameworks 5 years later. *Child Development, 84*(5), 1526–1541.

Gunderson, E. W., Kirkpatrick, M. G., Willing, L. M., & Holstege, C. P. (2013). Intranasal substituted cathinone "bath salts" psychosis potentially exacerbated by diphenhydramine. *Journal of Addiction Medicine, 7*(3), 163–168. doi:10.1097/ADM.0b013e31829084d5

Gunn, A., Bennett, S., Evans, L., Peterson, B., & Welsh, J. (2013). Autobiographies in preservice teacher education: A snapshot tool for building a culturally responsive pedagogy. *International Journal Of Multicultural Education, 15*(1), 1–20.

Gunzburger, D. W. (1977). Moral judgment and distributive justice. *Human Development (0018716X), 20*(3), 160–170.

Gust, L. V. (2012). Can policy reduce the collateral damage caused by the criminal justice system? Strengthening social capital in families and communities. *American Journal of Orthopsychiatry, 82*(2), 174–180. doi:10.1111/j.1939-0025.2012.01156.x

Guszkowska, M. (2014). The effect of exercise and childbirth classes on fear of childbirth and locus of labor pain control. Anxiety, Stress & Coping: An International Journal, 27(2), 176-189. doi:10.1080/10615806.2013.830107

Gutiérrez, K. D., & Rogoff, B. (2003). Cultural ways of learning: Individual traits or repertoires of practice. *Educational Researcher, 32*(5), 19–25.

Guttman, N. (2013). "My son is reliable": Young drivers' parents' optimism and views on the norms of parental involvement in youth driving. *Journal of Adolescent Research, 28*(2), 241–268. doi:10.1177/0743558411435853

Guyll, M., Madon, S., Prieto, L., & Scherr, K. C. (2010). The potential roles of self-fulfilling prophecies, stigma consciousness, and stereotype threat in linking Latino ethnicity and educational outcomes. *Journal of Social Issues, 66*(1), 113–130.

Härkönen, J. (2014). Birth order effects on educational attainment and educational transitions in West Germany. *European Sociological Review, 30*(2), 166-179.

Hébert, T., & Pagnani, A. (2010). Engaging gifted boys in new literacies. *Gifted Child Today, 33*(3), 36–45.

Ha, T., Dishion, T. J., Overbeek, G., Burk, W. J., & Engels, R. E. (2014). The blues of adolescent romance: Observed affective interactions in adolescent romantic relationships associated with depressive symptoms. *Journal of Abnormal Child Psychology, 42*(4), 551–562. doi:10.1007/s10802-013-9808-y

Haan, A. D., Deković, M., den Akker, A. L., Stoltz, S. J., & Prinzie, P. (2013). Developmental personality types from childhood to adolescence: Associations with parenting and adjustment. *Child Development, 84*(6), 2015–2030. doi:10.1111/cdev.12092

Hack, M., Schluchter, M., Forrest, C. B., Taylor, H., Drotar, D., Holmbeck, G., Youngstrom, E., Margevicius, S., & Andreias, L. (2012). Self-Reported Adolescent Health Status of Extremely Low Birth Weight Children Born 1992-1995. Pediatrics, 130(1), 46-53. doi:10.1542/peds.2011-3402

Hadjiachilleos, S., Valanides, N., & Angeli, C. (2013). The impact of cognitive and affective aspects of cognitive conflict on learners' conceptual change about floating and sinking. *Research In Science & Technological Education, 31*(2), 133–152. doi:10.1080/02635143.2013.811074

Haerens, L., Deforche, B., Maes, L., Cardon, G., Stevens, V., & De Bourdeaudhuij, I. (2006). Evaluation of a 2-year physical activity and healthy eating intervention in middle school children. *Health Education Research, 21*, 911–921.

Hafford, C. (2010). Sibling caretaking in immigrant families: Understanding cultural practices to inform child welfare practice and evaluation. *Evaluation and Program Planning, 33*(3), 294–302. doi:10.1016/j.evalprogplan.2009.05.003

Hagen, J. W., & Stanovich, K. G. (1977). Memory: Strategies of acquisition. In R. V. Kail, Jr., &

J. W. Hagen (Eds.), *Perspectives on the development of memory and cognition.* Hillsdale, NJ: Erlbaum.

Hagerman, R. J., & Lampe, M. E. (1999). Fragile X syndrome. In S. Goldstein & C. R. Reynolds (Eds.), *Handbook of neurodevelopmental and genetic disorders* (pp. 298–316). New York, NY: Guilford Press.

Hagger, M. S., Chatzisarantis, N. L. D., Barkoukis, V., Wang, C. K. J., & Baranowski, J. (2005). Perceived autonomy support in physical education and leisure-time physical activity: A cross-cultural evaluation of the trans-contextual model. *Journal of Educational Psychology, 97,*

Hahn, N., Jansen, P., & Heil, M. (2010). Preschoolers' mental rotation: Sex differences in hemispheric asymmetry. *Journal of Cognitive Neuroscience, 22*(6), 1244–1250.

Hahn-Holbrook, J., Holbrook, C., & Bering, J. (2010). Snakes, spiders, strangers: How the evolved fear of strangers may misdirect efforts to protect children from harm. In J. M. Lampinen & K. Sexton-Radek (Eds.), *Protecting children from violence: Evidence-based interventions* (pp. 263–289). New York, NY: Psychology Press.

Haidt, J. (2008). Morality. *Perspectives on Psychological Science, 3*(1), 65–72.

Haight, W. L. (1999). The pragmatics of caregiver–child pretending at home: Understanding culturally specific socialization practices. In A. Göncü (Ed.), *Children's engagement in the world: Sociocultural perspectives* (pp. 128–147). Cambridge, England: Cambridge University Press.

Haith, M. M. (1990). Perceptual and sensory processes in early infancy. *Merrill-Palmer Quarterly, 36,* 1–26.

Haith, M. M., Hazan, C., & Goodman, G. S. (1988). Expectation and anticipation of dynamic visual events by 3.5-month-old babies. *Child Development, 59,* 467–479.

Hale, D. R., Fitzgerald-Yau, N., & Mark Viner, R. (2014). A Systematic Review of Effective Interventions for Reducing Multiple Health Risk Behaviors in Adolescence. *American Journal Of Public Health, 104*(5), e19-e41. doi:10.2105/AJPH.2014.301874

Hale-Benson, J. E. (1986). *Black children: Their roots, culture, and learning styles.* Baltimore, MD: Johns Hopkins University Press.

Halford, G. S., & Andrews, G. (2006). Reasoning and problem solving. In W. Damon & R. M. Lerner (Series Eds.), & D. Kuhn & R. Siegler (Vol. Eds.), *Handbook of child psychology: Vol. 2. Cognition, perception, and language* (6th ed., pp. 557-608). New York, NY: Wiley.

Halgunseth, L. (2009). Family engagement, diverse families, and early childhood education programs: An integrated review of the literature. *Young Children, 64*(5), 56–58.

Halim, M., Ruble, D. N., Tamis-LeMonda, C. S., Zosuls, K. M., Lurye, L. E., & Greulich, F. K. (2014). Pink frilly dresses and the avoidance of all things "girly": Children's appearance rigidity and cognitive theories of gender development. *Developmental Psychology, 50*(4), 1091–1101. doi:10.1037/a0034906

Halim, M., Ruble, D., & Tamis-Lemonda, C. (2013). Four-year-olds' beliefs about how others regard males and females. *British Journal of Developmental Psychology, 31*(1), 128–135. doi:10.1111/j.2044-835X.2012.02084.x

Hall, E. C., Kronborg, H., Aagaard, H., & Brinchmann, B. (2013). The journey towards motherhood after a very preterm birth: Mothers' experiences in hospital and after home-coming. Journal of Neonatal Nursing, 19(3), 109–113. doi:10.1016/j.jnn.2012.08.002

Hall, W. A., Hauck, Y. L., Carty, E. M., Hutton, E. K., Fenwick, J., & Stoll, K. (2009). Childbirth fear,

anxiety, fatigue, and sleep deprivation in pregnant women. *Journal of Obstetric, Gynecologic, and Neonatal Nursing, 38,* 567–576.

Hallenbeck, M. J. (1996). The cognitive strategy in writing: Welcome relief for adolescents with learning disabilities. *Learning Disabilities Research and Practice, 11,* 107–119.

Halpern, D. F. (1992). *Sex differences in cognitive abilities* (2nd ed.). Hillsdale, NJ: Erlbaum.

Halpern, D. F. (1998). Teaching critical thinking for transfer across domains. *American Psychologist, 53,* 449–455.

Halpern, D. F. (2004). A cognitive-process taxonomy for sex differences in cognitive abilities. *Current Directions in Psychological Science, 13,* 135–139.

Halpern, D. F. (2006). Assessing gender gaps in learning and academic achievement. In P. A. Alexander & P. H. Winne (Eds.), *Handbook of educational psychology* (2nd ed., pp. 635–653). Mahwah, NJ: Erlbaum.

Halpern, D. F., & LaMay, M. L. (2000). The smarter sex: A critical review of sex differences in intelligence. *Educational Psychology Review, 12,* 229–246.

Halpern, D. F., Bendow, C. P., Geary, D. C., Gur, R. C., Hyde, J. S., & Gernsbacher, M. A. (2007). The science of sex differences in science and mathematics. *Psychological Science in the Public Interest, 8*(1), 1–51.

Hamers, J. H. M., & Ruijssenaars, A. J. J. M. (1997). Assessing classroom learning potential. In G. D. Phye (Ed.), *Handbook of academic learning: Construction of knowledge* (pp. 549-571). San Diego, CA: Academic Press.

Hamill, P. V., Drizd, T. A., Johnson, C. L., Reed, R. B., Roche, A. F., & Moore, W. M. (1979). Physical growth: National Center for Health Statistics percentiles. *American Journal of Clinical Nutrition, 32,* 607–629.

Hamilton, B. E., Martin, J. A, & Ventura, S. J. (2011). *Births: Preliminary data for 2010. National Vital Statistics Reports, 60*(2). Retrieved from http://www.cdc.gov/nchs/data/nvsr/nvsr60/nvsr60_02.pdf

Hamilton, J., Stange, J., Kleiman, E., Hamlat, E., Abramson, L., & Alloy, L. (2014). Cognitive vulnerabilities amplify the effect of early pubertal timing on interpersonal stress generation during adolescence. *Journal of Youth & Adolescence, 43*(5), 824-833. doi:10.1007/s10964-013-0015-5

Hamlen, K. R. (2011). Children's choices and strategies in video games. *Computers in Human Behavior, 27*(1), 532–539. doi:10.1016/j.chb.2010.10.001

Hammond, L. (2001). Notes from California: An anthropological approach to urban science education for language minority families. *Journal of Research in Science Teaching, 38*(9), 983–999.

Hamre, B. K., & Pianta, R. C. (2005). Can instructional and emotional support in the first-grade classroom make a difference for children at risk for school failure? *Child Development, 76,* 949–967.

Hamre, B., Hatfield, B., Pianta, R., & Jamil, F. (2014). Evidence for general and Domain-specific elements of teacher-child interactions: Associations with preschool children's development. *Child Development, 85*(3), 1257–1274. doi:10.1111/cdev.12184

Hankin, B. L., Oppenheimer, C., Jenness, J., Barrocas, A., Shapero, B. G., & Goldband, J. (2009). Developmental origins of cognitive vulnerabilities to depression: Review of processes contributing to stability and change across time. *Journal of Clinical Psychology, 65*(12), 1327–1338.

Hanley, P., Bennett, J., & Ratcliffe, M. (2014). The inter-relationship of science and religion: A typology of engagement. *International Journal of Science Education, 36*(7), 1210–1229. doi:10.1080/09500693.2013.853897

Hanlon, T. E., Simon, B. D., O'Grady, K. E., Carswell, S. B., & Callaman, J. M. (2009). The effectiveness of an after-school program targeting urban African American youth. *Education and Urban Society, 42*(1), 96–118. doi:10.1177/0013124509343144

Hannon, E. E., & Trehub, S. E. (2005). Metrical categories in infancy and adulthood. *Psychological Science, 16*, 48–55.

Hansen, J., & Kissel, B. (2009). Writing instruction for adolescent learners. In K. D. Wood & W. E. Blanton (Eds.), *Literacy instruction for adolescents: Research-based practice* (pp. 392–419). New York, NY: Guilford Press.

Hansen, M., & Markman, E. (2009). Children's use of mutual exclusivity to learn labels for parts of objects. *Developmental Psychology, 45*(2), 592–596.

Happé, F., & Frith, U. (2013). Annual research review: Towards a developmental neuroscience of atypical social cognition. *Journal of Child Psychology and Psychiatry.* doi:10.1111/jcpp.12162

Happé, F., & Frith, U. (2014). Annual research review: Towards a developmental neuroscience of atypical social cognition. *Journal of Child Psychology and Psychiatry, 55*(6), 553–577. doi:10.1111/jcpp.12162

Harach, L., & Kuczynski, L. (2005). Construction and maintenance of parent–child relationships: Bidirectional contributions from the perspectives of parents. *Infant and Child Development, 14*, 327–343.

Harden, S. M., Beauchamp, M. R., Pitts, B. H., Nault, E. M., Davy, B. M., Wen, Y., Weiss, P., & Estabrooks, P. A. (2014). Group-based lifestyle sessions for gestational weight gain management: A mixed method approach. American Journal of Health Behavior, 38(4), 560-569. doi:10.5993/AJHB.38.4.9

Hardy, I., Jonen, A., Möller, K., & Stern, E. (2006). Effects of instructional support within constructivist learning environments for elementary school students' understanding of "floating and sinking." *Journal of Educational Psychology, 98*, 307–326.

Hardy, L. (2013). An epidemic of cheating. *American School Board Journal, 200*(7), 16–19.

Hardy, S. A., Walker, L. J., Olsen, J. A., Woodbury, R. D., & Hickman, J. R. (2014). Moral identity as moral ideal self: Links to adolescent outcomes. *Developmental Psychology, 50*(1), 45–57. doi:10.1037/a0033598

Hareli, S., & Weiner, B. (2002). Social emotions and personality inferences: A scaffold for a new direction in the study of achievement motivation. *Educational Psychologist, 37*, 183–193.

Hargreaves, E. (2012). Teachers' classroom feedback: still trying to get it right. *Pedagogies, 7*(1), 1–15. doi:10.1080/1554480X.2012.630454

Harlow, H. F., & Zimmerman, R. R. (1959). Affectional responses in the infant monkey. *Science, 130*, 421–432.

Harnett, J. (2012). Reducing discrepancies between teachers' espoused theories and theories-in-use: An action research model of reflective professional development. *Educational Action Research, 20*(3), 367-384. doi:10.1080/09650792.2012.697397

Harper, G. W., & Riplinger, A. J. (2013). HIV prevention interventions for adolescents and young adults: What about the needs of gay and bisexual males? *AIDS and Behavior, 17*(3), 1082–1095. doi:10.1007/s10461-012-0178-1

Harradine, C. C., Coleman, M. B., & Winn, D. C. (2014). Recognizing academic potential in students of color: Findings of U-STARS~PLUS. *Gifted Child Quarterly, 58*(1), 24–34. doi:10.1177/0016986213506040

Harris, C. (2011). Oculomotor developmental pathology: An "evo-devo" perspective. In S. P. Liversedge, I. D. Gilchrist, S. Everling (Eds.), *The Oxford handbook of eye movements* (pp. 663–686). New York, NY: Oxford University Press.

Harris, C., Phillips, R., & Penuel, W. (2012). Examining teachers' instructional moves aimed at developing students' ideas and questions in learner-centered science classrooms. *Journal of Science Teacher Education, 23*(7), 769–788. doi:10.1007/s10972-011-9237-0

Harris, K. R., & Graham, S. (1992). Self-regulated strategy development: A part of the writing process. In M. Pressley, K. R. Harris, & J. T. Guthrie (Eds.), *Promoting academic competence and literacy in school* (pp. 277-309). San Diego, CA: Academic Press.

Harris, M. (1992). *Language experience and early language development: From input to uptake.* Hove, England: Erlbaum.

Harris, M. B. (1997). Preface: Images of the invisible minority. In M. B. Harris (Ed.), *School experiences of gay and lesbian youth: The invisible minority* (pp. xiv–xxii). Binghamton, NY: Harrington Park Press.

Harris, M. J., & Rosenthal, R. (1985). Mediation of interpersonal expectancy effects: 31 meta-analyses. *Psychological Bulletin, 97*, 363–386.

Harris, M., & Giannouli, V. (1999). Learning to read and spell in Greek: The importance of letter knowledge and morphological awareness. In M. Harris & G. Hatano (Eds.), *Learning to read and write: A cross-linguistic perspective.* Cambridge, England: Cambridge University Press.

Harris, P. L. (1989). *Children and emotion: The development of psychological understanding.* Oxford, England: Basil Blackwell.

Harris, P. L. (1989). *Children and emotion: The development of psychological understanding.* Oxford, England: Basil Blackwell.

Harris, P. L. (2006). Social cognition. In W. Damon & R. M. Lerner (Series Eds.), & D. Kuhn & R. Siegler (Vol. Eds.), *Handbook of child psychology: Vol. 2. Cognition, perception, and language* (6th ed., pp. 811–858). New York, NY: Wiley.

Harris, Y. R., & Graham, J. A. (2007). *The African American child: Development and challenges.* New York, NY: Springer.

Harrison, A. O., Wilson, M. N., Pine, C. J., Chan, S. Q., & Buriel, R. (1990). Family ecologies of ethnic minority children. *Child Development, 61*, 347–362.

Harrison, C. (2004). Giftedness in early childhood: The search for complexity and connection. *Roeper Review, 26*(2), 78–84.

Hart, B., & Risley, T. R. (1995). *Meaningful differences in the everyday experiences of young American children.* Baltimore, MD: Paul H. Brookes.

Hart, B., & Risley, T. R. (1999). *The social world of children learning to talk.* Baltimore, MD: Paul H. Brookes.

Hart, D. (1988). The adolescent self-concept in social context. In D. K. Lapsley & F. C. Power (Eds.), *Self, ego, and identity: Integrative approaches* (pp. 71–90). New York, NY: Springer-Verlag.

Hart, D., & Fegley, S. (1995). Prosocial behavior and caring in adolescence: Relations to self-understanding and social judgment. *Child Development, 66*, 1346–1359.

Hart, D., Atkins, R., & Donnelly, T. M. (2006). Community service and moral development. In M. Killen & J. G. Smetana (Eds.), *Handbook of moral development* (pp. 633–656). Mahwah, NJ: Erlbaum.

Hart, J. E., Mourot, J. E., & Aros, M. (2012). Children of same-sex parents: In and out of the closet. *Educational Studies, 38*(3), 277–281. doi:10.1080/03055698.2011.598677

Hart, S. (2011). *The impact of attachment.* New York, NY: Norton.

Hart, S. A., Soden, B., Johnson, W., Schatschneider, C., & Taylor, J. (2013). Expanding the environment: gene × school-level SES interaction on reading comprehension. *Journal of Child Psychology & Psychiatry, 54*(10), 1047–1055. doi:10.1111/jcpp.12083

Harter, S. (1992). The relationship between perceived competence, affect, and motivational orientation within the classroom: Processes and patterns of change. In A. K. Boggiano & T. S. Pittman (Eds.), *Achievement and motivation: A social-developmental perspective (pp. 77–115).* Cambridge, England: Cambridge University Press.

Harter, S. (1996). Teacher and classmate influences on scholastic motivation, self-esteem, and level of voice in adolescents. In J. Juvonen & K. Wentzel (Eds.), *Social motivation: Understanding children's school adjustment (pp. 11–42).* New York, NY: Cambridge University Press.

Harter, S. (1999). *The construction of the self.* New York, NY: Guilford Press.

Harter, S. (2006). The self. In W. Damon & R. M. Lerner (Eds. in Chief) & N. Eisenberg (Vol. Ed.), *Handbook of child psychology, Vol. 3. Social, emotional, and personality development* (6th ed., pp. 505–570). Hoboken, NJ: Wiley.

Harter, S. (2012). *The construction of the self: developmental and sociocultural foundations.* New York, NY: Guilford Press.

Harter, S., & Whitesell, N. R. (1989). Developmental changes in children's understanding of single, multiple, and blended emotion concepts. In C. Saarni & P. Harris (Eds.), *Children's understanding of emotion* (pp. 81–116). Cambridge, England: Cambridge University Press.

Harter, S., Stocker, C., & Robinson, N. S. (1996). The perceived directionality of the link between approval and self-worth: The liabilities of a looking glass self-orientation among young adolescents. *Journal of Research on Adolescence, 6*, 285–308.

Harter, S., Whitesell, N. R., & Junkin, L. J. (1998). Similarities and differences in domain-specific and global self-evaluations of learning-disabled, behaviorally disordered, and normally achieving adolescents. *American Educational Research Journal, 35*, 653–680.

Hartmann, A. S., Greenberg, J. L., & Wilhelm, S. (2013). The relationship between anorexia nervosa and body dysmorphic disorder. *Clinical Psychology Review, 33*(5), 675–685. doi:10.1016/j.cpr.2013.04.002

Hartmann, T., Krakowiak, K., & Tsay-Vogel, M. (2014). How violent video games communicate violence: A literature review and content analysis of moral disengagement factors. *Communication Monographs, 81*(3), 310–332. doi:10.1080/03637751.2014.922206

Hartup, W. W. (1983). Peer relations. In P. H. Mussen (Ed.), *Handbook of child psychology: Vol. IV. Socialization* (4th ed., pp. 91-152). New York, NY: Wiley.

Hartup, W. W. (1984). The peer context in middle childhood. In A. Collins (Ed.), *Development during middle childhood: The years from six to twelve.* Washington, DC: National Academy Press.

Hartup, W. W. (2009). Critical issues and theoretical viewpoints. In K. H. Rubin, W. M. Bukowski, & B. Laursen (Eds.) *Handbook of peer interactions, relationships, and groups* (pp. 3–19). New York, NY: Guilford Press.

Hartup, W. W., & Laursen, B. (1991). Relationships as developmental contexts. In R. Cohen & W. A. Siegel (Eds.), *Context and development* (pp. 253–279). Hillsdale, NJ: Erlbaum.

Harvey, S. (2011). Physical play with boys of all ages. In C. Haen (Ed.), *Engaging boys in treatment: Creative approaches to the therapy process* (pp. 91–113). New York, NY: Routledge/Taylor & Francis Group.

Haskill, A. M., & Corts, D. P. (2010). Acquiring language. In E. H. Sandberg & B. L. Spritz (Eds.), *A clinician's guide to normal cognitive development in childhood* (pp. 23–41). New York, NY: Routledge/Taylor & Francis.

Hatano, G., & Inagaki, K. (1996). Cognitive and cultural factors in the acquisition of intuitive biology.

In D. R. Olson & N. Torrance (Eds.), *The hand-book of education and human development: New models of learning, teaching, and schooling* (pp. 683–708). Cambridge, MA: Blackwell.

Hatfield, E., Cacioppo, J. T., & Rapson, R. L. (1994). *Emotional contagion.* Cambridge, England: Cambridge University Press.

Hatton, C. (1998). Pragmatic language skills in people with intellectual disabilities: A review. *Journal of Intellectual and Developmental Disability, 23*(1), 79–100. doi:10.1080/13668259800033601

Hauser-Cram, P., & Mitchell, D. B. (2012). Early childhood education. In K. R. Harris, S. Graham, T. Urdan, A. G. Bus, S. Major, & H. L. Swanson (Eds.), *APA educational psychology handbook, Vol. 3: Application to teaching and learning* (pp. 3–22). Washington, DC: American Psychological Association. doi:10.1037/13275-001

Haviland, J. M., & Lelwica, M. (1987). The induced affect response: 10-week-old infants' responses to three emotional expressions. *Developmental Psychology, 23,* 97–104.

Hawkins, B. L., Ryan, J. B., Cory, A., & Donaldson, M. C. (2014). Effects of equine-assisted therapy on gross motor skills of two children with autism spectrum disorder. *Therapeutic Recreation Journal, 48*(2), 135–149.

Hawkins, F. P. L. (1997). *Journey with children: The autobiography of a teacher.* Niwot, CO: University Press of Colorado.

Haworth, C. A., & Plomin, R. (2012). Genetics and education: Toward a genetically sensitive classroom. In K. R. Harris, S. Graham, T. Urdan, C. B. McCormick, G. M. Sinatra, & J. Sweller (Eds.), *APA educational psychology handbook, Vol. 1: Theories, constructs, and critical issues* (pp. 529–559). Washington, DC: American Psychological Association. doi:10.1037/13273-018

Hawthorne, N. (1892). *The scarlet letter: A romance.* Philadelphia, PA: H. Altemus Co.

Hay, D. F., Nash, A., Caplan, M., Swartzentruber, J., Ishikawa, F., & Vespo, J. (2011). The emergence of gender differences in physical aggression in the context of conflict between young peers. *British Journal of Developmental Psychology, 29*(2), 158–175. doi:10.1111/j.2044-835X.2011.02028.x

Hay, D. F., Perra, O., Hudson, K., Waters, C. S., Mundy, L., Phillips, R., Goodyer, I., Harold, G., Thapar, A., & van Goozen, S. (2010). Identifying early signs of aggression: Psychometric properties of the Cardiff Infant Contentiousness Scale. *Aggressive Behavior, 36*(6), 351–357. doi:10.1002/ab.20363

Hayashi, A., Karasawa, M., & Tobin, J. (2009). The Japanese preschool's pedagogy of feeling: Cultural strategies for supporting young children's emotional development. *Journal of the Society for Psychological Anthropology, 37*(1), 32–49.

Hayes, B., & Rehder, B. (2012). The development of causal categorization. *Cognitive Science, 36*(6), 1102–1128. doi:10.1111/j.1551-6709.2012.01244.x

Hayes, D. P., & Grether, J. (1983). The school year and vacations: When do students learn? *Cornell Journal of Social Relations, 17*(1), 56–71.

Hayne, H., & Simcock, G. (2009). Memory development in toddlers. In M. L. Courage & N. Cowan (Eds.), *The development of memory in infancy and childhood* (pp. 43–68). New York, NY: Psychology Press.

Haynes, J., & Zacarian, D. (2010). *Teaching English language learners across the content areas.* Alexandria, VA: ASCD.

Haywood, H. C., & Lidz, C. S. (2007). *Dynamic assessment in practice: Clinical and educational applications.* Cambridge, England: Cambridge University Press.

Hazlett, H. C., Gaspar De Alba, M., & Hooper, S. R. (2011). Klinefelter syndrome. In S. Goldstein &

C. R. Reynolds (Eds.), *Handbook of neurodevelopmental and genetic disorders in children* (2nd ed., pp. 382–397). New York, NY: Guilford Press.

Headden, S. (2013). The promise of personalized learning. *Education Next, 13*(4), 14–20.

Healy, K. L., Sanders, M. R., & Iyer, A. (2014). Facilitative parenting and children's social, emotional and behavioral adjustment. *Journal of Child and Family Studies.* doi:10.1007/s10826-014-9980-x

Heath, S. B. (1980). Questioning at home and at school: A comparative study. In G. Spindler (Ed.), *The ethnography of schooling: Educational anthropology in action* (pp. 20–47). New York, NY: Holt, Rinehart & Winston.

Heath, S. B. (1983). *Ways with words: Language, life, and work in communities and classrooms.* Cambridge, England: Cambridge University Press.

Heath, S. B. (1989). Oral and literate traditions among Black Americans living in poverty. *American Psychologist, 44,* 367–373.

Heatherton, T. F. (2011). Neuroscience of self and self-regulation. *Annual Review of Psychology, 62,* 363–390.

Hecht, S. A., Close, L., & Santisi, M. (2003). Sources of individual differences in fraction skills. *Journal of Experimental Child Psychology, 86,* 277–302.

Heckenhausen, H. (1984). Emergent achievement behavior: Some early developments. In J. Nicholls (Ed.), *Advances in achievement motivation* (pp. 1–32). Greenwich, CT: JAI Press.

Hedegaard, M., & Fleer, M. (2013). *Play, learning, and children's development: Everyday life in families and transition to school.* New York, NY US: Cambridge University Press.

Hedges, L. V., & Nowell, A. (1995). Sex differences in mental test scores, variability, and numbers of high-scoring individuals. *Science, 269,* 41–45.

Hedin, L. (2014). A sense of belonging in a changeable everyday life—A follow-up study of young people in kinship, network, and traditional foster families. *Child & Family Social Work, 19*(2), 165–173. doi:10.1111/j.1365-2206.2012.00887.x

Heerboth, M. K., & Mason, K. (2012). Educational materials can induce stereotype threat in elementary school students: Evidence for impaired math performance following exposure to a token. *Psychology Journal, 9*(4), 120–128.

Hegarty, M., & Kozhevnikov, M. (1999). Types of visual-spatial representations and mathematical problem solving. *Journal of Educational Psychology, 91,* 684–689.

Heilbronner, N. N. (2013). The STEM pathway for women: What has changed? *Gifted Child Quarterly, 57*(1), 39–55. doi:10.1177/0016986212460085

Heilig, J. (2011). Understanding the interaction between high-stakes graduation tests and English learners. *Teachers College Record, 113*(12), 2633–2669.

Heineman, K. R., Middelburg, K. J., & Hadders-Algra, M. (2010). Development of adaptive motor behaviour in typically developing infants. *Acta Paediatrica, 99*(4), 618–624.

Helibronner, N. (2013). Creating and delivering differentiated science content through wikis. *Science Scope, 36*(5), 24–34.

Hellal, P., & Lorch, M. P. (2013). The modern beginnings of research into developmental language disorders. In C. R. Marshall (Ed.), *Current issues in developmental disorders* (pp. 173–192). New York, NY: Psychology Press.

Hellenga, K. (2002). Social space, the final frontier: Adolescents on the Internet. In J. T. Mortimer & R. W. Larson (Eds.), *The changing adolescent experience: Societal trends and the transition to adulthood* (pp. 208–249). Cambridge, England: Cambridge University Press.

Helth, T., & Jarden, M. (2013). Fathers' experiences with the skin-to-skin method in NICU: Competent parenthood and redefined gender roles.

Journal of Neonatal Nursing, 19(3), 114–121. doi:10.1016/j.jnn.2012.06.001

Helwig, C. C., & Jasiobedzka, U. (2001). The relation between law and morality: Children's reasoning about socially beneficial and unjust laws. *Child Development, 72,* 1382–1393.

Helwig, C. C., Zelazo, P. D., & Wilson, M. (2001). Children's judgments of psychological harm in normal and noncanonical situations. *Child Development, 72,* 66–81.

Hemelt, S., & Marcotte, D. (2013). High school exit exams and dropout in an era of increased accountability. *Journal of Policy Analysis & Management, 32*(2), 323–349. doi:10.1002/pam.21688

Hemmer, I., Hemmer, M., Kruschel, K., Neidhardt, E., Obermaier, G., & Uphues, R. (2013). Which children can find a way through a strange town using a streetmap? Results of an empirical study on children's orientation competence. *International Research in Geographical & Environmental Education, 22*(1), 23–40. doi:10.1080/10382046.2012.759436

Hemphill, L., & Snow, C. (1996). Language and literacy development: Discontinuities and differences. In D. R. Olson & N. Torrance (Eds.), *The handbook of education and human development: New models of learning, teaching, and schooling* (pp. 173–201). Cambridge, MA: Blackwell.

Hemphill, S. A., & Schneider, S. (2013). Excluding students from school: A re-examination from a children's rights perspective. *International Journal of Children's Rights, 21*(1), 88–96. doi:10.1163/15718182-55680008

Henderson, D., & Zipin, L. (2010). Bringing clay to life: Developing student literacy through clay animation artwork to tell life-based stories. In B. Prosser, B. Lucas, & A. Reid (Eds.), *Connecting lives and learning: Renewing pedagogy in the middle years* (pp. 20–39). Adelaide, South Australia: Wakefield Press.

Henderson, J. (2009). Paying for performance: Giving students cash incentives for learning. *Education Update, 51*(3), 1, 6–7.

Henderson, N. D. (1982). Human behavior genetics. *Annual Review of Psychology, 33,* 403–440.

Hennessey, B. A. (1995). Social, environmental, and developmental issues and creativity. *Educational Psychology Review, 7,* 163–183.

Henriksen, R. C., Jr., & Paladino, D. A. (2009). Identity development in a multiple heritage world. In R. C. Henriksen & D. A. Paladino (Eds.), *Counseling multiple heritage individuals, couples, and families* (pp. 25-43). Alexandria, VA: American Counseling Association.

Henry, L. A., & Norman, T. (1996). The relationships between memory performance, use of simple memory strategies and metamemory in young children. *International Journal of Behavioral Development, 19*(1), 177–200. doi:10.1080/016502596386018

Hernandez, D. J. (2010). Internationally comparable indicators for children of immigrants. *Child Indicators Research, 3,* 409–411.

Hernandez, D. J., Denton, N. A., & Macartney, S. E. (2010). Children of immigrants and the future of America. In E. L. Grigorenko & R. Takanishi (Eds.), *Immigration, diversity, and education* (pp. 7–25). New York, NY: Routledge.

Herrell, A., & Jordan, M. (2004). *Fifty strategies for teaching English language learners* (2nd ed.). Upper Saddle River, NJ: Merrill/Prentice Hall.

Hersh, C. A., Stone, B. J., & Ford, L. (1996). Learning disabilities and learned helplessness: A heuristic approach. *International Journal of Neuroscience, 84,* 103–113.

Hespos, S. J., Dora, B., Rips, L. J., & Christie, S. (2012). Infants make quantity discriminations for substances. *Child Development, 83*(2), 554–567.

Hess, R. D., & Azuma, M. (1991). Cultural support for learning: Contrasts between Japan and the United States. *Educational Researcher, 29*(9), 2–8.

Hess, R. D., & Holloway, S. D. (1984). Family and school as educational institutions. In R. D. Parke, R. N. Emde, H. P. McAdoo, & G. P. Sackett (Eds.), *Review of child development research: Vol. 7. The family* (pp. 179–222). Chicago: University of Chicago Press.

Hetherington, E. M., & Clingempeel, W. G. (1992). Coping with marital transitions: A family systems perspective. *Monographs of the Society for Research in Child Development, 57*(2–3, Serial No. 227).

Hetherington, E. M., Bridges, M., & Insabella, G. M. (1998). What matters? What does not? Five perspectives on the association between marital transitions and children's adjustment. *American Psychologist, 53*, 167–184.

Hetherington, E. M., Cox, M., & Cox, R. (1978). The aftermath of divorce. In J. H. Stevens, Jr., & M. Matthews (Eds.), *Mother–child, father–child relations* (pp. 110–155). Washington, DC: National Association for the Education of Young Children.

Hettinger, H. R., & Knapp, N. F. (2001). Potential, performance, and paradox: A case study of J.P., a verbally gifted, struggling reader. *Journal for the Education of the Gifted, 24*, 248–289.

Hibel, L. C., Granger, D. A., Blair, C., & Cox, M. J. (2011). Maternal sensitivity buffers the adrenocortical implications of intimate partner violence exposure during early childhood. *Development And Psychopathology, 23*(2), 689–701. doi:10.1017/S0954579411000010

Hickendorff, M., van Putten, C. M., Verhelst, N. D., & Heiser, W. J. (2010). Individual differences in strategy use on division problems: Mental versus written computation. *Journal of Educational Psychology, 102*(2), 438–452. doi:10.1037/a0018177

Hickey, D. T. (1997). Motivation and contemporary socio-constructivist instructional perspectives. *Educational Psychologist, 32*, 175–193.

Hickey, D. T., & Granade, J. B. (2004). The influence of sociocultural theory on our theories of engagement and motivation. In D. M. McInerney & S. Van Etten (Eds.), *Big theories revisited* (pp. 223–247). Greenwich, CT: Information Age.

Hickey, T. L., & Peduzzi, J. D. (1987). Structure and development of the visual system. In P. Salapatek & L. Cohen (Eds.), *Handbook of infant perception: Vol. 1. From sensation to perception (pp. 1–42)*. New York, NY: Academic Press.

Hidi, S., & Renninger, K. A. (2006). The four-phase model of interest development. *Educational Psychologist, 41*, 111–127.

Hidi, S., Renninger, K. A., & Krapp, A. (2004). Interest, a motivational variable that combines affecting and cognitive functioning. In D. Y. Dai & R. J. Sternberg (Eds.), *Motivation, emotion, and cognition: Integrative perspectives on intellectual functioning and development* (pp. 89–115). Mahwah, NJ: Erlbaum.

Hiebert, E. H., & Raphael, T. E. (1996). Psychological perspectives on literacy and extensions to educational practice. In D. C. Berliner & R. C. Calfee (Eds.), *Handbook of educational psychology* (pp. 550–602). New York, NY: Macmillan.

Hiebert, J., & Wearne, D. (1992). Links between teaching and learning place value with understanding in first grade. *Journal for Research in Mathematics Education, 23*(2), 98–122. doi:10.2307/749496

Higgins, A. (1995). Educating for justice and community: Lawrence Kohlberg's vision of moral education. In W. M. Kurtines & J. L. Gewirtz (Eds.), *Moral development: An introduction (pp. 49–81)*. Boston: Allyn & Bacon.

Higgins, E., & Scholer, A. A. (2015). Goal pursuit functions: Working together. In M. Mikulincer, P. R. Shaver, E. Borgida, J. A. Bargh (Eds.), *APA handbook of personality and social psychology, Volume 1: Attitudes and social cognition* (pp. 843–889). Washington, DC: American Psychological Association. doi:10.1037/14341-027

Hilbert, D., & Eis, S. (2014). Early intervention for emergent literacy development in a collaborative community pre-kindergarten. *Early Childhood Education Journal, 42*(2), 105–113. doi:10.1007/s10643-013-0588-3

Hildenbrand, A. K., Daly, B. P., Nicholls, E., Brooks-Holliday, S., & Kloss, J. D. (2013). Increased risk for school violence-related behaviors among adolescents with insufficient sleep. *Journal of School Health, 83*(6), 408-414. doi:10.1111/josh.12044

Hill, D. (2013). Three mentor texts that support code-switching pedagogies. *Voices from the Middle, 20*(4), 10–15.

Hill, P. L., & Lapsley, D. K. (2011). Adaptive and maladaptive narcissism in adolescent development. In C. T. Barry, P. K. Kerig, K. K. Stellwagen, & T. D. Barry (Eds.), *Narcissism and Machiavellianism in youth: Implications for the development of adaptive and maladaptive behavior* (pp. 89–105). Washington, DC: American Psychological Association.

Hill, P. R., Hogben, J. H., & Bishop, D. V. M. (2005). Auditory frequency discrimination in children with specific language impairment: A longitudinal study. *Journal of Speech, Language and Hearing Research, 48*, 1136–1146.

Hilt, L. M., & Nolen-Hoeksema, S. (2009). The emergence of gender differences in depression in adolescence. In S. Nolen-Hoeksema, & L. M. Hilt (Eds.), *Handbook of depression in adolescents* (pp. 111–135). New York, NY: Routledge.

Hilt, L. M., Cha, C. B., & Nolen-Hoeksema, S. (2008). Nonsuicidal self-injury in young adolescent girls: Moderators of the distress-function relationship. *Journal of Consulting and Clinical Psychology, 76*(1), 63–71.

Hinduja, S., & Patchin, J. W. (2011, February). High-tech cruelty. *Educational Leadership, 68*(5), 48–52.

Hinkley, J. W., McInerney, D. M., & Marsh, H. W. (2001, April). *The multi-faceted structure of school achievement motivation: A case for social goals*. Paper presented at the annual meeting of the American Educational Research Association, Seattle, WA.

Hinnant, J., Nelson, J. A., O'Brien, M., Keane, S. P., & Calkins, S. D. (2013). The interactive roles of parenting, emotion regulation and executive functioning in moral reasoning during middle childhood. *Cognition and Emotion, 27*(8), 1460–1468. doi:10.1080/02699931.2013.789792

Hirschfield, P. (2009). Another way out: The impact of juvenile arrests on high school dropout. *Sociology of Education, 82*(4), 368–393. doi:10.1177/003804070908200404

Hirsh-Pasek, K., & Golinkoff, R. M. (1996). *The origins of grammar: Evidence from early language comprehension*. Cambridge, MA: MIT Press.

Hirsh-Pasek, K., Golinkoff, R. M., Berk, L. E., & Singer, D. G. (2009). *A mandate for playful learning in preschool: Presenting the evidence*. New York, NY: Oxford University Press.

Ho, C. S., & Fuson, K. C. (1998). Children's knowledge of teen quantities as tens and ones: Comparisons of Chinese, British, and American kindergartners. *Journal of Educational Psychology, 90*, 536–544.

Ho, D. Y. F. (1994). Cognitive socialization in Confucian heritage cultures. In P. M. Greenfield & R. R. Cocking (Eds.), *Cross-cultural roots of minority child development (pp. 285–313)*. Hillsdale, NJ: Erlbaum.

Hobson, P. (2004). *The cradle of thought: Exploring the origins of thinking*. Oxford, England: Oxford University Press.

Hoekstra, R. A., Bartels, M., & Boomsma, D. I. (2007). Longitudinal genetic study of verbal and nonverbal IQ from early childhood to young adulthood. *Learning and Individual Differences, 17*, 97–114.

Hoerr, T. R. (2003). Distributed intelligence and why schools need to foster it. *Independent School, 63*, 76–83.

Hoff, E., & Naigles, L. (2002). How children use input to acquire a lexicon. *Child Development, 73*, 418–433.

Hoffman, M. L. (1975). Altruistic behavior and the parent–child relationship. *Journal of Personality and Social Psychology, 31*, 937–943.

Hoffman, M. L. (1979). Development of moral thought, feeling, and behavior. *American Psychologist, 34*(10), 958–966. doi:10.1037/0003-066X.34.10.958

Hoffman, M. L. (1981). Is altruism part of human nature? *Journal of Personality and Social Psychology, 40*, 121–137.

Hoffman, M. L. (1988). Moral development. In M. H. Bornstein & M. E. Lamb (Eds.), *Developmental psychology: An advanced textbook* (2nd ed., pp. 497–548). Hillsdale, NJ: Erlbaum.

Hoffman, M. L. (1991). Empathy, social cognition, and moral action. In W. M. Kurtines & J. L. Gewirtz (Eds.), *Moral behavior and development: Vol. 1. Theory (pp. 275–301)*. Hillsdale, NJ: Erlbaum.

Hoffman, M. L. (1994). Discipline and internalization. *Developmental Psychology, 30*, 26–28.

Hoffman, M. L. (2000). *Empathy and moral development: Implications for caring and justice*. New York, NY: Cambridge University Press.

Hogg, L. (2011). Funds of knowledge: An investigation of coherence within the literature. *Teaching and Teacher Education, 27*(3), 666–677. doi:10.1016/j.tate.2010.11.005

Hoglund, W. G., & Chisholm, C. A. (2014). Reciprocating risks of peer problems and aggression for children's internalizing problems. *Developmental Psychology, 50*(2), 586–599. doi:10.1037/a0033617

Hokoda, A., & Fincham, F. D. (1995). Origins of children's helplessness and mastery achievement patterns in the family. *Journal of Educational Psychology, 87*, 375–385.

Holland, A. S., & McElwain, N. L. (2013). Maternal and paternal perceptions of coparenting as a link between marital quality and the parent–toddler relationship.*Journal of Family Psychology, 27*(1), 117–126. doi:10.1037/a0031427.

Holland, J. M. (2011). Career development planning: Getting students on the right track. *Techniques: Connecting Education & Careers, 86*(2), 8–9.

Hollenbaugh, E. E., & Ferris, A. L. (2014). Facebook self-disclosure: Examining the role of traits, social cohesion, and motives. *Computers In Human Behavior, 30*, 50–58. doi:10.1016/j.chb.2013.07.055

Holler, K. A., & Greene, S. M. (2010). Developmental changes in children's executive functioning. In E. J. Sandberg & B. L. Spritz (Eds.), *A clinician's guide to normal cognitive development in childhood* (pp. 215–238). New York, NY: Routledge.

Hollingsworth, H. L., & Buysse, V. (2009). Establishing friendships in early childhood inclusive settings: What roles do parents and teachers play? *Journal of Early Intervention, 31*(4), 287–307. doi:10.1177/1053815109352659

Holloway, S. D. (2000). *Contested childhood: Diversity and change in Japanese preschools*. New York, NY: Routledge.

Holm, S. M., Forbes, E. E., Ryan, N. D., Phillips, M. L., Tarr, J. A., & Dahl, R. E. (2009). Reward-related brain function and sleep in pre/early pubertal and mid/late pubertal adolescents. *Journal of Adolescent Health, 45*, 326–334.

Holt, N. L., Tink, L. N., Mandigo, J. L., & Fox, K. R. (2008). Do youth learn life skills through their involvement in high school sport? A case study. *Canadian Journal of Education, 31*(2), 281–304.

Holtz, P., & Appel, M. (2011). Internet use and video gaming predict problem behavior in early adolescence. *Journal of Adolescence, 34*(1), 49–58. doi:10.1016/j.adolescence.2010.02.004

Hong, J. S. (2010). Understanding Vietnamese youth gangs in America: An ecological systems analysis. *Aggression and Violent Behavior, 15*(4), 253–260. doi:10.1016/j.avb.2010.01.003

Honig, A. S. (2009). Understanding and working with non-compliant and aggressive young children. *Early Child Development and Care, 179*(8), 1007–1023. doi:10.1080/03004430701726217

Hoover-Dempsey, K. V., & Sandler, H. M. (1997). Why do parents become involved in their children's education? *Review of Educational Research, 67,* 3–42.

Hoppe, C., Fliessbach, K., Stausberg, S., Stojanovic, J., Trautner, P., Elger, C. E., & Weber, B. (2012). A key role for experimental task performance: Effects of math talent, gender and performance on the neural correlates of mental rotation. *Brain & Cognition, 78*(1), 14–27. doi:10.1016/j.bandc.2011.10.008

Horn, J. L. (2008). Spearman, *g*, expertise, and the nature of human cognitive capability. In P. C. Kyllonen, R. D. Roberts, & L. Stankov (Eds.), Extending intelligence: Enhancement and new constructs (pp. 185–230). New York, NY: Erlbaum/Taylor & Francis.

Horn, J. L., & Noll, J. (1997). Human cognitive capabilities: Gf-Gc theory. In D. P. Flanagan, J. L. Genshaft, & P. L. Harrison (Eds.), *Contemporary intellectual assessment: Theories, tests, and issues* (pp. 53–91). New York, NY: Guilford Press.

Hornstra, L., van der Veen, I., Peetsma, T., & Volman, M. (2013). Developments in motivation and achievement during primary school: A longitudinal study on group-specific differences. *Learning and Individual Differences, 23,* 195–204. doi:10.1016/j.lindif.2012.09.004

Horowitz, F. D., Darling-Hammond, L., & Bransford, J. (with Comer, J., Rosebrock, K., Austin, K., & Rust, F.) (2005). Educating teachers for developmentally appropriate practice. In L. Darling-Hammond & J. Bransford (Eds.), *Preparing teachers for a changing world: What teachers should learn and be able to do* (pp. 88–125). San Francisco, CA: Jossey-Bass/Wiley.

Horst, J. S., Oakes, L. M., & Madole, K. L. (2005). What does it look like and what can it do? Category structure influences how infants categorize. *Child Development, 76,* 614–631.

Hosenbocus, S., & Chahal, R. (2012). A review of executive function deficits and pharmacological management in children and adolescents. *Journal of The Canadian Academy of Child and Adolescent Psychiatry / Journal De L'académie Canadienne De Psychiatrie De L'enfant Et De L'adolescent, 21*(3), 223–229.

Hoskyn, M., & Tzoneva, I. (2008). Relations between working memory and emergent writing among preschool-aged children. *Exceptionality Education Canada, 18*(1), 33–58.

Howard, G. R. (2007). As diversity grows, so must we. *Educational Leadership, 64*(6), 16–22.

Howe, C. (2009). Collaborative group work in middle childhood. *Human Development, 52,* 215–239.

Howe, C. A., Freedson, P. S., Alhassan, S. S., Feldman, H. A., & Osganian, S. K. (2012). A recess intervention to promote moderate-to-vigorous physical activity. *Pediatric Obesity, 7*(1), 82–88. doi:10.1111/j.2047-6310.2011.00007.x

Howe, D. (2006). Disabled children, parent–child interaction and attachment. *Child and Family Social Work, 11,* 95–106.

Howe, M. L., Courage, M. L., & Rooksby, M. (2009). The genesis and development of autobiographical memory. In M. L. Courage & N. Cowan (Eds.), *The development of memory in infancy and childhood* (pp. 177–196). New York, NY: Psychology Press.

Howe, N., Recchia, H., Della Porta, S., & Funamoto, A. (2012). "The driver doesn't sit, he stands up like the Flintstones!": Sibling teaching during teacher-directed and self-guided tasks. *Journal of Cognition & Development, 13*(2), 208-231. doi:10.1080/15248372.2011.577703

Howell, J. C. (2000, August). *Youth gang programs and strategies*. Washington, DC: U.S. Department of Justice, Office of Juvenile Justice and Delinquency Prevention.

Howell, J. C., & Lynch, J. P. (2000, August). Youth gangs in schools. *Juvenile Justice Bulletin* (OJJDP Publication NCJ-183015). Washington, DC: U.S. Department of Justice, Office of Juvenile Justice and Delinquency Prevention.

Howes, C. (1988). The peer interactions of young children. *Monographs of the Society for Research in Child Development, 53*(1, Serial No. 217).

Howes, C. (1999). Attachment relationships in the context of multiple caregivers. In J. Cassidy & P. R. Shaver (Eds.), *Handbook of attachment: Theory, research, and clinical applications* (pp. 671–687). New York, NY: Guilford Press.

Howes, C., & Matheson, C. C. (1992). Sequences in the development of competent play with peers: Social and social-pretend play. *Developmental Psychology, 28,* 961–974.

Howes, C., & Ritchie, S. (1998). Changes in child–teacher relationships in a therapeutic preschool program. *Early Education and Development, 9,* 411–422.

Howes, C., Fuligni, A., Hong, S., Huang, Y., & Lara-Cinisomo, S. (2013). The preschool instructional context and child–teacher relationships. *Early Education & Development, 24*(3), 273–291. doi:10.1080/10409289.2011.649664

Howes, C., Smith, E., & Galinsky, E. (1995). *The Florida child care quality improvement study*. New York, NY: Families and Work Institute.

Howie, J. D. (2002, April). *Effects of audience, gender, and achievement level on adolescent students' communicated attributions and affect in response to academic success and failure*. Paper presented at the annual meeting of the American Educational Research Association, New Orleans, LA.

Hoyte, F., Torr, J., & Degotardi, S. (2014). The language of friendship: Genre in the conversations of preschool children. *Journal of Early Childhood Research, 12*(1), 20–34. doi:10.1177/1476718X13492941

Hrabok, M., & Kerns, K. A. (2010). The development of self-regulation: A neuropsychological perspective. In B. W. Sokol, U. Müeller, J. I. M. Carpendale, A. R. Young, & G. Iarocci (Eds.), *Self and social regulation: Social interaction and the development of social understanding and executive functions* (pp. 129–154). New York, NY: Oxford University Press.

Hromek, R., & Roffey, S. (2009). Promoting social and emotional learning with games: "It's fun and we learn things." *Simulation and Gaming, 40*(5), 626–644.

Huang, B. (2014). The effects of age on second language grammar and speech production. *Journal of Psycholinguistic Research, 43*(4), 397-420. doi:10.1007/s10936-013-9261-7

Huang, C. Y., Costeines, J., Kaufman, J. S., & Ayala, C. (2013). Parenting stress, social support, and depression for ethnic minority adolescent mothers: Impact on child development. *Journal of Child and Family Studies.* doi:10.1007/s10826-013-9807-1

Huang, Y., Hsu, C., Su, Y., & Liu, C. (2014). Empowering classroom observation with an e-book reading behavior monitoring system using sensing technologies. *Interacting With Computers, 26*(4), 372-387.

Hubbard, J. A., Morrow, M. T., Romano, L. J., & McAuliffe, M. D. (2010). The role of anger in children's reactive versus proactive aggression: Review of findings, issues of measurement, and implications for intervention. In W. F. Arsenio & E. A. Lemerise (Eds.), *Emotions, aggression, and morality in children: Bridging development and psychopathology* (pp. 201–217). Washington, DC: American Psychological Association. doi:10.1037/12129-01

Hubbard, T. L. (2013). Phenomenal causality II: Integration and implication. *Axiomathes: An International Journal in Ontology & Cognitive Systems, 23*(3), 485–524. doi:10.1007/s10516-012-9200-5

Hubel, D., & Wiesel, T. (1965). Binocular interaction in striate cortex of kittens reared with artificial squint. *Journal of Neurophysiology, 28,* 1041–1059.

Hudley, A. H. C. (2009). African American English. In H. A. Neville, B. M. Tynes, & S. O. Utsey (Eds.), *Handbook of African American psychology* (pp. 199–210).Thousand Oaks, CA: Sage.

Hudley, A. H. C., & Mallinson, C. (2011). *Understanding English language variation in U.S. schools*. New York, NY: Teachers College Press.

Hudson, J. A., & Mayhew, E. M. Y. (2009). The development of memory for recurring events. In M. L. Courage & N. Cowan (Eds.), *The development of memory in infancy and childhood* (pp. 69–91). New York, NY: Psychology Press.

Hudson, J., Lester, K., Lewis, C., Tropeano, M., Creswell, C., Collier, D., et al. (2013). Predicting outcomes following cognitive behaviour therapy in child anxiety disorders: the influence of genetic, demographic and clinical information. *Journal of Child Psychology & Psychiatry, 54*(10), 1086–1094.

Huebner, A. J., & Mancini, J. A. (2005). *Adjustment among adolescents in military families when a parent is deployed: A final report submitted to the Military Family Research Institute and Department of Defense Quality of Life Office. Falls Church: Virginia Tech Department of Human Development*. Falls Church, VA: Virginia Tech Department of Human Development. Retrieved from http://www.juvenilecouncil.gov/materials/june_8_2007/MFRI%20final%20report%20JUNE%202005.pdf

Huebner, C. E., & Payne, K. (2010). Home support for emergent literacy: Follow-up of a community-based implementation of dialogic reading. *Journal of Applied Developmental Psychology, 31*(3), 195–201.

Huennekens, M. E., & Xu, Y. (2010). Effects of a cross-linguistic storybook intervention on the second language development of two preschool English language learners. *Early Childhood Education Journal, 38*(1), 19–26.

Huesmann, L. R., Dubow, E. F., & Boxer, P. (2011). The transmission of aggressiveness across generations: Biological, contextual, and social learning processes. In P. R. Shaver & M. Mikulincer (Eds.), *Human aggression and violence: Causes, manifestations, and consequences. Herzilya series on personality and social psychology* (pp. 123–142). Washington, DC: American Psychological Association. doi:10.1037/12346-007

Hufton, N., Elliott, J., & Illushin, L. (2002). Achievement motivation across cultures: Some puzzles and their implications for future research. *New Directions for Child and Adolescent Development, 96,* 65–85.

Hughes, D. (2003). Correlates of African American and Latino parents' messages to children about ethnicity and race: A comparative study of racial socialization. *American Journal of Community Psychology, 31,* 15–33.

Hughes, F. P. (2010). *Children, play, and development* (4th ed.). Los Angeles, CA: Sage.

Hughes, J., & Kwok, O. (2007). Influence of student–teacher and parent–teacher relationships on lower achieving readers' engagement and achievement in the primary grades. *Journal of Educational Psychology, 99,* 39–51.

Huizink, A. C., Mulder, E. J. H., & Buitelaar, J. K. (2004). Prenatal stress and risk for psychopathology: Special effects or induction of general susceptibility? *Psychological Bulletin, 130,* 115–142.

Hulit, L. M., & Howard, M. R. (2006). *Born to talk* (4th ed.). Boston, MA: Allyn & Bacon.

Hulme, C., & Snowling, M. J. (2013). Learning to read: What we know and what we need to understand better. *Child Development Perspectives, 7*(1), 1–5. doi:10.1111/cdep.12005

Humphreys, A. P., & Smith, P. K. (1987). Rough-and-tumble play, friendship, and dominance in school children: Evidence for continuity and change with age. *Child Development, 58,* 201–212.

Humphreys, C., Lowe, P., & Williams, S. (2008). Sleep disruption and domestic violence: Exploring the interconnections between mothers and children. *Child and Family Social Work, 14,* 6–14.

Hunninus, S., & Bekkering, H. (2010). The early development of object knowledge: A study of infants' visual anticipations during action observation. *Developmental Psychology, 46*(2), 446–454.

Huotilainen, M. (2013). A new dimension on foetal language learning. *Acta Paediatrica, 102*(2), 102–103. doi:10.1111/apa.12122

Hursh, D. (2007). Assessing No Child Left Behind and the rise of neoliberal education policies. *American Educational Research Journal, 44,* 493–518.

Husman, J., & Freeman, B. (1999, April). *The effect of perceptions of instrumentality on intrinsic motivation.* Paper presented at the annual meeting of the American Educational Research Association, Montreal, Canada.

Hussong, A., Chassin, L., & Hicks, R. (1999, April). *The elusive relation between negative affect and adolescent substance use: Does it exist?* Paper presented at the biennial meeting of the Society for Research in Child Development, Albuquerque, NM.

Huston, A. C., Donnerstein, E., Fairchild, H., Feshbach, N. D., Katz, P. A., Murray, J. P., et al. (1992). *Big world, small screen: The role of television in American society.* Lincoln, NE: University of Nebraska Press.

Hutchins, D. J., Greenfield, M. D., Epstein, J. L., Sanders, G., & Galindo, C. L. (2012). *Multicultural partnerships: Involve all families.* Larchmont, NY: Eye on Education.

Hutman, T., & Dapretto, M. (2009). The emergence of empathy during infancy. *Cognition, Brain, Behavior, 13*(4), 367–390.

Huttenlocher, J., Jordan, N. C., & Levine, S. C. (1994). A mental model for early arithmetic. *Journal of Experimental Psychology: General, 123,* 284–296.

Huttenlocher, J., Newcombe, N., & Vasilyeva, M. (1999). Spatial scaling in young children. *Psychological Science, 10,* 393–398.

Huttenlocher, P. R. (1990). Morphometric study of human cerebral cortex development. *Neuropsychologia, 28,* 517–527.

Hwang, W.-C. (2006). Acculturative family distancing: Theory, research, and clinical practice. *Psychotherapy: Theory, Research, Practice, Training, 43,* 397–409.

Hyde, C., & Wilson, P. H. (2011). Dissecting online control in developmental coordination disorder: A kinematic analysis of double-step reaching. *Brain and Cognition, 75*(3), 232–241. doi:10.1016/j.bandc.2010.12.004

Hyde, J. S., Mezulis, A. H., & Abramson, L. Y. (2008). The ABCs of depression: Integrating affective, biological, and cognitive models to explain the emergence of the gender difference in depression. *Psychological Review, 115*(2), 291–313.

Hyde, K. L., & Peretz, I. (2004). Brains that are out of tune but in time. *Psychological Science, 15,* 356–360.

Hye-Kyung, K. (2014). Influence of culture and community perceptions on birth and perinatal care of immigrant women: Doulas' perspective. *Journal of Perinatal Education, 23*(1), 25-32. doi:10.1891/1058-1243.23.1.25

Hyman, I., Kay, B., Tabori, A., Weber, M., Mahon, M., & Cohen, I. (2006). Bullying: Theory, research, and interventions. In C. M. Evertson & C. S. Weinstein (Eds.), *Handbook of classroom management: Research, practice, and contemporary issues* (pp. 855–884). Mahwah, NJ: Erlbaum.

Hynd, C. (1998). Conceptual change in a high school physics class. In B. Guzzetti & C. Hynd (Eds.), *Perspectives on conceptual change: Multiple ways to understand knowing and learning in a complex world* (pp. 27–36). Mahwah, NJ: Erlbaum.

Hyson, M. C., Hirsh-Pasek, K., Rescorla, L., Cone, J., & Martell-Boinske, L. (1991). Ingredients of parental "pressure" in early childhood. *Journal of Applied Developmental Psychology, 12*(3), 347–365.

Hyvönen, P., & Kangas, M. (2007). From bogey mountains to funny houses: Children's desires for play environment. *Australian Journal of Early Childhood, 32*(3), 39–47.

Igoa, C. (1995). *The inner world of the immigrant child.* Mahwah, NJ: Erlbaum.

Iivonen, S. S., & Sääkslahti, A. K. (2014). Preschool children's fundamental motor skills: a review of significant determinants. *Early Child Development & Care, 184*(7), 1107-1126. doi:10.1080/03004430.2013.837897

Imhof, M. (2001, March). *In the eye of the beholder: Children's perception of good and poor listening behavior.* Paper presented at the annual meeting of the International Listening Association, Chicago.

Immordino-Yang, M. H., & Damasio, A. (2007). We feel, therefore we learn: The relevance of affective and social neuroscience to education. *Mind, Brain, and Education, 1,* 3–10.

Inhelder, B., & Piaget, J. (1958). *The growth of logical thinking from childhood to adolescence* (A. Parsons & S. Milgram, Trans.). New York, NY: Basic Books.

Insana, S. P., Foley, K. P., Montgomery-Downs, H. E., Kolko, D. J., & McNeil, C. B. (2013). Children exposed to intimate partner violence demonstrate disturbed sleep and impaired functional outcomes. *Psychological Trauma: Theory, Research, Practice, and Policy.* doi:10.1037/a0033108

Institute of Education Sciences. (2006). *Character education.* Retrieved from http://ies.ed.gov/ncee/wwc/reports/character_education/index.asp

Intrator, S. M., & Siegel, D. (2008). Project Coach: Youth development and academic achievement through sport. *Journal of Physical Education, Recreation, and Dance, 79*(7), 17–23.

Intravia, J., Wolff, K. T., Stewart, E. A., & Simons, R. L. (2014). Neighborhood-level differences in police discrimination and subcultural violence: A multilevel examination of adopting the code of the street. *Journal of Crime & Justice, 37*(1), 42–60. doi:10.1080/0735648X.2013.832480

Irujo, S. (1988). An introduction to intercultural differences and similarities in nonverbal communication. In J. S. Wurzel (Ed.), *Toward multiculturalism: A reader in multicultural education.* Yarmouth, ME: Intercultural Press.

Isabella, R. A., & Belsky, J. (1991). Interactional synchrony and the origins of infant-mother attachment: A replication study. *Child Development, 62,* 373–384.

Iselin, A., Mulvey, E., Loughran, T., Chung, H., & Schubert, C. (2012). A longitudinal examination of serious adolescent offenders' perceptions of chances for success and engagement in behaviors accomplishing goals. *Journal of Abnormal Child Psychology, 40*(2), 237–249.

Isik-Ercan, Z., Zeynep Inan, H., Nowak, J. A., & Kim, B. (2014). "We put on the glasses and Moon comes closer!" Urban second graders exploring the earth, the sun and moon through 3D technologies in a science and literacy unit. *International Journal of Science Education, 36*(1), 129–156. doi:10.1080/09500693.2012.739718

Israel, M., Maynard, K., & Williamson, P. (2013). Promoting literacy- Embedded, authentic STEM Instruction for students with disabilities and other struggling learners. *Teaching Exceptional Children, 45*(4), 18–25.

Iuculano, T., Rosenberg-Lee, M., Supekar, K., Lynch, C. J., Khouzam, A., Phillips, J., Uddin, L., & Menon, V. (2014). Brain organization underlying superior mathematical abilities in children with autism. *Biological Psychiatry, 75*(3), 223–230. doi:10.1016/j.biopsych.2013.06.018

Iyengar, S. S., & Lepper, M. R. (1999). Rethinking the value of choice: A cultural perspective on intrinsic motivation. *Journal of Personality and Social Psychology, 76,* 349–366.

Iyer, S., & Oiler, D. (2008). Prelinguistic vocal development in infants with typical hearing and infants with severe-to-profound hearing loss. *Volta Review, 108*(2), 115–138.

Järvelä, S., Järvenoja, H., & Malmberg, J. (2012). How elementary school students' motivation is connected to self-regulation. *Educational Research and Evaluation, 18*(1), 65–84. doi:10.1080/13803611.2011.641269

Jackson, M. (2013). The special educational needs of adolescents living with chronic illness: a literature review. *International Journal of Inclusive Education, 17*(6), 543–554. doi:10.1080/13603116.2012.676085

Jacobs, J. E., Davis-Kean, P., Bleeker, M., Eccles, J. S., & Malanchuk, O. (2005). "I can, but I don't want to": The impact of parents, interests, and activities on gender differences in math. In A. M. Gallagher & J. C. Kaufman (Eds.), *Gender differences in mathematics: An integrative psychological approach* (pp. 246–263). Cambridge, England: Cambridge University Press.

Jacobs, J. E., Lanza, S., Osgood, D. W., Eccles, J. S., & Wigfield, A. (2002). Changes in children's self-competence and values: Gender and domain differences across grades one through twelve. *Child Development, 73,* 509–527.

Jacobs, J. E., Lanza, S., Osgood, D. W., Eccles, J. S., & Wigfield, A. (2002). Changes in children's self-competence and values: Gender and domain differences across grades one through twelve. *Child Development, 73,* 509–527.

Jacobs, K., & Sillars, A. (2012). Sibling support during post-divorce adjustment: An idiographic analysis of support forms, functions, and relationship types. *Journal of Family Communication, 12*(2), 167–187. doi:10.1080/15267431.2011.584056

Jacobsen, B., Lowery, B., & DuCette, J. (1986). Attributions of learning disabled children. *Journal of Educational Psychology, 78,* 59–64.

Jadcherla, S. R., Gupta, A., Stoner, E., Fernandez, S., & Shaker, R. (2007). Pharyngeal swallowing: Defining pharyngeal and supper esophageal sphincter relationships in human neonates. *Journal of Pediatrics, 151,* 597–603.

Jaddoe, V. W. V. (2009). Antenatal education programmes: Do they work? *Lancet, 374*(9693), 863–864.

Jago, C. (2014). Writing Is TAUGHT Not CAUGHT. *Educational Leadership, 71*(7), 16–21.

Jahromi, L., Guimond, A., Umaña-Taylor, A., Updegraff, K., & Toomey, R. (2014). Family Context, Mexican-Origin Adolescent Mothers' Parenting Knowledge, and Children's Subsequent Developmental Outcomes. *Child Development, 85*(2), 593-609.

Jalongo, M. R. (2008). *Learning to listen, listening to learn: Building essential skills in young children.* Washington, DC: National Association for the Education of Young Children Press.

Jalongo, M. R., Isenberg, J. P., & Gerbracht, G. (1995). *Teachers' stories: From personal narrative to professional insight.* San Francisco, CA: Jossey-Bass.

Jambon, M., & Smetana, J. G. (2014). Moral complexity in middle childhood: Children's evaluations of necessary harm. *Developmental Psychology, 50*(1), 22–33. doi:10.1037/a0032992

Janssen, A., & Erickson-Schroth, L. (2013). A new generation of gender: Learning patience from our gender nonconforming patients. *Journal of The American Academy of Child & Adolescent Psychiatry, 52*(10), 995–997. doi:10.1016/j.jaac.2013.07.010

Janssen, M., Bakker, J. A., Bosman, A. T., Rosenberg, K., & Leseman, P. M. (2012). Differential trust between parents and teachers of children from low-income and immigrant backgrounds. *Educational Studies, 38*(4), 383–396. doi:10.1080/03055698.2011.643103

Janssen, P. A., Saxell, L., Page, L. A., Klein, M. C., Liston, R. M., & Shoo, K. L. (2009). Outcomes of planned home birth with registered midwife versus planned hospital birth with midwife or physician. *Canadian Medical Association Journal, 181*(6–7), 377–383.

Jarrold, C., & Citroën, R. (2013). Reevaluating key evidence for the development of rehearsal: Phonological similarity effects in children are subject to proportional scaling artifacts. *Developmental Psychology, 49*(5), 837–847. doi:10.1037/a0028771

Jaswal, V. K., & Dodson, C. S. (2009). Metamemory development: Understanding the role of similarity in false memories. *Child Development, 80*(3), 629–635.

Jaswal, V. K., & Markman, E. M. (2001). Learning proper and common names in inferential versus ostensive contexts. *Child Development, 72*, 768–786.

Jeffrey, R. (2009/2010). First steps to a healthier school. *Educational Leadership, 67*(4), 82–83.

Jelalian, E., Wember, Y. M., Bungeroth, H., & Birmaher, V. (2007). Practitioner review: Bridging review: Bridging the gap between research and clinical practice in pediatric obesity. *Journal of Child Psychology and Psychiatry, 48*, 115–127.

Jenkins, J. M., Turrell, S. L., Kogushi, Y., Lollis, S., & Ross, H. S. (2003). A longitudinal investigation of the dynamics of mental state talk in families. *Child Development, 74*, 905–920.

Jenkins, S., Bax, M., & Hart, H. (1980). Behavior problems in preschool children. *Journal of Child Psychology and Psychiatry, 21*, 5–18.

Jenlink, C. L. (1994, April). *Music: A lifeline for the self-esteem of at-risk students.* Paper presented at the annual meeting of the American Educational Research Association, New Orleans, LA.

Jenny, S., & Armstrong, T. (2013). Distance running and the elementary-age child. (cover story). JO-PERD: *The Journal of Physical Education, Recreation & Dance, 84*(3), 17–25.

Jensen, A. R. (2007). Book review: *Howard Gardner under fire: The rebel psychologist faces his critics. Intelligence, 36*, 96–97.

Jensen, M. M. (2005). *Introduction to emotional and behavioral disorders: Recognizing and managing problems in the classroom.* Upper Saddle River, NJ: Merrill Prentice Hall.

Jeon, L., Buettner, C. K., & Hur, E. (2014). Examining pre-school classroom quality in a statewide quality rating and improvement system. *Child & Youth Care Forum, 43*(4), 469–487. doi:10.1007/s10566-014-9248-z

Jeong, Y., Levine, S. C., & Huttenlocher, J. (2007). The development of proportional reasoning: Effect of continuous versus discrete quantities. *Journal of Cognition and Development, 8*(2), 237–256.

Jerome, E. M., Hamre, B. K., & Pianta, R. C. (2009). Teacher–child relationships from kindergarten to sixth grade: Early childhood predictors of teacher-perceived conflict and closeness. *Social Development, 18*(4), 915–945. doi:10.1111/sode.2009.18.issue-410.1111/j.1467-9507.2008.00508.x

Jessor, R., & Jessor, S. L. (1977). *Problem behavior and psychosocial development: A longitudinal study of youth.* San Diego, CA: Academic Press.

Jia, J., Chen, Y., Ding, Z., Bai, Y., Yang, B., Li, M., & Qi, J. (2013). Effects of an intelligent web-based English instruction system on students' academic performance. *Journal of Computer Assisted Learning, 29*(6), 556–568. doi:10.1111/jcal.12016

Jimenez, B., & Kemmery, M. (2013). Building the early numeracy skills of students with moderate intellectual disability. *Education & Training*

In Autism & Developmental Disabilities, 48(4), 479–490.

Jimerson, S., Egeland, B., & Teo, A. (1999). A longitudinal study of achievement trajectories: Factors associated with change. *Journal of Educational Psychology, 91*, 116–126.

Jin, M., Jacobvitz, D., Hazen, N., & Jung, S. (2012). Maternal sensitivity and infant attachment security in Korea: Cross-cultural validation of the Strange Situation. *Attachment & Human Development, 14*(1), 33–44. doi:10.1080/14616734.2012.636656

Jing, J. (2013). Teaching English reading through MI theory in primary schools. *English Language Teaching, 6*(1), 132–140. doi:10.5539/elt.v6n1p132

Jipson, J. L., & Callanan, M. A. (2003). Mother-child conversation and children's understanding of biological and nonbiological changes in size. *Child Development, 74*, 629–644.

Joanisse, M. F. (2007). Phonological deficits and developmental language impairments: Evidence from connectionist models. In D. Mareschal, S. Sirois, G. Westermann, & M. H. Johnson (Eds.), *Neuro-constructivism: Vol. 2. Perspectives and prospects* (pp. 205–229). Oxford, England: Oxford University Press.

John, O. P., Caspi, A., Robins, R. W., Moffitt, T. E., & Stouthamer-Loeber, M. (1994). The "Little Five": Exploring the five-factor model of personality in adolescent boys. *Child Development, 65*, 160–178.

Johnson, D. (2013). Technology skills every teacher needs. *Educational Leadership, 70*(6), 84–85.

Johnson, D. W., Johnson, R., Dudley, B., Ward, M., & Magnuson, D. (1995). The impact of peer mediation training on the management of school and home conflicts. *American Educational Research Journal, 32*, 829–844.

Johnson, J. S., & Newport, E. L. (1989). Critical period effects in second language learning: The influence of maturational state on acquisition of English as a second language. *Cognitive Psychology, 21*, 60–99.

Johnson, K. E., Alexander, J. M., Spencer, S., Leibham, M. E., & Neitzel, C. (2004). Factors associated with the early emergence of intense interests within conceptual domains. *Cognitive Development, 19*, 325–343.

Johnson, S. B., Riley, A. W., Granger, D. A., & Riis, J. (2013). The science of early life toxic stress for pediatric practice and advocacy. *Pediatrics, 131*(2), 319–327. doi:10.1542/peds.2012-0469

Johnson, S. C., Dweck, C. S., Chen, F. S., Stern, H. L., Ok, S., & Barth, M. (2010). At the intersection of social and cognitive development: Internal working models of attachment in infancy. *Cognitive Science, 34*(5), 807–825.

Johnson, S., & Fiarman, S. (2012). The potential of peer review. *Educational Leadership, 70*(3), 20–25.

Johnson, W., Deary, I. J., & Iacono, W. G. (2009). Genetic and environmental transactions underlying educational attainment. *Intelligence, 37*, 466–478.

Johnston, D. (1995). Jailed mothers. In K. Gabel & D. Johnston (Eds.), *Children of incarcerated parents* (pp. 41–55). New York, NY: Lexington Books.

Johnston, D. (2012). Services for children of incarcerated parents. *Family Court Review, 50*(1), 91–105. doi:10.1111/j.1744-1617.2011.01431.x

Johnston, J. R. (1997). Specific language impairment, cognition and the biological basis of language. In M. Gopnik (Ed.), *The inheritance and innateness of grammars* (pp. 161–180). New York, NY: Oxford University Press.

Johnston, L. D., O'Malley, P. M., Bachman, J. G., & Schulenberg, J. E. (2007). *Monitoring the Future national results on adolescent drug use: Overview of key findings, 2006* (NIH Publication No.

07-6202). Bethesda, MD: National Institute on Drug Abuse.

Johnston, P., & Afflerbach, P. (1985). The process of constructing main ideas from text. *Cognition and Instruction, 2*, 207–232.

Jones, L. (2012). Measuring resiliency and its predictors in recently discharged foster youth. *Child & Adolescent Social Work Journal, 29*(6), 515–533. doi:10.1007/s10560-012-0275-z

Jones, S., Bub, K., & Raver, C. (2013). Unpacking the black box of the Chicago School Readiness Project Intervention: The mediating roles of teacher–child relationship quality and self-regulation. *Early Education & Development, 24*(7), 1043–1064. doi:10.1080/10409289.2013.825188

Jordan, A. B. (2005). Learning to use books and television. *American Behavioral Scientist, 48*(5), 523–538.

Jordan, N. C., Glutting, J., & Ramineni, C. (2010). The importance of number sense to mathematics achievement in first and third grades. *Learning and Individual Differences, 20*(2), 82–88.

Jordan, N. C., Hanich, L. B., & Kaplan, D. (2003). A longitudinal study of mathematical competencies in children with specific mathematics difficulties versus children with comorbid mathematics and reading difficulties. *Child Development, 74*, 834–850.

Jorde, L. B., Carey, J. C., & Bamshad, M. J. (2010). *Medical genetics* (4th ed.). Philadelphia, PA: Mosby Elsevier.

Joseph, N. (2010). Metacognition needed: Teaching middle and high school students to develop strategic learning skills. *Preventing School Failure, 54*(2), 99–103.

Josephson, A. M. (2013). Family intervention as a developmental psychodynamic therapy. *Child and Adolescent Psychiatric Clinics Of North America, 22*(2), 241–260. doi:10.1016/j.chc.2012.12.006

Joshi, C., Torvaldsen, S., Hodgson, R., & Hayen, A. (2014). Factors associated with the use and quality of antenatal care in Nepal: a population-based study using the demographic and health survey data. *BMC Pregnancy & Childbirth, 14*(1), 1-21. doi:10.1186/1471-2393-14-94

Josselson, R. (1988). The embedded self: I and Thou revisited. In D. K. Lapsley & F. C. Power (Eds.), *Self, ego, and identity: Integrative approaches* (pp. 91–106). New York, NY: Springer-Verlag.

Jovanovic, J., & King, S. S. (1998). Boys and girls in the performance-based science classroom: Who's doing the performing? *American Educational Research Journal, 35*, 477–496.

Juel, C. (1991). Beginning reading. In R. Barr, M. L. Kamil, P. B. Mosenthal, & P. Pearson (Eds.), *Handbook of reading research* (Vol. 2, pp. 759–788). Hillsdale, NJ: Erlbaum.

Julian, M. M. (2013). Age at adoption from institutional care as a window into the lasting effects of early experiences. *Clinical Child and Family Psychology Review.* doi:10.1007/s10567-013-0130-6

Jung, J., & Recchia, S. (2013). Scaffolding infants' play through empowering and individualizing teaching practices. *Early Education and Development, 24*(6), 829–850. doi:10.1080/10409289.2013.744683

Juon, H., Evans-Polce, R., & Ensminger, M. (2013). Early life conditions of overall and cause-specific mortality among inner-city African Americans. *American Journal of Public Health, 103*(6), e1–e7. doi:10. 2105/AJPH.2013.301228

Jusczyk, P. W. (1995). Language acquisition: Speech sounds and phonological development. In J. L. Miller & P. D. Eimas (Eds.), *Handbook of perception and cognition: Vol. 11. Speech, language, and communication* (pp. 263-301). Orlando, FL: Academic Press.

Jusczyk, P. W. (1997). Finding and remembering words: Some beginnings by English-learning infants. *Current Directions in Psychological Science, 6,* 170–174.

Juster, N. (1961). *The phantom tollbooth.* New York, NY: Random House.

Justice, J. (1984). Can socio-cultural information improve health planning? A case study of Nepal's assistant nurse-midwife. *Social Science and Medicine, 19*(3), 193–198.

Juvonen, J. (1991). Deviance, perceived responsibility, and negative peer reactions. *Developmental Psychology, 27,* 672–681.

Juvonen, J. (2000). The social functions of attributional face-saving tactics among early adolescents. *Educational Psychology Review, 12,* 15–32.

Juvonen, J. (2006). Sense of belonging, social bonds, and school functioning. In P. A. Alexander & P. H. Winne (Eds.), *Handbook of educational psychology* (2nd ed., pp. 655–674). Mahwah, NJ: Erlbaum.

Juvonen, J., & Graham, S. (2014). Bullying in schools: The power of bullies and the plight of victims. *Annual Review of Psychology, 65*(1), 159–185.

Juvonen, J., Nishina, A., & Graham, S. (2000). Peer harassment, psychological adjustment, and school functioning in early adolescence. *Journal of Educational Psychology, 92,* 349–359.

Kärtner, J., Keller, H., & Chaudhary, N. (2010). Cognitive and social influences on early prosocial behavior in two sociocultural contexts. *Developmental Psychology, 46*(4), 905–914. doi:10.1037/a0019718

Kağitçibaşi, Ç. (2007). *Family, self, and human development across cultures: Theory and applications* (2nd ed.). Mahwah, NJ: Erlbaum.

Kagan, J. (1981). *The second year: The emergence of self-awareness.* Cambridge, MA: Harvard University Press.

Kagan, J. (1984). *The nature of the child.* New York, NY: Basic Books.

Kagan, J. (1984). *The nature of the child.* New York, NY: Basic Books.

Kagan, J. (2010). Emotions and temperament. In M. H. Bornstein (Ed.), *Handbook of cultural developmental science* (pp. 175–194). New York, NY: Psychology Press.

Kagan, J. K., & Fox, N. A. (2006). Biology, culture, and temperamental biases. In W. Damon & R. M. Lerner (Eds. in Chief) & N. Eisenberg (Vol. Ed.), *Handbook of child psychology, Vol. 3. Social, emotional, and personality development* (6th ed., pp. 167–225). Hoboken, NJ: Wiley.

Kagan, J., Snidman, N., Vahn, V., & Towsley, S. (2007). The preservation of two infant temperaments into adolescence. *Monographs of the Society for Research in Child Development, 72,* 1–80.

Kahlenberg, S. G., & Hein, M. M. (2010). Progression on Nickelodeon? Gender-role stereotypes in toy commercials. *Sex Roles, 62*(11–12), 830–847. doi:10.1007/s11199-009-9653-1

Kail, R. (1990). *The development of memory in children* (3rd ed.). New York, NY: Freeman.

Kail, R. V. (2013). Influences of credibility of testimony and strength of statistical evidence on children's and adolescents' reasoning. *Journal of Experimental Child Psychology, 116*(3), 747-754. doi:10.1016/j.jecp.2013.04.004

Kail, R. V., McBride-Chang, C., Ferrer, E., Cho, J., & Shu, H. (2013). Cultural differences in the development of processing speed. *Developmental Science, 16*(3), 476–483. doi:10.1111/desc.12039

Kalashnikova, M., & Mattock, K. (2014). Maturation of executive functioning skills in early sequential bilingualism. *International Journal of Bilingual Education & Bilingualism, 17*(1), 111–123. doi:10.1080/13670050.2012.746284

Kamps, D. M. (2002). Preventing problems by improving behavior. In B. Algozzine & P. Kay (Eds.), *Preventing problem behaviors: A handbook of successful prevention strategies* (pp. 11–36). Thousand Oaks, CA, US: Corwin Press.

Kan, K., Wicherts, J. M., Dolan, C. V., & van der Maas, H. J. (2013). On the nature and nurture of intelligence and specific cognitive abilities: The more heritable, the more culture dependent. *Psychological Science, 24*(12), 2420–2428. doi:10.1177/0956797613493292

Kanazawa, S. (2012). Intelligence, birth order, and family size. *Personality and Social Psychology Bulletin, 38*(9), 1157–1164. doi:10.1177/0146167212445911

Kanner, A. D., Feldman, S. S., Weinberger, D. A., & Ford, M. E. (1987). Uplifts, hassles, and adaptational outcomes in early adolescents. *Journal of Early Adolescence, 7,* 371–394.

Kapka, S. (2013). A Hospital-Based, Healthy Pregnancy Promotion Program to Empower the Socially at Risk: The Healthy Beginnings Program. Journal of Obstetric, Gynecologic & Neonatal Nursing, 42S4. doi:10.1111/1552-6909.12050

Kaplan, A., & Midgley, C. (1997). The effect of achievement goals: Does level of perceived academic competence make a difference? *Contemporary Educational Psychology, 22,* 415–435.

Kaplan, J. S. (2012). The effects of shared environment on adult intelligence: A critical review of adoption, twin, and MZA studies. *Developmental Psychology, 48*(5), 1292–1298. doi:10.1037/a0028133

Kapp-Simon, K., & Simon, D. J. (1991). Meeting the challenge: Social skills training for teens with special needs. *Connections: The Newsletter of the National Center for Youth and Disabilities, 2*(2), 1–5.

Kar, B., & Srinivasan, N. (2013). Development of selection and control. In B. Kar (Ed.), *Cognition and brain development: Converging evidence from various methodologies* (pp. 11–32). Washington, DC: American Psychological Association. doi:10.1037/14043-002

Karabenick, S. A., & Sharma, R. (1994). Seeking academic assistance as a strategic learning resource. In P. R. Pintrich, D. R. Brown, & C. E. Weinstein (Eds.), *Student motivation, cognition, and learning: Essays in honor of Wilbert J. McKeachie.* Hillsdale, NJ: Erlbaum.

Karcher, M. (2009). Increases in academic connectedness and self-esteem among high-school students who serve as cross-age peer mentors. *Professional School Counseling, 12*(4), 292–299.

Karmiloff-Smith, A. (1979). Language development after five. In P. Fletcher & M. Garman (Eds.), *Language acquisition: Studies in first language development (pp. 307-322).* Cambridge, England: Cambridge University Press.

Karmiloff-Smith, A. (2012). From constructivism to neuroconstructivism: The activity-dependent structuring of the human brain. In E. Martí & C. Rodríguez (Eds.), *After Piaget* (pp. 1–14). Piscataway, NJ: Transaction Publishers.

Karmiloff-Smith, A. (2013). From constructivism to neuroconstructivism: Did we still fall into the foundationalism/encodingism trap? Commentary on "Stepping off the pendulum: Why only an action-based approach can transcend the nativist–empiricist debate" by J. Allen and M. Bickhard. *Cognitive Development, 28*(2), 154-158. doi:10.1016/j.cogdev.2013.01.007

Karniol, R. (2010). *Social development as preference management: How infants, children, and parents get what they want from one another.* New York, NY: Cambridge University Press.

Karpov, Y. V., & Haywood, H. C. (1998). Two ways to elaborate Vygotsky's concept of mediation: Implications for instruction. *American Psychologist, 53,* 27–36.

Kaslow, F. W. (2000). Families experiencing divorce. In W. C. Nichols, M. A. Pace-Nichols, D. S. Becvar, & Y. A. Napier (Eds.), *Handbook of family development and intervention* (pp. 341–368). New York, NY: Wiley.

Katkovsky, W., Crandall, V. C., & Good, S. (1967). Parental antecedents of children's beliefs in internal-external control of reinforcements in intellectual achievement situations. *Child Development, 38,* 765–776.

Katz, E. W., & Brent, S. B. (1968). Understanding connectives. *Journal of Verbal Learning and Verbal Behavior, 7,* 501–509.

Katz, L. F., & Gottman, J. M. (1991). Marital discord and child outcomes: A social psychophysiological approach. In J. Garber & K. A. Dodge (Eds.), *The development of emotion regulation and dysregulation (pp.129-155).* Cambridge, England: Cambridge University Press.

Katz, S. L., Selman, R. L., & Mason, J. R. (2008). A study of teasing in the real world through the eyes of a practice-inspired researcher. *Educational Action Research, 16*(4), 469–480.

Kaufmann, L. (2008). Discalculia: Neuroscience and education. *Educational Research, 50*(2), 163–175.

Kavšek, M. (2013). The comparator model of infant visual habituation and dishabituation: Recent insights. *Developmental Psychobiology, 55*(8), 793–808. doi:10.1002/dev.21081

Kawabata, Y., Crick, N. R., & Hamaguchi, Y. (2010). The role of culture in relational aggression: Associations with social-psychological adjustment problems in Japanese and US school-aged children. *International Journal of Behavioral Development, 34*(4), 354–362. doi:10.1177/0165025409339151

Kaya, E., & Geban, Ö. (2012). Facilitating conceptual change in rate of reaction concepts using conceptual change oriented instruction. *Education & Science/Egitim Ve Bilim, 37*(163), 216–225.

Kaya, S., & Kablan, Z. (2013). Assessing the relationship between learning strategies and science achievement at the primary school level. *Journal of Baltic Science Education, 12*(4), 525–534.

Kaya, S., & Kablan, Z. (2013). Assessing the relationship between learning strategies and science achievement at the primary school level. *Journal of Baltic Science Education, 12*(4), 525–534.

Kayama, M., & Haight, W. (2013). The experiences of Japanese elementary-school children living with "developmental disabilities": Navigating peer relationships. *Qualitative Social Work: Research And Practice, 12*(5), 555–571. doi:10.1177/1473325012439321

Kazdin, A. E. (1997). Conduct disorder across the lifespan. In S. S. Luthar, J. A. Burack, D. Cicchetti, & J. R. Weisz (Eds.), *Developmental psychopathology: Perspectives on adjustment, risk, and disorder* (pp. 248–272). Cambridge, England: Cambridge University Press.

Kearins, J. M. (1981). Visual spatial memory in Australian Aboriginal children of desert regions. *Cognitive Psychology, 13,* 434–460.

Keating, D. P. (2012). Cognitive and brain development in adolescence. *Enfance, 64*(3), 267–279. doi:10.4074/S0013754512003035

Keefer, K. V., Holden, R. R., & Parker, J. A. (2013). Longitudinal assessment of trait emotional intelligence: Measurement invariance and construct continuity from late childhood to adolescence. *Psychological Assessment, 25*(4), 1255–1272. doi:10.1037/a0033903

Keeley, P. (2012). Food for plants: A bridging concept. *Science & Children, 49*(8), 26–29.

Keenan, J. M., & Meenan, C. E. (2014). Test differences in diagnosing reading comprehension deficits. *Journal of Learning Disabilities, 47*(2), 125–135. doi:10.1177/0022219412439326

Kehoe, C. E., Havighurst, S. S., & Harley, A. E. (2014). Tuning in to teens: Improving parent emotion socialization to reduce youth internalizing difficulties. *Social Development, 23*(2), 413-431. doi:10.1111/sode.12060

Keil, F. C. (1989). *Concepts, kinds, and cognitive development.* Cambridge, MA: MIT Press.

Keil, F. C. (1994). The birth and nurturance of concepts by domains: The origins of concepts of living things. In L. A. Hirschfeld & S. A. Gelman (Eds.), *Mapping the mind: Domain specificity in cognition and culture*. New York, NY: Cambridge University Press.

Keil, F. C. (2010). The feasibility of folk science. *Cognitive Science, 34*(5), 826–862. doi:10.1111/j.1551-6709.2010.01108.x

Keil, F. C. (2012). Does folk science develop? In J. Shrager & S. Carver (Eds.), *The journey from child to scientist: Integrating cognitive development and the education sciences* (pp. 67–86). Washington, DC: American Psychological Association. doi:10.1037/13617-003

Keil, F. C., & Silberstein, C. S. (1996). Schooling and the acquisition of theoretical knowledge. In D. R. Olson & N. Torrance (Eds.), *The handbook of education and human development: New models of learning, teaching, and schooling* (pp. 621-645). Cambridge, MA: Blackwell.

Keir, A. K., & Wilkinson, D. (2013). Towards evidence based medicine for paediatricians. *Archives of Disease in Childhood, 98*(5), 386–388. doi:10.1136/archdischild-2013-303791

Kelemen, D. (1999). Why are rocks pointy? Children's preference for teleological explanations of the natural world. *Developmental Psychology, 35,* 1440–1452.

Kelemen, D. (2004). Are children "intuitive theists"?: Reasoning about purpose and design in nature. *Psychological Science, 15,* 295–301.

Keller, H. (2003). Socialization for competence: Cultural models of infancy. *Human Development, 46,* 288–311.

Keller, H. (2011). Culture and Cognition: Developmental Perspectives. *Journal of Cognitive Education & Psychology, 10*(1), 3–8. doi:10.1891/19458959.10.1.3

Keller, T. A., & Just, M. A. (2009). Altering cortical connectivity: Remediation-induced changes in the white matter of poor readers. *Neuron, 64*(5), 624–631.

Kellogg, R. (1967). *The psychology of children's art.* New York, NY: CRM–Random House.

Kelly, J. B. (2007). Children's living arrangements following separation and divorce: Insights from empirical and clinical research. *Family Process, 46,* 35–52.

Kelly, J. B., & Lamb, M. E. (2000). Using child development research to make appropriate custody and access decisions for young children. *Family and Conciliation Courts Review, 38*(3), 297–311.

Kelly, K., & Bailey, A. L. (2013). Dual development of conversational and narrative discourse: Mother and child interactions during narrative co-construction. *Merrill-Palmer Quarterly, 59*(4), 426–460. doi:10.1353/mpq.2013.0019

Keltikangas-Järvinen, L. L., Jokela, M. M., Hintsanen, M. M., Salo, J. J., Hintsa, T. T., Alatupa, S. S., & Lehtimäki, T. T. (2010). Does genetic background moderate the association between parental education and school achievement? *Genes, Brain & Behavior, 9*(3), 318–324. doi:10.1111/j.1601-183X.2009.00561.x

Kemler Nelson, D. G., Egan, L. C., & Holt, M. B. (2004). When children ask, "What is it?" what do they want to know about artifacts? *Psychological Science, 15,* 384–389.

Kemper, S. (1984). The development of narrative skills: Explanations and entertainments. In S. Kuczaj (Ed.), *Discourse development: Progress in cognitive development research* (pp. 99-122). New York, NY: Springer-Verlag.

Kenneady, D., & Oswalt, S. B. (2014). Is Cass's model of homosexual identity formation relevant to today's society? *American Journal of Sexuality Education, 9*(2), 229–246. doi:10.1080/15546128.2014.900465

Kennedy Root, A. K., & Denham, S. A. (2010). The role of gender in the socialization of emotion: Key concepts and critical issues. In A. Kennedy Root & S. A. Denham (Eds.), *The role of gender in the socialization of emotion: Key concepts and critical issues. New Directions for Child and Adolescent Development, 128,* 1–9. San Francisco, CA: Jossey-Bass.

Kennedy, K., & Romo, H. (2013). "All Colors and Hues": An autoethnography of a multiethnic family's strategies for bilingualism and multiculturalism. *Family Relations, 62*(1), 109–124. doi:10.1111/j.1741-3729.2012.00742.x

Kentucky Department of Education. (2012, November 2). *First results from Unbridled Learning Accountability Model released: College/career readiness is a bright spot in data.* News release No. 12-077. Retrieved from http://education.ky.gov/comm/Documents/R077data.pdf

Keogh, B. K. (2003). *Temperament in the classroom: Understanding individual differences.* Baltimore, MD: Paul H. Brookes.

Keogh, B. K., & MacMillan, D. L. (1996). Exceptionality. In D. C. Berliner & R. C. Calfee (Eds.), *Handbook of educational psychology.* New York, NY: Macmillan.

Kerewsky, W., & Lefstein, L. M. (1982). Young adolescents and their community: A shared responsibility. In L. M. Lefstein et al. (Eds.), *3:00 to 6:00 p.m.: Young adolescents at home and in the community.* Carrboro, NC: Center for Early Adolescence.

Kerns, L. L., & Lieberman, A. B. (1993). *Helping your depressed child.* Rocklin, CA: Prima.

Kersey, K. C., & Masterson, M. L. (2009). Teachers connecting with families: In the best interest of children. *Young Children, 64*(5), 34–38.

Kessels, U., Heyder, A., Latsch, M., & Hannover, B. (2014). How gender differences in academic engagement relate to students' gender identity. *Educational Research, 56*(2), 220–229. doi:10.1080/0131881.2014.898916

Khalid, T. (2010). An integrated inquiry activity in an elementary teaching methods classroom. *Science Activities, 47*(1), 29–34.

Kiang, L., & Fuligni, A. J. (2010). Meaning in life as a mediator of ethnic identity and adjustment among adolescents from Latin, Asian, and European American backgrounds. *Journal of Youth and Adolescence, 39*(11), 1253–1264.

Kienbaum, J., & Wilkening, F. (2009). Children's and adolescents' intuitive judgments about distributive justice: Integrating need, effort, and luck. *European Journal of Developmental Psychology, 6*(4), 481–498.

Kievit, R. A., van Rooijen, H., Wicherts, J. M., Waldorp, L. J., Kan, K., Scholte, H., & Borsboom, D. (2012). Intelligence and the brain: A model-based approach. *Cognitive Neuroscience, 3*(2), 89–97. doi:10.1080/17588928.2011.628383

Killen, M., & Nucci, L. P. (1995). Morality, autonomy, and social conflict. In M. Killen & D. Hart (Eds.), *Morality in everyday life: Developmental perspectives* (pp. 52–86). Cambridge, England: Cambridge University Press.

Killen, M., & Smetana, J. G. (2010). Future directions: Social development in the context of social justice. *Social Development, 19*(3), 642–657. doi:10.1111/j.1467-9507.2009.00548.x

Killen, M., Margie, N. G., & Sinno, S. (2006). Morality in the context of intergroup relationships. In M. Killen & J. G. Smetana (Eds.), *Handbook of moral development* (pp. 155–183). Mahwah, NJ: Erlbaum.

Killen, M., Mulvey, K., & Hitti, A. (2013). Social exclusion in childhood: A developmental intergroup perspective. *Child Development, 84*(3), 772–790. doi:10.1111/cdev.12012

Killip, S., Bennett, J. M., & Chambers, M. D. (2007). Iron deficiency anemia. *American Family Physician, 75,* 671–678.

Kim, D., Solomon, D., & Roberts, W. (1995, April). *Classroom practices that enhance students' sense of community.* Paper presented at the annual meeting of the American Educational Research Association, San Francisco.

Kim, J. (2011). *Relationships among and between ELL status, demographic characteristics, enrollment history, and school persistence (CRESST Report 810).* Los Angeles, CA: University of California, National Center for Research on Evaluation, Standards, and Student Testing (CRESST).

Kim, J., & Cicchetti, D. (2009). Mean-level change and intraindividual variability in self-esteem and depression among high-risk children. *International Journal of Behavioral Development, 33*(3), 202–214.

Kim, J., Schallert, D. L., & Kim, M. (2010). An integrative cultural view of achievement motivation: Parental and classroom predictors of children's goal orientations when learning mathematics in Korea. *Journal of Educational Psychology, 102*(2), 418–437. doi:10.1037/a0018676

Kim, M., Bednarz, R., & Kim, J. (2012). The ability of young Korean children to use spatial representations. *International Research in Geographical & Environmental Education, 21*(3), 261–277. doi:10.1080/10382046.2012.698089

Kim, S., Kim, S., & Kamphaus, R. W. (2010). Is aggression the same for boys and girls? Assessing measurement invariance with confirmatory factor analysis and item response theory. *School Psychology Quarterly, 25*(1), 45–61. doi:10.1037/a0018768

Kim, Y., Petscher, Y., Schatschneider, C., & Foorman, B. (2010). Does growth rate in oral reading fluency matter in predicting reading comprehension achievement? *Journal of Educational Psychology, 102*(3), 652–667.

Kim, Y.-S., Apel, K., & Al Otaiba, S. (2013). The relation of linguistic awareness and vocabulary to word reading and spelling for first-grade students participating in response to intervention. *Language, Speech & Hearing Services in Schools, 44*(4), 337–347. doi:10.1044/0161-1461(2013/12-0013)

Kim-Cohen, J., Moffitt, T. E., Caspi, A., & Taylor A. (2004). Genetic and environmental processes in young children's resilience and vulnerability to socioeconomic deprivation. *Child Development, 75,* 651–668.

King, A. (1999). Discourse patterns for mediating peer learning. In A. M. O'Donnell, A. King (Eds.), *Cognitive perspectives on peer learning* (pp. 87-115). Mahwah, NJ: Erlbaum.

King, G., Imms, C., Palisano, R., Majnemer, A., Chiarello, L., Orlin, M., Law, M., & Avery, L. (2013). Geographical patterns in the recreation and leisure participation of children and youth with cerebral palsy: A CAPE international collaborative network study. *Developmental Neurorehabilitation, 16*(3), 196–206. doi:10.3109/17518423.2013.773102

King, P. E., & Benson, P. L. (2006). Spiritual development and adolescent well-being and thriving. In E. C. Roehlkepartain, P. E. King, L. Wagener, & P. L. Benson (Eds.), *The handbook of spiritual development in childhood and adolescence* (pp. 384–398). Thousand Oaks, CA: Sage.

King, R., McInerney, D., & Watkins, D. (2012). Studying for the sake of others: The role of social goals in academic engagement. *Educational Psychology, 32*(6), 749–776. doi:10.1080/01443410.2012.730479

Kingery, J. N., Erdley, C. A., Marshall, K. C., Whitaker, K. G., & Reuter, T. R. (2010). Peer experiences of anxious and socially withdrawn youth: An integrative review of the developmental and clinical literature. *Clinical Child and Family Psychology Review, 13*(1), 91–128.

Kinney, H. C. (2009). Brainstem mechanisms underlying the sudden infant death syndrome: Evidence from human pathologic studies. *Developmental Psychobiology, 51*(3), 223–233.

Kirby, A., Edwards, L., & Hughes, A. (2008). Parents' concerns about children with specific learning difficulties: Insights gained from an online message centre. *Support for Learning, 23*(4), 193–200.

Kirby, D., & Laris, B. A. (2009). Effective curriculum-based sex and STD/HIV education programs for adolescents. *Child Development Perspectives, 3*(1), 21–29.

Kirby, J. R., Parrila, R. K., & Pfeiffer, S. L. (2003). Naming speed and phonological awareness as predictors of reading development. *Journal of Educational Psychology, 95,* 453–464.

Kirk, S., Beatty, S., Callery, P., Gellatly, J., Milnes, L., & Pryjmachuk, S. (2013). The effectiveness of self-care support interventions for children and young people with long-term conditions: a systematic review. *Child: Care, Health & Development, 39*(3), 305–324. doi:10.1111/j.1365-2214.2012.01395j.2047-6310.2011.00007.x

Kirkorian, H. L., Wartella, E. A., & Anderson, D. R. (2008). Media and young children's learning. *Future of Children, 18*(1), 39–61.

Kirschner, P. A., Sweller, J., & Clark, R. E. (2006). Why minimal guidance during instruction does not work: An analysis of the failure of constructivist, discovery, problem-based, experiential, and inquiry-based teaching. *Educational Psychologist, 41,* 75–86.

Kirshner, B. (2008). Guided participation in three youth activism organizations: Facilitation, apprenticeship, and joint work. *Journal of the Learning Sciences, 17,* 60–101.

Kisilevsky, B. S., Hains, S. M. J., Brown, C. A., Lee, C. T., Cowperthwaite, B., Stutzman, S. S., et al. (2009). Fetal sensitivity to properties of maternal speech and language. *Infant Behavior and Development, 32*(1), 59–71.

Kitamura, T., Shikai, N., Uji, M., Hiramura, H., Tanaka, N., & Shono, M. (2009). Intergenerational transmission of parenting style and personality: Direct influence or mediation? *Journal of Child and Family Studies, 18*(5), 541–556.

Kitayama, S., Duffy, S., & Uchida, Y. (2007). Self as cultural mode of being. In S. Kitayama & D. Cohen (Eds.), *Handbook of cultural psychology* (pp. 136–174). New York, NY: Guilford Press.

Kjellstrand, J. M., Cearley, J., Eddy, J., Foney, D., & Martinez, C. R. (2012). Characteristics of incarcerated fathers and mothers: Implications for preventive interventions targeting children and families. *Children and Youth Services Review, 34*(12), 2409–2415. doi:10.1016/j.childyouth.2012.08.008

Klaczynski, P. (2000). Motivated scientific reasoning biases, epistemological beliefs, and theory polarization: A two-process approach to adolescent cognition. *Child Development, 71,* 1347–1366.

Klahr, D. (1982). Non-monotone assessment of monotone development: An information processing analysis. In S. Strauss & R. Stavy (Eds.), *U-shaped behavioral growth* (pp. 63–86). New York, NY: Academic Press.

Klahr, D., & Robinson, M. (1981). Formal assessment of problem solving and planning processes in children. *Cognitive Psychology, 13,* 113–148.

Klapwijk, E. T., Goddings, A., Burnett Heyes, S., Bird, G., Viner, R. M., & Blakemore, S. (2013). Increased functional connectivity with puberty in the mentalising network involved in social emotion processing. *Hormones & Behavior, 64*(2), 314–322. doi:10.1016/j.yhbeh.2013.03.012

Klassen, T. P., MacKay, J. M., Moher, D., Walker, A., & Jones, A. L. (2000). Community-based injury prevention interventions. *The Future of Children, 10*(1), 83–110.

Klatzkin, A., Lieberman, A. F., & Van Horn, P. (2013). Child—Parent psychotherapy and historical trauma. In J. D. Ford, C. A. Courtois (Eds.), *Treating complex traumatic stress disorders in children and adolescents: Scientific foundations and therapeutic models* (pp. 295–314). New York, NY: Guilford Press.

Klausi, J. F., & Owen, M. T. (2009). Stable maternal cohabitation, couple relationship quality, and characteristics of the home environment in the child's first two years. *Journal of Family Psychology, 23*(1), 103–106.

Klein, B., Gorter, J., & Rosenbaum, P. (2013). Diagnostic shortfalls in early childhood chronic stress: a review of the issues. *Child: Care, Health & Development, 39*(6), 765–771. doi:10.1111/cch.12009

Klibanoff, R. S., Levine, S. C., Huttenlocher, J., Vasilyeva, M., & Hedges, L. V. (2006). Preschool children's mathematical knowledge: The effect of teacher "math talk." *Developmental Psychology, 42,* 59–69.

Klimes-Dougan, B., Pearson, T. E., Jappe, L., Mathieson, L., Simard, M. R., Hastings, P., & Zahn-Waxler, C. (2014). Adolescent emotion socialization: A longitudinal study of friends' responses to negative emotions. *Social Development, 23*(2), 395–412. doi:10.1111/sode.12045

Klinnert, M. D. (1984). The regulation of infant behavior by maternal facial expression. *Infant Behavior and Development, 7,* 447–465.

Knafo, A., & Plomin, R. (2006). Prosocial behavior from early to middle childhood: Genetic and environmental influences on stability and change. *Developmental Psychology, 42,* 771–786.

Knafo, A., & Uzefovsky, F. (2013). Variation in empathy: The interplay of genetic and environmental factors. In M. Legerstee, D. W. Haley, & M. H. Bornstein (Eds.), *The infant mind: Origins of the social brain* (pp. 97–120). New York, NY: Guilford Press.

Knafo, A., Zahn-Waxler, C., Van Hulle, C., Robinson, J. L., & Rhee, S. H. (2008). The developmental origins of a disposition toward empathy: Genetic and environmental contributions. *Emotion, 8*(6), 737–752. doi:10.1037/a0014179

Knapp, M. S., Turnbull, B. J., & Shields, P. M. (1990). New directions for educating the children of poverty. *Educational Leadership, 48*(1), 4–9.

Knapp, N. F. (2002). Tom and Joshua: Perceptions, conceptions and progress in meaning-based reading instruction. *Journal of Literacy Research, 34,* 59–98.

Knerr, W., Gardner, F., & Cluver, L. (2013). Improving positive parenting skills and reducing harsh and abusive parenting in low- and middle-income countries: A systematic review. *Prevention Science.* doi:10.1007/s11121-012-0314-1

Knifsend, C. A., & Juvonen, J. (2014). Social identity complexity, cross-ethnic friendships, and intergroup attitudes in urban middle schools. *Child Development, 85*(2), 709-721. doi:10.1111/cdev.12157

Knowles, Z., Parnell, D., Stratton, G., & Ridgers, N. (2013). Learning from the experts: Exploring playground experience and activities using a write and draw technique. *Journal of Physical Activity & Health, 10*(3), 406–415.

Knudson, R. E. (1992). The development of written argumentation: An analysis and comparison of argumentative writing at four grade levels. *Child Study Journal, 22,* 167–181.

Kochanska, G. (1993). Toward a synthesis of parental socialization and child temperament in early development of conscience. *Child Development, 64,* 325–347.

Kochanska, G. (2002). Mutually responsive orientation between mothers and their young children: A context for the early development of conscience. *Current Directions in Psychological Science, 11*(6), 191–195. doi:10.1111/1467-8721.00198

Kochanska, G., & Aksan, N. (2006). Children's conscience and self-regulation. *Journal of Personality, 74,* 1587–1618.

Kochanska, G., & Kim, S. (2013). Difficult temperament moderates links between maternal responsiveness and children's compliance and behavior problems in low-income families. *Journal of Child Psychology and Psychiatry, 54*(3), 323–332. doi:10.1111/jcpp.12002

Kochanska, G., & Kim, S. (2013). Early attachment organization with both parents and future behavior problems: from infancy to middle childhood. *Child Development, 84*(1), 283–296. doi:10.1111/j.1467-8624.2012.01852.x

Kochanska, G., & Kim, S. (2014). A complex interplay among the parent–child relationship, effortful control, and internalized, rule-compatible conduct in young children: Evidence from two studies. *Developmental Psychology, 50*(1), 8–21. doi:10.1037/a0032330

Kochanska, G., Casey, R. J., & Fukumoto, A. (1995). Toddlers' sensitivity to standard violations. *Child Development, 66,* 643–656.

Kochanska, G., Coy, K. C., & Murray, K. T. (2001). The development of self-regulation in the first four years of life. *Child Development, 72,* 1091–1111.

Kochanska, G., Gross, J. N., Lin, M.-H., & Nichols, K. E. (2002). Guilt in young children: Development, determinants, and relations with a broader system of standards. *Child Development, 73,* 461–482.

Kochanska, G., Koenig, J. L., Barry, R. A., Kim, S., & Yoon, J. E. (2010). Children's conscience during toddler and preschool years, moral self, and a competent, adaptive developmental trajectory. *Developmental Psychology, 46*(5), 1320–1332. doi:10.1037/a0020381

Kodluboy, D. W. (2004). Gang-oriented interventions. In J. C. Conoley & A. P. Goldstein (Eds.), *School violence intervention* (2nd ed., pp. 194–232). New York, NY: Guilford Press.

Koekoek, J., Knoppers, A., & Stegeman, H. (2009). How do children think they learn skills in physical education? *Journal of Teaching in Physical Education, 28,* 310–332.

Koenig, M. A., & Woodward, A. L. (2010). Sensitivity of 24-month-olds to the prior inaccuracy of the source: Possible mechanisms. *Developmental Psychology, 46*(4), 815–826.

Koenig, M. A., Clément, F., & Harris, P. L. (2004). Trust in testimony: Children's use of true and false statements. *Psychological Science, 15,* 694–698.

Koeppel, J., & Mulrooney, M. (1992). The Sister Schools Program: A way for children to learn about cultural diversity—When there isn't any in their school. *Young Children, 48*(1), 44–47.

Kohlberg, L. (1963). Moral development and identification. In H. Stevenson (Ed.), *Child psychology: The sixty-second yearbook of the National Society for the Study of Education* (pp. 277–332). Chicago, IL: University of Chicago Press.

Kohlberg, L. (1964). Development of moral character and moral ideology. In M. L. Hoffman & L. W. Hoffman (Eds.), *Review of child development research: Vol. 1* (pp. 383–432). New York, NY: Russell Sage Foundation.

Kohlberg, L. (1966). A cognitive developmental analysis of children's sex-role concepts and attitudes. In E. E. Maccoby (Ed.), *The development of sex differences* (pp. 82–173). Stanford, CA: Stanford University Press.

Kohlberg, L. (1969). Stage and sequence: The cognitive-developmental approach to socialization. In D. A. Goslin (Ed.), *Handbook of socialization theory and research* (pp. 347–480). Chicago, IL: Rand McNally.

Kohlberg, L. (1969). Stage and sequence: The cognitive-developmental approach to socialization. In D. A. Goslin (Ed.), *Handbook of socialization theory and research* (pp. 347–480). Chicago: Rand McNally.

Kohlberg, L. (1975). The cognitive-developmental approach to moral education. *Phi Delta Kappan, 57,* 670–677.

Kohlberg, L. (1976). Moral stages and moralization: The cognitive-developmental approach. In T. Lickona (Ed.), *Moral development and behavior: Theory, research, and social issues (pp. 31–53).* New York, NY: Holt, Rinehart & Winston.

Kohlberg, L. (1981). *The philosophy of moral development: Moral stages and the idea of justice.* San Francisco, CA: Harper & Row.

Kohlberg, L. (1984). *The psychology of moral development: The nature and validity of moral stages.* San Francisco, CA: Harper & Row.

Kohlberg, L. (1986). A current statement on some theoretical issues. In S. Modgil & C. Modgil (Eds.), *Lawrence Kohlberg: Consensus and controversy.* Philadelphia, PA: Falmer Press.

Kohlberg, L., & Candee, D. (1984). The relationship of moral judgment to moral action. In W. M. Kurtines & J. L. Gewirtz (Eds.), *Morality, moral behavior, and moral development (pp. 52-73).* New York, NY: Wiley.

Kohlberg, L., & Fein, G. G. (1987). Play and constructive work as contributors to development. In L. Kohlberg (Ed.), *Child psychology and childhood education: A cognitive-developmental view* (pp. 392–440). New York, NY: Longman.

Kohlberg, L., & Kramer, R. (1969). Continuities and discontinuities in childhood and adult moral development. *Human Development, 12,* 93–120.

Kohlberg, L., & Mayer, R. (1972). Development as the aim of education. *Harvard Educational Review, 42,* 449–496.

Kohlberg, L., Levine, C., & Hewer, A. (1983). Moral stages: A current formulation and a response to critics. *Contributions to Human Development, 10,* 1–174.

Kohler, F. W., Greteman, C., Raschke, D., & Highnam, C. (2007). Using a buddy skills package to increase the social interactions between a preschooler with autism and her peers. *Topics in Early Childhood Education, 27,* 155–163.

Koinis-Mitchell, D., McQuaid, E. L., Seifer, R., Kopel, S. J., Nassau, J. H., Klein, R. B., et al. (2009). Symptom perception in children with asthma: Cognitive and psychological factors. *Health Psychology, 28*(2), 226–237.

Kok, R., Linting, M., Bakermans-Kranenburg, M. J., IJzendoorn, M. H., Jaddoe, V. V., Hofman, A., Verhulst, F. C., & Tiemeier, H. (2013). Maternal sensitivity and internalizing problems: Evidence from two longitudinal studies in early childhood. *Child Psychiatry and Human Development.* doi:10.1007/s10578-013-0369-7

Kokkinaki, T., & Vitalaki, E. (2013). Comparing spontaneous imitation in grandmother-infant and mother-infant interaction: A three generation familial study. *International Journal of Aging & Human Development, 77*(2), 77–105. doi:10.2190/AG.77.2.a

Kong, L., Cui, Y., Qiu, Y., Han, S., Yu, Z., & Guo, X. (2013). Anxiety and depression in parents of sick neonates: A hospital-based study. *Journal of Clinical Nursing, 22*(7–8), 1163–1172.

Konner, M. (2010). *The evolution of childhood: Relationships, emotion, mind.* Cambridge, MA: Belknap Press/Harvard University Press.

Koob, A. (2009). *The root of thought: Unlocking glia—The brain cell that will help us sharpen our wits, heal injury, and treat brain disease.* Upper Saddle River, NJ: Pearson Education.

Koolschijn, P. P., & Crone, E. A. (2013). Sex differences and structural brain maturation from childhood to early adulthood. *Developmental Cognitive Neuroscience, 5,* 106–118. doi:10.1016/j.dcn.2013.02.003

Koops, L. H. (2010). "Deñuy Jàngal seen bopp" (They teach themselves): Children's music learning in The Gambia. *Journal of Research in Music Education, 58*(1), 18–36.

Kopp, C. B. (1982). Antecedents of self-regulation: A developmental perspective. *Developmental Psychology, 18,* 199–214.

Koren-Karie, N., Oppenheim, D., Dolev, S., Sher, E., & Etzion-Carasso, A. (2002). Mothers' insightfulness regarding their infants' internal experience: Relations with maternal sensitivity and infant attachment. *Developmental Psychology, 38*(4), 534–542.

Korkman, M., Lahti-Nuuttila, P., Laasonen, M., Kemp, S. L., & Holdnack, J. (2013). Neurocognitive development in 5- to 16-year-old North American children: A cross-sectional study. *Child Neuropsychology, 19*(5), 516–539.

Kosciw, J. G., Palmer, N. A., & Kull, R. M. (2014). Reflecting resiliency: Openness about sexual orientation and/or gender identity and its relationship to well-being and educational outcomes for LGBT students. *American Journal of Community Psychology.* doi:10.1007/s10464-014-9642-6

Koskinen, P. S., Blum, I. H., Bisson, S. A., Phillips, S. M., Creamer, T. S., & Baker, T. K. (2000). Book access, shared reading, and audio models: The effects of supporting the literacy learning of linguistically diverse students in school and at home. *Journal of Educational Psychology, 92,* 23–36.

Koss, K. J., George, M. W., Davies, P. T., Cicchetti, D., Cummings, E., & Sturge-Apple, M. L. (2013). Patterns of children's adrenocortical reactivity to interparental conflict and associations with child adjustment: A growth mixture modeling approach. *Developmental Psychology, 49*(2), 317–326. doi:10.1037/a0028246

Kotila, L. E., & Kamp Dush, C. M. (2012). Another baby? Father involvement and childbearing in fragile families. *Journal of Family Psychology, 26*(6), 976–986. doi:10.1037/a0030715

Koutsoftas, A., & Gray, S. (2013). A structural equation model of the writing process in typically-developing sixth grade children. *Reading & Writing, 26*(6), 941–966. doi:10.1007/s11145-012-9399-y

Kovack-Lesh, K. A., Horst, J. S., & Oakes, L. M. (2008). The cat is out of the bag: The joint influence of previous experience and looking behavior on infant categorization. *Infancy, 13*(4), 285–307.

Kovas, Y., Haworth, C. M. A., Dale, P. S., & Plomin, R. (2007). The genetic and environmental origins of learning abilities and disabilities in the early school years. *Monographs of the Society for Research in Child Development, 72*(3, Serial No. 288), 1–160.

Kozulin, A. (1986). Vygotsky in context. In L. S. Vygotsky, *Thought and language* (rev. ed.; A. Kozulin, Ed. and Trans.). Cambridge, MA: MIT Press.

Kozulin, A., Lebeer, J., Madella-Noja, A., Gonzalez, F., Jeffrey, I., Rosenthal, N., et al. (2010). Cognitive modifiability of children with developmental disabilities: A multicentre study using Feuerstein's Instrumental Enrichment—Basic program. *Research in Developmental Disabilities, 31,* 551–559.

Kraljević, J., Cepanec, M., & Šimleša, S. (2014). Gestural development and its relation to a child's early vocabulary. *Infant Behavior & Development, 37*(2), 192-202. doi:10.1016/j.infbeh.2014.01.004

Krampen, G. (2013). Subjective well-being of children in the context of educational transitions. *Europe's Journal of Psychology, 9*(4), 744–763. doi:10.5964/ejop.v9i4.668

Krasa, N., & Shunkwiler, S. (2009). *Number sense and number nonsense: Understanding the challenges of learning math.* Baltimore, MD: Paul H. Brookes.

Krashen, S. D. (1996). *Under attack: The case against bilingual education.* Culver City, CA: Language Education Associates.

Krebs, D. L., & Van Hesteren, F. (1994). The development of altruism: Toward an integrative model. *Developmental Review, 14,* 103–158.

Kreutzer, M. A., Leonard, C., & Flavell, J. H. (1975). An interview study of children's knowledge about memory. *Monographs of the Society for Research in Child Development, 40*(1, Serial No. 159).

Krishnakumar, A., Narine, L., Roopnarine, J. L., & Logie, C. (2014). Multilevel and cross-level effects of neighborhood and family influences on children's behavioral outcomes in Trinidad and Tobago: The intervening role of parental control. *Journal of Abnormal Child Psychology, 42*(6), 1057–1068. doi:10.1007/s10802-014-9852-2

Krispin, O., Sternberg, K. J., & Lamb, M. E. (1992). The dimensions of peer evaluation in Israel: A cross-cultural perspective. *International Journal of Behavioral Development, 15,* 299–314.

Kristjánsson, Á., Sigfúsdóttir, I. D., & Allegrante, J. P. (2010). Health behavior and academic achievement among adolescents: The relative contribution of dietary habits, physical activity, body mass index, and self-esteem. *Health Education and Behavior, 37*(1), 51–64.

Krivitski, E. C., McIntosh, D. E., Rothlisberg, B., & Finch, H. (2004). Profile analysis of deaf children using the Universal Nonverbal Intelligence Test. *Journal of Psychoeducational Assessment, 22,* 338–350.

Kroger, J. (2003). What transits in an identity status transition? *Identity: An International Journal of Theory and Research, 3,* 197–220.

Kroger, J. (2004). Identity in formation. In K. Hoover (Ed.), *The future of identity: Centennial reflections on the legacy of Erik Erikson* (pp. 61–76). Lanham, MD: Lexington Books.

Kronholz, J. (2011). Truants: The challenges of keeping kids in school. *Education Next, 11*(1), 32–38.

Kufeldt, K., Simard, M., & Vachon, J. (2003). Improving outcomes for children in care: Giving youth a voice. *Adoptions and Fostering, 27,* 8–19.

Kuhl, P. K. (2007). Is speech learning "gated" by the social brain? *Developmental Science, 10,* 110–120.

Kuhl, P. K., Conboy, B. T., Padden, D., Nelson, T., & Pruitt, J. (2005). Early speech perception and later language development: Implications for the "critical period." *Language Learning and Development, 1,* 237–264.

Kuhn, D. (1997). Constraints or guideposts? Developmental psychology and science education. *Review of Educational Research, 67,* 141–150.

Kuhn, D. (2001a). How do people know? *Psychological Science, 12,* 1–8.

Kuhn, D. (2001b). Why development does (and does not) occur: Evidence from the domain of inductive reasoning. In J. L. McClelland & R. S. Siegler (Eds.), *Mechanisms of cognitive development: Behavioral and neural perspectives* (pp. 221–249). Mahwah, NJ: Erlbaum.

Kuhn, D. (2007). Is direct instruction an answer to the right question? *Educational Psychologist, 42,* 109–113.

Kuhn, D. (2009). Adolescent thinking. In R. M. Lerner, & L. Steinberg (Eds.), *Handbook of adolescent psychology, Vol. 1: Individual bases of adolescent development* (3rd ed., pp. 152–186). Hoboken, NJ: John Wiley & Sons Inc.

Kuhn, D. (2011). What is scientific thinking and how does it develop? In U. Goswami (Ed.), *The Wiley-Blackwell handbook of childhood cognitive development* (2nd ed., pp. 497–523). Wiley-Blackwell.

Kuhn, D., & Dean, D., Jr. (2005). Is developing scientific thinking all about learning to control variables? *Psychological Science, 16,* 866–870.

Kuhn, D., & Franklin, S. (2006). The second decade: What develops (and how)? In W. Damon & R. M. Lerner (Series Eds.), & D. Kuhn & R. Siegler (Vol. Eds.), *Handbook of child psychology:*

Vol. 1. Cognition, perception, and language (6th ed., pp. 953–993). New York: Wiley.

Kuhn, D., & Park, S.-H. (2005). Epistemological understanding and the development of intellectual values. *International Journal of Educational Research, 43*, 111–124.

Kuhn, D., & Pearsall, S. (2000). Developmental origins of scientific thinking. *Journal of Cognition and Development, 1*, 113–129.

Kuhn, D., & Pease, M. (2010). The dual components of developing strategy use: Production and inhibition. In H. S. Waters & W. Schneider (Eds.), *Metacognition, strategy use, and instruction* (pp. 135–159). New York, NY: Guilford Press.

Kuhn, D., Amsel, E., & O'Loughlin, M. (1988). *The development of scientific thinking skills*. San Diego, CA: Academic Press.

Kuhn, D., Garcia-Mila, M., Zohar, A., & Andersen, C. (1995). Strategies of knowledge acquisition. *Monographs of the Society for Research in Child Development, 60*(4, Whole No. 245).

Kuhn, D., Pease, M., & Wirkala, C. (2009). Coordinating the effects of multiple variables: A skill fundamental to scientific thinking. *Journal of Experimental Child Psychology, 103*(3), 268–284.

Kulberg, A. (1986). Substance abuse: Clinical identification and management. *Pediatrics Clinics of North America, 33*, 325–361.

Kulkarni, B., Christian, P., LeClerq, S. C., & Khatry, S. K. (2009). Determinants of compliance to antenatal micronutrient supplementation and women's perceptions of supplement use in rural Nepal. *Public Health Nutrition, 13*(1), 82–90.

Kumasi, K. (2014). Connected Learning. *Teacher Librarian, 43*(3), 8–15.

Kunjufu, J. (2006). *An African centered response to Ruby Payne's poverty theory*. Chicago: African American Images.

Kunzinger, E. L., III (1985). A short-term longitudinal study of memorial development during early grade school. *Developmental Psychology, 21*, 642–646.

Kurtines, W. M., Berman, S. L., Ittel, A., & Williamson, S. (1995). Moral development: A co-constructivist perspective. In W. M. Kurtines & J. L. Gewirtz (Eds.), *Moral development: An introduction*. Boston, MA: Allyn & Bacon.

Kushner, M. A. (2009). A review of the empirical literature about child development and adjustment postseparation. *Journal of Divorce and Remarriage, 50*, 496–516.

Kutner, L. A., Olson, C. K., Warner, D. E., & Hertzog, S. M. (2008). Parents' and sons' perspectives on video game play: A qualitative study. *Journal of Adolescent Research, 23*(1), 76–96.

Kuvalja, M., Verma, M., & Whitebread, D. (2013). Patterns of co-occurring non-verbal behaviour and self-directed speech; a comparison of three methodological approaches. *Metacognition and Learning*. doi:10.1007/s11409-013-9106-7

Kuzucu, Y., Bontempo, D. E., Hofer, S. M., Stallings, M. C., & Piccinin, A. M. (2014). Developmental change and time-specific variation in global and specific aspects of self-concept in adolescence and association with depressive symptoms. *The Journal of Early Adolescence, 34*(5), 638–666. doi:10.1177/0272431613507498

Kwisthout, J., Vogt, P., Haselager, P., & Dijkstra, T. (2008). Joint attention and language evolution. *Connection Science, 20*(2–3), 155–171.

Kwok, O.-M., Hughes, J. N., & Luo, W. (2007). Role of resilient personality on lower achieving first grade students' current and future achievement. *Journal of School Psychology, 45*, 61–82.

Kwon, K., & Lease, A. M. (2009). Children's social identification with a friendship group: A moderating effect on intent to conform to norms. *Small Group Research, 40*(6), 694–719. doi:10.1177/1046496409346578

Kwon, K., Lease, A., & Hoffman, L. (2012). The impact of clique membership on children's social behavior and status nominations. *Social Development, 21*(1), 150–169. doi:10.1111/j.1467-9507.2011.00620.x

Kwong, T. E., & Varnhagen, C. K. (2005). Strategy development and learning to spell new words: Generalization of a process. *Developmental Psychology, 41*(1), 148–159.

Kwun Chiu, R., & Dennis Lo, Y. (2013). Clinical applications of maternal plasma fetal DNA analysis: translating the fruits of 15 years of research. *Clinical Chemistry & Laboratory Medicine, 51*(1), 197-204. doi:10.1515/cclm-2012-0601

Kyratzis, A., & Tarım, Ş. (2010). Using directives to construct egalitarian or hierarchical social organization: Turkish middle-class preschool girls' socialization about gender, affect, and context in peer group conversations. *First Language, 30*(3/4), 473–492. doi:10.1177/0142723710370547

Kyza, E. A. (2009). Middle-school students' reasoning about alternative hypotheses in a scaffolded, software-based inquiry investigation. *Cognition and Instruction, 27*(4), 277–311.

López, L. (2012). Assessing the phonological skills of bilingual children from preschool through kindergarten: Developmental progression and cross-language transfer. *Journal of Research in Childhood Education, 26*(4), 371–391. doi:10.1080/02568543.2012.711800

Lüftenegger, M., van de Schoot, R., Schober, B., Finsterwald, M., & Spiel, C. (2014). Promotion of students' mastery goal orientations: Does TARGET work? *Educational Psychology, 34*(4), 451–469. doi:10.1080/01443410.2013.814189

La Greca, A. M., Lai, B. S., Joormann, J., Auslander, B. B., & Short, M. A. (2013). Children's risk and resilience following a natural disaster: Genetic vulnerability, posttraumatic stress, and depression. *Journal of Affective Disorders, 151*(3), 860–867. doi:10.1016/j.jad.2013.07.024

La Paro, K. M., & Pianta, R. C. (2000). Predicting children's competence in the early school years: A meta-analytic review. *Review of Educational Research, 70*, 443–484.

Laboratory of Comparative Human Cognition. (1982). Culture and intelligence. In R. J. Sternberg (Ed.), *Handbook of human intelligence (pp. 642-719)*. Cambridge, England: Cambridge University Press.

Laborde, S., Lautenbach, F., Allen, M. S., Herbert, C., & Achtzehn, S. (2014). The role of trait emotional intelligence in emotion regulation and performance under pressure. *Personality & Individual Differences, 57*, 43–47. doi:10.1016/j.paid.2013.09.013

Lacourse, E. E., Boivin, M. M., Brendgen, M. M., Petitclerc, A. A., Girard, A. A., Vitaro, F. F., et al. (2014). A longitudinal twin study of physical aggression during early childhood: Evidence for a developmentally dynamic genome. *Psychological Medicine, 44*(12), 2617–2627. doi:10.1017/S0033291713003218

Ladd, G. W. (2005). *Children's peer relations and social competence: A century of progress*. New Haven, CT: Yale University Press.

Ladd, G. W., & Burgess, K. B. (1999). Charting the relationship trajectories of aggressive, withdrawn, and aggressive/withdrawn children during early grade school. *Child Development, 70*, 910–929.

Ladd, G. W., Herald-Brown, S. L., & Kochel, K. P. (2009). Peers and motivation. In K. R. Wentzel & A. Wigfield (Eds.), *Handbook of motivation at school* (pp. 323–348). New York, NY: Routledge.

Ladd, G., Ettekal, I., Kochenderfer-Ladd, B., Rudolph, K., & Andrews, R. (2014). Relations among chronic peer group rejection, maladaptive behavioral dispositions, and early adolescents' peer perceptions. *Child Development, 85*(3), 971-988. doi:10.1111/cdev.12214

Ladd, H. F., Muschkin, C. G., & Dodge, K. A. (2014). From birth to school: Early childhood initiatives and third-grade outcomes in North Carolina. *Journal of Policy Analysis and Management, 33*(1), 162–187. doi:10.1002/pam.21734

Ladegaard, H. J., & Bleses, D. (2003). Gender differences in young children's speech: The acquisition of sociolinguistic competence. *International Journal of Applied Linguistics, 13*(2), 222–233. doi:10.1111/1473-4192.00045

Ladson-Billings, G. (1994). *The dreamkeepers: Successful teachers of African American children*. San Francisco, CA: Jossey-Bass.

Ladson-Billings, G. (1995). But that's just good teaching! The case for culturally relevant pedagogy. *Theory into Practice, 34*(3), 159–165.

Lafay, A., Thevenot, C., Castel, C., & Fayol, M. (2013). The role of fingers in number processing in young children. *Frontiers in Psychology, 4*.

Lafontana, K. M., & Cillessen, A. H. N. (1998). The nature of children's stereotypes of popularity. *Social Development, 7*, 301–320.

Lagattuta, K. (2014). Linking past, present, and future: Children's ability to connect mental states and emotions across time. *Child Development Perspectives, 8*(2), 90–95. doi:10.1111/cdep.12065

Lahat, A., Helwig, C. C., & Zelazo, P. (2013). An event-related potential study of adolescents' and young adults' judgments of moral and social conventional violations. *Child Development, 84*(3), 955-969. doi:10.1111/cdev.12001

Lahman, M. K. E. (2008). Always othered: Ethical research with children. *Early Childhood Research, 6*(3), 281–300.

Lai, D., Tseng, Y., Hou, Y., & Guo, H. (2012). Gender and geographic differences in the prevalence of intellectual disability in children: Analysis of data from the national disability registry of Taiwan. *Research in Developmental Disabilities, 33*(6), 2301–2307. doi:10.1016/j.ridd.2012.07.001

Lai, M. H., Graham, J. W., Caldwell, L. L., Smith, E. A., Bradley, S. A., Vergnani, T., Matthews, C., & Wegner, L. (2013). Linking life skills and norms with adolescent substance use and delinquency in South Africa. *Journal of Research on Adolescence, 23*(1), 128–137. doi:10.1111/j.1532-7795.2012.00801.x

Laible, D. J., & Thompson, R. A. (2000). Mother–child discourse, attachment security, shared positive affect, and early conscience development. *Child Development, 71*(5), 1424–1440.

Laible, D. J., Murphy, T., & Augustine, M. (2014). Adolescents' aggressive and prosocial behaviors: Links with social information processing, negative emotionality, moral affect, and moral cognition. *The Journal of Genetic Psychology: Research and Theory on Human Development, 175*(3), 270–286. doi:10.1080/00221325.2014.885878

Lajoie, S. P., & Derry, S. J. (Eds.). (1993). *Computers as cognitive tools*. Mahwah, NJ: Erlbaum.

Laks, B. (2013). Why is there variation rather than nothing?. *Language Sciences, 39*, 31–53. doi:10.1016/j.langsci.2013.02.009

Laland, K., Odling-Smee, J., & Feldman, M. (2000). Niche construction, biological evolution, and cultural change. *Behavioral and Brain Sciences, 23*, 131–175.

Lalor, J., Begley, C., & Galavan, E. (2009). Recasting hope: A process of adaptation following fetal anomaly diagnosis. *Social Science and Medicine, 68*, 462–472.

Lamaze, F. (1958). *Painless childbirth*. London: Burke.

Lamb, M. E., & Ahnert, L. (2006). Nonparental child care: Context, concepts, correlates, and consequences. In W. Damon & R. M. Lerner (Series Eds.) & K. A. Renninger & I. E. Sigel (Vol. Eds.),

Handbook of child psychology: Vol. 3. Social, emotional, and personality development (6th ed., pp. 950–1016). New York, NY: Wiley.

Lamb, M. E., & Lewis, C. (2004). The development and significance of father–child relationships in two-parent families. In M. E. Lamb (Ed.), *The role of the father in child development* (4th ed., pp. 272–306). Hoboken, NJ: John Wiley.

Lamb, M. E., Chuang, S. S., & Cabrera, N. (2005). Promoting child adjustment by fostering positive paternal involvement. In R. M. Lerner, F. Jacobs, & D. Wertlieb (Eds.), *Applied developmental science: An advanced textbook* (pp. 179–200). Thousand Oaks, CA: Sage.

Lamb, M. E., Frodi, A. M., Hwang, C. P., Frodi, M., & Steinberg, J. (1982). Mother– and father–infant interactions involving play and holding in traditional and non-traditional Swedish families. *Developmental Psychology, 18,* 215–221.

Lamb, S., & Feeny, N. C. (1995). Early moral sense and socialization. In W. M. Kurtines & J. L. Gewirtz (Eds.), *Moral development: An introduction.* Boston, MA: Allyn & Bacon.

Lamborn, S. D., Mounts, N. S., Steinberg, L., & Dornbusch, S. M. (1991). Patterns of competence and adjustment among adolescents from authoritative, authoritarian, indulgent, and neglectful families. *Child Development, 62,* 1049–1065.

Lancy, D. F. (2008). *The anthropology of childhood: Cherubs, chattel, and changelings.* Cambridge, England: Cambridge University Press.

Land, G., & Jarman, B. (1992). *Breakpoint and beyond: Mastering the future—today.* New York, NY: HarperBusiness.

Landrum, T. J., & Kauffman, J. M. (2006). Behavioral approaches to classroom management. In C. M. Evertson & C. S. Weinstein (Eds.), *Handbook of classroom management: Research, practice, and contemporary issues* (pp. 47–71). Mahwah, NJ: Erlbaum.

Landry, S. H., & Smith, K. E. (2010). Early social and cognitive precursors and parental support for self-regulation and executive function: Relations from early childhood into adolescence. In B. W. Sokol, U. Müeller, J. I. M. Carpendale, A. R. Young, & G. Iarocci (Eds.), *Self and social regulation: Social interaction and the development of social understanding and executive functions* (pp. 386–417). New York, NY: Oxford University Press.

Landry, S., Zucker, T., Taylor, H., Swank, P., Williams, J., Assel, M., et al. (2014). Enhancing early child care quality and learning for toddlers at risk: The responsive early childhood program. *Developmental Psychology, 50*(2), 526–541.

Langacker, R. (1986). An introduction to cognitive grammar. *Cognitive Science, 10,* 1–40.

Langberg, J. M., Dvorsky, M. R., & Evans, S. W. (2013). What specific facets of executive function are associated with academic functioning in youth with attention-deficit/hyperactivity disorder? *Journal of Abnormal Child Psychology, 41*(7), 1145–1159. doi:10.1007/s10802-013-9750-z

Langdon, P. E., Clare, I. C. H., & Murphy, G. H. (2010). Developing an understanding of the literature relating to the moral development of people with intellectual disabilities. *Developmental Review, 30*(3), 273–293. doi:10.1016/j.dr.2010.01.001

Lange, G., & Pierce, S. H. (1992). Memory-strategy learning and maintenance in preschool children. *Developmental Psychology, 28,* 453–462.

Langfur, S. (2013). The You-I event: On the genesis of self-awareness. *Phenomenology and the Cognitive Sciences, 12*(4), 769–790. doi:10.1007/s11097-012-9282-y

Langhaug, L. F., Cheung, Y. B., Pascoe, S., Hayes, R., & Cowan, F. M. (2009). Differences in prevalence of common mental disorders as measured during four questionnaire delivery methods among young people in rural Zimbabwe. *Journal of Affective Disorders, 118,* 220–223.

Lansford, J. E. (2009). Parental divorce and children's adjustment. *Perspectives on Psychological Science, 4*(2), 140–152.

Lapan, R. T., Tucker, B., Kim, S.-K., & Kosciulek, J. F. (2003). Preparing rural adolescents for post-high school transitions. *Journal of Counseling and Development, 81,* 329–342.

Lapsley, D. K. (1993). Toward an integrated theory of adolescent ego development: The "new look" at adolescent egocentrism. *American Journal of Orthopsychiatry, 63,* 562–571.

Lapsley, D., & Carlo, G. (2014). Moral development at the crossroads: New trends and possible futures. *Developmental Psychology, 50*(1), 1–7. doi:10.1037/a0035225

Laranjo, J., Bernier, A., Meins, E., & Carlson, S. M. (2014). The roles of maternal mind-mindedness and infant security of attachment in predicting preschoolers' understanding of visual perspective taking and false belief. *Journal of Experimental Child Psychology, 125,* 48–62. doi:10.1016/j.jecp.2014.02.005

Lareau, A. (2003). *Unequal childhoods: Class, race, and family life.* Berkeley, CA: University of California Press.

Larner, M. B., Stevenson, C. S., & Behrman, R. E. (1998). Protecting children from abuse and neglect: Analysis and recommendations. *The Future of Children: Protecting Children from Abuse and Neglect, 8*(1), 4–22.

Larrain, A., Freire, P., & Howe, C. (2014). Science Teaching and Argumentation: One-sided versus dialectical argumentation in Chilean middle-school science lessons. *International Journal of Science Education, 36*(6), 1017–1036. doi:10.1080/09500693.2013.832005

Larson, R. W., Clore, G. L., & Wood, G. A (1999). The emotions of romantic relationships: Do they wreak havoc on adolescents? In W. Furman, B. B. Brown, & C. Feiring (Eds.), *The development of romantic relationships in adolescence* (pp. 19–49). Cambridge, England: Cambridge University Press.

Larson, R., & Richards, M. H. (1994). *Divergent realities: The emotional lives of mothers, fathers, and adolescents.* New York, NY: Basic Books.

Laski, E. V., & Siegler, R. S. (2014). Learning from number board games: You learn what you encode. *Developmental Psychology, 50*(3), 853–864. doi:10.1037/a0034321

Last, C. G., Hersen, M., Kazdin, A. E., Francis, G., & Grubb, H. J. (1987). Psychiatric illness in the mothers of anxious children. *American Journal of Psychiatry, 144,* 1580–1583.

Latsch, M., & Hannover, B. (2014). Smart girls, dumb boys!? How the discourse on "failing boys" impacts performances and motivational goal orientation in German school students. *Social Psychology, 45*(2), 112–126. doi:10.1027/1864-9335/a000167

Laupa, M., & Turiel, E. (1995). Social domain theory. In W. M. Kurtines & J. L. Gewirtz (Eds.), *Moral development: An introduction.* Boston, MA: Allyn & Bacon.

Laurent, H. K. (2014). Clarifying the contours of emotion regulation: Insights from parent–child stress research. *Child Development Perspectives, 8*(1), 30–35. doi:10.1111/cdep.12058

Lave, J., & Wenger, E. (1991). *Situated learning: Legitimate peripheral participation.* Cambridge, England: Cambridge University Press.

Lavenex, P., & Banta Lavenex, P. (2013). Building hippocampal circuits to learn and remember: Insights into the development of human memory. *Behavioural Brain Research, 254,* 8-21. doi:10.1016/j.bbr.2013.02.007

Law, A., & Fung, A. (2013). Different forms of online and face-to-face victimization among schoolchildren with pure and co-occurring dimensions of reactive and proactive aggression. *Computers In Human Behavior, 29*(3), 1224–1233

Law, Y. (2014). The role of structured cooperative learning groups for enhancing Chinese primary students' reading comprehension. *Educational Psychology, 34*(4), 470-494. doi:10.1080/01443410.2013.860216

Lawanto, O., Santoso, H., & Yang Liu, u. (2012). Understanding of the relationship between interest and expectancy for success in engineering design activity in grades 9–12. *Journal of Educational Technology & Society, 15*(1), 152–161.

Lawrence, B. K. (2009). Rural gifted education: A comprehensive literature review. *Journal for the Education of the Gifted, 32*(4), 461–494.

Laws, G., Bates, G., Feuerstein, M., Mason-Apps, E., & White, C. (2012). Peer acceptance of children with language and communication impairments in a mainstream primary school: Associations with type of language difficulty, problem behaviours and a change in placement organization. *Child Language Teaching and Therapy, 28*(1), 73–86. doi:10.1177/0265659011419234

Lazard, D. S., Innes-Brown, H., & Barone, P. (2014). Adaptation of the communicative brain to post-lingual deafness. Evidence from functional imaging. *Hearing Research, 307,* 136–143. doi:10.1016/j.heares.2013.08.006

Lazonder, A. W., & Kamp, E. (2012). Bit by bit or all at once? Splitting up the inquiry task to promote children's scientific reasoning. *Learning & Instruction, 22*(6), 458–464. doi:10.1016/j.learninstruc.2012.05.005

Lazonder, A., & Egberink, A. (2014). Children's acquisition and use of the control-of-variables strategy: effects of explicit and implicit instructional guidance. *Instructional Science, 42*(2), 291–304. doi:10.1007/s11251-013-9284-3

Leaper, C., & Friedman, C. K. (2007). The socialization of gender. In J. E. Grusec & P. D. Hastings (Eds.), *Handbook of socialization: Theory and research* (pp. 561–587). New York, NY: Guilford Press.

Leaper, C., & Smith, T. E. (2004). A meta-analytic review of gender variations in children's language use: Talkativeness, affiliative speech, and assertive speech. *Developmental Psychology, 40*(6), 993–1027. doi:10.1037/0012-1649.40.6.993

Learning First Alliance. (2001). *Every child learning: Safe and supportive schools.* Washington, DC: Learning First Alliance and Association for Supervision and Curriculum Development.

Lebrun, M., Moreau, P., McNally-Gagnon, A., Goulet, G., & Peretz, I. (2012). Congenital amusia in childhood: A case study. *Cortex: A Journal Devoted to the Study of the Nervous System And Behavior, 48*(6), 683–688. doi:10.1016/j.cortex.2011.02.018

Lederberg, A. R., Schick, B., & Spencer, P. E. (2013). Language and literacy development of deaf and hard-of-hearing children: Successes and challenges. *Developmental Psychology, 49*(1), 15–30. doi:10.1037/a0029558

Lee Smith, M., Gilmer, M. H., Salge, L. E., Dickerson, J. B., & Wilson, K. L. (2013). Who enrolls in teen parent education programs? An emphasis on personal and familial characteristics and services received. *Child & Adolescent Social Work Journal, 30*(1), 21–36. doi:10.1007/s10560-012-0276-y

Lee, C. D., & Slaughter-Defoe, D. T. (1995). Historical and sociocultural influences on African and American education. In J. A. Banks & C. A. M. Banks (Eds.), *Handbook of research on multicultural education (pp. 348–371).* New York, NY: Macmillan.

Lee, C., & Therriault, D. (2013). The cognitive underpinnings of creative thought: A latent variable analysis exploring the roles of intelligence and working memory in three creative thinking processes. *Intelligence, 41*(5), 306–320. doi:10.1016/j.intell.2013.04.008

Lee, E. J., & Lee, S. H. (2009). Effects of instructional rubrics on class engagement behaviors and the achievement of lesson objectives by students with mild mental retardation and their typical peers. *Education and Training in Developmental Disabilities, 44*(3), 396–408.

Lee, H. (1960). *To kill a mockingbird*. Philadelphia, PA: Lippincott.

Lee, I. (2013). The application of speech recognition technology for remediating the writing difficulties of students with learning disabilities. *Dissertation Abstracts International Section A, 73*.

Lee, J. (2009). Escaping embarrassment: Face-work in the rap cipher. *Social Psychology Quarterly, 72*(4), 306–324.

Lee, J. (2014). Universal factors of student achievement in high-performing Eastern and Western countries. *Journal of Educational Psychology, 106*(2), 364-374. doi:10.1037/a0035609

Lee, K., Cameron, C. A., Doucette, J., & Talwar, V. (2002). Phantoms and fabrications: Young children's detection of implausible lies. *Child Development, 73*, 1688–1702.

Lee, O. (1999). Science knowledge, world views, and information sources in social and cultural contexts: Making sense after a natural disaster. *American Educational Research Journal, 36*, 187–219.

Lee, P. (2013). Self-invented notation systems created by young children. *Music Education Research, 15*(4), 392–405. doi:10.1080/14613808.2013.829429

Lee, R., Zhai, F., Brooks-Gunn, J., Han, W., & Waldfogel, J. (2013). Head Start participation and school readiness: Evidence from the Early Childhood Longitudinal Study–Birth Cohort. *Developmental Psychology*. doi:10.1037/a0032280

Lee-Pearce, M. L., Plowman, T. S., & Touchstone, D. (1998). Starbase-Atlantis, a school without walls: A comparative study of an innovative science program for at-risk urban elementary students. *Journal of Education for Students Placed at Risk, 3*, 223–235.

Lefever, J. B., Nicholson, J. S., & Noria, C. W. (2007). Children's uncertain futures: Problems in school. In J. G. Borkowski, J. R. Farris, T. L. Whitman, S. S. Carothers, K. Weed, & D. A. Keogh (Eds.), *Risk and resilience: Adolescent mothers and their children grow up* (pp. 259–278). Mahwah, NJ: Erlbaum.

LeFevre, J.-A., Shwarchuk, S.-L., Smith-Chant, B. L., Fast, L., Kamawar, D., & Bisanz, J. (2009). Home numeracy experiences and children's math performance in the early school years. *Canadian Journal of Behavioural Sciences, 41*(2), 55–66.

Lefmann, T., & Combs-Orme, T. (2013). Early brain development for social work practice: Integrating neuroscience with Piaget's theory of cognitive development. *Journal of Human Behavior in the Social Environment, 23*(5), 640–647. doi:10.1080/10911359.2013.775936

Lefstein, L. M., & Lipsitz, J. (1995). *3:00 to 6:00 p.m.: Programs for young adolescents*. Minneapolis, MN: Search Institute.

Legare, C. H. (2014). The contributions of explanation and exploration to children's scientific reasoning. *Child Development Perspectives, 8*(2), 101–106. doi:10.1111/cdep.12070

Legare, C. H., Evans, E., Rosengren, K. S., & Harris, P. L. (2012). The coexistence of natural and supernatural explanations across cultures and development. *Child Development, 83*(3), 779–793. doi:10.1111/j.1467-8624.2012.01743.x

Legare, C. H., Gelman, S. A., & Wellman, H. M. (2010). Inconsistency with prior knowledge triggers children's causal explanatory reasoning. *Child Development, 81*(3), 929–944. doi:10.1111/j.1467-8624.2010.01443.x

Legaspi, B., & Straits, W. (2011). Living or nonliving? *Science and Children, 48*(8), 27–31.

Legerstee, M. (2013). The developing social brain: Social connections and social bonds, social loss, and jealousy in infancy. In M. Legerstee, D. W. Haley, M. H. Bornstein (Eds.), *The infant mind: Origins of the social brain* (pp. 223–247). New York, NY: Guilford Press.

Lehman, D. R., & Nisbett, R. E. (1990). A longitudinal study of the effects of undergraduate training on reasoning. *Developmental Psychology, 26*, 952–960.

Lehmann, M., & Hasselhorn, M. (2012). Rehearsal dynamics in elementary school children. *Journal of Experimental Child Psychology, 111*(3), 552–560. doi:10.1016/j.jecp.2011.10.013

Lehrer, J., & Petrakos, H. (2011). Parent and child perceptions of grade one children's out of school play. *Exceptionality Education International, 21*(2–3), 74–92.

Leichtman, M. D., & Ceci, S. J. (1995). The effects of stereotypes and suggestions on preschoolers' reports. *Developmental Psychology, 31*, 568–578.

Lein, L. (1975). Black American immigrant children: Their speech at home and school. *Council on Anthropology and Education Quarterly, 6*, 1–11.

Leman, P. J., & Björnberg, M. (2010). Conversation, development, and gender: A study of changes in children's concepts of punishment. *Child Development, 81*(3), 958–971. doi:10.1111/j.1467-8624.2010.01445.x

Lemery-Chalfant, K., Kao, K., Swann, G., & Goldsmith, H. (2013). Childhood temperament: Passive gene–environment correlation, gene–environment interaction, and the hidden importance of the family environment. Development and Psychopathology, 25(1), 51–63.

Leming, J. S. (2000). Tell me a story: An evaluation of a literature-based character education programme. *Journal of Moral Education, 29*, 413–427.

Lemmens, J. S., Valkenburg, P. M., & Peter, J. (2011). The effects of pathological gaming on aggressive behavior. *Journal of Youth and Adolescence, 40*(1), 38–47. doi:10.1007/s10964-010-9558-x

Lennox, C., & Siegel, L. S. (1998). Phonological and orthographic processes in good and poor spellers. In C. Hulme & R. Joshi (Eds.), *Reading and spelling: Development and disorders* (pp. 395–404). Mahwah, NJ: Erlbaum.

Lens, W. (2001). How to combine intrinsic task motivation with the motivational effects of the instrumentality of present tasks for future goals. In A. Efklides, J. Kuhl & R. Sorrentino (Eds.), *Trends and prospects in motivation research* (pp. 37–52). Dordrecht, The Netherlands: Kluwer.

Leonard, J., & Martin, D. B. (2013). *The brilliance of Black children in mathematics: Beyond the numbers and toward new discourse*. Charlotte, NC: IAP Information Age Publishing.

Leonard, L. B. (2009). Some reflections on the study of children with specific language impairment. *Child Language Teaching and Therapy, 25*(2), 169–171.

Leong, D., & Bodrova, E. (2012). Assessing and scaffolding make-believe play. *YC: Young Children, 67*(1), 28–34.

Leont'ev, A. N. (1959). *Problemy razvitiia psikhiki (Translated title: Problems of mental development)*. Oxford, England: Rsfsr Academy Pedagogical Sciences.

Lepage, J., Dunkin, B., Hong, D. S., & Reiss, A. L. (2013). Impact of cognitive profile on social functioning in prepubescent females with Turner syndrome. Child Neuropsychology, 19(2), 161–172. doi:10.1080/09297049.2011.647900

Lepola, J., Lynch, J., Laakkonen, E., Silvén, M., & Niemi, P. (2012). The role of inference making and other language skills in the development of narrative listening comprehension in 4-6-Year-Old Children. *Reading Research Quarterly, 47*(3), 259–282. doi:10.1002/rrq.020

Lessard, A., Fortin, L., Marcotte, D., Potvin, P., & Royer, É. (2009). Why did they not drop out? Narratives from resilient students. *The Prevention Researcher, 16*(3), 21–24.

Letiecq, B. L., Bailey, S. J., & Dahlen, P. (2008). Ambivalence and coping among custodial grandparents. In B. Hayslip & P. L. Kaminski (Eds.), *Parenting the custodial grandchild* (pp. 3–16). New York, NY: Springer.

Leung, A., & McBride-Chang, C. (2013). Game on? Online friendship, cyberbullying, and psychosocial adjustment in Hong Kong Chinese Children. *Journal of Social & Clinical Psychology, 32*(2), 159–185. doi:10.1521/jscp.2013.32.2.159

LeVay, S. (2011). *Gay, straight, and the reason why: The science of sexual orientation*. New York, NY: Oxford University Press.

Leve, L. D., DeGarmo, D. S., Bridgett, D. J., Neiderhiser, J. M., Shaw, D. S., Harold, G. T., et al. (2013). Using an adoption design to separate genetic, prenatal, and temperament influences on toddler executive function. *Developmental Psychology, 49*(6), 1045–1057. doi:10.1037/a0029390

Leventhal, T., Dupéré, V., & Brooks-Gunn, J. (2009). Neighborhood influences on adolescent development. In R. M. Lerner & L. Steinberg (Eds.), *Handbook of adolescent psychology, Vol. 2: Contextual influences on adolescent development* (3rd ed., pp. 411–443). Hoboken, NJ: Wiley.

Levine, E. (2010). The rigors and rewards of internships. *Educational Leadership, 68*(1), 44–48.

Levine, L. (1983). Mine: Self-definition in 2-year-old boys. *Developmental Psychology, 19*, 544–549.

Levine, M. (2006). *The price of privilege: How parental pressure and material advantage are creating a generation of disconnected and unhappy kids*. New York, NY: HarperCollins.

LeVine, R. A. (2004). Challenging expert knowledge: Findings from an African study of infant care and development. In U. P. Gielen & J. P. Roopnarine (Eds.), *Childhood and adolescence: Cross-cultural perspectives and applications* (pp. 149–165). Westport, CT: Praeger.

LeVine, R. A., & Norman, K. (2008). Attachment in anthropological perspective. In R. A. LeVine & R. S. New (Eds.), *Anthropology and child development: A cross-cultural reader* (pp. 127–142). Malden, MA: Blackwell Publishing.

Levitt, M. J., Guacci-Franco, N., & Levitt, J. L. (1993). Convoys of social support in childhood and early adolescence: Structure and function. *Developmental Psychology, 29*, 811–818.

Levstik, L. S. (2008). Building a sense of history in a first-grade classroom. In L. S. Levstik & K. C. Barton (Eds.), *Researching history education: Theory, method, and context* (pp. 30–60). New York, NY: Routledge.

Levy, E., & McNeill, D. (2013). Narrative development as symbol formation: Gestures, imagery and the emergence of cohesion. *Culture & Psychology, 19*(4), 548–569. doi:10.1177/1354067X13500328

Lewandowski, L. J., & Rieger, B. (2009). The role of a school psychologist in concussion. *Journal of Applied School Psychology, 25*(1), 95–110.

Lewandowski, R., Verdeli, H., Wickramaratne, P., Warner, V., Mancini, A., & Weissman, M. (2014). Predictors of positive outcomes in offspring of depressed parents and non-depressed parents across 20 years. *Journal of Child & Family Studies, 23*(5), 800–811.

Lewin, T. (2000, June 25). Growing up, growing apart: Fast friends try to resist the pressure to divide by race. *The New York Times*, pp. 1, 18–20.

Lewis, M. (1993). Self-conscious emotions: Embarrassment, pride, shame, and guilt. In M. Lewis & J. Haviland (Eds.), *The handbook of emotions* (pp. 563–573). New York, NY: Guilford Press.

Lewis, M. (2005). The child and its family: The social network model. *Human Development, 48*, 8–27.

Lewis, M. (2014). *The rise of consciousness and the development of emotional life.* New York, NY: Guilford Press.

Lewis, M., & Brooks-Gunn, J. (1979). *Social cognition and the acquisition of self.* New York, NY: Plenum.

Lewis, M., Feiring, C., & Rosenthal, S. (2000). Attachment over time. *Child Development, 71,* 707–720.

Lewis, P., Abbeduto, L., Murphy, M., Richmond, E., Giles, N., Bruno, L., et al. (2006). Cognitive, language and social-cognitive skills of individuals with fragile X with and without autism. *Journal of Intellectual Disability Research, 50,* 532–545.

Lewkowicz, D. J., & Hansen-Tift, A. M. (2012). Infants deploy selective attention to the mouth of a talking face when learning speech. *Proceedings of the National Academy of Sciences of the United States of America, 109*(5), 1431–1436. doi:10.1073/pnas.1114783109

Leyva, D., Hopson, S., & Nichols, A. (2012). Reading a note, reading a mind: children's notating skills and understanding of mind. *Reading & Writing, 25*(3), 701–716. doi:10.1007/s11145-011-9296-9

Li, J. (2004). High abilities and excellence: A cultural perspective. In L. V. Shavinina & M. Ferrari (Eds.), *Beyond knowledge: Extracognitive aspects of developing high ability* (pp. 187–208). Mahwah, NJ: Erlbaum.

Li, J. (2006). Self in learning: Chinese adolescents' goals and sense of agency. *Child Development, 77,* 482–501.

Li, J. J., & Lee, S. S. (2014). Negative emotionality mediates the association of 5-HTTLPR genotype and depression in children with and without ADHD. *Psychiatry Research, 215*(1), 163–169. doi:10.1016/j.psychres.2013.10.026

Li, J., & Fischer, K. W. (2004). Thought and affect in American and Chinese learners' beliefs about learning. In D. Y. Dai & R. J. Sternberg (Eds.), *Motivation, emotion, and cognition: Integrative perspectives on intellectual functioning and development* (pp. 385–418). Mahwah, NJ: Erlbaum.

Li, S., Jin, X., Yan, C., Wu, S., Jiang, F., & Shen, X. (2009). Factors associated with bed and room sharing in Chinese school-age children. *Child: Care, Health, and Development, 35*(2), 171–177.

Li, S.-C. (2007). Biocultural co-construction of developmental plasticity across the lifespan. In S. Kitayama & D. Cohen (Eds.), *Handbook of cultural psychology* (pp. 528–544). New York, NY: Guilford Press.

Liben, L. S. (2009). The road to understanding maps. *Current Directions in Psychological Science, 18*(6), 310–315.

Liben, L. S., & Downs, R. M. (1989b). Understanding maps as symbols: The development of map concepts in children. In H. W. Reese (Ed.), *Advances in child development and behavior* (Vol. 22, pp.145-201). San Diego, CA: Harcourt Brace Jovanovich.

Liben, L. S., & Downs, R. M. (2003). Investigating and facilitating children's graphic, geographic, and spatial development: An illustration of Rodney R. Cocking's legacy. *Journal of Applied Developmental Psychology, 24*(6), 663–679. doi:10.1016/j.appdev.2003.09.008

Liben, L. S., & Myers, L. J. (2007). Developmental changes in children's understanding of maps: What, when, and how? In J. M. Plumert & J. P. Spencer (Eds.), *The emerging spatial mind* (pp. 193–218). New York, NY: Oxford University Press.

Liben, L. S., Kastens, K. A., & Stevenson, L. M. (2002). Real-world knowledge through real-world maps: A developmental guide for navigating the educational terrain. *Developmental Review, 22,* 267–322.

Liben, L. S., Myers, L. J., Christensen, A. E., & Bower, C. A. (2013). Environmental scale map use in middle childhood: Links to spatial skills,

strategies, and gender. *Child Development, 84*(6), 2047–2063. doi:10.1111/cdev.12090

Lickona, T. (1991). Moral development in the elementary school classroom. In W. M. Kurtines & J. L. Gewirtz (Eds.), *Moral behavior and development: Vol. 3. Application.* Hillsdale, NJ: Erlbaum.

Licona, M. (2013). Mexican and Mexican-American children's funds of knowledge as interventions into deficit thinking: opportunities for praxis in science education. *Cultural Studies of Science Education, 8*(4), 859–872. doi:10.1007/s11422-013-9515-6

Lidz, C. S. (1991). Issues in the assessment of preschool children. In B. A. Bracken (Ed.), *The psychoeducational assessment of preschool children* (2nd ed., pp. 18–31). Boston, MA: Allyn & Bacon.

Lieberman, A. F., & Van Horn, P. (2013). Infants and young children in military families: A conceptual model for intervention. *Clinical Child and Family Psychology Review, 16*(3), 282–293. doi:10.1007/s10567-013-0140-4

Lieberman, D. A. (1997). Interactive video games for health promotion: Effects on knowledge, self-efficacy, social support, and health. In R. L. Street, Jr., W. R. Gold, & T. R. Manning (Eds.), *Health promotion and interactive technology: Theoretical applications and future directions* (pp. 103–120). Mahwah, NJ: Erlbaum.

Liebtag, E. (2013). Moving forward with Common Core State Standards implementation: Possibilities and potential problems. *Journal of Curriculum & Instruction, 7*(2), 56–70. doi:10.3776/joci.2013.v7n2p56-70

Lieven, E., & Stoll, S. (2010). Language. In M. H. Bornstein (Ed.), *Handbook of cultural developmental science* (pp. 143–160). New York, NY: Psychology Press.

Light, S. N., Coan, J. A., Zahn-Waxler, C., Frye, C., Goldsmith, H. H., & Davidson, R. J. (2009). Empathy is associated with dynamic change in prefrontal brain electrical activity during positive emotion in children. *Child Development, 80*(4), 1210–1231. doi:10.1111/j.1467-8624.2009.01326.x

Lightfoot, C. (1992). Constructing self and peer culture: A narrative perspective on adolescent risk taking. In L. T. Winegar & J. Valsiner (Eds.), *Children's development within social context: Vol. 2. Research and methodology* (pp. 229–245). Hillsdale, NJ: Erlbaum.

Lightfoot, D. (1999). *The development of language: Acquisition, change, and evolution.* Malden, MA: Blackwell.

Lillard, A. S. (1993). Pretend play skills and the child's theory of mind. *Child Development, 64,* 348–371.

Lillard, A. S. (1997). Other folks' theories of mind and behavior. *Psychological Science, 8,* 268–274.

Lillard, A. S. (1998). Playing with a theory of mind. In O. N. Saracho & B. Spodek (Eds.), *Multiple perspectives on play in early childhood education.* Albany, NY: State University of New York Press.

Lillard, A. S. (1999). Developing a cultural theory of mind: The CIAO approach. *Current Directions in Psychological Science, 8,* 57–61.

Lillard, A. S., Lerner, M. D., Hopkins, E. J., Dore, R. A., Smith, E. D., & Palmquist, C. M. (2012, August). The impact of pretend play on children's development: A review of the evidence. *Psychological Bulletin,* doi:10.1037/a0029321

Lillard, A. S., Lerner, M. D., Hopkins, E. J., Dore, R. A., Smith, E. D., & Palmquist, C. M. (2013). The impact of pretend play on children's development: A review of the evidence. *Psychological Bulletin, 139*(1), 1–34. doi:10.1037/a0029321

Lillemyr, O. F., Søbstad, F., Marder, K., & Flowerday, T. (2011). A multicultural perspective on play and learning in primary school. *International Journal of Early Childhood, 43*(1), 43–65. doi:10.1007/s13158-010-0021-7

Lin, Z. (2010). Interactive dynamic assessment with children learning EFL in kindergarten. *Early Childhood Education Journal, 37,* 279–287.

Lindberg, L. D., & Maddow-Zimet, I. (2012). Consequences of sex education on teen and young adult sexual behaviors and outcomes, *Journal of Adolescent Health, 51*(4), 332–333.

Lindberg, S., Linkersdörfer, J., Ehm, J., Hasselhorn, M., & Lonnemann, J. (2013). Gender differences in children's math self-concept in the first years of elementary school. *Journal of Education & Learning, 2*(3), 1–8. doi:10.5539/jel.v2n3p1

Linder, J. R., & Gentile, D. A. (2009). Is the television rating system valid? Indirect, verbal, and physical aggression in programs viewed by fifth grade girls and associations with behavior. *Journal of Applied Developmental Psychology, 30,* 286–297.

Lindfors, K., Elovainio, M., Wickman, S., Vuorinen, R., Sinkkonen, J., Dunkel, L., et al. (2007). Brief report: The role of ego development in psychosocial adjustment among boys with delayed puberty. *Journal of Research on Adolescence, 17*(4), 601–612.

Lindsey, E. W., & Colwell, M. J. (2013). Pretend and physical play: Links to preschoolers' affective social competence. *Merrill-Palmer Quarterly, 59*(3), 330-360.

Linn, M. C., & Muilenburg, L. (1996). Creating lifelong science learners: What models form a firm foundation? *Educational Researcher, 25*(5), 18–24.

Linn, M. C., Songer, N. B., & Eylon, B. (1996). Shifts and convergences in science learning and instruction. In D. C. Berliner & R. C. Calfee (Eds.), *Handbook of educational psychology (pp. 438-490).* New York, NY: Macmillan.

Linn, R. L., & Miller, M.D. (2005). *Measurement and assessment in teaching* (9th ed.). Upper Saddle River, NJ: Merrill/Prentice Hall.

Linnemeier, E. (2012). School-based conflict resolution education and peer mediation programs: The Western Justice Center Experience. *Dispute Resolution, 18*(4), 14–19.

Linnenbrink, E. A. (2005). The dilemma of performance-approach goals: The use of multiple goal contexts to promote students' motivation and learning. *Journal of Educational Psychology, 97,* 197–213.

Linnenbrink, E. A., & Pintrich, P. R. (2004). Role of affect in cognitive processing in academic contexts. In D. Y. Dia & R. J. Sternberg (Eds.), *Motivation, emotion, and cognition: Integrative perspectives on intellectual functioning and development* (pp. 57–87). Mahwah, NJ: Erlbaum.

Linver, M. R., Brooks-Gunn, J., & Kohen, D. E. (2002). Family processes as pathways from income to young children's development. *Developmental Psychology, 38,* 719–734.

Lippa, R. A. (2002). *Gender, nature, and nurture.* Mahwah, NJ: Erlbaum.

Lipson, M. Y. (1983). The influence of religious affiliation on children's memory for text information. *Reading Research Quarterly, 18,* 448–457.

Lipton, J. S., & Spelke, E. S. (2005). Preschool children's mapping of number words to nonsymbolic numerosities. *Child Development, 76,* 978–988.

Liu, C. H., Yang, Y., Fang, S., Snidman, N., & Tronick, E. (2013). Maternal regulating behaviors through face-to-face play in first- and second-generation Chinese American and European American mothers of infants. *Research in Human Development, 10*(4), 289–307.

Liu, D., Wellman, H. M., Tardif, T., & Sabbagh, M. A. (2008). Theory of mind development in Chinese children: A meta-analysis of false-belief understanding across cultures and languages. *Developmental Psychology, 44,* 523–531.

Liu, R. T., Kraines, M. A., Massing-Schaffer, M., & Alloy, L. B. (2014). Rejection sensitivity and depression: Mediation by stress generation. *Psychiatry:*

Interpersonal & Biological Processes, 77(1), 86–97. doi:10.1521/psyc.2014.77.1.86

Livingston, B. A. (2014). Bargaining behind the scenes: Spousal negotiation, labor, and work–family burnout. *Journal of Management, 40*(4), 949–977. doi:10.1177/0149206311428355

Lloyd, M. E., & Newcombe, N. S. (2009). Implicit memory in childhood: Reassessing developmental invariance. In M. L. Courage & N. Cowan (Eds.), *The development of memory in infancy and childhood* (pp. 93–113). New York, NY: Psychology Press.

Lloyd, M., MacDonald, M., & Lord, C. (2013). Motor skills of toddlers with autism spectrum disorders. *Autism, 17*(2), 133–146. doi:10.1177/1362361311402230

Lobel, A. (1979). *Frog and Toad are friends.* New York, NY: HarperCollins.

Lochman, J. E., Wayland, K. K., & White, K. J. (1993). Social goals: Relationship to adolescent adjustment and to social problem solving. *Journal of Abnormal Child Psychology, 21,* 1993.

Lochrie, A. S., Wysocki, T., Hossain, J., Milkes, A., Antal, H., Buckloh, L., J. Canas, J. Bobo, E., & Lang, J. (2013). The effects of a family-based intervention (FBI) for overweight/obese children on health and psychological functioning. *Clinical Practice in Pediatric Psychology, 1*(2), 159–170. doi:10.1037/cpp0000020

Locke, J. L. (1993). *The child's path to spoken language.* Cambridge, MA: Harvard University Press.

Lockhart, K. L., Chang, B., & Story, T. (2002). Young children's beliefs about the stability of traits: Protective optimism? *Child Development, 73,* 1408–1430.

Lodewyk, K. R., & Winne, P. H. (2005). Relations among the structure of learning tasks, achievement, and changes in self-efficacy in secondary students. *Journal of Educational Psychology, 97,* 3–12.

Loeb, S., Fuller, B., Kagan, S. L., & Carrol, B. (2004). Child care in poor communities: Early learning effects of type, quality, and stability. *Child Development, 75,* 47–65.

Logan, J. (2013). Contemporary adoptive kinship: A contribution to new kinship studies. *Child & Family Social Work, 18*(1), 35–45. doi:10.1111/cfs.12042

Logan, J. R., Hart, S. A., Cutting, L., Deater-Deckard, K., Schatschneider, C., & Petrill, S. (2013). Reading development in young children: Genetic and environmental influences. *Child Development, 84*(6), 2131–2144. doi:10.1111/cdev.12104

Logan, J., Petrill, S. A., Flax, J., Justice, L. M., Hou, L., Bassett, A. S., et al. (2011). Genetic covariation underlying reading, language and related measures in a sample selected for specific language impairment. *Behavior Genetics, 41*(5), 651–659. doi:10.1007/s10519-010-9435-0

Logsdon, B. J., Alleman, L. M., Straits, S. A., Belka, D. E., & Clark, D. (1997). *Physical education unit plans for grades 5–6* (2nd ed.). Champaign, IL: Human Kinetics.

London, M. L., Ladewig, P. A. W., Ball, J. W., Bindler, R. C., & Cowen, K. J. (2011). *Maternal and child nursing care* (3rd ed.). Upper Saddle River, NJ: Pearson.

London, M. L., Ladewig, P. W., Ball, J. W., & Bindler, R. C. (2007). *Maternal and child nursing care* (2nd ed.). Upper Saddle River, NJ: Pearson Prentice Hall.

Lonigan, C. J., Burgess, S. R., Anthony, J. L., & Barker, T. A. (1998). Development of phonological sensitivity in 2- to 5-year-old children. *Journal of Educational Psychology, 90,* 294–311.

Lonigro, A., Laghi, F., Baiocco, R., & Baumgartner, E. (2014). Mind reading skills and empathy: Evidence for nice and nasty ToM behaviours in school-aged children. *Journal of Child and Family Studies, 23*(3), 581–590. doi:10.1007/s10826-013-9722-5

Loo, S. K., Shtir, C., Doyle, A. E., Mick, E., McGough, J. J., McCracken, J., Biederman, J., Smalley, S., Cantor, R., Faraone, S., & Nelson, S. F. (2012). Genome-wide association study of intelligence: Additive effects of novel brain expressed genes. *Journal of the American Academy of Child & Adolescent Psychiatry, 51*(4), 432–440. doi:10.1016/j.jaac.2012.01.006

Loper, A., Phillips, V., Nichols, E., & Dallaire, D. H. (2013). Characteristics and effects of the co-parenting alliance between incarcerated parents and child caregivers. *Journal of Child and Family Studies.* doi:10.1007/s10826-012-9709-7

Lopez, A. M. (2003). Mixed-race school-age children: A summary of census 2000 data. *Educational Researcher, 32*(6), 25–37.

Lopez, E. C. (1997). The cognitive assessment of limited English proficient and bilingual children. In D. P. Flanagan, J. L. Genshaft, & P. L. Harrison (Eds.), *Contemporary intellectual assessment: Theories, tests, and issues* (pp. 503–516). New York, NY: Guilford Press.

Lopez, V. A., & Emmer, E. T. (2002). Influences of beliefs and values on male adolescents' decision to commit violent offenses. *Psychology of Men and Masculinity, 3,* 28–40.

Lorber, M. F., Del Vecchio, T., & Smith Slep, A. M. (2014). Infant externalizing behavior as a self-organizing construct. *Developmental Psychology, 50*(7), 1854–1861. doi:10.1037/a0036985

Lorch, R. R., Lorch, E. P., Freer, B., Dunlap, E. E., Hodell, E. C., & Calderhead, W. J. (2014). Using valid and invalid experimental designs to teach the control of variables strategy in higher and lower achieving classrooms. *Journal of Educational Psychology, 106*(1), 18–35. doi:10.1037/a0034375

Lorenz, R. C., Gleich, T., Beck, A., Pöhland, L., Raufelder, D., Sommer, W., et al. (2014). Reward anticipation in the adolescent and aging brain. *Human Brain Mapping.* doi:10.1002/hbm.22540

Losey, K. M. (1995). Mexican American students and classroom interaction: An overview and critique. *Review of Educational Research, 65,* 283–318.

Losh, M., Martin, G. E., Klusek, J., Hogan-Brown, A. L., & Sideris, J. (2012). Social communication and theory of mind in boys with autism and fragile X syndrome. *Frontiers in Psychology, 3.* doi:10.3389/fpsyg.2012.00266

Lotan, R. A. (2006). Managing groupwork in the heterogeneous classroom. In C. M. Evertson & C. S. Weinstein (Eds.), *Handbook of classroom management: Research, practice, and contemporary issues* (pp. 525–539). Mahwah, NJ: Erlbaum.

Lou, Y., Abrami, P. C., Spence, J. C., Poulsen, C., Chambers, B., & d'Apollonia, S. (1996). Within-class grouping: A meta-analysis. *Review of Educational Research, 66,* 423–458.

Loukas, A., Roalson, L. A., & Herrera, D. E. (2010). School connectedness buffers the effects of negative family relations and poor effortful control on early adolescent conduct problems. *Journal of Research on Adolescence, 20*(1), 13–22. doi:10.1111/j.1532-7795.2009.00632.x

Lovett, B. J., & Sparks, R. L. (2013). The identification and performance of gifted students with learning disability diagnoses: A quantitative synthesis. *Journal of Learning Disabilities, 46*(4), 304–316. doi:10.1177/0022219411421810

Lovett, S. B., & Flavell, J. H. (1990). Understanding and remembering: Children's knowledge about the differential effects of strategy and task variables on comprehension and memorization. *Child Development, 61,* 1842–1858.

Lubinski, D., & Bleske-Rechek, A. (2008). Enhancing development in intellectually talented populations. In P. C. Kyllonen, R. D. Roberts, & L. Stankov (Eds.), *Extending intelligence: Enhancement and new constructs* (pp. 109–132). New York, NY: Erlbaum/Taylor & Francis.

Luby, J. L. (2010). Preschool depression: The importance of identification of depression early in development. *Current Directions in Psychological Science, 19*(2), 91–95.

Luby, J., Belden, A., Sullivan, J., Hayen, R., McCadney, A., & Spitznagel, E. (2009). Shame and guilt in preschool depression: Evidence for elevations in self-conscious emotions in depression as early as age 3. *Journal of Child Psychology and Psychiatry, 50*(9), 1156–1166. doi:10.1111/j.1469-7610.2009.02077.x

Lucariello, J., Kyratzis, A., & Nelson, K. (1992). Taxonomic knowledge: What kind and when? *Child Development, 63,* 978–998.

Luckasson, R., Borthwick-Duffy, S., Buntinx, W. H. E., Coulter, D. L., Craig, E. M., Reeve, A., et al. (Eds.). (2002). *Mental retardation: Definition, classification, and systems of supports* (10th ed.). Washington, DC: American Association on Mental Retardation.

Luckner, J., & Sebald, A. (2013). Promoting self-determination of students who are eaf or hard of hearing. *American Annals of the Deaf, 158*(3), 377–386.

Ludwig, J., & Miller, D. L. (2007). Does Head Start improve children's life chances? Evidence from a regression discontinuity design. *Quarterly Journal of Economics, 122,* 159–208.

Ludwig-Körner, C. (2012). Anna Freud and her collaborators in the early post-war period. In N. T. Malberg, & J. Raphael-Leff (Eds.), *The Anna Freud tradition: Lines of development—Evolution of theory and practice over the decades* (pp. 17–29). London, England: Karnac Books.

Luehrman, M., & Unrath, K. (2006). Making theories of children's artistic development meaningful for preservice teachers. *Art Education, 59*(3), 6–12.

Lueptow, L. B. (1984). *Adolescent sex roles and social change.* New York, NY: Columbia University Press.

Lugo-Gil, J., & Tamis-LeMonda, C. S. (2008). Family resources and parenting quality: Links to children's cognitive development across the first 3 years. *Child Development, 79*(4), 1065–1085.

Lugo-Neris, M. J., Jackson, C., & Goldstein, H. (2010). Effects of a conversation facilitating Vocabulary acquisition of young English language learners. *Language, Speech & Hearing Services in Schools, 41*(3), 314–327. doi:10.1044/0161-1461(2009/07-0082)

Luijk, M. M., Mileva-Seitz, V. R., Jansen, P. W., van IJzendoorn, M. H., Jaddoe, V. V., Raat, H., Hofman, A., Verhulst, F., &Tiemeier, H. (2013). Ethnic differences in prevalence and determinants of mother–child bed-sharing in early childhood. *Sleep Medicine, 14*(11), 1092-1099. doi:10.1016/j.sleep.2013.04.019

Luijk, M. P. C. M., Saridjan, N., Tharner, A., van IJzendoorn, M. H., Bakermans-Kranenburg, M. J., Jaddoe, V. W. V., et al. (2010). Attachment, depression, and cortisol: Deviant patterns in insecure-resistant and disorganized infants. *Developmental Psychobiology, 52*(5), 441–452.

Luiselli, J. K. (2009). Aggression and noncompliance. In J. L. Matson (Ed.), *Applied behavior analysis for children with autism spectrum disorders* (pp. 175–187). New York, NY: Springer Science + Business Media. doi:10.1007/978-1-4419-0088-3_10

Luke, N., & Banerjee, R. (2012). Maltreated children's social understanding and empathy: A preliminary exploration of foster carers' perspectives. *Journal of Child and Family Studies, 21*(2), 237–246. doi:10.1007/s10826-011-9468-x

Lumeng, J. (2006). Childhood obesity prevention: Responsibilities of the family, schools, and community. In K. Freeark & W. S. Davidson II (Vol. Eds.), & H. E. Fitzgerald, R. Zucker, & K. Freeark

(Eds. in Chief), *The crisis in mental health: Critical issues and effective programs. Vol. 3: Issues for families, schools, and communities* (pp. 55–77). Westport, CT: Praeger.

Luna, B. (2009). The maturation of cognitive control and the adolescent brain. In F. Aboitiz & D. Cosmelli (Eds.), *From attention to goal-directed behavior: Neurodynamical, methodological, clinical trends* (pp. 249–274). Berlin, Germany: Springer.

Lundahl, B., Bettmann, J., Hurtado, M., & Goldsmith, D. (2014). Different histories, different stories: Using a narrative tool to assess children's internal worlds. *Child & Adolescent Social Work Journal, 31*(2), 143–161. doi:10.1007/s10560-013-0312-6

Luster, L. (1992). *Schooling, survival, and struggle: Black women and the GED.* Unpublished doctoral dissertation, Stanford University, School of Education, Stanford, CA.

Luthar, S. S., & Goldstein, A. S. (2008). Substance use and related behaviors among suburban late adolescents: The importance of perceived parent containment. *Development and Psychopathology, 20,* 591–614.

Luthar, S. S., & Latendresse, S. J. (2005). Children of the affluent: Challenges to well-being. *Current Directions in Psychological Science, 14,* 49–53.

Lutter, C., & Lutter, R. (2012). Fetal and early childhood undernutrition, mortality, and lifelong health. *Science, 337*(6101), 1495–1499. doi:10.1126/science.1224616

Luykx, A., Lee, O., Mahotiere, M., Lester, B., Hart, J., & Deaktor, R. (2007). Cultural and home influences on children's responses to science assessments. *Teachers College Record, 109,* 897–926.

Ly, J., Zhou, Q., Chu, K., & Chen, S. H. (2012). Teacher–child relationship quality and academic achievement of Chinese American children in immigrant families. *Journal of School Psychology, 50*(4), 535–553.

Lyman, E. T. (1981). The responsive classroom discussion: The inclusion of all students. In A. Anderson (Ed.), *Mainstreaming digest* (pp. 109–113). College Park, MD: University of Maryland Press.

Lynch, A., Lerner, R., & Leventhal, T. (2013). Adolescent academic achievement and school engagement: An examination of the role of school-wide peer culture. *Journal of Youth & Adolescence, 42*(1), 6–19.

Lyon, T. D., & Flavell, J. H. (1994). Young children's understanding of "remember" and "forget." *Child Development, 65,* 1357–1371.

Lyons, K. E., & Ghetti, S. (2013). I don't want to pick! Introspection on uncertainty supports early strategic behavior. *Child Development, 84*(2), 726–736. doi:10.1111/cdev.12004

Müeller, U., & Overton, W. F. (2010). Thinking about thinking—Thinking about measurement: A Rasch analysis of recursive thinking. *Journal of Applied Measurement, 11*(1), 78–90.

Müller, J., Achtergarde, S., Frantzmann, H., Steinberg, K., Skorozhenina, O., Beyer, T., Fürniss, T., & Postert, C. (2013). Inter-rater reliability and aspects of validity of the Parent-Infant Relationship Global Assessment Scale (PIR-GAS). *Child and Adolescent Psychiatry and Mental Health, 7.*

MacArthur, C., & Graham, S. (1987). Learning disabled students' composing with three methods: Handwriting, dictation, and word processing. *Journal of Special Education, 21,* 22–42.

Maccoby, E. E. (1984). Middle childhood in the context of the family. In W. A. Collins (Ed.), *Development during middle childhood* (pp. 184–239). Washington, DC: National Academy Press.

Maccoby, E. E. (2007). Historical overview of socialization research and theory. In J. E. Grusec & P. D. Hastings (Eds.), *Handbook of socialization: Theory and research* (pp. 13–41). New York, NY: Guilford.

Maccoby, E. E., & Jacklin, C. N. (1974). *The psychology of sex differences.* Stanford, CA: Stanford University Press.

MacDermott, S. T., Gullone, E., Allen, J. S., King, N. J., & Tonge, B. (2010). The emotion regulation index for children and adolescents (ERICA): A psychometric investigation. *Journal of Psychopathology and Behavioral Assessment, 32*(3), 301–314. doi:10.1007/s10862-009-9154-0

MacDonald, S., Uesiliana, K., & Hayne, H. (2000). Cross-cultural and gender differences in childhood amnesia. *Memory, 8,* 365–376.

Mace, F. C., Belfiore, P. J., & Hutchinson, J. M. (2001). Operant theory and research on self-regulation. In B. J. Zimmerman & D. H. Schunk (Eds.), *Self-regulated learning and academic achievement: Theoretical perspectives* (2nd ed., pp. 39–65). Mahwah, NJ: Lawrence Erlbaum Associates Publishers.

Mackey, W. C. (2001). Support for the existence of an independent man-to-child affiliative bond: Fatherhood as a biocultural invention. *Psychology of Men and Masculinity, 2,* 51–66.

Mackintosh, V. H., Myers, B. J., & Kennon, S. S. (2006). Children of incarcerated mothers and their caregivers: Factors affecting the quality of their relationship. *Journal of Child and Family Studies, 15*(5), 581–596. doi:10.1007/s10826-006-9030-4

Macklem, G. L. (2008). *Practitioner's guide to emotion regulation in school-aged children.* New York, NY: Springer Science + Business Media.

MacWhinney, B., & Chang, F. (1995). Connectionism and language learning. In C. Nelson (Ed.), *Basic and applied perspectives on learning, cognition, and development: The Minnesota Symposia on Child Psychology* (Vol. 28). Mahwah, NJ: Erlbaum.

Madden, K. L., Turnbull, D., Cyna, A. M., Adelson, P., & Wilkinson, C. (2013). Pain relief for childbirth: The preferences of pregnant women, midwives and obstetricians. *Women & Birth, 26*(1), 33–40. doi:10.1016/j.wombi.2011.12.002

Madden, N. A., & Slavin, R. E. (1983). Mainstreaming students with mild handicaps: Academic and social outcomes. *Review of Educational Research, 53,* 519–569.

Madigan, S., Atkinson, L., Laurin, K., & Benoit, D. (2013). Attachment and internalizing behavior in early childhood: A meta-analysis. *Developmental Psychology, 49*(4), 672–689.

Madkour, A., Harville, E., & Xie, Y. (2014). Neighborhood disadvantage, racial concentration and the birthweight of infants born to adolescent mothers. *Maternal & Child Health Journal, 18*(3), 663–671. doi:10.1007/s10995-013-1291-0

Maehr, M. L., & Zusho, A. (2009). Achievement goal theory: The past, present, and future. In K. R. Wenzel & A. Wigfield (Eds.), *Handbook of motivation at school. Educational psychology handbook series* (pp. 77–104). New York, NY: Routledge/Taylor & Francis Group.

Magnuson, K., & Berger, L. M. (2009). Family structure states and transitions: Associations with children's well-being during middle childhood. *Journal of Marriage and Family, 71,* 575–591.

Mahaffy, K. A., & Ward, S. K. (2002). The gendering of adolescents' childbearing and educational plans: Reciprocal effects and the influence of social context. *Sex Roles, 46,* 403–417.

Mahn, H., & John-Steiner, V. (2013). Vygotsky and sociocultural approaches to teaching and learning. In W. M. Reynolds, G. E. Miller, & I. B. Weiner (Eds.), *Handbook of psychology, Vol. 7: Educational psychology* (2nd ed., pp. 117–145). Hoboken, NJ: John Wiley & Sons Inc.

Mahoney J. L., & Parente, M. E. (2009). Should we care about adolescents who care for themselves? What we have learned and what we need to know about youth in self-care. *Child Development Perspectives, 3*(3), 189–195.

Maier, M. A., Bernier, A., Pekrun, R., Zimmermann, P., & Grossmann, K. E. (2004). Attachment working models as unconscious structures: An experimental test. *International Journal of Behavioral Development, 28*(2), 180–189.

Maier, M., Vitiello, V., & Greenfield, D. (2012). A multilevel model of child- and classroom-level psychosocial factors that support language and literacy resilience of children in Head Start. *Early Childhood Research Quarterly, 27*(1), 104–114. doi:10.1016/j.ecresq.2011.06.002

Main, L. F. (2012). Too much too soon? Common core math standards in the early years. *Early Childhood Education Journal, 40*(2), 73–77. doi:10.1007/s10643-011-0484-7

Main, M., & Cassidy, J. (1988). Categories of response to reunion with the parent at age 6: Predictable from infant attachment classification and stable over a 1-month period. *Developmental Psychology, 24,* 415–426.

Main, M., & Solomon, J. (1986). Discovery of an insecure-disorganized/disoriented attachment pattern. In T. B. Brazelton & M. W. Yogman (Eds.), *Affective development in infancy* (pp. 95–124). Norwood, NJ: Ablex.

Main, M., & Solomon, J. (1990). Procedures for identifying infants as disorganized/disoriented during the Ainsworth Strange Situation. In M. T. Greenberg, D. Cicchetti, & E. M. Cummings (Eds.), *Attachment in the preschool years* (pp. 121–160). Chicago, IL: University of Chicago Press.

Main, M., Kaplan, N., & Cassidy, J. (1985). Security in infancy, childhood, and adulthood: A move to the level of representation. *Monographs of the Society for Research in Child Development, 50,* 66–104.

Makarova, E., & Herzog, W. (2013). Hidden school dropout among immigrant students: a cross-sectional study. *Intercultural Education, 24*(6), 559–572. doi:10.1080/14675986.2013.867603

Maker, C. J. (1993). Creativity, intelligence, and problem solving: A definition and design for cross-cultural research and measurement related to giftedness. *Gifted Education International, 9*(2), 68–77.

Malatesta, C. Z., & Haviland, J. M. (1982). Learning display rules: The socialization of emotion expression in infancy. *Child Development, 53,* 991–1003.

Malberg, N., Stafler, N., & Geater, E. (2012). Putting the pieces of the puzzle together: A mentalization-based approach to early intervention in primary schools. *Journal of Infant, Child & Adolescent Psychotherapy, 11*(3), 190–204. doi:10.1080/15289168.2012.700623

Maldonado-Molina, M. M., Reingle, J. M., Tobler, A. L., Jennings, W. G., & Komro, K. A. (2010). Trajectories of physical aggression among Hispanic urban adolescents and young adults: An application of latent trajectory modeling from ages 12 to 18. *American Journal of Criminal Justice, 35*(3), 121–133. doi:10.1007/s12103-010-9074-2

Malinsky, K. P. (1997). Learning to be invisible: Female sexual minority students in America's public high schools. In M. B. Harris (Ed.), *School experiences of gay and lesbian youth: The invisible minority* (pp. 35–50). Binghamton, NY: Harrington Park Press.

Maller, S. J. (2000). Item invariance of four subtests of the Universal Nonverbal Intelligence Test across groups of deaf and hearing children. *Journal of Psychoeducational Assessment, 18,* 240–254.

Mallick, S. K., & McCandless, B. R. (1966). A study of catharsis of aggression. *Journal of Personality and Social Psychology, 4,* 591–596.

Malmberg, J., Järvenoja, H., & Järvelä, S. (2013). Patterns in elementary school students? strategic actions in varying learning situations. *Instructional Science, 41*(5), 933–954. doi:10.1007/s11251-012-9262-1

Malmberg, L. E., Stein, A., West, A., Simon, L., Barnes, J., Leach, P., et al. (2007). Parent–infant interaction: A growth model approach. *Infant Behavior and Development, 30,* 615–630.

Malone, D. M., Stoneham, Z., & Langone, J. (1995). Contextual variation of correspondences among measures of play and developmental level of preschool children. *Journal of Early Intervention, 18,* 199–215.

Malti, T., Eisenberg, N., Kim, H., & Buchmann, M. (2013). Developmental trajectories of sympathy, moral emotion attributions, and moral reasoning: The role of parental support. *Social Development, 22*(4), 773–793. doi:10.1111/sode.12031

Mana, A., Orr, E., & Mana, Y. (2009). An integrated acculturation model of immigrants' social identity. *Journal of Social Psychology, 149*(4), 450–473.

Mandel, D. R., Jusczyk, P. W., & Pisoni, D. B. (1995). Infants' recognition of the sound patterns of their own names. *Psychological Science, 6,* 314–317.

Mandel, E., Osana, H., & Venkatesh, V. (2013). Addressing the effects of reciprocal teaching on the receptive and expressive vocabulary of 1st-grade students. *Journal of Research in Childhood Education, 27*(4), 407–426. doi:10.1080/02568543.2013.824526

Mandel, E., Osana, H., & Venkatesh, V. (2013). Addressing the effects of reciprocal teaching on the receptive and expressive vocabulary of 1st-grade students. *Journal of Research in Childhood Education, 27*(4), 407–426. doi:10.1080/02568543.2013.824526

Mandler, J. M. (2007a). The conceptual foundations of animals and artifacts. In E. Margolis & S. Laurence (Eds.), *Creations of the mind: Theories of artifacts and their representation* (pp. 191–211). New York, NY: Oxford University Press.

Mandler, J. M. (2007b). On the origins of the conceptual system. *American Psychologist, 62,* 741–751.

Mandler, J. M., Fivush, R., & Reznick, J. S. (1987). The development of contextual categories. *Cognitive Development, 2,* 339–354.

Manfra, L., Dinehart, L., & Sembiante, S. (2014). Associations between counting ability in preschool and mathematic performance in first grade among a sample of ethnically diverse, low-income children. *Journal of Research in Childhood Education, 28*(1), 101–114. doi:10.1080/02568543.2013.850129

Mangelsdorf, S. C., Shapiro, J. R., & Marzolf, D. (1995). Developmental and temperamental differences in emotion regulation in infancy. *Child Development, 66,* 1817–1828.

Mann, W., Marshall, C. R., Mason, K., & Morgan, G. (2010). The acquisition of sign language: The impact of phonetic complexity on phonology. *Language Learning and Development, 6*(1), 60–86.

Mannion, A., Leader, G., & Healy, O. (2013). An investigation of comorbid psychological disorders, sleep problems, gastrointestinal symptoms and epilepsy in children and adolescents with autism spectrum disorder. *Research in Autism Spectrum Disorders, 7*(1), 35–42. doi:10.1016/j.rasd.2012.05.002

Manolitsis, G., Georgiou, G. K., & Parrila, R. (2011). Revisiting the home literacy model of reading development in an orthographically consistent language. *Learning & Instruction, 21*(4), 496–505. doi:10.1016/j.learninstruc.2010.06.005

Manuel, A., & Wade, T. D. (2013). Emotion regulation in broadly defined anorexia nervosa: Association with negative affective memory bias. *Behaviour Research and Therapy, 51*(8), 417–424. doi:10.1016/j.brat.2013.04.005

Manzi, C., Ferrari, L., Rosnati, R., & Benet-Martinez, V. (2014). Bicultural identity integration of transracial adolescent adoptees: Antecedents and outcomes. *Journal of Cross-Cultural Psychology, 45*(6), 888–904.

Maoz, H., Tsviban, L., Gvirts, H., Shamay-Tsoory, S., Levkovitz, Y., Watemberg, N., & Bloch, Y. (2014). Stimulants improve theory of mind in children with attention deficit/hyperactivity disorder. *Journal of Psychopharmacology, 28*(3), 212–219. doi:10.1177/0269881113492030

Mar, R. A., & Oatley, K. (2008). The function of fiction is the abstraction and simulation of social experience. *Perspectives on Psychological Science, 3,* 173–192.

Maraj, B. K. V., & Bonertz, C. M. (2007). Verbal-motor learning in children with Down syndrome. *Journal of Sport and Exercise Psychology, 29* (Supplement), 108.

March of Dimes. (2013). *Chromosomal abnormalities. Healthy babies, Healthy business quick references and fact sheets.* Retrieved from http://www.marchofdimes.com/hbhb_syndication/15530_1209.asp

Marchand, G. C., & Taasoobshirazi, G. (2013). Stereotype threat and women's performance in physics. *International Journal of Science Education, 35*(18), 3050-3061. doi:10.1080/09500693.2012.683461

Marchand, G., & Skinner, E. A. (2007). Motivational dynamics of children's help-seeking and concealment. *Journal of Educational Psychology, 99*(1), 65–82.

Marcia, J. (1991). Identity and self-development. In R. M. Lerner, A. C. Petersen, & J. Brooks-Gunn (Eds.), *Encyclopedia of adolescence* (Vol. 1, pp. 529–533). New York, NY: Garland.

Marcia, J. E. (1980). Identity in adolescence. In J. Adelson (Ed.), *Handbook of adolescent psychology (pp. 159–177).* New York, NY: Wiley.

Marcia, J. E. (1988). Common processes underlying ego identity, cognitive/moral development, and individuation. In D. K. Lapsley & F. C. Power (Eds.), *Self, ego, and identity: Integrative approaches* (pp. 211–225). New York, NY: Springer-Verlag.

Marcia, J., & Josselson, R. (2013). Eriksonian personality research and its implications for psychotherapy. *Journal of Personality, 81*(6), 617–629. doi:10.1111/jopy.12014

Marcovitch, S., Goldberg, S., Gold, A., Washington, J., Wasson, C., Krekewich, K., et al. (1997). Determinants of behavioral problems in Romanian children adopted in Ontario. *International Journal of Behavioral Development, 20,* 17–31.

Marcus, G. F. (1996). Why do children say "breaked"? *Current Directions in Psychological Science, 5,* 81–85.

Marcus, G. F., Vijayan, S., Bandi Rao, S., & Vishton, P. M. (1999). Rule learning by seven-month-old infants. *Science, 283,* 77–80.

Mares, M., Palmer, E., & Sullivan, T. (2008). Prosocial effects of media exposure. In S. L. Calvert & B. J. Wilson (Eds.), *The handbook of children, media, and development. Handbooks in communication and media* (pp. 268–289). Malden, MA: Blackwell Publishing. doi:10.1002/9781444302752.ch12

Mares, S. H. W., de Leeuw, R. N. H., Scholte, R. H. J., & Engels, R. C. M. E. (2010). Facial attractiveness and self-esteem in adolescence. *Journal of Clinical Child and Adolescent Psychology, 39*(5), 627–637.

Mareschal, D., Johnson, M. H., Sirois, S., Spratling, M. W., Thomas, M. S. C., & Westermann, G. (2007). *Neuroconstructivism: Vol. 1. How the brain constructs cognition.* Oxford, England: Oxford University Press.

Marinak, B. A., & Gambrell, L. B. (2010). Reading motivation: Exploring the elementary gender gap. *Literacy Research and Instruction, 49*(2), 129–141.

Markman, E. M. (1979). Realizing that you don't understand: Elementary school children's awareness of inconsistencies. *Child Development, 50*(3), 643–655.

Markman, E. M. (1989). *Categorization and naming in children: Problems of induction.* Cambridge, MA: MIT Press.

Markova, G., & Legerstee, M. (2012). Social pretence with mothers and peers at 15 months. *European Journal of Developmental Psychology, 9*(6), 711–722. doi:10.1080/17405629.2012.671714

Marks, D. F. (2011). IQ variations across time, race, and nationality: An artifact of differences in literacy skills. *Counselor Education and Supervision, 50*(3), 643–664.

Markstrom, C. A., Huey, E., Stiles, B. M., & Krause, A. L. (2010). Frameworks of caring and helping in adolescence: Are empathy, religiosity, and spirituality related constructs? *Youth & Society, 42*(1), 59–80. doi:10.1177/0044118X09333644

Markus, H. R., & Hamedani, M. G. (2007). Sociocultural psychology: The dynamic interdependence among self systems and social systems. In S. Kitayama & D. Cohen (Eds.), *Handbook of cultural psychology* (pp. 3–39). New York, NY: Guilford Press.

Marques, S. C. F., Oliveira, C. R., Pereira, C. M. F., & Outeiro, T. F. (2011). Epigenetics in neurodegeneration: A new layer of complexity. *Progress in Neuro-Psychopharmacology & Biological Psychiatry, 35*(2), 348–355. doi:10.1016/j.pnpbp.2010.08.008

Marquez, B., Marquez, J., Vincent, C. G., Pennefather, J., Sprague, J. R., Smolkowski, K., & Yeaton, P. (2014). The iterative development and initial evaluation of We Have Skills!, an innovative approach to teaching social skills to elementary students. *Education & Treatment of Children, 37*(1), 137–161.

Marsh, H. W. (1990a). Causal ordering of academic self-concept and academic achievement: A multiwave, longitudinal panel analysis. *Journal of Educational Psychology, 82,* 646–656.

Marsh, H. W. (1990b). A multidimensional, hierarchical model of self-concept: Theoretical and empirical justification. *Educational Psychology Review, 2,* 77–172.

Marsh, H. W., & Craven, R. (1997). Academic self-concept: Beyond the dustbowl. In G. D. Phye (Ed.), *Handbook of classroom assessment: Learning, achievement, and adjustment.* San Diego, CA: Academic Press.

Marsh, H. W., & Hau, K.-T. (2003). Big-fish-little-pond effect on academic self-concept: A cross-cultural (26-country) test of the negative effects of academically selective schools. *American Psychologist, 58,* 364–376.

Marsh, H. W., Parada, R. H., Yeung, A. S., & Healey, J. (2001). Aggressive school troublemakers and victims: A longitudinal model examining the pivotal role of self-concept. *Journal of Educational Psychology, 93,* 411–419.

Marshall, E., & Toohey, K. (2010). Representing family: Community funds of knowledge, bilingualism, and multimodality. *Harvard Educational Review, 80*(2), 221–241.

Marshall, N. L. (2004). The quality of early child care and children's development. *Current Directions in Psychological Science, 13,* 165–168.

Marshall, S. L., Parker, P. D., Ciarrochi, J., & Heaven, P. L. (2014). Is self-esteem a cause or consequence of social support? A 4-year longitudinal study. *Child Development, 85*(3), 1275–1291. doi:10.1111/cdev.12176

Martens, R., de Brabander, C., Rozendaal, J., Boekaerts, M., & van der Leeden, R. (2010). Inducing mind sets in self-regulated learning with motivational information. *Educational Studies, 36*(3), 311–327. doi:10.1080/03055690903424915

Martin, C. L., & Ruble, D. N. (2010). Patterns of gender development. *Annual Review of Psychology, 61,* 353–381. doi:10.1146/annurev.psych.093008.100511

Martin, J. L. (2009). Formation and stabilization of vertical hierarchies among adolescents: Towards a quantitative ethology of dominance among humans. *Social Psychology Quarterly, 72*(3), 241–264. doi:10.1177/019027250907200307

Martin, J., & Sokol, B. (2011). Generalized others and imaginary audiences: A neo-Meadian approach to adolescent egocentrism. *New Ideas in Psychology, 29*(3), 364–375. doi:10.1016/j.newideapsych.2010.03.006

Martin, K. A., & Torres, J. C. (2014). Where did I come from? US parents' and preschool children's participation in sexual socialisation. *Sex Education, 14*(2), 174–190. doi:10.1080/14681811.2013.856291

Martinez, C. R., & Forgatch, M. S. (2001). Preventing problems with boys' noncompliance: Effects of a parent-training intervention for divorcing mothers. *Journal of Consulting and Clinical Psychology, 69*, 416–428.

Martinez, M. E. (2010). *Learning and cognition: The design of the mind.* Upper Saddle River, NJ: Pearson Merrill.

Martino, S. C., Ellickson, P. L., Klein, D. J., McCaffrey, D., & Edelen, M. O. (2008). Multiple trajectories of physical aggression among adolescent boys and girls. *Aggressive Behavior, 34*, 61–75.

Marzecová, A., Bukowski, M., Correa, Á., Boros, M., Lupiáñez, J., & Wodniecka, Z. (2013). Tracing the bilingual advantage in cognitive control: The role of flexibility in temporal preparation and category switching. *Journal of Cognitive Psychology, 25*(5), 586–604. doi:10.1080/20445911.2013.809348

Masataka, N. (1992). Pitch characteristics of Japanese maternal speech to infants. *Journal of Child Language, 19*, 213–224.

Maschinot, B. (2008). *The changing face of the United States: The influence of culture on early child development.* Washington, DC: Zero to Three.

Mascolo, M. P., & Fischer, K. W. (2010). The dynamic development of thinking, feeling, and acting over the life span. In W. F. Overton, R. M. Lerner (Eds.), *The handbook of life-span development, Vol 1: Cognition, biology, and methods* (pp. 149-194). Hoboken, NJ: Wiley. doi:10.1002/9780470880166.hlsd001006

Mash, C., Bornstein, M. H., & Banerjee, A. (2014). Development of object control in the first year: Emerging category discrimination and generalization in infants' adaptive selection of action. *Developmental Psychology, 50*(2), 325–335. doi:10.1037/a0033234

Mason, L. (2003). Personal epistemologies and intentional conceptual change. In G. M. Sinatra & P. R. Pintrich (Eds.), *Intentional conceptual change* (pp. 199–236). Mahwah, NJ: Erlbaum.

Massey, C. M., & Gelman, R. (1988). Preschoolers' ability to decide whether a photographed unfamiliar object can move itself. *Developmental Psychology, 24*, 307–317.

Massey, D. S., & Denton, N. A. (1993). *American apartheid: Segregation and the making of the underclass.* Cambridge, MA: Cambridge University Press.

Massey, S. L. (2013). From the reading rug to the play center: Enhancing vocabulary and comprehensive language skills by connecting storybook reading and guided play. *Early Childhood Education Journal, 41*(2), 125–131. doi:10.1007/s10643-012-0524-y

Massimini, K. (2000). *Genetic disorders sourcebook* (2nd ed.). Detroit, MI: Omnigraphics.

Masur, E. F., McIntyre, C. W., & Flavell, J. H. (1973). Developmental changes in apportionment of study time among items in a multitrial free recall task. *Journal of Experimental Child Psychology, 15*, 237–246.

Mather, N. (2009). The intelligent testing of children with specific learning disabilities. In J. C. Kaufman (Ed.), *Intelligent testing: Integrating psychological theory and clinical practice* (pp. 30–52). New York, NY: Cambridge University Press.

Matheson, C., Olsen, R. J., & Weisner, T. (2007). A good friend is hard to find: Friendship among adolescents with disabilities. *American Journal on Mental Retardation, 112*(5), 319–329.

Mathieson, K., & Banerjee, R. (2010). Pre-school peer play: The beginnings of social competence. *Educational and Child Psychology. Special Issue: In-School Relationships and their Outcomes, 27*(1), 9–20.

Matjasko, J. L., Needham, B. L., Grunden, L. N., & Farb, A. F. (2010). Violent victimization and perpetration during adolescence: Developmental stage dependent ecological models. *Journal of Youth and Adolescence, 39*(9), 1053–1066. doi:10.1007/s10964-010-9508-7

Matson, J. L., & Fodstad, J. C. (2010). Teaching social skills to developmentally delayed preschoolers. In C. E. Schaefer (Ed.), *Play therapy for preschool children* (pp. 301–322). Washington, DC: American Psychological Association.

Matsuyama, A., & Moji, K. (2008). Perception of bleeding as a danger sign during pregnancy, delivery, and the postpartum period in rural Nepal. *Qualitative Health Research, 18*(2), 196–208.

Matthews, D. J. (2009). Developmental transitions in giftedness and talent: Childhood into adolescence. In F. D. Horowitz, R. F. Subotnik & D. J. Matthews (Eds.), *The development of giftedness and talent across the life span* (pp. 89–107). Washington, DC: American Psychological Association.

Matthews, D., Lieven, E., & Tomasello, M. (2007). How toddlers and preschoolers learn to uniquely identify referents for others: A training study. *Child Development, 78*, 1744–1759.

Maulana, R., Opdenakker, M., & Bosker, R. (2014). Teacher-student interpersonal relationships do change and affect academic motivation: A multilevel growth curve modelling. *British Journal of Educational Psychology, 84*(3), 459–482. doi:10.1111/bjep.12031

Mayer, D. L., & Dobson, V. (1982). Visual acuity development in infants and young children, as assessed by operant preferential looking. *Vision Research, 22*, 1141–1151.

Mayer, D., Sodian, B., Koerber, S., & Schwippert, K. (2014). Scientific reasoning in elementary school children: Assessment and relations with cognitive abilities. *Learning & Instruction, 29*, 43–55. doi:10.1016/j.learninstruc.2013.07.005

Mayer, R. E. (2004). Should there be a three-strikes rule against pure discovery learning? *American Psychologist, 59*, 14–19.

Mayer, R. E. (2010). Fostering scientific reasoning with multimedia instruction. In H. S. Waters & W. Schneider (Eds.), *Metacognition, strategy use, and instruction* (pp. 160–175). New York, NY: Guilford Press.

Mayer, R. E. (2012). Information processing. In K. R. Harris, S. Graham, T. Urdan, C. B. McCormick, G. M. Sinatra, & J. Sweller (Eds.), *APA educational psychology handbook, Vol. 1: Theories, constructs, and critical issues* (pp. 85–99). Washington, DC: American Psychological Association. doi:10.1037/13273-004

Mayer, S. J. (2005). The early evolution of Jean Piaget's clinical method. *History of Psychology, 8*(4), 362–382. doi:10.1037/1093-4510.8.4.362

Mayes, L. C., & Bornstein, M. H. (1997). The development of children exposed to cocaine. In S. S. Luthar, J. A. Burack, D. Cicchetti, & J. R. Weisz (Eds.), *Developmental psychopathology: Perspectives on adjustment, risk, and disorder* (pp. 166–188). Cambridge, England: Cambridge University Press.

Maynard, A. E. (2002). Cultural teaching: The development of teaching skills in Maya sibling interactions. *Child Development, 73*, 969–982.

Maynard, A. E. (2008). What we thought we knew and how we came to know it: Four decades of cross-cultural research from a Piagetian point of view. *Human Development, 51*, 56–65.

Maynard, B., Peters, K., Vaughn, M., & Sarteschi, C. (2013). Fidelity in after-school program intervention research: A systematic review. *Research on Social Work Practice, 23*(6), 613–623.

Mayseless, O. (2005). Ontogeny of attachment in middle childhood: Conceptualization of normative changes. In K. A. Kerns & R. A. Richardson (Eds.), *Attachment in middle childhood* (pp. 1–23). New York, NY: Guilford Press.

Mayworm, A. M., & Sharkey, J. D. (2014). Ethical considerations in a three-tiered approach to school discipline policy and practice. *Psychology in the Schools.* doi:10.1002/pits.21782

McAdams, D. P., & McLean, K. C. (2013). Narrative identity. *Current Directions in Psychological Science, 22*(3), 233–238.

McAdoo, H. P., & Martin, A. (2005). Families and ethnicity. In R. M. Lerner, F. Jacobs, & D. Wertlieb (Eds.), *Applied developmental science: An advanced textbook* (pp. 141–154). Thousand Oaks, CA: Sage.

McAlister, A., & Peterson, C. (2013). Siblings, theory of mind, and executive functioning in children aged 3-6 years: New longitudinal evidence. *Child Development, 84*(4), 1442–1458. doi:10.1111/cdev.12043

McAlpine, L., & Taylor, D. M. (1993). Instructional preferences of Cree, Inuit, and Mohawk teachers. *Journal of American Indian Education, 33*(1), 1–20.

McBride, D. (2013). Uplifting the family: African American parents' ideas of how to integrate religion into family health programming. *Journal of Child & Family Studies, 22*(1), 161–173. doi:10.1007/s10826-012-9654-5

McBride-Chang, C., & Treiman, R. (2003). Hong Kong Chinese kindergartners learn to read English analytically. *Psychological Science, 14*, 138–143.

McBrien, J. L. (2005a). *Discrimination and academic motivation in adolescent refugee girls.* Unpublished doctoral dissertation, Emory University, Atlanta, GA. *Dissertation Abstracts International Section A: Humanities and Social Sciences, 66*(5-A), 2055, pp. 1602.

McBrien, J. L. (2005b). Educational needs and barriers for refugee students in the United States: A review of the literature. *Review of Educational Research, 75*, 329–364.

McCabe, A., Tamis-Lemonda, C. S., Bornstein, M. H., Cates, C. B., Golinkoff, R., Guerra, A. W., et al. (2013). Multilingual children: Beyond myths and toward best practices. *Social Policy Support, 27*(4). Society for Research in Child Development.

McCall, R. B. (1993). Developmental functions for general mental performance. In D. K. Detterman (Ed.), *Current topics in human intelligence* (Vol. 3, pp. 3-29). Norwood, NJ: Ablex.

McCall, R. B., Kennedy, C. B., & Applebaum, M. I. (1977). Magnitude of discrepancy and the distribution of attention in infants. *Child Development, 48*, 772–786.

McCallum, R. S. (1999). A "baker's dozen" criteria for evaluating fairness in nonverbal testing. *The School Psychologist, 53*, 41–60.

McCallum, R. S., & Bracken, B. A. (1997). The Universal Nonverbal Intelligence Test. In D. P. Flanagan, J. L. Genshaft, & P. L. Harrison (Eds.), *Contemporary intellectual assessment: Theories, tests, and issues* (pp. 268–280). New York, NY: Guilford Press.

McCallum, R., & Bracken, B. A. (2012). The Universal Nonverbal Intelligence Test: A multidimensional nonverbal alternative for cognitive assessment. In D. P. Flanagan & P. L. Harrison (Eds.), *Contemporary intellectual assessment: Theories, tests, and issues* (3rd ed., pp. 357-375). New York, NY: Guilford Press.

McCann, T. M. (1989). Student argumentative writing knowledge and ability at three grade levels. *Research in the Teaching of English, 23,* 62–72.

Mccarney, D., Peters, L., Jackson, S., Thomas, M., & Kirby, A. (2013). Does poor handwriting conceal literacy potential in primary school children?. *International Journal of Disability, Development & Education, 60*(2), 105-118. doi:10.1080/10349 12X.2013.786561

McCarthy, B., & Grodsky, E. (2011). Sex and school: Adolescent sexual intercourse and education. *Social Problems, 58*(2), 213–234. doi:10.1525/sp.2011.58.2.213

McCarthy, M., & Kuh, G. D. (2005, September 9). Student engagement: A missing link in improving high schools. *Teachers College Record, 87*(9), 664–669.

McCarty, T. (2009). The impact of high-stakes accountability policies on Native American learners: evidence from research. *Teaching Education, 20*(1), 7–29.

McCarty, T. L., & Watahomigie, L. J. (1998). Language and literacy in American Indian and Alaska Native communities. In B. Pérez (Ed.), *Sociocultural contexts of language and literacy (pp. 79–110).* Mahwah, NJ: Erlbaum.

McCaslin, M., & Good, T. L. (1996). The informal curriculum. In D. C. Berliner & R. C. Calfee (Eds.), *Handbook of educational psychology.* New York, NY: Macmillan.

McClain, D., Schmertzing, L., & Schmertzing, R. (2012). Priming the pump: Implementing Response to Intervention in preschool. *Rural Special Education Quarterly, 31*(1), 33–45.

McClelland, J. L. (2001). Failures to learn and their remediation: A Hebbian account. In J. L. McClelland & R. S. Siegler (Eds.), *Mechanisms of cognitive development: Behavioral and neural perspectives* (pp. 97–121). Mahwah, NJ: Erlbaum.

McClelland, J. L., Fiez, J. A., & McCandliss, B. D. (2002). Teaching the /r/–/l/ discrimination to Japanese adults: Behavioral and neural aspects. *Physiology and Behavior, 77,* 657–662.

McCloskey, M. (1983). Naïve theories of motion. In D. Genter & A. L. Stevens (Eds.), *Mental models* (pp. 299–324). Hillsdale, NJ: Erlbaum.

McCloskey, R. (1948). *Blueberries for Sal.* New York, NY: Viking Press.

McClowry, S., Rodriguez, E., Tamis-LeMonda, C., Spellmann, M., Carlson, A., & Snow, D. (2013). Teacher/student interactions and classroom behavior: The role of student temperament and gender. *Journal of Research in Childhood Education, 27*(3), 283–301. doi:10.1080/02568543.2013.796330

McCombs, B. L., & Vakili, D. (2005). A learner-centered framework for e-learning. *Teachers College Record, 107*(8), 1582–1600.

McConney, M., & Perry, M. (2011). A change in questioning tactics: prompting student autonomy. *Investigations in Mathematics Learning, 3*(3), 26–45.

McCoy, K. (1994). *Understanding your teenager's depression.* New York, NY: Perigee.

McCreary, M. L., Slavin, L. A., & Berry, E. J. (1996). Predicting problem behavior and self-esteem among African-American adolescents. *Journal of Adolescent Research, 11,* 216–234.

McCrink, K., & Wynn, K. (2004). Large-number addition and subtraction by 9-month-old infants. *Psychological Science, 15,* 776–781.

McCrink, K., & Wynn, K. (2007). Ratio abstraction by 6-month-old infants. *Psychological Science, 18,* 740–745.

McCrink, K., & Wynn, K. (2009). Operational momentum in large-number addition and subtraction by 9-month-olds. *Journal of Experimental Child Psychology, 103*(4), 400–408.

McCubbin, L. D., & McCubbin, H. I. (2013). Resilience in ethnic family systems: A relational theory for research and practice. In D. S. Becvar (Ed.), *Handbook of family resilience* (pp. 175–195). New York, NY: Springer Science + Business Media. doi:10.1007/978-1-4614-3917-2_11

McCullough, M. E., Kurzban, R., & Tabak, B. A. (2011). Evolved mechanisms for revenge and forgiveness. In P. R. Shaver & M. Mikulincer (Eds.), *Human aggression and violence: Causes, manifestations, and consequences. Herzilya series on personality and social psychology* (pp. 221–239). Washington, DC: American Psychological Association. doi:10.1037/12346-012

McCutchen, D. (1987). Children's discourse skill: Form and modality requirements of schooled writing. *Discourse Processes, 10,* 267–286.

McDevitt, M., & Ostrowski, A. (2009). The adolescent unbound: Unintentional influence of curricula and ideological conflict seeking. *Political Communication, 26*(1), 11–29. doi:10.1080/10584600802622811

McDevitt, T. M. (1990). Encouraging young children's listening skills. *Academic Therapy, 25,* 569–577.

McDevitt, T. M., & Ford, M. E. (1987). Processes in young children's communicative functioning and development. In M. E. Ford & D. H. Ford (Eds.), *Humans as self-constructing systems: Putting the framework to work.* (pp. 145–175). Hillsdale, NJ: Erlbaum.

McDevitt, T. M., Jobes, R. D., Sheehan, E. P., & Cochran, K. (2010). Is it nature of nurture? Beliefs about child development held by students in psychology courses. *College Student Journal, 44*(2), 533–550.

McDevitt, T. M., Spivey, N., Sheehan, E. P., Lennon, R., & Story, R. (1990). Children's beliefs about listening: Is it enough to be still and quiet? *Child Development, 61,* 713–721.

McDonald, K. L., Baden, R. E., & Lochman, J. E. (2013). Parenting influences on the social goals of aggressive children. *Applied Developmental Science, 17*(1), 29–38. doi:10.1080/10888691.2013.748423

McDonald, K. L., Malti, T., Killen, M., & Rubin, K. H. (2014). Best friends' discussions of social dilemmas. *Journal of Youth and Adolescence, 43*(2), 233–244. doi:10.1007/s10964-013-9961-1

McDonnell, J. (2010). Employment training. In J. McDonnell, M. L. Hardman (Eds.), *Successful transition programs: Pathways for students with intellectual and developmental disabilities* (2nd ed., pp. 241–256). Thousand Oaks, CA: Sage Publications, Inc.

McDuffie, A., Kover, S. T., Hagerman, R., & Abbeduto, L. (2013). Investigating word learning in fragile X syndrome: A fast-mapping study. *Journal of Autism and Developmental Disorders, 43*(7), 1676–1691. doi:10.1007/s10803-012-1717-3

McFadden, K. E., & Tamis-LeMonda, C. S. (2013). Fathers in the U.S. In D. W. Shwalb, B. J. Shwalb, & M. E. Lamb (Eds.), *Fathers in cultural context* (pp. 250–276). New York, NY: Routledge/Taylor & Francis Group.

McGee, E., & Spencer, M. (2014). The development of coping skills for science, technology, engineering, and mathematics students: Transitioning from minority to majority environments. In C. Camp Yeakey, V. L. Sanders Thompson, & A. Wells (Eds.), *Urban ills: Twenty-first-century complexities of urban living in global contexts* (Vol. 1, pp. 351–378). Lanham, MD: Lexington Books/Rowman & Littlefield.

McGeown, S., & Medford, E. (2014). Using method of instruction to predict the skills supporting initial reading development: insight from a synthetic phonics approach. *Reading & Writing, 27*(3), 591–608. doi:10.1007/s11145-013-9460-5

McGonigle-Chalmers, M., Slater, H., & Smith, A. (2013). Rethinking private speech in preschoolers: The effects of social presence. *Developmental Psychology.* doi:10.1037/a0033909

McGowan, D. (2007). *Parenting beyond belief: On raising ethical, caring kids without religion.* New York, NY: AMACOM.

McGrady, P. B., & Reynolds, J. R. (2013). Racial mismatch in the classroom: Beyond black-white differences. *Sociology of Education, 86*(1), 3–17. doi:10.1177/0038040712444857

McGrew, K. S. (2005). The Cattell-Horn-Carroll theory of cognitive abilities: Past, present, and future. In D. P. Flanagan & P. L. Harrison (Eds.), *Contemporary intellectual assessment: Theories, tests, and issues* (2nd ed., pp. 136–181). New York, NY: Guilford Press.

McGue, M., Bouchard, T. J., Jr., Iacono, W. G., & Lykken, D. T. (1993). Behavioral genetics of cognitive ability: A life-span perspective. In R. Plomin & G. E. McClearn (Eds.), *Nature, nurture, and psychology (pp. 59-76).* Washington, DC: American Psychological Association.

McGuire, J. K., Anderson, C. R., Toomey, R. B., & Russell, S. T. (2010). School climate for transgender youth: A mixed method investigation of student experiences and school responses. *Journal of Youth and Adolescence, 39*(10), 1175–1188. doi:10.1007/s10964-010-9540-7

McHale, J. P., & Rasmussen, J. L. (1998). Coparental and family group-level dynamics during infancy: Early family precursors of child and family functioning during preschool. *Development and Psychopathology, 10,* 39–59.

McKean, C., Letts, C., & Howard, D. (2013). Functional reorganization in the developing lexicon: separable and changing influences of lexical and phonological variables on children's fast-mapping. *Journal of Child Language, 40*(2), 307–335. doi:10.1017/S0305000911000444

McKenzie, J. K. (1993). Adoption of children with special needs. *The Future of Children, 3*(1), 26–42.

McKeough, A. (1995). Teaching narrative knowledge for transfer in the early school years. In A. McKeough, J. Lupart, & A. Marini (Eds.), *Teaching for transfer: Fostering generalization in learning (pp. 156-176).* Mahwah, NJ: Erlbaum.

McKie, B. K., Butty, J., & Green, R. D. (2012). Reading, reasoning, and literacy: Strategies for early childhood education from the analysis of classroom observations. *Early Childhood Education Journal, 40*(1), 55–61. doi:10.1007/s10643-011-0489-2

McKinlay, A., Grace, R. C., Horwood, L. J., Fergusson, D. M., Ridder, E. M., & MacFarlane, M. R. (2008). Prevalence of traumatic brain injury among children, adolescents and young adults: Prospective evidence from a birth cohort. *Brain Injury, 22*(2), 175–181.

McLachlan, C., & Arrow, A. (2013). Promoting alphabet knowledge and phonological awareness in low socioeconomic child care settings: A quasi experimental study in five new zealand centers. *Reading and Writing.* doi:10.1007/s11145-013-9467-y

McLane, J. B., & McNamee, G. D. (1990). *Early literacy.* Cambridge, MA: Harvard University Press.

McLoyd, V. C. (1998a). Children in poverty: Development, public policy, and practice. In W. Damon (Series Ed.), & I. E. Sigel, & K. A. Renninger (Vol. Eds.), *Handbook of child psychology: Vol. 4. Child psychology in practice* (5th ed., pp. 135–208). New York, NY: Wiley.

McLoyd, V. C. (1998b). Socioeconomic disadvantage and child development. *American Psychologist, 53,* 185–204.

McLoyd, V. C., Aikens, N. L., & Burton, L. M. (2006). Childhood poverty, policy, and practice. In W. Damon & R. M. Lerner (Eds. in Chief) & K. A. Renninger & I. E. Sigel (Vol. Ed.), *Handbook of child psychology, Vol. 4. Child psychology in practice* (6th ed., pp. 700–775). Hoboken, NJ: Wiley.

McLoyd, V. C., Kaplan, R., Purtell, K. M., Bagley, E., Hardaway, C. R., & Smalls, C. (2009). Poverty and socioeconomic disadvantage in adolescence. In R. M. Lerner & L. Steinberg (Eds.), *Handbook of adolescent psychology. Vol. 2. Contextual influences on adolescent development* (3rd ed., pp. 444–491). Hoboken, NJ: Wiley.

McMahon, S. (1992). Book club: A case study of a group of fifth graders as they participate in a literature-based reading program. *Reading Research Quarterly, 27*, 292–294.

McMillan, B. (2013). Inuit legends, oral histories, art, and science in the collaborative development of lessons that foster two-way learning: The return of the sun in Nunavut. *Interchange, 43*(2), 129–145. doi: 10.1007/s10780-013-9189-8

McMillan, J., & Jarvis, J. (2013). Mental health and students with disabilities: A review of literature. *Australian Journal of Guidance & Counselling, 23*(2), 236–251. doi:10.1017/jgc.2013.14

McMurray, B., Horst, J. S., & Samuelson, L. K. (2012). Word learning emerges from the interaction of online referent selection and slow associative learning. *Psychological Review, 119*(4), 831–877. doi:10.1037/a0029872

McMurray, B., Kovack-Lesh, K., Goodwin, D., & McEchron, W. (2013). Infant directed speech and the development of speech perception: Enhancing development or an unintended consequence? *Cognition, 129*(2), 362–378. doi:10.1016/j.cognition.2013.07.015

McNeill, B., & Kirk, C. (2014). Theoretical beliefs and instructional practices used for teaching spelling in elementary classrooms. *Reading & Writing, 27*(3), 535–554. doi:10.1007/s11145-013-9457-0

McNeill, D. (1966). Developmental psycholinguistics. In F. Smith & G. A. Miller (Eds.), *The genesis of language (pp. 15-84)*. Cambridge, MA: MIT Press.

McNeill, D. (1970). *The acquisition of language: The study of developmental psycholinguistics.* Mervis, C. B., & Becerra, A. M. (2007). Language and communicative development in Williams syndrome. *Mental Retardation & Developmental Disabilities Research Reviews, 13*(1), 3–15. doi:10.1002/mrdd.20140

McWayne, C. M., Owsianik, M., Green, L. E., & Fantuzzo, J. W. (2008). Parenting behaviors and preschool children's social and emotional skills: A question of consequential validity of traditional parenting constructs for low-income African Americans. *Early Childhood Research Quarterly, 23*, 173–192.

Meadan, H., Angell, M.E., Stoner, J.B., & Daczewitz, M.E. (2014). Parent-implemented social-pragmatic communication intervention: A pilot study. *Focus on Autism & Other Developmental Disabilities, 29*(2), 95–110. doi:10.1177/1088357613517504

Meadows, S. (2010). *The child as a social person.* London, England: Routledge.

Mears, A. (2013). Ethnography as precarious work. *The Sociological Quarterly, 54*(1), 20–34. doi:10.1111/tsq.12005

Medrich, E. A. (1981). *The serious business of growing up: A study of children's lives outside the school.* Berkeley, CA: University of California Press.

Medwell, J., & Wray, D. (2014). Handwriting automaticity: the search for performance thresholds. *Language & Education: An International Journal, 28*(1), 34–51. doi:10.1080/09500782.2013.763819

Meece, J. L., & Holt, K. (1993). A pattern analysis of students' achievement goals. *Journal of Educational Psychology, 85*, 582–590.

Meehan, B. T., Hughes, J. N., & Cavell, T. A. (2003). Teacher–student relationships as compensatory resources for aggressive children. *Child Development, 74*, 1145–1157.

Meeusen, C. (2014). The parent–child similarity in cross-group friendship and anti-immigrant prejudice: A study among 15-year old adolescents and both their parents in Belgium. *Journal of*

Research in Personality, 50, 46–55. doi:10.1016/j.jrp.2014.03.001

Mega, C., Ronconi, L., & De Beni, R. (2014). What makes a good student? How emotions, self-regulated learning, and motivation contribute to academic achievement. *Journal of Educational Psychology, 106*(1), 121–131. doi:10.1037/a0033546

Megalakaki, O. (2008). Pupils' conceptions of force in inanimates and animates. *European Journal of Psychology of Education, 23*(3), 339–353.

Megalakaki, O., & Yazbek, H. (2013). Categorization activities performed by children with intellectual disability and typically developing children. *International Journal of Child Health and Human Development, 6*(3), 355–366.

Mehan, H. (1979). *Social organization in the classroom.* Cambridge, MA: Harvard University Press.

Mehler, J., Jusczyk, P., Lambertz, G., Halsted, N., Bertoncini, J., & Amiel-Tison, C. (1988). A precursor of language acquisition in young infants. *Cognition, 29*(2), 143–178.

Mehnert, J., Akhrif, A., Telkemeyer, S., Rossi, S., Schmitz, C. H., Steinbrink, J., Isabell Wartenburger, I., Obrig, H., & Neufang, S. (2013). Developmental changes in brain activation and functional connectivity during response inhibition in the early childhood brain. *Brain & Development, 35*(10), 894–904. doi:10.1016/j.braindev.2012.11.006

Mehr, S. A., Schachner, A., Katz, R. C., & Spelke, E. S. (2013). Two randomized trials provide no consistent evidence for nonmusical cognitive benefits of brief preschool music enrichment. *Plos ONE, 8*(12), 1–12. doi:10.1371/journal.pone.0082007

Mehta, C. M., & Strough, J. (2009). Sex segregation in friendships and normative contexts across the life span. *Developmental Review, 29*(3), 201–220.

Mehta, N., Baker, A. L., & Chong, J. (2013). Training foster parents in loyalty conflict: A training evaluation. *Children and Youth Services Review, 35*(1), 75–81. doi:10.1016/j.childyouth.2012.10.006

Meichenbaum, D. (1977). *Cognitive-behavior modification: An integrative approach.* New York, NY: Plenum Press.

Meichenbaum, D. (1985). Teaching thinking: A cognitive-behavioral perspective. In S. F. Chipman, J. W. Segal, & R. Glaser (Eds.), *Thinking and learning skills: Vol. 2. Research and open questions (pp. 407–426)*. Hillsdale, NJ: Erlbaum.

Meisels, S. J., Wen, X., & Beachy-Quick, K. (2010). Authentic assessment for infants and toddlers: Exploring the reliability and validity of the ounce scale. *Applied Developmental Science, 14*(2), 55–71. doi:10.1080/1088691003697911

Melde, C., Taylor, T. J., & Esbensen, F. (2009). "I got your back": An examination of the protective function of gang membership in adolescence. *Criminology: An Interdisciplinary Journal, 47*(2), 565–594. doi:10.1111/j.1745-9125.2009.00148.x

Mello, Z., Mallett, R., Andretta, J., & Worrell, F. (2012). Stereotype threat and school belonging in adolescents from diverse racial/ethnic backgrounds. *Journal of At-Risk Issues, 17*(1), 9–14.

Meloni, M. (2013). Moralizing biology: The appeal and limits of the new compassionate view of nature. *History of the Human Sciences, 26*(3), 82–106. doi:10.1177/0952695113492163

Meltzer, L. (2010). *Promoting executive function in the classroom.* New York, NY: Guilford Press.

Meltzer, L. (Ed.). (2007). *Executive function in education: From theory to practice.* New York, NY: Guilford Press.

Meltzer, L., & Krishnan, K. (2007). Executive function difficulties and learning disabilities: Understandings and misunderstandings. In L. Meltzer (Ed.), *Executive function in education: From theory to practice* (pp. 77–105). New York, NY: Guilford Press.

Meltzer, L., Pollica, L. S., & Barzillai, M. (2007). Executive function in the classroom: Embedding strategy instruction into daily teaching practices. In L. Meltzer (Ed.), *Executive function in education: From theory to practice* (pp. 165–193). New York, NY: Guilford Press.

Meltzoff, A. N. (2007). "Like me": A foundation for social cognition. *Developmental Science, 10*(1), 126–134.

Menard, S., & Grotpeter, J. K. (2014). Evaluation of Bully-Proofing Your School as an elementary school antibullying intervention. *Journal of School Violence, 13*(2), 188–209. doi:10.1080/15388220.2013.840641

Menary, K., Collins, P. F., Porter, J. N., Muetzel, R., Olson, E. A., Kumar, V., Steinbach, M, Lim, K,& Luciana, M. (2013). Associations between cortical thickness and general intelligence in children, adolescents and young adults. *Intelligence, 41*(5), 597–606. doi:10.1016/j.intell.2013.07.010

Mendez, L., Ogg, J., Loker, T., & Fefer, S. (2013). Including parents in the continuum of school-based mental health services: A review of intervention program research from 1995 to 2010. *Journal of Applied School Psychology, 29*(1), 1–36. doi:10.1080/15377903.2012.725580

Menghini, D., Finzi, A., Benassi, M., Bolzani, R., Facoetti, A., Giovagnoli, S., et al. (2010). Different underlying neurocognitive deficits in developmental dyslexia: A comparative study. *Neuropsychologia, 48*(4), 863–872.

Mennella, J. A., Jagnow, C. P., & Beauchamp, G. K. (2001). Prenatal and postnatal flavor learning by human infants. *Pediatrics, 107*, 88.

Menyuk, P., & Menyuk, D. (1988). Communicative competence: A historical and cultural perspective. In J. S. Wurzel (Ed.), *Toward multiculturalism: A reader in multicultural education (pp. 151-161)*. Yarmouth, ME: Intercultural Press.

Mercer, J. (2006). *Understanding attachment: Parenting, child care, and emotional development.* Westport, CT: Praeger.

Mero, D., & Hartzman, M. (2012). Breaking ranks in action: Collaboration is the foundation. *Principal Leadership, 12*(9), 18–19.

Merrill, E. C., & Conners, F. A. (2013). Age-related interference from irrelevant distracters in visual feature search among heterogeneous distracters. *Journal of Experimental Child Psychology, 115*(4), 640–654. doi:10.1016/j.jecp.2013.03.013

Merritt, E., Wanless, S., Rimm-Kaufman, S., Cameron, C., & Peugh, J. (2012). The contribution of teachers' emotional support to children's social behaviors and self-regulatory skills in first grade. *School Psychology Review, 41*(2), 141–159.

Mervis, C. B., & Becerra, A. M. (2007). Language and communicative development in Williams syndrome. *Mental Retardation & Developmental Disabilities Research Reviews, 13*(1), 3–15. doi:10.1002/mrdd.20140

Merz, E. C., McCall, R. B., & Wright, A. J. (2013). Attention and language as mediators of academic outcomes following early psychosocial deprivation. *International Journal of Behavioral Development, 37*(5), 451–459. doi:10.1177/0165025413490867

Mestre, M. V., Samper, P., Frías, M. D., & Tur, A. M. (2009). Are women more empathetic than men? A longitudinal study in adolescence. *The Spanish Journal of Psychology, 12*(1), 76–83.

Metcalfe, J., & Finn, B. (2013). Metacognition and control of study choice in children. *Metacognition & Learning, 8*(1), 19–46. doi:10.1007/s11409-013-9094-7

Meteyer, K. B., & Perry-Jenkins, M. (2009). Dyadic parenting and children's externalizing symptoms. *Family Relations, 58*, 289–302.

Metz, K. E. (2004). Children's understanding of scientific inquiry: Their conceptualizations of uncertainty in investigations of their own design. *Cognition and Instruction, 22,* 219–290.

Meyer, D. K., Turner, J. C., & Spencer, C. A. (1994, April). *Academic risk taking and motivation in an elementary mathematics classroom.* Paper presented at the annual meeting of the American Educational Research Association, New Orleans, LA.

Meyer, D. K., Turner, J. C., & Spencer, C. A. (1997). Challenge in a mathematics classroom: Students' motivation and strategies in project-based learning. *Elementary School Journal, 97,* 501–521.

Meyer, S., Raikes, H., Virmani, E. A., Waters, S., & Thompson, R. A. (2014). Parent emotion representations and the socialization of emotion regulation in the family. *International Journal of Behavioral Development, 38*(2), 164–173. doi:10.1177/0165025413519014

Meyers, D. T. (1987). The socialized individual and individual autonomy: An intersection between philosophy and psychology. In E. F. Kittay & D. T. Meyers (Eds.), *Women and moral theory.* Totowa, NJ: Rowman & Littlefield.

Micheli, L. J. (1995). Sports injuries in children and adolescents: Questions and controversies. *Clinics in Sports Medicine, 14,* 727–745.

Middleton, J. (2013). More than motivation: The combined effects of critical motivational variables on middle school mathematics Achievement. *Middle Grades Research Journal, 8*(1), 77–95.

Midgley, C. (Ed.). (2002). *Goals, goal structures, and patterns of adaptive learning.* Mahwah, NJ: Erlbaum.

Midgley, C., Kaplan, A., & Middleton, M. (2001). Performance-approach goals: Good for what, for whom, under what circumstances, and at what cost? *Journal of Educational Psychology, 93,* 77–86.

Miele, D., Son, L., & Metcalfe, J. (2013). Children's naive theories of intelligence influence their metacognitive judgments. *Child Development, 84*(6), 1879–1886. doi:10.1111/cdev.12101

Mielke, P., & Frontier, T. (2012). Keeping improvement in mind. *Educational Leadership, 70*(3), 10–13.

Mikolajewski, A. J., Allan, N. P., Hart, S. A., Lonigan, C. J., & Taylor, J. (2013). Negative affect shares genetic and environmental influences with symptoms of childhood internalizing and externalizing disorders. Journal of Abnormal Child Psychology, 41(3), 411–423. doi:10.1007/s10802-012-9681-0

Miksza, P., & Gault, B. M. (2014). Classroom music experiences of U.S. elementary school children: An analysis of the early childhood longitudinal study of 1998–1999. *Journal of Research in Music Education, 62*(1), 4–17. doi:10.1177/0022429413519822

Mikulincer, M., & Shaver, P. R. (2007). *Attachment in adulthood: Structure, dynamics, and change.* New York, NY: Guilford Press.

Mikulincer, M., & Shaver, P. R. (2013). Attachment orientations and meaning in life. In J. A. Hicks, & C. Routledge (Eds.), *The experience of meaning in life: Classical perspectives, emerging themes, and controversies* (pp. 287–304). New York, NY: Springer Science + Business Media. doi:10.1007/978-94-007-6527-6_22

Milanowicz, A., & Bokus, B. (2013). Gender and moral judgments: The role of who is speaking to whom. *Journal of Gender Studies, 22*(4), 423–443. doi:10.1080/09589236.2012.719314

Milardo, R. M. (2010). *The forgotten kin: Aunts and uncles.* New York, NY: Cambridge University Press.

Military Child Education Coalition. (2013). *A military parent's guide to school policies and transitions.* Harker Heights, TX: Author. Retrieved from http://www.militarychild.org/parents-and-students/resources

Miljkovitch, R., Danet, M., & Bernier, A. (2012). Intergenerational transmission of attachment representations in the context of single parenthood in France. *Journal of Family Psychology, 26*(5), 784–792. doi:10.1037/a0029627

Miller, E., & Carlsson-Paige, N. (2013, January 29). A tough critique of Common Core on early childhood education. *Washington Post.* Retrieved from http://www.washingtonpost.com/blogs/answer-sheet/wp/2013/01/29/a-tough-critique-of-common-core-on-early-childhood-education/

Miller, G. E. (1987). School interventions for dishonest behavior. *Special Services in the Schools, 3*(3–4), 21–36. doi:10.1300/J008v03n03_03

Miller, J. (2013). Resilience, violent extremism and religious education. *British Journal of Religious Education, 35*(2), 188–200. doi:10.1080/0141620 0.2012.740444

Miller, J. G. (1987). Cultural influences on the development of conceptual differentiation in person description. *British Journal of Developmental Psychology, 5,* 309–319.

Miller, J. G. (2007). Cultural psychology of moral development. In S. Kitayama & D. Cohen (Eds.), *Handbook of cultural psychology* (pp. 477–499). New York, NY: Guilford Press.

Miller, J. L., & Lossia, A. K. (2013). Prelinguistic infants' communicative system: Role of caregiver social feedback. *First Language, 33*(5), 524–544. doi:10.1177/0142723713503147

Miller, J. L., Lynn, C. H., Shuster, J. J., & Driscoll, D. J. (2013). A reduced-energy intake, well-balanced diet improves weight control in children with Prader-Willi syndrome. Journal of Human Nutrition and Dietetics, 26(1), 2–9. doi:10.1111/j.1365-277X.2012.01275.x

Miller, K. (1989). Measurement as a tool for thought: The role of measuring procedures in children's understanding of quantitative invariance. *Developmental Psychology, 25,* 589–600.

Miller, K. (2013). Variable input: What Sarah reveals about nonagreeing don't and theories of root infinitives. *Language Acquisition, 20*(4), 305–324. doi:10.1080/10489223.2013.828061

Miller, K. F., Smith, C. M., Zhu, J., & Zhang, H. (1995). Preschool origins of cross-national differences in mathematical competence: The role of number-naming systems. *Psychological Science, 6,* 56–60.

Miller, L. S. (1995). *An American imperative: Accelerating minority educational advancement.* New Haven, CT: Yale University Press.

Miller, N., & Maruyama, G. (1976). Ordinal position and peer popularity. *Journal of Personality and Social Psychology, 33,* 123–131.

Miller, P. J., & Goodnow, J. J. (1995). Cultural practices: Toward an integration of culture and development. In J. J. Goodnow & P. J. Miller (Eds.), *Cultural practices as contexts for development* (New Directions for Child Development, No. 67; pp. 5–16). San Francisco: Jossey-Bass.

Miller, P. M., Danaher, D. L., & Forbes, D. (1986). Sex-related strategies of coping with interpersonal conflict in children aged five to seven. *Developmental Psychology, 22,* 543–548.

Miller, R. B., & Brickman, S. J. (2004). A model of future-oriented motivation and self-regulation. *Educational Psychology Review, 16,* 9–33.

Mills, G. E. (2007). *Action research: A guide for the teacher researcher* (3rd ed.). Upper Saddle River, NJ: Pearson Merrill/Prentice Hall.

Mills, M., Watkins, R., Washington, J., Nippold, M., & Schneider, P. (2013). Structural and dialectal characteristics of the fictional and personal narratives of school-age African American children. *Language, Speech & Hearing Services in Schools, 44*(2), 211–223. doi:10.1044/0161-1461(2012/12-0021)

Mills, R. S. L., & Grusec, J. E. (1989). Cognitive, affective, and behavioral consequences of praising altruism. *Merrill-Palmer Quarterly, 35,* 299–326.

Mills, S., & Black, L. (2014). Ensuring children with Down's syndrome reach their full potential. British Journal of School Nursing, 9(2), 97-99.

Milner, H. R. (2006). Classroom management in urban classrooms. In C. M. Evertson & C. S. Weinstein (Eds.), *Handbook of classroom management: Research, practice, and contemporary issues* (pp. 491–522). Mahwah, NJ: Erlbaum.

Milner, H. R., & Ford, D. Y. (2007). Cultural considerations of culturally diverse elementary students in gifted education. *Roeper Review, 29*(3), 166–173.

Mingroni, M. A. (2007). Resolving the IQ paradox: Heterosis as a cause of the Flynn effect and other trends. *Psychological Review, 114,* 806–829.

Minnameier, G., & Schmidt, S. (2013). Situational moral adjustment and the happy victimizer. *European Journal of Developmental Psychology, 10*(2), 253–268. doi:10.1080/17405629.2013.765797

Minshawi, N. F., Hurwitz, S., Fodstad, J. C., Biebl, S., Morriss, D. H., & McDougle, C. J. (2014). The association between self-injurious behaviors and autism spectrum disorders. *Psychology Research & Behavior Management, 7,* 125–136. doi:10.2147/PRBM.S44635

Minshew, N. J., & Williams, D. L. (2007). The new neurobiology of autism: Cortex, connectivity, and neuronal organization. *Archives of Neurology, 64*(7), 945–950. doi:10.1001/archneur.64.7.945

Minskoff, E. H. (1980). Teaching approach for developing nonverbal communication skills in students with social perception deficits: II. Proxemic, vocalic, and artifactual cues. *Journal of Learning Disabilities, 13,* 203–208.

Minstrell, J., & Stimpson, V. (1996). A classroom environment for learning: Guiding students' reconstruction of understanding and reasoning. In L. Schauble & R. Glaser (Eds.), *Innovations in learning: New environments for education (pp. 175-202).* Mahwah, NJ: Erlbaum.

Mischel, W. (1974). Processes in delay of gratification. In L. Berkowitz (Ed.), *Advances in experimental social psychology* (Vol. 7, pp. 249–292). New York, NY: Academic Press.

Mischel, W., & Ebbesen, E. (1970). Attention in delay of gratification. *Journal of Personality and Social Psychology, 16,* 329–337.

Mischel, W., Shoda, Y., & Rodriguez, M. L. (1989). Delay of gratification in children. *Science, 244*(4907), 933–938. doi:10.1126/science.2658056

Missana, M., Grigutsch, M., & Grossmann, T. (2014). Developmental and individual differences in the neural processing of dynamic expressions of pain and anger. *Plos ONE, 9*(4), 1–13. doi:10.1371/journal.pone.0093728

Mitchell, E. A. (2009). What is the mechanism of SIDS? Clues from epidemiology. *Developmental Psychobiology, 51*(3), 216–222.

Mitchell, M. (2013). Women's use of complementary and alternative medicine in pregnancy: A journey to normal birth. British Journal of Midwifery, 21(2), 100-106.

Mitchell, M. L., & Brendtro, L. K. (2013). Victories over violence: The quest for safe schools and communities. *Reclaiming Children & Youth,* pp. 5–11.

Mitchell, S., Foulger, T. S., & Wetzel, K. (2009). Ten tips for involving families through internet-based communication. *Young Children, 64*(5), 46–49.

Mitru, G., Millrood, D., & Mateika, J. H. (2002). The impact of sleep on learning and behavior of adolescents. *Teachers College Record, 104,* 704–726.

Mittal, R., Russell, B., Britner, P., & Peake, P. (2013). Delay of gratification in two- and three-year-olds: Associations with attachment, personality, and temperament. *Journal of Child & Family Studies, 22*(4), 479–489. doi:10.1007/s10826-012-9600-6

Miura, I. T., & Okamoto, Y. (2003). Language supports for mathematics understanding and performance. In A. J. Baroody, A. Dowker (Eds.), *The development of arithmetic concepts and skills: Constructing adaptive expertise* (pp. 229–242). Mahwah, NJ: Lawrence Erlbaum Associates Publishers.

Miyake, K., Chen, S.-J., & Campos, J. J. (1985). Infant temperament, mother's mode of interaction, and attachment in Japan: An interim report. In I. Bretherton & E. Waters (Eds.), Growing points of attachment theory and research. *Monographs of the Society for Research in Child Development, 50*(1–2, Serial No. 209), 276–297.

Miyazaki, K., Makomaska, S., & Rakowski, A. (2012). Prevalence of absolute pitch: A comparison between Japanese and Polish music students. *Journal of the Acoustical Society of America, 132*(5), 3484–3493. doi:10.1121/1.4756956

Modestou, M., & Gagatsis, A. (2010). Cognitive and metacognitive aspects of proportional reasoning. *Mathematical Thinking and Learning, 12*(1), 36–53.

Moely, B. E., Santulli, K. A., & Obach, M. S. (1995). Strategy instruction, metacognition, and motivation in the elementary school classroom. In F. E. Weinert & W. Schneider (Eds.), *Memory performance and competencies: Issues in growth and development* (pp. 301–321). Hillsdale, NJ: Erlbaum.

Moffitt, T. E., Arseneault, L., Belsky, D., Dickson, N., Hancox, R. J., Harrington, H., et al. (2011). A gradient of childhood self-control predicts health, wealth, and public safety. *Proceedings of the National Academy of Sciences of the United States of America, 108*(7), 2693–2698. doi:10.1073/pnas.1010076108

Mohatt, G., & Erickson, F. (1981). Cultural differences in teaching styles in an Odawa school: A socio-linguistic approach. In H. T. Trueba, G. P. Guthrie, & K. H. Au (Eds.), *Culture and the bilingual classroom: Studies in classroom ethnography* (pp. 105–119). Rowley, MA: Newbury House.

Moje, E. B. (2000). "To be part of the story": The literacy practices of gangsta adolescents. *Teachers College Record, 102*(3), 651–690.

Moksnes, U. K., Espnes, G. A., & Haugan, G. (2014). Stress, sense of coherence and emotional symptoms in adolescents. *Psychology & Health, 29*(1), 32–49. doi:10.1080/08870446.2013.822868

Moksnes, U. K., Moljord, I. E. O., Espnes, G. A., & Byrne, D. G. (2010). The association between stress and emotional states in adolescents: The role of gender and self-esteem. *Personality and Individual Differences, 49*(5), 430–435.

Moll, L. C., Amanti, C., & Neff, D. (1992). Funds of knowledge for teaching: Using a qualitative approach to connect homes and classrooms. *Theory into Practice, 31*, 132–141. doi:10.1080/00405849209543534

Moll, L., Amanti, C., Neff, D., & González, N. (2005). Funds of knowledge for teaching: Using a qualitative approach to connect homes and classrooms. In N. González, L. C. Moll, & C. Amanti (Eds.), *Funds of knowledge: Theorizing practices in households, communities, and classrooms* (pp. 71–87). Mahwah, NJ: Erlbaum.

Montagu, A. (1999). Introduction. In A. Montagu (Ed.), *Race and IQ* (expanded ed., pp. 1–18). New York, NY: Oxford University Press.

Montague, M., Enders, C., & Dietz, S. (2011). Effects of cognitive strategy instruction on math problem solving of middle school students with learning disabilities. *Learning Disability Quarterly, 34*(4), 262–272.

Montemayor, R. (1982). The relationship between parent–adolescent conflict and the amount of time adolescents spend with parents, peers, and alone. *Child Development, 53*, 1512–1519.

Montessori, M. (1936). *The secret of childhood* (M. J. Costelloe, Trans.). New York, NY: Ballantine Books, 1966.

Montessori, M. (1949). *The absorbent mind* (M. J. Costelloe, Trans.). New York, NY: Holt, Rinehart & Winston.

Montgomery, H. (2009). *An introduction to childhood: Anthropological perspectives on children's lives.* Chichester, United Kingdom: Wiley.

Montgomery, K. S., Mackey, J., Thuett, K., Ginestra, S., Bizon, J. L., & Abbott, L. C. (2008). Chronic, low-dose prenatal exposure to methylmercury impairs motor and mnemonic function in adult C57/B6 mice. *Behavioural Brain Research, 191*, 55–61.

Montroy, J., Bowles, R., Skibbe, L., & Foster, T. (2014). Social skills and problem behaviors as mediators of the relationship between behavioral self-regulation and academic achievement. *Early Childhood Research Quarterly, 29*(3), 298–309. doi:10.1016/j.ecresq.2014.03.002

Moomaw, S. (2012). STEM begins in the early years. *School Science & Mathematics, 112*(2), 57–58. doi:10.1111/j.1949-8594.2011.00119.x

Moon, C., Lagercrantz, H., & Kuhl, P. (2013). Language experienced in utero affects vowel perception after birth: A two-country study. *Acta Paediatrica, 102*(2), 156–160. doi:10.1111/apa.12098

Moon, S. M., Feldhusen, J. F., & Dillon, D. R. (1994). Long term effects of an enrichment program based on the Purdue three-stage model. *Gifted Child Quarterly, 38*, 38–47.

Mooney, R. (2014). The preschool playground: A young child's experience of entering the emotional field. *Infant Observation, 17*(1), 35–49. doi:10.1080/13698036.2014.895220

Moore, C. (2010). The development of future-oriented decision-making. In B. W. Sokol, U. Müeller, J. I. M. Carpendale, A. R. Young, & G. Iarocci (Eds.), *Self and social regulation: Social interaction and the development of social understanding and executive functions* (pp. 270–286). New York, NY: Oxford University Press.

Moore, G. A., Cohn, J. F., & Campbell, S. B. (2001). Infant affective responses to mother's still face at 6 months differentially predict externalizing and internalizing behaviors at 18 months. *Developmental Psychology, 37*, 706–714.

Moore, K. L., & Persaud, T. V. N. (2008). *Before we are born: Essentials of embryology and birth defects* (7th ed.). Philadelphia, PA: Saunders/Elsevier.

Moore, K. L., Persaud, T. V. N., & Torchia, M. G. (2013). *Before we are born: Essentials of embryology and birth defects* (9th ed.). Philadelphia, PA: Saunders/Elsevier.

Moore, L. C. (2006). Learning by heart in Qur'anic and public schools in northern Cameroon. *Social Analysis, 50*(3), 109–126.

Moore, L. C. (2010). Learning in schools. In D. F. Lancy, J. Bock, & S. Gaskins (Eds.), *The anthropology of learning in childhood* (pp. 207–232). Lanham, MD: AltaMira Press/Rowman & Littlefield.

Moore, L. C. (2013). Qur'anic school sermons as a site for sacred and second language socialisation. *Journal of Multilingual & Multicultural Development, 34*(5), 445–458. doi:10.1080/01434632.2013.783036

Moore, P. S., Whaley, S. E., & Sigman, M. (2004). Interactions between mothers and children: Impacts of maternal and child anxiety. *Journal of Abnormal Psychology, 113*(3), 471–476.

Moore, R. (2013). Imitation and conventional communication. *Biology & Philosophy, 28*(3), 481–500. doi:10.1007/s10539-012-9349-8

Moran, S., & Gardner, H. (2006). Extraordinary achievements: A developmental and systems analysis. In W. Damon & R. M. Lerner (Series Eds.), & D. Kuhn & R. Siegler (Vol. Eds.), *Handbook of child psychology: Vol. 2. Cognition, perception, and language* (6th ed., pp. 905–949). New York, NY: Wiley.

Morawska, A., Laws, R., Moretto, N., & Daniels, L. (2014). Observing the mother–infant feeding interaction. *Early Child Development & Care, 184*(4), 522–536. doi:10.1080/03004430.2013.800051

Morelli, G. A., & Rothbaum, F. (2007). Situating the child in context: Attachment relationships and self-regulation in different cultures. In S. Kitayama & D. Cohen (Eds.), *Handbook of cultural psychology* (pp. 500–527). New York, NY: Guilford Press.

Moreno, M. A., Jelenchick, L. A., & Christakis, D. A. (2013). Problematic internet use among older adolescents: A conceptual framework. *Computers in Human Behavior, 29*(4), 1879–1887. doi:10.1016/j.chb.2013.01.053

Morgan, H. (2012). What teachers and schools can do to control the growing problem of school bullying. *Clearing House, 85*(5), 174–178. doi:10.1080/00098655.2012.677075

Morimoto, S., & Friedland, L. (2013). Cultivating success: Youth achievement, capital and civic engagement in the contemporary United States. *Sociological Perspectives, 56*(4), 523–546.

Morin, A. S., Maïano, C., Marsh, H. W., Nagengast, B., & Janosz, M. (2013). School life and adolescents' self-esteem trajectories. *Child Development, 84*(6), 1967–1988. doi:10.1111/cdev.12089

Moroney, S. K. (2006). Higher stages? Some cautions for Christian integration with Kohlberg's Theory. *Journal of Psychology and Theology, 34*(4), 361–371.

Morra, S., Gobbo, C., Marini, Z., & Sheese, R. (2008). *Cognitive development: Neo-Piagetian perspectives.* New York, NY: Erlbaum.

Morris, A. S., Cui, L., & Steinberg, L. (2013). Parenting research and themes: What we have learned and where to go next. In R. E. Larzelere, A. Morris, A. W. Harrist (Eds.), *Authoritative parenting: Synthesizing nurturance and discipline for optimal child development* (pp. 35–58). Washington, DC: American Psychological Association. doi:10.1037/13948-003

Morris, A., Silk, J. S., Morris, M. S., Steinberg, L., Aucoin, K. J., & Keyes, A. W. (2011). The influence of mother–child emotion regulation strategies on children's expression of anger and sadness. *Developmental Psychology, 47*(1), 213–225. doi:10.1037/a0021021

Morris, D. (1977). *Manwatching: A field guide to human behaviour.* New York, NY: Harry N. Abrams.

Morris, H. (2014). Socioscientific issues and multidisciplinarity in school science textbooks. *International Journal of Science Education, 36*(7), 1137–1158. doi:10.1080/09500693.2013.848493

Morrison, G. M., Furlong, M. J., D'Incau, B., & Morrison, R. L. (2004). The safe school: Integrating the school reform agenda to prevent disruption and violence at school. In J. C. Conoley & A. P. Goldstein (Ed.), *School violence intervention* (2nd ed., pp. 256–296). New York, NY: Guilford Press.

Morrongiello, B. A., Fenwick, K. D., Hillier, L., & Chance, G. (1994). Sound localization in newborn human infants. *Developmental Psychobiology, 27*, 519–538.

Mortimer, J. T., Shanahan, M., & Ryu, S. (1994). The effects of adolescent employment on school-related orientation and behavior. In R. K. Silbereisen & E. Todt (Eds.), *Adolescence in context: The interplay of family, school, peers and work in adjustment* (pp. 304–326). New York, NY: Springer-Verlag.

Mortimer, J. T., Shanahan, M., & Ryu, S. (1994). The effects of adolescent employment on school-related orientation and behavior. In R. K. Silbereisen & E. Todt (Eds.), *Adolescence in context: The interplay of family, school, peers and work in adjustment.* New York, NY: Springer-Verlag.

Morton, A. (1980). *Frames of mind: Constraints on the common-sense conception of the mental.* Oxford, England: Clarendon Press.

Mosier, K. L. (2013). Judgment and prediction. In J. D. Lee, A. Kirlik (Eds.), *The Oxford handbook of cognitive engineering* (pp. 68–87). New York, NY: Oxford University Press.

Mou, Y., & vanMarle, K. (2014). Two core systems of numerical representation in infants. *Developmental Review, 34*(1), 1–25. doi:10.1016/j.dr.2013.11.001

Muñoz-García, A., & Aviles-Herrera, M. (2014). Effects of academic dishonesty on dimensions of spiritual well-being and satisfaction: a comparative study of secondary school and university students. *Assessment & Evaluation in Higher Education, 39*(3), 349–363. doi:10.1080/0260293 8.2013.832729

Muennig, P., Schweinhart, L., Montie, J., & Neidell, M. (2009). Effect of a prekindergarten educational intervention on adult health: 37-year follow-up results of a randomized control trial. *American Journal of Public Health, 99*(5), 1431–1437.

Muftuler, L., Davis, E., Buss, C., Solodkin, A., Su, M., Head, K. M., Hasso, A. N., & Sandman, C. A. (2012). Development of white matter pathways in typically developing preadolescent children. *Brain Research.* doi:10.1016/j.brainres.2012.05.035

Muijs, D., Kyriakides, L., van der Werf, G., Creemers, B., Timperley, H., & Earl, L. (2014). State of the art – teacher effectiveness and professional learning. *School Effectiveness & School Improvement, 25*(2), 231–256. doi:10.1080/09243453.2014.885451

Muis, K. R. (2007). The role of epistemic beliefs in self-regulated learning. *Educational Psychologist, 42,* 173–190.

Mulcahey, C. (2009, July). Providing rich art activities for young children. *Young Children, 64*(4), 107–112.

Mullins, D., & Tisak, M. S. (2006). Moral, conventional, and personal rules: The perspective of foster youth. *Journal of Applied Developmental Psychology, 27,* 310–325.

Mullis, R. L., Graf, S. C., & Mullis, A. K. (2009). Parental relationships, autonomy, and identity processes of high school students. *The Journal of Genetic Psychology: Research and Theory on Human Development, 170*(4), 326–338.

Mundy, P., & Newell, L. (2007). Attention, joint attention, and social cognition. *Current Directions in Psychological Science, 16,* 269–274.

Munroe, R. L., & Munroe, P. J. (1992). Fathers in children's environments: A four culture study. In B. S. Hewlett (Ed.), *Father–child relations: Cultural and biosocial contexts* (pp. 213–230). New York, NY: Aldine de Gruyter.

Muramoto, Y., Yamaguchi, S., & Kim, U. (2009). Perception of achievement attribution in individual and group contexts: Comparative analysis of Japanese, Korean, and Asian-American results. *Asian Journal of Social Psychology, 12*(3), 199–210. doi:10.1111/j.1467-839X.2009.01285.x

Murdock, T. B. (1999). The social context of risk: Status and motivational predictors of alienation in middle school. *Journal of Educational Psychology, 91,* 62–75.

Muris, P., & Meesters, C. (2014). Small or big in the eyes of the other: On the developmental psychopathology of self-conscious emotions as shame, guilt, and pride. *Clinical Child and Family Psychology Review, 17*(1), 19–40. doi:10.1007/s10567-013-0137-z

Muris, P., & Meesters, C. (2014). Small or big in the eyes of the other: On the developmental psychopathology of self-conscious emotions as shame, guilt, and pride. *Clinical Child and Family Psychology Review, 17*(1), 19–40. doi:10.1007/s10567-013-0137-z

Muris, P., Meesters, C., & Rompelberg, L. (2006). Attention control in middle childhood: Relations to psychopathological symptoms and threat perception distortions. *Behaviour Research and Therapy, 45,* 997–1010.

Murnane, R. J. (2007, Fall). Improving the education of children living in poverty. *The Future of Children, 17*(2), 161–182.

Murphy, P. K. (2007). The eye of the beholder: The interplay of social and cognitive components in change. *Educational Psychologist, 42,* 41–53.

Murphy, P. K., & Alexander, P. A. (2008). Examining the influence of knowledge, beliefs, and motivation in conceptual change. In S. Vosniadou (Ed.), *International handbook of research on conceptual change* (pp. 583–616). New York, NY: Taylor & Francis.

Murphy, P. K., & Mason, L. (2006). Changing knowledge and beliefs. In P. A. Alexander & P. H. Winne (Eds.), *Handbook of educational psychology* (2nd ed., pp. 305–324). Mahwah, NJ: Erlbaum.

Mussolin, C., Mejias, S., & Noël, M. (2010). Symbolic and nonsymbolic number comparison in children with and without dyscalculia. *Cognition, 115*(1), 10–25.

Mustanski, B. S., Viken, R. J., Kaprio, J., Pulkkinen, L., & Rose, R. (2004). Genetic and environmental influences on pubertal influences on pubertal development: Longitudinal data from Finnish twins at ages 11 and 14. *Developmental Psychology, 40,* 1188–1198.

Muter, V. (1998). Phonological awareness: Its nature and its influence over early literacy development. In C. Hulme & R. M. Joshi (Eds.), *Reading and spelling: Development and disorders (pp. 113-125).* Mahwah, NJ: Erlbaum.

Mweru, M., & murungi, C. (2013). What can schools learn from children about use of culturally relevant methods and materials? *Journal of Emerging Trends in Educational Research & Policy Studies, 4*(3), 491–498.

Myatchin, I., & Lagae, L. (2013). Developmental changes in visuo-spatial working memory in normally developing children: Event-related potentials study. *Brain & Development, 35*(9), 853–864. doi:10.1016/j.braindev.2012.11.005

Myers, B. J., Smarsh, T. M., Amlund-Hagen, K., & Kennon, S. (1999). Children of incarcerated mothers. *Journal of Child and Family Studies, 8*(1), 11–25. doi:10.1023/A:1022990410036

Myers, L. L. (2013). Substance use among rural African American adolescents: Identifying risk and protective factors. *Child & Adolescent Social Work Journal, 30*(1), 79–93. doi:10.1007/s10560-012-0280-2

Myles, B. M., & Simpson, R. L. (2001). Understanding the hidden curriculum: An essential social skill for children and youth with Asperger syndrome. *Intervention in School and Clinic, 36*(5), 279–286.

Myrberg, E., & Rosén, M. (2009). Direct and indirect effects of parents' education on reading achievement among third graders in Sweden. *British Journal of Educational Psychology, 79*(4), 695–711.

Nærde, A., Ogden, T., Janson, H., & Daae Zachrisson, H. (2014). Normative development of physical aggression from 8 to 26 Months. *Developmental Psychology, 50*(6), 1710–1720. doi:10.1037/a0036324

Naar-King, S., Montepiedra, G., Garvie, P., Kammerer, B., Malee, K., Sirois, P. A., Aaron, L., & Nichols, S. L. (2013). Social ecological predictors of longitudinal HIV treatment adherence in youth with perinatally acquired HIV. *Journal of Pediatric Psychology, 38*(6), 664–674. doi:10.1093/jpepsy/jst017

Nabors, L. A., Little, S. G., Akin-Little, A., & Iobst, E. A. (2008). Teacher knowledge of and confidence in meeting the needs of children with chronic medical conditions: Pediatric psychology's contribution to education. *Psychology in the Schools, 45*(3), 217–226.

Naegele, J. R., & Lombroso, P. J. (2001). Genetics of central nervous system developmental disorders. *Child and Adolescent Psychiatric Clinics of North America, 10,* 225–239.

Naglieri, J. A., & Conway, C. (2009). The Cognitive Assessment System. In J. A. Naglieri & S. Goldstein (Eds.), *Practitioner's guide to assessing intelligence and achievement* (pp. 27–59). Hoboken, NJ: Wiley.

Naglieri, J. A., & Otero, T. M. (2012). The Cognitive Assessment System: From theory to practice. In D. P. Flanagan, P. L. Harrison (Eds.), *Contemporary intellectual assessment: Theories, tests, and issues* (3rd ed., pp. 376–399). New York, NY: Guilford Press.

Naglieri, J. A., De Lauder, B. Y., Goldstein, S., & Schwebech, A. (2006). WISC-III and CAS: Which correlates higher with achievement for a clinical sample? *School Psychology Quarterly, 21*(1), 62–76.

Nagy, E. (2008). Innate intersubjectivity: Newborns' sensitivity to communication disturbance. *Developmental Psychology, 44*(6), 1779–1784.

Nail, M. H. (2007). Reaching out to families with student-created newsletters. *Kappa Delta Pi Record, 44*(1), 39-41.

Nakata, N., & Trehub, S. E. (2004). Infants' responsiveness to maternal speech and singing. *Infant Behavior and Development, 27,* 455–464.

Nalkur, P. G. (2009). A cultural comparison of Tanzanian street children, former street children, and school-going children. *Journal of Cross-Cultural Psychology, 40*(6), 1012–1027. doi:10.1177/0022022109346954

Nanu, C., Tăut, D., & Băban, A. (2013). Appearance esteem and weight esteem in adolescence. Are they different across age and gender? *Cognition, Brain, Behavior: An Interdisciplinary Journal, 17*(3), 189–200.

Narayanan, U., & Warren, S. T. (2006). Neurobiology of related disorders: Fragile X syndrome. In S. O. Moldin & J. L. R. Rubenstein (Eds.), *Understanding autism: From basic neuroscience to treatment* (pp. 113–131). Boca Raton, FL: CRC Press.

Narváez, D. (1998). The influence of moral schemas on the reconstruction of moral narratives in eighth graders and college students. *Journal of Educational Psychology, 90,* 13–24.

Narváez, D., & Rest, J. (1995). The four components of acting morally. In W. M. Kurtines & J. L. Gewirtz (Eds.), *Moral development: An introduction.* Boston: Allyn & Bacon.

Nash, K., Schiller, B., Gianotti, L. R., Baumgartner, T., & Knoch, D. (2013). Electrophysiological indices of response inhibition in a go/no go task predict self-control in a social context. *Plos ONE, 8*(11), 1–7. doi:10.1371/journal.pone.0079462

Natarajan, G., Shankaran, S., Laptook, A. R., Pappas, A., Bann, C. M., McDonald, S. A., Das, A., Higgins, R. A., Hintz, S. R., & Vohr, B. R. (2013). Apgar scores at 10 min and outcomes at 6–7 years following hypoxic-ischaemic encephalopathy. *Archives of Disease in Childhood—Fetal & Neonatal Edition, 98*(6), F473–F479. doi:10.1136/archdischild-2013-303692

Nation, K., & Hulme, C. (1998). The role of analogy in early spelling development. In C. Hulme & R. Joshi (Eds.), *Reading and spelling: Development and disorders* (pp. 433–445). Mahwah, NJ: Lawrence Erlbaum.

National Association for the Education of Young Children. (1997). *Developmentally appropriate practice in early childhood programs serving children from birth through age 8.* Washington, DC: Author.

National Association for the Education of Young Children. (2009). *Developmentally appropriate practice in early childhood programs serving children birth through age 8.* Retrieved from http://208.118.177.216/about/positions/pdf/PSDAP.pdf

National Association for the Education of Young Children. (2012). *The Common Core State Standards: Caution and opportunity for early childhood education*. Washington, DC: Author. Retrieved from https://www.naeyc.org/files/naeyc/11_CommonCore1_2A_rv2.pdf

National Association of Secondary School Principals. (2004). *Breaking ranks II: Strategies for leading high school reform*. Reston, VA: Author.

National Board for Professional Teaching Standards. (2001). *NBTS Middle childhood generalist standards* (2nd ed.). Retrieved from http://www.nbpts.org/the_standards/standards_by_cert?ID=27&x=57&y=9

National Center for Education Statistics (2012). *Average National Assessment of Educational Progress (NAEP) reading scale score, by grade and selected student and school characteristics: Selected years, 1992 through 2011*. Retrieved from http://nces.ed.gov/programs/digest/d12/tables/dt12_142.asp

National Center for Education Statistics. (2007). *Digest of education statistics. Table 183. Graduation rates and postsecondary attendance rates of recent high school students, by selected high school characteristics: 1999–2000*. National Center for Education Statistics, Institute of Education Sciences, U.S. Department of Education. Retrieved from http://nces.ed.gov/programs/digest/d05/tables/dt05_183.asp

National Center for Education Statistics. (2014). *Fast facts: English language learners*. Retrieved from http://nces.ed.gov/fastfacts/display.asp?id=96

National Center for Missing and Exploited Children. (2004). *HDOP: Help delete online predators*. Retrieved from http://www.missingkids.com/adcouncil

National Center on Linguistic and Cultural Responsiveness. (2014). *Gathering information on language that families share*. Retrieved from http://eclkc.ohs.acf.hhs.gov/hslc/tta-system/cultural-linguistic/docs/dll_background_info.pdf

National Clearinghouse for English Language Acquisition. (2006). *Resources about secondary English language learners*. Retrieved from http://www.ncela.gwu.edu/resabout/ells/intro

National Dissemination Center for Children with Disabilities. (2013). *Intellectual disability*. Retrieved from http://nichcy.org/disability/specific/intellectual#causes

National Drug Intelligence Center. (2008). *Attorney General's report to Congress on the growth of violent street gangs in suburban areas*. Retrieved from http://www.usdoj.gov/ndic/pubs27/27612/estimate.htm

National Governors Association and Council of Chief State School Officers. (2014). *Common Core State Standards Initiative: Preparing America's students for college and career*. Retrieved from http://www.corestandards.org

National Institute of Mental Health. (2008a). *Autism spectrum disorders (Pervasive developmental disorders)*. Retrieved from http://www.nimh.nih.gov/health/publications/autism/summary.shtml

National Institute of Mental Health. (2008b). *Suicide in the U.S.: Statistics and prevention*. Retrieved from http://www.nimh.nih.gov/health/publications/suicide-in-the-us-statistics-and-prevention.shtml#races

National Institute on Drug Abuse. (2003). *Preventing drug use among children and adolescents: A research-based guide for parents, educators, and community leaders*. Bethesda, MD: U.S. Department of Health and Human Services, National Institutes of Health, National Institute on Drug Abuse.

National Institute on Drug Abuse. (2009). *Principles of drug addiction treatment: A research-based guide* (2nd ed.). Retrieved from http://www.drugabuse.gov/PODAT/PODATIndex.html

National Institute on Drug Abuse. (2010a). *Alcohol*. Retrieved from http://www.drugabuse.gov/drugpages/alcohol.html

National Institute on Drug Abuse. (2010b). *Cocaine*. Retrieved from http://www.drugabuse.gov/drugpages/cocaine.html

National Institute on Drug Abuse. (2010c). *Inhalants*. Retrieved from http://www.drugabuse.gov/drugpages/inhalants.html

National Institute on Drug Abuse. (2010d). *Marijuana*. Retrieved from http://www.drugabuse.gov/drugpages/marijuana.html

National Institute on Drug Abuse. (2010e). *MDMA (Ecstasy)*. Retrieved from http://www.drugabuse.gov/drugpages/mdma.html

National Institute on Drug Abuse. (2010f). *Methamphetamines*. Retrieved from http://www.drugabuse.gov/drugpages/methamphetamine.html

National Institute on Drug Abuse. (2010g). *Prescription drugs*. Retrieved from http://www.drugabuse.gov/drugpages/prescription.html

National Institute on Drug Abuse. (2010h). *Steroids (anabolic)*. Retrieved from http://www.drugabuse.gov/drugpages/steroids.html

National Research Council. (1999). *How people learn: Brain, mind, experience, and school*. Washington, DC: Author.

National Science Teachers Association. (2014). NSTA position statement: Early childhood science education. *Science & Children, 51*(7), 10–12.

NCSS Task Force on Ethnic Studies Curriculum Guidelines. (1992). Curriculum guidelines for multicultural education. *Social Education, 56*, 274–294.

Neal, J., Neal, Z. P., & Cappella, E. (2014). I know who my friends are, but do you? Predictors of self-reported and peer-inferred relationships. *Child Development, 85*(4), 1366–1372. doi:10.1111/cdev.12194

Needham, B. L., & Austin, E. L. (2010). Sexual orientation, parental support, and health during the transition to young adulthood. *Journal of Youth and Adolescence, 39*(10), 1189–1198. doi:10.1007/s10964-010-9533-6

Needham-Penrose, J., & Friedman, H. L. (2012). Moral identity versus moral reasoning in religious conservatives: Do Christian evangelical leaders really lack moral maturity? *The Humanistic Psychologist, 40*(4), 343–363. doi:10.1080/08873267.2012.724256

Neinstein, L. S. (2004). *Substance abuse—Stimulants/inhalants/opioids/anabolic steroids/designer and club drugs. Adolescent health curriculum*. Retrieved from http://www.usc.edu/student-affairs/Health_Center/adolhealth/content/b8subs3.html

Neisser, U. (1976). *Cognition and reality*. San Francisco, CA: Freeman.

Neisser, U. (1998a). Introduction: Rising test scores and what they mean. In U. Neisser (Ed.), *The rising curve: Long-term gains in IQ and related measures* (pp. 3–22). Washington, DC: American Psychological Association.

Neisser, U. (Ed.). (1998b). *The rising curve: Long-term gains in IQ and related measures*. Washington, DC: American Psychological Association.

Neisser, U., Boodoo, G., Bouchard, T. J., Boykin, A. W., Brody, N., Ceci, S. J., Halpern, D., Loehlin, J., Perloff, R., Sternberg, R,. & Urbina, S. (1996). Intelligence: Knowns and unknowns. *American Psychologist, 51*, 77–101.

Nelson, B. B., Chung, P. J., Forness, S. R., Pillado, O., Savage, S., Duplessis, H. M., Hayslip, W., & Hataoka, S. H. (2013). Developmental and Health Services in Head Start Preschools: A Tiered Approach to Early Intervention. *Academic Pediatrics, 13*(2), 145–151.

Nelson, C. A. (2005, April). *Brain development and plasticity: Examples from the study of early institutional rearing*. Invited address at the Developmental Science Teaching Institute at the biennial meeting of the Society for Research in Child Development, Atlanta.

Nelson, C. A., III, Thomas, K. M., & de Haan, M. (2006). Neural bases of cognitive development. In D. Kuhn & R. Siegler (Vol. Eds.), & W. Damon, & R. M. Lerner (Series Eds.), *Handbook of child psychology. Vol. 2: Cognition, perception, and language* (6th ed., pp. 3–57). New York, NY: Wiley.

Nelson, K. (1973). Structure and strategy in learning to talk. *Monographs of the Society for Research in Child Development, 38*(1–2, Serial No. 149).

Nelson, K. (1996a). *Language in cognitive development: The emergence of the mediated mind*. Cambridge, England: Cambridge University Press.

Nelson, K. (1996b). Memory development from 4 to 7 years. In A. J. Sameroff & M. M. Haith (Eds.), *The 5 to 7 shift* (pp. 141–160). Chicago, IL: University of Chicago Press.

Nelson, K. (1997). Event representations then, now, and next. In P. van den Broek, P. J. Bauer, & T. Bourg (Eds.), *Developmental spans in event representation and comprehension: Bridging fictional and actual events* (pp. 1–26). Mahwah, NJ: Erlbaum.

Nelson, K. (2005). Evolution and development of human memory systems. In B. J. Ellis & D. F. Bjorklund (Eds.), *Origins of the social mind: Evolutionary psychology and child development* (pp. 354–382). New York, NY: Guilford Press.

Nelson, S. W., & Guerra, P. L. (2009). For diverse families, parent involvement takes on a new meaning. *Journal of Staff Development, 30*(4), 65–66.

Nesteruk, O., Marks, L., & Garrison, M. E. B. (2009). Immigrant parents' concerns regarding their children's education in the United States. *Family and Consumer Sciences Research Journal, 37*(4), 422–441.

Nettelbeck, T., & Wilson, C. (2005). Intelligence and IQ: What teachers should know. *Educational Psychology, 25*(6), 609–630.

Neuman, S. B., Kaefer, T., Pinkham, A., & Strouse, G. (2014). Can babies learn to read? A randomized trial of baby media. *Journal of Educational Psychology*. doi:10.1037/a0035937

Neville, H. J., & Bavelier, D. (2001). Variability of developmental plasticity. In J. L. McClelland & R. S. Siegler (Eds.), *Mechanisms of cognitive development: Behavioral and neural perspectives* (pp. 271–287). Mahwah, NJ: Erlbaum.

Newcomb, A. F., & Bagwell, C. L. (1995). Children's friendship relations: A meta-analysis review. *Psychological Bulletin, 117*, 306–347.

Newcomb, A. F., & Brady, J. E. (1982). Mutuality in boys' friendship relations. *Child Development, 53*, 392–395.

Newcombe, N. S., Sluzenski, J., & Huttenlocher, J. (2005). Preexisting knowledge versus on-line learning: What do young infants really know about spatial location? *Psychological Science, 16*, 222–227.

Newell, D. A. (2012). Risk and protective factors for secondary girls of incarcerated parents. *Family Court Review, 50*(1), 106–112. doi:10.1111/j.1744-1617.2011.01432.x

Newkirk, T. (2002). *Misreading masculinity: Boys, literacy, and popular culture*. Portsmouth, NH: Heinemann.

Newland, J., & Treloar, C. (2013). Peer education for people who inject drugs in New South Wales: Advantages, unanticipated benefits and challenges. *Drugs: Education, Prevention & Policy, 20*(4), 304–311. doi:10.3109/09687637.2012.761951

Newman, A. J., Supalla, T., Hauser, P. C., Newport, E. L., & Bavelier, D. (2010). Prosodic and narrative processing in American Sign Language: An fMRI study. *NeuroImage, 52*(2), 669–676.

Newman, J., & Hubner, J. (2012). Designing challenging science experiences for high-ability learners through partnerships with university professors. *Gifted Child Today, 35*(2), 102–115. doi:10.1177/1076217511436093

Newman, L. S. (1990). Intentional and unintentional memory in young children: Remembering vs. playing. *Journal of Experimental Child Psychology, 50,* 243–258.

Newman, R. S., & Schwager, M. T. (1992). Student perceptions and academic help seeking. In D. Schunk & J. Meece (Eds.), *Student perceptions in the classroom (pp. 123–146).* Hillsdale, NJ: Erlbaum.

Newport, E. L. (1990). Maturational constraints on language learning. *Cognitive Science, 14,* 11–28.

Newson, J., & Newson, E. (1975). Intersubjectivity and the transmission of culture: On the origins of symbolic functioning. *Bulletin of the British Psychological Society, 28,* 437–446.

Nguyen, L., & Gu, Y. (2013). Strategy-based instruction: A learner-focused approach to developing learner autonomy. *Language Teaching Research, 17*(1), 9-30. doi:10.1177/1362168812457528

Ni, Y., & Zhou, Y.-D. (2005). Teaching and learning fraction and rational numbers: The origins and implications of whole number bias. *Educational Psychologist, 40,* 27–52.

NICHD Early Child Care Research Network. (2002). Early child care and children's development prior to school entry: Results from the NICHD study of early child care. *American Educational Research Journal, 39*(1), 133–164.

NICHD Early Child Care Research Network. (2006a). Child-care effect sizes for the NICHD Study of Early Child Care and Youth Development. *American Psychologist, 61,* 99–116.

NICHD Early Child Care Research Network. (2006b). Infant–mother attachment classification: Risk and protection in relation to changing maternal caregiving quality. *Developmental Psychology, 42,* 38–58.

Nicholls, J. G. (1984). Conceptions of ability and achievement motivation. In R. Ames & C. Ames (Eds.), *Research on motivation in education: Vol. 1. Student motivation (pp. 39–73).* San Diego, CA: Academic Press.

Nicholls, J. G. (1990). What is ability and why are we mindful of it? A developmental perspective. In R. J. Sternberg & J. Kolligian (Eds.), *Competence considered.* New Haven, CT: Yale University Press.

Nicholls, J. G., Cobb, P., Yackel, E., Wood, T., & Wheatley, G. (1990). Students' theories of mathematics and their mathematical knowledge: Multiple dimensions of assessment. In G. Kulm (Ed.), *Assessing higher order thinking in mathematics (pp. 137–154).* Washington, DC: American Association for the Advancement of Science.

Nichols, E., & Loper, A. (2012). Incarceration in the household: Academic outcomes of adolescents with an incarcerated household member. *Journal of Youth and Adolescence, 41*(11), 1455–1471. doi:10.1007/s10964-012-9780-9

Nichols, M. L., & Ganschow, L. (1992). Has there been a paradigm shift in gifted education? In N. Coangelo, S. G. Assouline, & D. L. Ambroson (Eds.), *Talent development: Proceedings from the 1991 Henry B. and Jocelyn Wallace National Research Symposium on Talent Development.* New York, NY: Trillium.

Nichter, M., Nichter, M., Muramoto, M., Adrian, S., Goldade, K., Tesler, L., et al. (2007). Smoking among low-income pregnant women: An ethnographic analysis. *Health Education and Behavior, 34*(5), 748–764.

Nickerson, R. S. (2010). *Mathematical reasoning: Patterns, problems, conjectures, and proofs.* New York, NY: Psychology Press.

Nicolaidou, I. (2013). E-portfolios supporting primary students' writing performance and peer feedback. *Computers & Education, 68,* 404–415. doi:10.1016/j.compedu.2013.06.004

Nicolopoulou, A., & Richner, E. S. (2007). From actors to agents to persons: The development of character representation in young children's narratives. *Child Development, 78,* 412–429.

Nicolson, S., & Shipstead, S. G. (2002). *Through the looking glass: Observations in the early childhood classroom* (3rd ed.). Upper Saddle River, NJ: Merrill/Prentice Hall.

Nielsen, M. (2012). Imitation, pretend play, and childhood: Essential elements in the evolution of human culture? *Journal of Comparative Psychology, 126*(2), 170–181. doi:10.1037/a0025168

Nieto, S. (1995). *Affirming diversity* (2nd ed.). White Plains, NY: Longman.

Nihiser A. J., Lee S. M., Wechsler H., McKenna M., Odom E., Reinold C., Thompson D., & Grummer-Strawn L. (2009). BMI measurement in schools. *Pediatrics, 124*(Suppl. 1), S89–S97. doi: 10.1542

Nilsson, D. E., & Bradford, L. W. (1999). Neurofibromatosis. In S. Goldstein & C. R. Reynolds (Eds.), *Handbook of neurodevelopmental and genetic disorders* (pp. 350–367). New York, NY: Guilford Press.

Nippold, M. A., & Taylor, C. L. (1995). Idiom understanding in youth: Further examination of familiarity and transparency. *Journal of Speech and Hearing Research, 38,* 426–433.

Nisbett, R. (2013). Schooling makes you smarter. *American Educator, 37*(1), 10–39.

Nisbett, R. E. (2003). *The geography of thought: How Asians and Westerners think differently—and why.* New York, NY: Free Press.

Nisbett, R. E. (2009). *Intelligence and how to get it: Why schools and cultures count.* New York: W. W. Norton.

Nisbett, R. E., Aronson, J., Blair, C., Dickens, W., Flynn, J., Halpern, D. F., & Turkheimer, E. (2012). Group differences in IQ are best understood as environmental in origin. *American Psychologist, 67*(6), 503–504. doi:10.1037/a0029772

Noam, G. G., & Bernstein-Yamashiro, B. (2013). Youth development practitioners and their relationships in schools and after-school programs. *New Directions for Youth Development, 2013*(137), 57–68. doi:10.1002/yd.20048

Noffke, S. (1997). Professional, personal, and political dimensions of action research. *Review of Research in Education, 22,* 305–343.

Nokes, J. D., Dole, J. A., & Hacker, D. J. (2007). Teaching high school students to use heuristics while reading historical texts. *Journal of Educational Psychology, 99,* 492–504.

Nolen-Hoeksema, S., Morrow, J., & Fredrickson, B. L. (1993). Response styles and the duration of episodes of depressed moods. *Journal of Abnormal Psychology, 102,* 20–28.

Nolte, K., Krüger, P. E., Els, P., & Nolte, H. (2013). Three dimensional musculoskeletal modelling of the abdominal crunch resistance training exercise. *Journal of Sports Sciences, 31*(3), 264-275.

Nomura, Y., Fifer, W., & Brooks-Gunn, J. (2005). *The role of perinatal factors for risk of co-occurring psychiatric and medical disorders in adulthood.* Paper presented at the biennial meeting of the Society for Research in Child Development, Atlanta, GA.

Nordahl, K., Janson, H., Manger, T., & Zachrisson, H. (2014). Family concordance and gender differences in parent-child structured interaction at 12 months. *Journal of Family Psychology, 28*(2), 253–259. doi:10.1037/a0035977

Norenzayan, A. (2014). Does religion make people moral? *Behaviour, 151*(2/3), 365–384. doi:10.1163/1568539X-00003139

North Central Regional Educational Laboratory. (2008). *Implementing the No Child Left Behind Act: Implications for rural schools and districts.* Retrieved from http://www.ncrel.org/policy/pubs/html/implicate/challenge.htm

Norton, N. L. (2014). Young children manifest spiritualities in their hip-hop writing. *Education & Urban Society, 46*(3), 329-351. doi:10.1177/0013124512446216.

Nucci, L. P. (2001). *Education in the moral domain.* Cambridge, England: Cambridge University Press.

Nucci, L. P. (2006). Education for moral development. In M. Killen & J. G. Smetana (Eds.), *Handbook of moral development* (pp. 657–681). Mahwah, NJ: Erlbaum.

Nucci, L. P. (2009). *Nice is not enough: Facilitating moral development.* Upper Saddle River, NJ: Pearson Education.

Nucci, L. P., & Weber, E. K. (1991). The domain approach to values education: From theory to practice. In W. M. Kurtines & J. L. Gewirtz (Eds.), *Handbook of moral behavior and development: Vol. 3. Application* (pp. 251–266). Hillsdale, NJ: Erlbaum.

Nucci, L. P., & Weber, E. K. (1995). Social interactions in the home and the development of young children's conceptions of the personal. *Child Development, 66,* 1438–1452.

Nugent, J. (2013). The competent newborn and the Neonatal Behavioral Assessment Scale: T. Berry Brazelton's legacy. *Journal of Child and Adolescent Psychiatric Nursing, 26*(3), 173–179. doi:10.1111/jcap.12043

Nuijens, K. L., Teglasi, H., & Hancock, G. R. (2009). Self-perceptions, discrepancies between self- and other-perceptions, and children's self-reported emotions. *Journal of Psychoeducational Assessment, 27*(6), 477–493.

Nunner-Winkler, G. (2007). Development of moral motivation from childhood to early adulthood. *Journal of Moral Education, 36*(4), 399–414. doi:10.1080/03057240701687970

Nuttall, R. L., Casey, M. B., & Pezaris, E. (2005). Spatial ability as mediator of gender differences on mathematics tests. In A. M. Gallagher & J. C. Kaufman (Eds.), *Gender differences in mathematics: An integrative psychological approach* (pp. 121–142). Cambridge, England: Cambridge University Press.

Nwokah, E. E., Burnette, S. E., & Graves, K. N. (2013). Joke telling, humor creation, and humor recall in children with and without hearing loss. *Humor: International Journal of Humor Research, 26*(1), 69–96. doi:10.1515/humor-2013-0005

Nwokah, E. E., Burnette, S. E., & Graves, K. N. (2013). Joke telling, humor creation, and humor recall in children with and without hearing loss. *Humor: International Journal of Humor Research, 26*(1), 69–96. doi:10.1515/humor-2013-0005

Øberg, G., Blanchard, Y., & Obstfelder, A. (2014). Therapeutic encounters with preterm infants: interaction, posture and movement. *Physiotherapy Theory & Practice, 30*(1), 1-5. doi:10.3109/09593985.2013.806621

O'Brennan, L. M., & Furlong, M. J. (2010). Relations between students' perceptions of school connectedness and peer victimization. *Journal of School Violence, 9*(4), 375–391. doi:10.1080/15388220.2010.509009

O'Connell, D. C., & Kowal, S. (2008). *Communicating with one another: Toward a psychology of spontaneous spoken discourse.* New York, NY: Springer Science + Business Media.

O'Connor, E., & McCartney, K. (2006). Testing associations between young children's relationships with mothers and teachers. *Journal of Educational Psychology, 98,* 87–98.

O'Connor, J. (2012). Is it good to be gifted? The social construction of the gifted child. *Children & Society, 26*(4), 293–303. doi:10.1111/j.1099-0860.2010.00341.x

O'Connor, T. G., & Hirsch, N. (1999). Intra-individual differences and relationship-specificity of mentalising in early adolescence. *Social Development, 8*(2), 256–274. doi:10.1111/1467-9507.00094

O'Flaherty, J. Liddy, M.,Tansey, L., Roche, C. (2011). Educating engaged citizens: Four projects from Ireland. *Education + Training, 53*(4), 267–283.

O'Grady, W. (1997). *Syntactic development*. Chicago: University of Chicago Press.

O'Keefe, P. A. (2013). Mindsets and self-evaluation: How beliefs about intelligence can create a preference for growth over defensiveness. In S. Kaufman (Ed.), *The complexity of greatness: Beyond talent or practice* (pp. 119–134). New York, NY: Oxford University Press.

O'Leary, K. D., & O'Leary, S. G. (Eds.). (1972). *Classroom management: The successful use of behavior modification*. New York, NY: Pergamon Press.

O'Leary, S. G., & Vidair, H. B. (2005). Marital adjustment, child-rearing disagreements, and overreactive parenting: Predicting child behavior problems. *Journal of Family Psychology, 19*, 208–216.

O'Malley, P. M., & Bachman, J. G. (1983). Self-esteem: Change and stability between ages 13 and 23. *Developmental Psychology, 19*, 257–268.

O'Neill, G., & Miller, P. (2013). A show of hands: Relations between young children's gesturing and executive function. *Developmental Psychology, 49*(8), 1517–1528. doi:10.1037/a0030241

O'Neill, S., Fleer, M., Agbenyega, J., Ozanne-Smith, J., & Urlichs, M. (2013). A cultural-historical construction of safety education programs for preschool children: Findings from SeeMore Safety, the pilot study. *Australasian Journal of Early Childhood, 38*(2), 74–84.

O'Reilly, F., & Matt, J. (2012). The selection of gifted students: Did Malcolm Gladwell overstate the role of relative age in the gifted program selection process? *Gifted Child Today, 35*(2), 122–127. doi:10.1177/1076217512437733

O'Sullivan-Lago, R., & de Abreu, G. (2010). The dialogical self in a cultural contact zone: Exploring the perceived 'cultural correction' function of schooling. *Journal of Community and Applied Social Psychology, 20*, 275–287.

O'Toole, M. E. (2000). *The school shooter: A threat assessment perspective*. Quantico, VA: Federal Bureau of Investigation. Retrieved from http://www.fbi.gov/publications/school/school2.pdf

Oakes, J., & Guiton, G. (1995). Matchmaking: The dynamics of high school tracking decisions. *American Educational Research Journal, 32*, 3–33.

Obadina, S. (2013). Understanding attachment in abuse and neglect: implications for child development. *British Journal of School Nursing, 8*(6), 290-295.

Obradović, J., Long, J. D., Cutuli, J. J., Chan, C., Hinz, E., Heistad, D., et al. (2009). Academic achievement of homeless and highly mobile children in an urban school district: Longitudinal evidence on risk, growth, and resilience. *Development and Psychopathology, 21*(2), 493–518.

Ochs, E. (2002). Becoming a speaker of culture. In C. Kramsch (Ed.), *Language acquisition and language socialization* (pp. 99–120). London, England: Continuum.

Ochs, E., & Schieffelin, B. (1995). The impact of language socialization on grammatical development. In P. Fletcher & B. MacWhinney (Eds.), *The handbook of child language* (pp. 73-94). Cambridge, MA: Blackwell.

Ogbu, J. U. (1994). From cultural differences to differences in cultural frames of reference. In P. M. Greenfield & R. R. Cocking (Eds.), *Cross-cultural roots of minority child development* (pp. 365–391). Hillsdale, NJ: Erlbaum.

Ogbu, J. U. (1999). Beyond language: Ebonics, proper English, and identity in a Black-American speech community. *American Educational Research Journal, 36*, 147–184.

Ogbu, J. U. (2003). *Black American students in an affluent suburb: A study of academic disengagement*. Mahwah, NJ: Erlbaum.

Ogden, E. H., & Germinario, V. (1988). *The at-risk student: Answers for educators*. Lancaster, PA: Technomic.

Ogliari, A., Spatola, C. A., Pesenti-Gritti, P., Medda, E., Penna, L., Stazi, M. A., et al. (2010). The role of genes and environment in shaping co-occurrence of DSM-IV defined anxiety dimensions among Italian twins aged 8–17. *Journal of Anxiety Disorders, 24*(4), 433–439.

Oguntoyinbo, L. (2009). Disappearing act. *Diverse Issues in Higher Education, 26*(16), 14–15.

Ohye, B., Rauch, P., & Bostic, J. (2012*). Educator toolkit to increase awareness and support to military children in schools*. Red Sox Foundation and Massachusetts General Hospital. Retrieved from http://www.homebaseprogram.org/community-education/tool-kits.aspx

Okagaki, L. (2001). Triarchic model of minority children's school achievement. *Educational Psychologist, 36*, 9–20.

Okita, S. Y. (2014). Learning from the folly of others: Learning to self-correct by monitoring the reasoning of virtual characters in a computer-supported mathematics learning environment. *Computers & Education, 71*, 257–278. doi:10.1016/j.compedu.2013.09.018

Okoza, J., Aluede, O., & Owens-Sogolo, O. (2013). Assessing students' metacognitive awareness of learning strategies among secondary school students in Edo State, Nigeria. *Research in Education*, (90), 82–97. doi:10.7227/RIE.90.1.6

Olive, T., Favart, M., Beauvais, C., & Beauvais, L. (2009). Children's cognitive effort and fluency in writing: Effects of genre and of handwriting automatisation. *Learning and Instruction, 19*(4), 299–308.

Ollendick, T. H., Costa, N. M., & Benoit, K. E. (2010). Interpersonal processes and the anxiety disorders of childhood. In J. G. Beck (Ed.), *Interpersonal processes in the anxiety disorders: Implications for understanding psychopathology and treatment* (pp. 71–95). Washington, DC: American Psychological Association.

Oller, J. r., Oller, S. D., & Oller, S. N. (2014). *Milestones: Normal speech and language development across the life span* (2nd ed.). San Diego, CA: Plural Publishing.

Olmedo, I. M. (2009). Blending borders of language and culture: Schooling in La Villita. *Journal of Latinos and Education, 8*(1), 22–37.

Olowokere, A. E., & Okanlawon, F. A. (2014). The effects of a school-based psychosocial intervention on resilience and health outcomes among vulnerable children. *The Journal of School Nursing, 30*(3), 206–215. doi:10.1177/1059840513501557

Olshansky, B., O'Connor, S., & O'Byrne, S. (2006, April). *Picture writing: Fostering literacy through art—diverse perspectives*. Paper presented at the annual meeting of the American Educational Research Association, San Francisco, CA.

Olson, C. K. (2010). Children's motivations for video game play in the context of normal development. *Review of General Psychology, 14*(2), 180–187. doi:10.1037/a0018984

Olson, C., Kim, J., Scarcella, R., Kramer, J., Pearson, M., van Dyk, D., et al. (2012). Enhancing the interpretive reading and analytical writing of mainstreamed English learners in secondary school: Results from a randomized field trim using a cognitive strategies approach. *American Educational Research Journal, 49*(2), 323–355. doi:10.3102/0002831212439434

Olson, J. A. (2012). Geography, GIS and gaming: Learning tools or just for fun? *Journal of Map & Geography Libraries, 8*(3), 290–294. doi:10.1080/15420353.2012.696533

Olson, R. K. (2008). Genetic and environmental influences on word-reading skills. In E. L. Grigorenko & A. J. Naples (Eds.), *Single-word reading: Behavioral and biological perspectives. New directions in communication disorders research: Integrative approaches* (pp. 233–253). Mahwah, NJ: Erlbaum.

Olswang, L. B., Feuerstein, J. L., Pinder, G., & Dowden, P. (2013). Validating dynamic assessment of triadic gaze for young children with severe disabilities. *American Journal of Speech-Language Pathology, 22*(3), 449–462.

Olszewski-Kubilius, P., Lee, S., & Thomson, D. (2014). Family environment and social development in gifted students. *Gifted Child Quarterly, 58*(3), 199–216. doi:10.1177/0016986214526430

Oltmanns, T. F., & Emery, R. E. (2007). *Abnormal psychology* (5th ed.). Upper Saddle River, NJ: Pearson Prentice Hall.

Ongley, S. F., & Malti, T. (2014). The role of moral emotions in the development of children's sharing behavior. *Developmental Psychology, 50*(4), 1148–1159. doi:10.1037/a0035191

Oortwijn, M. B., Boekaerts, M., Vedder, P., & Fortuin, J. (2008). The impact of a cooperative learning experience on pupils' popularity, non-cooperativeness, and interethnic bias in multiethnic elementary schools. *Educational Psychology, 28*(2), 211–221.

Opfer, J. E., & Siegler, R. S. (2004). Revisiting preschoolers' living things concept: A microgenetic analysis of conceptual change in basic biology. *Cognitive Psychology, 49*(4), 301–332. doi:10.1016/j.cogpsych.2004.01.002

Organization of Teratology Information Specialists. (2013a). *Isotretinoin (Accutane®) and pregnancy*. Retrieved from http://www.mothertobaby.org/files/isotretinoin.pdf

Organization of Teratology Information Specialists. (2013b). Marijuana and pregnancy. Retrieved from http://www.mothertobaby.org/files/marijuana.pdf

Organization of Teratology Information Specialists. (2013c). Methamphetamine/Dextroamphetamine and pregnancy. Retrieved from http://www.mothertobaby.org/files/methamphetamine.pdf

Organization of Teratology Information Specialists. (2013d). Toxoplasmosis and pregnancy. Retrieved from http://www.mothertobaby.org/files/toxoplasmosis.pdf

Orme, J. G., & Buehler, C. (2001). Foster family characteristics and behavioral and emotional problems of foster children: A narrative review. *Family Relations, 50*, 3–15.

Ormrod, J. E. (2008). *Human learning* (5th ed.). Upper Saddle River, NJ: Merrill/Prentice Hall.

Ormrod, J. E. (2011). *Educational psychology: Developing learners* (7th ed.). Boston: Pearson/Allyn & Bacon.

Ormrod, J. E., & McGuire, D. J. (2007). *Case studies: Applying educational psychology* (2nd ed.). Upper Saddle River, NJ: Merrill/Prentice Hall.

Ormrod, J. E., Jackson, D. L., Kirby, B., Davis, J., & Benson, C. (1999, April). *Cognitive development as reflected in children's conceptions of early American history*. Paper presented at the annual meeting of the American Educational Research Association, Montreal, Canada.

Ornstein, P. A., Grammer, J. K., & Coffman, J. L. (2010). Teachers' "mnemonic style" and the development of skilled memory. In H. S. Waters, & W. Schneider (Eds.), *Metacognition, strategy use, and instruction.* (pp. 23–53). New York, NY: Guilford Press.

Ornstein, R. (1997). *The right mind: Making sense of the hemispheres*. San Diego, CA: Harcourt Brace.

Ortlieb, E. (2013). Using anticipatory reading guides to improve elementary students' comprehension. *International Journal of Instruction, 6*(2), 145–162.

Ortony, A., Turner, T. J., & Larson-Shapiro, N. (1985). Cultural and instructional influences on figurative comprehension by inner city children. *Research in the Teaching of English, 19*(1), 25–36.

Osório, A., Meins, E., Martins, C., Martins, E., & Soares, I. (2012). Child and mother mental-state talk in shared pretense as predictors of children's social symbolic play abilities at age 3. *Infant Behavior & Development, 35*(4), 719–726. doi:10.1016/j.infbeh.2012.07.012

Oser, F. K., Althof, W., & Higgins-D'Alessandro, A. (2008). The Just Community approach to moral education: system change or individual change? *Journal of Moral Education, 37*(3), 395–415. doi:10.1080/03057240802227551

Ostad, S. (2013). Private speech use in arithmetical calculation: Contributory role of phonological awareness in children with and without mathematical difficulties. *Journal of Learning Disabilities, 46*(4), 291–303. doi:10.1177/0022219411419013

Ostenson, J. U. (2014). Reconsidering the checklist in teaching internet source evaluation. *Portal: Libraries & The Academy, 14*(1), 33–50.

Osterman, K. F. (2000). Students' need for belonging in the school community. *Review of Educational Research, 70,* 323–367.

Ota, C. L., & Austin, A. (2013). Training and mentoring: Family child care providers' use of linguistic inputs in conversations with children. *Early Childhood Research Quarterly.* doi:10.1016/j.ecresq.2013.04.001

Otgaar, H., Verschuere, B., Meijer, E. H., & van Oorsouw, K. (2012). The origin of children's implanted false memories: Memory traces or compliance? *Acta Psychologica, 139*(3), 397–403. doi:10.1016/j.actpsy.2012.01.002

Otis, N., Grouzet, F. M. E., & Pelletier, L. G. (2005). Latent motivational change in an academic setting: A 3-year longitudinal study. *Journal of Educational Psychology, 97,* 170–183.

Otto, B. (2010). *Language development in early childhood* (3rd ed.). Upper Saddle River, NJ: Merrill Pearson.

Owens, R. E., Jr. (2008). *Language development* (7th ed.). Boston, MA: Allyn & Bacon.

Owens, R. E., Jr. (2012). *Language development* (8th ed.). Boston, MA: Pearson.

Oyserman, D., & Lee, S. W.-S. (2007). Priming "culture": Culture as situated cognition. In S. Kitayama & D. Cohen (Eds.), *Handbook of cultural psychology* (pp. 255–279). New York, NY: Guilford Press.

Oyserman, D., & Markus, H. R. (1993). The sociocultural self. In J. Suls (Ed.), *Psychological perspectives on the self* (Vol. 7, pp. 187–220). Mahwah, NJ: Erlbaum.

Ozdemir, A. (2008). Shopping malls: Measuring interpersonal distance under changing conditions and across cultures. *Field Methods, 20*(3), 226–248.

Ozechowski, T. J., & Waldron, H. B. (2010). Assertive outreach strategies for narrowing the adolescence substance abuse treatment gap: Implications for research, practice, and policy. *Journal of Behavioral Health Services and Research, 37*(1), 40–63.

Ozonoff, S. (2010). Autism spectrum disorders. In K. O. Yeates, M. D. Ris, H. G. Taylor, & B. F. Pennington (Eds.), *Pediatric neuropsychology: Research, theory, and practice* (pp. 418–446). New York, NY: Guilford Press.

Pérez, B. (Ed.). (1998). *Sociocultural contexts of language and literacy.* Mahwah, NJ: Erlbaum.

Padilla, A. M. (2006). Second language learning: Issues in research and teaching. In P. A. Alexander & P. H. Winne (Eds.), *Handbook of educational psychology* (2nd ed., pp. 571–591). Mahwah, NJ: Erlbaum.

Padilla, M. J. (1991). Science activities, process skills, and thinking. In S. M. Glynn, R. H. Yeany, & B. K. Britton (Eds.), *The psychology of learning science* (pp. 205-217). Hillsdale, NJ: Erlbaum.

Padilla-Walker, L. M., & Carlo, G. (2007). Personal values as a mediator between parent and peer expectations and adolescent behaviors. *Journal of Family Psychology, 21,* 538–541.

Padilla-Walker, L. M., & Carlo, G. (2014). *Prosocial development: A multidimensional approach.* New York, NY: Oxford University Press. doi:10.1093/acprof:oso/9780199964772.001.0001

Padilla-Walker, L. M., Carlo, G., Christensen, K. J., & Yorgason, J. B. (2012). Bidirectional relations between authoritative parenting and adolescents' prosocial behaviors. *Journal of Research on Adolescence, 22*(3), 400–408. doi:10.1111/j.1532-7795.2012.00807.x

Paget, K. F., Kritt, D., & Bergemann, L. (1984). Understanding strategic interactions in television commercials: A developmental study. *Journal of Applied Developmental Psychology, 5,* 145–161.

Pahl, K., & Way, N. (2006). Longitudinal trajectories of ethnic identity among urban Black and Latino adolescents. *Child Development, 77,* 1403–1415.

Paikoff, R. L., & Brooks-Gunn, J. (1991). Do parent-child relationships change during puberty? *Psychological Bulletin, 110,* 47–66.

Palacios, J., & Sánchez-Sandoval, Y. (2005). Beyond adopted/nonadopted comparisons. In D. M. Brodzinsky & J. Palacios (Eds.), *Psychological issues in adoption: Research and practice* (pp. 117–144). Westport, CT: Praeger/Greenwood.

Palaiologou, I. (2014). 'Do we hear what children want to say?' Ethical praxis when choosing research tools with children under five. *Early Child Development and Care, 184*(5), 689–705. doi:10.1080/03004430.2013.809341.

Palermo, D. S. (1974). Still more about the comprehension of "less." *Developmental Psychology, 10,* 827–829.

Paley, V. G. (1984). *Boys and girls: Superheroes in the doll corner.* Chicago: University of Chicago Press.

Paley, V. G. (2007). Goldilocks and her sister: An anecdotal guide to the doll corner. *Harvard Educational Review, 77*(2), 144–151.

Palincsar, A. S., & Brown, A. L. (1984). Reciprocal teaching of comprehension-fostering and comprehension-monitoring activities. *Cognition and Instruction, 1,* 117–175.

Palincsar, A. S., & Brown, A. L. (1989). Classroom dialogues to promote self-regulated comprehension. In J. Brophy (Ed.), *Advances in research on teaching* (Vol. 1, pp. 36-67). Greenwich, CT: JAI Press.

Palincsar, A. S., & Herrenkohl, L. R. (1999). Designing collaborative contexts: Lessons from three research programs. In A. M. O'Donnell & A. King (Eds.), *Cognitive perspectives on peer learning* (pp. 151–177). Mahwah, NJ: Erlbaum.

Palkovitz, R., Fagan, J., & Hull, J. (2013). Coparenting and children's well-being. In N. J. Cabrera & C. S. Tamis-LeMonda (Eds.), *Handbook of father involvement: Multidisciplinary perspectives* (2nd ed., pp. 202–219). New York, NY: Routledge/Taylor & Francis Group.

Pallante, D. H., & Kim, Y. (2013). The effect of a multicomponent literacy instruction model on literacy growth for kindergartners and first-grade students in Chile. *International Journal of Psychology, 48*(5), 747–761. doi:10.1080/00207594.2012.719628

Pallotta, J., & Mazzola, F., Jr. (Illustrator). (1986). *The ocean alphabet book.* Watertown, MA: Charlesbridge.

Palmer, E. L. (1965). Accelerating the child's cognitive attainments through the inducement of cognitive conflict: An interpretation of the Piagetian position. *Journal of Research in Science Teaching, 3,* 324.

Palmer, R. C., Knopik, V. S., Rhee, S., Hopfer, C. J., Corley, R. C., Young, S. E., Stallings, M. C., & Hewitt, J. K. (2013). Prospective effects of adolescent indicators of behavioral disinhibition on DSM-IV alcohol, tobacco, and illicit drug dependence in young adulthood. *Addictive Behaviors, 38*(9), 2415–2421. doi:10.1016/j.addbeh.2013.03.021

Pan, B. A., Rowe, M. L., Singer, J. D., & Snow, C. E. (2005). Maternal correlates of growth in toddler vocabulary production in low-income families. *Child Development, 76,* 763–782.

Pan-Skadden, J., Wilder, D. A., Sparling, J., Severtson, E., Donaldson, J., Postma, N., et al. (2009). The use of behavioral skills training and in-situ training to teach children to solicit help when lost: A preliminary investigation. *Education and Treatment of Children, 32*(3), 359–370.

Panadero, E., Tapia, J., & Huertas, J. (2012). Rubrics and self-assessment scripts effects on self-regulation, learning and self-efficacy in secondary education. *Learning & Individual Differences, 22*(6), 806–813. doi:10.1016/j.lindif.2012.04.007

Panahon, C. J., & Martens, B. K. (2013). A comparison of noncontingent plus contingent reinforcement to contingent reinforcement alone on students' academic performance. *Journal of Behavioral Education, 22*(1), 37–49. doi:10.1007/s10864-012-9157-x

Pang, V. (2007). Asian Pacific American cultural capital: Understanding diverse parents and students. In S. J. Paik, H. J. Walberg (Eds.), *Narrowing the achievement gap strategies for educating Latino, Black, and Asian students* (pp. 49-64). New York, NY: Springer Science + Business Media.

Pangrazi, R. P., & Beighle, A. (2010). *Dynamic physical education for elementary school children* (16th ed.). San Francisco, CA: Pearson Benjamin Cummings.

Panksepp, J. (1998). Attention deficit hyperactivity disorders, psychostimulants, and intolerance of childhood playfulness: A tragedy in the making? *Current Directions in Psychological Science, 7,* 91–98.

Panter, J. E., & Bracken, B. A. (2013). Preschool assessment. In K. F. Geisinger, B. A. Bracken, J. F. Carlson, J. C. Hansen, N. R. Kuncel, S. P. Reise, & M. C. Rodriguez (Eds.), *APA handbook of testing and assessment in psychology, Vol. 3: Testing and assessment in school psychology and education* (pp. 21–37). Washington, DC: American Psychological Association. doi:10.1037/14049-002

Papandreou, M. (2014). Communicating and thinking through drawing activity in early childhood. *Journal of Research in Childhood Education, 28*(1), 85–100. doi:10.1080/02568543.2013.851131

Paradise, R., & Rogoff, B. (2009). Side by side: Learning by observing and pitching in. *Ethos, 37*(1), 102–138.

Parent, J., Jones, D. J., Forehand, R., Cuellar, J., & Shoulberg, E. K. (2013). The role of coparents in African American single-mother families: The indirect effect of coparent identity on youth psychosocial adjustment. *Journal of Family Psychology, 27*(2), 252–262. doi:10.1037/a0031477

Paris, D. (2009). "They're in my culture, they speak the same way": African American language in multiethnic high schools. *Harvard Educational Review, 79*(3), 428–447.

Paris, S. G., & Ayres, L. R. (1994). *Becoming reflective students and teachers with portfolios and authentic assessment.* Washington, DC: American Psychological Association.

Paris, S. G., & Byrnes, J. P. (1989). The constructivist approach to self-regulation and learning in the classroom. In B. J. Zimmerman & D. H. Schunk (Eds.), *Self-regulated learning and academic achievement: Theory, research, and practice* (pp. 168–200). New York, NY: Springer-Verlag.

Paris, S. G., & Cunningham, A. E. (1996). Children becoming students. In D. C. Berliner & R. C. Calfee (Eds.), *Handbook of educational psychology* (pp. 117–146). New York, NY: Macmillan.

Paris, S. G., & Turner, J. C. (1994). Situated motivation. In P. R. Pintrich, D. R. Brown, & C. E. Weinstein (Eds.), *Student motivation, cognition, and learning: Essays in honor of Wilbert J. McKeachie* (pp. 213–238). Mahwah, NJ: Erlbaum.

Paris, S. G., & Upton, L. R. (1976). Children's memory for inferential relationships in prose. *Child Development, 47,* 660–668.

Paris, S. G., Morrison, F. J., & Miller, K. F. (2006). Academic pathways from preschool through elementary school. In P. A. Alexander & P. H. Winne (Eds.), *Handbook of educational psychology* (2nd ed., pp. 61–85). Mahwah, NJ: Erlbaum.

Paris, S. G., Yeung, A., Wong, H., & Luo, S. (2012). Global perspectives on education during middle childhood. In K. R. Harris, S. Graham, T. Urdan, A. G. Bus, S. Major, & H. L. Swanson (Eds.), *APA educational psychology handbook, Vol. 3: Application to teaching and learning* (pp. 23–41). Washington, DC: American Psychological Association. doi:10.1037/13275-002

Parish, P., & Sweat, L. (2003). *Amelia Bedelia goes camping.* New York, NY: HarperCollins.

Park, L. E., Crocker, J., & Vohs, K. D. (2006). Contingencies of self-worth and self-validation goals: Implications for close relationships. In K. D. Vohs & E. J. Finkel (Eds.), *Self and relationships: Connecting intrapersonal and interpersonal processes* (pp. 84–103). New York, NY: Guilford Press.

Parke, R. D., & Buriel, R. (2006). Socialization in the family: Ethnic and ecological perspectives. In W. Damon & R. M. Lerner (Eds. in Chief) & N. Eisenberg (Vol. Ed.), *Handbook of child psychology: Vol. 3. Social, emotional, and personality development* (6th ed., pp. 429–504). Hoboken, NJ: Wiley.

Parke, R. D., & Clarke-Stewart, A. (2011). *Social development.* Hoboken, NJ: Wiley.

Parke, R. D., Ornstein, P. A., Rieser, J. J., & Zahn-Waxler, C. (1994). The past as prologue: An overview of a century of developmental psychology. In R. D. Parke, P. A. Ornstein, J. J. Rieser, & C. Zahn-Waxler (Eds.), *A century of developmental psychology* (pp. 1–70). Washington, DC: American Psychological Association.

Parker, J. G. (1986). Becoming friends: Conversational skills for friendship formation in young children. In J. M. Gottman & J. G. Parker (Eds.), *Conversations of friends: Speculations on affective development* (pp. 103–138). Cambridge, England: Cambridge University Press.

Parker, J. G., & Gottman, J. M. (1989). Social and emotional development in a relational context: Friendship interaction from early childhood to adolescence. In T. J. Berndt & G. W. Ladd (Eds.), *Peer relations in child development* (pp. 95–131). New York: Wiley.

Parker, J. G., Kruse, S. A., & Aikins, J. W. (2010). When friends have other friends: Friendship jealousy in childhood and early adolescence. In S. L. Hart & M. Legerstee (Eds.), *Handbook of jealousy: Theory, research, and multidisciplinary approaches* (pp. 516–546). Chichester, UK/Malden, MA: Wiley-Blackwell. doi:10.1002/9781444323542.ch22

Parker, W. D. (1997). An empirical typology of perfectionism in academically talented children. *American Educational Research Journal, 34,* 545–562.

Parkhurst, J. T., & Hopmeyer, A. (1998). Socio-metric popularity and peer-perceived popularity: Two distinct dimensions of peer status. *Journal of Early Adolescence, 18,* 125–144.

Parkhurst, J., & Gottman, J. M. (1986). How young children get what they want. In J. M. Gottman & J. G. Parker (Eds.), *Conversations of friends: Speculations on affective development* (pp. 315–345). Cambridge, England: Cambridge University Press.

Parks, C. P. (1995). Gang behavior in the schools: Reality or myth? *Educational Psychology Review, 7,* 41–68.

Partanen, E., Kujala, T., Näätänen, R., Liitola, A., Sambeth, A., & Huotilainen, M. (2013). Learning-induced neural plasticity of speech processing before birth. *PNAS Proceedings of the National Academy of Sciences of the United States of America, 110*(37), 15145–15150. doi:10.1073/pnas.1302159110

Partanen, E., Pakarinen, S., Kujala, T., & Huotilainen, M. (2013). Infants' brain responses for speech sound changes in fast multifeature MMN paradigm. *Clinical Neurophysiology, 124*(8), 1578–1585. doi:10.1016/j.clinph.2013.02.014

Parten, M. B. (1932). Social participation among preschool children. *Journal of Abnormal and Social Psychology, 27,* 243–269.

Pascarella, E. T., & Terenzini, P. T. (1991). *How college affects students: Findings and insights from twenty years of research.* San Francisco: Jossey-Bass.

Pascual-Leone, J. (1970). A mathematical model for the transition rule in Piaget's developmental stages. *Acta Psychologica, 32,* 301–345.

Pascual-Leone, J. (2013). Can we model organismic causes of working memory, efficiency and fluid intelligence? A meta-subjective perspective. *Intelligence,* doi:10.1016/j.intell.2013.06.001

Pasta, T., Mendola, M., Longobardi, C., Prino, L., & Gastaldi, F. (2013). Attributional style of children with and without specific learning disability. *Electronic Journal of Research in Educational Psychology, 11*(3), 649–664. doi:10.14204/ejrep.31.13064'

Patall, E. A., Cooper, H., & Wynn, S. (2008, March). *The importance of providing choices in the classroom.* Paper presented at the annual meeting of the American Educational Research Association, New York.

Patel, F. V. (2014). Advisory programs in middle and high schools. *Dissertation Abstracts International Section A, 74.*

Patnode, C. D., O'Connor, E., Rowland, M., Burda, B. U., Perdue, L. A., & Whitlock, E. P. (2014). Primary care behavioral interventions to prevent or reduce illicit drug use and nonmedical pharmaceutical use in children and adolescents: A systematic evidence review for the U.S. Preventive Services Task Force. *Annals Of Internal Medicine, 160*(9), 612-620.

Patrick, R. B., & Gibbs, J. C. (2012). Inductive discipline, parental expression of disappointed expectations, and moral identity in adolescence. *Journal of Youth and Adolescence, 41*(8), 973–983. doi:10.1007/s10964-011-9698-7

Patterson, C. J. (1995). Sexual orientation and human development: An overview. *Developmental Psychology, 31,* 3–11.

Patterson, C. J. (2009). Children of lesbian and gay parents: Psychology, law, and policy. *American Psychologist, 64*(8), 727–736.

Patterson, C. J., & Hastings, P. D. (2007). Socialization in the context of family diversity. In J. E. Grusec & P. D. Hastings (Eds.), *Handbook of socialization: Theory and research* (pp. 328–351). New York, NY: Guilford.

Patterson, G. R., & Reid, J. B. (1970). Reciprocity and coercion: Two facets of social systems. In C. Neuringer & J. Michael (Eds.), *Behavior modification in clinical psychology.* New York, NY: Appleton-Century-Crofts.

Patterson, G. R., DeBaryshe, B. D., & Ramsey, E. (1989). A developmental perspective on antisocial behavior. *American Psychologist, 44,* 329–335.

Patterson, J., & Vakili, S. (2014). Relationships, environment, and the brain: How emerging research is changing what we know about the impact of families on human development. *Family Process, 53*(1), 22-32. doi:10.1111/famp.12057

Patterson, J., & Vakili, S. (2014). Relationships, Environment, and the Brain: How Emerging Research is Changing What We Know about the Impact of Families on Human Development. *Family Process, 53*(1), 22-32. doi:10.1111/famp.12057

Patton, D. (2013). Connected, known and protected: African American adolescent males navigating community violence. *Dissertation Abstracts International Section A, 74* (1-A)(E).

Patton, J. R., Blackbourn, J. M., & Fad, K. (1996). *Exceptional individuals in focus* (6th ed.). Upper Saddle River, NJ: Merrill/Prentice Hall.

Paul, R. (1990). Comprehension strategies: Interactions between world knowledge and the development of sentence comprehension. *Topics in Language Disorders, 10*(3), 63–75.

Paulus, M. (2014). The emergence of prosocial behavior: Why do infants and toddlers help, comfort, and share? *Child Development Perspectives, 8*(2), 77–81. doi:10.1111/cdep.12066

Pawlas, G. E. (1994). Homeless students at the school door. *Educational Leadership, 51*(8), 79–82.

Payne, R. K., DeVol, P., & Smith, R. D. (2006). *Bridges out of poverty: Strategies for professionals and communities.* Highlands, TX: aha! Process.

Pea, R. D. (1993). Practices of distributed intelligence and designs for education. In G. Salomon (Ed.), *Distributed cognitions: Psychological and educational considerations.* Cambridge, England: Cambridge University Press.

Peak, L. (2001). Learning to become part of the group: The Japanese child's transition to preschool. In H. Shimizu & R. A. Levine (Eds.), *Japanese frames of mind: Cultural perspectives on human development* (pp. 143–169). New York, NY: Cambridge University Press.

Pears, K. C., Fisher, P. A., Kim, H. K., Bruce, J., Healey, C. V., & Yoerger, K. (2013). Immediate effects of a school readiness intervention for children in foster care. *Early Education and Development, 24*(6), 771–791. doi:10.1080/10409289.2013.736037

Pearson, B. Z., Velleman, S. L., Bryant, T. J., & Charko, T. (2009). Phonological milestones for African American English-speaking children learning Mainstream American English as a second dialect. *Language, Speech, and Hearing Services in Schools, 40*(3), 229–244.

Pearson, B., Conner, T., & Jackson, J. E. (2013). Removing obstacles for African American English-Speaking children through greater understanding of language difference. *Developmental Psychology, 49*(1), 31–44. doi:10.1037/a0028248

Pearson, P. D., Hansen, J., & Gordon, C. (1979). The effect of background knowledge on young children's comprehension of explicit and implicit information. *Journal of Reading Behavior, 11,* 201–209.

Pederson, D. R., Rook-Green, A., & Elder, J. L. (1981). The role of action in the development of pretend play in young children. *Developmental Psychology, 17,* 756–759.

Pedro-Carroll, J. L. (2005). Fostering resilience in the aftermath of divorce: The role of evidence-based programs for children. *Family Court Review, 43,* 52–64.

Pei-Ying, T., Sufen, C., Huey-Por, C., & Wen-Hua Chang4, s. (2013). Effects of prompting critical reading of science news on seventh graders' cognitive achievement. *International Journal of Environmental & Science Education, 8*(1), 85–107.

Pellegrini, A. D. (1996). *Observing children in their natural worlds: A methodological primer.* Mahwah, NJ: Erlbaum.

Pellegrini, A. D. (2002). Bullying, victimization, and sexual harassment during the transition to middle school. *Educational Psychologist, 37,* 151–163.

Pellegrini, A. D. (2006). The development and function of rough-and-tumble play in childhood and adolescence: A sexual selection theory perspective. In A. Göncü & S. Gaskins (Eds.), *Play and development: Evolutionary, sociocultural, and functional perspectives* (pp. 77–98) Mahwah, NJ: Erlbaum.

Pellegrini, A. D. (2013). Object use in childhood: development and possible functions. *Behaviour, 150*(8), 813–843. doi:10.1163/1568539X-00003086

Pellegrini, A. D., & Bjorklund, D. F. (1997). The role of recess in children's cognitive performance. *Educational Psychologist, 32,* 35–40.

Pellegrini, A. D., & Bohn, C. M. (2005). The role of recess in children's cognitive performance and school adjustment. *Educational Researcher, 34*(1), 13–19.

Pellegrini, A. D., & Horvat, M. (1995). A developmental contextualist critique of attention deficit hyperactivity disorder. *Educational Researcher, 24*(1), 13–19.

Pellegrini, A. D., Bartini, M., & Brooks, F. (1999). School bullies, victims, and aggressive victims: Factors relating to group affiliation and victimization in early adolescence. *Journal of Educational Psychology, 91,* 216–224.

Peltzer, K. (2010). Early sexual debut and associated factors among in-school adolescents in eight African countries. *Acta Paediatrica, 99*(8), 1242–1247. doi:10.1111/j.1651-2227.2010.01874. xdoi:10.1177/0165025410368943

Pence, K. L., & Justice, L. M. (2008). *Language development from theory to practice.* Upper Saddle River, NJ: Merrill/Prentice Hall.

Pener-Tessler, R., Avinun, R., Uzefovsky, F., Edelman, S., Ebstein, R. P., & Knafo, A. (2013). Boys' serotonin transporter genotype affects maternal behavior through self-control: A case of evocative gene–environment correlation. Development and Psychopathology, 25(1), 151–162.

Pennequin, V., Sorel, O., Nanty, I., & Fontaine, R. (2010). Metacognition and low achievement in mathematics: The effect of training in the use of metacognitive skills to solve mathematical word problems. *Thinking & Reasoning, 16*(3), 198–220. doi:10.1080/13546783.2010.509052

Pennington, B. F., & Bennetto, L. (1993). Main effects of transactions in the neuropsychology of conduct disorder. Commentary on "The neuropsychology of conduct disorder." *Development and Psychopathology, 5,* 153–164.

Pennisi, E. (2012, September). How genome is much more than genes. Science Now. Retrieved from http://news.sciencemag.org/sciencenow/2012/09/human-genome-is-much-more-than-j.html

Pentimonti, J. M., & Justice, L. M. (2010). Teachers' use of scaffolding strategies during read alouds in the preschool classroom. *Early Childhood Education, 37,* 241–248.

Peper, J. S., & Dahl, R. E. (2013). The teenage brain: Surging hormones—Brain-behavior interactions during puberty. *Current Directions in Psychological Science, 22*(2), 134–139. doi:10.1177/0963721412473755

Peregoy, S. F., & Boyle, O. F. (2008). *Reading, writing, and learning in ESL: A resource book for teaching K–12 English learners.* Boston, MA: Pearson Education/Allyn & Bacon.

Perels, F., Merget-Kullmann, M., Wende, M., Schmitz, B., & Buchbinder, C. (2009). Improving self-regulated learning of preschool children: Evaluation of training for kindergarten teachers. *British Journal of Educational Psychology, 79*(2), 311–327.

Perez, S. M., & Gauvain, M. (2009). Mother-child planning, child emotional functioning, and children's transition to first grade. *Child Development, 80*(3), 776–791.

Perfetti, C. A. (1985). Reading ability. In R. J. Sternberg (Ed.), *Human abilities: An information-processing approach (pp. 59-81).* New York, NY: Freeman.

Perfetti, C. A., & McCutchen, D. (1987). Schooled language competence: Linguistic abilities in reading and writing. In S. Rosenberg (Ed.), *Advances in applied psycholinguistics* (p. 105). Cambridge, England: Cambridge University Press.

Perkins, D. N. (1992). *Smart schools: From training memories to educating minds.* New York, NY: Free Press/Macmillan.

Perkins, D. N. (1995). *Outsmarting IQ: The emerging science of learnable intelligence.* New York: Free Press.

Perkinson-Gloor, N., Lemola, S., & Grob, A. (2013). Sleep duration, positive attitude toward life, and academic achievement: The role of daytime tiredness, behavioral persistence, and school start times. *Journal of Adolescence, 36*(2), 311–318. doi:10.1016/j.adolescence.2012.11.008

Perner, J., & Wimmer, H. (1985). "John *thinks* that Mary *thinks* that?" Attribution of second-order beliefs by 5- to 10-year-old children. *Journal of Experimental Child Psychology, 39,* 437–471.

Perone, S., & Spencer, J. P. (2014). The co-development of looking dynamics and discrimination performance. Developmental Psychology, 50(3), 837-852. doi:10.1037/a0034137

Perovic, A., Vuksanović, J., Petrović, B., & Avramović-Ilić, I. (2014). The acquisition of passives in Serbian. *Applied Psycholinguistics, 35*(1), 1–26. doi:10.1017/S0142716412000240

Perreira, K. M., Kiang, L., & Potochnick, S. (2013). Ethnic discrimination: Identifying and intervening in its effects on the education of immigrant children. In E. L. Grigorenko (Ed.), *U.S. immigration and education: Cultural and policy issues across the lifespan* (pp. 137–161). New York, NY: Springer Publishing Co.

Perren, J., Grove, N., & Thornton, J. (2013). Three empowering curricular innovations for service-learning in ESL programs. *TESOL Journal, 4*(3), 463–486. doi:10.1002/tesj.95

Perry, N. E. (1998). Young children's self-regulated learning and contexts that support it. *Journal of Educational Psychology, 90,* 715–729.

Perry, N. E., VandeKamp, K. O., Mercer, L. K., & Nordby, C. J. (2002). Investigating teacher–student interactions that foster self-regulated learning. *Educational Psychologist, 37,* 5–15.

Persellin, D., & Bateman, L. (2009). A comparative study on the effectiveness of two song-teaching methods: Holistic vs. phrase-by-phrase. *Early Child Development and Care, 179*(6), 799–806.

Pescarmona, I. (2014). Learning to participate through Complex Instruction. *Intercultural Education, 25*(3), 187–196. doi:10.1080/14675986.2014.905360

Peters, A. M. (1983). *The units of language acquisition.* New York, NY: Cambridge University Press.

Peterson, B. E., & Stewart, A. J. (1996). The antecedents and contexts of generativity motivation at midlife. *Psychology and Aging, 11*(1), 21–33.

Peterson, C. C. (2002). Drawing insight from pictures: The development of concepts of false drawing and false belief in children with deafness, normal hearing, and autism. *Child Development, 73,* 1442–1459.

Peterson, C., Maier, S. F., & Seligman, M. E. P. (1993). *Learned helplessness: A theory for the age of personal control.* New York, NY: Oxford University Press.

Peterson, J., Puhl, R. M., & Luedicke, J. (2012). An experimental assessment of physical educators' expectations and attitudes: The importance of student weight and gender. *Journal of School Health, 82*(9), 432–440. doi:10.1111/j.1746-1561.2012.00719.x

Peterson, L. (1980). Developmental changes in verbal and behavioral sensitivity to cues of social norms of altruism. *Child Development, 51,* 830–838.

Peterson, R. L., & Pennington, B. F. (2010). Reading disability. In K. O. Yeates, M. D. Ris, H. G. Taylor, & B. F. Pennington (Eds.), *Pediatric neuropsychology:*

Research, theory, and practice (2nd ed., pp. 324–362). New York, NY: Guilford Press.

Peterson, S. (2014). Award-winning authors and illustrators talk about writing and teaching writing. *Reading Teacher, 67*(7), 498–506. doi:10.1002/trtr.1249

Petitto, A. L. (1985). Division of labor: Procedural learning in teacher-led small groups. *Cognition and Instruction, 2,* 233–270.

Petitto, L. A. (1997). In the beginning: On the genetic and environmental factors that make early language acquisition possible. In M. Gopnik (Ed.), *The inheritance and innateness of grammars (pp. 45-69).* New York, NY: Oxford University Press.

Petrill, S. A., & Wilkerson, B. (2000). Intelligence and achievement: A behavioral genetic perspective. *Educational Psychology Review, 12,* 185–199.

Petrill, S. A., Lipton, P. A., Hewitt, J. K., Plomin, R., Cherny, S. S., Corley, R., et al. (2004). Genetic and environmental contributions to general cognitive ability through the first 16 years of life. *Developmental Psychology, 40,* 805–812.

Pettigrew, J. (2013). "I'll take what I can get": Identity development in the case of a stepfather. *Journal of Divorce & Remarriage, 54*(1), 25–42. doi:10.1080/10502556.2012.725360

Pfefferbaum, B., Pfefferbaum, R. L., & Norris, F. H. (2010). Community resilience and wellness for the children exposed to Hurricane Katrina. In R. P. Kilmer, V. Gil-Rivas, R. G. Tedeschi, & L. G. Calhoun (Eds.), *Helping families and communities recover from disaster: Lessons learned from Hurricane Katrina and its aftermath* (pp. 265–285). Washington, DC: American Psychological Association.

Pfeifer, J. H., Brown, C. S., & Juvonen, J. (2007). Prejudice reduction in schools. Teaching tolerance in schools: Lessons learned since *Brown v. Board of Education* about the development and reduction of children's prejudice. *Social Policy Report, 21*(2), 1, 3–13, 20–23. Ann Arbor, MI: Society for Research in Child Development.

Phares, V., Fields, S., & Kamboukos, D. (2009). Fathers' and mothers' involvement with their adolescents. *Journal of Child and Family Studies, 28,* 1–9.

Phasha, T. N. (2008). The role of the teacher in helping learners overcome the negative impact of child sexual abuse. *School Psychology International, 29*(3), 303–327.

Phelan, P., Yu, H. C., & Davidson, A. L. (1994). Navigating the psychosocial pressures of adolescence: The voices and experiences of high school youth. *American Educational Research Journal, 31,* 415–447.

Phillips, D., & Zimmerman, M. (1990). The developmental course of perceived competence and incompetence among competent children. In R. Sternberg & J. Kolligian (Eds.), *Competence considered* (pp. 41–66). New Haven, CT: Yale University Press.

Phillips, M. (1997). What makes schools effective? A comparison of the relationships of communitarian climate and academic climate to mathematics achievement and attendance during middle school. *American Educational Research Journal, 34,* 633–662.

Phinney, J. S. (1989). Stages of ethnic identity development in minority group adolescents. *Journal of Early Adolescence, 9,* 34–49.

Phinney, J. S. (1990). Ethnic identity in adolescents and adults: Review of research. *Psychological Bulletin, 108,* 499–514.

Phinney, J. S., & Tarver, S. (1988). Ethnic identity search and commitment in Black and White eighth graders. *Journal of Early Adolescence, 8,* 265–277.

Phinney, J. S., Cantu, C. L., & Kurtz, D. A. (1997). Ethnic and American identity as predictors of self-esteem among African American, Latino, and White adolescents. *Journal of Youth and Adolescence, 26,* 165–185.

Piaget, J. (1928). *Judgment and reasoning in the child* (M. Warden, Trans.). New York, NY: Harcourt, Brace.

Piaget, J. (1929). *The child's conception of the world*. New York, NY: Harcourt, Brace.

Piaget, J. (1940). Le mécanisme du développement mental et les lois du groupement des opérations. *Archives de Psychologie, 28,* 215–285.

Piaget, J. (1950). *Introduction à l'épistémologie génétique*. Paris: Presses Universitaires de France.

Piaget, J. (1952a). *The child's conception of number* (C. Gattegno & F. M. Hodgson, Trans.). London, England: Routledge & Kegan Paul.

Piaget, J. (1952b). *The origins of intelligence in children*. New York, NY: International Universities Press.

Piaget, J. (1954). *The construction of reality in the child*. New York, NY: Basic Books.

Piaget, J. (1959). *The language and thought of the child* (3rd ed.; M. Gabain, Trans.). London, England: Routledge & Kegan Paul.

Piaget, J. (1960a). *The child's conception of physical causality* (M. Gabain, Trans.). Paterson, NJ: Littlefield, Adams.

Piaget, J. (1960b). The definition of stages of development. In J. M. Tanner & B. Inhelder (Eds.), *Discussions on child development: A consideration of the biological, psychological and cultural approaches to the understanding of human development and behavior: Vol. 4. The proceedings of the fourth meeting of the World Health Organization Study Group on the Psychobiological Development of the Child, Geneva, 1956* (pp. 116–135). New York, NY: International Universities Press.

Piaget, J. (1962). *Play, dreams, and imitation in childhood*. New York, NY: W. W. Norton.

Piaget, J. (1971). The theory of stages in cognitive development. In D. R. Green (Ed.), *Measurement and Piaget* (pp. 1–11). New York, NY: McGraw-Hill.

Piaget, J. (1972). Intellectual evolution from adolescence to adulthood. *Human Development, 15,* 1–12.

Piaget, J. (1985). *The equilibration of cognitive structures: The central problem of intellectual development*. Chicago: University of Chicago Press.

Pianta, R. C., Belsky, J., Houts, R., & Morrison, F. (2007). Opportunities to learn in America's elementary classrooms. *Science, 315*(5820), 1795–1796.

Pianta, R. C., Hamre, B., & Stuhlman, M. (2003). Relationships between teachers and children. In W. M. Reynolds & G. E. Miller (Eds.), *Handbook of psychology: Educational psychology* (Vol. 7, pp. 199–234). New York, NY: Wiley.

Piasta, S., Pelatti, C., & Miller, H. (2014). Mathematics and science learning opportunities in preschool classrooms. *Early Education & Development, 25*(4), 445–468. doi:10.1080/10409289.2013.817753

Piirto, J. (1999). *Talented children and adults: Their development and education* (2nd ed.). Upper Saddle River, NJ: Merrill/Prentice Hall.

Pillow, B. H. (2002). Children's and adults' evaluation of the certainty of deductive inferences, inductive inferences, and guesses. *Child Development, 73,* 779–792.

Pilyoung, K., Evans, G. W., Angstadt, M., Shaun Ho, S. S., Sripada, C. S., Swain, J. E., Liberzon, I., & Luan Phan, K. K. (2013). Effects of childhood poverty and chronic stress on emotion regulatory brain function in adulthood. *Proceedings of the National Academy of Sciences of the United States of America, 110*(46), 18442–18447. doi:10.1073/pnas.1308240110

Pine, K. J., Lufkin, N., Kirk, E., & Messer, D. (2007). A microgenetic analysis of the relationship between speech and gesture in children: Evidence for semantic and temporal asynchrony. *Language and Cognitive Processes, 22*(2), 234–246.

Pinel, P., & Dehaene, S. (2009). Beyond hemispheric dominance: Brain regions underlying the joint lateralization of language and arithmetic to the left hemisphere. *Journal of Cognitive Neuroscience, 22*(1), 48–66.

Pinker, S. (1984). *Language learnability and language development*. Cambridge, MA: Harvard University Press.

Pinker, S. (1987). The bootstrapping problem in language acquisition. In B. MacWhinney (Ed.), *Mechanisms of language acquisition* (pp. 399–441). Hillsdale, NJ: Erlbaum.

Pinquart, M., Feußner, C., & Ahnert, L. (2013). Meta-analytic evidence for stability in attachments from infancy to early adulthood. *Attachment & Human Development, 15*(2), 189–218. doi:10.1080/14616734.2013.746257

Pintrich, P. R., & Schunk, D. H. (2002). *Motivation in education: Theory, research, and applications* (2nd ed.). Upper Saddle River, NJ: Merrill/Prentice Hall.

Pipher, M. (1994). *Reviving Ophelia: Saving the selves of adolescent girls*. New York, NY: Putnam.

Pipher, M. (1994). *Reviving Ophelia: Saving the selves of adolescent girls*. New York, NY: Putnam.

Plomin, R., & Petrill, S. A. (1997). Genetics and intelligence: What's new? *Intelligence, 24,* 53–77.

Plomin, R., Fulker, D. W., Corley, R., & DeFries, J. C. (1997). Nature, nurture, and cognitive development from 1 to 16 years: A parent–offspring adoption study. *Psychological Science, 8,* 442–447.

Plomin, R., Owen, M. J., & McGuffin, P. (1994). The genetic basis of complex human behaviors. *Science, 24,* 1733–1739.

Poel, E. W. (2007). Enhancing what students can do. *Educational Leadership, 64,* 64–66.

Pokhrel, P., Herzog, T. A., Black, D. S., Zaman, A., Riggs, N. R., & Sussman, S. (2013). Adolescent neurocognitive development, self-regulation, and school-based drug use prevention. *Prevention Science.* doi:10.1007/s11121-012-0345-7

Polat, N., & Mahalingappa, L. (2013). Pre- and in-service teachers' beliefs about ELLs in content area classes: a case for inclusion, responsibility, and instructional support. *Teaching Education, 24*(1), 58–83. doi:10.1080/10476210.2012.713930

Pollack, W. S. (2010). Gender issues: Modern models of young male resilient mental health. In J. E. Grant, M. N. Potenza (Eds.), *Young adult mental health* (pp. 96–109). New York, NY: Oxford University Press.

Pollitt, E., & Oh, S. (1994). Early supplemental feeding, child development and health policy. *Food & Nutrition Bulletin, 15,* 208–214.

Pomerantz, E. M., & Wang, Q. (2009). The role of parental control in children's development in Western and East Asian countries. *Current Directions in Psychological Science, 18*(5), 285–289.

Pomerantz, E. M., Altermatt, E. R., & Saxon, J. L. (2002). Making the grade but feeling distressed: Gender differences in academic performance and internal distress. *Journal of Educational Psychology, 94,* 396–404.

Ponder, J., Vander Veldt, M., & Lewis-Ferrell, G. (2011). Lessons from the journey: Exploring citizenship through active civic involvement. In B. D. Schultz (Ed.), *Listening to and learning from students: Possibilities for teaching, learning, and curriculum* (pp. 115–130). Greenwich, CT: IAP Information Age Publishing.

Poresky, R. H., Daniels, A. M., Mukerjee, J., & Gunnell, K. (1999, April). *Community and family influences on adolescents' use of alcohol and other drugs: An exploratory ecological analysis.* Paper presented at the biennial meeting of the Society for Research in Child Development, Albuquerque, NM.

Portes, P. R. (1996). Ethnicity and culture in educational psychology. In D. C. Berliner & R. C. Calfee (Eds.), *Handbook of educational psychology* (pp. 331–357). New York, NY: Macmillan.

Posada, G. (2013). Piecing together the sensitivity construct: Ethology and cross-cultural research. *Attachment & Human Development, 15*(5–6), 637–656. doi:10.1080/14616734.2013.842753

Posner, M. I. (Ed.). (2004). *Cognitive neuroscience of attention*. New York, NY: Guilford Press.

Posner, M. I., & Rothbart, M. K. (2007). *Educating the human brain*. Washington, DC: American Psychological Association.

Posner, M. I., & Rothbart, M. K. (2013). Development of attention networks. In B. Kar (Ed.), *Cognition and brain development: Converging evidence from various methodologies* (pp. 61–83). Washington, DC: American Psychological Association. doi:10.1037/14043-004

Potvin, M., Snider, L., Prelock, P., Kehayia, E., & Wood-Dauphinee, S. (2013). Recreational participation of children with high functioning autism. *Journal of Autism and Developmental Disorders, 43*(2), 445–457. doi:10.1007/s10803-012-1589-6

Poulin, F., & Boivin, M. (1999). Proactive and reactive aggression and boys' friendship quality in mainstream classrooms. *Journal of Emotional and Behavioral Disorders, 7,* 168–177.

Poulin-Dubois, D., Frenkiel-Fishman, S., Nayer, S., & Johnson, S. (2006). Infants' inductive generalization of bodily, motion, and sensory properties to animals and people. *Journal of Cognition and Development, 7*(4), 431–453.

Powell, M. P., & Schulte, T. (1999). Turner syndrome. In S. Goldstein & C. R. Reynolds (Eds.), *Handbook of neurodevelopmental and genetic disorders* (pp. 277–297). New York, NY: Guilford Press.

Power, F. C., Higgins, A., & Kohlberg, L. (1989). *Lawrence Kohlberg's approach to moral education*. New York, NY: Columbia University Press.

Power, F., & Power, A. R. (2006). Cheating. In G. G. Bear, K. M. Minke (Eds.), *Children's needs III: Development, prevention, and intervention* (pp. 185–197). Washington, DC, US: National Association of School Psychologists.

Powers, N., & Trevarthen, C. (2009). Voices of shared emotion and meaning: Young infants and their mothers in Scotland and Japan. In S. Malloch & C. Trevarthen (Eds.), *Communicative musicality: Exploring the basis of human companionship* (pp. 209–240). New York, NY: Oxford University Press.

Pressley, M. (1982). Elaboration and memory development. *Child Development, 53,* 296–309.

Pressley, M., & Hilden, K. (2006). Cognitive strategies: Production deficiencies and successful strategy instruction everywhere. In W. Damon & R. M. Lerner (Series Eds.), & D. Kuhn & R. Siegler (Vol. Eds.), *Handbook of child psychology: Vol. 2. Cognition, perception, and language* (6th ed., pp. 511-556). New York, NY: Wiley.

Pressley, M., Almasi, J., Schuder, T., Bergman, J., Hite, S., El-Dinary, P. B., et al. (1994). Transactional instruction of comprehension strategies: The Montgomery County Maryland SAIL program. *Reading and Writing Quarterly, 10,* 5–19.

Pressley, M., Borkowski, J. G., & Schneider, W. (1987). Cognitive strategies: Good strategy users coordinate metacognition and knowledge. In R. Vasta (Ed.), *Annals of child development* (Vol. 4, pp. 89–129). Greenwich, CT: JAI Press.

Pressley, M., El-Dinary, P. B., Marks, M. B., Brown, R., & Stein, S. (1992). Good strategy instruction is motivating and interesting. In K. A. Renninger, S. Hidi, & A. Krapp (Eds.), *The role of interest in learning and development*. Hillsdale, NJ: Erlbaum.

Pribilsky, J. (2001). Nervios and "modern childhood": Migration and shifting contexts of child life in the Ecuadorian Andes. *Childhood, 8*(2), 251–273.

Price, G. R., Mazzocco, M. M., & Ansari, D. (2013). Why mental arithmetic counts: Brain activation during single digit arithmetic predicts high school math scores. *Journal of Neuroscience, 33*(1), 156–163. doi:10.1523/JNEUROSCI.2936-12.2O13

Price, J. R., Roberts, J. E., & Jackson, S. C. (2006). Structural development of the fictional narratives of African American preschoolers. *Language, Speech, and Hearing Services in Schools, 37*, 178–190.

Price-Williams, D. R., Gordon, W., & Ramirez, M. (1969). Skill and conservation. *Developmental Psychology, 1*, 769.

Priddis, L., Landy, S., Moroney, D., & Kane, R. (2014). An exploratory study of aggression in school-age children: Underlying factors and implications for treatment. *Australian Journal of Guidance & Counselling, 24*(1), 18–35. doi:10.1017/jgc.2013.12

Priebe, S., Keenan, J., & Miller, A. (2012). How prior knowledge affects word identification and comprehension. *Reading & Writing, 25*(1), 131–149. doi:10.1007/s11145-010-9260-0

Prinstein, M. J., Rancourt, D., Guerry, J. D., & Browne, C. B. (2009). Peer reputations and psychological adjustment. In K. H. Rubin, W. M. Bukowski, & B. Laursen (Eds.), *Handbook of peer interactions, relationships, and groups* (pp. 548–567). New York, NY: Guilford Press.

Proctor, C. P., August, D., Carlo, M. S., & Snow, C. (2006). The intriguing role of Spanish language vocabulary knowledge in predicting English reading comprehension. *Journal of Educational Psychology, 98*, 159–169.

Proctor, R. W., & Dutta, A. (1995). *Skill acquisition and human performance.* Thousand Oaks, CA: Sage.

Project Coach (2013). *Project Coach.* Retrieved from http://projectcoach.smith.edu/about

Protzko, J., Aronson, J., & Blair, C. (2013). How to make a young child smarter: Evidence from the database of raising intelligence. *Perspectives on Psychological Science (Sage Publications Inc.), 8*(1), 25–40. doi:10.1177/1745691612462585

Provasnik, S., KewalRamani, A., Coleman, M. M., Gilbertson, L., Herring, W., & Xie, Q. (2007). *Status of education in rural America* (NCES 2007-040). Washington, DC: National Center for Education Statistics, Institute of Education Sciences, U.S. Department of Education.

Provost, B., Lopez, B. R., & Heimerl, S. (2007). A comparison of motor delays in young children: Autism spectrum disorder, developmental delay, and developmental concerns. *Journal of Autism and Developmental Disorders, 37*(2), 321–328.

Prows, C. A., Hopkin, R. J., Barnoy, S., & Van Riper, M. (2013). An update of childhood genetic disorders. Journal of Nursing Scholarship, 45(1), 34–42. doi:10.1111/jnu.12003

Pruden, S. M., Hirsh-Pasek, K., Golinkoff, R. M., & Hennon, E. A. (2006). The birth of words: Ten-month-olds learn words through perceptual salience. *Child Development, 77*, 266–280.

Pruett, K., & Pruett, M. K. (2009). *Partnership parenting: How men and women parent differently— Why it helps your kids and can strengthen your marriage.* Cambridge, MA: Da Capo Press.

Pugh, K. J. (2011). Transformative experience: An integrative construct in the spirit of Deweyan pragmatism. *Educational Psychologist, 46*(2), 107–121. doi:10.1080/00461520.2011.558817

Pulkkinen, L. (1982). Self-control and continuity from childhood to adolescence. In P. B. Baltes & O. G. Brim (Eds.), *Life-span development and behavior* (Vol. 4). Orlando, FL: Academic Press.

Pulos, S. (1997). Adolescents' implicit theories of physical phenomena: A matter of gravity. *International Journal of Behavioral Development, 20*, 493–507.

Pulos, S., & Linn, M. C. (1981). Generality of the controlling variables scheme in early adolescence. *Journal of Early Adolescence, 1*, 26–37.

Pulverman, R., Song, L., Hirsh-Pasek, K., Pruden, S. M., & Golinkoff, R. M. (2013). Preverbal infants' attention to manner and path: Foundations for learning relational terms. *Child Development, 84*(1), 241–252. doi:10.1111/cdev.12030

Puntambekar, S., & Hübscher, R. (2005). Tools for scaffolding students in a complex learning environment: What have we gained and what have we missed? *Educational Psychologist, 40*, 1–12.

Puranik, C., Petscher, Y., & Lonigan, C. (2013). Dimensionality and reliability of letter writing in 3- to 5-year-old preschool children. *Learning & Individual Differences, 28*, 133–141. doi:10.1016/j.lindif.2012.06.011

Purcell-Gates, V. (1995). *Other people's words: The cycle of low literacy.* Cambridge, MA: Harvard University Press.

Purdie, N., & Hattie, J. (1996). Cultural differences in the use of strategies for self-regulated learning. *American Educational Research Journal, 33*, 845–871.

Putallaz, M., & Gottman, J. M. (1981). Social skills and group acceptance. In S. R. Asher & J. M. Gottman (Eds.), *The development of children's friendships* (pp. 116–149). New York, NY: Cambridge University Press.

Putallaz, M., & Heflin, A. H. (1986). Toward a model of peer acceptance. In J. M. Gottman & J. G. Parker (Eds.), *Conversations of friends: Speculations on affective development* (pp. 292–314). Cambridge, England: Cambridge University Press.

Puustinen, M., Lyyra, A., Metsäpelto, R., & Pulkkinen, L. (2008). Children's help seeking: The role of parenting. *Learning and Instruction, 18*(2), 160–171.

Qian, G., & Pan, J. (2002). A comparison of epistemological beliefs and learning from science text between American and Chinese high school students. In B. K. Hofer & P. R. Pintrich (Eds.), *Personal epistemology: The psychology of beliefs about knowledge and knowing* (pp. 365–385). Mahwah, NJ: Erlbaum.

Quinn, P. C. (2002). Category representation in young infants. *Current Directions in Psychological Science, 11*, 66–70.

Quinn, P. C. (2007). On the infant's prelinguistic conception of spatial relations: Three developmental trends and their implications for spatial language learning. In J. M. Plumert & J. P. Spencer (Eds.), *The emerging spatial mind* (pp. 117–141). New York, NY: Oxford University Press.

Quinn, S., & Oldmeadow, J. (2013). Is the igeneration a "we" generation? Social networking use among 9- to 13-year-olds and belonging. *British Journal of Developmental Psychology, 31*(1), 136–142. doi:10.1111/bjdp.12007

Rönnau-Böse, M., & Fröhlich-Gildhoff, K. (2009). The promotion of resilience: A person-centered perspective of prevention in early childhood institutions. *Person-Centered and Experiential Psychotherapies, 8*(4), 299–318.

Raccanello, D., Brondino, M., & Bernardi, B. (2013). Achievement emotions in elementary, middle, and high school: How do students feel about specific contexts in terms of settings and subject-domains? *Scandinavian Journal of Psychology, 54*(6), 477–484. doi:10.1111/sjop.12079

Raevuori, A., Dick, D. M., Keski-Rahkonen, A., Pulkkinen, L., Rose, R. J., Rissanen, A., et al. (2007). Genetic and environmental factors affecting self-esteem from age 14 to 17: A longitudinal study of Finnish twins. *Psychological Medicine, 37*, 1625–1633.

Raghupathy, S., Klein, C., & Card, J. (2013). Online activities for enhancing sex education curricula: Preliminary evidence on the effectiveness of the abstinence and contraception education storehouse. *Journal of HIV/AIDS & Social Services, 12*(2), 160–171. doi:10.1080/15381501.2013.790749

Rahman, K. (2013). Belonging and learning to belong in school: the implications of the hidden curriculum for indigenous students. *Discourse: Studies in The Cultural Politics of Education, 34*(5), 660–672. doi:10.1080/01596306.2013.728362

Rahman, Q., & Wilson, G. D. (2003). Sexual orientation and the 2nd to 4th finger length ratio: Evidence for organising effects of sex hormones or developmental instability? *Psychoneuroendocrinology, 28*, 288–303.

Raikes, H., Virmani, E. A., Thompson, R. A., & Hatton, H. (2013). Declines in peer conflict from preschool through first grade: Influences from early attachment and social information processing. *Attachment & Human Development, 15*(1), 65–82. doi:10.1080/14616734.2012.728381

Raine, A., & Scerbo, A. (1991). Biological theories of violence. In J. S. Milner (Ed.), *Neuropsychology of aggression* (pp. 1–25). Boston, MA: Kluwer Academic Press.

Rakes, C. R., Valentine, J. C., McGatha, M. B., & Ronau, R. N. (2010). Methods of instructional improvement in algebra: A systematic review and meta-analysis. *Review of Educational Research, 80*(3), 372–400.

Rakic, P. (1995). Corticogenesis in human and non-human primates. In M. S. Gazzaniga (Ed.), *The cognitive neurosciences* (pp. 127–145). Cambridge, MA: MIT Press.

Rakow, S. (2012). Helping gifted learners SOAR. *Educational Leadership, 69*(5), 34–40.

Ramírez, E., Ortega, A., Chamorro, A., & Colmenero, J. (2014). A program of positive intervention in the elderly: Memories, gratitude and forgiveness. *Aging & Mental Health, 18*(4), 463–470. doi:10.1080/13607863.2013.856858

Ramírez, N., Lieberman, A. M., & Mayberry, R. I. (2013). The initial stages of first-language acquisition begun in adolescence: When late looks early. *Journal of Child Language, 40*(2), 391–414. doi:10.1017/S0305000911000535

Ramaswamy, V., & Bergin, C. (2009). Do reinforcement and induction increase prosocial behavior? Results of a teacher-based intervention in preschools. *Journal of Research in Childhood Education, 23*(4), 527–538.

Ramey, C. T., Campbell, F. A., Burchinal, M., Skinner, M. L., Gardner, D. M., & Ramey, S. L. (2000). Persistent effects of early childhood education on high-risk children and their mothers. *Applied Developmental Science, 4*(1), 2–14.

Ramey, S. L., & Ramey, C. T. (1999). Early experience and early intervention for children "at risk" for developmental delay and mental retardation. *Mental Retardation and Developmental Disabilities Research Reviews, 5*(1), 1–10.

Ramirez, A. Y. F., & Soto-Hinman, I. (2009). A place for all families. *Educational Leadership, 66*(7), 79–82.

Ramos Olazagasti, M. A., Klein, R. G., Mannuzza, S., Belsky, E., Hutchison, J. A., Lashua-Shriftman, E. C., & Castellanos, F. (2013). Does childhood attention-deficit/hyperactivity disorder predict risk-taking and medical illnesses in adulthood? *Journal of the American Academy of Child & Adolescent Psychiatry, 52*(2), 153–162. doi:10.1016/j.jaac.2012.11.012

Randell, A. C., & Peterson, C. C. (2009). Affective qualities of sibling disputes, mothers' conflict attitudes, and children's theory of mind development. *Social Development, 18*(4), 857–874.

Rao, K., Ok, M., & Bryant, B. (2014). A review of research on universal design educational models. Remedial & Special Education, 35(3), 153-166. doi:10.1177/0741932513518980

Raposa, E., Hammen, C., O'Callaghan, F., Brennan, P., & Najman, J. (2014). Early adversity and health outcomes in young adulthood: The role of ongoing stress. *Health Psychology, 33*(5), 410–418.

Rapport, M. D., Orban, S. A., Kofler, M. J., & Friedman, L. M. (2013). Do programs designed to train working memory, other executive functions, and attention benefit children with ADHD? A meta-analytic review of cognitive, academic, and behavioral outcomes. *Clinical Psychology Review.* doi:10.1016/j.cpr.2013.08.005

Rasmussen, M., & Laumann, K. (2013). The academic and psychological benefits of exercise in healthy children and adolescents. *European Journal of Psychology of Education, 28*(3), 945–962. doi:10.1007/s10212-012-0148-z

Rassin, M., Klug, E., Nathanzon, H., Kan, A., & Silner, D. (2009). Cultural differences in child delivery: Comparisons between Jewish and Arab women. *International Nursing Review, 56,* 123–130.

Rattan, A., Good, C., & Dweck, C. S. (2012). "It's ok—Not everyone can be good at math": Instructors with an entity theory comfort (and demotivate) students. *Journal of Experimental Social Psychology, 48*(3), 731–737. doi:10.1016/j.jesp.2011.12.012

Rattanavich, S. (2013). Comparison of effects of teaching English to Thai undergraduate teacher-students through cross-curricular thematic instruction program based on Multiple Intelligence Theory and conventional Instruction. *English Language Teaching, 6*(9), 1–18. doi:10.5539/elt.v6n9p1

Ratz, C. (2013). Do students with Down syndrome have a specific learning profile for reading?. *Research In Developmental Disabilities, 34*(12), 4504–4514. doi:10.1016/j.ridd.2013.09.031

Rauer, A. J., Pettit, G. S., Lansford, J. E., Bates, J. E., & Dodge, K. A. (2013). Romantic relationship patterns in young adulthood and their developmental antecedents. *Developmental Psychology, 49*(11), 2159–2171. doi:10.1037/a0031845

Raval, V. (2013). Fight or flight? Competing discourses of individualism and collectivism in runaway boys' interpersonal relationships in India. *Journal of Social & Personal Relationships, 30*(4), 410–429. doi:10.1177/0265407512458655

Raver, C. (2012). Low-income children's self-regulation in the classroom: Scientific inquiry for social change. *American Psychologist, 67*(8), 681–689. doi:10.1037/a0030085

Ravid, D., & Geiger, V. (2009). Promoting morphological awareness in Hebrew-speaking grade-schoolers: An intervention study using linguistic humor. *First Language, 29*(1), 81–112.

Ravid, D., & Zilberbuch, S. (2003). Morphosyntactic constructs in the development of spoken and written Hebrew text production. *Journal of Child Language, 30,* 395–418.

Ray, J. A., Prewitt-Kinder, J., & George, S. (2009). Partnering with families of children with special needs. *Young Children, 64*(5), 16–22.

Rayner, K., Foorman, B. R., Perfetti, C. A., Pesetsky, D., & Seidenberg, M. S. (2001). How psychological science informs the teaching of reading. *Psychological Science in the Public Interest, 2,* 31–74.

Recchia, H. E., & Howe, N. (2009). Associations between social understanding, sibling relationship quality, and siblings' conflict strategies and outcomes. *Child Development, 80*(5), 1564–1578.

Recchia, H. E., Wainryb, C., Bourne, S., & Pasupathi, M. (2014). The construction of moral agency in mother–child conversations about helping and hurting across childhood and adolescence. *Developmental Psychology, 50*(1), 34–44. doi:10.1037/a0033492

Recchia, S. L., & Dvorakova, K. (2012). How three young toddlers transition from an infant to a toddler child care classroom: Exploring the influence of peer relationships, teacher expectations, and changing social contexts. *Early Education And Development, 23*(2), 181–201. doi:10.1080/10409289.2012.630824

Recchia, S. L., & Shin. M. (2012). In and out of synch: Infant childcare teachers' adaptations to infants' developmental changes. *Early Child Development and Care, 182*(12), 1545–1562.

Recker, N., Clark, L., & Foote, R. A. (2008, June). About my families and me. *Journal of Extension, 46*(3).

Rees, S., Harding, R., & Inder, T. (2006). The developmental environment and the origins of neurological disorders. In P. Gluckman & M. Hanson (Ed.), *Developmental origins of health and disease* (pp. 379–391). New York, NY: Cambridge University Press.

Reese, E., Hayne, H., & MacDonald, S. (2008). Looking back to the future: Māori and Pakeha mother–child birth stories. *Child Development, 79*(1), 114–125.

Reese, E., Sparks, A., & Leyva, D. (2010). A review of parent interventions for preschool children's language and emergent literacy. *Journal of Early Childhood Literacy, 10*(1), 97–117.

Reese, E., Yan, C., Fiona, J., & Hayne, H. (2010). Emerging identities: Narrative and self from early childhood to early adolescence. In K. C. McLean & M. Pasupathi (Eds.), *Narrative development in adolescence: Creating the storied self* (pp. 23–43). New York, NY: Springer Science + Business Media.

Reese, E., Yan, C., Jack, F., & Hayne, H. (2010). Emerging identities: Narrative and self from early childhood to early adolescence. In K. C. McLean & M. Pasupathi (Eds.), *Narrative development in adolescence: Creating the storied self. Advancing responsible adolescent development* (pp. 23–43). New York, NY: Springer Science + Business Media.

Reese, L., Garnier, H., Gallimore, R., & Goldenberg, C. (2000). Longitudinal analysis of the antecedents of emergent Spanish literacy and middle-school English reading achievement of Spanish-speaking students. *American Educational Research Journal, 37,* 633–662.

Reese, S. (1996). KIDMONEY: Children as big business. *Technos Quarterly, 5*(4), 1–7. Retrieved from http://www.ait.net/technos/tq_05/4reesephp

Reeve, J., Bolt, E., & Cai, Y. (1999). Autonomy-supportive teachers: How they teach and motivate students. *Journal of Educational Psychology, 91,* 537–548.

Reeve, J., Deci, E. L., & Ryan, R. M. (2004). Self-determination theory: A dialectical framework for understanding sociocultural influences on student motivation. In D. M. McInerney & S. Van Etten (Eds.), *Big theories revisited* (pp. 31–60). Greenwich, CT: Information Age.

Regev, R., & Ehrenberg, M. F. (2012). A pilot study of a support group for children in divorcing families: Aiding community program development and marking pathways to resilience. *Journal of Divorce & Remarriage, 53*(3), 220–230. doi:10.1080/10502556.2012.663271

Regmi, K., & Madison, J. (2009). Contemporary childbirth practices in Nepal: Improving outcomes. *British Journal of Midwifery, 17*(6), 382–387.

Reich, P. A. (1986). *Language development.* Englewood Cliffs, NJ: Prentice Hall.

Reid, N. (1989). Contemporary Polynesian conceptions of giftedness. *Gifted Education International, 6*(1), 30–38.

Reigosa-Crespo, V., Valdés-Sosa, M., Butterworth, B., Estévez, N., Rodríguez, M., Santos, E., et al. (2012). Basic numerical capacities and prevalence of developmental dyscalculia: The Havana Survey. *Developmental Psychology, 48*(1), 123–135. doi:10.1037/a0025356

Reilly, D., & Neumann, D. (2013). Gender-role differences in spatial ability: A meta-analytic review. *Sex Roles, 68*(9/10), 521–535. doi:10.1007/s11199-013-0269-0

Reimer, J., Paolitto, D. P., & Hersh, R. H. (1983). *Promoting moral growth: From Piaget to Kohlberg* (2nd ed.). White Plains, NY: Longman.

Reiner, M., Slotta, J. D., Chi, M. T. H., & Resnick, L. B. (2000). Naïve physics reasoning: A commitment to substance-based conceptions. *Cognition and Instruction, 18,* 1–34.

Reinke, W., Herman, K., & Stormont, M. (2013). Classroom-level positive behavior supports in schools implementing SW-PBIS: Identifying areas for enhancement. *Journal of Positive Behavior Interventions, 15*(1), 39–50. doi:10.1177/1098300712459079

Reis, S. M. (2011). Self-regulated learning and academically talented students. In J. L. Jolly, D. J. Treffinger, T. F. Inman, & J. F. Smutny (Eds.), *Parenting gifted children: The authoritative guide from the National Association for Gifted Children* (pp. 42–52). Waco, TX: Prufrock Press.

Reiss, D. (2005). The interplay between genotypes and family relationships: Reframing concepts of development and prevention. *Current Directions in Psychological Science, 14,* 139–143.

Reissland, N. (2006). Teaching a baby the language of emotions: A father's experience. *Zero to Three, 27*(1), 42–47.

Rendle-Short, J., & Moses, K. (2010). Taking an interactional perspective: Examining children's talk in the Australian Aboriginal community of Yakanarra. *Australian Journal of Linguistics, 30*(4), 397–421. doi:10.1080/07268602.2010.518553

Renk, K., White, R. W., Scott, S., & Middleton, M. (2009). Evidence-based methods of dealing with social deficits in conduct disorder. In J. L. Matson (Ed.), *Social behavior and skills in children* (pp. 187–218). New York, NY: Springer Science Business Media.

Repacholi, B. M., & Gopnik, A. (1997). Early reasoning about desires: Evidence from 14- and 18-month-olds. *Developmental Psychology, 33,* 12–21.

Repetti, R., & Wang, S.-W. (2010). Parent employment and chaos in the family. In G. W. Evans & T. D. Wachs (Eds.), *Chaos and its influence on children's development: An ecological perspective* (pp. 191–208). Washington, DC: American Psychological Association.

Rest, J. R., Narváez, D., Bebeau, M., & Thoma, S. (1999). A neo-Kohlbergian approach: The DIT and schema theory. *Educational Psychology Review, 11,* 291–324.

Reston, J. (2007). Reflecting on admission criteria. In G. E. Mills, *Action research: A guide for the teacher researcher* (3rd ed., pp. 141–142). Upper Saddle River, NJ: Pearson Merrill/Prentice Hall.

Reutzel, D., Child, A., Jones, C. D., & Clark, S. K. (2014). Explicit instruction in core reading programs. *Elementary School Journal, 114*(3), 406–430.

Revelle, G. (2013). Applying developmental theory and research to the creation of educational games. *New Directions for Child & Adolescent Development, 2013*(139), 31–40. doi:10.1002/cad.20029

Reyes, I., & Azuara, P. (2008). Emergent biliteracy in young Mexican immigrant children. *Reading Research Quarterly, 43*(4), 374–398.

Reyna, C. (2000). Lazy, dumb, or industrious: When stereotypes convey attribution information in the classroom. *Educational Psychology Review, 12,* 85–110.

Reyna, V. F., & Farley, F. (2006). Risk and rationality in adolescent decision making: Implications for theory, practice, and public policy. *Psychological Science in the Public Interest, 7,* 1–44.

Reynolds, A. J., Englund, M. M., Ou, S., Schweinhart, L. J., & Campbell, F. A. (2010). Paths of effects of preschool participation to educational attainment at age 21: A three-study analysis. In A. J. Reynolds, A. J. Rolnick, M. M. Englund, J. A. Temple (Eds.), *Childhood programs and practices in the first decade of life: A human capital integration* (pp. 415–452). New York, NY: Cambridge University Press. doi:10.1017/CBO9780511762666.022

Reynolds, M., Floyd, R., & Niileksela, C. (2013). How well is psychometric g indexed by global composites? Evidence from three popular intelligence tests. *Psychological Assessment, 25*(4), 1314–1321. doi:10.1037/a0034102

Reznick, J. S. (2009). Working memory in infants and toddlers. In M. L. Courage & N. Cowan (Eds.), *The development of memory in infancy and childhood* (pp. 343–365). New York, NY: Psychology Press.

Reznick, J. S., & Goldfield, B. A. (1992). Rapid change in lexical development in comprehension and production. *Developmental Psychology, 28,* 408–414.

Rhoads, D. (1956). *The corn grows ripe.* Illustrated by Jean Charlot. New York, NY: Viking Press.

Rhodes, J. E., & Lowe, S. R. (2009). Mentoring in adolescence. In R. M. Lerner & L. Steinberg (Eds.), *Handbook of adolescent psychology. Vol. 2. Contextual influences on adolescent development* (3rd ed., pp. 152–190). Hoboken, NJ: Wiley.

Rhodes, M., & Wellman, H. (2013). Constructing a new theory from old ideas and new evidence. *Cognitive Science, 37*(3), 592–604. doi:10.1111/cogs.12031

Ricci, D., Romeo, D. M. M., Serrao, F., Cesarini, L., Gallini, F., Cota, F., et al. (2008). Application of a neonatal assessment of visual function in a population of low risk full-term newborn. *Early Human Development, 84,* 277–280.

Ricciuti, H. N. (1993). Nutrition and mental development. *Current Directions in Psychological Science, 2,* 43–46.

Rice, M. L. (2013). Language growth and genetics of specific language impairment. *International Journal of Speech-Language Pathology, 15*(3), 223–233.

Rice, M., Hadley, P. A., & Alexander, A. L. (1993). Social biases toward children with speech and language impairments: A correlative causal model of language limitations. *Applied Psycholinguistics, 14,* 445–471.

Richard, J. F., & Schneider, B. H. (2005). Assessing friendship motivation during preadolescence and early adolescence. *Journal of Early Adolescence, 25*(3), 367–385.

Richards, J. E., & Turner, E. D. (2001). Extended visual fixation and distractibility in children from six to twenty-four months of age. *Child Development, 72,* 963–972.

Richards, K., & Levesque-Bristol, C. (2014). Student learning and motivation in physical education. *Strategies (08924562), 27*(2), 43–45.

Richardson, W. (2011, February). Publishers, participants all. *Educational Leadership, 68*(5), 22–26.

Riches, N. G. (2013). Treating the passive in children with specific language impairment: A usage-based approach. *Child Language Teaching & Therapy, 29*(2), 155–169. doi:10.1177/0265659012466667

Richman, G., Hope, T., & Mihalas, S. (2010). Assessment and treatment of self-esteem in adolescents with ADHD. In M. H. Guindon (Ed.), *Self-esteem across the lifespan: Issues and interventions* (pp. 111–123). New York, NY: Routledge/Taylor & Francis Group.

Richman, S. B., & Mandara, J. (2013). Do socialization goals explain differences in parental control between black and white parents?. *Family Relations: An Interdisciplinary Journal of Applied Family Studies, 62*(4), 625–636. doi:10.1111/fare.12022

Richmond, K., Carroll, K., & Denboske, K. (2010). Gender identity disorder: Concerns and controversies. In J. C. Chrisler & D. R. McCreary (Eds.), *Handbook of gender research in psychology, Vol. 2: Gender research in social and applied psychology* (pp. 111–131). New York, NY: Springer Science + Business Media. doi:10.1007/978-1-4419-1467-5_6

Ricketts, H., & Anderson, P. (2008). The impact of poverty and stress on the interaction of Jamaican caregivers with young children. *International Journal of Early Years Education, 16*(1), 61–74.

Ridenour, T. A., Clark, D. B., & Cottler, L. B. (2009). The illustration-based assessment of liability and exposure to substance use and antisocial behavior for children. *The American Journal of Drug and Alcohol Abuse, 35*(4), 242–252.

Riemer, F. J., & Blasi, M. (2008). Rethinking relationships, reconfiguring teacher research: Teachers as ethnographers of culture, childhood, and classrooms. *Action in Teacher Education, 29*(4), 53–65.

Rihtman, T., Tekuzener, E., Parush, S., Tenenbaum, A., Bachrach, S. J., & Ornoy, A. (2010). Are the cognitive functions of children with Down syndrome related to their participation? *Developmental Medicine & Child Neurology, 52*(1), 72–78.

Riley, J. (2014). Teaching contemporary case studies. *Teaching Geography, 39*(1), 19–21.

Rimm-Kaufman, S. E., Early, D. M., Cox, M. J., Saluja, G., Pianta, R. C., Bradley, R. H., et al. (2002). Early behavioral attributes and teachers' sensitivity as predictors of competent behavior in the kindergarten classroom. *Journal of Applied Developmental Psychology, 23*(4), 451–470.

Rine, R., & Wiener-Vacher, S. (2013). Evaluation and treatment of vestibular dysfunction in children. *Neurorehabilitation, 32*(3), 507–518.

Rinehart, S. D., Stahl, S. A., & Erickson, L. G. (1986). Some effects of summarization training on reading and studying. *Reading Research Quarterly, 21,* 422–438.

Riojas-Cortez, M., Huerta, M. E., Flores, B. B., Perez, B., & Clark, E. R. (2008). Using cultural tools to develop scientific literacy of young Mexican American preschoolers. *Early Child Development and Care, 178*(5), 527–536.

Riordan, D., Morris, C., Hattie, J., & Stark, C. (2012). Family size and perinatal circumstances, as mental health risk factors in a Scottish birth cohort. *Social Psychiatry and Psychiatric Epidemiology, 47*(6), 975–983. doi:10.1007/s00127-011-0405-5

Rios-Aguilar, C. González-Canche, M., Moll, L. C. (2010). *The study of Arizona's teachers of English Language learners.* Retrieved from http://http://civilrightsproject.ucla.edu/research/k-12-education/language-minority-students/a-study-of-arizonas-teachers-of-english-language-learners.

Rishel, C., Cottrell, L., & Kingery, T. (2012). Preventing adolescent risk behavior in the rural context: An integrative analysis of adolescent, parent, and provider perspectives. *Journal of Family Social Work, 15*(5), 401–416. doi:10.1080/10522158.2012.719487

Rittle-Johnson, B. (2006). Promoting transfer: Effects of self-explanation and direct instruction. *Child Development, 77,* 1–15.

Rittle-Johnson, B., & Koedinger, K. R. (2005). Designing knowledge scaffolds to support mathematical problem solving. *Cognition and Instruction, 23,* 313–349.

Rittle-Johnson, B., & Siegler, R. S. (1999). Learning to spell: Variability, choice, and change in children's strategy use. *Child Development, 70,* 332–348.

Ritts, V., Patterson, M. L., & Tubbs, M. E. (1992). Expectations, impressions, and judgments of physically attractive students: A review. *Review of Educational Research, 62,* 413–426.

Rizzo, K., & Bosacki, S. (2013). Social cognitive theory and practice of moral development in educational settings. In B. J. Irby, G. Brown, R. Lara-Alecio, S. Jackson (Eds.), *The handbook of educational theories* (pp. 595–606). Charlotte, NC, US: IAP Information Age Publishing.

Rizzo, V. (2009). The Howard Gardner School for Discovery. In J.-Q. Chen, S. Moran, & H. Gardner, H. (Eds.), *Multiple intelligences around the world* (pp. 3–16). San Francisco, CA: Jossey-Bass.

Rizzolatti, G., & Fabbri-Destro, M. (2010). Mirror neurons: From discovery to autism. *Experimental Brain Research, 200*(3–4), 223–237. doi:10.1007/s00221-009-2002-3

Robbers, M. L. P. (2008). The caring equation: An intervention program for teenage mothers and their male partners. *Children and Schools, 30*(1), 37–47.

Robbins, V., Dollard, N., Armstrong, B. J., Kutash, K., & Vergon, K. S. (2008). Mental health needs of poor suburban and rural children and their families. *Journal of Loss and Trauma, 13,* 94–122.

Robbins, W. J., Brody, S., Hogan, A. G., Jackson, C. M., & Green, C. W. (Eds.). (1928). *Growth.* New Haven, CT: Yale University Press.

Roberts, D. F., & Foehr, U. G. (2008). Trends in media use. *Future of Children, 18*(1), 11–37.

Roberts, D. F., Christenson, P., Gibson, W. A., Mooser, L., & Goldberg, M. E. (1980). Developing discriminating consumers. *Journal of Communication, 30,* 94–105.

Roberts, K. L. (2013). Comprehension strategy instruction during parent–child shared reading: An intervention study. *Literacy Research and Instruction, 52*(2), 106–129. doi:10.1080/19388071.2012.754521

Roberts, M. C., Brown, K. J., Boles, R. E., & Mashunkashey, J. O. (2004). Prevention of injuries: Concepts and interventions for pediatric psychology in the schools. In R. T. Brown (Ed.), *Handbook of pediatric psychology in school settings* (pp. 65–80). Mahwah, NJ: Erlbaum.

Roberts, T. A. (2005). Articulation accuracy and vocabulary size contributions to phonemic awareness and word reading in English language learners. *Journal of Educational Psychology, 97,* 601–616.

Roberts, W., Strayer, J., & Denham, S. (2014). Empathy, anger, guilt: Emotions and prosocial behaviour. *Canadian Journal of Behavioural Science/Revue Canadienne Des Sciences Du Comportement,* doi:10.1037/a0035057

Robertson, S., von Hapsburg, D., Hay, J. S., Champlin, C., & Werner, L. (2013). The effect of hearing loss on the perception of infant- and adult-directed speech. *Journal of Speech, Language & Hearing Research, 56*(4), 1108–1119. doi:10.1044/1092-4388(2012/12-0110)

Robins, R. W., & Trzesniewski, K. H. (2005). Self-esteem development across the lifespan. *Current Directions in Psychological Science, 14,* 158–162.

Robinson-Cimpian, J. P., Lubienski, S., Ganley, C. M., & Copur-Gencturk, Y. (2014). Teachers' perceptions of students' mathematics proficiency may exacerbate early gender gaps in achievement. *Developmental Psychology, 50*(4), 1262-1281. doi:10.1037/a0035073

Rocha, N., de Campos, A., dos Santos Silva, F., & Tudella, E. (2013). Adaptive actions of young infants in the task of reaching for objects. *Developmental Psychobiology, 55*(3), 275–282. doi:10.1002/dev.21026

Rochat, P., & Bullinger, A. (1994). Posture and functional action in infancy. In A. Vyt, H. Bloch, & M. H. Bornstein (Eds.), *Early child development in the French tradition: Contributions from current research.* Hillsdale, NJ: Erlbaum.

Roche, B., Cassidy, S., & Stewart, I. (2013). Nurturing genius: Using relational frame theory to address a foundational aim of psychology. In T. B. Kashdan & J. Ciarrochi (Eds.), *Mindfulness, acceptance, and positive psychology: The seven foundations of well-being* (pp. 267–302). Oakland, CA: Context Press/New Harbinger Publications.

Roche, K. M., Ghazarian, S. R., & Fernandez-Esquer, M. (2012). Unpacking acculturation: Cultural orientations and educational attainment among Mexican-origin youth. *Journal of Youth and Adolescence, 41*(7), 920–931. doi:10.1007/s10964-011-9725-8

Roderick, M., & Camburn, E. (1999). Risk and recovery from course failure in the early years of high school. *American Educational Research Journal, 36,* 303–343.

Rodkin, P. C., Ryan, A. M., Jamison, R., & Wilson, T. (2013). Social goals, social behavior, and social status in middle childhood. *Developmental Psychology, 49*(6), 1139–1150. doi:10.1037/a0029389

Rodriguez, G. (2013). Power and agency in education: Exploring the pedagogical dimensions of funds of knowledge. *Review of Research in Education, 37*(1), 87–120. doi:10.3102/0091732X12462686

Roebers, C. M., Krebs, S. S., & Roderer, T. (2014). Metacognitive monitoring and control in elementary school children: Their interrelations and their role for test performance. *Learning & Individual Differences, 29*,141-149. doi:10.1016/j.lindif.2012.12.003

Roediger, H., McDermott, K. B., & McDaniel, M. A. (2011). Using testing to improve learning and memory. In M. Gernsbacher, R. W. Pew, L. M. Hough, & J. R. Pomerantz (Eds.), *Psychology and the real world: Essays illustrating fundamental contributions to society* (pp. 65–74). New York, NY: Worth Publishers.

Roediger, H., Putnam, A. L., & Smith, M. A. (2011). Ten benefits of testing and their applications to educational practice. In J. P. Mestre, B. H. Ross (Eds.), *The psychology of learning and motivation (Vol. 55): Cognition in education* (pp. 1–36). San Diego, CA US: Elsevier Academic Press. doi:10.1016/B978-0-12-387691-1.00001-6

Roeper, T. (2012). Minimalism and bilingualism: How and why bilingualism could benefit children with SLI. *Bilingualism: Language & Cognition, 15*(1), 88–101. doi:10.1017/S1366728911000605

Roeser, R. W., Midgley, C., & Urdan, T. C. (1996). Perceptions of school psychological environment and early adolescents' psychological and behavioral functioning in school: The mediating role of goals and belonging. *Journal of Educational Psychology, 88,* 408–422.

Roffwarg, H. P., Muzio, J. N., & Dement, W. C. (1966). Ontogenetic development of the human sleep-dream cycle. *Science, 152,* 604–619.

Rogers, L. O., Zosuls, K. M., Halim, M., Ruble, D., Hughes, D., & Fuligni, A. (2012). Meaning making in middle childhood: An exploration of the meaning of ethnic identity. *Cultural Diversity and Ethnic Minority Psychology, 18*(2), 99–108. doi:10.1037/a0027691

Rogoff, B. (1990). *Apprenticeship in thinking: Cognitive development in social context.* New York, NY: Oxford University Press.

Rogoff, B. (1991). Social interaction as apprenticeship in thinking: Guidance and participation in spatial planning. In L. B. Resnick, J. M. Levine, & S. D. Teasley (Eds.), *Perspectives on socially shared cognition* (pp. 349–364). Washington, DC: American Psychological Association.

Rogoff, B. (1994, April). *Developing understanding of the idea of communities of learners.* Paper presented at the annual meeting of the American Educational Research Association, New Orleans, LA.

Rogoff, B. (2003). *The cultural nature of human development.* New York, NY: Oxford University Press.

Rogoff, B., & Morelli, G. (1989). Perspectives on children's development from cultural psychology. *American Psychologist, 44,* 343–348.

Rogoff, B., Mistry, J., Göncü, A., & Mosier, C. (1993). Guided participation in cultural activity by toddlers and caregivers. *Monographs of the Society for Research in Child Development, 58*(8, Serial No. 236).

Rogoff, B., Moore, L., Najafi, B., Dexter, A., Correa-Chávez, M., & Solís, J. (2007). Children's development of cultural repertoires through participation in everyday routines and practices. In J. E. Grusec & P. D. Hastings (Eds.), *Handbook of socialization: Theory and research* (pp. 490–515). New York, NY: Guilford Press.

Rogoff, B., Morelli, G. A., & Chavajay, P. (2010). Children's integration in communities and segregation from people of differing ages. *Perspectives on Psychological Science, 5*(4), 431–440.

Rohde, M. C., Corydon, T. J., Hansen, J., Bak Pedersen, C., Schmidt, S., Gregersen, N., & Banner, J. (2013). Heat stress and sudden infant death syndrome–Stress gene expression after exposure to moderate heat stress. *Forensic Science International, 232*(1-3), 16-24.

Rohner, R. P., & Rohner, E. C. (1981). Parental acceptance-rejection and parental control: Cross-cultural codes. *Ethnology, 20,* 245–260.

Roid, G. (2003). *Stanford-Binet Intelligence Scales* (5th ed.). Itasca, IL: Riverside.

Roid, G. H., & Pomplun, M. (2012). The Stanford-Binet Intelligence Scales, Fifth Edition. In D. P. Flanagan, & P. L. Harrison (Eds.), *Contemporary intellectual assessment: Theories, tests, and issues* (3rd ed.; pp. 249–268). New York, NY: Guilford Press.

Roid, G. H., & Tippin, S. M. (2009). Assessment of intellectual strengths and weaknesses with the Stanford-Binet Intelligence Scales–Fifth Edition (SB5). In J. A. Naglieri & S. Goldstein (Eds.), *Practitioner's guide to assessing intelligence and achievement* (pp. 127–). Hoboken, NJ: Wiley.

Rojek, J., Petrocelli, M., & Oberweis, T. (2010). Recent patterns in gang prevalence: A two state comparison. *Journal of Gang Research, 18*(1), 1–18.

Rollison, J., Banks, D., Martin, A. J., Owens, C., Thomas, N., Dressler, K. J., & Wells, M. (2013). Improving school-justice partnerships: Lessons learned from the Safe Schools/Healthy Students Initiative. *Family Court Review, 51*(3), 445–451. doi:10.1111/fcre.12041

Rolls, C., & Chamberlain, M. (2004). From east to west: Nepalese women's experiences. *International Council of Nurses, 51,* 176–184.

Romero, A. J., & Roberts, R. E. (2003). The impact of multiple dimensions of ethnic identity on discrimination and adolescents' self-esteem. *Journal of Applied Social Psychology, 33,* 2288–2305.

Romero, A., Edwards, L., Fryberg, S., & Orduña, M. (2014). Resilience to discrimination stress across ethnic identity stages of development. *Journal of Applied Social Psychology, 44*(1), 1–11.

Romero-Little, M. (2011). Learning the community's curriculum: The linguistic, social, and cultural resources of American Indian and Alaska Native children. In M. C. Sarche, P. Spicer, P. Farrell, & H. E. Fitzgerald (Eds.), *American Indian and Alaska Native children and mental health: Development, context, prevention, and treatment* (pp. 89–99). Santa Barbara, CA: Praeger/ABC-CLIO.

Rondan, C., & Deruelle, C. (2007). Global and configural visual processing in adults with autism and Asperger syndrome. *Research in Developmental Disabilities, 28,* 197–206.

Roos, S., Hodges, E. E., & Salmivalli, C. (2014). Do guilt- and shame-proneness differentially predict prosocial, aggressive, and withdrawn behaviors during early adolescence? *Developmental Psychology, 50*(3), 941–946. doi:10.1037/a0033904

Roosa, M. W., Weaver, S. R., White, R. M. B., Tein, J.-Y., Knight, G. P., Gonzales, N., & Saenz, D. (2009). Family and neighborhood fit or misfit and the adaptation of Mexican Americans. *American Journal of Community Psychology, 44,* 15–27.

Root-Bernstein, R., & Root-Bernstein, M. (2013). The art & craft of science. *Educational Leadership, 70*(5), 16–21.

Roscigno, V. J., Karafin, D. L., & Tester, G. (2009). The complexities and processes of racial housing discrimination. *Social Problems, 56*(1), 49–69.

Rose, A. J., & Smith, R. L. (2009). Sex differences in peer relationships. In K. H. Rubin, W. M. Bukowski, & B. Laursen (Eds.), *Handbook of peer interactions, relationships, and groups* (pp. 379–393). New York, NY: Guilford Press.

Roseboom, T., de Rooij, S., & Painter, R. (2006). The Dutch famine and its long-term consequences for adult health. *Early Human Development, 82*(8), 485–491.

Rosen, L., Mark Carrier, L., & Cheever, N. (2013). Facebook and texting made me do it: Media-induced task-switching while studying. *Computers in Human Behavior, 29*(3), 948–958. doi:10.1016/j.chb.2012.12.001

Rosenblum, K. L., & Muzik, M. (2014). STRoNG intervention for military families with young children. *Psychiatric Services, 65*(3), 399.

Rosende-Vázquez, M., & Vieiro-Iglesias, P. (2013). Inferential processes in children with Down syndrome. *RELIEVE—Revista Electrónica De Investigación Y Evaluación Educativa, 19*(1), 1–12. doi:10.7203/relieve.19.1.2612

Rosenkoetter, L. I., Rosenkoetter, S. E., Ozretich, R. A., & Acock, A. C. (2004). Mitigating the harmful effects of violent television. *Applied Developmental Psychology, 25,* 25–47.

Rosenshine, B., & Meister, C. (1992). The use of scaffolds for teaching higher-level cognitive strategies. *Educational Leadership, 49*(7), 26–33.

Rosenshine, B., Meister, C., & Chapman, S. (1996). Teaching students to generate questions: A review of the intervention studies. *Review of Educational Research, 66,* 181–221.

Rosenthal, R. (1994). Interpersonal expectancy effects: A 30-year perspective. *Current Directions in Psychological Science, 3,* 176–179.

Rostad, K., & Pexman, P. M. (2014). Developing appreciation for ambivalence: The understanding of concurrent conflicting desires in 4- to 7-year-old children. *Canadian Journal of Experimental Psychology/Revue Canadienne De Psychologie Expérimentale, 68*(2), 122–132. doi:10.1037/cep0000016

Rotenberg, K. J., & Boulton, M. (2013). Interpersonal trust consistency and the quality of peer relationships during childhood. *Social Development, 22*(2), 225–241. doi:10.1111/sode.12005

Rothbart, M. K. (2007). Temperament, development, and personality. *Current Directions in Psychological Science, 16,* 207–212.

Rothbart, M. K. (2012). Advances in temperament: History, concepts, and measures. In M. Zentner & R. L. Shiner (Eds.), *Handbook of temperament* (pp. 3–20). New York, NY: Guilford Press.

Rothbart, M. K., & Bates, J. E. (2006). Temperament. In W. Damon & R. M. Lerner (Eds. in Chief) & N. Eisenberg (Vol. Ed.), *Handbook of child psychology, Vol. 3. Social, emotional, and personality development* (6th ed., pp. 99–225). Hoboken, NJ: Wiley.

Rothbart, M. K., Hanley, D., & Albert, M. (1986). Gender differences in moral reasoning. *Sex Roles, 15,* 645–653.

Rothbart, M. K., Posner, M. I., & Kieras, J. (2006). Temperament, attention, and the development of self-regulation. In K. McCartney & D. Phillips (Eds.), *Blackwell handbook of early childhood development* (pp. 338–357). Malden, MA: Blackwell.

Rothbart, M. K., Sheese, B. E., & Conradt, E. D. (2009). Childhood temperament. In P. J. Corr, & G. Matthews (Eds.), *The Cambridge handbook of personality psychology* (pp. 177–190). New York, NY: Cambridge University Press.

Rothbaum, F., Nagaoka, R., & Ponte, I. C. (2006). Caregiver sensitivity in cultural context: Japanese and U.S. teachers' beliefs about anticipating and responding to children's needs. *Journal of Research in Childhood Education, 21*(1), 23–40.

Rothbaum, F., Pott, M., Azuma, H., Miyake, K., & Weisz, J. (2000). The development of close relationships in Japan and the United States: Paths of symbiotic harmony and generative tension. *Child Development, 71*(5), 1121–1142. doi:10.1111/1467-8624.00214

Rothenberg, C., & Fisher, D. (2007). *Teaching English language learners: A differentiated approach.* Upper Saddle River, NJ: Pearson Merrill.

Rothrauff, T. C., Cooney, T. M., & An, J. S. (2009). Remembered parenting styles and adjustment in middle and late adulthood. *Journal of Gerontology, 64B*(1), 137–146.

Rothstein-Fisch, C., & Trumbull, E. (2008). *Managing diverse classrooms: How to build on students' strengths.* Alexandria, VA: Association for Supervision and Curriculum Development.

Rothstein-Fisch, C., Trumbull, E., & Garcia, S. G. (2009). Making the implicit explicit: Supporting teachers to bridge cultures. *Early Childhood Research Quarterly, 24,* 474–486. doi:10.1016/j.ecresq.2009.08.006

Rovee-Collier, C. (1999). The development of infant memory. *Current Directions in Psychological Science, 8,* 80–85.

Rovee-Collier, C., & Cuevas, K. (2009). Multiple memory systems are unnecessary to account for infant memory development: An ecological model. *Developmental Psychology, 45*(1), 160–174. doi:10.1037/a0014538

Rowe, D. C., Almeida, D. M., & Jacobson, K. C. (1999). School context and genetic influences on aggression in adolescence. *Psychological Science, 10,* 277–280.

Rowe, D. W., & Harste, J. C. (1986). Metalinguistic awareness in writing and reading: The young child as curricular informant. In D. B. Yaden, Jr., & S. Templeton (Eds.), *Metalinguistic awareness and beginning literacy: Conceptualizing what it means to read and write (pp.235-256).* Portsmouth, NH: Heinemann.

Rowe, E., Miller, C., Ebenstein, L., & Thompson, D. (2012). Cognitive predictors of reading and math achievement among gifted referrals. *School Psychology Quarterly, 27*(3), 144–153. doi:10.1037/a0029941

Rowe, M. B. (1974). Wait-time and rewards as instructional variables, their influence on language, logic, and fate control: Part one—wait time. *Journal of Research in Science Teaching, 11,* 81–94.

Rowe, M. B. (1978). *Teaching science as continuous inquiry.* New York, NY: McGraw-Hill.

Rowe, M. B. (1987). Wait-time: Slowing down may be a way of speeding up. *American Educator, 11,* 38–43, 47.

Rowland, T. W. (1990). *Exercise and children's health.* Champaign, IL: Human Kinetics.

Roy, A. L., & Raver, C. C. (2014). Are all risks equal? Early experiences of poverty-related risk and children's functioning. *Journal of Family Psychology, 28*(3), 391–400. doi:10.1037/a0036683

Rozalski, M. E., & Yell, M. L. (2004). Law and school safety. In: J. C. Conoley & A. P. Goldstein (Eds.), *School violence intervention* (2nd ed., pp. 507–523). New York, NY: Guilford Press.

Rozendaal, E., Buijzen, M., & Valkenburg, P. M. (2012). Think-aloud process superior to thought-listing in increasing children's critical processing of advertising. *Human Communication Research, 38*(2), 199–221. doi:10.1111/j.1468-2958.2011.01425.x

Rozendaal, M., & Baker, A. (2010). The acquisition of reference: Pragmatic aspects and the influence of language input. *Journal of Pragmatics, 42*(7), 1866–1879. doi:10.1016/j.pragma.2009.05.013

Rubie-Davies, C. M. (2007). Classroom interactions: Exploring the practices of high- and low- expectation teachers. *British Journal of Educational Psychology, 77,* 289–306.

Rubin, K. H., Bowker, J. C., & Kennedy, A. E. (2009). Avoiding and withdrawing from the peer group. In K. H. Rubin, W. M. Bukowski, & B. Laursen (Eds.), *Handbook of peer interactions, relationships, and groups* (pp. 303–321). New York, NY: Guilford Press.

Rubin, K. H., Bukowski, W. M., & Parker, J. G. (2006). Peer interactions, relationships, and groups. In W. Damon & R. M. Lerner (Series Eds.) & N. Eisenberg (Vol. Ed.), *Handbook of child psychology: Vol. 3. Social, emotional, and personality development* (6th ed., pp. 571–645). New York, NY: Wiley.

Rubin, K. H., Lynch, D., Coplan, R., Rose-Krasnor, L., & Booth, C. L. (1994). "Birds of a feather": Behavioral concordances and preferential personal attraction in children. *Child Development, 65,* 1778–1785.

Rubin, K., Fein, G., & Vandenberg, B. (1983). Play. In E. M. Hetherington (Ed.), *Handbook of child psychology: Vol. 4. Socialization, personality, and social development* (pp. 693–774). New York, NY: Wiley.

Ruble, D. N., Martin, C. L., & Berenbaum, S. A. (2006). Gender development. In W. Damon & R. M. Lerner (Eds. in Chief) & N. Eisenberg (Vol. Ed.), *Handbook of child psychology, Vol. 3. Social, emotional, and personality development* (6th ed., pp. 858–932). Hoboken, NJ: Wiley.

Ruble, D. N., Taylor, L. J., Cyphers, L., Greulich, F. K., Lurye, L. E., & Shrout, P. E. (2007). The role of gender constancy in early gender development. *Child Development, 78,* 1121–1136.

Ruby, P., & Decety, J. (2001). Effect of subjective perspective taking during simulation of action: A PET investigation of agency. *Nature and Neuroscience, 4,* 546–550.

Rudasill, K. M., Gallagher, K. C., & White, J. M. (2010). Temperamental attention and activity, classroom emotional support, and academic achievement in third grade. *Journal of School Psychology, 48*(2), 113–134.

Rudasill, K., Pössel, P., Winkeljohn Black, S., & Niehaus, K. (2014). Teacher support mediates concurrent and longitudinal associations between temperament and mild depressive symptoms in sixth grade. *Early Child Development & Care, 184*(6), 803-818. doi:10.1080/03004430.2013.821610

Rudlin, C. R. (1993). Growth and sexual development: What is normal, and what is not? *Journal of the American Academy of Physician Assistants, 6,* 25–35.

Rudolph, K. D., Caldwell, M. S., & Conley, C. S. (2005). Need for approval and children's well-being. *Child Development, 76,* 309–323.

Rudy, D., & Grusec, J. E. (2006). Authoritarian parenting in individualistic and collectivist groups: Associations with maternal emotion and cognition and children's self-esteem. *Journal of Family Psychology, 20,* 68–78.

Rudy, D., Carlo, G., Lambert, M., & Awong, T. (2014). Undergraduates' perceptions of parental relationship-oriented guilt induction versus harsh psychological control: Does cultural group status moderate their associations with self-esteem? *Journal of Cross-Cultural Psychology, 45*(6), 905–920.

Rueger, S., Chen, P., Jenkins, L., & Choe, H. (2014). Effects of perceived support from mothers, fathers, and teachers on depressive symptoms during the transition to middle school. *Journal of Youth & Adolescence, 43*(4), 655–670.

Ruff, H. A., & Lawson, K. R. (1990). Development of sustained, focused attention in young children during free play. *Developmental Psychology, 26,* 85–93.

Ruitenberg, M. L., Abrahamse, E. L., & Verwey, W. B. (2013). Sequential motor skill in preadolescent children: The development of automaticity. *Journal of Experimental Child Psychology, 115*(4), 607–623. doi:10.1016/j.jecp.2013.04.005

Ruiz-Gallardo, J., Verde, A., & Valdés, A. (2013). Garden-based learning: An experience with "at risk" secondary education students. *Journal of Environmental Education, 44*(4), 252–270. doi:10.1080/00958964.2013.786669

Rule, A. C. (2007). Mystery boxes: Helping children improve their reasoning. *Early Childhood Education Journal, 35*(1), 13–18.

Rumberger, R. W. (1995). Dropping out of middle school: A multilevel analysis of students and schools. *American Educational Research Journal, 32,* 583–625.

Rumi, H., Toshihiro, K., & Kenryu, N. (2013). Development of handwriting patterns in elementary school children using digital. *Japanese Journal of Developmental Psychology, 24*(1), 13–21.

Rusby, J. C., Jones, L., Crowley, R., & Smolkowski, K. (2013). The child care ecology inventory: A domain-specific measure of home-based child care quality to promote social competence for school readiness. *Early Childhood Research Quarterly, 28*(4), 947–959. doi:10.1016/j.ecresq.2013.02.003

Rush, C. (2012). Transana video analysis software as a tool for consultation: Applications to improving PTA meeting leadership. *Journal of Educational & Psychological Consultation, 22*(4), 300–313. doi:10.1080/10474412.2012.706129

Rushton, J. P., Fulkner, D. W., Neal, M. C., Nias, D. K. B., & Eysenck, H. J. (1986). Altruism and aggression: The heritability of individual differences. *Journal of Personality and Social Psychology, 50,* 1192–1198.

Russell, A., & Finnie, V. (1990). Preschool children's social status and maternal instructions to assist group entry. *Developmental Psychology, 26*(4), 603–611. doi:10.1037/0012-1649.26.4.603

Rutland, A., Cameron, L., Jugert, P., Nigbur, D., Brown, R., Watters, C., & Hossain, R., Landau, A., & Le Touze, D. (2012). Group identity and peer relations: A longitudinal study of group identity, perceived peer acceptance, and friendships amongst ethnic minority English children. *British Journal of Developmental Psychology, 30*(2), 283–302. doi:10.1111/j.2044-835X.2011.02040.x

Rutland, A., Killen, M., & Abrams, D. (2010). A new social-cognitive developmental perspective on prejudice: The interplay between morality and group identity. *Perspectives on Psychological Science, 5*(3), 279–291. doi:10.1177/1745691610369468

Rutter, M. (2005). Adverse preadoption experiences and psychological outcomes. In D. M. Brodzinsky & J. Palacios (Eds.), *Psychological issues in adoption: Research and practice* (pp. 67–92). Westport, CT: Praeger/Greenwood.

Rutter, M. (2013). Annual research review: Resilience—Clinical implications. Journal of Child Psychology And Psychiatry, 54(4), 474–487.

Rutter, M. L. (1997). Nature–nurture integration: The example of antisocial behavior. *American Psychologist, 52,* 390–398.

Ryan, R. M., & Deci, E. L. (2000). Self-determination theory and the facilitation of intrinsic motivation, social development, and well-being. *American Psychologist, 55,* 68–78.

Ryan, R. M., & Deci, E. L. (2009). Promoting self-determined school engagement. In K. R. Wentzel & A. Wigfield (Eds.), *Handbook of motivation at school* (pp. 171–195). New York, NY: Routledge.

Ryan, R. M., & Kuczkowski, R. (1994). The imaginary audience, self-consciousness, and public individuation in adolescence. *Journal of Personality, 62,* 219–237.

Ryan, R. M., & Lynch, J. H. (1989). Emotional autonomy versus detachment: Revisiting the vicissitudes of adolescence and young adulthood. *Child Development, 60,* 340–356.

Ryan, R. M., Connell, J. P., & Grolnick, W. S. (1992). When achievement is *not* intrinsically motivated: A theory of internalization and self-regulation in school. In A. K. Boggiano & T. S. Pittman (Eds.), *Achievement and motivation: A social-developmental perspective (pp. 167–188).* Cambridge, England: Cambridge University Press.

Ryan, R. M., Stiller, J. D., & Lynch, J. H. (1994). Representations of relationships to teachers, parents, and friends as predictors of academic motivation and self-esteem. *Journal of Early Adolescence, 14,* 226–249.

Rycus, J. S., Freundlich, M., Hughes, R. C., Keefer, B., & Oakes, E. J. (2006). Confronting barriers to adoption success. *Family Court Review, 44,* 210–230.

Sénéchal, M., & LeFevre, J.-A. (2002). Parental involvement in the development of children's reading skill: A five-year longitudinal study. *Child Development, 73,* 445–460.

Saarni, C., Campos, J. J., Camras, L. A., & Witherington, D. (2006). Emotional development: Action, communication, and understanding. In W. Damon & R. M. Lerner (Eds. in Chief) & N. Eisenberg (Vol. Ed.), *Handbook of child psychology, Vol. 3. Social, emotional, and personality development* (6th ed., pp. 226–299). Hoboken, NJ: Wiley.

Sabol, T. J., & Pianta, R. C. (2012). Recent trends in research on teacher–child relationships. *Attachment & Human Development, 14*(3), 213–231. doi:10.1080/14616734.2012.672262

Sachdeva, S., Singh, P., & Medin, D. (2011). Culture and the quest for universal principles in moral reasoning. *International Journal of Psychology, 46*(3), 161–176. doi:10.1080/00207594.2011.568486

Sadeh, A., Gruber, R., & Raviv, A. (2002). Sleep, neurobehavioral functioning, and behavior problems in school-age children. *Child Development, 73,* 405–417.

Sadler, T. W. (2010). *Langman's medical embryology* (11th ed.). Baltimore, MD: Lippincott Williams & Wilkins.

Safe Motherhood Network Federation. (2010). *Safe motherhood in Nepal.* Retrieved from *http://www.safemotherhood.org.np/index.php*

Saffran, J. R., & Griepentrog, G. J. (2001). Absolute pitch in infant auditory learning: Evidence for developmental reorganization. *Developmental Psychology, 37,* 74–85.

Saine, N. L., Lerkkanen, M., Ahonen, T., Tolvanen, A., & Lyytinen, H. (2013). Long-term intervention effects of spelling development for children with compromised preliteracy skills. *Reading & Writing Quarterly, 29*(4), 333–357. doi:10.1080/10573569.2013.741962

Salley, B., Panneton, R. K., & Colombo, J. (2013). Separable attentional predictors of language outcome. *Infancy, 18*(4), 462–489. doi:10.1111/j.1532-7078.2012.00138.x

Salley, C. G., Vannatta, K., Gerhardt, C. A., & Noll, R. B. (2010). Social self-perception accuracy: Variations as a function of child age and gender. *Self and Identity, 9*(2), 209–223.

Sallquist, J., Didonato, M., Hanish, L., Martin, C., & Fabes, R. (2012). The importance of mutual positive expressivity in social adjustment: Understanding the role of peers and gender. *Emotion (15283542), 12*(2), 304–313.

Salmani Nodoushan, M. (2009). The Shaffer-Gee perspective: Can epistemic games serve education?. *Teaching and Teacher Education, 25*(6), 897–901. doi:10.1016/j.tate.2009.01.013

Salmon, A. K., & Lucas, T. (2011). Exploring young children's conceptions about thinking. *Journal of Research in Childhood Education, 25*(4), 364–375. doi:10.1080/02568543.2011.605206

Salmon, D., & Rickaby, C. (2014). City of one: A Qualitative study examining the participation of young people in care in a theatre and music initiative. *Children & Society, 28*(1), 30-41. doi:10.1111/j.1099-0860.2012.00444.x

Salomo, D., & Liszkowski, U. (2013). Sociocultural settings influence the emergence of prelinguistic deictic gestures. *Child Development, 84*(4), 1296–1307. doi:10.1111/cdev.12026

Salomo, D., & Liszkowski, U. (2013). Sociocultural settings influence the emergence of prelinguistic deictic gestures. *Child Development, 84*(4), 1296–1307.

Saltz, E. (1971). *The cognitive bases of human learning.* Homewood, IL: Dorsey.

Saltz, J. B., & Nuzhdin, S. V. (2014). Genetic variation in niche construction: implications for development and evolutionary genetics. *Trends In Ecology & Evolution, 29*(1), 8-14. doi:10.1016/j.tree.2013.09.011

Salvas, M., Vitaro, F., Brendgen, M., Dionne, G., Tremblay, R. E., & Boivin, M. (2014). Friendship conflict and the development of generalized physical aggression in the early school years: A genetically informed study of potential moderators. *Developmental Psychology, 50*(6), 1794–1807. doi:10.1037/a0036419

Sameroff, A. (2009). The transactional model. In A. Sameroff (Ed.), *The transactional model of development: How children and contexts shape each other* (pp. 3–21). Washington, DC: American Psychological Association.

Sampson, V., Enderle, P., Grooms, J., & Witte, S. (2013). Writing to learn by learning to write during the school science laboratory: Helping middle and high school students develop argumentative writing skills as they learn core ideas. *Science Education, 97*(5), 643–670. doi:10.1002/sce.21069

Samson, A., Phillips, J., Parker, K., Shah, S., Gross, J., & Hardan, A. (2014). Emotion dysregulation and the core features of autism spectrum disorder. *Journal of Autism & Developmental Disorders, 44*(7), 1766–1772. doi:10.1007/s10803-013-2022-5

Samuels, B., & Blitz, C. (2014). A call to action promoting effective interventions for children in child welfare using neuroscience. *Social Policy Report, 28*(1), 28–31.

Samuels, G. M. (2009a). Ambiguous loss of home: The experience of familial (im)permanence among young adults with foster care backgrounds. *Children and Youth Services Review, 31,* 1229–1239.

Sanchez, C. E., Richards, J. E. and Almli, C. R. (2012), Neurodevelopmental MRI brain templates for children from 2 weeks to 4 years of age. *Developmental Psychobiology, 54,* 77–91. doi: 10.1002/dev.20579

Sanchez, F., & Anderson, M. L. (1990). Gang mediation: A process that works. *Principal, 69*(4), 54–56.

Sandamas, G., Foreman, N., & Coulson, M. (2009). Interface familiarity restores active advantage in a virtual exploration and reconstruction task in children. *Spatial Cognition and Computation, 9*(2), 96–108.

Sanders, M., & Mazzucchelli, T. (2013). The promotion of self-regulation through parenting interventions. *Clinical Child & Family Psychology Review, 16*(1), 1–17. doi:10.1007/s10567-013-0129-z

Sanders, W. H. (2010). Walking alongside children as they form compassion. *Exchange, 32*(3), 50–53.

Sands, D. J., & Wehmeyer, M. L. (Eds.). (1996). *Self-determination across the life span: Independence and choice for people with disabilities.* Baltimore, MD: Paul H. Brookes.

Santamaria, L. J. (2009). Culturally responsive differentiated instruction: Narrowing gaps between best pedagogical practices benefiting all learners. *Teachers College Record, 111*(1), 214–247.

Santelli, J. S., Orr, M., Lindberg, L. D., & Diaz, D. C. (2009). Changing behavioral risk for pregnancy among high school students in the United States, 1991–2007. *Journal of Adolescent Health, 45*(1), 25–32.

Santo, J., Bukowski, W. M., Stella-Lopez, L., Carmago, G., Mayman, S. B., & Adams, R. E. (2013). Factors underlying contextual variations in the structure of the self: Differences related to SES, gender, culture, and "majority/nonmajority" status during early adolescence. *Journal of Research on Adolescence (Wiley-Blackwell), 23*(1), 69–80. doi:10.1111/j.1532-7795.2012.00793.x

Santos, A. J., Vaughn, B. E., Peceguina, I., & Daniel, J. R. (2014). Longitudinal stability of social competence indicators in a Portuguese sample: Q-sort profiles of social competence, measures of social engagement, and peer sociometric acceptance. *Developmental Psychology, 50*(3), 968–978. doi:10.1037/a0034344

Saracho, O. N. (2014). Theory of mind: Understanding young children's pretence and mental states. *Early Child Development and Care, 184*(8), 1281–1294. doi:10.1080/03004430.2013.865617

Sarahan, N., & Copas, R. (2014). Autism assets. *Reclaiming Children & Youth, 22*(4), 34–37.

Sarnecka, B. W., & Wright, C. E. (2013). The idea of an exact number: Children's understanding of cardinality and equinumerosity. *Cognitive Science, 37*(8), 1493–1506. doi:10.1111/cogs.12043

Sarrazin, J., & Cyr, F. (2007). Parental conflicts and their damaging effects on children. *Journal of Divorce and Remarriage, 47,* 77–93.

Satcher, D. (2010). Taking charge of school wellness. *Educational Leadership, 67*(4), 38–43.

Sattler, J. M. (2001). *Assessment of children: Cognitive applications* (4th ed.). San Diego, CA: Author.

Savin-Williams, R. C. (1989). Gay and lesbian adolescents. *Marriage and Family Review, 14*(3–4), 197–216.

Savin-Williams, R. C. (2005). *The new gay teenager.* Cambridge, MA: Harvard University Press.

Savin-Williams, R. C., & Diamond, L. M. (1997). Sexual orientation as a developmental context for lesbians, gays, and bisexuals: Biological perspectives. In N. L. Segal, G. E. Weisfeld, & C. C. Weisfeld (Eds.), *Uniting psychology and biology: Integrative perspectives on human development* (pp. 217–238). Washington, DC: American Psychological Association.

Sawyer, M. G., Pfeiffer, S., Spence, S. H., Bond, L., Graetz, B., Kay, D., Patton, G., & Sheffield, J. (2010). School-based prevention of depression: A randomised controlled study of the *beyond blue* schools research initiative. *Journal of Child Psychology and Psychiatry, 51*(2), 199–209.

Sawyer, R. J., Graham, S., & Harris, K. R. (1992). Direct teaching, strategy instruction, and strategy instruction with explicit self-regulation: Effects on the composition skills and self-efficacy of students with learning disabilities. *Journal of Educational Psychology, 84,* 340–352.

Saxe, G. B. (1988). The mathematics of child street vendors. *Child Development, 59*(5), 1415–1425.

Sayer, E., Beaven, A., Stringer, P., & Hermena, E. (2013). Investigating sense of community in primary schools. *Educational & Child Psychology, 30*(1), 9–25.

Sayer, E., Beaven, A., Stringer, P., & Hermena, E. (2013). Investigating sense of community in primary schools. *Educational and Child Psychology, 30*(1), 9–25.

Scardamalia, M., & Bereiter, C. (1986). Writing. In R. F. Dillon & R. J. Sternberg (Eds.), *Cognition and instruction* (pp. 59–81). San Diego, CA: Academic Press.

Scarr, S. (1992). Developmental theories for the 1990s: Development and individual differences. *Child Development, 63,* 1–19.

Scarr, S., & McCartney, K. (1983). How people make their own environments: A theory of genotype environment effects. *Child Development, 54,* 424–435.

Schaefer-McDaniel, N. (2007). "They be doing illegal things": Early adolescents talk about their inner-city neighborhoods. *Journal of Adolescent Research, 22,* 413–436.

Schaffer, H. R. (1996). *Social development*. Cambridge, MA: Blackwell.

Schauble, L. (1990). Belief revision in children: The role of prior knowledge and strategies for generating evidence. *Journal of Experimental Child Psychology, 49,* 31–57.

Schellenberg, E. G. (2006). Long-term positive associations between music lessons and IQ. *Journal of Educational Psychology, 98,* 457–468.

Scherer, M. (2011, February). Transforming education with technology. *Educational Leadership, 68*(5), 17–21.

Scherer, N., & Olswang, L. (1984). Role of mothers' expansions in stimulating children's language production. *Journal of Speech and Hearing Research, 27,* 387–396.

Schiefele, U. (2009). Situational and individual interest. In K. R. Wentzel & A. Wigfield (Eds.), *Handbook of motivation at school* (pp. 197–222). New York, NY: Routledge.

Schieffelin, B. B. (1985). The acquisition of Kaluli. In D. I Slobin (Ed.), *The crosslinguistic study of language acquisition* (pp. 525–593). Hillsdale, NJ: Erlbaum.

Schieffelin, B. B. (1990). *The give and take of everyday life: Language socialization of Kaluli children*. New York, NY: Cambridge University Press.

Schilling, T. A. (2008). An examination of resilience processes in context: The case of Tasha. *Urban Review, 40,* 296–316.

Schinke, S. P., Moncher, M. S., & Singer, B. R. (1994). Native American youths and cancer risk prevention. *Journal of Adolescent Health, 15,* 105–110.

Schlaefli, A., Rest, J. R., & Thoma, S. J. (1985). Does moral education improve moral judgment? A meta-analysis of intervention studies using the defining issues test. *Review of Educational Research, 55,* 319–352.

Schlam, T. R., Wilson, N. L., Shoda, Y., Mischel, W., & Ayduk, O. (2013). Preschoolers' delay of gratification predicts their body mass 30 years later. *Journal of Pediatrics, 162*(1), 90–93. doi:10.1016/j.jpeds.2012.06.049

Schlegel, A., & Barry, H. L., III. (1980). The evolutionary significance of adolescent initiation ceremonies. *American Ethnologist, 7*(4), 696–715.

Schleppenbach, M., Perry, M., Miller, K. F., Sims, L., & Fang, G. (2007). The answer is only the beginning: Extended discourse in Chinese and U.S. mathematics classrooms. *Journal of Educational Psychology, 99,* 380–396.

Schlottmann, A., Ray, E. D., & Surian, L. (2012). Emerging perception of causality in action-and-reaction sequences from 4 to 6 months of age: Is it domain-specific? *Journal of Experimental Child Psychology, 112*(2), 208–230. doi:10.1016/j.jecp.2011.10.011

Schmitow, C., & Stenberg, G. (2013). Social referencing in 10-month-old infants. *European Journal of Developmental Psychology, 10*(5), 533–545. doi:10.1080/17405629.2013.763473

Schneider, M., & Hardy, I. (2013). Profiles of inconsistent knowledge in children's pathways of conceptual change. *Developmental Psychology, 49*(9), 1639–1649. doi:10.1037/a0030976

Schneider, W., & Lockl, K. (2002). The development of metacognitive knowledge in children and adolescents. In T. J. Perfect & B. L. Schwartz (Eds.), *Applied metacognition* (pp. 224–257). Cambridge, England: Cambridge University Press.

Schneider, W., & Pressley, M. (1989). *Memory development between 2 and 20*. New York, NY: Springer-Verlag.

Schneider, W., & Shiffrin, R. M. (1977). Controlled and automatic human information processing: I. Detection, search, and attention. *Psychological Review, 84,* 1–66.

Schoenfeld, A. H. (1988). When good teaching leads to bad results: The disasters of "well-taught" mathematics courses. *Educational Psychologist, 23,* 145–166.

Schofield, G., & Beek, M. (2009). Growing up in foster care: Providing a secure base through adolescence. *Child and Family Social Work, 14,* 255–266.

Schommer, M. (1994b). Synthesizing epistemological belief research: Tentative understandings and provocative confusions. *Educational Psychology Review, 6,* 293–319.

Schonert-Reichl, K. A. (1993). Empathy and social relationships in adolescents with behavioral disorders. *Behavioral Disorders, 18,* 189–204.

Schramm, D. G., Harris, S. M., Whiting, J. B., Hawkins, A. J., Brown, M., & Porter, R. (2013). Economic costs and policy implications associated with divorce: Texas as a case study. *Journal of Divorce & Remarriage, 54*(1), 1–24. doi:10.1080/1050255 6.2012.725354

Schraw, G., Flowerday, T., & Lehman, S. (2001). Increasing situational interest in the classroom. *Educational Psychology Review, 13,* 211–224.

Schraw, G., Potenza, M. T., & Nebelsick-Gullet, L. (1993). Constraints on the calibration of performance. *Contemporary Educational Psychology, 18,* 455–463.

Schreibman, L. (2008). Treatment controversies in autism. *Zero to Three, 28*(4), 38–45.

Schuchardt, K., Gebhardt, M., & Mäehler, C. (2010). Working memory functions in children with different degrees of intellectual disability. *Journal of Intellectual Disability Research, 54*(4), 346–353.

Schuengel, C., de Schipper, J., Sterkenburg, P. S., & Kef, S. (2013). Attachment, intellectual disabilities and mental health: Research, assessment and intervention. *Journal of Applied Research in Intellectual Disabilities, 26*(1), 34–46. doi:10.1111/jar.12010

Schultz, G. F., & Switzky, H. N. (1990). The development of intrinsic motivation in students with learning problems: Suggestions for more effective instructional practice. *Preventing School Failure, 34*(2), 14–20.

Schultz, J., Lieberman, L., Ellis, M., & Hilgenbrinck, L (2013). Ensuring the success of deaf students in Inclusive Physical Education. *Journal of Physical Education, Recreation & Dance, 84*(5), 51–56.

Schulz, L. E., Goodman, N. D., Tenenbaum, J. B., & Jenkins, A. C. (2008). Going beyond the evidence: Abstract laws and preschoolers' responses to anomalous data. *Cognition, 109,* 211–223.

Schunk, D. H. (1996). Goal and self-evaluative influences during children's cognitive skill learning. *American Educational Research Journal, 33,* 359–382.

Schunk, D. H. (2012). Social cognitive theory. In K. R. Harris, S. Graham, T. Urdan, C. B. McCormick, G. M. Sinatra, & J. Sweller (Eds.), *APA educational psychology handbook, Vol. 1: Theories, constructs, and critical issues* (pp. 101–123). Washington, DC: American Psychological Association. doi:10.1037/13273-005

Schunk, D. H., & Hanson, A. R. (1985). Peer models: Influence on children's self-efficacy and achievement. *Journal of Educational Psychology, 77,* 313–322.

Schunk, D. H., & Pajares, F. (2004). Self-efficacy in education revisited: Empirical and applied evidence. In D. M. McNerney & S. Van Etten (Eds.), *Big theories revisited* (pp. 115–138). Greenwich, CT: Information Age.

Schunk, D. H., & Pajares, F. (2009). Self-efficacy theory. In K. R. Wentzel & A. Wigfield (Eds.), *Handbook of motivation at school* (pp. 35–53). New York, NY: Routledge.

Schunk, D. H., & Rice, J. (1989). Learning goals and children's reading comprehension. *Journal of Reading Behavior, 21,* 279–293.

Schutz, P. A. (1994). Goals as the transactive point between motivation and cognition. In P. R. Pintrich, D. R. Brown, & C. E. Weinstein (Eds.), *Student motivation, cognition, and learning: Essays in honor of Wilbert J. McKeachie* (pp. 113–133). Hillsdale, NJ: Erlbaum.

Schwartz, J. L., Yarushalmy, M., & Wilson, B. (Eds.) (1993). *The geometric supposer: What is it a case of?* Hillsdale, NJ: Erlbaum.

Schwartz, M., & Shaul, Y. (2013). Narrative development among language-minority children: The role of bilingual versus monolingual preschool education. *Language, Culture and Curriculum, 26*(1), 36–51. doi:10.1080/07908318.2012.760568

Schwartz, P. D., Maynard, A. M., & Uzelac, S. M. (2008). Adolescent egocentrism: A contemporary view. *Adolescence, 43*(171), 441–448.

Schwartz, S. J., Syed, M., Yip, T., Knight, G. P., Umaña-Taylor, A. J., Rivas-Drake, D., & Lee, R. M. (2014). Methodological issues in ethnic and racial identity research with ethnic minority populations: Theoretical precision, measurement issues, and research designs. *Child Development, 85*(1), 58–76. doi:10.1111/cdev.12201

Schwarz, C. V., & White, B. Y. (2005). Metamodeling knowledge: Developing students' understanding of scientific modeling. *Cognition and Instruction, 23,* 165–205.

Schweinhart, L. J. (2006). The High/Scope approach: Evidence that participatory learning in early childhood contributes to human development. In N. F. Watt, C. Ayoub, R. H. Bradley, J. E. Puma, & W. A. LeBoeuf (Eds.), *The crisis in youth mental health: Critical issues and effective programs, Vol. 4: Early intervention programs and policies* (pp. 207–227). Westport, CT: Praeger Publishers/Greenwood Publishing Group.

Schweinhart, L. J., & Weikart, D. P. (1993, November). Success by empowerment: The High/Scope Perry Preschool Study through age 27. *Young Children, 48,* 54–58.

Schweinle, A., Berg, P., & Sorenson, A. (2013). Preadolescent perceptions of challenging and difficult course activities and their motivational distinctions. *Educational Psychology, 33*(7), 797–816. doi:10.1080/01443410.2013.785049

Schwenck, C., Göhle, B., Hauf, J., Warnke, A., Freitag, C. M., & Schneider, W. (2014). Cognitive and emotional empathy in typically developing children: The influence of age, gender, and intelligence. *European Journal of Developmental Psychology, 11*(1), 63–76. doi:10.1080/17405629.2013.808994

Scott-Little, M., & Holloway, S. (1992). Child care providers' reasoning about misbehaviors: Relation to classroom control strategies and professional training. *Early Childhood Research Quarterly, 7,* 595–606.

Scrimin, S., Moscardino, U., & Natour, M. (2014). Socio-ecological correlates of mental health among ethnic minorities in areas of political conflict: A study of Druze adolescents in Israel. *Transcultural Psychiatry, 51*(2), 209–227. doi:10.1177/1363461513520342

Sear, R., & Mace, R. (2008). Who keeps children alive? A review of the effects of kin on child survival. *Evolution and Human Behavior, 29,* 1–18.

Seaton, E., Yip, T., Morgan-Lopez, A., & Sellers, R. (2012). Racial discrimination and racial socialization as predictors of African American adolescents' racial identity development using latent transition analysis. *Developmental Psychology, 48*(2), 448–458.

Seaton, M., Parker, P., Marsh, H., Craven, R., & Yeung, A. (2014). The reciprocal relations between self-concept, motivation and achievement: juxtaposing academic self-concept and achievement goal orientations for mathematics success. *Educational Psychology, 34*(1), 49–72. doi:10.1080/01443410.2013.825232

Sebire, S. J., Jago, R., Fox, K. R., Edwards, M. J., & Thompson, J. (2013). Testing a self-determination theory model of children's physical activity motivation: A cross-sectional study. *The International Journal of Behavioral Nutrition and Physical Activity, 10.* doi:10.1186/1479-5868-10-111

Segal, N. L. (2012). *Born together—reared apart: The landmark Minnesota Twin Study.* Cambridge, MA: Harvard University Press. doi:10.4159/harvard.9780674065154

Seibert, A. C., & Kerns, K. A. (2009). Attachment figures in middle childhood. *International Journal of Behavioral Development, 33*(4), 347–355.

Seiver, E., Gopnik, A., & Goodman, N. D. (2013). Did she jump because she was the big sister or because the trampoline was safe? Causal inference and the development of social attribution. *Child Development, 84*(2), 443–454. doi:10.1111/j.1467-8624.2012.01865.x

Sejnost, R. L., & Thiese, S. M. (2010). *Building content literacy: Strategies for the adolescent learner.* Thousand Oaks, CA: Corwin Press.

Selfe, L. (1977). *Nadia: A case of extraordinary drawing ability in an autistic child.* London: Academic Press.

Selfe, L. (1995). Nadia reconsidered. In C. Golomb (Ed.), *The development of artistically gifted children: Selected case studies* (pp. 197–236). Hillsdale, NJ: Erlbaum.

Seligman, M. E. P. (1991). *Learned optimism.* New York, NY: Knopf.

Selman, R. L. (1980). *The growth of interpersonal understanding: Developmental and clinical analysis.* New York, NY: Academic Press.

Selman, R. L. (2003). *The promotion of social awareness: Powerful lessons from the partnership of developmental theory and classroom practice.* New York, NY: Russell Sage Foundation.

Selman, R. L., & Byrne, D. F. (1974). A structural-developmental analysis of levels of role taking in middle childhood. *Child Development, 45,* 803–806.

Selman, R. L., & Schultz, L. J. (1990. *Making a friend in youth: Developmental theory and pair therapy.* Chicago: University of Chicago Press.

Semrud-Clikeman, M., Fine, J., & Bledsoe, J. (2013). Comparison among children with children with autism spectrum disorder, nonverbal learning disorder and typically developing children on measures of executive functioning. *Journal of Autism and Developmental Disorders.* doi:10.1007/s10803-013-1871-2

Senghas, A., & Coppola, M. (2001). Children creating language: How Nicaraguan Sign Language acquired a spatial grammar. *Psychological Science, 12,* 323–328.

Senn, N. (2012). Effective approaches to motivate and engage reluctant boys in literacy. *Reading Teacher, 66*(3), 211–220. doi:10.1002/TRTR.01107

Seo, H. (2014). Promoting the self-determination of elementary and secondary students with disabilities: Perspectives of general and special educators in Korea. *Education & Training In Autism & Developmental Disabilities, 49*(3), 277–289.

Serpell, R. (2011). Social responsibility as a dimension of intelligence, and as an educational goal: Insights from programmatic research in an African society. *Child Development Perspectives, 5*(2), 126–133. doi:10.1111/j.1750-8606.2011.00167.x

Serpell, R., Baker, L., & Sonnenschein, S. (2005). *Becoming literate in the city: The Baltimore Early Childhood Project.* Cambridge, England: Cambridge University Press.

Setoh, P., Wu, D., Baillargeon, R., & Gelman, R. (2013). Young infants have biological expectations about animals. *PNAS Proceedings of the National Academy of Sciences of the United States of America, 110*(40), 15937–15942.

Seuss, Dr. (1968). *The foot book.* New York, NY: Random House.

Sewell, A. (2011). Exploring the development of a community of learners in four primary classrooms. *New Zealand Journal Of Educational Studies, 46*(2), 61–74.

Sewell, A., St George, A., & Cullen, J. (2013). The distinctive features of joint participation in a community of learners. *Teaching & Teacher Education, 31,* 46–55. doi:10.1016/j.tate.2012.11.00

Shahaeian, A., Nielsen, M., Peterson, C., & Slaughter, V. (2014). Cultural and family influences on children's theory of mind development: A comparison of Australian and Iranian school-age children. *Journal of Cross-Cultural Psychology, 45*(4), 555–568.

Shahinfar, A., Kupersmidt, J. B., & Matza, L. S. (2001). The relation between exposure to violence and social information processing among incarcerated adolescents. *Journal of Abnormal Psychology, 110,* 136–141.

Shanahan, T., & Tierney, R. J. (1990). Reading-writing connection: The relations among three perspectives. In J. Zutell & S. McCormick (Eds.), *Literacy theory and research: Analyses from multiple paradigms. Thirty-ninth yearbook of the National Reading Conference.* Chicago, IL: National Reading Conference.

Shapiro, E. S., & Manz, P. H. (2004). Collaborating with schools in the provision of pediatric psychological services. In R. T. Brown (Ed.), *Handbook of pediatric psychology in school settings* (pp. 49–64). Mahwah, NJ: Erlbaum.

Share, D. L., & Gur, T. (1999). How reading begins: A study of preschoolers' print identification strategies. *Cognition and Instruction, 17,* 177–213.

Sharkey, J. D., Shekhtmeyster, Z., Chavez-Lopez, L., Norris, E., & Sass, L. (2010). The protective influence of gangs: Can schools compensate? *Aggression and Violent Behavior,* doi:10.1016/j.avb.2010.11.001

Shatz, M., & Gelman, R. (1973). The development of communication skills: Modifications in the speech of young children as a function of listener. *Monographs of the Society for Research in Child Development, 38*(5, Serial No. 152), 1–37. doi:10.2307/1165783

Shavinina, L. V., & Ferrari, M. (2004). Extracognitive facets of developing high ability: Introduction to some important issues. In L. V. Shavinina & M. Ferrari (Eds.), *Beyond knowledge: Extracognitive aspects of developing high ability* (pp. 3–13). Mahwah, NJ: Erlbaum.

Shaw, D. (2013). Future directions for research on the development and prevention of early conduct problems. *Journal of Clinical Child & Adolescent Psychology, 42*(3), 418–428.

Shaw, G. B. (1916). *Androcles and the lion; Overruled; Pygmalion.* New York, NY: Brentano.

Shayne, R., & Miltenberger, R. G. (2013). Evaluation of behavioral skills training for teaching functional assessment and treatment selection skills to parents. *Behavioral Interventions, 28*(1), 4–21. doi:10.1002/bin.1350

Shaywitz, S. E. (2004). *Overcoming dyslexia.* New York, NY: Knopf.

Shear, K., & Shair, H. (2005). Attachment, loss, and complicated grief. *Developmental Psychobiology, 47*(3), 253–267. doi:10.1002/dev.20091

Shechtman, Z., & Ifargan, M. (2009). School-based integrated and segregated interventions to reduce aggression. *Aggressive Behavior, 35,* 342–356.

Sheehan, E. P., & Smith, H. V. (1986). Cerebral lateralization and handedness and their effects on verbal and spatial reasoning. *Neuropsychologia, 24,* 531–540.

Sheets, R. H. (1999). Human development and ethnic identity. In R. H. Sheets & E. R. Hollins (Eds.), *Racial and ethnic identity in school practices: Aspects of human development* (pp. 91–101). Mahwah, NJ: Erlbaum.

Sheffield, E., Stromswold, K., & Molnar, D. (2005, April). *Do prematurely born infants catch up?* Paper presented at the biennial meeting of the Society for Research in Child Development, Atlanta, GA.

Sheldon, J., Arbreton, A., Hopkins, L., & Grossman, J. B. (2010). Investing in success: Key strategies for building quality in after-school programs. *American Journal of Community Psychology, 45*(3–4), 394–404.

Sheldon, K. M. (2013). Motivation: Internalized motivation in the classroom. In J. J. Froh, A. C. Parks (Eds.), *Activities for teaching positive psychology: A guide for instructors* (pp. 155–160). Washington, DC: American Psychological Association. doi:10.1037/14042-025

Shellenberg, E. G., & Trehub, S. E. (2003). Good pitch memory is widespread. *Psychological Science, 14,* 262–266.

Shen, Z. (2009). Multiple intelligences theory on the mainland of China. In J.-Q. Chen, S. Moran, & H. Gardner (Eds.), *Multiple intelligences around the world* (pp. 55–65). San Francisco, CA: Jossey-Bass.

Shenfield, T., Trehub, S. E., & Nakata, T. (2003). Maternal singing modulates infant arousal. *Psychology of Music, 31,* 365–375.

Shenkin, S. D., Starr, J. M., & Deary, I. J. (2004). Birth weight and cognitive ability in childhood: A systematic review. *Psychological Bulletin, 130,* 989–1013.

Shepard, R. N., & Metzler, J. (1971). Mental rotation of three-dimensional objects. *Science, 171,* 701–703.

Sheridan, M. D. (1975). *Children's developmental progress from birth to five years: The Stycar Sequences.* Windsor, England: NFER.

Sherif, M., Harvey, O. J., White, B. J., Hood, W. R., & Sherif, C. (1961). *Inter-group conflict and cooperation: The Robbers Cave experiment.* Norman, OK: University of Oklahoma Press.

Sherry, J. L. (2013). Formative research for STEM educational games: Lessons from the Children's Television Workshop. *Zeitschrift Für Psychologie, 221*(2), 90–97. doi:10.1027/2151-2604/a000134

Sherry, J. L., Lucas, K., Greenberg, B. S., & Holmstrom, A. (2013). Child development and genre preference: Research for educational game design. *Cyberpsychology, Behavior & Social Networking, 16*(5), 335–339. doi:10.1089/cyber.2012.0242

Sherwen, L. N., Scoloveno, M. A., & Weingarten, C. T. (1999). *Maternity nursing: Care of the childbearing family* (3rd ed.). Stamford, CT: Appleton & Lange.

Shevell, M. (2009). The tripartite origins of the tonic neck reflex. *Neurology, 72,* 850–853.

Shi, B., & Xie, H. (2014). Moderating effects of group status, cohesion, and ethnic composition on socialization of aggression in children's peer groups. *Developmental Psychology.* doi:10.1037/a0037177

Shi, R., & Werker, J. F. (2001). Six-month-old infants' preference for lexical words. *Psychological Science, 12,* 70–75.

Shields, M. K., & Behrman, R. E. (2004). Children of immigrant families: Analysis and recommendations. *The Future of Children, 14*(2), 4–15.

Shih, S. (2009). An examination of factors related to Taiwanese adolescents' reports of avoidance strategies. *Journal of Educational Research (Washington, D.C.), 102*(5), 377–388.

Shilubane, H., Ruiter, R., Bos, A., den Borne, B., James, S., & Reddy, P. (2014). Psychosocial correlates of suicidal ideation in rural South African Adolescents. *Child Psychiatry & Human Development, 45*(2), 153–162.

Shing, R. (2013). Relationships between early language skills and future literacy development in Hong Kong. *Early Child Development & Care, 183*(10), 1397–1406. doi:10.1080/03004430.2013 .788820

Shoda, Y., Mischel, W., & Peake, P. K. (1990). Predicting adolescent cognitive and self-regulatory competencies from preschool delay of gratification: Identifying diagnostic conditions. *Developmental Psychology, 26*(6), 978–986. doi:10.1037/0012-1649.26.6.978

Shogren, K. A., Kennedy, W., Dowsett, C., & Little, T. D. (2014). Autonomy, psychological empowerment, and self-realization: Exploring data on self-determination from NLTS2. *Exceptional Children, 80*(2), 221–235.

Shonkoff, J. P. & Phillips, D. A. (Eds.). (2000). *From neurons to neighborhoods: The science of early childhood development.* Washington, DC: National Academy of Sciences.

Shonkoff, J. P., & Richter, L. (2013). The powerful reach of early childhood development: A science-based foundation for sound investment. In P. Britto, P. L. Engle, C. M. Super (Eds.), *Handbook of early childhood development research and its impact on global policy* (pp. 24–34). New York, NY: Oxford University Press. doi:10.1093/ acprof:oso/9780199922994.003.0002

Short, E. J., & Ryan, E. B. (1984). Metacognitive differences between skilled and less skilled readers: Remediating deficits through story grammar and attribution training. *Journal of Educational Psychology, 76,* 225–235.

Short, M., Gradisar, M., Lack, L., Wright, H., Dewald, J., Wolfson, A., & Carskadon, M. (2013). A cross-cultural comparison of sleep duration between U.S. and Australian adolescents: The effect of school start time, parent-set bedtimes, and extracurricular load. *Health Education & Behavior, 40*(3), 323–330. doi:10.1177/1090198112451266

Shoshani, A., & Steinmetz, S. (2013). Positive psychology at school: A school-based intervention to promote adolescents' mental health and well-being. *Journal of Happiness Studies.* doi:10.1007/ s10902-013-9476-1

Shreyar, S., Zolkower, B., & Pérez, S. (2010). Thinking aloud together: A teacher's semiotic mediation of a whole-class conversation about percents. *Educational Studies in Mathematics, 73,* 21–53.

Shrum, W., & Cheek, N. H. (1987). Social structure during the school years: Onset of the degrouping process. *American Sociological Review, 52,* 218–223.

Shultz, T. R. (1974). Development of the appreciation of riddles. *Child Development, 45,* 100–105.

Shultz, T. R., & Horibe, F. (1974). Development of the appreciation of verbal jokes. *Developmental Psychology, 10,* 13–20.

Shumsky, E. (2013). Discussion of Jane R. Lewis's "Hair-pulling, culture, and unmourned death." *International Journal of Psychoanalytic Self Psychology, 8*(2), 218–224. doi:10.1080/15551024.20 13.768751

Shweder, R. A., Goodnow, J., Hatano, G., LeVine, R. A., Markus, H., & Miller, P. (1998). The cultural psychology of development: One mind, many mentalities. In W. Damon (Series Ed.) & R. M. Lerner (Vol. Ed.), *Handbook of child psychology: Vol. 1. Theoretical models of human development* (5th ed., pp. 865–937). New York, NY: Wiley.

Shweder, R. A., Mahapatra, M., & Miller, J. G. (1987). Culture and moral development. In J. Kagan & S. Lamb (Eds.), *The emergence of morality in young*

children (pp. 1–83). Chicago, IL: University of Chicago Press.

Sieber, J. E., O'Neil, H. F., & Tobias, S. (1977). *Anxiety, learning, and instruction.* Oxford England.

Siegel, D. J. (2001). Toward an interpersonal neurobiology of the developing mind: Attachment relationships, "mindsight," and neural integration. *Infant Mental Health Journal, 22,* 67–94.

Sieger, K., & Renk, K. (2007). Pregnant and parenting adolescents: A study of ethnic identity, emotional and behavioral functioning, child characteristics, and social support. *Journal of Youth and Adolescence, 36*(4), 567–581.

Siegler, R. S. (1989). Mechanisms of cognitive growth. *Annual Review of Psychology, 40,* 353–379.

Siegler, R. S. (2006). Microgenetic analyses of learning. In W. Damon & R. M. Lerner (Eds. in Chief) & D. Kuhn & R. S. Siegler (Vol. Eds.), *Handbook of child psychology: Vol. 2. Cognition, perception, and language* (6th ed., pp. 464–510). Hoboken, NJ: Wiley.

Siegler, R. S., & Alibali, M. W. (2005). *Children's thinking* (4th ed.). Upper Saddle River, NJ: Prentice Hall.

Siegler, R. S., & Jenkins, E. (1989). *How children discover new strategies.* Hillsdale, NJ: Erlbaum.

Sigelman, C. (2012). Age and ethnic differences in cold weather and contagion theories of colds and flu. *Health Education & Behavior, 39*(1), 67–76. doi:10.1177/1090198111407187

Sigman, M., & Whaley, S. E. (1998). The role of nutrition in the development of intelligence. In U. Neisser (Ed.), *The rising curve: Long-term gains in IQ and related measures* (pp. 155–182). Washington, DC: American Psychological Association.

Sigurdson, J. F., Wallander, J. J., & Sund, A. M. (2014). Is involvement in school bullying associated with general health and psychosocial adjustment outcomes in adulthood? *Child Abuse & Neglect.* doi:10.1016/j.chiabu.2014.06.001

Silcock, P. (2013). Should the Cambridge Primary Review be wedded to Vygotsky? *Education 3-13, 41*(3), 316–329. doi:10.1080/03004279.2011.586641

Silinskas, G., Niemi, P., Lerkkanen, M., & Nurmi, J. (2013). Children's poor academic performance evokes parental homework assistance—but does it help? *International Journal of Behavioral Development, 37*(1), 44–56. doi:10.1177/0165025412456146

Silva, M., Lopes, J., & Silva, A. (2013). Using senses and sensors in the environment to develop abstract thinking: A theoretical and instrumental framework. *Problems of Education in the 21St Century, 53,* 99–119.

Silverman, I. W. (2012). A critical review of committed compliance. *Journal of Early Childhood & Infant Psychology, 8,* 57–73.

Silverman, L. K. (1994). The moral sensitivity of gifted children and the evolution of society. *Roeper Review, 17*(2), 110–116.

Silvetti, M., Wiersema, J. R., Sonuga-Barke, E., & Verguts, T. (2013). Deficient reinforcement learning in medial frontal cortex as a model of dopamine-related motivational deficits in ADHD. *Neural Networks, 46,* 199–209. doi:10.1016/ j.neunet.2013.05.008

Simmons, C. (2014). Playing with popular culture – an ethnography of children's sociodramatic play in the classroom. *Ethnography & Education, 9*(3), 270–283. doi:10.1080/17457823.2014.904753

Simmons, D. C., Taylor, A. B., Oslund, E. L., Simmons, L. E., Coyne, M. D., Little, M. E., et al. (2013). Predictors of at-risk kindergarteners' later reading difficulty: Examining learner-by-intervention interactions. *Reading and Writing.* doi:10.1007/ s11145-013-9452-5

Simons, R. L., Robertson, J. F., & Downs, W. R. (1989). The nature of the association between parental rejection and delinquent behavior. *Journal of Youth and Adolescence, 18,* 297–310.

Simons, R. L., Whitbeck, L. B., Conger, R. D., & Conger, K. J. (1991). Parenting factors, social skills, and value commitments as precursors to school failure, involvement with deviant peers, and delinquent behavior. *Journal of Youth and Adolescence, 20,* 645–664.

Simons-Morton, B., & Chen, R. (2009). Peer and parent influences on school engagement among early adolescents. *Youth and Society, 41(1),* 3–25.

Simonton, D. K. (2001). Talent development as a multidimensional, multiplicative, and dynamic process. *Current Directions in Psychological Science, 10,* 39–42.

Simos, P. G., Fletcher, J. M., Sarkari, S., Billingsley, R. L., Denton, C., & Papanicolaou, A. C. (2007). Altering the brain circuits for reading through intervention: A magnetic source imaging study. *Neuropsychology, 21,* 485–496.

Simpkins, S. D., Delgado, M. Y., Price, C. D., Quach, A., & Starbuck, E. (2013). Socioeconomic status, ethnicity, culture, and immigration: Examining the potential mechanisms underlying Mexican-origin adolescents' organized activity participation. *Developmental Psychology, 49*(4), 706–721. doi:10.1037/a0028399

Simpson, J. S., & Parsons, E. C. (2009). African American perspectives and informal science educational experiences. *Science Education, 93*(2), 293–321.

Sims, M. (1993). How my question keeps evolving. In M. Cochran-Smith & S. L. Lytle (Eds.), *Inside/ outside: Teacher research and knowledge* (pp. 283–289). New York, NY: Teachers College Press.

Singer, E., & Doornenbal, J. (2006). Learning morality in peer conflict: A study of schoolchildren's narratives about being betrayed by a friend. *Childhood, 13*(2), 225–245.

Singer, J., Marx, R. W., Krajcik, J., & Chambers, J. C. (2000). Constructing extended inquiry projects: Curriculum materials for science education reform. *Educational Psychologist, 35,* 165–178.

Singh, A. A., Meng, S. E., & Hansen, A. W. (2014). "I am my own gender": Resilience strategies of trans youth. *Journal of Counseling & Development, 92*(2), 208–218. doi:10.1002/j.1556-6676.2014.00150.x

Sinnott, J. D. (2009). Cognitive development as the dance of adaptive transformation: Neo-Piagetian perspectives on adult cognitive development. In M. C. Smith & N. DeFrates-Densch (Eds.), *Handbook of research on adult learning and development* (pp. 103–134). New York, NY: Routledge/ Taylor & Francis.

Sipe, R. B. (2006). Grammar matters. *English Journal, 95,* 15–17.

Sirois, S., Buckingham, D., & Shultz, T. R. (2000). Artificial grammar learning by infants: An auto-associator perspective. *Developmental Science, 3,* 442–456.

Siry, C., & Max, C. (2013). The Collective construction of a science unit: Framing curricula as emergent from kindergarteners' wonderings. *Science Education, 97*(6), 878–902. doi:10.1002/sce.21076

Sitko, B. M. (1998). Knowing how to write: Metacognition and writing instruction. In D. J. Hacker, J. Dunlosky, & A. C. Graesser (Eds.), *Metacognition in educational theory and practice* (pp. 93–115). Mahwah, NJ: Erlbaum.

Sjostrom, L., & Stein, N. (1996). *Bully proof: A teacher's guide on teasing and bullying for use with fourth and fifth grade students.* Wellesley, MA: Wellesley College Center for Women.

Skarakis-Doyle, E., & Dempsey, L. (2008). The detection and monitoring of comprehension errors by preschool children with and without language impairment. *Journal of Speech, Language, and Hearing Research, 51*(5), 1227–1243.

Skiba, R. J. (2014). The failure of zero tolerance. *Reclaiming Children & Youth, 22*(4), 27–33.

Skibbe, L. E., Bindman, S. W., Hindman, A. H., Aram, D., & Morrison, F. J. (2013). Longitudinal relations between parental writing support and preschoolers' language and literacy skills. *Reading Research Quarterly, 48*(4), 387–401. doi:10.1002/rrq.55

Skinner, B. F. (1953). *Science and human behavior.* New York, NY: Macmillan.

Skinner, B. F. (1957). *Verbal behavior.* New York, NY: Appleton-Century-Crofts.

Skinner, B. F. (1968). *The technology of teaching.* New York, NY: Appleton-Century-Crofts.

Slater, A. M., Bremner, J., Johnson, S. P., & Hayes, R. A. (2011). The role of perceptual processes in infant addition/subtraction experiments. In L. M. Oakes, C. H. Cashon, M. Casasola, & D. H. Rakison (Eds.), *Infant perception and cognition: Recent advances, emerging theories, and future directions* (pp. 85–110). New York, NY: Oxford University Press.

Slavin, R. E. (1990). *Cooperative learning: Theory, research, and practice.* Upper Saddle River, NJ: Prentice Hall.

Slavin, R. E., & Cheung, A. (2005). A synthesis of research on language of reading instruction for English language learners. *Review of Educational Research, 75,* 247–284.

Slavin, R., Lake, C., & Groff, C. (2009). Effective programs in middle and high school mathematics: A best-evidence synthesis. *Review of Educational Research, 79*(2), 839–911. doi:10.3102/0034654308330968

Sleeter, C. E., & Grant, C. A. (1999). *Making choices for multicultural education: Five approaches to race, class, and gender* (3rd ed.). Upper Saddle River, NJ: Merrill/Prentice Hall.

Slesnick, N., Feng, X., Brakenhoff, B., & Brigham, G. (2014). Parenting under the influence: The effects of opioids, alcohol and cocaine on mother–child interaction. *Addictive Behaviors, 39*(5), 897-900.

Slobin, D. I. (1985). *Crosslinguistic evidence for the language-making capacity.* Hillsdale, NJ: Erlbaum.

Slotkin, T. A. (2008). If nicotine is a developmental neurotoxicant in animal studies, dare we recommend nicotine replacement therapy in pregnant women and adolescents? *Neurotoxicology and Teratology, 20,* 1–19.

Smart, C., Neale, B., & Wade, A. (2001). *The changing experience of childhood: Families and divorce.* Cambridge, England: Polity.

Smetana, J. G. (1981). Preschool children's conceptions of moral and social rules. *Child Development, 52,* 1333–1336.

Smetana, J. G. (2006). Social-cognitive domain theory: Consistencies and variations in children's moral and social judgments. In M. Killen & J. G. Smetana (Eds.), *Handbook of moral development* (pp. 119–153). Mahwah, NJ: Lawrence.

Smetana, J. G., & Braeges, J. L. (1990). The development of toddlers' moral and conventional judgments. *Merrill-Palmer Quarterly, 36,* 329–346.

Smetana, J. G., & Killen, M. (2008). Moral cognitions, emotions, and neuroscience: An integrative developmental view. *European Journal of Developmental Science, 2*(3), 324–339.

Smetana, J. G., & Villalobos, M. (2009). Social cognitive development in adolescence. In R. M. Lerner & L. Steinberg (Eds.), *Handbook of adolescent psychology. Vol. 1: Individual bases of adolescent development* (3rd ed., pp. 187–228). Hoboken, NJ: Wiley.

Smetana, J. G., Killen, M., & Turiel, E. (1991). Children's reasoning about interpersonal and moral conflicts. *Child Development, 62,* 629–644.

Smetana, J. G., Metzger, A., Gettman, D. C., & Campione-Barr, N. (2006). Disclosure and secrecy in adolescent–parent relationships. *Child Development, 77,* 201–217.

Smilansky, S. (1968). *The effects of sociodramatic play on disadvantaged preschool children.* Oxford, England: Wiley.

Smit, J., van Eerde, H. A., & Bakker, A. (2013). A conceptualisation of whole-class scaffolding. *British Educational Research Journal, 39*(5), 817-834. doi:10.1002/berj.3007

Smith, A., & Thomson, M. (2014). Alternative education programmes: Synthesis and psychological perspectives. *Educational Psychology in Practice, 30*(2), 111–119. doi:10.1080/02667363.2014.891101

Smith, A., Andrews, J., Ausbrooks, M., Gentry, M., & Jacobowitz, E. (2013). A metalinguistic awareness test for ASL/English bilingual deaf children: The TASLA-R. *Journal of Language Teaching & Research, 4*(5), 885–899. doi:10.4304/jltr.4.5.885-899

Smith, C. B., Battin, M. P., Francis, L. P., & Jacobson, J. A. (2007). Should rapid tests for HIV infection now be mandatory during pregnancy? Global differences in scarcity and a dilemma of technological advance. *Developing World Bioethics, 7*(2), 86–103.

Smith, C. E., Fischer, K. W., & Watson, M. W. (2009). Toward a refined view of aggressive fantasy as a risk factor for aggression: Interaction effects involving cognitive and situational variables. *Aggressive Behavior, 35*(4), 313–323.

Smith, C. L. (2007). Bootstrapping processes in the development of students' commonsense matter theories: Using analogical mappings, thought experiments, and learning to measure to promote conceptual restructuring. *Cognition and Instruction, 25,* 337–398.

Smith, E. P., Boutte, G. S., Zigler, E., & Finn-Stevenson, M. (2004). Opportunities for schools to promote resilience in children and youth. In K. I. Maton, C. J. Schellenbach, B. J. Leadbeater, & A. L. Solarz (Eds.), *Investing in children, youth, families, and communities: Strengths-based research and policy* (pp. 213–231). Washington, DC: American Psychological Association.

Smith, H. (2008). Searching for kinship: The creation of street families among homeless youth. *American Behavioral Scientist, 51*(6), 756–771.

Smith, J. T. (1999). Sickle cell disease. In S. Goldstein & C. R. Reynolds (Eds.), *Handbook of neurodevelopmental and genetic disorders* (pp. 368–384). New York, NY: Guilford Press.

Smith, J., Boone, A., Gourdine, R. M., & Brown, A. W. (2013). Fictions and facts about parents and parenting older first-time entrants to foster care. *Journal of Human Behavior in the Social Environment, 23*(2), 211–219. doi:10.1080/10911359.2013.747400

Smith, M. J., & Perkins, K. (2008). Attending to the voice of adolescents who are overweight to promote mental health. *Archives of Psychiatric Nursing, 22*(6), 391–393.

Smith, M., Roediger III, H., & Karpicke, J. (2013). Covert retrieval practice benefits retention as much as overt retrieval practice. *Journal of Experimental Psychology. Learning, Memory & Cognition, 39*(6), 1712–1725. doi:10.1037/a0033569

Smith, N. R., Cicchetti, L., Clark, M. C., Fucigna, C., Gordon-O'Connor, B., Halley, B. A., et al. (1998). *Observation drawing with children: A framework for teachers.* New York, NY: Teachers College Press.

Smith, R. E., & Smoll, F. L. (1997). Coaching the coaches: Youth sports as a scientific and applied behavioral setting. *Current Directions in Psychological Science, 6,* 16–21.

Smith, S. (2013). Would you step through my door? *Educational Leadership, 70*(8), 76–78.

Smith-Lock, K. M., Leitao, S., Lambert, L., & Nickels, L. (2013). Effective intervention for expressive grammar in children with specific language impairment. *International Journal of Language & Communication Disorders, 48*(3), 265–282. doi:10.1111/1460-6984.12003

Smitherman, G. (1994). "The blacker the berry the sweeter the juice": African American student writers. In A. H. Dyson & C. Genishi (Eds.), *The need for story: Cultural diversity in classroom and community* (pp. 80-101). Urbana, IL: National Council of Teachers of English.

Smitherman, G. (2007). The power of the rap: The Black idiom and the new Black poetry. In H. S. Alim & J. Baugh (Eds.), *Talkin Black talk: Language, education, and social change* (pp. 77–91). New York, NY: Teachers College Press.

Smithsonian National Museum of Natural History. (2010). *Volcanoes and hot spots.* Retrieved from http://www.mnh.si.edu/earth/main_frames.html

Smutny, J. F., & von Fremd, S. E. (2009). *Igniting creativity in gifted learners, K–6: Strategies for every teacher.* Thousand Oaks, CA: Corwin Press.

Smutny, J. F., von Fremd, S. E., & Artabasy, J. (2009). Creativity: A gift for the gifted. In J. F. Smutny, & S. E. von Fremd (Eds.), *Igniting creativity in gifted learners, K–6: Strategies for every teacher* (pp. 5–17). Thousand Oaks, CA: Corwin Press.

Snedeker, J., Geren, J., & Shafto, C. L. (2007). Starting over: International adoption as a natural experiment in language development. *Psychological Science, 18,* 79–87.

Snow, C. E., & Van Hemel, S. B. (Eds.) (2008). *Early childhood assessment: Why, what, and how/ Committee on Developmental Outcomes and Assessment of Young Children.* Washington, DC: National Research Council.

Snow, C. W., & McGaha, C. G. (2003). *Infant development* (3rd ed.). Upper Saddle River, NJ: Prentice Hall.

Snow, K., & Mann-Feder, V. (2013). Peer-centered practice: A theoretical framework for intervention with young people in and from care. *Child Welfare, 92*(4), 75–93.

Snyder, K. E., Nietfeld, J. L., & Linnenbrink-Garcia, L. (2011). Giftedness and metacognition: A short-term longitudinal investigation of metacognitive monitoring in the classroom. *Gifted Child Quarterly, 55*(3), 181–193. doi:10.1177/0016986211412769

Snyder, K., Malin, J., Dent, A., & Linnenbrink-Garcia, L. (2014). The message matters: The role of implicit beliefs about and failure experiences in academic self-handicapping. *Journal of Educational Psychology, 106*(1), 230–241. doi:10.1037/a0034553\

Snyder, L., & Caccamise, D. (2010). Comprehension processes for expository text: Building meaning and making sense. In M. A. Nippold & C. M. Scott (Eds.), *Expository discourse in children, adolescents, and adults: Development and disorders* (pp. 13–39). New York, NY: Psychology Press.

Society for Research in Child Development. (2007). *Ethical standards for research with children.* First published in the 1990–91 Directory and Fall 1991 Newsletter. Retrieved from http://www.srcd.org/ethicalstandards.html

Soet, J. E., Brack, G. A., & Dilorio, C. (2003). Prevalence and predictors of women's experience of psychological trauma during childbirth. *Birth, 30* (1), 36–46.

Sokol, S. (1978). Measurement of infant visual acuity from pattern reversal evoked potentials. *Vision Research, 18*(1), 33–39. doi:10.1016/0042-6989(78)90074-3

Solem, M. (2013). Understanding parenting as situated in the larger sociocultural context in clinical social work. *Child & Adolescent Social Work Journal, 30*(1), 61–78. doi:10.1007/s10560-012-0278-9

Solity, J., & Vousden, J. (2009). Real books vs reading schemes: A new perspective from instructional psychology. *Educational Psychology, 29*(4), 469–511.

Solomon, D., Watson, M. S., Delucchi, K. L., Schaps, E., & Battistich, V. (1988). Enhancing children's prosocial behavior in the classroom. *American Educational Research Journal, 25,* 527–554.

Solomon, D., Watson, M., Battistich, E., Schaps, E., & Delucchi, K. (1992). Creating a caring community: Educational practices that promote children's prosocial development. In F. K. Oser, A. Dick, & J. L. Patry (Eds.), *Effective and responsible teaching: The new synthesis (pp. 383–395)*. San Francisco, CA: Jossey-Bass.

Somerville, L. H., Jones, R. M., & Casey, B. J. (2010). A time of change: Behavioral and neural correlates of adolescent sensitivity to appetitive and aversive environmental cues. *Brain and Cognition, 72,* 124–133.

Sonnenschein, S. (1988). The development of referential communication: Speaking to different listeners. *Child Development, 59,* 694–702.

Sophian, C. (2013). Vicissitudes of children's mathematical knowledge: Implications of developmental research for early childhood mathematics education. *Early Education and Development, 24*(4), 436–442. doi:10.1080/10409289.2013.773255

Sophian, C., & Vong, K. I. (1995). The parts and wholes of arithmetic story problems: Developing knowledge in the preschool years. *Cognition and Instruction, 13,* 469–477.

Sorenson, R., & Goldsmith, L. (2012). The pressure of high stakes testing. *Principal Matters, 91,* 48–52.

Sorsana, C., Guizard, N., & Trognon, A. (2013). Preschool children's conversational skills for explaining game rules: Communicative guidance strategies as a function of type of relationship and gender. *European Journal of Psychology of Education, 28*(4), 1453–1475. doi:10.1007/s10212-013-0175-4

Sotelo-Dynega, M., Flanagan, D. P., & Alfonso, V. C. (2011). Overview of specific learning disabilities. In D. P. Flanagan, V. C. Alfonso (Eds.), *Essentials of specific learning disability identification* (pp. 1-19). Hoboken, NJ: Wiley.

Sousa, D. A. (2009). *How the gifted brain works* (2nd ed.). Thousand Oaks, CA: Corwin.

South, D. (2007). What motivates unmotivated students? In G. E. Mills (Ed.), *Action research: A guide for the teacher researcher* (3rd ed., pp. 1–2). Upper Saddle River, NJ: Pearson Merrill/Prentice Hall.

Sowell, E. R., Delis, D., Stiles, J., & Jernigan, T. L. (2001). Improved memory functioning and frontal lobe maturation between childhood and adolescence: A structural MRI study. *Journal of the International Neuropsychological Society, 7,* 312–322.

Spangler, G. (2013). Individual dispositions as precursors of differences in attachment quality: Why maternal sensitivity is nevertheless important. *Attachment & Human Development, 15*(5-6), 657–672. doi:10.1080/14616734.2013.842065

Sparks, A., Lee, M., & Spjeldnes, S. (2012). Evaluation of the high school relationship curriculum connections: Dating and emotions. *Child & Adolescent Social Work Journal, 29*(1), 21–40. doi:10.1007/s10560-011-0244-y

Spearman, C. (1904). General intelligence, objectively determined and measured. *American Journal of Psychology, 15,* 201–293.

Spearman, C. (1927). *The abilities of man: Their nature and measurement.* New York, NY: Macmillan.

Spector, R. E. (2004). Cultural diversity in health and illness (6th ed.). Upper Saddle River, NJ: Prentice Hall.

Spelke, E. S. (1994). Initial knowledge: Six suggestions. *Cognition, 50,* 431–445.

Spelke, E. S. (2000). Core knowledge. *American Psychologist, 55,* 1233–1243.

Spelke, E. S. (2005). Sex differences in intrinsic aptitude for mathematics and science? A critical review. *American Psychologist, 60,* 950–958.

Spelke, E. S., & Kinzler, K. D. (2007). Core knowledge. *Developmental Science, 10*(1), 89–96.

Spencer, M. B. (2006). Phenomenology and ecological systems theory: Development of diverse groups. In W. Damon & R. M. Lerner (Eds. in Chief) & R. M. Lerner (Vol. Ed.), *Handbook of child psychology, Vol. 1. Theoretical models of human development* (6th ed., pp. 829–893). Hoboken, NJ: Wiley.

Spencer, M. B. (2014). Pursuing identity-focused resiliency research post-Brown v. Board of Education 1954. In R. M. Lerner, A. C. Petersen, R. K. Silbereisen, & J. Brooks-Gunn (Eds.), *The developmental science of adolescence: History through autobiography* (pp. 482–493). New York, NY: Psychology Press.

Spencer, M. B., & Markstrom-Adams, C. (1990). Identity processes among racial and ethnic minority children in America. *Child Development, 61,* 290–310.

Spencer, M. B., & Spencer, T. R. (2014). Invited commentary: Exploring the promises, intricacies, and challenges to positive youth development. *Journal Of Youth And Adolescence,* doi:10.1007/s10964-014-0125-8

Spencer, M. B., Noll, E., Stoltzfus, J., & Harpalani, V. (2001). Identity and school adjustment: Revisiting the "acting White" assumption. *Educational Psychologist, 36,* 21–30.

Spencer, M., & Swanson, D. (2013). Opportunities and challenges to the development of healthy children and youth living in diverse communities. *Development and Psychopathology, 25*(4, Pt 2), 1551–1566. doi:10.1017/S095457941300076X

Spencer, M., Dupree, D., Tinsley, B., McGee, E. O., Hall, J., Fegley, S. G., & Elmore, T. (2012). Resistance and resiliency in a color conscious society: Implications for learning and teaching. In K. R. Harris, S. Graham, T. Urdan, C. B. McCormick, G. M. Sinatra, & J. Sweller (Eds.), *APA educational psychology handbook, Vol. 1: Theories, constructs, and critical issues* (pp. 461–494). Washington, DC: American Psychological Association. doi:10.1037/13273-016

Sperling, M. (1996). Revisiting the writing-speaking connection: Challenges for research on writing and writing instruction. *Review of Educational Research, 66,* 53–86.

Speybroeck, S., Kuppens, S., Damme, J., Petegem, P., Lamote, C., Boonen, T., & Bilde, J. (2012). The role of teachers' expectations in the association between children's SES and performance in kindergarten: A moderated mediation analysis. *Plos ONE, 7*(4), 1–8. doi:10.1371/journal.pone.0034502

Spicker, H. H. (1992). Identifying and enriching: Rural gifted children. *Educational Horizons, 70*(2), 60–65.

Spiegel, C., & Halberda, J. (2011). Rapid fast-mapping abilities in 2-year-olds. *Journal of Experimental Child Psychology, 109*(1), 132–140. doi:10.1016/j.jecp.2010.10.013

Spinath, B., & Steinmayr, R. (2008). Longitudinal analysis of intrinsic motivation and competence beliefs: Is there a relation over time? *Child Development, 79*(5), 1555–1569. doi:10.1111/j.1467-8624.2008.01205.x

Spinath, B., & Steinmayr, R. (2012). The roles of competence beliefs and goal orientations for change in intrinsic motivation. *Journal of Educational Psychology, 104*(4), 1135–1148. doi:10.1037/a0028115

Spinath, F. M., Price, T. S., Dale, P. S., & Plomin, R. (2004). The genetic and environmental origins of language disability and ability. *Child Development, 75,* 445–454.

Spirito, A., Valeri, S., Boergers, J., & Donaldson, D. (2003). Predictors of continued suicidal behaviors in adolescents following a suicide attempt. *Journal of Clinical Child and Adolescent Psychology, 32,* 284–289.

Spivey, N. N. (1997). *The constructivist metaphor: Reading, writing, and the making of meaning.* San Diego, CA: Academic Press.

Sprafkin, C., Serbin, L. A., Denier, C., & Connor, J. M. (1983). Sex-differentiated play: Cognitive consequences and early interventions. In M. B. Liss (Ed.), *Social and cognitive skills: Sex roles and children's play (pp. 167–192)*. San Diego, CA: Academic Press.

Springen, K. (2014). Occupy summer. *School Library Journal, 60*(3), 32.

Springer, A. E., Tanguturi, Y., Ranjit, N., Skala, K. A., & Kelder, S. H. (2013). Physical activity during recess in low-income third-grade Texas students. *American Journal of Health Behavior, 37*(3), 318–324. doi:10.5993/AJHB.37.3.4

Spritz, B. L., Fergusson, A. S., & Bankoff, S. M. (2010). False beliefs and the development of deception. In E. H. Sandberg & B. L. Spritz (Eds.), *A clinician's guide to normal cognitive development in childhood* (pp. 101–120). New York, NY: Routledge/Taylor & Francis.

Squires, J. (2012). Assessing young children's social and emotional development. In S. Summers & R. Chazan-Cohen (Eds.), *Understanding early childhood mental health: A practical guide for professionals* (pp. 99–123). Baltimore, MD: Paul H Brookes Publishing.

Sroufe, L. A. (1983). Infant-caregiver attachment and patterns of adaptation in preschool: The roots of maladaptation and competence. In M. Perlmutter (Ed.), Development and policy concerning children with special needs. *Minnesota Symposium on Child Psychology, 16,* 41–83. Hillsdale, NJ: Erlbaum.

Sroufe, L. A., Egeland, B., Carlson, E., & Collins, W. (2005). *Minnesota study of risk and adaptation from birth to maturity: The development of the person.* New York, NY: Guilford Press.

St. James-Roberts, I., & Plewis, I. (1996). Individual differences, daily fluctuations, and developmental changes in amounts of infant waking, fussiness, crying, feeding, and sleeping. *Child Development, 67,* 2527–2540.

Staff, J., Messersmith, E. E., & Schulenberg, J. E. (2009). Adolescents and the world of work. In R. M. Lerner & L. Steinberg (Eds.), *Handbook of adolescent psychology, Vol. 2: Contextual influences on adolescent development* (pp. 270–313). Hoboken, NJ: Wiley.

Stainthorp, R., Stuart, M., Powell, D., Quinlan, P., & Garwood, H. (2010). Visual processing deficits in children with slow RAN performance. *Scientific Studies of Reading, 14*(3), 266–292.

Standage, M., Cumming, S. P., & Gillison, F. B. (2013). A cluster randomized controlled trial of the be the best you can be intervention: Effects on the psychological and physical well-being of school children. *BMC Public Health, 13*(1), 1–10. doi:10.1186/1471-2458-13-666

Stanovich, K. E. (1999). The sociopsychometrics of learning disabilities. *Journal of Learning Disabilities, 32,* 350–361.

Stanovich, K. E. (2000). *Progress in understanding reading: Scientific foundations and new frontiers.* New York, NY: Guilford Press.

Stanovich, K. E., West, R. F., & Toplak, M. E. (2012). Judgment and decision making in adolescence: Separating intelligence from rationality. In V. F. Reyna, S. B. Chapman, M. R. Dougherty, & J. Confrey (Eds.), *The adolescent brain: Learning, reasoning, and decision making* (pp. 337–378). Washington, DC: American Psychological Association. doi:10.1037/13493-012

Stanton-Chapman, T. L. (2014). Promoting positive peer interactions in the preschool classroom: The role and the responsibility of the teacher in supporting children's sociodramatic play. *Early Childhood Education Journal.* doi:10.1007/s10643-014-0635-8

Stanutz, S., Wapnick, J., & Burack, J. (2014). Pitch discrimination and melodic memory in children with autism spectrum disorders. *Autism: The International Journal of Research & Practice, 18*(2), 137–147. doi:10.1177/1362361312462905

Starke, M., Wikland, K. A., & Möller, A. (2003). Parents' descriptions of development and problems associated with infants with Turner syndrome: A retrospective study. *Journal of Paediatrics and Child Health, 39,* 293–298.

Stathi, S., Cameron, L., Hartley, B., & Bradford, S. (2014). Imagined contact as a prejudice-reduction intervention in schools: The underlying role of similarity and attitudes. *Journal of Applied Social Psychology.* doi:10.1111/jasp.12245

Staub, D. (1998). *Delicate threads: Friendships between children with and without special needs in inclusive settings.* Bethesda, MD: Woodbine House.

Steegen, S., & De Neys, W. (2012). Belief inhibition in children's reasoning: Memory-based evidence. *Journal of Experimental Child Psychology, 112*(2), 231–242. doi:10.1016/j.jecp.2012.01.006

Steele, C. M. (1997). A threat in the air: How stereotypes shape intellectual identity and performance. *American Psychologist, 52,* 613–629.

Steenpaß, A., & Steinbring, H. (2014). Young students' subjective interpretations of mathematical diagrams: elements of the theoretical construct "frame-based interpreting competence." *Zdm, 46*(1), 3–14. doi:10.1007/s11858-013-0544-0

Steensma, T. D., Kreukels, B. C., de Vries, A. C., & Cohen-Kettenis, P. T. (2013). Gender identity development in adolescence. *Hormones and Behavior, 64*(2), 288–297. doi:10.1016/j.yhbeh.2013.02.020

Stein, N. L. (1982). What's in a story: Interpreting the interpretations of story grammars. *Discourse Processes, 5,* 319–335.

Steinberg, L. (1986). Latchkey children and susceptibility to peer pressure: An ecological analysis. *Developmental Psychology, 22,* 433–439.

Steinberg, L. (2007). Risk taking in adolescence: New perspectives from brain and behavioral science. *Current Directions in Psychological Science, 16,* 55–59.

Steinberg, L., Blinde, P. L., & Chan, K. S. (1984). Dropping out among language minority youth. *Review of Educational Research, 54,* 113–132.

Steinberg, L., Brown, B. B., Cider, M., Kaczmarek, N., & Lazzaro, C. (1988). *Noninstructional influences on high school student achievement: The contributions of parents, peers, extracurricular activities, and part-time work.* Madison, WI: National Center on Effective Secondary Schools. (ERIC Document Reproduction Service No. ED 307 509)

Steinberg, L., Elmen, J., & Mounts, N. (1989). Authoritative parenting, psychosocial maturity, and academic success among adolescents. *Child Development, 60,* 1424–1436.

Steinberg, L., Lamborn, S., Darling, N., Mounts, S., & Dornbusch, S. (1994). Over time change in adjustment and competence among adolescents from authoritative, authoritarian, indulgent, and neglectful families. *Child Development, 65,* 754–770.

Stenberg, C. R., & Campos, J. J. (1990). The development of anger expressions in infancy. In N. L. Stein, B. Leventhal, & T. Trabasso (Eds.), *Psychological and biological approaches to emotion* (pp. 247–282). Hillsdale, NJ: Erlbaum.

Stephan, K. E., Fink, G. R., & Marshall, J. C. (2007). Mechanisms of hemispheric specialization: Insights from analyses of connectivity. *Neuropsychologia, 45,* 209–228.

Stern, D. N. (1977). *The first relationship: Mother and infant.* Cambridge, MA: Harvard University Press.

Stern, W. (1912). *Die psychologischen Methoden der Intelligenzprufung.* Leipzig, Germany: Barth.

Sternberg, R. J. (1985). *Beyond IQ: A triarchic theory of human intelligence.* Cambridge, England: Cambridge University Press.

Sternberg, R. J. (1996). Myths, countermyths, and truths about intelligence. *Educational Researcher, 25*(2), 11–16.

Sternberg, R. J. (1997). The concept of intelligence and its role in lifelong learning and success. *American Psychologist, 52,* 1030–1037.

Sternberg, R. J. (2002). Raising the achievement of all students: Teaching for successful intelligence. *Educational Psychology Review, 14,* 383–393.

Sternberg, R. J. (2003a). "My house is a very very very fine house"—But it is not the only house. In H. Nyborg (Ed.), *The scientific study of general intelligence: Tribute to Arthur Jensen* (pp. 373–395). Oxford, England: Elsevier.

Sternberg, R. J. (2003b). *Wisdom, intelligence, and creativity synthesized.* Cambridge, England: Cambridge University Press.

Sternberg, R. J. (2005). The triarchic theory of successful intelligence. In D. P. Flanagan & P. L. Harrison (Eds.), *Contemporary intellectual assessment: Theories, tests, and issues* (2nd ed., pp. 103–119). New York, NY: Guilford Press.

Sternberg, R. J. (2009). The theory of successful intelligence as a basis for new forms of ability testing at the high school, college, and graduate school levels. In J. C. Kaufman (Ed.), *Intelligent testing: Integrating psychological theory and clinical practice* (pp. 113–147). New York, NY: Cambridge University Press.

Sternberg, R. J. (2012). Intelligence in its cultural context. In M. J. Gelfand, C. Ciu, & Y. Hong (Eds.), *Advances in culture and psychology* (Vol. 2, pp. 205–248). New York, NY: Oxford University Press.

Sternberg, R. J. (2013). Contemporary theories of intelligence. In W. M. Reynolds, G. E. Miller, I. B. Weiner (Eds.), *Handbook of psychology, Vol. 7: Educational psychology* (2nd ed., pp. 23–44). Hoboken, NJ: John Wiley & Sons Inc.

Sternberg, R. J., & Grigorenko, E. L. (2000). Theme-park psychology: A case study regarding human intelligence and its implications for education. *Educational Psychology Review, 12,* 247–268.

Sternberg, R. J., Forsythe, G. B., Hedlund, J., Horvath, J. A., Wagner, R. K., Williams, W. M., Snook, S., & Grigorenko, E. (2000). *Practical intelligence in everyday life.* Cambridge, England: Cambridge University Press.

Sternberg, R. J., Grigorenko, E. L., & Bridglall, B. L. (2007). Intelligence as a socialized phenomenon. In E. W. Gordon & B. L. Bridglall (Eds.), *Affirmative development: Cultivating academic ability* (pp. 49–72). Lanham, MD: Rowman.

Sternberg, R. J., Jarvin, L., & Grigorenko, E. L. (2009). *Teaching for wisdom, intelligence, creativity, and success.* Thousand Oaks, CA: Corwin.

Sternberg, R. J., Torff, B., & Grigorenko, E. L. (1998). Teaching for successful intelligence raises school achievement. *Phi Delta Kappa, 79,* 667–669.

Sterponi, L. (2010). Learning communicative competence. In D. F. Lancy, J. Bock, & S. Gaskins (Eds.), *The anthropology of learning in childhood* (pp. 235–259). Lanham, MD: AltaMira Press/Rowman & Littlefield

Stevens, P., & Smith, R. L. (2013). *Substance abuse counseling: Theory and practice* (5th ed.). Boston, MA: Pearson.

Stevens, R. J., & Slavin, R. E. (1995). The cooperative elementary school: Effects of students' achievement, attitudes, and social relations. American *Educational Research Journal, 32,* 321–351.

Stevenson, M. M., Braver, S. L., Ellman, I. M., & Votruba, A. M. (2013). Fathers, divorce, and child custody. In N. J. Cabrera & C. S. Tamis-LeMonda (Eds.), *Handbook of father involvement: Multidisciplinary perspectives* (2nd ed., pp. 379–396). New York, NY: Routledge/Taylor & Francis Group.

Stevick, R. A. (2007). *Growing up Amish: The teenage years.* Baltimore, MD: Johns Hopkins University Press.

Stewart, L., & Pascual-Leone, J. (1992). Mental capacity constraints and the development of moral reasoning. *Journal of Experimental Child Psychology, 54,* 251–287.

Stewart, M. (2013). Giving voice to Valeria's story: Support, value, and agency for immigrant adolescents. *Journal of Adolescent & Adult Literacy, 57*(1), 42–50. doi:10.1002/jaal.217

Stice, E., Marti, C., & Rohde, P. (2013). Prevalence, incidence, impairment, and course of the proposed DSM-5 eating disorder diagnoses in an 8-year prospective community study of young women. *Journal of Abnormal Psychology, 122*(2), 445–457. doi:10.1037/a0030679

Stiggins, R. (2007). Assessment through students' eyes. *Educational Leadership, 64*(8), 22–26.

Stiles, J. (2008). *The fundamentals of brain development: Integrating nature and nurture.* Cambridge, MA: Harvard University Press.

Stipek, D. (2002). At what age should children enter kindergarten? A question for policy makers and parents. *Social Policy Report, 16*(1), 3–16. Ann Arbor, MI: Society for Research in Child Development.

Stipek, D. J. (1993). *Motivation to learn: From theory to practice* (2nd ed.). Needham Heights, MA: Allyn & Bacon.

Stipek, D. J. (1993). *Motivation to learn: From theory to practice* (2nd ed.). Needham Heights, MA: Allyn & Bacon.

Stipek, D. J. (1996). Motivation and instruction. In D. C. Berliner & R. C. Calfee (Eds.), *Handbook of educational psychology.* New York, NY: Macmillan.

Stipek, D. J., & Kowalski, P. S. (1989). Learned helplessness in task-orienting versus performance-orienting testing conditions. *Journal of Educational Psychology, 81,* 384–391.

Stipek, D. J., Recchia, S., & McClintic, S. M. (1992). Self-evaluation in young children. *Monographs of the Society for Research in Child Development, 57*(2, Serial No. 226).

Stocco, A., Yamasaki, B., Natalenko, R., & Prat, C. S. (2014). Bilingual brain training: A neurobiological framework of how bilingual experience improves executive function. *International Journal of Bilingualism, 18*(1), 67-92. doi:10.1177/1367006912456617

Stoicovy, C., Fee, R., & Fee, J. (2012). Culturally responsive instruction Leaves No Child Behind: The Story of Juan, a Pacific Island special needs student. *International Journal of Multicultural Education, 14*(1), 1–19.

Stormont, M. (2001). Social outcomes of children with AD/HD: Contributing factors and implications for practice. *Psychology in the Schools, 38,* 521–531.

Straehler-Pohl, H., Fernández, S., Gellert, U., & Figueiras, L. (2014). School mathematics registers in a context of low academic expectations. *Educational Studies in Mathematics, 85*(2), 175–199. doi:10.1007/s10649-013-9503-5

Strand-Cary, M., & Klahr, D. (2008). Developing elementary science skills: Instructional effectiveness and path independence. *Cognitive Development, 23,* 488–511.

Straus, M. A. (2000). The benefits of never spanking: New and more definitive evidence. In M. A. Straus (Ed.), *Beating the devil out of them: Corporal punishment by American families and its effects on children*. New Brunswick, NJ: Transaction Publications.

Strayer, F. F. (1991). The development of agonistic and affiliative structures in preschool play groups. In J. Silverberg & P. Gray (Eds.), *To fight or not to fight: Violence and peacefulness in humans and other primates*. Oxford, England: Oxford University Press.

Streissguth, A. P., Barr, H. M., Sampson, P. D., & Bookstein, F. L. (1994). Prenatal alcohol and offspring development: The first fourteen years. *Drug and Alcohol Dependence, 36*, 89–99.

Streri, A., Coulon, M., & Guellaï, B. (2013). The foundations of social cognition: Studies on face/voice integration in newborn infants. *International Journal of Behavioral Development, 37*(2), 79–83. doi:10.1177/0165025412465361

Stricklin, K. (2011). Hands-on reciprocal teaching: A comprehension technique. *The Reading Teacher, 64*(8), 620–625. doi:10.1598/RT.64.8.8

Strozer, J. R. (1994). *Language acquisition after puberty*. Washington, DC: Georgetown University Press.

Strzelecka, J. (2014). Electroencephalographic studies in children with autism spectrum disorders. *Research in Autism Spectrum Disorders, 8*(3), 317–323. doi:10.1016/j.rasd.2013.11.010

Styne, D. M. (2003). The regulation of pubertal growth. *Hormone Research, 60*(Suppl.1), 22–26.

Suárez-Orozco, C., Suárez-Orozco, M. M., & Todorova, I. (2008). *Learning a new land: Immigrant students in American society*. Cambridge, MA: Belknap Press.

Su, W., Mrug, S., & Windle, M. (2010). Social cognitive and emotional mediators link violence exposure and parental nurturance to adolescent aggression. *Journal of Clinical Child and Adolescent Psychology, 39*(6), 814–824. doi:10.1080/15374416.2010.517163

Subrahmanyam, K., & Greenfield, P. (2012). Digital media and youth: Games, Internet, and development. In D. G. Singer, J. L. Singer (Eds.), *Handbook of children and the media* (2nd ed., pp. 75–96). Thousand Oaks, CA: Sage Publications, Inc.

Sudhalter, V., & Braine, M. D. (1985). How does comprehension of passives develop? A comparison of actional and experiential verbs. *Journal of Child Language, 12*, 455–470.

Suh, S., Suh, J., & Houston, I. (2007). Predictors of categorical at-risk high school dropouts. *Journal of Counseling & Development, 85*, 196–203.

Suhr, D. D. (1999). *An investigation of mathematics and reading achievement of 5- through 14-year-olds using latent growth curve methodology*. Unpublished doctoral dissertation, University of Northern Colorado, Greeley.

Suina, J. H., & Smolkin, L. B. (1994). From natal culture to school culture to dominant society culture: Supporting transitions for Pueblo Indian students. In P. M. Greenfield & R. R. Cocking (Eds.), *Cross-cultural roots of minority child development* (pp. 115–130). Mahwah, NJ: Erlbaum.

Sukhram, D., & Hsu, A. (2012). Developing reading partnerships between parents and children: A reflection on the reading together program. *Early Childhood Education Journal, 40*(2), 115–121. doi:10.1007/s10643-011-0500-y

Sullivan, F. M., & Barlow, S. M. (2001). Review of risk factors for sudden infant death syndrome. *Paediatric and Perinatal Epidemiology, 15*, 144–200.

Sullivan, H. S. (1953). *The interpersonal theory of psychiatry*. New York, NY: Norton.

Sullivan, J. R., & Conoley, J. C. (2004). Academic and instructional interventions with aggressive students. In J. C. Conoley & A. P. Goldstein (Eds.), *School violence intervention* (2nd ed., pp. 235–255). New York, NY: Guilford Press.

Sullivan, M. W., & Lewis, M. (2003). Contextual determinants of anger and other negative expressions in young infants. *Developmental Psychology, 39*, 693–705.

Sullivan, R. C. (1994). Autism: Definitions past and present. *Journal of Vocational Rehabilitation, 4*, 4–9.

Sullivan-DeCarlo, C., DeFalco, K., & Roberts, V. (1998). Helping students avoid risky behavior. *Educational Leadership, 56*(1), 80–82.

Sulzby, E. (1985). Children's emergent reading of favorite storybooks: A developmental study. *Reading Research Quarterly, 20*, 458–481.

Sulzby, E. (1986). Children's elicitation and use of metalinguistic knowledge about word during literacy interactions. In D. Yaden & S. Templeton (Eds.), *Metalinguistic awareness and beginning literacy: Conceptualizing what it means to read and write* (pp. 219–233). Portsmouth, NH: Heinemann Educational Books.

Summers, A., Gatowski, S., & Dobbin, S. (2012). Terminating parental rights: The relation of judicial experience and expectancy-related factors to risk perceptions in child protection cases. *Psychology, Crime & Law, 18*(1), 95–112. doi:10.1080/1068316X.2011.589388

Sun, L., & Nippold, M. A. (2012). Narrative writing in children and adolescents: Examining the literate lexicon. *Language, Speech & Hearing Services in Schools, 43*(1), 2–13. doi:10.1044/0161-1461(2011/10-0099)

Sundqvist, A., Lyxell, B., Jönsson, R., & Heimann, M. (2014). Understanding minds: Early cochlear implantation and the development of theory of mind in children with profound hearing impairment. *International Journal of Pediatric Otorhinolaryngology, 78*(3), 538–544. doi:10.1016/j.ijporl.2013.12.039

Suskind, R. (1998). *A hope in the unseen: An American odyssey from the inner city to the Ivy League*. New York, NY: Broadway Books.

Susman, E. J., Inoff-Germain, G., Nottelmann, E. D., Loriaux, D. L., Cutler, J., Gordon, B., et al. (1987). Hormones, emotional dispositions, and aggressive attributes in young adolescents. *Child Development, 58*, 1114–1134.

Sutherland, S. L., & Friedman, O. (2013). Just pretending can be really learning: Children use pretend play as a source for acquiring generic knowledge. *Developmental Psychology, 49*(9), 1660–1668. doi:10.1037/a0030788

Suttles, G. D. (1970). Friendship as a social institution. In G. J. McCall, M. McCall, N. K. Denzin, G. D. Scuttles, & S. Kurth (Eds.), *Social relationships* (pp. 95–135). Chicago, IL: Aldine de Gruyter.

Sutton-Smith, B. (1986). The development of fictional narrative performances. *Topics in Language Disorders, 7*(1), 1–10.

Sutton-Smith, B. (Ed.). (1979). *Play and learning*. New York, NY: Gardner Press.

Suzuki, L. A., Naqvi, S., & Hill, J. S. (2014). Assessing intelligence in a cultural context. In F. L. Leong, L. Comas-Díaz, G. C. Nagayama Hall, V. C. McLoyd, & J. E. Trimble (Eds.), *APA handbook of multicultural psychology, Vol. 1: Theory and research* (pp. 247–266). Washington, DC: American Psychological Association. doi:10.1037/14189-013

Suzuki, L. A., Onoue, M., & Hill, J. S. (2013). Clinical assessment: A multicultural perspective. In K. F. Geisinger, B. A. Bracken, J. F. Carlson, J. C. Hansen, N. R. Kuncel, S. P. Reise, & M. C. Rodriguez (Eds.), *APA handbook of testing and assessment in psychology, Vol. 2: Testing and assessment in clinical and counseling psychology* (pp. 193–212). Washington, DC: American Psychological Association. doi:10.1037/14048-012

Svanberg, P. O., Mennet, L., & Spieker, S. (2010). Promoting a secure attachment: A primary prevention practice model. *Clinical Child Psychology and Psychiatry, 15*(3), 363–378.

Svinicki, M. (2013). Which is better for student learning: Learning goals, performance goals, or a little bit of both? *National Teaching & Learning Forum, 22*(2), 11–12. doi:10.1002/ntlf.20007

Svirsky, M. A., Robbins, A. M., Kirk, K. I., Pisoni, D. B., & Miyamoto, R. T. (2000). Language development in profoundly deaf children with cochlear implants. *Psychological Science, 11*, 153–158.

Swain, J. E., Konrath, S., Dayton, C. J., Finegood, E. D., & Ho, S. (2013). Toward a neuroscience of interactive parent–infant dyad empathy. *Behavioral and Brain Sciences, 36*(4), 438–439. doi:10.1017/S0140525X12002063

Swanborn, M. S. L., & de Glopper, K. (1999). Incidental word learning while reading: A meta-analysis. *Review of Educational Research, 69*, 261–285.

Swanson, D. P., Cunningham, M., Youngblood, J. II, & Spencer, M. B. (2009). Racial identity development during childhood. In H. A. Neville, B. M. Tynes, S. O. Utsey (Eds.), *Handbook of African American psychology* (pp. 269–281). Thousand Oaks, CA: Sage Publications.

Swanson, H. (2011). Working memory, attention, and mathematical problem solving: A longitudinal study of elementary school children. *Journal of Educational Psychology, 103*(4), 821–837. doi:10.1037/a0025114

Swanson, H. L., & Jerman, O. (2006). Math disabilities: A selective meta-analysis of the literature. *Review of Educational Research, 76*, 249–274.

Swanson, H. L., & Lussier, C. M. (2001). A selective synthesis of the experimental literature on dynamic assessment. *Review of Educational Research, 71*, 321–363.

Swanson, H. L., Jerman, O., & Zheng, X. (2008). Growth in working memory and mathematical problem solving in children at risk and not at risk for serious math difficulties. *Journal of Educational Psychology, 100*, 343–379.

Swenson, L. P., & Rose, A. J. (2009). Friends' knowledge of youth internalizing and externalizing adjustment: Accuracy, bias, and the influences of gender, grade, positive friendship quality, and self-disclosure. *Journal of Abnormal Child Psychology, 37*(6), 887–901. doi:10.1007/s10802-009-9319-z

Swim, J. K., & Stangor, C. (Eds.). (1998). *Prejudice: The target's perspective* (pp. 220–241). San Diego, CA: Academic Press.

Sylva, K., Melhuish, E., Sammons, P., Siraj-Blatchford, I., & Taggart, B. (2004). *Effective pre-school education*. London, England: Institute of Education, University of London.

Symon, A., Winter, C., Inkster, M. & Donnan, P. T. (2009). Outcomes for births booked under and independent midwife and births in NHS maternity units: Matched comparison study. *British Medical Journal, 338*, 1–9.

Szielasko, A. L., Symons, D. K., & Lisa Price, E. E. (2013). Development of an attachment-informed measure of sexual behavior in late adolescence. *Journal of Adolescence, 36*(2), 361–370. doi:10.1016/j.adolescence.2012.12.008

Szyf, M., & Bick, J. (2013). DNA methylation: A mechanism for embedding early life experiences in the genome. *Child Development, 84*(1), 49–57. doi:10.1111/j.1467-8624.2012.01793.x

Szynal-Brown, C., & Morgan, R. R. (1983). The effects of reward on tutor's behaviors in a cross-age tutoring context. *Journal of Experimental Child Psychology, 36*, 196–208.

Téllez, K., & Waxman, H. (2010). A review of research on effective community programs for English Language Learners. *School Community Journal, 20*(1), 103–119.

Tabak, I., & Weinstock, M. (2008). A sociocultural exploration of epistemological beliefs. In M. S. Khine (Ed.), *Knowing, knowledge and beliefs: Epistemological studies across diverse cultures* (pp. 177–195). New York, NY: Springer Science + Business Media.

Taffoni, F., Tamilia, E., Focaroli, V., Formica, D., Ricci, L., Di Pino, G., et al. (2014). Development of goal-directed action selection guided by intrinsic motivations: An experiment with children. *Experimental Brain Research, 232*(7), 2167–2177. doi:10.1007/s00221-014-3907-z

Takahashi, K. (1990). Are the key assumptions of the "Strange Situation" procedure universal? A view from Japanese research. *Human Development, 33,* 23–30.

Taki, Y., Thyreau, B., Hashizume, H., Sassa, Y., Takeuchi, H., Wu, K., Kotozaki, Y., Nouchi, R., Asano, M., Asano, K., Fukuda, H.,& Kawashima, R. (2013). Linear and curvilinear correlations of brain white matter volume, fractional anisotropy, and mean diffusivity with age using voxel-based and region-of-interest analyses in 246 healthy children. *Human Brain Mapping, 34*(8), 1842–1856.

Taliaferro, L. A., & Muehlenkamp, J. J. (2014). Risk and protective factors that distinguish adolescents who attempt suicide from those who only consider suicide in the past year. *Suicide & Life-Threatening Behavior, 44*(1), 6–22. doi:10.1111/sltb.12046

Tamburrini, J. (1982). Some educational implications of Piaget's theory. In S. Modgil & C. Modgil (Eds.), *Jean Piaget: Consensus and controversy.* New York, NY: Praeger.

Tamis-LeMonda, C. S., & Song, L. (2013). Parent-infant communicative interactions in cultural context. In R. M. Lerner, M. Easterbrooks, J. Mistry, & I. B. Weiner (Eds.), *Handbook of psychology, Vol. 6: Developmental psychology* (2nd ed., pp. 143–170). Hoboken, NJ: John Wiley & Sons Inc.

Tan, E. T., & Goldberg, W. A. (2009). Parental school involvement in relation to children's grades and adaptation to school. *Journal of Applied Developmental Psychology, 30,* 442–453.

Tangney, J. P., & Dearing, R. L. (2002). *Shame and guilt.* New York, NY: Guilford Press.

Tannen, D. (1990). *You just don't understand: Talk between the sexes.* New York, NY: Ballantine.

Tanner, J. M. (1990). *Foetus into man: Physical growth from conception to maturity* (Rev. ed.). Cambridge, MA: Harvard University Press.

Tarman, B., & Tarman, I. (2011). Teachers' involvement in children's play and social interaction. *Ilkogretim Online, 10*(1), 325–337.

Tas, Y., & Cakir, B. (2014). An investigation of science active learning strategy use in relation to motivational beliefs. *Mevlana International Journal of Education, 4*(1), 55–66. doi:10.13054/mije.13.55.4.1

Task Force on Sudden Infant Death Syndrome. (2011). SIDS and other sleep-related infant deaths: Expansions of recommendations for a safe infant sleeping environment. *Pediatrics, 128*(5), 1341–1367. doi: 10.1542/peds.2011-2285.

Tasker, F. (2013). Lesbian and gay parenting post-heterosexual divorce and separation. In A. E. Goldberg, K. R. Allen (Eds.), *LGBT-parent families: Innovations in research and implications for practice* (pp. 3–20). New York, NY: Springer Science + Business Media.

Tassoni, P. (2013). Side by side. *Nursery World, 112*(4312), 20–22.

Tatum, A. W. (2008). Toward a more anatomically complete model of literacy instruction: A focus on African American male adolescents and teens. *Harvard Educational Review, 78*(1), 155–180.

Tatum, B. D. (1997). *Why are all the black kids sitting together in the cafeteria? and other conversations about race.* New York, NY: Basic Books.

Taumoepeau, M., & Ruffman, T. (2008). Stepping stones to others' minds: Maternal talk relates to child mental state language and emotion understandings at 15, 24, and 33 months. *Child Development, 79,* 284–302.

Taylor, J. M. (1994). *MDMA frequently asked questions list.* Retrieved from http://ibbserver.ibb.uu.nl/jboschma/ecstasy/xtc01

Taylor, L. K., Merrilees, C. E., Goeke-Morey, M. C., Shirlow, P., Cairns, E., & Cummings, E. (2014). Political violence and adolescent out-group attitudes and prosocial behaviors: Implications for positive inter-group relations. *Social Development.* doi:10.1111/sode.12074

Taylor, M., Esbensen, B. M., & Bennett, R. T. (1994). Children's understanding of knowledge acquisition: The tendency for children to report that they have always known what they have just learned. *Child Development, 65,* 1581–1604.

Taylor, W. C., Beech, B. M., & Cummings, S. S. (1998). Increasing physical activity levels among youth: A public health challenge. In D. K. Wilson, J. R. Rodrigue, & W. C. Taylor (Eds.), *Health-promoting and health-compromising behaviors among minority adolescents* (pp. 107–128). Washington, DC: American Psychological Association.

Telingator C. (2013). Clinical work with children and adolescents growing up with lesbian, gay, and bisexual parents. In A. E. Goldberg & K. R. Allen (Eds.), *LGBT-parent families: Innovations in research and implications for practice* (e-book, pp. 261–274). New York, NY: Springer Science + Business Media.

Tellegren, A., Lykken, D. T., Bouchard, T. J., & Kagan, J., Snidman, N., Vahn, V., & Towsley, S. (2007). The preservation of two infant temperaments into adolescence. *Monographs of the Society for Research in Child Development, 72,* 1–80.

Temple, J., Reynolds, A., & Arteaga, I. (2010). Low birth weight, preschool education, and school remediation. *Education and Urban Society, 42*(6), 705–729. doi:10.1177/0013124510370946

Tennenbaum, H. R., & Leaper, C. (2002). Are parents' gender schemas related to their children's gender-related cognitions? A meta-analysis. *Developmental Psychology, 38,* 615–630.

Tennyson, R. D., & Cocchiarella, M. J. (1986). An empirically based instructional design theory for teaching concepts. *Review of Educational Research, 56,* 40–71.

Terman, L. M. (1916). *The measurement of intelligence.* Boston, MA: Houghton Mifflin.

Terman, L. M., & Merrill, M. A. (1972). *Stanford-Binet Intelligence Scale* (3rd ed.). Boston, MA: Houghton Mifflin.

Terry, A. W. (2000). An early glimpse: Service learning from an adolescent perspective. *Journal of Secondary Gifted Education, 11*(3), 115–134.

Terry, A. W. (2001). *A case study of community action service learning on young, gifted adolescents and their community* (Doctoral dissertation, University of Georgia, 2000). *Dissertation Abstracts International, 61*(08), 3058.

Terry, A. W. (2003). Effects of service learning on young, gifted adolescents and their community. *Gifted Child Quarterly, 47*(4), 295–308.

Terry, A. W. (2008). Student voices, global echoes: Service-learning and the gifted. *Roeper Review, 30,* 45–51.

Terry, A., & Panter, T. (2010). Students make sure the Cherokees are not removed . . . again: A study of service-learning and artful learning in teaching history. *Journal for the Education of the Gifted, 34*(1), 156–176.

Terry, J., Smith, B., & McQuillin, S. (2014). Teaching evidence-based practice in service-learning: A model for education and service. *Journal on Excellence in College Teaching, 25*(1), 55–69.

Teti, D. M., Gelfand, D., Messinger, D. S., & Isabella, R. (1995). Maternal depression and the quality of early attachment: An examination of infants, preschoolers and their mothers. *Developmental Psychology, 31,* 364–376.

Tharp, R. G. (1989). Psychocultural variables and constants: Effects on teaching and learning in schools. *American Psychologist, 44,* 349–359.

Tharp, R. G. (1994). Intergroup differences among Native Americans in socialization and child cognition: An ethnogenetic analysis. In P. M. Greenfield & R. R. Cocking (Eds.), *Cross-cultural roots of minority child development* (pp. 87–105). Hillsdale, NJ: Erlbaum.

Thatch, L V. L. (2008). *A case study of an elementary science teacher's efforts to transform students' scientific communication from "informal science talk" to "formal science talk."* Ph.D. dissertation, The University of Texas at Austin, United States–Texas. Retrieved August 30, 2010, from Dissertations & Theses: A&I. (Publication No. AAT 3315081)

Thatcher, K. L. (2010). The development of phonological awareness with specific language-impaired and typical children. *Psychology in the Schools, 47*(5), 467–480.

The Freedom Writers (with Gruwell, E.). (1999). *The Freedom Writers diary: How a teacher and 150 teens used writing to change themselves and the world around them.* New York, NY: Broadway Books.

Thelen, E., & Smith, L. B. (2006). Dynamic systems theories. In W. Damon & R. M. Lerner (Eds. in Chief) & R. M. Lerner (Vol. Ed.), *Handbook of child psychology: Vol. 1. Theoretical models of human development* (6th ed., pp. 258–312). Hoboken, NJ: Wiley.

Thomas, A., & Chess, S. (1977). *Temperament and development.* New York, NY: Brunner/Mazel.

Thomas, H. (2006). Obesity prevention programs for children and youth: Why are their results so modest? *Health Education Research, 21,* 783–795.

Thomas, J. (2012). Language play for infants: Man in the moon for male caregivers. *Aplis, 25*(2), 71–75.

Thomas, M. C., Forrester, N. A., & Ronald, A. (2013). Modeling socioeconomic status effects on language development. *Developmental Psychology, 49*(12), 2325–2343. doi:10.1037/a0032301

Thomas, R. M. (2005). *High-stakes testing: Coping with collateral damage.* Mahwah, NJ: Erlbaum.

Thomas, S., & Oldfather, P. (1997). Intrinsic motivations, literacy, and assessment practices: "That's my grade. That's me." *Educational Psychologist, 32,* 107–123.

Thompson, M., & Grace, C. O. (with L. J. Cohen). (2001). *Best friends, worst enemies: Understanding the social lives of children.* New York, NY: Ballantine.

Thompson, R. (2014). Stress and child development. *Future of Children, 24*(1), 41–59.

Thompson, R. A. (1994b). The role of the father after divorce. *The Future of Children: Children and Divorce, 4*(1), 210–235.

Thompson, R. A. (2006). The development of the person: Social understanding, relationships, conscience, self. In W. Damon & R. M. Lerner (Eds. in Chief) & N. Eisenberg (Vol. Ed.), *Handbook of child psychology, Vol. 3. Social, emotional, and personality development* (6th ed., pp. 24–98). Hoboken, NJ: Wiley.

Thompson, R. A. (2012). Whither the preconventional child? Toward a life-span moral development theory. *Child Development Perspectives, 6*(4), 423–429. doi:10.1111/j.1750-8606.2012.00245.x

Thompson, R. A., & Newton, E. K. (2010). Emotions in early conscience. In W. F. Arsenio & E. A. Lemerise (Eds.), *Emotions, aggression, and morality in children: Bridging development and psychopathology* (pp. 13–31). Washington, DC: American Psychological Association.

Thompson, R. A., & Virmani, E. A. (2010). Self and personality. In M. H. Bornstein (Ed.), *Handbook of cultural developmental science* (pp. 195–207). New York, NY: Psychology Press.

Thompson, R. A., Easterbrooks, M. A., & Padilla-Walker, L. M. (2003). Social and emotional development in infancy. In R. M. Lerner, M. A. Easterbrooks, & J. Mistry (Vol. Eds.), & I. B. Weiner (Editor-in-Chief), *Handbook of psychology. Vol. 6: Developmental psychology* (pp. 91–112). Hoboken, NJ: Wiley.

Thompson, R. H., Cotnoir-Bichelman, N. M., McKerchar, P. M., Tate, T. L., & Dancho, K. A. (2007). Enhancing early communication through infant sign training. *Journal of Applied Behavior Analysis, 40*, 15–23.

Thompson-Schill, S. L., Ramscar, M., & Chrysikou, E. G. (2009). Cognition without control: When a little frontal lobe goes a long way. *Current Directions in Psychological Science, 18*(5), 259–263.

Thomson, D. M. (2010). Marshmallow power and frooty treasures: Disciplining the child consumer through online cereal advergaming. *Critical Studies in Media Communication, 27*(5), 438–454. doi:10.1080/15295030903583648

Thorkildsen, T. A. (1995). Conceptions of social justice. In W. M. Kurtines & J. L. Gewirtz (Eds.), *Moral development: An introduction*. Boston, MA: Allyn & Bacon.

Thornberg, R. (2008). "It's not fair!"—Voicing pupils' criticisms of school rules. *Children & Society, 22*(6), 418–428. doi:10.1111/j.1099-0860.2007.00121.x

Thornberg, R. (2010). A study of children's conceptions of school rules by investigating their judgments of transgressions in the absence of rules. *Educational Psychology, 30*(5), 583–603. doi:10.1080/01443410.2010.492348

Thorndike, R., Hagen, E., & Sattler, J. (1986). *Stanford-Binet Intelligence Scale* (4th ed.). Chicago, IL: Riverside.

Throndsen, I. (2011). Self-regulated learning of basic arithmetic skills: A longitudinal study. *British Journal of Educational Psychology, 81*(4), 558–578. doi:10.1348/2044-8279.002008

Tiedemann, J. (2000). Parents' gender stereotypes and teachers' beliefs as predictors of children's concept of their mathematical ability in elementary school. *Journal of Educational Psychology, 92*, 144–151.

Tierney, A. L., & Nelson, C. A. III. (2009). Brain development and the role of experience in the early years. *Zero to Three, 30*(2), 9–13.

Tilley, S., & Taylor, L. (2013). Understanding curriculum as lived: teaching for social justice and equity goals. *Race, Ethnicity & Education, 16*(3), 406–429. doi:10.1080/13613324.2011.645565

Timler, G. R., Olswang, L. B., & Coggins, L. E. (2005). "Do I know what I need to do?" A social communication intervention for children with complex clinical profiles. *Language, Speech, and Hearing Services in Schools, 36*, 73–85.

Tisak, M. S. (1993). Preschool children's judgments of moral and personal events involving physical harm and property damage. *Merrill-Palmer Quarterly: Journal of Developmental Psychology, 39*(3), 375–390.

Tisak, M. S., & Turiel, E. (1984). Children's conceptions of moral and prudential rules. *Child Development, 55*(3), 1030–1039. doi:10.2307/1130154

Tobias, J. W., & Andreasen, J. B. (2013). Developing multiplicative thinking from additive reasoning. *Teaching Children Mathematics, 20*(2), 102–109.

Tobin, J. J., Wu, D. T. H., & Davidson, D. H. (1991). *Preschool in three cultures: Japan, China, and the United States*. New Haven, CT: Yale University Press.

Tobin, M., & Hill, E. W. (2012). The development of reading skills in young partially sighted readers. *British Journal of Special Education, 39*(2), 80–86. doi:10.1111/j.1467-8578.2012.00540.x

Toga, A. W., & Thompson, P. M. (2003). Mapping brain asymmetry. *Nature Review Neuroscience, 4*, 37–48.

Tolani, N., & Brooks-Gunn, J. (2006). Are there socioeconomic disparities in children's mental health? In H. E. Fitzgerald, B. M. Lester, & B. Zuckerman (Vol. Eds.), & H. E. Fitzgerald, R. Zucker, & K. Freeark (Eds. in Chief), *The crisis in youth mental health: Critical issues and effective programs* (Vol. 1, pp. 277–303). Westport, CT: Praeger.

Toldson, I., & Lemmons, B. (2013). Social demographics, the school environment, and parenting practices associated with parents' participation in schools and academic success among black, Hispanic, and white Students. *Journal of Human Behavior in the Social Environment, 23*(2), 237–255. doi:10.1080/10911359.2013.747407

Tomasello, M. (1999). *The cultural origins of human cognition*. Cambridge, MA: Harvard University Press.

Tomasello, M., Carpenter, M., & Liszkowski, U. (2007). A new look at infant pointing. *Child Development, 78*, 705–722.

Tompkins, G. E., & McGee, L. M. (1986). Visually impaired and sighted children's emerging concepts about written language. In D. B. Yaden, Jr., & S. Templeton (Eds.), *Metalinguistic awareness and beginning literacy: Conceptualizing what it means to read and write (pp. 259–275)*. Portsmouth, NH: Heinemann.

Tompkins, V., Guo, Y., & Justice, L. (2013). Inference generation, story comprehension, and language skills in the preschool years. *Reading & Writing, 26*(3), 403–429. doi:10.1007/s11145-012-9374-7

Tong, S., Baghurst, P., Vimpani, G., & McMichael, A. (2007). Socioeconomic position, maternal IQ, home environment, and cognitive development. *Journal of Pediatrics, 151*(3), 284–288.e1.

Tong, X., Deacon, S., & Cain, K. (2014). Morphological and syntactic awareness in poor comprehenders: Another piece of the puzzle. *Journal of Learning Disabilities, 47*(1), 22–33. doi:10.1177/0022219413509971

Tong, X., Shigetomi, E., Looger, L. L., & Khakh, B. S. (2013). Genetically encoded calcium indicators and astrocyte calcium microdomains. *The Neuroscientist, 19*(3), 274–291. doi:10.1177/1073858412468794

Topping, K., Dekhinet, R., & Zeedyk, S. (2013). Parent–infant interaction and children's language development. *Educational Psychology, 33*(4), 391–426. doi:10.1080/01443410.2012.744159

Torges, C., Stewart, A., & Duncan, L. (2009). Appreciating life's complexities: Assessing narrative ego integrity in late midlife. *Journal of Research in Personality, 43*(1), 66–74.

Torrance, E. (1981). Empirical validation of criterion-referenced indicators of creative ability through a longitudinal study. *Creative Child & Adult Quarterly, 6*(3), 136–140.

Torrance, E. P. (1995). Insights about creativity: Questioned, rejected, ridiculed, ignored. *Educational Psychology Review, 7*, 313–322.

Torres, D. (2013). Understanding how family socioeconomic status mediates the maternal intelligence–child cognitive outcomes relationship: A moderated mediation analysis. *Biodemography & Social Biology, 59*(2), 157–177. doi:10.1080/19485565.2013.833804

Torres, M. E., Smithwick, J., Luchok, K. J., & Rodman-Rice, G. (2012). Reducing maternal and child health disparities among Latino immigrants in South Carolina through a tailored, culturally appropriate and participant-driven initiative. *Californian Journal of Health Promotion, 10*(2), 1-14.

Torres-Guzmán, M. E. (1998). Language, culture, and literacy in Puerto Rican communities. In B. Pérez (Ed.), *Sociocultural contexts of language and literacy*. Mahwah, NJ: Erlbaum.

Torres-Guzmán, M. E. (1998). Language, culture, and literacy in Puerto Rican communities. In B. Pérez (Ed.), *Sociocultural contexts of language and literacy*. Mahwah, NJ: Erlbaum.

Torres-Guzmán, M. E. (2011). Methodologies and teacher stances: How do they interact in classrooms? *International Journal of Bilingual Education and Bilingualism, 14*(2), 225–241. doi:10.1080/13670050.2010.539675

Tourniaire, F., & Pulos, S. (1985). Proportional reasoning: A review of the literature. *Educational Studies in Mathematics, 16*, 181–204.

Towne, J. (2009). A dropout's guide to education reform. *Education Week, 29*(8), 25.

Träff, U. (2013). The contribution of general cognitive abilities and number abilities to different aspects of mathematics in children. *Journal of Experimental Child Psychology, 116*(2), 139–156. doi:10.1016/j.jecp.2013.04.007

Tracy, B., Reid, R., & Graham, S. (2009). Teaching young students strategies for planning and drafting stories: The impact of self-regulated strategy development. *Journal of Educational Research, 102*(5), 323–331.

Trainor, L. J., & Trehub, S. E. (1992). A comparison of infants' and adults' sensitivity to Western tonal structure. *Journal of Experimental Psychology: Human Perception and Performance, 19*, 615–626.

Trawick-Smith, J. (2010). *Early childhood development: A multicultural perspective* (5th ed.). Upper Saddle River, NJ: Merrill/Pearson.

Trawick-Smith, J. (2014). *Early childhood development: A multicultural perspective* (6th ed.). Boston, MA: Pearson.

Treffert, D. A. (2014). Savant syndrome: Realities, myths and misconceptions. *Journal of Autism and Developmental Disorders, 44*(3), 564–571. doi:10.1007/s10803-013-1906-8

Treffert, D. A., & Wallace, G. L. (2002). Islands of genius. *Scientific American, 286*(6), 76–85.

Treiman, R. (1998). Beginning to spell in English. In C. Hulme & R. M. Joshi (Eds.), *Reading and spelling: Development and disorders*. Mahwah, NJ: Erlbaum.

Treiman, R., & Kessler, B. (2013). Learning to use an alphabetic writing system. *Language Learning And Development, 9*(4), 317–330. doi:10.1080/15475441.2013.812016

Treiman, R., Cohen, J., Mulqueeny, K., Kessler, B., & Schechtman, S. (2007). Young children's knowledge about printed names. *Child Development, 78*, 1458–1471.

Trelease, J. (1982). *The read-aloud handbook*. New York, NY: Penguin Books.

Tremarche, P., Robinson, E., & Graham, L. (2007). Physical education and its effects on elementary testing results. *Physical Educator, 64*(2), 58–64.

Tremblay, R. E., Nagin, D. S, Seguin, J. R., Zoccolillo, M., Zelazo, P. D., Boivin, M., et al. (2004). Physical aggression during early childhood: Trajectories and predictors. *Pediatrics, 114*, E43–E50.

Trevarthen, C., & Hubley, P. (1978). Secondary intersubjectivity: Confidence, confiding and acts of meaning in the first year. In A. Lock (Ed.), *Action, gesture, and symbol: The emergence of language (pp. 183-230)*. London: Academic Press.

Triandis, H. C. (1995). *Individualism and collectivism*. Boulder, CO: Westview Press.

Trommsdorff, G. (2012). Development of "agentic" regulation in cultural context: The role of self and world views. *Child Development Perspectives, 6*(1), 19–26. doi:10.1111/j.1750-8606.2011.00224.x

Trommsdorff, G., & Heikamp, T. (2013). Socialization of emotions and emotion regulation in cultural context. In S. Barnow & N. Balkir (Eds.), *Cultural variations in psychopathology: From research to practice* (pp. 67–92). Cambridge, MA: Hogrefe Publishing.

Tronick, E. Z., Als, H., Adamson, L., Wise, S., & Brazelton, B. (1978). The infants' response to entrapment between contradictory messages in face-to-face interaction. *American Academy of Child Psychiatry, 1,* 1–13.

Tronick, E. Z., Cohn, J., & Shea, E. (1986). The transfer of affect between mother and infant. In T. B. Brazelton & M. W. Yogman (Eds.), *Affective development in infancy* (pp. 11–25). Norwood, NJ: Ablex.

Trost, S. G., & van der Mars, H. (2009/2010). Why we should not cut P.E. *Educational Leadership, 67*(4), 60–65.

Trzaskowski, M., Yang, J., Visscher, P., & Plomin, R. (2014). DNA evidence for strong genetic stability and increasing heritability of intelligence from age 7 to 12. *Molecular Psychiatry, 19*(3), 380–384. doi:10.1038/mp.2012.191

Tsantefski, M., Parkes, A., Tidyman, A., & Campion, M. (2013). An extended family for life for children affected by parental substance dependence. *Family Matters, (93),* 74-83.

Tse, L. (2001). *Why don't they learn English: Separating fact from fallacy in the U.S. language debate.* New York, NY: Teachers College Press.

Tsethlikai, M., & Rogoff, B. (2013). Involvement in traditional cultural practices and American Indian children's incidental recall of a folktale. *Developmental Psychology, 49*(3), 568-578. doi:10.1037/a0031308

Tsubota, Y., & Chen, Z. (2012). How do young children's spatio-symbolic skills change over short time scales? *Journal of Experimental Child Psychology, 111*(1), 1–21. doi:10.1016/j.jecp.2011.06.005

Tsui, J. M., & Mazzocco, M. M. M. (2007). Effects of math anxiety and perfectionism on timed versus untimed math testing in mathematically gifted sixth graders. *Roeper Review, 29*(2), 132–139.

Tucker, C., & Kazura, K. (2013). Parental responses to school-aged children's sibling conflict. *Journal of Child and Family Studies.* doi:10.1007/s10826-013-9741-2

Tucker, J. S., Ellickson, P. L., & Klein, D. J. (2008). Growing up in a permissive household: What deters at-risk adolescents from heavy drinking. *Journal of Studies on Alcohol and Drugs, 69*(4), 528–528-534.

Tucker, V., & Schwartz, I. (2013). Parents' perspectives of collaboration with school professionals: Barriers and facilitators to successful partnerships in planning for students with ASD. *School Mental Health, 5*(1), 3–14. doi:10.1007/s12310-012-9102-0

Tucker-Drob, E. M., & Harden, K. (2012). Early childhood cognitive development and parental cognitive stimulation: Evidence for reciprocal gene–environment transactions. *Developmental Science, 15*(2), 250–259. doi:10.1111/j.1467-7687.2011.01121.x

Tucker-Drob, E., & Harden, K. (2012). Intellectual interest mediates gene × socioeconomic status interaction on adolescent academic achievement. *Child Development, 83*(2), 743–757. doi:10.1111/j.1467-8624.2011.01721.x

Tunmer, W. E., Pratt, C., & Herriman, M. L. (Eds.). (1984). *Metalinguistic awareness in children: Theory, research, and implications.* Berlin, Germany: Springer-Verlag.

Turati, C., Gava, L., Valenza, E., & Ghirardi, V. (2013). Number versus extent in newborns' spontaneous preference for collections of dots. *Cognitive Development, 28*(1), 10–20. doi:10.1016/j.cogdev.2012.06.002

Turiel, E. (1983). *The development of social knowledge: Morality and convention.* Cambridge, England: Cambridge University Press.

Turiel, E. (1998). The development of morality. In W. Damon (Series Ed.) & N. Eisenberg (Vol. Ed.), *Handbook of child psychology: Vol. 3. Social, emotional, and personality development* (pp. 863–932). New York, NY: Wiley.

Turiel, E. (2002). *The culture of morality: Social development, context, and conflict.* Cambridge, England: Cambridge University Press.

Turiel, E. (2006a). The development of morality. In W. Damon & R. M. Lerner (Eds. in Chief) & N. Eisenberg (Vol. Ed.), *Handbook of child psychology, Vol. 3. Social, emotional, and personality development* (6th ed., pp. 789–857). Hoboken, NJ: Wiley.

Turiel, E. (2006b). Thought, emotions, and social interactional processes in moral development. In M. Killen & J. G. Smetana (Eds.), *Handbook of moral development* (pp. 7–35). Mahwah, NJ: Erlbaum.

Turiel, E. (2008a). The development of children's orientations toward moral, social, and personal orders: More than a sequence in development. *Human Development, 51,* 21–39.

Turiel, E. (2008b). Thought about actions in social domains: Morality, social conventions, and social interactions. *Cognitive Development, 23*(1), 136–154. doi:10.1016/j.cogdev.2007.04.001

Turiel, E., & Killen, M. (2010). Taking emotions seriously: The role of emotions in moral development. In W. F. Arsenio & E. A. Lemerise (Eds.), *Emotions, aggression, and morality in children: Bridging development and psychopathology* (pp. 33–52). Washington, DC: American Psychological Association.

Turiel, E., Killen, M., & Helwig, C. C. (1987). Morality: Its structure, function, and vagaries. In J. Kagan & S. Lamb (Eds.), *The emergence of morality in young children* (pp. 155–243). Chicago, IL: University of Chicago Press.

Turiel, E., Smetana, J. G., & Killen, M. (1991). Social contexts in social cognitive development. In W. M. Kurtines & J. L. Gewirtz (Eds.), *Moral behavior and development: Vol. 2. Research* (pp. 307–332). Hillsdale, NJ: Erlbaum.

Turkanis, C. G. (2001). Creating curriculum with children. In B. Rogoff, C. G. Turkanis, & L. Bartlett (Eds.), *Learning together: Children and adults in a school community* (pp. 91–102). New York, NY: Oxford University Press.

Turkheimer, E. (2000). Three laws of behavior genetics and what they mean. *Current Directions in Psychological Science, 9,* 160–164.

Turkheimer, E., Haley, A., Waldron, M., D'Onofrio, B., & Gottesman, I. I. (2003). Socioeconomic status modifies heritability of IQ in young children. *Psychological Science, 14,* 623–628.

Turnbull, A. P., Pereira, L., & Blue-Banning, M. (2000). Teachers as friendship facilitators: Re-Chin, J. (2014). Young children's trust beliefs in peers: Relations to social competence and interactive behaviors in a peer group. *Early Education and Development, 25*(5), 601–618. doi:10.1080/10409289.2013.836698

Turnbull, A. P., Turnbull, R., & Wehmeyer, M. L. (2010). *Exceptional lives: Special education in today's schools* (6th ed.). Upper Saddle River, NJ: Merrill Pearson.

Turner, K. L., & Brown, C. S. (2007). The centrality of gender and ethnic identities across individuals and contexts. *Social Development, 16,* 700–719.

Turner, S. L., & Conkel, J. L. (2010). Evaluation of a career development skills intervention with adolescents living in an inner city. *Journal of Counseling and Development, 88,* 457–465.

Turns, B., & Kimmes, J. (2014). "I'm NOT the Problem!" Externalizing children's "problems" using play therapy and developmental considerations. *Contemporary Family Therapy: An International Journal, 36*(1), 135–147. doi:10.1007/s10591-013-9285-z

Tuvblad, C., Bezdjian, S., Raine, A., & Baker, L. (2013). Psychopathic personality and negative parent-to-child affect: A longitudinal cross-lag twin study. *Journal of Criminal Justice, 41*(5), 331–341.

Tuvblad, C., Bezdjian, S., Raine, A., & Baker, L. A. (2014). The heritability of psychopathic personality in 14- to 15-year-old twins: A multirater, multimeasure approach. *Psychological Assessment,* doi:10.1037/a0036711

Tversky, A., & Kahneman, D. (1990). Judgment under uncertainty: Heuristics and biases. In P. K. Moser (Ed.), *Rationality in action: Contemporary approaches* (pp. 171–188). New York, NY: Cambridge University Press.

Tynes, B. M. (2007). Role taking in online "classrooms": What adolescents are learning about race and ethnicity. *Developmental Psychology, 43*(6), 1312–1320.

Tzilos, G., Hess, L., Kao, J., & Zlotnick, C. (2013). Characteristics of perinatal women seeking treatment for marijuana abuse in a community-based clinic. *Archives of Women's Mental Health.* doi:10.1007/s00737-013-0358-7

Tzuriel, D. (2000). Dynamic assessment of young children: Educational and intervention perspectives. *Educational Psychology Review, 12,* 385–435.

U. S. Census Bureau. (2013b). *Table C4. Children with grandparents by presence of parents, sex, race, and Hispanic origin for selected characteristics: 2012.* Retrieved from http://www.census.gov/hhes/families/data/cps2012.html.

U.S. Census Bureau. (2013a). *Table C3. Living arrangements of children under 18 years and marital status of parents, by age, sex, race, and Hispanic origin and selected characteristics of the child for all children: 2012.* Retrieved from http://www.census.gov/hhes/families/data/cps2012.html

U.S. Department of Agriculture Center for Nutrition Policy and Promotion. (2013). *Getting started with MyPlate.* Retrieved from http://www.choosemyplate.gov/downloads/GettingStartedWithMyPlate.pdf

U.S. Department of Education (2004). *Building the legacy: IDEA 2004.* from http://idea.ed.gov/explore/view/p/,root,regs,300,A,300%252E8

U.S. Department of Education. (1993). *National excellence: A case for developing America's talent.* Washington, DC: Office of Educational Research and Improvement.

U.S. Department of Energy Office of Science. (2008). *Genomics and its impact on science and society.* Retrieved from http://www.ornl.gov/sci/techresources/Human_Genome/publicat/primer/

U.S. Department of Health and Human Services, Administration for Children and Families, Administration on Children, Youth and Families, Children's Bureau. (2012). *Child maltreatment 2011.* Retrieved from http://www.acf.hhs.gov/programs/cb/research-data-technology/statistics-research/child-maltreatment

U.S. Department of Health and Human Services. (2000). *Eating disorders.* Retrieved from http://4women.gov/owh/pub/factsheets/eatingdis.htm

U.S. Department of Health and Human Services. (2007). *The AFCARS Report: Preliminary FY 2005 estimates as of September 2006.* Retrieved from http://www.acf.hhs.gov/programs/cb/stats_research/afcars/tar/report13.htm

U.S. Department of Justice Drug Enforcement Administration. (2011). *Drugs of abuse.* Retrieved from http://www.justice.gov/dea/pr/multimedia-library/publications/drug_of_abuse.pdf http://www.justice.gov/dea/druginfo/factsheets.shtml

U.S. Department of Labor. (2013). *Employment characteristics of families summary.* Retrieved from http://www.bls.gov/news.release/famee.nr0.htm

U.S. Department of State. (2013). *Intercountry adoption.* Retrieved from http://adoption.state.gov/about_us/statistics.php

U.S. Drug Enforcement Administration. (2002). *Team up: A drug prevention manual for high school athletic coaches*. Washington, DC: U.S. Department of Justice Drug Enforcement Administration.

U.S. Secret Service National Threat Assessment Center, in collaboration with the U.S. Department of Education. (2000, October). *Safe school initiative: An interim report on the prevention of targeted violence in schools*. Retrieved from http://cecp.air.org/download/ntac_ssi_report.pdf

Uji, M., Sakamoto, A., Adachi, K., & Kitamura, T. (2014). The impact of authoritative, authoritarian, and permissive parenting styles on children's later mental health in Japan: Focusing on parent and child gender. *Journal of Child and Family Studies, 23*(2), 293-302. doi:10.1007/s10826-013-9740-3

Ullman, E. (2010a, March). Closing the STEM gender gap. *Education Update, 52*(3), 1, 6–7.

Ullman, E. (2010b). Providing professional development to educators in rural areas. *Education Update, 52*(1), 1, 4–5.

Ullrich-French, S., & Smith, A. L. (2006). Perceptions of relationships with parents and peers in youth sport: Independent and combined prediction of motivational outcome. *Psychology of Sport and Exercise, 7,* 193–214.

Ulusoy, Y., & Duy, B. (2013). Effectiveness of a psycho-education program on learned helplessness and irrational beliefs. *Educational Sciences: Theory & Practice, 13*(3), 1440–1446. doi:10.12738/estp.2013.3.1469

Umaña-Taylor, A. J., & Alfaro, E. C. (2006). Ethnic identity among U.S. Latino adolescents: Theory, measurement, and implications for well-being. In K. Freeark & W. S. Davidson II (Vol. Eds.), & H. E. Fitzgerald, R. Zucker, & K. Freeark (Eds. in Chief), *The crisis in youth mental health: Vol. 3: Critical issues and effective programs* (pp. 195–211). Westport, CT: Praeger.

United Nations Children's Fund (n.d.). *A summary of the rights under the Convention on the Rights of the Child*. Retrieved from http://www.unicef.org/crc/files/Rights_overview.pdf

Upegui-Hernández, D. (2012). "Because I'm neither Gringa nor Latina": Conceptualizing multiple identities within transnational social fields. In R. Josselson, M. Harway (Eds.), *Navigating multiple identities: Race, gender, culture, nationality, and roles* (pp. 227–253). New York, NY: Oxford.

Urban, J., Carlson, E., Egeland, B., & Sroufe, L. A. (1991). Patterns of individual adaptation across childhood. *Development and Psychopathology, 3,* 445–460.

Urdan, T. (1997). Achievement goal theory: Past results, future directions. In M. L. Maehr & P. R. Pintrich (Eds.), *Advances in motivation and achievement* (Vol. 10, pp. 99–141). Greenwich, CT: JAI Press.

Urdan, T. (2004). Predicators of academic self-handicapping and achievement: Examining achievement goals, classroom goal structures, and culture. *Journal of Educational Psychology, 96,* 251–264.

Urdan, T. (2012). Factors affecting the motivation and achievement of immigrant students. In K. R. Harris, S. Graham, T. Urdan, S. Graham, J. M. Royer, & M. Zeidner (Eds.), *APA educational psychology handbook, Vol. 2: Individual differences and cultural and contextual factors* (pp. 293–313). Washington, DC US: American Psychological Association. doi:10.1037/13274-012

Urdan, T., Ryan, A. M., Anderman, E. M., & Gheen, M. H. (2002). Goals, goal structures, and avoidance behaviors. In C. Midgley (Ed.), *Goals, goal structures, and patterns of adaptive learning* (pp. 55–83). Mahwah, NJ: Erlbaum.

Ursache, A., & Raver, C. (2014). Trait and state anxiety: Relations to executive functioning in an at-risk sample. *Cognition & Emotion, 28*(5), 845–855. doi:10.1080/02699931.2013.855173

Ursache, A., Blair, C., & Raver, C. (2012). The promotion of self-regulation as a means of enhancing school readiness and early achievement in children at risk for school failure. *Child Development Perspectives, 6*(2), 122–128. doi:10.1111/j.1750-8606.2011.00209.x

Usinger, J., & Smith, M. (2010). Career development in the context of self-construction during adolescence. *Journal of Vocational Behavior, 76*(3), 580–591. doi:10.1016/j.jvb.2010.01.010

Uvaas, T. (2010). *Improving transitions to high school: Examining the effectiveness of a school connectedness program* (ProQuest Information & Learning). Retrieved from http://www.csa.com. (2010-99041-034)

Véronneau, M., & Dishion, T. J. (2011). Middle school friendships and academic achievement in early adolescence: A longitudinal analysis. *The Journal of Early Adolescence, 31*(1), 99–124. doi:10.1177/0272431610384485

Valdés, G., Bunch, G., Snow, C., & Lee, C. (with Matos, L.). (2005). Enhancing the development of students' language(s). In L. Darling-Hammond & J. Bransford (Eds.), *Preparing teachers for a changing world: What teachers should learn and be able to do* (pp. 126–168). San Francisco, CA: Jossey-Bass/Wiley.

Valiente, C., Lemery-Chalfant, K., Swanson, J., & Reiser, M. (2008). Prediction of children's academic competence from their effortful control, relationships, and classroom participation. *Journal of Educational Psychology, 100*(1), 67–77.

Vallotton, C. D. (2012). Infant signs as intervention? Promoting symbolic gestures for preverbal children in low-income families supports responsive parent–child relationships. *Early Childhood Research Quarterly, 27*(3), 401–415. doi:10.1016/j.ecresq.2012.01.003

Vallotton, C. D., & Ayoub, C. C. (2010). Symbols build communication and thought: The role of gestures and words in the development of engagement skills and social-emotional concepts during toddlerhood. *Social Development, 19*(3), 601–626. doi:10.1111/j.1467-9507.2009.00549.x

Van den Broek, P., Bauer, P. J., & Bourg, T. (Eds.). (1997). *Developmental spans in event comprehension and representation: Bridging fictional and actual events*. Mahwah, NJ: Erlbaum.

van den Broek, P., Lynch, J. S., Naslund, J., Ievers-Landis, C. E., & Verduin, K. (2003). The development of comprehension of main ideas in narratives: Evidence from the selection of titles. *Journal of Educational Psychology, 95,* 707–718.

van den Heuvel, M. P., Stam, C. J., Kahn, R. S., & Hulshoff Pol, H. E. (2009). Efficiency of functional brain networks and intellectual performance. *Journal of Neuroscience, 29*(23), 7619–7624.

Van der Graaff, J., Branje, S., De Wied, M., Hawk, S., Van Lier, P., & Meeus, W. (2014). Perspective taking and empathic concern in adolescence: Gender differences in developmental changes. *Developmental Psychology, 50*(3), 881–888. doi:10.1037/a0034325

Van der Schoot, M., Reijntjes, A., & Lieshout, E. (2012). How do children deal with inconsistencies in text? An eye fixation and self-paced reading study in good and poor reading comprehenders. *Reading & Writing, 25*(7), 1665–1690. doi:10.1007/s11145-011-9337-4

van der Ven, S. G., Boom, J., Kroesbergen, E. H., & Leseman, P. M. (2012). Microgenetic patterns of children's multiplication learning: Confirming the overlapping waves model by latent growth modeling. *Journal of Experimental Child Psychology, 113*(1), 1–19. doi:10.1016/j.jecp.2012.02.001

Van Dooren, W., De Bock, D., Hessels, A., Janssens, D., & Verschaffel, L. (2005). Not everything is proportional: Effects of age and problem type on propensities for overgeneralization. *Cognition and Instruction, 23,* 57–86.

van Hof-van Duin, J., & Mohn, G. (1986). The development of visual acuity in normal full-term and preterm infants. *Vision Research, 26,* 909–916.

van IJzendoorn, M. H., Goldberg, S., Kroonenberg, P. M., & Frenkel, O. J. (1992). The relative effects of maternal and child problems on the quality of attachment: A meta-analysis of attachment in clinical samples. *Child Development, 63,* 840–858.

van Kraayenoord, C. E., & Paris, S. G. (1997). Children's self-appraisal of their work samples and academic progress. *Elementary School Journal, 97,* 523–537.

Van Leijenhorst, L., & Crone, E. A. (2010). Paradoxes in adolescent risk taking. In P. D. Zelazo, M. Chandler, & E. Crone (Eds.), *Developmental social cognitive neuroscience. The Jean Piaget symposium series* (pp. 209–225). New York, NY: Psychology Press.

Van Ouytsel, J., Walrave, M., & Ponnet, K. (2014). How schools can help their students to strengthen their online reputations. *Clearing House, 87*(4), 180–185. doi:10.1080/00098655.2014.909380

van Soelen, I. C., Brouwer, R. M., van Leeuwen, M., Kahn, R. S., Pol, H., & Boomsma, D. I. (2011). Heritability of verbal and performance intelligence in a pediatric longitudinal sample. *Twin Research And Human Genetics, 14*(2), 119–128. doi:10.1375/twin.14.2.119

van Staden, A. (2013). An evaluation of an intervention using sign language and multi-sensory coding to support word learning and reading comprehension of deaf signing children. *Child Language Teaching & Therapy, 29*(3), 305–318. doi:10.1177/0265659013479961

van Tuijl, L. A., de Jong, P. J., Sportel, B., de Hullu, E., & Nauta, M. H. (2014). Implicit and explicit self-esteem and their reciprocal relationship with symptoms of depression and social anxiety: A longitudinal study in adolescents. *Journal of Behavior Therapy & Experimental Psychiatry, 45*(1), 113–121. doi:10.1016/j.jbtep.2013.09.007

VanderLaan, D. P., Blanchard, R., Wood, H., & Zucker, K. J. (2014). Birth order and sibling sex ratio of children and adolescents referred to a gender identity service. *Plos ONE, 9*(3), 1–9. doi:10.1371/journal.pone.0090257

Vandermaas-Peeler, M., Nelson, J., Bumpass, C., & Sassine, B. (2009). Social contexts of development: Parent-child interactions during reading and play. *Journal of Early Childhood Literacy, 9*(3), 295–317.

Vanderwert, R. E., & Nelson, C. A. (2014). The use of near-infrared spectroscopy in the study of typical and atypical development. *Neuroimage, 85*(Part 1), 264–271. doi:10.1016/j.neuroimage.2013.10.009

VanSledright, B., & Limón, M. (2006). Learning and teaching social studies: A review of cognitive research in history and geography. In P. A. Alexander & P. H. Winne (Eds.), *Handbook of educational psychology* (2nd ed., pp. 545–570). Mahwah, NJ: Erlbaum.

Vansteenkiste, M., Lens, W., & Deci, E. L. (2006). Intrinsic versus extrinsic goal contents in self-determination theory: Another look at the quality of academic motivation. *Educational Psychologist, 41,* 19–31.

Vassallo, S. (2013). Considering class-based values related to guardian involvement and the development of self-regulated learning. *New Ideas in Psychology, 31*(3), 202–211. doi:10.1016/j.newideapsych.2011.12.002

Vaughan, D., Cleary, B., & Murphy, D. (2014). Delivery outcomes for nulliparous women at the extremes of maternal age - a cohort study. *BJOG: An International Journal Of Obstetrics & Gynaecology, 121*(3), 261-268. doi:10.1111/1471-0528.12311

Vaughan, M. D., & Rodriguez, E. M. (2013). The influence of Erik Erikson on positive psychology theory and research. In J. D. Sinnott (Ed.), *Positive psychology: Advances in understanding adult motivation* (pp. 231–245). New York, NY: Springer Science + Business Media. doi:10.1007/978-1-4614-7282-7_15

Vaughn, B. E., Egeland, B., Sroufe, L. A., & Waters, E. (1979). Individual differences in infant-mother attachment at twelve and eighteen months: Stability and change in families under stress. *Child Development, 50*, 971–975.

Vaughn, B. E., Kopp, C. B., & Krakow, J. B. (1984). The emergence and consolidation of self-control from eighteen to thirty months of age: Normative trends and individual differences. *Child Development, 55*, 990–1004.

Vaughn, B. E., Shin, N., Kim, M., Coppola, G., Krzysik, L., Santos, A. J., et al. (2009). Hierarchical models of social competence in preschool children: A multisite, multinational study. *Child Development, 80*(6), 1775–1796. doi:10.1111/j.1467-8624.2009.01367.x

Vaughn, S., Klingner, J. K., Swanson, E. A., Boardman, A. G., Roberts, G., Mohammed, S. S., & Stillman-Spisak, S. J. (2011). Efficacy of collaborative strategic reading with middle school students. *American Educational Research Journal, 48*(4), 938–964. doi:10.3102/0002831211410305

Vavra, E. (1987). Grammar and syntax: The student's perspective. *English Journal, 76*, 42–48.

Vedamurthy, I., Suttle, C. M., Alexander, J., & Asper, L. J. (2008). A psychophysical study of human binocular interactions in normal and amblyopic visual systems. *Vision Research, 48*(14), 1522–1531.

Venta, A., Shmueli-Goetz, Y., & Sharp, C. (2014). Assessing attachment in adolescence: A psychometric study of the Child Attachment Interview. *Psychological Assessment, 26*(1), 238–255. doi:10.1037/a0034712

Venter, E., & Rambau, E. (2011). The effect of a latchkey situation on a child's educational success. *South African Journal of Education, 31*(3), 345–356.

Vereen, L. G., Hill, N. R., & Butler, S. (2013). The use of humor and storytelling with African American men: Innovative therapeutic strategies for success in counseling. *International Journal for the Advancement of Counselling, 35*(1), 57–63. doi:10.1007/s10447-012-9165-5

Vermeer, H. J., Boekaerts, M., & Seegers, G. (2000). Motivational and gender differences: Sixth-grade students' mathematical problem-solving behavior. *Journal of Educational Psychology, 92*, 308–315.

Vickery, J. (2014). The role of after-school digital media clubs in closing participation gaps and expanding social networks. *Equity & Excellence In Education, 47*(1), 78–95. doi:10.1080/10665684.2013.866870

Victor, E. (2012). Mental health and hooking up: A self-discrepancy perspective. *New School Psychology Bulletin, 9*(2), 24-34.

Villegas, A. M., & Lucas, T. (2007). The culturally responsive teacher. *Educational Leadership, 64*(6), 28–33.

Vlachou, A., Eleftheriadou, D., & Metallidou, P. (2014). Do learning difficulties differentiate elementary teachers' attributional patterns for students' academic failure? A comparison between Greek regular and special education teachers. *European Journal of Special Needs Education, 29*(1), 1–15. doi:10.1080/08856257.2013.830440

Vlismas, W., Malloch, S., & Burnham, D. (2013). The effects of music and movement on mother-infant interactions. *Early Child Development and Care, 183*(11), 1669–1688. doi:10.1080/03004430.2012.746968

Vohr, B., Topol, D., Watson, V., St Pierre, L., & Tucker, R. (2014). The importance of language in the home for school-age children with permanent hearing loss. *Acta Paediatrica, 103*(1), 62–69. doi:10.1111/apa.12441

Volker, M. A., Lopata, C., & Cook-Cottone, C. (2006). Assessment of children with intellectual giftedness and reading disabilities. *Psychology in the Schools, 43*, 855–869.

Volling, B. L. (2001). Early attachment relationships as predictors of preschool children's emotion regulation with a distressed sibling. *Early Education and Development, 12*(2), 185–207.

Vollmer, T. R., & Hackenberg, T. D. (2001). Reinforcement contingencies and social reinforcement: Some reciprocal relations between basic and applied research. *Journal of Applied Behavior Analysis, 34*, 241–253.

Volterra, A., Liaudet, N., & Savtchouk, I. (2014). Astrocyte Ca2+ signalling: an unexpected complexity. *Nature Reviews Neuroscience, 15*(5), 327-335. doi:10.1038/nrn3725

Volterra, V., Caselli, M. C., Capirci, O., & Pizzuto, E. (2005). Gesture and the emergence and development of language. In M. Tomasello & D. I. Slobin (Eds.), *Beyond nature–nurture: Essays in honor of Elizabeth Bates* (pp. 3–40). Mahwah, NH: Erlbaum.

von Károlyi, C. (2013). From Tesla to Tetris: Mental rotation, vocation, and gifted education. *Roeper Review, 35*(4), 231–240. doi:10.1080/02783193.2013.829547

Vorrath, H. (1985). *Positive peer culture.* New York, NY: Aldine de Gruyter.

Vorstius, C., Radach, R., Mayer, M. B., & Lonigan, C. J. (2013). Monitoring local comprehension monitoring in sentence reading. *School Psychology Review, 42*(2), 191–206.

Vosniadou, S. (1991). Conceptual development in astronomy. In S. M. Glynn, R. H. Yeany, & B. K. Britton (Eds.), *The psychology of learning science* (pp. 149–177). Hillsdale, NJ: Erlbaum.

Vosniadou, S. (2009). Science education for young children: A conceptual-change point of view. In O. A. Barbarin & B. H. Wasik (Eds.), *Handbook of child development and early education: Research to practice* (pp. 544–557). New York, NY: Guilford Press.

Vosniadou, S., & Brewer, W. F. (1992). Mental models of the earth: A study of conceptual change in childhood. *Cognitive Psychology, 24*, 535–585. doi:10.1016/0010-0285(92)90018-W

Vosniadou, S., & Mason, L. (2012). Conceptual change induced by instruction: A complex interplay of multiple factors. In K. R. Harris, S. Graham, T. Urdan, S. Graham, J. M. Royer, & M. Zeidner (Eds.), *APA educational psychology handbook, Vol. 2: Individual differences and cultural and contextual factors* (pp. 221–246). Washington, DC: American Psychological Association. doi:10.1037/13274-009

Voutsina, C. (2012). A micro-developmental approach to studying young children's problem solving behavior in addition. *Journal of Mathematical Behavior, 31*(3), 366–381. doi:10.1016/j.jmathb.2012.03.002

Vozzola, E. C. (2014). *Moral development: Theory and applications.* New York, NY: Routledge/Taylor & Francis Group.

Vrijsen, J. N., Becker, E. S., Arias-Vásquez, A., van Dijk, M. K., Speckens, A., & Oostrom, I. (2014). What is the contribution of different cognitive biases and stressful childhood events to the presence and number of previous depressive episodes? *Psychiatry Research, 217*(3), 134–142. doi:10.1016/j.psychres.2014.02.033

Vuksanovic, J., & Bjekic, J. (2013). Developmental relationship between language and joint attention in late talkers. *Research in Developmental Disabilities, 34*(8), 2360–2368. doi:10.1016/j.ridd.2013.04.017

Vygotsky, L. (1993). *The collected works of L. S. Vygotsky, Vol. 2: The fundamentals of defectology (abnormal psychology and learning disabilities).* (Translated by J. E. Knox, & C. B. Stevens; Edited by R. W. Rieber & A. S. Carton). New York, NY: Plenum Press.

Vygotsky, L. S. (1934/1986). *Thought and language* (rev. ed.; A. Kozulin, Ed. and Trans.). Cambridge, MA: MIT Press. (Original work published 1934)

Vygotsky, L. S. (1962). *Thought and language* (E. Haufmann & G. Vakar, Eds. and Trans.). Cambridge, MA: MIT Press.

Vygotsky, L. S. (1966). [Imaginary] play and its role in the mental development of the child. *Soviet Psychology, 5*(3), 6–18. (Original work published 1931)

Vygotsky, L. S. (1978). *Mind in society: The development of higher psychological processes* (M. Cole, V. John-Steiner, S. Scribner, & E. Souberman, Eds.). Cambridge, MA: Harvard University Press.

Vygotsky, L. S. (1987a). The problem and the method of investigation. In R. W. Rieber & A. S. Carton (Eds.), *Collected works of L. S. Vygotsky: Vol. 1. Problems of general psychology* (pp. 167–241). New York, NY: Plenum Press.

Vygotsky, L. S. (1997a). Analysis of higher mental functions. In R. W. Rieber (Ed.), *Collected works of L. S. Vygotsky: Vol. 4. The history of the development of higher mental functions* (pp. 65–82). New York, NY: Plenum Press.

Vygotsky, L. S. (1997b). *Educational psychology.* Boca Raton, FL: St. Lucie Press.

Vygotsky, L. S. (1997c). The development of mnemonic and mnemotechnical functions. In R. W. Rieber (Ed.), *Collected works of L. S. Vygotsky: Vol. 4. The history of the development of higher mental functions* (pp. 179–190). New York, NY: Plenum (Originally published 1982–1984).

Vygotsky, L. S. (1997d). The historical meaning of the crisis in psychology: A methodological investigation. In R. W. Rieber & J. Wollock (Eds.), *Collected works of L. S. Vygotsky: Vol. 3. Problem of the theory and history of psychology* (pp. 233–343). New York, NY: Plenum Press.

Vygotsky, L. S. (1997e). Research method. In R. W. Rieber (Ed.), *Collected works of L. S. Vygotsky: Vol. 4. The history of the development of higher mental functions* (pp. 27–63). New York, NY: Plenum. (Originally published 1982–1984)

Vygotsky, L. S. (1997f). Genesis of higher mental functions. In R. W. Rieber (Ed.), *Collected works of L. S. Vygotsky: Vol. 4. The history of the development of higher mental functions* (pp. 97–119). New York, NY: Plenum Press.

Vygotsky, L. S. (1987b). An experimental study of concept development. In R. W. Rieber & A. S. Carton (Eds.), *Collected works of L. S. Vygotsky: Vol. I. Problems of general psychology* (pp. 121–166). New York, NY: Plenum.

Wölfer, R., & Scheithauer, H. (2014). Social influence and bullying behavior: Intervention-based network dynamics of the fairplayer.manual bullying prevention program. *Aggressive Behavior, 40*(4), 309–319. doi:10.1002/ab.21524

Waddington, C. H. (1957). *The strategy of the genes.* London, England: Allyn & Bacon.

Wagener, U. (2013). Young children's self-regulated learning: A reflection on Pintrich's model from a microanalytic perspective. *Journal of Cognitive Education and Psychology, 12*(3), 306-322. doi:10.1891/1945-8959.12.3.306

Wagley, C. (1977). *Welcome of tears: The Tapirapé Indians of central Brazil.* New York, NY: Oxford University Press.

Wagner, L. (2010). Inferring meaning from syntactic structures in acquisition: The case of transitivity and telicity. *Language & Cognitive Processes, 25*(10), 1354-1379. doi:10.1080/01690960903488375

Wagner, L., Greene-Havas, M., & Gillespie, R. (2010). Development in children's comprehension of linguistic register. *Child Development, 81*(6), 1678-1686. doi:10.1111/j.1467-8624.2010.01502.x

Wagner, S., Forer, B., Cepeda, I., Goelman, H., Maggi, S., D'angiulli, A., et al. (2013). Perceived stress and Canadian early childcare educators. *Child & Youth Care Forum, 42*(1), 53–70. doi:10.1007/s10566-012-9187-5

Wahlsten, D., & Gottlieb, G. (1997). The invalid separation of effects of nature and nurture: Lessons from animal experimentation. In R. J. Sternberg & E. L. Grigorenko (Eds.), *Intelligence, heredity, and environment* (pp. 163–192). Cambridge, England: Cambridge University Press.

Wahlstrom, D., Breaux, K. C., Zhu, J., & Weiss, L. G. (2012). The Wechsler Preschool and Primary Scale of Intelligence—Third Edition, the Wechsler Intelligence Scale for Children—Fourth Edition, and the Wechsler Individual Achievement Test—Third Edition. In D. P. Flanagan, & P. L. Harrison (Eds.), *Contemporary intellectual assessment: Theories, tests, and issues* (3rd ed., pp. 224–248). New York, NY US: Guilford Press.

Wahlstrom, K., Davison, M., Choi, J., & Ross, J. (2001). *Minneapolis public schools start time study.* Center for Applied Research and Educational Improvement. Retrieved from http://www.cehd.umn.edu/carei/Reports/docs/SST-2001ES.pdf

Wainryb, C. (2006). Moral development in culture: Diversity, tolerance, and justice. In M. Killen & J. G. Smetana (Eds.), *Handbook of moral development* (pp. 211–240). Mahwah, NJ: Erlbaum.

Waisbren, S. E., & Antshel, K. M. (2013). Phenylketonuria. In I. Baron & C. Rey-Casserly (Eds.), *Pediatric neuropsychology: Medical advances and lifespan outcomes* (pp. 219-236). New York, NY: Oxford University Press.

Wakeel, F., Wisk, L. E., Gee, R., Chao, S. M., & Witt, W. P. (2013). The balance between stress and personal capital during pregnancy and the relationship with adverse obstetric outcomes: Findings from the 2007 Los Angeles Mommy and Baby (Lamb) study. Archives Of Women's Mental Health. doi:10.1007/s00737-013-0367-6

Wakeman, S., Karvonen, M., & Ahumada, A. (2013). Changing instruction to increase achievement for students with moderate to severe intellectual disabilities. *Teaching Exceptional Children, 46*(2), 6–13.

Walker, A. (2012). Collaborating with the community: Lessons from a rural school district. *TESOL Journal, 3*(3), 469–487. doi:10.1002/tesj.25

Walker, C. M., & Gopnik, A. (2013). Pretense and possibility—A theoretical proposal about the effects of pretend play on development: Comment on Lillard et al. (2013). *Psychological Bulletin, 139*(1), 40–44. doi:10.1037/a0030151

Walker, E. A., McGregor, K. K., Bacon, S., & Tobey, E. (2013). Word learning processes in children with cochlear implants. *Journal of Speech, Language & Hearing Research, 56*(2), 375-387. doi:10.1044/1092-4388(2012/11-0343)

Walker, H. M., Horner, R. H., Sugai, G., Bullis, M., Sprague, J. R., Bicker, D., & Kaufman, M. J. (1996). Integrated approaches to preventing antisocial behavior patterns among school-age children and youth. *Journal of Emotional and Behavioral Disorders, 4,* 194–209.

Walker, L. J. (1991). Sex differences in moral reasoning. In W. M. Kurtines & J. L. Gewirtz (Eds.), *Handbook of moral behavior and development: Vol. 2. Research* (pp. 333–364). Hillsdale, NJ: Erlbaum.

Walker, L. J. (1995). Sexism in Kohlberg's moral psychology? In W. M. Kurtines & J. L. Gewirtz (Eds.), *Moral development: An introduction* (pp. 83–107). Boston, MA: Allyn & Bacon.

Walker, L. J. (2006). Gender and morality. In M. Killen & J. G. Smetana (Eds.), *Handbook of moral development* (pp. 93–115). Mahwah, NJ: Erlbaum.

Walker, L. J., & Reimer, K. S. (2006). The relationship between moral and spiritual development. In E. C. Roehlkepartain, P. E. King, L. Wagener, & P. L. Benson (Eds.), *The handbook of spiritual development in childhood and adolescence* (pp. 224–238). Thousand Oaks, CA:

Walker, S. (2009). Sociometric stability and the behavioral correlates of peer acceptance in early childhood. *The Journal of Genetic Psychology: Research and Theory on Human Development, 170*(4), 339–358. doi:10.1080/00221320903218364

Walker, S. P., Wachs, T. D., Gardner, J. M., Lozoff, B., Wasserman, G. A., Pollitt, et al. (2007). Child development: Risks factors for adverse outcomes in developing countries. *Lancet, 369*(9556), 145–157.

Walkley, M., & Cox, T. L. (2013). Building trauma-informed schools and communities. *Children & Schools, 35*(2), 123–126.

Wallander, J. L., Eggert, K. M., & Gilbert, K. K. (2004). Adolescent health-related issues. In R. T. Brown (Ed.), *Handbook of pediatric psychology in school settings* (pp. 503–520). Mahwah, NJ: Erlbaum.

Wallerstein, J. S., & Kelly, J. B. (1980). *Surviving the break-up: How children and parents cope with divorce.* New York, NY: Basic Books.

Wallerstein, J., & Lewis, J. M. (2007). Sibling outcomes and disparate parenting and stepparenting after divorce: Report from a 10-year longitudinal study. *Psychoanalytic Psychology, 24*(3), 445–458.

Wallingford, J., Niswander, L., Shaw, G., & Finnell, R. (2013). The continuing challenge of understanding, preventing, and treating neural tube defects. *Science, 339*(6123), 1047. doi:10.1002/bdra.20676

Walsh, E. M. (2013). An examination of climate scientists' participation in education: Implications for supporting the teaching and learning of socially controversial science. *Dissertation Abstracts International Section A, 73.*

Walters, G. C., & Grusec, J. E. (1977). *Punishment.* San Francisco, CA: Freeman.

Wang, H., & Olson, N. (2009). *A journey to unlearn and learn in multicultural education.* New York, NY: Peter Lang.

Wang, J., & Lin, E. (2005). Comparative studies on U.S. and Chinese mathematics learning and the implications for standards-based mathematics teaching reform. *Educational Researcher, 34*(5), 3–13.

Wang, M., & Eccles, J. (2013). School context, achievement motivation, and academic engagement: A longitudinal study of school engagement using a multidimensional perspective. *Learning & Instruction, 28,* 12–23. doi:10.1016/j.learninstruc.2013.04.002

Wang, P. P., & Baron, M. A. (1997). Language and communication: Development and disorders. In M. L. Batshaw (Ed.), *Children with disabilities* (4th ed.). Baltimore, MD: Paul H. Brookes.

Wang, Q. (2006). Culture and the development of self-knowledge. *Current Directions in Psychological Science, 15,* 182–187.

Wang, Q. (2013). *The autobiographical self in time and culture.* New York, NY: Oxford University Press. doi:10.1093/acprof:oso/9780199737833.001.0001

Wang, Q., & Pomerantz, E. M. (2009). The motivational landscape of early adolescence in the United States and China: A longitudinal investigation. *Child Development, 80*(4), 1272–1287.

Wang, Q., & Ross, M. (2007). Culture and memory. In S. Kitayama & D. Cohen (Eds.), *Handbook of cultural psychology* (pp. 645–667). New York, NY: Guilford Press.

Wang, T.-H. (2010). Web-based dynamic assessment: Taking assessment as teaching and learning strategy for improving students' e-learning effectiveness. *Computers and Education, 5,* 1157–1166.

Wang, Y., & Lim, H. (2012). The global childhood obesity epidemic and the association between socio-economic status and childhood obesity. *International Review of Psychiatry, 24*(3), 176–188. doi:10.3109/09540261.2012.688195

Wang, Z., & Deater-Deckard, K. (2013). Resilience in gene–environment transactions. In S. Goldstein, R. B. Brooks (Eds.), *Handbook of resilience in children* (2nd ed., pp. 57–72). New York, NY: Springer Science + Business Media. doi:10.1007/978-1-4614-3661-4_4

Ward, R. A., & Spitze, G. (1998). Sandwiched marriages: The implications of child and parent relations for marital quality in midlife. *Social Forces, 77,* 647–666.

Ward, S., & Parker, M. (2013). The voice of youth: atmosphere in positive youth development program. *Physical Education & Sport Pedagogy, 18*(5), 534–548. doi:10.1080/17408989.2012.726974

Ward, T., & Durrant, R. (2011). Evolutionary psychology and the rehabilitation of offenders: Constraints and consequences. *Aggression and Violent Behavior.* doi:10.1016/j.avb.2011.02.011

Warming, H. (2011). Getting under their skins? Accessing young children's perspectives through ethnographic fieldwork. *Childhood: A Global Journal of Child Research, 18*(1), 39–53. doi:10.1177/0907568210364666

Warnick, B., Johnson, B., & Rocha, S. (2010). Tragedy and the Meaning of School Shootings. *Educational Theory, 60*(3), 371–390.

Warton, P. M., & Goodnow, J. J. (1991). The nature of responsibility: Children's understanding of "your job." *Child Development, 62,* 156–165.

Wasik, B. A., & Bond, M. A. (2001). Beyond the pages of a book: Interactive book reading and language development in preschool classrooms. *Journal of Educational Psychology, 93,* 243–250.

Wasik, B. A., Karweit, N., Burns, L., & Brodsky, E. (1998, April). *Once upon a time: The role of rereading and retelling in storybook reading.* Paper presented at the annual meeting of the American Educational Research Association, San Diego, CA.

Water Educational Training Science Project. (2010). *Wet science lesson #6: There is acid in my rain!* Retrieved from http://www.cloudnet.com/~edrbsass/edsci.htm#wetlands

Waterhouse, L. (2006). Multiple intelligences, the Mozart Effect, and Emotional Intelligence: A critical review. *Educational Psychologist, 41*(4), 207–225. doi:10.1207/s15326985ep4104_1

Waterhouse, L., & Gillberg, C. (2014). Why autism must be taken apart. *Journal of Autism & Developmental Disorders, 44*(7), 1788–1792. doi:10.1007/s10803-013-2030-5

Waters, E., Merrick, S., Treboux, D., Crowell, J., & Albersheim, L. (2000). Attachment security in infancy and early adulthood: A twenty-year longitudinal study. *Child Development, 71,* 684–689.

Waters, H. S. (1982). Memory development in adolescence: Relationships between metamemory, strategy use, and performance. *Journal of Experimental Child Psychology, 33,* 183–195.

Waters, H., & Waters, T. A. (2010). Bird experts: A study of child and adult knowledge utilization. In H. Waters & W. Schneider (Eds.), *Metacognition, strategy use, and instruction* (pp. 113-134). New York, NY: Guilford Press.

Waters, N. (2013). What goes up must come down! A primary care approach to preventing injuries amongst highflying cheerleaders. *Journal of the American Academy of Nurse Practitioners, 25*(2), 55–64. doi:10.1111/1745-7599.12000

Waters, S. F., Virmani, E. A., Thompson, R. A., Meyer, S., Raikes, H. A., & Jochem, R. (2010). Emotion regulation and attachment: Unpacking two constructs and their association. *Journal of Psychopathology and Behavioral Assessment, 32*(1), 37–47.

Watkins, M. W., & Beaujean, A. (2013). Bifactor structure of the Wechsler Preschool and Primary Scale of Intelligence—Fourth Edition. *School Psychology Quarterly.* doi:10.1037/spq0000038

Watson, M., & Battistich, V. (2006). Building and sustaining caring communities. In C. M. Evertson & C. S. Weinstein (Eds.), *Handbook of classroom management: Research, practice, and contemporary issues* (pp. 253–279). Mahwah, NJ: Erlbaum.

Waxman, S., Fu, X., Arunachalam, S., Leddon, E., Geraghty, K., & Song, H. (2013). Are nouns learned before verbs? Infants provide insight into a longstanding debate. *Child Development Perspectives, 7*(3), 155-159. doi:10.1111/cdep.12032

Way, N. (1998). *Everyday courage: The lives and stories of urban teenagers.* New York, NY: New York University Press.

Weaver-Hightower, M. (2003). The "boy turn" in research on gender and education. *Review of Educational Research, 73,* 471–498.

Webb, N. M., & Farivar, S. (1994). Promoting helping behavior in cooperative small groups in middle school mathematics. *American Educational Research Journal, 31,* 369–395.

Webb, N. M., & Palincsar, A. S. (1996). Group processes in the classroom. In D. C. Berliner & R. C. Calfee (Eds.), *Handbook of educational psychology (pp. 841-873).* New York, NY: Macmillan.

Webber, J., Scheuermann, B., McCall, C., & Coleman, M. (1993). Research on self-monitoring as a behavior management technique in special education classrooms: A descriptive review. *Remedial and Special Education, 14*(2), 38–56.

Wechsler, D. (2002). *Wechsler Preschool and Primary Scale of Intelligence–Third Edition.* San Antonio, TX: Psychological Corporation.

Wechsler, D. (2003). *Wechsler Intelligence Scale for Children* (4th ed.). San Antonio, TX: Psychological Corporation.

Wechsler, D. (2012). *Wechsler Preschool and Primary Scale of Intelligence—fourth edition technical manual and interpretive manual.* San Antonio, TX: Psychological Corporation.

Weeks, T. L., & Pasupathi, M. (2010). Autonomy, identity, and narrative construction with parents and friends. In K. C. McLean, & M. Pasupathi (Eds.), *Narrative development in adolescence: Creating the storied self. Advancing responsible adolescent development* (pp. 65–91). New York, NY: Springer Science + Business Media. doi:10.1007/978-0-387-89825-4_4

Weinberg, R. A. (1989). Intelligence and IQ: Landmark issues and great debates. *American Psychologist, 44,* 98–104.

Weiner, B. (1984). Principles for a theory of student motivation and their application within an attributional framework. In R. Ames & C. Ames (Eds.), *Research on motivation in education: Vol. 1. Student motivation.* San Diego, CA: Academic Press.

Weiner, B. (1986). *An attributional theory of motivation and emotion.* New York, NY: Springer-Verlag.

Weiner, B. (2000). Intrapersonal and interpersonal theories of motivation from an attributional perspective. *Educational Psychology Review, 12,* 1–14.

Weiner, B. (2004). Attribution theory revisited: Transforming cultural plurality into theoretical unity. In D. M. McNerney & S. Van Etten (Eds.), *Big theories revisited* (pp. 13–29). Greenwich, CT: Information Age.

Weinert, S. (2009). Implicit and explicit modes of learning: Similarities and differences from a developmental perspective. *Linguistics, 47*(2), 241–271.

Weinstein, C. E., Ridley, D., & Dahl, T. (1988). Helping students develop strategies for effective learning. *Educational Leadership, 46,* 17–19.

Weinstein, R. S. (1993). Children's knowledge of differential treatment in school: Implications for motivation. In T. M. Tomlinson (Ed.), *Motivating students to learn: Overcoming barriers to high achievement.* Berkeley, CA: McCutchan.

Weinstein, R. S., Madison, S. M., & Kuklinski, M. R. (1995). Raising expectations in schooling: Obstacles and opportunities for change. *American Educational Research Journal, 32,* 121–159.

Weisgram, E. S., Bigler, R. S., & Liben, L. S. (2010). Gender, values, and occupational interests among children, adolescents, and adults. *Child Development, 81*(3), 778–796. doi:10.1111/j.1467-8624.2010.01433.x

Weisleder, A., & Fernald, A. (2013). Talking to children matters: Early language experience strengthens processing and builds vocabulary. *Psychological Science, 24*(11), 2143–2152. doi:10.1177/0956797613488145

Weisner, T. S., & Gallimore, R. (1977). My brother's keeper: Child and sibling caregiving. *Current Anthropology, 18,* 169–190.

Weissbourd, R. (2011). The overpressured student. *Educational Leadership, 68*(5), 22–27.

Wellman, H. M. (1990). *The child's theory of mind.* Cambridge, MA: MIT Press.

Wellman, H. M., & Estes, D. (1986). Early understanding of mental entities: A reexamination of childhood realism. *Child Development, 57,* 910–923.

Wellman, H. M., & Gelman, S. A. (1998). Knowledge acquisition in foundational domains. In W. Damon (Series Ed.), & D. Kuhn & R. S. Siegler (Vol. Eds.), *Handbook of child psychology: Vol. 2. Cognition, perception, and language* (5th ed., pp. 523–573). New York, NY: Wiley.

Wellman, H. M., & Hickling, A. K. (1994). The mind's "I": Children's conception of the mind as an active agent. *Child Development, 65,* 1564–1580.

Wellman, H. M., Cross, D., & Watson, J. (2001). Meta-analysis of theory-of-mind development: The truth about false belief. *Child Development, 72,* 655–684.

Wellman, H. M., Fang, F., Liu, D., Zhu, L., & Zhu, G. (2006). Scaling of theory-of-mind understandings in Chinese children. *Psychological Science, 17,* 1075–1081.

Wellman, H. M., Phillips, A. T., & Rodriguez, T. (2000). Young children's understanding of perception, desire, and emotion. *Child Development, 71,* 895–912.

Welsh, M. C. (1991). Rule-guided behavior and self-monitoring on the tower of Hanoi disk-transfer task. *Cognitive Development, 4,* 59–76.

Welsh, M. G. (2011). Growing up in a same-sex parented family: The adolescent voice of experience. *Journal of GLBT Family Studies, 7*(1–2), 49–71. doi:10.1080/1550428X.2010.537241

Wen, M. (2008). Family structure and children's health and behavior. *Journal of Family Issues, 29*(11), 1492–1519.

Wentzel, K. R. (1999). Social-motivational processes and interpersonal relationships: Implications for understanding motivation at school. *Journal of Educational Psychology, 91,* 76–97.

Wentzel, K. R. (2000). What is it that I'm trying to achieve? Classroom goals from a content perspective. *Contemporary Educational Psychology, 25,* 105–115.

Wentzel, K. R. (2009). Peers and academic functioning at school. In K. H. Rubin, W. M. Bukowski, & B. Laursen (Eds.), *Handbook of peer interactions, relationships, and groups. Social, emotional, and personality development in context* (pp. 531–547). New York: Guilford Press.

Wentzel, K. R. (2014). Prosocial behavior and peer relations in adolescence. In L. M. Padilla-Walker, G. Carlo (Eds.), *Prosocial development: A multidimensional approach* (pp. 178–200). New York, NY: Oxford University Press.

Wentzel, K. R., & Wigfield, A. (1998). Academic and social motivational influences on students' academic performance. *Educational Psychology Review, 10,* 155–175.

Werbner, P. (2009). The hidden lion: Tswapong girls' puberty rituals and the problem of history. *American Ethnologist, 36*(3), 441–458.

Werker, J. F., & Lalonde, C. E. (1988). Cross-language speech perception: Initial capabilities and developmental change. *Developmental Psychology, 24,* 672–683.

Werker, J. F., & Tees, R. C. (1999). Influences on infant speech processing: Toward a new synthesis. *Annual Review of Psychology, 50,* 509–535.

Werker, J. F., & Tees, R. C. (1999). Influences on infant speech processing: Toward a new synthesis. *Annual Review of Psychology, 50,* 509–535.

Werker, J. F., Maurer, D. M., & Yoshida, K. A. (2010). Perception. In M. H. Bornstein (Ed.), *Handbook of cultural developmental science* (pp. 89–125). New York, NY: Psychology Press.

Werner, E. E., & Smith, R. S. (2001). *Journeys from childhood to midlife: Risk, resilience, and recovery.* Ithaca, NY: Cornell University Press.

Wery, J., & Thomson, M. (2013). Motivational strategies to enhance effective learning in teaching struggling students. *Support for Learning, 28*(3), 103–108. doi:10.1111/1467-9604.12027

Wesley, M. J., & Bickel, W. K. (2013). Remember the future ii: Meta-analyses and functional overlap of working memory and delay discounting. *Biological Psychiatry.* doi:10.1016/j.biopsych.2013.08.008

West, A. E., & Weinstein, S. M. (2012). Bipolar disorder: School-based cognitive-behavioral interventions. In R. B. Mennuti, R. W. Christner, & A. Freeman (Eds.), *Cognitive-behavioral interventions in educational settings: A handbook for practice* (2nd ed., pp. 239–274). New York, NY: Routledge/Taylor & Francis Group.

Wheeler, S. (2014). Organised activities, educational activities and family activities: How do they feature in the middle-class family's weekend? *Leisure Studies, 33*(2), 215–232. doi:10.1080/02614367.2013.833972

White, B. A., Jarrett, M. A., & Ollendick, T. H. (2013). Self-regulation deficits explain the link between reactive aggression and internalizing and externalizing behavior problems in children. *Journal of Psychopathology and Behavioral Assessment, 35*(1), 1–9. doi:10.1007/s10862-012-9310-9

White, B. Y., & Frederiksen, J. (2005). A theoretical framework and approach for fostering metacognitive development. *Educational Psychologist, 40,* 211–223.

White, B. Y., & Frederiksen, J. R. (1998). Inquiry, modeling, and metacognition: Making science accessible to all students. *Cognition and Instruction, 16,* 3–118.

White, R. (1959). Motivation reconsidered: The concept of competence. *Psychological Review, 66,* 297–333.

White, S., Brislin, S., Sinclair, S., Fowler, K., Pope, K., & Blair, R. (2013). The relationship between large cavum septum pellucidum and antisocial behavior, callous-unemotional traits and psychopathy in adolescents. *Journal of Child Psychology & Psychiatry, 54*(5), 575–581.

Whitehead, D., & Murphy, F. (2014). Mind Your Language. *Journal of Adolescent & Adult Literacy, 57*(6), 492–502. doi:10.1002/jaal.272

Whitehurst, G. J., Arnold, D. S., Epstein, J. N., Angell, A. L., Smith, M., & Fischel, J. E. (1994). A picture book reading intervention in day care and home for children from low-income families. *Developmental Psychology, 30,* 679–689.

Whiting, B. B., & Edwards, C. P. (1988). *Children of different worlds*. Cambridge, MA: Harvard University Press.

Whiting, B. B., & Whiting, J. W. M. (1975). *Children of six cultures: A psycho-cultural analysis*. Cambridge, MA: Harvard University Press.

Whitley, B. E., Jr., & Frieze, I. H. (1985). Children's causal attributions for success and failure in achievement settings: A meta-analysis. *Journal of Educational Psychology, 77*, 608–616.

Wiebler, L. R. (2013). Developmental differences in response to trauma. In E. Rossen & R. Hull (Eds.), *Supporting and educating traumatized students: A guide for school-based professionals* (pp. 37–47). New York, NY: Oxford University Press.

Wieder, S., Greenspan, S., & Kalmanson, B. (2008). Autism assessment and intervention: The developmental individual-difference, relationship-based DIR®/Floortime™ model. *Zero to Three, 28*(4), 31–37.

Wigfield, A. (1994). Expectancy-value theory of achievement motivation: A developmental perspective. *Educational Psychology Review, 6*, 49–78.

Wigfield, A., & Eccles, J. (2000). Expectancy-value theory of achievement motivation. *Contemporary Educational Psychology, 25*, 68–81.

Wigfield, A., Byrnes, J. P., & Eccles, J. S. (2006). Development during early and middle adolescence. In P. A. Alexander & P. H. Winne (Eds.), *Handbook of educational psychology* (2nd ed., pp. 87–113). Mahwah, NJ: Erlbaum.

Wigfield, A., Eccles, J. S., & Pintrich, P. R. (1996). Development between the ages of 11 and 25. In D. C. Berliner & R. C. Calfee (Eds.), *Handbook of educational psychology (pp. 148–185)*. New York, NY: Macmillan.

Wigfield, A., Eccles, J. S., & Pintrich, P. R. (1996). Development between the ages of 11 and 25. In D. C. Berliner & R. C. Calfee (Eds.), *Handbook of educational psychology*. New York, NY: Macmillan.

Wigfield, A., Eccles, J. S., & Pintrich, P. R. (1996). Development between the ages of 11 and 25. In D. C. Berliner & R. C. Calfee (Eds.), *Handbook of educational psychology* (pp. 148–185). New York, NY.

Wigfield, A., Eccles, J., Mac Iver, D., Reuman, D., & Midgley, C. (1991). Transitions at early adolescence: Changes in children's domain-specific self-perceptions and general self-esteem across the transition to junior high school. *Developmental Psychology, 27*, 552–565.

Wigfield, A., Tonks, S., & Eccles, J. S. (2004). Expectancy value theory in cross-cultural perspective. In D. M. McNerney & S. Van Etten (Eds.), *Big theories revisited* (pp. 165–198). Greenwich, CT: Information Age.

Wiggins, G. (2012). 7 keys to effective feedback. *Educational Leadership, 70*(1), 10–16.

Wiig, E. H., Gilbert, M. F., & Christian, S. H. (1978). Developmental sequences in perception and interpretation of ambiguous sentences. *Perceptual and Motor Skills, 46*, 959–969.

Wilcox, S. (1994). Struggling for a voice: An interactionist view of language and literacy in Deaf education. In V. John-Steiner, C. P. Panofsky, & L. W. Smith (Eds.), *Sociocultural approaches to language and literacy: An interactionist perspective*. Cambridge, England: Cambridge University Press.

Wilhelm, J., Jackson, C., Sullivan, A., & Wilhelm, R. (2013). Examining differences between preteen groups' spatial-scientific understandings: A quasi-experimental study. *Journal of Educational Research, 106*(5), 337–351. doi:10.1080/00220671.2012.753

Wilk, B., Pender, N., Volterman, K., Bar-Or, O., & Timmons, B. W. (2013). Influence of pubertal stage on local sweating patterns of girls exercising in the heat. *Pediatric Exercise Science, 25*(2), 212–220.

Willard, N. E. (2007). *Cyberbullying and cyberthreats: Responding to the challenge of online social aggression, threats, and distress*. Champaign, IL: Research Press.

Willats, J. (1995). An information-processing approach to drawing development. In C. Lange-Kuttner & G. V. Thomas (Eds.), *Drawing and looking: Theoretical approaches to pictorial representation in children* (pp. 27–43). New York, NY: Harvester Wheatsheaf.

Willatts, P. (1990). Development of problem solving strategies in infancy. In D. F. Bjorklund (Ed.), *Children's strategies* (pp. 23–66). Hillsdale, NJ: Erlbaum.

Willcock, E., Imuta, K., & Hayne, H. (2011). Children's human figure drawings do not measure intellectual ability. *Journal of Experimental Child Psychology, 110*(3), 444–452. doi:10.1016/j.jecp.2011.04.013

Williams, H. L., & Conway, M. A. (2009). Networks of autobiographical memories. In P. Boyer & J. V. Wertsch (Eds.), *Memory in mind and culture* (pp. 33–61). New York, NY: Cambridge University Press.

Williams, J. L., & Smalls-Glover, C. (2014). Content and attributions of caregiver racial socialization as predictors of African American adolescents' private racial regard. *Journal of Black Psychology, 40*(1), 69–80. doi:10.1177/0095798412471681

Williams, J., & Bryan, J. (2013). Overcoming adversity: High-achieving African American youth's perspectives on educational resilience. *Journal of Counseling & Development, 91*(3), 291–300.

Williams, J., & Williamson, K. (1992). "I wouldn't want to shoot nobody": The out-of-school curriculum as described by urban students. *Action in Teacher Education, 14*(2), 9–15.

Williams, K. E., Ciarrochi, J., & Heaven, P. L. (2012). Inflexible parents, inflexible kids: A 6-year longitudinal study of parenting style and the development of psychological flexibility in adolescents. *Journal of Youth and Adolescence, 41*(8), 1053–1066. doi:10.1007/s10964-012-9744-0

Williams, K. M. (2001). What derails peer mediation? In J. N. Burstyn, G. Bender, R. Casella, H. W. Gordon, D. P. Guerra, K. V. Luschen, Stevens, R., & Williams, K. M. (Eds.), *Preventing violence in schools: A challenge to American democracy* (pp. 199–208). Mahwah, NJ: Erlbaum.

Williams, R. L. (2013). Overview of the Flynn effect. *Intelligence, 41*(6), 753–764. doi:10.1016/j.intell.2013.04.010

Williams, R. W., & Herrup, K. (1998). The control of neuron number. *Annual Review of Neuroscience, 11*, 423–453.

Williams, T. T., & Sánchez, B. (2013). Identifying and decreasing barriers to parent involvement for inner-city parents. *Youth & Society, 45*(1), 54–74. doi:10.1177/0044118X11409066

Williams, T. T., Mance, G., Caldwell, C., & Antonucci, T. C. (2012). The role of prenatal stress and maternal emotional support on the postpartum depressive symptoms of African American adolescent fathers. *Journal of Black Psychology, 38*(4), 455–470. doi:10.1177/0095798411433842

Williford, A. P., Whittaker, J., Vitiello, V. E., & Downer, J. T. (2013). Children's engagement within the preschool classroom and their development of self-regulation. *Early Education and Development, 24*(2), 162–187. doi:10.1080/10409289.2011.628270

Willingham, D. (2012). Why does family wealth affect learning? *American Educator, 36*(1), 33–39.

Wilson, B. (1997). Types of child art and alternative developmental accounts: Interpreting the interpreters. *Human Development, 40*, 155–168.

Wilson, B. J. (2008). Media and children's aggression, fear, and altruism. *Future of Children, 18*(1), 87–118.

Wilson, B. L., & Corbett, H. D. (2001). *Listening to urban kids: School reform and the teachers they want*. Albany, NY: State University of New York Press.

Wilson, C., Robertson, S. J., Herlong, L. H., & Haynes, S. N. (1979). Vicarious effects of time-out in the modification of aggression in the classroom. *Behavior Modification, 3*(1), 97–111. doi:10.1177/014544557931006

Wilson, D. K., Nicholson, S. C., & Krishnamoorthy, J. S. (1998). The role of diet in minority adolescent health promotion. In D. K. Wilson, J. R. Rodrigue, & W. C. Taylor (Eds.), *Health-promoting and health-compromising behaviors among minority adolescents* (pp. 129–151). Washington, DC: American Psychological Association.

Wilson, D. M. (2012). Struggling in suburbia. *Teaching Tolerance, 42*, 40–43.

Wilson, H. K., Pianta, R. C., & Stuhlman, M. (2007). Typical classroom experiences in first grade: The role of classroom climate and functional risk in the development of social competencies. *Elementary School Journal, 108*(2), 81–96.

Wilson, L. (2007). Great American schools: The power of culture and passion. *Educational Horizons, 86*(1), 33–44.

Wimmer, H., & Perner, J. (1983). Beliefs about beliefs: Representation and constraining function of wrong beliefs in young children's understanding of deception. *Cognition, 13*, 103–128.

Wimmer, M. C., & Howe, M. L. (2009). The development of automatic associative processes and children's false memories. *Journal of Experimental Child Psychology, 104*, 447–465.

Winberg, J. (2005). Mother and newborn baby: Mutual regulation of physiology and behavior—A selective review. *Developmental Psychobiology, 47*, 219–229.

Winkler-Rhoades, N., Carey, S. C., & Spelke, E. S. (2013). Two-year-old children interpret abstract, purely geometric maps. *Developmental Science, 16*(3), 365–376. doi:10.1111/desc.12038

Winne, P. H. (1995a). Inherent details in self-regulated learning. *Educational Psychologist, 30*, 173–187.

Winne, P. H. (1995b). Self-regulation is ubiquitous but its forms vary with knowledge. *Educational Psychologist, 30*, 223–228.

Winner, E. (1997). Exceptionally high intelligence and schooling. *American Psychologist, 52*, 1070–1081.

Winner, E. (2000). The origins and ends of giftedness. *American Psychologist, 55*, 159–169.

Winner, E. (2006). Development in the arts: Drawing and music. In D. Kuhn, R. S. Siegler, W. Damon, & R. M. Lerner (Eds.), *Handbook of child psychology: Vol. 2, Cognition, perception, and language* (6th ed., pp. 859–904). Hoboken, NJ: John Wiley & Sons.

Winsler, A., & Naglieri, J. (2003). Overt and covert verbal problem-solving strategies: Developmental trends in use, awareness, and relations with task performance in children aged 5 to 17. *Child Development, 74*, 659–678.

Winsler, A., Díaz, R. M., Espinosa, L., & Rodriguez, J. L. (1999). When learning a second language does not mean losing the first: Bilingual language development in low-income, Spanish-speaking children attending bilingual preschool. *Child Development, 70*, 349–362.

Winston, P. (1973). Learning to identify toy block structures. In R. L. Solso (Ed.), *Contemporary issues in cognitive psychology: The Loyola Symposium*. Washington, DC: V. H. Winston.

Winterdyk, J., & Ruddell, R. (2010). Managing prison gangs: Results from a survey of U.S. prison systems. *Journal of Criminal Justice, 38*(4), 730–736. doi:10.1016/j.jcrimjus.2010.04.047

Witkow, M. R., & Fuligni, A. J. (2007). Achievement goals and daily school experiences among adolescents with Asian, Latino, and European American backgrounds. *Journal of Educational Psychology, 99,* 584–596.

Witt, A., & Vinter, A. (2013). Children with intellectual disabilities may be impaired in encoding and recollecting incidental information. *Research in Developmental Disabilities, 34*(2), 864–871. doi:10.1016/j.ridd.2012.11.003

Wittmer, D. (2012). The wonder and complexity of infant and toddler peer relationships. *Young Children, 67*(4), 16–25.

Wittmer, D. S., & Honig, A. S. (1994). Encouraging positive social development in young children. *Young Children, 49*(5), 4–12.

Witvliet, M., van Lier, P. A. C., Cuijpers, P., & Koot, H. M. (2010). Change and stability in childhood clique membership, isolation from cliques, and associated child characteristics. *Journal of Clinical Child and Adolescent Psychology, 39*(1), 12–24. doi:10.1080/15374410903401161

Wodrich, D. L., Tarbox, J., Balles, J., & Gorin, J. (2010). Medical diagnostic consultation concerning mental retardation: An analogue study of school psychologists' attitudes. *Psychology in the Schools, 47*(3), 246–256.

Wolcott, H. F. (1999). *Ethnography: A way of seeing.* Walnut Creek, CA: AltMira.

Wolf, M., & Bowers, P. G. (1999). The double-deficit hypothesis for the developmental dyslexias. *Journal of Educational Psychology, 91,* 415–438.

Wolfe, D. A., & Wekerle, C. (1997). Pathways to violence in teen dating relationships. In D. Cicchetti & S. L. Toth (Eds.), Developmental perspectives on trauma: Theory, research, and intervention. *Rochester Symposium on Developmental Psychology, 8,* 315–341. Rochester, NY: University of Rochester Press.

Wolfe, M. B. W., & Goldman, S. R. (2005). Relations between adolescents' text processing and reasoning. *Cognition and Instruction, 23,* 467–502.

Wolff, P. G. (1966). The causes, controls, and organization of behavior in the neonate. *Psychological Issues, 5*(1, Serial No. 17).

Wolfson, A. R., & Carskadon, M. A. (2005). A survey of factors influencing high school start times. *NASSP Bulletin, 89*(642), 47–66.

Wolke, D. D., Lereya, S. T., Fisher, H. L., Lewis, G. G., & Zammit, S. S. (2014). Bullying in elementary school and psychotic experiences at 18 years: A longitudinal, population-based cohort study. *Psychological Medicine, 44*(10), 2199–2211. doi:10.1017/S0033291713002912

Wolock, I., Sherman, P., Feldman, L. H., & Metzger, B. (2001). Child abuse and neglect referral patterns: A longitudinal study. *Children and Youth Services Review, 23,* 21–47.

Wong, H., & Edwards, P. (2013). Nature or nurture: A systematic review of the effect of socio-economic status on the developmental and cognitive outcomes of children born preterm. *Maternal & Child Health Journal, 17*(9), 1689–1700. doi:10.1007/s10995-012-1183-8

Wong, S. C. (1993). Promises, pitfalls, and principles of text selection in curricular diversification: The Asian-American case. In T. Perry & J. W. Fraser (Eds.), *Freedom's plow: Teaching in the multicultural classroom.* New York, NY: Routledge.

Wong-Lo, M., & Bai, H. (2013). Recommended practices: Cultivating a culturally responsive learning environment for Chinese immigrants and Chinese American students. *Preventing School Failure, 57*(1), 17–21. doi:10.1080/1045988X.2013.731272

Wood, A. C., Saudino, K. J., Rogers, H., Asherson, P., & Kuntsi, J. (2007). Genetic influences on mechanically-assessed activity level in children. *Journal of Child Psychology and Psychiatry, 48,* 695–702.

Wood, A., & Wood, B. (2001). *Alphabet adventure.* New York: Scholastic Books.

Wood, C. (2007). *Yardsticks: Children in the classroom ages 4—14.* Turner Falls, MA: Northeast Foundation for Children, Inc.

Wood, C., Kemp, N., Waldron, S., & Hart, L. (2014). Grammatical understanding, literacy and text messaging in school children and undergraduate students: A concurrent analysis. *Computers & Education, 70,* 281–290. doi:10.1016/j.compedu.2013.09.003

Wood, D., Bruner, J. S., & Ross, G. (1976). The role of tutoring in problem-solving. *Journal of Child Psychology and Psychiatry, 17,* 89–100.

Wood, J. W. (1998). *Adapting instruction to accommodate students in inclusive settings* (3rd ed.). Upper Saddle River, NJ: Merrill/Prentice Hall.

Wood, M. B., Olson, A. M., Freiberg, E. J., & Vega, R. I. (2013). Fractions as subtraction: An activity-oriented perspective from elementary children. *School Science & Mathematics, 113*(8), 390–399. doi:10.1111/ssm.12040

Woods, A., Graber, K., & Daum, D. (2012). Children's recess physical activity: Movement patterns and preferences. *Journal of Teaching in Physical Education, 31*(2), 146–162.

Woodson, J. (2009). *Peace, Locomotion.* New York, NY: G.P. Putnam's Sons.

Woodward, A. L., Markman, E. M., & Fitzsimmons, C. M. (1994). Rapid word learning in 13- and 18-month-olds. *Developmental Psychology, 30,* 553–566.

Woody, J. D., D'Souza, H. J., & Russel, R. (2003). Emotions and motivations in first adolescent intercourse: An exploratory study based on object relations theory. *Canadian Journal of Human Sexuality, 12*(1), 35–51.

Woolley, J. D. (1995). The fictional mind: Young children's understanding of pretense, imagination, and dreams. *Developmental Review, 15,* 172–211.

World Health Organization. (2000). *Obesity: Preventing and managing the global epidemic* (WHO Report No. 894). Geneva: Author.

Worley, J. (2012). To speak in a clear voice. *Tribal College Journal, 23*(3), 60–61.

Wouters, S., Doumen, S., Germeijs, V., Colpin, H., & Verschueren, K. (2013). Contingencies of self-worth in early adolescence: The antecedent role of perceived parenting. *Social Development, 22*(2), 242–258. doi:10.1111/sode.12010

Wright, B. C., & Mahfoud, J. (2012). A child-centred exploration of the relevance of family and friends to theory of mind development. *Scandinavian Journal of Psychology, 53*(1), 32–40. doi:10.1111/j.1467-9450.2011.00920.x

Wright, R. (2009). Methods for improving test scores: The good, the bad, and the ugly. *Kappa Delta Pi Record, 45*(3), 116–121.

WritersCorps. (2003). *Paint me like I am: Teen poems from WritersCorps.* New York, NY: HarperTempest.

Wu, H., & Chu, S. (2012). Self-determination of young children with special needs from culturally and linguistically diverse backgrounds. *Preventing School Failure, 56*(3), 149–156. doi:10.1080/1045988X.2011.619221

Wu, P., Liu, X., & Fan, B. (2010). Factors associated with initiation of ecstasy use among US adolescents: Findings from a national survey. *Drug and Alcohol Dependence, 106*(2-3), 193–198.

Wu, R., Gopnik, A., Richardson, D. C., & Kirkham, N. Z. (2011). Infants learn about objects from statistics and people. *Developmental Psychology, 47*(5), 1220–1229. doi:10.1037/a0024023

Wu, W., West, S. G., & Hughes, J. N. (2010). Effect of grade retention in first grade on psychosocial outcomes. *Journal of Educational Psychology, 102*(1), 135–152.

Wulczyn, F. (2009). Epidemiological perspectives on maltreatment prevention. *Future of Children, 19*(2), 39–66.

Wynbrandt, J., & Ludman, M. D. (2000). *The encyclopedia of genetic disorders and birth defects* (2nd ed.). New York, NY: Facts on File.

Wynn, K. (1990). Children's understanding of counting. *Cognition, 36,* 155–193.

Wynn, K. (1992). Addition and subtraction by human infants. *Nature, 358,* 749–750.

Wynn, K. (1995). Infants possess a system of numerical knowledge. *Current Directions in Psychological Science, 4,* 172–177.

Xie, Y., & Reider, D. (2014). Integration of innovative technologies for enhancing students' motivation for science learning and career. *Journal of Science Education & Technology, 23*(3), 370–380. doi:10.1007/s10956-013-9469-1

Xu, F., & Kushnir, T. (2013). Infants are rational constructivist learners. *Current Directions in Psychological Science, 22*(1), 28–32.

Xu, F., & Spelke, E. S. (2000). Large number discrimination in 6-month-old infants. *Cognition, 74,* B1–B11.

Xu, L., & Clarke, D. (2012). What does distributed cognition tell us about student learning of science? *Research in Science Education, 42*(3), 491–510. doi:10.1007/s11165-011-9207-8

Xu, M.-Q., Sun, W.-S., Liu, B. X., Feng, G.-Y., Yu, L., Yang, L., et al. (2009). Prenatal malnutrition and adult schizophrenia: Further evidence from the 1959–1961 Chinese famine. *Schizophrenia Bulletin, 35*(3), 568–576.

Xu, Y., Farver, J. A. M., Chang, L., Zhang, Z., & Yu, L. (2007). Moving away or fitting in? understanding shyness in Chinese children. *Merrill-Palmer Quarterly: Journal of Developmental Psychology, 53*(4), 527–556.

Xue, J. J., Ooh, J. J., & Magiati, I. I. (2014). Family functioning in Asian families raising children with autism spectrum disorders: The role of capabilities and positive meanings. *Journal of Intellectual Disability Research, 58*(5), 406–420. doi:10.1111/jir.12034

Yaden, D. B., Jr., & Templeton, S. (Eds.). (1986). *Metalinguistic awareness and beginning literacy: Conceptualizing what it means to read and write.* Portsmouth, NH: Heinemann.

Yakovlev, P. I., & Lecours, A. R. (1967). The myelogenetic cycles of regional maturation of the brain. In A. Minkowski (Ed.), *Regional development of the brain in early life* (pp. 3–70). Oxford, England: Blackwell Scientific.

Yang, F., & Tsai, C. (2010). Reasoning about science-related uncertain issues and epistemological perspectives among children. *Instructional Science, 38*(4), 325–354.

Yang, P. P., Jong, Y. J., Hsu, H. Y., & Lung, F. W. (2011). Role of assessment tests in the stability of intelligence scoring of preschool children with uneven/delayed cognitive profile. *Journal of Intellectual Disability Research, 55*(5), 453–461. doi:10.1111/j.1365-2788.2

Yardley, A. (2014). Children describing the world: Mixed-method research by child practitioners developing an intergenerational dialogue. *Educational & Child Psychology, 31*(1), 48-62.

Yasri, P., & Mancy, R. (2010). *Perceptions of the relationship between evolutionary theory and biblical explanations of the origins of life and their effects on the learning of evolution among high school students:* International Conference of the Learning Sciences (29 June–2 July), Chicago, IL.

Yates, M., & Youniss, J. (1996). A developmental perspective on community service in adolescence. *Social Development, 5,* 85–111.

Yau, J., & Smetana, J. G. (2003). Conceptions of moral, social-conventional, and personal events among Chinese preschoolers in Hong Kong. *Child Development, 74,* 647–658.

Yeager, E. A., Foster, S. J., Maley, S. D., Anderson, T., Morris, J. W., III, & Davis, O. L., Jr. (1997,

March). *The role of empathy in the development of historical understanding.* Paper presented at the annual meeting of the American Educational Research Association, Chicago.

Yermolayeva, Y., & Rakison, D. H. (2013). Connectionist modeling of developmental changes in infancy: Approaches, challenges, and contributions. *Psychological Bulletin,* doi:10.1037/a0032150

Yildirim, K., Rasinski, T., Ates, S., Fitzgerald, S., Zimmerman, B., & Yildiz, M. (2014). The relationship between reading fluency and vocabulary in fifth grade Turkish students. *Literacy Research & Instruction, 53*(1), 72-89. doi:10.1080/19388071.2013.812166

Yim, D., & Rudoy, J. (2013). Implicit statistical learning and language skills in bilingual children. *Journal of Speech, Language, and Hearing Research, 56*(1), 310–322.

Ying, Y.-W., & Han, M. (2007). The longitudinal effect of intergenerational gap in acculturation on conflict and mental health in Southeast Asian American adolescents. *American Journal of Orthopsychiatry, 77,* 61–66.

Yoo, Y., Popp, J., & Robinson, J. (2013). Maternal distress influences young children's family representations through maternal view of child behavior and parent–child interactions. *Child Psychiatry and Human Development.* doi:10.1007/s10578-013-0377-7

Yoon, C. (2009). Self-regulated learning and instructional factors in the scientific inquiry of scientifically gifted Korean middle school students. *Gifted Child Quarterly, 53*(3), 203–216.

Yoon, E., Chang, C., Kim, S., Clawson, A., Cleary, S., Hansen, M., et al. (2013). A meta-analysis of acculturation/enculturation and mental health. *Journal of Counseling Psychology, 60*(1), 15–30. doi:10.1037/a0030652

Young, A. G., Alibali, M. W., & Kalish, C. W. (2012). Disagreement and causal learning: Others' hypotheses affect children's evaluations of evidence. *Developmental Psychology, 48*(5), 1242-1253. doi:10.1037/a0027540

Young, G. (2012). A unitary Neo-Piagetian/Neo-Eriksonian model of development: Fundamental assumptions and meta-issues. *New Ideas in Psychology, 30*(2), 241–249. doi:10.1016/j.newideapsych.2011.11.002

Young, J. M., Howell, A. N., & Hauser-Cram, P. (2005, April). *Predictors of mastery motivation in children with disabilities born prematurely.* Paper presented at the biennial meeting of the Society for Research in Child Development, Atlanta, GA.

Young-Suk, K., Al Otaiba, S., Folsom, J. S., Greulich, L., & Puranik, C. (2014). Evaluating the dimensionality of first-grade written composition. *Journal of Speech, Language & Hearing Research, 57*(1), 199–211. doi:10.1044/1092-4388(2013/12-0152)

Young-Suk, K., Apel, K., Al Otaiba, S., Nippold, M., & Joffe, V. (2013). The relation of linguistic awareness and vocabulary to word reading and spelling for first-grade students participating in response to intervention. *Language, Speech & Hearing Services in Schools, 44*(4), 337–347. doi:10.1044/0161-1461(2013/12-0013)

Youngblood, J., II, & Spencer, M. B. (2002). Integrating normative identity processes and academic support requirements for special needs adolescents: The application of an identity-focused cultural ecological (ICE) perspective. *Applied Developmental Science, 6,* 95–108.

Youniss, J. (1983). Social construction of adolescence by adolescents and their parents. In H. D. Grotevant & C. R. Cooper (Eds.), *Adolescent development in the family: New directions for child development* (No. 22). San Francisco: Jossey-Bass.

Youniss, J., & Yates, M. (1999). Youth service and moral-civic identity: A case of everyday morality. *Educational Psychology Review, 11,* 361–376.

Ysseldyke, J. E., & Algozzine, B. (1984). *Introduction to special education.* Boston, MA: Houghton Mifflin.

Yuill, N. (2009). The relation between ambiguity understanding and metalinguistic discussion of joking riddles in good and poor comprehenders: Potential for intervention and possible processes of change. *First Language, 29*(1), 65–79.

Zaff, J. F., Ginsberg, K., Boyd, M. J., & Kakli, Z. (2014). Reconnecting disconnected youth: Examining the development of productive engagement. *Journal of Research on Adolescence, 24*(3), 526–540. doi:10.1111/jora.12109

Zahn-Waxler, C. (1991). The case for empathy: A developmental perspective. *Psychological Inquiry, 2*(2), 155–158. doi:10.1207/s15327965pli0202_16

Zahn-Waxler, C., & Kochanska, G. (1990). The origins of guilt. In R. A. Dientsbier (Series Ed.), & R. A. Thompson (Vol. Ed.), *The 36th Annual Nebraska Symposium on Motivation: Socioemotional development. Current theory and research in motivation* (Vol. 36, pp. 183–258). Lincoln, NE: University of Nebraska Press.

Zahn-Waxler, C., & Robinson, J. (1995). Empathy and guilt: Early origins of feelings of responsibility. In J. P. Tangney & K. W. Fischer (Eds.), *Self-conscious emotions: The psychology of shame, guilt, embarrassment, and pride* (pp. 143–173). New York, NY: Guilford Press.

Zahn-Waxler, C., Radke-Yarrow, M., Wagner, E., & Chapman, M. (1992). Development of concern for others. *Developmental Psychology, 28,* 126–136.

Zajdel, R. T., Bloom, J., Fireman, G., & Larsen, J. T. (2013). Children's understanding and experience of mixed emotions: The roles of age, gender, and empathy. *The Journal of Genetic Psychology: Research and Theory on Human Development, 174*(5), 582–603. doi:10.1080/00221325.2012.732125

Zajicek-Farber, M. L., Mayer, L. M., & Daughtery, L. G. (2012). Connections among parental mental health, stress, child routines, and early emotional behavioral regulation of preschool children in low-income families. *Journal of the Society for Social Work and Research, 3*(1). doi:10.5243/jsswr.2012.3

Zajonc, R. B., & Mullally, P. R. (1997). Birth order: Reconciling conflicting effects. *American Psychologist, 52,* 685–699.

Zakar, T., & Mesiano, S. (2011). How does progesterone relax the uterus in pregnancy?*The New England Journal of Medicine, 364*(10), 972–973. doi:http://dx.doi.org/10.1056/NEJMcibr1100071

Zamarian, L., Ischebeck, A., & Delazer, M. (2009). Neuroscience of learning arithmetic—Evidence from brain imaging studies. *Neuroscience and Biobehavioral Reviews, 33*(6), 909–925.

Zambo, D. (2003, April). *Thinking about reading: Talking to children with learning disabilities.* Paper presented at the annual meeting of the American Educational Research Association, Chicago.

Zambo, D., & Brem, S. K. (2004). Emotion and cognition in students who struggle to read: New insights and ideas. *Reading Psychology, 25,* 1–16.

Zampini, L., Suttora, C., D'Odorico, L., & Zanchi, P. (2013). Sequential reasoning and listening text comprehension in preschool children. *European Journal of Developmental Psychology, 10*(5), 563–579. doi:10.1080/17405629.2013.766130

Zeanah, C. H. (2000). Disturbances of attachment in young children adopted from institutions. *Journal of Developmental and Behavioral Pediatrics, 21,* 230–236.

Zehr, J. L., Culbert, K. M., Sisk, C. L., & Klump, K. L. (2007). An association of early puberty with disordered eating and anxiety in a population of undergraduate women and men. *Hormones and Behavior, 52,* 427–435.

Zelazo, P. D., Müller, U., Frye, D., & Marcovitch, S. (2003). The development of executive function in early childhood. *Monographs of the Society for Research in Child Development, 68*(3, Serial No. 274).

Zentner, M., & Eerola, T. (2010). Rhythmic engagement with music in infancy. *Proceedings of the National Academy of Sciences of the United States of America, 107*(13), 5768–5773.

Zero to Three: National Center for Infants, Toddlers, and Families. (2002). *Temperament.* Retrieved from http://www.zerotothree.org/Archive/TEMPERAM.HTM

Zero to Three: National Center for Infants, Toddlers, and Families. (2010). *It's too mushy! It's too spicy! The peas are touching the chicken! (Or, how to handle your picky eater).* Retrieved from http://www.zerotothree.org/site/PageServer?pagename?ter_key_health_picky

Zhang, L., Li, X., Kaljee, L., Fang, X., Lin, X., Zhao, G., et al. (2009). "I felt I have grown up as an adult": Caregiving experience of children affected by HIV/AIDS in China. *Child: Care, Health, and Development, 35*(4), 542–550.

Zhang, M., & Kong L. (2012). An exploration of reasons for Shanghai's success in the OECD Program for International Student Assessment (PISA) 2009. *Frontiers of Education In China, 7*(1), 124-162. doi:10.3868/s110-001-012-0007-3

Zhou, D., Lebel, C., Evans, A., & Beaulieu, C. (2013). Cortical thickness asymmetry from childhood to older adulthood. *NeuroImage, 83,* 66–74.

Zhou, N., Lam, S., & Chan, K. (2012). The Chinese classroom paradox: A cross-cultural comparison of teacher controlling behaviors. *Journal of Educational Psychology, 104*(4), 1162–1174. doi:10.1037/a0027609

Zhou, Q., Chen, S. H., & Main, A. (2012). Commonalities and differences in the research on children's effortful control and executive function: A call for an integrated model of self-regulation. *Child Development Perspectives, 6*(2), 112–121. doi:10.1111/j.1750-8606.2011.00176.x

Zhou, Q., Eisenberg, N., Losoya, S. H., Fabes, R. A., Reiser, M., Guthrie, I. K., et al. (2002). The relations of parental warmth and positive expressiveness to children's empathy-related responding and social functioning: A longitudinal study. *Child Development, 73,* 893–915.

Zhu, X., Sun, H., Chen, A., & Ennis, C. (2012). Measurement invariance of expectancy-value questionnaire in physical education. *Measurement in Physical Education & Exercise Science, 16*(1), 41–54. doi:10.1080/1091367X.2012.639629

Ziegert, D. I., Kistner, J. A., Castro, R., & Robertson, B. (2001). Longitudinal study of young children's responses to challenging achievement situations. *Child Development, 72,* 609–624.

Ziegert, J. C., & Hanges, P. J. (2005). Employment discrimination: The role of implicit attitudes, motivation, and a climate or racial bias. *Journal of Applied Psychology, 90,* 553–562.

Ziegler, S. G. (1987). Effects of stimulus cueing on the acquisition of groundstrokes by beginning tennis players. *Journal of Applied Behavior Analysis, 20,* 405–411.

Zigler, E. (2003). Forty years of believing in magic is enough. *Social Policy Report, 17*(1), 10. Ann Arbor, MI: Society for Research in Child Development.

Zigler, E. F., & Finn-Stevenson, M. (1992). Applied developmental psychology. In M. H. Bornstein & M. E. Lamb (Eds.), *Developmental psychology: An advanced textbook (pp. 677-729).* Hillsdale, NJ: Erlbaum.

Zigler, E., & Styfco, S. J. (2010). *The hidden history of Head Start.* New York: Oxford University Press.

Zigmond, N., Kloo, A., & Volonino, V. (2009). What, where, and how? Special education in the climate of full inclusion. *Exceptionality, 17*, 189–204.

Zilberstein, K., & Messer, E. A. (2010). Building a secure base: Treatment of a child with disorganized attachment. *Clinical Social Work Journal, 38*(1), 85–97.

Zimmer-Gembeck, M., & Skinner, E. (2008). Adolescents coping with stress: development and diversity. *Prevention Researcher, 15*(4), 3–7.

Zimmerman, B. J. (2004). Sociocultural influence and students' development of academic self-regulation: A social-cognitive perspective. In D. M. McNerney & S. Van Etten (Eds.), *Big theories revisited* (pp. 139–164). Greenwich, CT: Information Age.

Zimmerman, B. J., & Cleary, T. J. (2009). Motives to self-regulate learning. In K. R. Wentzel & A. Wigfield (Eds.), *Handbook of motivation at school* (pp. 247–264). New York, NY: Routledge.

Zimmerman, B. J., & Risemberg, R. (1997). Self-regulatory dimensions of academic learning and motivation. In G. D. Phye (Ed.), *Handbook of academic learning: Construction of knowledge* (pp. 105-125). San Diego, CA: Academic Press.

Zimmerman, B. J., & Schunk, D. H. (2004). Self-regulating intellectual processes and outcomes; A social cognitive perspective. In D. Y. Dai & R. J. Sternberg (Eds.), *Motivation, emotion, and cognition: Integrative perspectives on intellectual functioning and development* (pp. 323–349). Mahwah, NJ: Erlbaum.

Zimmerman, C. (2007). The development of scientific thinking skills in elementary and middle school. *Developmental Review, 27*, 172–223.

Ziol-Guest, K. M., & Kalil, A. (2012). Health and medical care among the children of immigrants. *Child Development, 83*(5), 1494–1500. doi:10.1111/j.1467-8624.2012.01795.x

Ziv, M., Smadja, M., & Aram, D. (2013). Mothers' mental-state discourse with preschoolers during storybook reading and wordless storybook telling. *Early Childhood Research Quarterly, 28*(1), 177–186. doi:10.1016/j.ecresq.2012.05.005

Zosuls, K. M., Field, R. D., Martin, C., Andrews, N. Z., & England, D. E. (2014). Gender-based relationship efficacy: Children's self-perceptions in intergroup contexts. *Child Development, 85*(4), 1663–1676. doi:10.1111/cdev.12209

Zucker, T. A., Cabell, S. Q., Justice, L. M., Pentimonti, J. M., & Kaderavek, J. N. (2013). The role of frequent, interactive prekindergarten shared reading in the longitudinal development of language and literacy skills. *Developmental Psychology, 49*(8), 1425-1439. doi:10.1037/a0030347

Zuckerman, M. U. (2007). *Sensation seeking and risky behavior.* Washington, DC: American Psychological Association.

Zumbrunn, S., & Bruning, R. (2013). Improving the writing and knowledge of emergent writers: The effects of self-regulated strategy development. *Reading & Writing, 26*(1), 91–110. doi:10.1 bv007/s11145-012-9384-5

Photo Credits